THE 114TH CONGRESS, 2015–2016*

UNITED STATES HOUSE OF REPRESENTATIVES

2014 Election Results: Republicans gained at least 10 seats*

Democrats: 186 | Republicans: 244 | Undecided: 5

Democrat

Republican

Undecided

American Politics Today

FOURTH EDITION

W. W. Norton & Company has been independent since its founding in 1923, when William Warder Norton and Mary D. Herter Norton first published lectures delivered at the People's Institute, the adult education division of New York City's Cooper Union. The firm soon expanded its program beyond the Institute, publishing books by celebrated academics from America and abroad. By midcentury, the two major pillars of Norton's publishing program—trade books and college texts—were firmly established. In the 1950s, the Norton family transferred control of the company to its employees, and today—with a staff of four hundred and a comparable number of trade, college, and professional titles published each year—W. W. Norton & Company stands as the largest and oldest publishing house owned wholly by its employees.

Editor: Peter Lesser
Project Editors: Linda Feldman and Sandy Lifland
Editorial Assistants: Samantha Held and Sarah Wolf
Managing Editor, College: Marian Johnson
Managing Editor, College Digital Media: Kim Yi
Senior Production Supervisor, College: Ashley Horna
Media Editor: Toni Magyar
Media Editorial Assistant: Michael Jaoui
Marketing Manager, Political Science: Erin Brown
Text Designer: Jillian Burr
Photo Editor: Evan Luberger
Photo Researcher: Jane Miller
Permissions Manager: Megan Jackson
Composition: Cenveo® Publisher Services
Manufacturing: R. R. Donnelley—Roanoke

Permission to use copyrighted material is included in the credits section of this book on page A73.

Library of Congress Cataloging-in-Publication Data

Bianco, William T., 1960-
  American politics today / William T. Bianco.—Fourth edition.
    pages cm
  Includes bibliographical references and index.
  ISBN 978-0-393-93700-8
  1. United States—Politics and government—Textbooks. I. Title.
  JK275.B54   2015
  320.473—dc23   2014044205

W. W. Norton & Company, Inc., 500 Fifth Avenue, New York, NY 10110-0017

wwnorton.com

W. W. Norton & Company Ltd., Castle House, 75/76 Wells Street, London W1T 3QT

1 2 3 4 5 6 7 8 9 0

For our families,
Regina, Anna, and Catherine,
Sarah, Neal, Katherine, and Sophia,
who encouraged, empathized, and
helped, with patience,
grace, and love.

ABOUT THE AUTHORS

WILLIAM T. BIANCO

William T. Bianco is professor of political science at Indiana University, Bloomington. His research focuses on congressional institutions, representation, and international cooperation in crewed spaceflight. He received his undergraduate degree from SUNY Stony Brook and his MA and Ph.D. from the University of Rochester. He is the author of *Trust: Representatives and Constituents; American Politics: Strategy and Choice*; and numerous articles on American politics. His research and graduate students have received funding from the National Science Foundation and the national Council for Eurasian and Eastern European Research. He has also served as a consultant to congressional candidates and party campaign committees, as well as to the U.S. Department of Energy, the U.S. Department of Health and Human Services, and other state and local government agencies. He was also a Fulbright Senior Scholar in Moscow, Russia, during 2011–12.

DAVID T. CANON

David T. Canon is professor of political science at the University of Wisconsin, Madison. His teaching and research interests focus on American political institutions, especially Congress, and racial representation. He is the author of *Actors, Athletes, and Astronauts: Political Amateurs in the U.S. Congress; Race, Redistricting, and Representation: The Unintended Consequences of Black Majority Districts* (winner of the Richard F. Fenno Prize); *The Dysfunctional Congress?* (with Kenneth Mayer); and various articles and book chapters. He recently finished a term as the Congress editor of *Legislative Studies Quarterly*. He is an AP consultant and has taught in the University of Wisconsin Summer AP Institute for U.S. Government & Politics since 1997. Professor Canon is the recipient of a University of Wisconsin Chancellor's Distinguished Teaching Award.

CONTENTS IN BRIEF

PART I: FOUNDATIONS

1. Understanding American Politics   2
2. The Constitution and the Founding   28
3. Federalism   66
4. Civil Liberties   104
5. Civil Rights   150

PART II: POLITICS

6. Public Opinion   198
7. The Media   236
8. Political Parties   268
9. Elections   304
10. Interest Groups   350

PART III: INSTITUTIONS

11. Congress   386
12. The Presidency   434
13. The Bureaucracy   472
14. The Courts   508

PART IV: POLICY

15. Economic Policy   552
16. Social Policy   594
17. Foreign Policy   634

APPENDIX

The Declaration of Independence   A1
The Articles of Confederation   A3
The Constitution of the United States of America   A6
Amendments to the Constitution   A11
The Federalist Papers   A15

Glossary   **A21**
Endnotes   **A31**

CONTENTS

Preface xxi

Features of the Text and Media Package xxv

Acknowledgments xxvii

PART I: FOUNDATIONS

1. UNDERSTANDING AMERICAN POLITICS 2

Making Sense of American Government and Politics 5

Why Do We Have a Government? 6

Forms of Government 8

What Is Politics? 9

Politics Is Conflictual 9

Political Process Matters 13

Politics Is Everywhere 14

Sources of Conflict in American Politics 16

Economic Interests 16

Cultural Values 17

Racial, Gender, and Ethnic Differences 18

Ideology 19

Resolving Conflict: Democracy and American Political Values 21

Conclusion 24

STUDY GUIDE 25

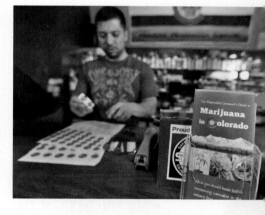

2. THE CONSTITUTION AND THE FOUNDING 28

The Historical Context of the Constitution 31

The Articles of Confederation: The First Attempt at Government 31

Political Theories of the Framers 35

Economic Interests 36

The Politics of Compromise at the Constitutional Convention 37

Majority Rule versus Minority Rights 38

Small States versus Large States 39

Legislative Power versus Executive Power 40

National Power versus State and Local Power 42

Slave States versus Nonslave States 43

Ratification 45

The Antifederalists' Concerns 46

The Federalists' Strategies 47

The Constitution: A Framework for Government 48

Exclusive Powers 48

Shared Powers 51

Negative or Checking Powers 53

Is the Constitution a "Living" Document? 55

Ambiguity 55

Changing the Constitution 57

Multiple Interpreters 59

Conclusion 61

STUDY GUIDE 63

3. FEDERALISM 66

What Is Federalism and Why Does It Matter? 69

Levels of Government and Their Degrees of Autonomy 69

A Comparative Perspective 70

Balancing National and State Power in the Constitution 71

A Strong National Government 72

State Powers and Limits on National Power 72

Clauses that Favor Both Perspectives 73

The Evolving Concept of Federalism 74

The Early Years 75

Dual Federalism 77

Cooperative Federalism 80

Federalism Today 83

Cooperative Federalism Lives On: Fiscal Federalism 83

The Rise of Coercive Federalism 86

The States Fight Back 89

Fighting for States' Rights: The Role of the Modern Supreme Court 90

Assessing Federalism 95

Ideological Complexities 95

Advantages of a Strong Role for the States 96

Disadvantages of Too Much State Power 98

Conclusion 100

STUDY GUIDE 101

4. CIVIL LIBERTIES 104

Defining Civil Liberties 106

Balancing Interests 107

Drawing Lines 108

The Origins of Civil Liberties 109

Origins of the Bill of Rights 109

Selective Incorporation and the Fourteenth Amendment 111

Freedom of Religion 112

The Establishment Clause and Separation of Church and State 114

The Free Exercise Clause 116

Freedom of Speech, Assembly, and the Press 119

Generally Protected Expression 120

Less Protected Speech and Publications 127

The Right to Bear Arms 130

Law, Order, and the Rights of Criminal Defendants 132

The Fourth Amendment: Unreasonable Searches and Seizures 133

The Fifth Amendment: Self-Incrimination 138

The Sixth Amendment: The Right to Legal Counsel and a Jury Trial 140

The Eighth Amendment: Cruel and Unusual Punishment 141

Privacy Rights 142

Abortion Rights 143

Gay Rights 145

Conclusion 145

STUDY GUIDE 146

5. CIVIL RIGHTS 150

The Context of Civil Rights 153

African Americans 154

Native Americans, Latinos, and Asian Americans 156

Women and Civil Rights 158

Gays and Lesbians 159

A Color-Blind Society? 160

The Racial Divide Today 162

Differences in Voting Access 162

Socioeconomic Indicators 163

Criminal Justice and Hate Crimes 165

Key Players in the Conflict Over Civil Rights 166

The Courts 170

Congress 181

The President 184

Civil Rights Issues Today 187

Affirmative Action 187

Multicultural Issues 190

Conclusion 193

STUDY GUIDE 195

PART II: POLITICS

6. PUBLIC OPINION 198

What Is Public Opinion? 200

Early Theories of Public Opinion 201

Contemporary Theory of Public Opinion 202

How People Form Opinions 203

Personal Knowledge and Considerations 205

Where Do Opinions Come From? 206

Socialization: Family and Communities 206

Events 208

Group Identity 209

Politicians and Other Political Actors 211

Measuring Public Opinion 212

Problems in Measuring Public Opinion 214

How Useful Are Surveys? 218

Characteristics of American Public Opinion 219

Ideological Polarization 219

Evaluations of Government and Officeholders 221

Policy Preferences 224

Does Public Opinion Matter? 229

Public Opinion Is Relevant 230

Public Opinion Can Influence Government 230

Conclusion 231

STUDY GUIDE 233

7. THE MEDIA 236

The News Media in America 238

Historical Overview 239

Media Sources 242

Political Reporting: Sources, Leaks, and Shield Laws 247

Staging the News 250

Revealing Sources 250

How Do Americans Use the Media to Learn about Politics? 251

Does the Source Matter? 253

Media Effects on American Citizens and Government Policy 254

Theories of Media Influence 255

Assessing Media Coverage of American Politics 258

Media Bias 258

Where Else Does Media Coverage Fall Short? 262

The Effect of Market Forces 263

Conclusion 264

STUDY GUIDE 265

8. POLITICAL PARTIES 268

What Are Political Parties? 270

History of American Political Parties 271

The Evolution of American Political Parties 272

Realignments 275

Modern American Political Parties 275

The Party Organization 275

The Party in Government 278

The Party in the Electorate 280

The Role of Political Parties in American Politics 285

Organizing Elections 285

Cooperation in Government 292

Minor Parties 295

Effects on Election Outcomes 295

Unique Issues Facing Minor Parties 296

What Kind of Democracy Do American Political Parties Create? 297

Recruiting Good Candidates 297

Working Together in Campaigns 297

Working Together in Office 298

Providing Accountability 299

Citizens' Behavior 299

Conclusion 300

STUDY GUIDE 301

9. ELECTIONS 304

How Do American Elections Work? 306

Functions of Elections 307

Two Stages of Elections 308

Constituencies: Who Chooses Representatives? 309

Presidential Elections 311

Electoral Campaigns 318

Setting the Stage 318

Before the Campaign 319

The General Election Campaign 321

Campaign Advertising: Getting the Word Out 326

Campaign Finance 328

How Do Voters Decide? 332

The Decision to Vote 334

How Do People Vote? 335

Voting in Normal and Nationalized Elections 337

Understanding the 2014 Election 340

The Path to 2014: The 2010 and 2012 Elections 340

Analyzing the 2014 Elections 344

Conclusion 346

STUDY GUIDE 347

10. INTEREST GROUPS 350

The Interest Group Universe 352

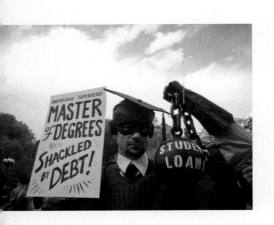

The Business of Lobbying 354

Organizational Structures 357

Staff 359

Membership 360

Resources 361

Getting Organized 363

The Logic of Collective Action 363

Interest Group Strategies 365

Inside Strategies 365

Outside Strategies 368

Choosing Strategies 376

How Much Power Do Interest Groups Have? 376

What Determines When Interest Groups Succeed? 378

How Groups Succeed 380

Conclusion 381

STUDY GUIDE 383

PART III: INSTITUTIONS

11. CONGRESS 386

Congress's Place in Our Constitutional System 389

Congress and the People 390

Representation and the Constituency 391

The Electoral Connection 395

Redistricting 398

Congress's Image Problem 401

The Incumbency Advantage and Its Sources 403

In the District: Home Style 404

Campaign Fund-Raising 405

Constituency Service 405

The Structure of Congress 407

Informal Structures 408

Formal Structures 410

How a Bill Becomes a Law 417

The Conventional Process 417

Deviations From the Conventional Process 423

Differences in the House and Senate Legislative Processes 423

Oversight 425

Congressional Reform 427

Conclusion 428

STUDY GUIDE 430

12. THE PRESIDENCY 434

Presidential Power: Yesterday and Today 436

Early Years through World War I 437

The Great Depression through the Present 438

The President's Job Description 440

Head of the Executive Branch 441

The President as Politician 450

Presidential Succession 453

The Executive Branch 455

The Executive Office of the President 455

The Vice President 456

The President's Cabinet 457

The American Public and the President 458

Gauging Presidential Popularity 459

Explaining Presidential Approval 460

Assessing Presidential Power 462

Presidents and Unilateral Action 463

Control over the Interpretation and Implementation of Laws 465

Congressional Responses to Unilateral Action 466

Conclusion 467

STUDY GUIDE 469

13. THE BUREAUCRACY 472

What Is the Federal Bureaucracy? 474

What Do Bureaucrats Do? 474

Bureaucratic Expertise and Its Consequences 480

How Has the American Bureaucracy Grown? 483

The Beginning of America's Bureaucracy 484

Building a New American State: The Progressive Era 485

The New Deal, the Great Society, and the Reagan Revolution 485

The Modern Federal Bureaucracy 487

The Structure of the Federal Government 488

The Size of the Federal Government 490

The Human Face of the Bureaucracy 493

Civil Service Regulations 494

Limits on Political Activity 495

Political Appointees and the Senior Executive Service 496

Controlling the Bureaucracy 497

Agency Organization 498

Monitoring 498

Correcting Violations 501

The Consequences of Control 502

Conclusion 504

STUDY GUIDE 505

14. THE COURTS 508

The Development of an Independent and Powerful Federal Judiciary 511

The Founders' Views of the Courts: The Weakest Branch? 511

Judicial Review and Marbury v. Madison 513

Judicial Review in Practice 514

The American Legal and Judicial System 515

Court Fundamentals 516

Structure of the Court and Federalism 519

How Judges Are Selected 523

Access to the Supreme Court 528

The Court's Workload 528

Rules of Access 531

The Court's Criteria 531

Internal Politics 533

Hearing Cases before the Supreme Court 534

Briefs 534

Oral Argument 535

Conference 536

Opinion Writing 536

Supreme Court Decision Making 538

Legal Factors 538

Political Factors 540

The Role of the Court as a Policy Maker 545

Compliance and Implementation 545

Relations with the Other Branches 545

Conclusion 548

STUDY GUIDE 549

PART IV: POLICY

15. ECONOMIC POLICY 552

Goals of Economic Policy 555

Full Employment 555

Stable Prices 556

Promote the Free Market and Growth 557

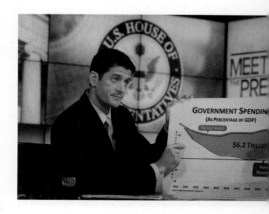

Balanced Budgets 558

Balance of Payments, or the Current Account 560

Trade-offs between Economic Goals 561

The Key Players in Economic Policy Making 561

Congress 561

The President 565

The Bureaucracy 567

How Economic Policy Makers Interact: The 2008 Economic Crisis 569

Tools and Theories of Economic Policy 572

Fiscal Policy 572

Monetary Policy 578

Regulatory Policy 582

Trade Policy and the Balance of Payments 584

The Politics of Trade Policy 588

Conclusion 589

STUDY GUIDE 591

16. SOCIAL POLICY 594

The History and Background of Social Policy 597

Poverty and Income Inequality 600

The Key Players in Social Policy Making 604

Congress and the President 604

The Bureaucracy 605

The States 605

Interest Groups 606

The Policy-Making Process 606

Social Policy Today 610

Social Security 610

Health Care 617

Income Support and Welfare 624

Education 626

Conclusion 630

STUDY GUIDE 631

17. FOREIGN POLICY 634

What Is Foreign Policy? 637

Foreign Policy Principles and Perspectives 637

History of American Foreign Policy 639

Foreign Policy Makers 646

The President and the Executive Branch 647

Congress 649

The Federal Courts 650

Groups outside the Federal Government 653

The Tools of Foreign Policy 657

Diplomacy 657

Trade and Economic Policies 657

Foreign Aid 659

Alliances and Treaties 661

Military Force 661

The Politics of Foreign Policy Today 662

Managing International Trade: China 662

Fighting Terrorism: Afghanistan 665

Preventing the Spread of Weapons of Mass Destruction: North Korea 666

Conclusion 668

STUDY GUIDE 669

APPENDIX

The Declaration of Independence A1

The Articles of Confederation A3

The Constitution of the United States of America A6

Amendments to the Constitution A11

The Federalist Papers A15

Glossary A21

Endnotes A31

Answer Key A71

Credits A73

Index A75

PREFACE

This book is based on three simple premises: politics is conflictual, political process matters, and politics is everywhere. It reflects our belief that politics is explainable, that political outcomes can be understood in terms of decisions made by individuals—and that the average college undergraduate can make sense of the political world in these terms. It focuses on contemporary American politics, the events and outcomes that our students have lived through and know something about. The result, we believe, is a book that provides an accessible but rigorous account of the American political system.

American Politics Today is also the product of our dissatisfaction with existing texts. Twenty-five years ago we were assistant professors at the same university, assigned to teach the introductory class in alternate semesters. Though our graduate training was quite different, we found that we shared a deep disappointment with available texts. Their wholesale focus on grand normative concepts such as civic responsibility or their use of analytic themes such as collective action left students with little idea of how American politics really works, how events in Washington, D.C., affect their everyday lives, and how to piece together all the facts about American politics into a coherent explanation of why things happen as they do. These texts did not engender excitement, fascination, or even passing interest. What they did was put students to sleep.

The first three editions of this book broke new ground in both approach and content. In the Fourth Edition, our themes continue to embody our belief that we can move beyond simply describing what happens in political life to predicting and explaining behavior and outcomes—and that we can do so in an introductory class. In part we wish to counter the widespread belief among students that politics is too complicated, too chaotic, or too secretive to make sense of. More than that, we want to empower our students, to demonstrate that everyday American politics is relevant to their lives. This emphasis is also a response to the typical complaint about American government textbooks—that they are full of facts but devoid of useful information, and that after students finish reading, they are no better able to answer "why" questions than they were before they cracked the book.

In this edition, we maintain our central focus on conflict and compromise in American politics—identifying what Americans agree and disagree about and assessing how conflict shapes American politics, from campaign platforms to policy outcomes. Though this emphasis seems especially timely given the budget crisis of 2013, the hotly contested midterm elections in 2014, and the intense debates (and often stalemates) in Congress over health care reform, immigration, and economic opportunity, our aim is to go beyond these events to identify a fundamental constant in American politics: the reality that much of politics is driven by disagreements over the scope and form of government policy, and that compromise is an essential component of virtually all significant changes in government policy. Indeed, it is impossible to imagine politics without conflict. Conflict was embedded in the American political system by the Founders, who set up a system of checks and balances to make sure that no single group could dominate. The Constitution's division of power guarantees that enacting and implementing laws will involve conflict and compromise. Accordingly, despite the general dislike people have for conflict, our students must recognize that conflict and compromise lie at the heart of politics.

Throughout the text, we emphasize common sense, showing students that politics inside the Beltway is often strikingly similar to the students' own everyday interactions. For example, what sustains policy compromises made by members of Congress? The fact that the members typically have long careers, that they interact frequently with each other, and that they only deal with colleagues who have kept their word in the past. These strategies are not unique to the political world. Rather, they embody rules of thumb that most people follow (or are at least aware of) in their everyday interactions. In short, we try to help students understand American politics by emphasizing how it is not all that different from the world they know.

This focus on common sense is coupled with many references to the political science literature. We believe that contemporary research has something to say about prediction and explanation of events that students care about—and that these insights can be taught without turning students into formal theorists or statisticians. This emphasis has the secondary benefit of tying the introductory course to the wider political science discipline, including the American politics subfield and work on democracies more generally. To this end we include a link in each chapter to an online feature ("What Do Political Scientists Do?") that talks about a specific piece of research, setting out the author's research question and showing how he or she went about answering it. These boxes are augmented by videos in which the authors discuss their research, as well as how they came to be interested in politics and political science. Together, the boxes and videos allow us to offer deeper explanations of political phenomena, as well as reinforce our argument that political science research is both understandable and relevant.

The Fourth Edition builds on these strengths. First, we have worked to streamline and improve the presentation of text and graphics. The result is a text that is even more accessible to students. We also have improved the pedagogy by revising already extensive review and quiz material at the conclusion of every chapter and added smart new graphics—"How It Works In Practice," and many new figures and tables—within the chapters. In the Fourth Edition, new or revised chapter openers use contemporary stories and examples (from student loans to marijuana legalization to the threats posed by ISIL) to highlight the conflict and compromise theme. We refer to these openers throughout the chapters to illustrate and extend our discussion. You also might be happy to know that we did all of this while cutting the length of the book by 10 percent!

We do not frame the text in terms of any one theory or approach. We present the essential insights of contemporary research, motivated by real-world political phenomena and explained using text or simple diagrams. This approach gives students a set of tools for understanding politics, provides an introduction to the political science literature, and matches up well with students' common-sense intuitions about everyday life. Moreover, by showing that academic scholarship is not a blind alley or irrelevant, this approach helps to bridge the gap between an instructor's teaching and his or her research.

The text continues to be ruthlessly contemporary. Although we do not ignore American history, our stress is on contemporary politics—on the debates, actions, and outcomes that most college students are aware of. Focusing on recent events emphasizes the utility of the concepts and insights that we develop in the text. It also goes a long way toward establishing the relevance of the intro class. The new edition discusses the rapidly changing acceptance of same-sex marriage, attempts to address sexual assaults in the military, and debates over income inequality—all issues that affect everyone's lives.

Finally, our book offers an individual-level perspective on America's government. The essential message is that politics—elections, legislative proceedings, regulatory choices, and everything else we see—is a product of the decisions made by real flesh-and-blood people. This approach grounds our discussion of politics in the real world. Many texts focus on abstractions such as "the eternal debate," "the great questions," or "the pulse of democracy." The problem with these constructs is that they don't explain where the debate, the questions, or even democracy come from. Nor do they help students understand what's going on in Washington, D.C., and elsewhere, as it's not obvious that the participants care much about these sorts of abstractions—quite the opposite, in fact.

We replace these constructs with a focus on real people and actual choices. The primary goal is to make sense of American politics by understanding why politicians, bureaucrats, judges, and citizens act as they do. That is, we are grounding our description of American politics at the most fundamental level— an individual facing a decision. How, for example, does a voter choose among candidates? Stated that way, it is reasonably easy to talk about where the choice came from, how the individual might evaluate different options, and why one choice might look better than the others. Voters' decisions may be understood by examining the different feasible strategies they employ (issue voting, retrospective evaluations, stereotyping, etc.) and by asking ourselves why some voters use one strategy while others use a different one.

By focusing on individuals and choices, we can place students in the shoes of the decision makers, and in so doing, give them insight into why people act as they do. We can discuss, for example, why a House member might favor enacting wasteful pork-barrel spending, even though a proposal full of such projects will make his constituents economically worse off—and why constituents might reward such behavior, even if they suspect the truth. By taking this approach, we are not trying to let legislators off the hook. Rather, we believe that any real understanding of the political process must begin with a sense of the decisions the participants make and why they make them.

Focusing on individuals also segues naturally into a discussion of consequences, allowing us to move from examining decisions to describing and evaluating outcomes. In this way, we can show students how large-scale outcomes in politics, such as inefficient programs, don't happen by accident or because of malfeasance. Rather, they are the predictable results of choices made by individuals (here, politicians and voters).

The policy chapters in the Full and Essentials Editions also represent a distinctive feature of this book. The discussion of policy at the end of an intro class often fits awkwardly with the material covered earlier. It is supposed to be a culmination of the semester-long discussion of institutions, politicians, and political behavior, but instead it often becomes an afterthought that gets discarded when time runs out in the last few weeks of class. Our policy chapters explicitly draw on previous chapters' discussions of the actors that shape policy: the president, Congress, the courts, interest groups, and parties. By doing so, these chapters show how all the pieces of the puzzle fit together.

Finally, this book reflects our experience as practicing scholars and teachers, as well as interactions with more than fifteen thousand students in introductory classes at several universities. Rather than thinking of the intro class as a service obligation, we believe it offers a unique opportunity for faculty to develop a broader sense of American politics and American political science, while at the same time giving students the tools they need to behave as knowledgeable citizens or enthusiastic political science majors. We hope that it works for you as well as it does for us.

FEATURES OF THE TEXT AND MEDIA PACKAGE

THE BOOK'S "THREE KEY IDEAS"—politics is conflictual, political process matters, and politics is everywhere—are fully integrated throughout the text.

▶ **Politics Is Conflictual** and conflict and compromise are a normal, healthy part of politics. The questions debated in elections and the policy options considered by people in government are generally marked by disagreement at all levels. Making policy typically involves important issues on which people disagree, sometimes strongly; so compromise, bargaining, and tough choices about trade-offs are often necessary.

▶ **Political Process Matters** because it is the mechanism we have established to resolve conflicts and achieve compromise. Governmental actions result from conscious choices made by voters, elected officials, and bureaucrats. The media often cover political issues in the same way they do sporting events, and though this makes for entertaining news, it also leads citizens to overlook the institutions, rules, and procedures that have a decisive influence on American life. Politics really is not just a game.

▶ **Politics Is Everywhere** in that the results of the political process affect all aspects of Americans' everyday lives. Politics governs what people can and cannot do, their quality of life, and how they think about events, other people, and situations.

NEW AND REVISED CONFLICT AND COMPROMISE CHAPTER OPENERS

reflect our "politics is conflictual" emphasis. Each chapter begins with an example of conflict in American politics, from debates over what the Constitution means to disagreements within the Democratic and Republican parties. In the Fourth Edition, all of these openers are new or have been revised to reflect recent events. Within each chapter and especially in the chapter conclusions, we return to the examples, showing how disagreements and efforts to mitigate them shape every area of American politics.

ORGANIZATION AROUND CHAPTER GOALS stresses learning objectives and mastery of core material.

▶ **Chapter Goals** appear at the beginning of the chapter and then recur at the start of the relevant sections throughout the chapter to create a more active reading experience that emphasizes important learning objectives.

▶ **Extensive end-of-chapter review sections organized around the Chapter Goals** include section summaries, practice quiz questions, key terms, and suggested reading lists. Students have everything they need to master the material in each section of the chapter.

BOXED FEATURES reinforce the three key ideas while introducing other important ways to think about American politics.

▶ **"How It Works" graphics** show how the political process works and how it resolves (or fails to resolve) conflicts. These complement the chapter-opening stories, depicting the processes that underlie the conflicts and compromises we see in American politics. **NEW "How It Works In Practice"** sections show how these processes play out in real political situations. Critical-thinking questions ask students to consider the implications of the process and how it affects the outcome.

▶ **"You Decide" features** present a controversial issue and encourage students to consider the possible trade-offs involved in proposed solutions. Each feature concludes with two critical-thinking questions.

▶ **"Nuts & Bolts" figures provide students with concise explanations of key concepts**, like the difference between civil liberties and civil rights, different kinds of gerrymanders, and brief summaries of campaign finance rules. These features provide an easy way for quick study and review.

▶ In each chapter, students will find a link to online **"What Do Political Scientists Do?" boxes and videos** that explain in an engaging, journalistic style how political scientists identify research topics and conduct their studies, as well as what makes this research and analysis important to the lives of ordinary people.

TOOLS FOR A DYNAMIC CLASSROOM

▶ **Norton Coursepacks are free and open with no access codes,** allowing you to easily bring Norton's high-quality digital content into your existing learning management system. The content is fully editable and is yours to keep forever. The Norton Coursepack for *American Politics Today,* Fourth Edition contains the following activities and quizzes:

- **A new tutorial helping students interpret charts and graphs** that provides students with extra practice and guidance interpreting common representations of data that they will encounter in this textbook and in the world,

- **Pre-and post-test chapter quizzes** that assess student knowledge of core concepts,

- **Video exercises** that engage students and help them retain and apply information through significant events,

- **"How It Works" and "How It Works In Practice" animated graphics** that guide students through understanding political processes and institutions,

- **Simulations** that show students how concepts work in the real world,

- **"By the Numbers" activities** that give students more practice with quantitative skills and more familiarity with how political scientists know what they know, and

- **"You Decide" exercises** that present students with multiple sides of contemporary debates and ask them to consider and refine their own views based on what they've learned.

▶ **Test bank** contains more than 1,800 questions tagged to chapter-learning objectives and keyed to Bloom's taxonomy.

▶ **Instructor's manual** includes chapter outlines, class activities, and discussion questions.

▶ **Instructor PowerPoints** contains fully customizable lecture slides with clicker questions and "How It Works" and "How It Works In Practice" animated PowerPoint slides for optimal classroom presentation.

ACKNOWLEDGMENTS

This edition of *American Politics Today* is again dedicated to our families. Our wives, Regina and Sarah, have continued to accommodate our deadlines and schedules and have again served as our most accurate critics and sources of insight and inspiration. Our five children, several of whom are now undergraduates themselves, have again been forced to contend with politics and textbook writing as a perennial topic of conversation and have responded with critiques and insights of their own, which appear throughout the text.

Our colleagues at Indiana University and the University of Wisconsin (and before that, Duke University for both of us) provided many opportunities to talk about American politics and teaching this course.

Bill thanks his colleagues at Indiana University and elsewhere, including Christine Barbour, John Brehm, Ted Carmines, Chris DeSante, Mike Ensley, Bernard Fraga, Russ Hansen, Matthew Hayes, Jeff Hill, Yanna Krupnikov, Lin Ostrom, Regina Smyth, Will Winecoff, and Gerry Wright, for sharp insights and encouragement at crucial moments. He is also grateful to the legion of teaching assistants who have helped him organize and teach the intro class at three universities. Finally, he thanks the students at the Higher School of Economics in Moscow, Russia, where he taught the introductory class as a Fulbright Scholar in 2012.

David gives special thanks to Ken Mayer, whose daily "reality checks" and consistently thoughtful professional and personal advice are greatly appreciated. Barry Burden, Ben Marquez, Don Moynihan, Ryan Owens, Ellie Powell, Howard Schweber, Byron Shafer, Alex Tahk, Dave Weimer, Kathy Walsh, Susan Yackee, and all the great people at Wisconsin have provided a wonderful community within which to teach and research American politics. John Coleman, who has moved on to become a dean at the University of Minnesota, also deserves special thanks as a former member of the intro American team and good friend and colleague. David would also like to thank the students at the University of Debrecen in Hungary, where he taught American politics as a Fulbright Scholar in 2003–04, and the Eberhard Karls University of Tübingen, Germany, where he taught as a Fulbright Scholar in 2011–12. The Hungarian students' unique perspective on democracy, civil liberties, and the role of government required David to think about American politics in a different way. The German students' views on the role of political parties, campaigns, and the social welfare state also provided a strong contrast to the views of his American students.

Both of us are grateful to the political science faculty at Duke University, who, in addition to providing us with our first academic jobs, worked to construct a hospitable and invigorating place to research and to teach. In particular, Rom Coles, Ruth Grant, John Aldrich, Tom Spragens, Taylor Cole, and David Barber were model colleagues and scholars. We both learned to teach by watching them, and we are better instructors and scholars for it.

The outstanding people at W. W. Norton made this a much better book than we could have produced on our own. Steve Dunn was responsible for getting the process started and providing good counsel from beginning to end. Roby Harrington has been a source of constant encouragement and feedback. Peter Lesser's combination of wit, insight, and expertise is evident on every page of the book. Toni Magyar's clear vision for the electronic media and for the textbook itself was a major help. Linda Feldman and Sandy Lifland were superb project editors, bringing to the project their talent for clarity of words and visuals. Sarah Wolf, Samantha Held, and Michael Jaoui made sure everyone had the right versions of everything and kept schedules and priorities clear. Jane Miller and Evan Luberger put together an excellent photo program. Megan Jackson cleared reprint permissions for the figures and tables. Ashley Horna handled production with efficiency and good humor. Jillian Burr created a beautiful design for the book's interior and cover. We also would like to thank Aaron Javsicas and Ann Shin for their outstanding work on earlier editions. The entire crew at Norton has been incredibly professional and supportive. We feel very fortunate to work with them.

We are also indebted to the many reviewers who have commented on the text.

FIRST EDITION REVIEWERS

Dave Adler, *Idaho State University*
Rick Almeida, *Francis Marion University*
Jim Bailey, *Arkansas State University, Mountain Home*
Todd Belt, *University of Hawaii, Hilo*
Scott Buchanan, *Columbus State University*
Randy Burnside, *Southern Illinois University, Carbondale*
Carolyn Cocca, *SUNY College at Old Westbury*
Tom Dolan, *Columbus State University*
Dave Dulio, *Oakland University*
Matt Eshbaugh-Soha, *University of North Texas*
Kevin Esterling, *University of California, Riverside*
Peter Francia, *East Carolina University*
Scott Frisch, *California State University, Channel Islands*
Sarah Fulton, *Texas A&M University*
Keith Gaddie, *University of Oklahoma*
Joe Giammo, *University of Arkansas, Little Rock*
Kate Greene, *University of Southern Mississippi*
Steven Greene, *North Carolina State University*
Phil Habel, *Southern Illinois University, Carbondale*
Charles Hartwig, *Arkansas State University, Jonesboro*
Ted Jelen, *University of Nevada, Las Vegas*
Jennifer Jensen, *Binghamton University (SUNY)*
Terri Johnson, *University of Wisconsin, Green Bay*
Luke Keele, *Ohio State University*
Linda Keith, *University of Texas, Dallas*
Chris Kelley, *Miami University*
Jason Kirksey, *Oklahoma State University*
Jeffrey Kraus, *Wagner College*
Chris Kukk, *Western Connecticut State University*
Mel Kulbicki, *York College*
Joel Lieske, *Cleveland State University*
Steve Light, *University of North Dakota*
Baodong (Paul) Liu, *University of Utah*
Ken Long, *Saint Joseph College, Connecticut*
Michael Lynch, *University of Kansas*
Cherie Maestas, *Florida State University*
Tom Marshall, *University of Texas, Arlington*
Scott McClurg, *Southern Illinois University, Carbondale*
Jonathan Morris, *East Carolina University*
Jason Mycoff, *University of Delaware*
Sean Nicholson-Crotty, *University of Missouri, Columbia*
Timothy Nokken, *Texas Tech University*
Sandra O'Brien, *Florida Gulf Coast University*

John Orman, *Fairfield University*
L. Marvin Overby, *University of Missouri, Columbia*
Catherine Paden, *Simmons College*
Dan Ponder, *Drury University*
Paul Posner, *George Mason University*
David Redlawsk, *University of Iowa*
Russell Renka, *Southeast Missouri State University*
Travis Ridout, *Washington State University*
Andy Rudalevige, *Dickinson College*
Denise Scheberle, *University of Wisconsin, Green Bay*
Tom Schmeling, *Rhode Island College*
Pat Sellers, *Davidson College*
Dan Smith, *Northwest Missouri State University*
Dale Story, *University of Texas, Arlington*
John Vile, *Middle Tennessee State University*
Mike Wagner, *University of Nebraska*
Dave Wigg, *St. Louis Community College*
Maggie Zetts, *Purdue University*

SECOND EDITION REVIEWERS

Danny Adkison, *Oklahoma State University*
Hunter Bacot, *Elon College*
Tim Barnett, *Jacksonville State University*
Robert Bruhl, *University of Illinois, Chicago*
Daniel Butler, *Yale University*
Jennifer Byrne, *James Madison University*
Jason Casellas, *University of Texas, Austin*
Jeffrey Christiansen, *Seminole State College*
Richard Conley, *University of Florida*
Michael Crespin, *University of Georgia*
Brian DiSarro, *California State University, Sacramento*
Ryan Emenaker, *College of the Redwoods*
John Evans, *California State University, Northridge*
John Fliter, *Kansas State University*
Jimmy Gleason, *Purdue University*
Dana Glencross, *Oklahoma City Community College*
Jeannie Grussendorf, *Georgia State University*
Phil Habel, *Southern Illinois University, Carbondale*
Lori Han, *Chapman University*
Katy Harriger, *Wake Forest University*
Richard Himelfarb, *Hofstra University*
Doug Imig, *University of Memphis*
Daniel Klinghard, *College of the Holy Cross*
Eddie Meaders, *University of North Texas*
Kristy Michaud, *California State University, Northridge*
Kris Miler, *University of Illinois, Urbana-Champaign*
Melinda Mueller, *Eastern Illinois University*

Michael Mundt, *Oakton Community College*
Emily Neff-Sharum, *University of North Carolina, Pembroke*
David Nice, *Washington State University*
Tim Nokken, *Texas Tech University*
Stephen Nuño, *Northern Arizona University*
Richard Powell, *University of Maine, Orono*
Travis Ridout, *Washington State University*
Sara Rinfret, *University of Wisconsin, Green Bay*
Martin Saiz, *California State University, Northridge*
Gabriel Ramon Sanchez, *University of New Mexico*
Charles Shipan, *University of Michigan*
Dan Smith, *Northwest Missouri State University*
Rachel Sondheimer, *United States Military Academy*
Chris Soper, *Pepperdine University*
Walt Stone, *University of California, Davis*
Greg Streich, *University of Central Missouri*
Charles Walcott, *Virginia Tech*
Rick Waterman, *University of Kentucky*
Edward Weber, *Washington State University*
Jack Wright, *Ohio State University*

THIRD EDITION REVIEWERS

Steve Anthony, *Georgia State University*
Marcos Arandia, *North Lake College*
Richard Barberio, *SUNY College at Oneonta*
Jody Baumgartner, *East Carolina University*
Brian Berry, *University of Texas, Dallas*
David Birch, *Lone Star College, Tomball*
Eileen Burgin, *University of Vermont*
Randolph Burnside, *Southern Illinois University, Carbondale*
Kim Casey, *Northwest Missouri State University*
Christopher Chapp, *University of Wisconsin, Whitewater*
Daniel Coffey, *University of Akron*
William Corbett, *University of Texas at El Paso*
Jonathan Day, *Western Illinois University*
Rebecca Deen, *University of Texas, Arlington*
Brian DiSarro, *California State University, Sacramento*
Nelson Dometrius, *Texas Tech University*
Stan Dupree, *College of the Desert*
David Edwards, *University of Texas, Austin*
Ryan Emenaker, *College of the Redwoods*
John Evans, *University of Wisconsin, Eau Claire*
Brandon Franke, *Blinn College, Bryan*
Rodd Freitag, *University of Wisconsin, Eau Claire*
Donna Godwin, *Trinity Valley Community College*
Craig Goodman, *Texas Tech University*

Amy Gossett, *Lincoln University*
Tobin Grant, *Southern Illinois University*
Stephanie Hallock, *Harford Community College*
Alexander Hogan, *Lone Star College, CyFair*
Marvin King, *University of Mississippi*
Timothy LaPira, *James Madison University*
Mary Linder, *Grayson University*
Christine Lipsmeyer, *Texas A&M University*
Michael Lyons, *Utah State University*
Jill Marshall, *University of Texas, Arlington*
Thomas Masterson, *Butte College*
Daniel Matisoff, *Georgia Institute of Technology*
Jason McDaniel, *San Francisco State University*
Mark McKenzie, *Texas Tech University*
Leonard McNeil, *Contra Costa College*
Melissa Merry, *University of Louisville*
Ann Mezzell, *Lincoln University*
Eric Miller, *Blinn College, Bryan*
Jonathan Morris, *East Carolina University*
Leah Murray, *Weber State University*
Farzeen Nasri, *Ventura College*
Brian Newman, *Pepperdine University*
David Nice, *Washington State University*
Stephen Nichols, *Cal State University, San Marcos*
Tim Nokken, *Texas Tech University*
Barbara Norrander, *University of Arizona*
Andrew Reeves, *Boston University*
Michelle Rodriguez, *San Diego Mesa College*
Dan Smith, *Northwest Missouri State University*
Christopher Soper, *Pepperdine University*
Jim Startin, *University of Texas, San Antonio*
Jeffrey Stonecash, *Syracuse University*
Linda Trautman, *Ohio University*
Kevin Unter, *University of Louisiana, Monroe*
Michelle Wade, *Northwest Missouri State University*
Michael Wagner, *University of Nebraska, Lincoln*
Adam Warber, *Clemson University*
Wayne Wolf, *South Suburban College*

FOURTH EDITION REVIEWERS

Rickert Althaus, *Southeast Missouri State University*
Eric K. Austin, *Montana State University*
Evelyn Ballard, *Houston Community College Southeast*
Jim Battista, *SUNY-Buffalo*
Kenneth C. Blanchard Jr., *Northern State University*
Heidi Brockmann, *United States Military Academy*
Adriana Buliga-Stoian, *Mount Mercy University*

Abbe Allen DeBolt, *Sandhills Community College*
John C. Evans, *University of Wisconsin - Eau Claire*
Babette Faehmel, *Schenectady County Community College*
Daniel Fuerstman, *State College of Florida*
Stephanie Hallock, *Harford Community College*
John Hitt, *North Lake College*
Debra Jenke, *Angelina College*
Ronald A. Kuykendall, *Trident Technical College*
Paul Lewis, *Arizona State University*
Mary Linder, *Grayson College*
Michael Lyons, *Utah State University*
Wendy Martinek, *SUNY-Binghamton*
Melissa Merry, *University of Louisville*
Javan "J. D." Mesnard, *Mesa Community College*
Monique Mironesco, *University of Hawai'i, West O'ahu*
Tim Nokken, *Texas Tech University*
David Parker, *Montana State University*
Sylvia Peregrino, *El Paso Community College*
Blayne Primozich, *El Paso Community College*
Bryan Rasmussen, *Collin College*

Suzanne M. Robbins, *George Mason University*
Susan Roomberg, *University of Texas at San Antonio*
Michael Shamgochian, *Worcester State University*
Geoffrey Shine, *Wharton County Junior College*
Rachel Milstein Sondheimer, *United State Military Academy*
Gregory Streich, *University of Central Missouri*
Jeremy Teigen, *Ramapo College*
Dave Wells, *Arizona State University*

It is a humbling experience to have so many smart people involved in the process. Their reviews were often critical, but always insightful, and we have been fortunate to have them guide our revisions. In many cases, the improvements in this edition are the direct result of their suggestions. They have our profound thanks.

William T. Bianco
David T. Canon
November 2014

American Politics Today

FOURTH EDITION

1

Understanding American Politics

The Responsible Consumer's Guide to

Marijuana
in ◐olorado

Proud

UNTIL RECENTLY, THE POSSESSION AND SALE OF MARIJUANA was a serious crime under federal and state law, one that put many Americans in prison. Over the last decade, however, laws at the state level have been weakened, ignored, or even abolished. As of late 2014, 23 states had decriminalized the use of marijuana for medical purposes. Four states—Alaska, Colorado, Oregon, and Washington—had legalized the growth, sale, and possession of marijuana, and many other states were considering legalization through legislation or referenda.

The legalization of marijuana illustrates one of the central themes of this book: politics is conflictual. The changes in state law do not imply that all or even most Americans favor decriminalization. Recent national polls show that Americans are almost equally divided on legalization, with a sharp split between Republicans (generally opposed) and Democrats (generally in favor). Moreover, most of the states that have made moves toward decriminalization and legalization are either moderately to strongly Democratic (Washington, Colorado) or Republican with a libertarian bent (Alaska, Maine). If the rift between the parties on this issue persists, it will likely limit the number of states that change their laws, as well as affect whether those states will only allow medical marijuana or will also approve its recreational use.

CONFLICT & COMPROMISE
in American Politics

CHAPTER *goals*

Describe the basic functions of government.
► PAGES 5–8

Define politics and identify three key ideas that help explain politics.
► PAGES 9–16

Identify major sources of conflict in American politics.
► PAGES 16–21

Explain how the American values of democracy, liberty, and equality work to resolve political conflict.
► PAGES 21–23

Marijuana legalization also illustrates a second theme of the book: the political process matters. At present, the legality of marijuana depends on where you live, which follows from the fact that each state has its own criminal code. Moreover, even as legalization occurs at the state level, federal laws that criminalize marijuana are still in place. While it is highly unlikely that federal agents will seek to arrest marijuana producers and buyers in states where legalization has occurred, they could. In fact, federal banking regulators had to issue a special notice informing banks that they could do business with marijuana producers and retailers without putting themselves in legal jeopardy. In other words, the legality of marijuana is still in question—even in the states that have changed their laws. This complexity is the result of a provision in our Constitution called federalism that gives the federal government power over the states in many areas, but limits the federal government's ability to override state laws (see Chapter 3). As a result, the rights you have and the laws you are subject to vary across the 50 states.

The legalization of marijuana shows how digging below the surface of political events can help to explain why things happen in American politics—and why conflict is natural. Our goal is to give you a similar understanding of American politics more broadly. Much of that understanding will come from the idea that politics is conflictual. People shy away from conflict in their personal lives and tend to see conflict in politics as a problem. Yet, ironically, they often view political compromise as "selling out," "caving in," or giving up on core values and principles. Because Americans disagree on what to do about many issues, conflict is actually an essential part of politics, and compromise is usually needed to enact changes in government policy or to resolve deep conflicts.

CONFLICTS WITHIN THE government—say, between the Democrats and Republicans in Congress—often reflect real divisions among American citizens about what government should do about certain issues. Groups on all sides of controversial issues pressure the government to enact their preferred policies.

MAKING SENSE OF AMERICAN GOVERNMENT AND POLITICS

The premise of this book is simple: *American politics makes sense.* What happens in elections, in Washington, D.C., and everywhere else—even the legalization of marijuana—has a logical and often simple explanation.

This claim may seem unrealistic or even naive. On the surface, American politics is full of bewildering complexities, from the powers explicitly set forth in the Constitution to the unwritten rules that govern how Congress works. Many policy questions, from confronting economic crises to deciding what to do about climate change, seem hopelessly intractable. As our chapter opening story suggested, conflict between state and national laws may create confusion about what is legal or illegal. Election outcomes may look random or even chaotic.

Many people, we believe, have given up on American politics because they don't understand the political process, feel helpless to influence election outcomes or policy making, and believe that politics is irrelevant to their lives. As in the case of legalizing marijuana, many people are thrilled but others are angry about changes in the law and see this as more evidence that politicians are not listening to them. Since you are taking a class on American politics, we hope you have not given up on politics entirely. It is *not* our goal to turn you into a political junkie or a policy expert. And it isn't necessary to be completely immersed in politics to make sense of it, but we hope that after finishing this book you will have a basic understanding of the political process.

One goal of this book is to help you take an active role in the political process. A functioning democracy allows citizens to defer complicated policy decisions to their elected leaders, but it also requires citizens to monitor what those politicians are doing and to hold them accountable at the voting booth. This book will help you accomplish this important duty by providing the analytical skills you need to make sense of politics, even when it initially appears senseless.

We are not going to spend much time talking about how American politics should be. Rather, our focus will be on explaining American politics as it is. Here are some other questions we will examine:

▶ Why do some people participate in the political system while others do not?

▶ How does the Constitution structure our rights and liberties and the broader political system?

▶ Why do people vote as they do?

▶ Why do so many people mistrust politicians and the political system?

▶ Why do most members of Congress get reelected?

▶ How do Supreme Court justices decide cases?

▶ Why do presidents sometimes appear all-powerful but look powerless at other times?

▶ How much do the media, interest groups, judges, and bureaucrats influence policy decisions and why?

We will answer these questions and many others by applying three key ideas about the nature of politics: politics is conflictual, political process matters, and politics is everywhere. But first, we begin with an even more basic question: Why do we have a government?

TWO IMPORTANT GOVERNMENT FUNCTIONS described in the Constitution are to "provide for the common defence" and "insure domestic Tranquility." The military and local police are two of the most commonly used forces the government maintains to fulfill those roles.

WHY DO WE HAVE A GOVERNMENT?

government The system for implementing decisions made through the political process.

As we prepare to address this question, let's agree on a definition: **government** is the system for implementing decisions made through the political process. All countries have some form of government, which in general serves two broad purposes: to provide order and to promote the general welfare.

TO PROVIDE ORDER At a basic level, the answer to the question "Why do we have a government?" seems obvious: without government there would be chaos.

As the seventeenth-century British philosopher Thomas Hobbes said, life in the "state of nature" (that is, without government) would be "solitary, poor, nasty, brutish, and short."[1] Without government there would be no laws—people could do whatever they wanted. Even if people tried to develop informal rules, there would be no way to guarantee enforcement of those rules.

The Founders of the United States noted this crucial role in the document's preamble: two of the central goals of government are to "provide for the common defence" and to "insure domestic Tranquility." The former refers to military protection against foreign invasion and the defense of our nation's common security interests. The latter refers to law enforcement within the nation, which today includes the National Guard, Federal Bureau of Investigation (FBI), Department of Homeland Security, state and local police, and the courts. So at a minimal level, government is necessary to provide security.

However, there's more to it than that. The Founders cited the desire to "establish Justice . . . and secure the Blessings of Liberty to ourselves and our Posterity." But do we need government to do these things? It may be obvious that the police power of the nation is required to prevent anarchy, but can't people have justice and liberty without government? In a perfect world, maybe, but the Founders had a more realistic view of human nature. As James Madison, one of the founding fathers (and the fourth president of the United States), said, "But what is government itself, but the greatest of all reflections on human nature? If men were angels, no government would be necessary. If angels were to govern men, neither external nor internal controls on government would be necessary."[2] Furthermore, Madison continued, people have a variety of interests that have "divided mankind into parties, inflamed them with mutual animosity, and rendered them much more disposed to vex and oppress each other than to co-operate for their common good."[3] That is, without government, we would quickly be headed toward Hobbes's nasty and brutish state of nature.

Madison's view of human nature might sound pessimistic, but it was also realistic. He assumed that people were self-interested: we want what is best for ourselves and for our families, and to satisfy those interests we tend to form groups with like-minded people. Madison saw these groups, which he called **factions**, as being opposed to the public good, and his greatest fear was of tyranny by a faction imposing its will on the rest of the nation. For example, if one group took power and established an official state religion, that faction would be tyrannizing people who practiced a different religion. This type of oppression is precisely why many of the early American colonists fled Europe in the first place.

So government is necessary to avoid the anarchy of the state of nature, and the right kind of government is needed to avoid oppression by whoever controls the policy-making process. As we will discuss in Chapters 2 and 3, America's government seeks to control the effects of factions by dividing government power in three main ways. First, the **separation of powers** divides the government into three branches—judicial, executive, and legislative—and assigns distinct duties to each branch. Second, the system of **checks and balances** gives each branch some power over the other two. (For example, the president can veto legislation passed by Congress; Congress can impeach the president; and the Supreme Court has the power to interpret laws written by Congress to determine whether they are constitutional.) Third, **federalism** divides power yet again by allotting different responsibilities to local, state, and national government. With power divided in this fashion, Madison reasoned, no single faction could dominate the government.

TO PROMOTE THE GENERAL WELFARE The preamble to the Constitution also states that the federal government exists to "promote the general Welfare." This means tackling the hard problems that Americans cannot solve on their own, such as taking care of the poor, the sick, or the aged, and dealing with global issues like climate change, terrorist threats, and poverty in other countries. However, government intervention is not inevitable—people can decide that these problems aren't worth solving. But if people *do* want to address these large problems, government action is necessary because **public goods** such as these are not efficiently provided by the free market, either because of **collective action problems** or other reasons.

It is easy for two people or even a small group to tackle a common problem without the help of government, but 1,000 people (to say nothing of the more than 320 million in the United States today) would have a very difficult time. They would suffer from the **free rider problem**—that is, because it is in everyone's own interest to let someone else do the work while shirking the work oneself, the danger is that no one will contribute, even though everyone wants the outcome that collective contributions would create. A government representing 320 million people can provide public goods, such as protecting the environment or defending the nation, that all those people acting on their own would be unable to provide, so they elect leaders and pay taxes to provide those public goods.

factions Groups of like-minded people who try to influence the government. American government is set up to avoid domination by any one of these groups.

separation of powers The division of government power across the judicial, executive, and legislative branches.

checks and balances A system in which each branch of government has some power over the others.

federalism The division of power across the local, state, and national levels of government.

public goods Services or actions (such as protecting the environment) that, once provided to one person, become available to everyone. Government is typically needed to provide public goods because they will be underprovided by the free market.

collective action problems Situations in which the members of a group would benefit by working together to produce some outcome, but each individual is better off refusing to cooperate and reaping benefits from those who do the work.

free rider problem The incentive to benefit from others' work without making a contribution, which leads individuals in a collective action situation to refuse to work together.

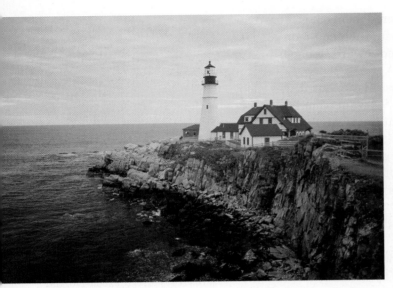

Collective action problems are common in modern society. Education is a great example. You benefit personally from your college education in terms of the knowledge and experience you gain, and perhaps from the higher salary you will earn because of your college degree. However, society also benefits from your education. Your employer will benefit from your knowledge and skills, as will people you interact with. If education were solely provided by the free market, those who could afford schooling would be educated, but the rest would not, leaving a large segment of society with little or no education and therefore unemployable. So, public education, like many important services, benefits all levels of society and must be provided by the government for the general welfare.

A LIGHTHOUSE IS A CLASSIC example of a public good—a service or product that could not be produced by private markets because once the good is provided, anyone can benefit from it without paying. Supplying public goods is one way that the government promotes the public welfare.

Now that we understand *why* we have a government, the next question is: *What* does the government do to "insure domestic Tranquility" and "promote the general Welfare"? Many visible components of the government promote these goals, from the police and armed services to the Internal Revenue Service, Federal Reserve, Postal Service, Social Security Administration, National Aeronautics and Space Administration, Department of Education, and the Food and Drug Administration. In fact, it is hard to find an aspect of everyday life that does not involve the government in some way, either as a provider of public goods, such as national defense, interstate highways, and national parks, as a protector of civil liberties, as an enforcer of laws and property rights, or as a regulator of individual or corporate behavior.

FORMS OF GOVERNMENT

While all governments must provide order and promote the general welfare, there are different types of governments. Greek political philosopher Aristotle, writing in the fourth century BC, developed a classification scheme for governments that is still surprisingly useful today. Aristotle distinguished three pure types of government based on the number of rulers versus the number of people ruled: monarchy (rule by one), aristocracy (rule by the few), and polity (rule by the many—such as the general population).

Additional distinctions can be made within Aristotle's third type—constitutional republican governments—based on how they allocate power among the executive, legislative, and judicial branches. Presidential systems such as we have in the United States tend to follow a separation of power among the three branches, while parliamentary systems such as the one in the United Kingdom elect the chief executive from the legislature so there is much closer coordination between those two branches.

We can further refine Aristotle's third type by considering the relationships among different levels of the government. In a federal system such as the United States, power is shared among the local, state, and national levels of government. In a unitary system, all power is held at the national level. A confederation is a less common form of government in which states retain their sovereignty and autonomy but form a loose association at the national level.

WHAT IS POLITICS?

We define **politics** as the process that determines what government does. You may consider politics the same thing as government, but we view politics as being much broader; it includes ways of behaving and making decisions that are common in everyday life. Many aspects of our discussion of politics will probably sound familiar because your life involves politics on a regular basis. This may sound a little abstract, but it should become clear in light of the three key ideas of this book (see the How It Works graphic in this chapter).

politics The process that determines what government does.

First, *politics is conflictual.* As the debate over legalizing marijuana illustrates, the questions debated in election campaigns and in Washington and the options considered by policy makers generally involve disagreement at all levels. The federal government does not spend much time resolving issues that everyone agrees should be decided in a particular way. Rather, making government policy involves issues on which people disagree, sometimes strongly, which makes compromise difficult—and this is a normal, healthy part of politics. Although compromise may be difficult, it is often necessary to produce an outcome that can be enacted and implemented.

Second, *political process matters.* Governmental actions don't happen by accident—they result from conscious choices made by elected officials and bureaucrats. Politics, as the process that determines what governments do, puts certain individuals into positions of power and makes the rules that structure their choices. The media often cover political campaigns the way they would report on a boxing match or the Super Bowl, focusing on the competition, rivalries, and entertaining stories, which can lead people to overlook the institutions, rules, and procedures that have a decisive influence on politics. Indeed, the political process is the mechanism for resolving conflict. The most obvious example of the political process at work is elections, which democracies use to resolve a fundamental conflict in society: deciding who should lead the country.

Third, *politics is everywhere.* Decisions about what government should do or who should be in charge are integral to society, and they influence the everyday lives of all Americans. Politics helps to determine what people can and cannot do, their quality of life, and how they think about events, people, and situations. Moreover, people's political thought and behavior are driven by the same types of calculations and decision-making rules that shape beliefs and actions in other parts of life. For example, deciding which presidential candidate to vote for is similar to deciding which college to attend. In the first instance, you might consider issue positions, character, and leadership ability, while in the latter you would weigh which school fits your academic goals, how much tuition you can afford, and where different schools are located. In both cases you are making a decision that will satisfy the criteria most important to you.

POLITICS IS CONFLICTUAL

Political scientists have long recognized the central role of conflict in politics. In fact, one prominent theory in the mid-twentieth century saw conflict between interest groups as explaining most outcomes in American politics. The political scientist E. E. Schattschneider argued that the scope of political conflict—that is, how many people are involved in the fight—determines who wins in politics. Others have argued that some conflict is essential for small-group decision making: if nobody challenges a widely shared but flawed view, people may convince themselves that the obvious flaws are not a problem. Bureaucratic politics, congressional politics, elections, and even Supreme Court decision making have all been studied through the lens of political conflict.[4]

Despite the consensus that conflict in politics is essential, most people do not like conflict, either in their personal lives or in politics. You probably have heard people say that the three topics one should not discuss in polite company are money, religion, and politics. Rather than talking about controversial subjects, many people simply avoid them. Indeed, since the 1950s, political scientists have found strong evidence that people avoid discussing politics in order to maintain social harmony.[5]

Many people apply their disdain for conflict to politicians as well. "Why is there so much partisan bickering?" our students frequently ask. "Why can't they just get along?" Many such comments were voiced during negotiations over the debt limit and government shutdown in 2013, and during many other legislative fights in recent years.

This dislike of conflict, and of politics more generally, produces a desire for what political scientists John Hibbing and Elizabeth Theiss-Morse call "stealth democracy"—that is, nondemocratic practices such as running government like a business or taking action without political debate. In essence, this idea reflects the hope that everything would be better if we could just take the politics out of politics. Hibbing and Theiss-Morse argue that, to combat this belief, we need to do a better job of educating people about conflict and policy differences, and that the failure to do so "is encouraging students to conclude that real democracy is unnecessary and stealth democracy will do just fine."[6] Conflict cannot be avoided in politics; ignoring fundamental disagreements will not make conflict go away.

Instead of pretending that we agree on most policies and that conflict is unnecessary, Americans must recognize that political conflict is inevitable because it is rooted in our disagreements on policy questions. It is wrong-headed to claim

CONFLICT IS INHERENT IN AMERICAN politics, a fact that has been driven home by the ongoing national debate over health care reform. Here, both supporters and opponents of the Affordable Care Act demonstrate in front of the Supreme Court as the justices hear legal arguments over the constitutionality of the act.

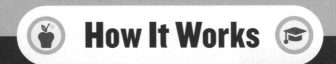 **How It Works**

THREE KEY IDEAS FOR UNDERSTANDING POLITICS

POLITICS IS CONFLICTUAL

Conflict and compromise are natural parts of politics.

Political conflict over issues like the national debt, abortion, and health care reflects disagreements among the American people and often requires compromises within government.

POLITICAL PROCESS MATTERS

How political conflicts are resolved is important.

Elections determine who represents citizens in government. Rules and procedures determine who has power in Congress and other branches of government.

POLITICS IS EVERYWHERE

What happens in government affects our lives in countless ways.

Policies related to jobs and the economy, food safety and nutrition, student loans, and many other areas shape our everyday lives. We see political information in the news and encounter political situations in many areas of our lives.

POP QUIZ

1 The rule that the president must receive a majority of votes in the electoral college (not just the most votes from citizens) illustrates the idea that

  a politics is conflictual.

  b political process matters.

  c politics is everywhere.

  d the government has police powers.

  e the government promotes the general welfare.

2 The fact that virtually no one got exactly what they wanted in the recent health care law (the Affordable Care Act) illustrates the idea that

  a politics is conflictual.

  b political process matters.

  c politics is everywhere.

  d the government has police powers.

  e the government promotes the general welfare.

Answers: 1.b; 2.a

WHEN EVERYONE (OR ALMOST
everyone) agrees about what
government should do to
solve a problem, the issue is
generally dealt with quickly and
without much conflict. In the
1980s, general consensus was
reached over how to deal with
chlorofluorocarbons (chemicals
once used in aerosol cans), and
they were banned. Controversial
issues, on the other hand, tend
to stay with us and result in
protracted political conflict.

that there would be no conflict in politics if politicians would just listen to the public—after all, Americans themselves are generally divided on what public policy should look like.

The argument over abortion is a good example. Abortion rights have been a perennial topic of debate since a 1973 Supreme Court decision held that state laws banning abortion were unconstitutional. Surveys about abortion rights show that public opinion spans a wide range of policy options, with little agreement about which policy is best. (In Chapter 6, we will examine the political implications of this kind of broad disagreement.) Such conflicts reflect intense differences of opinion that are rooted in self-interest, ideology, and personal beliefs. Moreover, in such situations, no matter what Congress does, many people will be unhappy with the result. You might expect that politicians will ultimately find a compromise that satisfies everyone, but this is not always true. In many cases, no single policy choice satisfies even a slight majority of elected officials or citizens.

The idea that conflict is nearly always a part of politics should be no surprise. Situations in which everyone (or almost everyone) agrees about what government should be doing are easy to resolve: either a popular new policy is enacted or an unpopular issue is avoided, and the debate moves off the political agenda. Although issues where there is consensus resolve quickly and disappear, conflictual issues remain on the agenda as the winners try to extend their gains and the losers work to roll back policies. Thus, one reason that abortion rights is a perennial issue in campaigns and congressional debates is that there is no national consensus on when to allow abortions, no indication that the issue is becoming less important to citizens or elected officials, and no sign of a compromise policy that would attract widespread support.

An important consequence of the inevitable conflicts in American politics is that compromise and bargaining are essential to getting things done. Politicians who bargain with opponents are not necessarily abandoning their principles; striking a deal may be the only way to make some of the policy changes they want. Moreover, agreement sometimes exists even in the midst of controversy. For example, surveys that measure attitudes about abortion find widespread support for measures such as prohibiting government funding for abortions, requiring parental notification when a minor has an abortion, or requiring doctors who perform the procedure to present their patients with information on alternatives such as adoption.

Another consequence of conflict is that it is almost impossible to get exactly what you want from the political process. Even when a significant percentage of the population is united behind common goals—such as supporters of Barack Obama after the 2012 election, who favored immigration reform and additional control on handguns, or Tea Party sympathizers, who wanted to shrink government and repeal Obamacare—these individuals almost always find that they need to accept something short of their ideal to attract enough support to implement policy change. Tea Party sympathizers, for example, had to accept that Obamacare was here to stay, at least for the moment. The need for compromise does not mean that change is impossible, only that what is achievable often falls short of individuals' demands.

Finally, it is important to note that we are not arguing that all conflict is good. For example, the scream fests on cable news and obstruction for the sake of obstruction in Congress do not serve the greater public good. Our point here—as it is throughout this book—is simply that conflict and compromise are inherent parts of politics.

POLITICAL PROCESS MATTERS

The political process is often described like a sporting event, with a focus on strategies and ultimately on "winning." In fact, a political news show on CNN has a daily segment titled "The Play of the Day." This focus overlooks an important point: politics is the process that determines what government does, none of which is inevitable. Public policy—everything from defending the nation to spending on Medicare—is up for grabs. And the political process determines these government actions. It is not just a game.

Elections are an excellent example of the importance of the political process. Elections allow voters to give fellow citizens the power to enact laws, write budgets, and appoint senior bureaucrats and federal judges—so it does matter who gets elected. After the 2008 election, when Democrats captured control of Congress and the presidency, they enacted a massive economic stimulus package and new policies for alternative energy, global warming, education, health care, regulation of the mortgage and financial sectors, and the plan for fighting the wars in Iraq and Afghanistan. Clearly, political process matters: if the 2008 election had gone the other way, policies in all these important areas would have been significantly different. Obama's reelection in 2012 meant that these changes would be almost impossible to undo, at least until the next presidential election in 2016. Again, elections matter.

Yet, politics is more than elections. As you will see, many members of the federal bureaucracy have influence over what government does by virtue of their roles in developing and implementing government policies. The same is true for federal judges, who review government actions to see if they are consistent with the Constitution and other federal laws. These individuals' decisions are part of the political process, even though they are not elected to their positions.

Ordinary citizens are also part of politics. They can vote; donate time or money to interest groups, party organizations, or individual candidates; or demand action from these groups or individuals. Such actions can influence government policy, either by determining who holds the power to change policy directly or by signaling to policy makers which options have public support.

Another important element of politics is the web of rules and procedures that determines who has the power to make choices about government policy. These rules range from the requirement that the president must have been born in the United States, to the rules that structure debates and voting in the House and the Senate, to the procedures for approving new federal regulations. Seemingly innocuous rules can have an enormous impact on what can or does happen, which means that choices about these rules are actually choices about outcomes.

Consider the cloture rule for ending debate in the Senate. It states that 60 out of 100 votes are needed to enact a new law, not just a simple majority of 51. Since the 2012 election, many significant proposals, such as gun control legislation, failed to advance in the Senate— although the measures had majority support, they could not pass the 60-vote hurdle. The Democratic majority in the Senate complained bitterly about the Republicans'

THE POLITICAL PROCESS MATTERED in the 2012 presidential election, from determining who the candidates would be, to affecting which states received the most attention from the campaigns. Here, President Barack Obama is shown debating Governor Mitt Romney. In this town hall–style debate, the public asked the candidates questions on domestic and foreign policy issues.

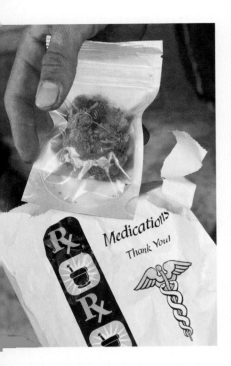

ORDINARY CITIZENS CAN INFLUENCE government policy. For example, in a citizen initiative, voters approved the Arizona Medical Marijuana Act, which legalized the use of medical marijuana. Pictured here is a legal prescription for marijuana from a medical marijuana dispensary in Glendale, Arizona.

willingness to block their initiatives. Even so, it is important to remember that the Democrats had behaved in exactly the same way from 2003 to 2007 during Republican George W. Bush's presidency, when Democrats were the minority party in the Senate.

As the cloture example implies, the ability to determine political rules empowers the people who make those choices. To paraphrase a favorite saying of former Representative John Dingell (D-MI), whose 60 years of service in Congress was a record, "If you let me decide procedure and I let you decide substance, I'll [beat] you every time."

POLITICS IS EVERYWHERE

Even though most Americans have little interest in politics, most of us encounter it every day. When you read the newspaper, watch TV, surf the Web, or listen to the radio you'll almost surely encounter a political story. When you are walking down the street, you may see billboards, bumper stickers, or T-shirts advertising a candidate, a political party, an interest group, or an issue position. Someone may ask you to sign a petition. You may walk past a homeless person and wonder whether a winning candidate followed through on her promise to help. You may glance at a headline about the continued violence in Iraq and Afghanistan and wonder whether members of Congress and the president were right to bring home our troops.

Many people have an interest in putting politics in front of us on a daily basis. Interest groups, political parties, and candidates work to raise public awareness of the political process and to shape what people know and want. Moreover, the news media offer extensive coverage of politics in stories about elections and governing and how government policies affect ordinary Americans. Through efforts like these, politics really is everywhere.

THE IDEA THAT "POLITICS IS everywhere" is evident when government policies influence highly personal decisions, such as those pertaining to marriage. Same-sex marriage has been controversial, and many states have passed laws and constitutional amendments defining marriage as being between a man and a woman. But in 2013, the Supreme Court ruled that the federal Defense of Marriage Act, which restricted marriage to heterosexual couples, was unconstitutional.

Politics is also a fundamental part of how Americans think about themselves. Virtually all of us can name our party identification (Democrat, Republican, or Independent)[7] and can place our views on a continuum between liberal and conservative.[8] Indeed, Americans often see the world through a partisan or ideological lens. For example, people are more likely to see economic conditions as favorable when the president is from their party.[9]

Politics is everywhere in another important way, too: actions by the federal government touch virtually every aspect of your life. Figure 1.1 shows a timeline for a typical college student on a typical day. As you can see, from the moment this student wakes up until the end of the day, his or her actions are influenced by federal programs, spending, and regulations. As you will see in later chapters, it's not surprising that the federal government touches your everyday life in many ways. The federal government is extraordinarily large regardless of whether you measure spending (nearly $4 trillion a year), number of employees (nearly 10 million if you include contractors and postal service workers), or new regulations (over 80,000 pages per year).[10]

Moreover, the idea that politics is everywhere has a deeper meaning: people's political behavior is similar to their behavior in the rest of their lives. For example, many voters form judgments about candidates by focusing on the candidates' appearance, including ethnic background, gender, or age. Such stereotyping also shapes people's judgments about individuals whom they meet in other areas of life. Also, consider that convincing like-minded individuals to contribute to a group's lobbying efforts is no easy task. Each would-be contributor of time or money also has the opportunity to be a free rider who refuses to participate yet reaps the benefits of others' participation. Because of these difficulties, some

FIGURE » 1.1

GOVERNMENT IN A STUDENT'S DAILY LIFE

On a typical day, the government plays a critical role in a student's daily life through federal programs, regulation, and spending.

Read weather reports that use data from National Weather Service

Ride home from school on federally subsidized mass transit

Eat cereal regulated by Food and Drug Administration

Drive past post office, military recruitment office, and environmental cleanup site

Call friend on cell phone whose operation is regulated by Federal Communications Commission

Wake Up   **Morning**   **Afternoon**   **Evening**   **Sleep**

Wake up in dorm funded by federal program

Check e-mail using Internet developed with federal funding

Attend lecture by professor whose research receives federal funding

Watch TV program on station that has federal license

Get dressed in clothing subject to import tariffs and regulations

Drive to school in car whose design is shaped by federal regulations

Pay bursar bill using federally funded student loan

groups of people with common goals remain unorganized. College students are a good example: many want more student aid and lower interest rates on government-subsidized student loans, but they fail to organize politically toward those ends.

Similar collective action problems occur when you live with roommates and need to keep common areas neat and clean: everyone has an interest in a clean area, but each person is inclined to let someone else do the work. The same principles help us to understand campus protests of tuition hikes, alcohol bans, or changes in graduation requirements in terms of which kinds of issues and circumstances foster cooperation. In each case, individual free riders acting in their own self-interest may undermine the outcome that most people prefer.

This similarity between behavior in political situations and in the rest of life is no surprise; everything that happens in politics is the result of individuals' choices. And the connections between politics and everyday life mean you already know more about politics than you realize.

WHAT DO POLITICAL SCIENTISTS DO?

To learn about how political scientists conduct research, visit **wwnpag.es/wdpsd**

> IDENTIFY MAJOR SOURCES OF CONFLICT IN AMERICAN POLITICS

SOURCES OF CONFLICT IN AMERICAN POLITICS

Where does political conflict come from? As mentioned earlier, most people avoid conflict, so you might think politicians would try to minimize it. The reality is that conflict must be addressed in order to find compromise and enact policy. Sometimes, however, disagreements resist resolution because of inherent differences among people and their opinions about government and politics.

ECONOMIC INTERESTS

People's economic interests today vary widely, and they constitute a source of conflict in politics. In contrast, relative economic equality was a defining characteristic of our nation's early history—at least among white men, since small landowners, businessmen, craftsmen, and their families constituted a large majority of the nation's population. Compared to our European counterparts, the United States has been relatively free from class-based politics. Over time, our nation has become more stratified by class, to the point that the United States has one of the highest levels of income inequality among developed nations.[11] Nonetheless, a commitment to the **free market** (an economic system based on competition among businesses without government interference) and to **economic individualism** (the autonomy of individuals to manage their own financial decisions without government interference) remains central to our national identity.

Despite this basic consensus on economic principles and a history relatively free of class-based politics, there are important differences among American citizens, interest groups, and political parties in terms of their economic interests and favored economic policies. As we discuss in Chapter 8, Democratic politicians and activists tend to favor more **redistributive tax policies** (that is, tax policies,

free market An economic system based on competition among businesses without government interference.

economic individualism The autonomy of individuals to manage their own financial decisions without government interference.

redistributive tax policies Policies, generally favored by Democratic politicians, that use taxation to attempt to create greater social equality (for example, higher taxation of the rich to provide programs for the poor).

such as taxing the rich at higher percentages than the middle class or the poor, that attempt to create greater social equality) and social spending on programs for the poor. Democrats are also more inclined to regulate industry to protect the environment and worker and product safety, but they tend to favor fewer restrictions on the personal behavior of individuals. Republicans favor lower taxes and less spending on social policies. They are also more supportive than Democrats of the free market and less inclined to interfere with business interests, although many Republicans favor regulation of individual behaviors, such as abortion rights and gay marriage.

CULTURAL VALUES

Another source of conflict in American politics is differing cultural values. For example, political analysts often focus attention on the **culture wars** in the United States between "red-state" Americans, who tend to have strong religious beliefs, and "blue-state" Americans, who tend to be more secular. (The color coding of the states comes from the election-night maps on television that show the states carried by Republican candidates in red and those won by Democrats in blue—but see Figure 1.2, "Purple America," for a more nuanced take on this).

culture wars Political conflict in the United States between "red-state" Americans, who tend to have strong religious beliefs, and "blue-state" Americans, who tend to be more secular.

Although the precise makeup and impact of "values voters" is still debated, there is no doubt that many Americans disagree on cultural and moral issues. These include the broad category of "family values" (such as whether and how to regulate pornography, gambling, and media obscenity and violence); whether to supplement the teaching of evolution in public schools with intelligent design and creationism; same-sex marriage; abortion; school prayer; the war on drugs; gun control; school vouchers; the federal Common Core curriculum for K–12 schools; and religious displays in public places. These are all hot-button issues that interest groups and activists on all sides attempt to keep at the top of the policy agenda.

RACIAL, GENDER, AND ETHNIC DIFFERENCES

CIVIL AND VOTING RIGHTS POLICIES contributed to the realignment of the South in the second half of the twentieth century, as more whites began supporting the Republican Party, and the Democratic Party came to be seen as the champion of minority rights. Here, blacks and whites in Alabama wait in line together to vote at a city hall after enactment of the 1965 Voting Rights Act.

Many political differences are correlated with racial, gender, and ethnic differences. For example, over the last generation, about 90 percent of African Americans have been strong supporters of Democratic candidates. Other racial groups have been less cohesive in their voting, with their support for a particular party ranging from 55 to 70 percent. Whites tend to vote Republican; Latinos tend to vote Democratic, with the exception of Cuban Americans, who tend to vote Republican; Asian Americans tend to support Democrats with about 70 percent of the vote. A gender gap in national politics is also evident, with women being somewhat more likely to vote for Democrats and men for Republicans.[12] Because these tendencies are not fixed, however, the political implications of racial, gender, and ethnic differences can change over time.

One of the enduring debates in American politics concerns whether ethnic and racial differences *should* be tied to political interests. One perspective reflects the melting pot image of America, which holds that as different racial and ethnic groups come to this country, they should mostly leave their native languages and customs behind. This perspective focuses on assimilation into American culture, with the belief that while immigrant groups will maintain some traditions from their native country, our common bonds as Americans are more important. Supporters of this view usually advocate making English the country's official language, oppose bilingual public education, and, if they favor immigration at all, prefer that it be restricted to well-off people from English-speaking countries.

However, there are varied alternatives to the melting pot view. These range from racial separatists such as the Nation of Islam, whose members see white-dominated society as oppressive and discriminatory, to multiculturalists, who argue that there is strength in diversity and embrace a "tossed salad" version of assimilation (that is, each ingredient remains distinct, but contributes to the overall quality of the salad).[13] In general, people holding this viewpoint favor less restrictive immigration laws and oppose policies that encourage immigrants to assimilate.

This debate over culture is one reason why recent discussions about immigration law have been so conflictual—the two sides start from very different premises about the value of diversity. But regardless of how this debate is resolved, our multiracial makeup is clear, as Table 1.1 shows. In fact, trends in population growth suggest that by 2042, whites will no longer constitute a majority of the U.S. population. The extent to which this diversity continues to be a source of political conflict depends on the broader role of race in our society. As long as there are racial differences in employment, education, health, housing, and crime, and as long as racial discrimination is present in our society, race will continue to be a source of political conflict.

Many of the same observations apply to gender and politics. The women's movement is usually viewed as beginning in 1848 at the first Women's Rights Convention at Seneca Falls, New York. The fight for women's suffrage and legal rights dominated the movement through the late nineteenth and early twentieth centuries. In the 1960s and 1970s, feminism and the women's liberation movement highlighted a broad range of issues: workplace issues such as maternity leave, equal pay, and sexual harassment; reproductive rights and abortion; domestic violence; and sexual violence. While progress has occurred on many fronts, gender remains an important source of political disagreement and identity politics.

TABLE » 1.1

THE RACIAL COMPOSITION OF THE UNITED STATES, 2012

Only about 75 percent of Americans describe themselves as white. Moreover, the proportion of Hispanics and Latinos in the population is 16.9 percent and rising, although this category contains many distinct subgroups.

RACE	NUMBER	PERCENT
Total U.S. population	**313,914,040**	**100**
White	231,992,377	73.9
Hispanic or Latino (any race)	52,961,017	16.9
Mexican	34,038,599	10.8
Puerto Rican	4,970,604	1.6
Cuban	1,957,557	0.6
Dominican	1,656,960	0.5
Other, Hispanic, or Latino	10,337,297	3.2
Black or African American	39,623,138	12.6
Asian	15,555,530	4.9
American Indian and Alaska Native	2,563,505	0.8
Native Hawaiian and Other Pacific Islander	543,198	0.1
Some other race	14,562,678	4.8
Two or more races	9,073,614	2.7

SOURCE: U.S. Census Bureau, 2012 American Community Survey. http://factfinder2.census.gov/faces/tableservices/jsf/pages/productview .xhtml?pid=ACS_12_1YR_B02001&prodType=table (accessed 4/8/14).

IDEOLOGY

Another source of differences in interests is **ideology**: a cohesive set of ideas and beliefs that allows an individual to organize and evaluate the political world. Ideology may seem most obviously related to political interests through political parties, since Republicans tend to be **conservative** and Democrats tend to be **liberal**. While this is true in a relative sense (most Republicans are more conservative than most Democrats), few Americans consider their own views ideologically extreme.[14]

Ideology shapes specific beliefs. Conservatives promote traditional social practices and favor lower taxes, a free market, and more-limited government, whereas liberals support social tolerance, stronger government programs, and more market regulation. However, the picture gets cloudy if we look more closely. **Libertarians**, for example, prefer very limited government—that is, they believe that the government should provide for the national defense and should only have a few other narrowly defined responsibilities. Because they are at the extreme end of the ideological continuum on this issue, libertarians are generally conservative on issues such as social welfare policy, environmental policy, and government funding for education, and generally liberal on issues involving personal liberty such as free speech, abortion, and the legalization of drugs. For libertarians, the consistent ideological theme is limiting the role of government in our lives.

ideology A cohesive set of ideas and beliefs used to organize and evaluate the political world.

conservative One side of the ideological spectrum defined by support for lower taxes, a free market, and a more-limited government; generally associated with Republicans.

liberal One side of the ideological spectrum defined by support for stronger government programs and more market regulation; generally associated with Democrats.

libertarians Those who prefer very limited government and therefore tend to be conservative on issues such as welfare policy, environmental policy, and public support for education, but liberal on issues of personal liberty such as free speech, abortion, and the legalization of drugs.

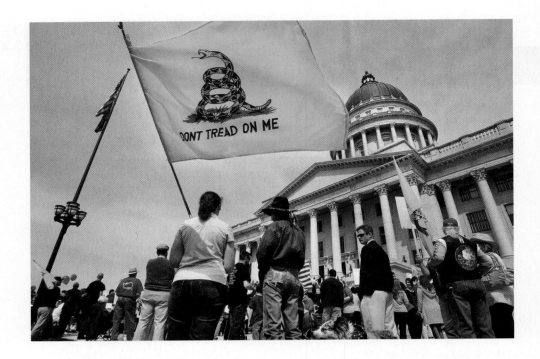

Personal ideologies are not always consistent. Someone can be both a fiscal conservative (favoring balanced budgets) and a social liberal (favoring the pro-choice position on abortion and marital rights for gay men and lesbians), or a liberal on foreign policy issues (supporting humanitarian aid and opposing the war in Afghanistan) and a conservative on moral issues (being pro-life on abortion and opposing stem-cell research). Ideology is a significant source of conflict in politics, and it does not always operate in a straightforward manner. In Chapter 6, we explore whether America is becoming more ideological and polarized, deepening our conflicts and making compromise more difficult.

Even so, there are clear areas of agreement in American politics, even on issues that once divided us. For example, while there is still considerable disagreement over same-sex marriage, public opinion has clearly shifted toward making such unions legal. Along the same lines, two generations ago, Americans were divided on the legality of mixed-race marriage, while today very few people would object. Thus, even though conflict is a constant in American politics, it is wrong to say that we are divided into two groups, red and blue, that oppose each other on all issues of significance.

Figure 1.2 illustrates this finding with data from the 2012 presidential election. The map shows the relative strength by state of Mitt Romney and Barack Obama, with the reddest states showing the strongest Republican support and the bluest states showing the Democratic strongholds. As you can see, however, most of the country is purple, which indicates a geographic intermixing between the parties and their associated ideological beliefs. One interesting thing about the purple map is that, even in very Republican states such as Texas, Mississippi, and Alabama, there are some very blue areas and, in strong Democratic states such as California and New York, there are plenty of red counties. Thus, the typical "red and blue" map of the United States that you see on election night is misleading on two levels: the country is much more purple than red or blue and within most states there is a great deal of partisan diversity.

FIGURE » 1.2

PURPLE AMERICA: THE 2012 PRESDENTIAL ELECTION

The media create maps of the country on election night to indicate which states voted Republican (shown in red) and which states voted Democratic (shown in blue). But the reality is that in all states, some people were voting Republican while others were voting Democratic, hence leading to the "purple" shown on the map.

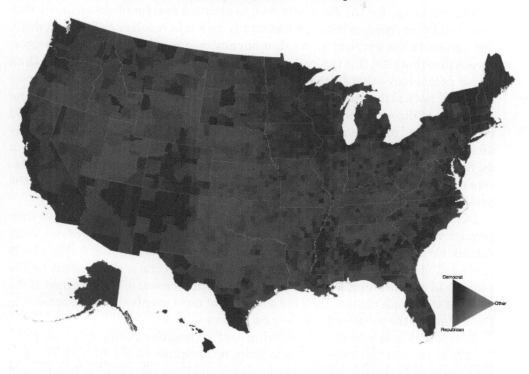

SOURCE: Provided by Robert J. Vanderbei, Princeton University, "2012 Presidential Election, Purple America," www.princeton.edu/~rvdb/JAVA/election2012 (accessed 11/10/12).

RESOLVING CONFLICT: DEMOCRACY AND AMERICAN POLITICAL VALUES

EXPLAIN HOW THE AMERICAN VALUES OF DEMOCRACY, LIBERTY, AND EQUALITY WORK TO RESOLVE POLITICAL CONFLICT

For any political system to survive, it must have the means to resolve conflict. One mechanism used by authoritarian governments is to suppress conflict though violence and limiting freedom. Some former Communist governments, such as North Korea and to a lesser extent China (China has some economic freedom but no political freedom), fascist governments, such as Hitler's Germany or Mussolini's Italy, or theocracies (which are governed by religiously based laws), such as Iran, all fit this description.

The alternative is to embrace conflict as a natural consequence of the differences between people and to embrace the political freedom to express views based on those differences. To the Founders, **liberty** was the central principle for their

liberty Political freedom, such as the freedom of speech, press, assembly, and religion. These and other legal and due process rights protecting individuals from government control are outlined in the Bill of Rights of the U.S. Constitution.

new government: they believed that people must have the freedom to express their political views. The Bill of Rights of the Constitution, discussed in Chapter 4, outlines the nature of those liberties: the freedom of speech, press, assembly, and religion, as well as many legal and due process rights protecting individuals from government control. James Madison recognized this essential trade-off between liberty and conflict. He argued that suppressing conflict by limiting freedom was "worse than the disease" (worse than conflict). Therefore, any political system with political freedom will have conflict.

The challenge for the Founders was to create a system of government that would embrace freedom while providing the means to resolve conflict: in a word, democracy. In the simplest terms, **democracy** means government by the people. As put into practice, this typically means representative democracy rather than direct democracy—that is, the people elect representatives who decide policies and pass laws rather than determining those things directly. There are some examples of direct democracy in the United States, such as the New England town meeting[15] and the referendum process, in which people in a state directly determine policy. But for the most part, Americans elect politicians to represent us, from school board and city council members at the local level, to state legislators and governors at the state level, to U.S. House members, Senators, and the president at the national level.

Democracy means resolving conflict through voting and elections rather than through violence or coercion. When the second president of the United States, John Adams, turned over power to his bitter rival, Thomas Jefferson, after losing a hotly contested election in 1800, it demonstrated that democratic government by the people had real meaning. Democracy depends on the consent of the governed: if the views of the people change, then the government must eventually be responsive to those views or the people will choose new leaders.

Democracy also means that resolving conflict requires compromise. In a dictatorship, totalitarian state, or a monarchy, no compromise is required. The government simply chooses its preferred policies and implements them. Any dissent is either ignored or quashed. Representative democracies must be more open to dissent, or they lose legitimacy. Given the broad range of interests outlined in the previous section, no single group can get its way all of the time. Having a functioning democracy means compromising on issues that we may care deeply about.

Despite the need for compromise, democracies are vulnerable to majority tyranny—that is, the majority that wins an election may suppress the liberties of the minority that loses. The Founders were very concerned about this tension between majority rule and minority rights. Our elaborate system of separation of powers and checks and balances (see Chapter 2) protects against majority tyranny.

Another principle of democracy is **equality**. Even though the Declaration of Independence boldly declared "all men are created equal," this did not mean that all people were entitled to the same income or even the same social status. Instead, the most widely embraced notion of equality is the equality of opportunity—that is, everyone should have the same chance to realize his or her potential. People will have different talents and abilities, but everyone should have an equal opportunity to pursue his or her interests.

Political equality also means that people are treated the same in the political system. Everyone has one vote in an election, and everyone is equal in the eyes of the law. In practice, that has not always been true. In our early history, only white men could vote, and in many states those men needed to be property owners in order to vote. Slowly, political equality expanded as property requirements were

democracy Government by the people. In most contexts, this means representative democracy in which the people elect leaders to enact policies. Democracies must have fair elections with at least two alternatives.

equality In the context of American politics, equality means equality before the law, political equality (one person, one vote), and equality of opportunity (the equal chance for everyone to realize their potential), but not material equality (equal income or wealth).

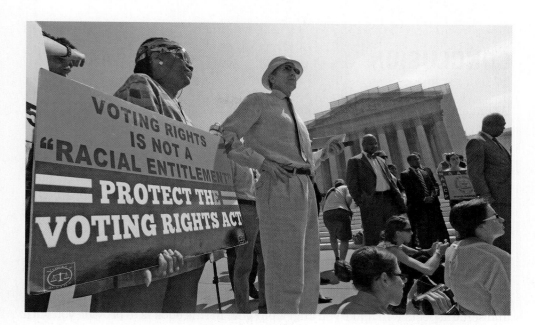

SUPPORTERS OF THE VOTING RIGHTS Act gather in front of the Supreme Court building in June 2013. Enacted in 1965, the act was intended to eliminate discrimination against black voters. In 2013, the Supreme Court ruled that federal review of state voting rules in certain areas of the country was no longer necessary, opening the door to new rules that would again serve to disenfranchise minority voters.

dropped, black men (in 1870, but restrictions persisted into the 1960s), women (in 1919), and 18- to 20-year-olds (in 1971) got the right to vote (for more on the expansion of the right to vote, see Chapter 5). Today, although wealthy people clearly can have their voices heard more easily than poor people (through campaign contributions or independent expenditures on political ads), the notion of political equality is central to our democracy.

Like democracy, political equality also contributes to resolving conflict. First, if people know that they will be treated equally by the political system, they are more likely to respect the system. Indeed, one of the triggers for revolutions around the world is reaction against rigged elections (for example, protests in Pakistan after the 2013 general elections). If people believe that the principle of "one person, one vote" is being ignored, they are less likely to respect election results. Second, political equality also suggests a consensus on basic values. As Louis Hartz famously argued in 1955, America is rooted in a consensus on the basic values of liberty, limited government, and property rights.[16] This basic agreement on core principles limited the scope of conflict so that the United States never had the extreme politics that were commonly observed in Europe. Americans have been more willing to grant each other political equality because there is more agreement on the basic boundaries of political debate. Again, this consensus does not imply there is no conflict—quite the contrary. However, conflict is easier to resolve if it is over a narrower range of options.

The American political values of democracy, liberty, and equality are central to thinking about and understanding American politics. Not surprisingly, they will come up throughout this book. You also might want to look out for them when you are watching the news or reading about national politics—you will find consistent references to these values throughout the media. When President Obama talks about the need to provide health care for all Americans, he is emphasizing equality. When supporters of gun rights speak out against gun control laws, they are exercising their liberties of speech and the right to bear arms. And continuous media coverage of the upcoming presidential election of 2016 is a reminder of the importance of elections in a democracy.

CONCLUSION

By understanding that politics is conflictual, that it is rooted in process, and that it is everywhere, you will see that modern American political life makes more sense than you might have thought. Along the way, you will learn important "nuts and bolts" of the American political process as well as some political history. In general, however, your reading in this book will focus on contemporary questions, debates, and examples to illustrate broader points about our nation's political system. After all, American politics in its current form is the politics that will have the greatest impact on your life. To return to the story at the beginning of the chapter, regardless of how you feel about the legalization of marijuana, you need to know how things work in order to understand why your preferred outcome won or lost—and to determine what actions you might take to help your cause.

Although you will no doubt disagree with some aspects of American politics, and some aspects will make you angry, our goal in this book is to provide you with the tools to understand *why* government operates as it does. We are not arguing that the federal government is perfect or that imperfect responses to policy problems are inevitable. Rather, we believe that any attempt to explain these outcomes, or to devise ways to prevent similar problems, requires an understanding of why they happened in the first place. After reading this book, you will have a better sense of how American politics works.

MAKING SENSE OF AMERICAN GOVERNMENT AND POLITICS

▶ *Describe the basic functions of government.* **(Pages 5–8)**

SUMMARY

Forms of government can be characterized by the number of people who hold power (many versus few) and the number of levels over which power is distributed (national versus state versus local). Government exists primarily to provide order, although it must do so while avoiding oppression by the rulers. Government also needs to provide public goods because they will be underprovided by the free market.

KEY TERMS

government (p. 6)
factions (p. 7)
separation of powers (p. 7)
checks and balances (p. 7)
federalism (p. 7)
public goods (p. 7)
collective action problems (p. 7)
free rider problem (p. 7)

CRITICAL THINKING AND DISCUSSION

What are some examples from your life that illustrate that "politics is everywhere"? How do government policies affect the things you do every day? Can you think of past decisions or experiences that you may not have viewed as political, but that illustrate this idea as well?

PRACTICE QUIZ QUESTIONS

1. What did Aristotle call "a government ruled by the many"?
   - A monarchy
   - B aristocracy
   - C polity
   - D unitary system
   - E democracy

2. Which term describes giving each branch of government power over the other two?
   - A separation of powers
   - B checks and balances
   - C federalism
   - D plutocracy
   - E unitary system

3. Which term describes the inability to get individuals to cooperate to achieve a common goal?
   - A positive externality
   - B the Samaritan's dilemma
   - C collective action problem
   - D principal-agent problem
   - E public goods

WHAT IS POLITICS?

▶ *Define politics and identify three key ideas that help explain politics.* **(Pages 9–16)**

SUMMARY

Conflict cannot be avoided in politics: the American people disagree on nearly every issue on which politicians make policy decisions. Compromise and bargaining are essential to enacting policy, but this means that it is almost impossible to get exactly what you want from the political process. Policy outcomes are also influenced by the policy process itself—different procedures of making policy can lead to different outcomes. Whether it is on the news or influencing most aspects of your life, politics is all around us.

KEY TERM

politics (p. 9)

CRITICAL THINKING AND DISCUSSION

Consider the observation by former Representative John Dingell (D-MI) that "If you let me decide procedure and I let you decide substance, I'll [beat] you every time." Do you think Dingell is right? What are some instances in which process was more important than substance in determining an outcome?

PRACTICE QUIZ QUESTIONS

4. What is the main reason why politicians have a hard time resolving the issue of abortion?
   - A Politicians don't listen to the people.
   - B The parties are divided on what abortion policy should look like.
   - C Politicians don't know what their constituents' views are.
   - D The country is divided on what abortion policy should look like.
   - E Abortion is a relatively new issue.

5. Which concept describes the idea that actions by the government touch most aspects of your life?

   Ⓐ Politics is understandable.

   Ⓑ Politics is conflictual.

   Ⓒ Political process matters.

   Ⓓ Politics is everywhere.

   Ⓔ People have different interests.

6. Rules such as those regulating debate in the Senate, or limiting who can vote in elections, serve as evidence that _____.

   Ⓐ politics is understandable

   Ⓑ politics is conflictual

   Ⓒ political process matters

   Ⓓ politics is everywhere

   Ⓔ people have different interests

SOURCES OF CONFLICT IN AMERICAN POLITICS

▶ *Identify major sources of conflict in American politics.* **(Pages 16–21)**

SUMMARY

Although Americans generally agree on a free market system, there is considerable conflict over how much the government should support tax policies that redistribute wealth. Conflict also arises on cultural grounds, pitting religious "red-state" Americans against the more secular "blue-state" Americans. There is also disagreement on the extent to which racial, gender, and ethnic diversity should be celebrated or minimized. Lastly, although Americans are not as polarized as one would think, liberals and conservatives come into conflict on ideological grounds.

KEY TERMS

free market (p. 16)
economic individualism (p. 16)
redistributive tax policies (p. 16)
culture wars (p. 17)
ideology (p. 19)
conservative (p. 19)
liberal (p. 19)
libertarians (p. 19)

CRITICAL THINKING AND DISCUSSION

What are your views on the role of conflict in politics? What types of issues are most likely to be resolved through political conflict and compromise, and which issues are more resistant to compromise?

PRACTICE QUIZ QUESTIONS

7. Democrats tend to favor _____ tax policies and are _____ inclined to regulate industry.

   Ⓐ redistributive; more

   Ⓑ conservative; more

   Ⓒ redistributive; less

   Ⓓ conservative; less

   Ⓔ regressive; less

8. Which issue is commonly associated with the culture wars?

   Ⓐ the national debt

   Ⓑ environmental regulation

   Ⓒ affirmative action

   Ⓓ the tax code

   Ⓔ same-sex marriage

9. An individual who opposes government social welfare policy and supports the legalization of drugs is most likely a _____.

   Ⓐ libertarian

   Ⓑ socialist

   Ⓒ Democrat

   Ⓓ Republican

   Ⓔ centrist

RESOLVING CONFLICT: DEMOCRACY AND AMERICAN POLITICAL VALUES

▶ *Explain how the American values of democracy, liberty, and equality work to resolve political conflict.* **(Pages 21–23)**

SUMMARY

Democracy, liberty, and equality are American political values that are essential for understanding how conflict is resolved. Representative democracies resolve conflict through elections rather than through violence. Although liberty ensures that people will have the freedom to express differing views—which can lead to conflict—democracy is the best system for resolving those conflicts. Political equality ensures that everyone is treated the same before the law and that all votes are equal, and the equality of opportunity means that every person has an equal chance to realize his or her potential.

KEY TERMS

liberty (p. 21)
democracy (p. 22)
equality (p. 22)

CRITICAL THINKING AND DISCUSSION

One could argue that a dictatorship is a much more efficient way to deal with conflict than the messiness of democracy. Given that having freedom means more conflict, would we be better off with less freedom? Or is the messiness of democracy worth it?

PRACTICE QUIZ QUESTIONS

10. Which type of equality is *not* typically agreed upon in American politics?

 A equality of opportunity

 B equality before the law

 C political equality

 D one person, one vote

 E material equality (such as equal income)

11. What did James Madison argue was "worse than the disease"?

 A giving too much power to state legislatures

 B allowing people to have too much freedom, which would lead to chaos

 C giving up liberty to get rid of conflict

 D allowing politicians to exercise their judgment rather than listen to the people

 E taking cod liver oil to treat various ailments

SUGGESTED READING

Dahl, Robert. *On Democracy*. New Haven, CT: Yale University Press, 1998.

Fiorina, Morris P., with Samuel J. Abrams and Jeremy C. Pope. *Culture War? The Myth of a Polarized America*, 2nd ed. New York: Pearson, Longman, 2006.

Gutman, Amy. *Identity in Democracy*. Princeton, NJ: Princeton University Press, 2003.

Schattschneider, E. E. *The Semisovereign People: A Realist's View of Democracy in America*. New York: Holt, Rinehart, and Winston, 1960.

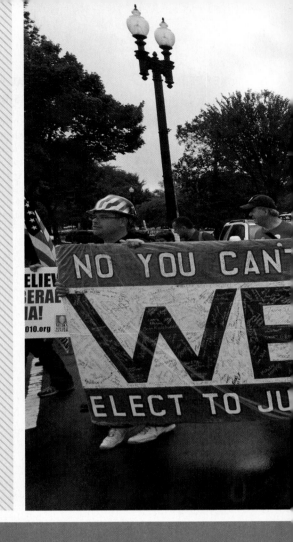

The Constitution and the Founding

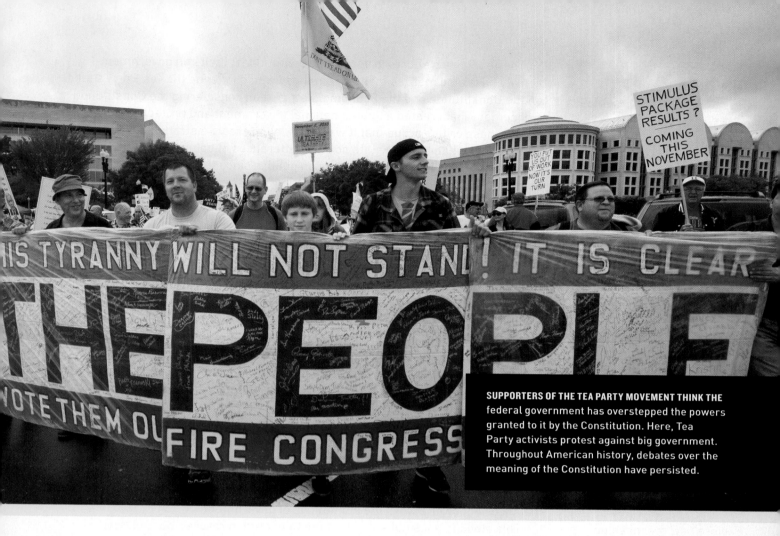

SUPPORTERS OF THE TEA PARTY MOVEMENT THINK THE federal government has overstepped the powers granted to it by the Constitution. Here, Tea Party activists protest against big government. Throughout American history, debates over the meaning of the Constitution have persisted.

ECENTLY, THE CONSTITUTION ITSELF HAS BECOME the focus of political debate and conflict. Starting in the 2010 midterm elections and continuing through the 2012 presidential election and the 2014 midterms, a popular movement known as the Tea Party has supported candidates who endorse a return to the Constitution's founding principles. Although the range of views within the Tea Party movement is vast, its supporters generally see the expansion of federal power—which began with Teddy Roosevelt, exploded during the New Deal of the 1930s and Great Society of the 1960s, and continues today with President Obama's health care reform—as constitutional overreach. Many Tea Party supporters see Social Security, Medicare, and the Federal Reserve System as unconstitutional because such policies are not expressly permitted by the Constitution. Jim DeMint, head of the conservative Heritage Foundation and a leading Tea Partier, wrote in 2010, "If President Obama's motto is 'Yes, we can,' the Constitution's is 'No, you can't.' . . . Although the Constitution does give some defined powers to the federal government, it is overwhelmingly a document of limits, and those limits must be respected."[1]

To draw more attention to the Constitution, members of Congress took turns reading the document from the floor at the start of the new session of the House of Representatives in 2011. It was the first time in U.S. history that the entire Constitution had been read aloud in Congress. But even this simple gesture proved to be controversial: former Representative Jesse Jackson, Jr. (D-Ill.) objected to the "whitewashing" of the document, as the reading excluded all portions of the Constitution that alluded to slavery.[2]

CONFLICT & COMPROMISE

in American Politics

CHAPTER *goals*

Describe the historical circumstances that led to the Constitutional Convention of 1787.

▶ PAGES 31–37

Analyze the major issues debated by the framers of the Constitution.

▶ PAGES 37–45

Contrast the arguments of the Federalists with those of the Antifederalists.

▶ PAGES 45–48

Outline the major provisions of the Constitution.

▶ PAGES 48–55

Explore how the meaning of the Constitution has evolved.

▶ PAGES 55–61

The Tea Party's efforts to establish constitutional limits on government activity have also met resistance from those who challenge the Tea Party's take on the Constitution and the Founding. Rather than considering the Constitution a document that created a limited national government and protected state power, these critics argue that it was intended to create a strong national government while limiting state power.[3] Differences of opinion about the Constitution have been part of American politics since the debates between the Federalists and Antifederalists over the ratification of the document. Unfortunately, the Constitution itself provides few definitive answers because its language was intentionally written to be general so it would stand the test of time. Consequently, in every major political debate in our history, both sides have claimed to ground their views in the Constitution. Abolitionists and secessionists during the pre–Civil War period, New Deal supporters and opponents, and civil rights activists and segregationists all claimed to have the Constitution on their side, whether the dispute was over a broad or narrow interpretation of the commerce clause, the Fourteenth Amendment, or the Tenth Amendment. Today's vigorous debate about the proper scope of the national government's powers is only the most recent chapter in this perpetual conflict.

The Constitution provides the basis for resolving conflict through elections and representative government rather than by taking up arms. Losers of one round of elections know that they have an opportunity to compete in the next election and that their voices can be heard in another part of the government. The peaceful transition of power and the stability in our political system may be attributed to the hallmark characteristic of U.S. constitutional government: the separation of power across the levels of government (national, state, and local) and within government (legislative, executive, and judicial), and the checks and balances of power across the institutions of government.

This stability does not mean that the Constitution *resolves* our political conflicts. The Founders recognized that self-interest and conflict are inherent parts of human nature and cannot be eliminated, so they attempted to control conflict by dispersing power across different parts of government. This means

THE FOUNDERS WANTED TO CREATE a constitution that was general enough to stand the test of time. Their approach succeeded, and the U.S. Constitution is the oldest written constitution still in use today. However, by leaving some passages open to interpretation, they also set the stage for conflict over the meaning of the Constitution. This painting depicts the signing of the document at the Constitutional Convention of 1787.

that parts of the political system are always competing with one another in pursuit of various interests: for example, Republicans in Congress may want to cut spending to balance the budget whereas a Democratic president may want to achieve that goal by using a mix of spending cuts and tax increases. This creates a conflictual process that is often criticized as being mired in "gridlock" and "partisan bickering." But that is the system our Founders created. Think about it this way: dictatorships do not have political conflict because dissenters are sent to jail or shot. We experience political conflict because there is free and open competition between different interests and ideas.

THE HISTORICAL CONTEXT OF THE CONSTITUTION

DESCRIBE THE HISTORICAL CIRCUMSTANCES THAT LED TO THE CONSTITUTIONAL CONVENTION OF 1787

The Constitution was created through conflict and compromise, and understanding the historical context can help clarify *why* the framers made the specific choices they did. The first event that led many American colonists to question the fairness of British rule and shape their ideas about self-governance was the Stamp Act of 1765, which imposed a tax on many publications and legal documents in the colonies. The British Parliament enacted the tax to help pay for the French and Indian War (1754–1763), which those lawmakers thought was only reasonable because the American colonies were benefiting from the protection of British troops. However, many colonists saw this as unfair "taxation without representation" because they had no representation in the British Parliament and thus had no say in the passage of the act. A series of escalating events moved the colonies closer to the inevitable break with Great Britain. These included the British-imposed Tea Act (1773) and the Boston Tea Party later that year, in which colonists dumped tea from the British East India Company into the harbor rather than pay the new tax. The British Parliament responded to the tea party with the Coercive Acts (or Intolerable Acts) of 1774 in a series of moves aimed at making sure the colonists paid for the tea they had destroyed and designed to break the pattern of the colonists' resistance to British rule. Attempts at a political solution failed, so the Continental Congress declared independence from Britain on July 4, 1776.[4]

THE ARTICLES OF CONFEDERATION: THE FIRST ATTEMPT AT GOVERNMENT

Throughout the Revolutionary and early post–Revolutionary era, the future of the American colonies was very much in doubt. While many Americans were eager to sever ties with the oppressive British government and establish a new nation that rejected the trappings of royalty, there was still a large contingent of Tories (supporters of the British monarchy) and probably an even larger group of Americans who wished the conflict would just go away. Although public opinion on the matter is impossible to know, John Adams, the second president of the United States, estimated that the Second Continental Congress was about equally

The sequence of important events leading to independence and the writing and ratification of the Constitution.

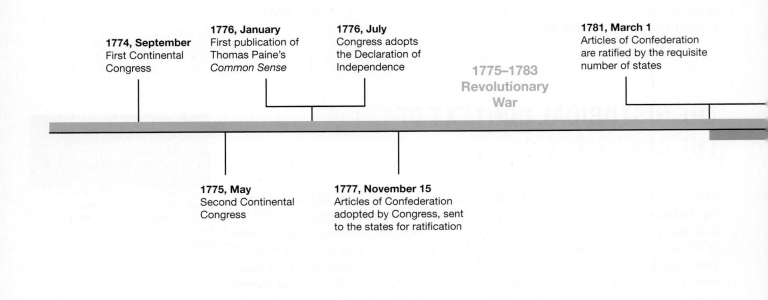

1774, September
First Continental Congress

1776, January
First publication of Thomas Paine's *Common Sense*

1776, July
Congress adopts the Declaration of Independence

1775–1783
Revolutionary War

1781, March 1
Articles of Confederation are ratified by the requisite number of states

1775, May
Second Continental Congress

1777, November 15
Articles of Confederation adopted by Congress, sent to the states for ratification

Articles of Confederation
Sent to the states for ratification in 1777, these were the first attempt at a new American government. It was later decided that the Articles restricted national government too much, and they were replaced by the Constitution.

limited government A political system in which the powers of the government are restricted to prevent tyranny by protecting property and individual rights.

divided between Tories, "true blue" revolutionaries, and "those too cautious or timid to take a position one way or the other."[5] This context of uncertainty and conflict made the Founders' task of creating a lasting republic extremely difficult.

The first attempt to structure an American government, the **Articles of Confederation**, swung too far in the direction of **limited government**. The Articles were written in the summer of 1776 during the Second Continental Congress, which also authorized and approved the Declaration of Independence. The Articles were submitted to all 13 states in 1777 for approval, but they did not take effect until the last state ratified them in 1781. However, in the absence of any alternative, the Articles of Confederation served as the basis for organizing the government during the Revolutionary War (see Figure 2.1).

In their zeal to reject monarchy, the authors of the Articles did not even include a president or any other executive leader. Instead, they assigned all national power to a Congress in which each state had a single vote. Members of Congress were elected by state legislatures rather than directly by the people. There was no judicial branch; all legal matters were left to the states, with the exception of disputes among the states, which would be resolved by special panels of judges appointed on an as-needed basis by Congress. To limit the power of government, the authors of the Articles gave each state veto power over any changes to the Articles and required approval from 9 of the 13 states on any legislation. Even more important, the states maintained autonomy and did not sacrifice any significant power to the national government. For example, both the national government and the states could make treaties and coin money.

FIGURE » 2.1

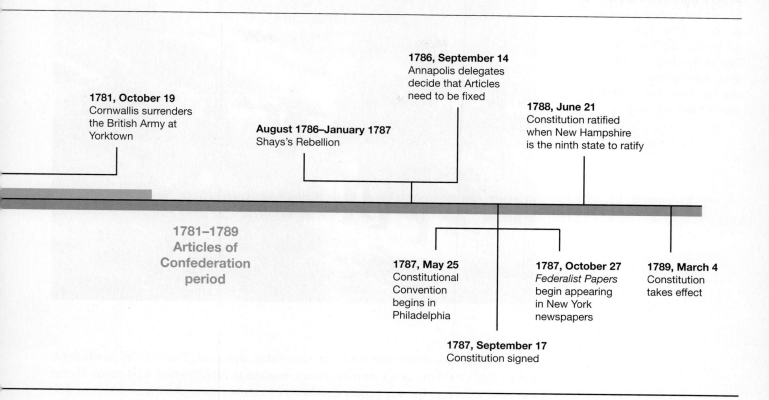

1786, September 14
Annapolis delegates
decide that Articles
need to be fixed

1781, October 19
Cornwallis surrenders
the British Army at
Yorktown

August 1786–January 1787
Shays's Rebellion

1788, June 21
Constitution ratified
when New Hampshire
is the ninth state to ratify

1781–1789
Articles of
Confederation
period

1787, May 25
Constitutional
Convention
begins in
Philadelphia

1787, October 27
Federalist Papers
begin appearing
in New York
newspapers

1789, March 4
Constitution
takes effect

1787, September 17
Constitution signed

Congress also lacked any real authority over the states. For example, Congress could suggest the amount of money each state owed to support the Revolutionary army but could not enforce payment. General George Washington's troops were in dire straits, lacking basic food and clothing—to say nothing about the arms and munitions they needed to defeat the British. At first, Congress tried to compel the states to support their own troops, but this appeal failed. Desperate for funds, in 1781 Congress tried to give itself the power to raise taxes, but the measure was vetoed by Rhode Island, which represented less than 2 percent of the nation's population! If France had not come to the aid of the American army with much-needed funds and troops, the weakness of the national government could have led to defeat.[6]

After the Revolutionary War ended with the British surrender at Yorktown in October 1781, the inability to raise revenue through taxes continued to plague Congress. The new government owed millions of dollars in war debts to foreign governments and domestic creditors, so Congress devised a plan to repay the debts over 25 years; but again, it had no way to make the states pay their share. Instead, Congress proposed an amendment to the Articles that would allow it to collect import duties, but New York, the busiest seaport in the nation, did not want to share its revenue and vetoed the amendment. Foreign trade also suffered because of the weak national government. If a foreign government negotiated a trade arrangement with Congress, it could be vetoed or amended by a state government, so that a foreign country wanting to conduct business with the United States might have to negotiate separate agreements with Congress and each state legislature. Even trade among the states was complicated and inefficient: each state could make its own currency, exchange rates varied, and many states charged tolls and fees to export goods across state lines. (Just imagine how difficult interstate commerce would be today if you had to exchange currency at every state line and if the value of your currency varied depending on which state you were in.)

A small group of leaders decided that something had to be done. A group from Virginia urged state legislatures to send delegates to a convention on interstate commerce in Annapolis, Maryland, in September 1786. Only five sent delegates. However, Alexander Hamilton and James Madison salvaged success from the convention by getting those delegates to agree to convene again in Philadelphia the following May. Delegates to the Annapolis Convention also agreed that the next convention would examine the defects of the current government and "devise such further provisions as shall appear to them necessary to render the Constitution of the Federal Government adequate to the exigencies of the Union."[7]

The issues that motivated the Annapolis Convention gained new urgency as events unfolded over the next several months. In the years after the war, economic chaos led to a depression, and many farmers lost their land because they could not pay their debts or state taxes. Frustration mounted, and early in 1787 a former captain in the Revolutionary army, Daniel Shays, led a force of a thousand farmers in an attempt to take over the Massachusetts state government arsenal in Springfield. Their goal was to force the state courts to stop prosecuting debtors and taking their land, but the rebels were repelled by a state militia. Similar protests on a smaller scale took place in Pennsylvania and Virginia. Some state legislatures gave in to the debtors' demands, causing national leaders to fear that Shays's Rebellion had exposed fundamental discontent with the new government. The very future of the fledgling nation was at risk.

POLITICAL THEORIES OF THE FRAMERS

Although the leaders who gathered in Philadelphia in the summer of 1787 to write the Constitution were chastened by the failure of the Articles of Confederation, these men still shared many of the principles that had motivated the Revolution. There continued to be broad consensus on three key principles: (1) popular control of government through a republican democracy, (2) a rejection of **monarchy**, and (3) limitations on government power that would protect individual rights and personal property (that is, protect against tyranny).

REPUBLICANISM First among these principles was rejection of monarchy in favor of a form of government based on self-rule. In its broadest sense, **republicanism** is the ideology of any state that is not a monarchy. As understood by the framers, it is a government in which elected leaders would represent the views of the people. Thomas Paine, an influential political writer of the Revolutionary era, wrote a pamphlet entitled *Common Sense* in 1776 that was a widely read[8] indictment of monarchy and an endorsement of the principles that fueled the Revolution and underpinned the framers' thinking. Paine wrote that a monarchy was the "most bare-faced falsity ever imposed on mankind" and that the common interests of the community should be served by elected representatives.

The Founders' views of republicanism, together with liberal principles of liberty and individual rights, shaped their vision of the proper form of government. The best expression of these principles is found in the Declaration of Independence:

> We hold these truths to be self-evident, that all men are created equal, that they are endowed by their Creator with certain unalienable Rights, that among these are Life, Liberty, and the pursuit of Happiness. That to secure these rights, Governments are instituted among Men, deriving their just powers from the consent of the governed. That whenever any Form of Government becomes destructive of these ends, it is the Right of the People to alter or to abolish it, and to institute new Government.

Three crucial ideas are packed into this passage: equality, self-rule, and natural rights. Equality was not given much attention in the Constitution (in later chapters we discuss how the problem of slavery was handled), but the notion that a government gains its legitimacy from the **"consent of the governed"** and that its central purpose is to uphold the "unalienable" or **natural rights** of the people were central to the framers. The "right of the people to alter or abolish" a government that did not protect these rights served both to justify the revolt against the British and to remind the framers of their continuing obligation to make sure that those needs were met. The leaders who met in Philadelphia thought the Articles of Confederation had become "destructive to those ends" and therefore needed to be altered.

Paine, Jefferson, Madison, and other political thinkers of the American Founding broke new ground in laying out the principles of republican democracy, but they also built on the ideas of political philosophers of their era. As mentioned in Chapter 1, Thomas Hobbes argued that government was necessary to prevent people from living in an anarchic "state of nature" in which life would be "nasty, brutish, and short." However, Hobbes's central conclusion was undemocratic: he believed that a single king must rule because any other form of government would produce warring factions. Another influential seventeenth-century philosopher, John Locke, took the notion of the consent of the governed in determining

monarchy A form of government in which power is held by a single person, or monarch, who comes to power through inheritance rather than election.

republicanism As understood by James Madison and the framers, the belief that a form of government in which the interests of the people are represented through elected leaders is the best form of government. Our form of government is known as a republican democracy.

"consent of the governed" The idea that government gains its legitimacy through regular elections in which the people living under that government participate to elect their leaders.

natural rights Also known as "unalienable rights," the Declaration of Independence defines them as "Life, Liberty, and the pursuit of Happiness." The Founders believed that upholding these rights should be the government's central purpose.

SEVENTEENTH-CENTURY POLITICAL philosopher John Locke greatly influenced the Founders. Many ideas discussed in Locke's writing appear in the Declaration of Independence and the Constitution.

a government's legitimacy in a more democratic direction. He discussed many of the ideas that later appeared in the Declaration of Independence and the Constitution, including natural rights, property rights, the need for a vigorous executive branch that would be checked by a legislative branch, and self-rule through elections.[9] Baron de Montesquieu, an eighteenth-century political thinker, also influenced the framers. Although he did not use the term "separation of powers," Montesquieu argued in *The Spirit of the Laws* (1748) that no two, let alone three, functions of government (judicial, legislative, and executive) should be controlled by one branch. He also argued that in order to preserve liberty, one branch of government should be able to check the excesses of the other branches.

HUMAN NATURE AND ITS IMPLICATIONS FOR DEMOCRACY The most comprehensive statement of the framers' political philosophy and democratic theory was a series of essays written by James Madison, Alexander Hamilton, and John Jay entitled the *Federalist Papers*. These essays explained and justified the framework of government created by the Constitution; they also revealed the framers' view of human nature and its implications for democracy. The framers' view of human nature as basically being driven by self-interest led to Madison's assessment that "[i]n framing a government which is to be administered by men over men, the great difficulty lies in this: you must first enable the government to control the governed; and in the next place oblige it to control itself." This analysis, which comes from *Federalist 51,* is often considered the clearest articulation of the need for republican government and a system of separated powers. In *Federalist 10,* Madison described the central problem for government as the need to control factions.

Madison argued that governments cannot control the causes of factions, because differences of opinion—based on the fallibility of reason; differences in wealth, property, and native abilities; and attachments to different leaders—are part of human nature. The only way to eliminate factions would be to either remove liberty or try to make everyone the same. The first remedy Madison called "worse than the disease," and the second he found "as impracticable as the first would be unwise." Because people are driven by self-interest, which sometimes conflicts with the common good, government must, however, try to control the effects of factions. This was the task facing the framers at the Constitutional Convention.

ECONOMIC INTERESTS

Political ideas were central to the framers' thinking at the Constitutional Convention, but economic interests were equally important. First, while there were certainly class differences among Americans in the late eighteenth century, they were insignificant compared to the inequalities found in Europe. America did not have the history of feudalism that had created tremendous inequality in Europe between landowners and propertyless serfs who worked the land. In contrast, most Americans owned small farms or worked as middle-class artisans and craftsmen. Thus, while political equality did not figure prominently in the Constitution, citizens' relative economic equality did influence the context of debates at the Constitutional Convention.

Second, despite Americans' general economic equality, there were significant regional economic differences. The South was largely agricultural, with cotton and tobacco plantations that depended on slave labor. The South favored free trade because of its export-based economy (bolstered by westward expansion) and the slave trade. The middle Atlantic and northern states, however, had smaller farms and a broad economic base of manufacturing, fishing, and trade. These states favored government-managed trade and commercial development.

Despite these differences, the diverse population favored a stronger national government and reform of the Articles of Confederation (see Nuts & Bolts 2.1). Creditors wanted a government that could pay off its debts to them, southern farmers wanted free trade that could only be efficiently promoted by a central government, and manufacturers and traders wanted a single national currency and uniform interstate commerce regulations. However, there was a deep division between the supporters of empowering the national government and those who still favored strong state governments and a weak national government. These two groups became known as the **Federalists** and the **Antifederalists**. Now the stage was set for a productive but contentious convention.

Federalists Those at the Constitutional Convention who favored a strong national government and a system of separated powers.

Antifederalists Those at the Constitutional Convention who favored strong state governments and feared that a strong national government would be a threat to individual rights.

THE POLITICS OF COMPROMISE AT THE CONSTITUTIONAL CONVENTION

ANALYZE THE MAJOR ISSUES DEBATED BY THE FRAMERS OF THE CONSTITUTION

The central players at the convention were James Madison, Gouverneur Morris, Edmund Randolph, James Wilson, Benjamin Franklin, and George Washington, who was the unanimous choice to preside over the convention. Several of the important leaders of the Revolution were not present. Patrick "Give me Liberty, or give me Death!" Henry was selected to attend but declined to do so, as he opposed any changes in the Articles, saying he "smelled a rat." Thomas Jefferson and John Adams were working overseas as U.S. diplomats, and Thomas Paine was back in England, so they did not attend. Moreover, John Hancock and Samuel Adams were not selected to attend. The delegates met in secret to encourage open, uncensored debate.

Although there was broad consensus among the delegates that the Articles of Confederation needed to be changed, there were many tensions over the issues that required political compromise. Among them were the following:

▶ majority rule versus minority rights,

▶ large states versus small states,

▶ legislative power versus executive power (and how to elect the executive),

▶ national power versus state and local power, and

▶ slave states versus nonslave states.

These complex competing interests meant that the delegates had to focus on pragmatic, achievable solutions rather than on proposals that represented particular groups' ideals but that could not gain majority support. Robert Dahl, a leading democratic theorist of the twentieth century, argues that it was impossible for the Constitution to "reflect a coherent, unified theory of government" because so much compromising and vote trading was required to find common ground.[10] Instead, the delegates tackled the problems one at a time, holding lengthy debates and multiple votes on most issues.

JAMES MADISON ARGUED THAT IT is beneficial to put the interests of one group in competition with the interests of other groups, so that no one group can dominate government. He hoped to achieve this through the separation of powers across different branches of the national government and across the national, state, and local levels.

MAJORITY RULE VERSUS MINORITY RIGHTS

A central problem for any representative democracy is protecting minority rights within a system ruled by the majority. The framers did not think of this issue in terms of racial and ethnic minorities (as we might today), but in terms of regional and economic minorities. How could the framers be sure that small landowners and poorer people would not impose onerous taxes on the wealthier minority? How could they guarantee that dominant agricultural interests would not impose punitive tariffs on manufacturing while allowing free export of farmed commodities? The answers to these questions can be found in Madison's writings on the problem of factions.

Madison defined a faction as a group motivated by selfish interests against the common good. If these interests prevailed, it could produce the very kind of tyranny that the Americans had fought to escape during the Revolutionary War. Madison was especially concerned about tyranny by majority factions because, in a democracy, minority tyranny would be controlled by the republican principle: the majority could simply vote out the minority faction. If, on the other hand, the majority always rules, majority tyranny could be a real problem. Given the understanding of selfish human nature that Madison so clearly outlined, a populist, majoritarian democracy would not necessarily produce the common good. On the other hand, if too many protections were provided to minority and regional interests, the collective interest would not be served because constructive changes could be vetoed too easily, as under the Articles of Confederation.

Madison's solution to this problem provided the justification for our form of government. He argued that to control majority tyranny, factions must be set against one another to counter each other's ambitions and prevent the tyranny of any single majority faction. This was to be accomplished through the "double protection" of the separation of powers within the national government in the form of checks and balances, and also by further dividing power across the levels of state and local governments.

COMPARING THE ARTICLES OF CONFEDERATION AND THE CONSTITUTION

Issue	Articles of Confederation	Constitution
Legislature	Unicameral Congress	Bicameral Congress divided into the House of Representatives and the Senate
Members of Congress	Between two and seven per state	Two senators per state; representatives apportioned according to population of each state
Voting in Congress	One vote per state	One vote per representative or senator
Selection of members	Appointed by state legislatures	Representatives elected by popular vote; senators appointed by state legislatures
Executive	None	President
National judiciary	Maritime judiciary established, no general federal courts	Supreme Court; Congress authorized to establish national judiciary
Amendments to the document	When approved by all states	When approved by two-thirds of each house of Congress and three-fourths of the states
Power to coin money	Federal government and the states	Federal government only
Taxes	Apportioned by Congress, collected by the states	Apportioned and collected by Congress
Ratification	Unanimous consent required	Consent of nine states required

Madison also argued that additional protection against majority tyranny would come from the "size principle." That is, the new nation would be a large and diverse republic in which majority interests would be less likely to organize, and therefore less able to dominate. According to Madison, "Extend the sphere, and you take in a greater variety of parties and interests; you make it less probable that a majority of the whole will have a common motive to invade the rights of other citizens; or if such a common motive exists, it will be more difficult for all who feel it to discover their own strength, and to act in unison with each other."[11] This insight provides the basis for modern **pluralism**, a political theory that makes the same argument about the cross-cutting interests of groups today.

The precise contours of Madison's solution still had to be hammered out at the convention, but the general principle pleased both the Antifederalists and the Federalists. State governments would maintain some autonomy, but the national government would become stronger than it had been under the Articles. The issue was striking the appropriate balance: none of the framers favored a pure populist majoritarian democracy, and few wanted to protect minority rights to the extent that the Articles had.

pluralism The idea that having a variety of parties and interests within a government will strengthen the system, ensuring that no group possesses total control.

SMALL STATES VERSUS LARGE STATES

The question of the appropriate balance came to an immediate head in a debate between small-population and large-population states over representation in the national legislature. Under the Articles, every state had a single vote, but this

FIGURE » 2.2

CONNECTICUT'S PIVOTAL PLACE AT THE CONSTITUTIONAL CONVENTION

As the seventh of the thirteen states in terms of population, Connecticut was in a perfect position to offer a compromise that would appeal to both the small and large states. If representation in Congress had been based on population, the four largest states could have outvoted the nine smallest states.

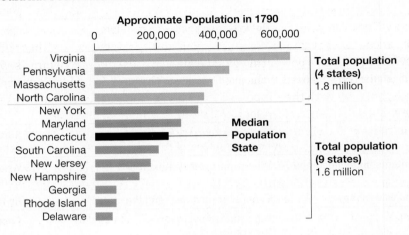

Virginia Plan A plan proposed by the larger states during the Constitutional Convention that based representation in the national legislature on population. The plan also included a variety of other proposals to strengthen the national government.

New Jersey Plan A plan that was in response to the Virginia Plan, in which smaller states at the Constitutional Convention proposed that each state should receive equal representation in the national legislature, regardless of size.

Great Compromise A compromise between the large and small states, proposed by Connecticut, in which Congress would have two houses: a Senate with two legislators per state and a House of Representatives in which each state's representation would be based on population (also known as the Connecticut Compromise).

did not seem fair to large states. They were pushing for representation based on population. This proposal, along with others that would strengthen the national government, was the **Virginia Plan**. The small states countered with the **New Jersey Plan**, which proposed maintaining equal representation for every state. Rhode Island, the smallest state, was so concerned about small-state power that it boycotted the convention. Tensions were running high; this issue appeared to have all the elements of a deal breaker, and there seemed to be no way to resolve the impasse.

Just as it appeared that the convention might grind to a halt before it really got started, Connecticut proposed what became known as the **Great Compromise**, or Connecticut Compromise. The plan suggested establishing a Congress with two houses: the Senate would have two senators from each state, and in the House of Representatives each state's number of representatives would be based on its population. Interestingly, Connecticut's population was ranked seventh of the thirteen states (see Figure 2.2). It was in a perfect position to offer a compromise because it did not have strong vested interests in the plans offered by either the small states or the large states.

LEGISLATIVE POWER VERSUS EXECUTIVE POWER

An equally difficult challenge was how to divide power at the national level. Here the central issues revolved around the executive—the president. How much power should the president have relative to the legislative branch? (The courts also figured here, but they were less central to the discussions.) And how would the president be elected?

LIMITING PRESIDENTIAL POWER The delegates knew what they did not want: the king of England and his colonial governors were viewed as tramplers of liberty. But many delegates rejected outright the idea of a single executive because they believed it was impossible to have an executive who would not be oppressive. Edmund Randolph proposed a three-person executive for this reason, arguing that a single executive would be the "fetus of monarchy." The Virginia Plan envisioned a single executive who would share some legislative power with federal judges in a Council of Revision with the power to veto legislation passed by Congress (however, the veto could be overridden by a simple majority vote in Congress). The delegates finally agreed on the single executive because he would have the most "energy, dispatch, and responsibility for the office," but they constrained the president's power through the system of checks and balances. One significant power they granted to the executive was the veto. It could be overridden by Congress, but only with the support of two-thirds of both chambers. This requirement gave the president a significant role in the legislative process.

In addition to Hamilton, the other New Yorkers also favored a strong executive. This was probably because the governorship of New York closely resembled the type of executive that the Constitution envisioned. The governor of New York was elected by the people rather than by the legislature, served for three years, and was eligible for reelection. The office also had a legislative veto power and considerable control over appointments to politically controlled jobs. The arguments the New Yorkers made on behalf of the strong executive relied heavily on the philosophy of John Locke. Locke saw the general superiority of a government of laws created by legislatures, but he also saw the need for an executive with more flexible leadership powers, or what he called "prerogative powers." Legislatures are unable, Locke wrote, "to foresee, and so by laws to provide for all accidents and necessities." They also are, by virtue of their size and unwieldiness, too slow to alter and adapt the law in times of crisis, when the executive could step in to pursue policies in the public's interest.

Although there was support for this view, the Antifederalists were concerned that if such powers were viewed as open-ended, they could give rise to the type of oppressive leader the framers were trying to avoid. Madison attempted to reassure the opponents of executive power, arguing that any prerogative powers would have to be clearly enumerated in the Constitution. In fact, the Constitution explicitly provides only one extraordinary executive power: the right to grant reprieves and pardons, which means that the president can forgive any crimes against the federal government.

SELECTING THE PRESIDENT The second contentious issue concerning the executive was the method of selecting a president. The way the president was elected incorporated the issues of majority rule and minority rights, state versus national power, and the nature of executive power itself. Would the president be elected by the nation as a whole, by the states, or by coalitions within Congress? If the state-level governments played a central role, would this mean that the president could not speak for national interests? If Congress elected the president, could the executive still provide a check on the legislative branch?

Most Americans do not realize that (1) our presidential system is unique, and (2) we came close to having a parliamentary system, which is the form of government that exists in most other established democracies. In a **parliamentary system**, the executive branch depends on the support of the legislative branch. The Virginia Plan proposed that Congress elect the president, just as Parliament elects the British prime minister. However, facing lingering concerns that a congressionally elected president would be too beholden to that body, a committee of

parliamentary system
A system of government in which legislative and executive power are closely joined. The legislature (parliament) selects the chief executive (prime minister) who forms the cabinet from members of the parliament.

framers subsequently made the following recommendations: that the president be selected by an electoral college, representation in which would be based on the number of representatives and senators each state has in Congress, and that members of each state's legislature would determine the method for choosing their state's electors.[12] The delegates ultimately approved this recommendation.

Why did the delegates favor this complicated, indirect way of electing the president? As with good compromises, all sides could claim victory to some extent. Advocates of state power were happy because state legislatures played a central role in presidential elections; those who worried about the direct influence of the people liked the indirect manner of election; and proponents of strong executive power were satisfied that the president would not simply be an agent of Congress.

However, the solution had its flaws and did not work out the way the framers intended. First, if the Electoral College was supposed to provide an independent check on the voters, it never played this role because the framers did not anticipate the quick emergence of political parties. Electors became agents of the parties, as they remain today, rather than independent actors who would use their judgment to pick the most qualified candidate for president. Second, the emergence of parties created a serious technical error in the Constitution: the provision that gave each elector two votes and elected the candidate with the most votes as president and the second-place finisher as vice president. With electors acting as agents of parties, they ended up casting one vote each for the presidential and vice-presidential candidate of their own party. This created a tie in the 1800 presidential election when Thomas Jefferson and Aaron Burr each received 73 electoral votes. The problem was fixed by the Twelfth Amendment, which required that electors cast separate ballots for president and vice president.

NATIONAL POWER VERSUS STATE AND LOCAL POWER

Tensions over the balance of power cut across virtually every debate at the convention. The issues included presidential versus legislative power, whether the national government could supersede state laws, apportionment in the legislature, slavery, regulation of commerce and taxation, and the amending process. The overall compromise that addressed these tensions was the second of Madison's "double protections," the system of federalism, which divided power between autonomous levels of government that controlled different areas of policy.

Federalism is such an important topic that we devote the entire next chapter to it, but two brief points about it are important here. First, federalism is an example of how careful compromises can alter the Constitution's meaning by changing a single word. The Tenth Amendment, which was added as part of the Bill of Rights shortly after ratification, was a concession to the Antifederalists who were concerned that the national government would gain too much power in the new political system. The Tenth Amendment says, "The powers not delegated to the United States by the Constitution, nor prohibited by it to the States, are reserved to the States respectively, or to the people." This definition of **reserved powers** was viewed as setting outer limits on the reach of national power.

However, the Antifederalists were not happy with this wording because of the removal of a single word; they wanted the Tenth Amendment to read, "The powers not *expressly* delegated to the United States." The new wording would have more explicitly restricted national power. With the word "expressly" removed, the amendment became much more ambiguous and less restrictive of national power.

reserved powers As defined in the Tenth Amendment, powers that are not given to the national government by the Constitution, or not prohibited to the states, are reserved by the states or the people.

Indeed, the Supreme Court did not use the amendment to strike down an act of Congress until 1871. However, between 1918 and 1937 and then again starting in the 1990s, the Supreme Court has frequently invoked the Tenth Amendment to nullify various laws passed by Congress as unconstitutional intrusions on the reserved powers of the states (see the discussion in Chapter 3 of the Supreme Court's recent preference for state-centered federalism). As noted in the chapter opener, the Tea Party has relied on the Tenth Amendment to support its arguments against national power. For example, Tea Partiers argue that the states and the private sector, not the national government, should have the primary responsibility for health care policy.

Second, the **national supremacy clause** of the Constitution (Article VI) says that any national law is the supreme law of the land and takes precedence over any state law that conflicts with it. This is especially important in areas where the national and state governments have overlapping responsibilities for policy.

national supremacy clause Part of Article VI, Section 2, of the Constitution stating that the Constitution and the laws and treaties of the United States are the "supreme Law of the Land," meaning national laws take precedence over state laws if the two conflict.

SLAVE STATES VERSUS NONSLAVE STATES

Slavery was another nearly insurmountable issue for the delegates. Southern states would not agree to any provisions limiting slavery. Although the nonslave states opposed the practice, they were not willing to scuttle the entire Constitution by taking a principled stand. Even after these basic divisions had been recognized, many unresolved issues remained. Could the importation of slaves be restricted in the future? How would northern states deal with runaway slaves? Most important in terms of the politics of the issue, how would the slave population be counted for the purpose of slave states' representation in Congress?

The deals that the convention delegates cut on the issue of slavery illustrate the two most common forms of compromise: splitting the difference and logrolling (trading votes). Splitting the difference is familiar to anyone who has haggled over the price of a car or bargained for something at a flea market; you end up meeting halfway, or splitting the difference. Logrolling occurs when politicians trade votes for one another's pet projects.

A SLAVE AUCTION IN VIRGINIA. Slavery proved problematic at the Constitutional Convention: Would there be limits on the importation of slaves? How would runaway slaves be dealt with by nonslave states? And how would slaves be counted for the purposes of congressional representation?

The delegates went through similar negotiations over how slaves would be counted for purposes of states' congressional representation. The states had been through this debate once before, when they addressed the issue of taxation under the Articles of Confederation. At that point, the slave states had argued that slaves should not be counted because they did not receive the same benefits as citizens and were not the same burden to the government. Nonslave states had countered that slaves should be counted the same way as citizens when determining a state's fair share of the tax burden. The sides had reached a compromise by agreeing that slaves would count as three-fifths of all other persons for purposes of taxation. The arguments over the issue of representation became even more contentious at the Constitutional Convention, where the positions were reversed, with slave states arguing that slaves should be counted like everyone else for the purposes of determining the number of House representatives for each state. Once again, both sides managed to agree on the **Three-Fifths Compromise**.

The other two issues, the importation of slaves and dealing with runaway slaves, were handled by logrolling combined with an element of splitting the difference. Logrolling is more likely to occur than splitting the difference when the issue cannot be neatly divided. For example, northern states either would be obligated to return runaway slaves to their southern owners or they would not. There was no way to

Three-Fifths Compromise
The states' decision during the Constitutional Convention to count each slave as three-fifths of a person in a state's population for the purposes of determining the number of House members and the distribution of taxes.

2.2 NUTS *& bolts*

MAJOR COMPROMISES AT THE CONSTITUTIONAL CONVENTION

Conflict	Position of the Large States	Position of the Small States	Compromise
Apportionment in Congress	By population	State equality	Great Compromise created the Senate and House
Method of election to Congress	By the people	By the states	House elected by the people; Senate elected by the state legislatures
Electing the executive (president)	By Congress	By the states	By the electoral college
Who decides federal–state conflicts?	Some federal authority	State courts	State courts to decide*
	Position of the Slave States	**Position of the Nonslave States**	**Compromise**
Control over commerce	By the states	By Congress	By Congress, but with 20-year exemption for the importation of slaves
Counting slaves toward apportionment	Counted 1:1 like citizens	Not counted	Three-Fifths Compromise
	Position of the Federalists	**Position of the Antifederalists**	**Compromise**
Protection for individual rights	Secured by state constitutions; national Bill of Rights not needed	National Bill of Rights needed	Bill of Rights passed by the first Congress; ratified by all states as of December 1791

*This was changed by the Judiciary Act of 1789, which provided for appeals from state to federal courts.

split the difference. On issues with no clear middle ground, opposing sides will look for other issues on which they can trade votes. The nonslave states wanted more national government control over commerce and trade than was provided under the Articles, a change that the slave states opposed. So a logroll—or vote trade—developed as a way to compromise the competing regional interests of slavery and regulation of commerce. Northern states agreed to return runaway slaves (the Fugitive Slave Clause), and southern states agreed to allow Congress to regulate commerce and tax imports with a simple majority vote (rather than the supermajority required under the Articles).

The importation of slaves was included as part of this logroll, along with some split-the-difference negotiating. Northern states wanted to allow future Congresses to ban the importation of slaves; southern states wanted to allow the importation of slaves to continue indefinitely, arguing that slavery was essential to produce their labor-intensive crops. After much negotiation among the states, the final language of the Article resulting from this part of the logroll prevented a constitutional amendment from banning the slave trade until 1808.[13]

From a modern perspective, it is difficult to understand how the framers could have taken such a purely political approach to the moral issue of slavery. Many of the delegates believed slavery was immoral, yet they were willing to negotiate for the southern states' support of the Constitution. Some southern delegates were apologetic about slavery, even as they argued for protecting their interests. Many constitutional scholars view the convention's treatment of slavery as its central failure. In fairness to the delegates, the issue of slavery could not be settled since the goal was to create a document that all states would support. However, the delegates' inability to resolve this issue meant that it would simmer below the surface for the next 70 years, finally boiling over into the bloodiest of all American wars, the Civil War.

The convention ended on a relatively harmonious note with Benjamin Franklin moving for adoption. Franklin's motion was worded ambiguously to allow those who still had reservations to sign the Constitution anyway. Franklin's motion was in the "following convenient form," "Done in Convention by the unanimous consent of the States present the 17th of September. . . . In Witness whereof we have hereunto subscribed our names." His clever wording meant that the signers were only bearing witness to the approval by the states and therefore could still, in good faith, oppose substantial parts of the document. Franklin's motion passed with 10 ayes, no nays, and one delegation divided. All but three of the remaining delegates signed.

UNION AND CONFEDERATE TROOPS clash in close combat in the Battle of Cold Harbor, Virginia, in June 1864. The inability of the framers to resolve the issue of slavery allowed tensions over the issue to grow throughout the early nineteenth century, culminating in the Civil War.

RATIFICATION

> CONTRAST THE ARGUMENTS OF THE FEDERALISTS WITH THOSE OF THE ANTIFEDERALISTS

Article VII of the Constitution, which described the process for ratifying the document, was also designed to maximize its chance of success. Only nine states were needed to ratify, rather than the unanimity rule that had applied to changing the Articles of Confederation. Equally important, ratification votes would be taken in state conventions set up specifically for that purpose, bypassing the state legislatures, which would be more likely to resist some of the Constitution's state–federal power-sharing arrangements.

The near-unanimous approval at the Constitutional Convention's end masked the very strong opposition that remained. Many delegates simply left the convention when it became clear that things were not going their way (overall, 74 delegates were elected to go, 55 attended, and 39 signed the Constitution). Rhode Island sent no delegates and refused to appoint a ratification convention. More ominously, New York seemed dead set against the Constitution, and Pennsylvania, Virginia, and Massachusetts were split. The ratifying conventions in each state subjected the Constitution to intense scrutiny, as attendees examined every sentence for possible objections. A national debate raged over the next nine months.

THE ANTIFEDERALISTS' CONCERNS

The Antifederalists were most worried about the role of the president, the transfer of power from the states to the national government, and the lack of specific guarantees of civil liberties. In short, they feared that the national government would become tyrannical. The doubts about the single central executive were expressed by Patrick Henry, a leading Antifederalist. Speaking to the Virginia ratifying convention, Henry was mocking in his indictment, "Your president may easily become a king.... There will be no checks, no real balances in this government."[14] Even Thomas Jefferson complained that the president would control the armed forces and could be reelected indefinitely.[15] State power and the ability to regulate commerce were also central concerns. States such as New York would lose substantial revenue if they could no longer charge tariffs on goods that came into their ports. Other states were concerned that they would pay a disproportionate share of national taxes.

THIS ENGRAVING BY AMOS Doolittle entitled "The Looking Glass for 1787" satirizes some of the issues raised in the debate over the ratification of the Constitution. The wagon in the center is carrying Connecticut and sinking into the mud under the weight of debts and paper money as "Federalists" and "Antifederalists" try to pull it out.

The Antifederalists' foremost objection was to the lack of protections for civil liberties in the new political system. During the last week of the convention, Elbridge Gerry and George Mason offered a resolution "to prepare a Bill of Rights." However, the resolution was unanimously defeated by the state delegations. Some believed that the national government posed no threat to liberties, such as freedom of the press, because it did not have the power to restrict them in the first place. Others thought that because it would be impossible to enumerate all rights, it was better to list none at all. Federalists such as Roger Sherman argued that state constitutions, most of which protected freedom of speech, freedom of the press, right to a trial by jury, and other civil liberties, would be sufficient to protect liberty. However, many Antifederalists still wanted assurances that the *national* government would not trample their rights.

THE FEDERALISTS' STRATEGIES

The Federalists counterattacked on several fronts. First, supporters of the Constitution gained the upper hand in the debate by claiming the term "federalist." It is a common tactic in debates to co-opt a strong point of the opposing side as a positive for your side. The opponents to the Constitution probably had a stronger claim than its supporters to being federalists—that is, those who favor and emphasize the autonomous power of the state governments. Today, for example, the Federalist Society is a conservative group organized around the principles of states' rights and limited government. By calling themselves Federalists, the supporters of the Constitution asserted that they were the true protectors of states' interests, which irritated the Antifederalists to no end. The Antifederalists also had the rhetorical disadvantage of having "anti" attached to their name, thereby being defined in terms of their opponents' position rather than their own. But the problem was more than just rhetorical: the Federalists pointed out that the Antifederalists did not have their own

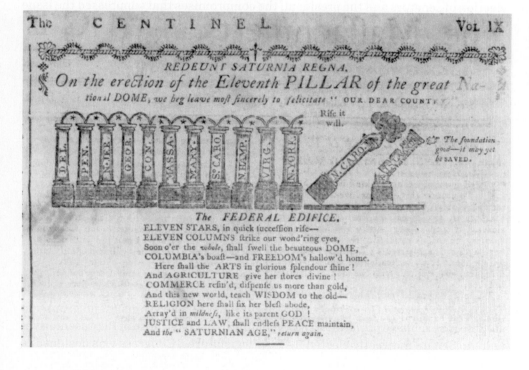

THIS POLITICAL CARTOON FROM 1788 depicts the erection of the "eleventh pillar in the great national dome" when New York became the eleventh state to ratify the Constitution, leaving only North Carolina and Rhode Island (shown as still wobbling in this cartoon) to ratify the document.

plan to solve the problems created by the Articles and therefore were cast as defenders of the status quo, which the Federalists viewed as unsustainable.

Second, the Federalists published the *Federalist Papers.* Although originally published in New York newspapers, they were widely read throughout the nation. The *Federalist Papers* were essentially one-sided arguments aimed at changing public opinion. The authors downplayed potentially unpopular aspects of the new system, such as the power of the president, while emphasizing points they knew would appeal to the opposition. Despite their biased arguments, the *Federalist Papers* are the best comprehensive discussion of the political theory underlying the Constitution and the framers' interpretations of many of its key provisions.

Third, the Federalists agreed that the new Congress's first order of business would be to add a **Bill of Rights** to the Constitution to protect individual rights and liberties. This promise was essential for securing the support of New York, Massachusetts, and Virginia. The ninth state, New Hampshire, ratified the Constitution on June 21, 1788, but New York and Virginia were still dragging their heels, and their support was viewed as necessary for the legitimacy of the United States, even if it technically was not needed. By the end of the summer, both Virginia and New York finally voted for ratification. Rhode Island and North Carolina refused to ratify until Congress made good on its promise of a Bill of Rights. The first Congress submitted 12 amendments to the states, and 10 were ratified by all the states as of December 15, 1791.

Bill of Rights The first 10 amendments to the Constitution; they protect individual rights and liberties.

OUTLINE THE MAJOR PROVISIONS OF THE CONSTITUTION

THE CONSTITUTION: A FRAMEWORK FOR GOVERNMENT

The Constitution certainly has its flaws (some of which have been corrected through amendments), primarily its undemocratic qualities such as the indirect election of senators and the president, the compromises that suppressed the issue of slavery (indeed, the words "slave" and "slavery" do not appear in the Constitution), and the absence of any general statement about citizens' right to vote. However, given the delegates' political context and the various factions that had to be satisfied, the Constitution's accomplishments are substantial.

The document's longevity is testimony to the framers' foresight in crafting a flexible framework for government. Perhaps its most important feature is the system of separation of powers and checks and balances that prevent majority tyranny, while maintaining sufficient flexibility for decisive leadership during times of crisis (such as the Civil War, the Great Depression, and World War II). The system of checks and balances means that each branch of national government has certain exclusive powers, some shared powers, and the ability to check the other two branches (see How It Works: Checks and Balances).

EXCLUSIVE POWERS

The framers viewed Congress as the "first branch" of government and granted it significant exclusive powers. With the popularly elected House of Representatives and the Senate indirectly elected by state legislatures, Congress was designed to

CHECKS AND BALANCES

EXECUTIVE

The Senate approves presidential nominations, and Congress can pass laws over the president's veto.

The Court interprets actions by the executive.

IN THE CONSTITUTION

If one branch tries to assert too much power, the other branches have certain key powers that allow them to fight back and restore the balance. (In addition to the powers noted in the diagram, the Congress can impeach the president and remove him or her from office.)

President can veto congressional legislation.

President nominates judges.

LEGISLATIVE

JUDICIAL

The Court interprets the laws passed by Congress.

The Senate confirms the president's nominations. Congress can impeach and remove judges from office.

How It Works
In Practice

CHECKS AND BALANCES IN THE WAR ON TERROR

Since shortly after the attacks of September 11, 2001, the president, acting on his power as commander in chief, authorized the Guantánamo Bay detention center in Cuba to be used as a place to detain, interrogate, and try prisoners related to the war on terror. There have been allegations of human rights violations, including torture. The controversies and policies surrounding Guantánamo show how checks and balances work in practice.

■ EXECUTIVE ACTIONS ■ JUDICIAL ACTIONS ■ LEGISLATIVE ACTIONS

President George W. Bush asserts that Guantánamo is outside the legal jurisdiction of the U.S. and that the prisoners held there do not have protections guaranteed to prisoners of war under the Geneva Convention.

Two days after taking office, President Obama signs an order to close the center by the end of the year and to suspend all Guantánamo military commission hearings for 120 days.

A few months later, Congress votes to block funds needed for the transfer or release of prisoners held at the facility.

The Supreme Court disagrees in *Hamdan v. Rumsfeld* on June 29, 2006, ruling that the detainees were entitled to basic legal rights and that the Geneva Convention did apply.

A week later, a military court judge overturns the order to suspend hearings at Guantánamo.

More than 100 prisoners go on a hunger strike in 2013. The U.S. government force-feeds them rather than letting them die, leading to renewed calls to close the facility.

First prisoners are taken to Guantánamo on January 11, 2002.

The detention center is increasingly controversial as Amnesty International, a human rights organization, calls it "the gulag of our time," and in 2006, the United Nations urges the U.S. to close the facility.

President Obama wants to move Guantánamo prisoners to a federal prison in Illinois.

POP QUIZ

1 How can the president (the executive branch) stop Congress (the legislative branch) from asserting too much power?

  a by declaring laws unconstitutional
  b by impeaching members of Congress
  c by vetoing legislation
  d by holding hearings
  e through nominations

2 How did the Supreme Court "check" the Bush administration in cases involving the rights of terror suspects?

  a by declaring presidential/executive branch acts unconstitutional
  b by impeaching the president
  c by passing legislation
  d through nominations
  e through ratification

be both the voice of the people and an institution more removed from the people, with a significant role in domestic and foreign policy. Congress was given the power to raise revenue for the federal government through taxes and borrowing, regulate interstate and foreign commerce, coin money, establish post offices and roads, grant patents and copyrights, create the system of federal courts, declare war, "raise and support armies," make rules for the military, and create and maintain a navy. Most important is the so-called power of the purse—control over taxation and spending—given to Congress in Article I, Section 8, of the Constitution: "No money shall be drawn from the Treasury, but in consequence of appropriations made by law." Or as Madison put it, "the legislative department alone has access to the pockets of the people."

Congress's exclusive powers take on additional significance through the **necessary and proper clause**, also known as the elastic clause. It gives Congress the flexibility to "make all Laws which shall be necessary and proper for carrying into Execution the foregoing Powers, and all other Powers vested by this Constitution in the Government of the United States, or in any Department or Officer thereof." This broad grant of power meant that Congress could pass laws related to any of its exclusive powers. For example, although the Constitution did not explicitly mention Congress's right to compel people to serve in the military, its power to enact a draft was clearly given by the necessary and proper clause, in conjunction with its power to "raise and support armies."

Congress's exclusive powers are more numerous and specific than the limited powers granted to the president. The president is the commander in chief of the armed forces and has power to receive ambassadors and foreign ministers and to issue pardons. The president's most important powers are contained in the executive powers clause that says, "The executive power shall be vested in a President of the United States of America," and in the directive to ensure "that the laws are faithfully executed." As we see later in the chapter, these Article II clauses impart most of the president's power.

The courts did not receive nearly as much attention in the Constitution as either Congress or the president. Alexander Hamilton argued in *Federalist 78* that the Supreme Court would be the "least dangerous branch," because it had "neither the power of the purse nor the sword." The most important positive powers that the framers gave the Supreme Court were lifetime tenure for justices in good behavior and relative independence from the other two branches. The critical negative power of judicial review, the ability to strike down the laws and actions of other branches, will be discussed below.

SHARED POWERS

Along with dividing the exclusive powers between branches, checks and balances designate some shared powers. These are areas where no branch has exclusive control. For example, the president has the power to negotiate treaties and make appointments to the federal courts and other government offices, but these executive actions are to be undertaken with the "advice and consent" of the Senate, which means they were intended to be shared powers. In the twentieth century, these particular powers became executive-centered, with the Senate providing almost no advice to the president and routinely giving its consent (often disapprovingly called "rubber-stamping"). However, the Senate can assert its shared power, as shown by the Senate's relatively recent blocking of several of President George W. Bush's and President Obama's lower-court nominees.

necessary and proper clause Part of Article I, Section 8, of the Constitution that grants Congress the power to pass all laws related to one of its expressed powers; also known as the elastic clause.

JANET YELLEN TESTIFIES BEFORE the Senate Banking Committee at her confirmation hearings to become chair of the Federal Reserve. The president and the Senate share the appointment power to many federal offices: the president makes the nominations, and the Senate provides its "advice and consent."

The war powers, which include decisions about when and how to use military force, were also intended to be shared but have become executive-dominated powers. The framers disagreed about who should control the war powers. Some wanted to keep the arrangement set up by the Articles of Confederation in which nine of the thirteen states had to agree before Congress could declare war. Another group wanted to follow the British system in which the executive branch controlled war powers, whereas others argued that the president should have the power to repel a sudden attack but that Congress should have the power to declare war. The ultimate compromise that the framers reached shows checks and balances at work, with the president serving as the commander in chief of the armed forces, and Congress having the power to declare war and to appropriate the funds to conduct a war. At the Constitutional Convention, the original proposal gave Congress the power to "make war" rather than "declare war." Clearly this would have been a far more significant grant of power, suggesting an ongoing role for Congress in the conduct of a war.

One other goal of the Founders in making the war powers a shared power was to ensure civilian control of the military. By providing a role for both Congress and the president, the Constitution made it more likely that this important democratic principle would be maintained. One critical event occurred before the Constitution was written when George Washington resigned his commission as commander in chief of the Continental Army. Congress had given Washington complete authority over conduct of the Revolutionary War, and many in Congress wanted him to continue to rule, almost as a king. Washington knew that it was critical for the new nation to have democratically elected leaders control the military. By resigning his commission, he made it clear that any future leadership role he would play (and it was widely assumed by the Founders that he would be the first president) would be as a civilian rather than a general.

Since very early in our nation's history, the president has taken a lead role in the war powers, making the decision to use military force. Presidents have authorized the use of American troops on hundreds of occasions, but Congress has declared war

THIS PAINTING, WHICH HANGS IN the Capitol rotunda, shows General George Washington resigning his commission as commander in chief of the Continental Army. This set the precedent that democratically elected officials would control the United States military.

only five times. Of these, Congress debated the merits of entering only one war, the War of 1812. The other "declarations" recognized a state of war that already existed. (For example, after Japan bombed Pearl Harbor, Hawaii, in 1941, Congress's subsequent declaration of war formally recognized what everyone already knew.) As the 2003 invasion of Iraq demonstrated, if a president is intent on going to war, Congress must go along or get out of the way.

In a few instances, however, Congress wanted to declare war and the president resisted. For example, in 1895 and 1896 when Grover Cleveland was president, tensions mounted in the United States over Cuba's struggle for independence from Spain. Congressional leaders tried to convince Cleveland of the merits of entering the war to help Cuba, but he refused, saying, "I will not mobilize the army. I happen to know that we can buy the Island of Cuba from Spain for $100 million and a war will cost vastly more than that. . . . It would be an outrage to declare war."[16]

Examples such as this are unusual. It would be impossible today for Congress to declare war without a willing commander in chief. However, since the Vietnam War, Congress has tried to redress the imbalance in the war powers in other ways. In 1970, during the Vietnam War, Congress passed a resolution that prevented any funds from supporting ground troops in Laos or Cambodia (nations that bordered Vietnam). In the 1980s, Democrats in Congress prevented President Ronald Reagan from using any appropriated funds to support the Contra rebels in their fight against the Sandinista government in Nicaragua.[17] In 2013, Congress was strongly opposed to a military strike against Syria in response to its use of chemical weapons against its own people. A showdown with President Obama was averted when Syria agreed to allow weapons inspectors to destroy their chemical weapons stockpile. The Republican House has also been extremely critical of President Obama's relatively limited response to the crisis in Ukraine. These examples show that although the president continues to dominate the war powers, Congress can assert its power when it has the will—just as it can by advising the president in treaty negotiations or by withholding approval of the president's nominees for appointed positions.

CONGRESS ALONE HAS "THE POWER of the purse" to fund government programs. Although President Obama ordered the "troop surge" in Afghanistan, Congress had to continue appropriating money to pay for the war.

NEGATIVE OR CHECKING POWERS

The last part of the system of checks and balances is the negative power that the branches have over one another. These powers are especially important to ensure that no single branch dominates the national government.

CONGRESSIONAL CHECKS Congress has two important negative checks on the other two branches: impeachment and the power of the purse. **Impeachment** was based on the British practice of removing unpopular or corrupt ministers of the king through a vote of no confidence, but the framers made one important change. The president, vice president, or other "officers of the United States" (including federal judges) could not be removed for political reasons, but only for abuses of power—specifically, "Treason, Bribery, or other High Crimes or Misdemeanors." The framers placed this central check with Congress as part of the overall move toward centralizing power at the national level.

Through the **power of the purse**, Congress can punish executive agencies by freezing or cutting their funding or holding hearings on, investigations of, or audits of their operations to make sure money is being spent properly. Congress can also

impeachment A negative or checking power over the other branches that allows Congress to remove the president, vice president, or other "officers of the United States" (including federal judges) for abuses of power.

power of the purse The constitutional power of Congress to raise and spend money. Congress can use this as a negative or checking power over the other branches by freezing or cutting their funding.

THE CONSTITUTION ATTEMPTS to strike a balance between protecting our civil liberties from government intrusion and providing for a government strong enough to protect our national security. There has been much controversy around revelations that the National Security Administration (NSA) has used electronic surveillance to gather data about people living in the United States. Information about this program was leaked by Edward Snowden, a staffer at the NSA.

freeze judges' salaries to show displeasure with court decisions, and it has the power to limit the issues that federal courts can consider. Congress can also limit the discretion of judges in other ways, such as by setting federal sentencing guidelines that recommend a range of years in prison that should be served for various crimes. Even today, the system of checks and balances is not fixed in stone but evolves according to the changing political climate.

PRESIDENTIAL CHECKS The framers placed important checks on congressional power as well, and the president's most important check on Congress is the veto. Again, there was very little agreement on this topic. The Antifederalists argued that it was "a political error of the greatest magnitude, to allow the executive power a negative, or in fact any kind of control over the proceedings of the legislature." But the Federalists worried that Congress would slowly strip away presidential powers and leave the president too weak. In the end, the Federalist view that the president needed some protections against the "depredations" of the legislature won the day. However, the veto has developed into a major policy-making tool for the president, which is probably broader than the check against "depredations" envisioned by the framers.

The president does not have any formal check on the courts other than the power to appoint judges. However, presidents have, at various times, found unconventional ways to try to influence the courts. For example, Franklin D. Roosevelt tried to "pack the Court" by expanding the size of the Supreme Court with justices who would be sympathetic with his New Deal policies. More recently, George W. Bush attempted to expand the reach of executive power in the War on Terror by taking over some functions within the executive branch that the courts had previously performed. However, the Supreme Court struck down some of these policies as unconstitutional violations of defendants' due process rights. President Obama changed many of Bush's policies, such as harsh interrogation methods and excessive secrecy. But other Bush-era policies were either more difficult to change than Obama anticipated, such as the detainment of enemy combatants in the prison at Guantánamo Bay, or deemed necessary to fight terrorism, such as indefinite detention without trial for suspected terrorists who were arrested outside combat areas.[18] Critics claim that the expansion of executive power in order to fight terrorism has threatened the institutional balance of power by giving the president too much control over functions previously carried out by the courts.[19]

judicial review The Supreme Court's power to strike down a law or executive branch action that it finds unconstitutional.

JUDICIAL REVIEW The Constitution did not provide the Supreme Court with any negative checks on the other two branches. Instead, the court itself (in the landmark decision of *Marbury v. Madison* in 1803) established the practice of **judicial review**, the ability of the Supreme Court to strike down a law or an executive branch action as unconstitutional. According to Madison's notes, nine of the eleven framers who spoke on the topic clearly favored explicitly granting the Supreme Court the power of judicial review, but the issue was not resolved at the convention. In several states, assertive courts had struck down state laws, and delegates from those states resisted giving an unelected national court similar power over the entire country. Although judicial review is not explicitly mentioned in the Constitution, supporters of the practice point to the supremacy clause, which states that the "Constitution, and the Laws of the United States which shall be made in Pursuance thereof . . . shall be the supreme Law of the Land."

As Chief Justice John Marshall argued in *Marbury v. Madison,* to enforce the Constitution as the supreme law of the land, the Court must determine which laws are "in pursuance thereof." Critics of judicial review argue that the Constitution is supreme because it gains its legitimacy from the people, and therefore elected officials—Congress and the president—should be the primary interpreters of the Constitution rather than the courts. This dispute may never be fully resolved, but Marshall's bold assertion of judicial review made the Supreme Court an equal partner in the system of separate powers and checks and balances rather than "the least dangerous branch" that the framers described.

IS THE CONSTITUTION A "LIVING" DOCUMENT?

EXPLORE HOW THE MEANING OF THE CONSTITUTION HAS EVOLVED

Polls suggest that many Americans are unfamiliar with the Constitution's basic provisions. Indeed, a national poll found that only 42 percent of the public could name the three branches of government, although 73 percent could identify the Three Stooges (Larry, Moe, and Curly). In another survey, 24 percent of the public could not name any First Amendment rights, 52 percent did not know that the Senate has 100 members, and 16 percent thought that the Constitution created a Christian nation.[20]

In the face of such public ignorance, can the Constitution provide the blueprint for modern democratic governance? If so, how has it remained relevant after more than 200 years? The answer to the first question, in our opinion, is clearly yes. Although the United States falls short on many measures of an ideal democracy, the Constitution remains relevant in part because it embodies many of the central values of American citizens: liberty and freedom, majority rule and minority rights, equal protection for all citizens under the laws, and a division of power across and within levels of government. The Constitution presents a list of substantive values, largely within the Bill of Rights, aimed at legally protecting certain individual rights that we still consider basic and necessary. The Constitution also sets out the institutional framework within which the government operates.

But these observations beg the question of *why* the Constitution remains relevant today. Why does this framework of government still work? How can the framers' values still be meaningful to us? There are at least three components of the Constitution that allow it to continue as a "living document": the ambiguity in central passages that permits flexible interpretation, the amending process, and the document's own designation of multiple interpreters of the Constitution. These factors have allowed the Constitution to evolve with the changing values and norms of the nation (see the You Decide feature).

WHAT DO POLITICAL SCIENTISTS DO?

For more about the Constitution as a "living" document, visit **wwnpag.es/wdpsd**

AMBIGUITY

The Constitution's inherent ambiguity is a characteristic that has kept the document relevant to this day. Key passages were written in very general language, which has allowed the Constitution to evolve along with changing norms, values, and political contexts. This ambiguity was a political necessity: not only were the

A LIVING CONSTITUTION?

Should the Constitution be viewed as a flexible framework or a document that has fixed meaning? Those who think the former argue that a dynamic and modern society cannot be bound by ideas rooted in the late eighteenth century. Proponents of the other side of the debate fear that flexibility is a recipe for arbitrary law based on Supreme Court justices' individual preferences and biases. They offer an alternative perspective, called "originalism," that says constitutional interpretation must be based on the original meaning of the document and its amendments. The Tea Party strongly supports this perspective in its emphasis on the Constitution and its founding principles.

Justice Clarence Thomas is perhaps the strongest advocate of the originalist view. He wrote, "Let me put it this way; there are really only two ways to interpret the Constitution—try to discern as best we can what the framers intended or make it up."[a] Former Chief Justice William Rehnquist, although generally adhering to the originalist view, took a more nuanced approach. He favorably cites a 1920 Supreme Court opinion by Oliver Wendell Holmes, "When we are dealing with words that also are a constituent act, like the Constitution of the United States, we must realize that they have called into life a being the development of which could not have been foreseen completely by the most gifted of its begetters."[b] John Marshall in *McCulloch v. Maryland*, also endorses this view, saying the Constitution was "intended to endure for ages to come, and consequently to be adapted to the various crises of human affairs." Rehnquist says that "scarcely anyone would disagree" with the idea that the Constitution was written broadly enough to allow principles such as the prohibition against illegal searches and seizures to apply to technologies, such as the telephone or the Internet, which could not have been envisioned by the framers.[c]

However, according to this view, the *meaning* of the Constitution cannot change with the times. Rehnquist writes, "mere change in public opinion since the adoption of the Constitution, unaccompanied by a constitutional amendment, should not change the meaning of the Constitution. A merely temporary majoritarian groundswell should not abrogate some individual liberty truly protected by the Constitution."[d] Therefore, recent rulings restricting the death penalty (which is clearly endorsed by the Constitution), expanding gay rights, or allowing a child to testify remotely against her sexual abuser rather than having to confront him directly in court (as guaranteed by the Sixth Amendment) would all be inconsistent with the originalist view. This view would also hold that anything other than relying on the meaning of the words of the Constitution allows justices to "legislate from the bench," which is undemocratic given that the judges are not elected.

Proponents of a living constitution argue for a more flexible view. Justice Thurgood Marshall advocated a living constitution,

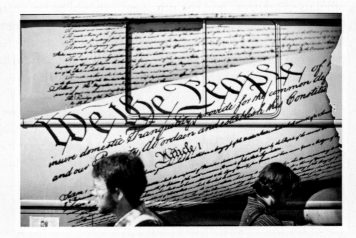

There is a vigorous debate among justices of the Supreme Court as to whether the Constitution is a living document or whether it should be interpreted more strictly according to the orginal intent of the framers.

noting that the framers "could not have imagined, nor would they have accepted, that the document they were drafting would one day be construed by a Supreme Court to which had been appointed a woman and the descendent of an African slave."[e] If the meaning of the Constitution is fixed, then the Court would have to uphold a state law allowing the death penalty for horse stealing, which was common during the Founding era. Executing horse thieves, or more realistically, children and the mentally impaired (which *was* allowed in many states until 2005), is unacceptable in a modern society, even if it would be allowed by a strict reading of the Constitution.

Answering the question about how justices should interpret the Constitution ultimately depends on one's broader views of the proper role of the Court within a representative democracy. Should justices be constrained by the original meaning of the Constitution, or should that meaning evolve over time? You decide.

CRITICAL THINKING QUESTIONS

1. If you were on the Supreme Court, would you adopt an originalist or a living constitution approach? Justify your position.

2. Based on the originalist view, should a state be allowed to execute whomever it wants to, including minors (or horse thieves)? Based on the living constitution approach, should limits be placed on justices to prevent them from "legislating from the bench"?

framers aware that the document would need to survive for generations, but in many instances the language that they chose was simply the only wording that all the framers could agree on.

Three of the most important parts of the Constitution are also among its most ambiguous: the necessary and proper (or elastic) clause, the **executive powers clause**, and the **commerce clause**. As discussed earlier, the necessary and proper clause gives Congress the power to enact laws that are related to its **enumerated powers**, or those that are explicitly granted. But what does "necessary and proper" mean? For the most part, Congress gets to answer that question.

The executive powers clause is even more vague: Article II begins with the words "The executive Power shall be vested in a President of the United States of America." This sentence has served to justify a broad range of presidential actions because it does not define any boundaries for the "executive powers" it grants. The vague wording was necessary because the Constitutional Convention delegates could not agree on a definition of executive power. The wording also had the desirable consequence of making the clause flexible enough to serve the country both in times that require strong presidential action (such as the Civil War, the Great Depression, or World War II), and in times when the president was not as central (such as the "golden age of Congress" in the late nineteenth century).

Perhaps the best illustration of the importance of ambiguity in the Constitution is the commerce clause, which gives Congress "the power to regulate commerce . . . among the several States." What is "commerce," and what exactly does "among the states" mean? Different interpretations have reflected prevailing norms of the time. In the nineteenth century, when the national government was relatively weak and more power was held at the state level, the Supreme Court interpreted the clause to mean that Congress could not regulate commerce that was entirely within the boundaries of a single state (intrastate, as opposed to interstate, commerce). Because manufacturing typically occurred within the boundaries of a given state, this ruling led to a distinction between manufacturing and commerce, which had significant implications. For example, Congress could not regulate working hours, worker safety, or child labor given that these were defined as part of manufacturing rather than commerce. In the New Deal era of the mid-1930s, the Court adopted a more expansive interpretation of the commerce clause that largely obliterated the distinction between intrastate and interstate commerce. This view was strengthened in the 1960s when the Supreme Court upheld a civil rights law that, among other things, prevented owners of hotels and restaurants from discriminating against African Americans. As we discuss more fully in Chapter 3, for nearly 60 years this interpretation held. More recently the Supreme Court has tightened the scope of Congress's powers to regulate commerce, but the clause still serves as the basis for most important national legislation. The commerce clause has been unchanged since 1789, but its ambiguous wording has been used to justify or restrict a varying array of legislation.

executive powers clause Part of Article II, Section 1, of the Constitution that states, "The executive Power shall be vested in a President of the United States of America." This broad statement has been used to justify many assertions of presidential power.

commerce clause Part of Article I, Section 8, of the Constitution that gives Congress "the power to regulate Commerce . . . among the several States." The Supreme Court's interpretation of this clause has varied, but today it serves as the basis for much of Congress's legislation.

enumerated powers Powers explicitly granted to Congress, the president, or the Supreme Court in the first three articles of the Constitution. Examples include Congress's power to "raise and support armies" and the president's power as commander in chief.

CHANGING THE CONSTITUTION

The most obvious way that the Constitution keeps up with the times is by allowing for changes to its language. The framers broadly supported the idea behind Article V, which lays out the formal process for amending the Constitution: the people must control their own political system, which included the ability to change it through a regular, nonviolent process. George Washington called constitutional amendments "explicit and authentic acts," and Thomas Jefferson was adamant that each generation needed to have the power to change the Constitution. Toward the end of his life, he wrote in a letter to James Madison:

> Some men look at constitutions with sanctimonious reverence, and deem them like the ark of the covenant, too sacred to be touched. They ascribe to the men of the preceding age a wisdom more than human, and suppose what they did to be beyond amendment. I knew that age well; I belonged to it and labored with it.... It was very like the present.... Let us not weakly believe that one generation is not as capable as another of taking care of itself.[21]

PROPOSAL AND RATIFICATION Although there was strong consensus on including in the Constitution a set of provisions for amending it, there was no agreement on how this should be done. The Virginia Plan envisioned a relatively easy process of changing the Constitution "whensoever it shall seem necessary" by means of ratification by the people, whereas the New Jersey Plan proposed a central role for state governments. Madison suggested the plan that was eventually adopted, which once again accommodated both those who wanted a stronger national government and those who favored the states.

Article V describes the two steps necessary to change the Constitution: proposal and ratification. Congress may *propose* an amendment that has the approval of two-thirds of the members in both houses, or an amendment may be proposed by a national convention that has been called by two-thirds of the states' legislatures. In either case, the amendment must be *ratified* by three-fourths of the states' legislatures or state conventions (see Figure 2.3). A national convention has never been used to propose an amendment, and every amendment except for the Twenty-First, which repealed Prohibition, has been ratified by state legislatures rather than state conventions.

A RANGE OF AMENDMENTS Amendments have ranged from fairly narrow, technical corrections of errors in the original document (Eleventh and Twelfth Amendments), to important topics such as the abolition of slavery (Thirteenth Amendment), mandating equal protection of the laws for all

AMENDING THE CONSTITUTION IS DIFFICULT and can be controversial. Some amendments that are widely accepted today, like the Nineteenth Amendment giving women the right to vote, were intensely debated prior to their ratification.

FIGURE » 2.3

AMENDING THE CONSTITUTION

This flowchart shows how amendments to the Constitution can be proposed and ratified, and the frequency with which each method has been used.

Proposal	Ratification	Frequency of Use
Congress proposes amendment by at least a two-thirds vote	By at least three-fourths of the state legislatures	All but once
	By at least three-fourths of state conventions called for the purpose of ratifying the amendment	Once
Amendment is proposed by a national convention that is called by at least two-thirds of the state legislatures	By at least three-fourths of the state legislatures	Never
	By at least three-fourths of state conventions called for the purpose of ratifying the amendment	Never

citizens (Fourteenth Amendment), providing for the popular election of senators (Seventeenth Amendment), giving blacks and then women the right to vote (Fifteenth and Nineteenth Amendments), and allowing a national income tax (Sixteenth Amendment). Potential constitutional amendments have addressed many other issues, with more than 10,000 proposed; of those, 33 were sent to the states and 27 have made it through the amending process (the first 10 came at once in the Bill of Rights). Table 2.1 shows several amendments that were introduced but not ratified.

MULTIPLE INTERPRETERS

The final way that the Constitution maintains its relevance is through changing views of the document by multiple interpreters. As we pointed out in the previous discussion of the commerce clause, there have been significant changes in the way the Constitution structures the policy-making process, even though the pertinent text of the Constitution has not changed.[22] This point is best understood by examining the concept of **implied powers**—that is, powers that are not explicitly stated in the Constitution but can be inferred from an enumerated power. The Supreme Court often defines the boundaries of implied powers, but Congress, the president, and the public can also play key roles.

Three of the earliest examples of implied powers show the president, the Supreme Court, and Congress each interpreting the Constitution and contributing to its evolving meaning. The first involved the question of how active the president should be in stating national foreign policy principles. In issuing his famous proclamation of neutrality in 1793, George Washington unilaterally set forth a national foreign policy, even though the president's power to do so is not explicitly

implied powers Powers supported by the Constitution that are not expressly stated in it.

TABLE » 2.1

AMENDMENTS INTRODUCED IN CONGRESS THAT DID NOT PASS

Many proposed constitutional amendments have almost no chance of passing. Indeed, most of those listed here did not even make it to the floor of the House or Senate for a vote. Why do you think a member of Congress would propose an amendment that he or she knew would fail?

113th Congress (2013–2014)	No treaty, executive order, or agreement with another nation can diminish the rights of U.S. citizens.
	All laws that apply to U.S. citizens must apply equally to U.S. senators and representatives.
112th Congress (2011–2012)	Impose 12-year term limits for the House and Senate.
	Amend the First Amendment to allow limitations on federal campaign contributions and expenditures.
	Protect the right of parents to raise and educate their children without interference from government.
	Require that the federal budget is balanced.
111th Congress (2009–2010)	Abolish the electoral college and provide for the direct election of the president and vice president.
	Provide a high-quality education to all citizens of the United States.
	Repeal the Sixteenth Amendment (prohibit an income tax).
110th Congress (2007–2008)	Repeal the Twenty-Second Amendment (abolish term limits for the president).
	Provide the right to a clean, safe, and sustainable environment for all persons.
	Permit voluntary school prayer.
109th Congress (2005–2006)	Make the filibuster in the Senate a part of the Constitution.
	Provide for continuity of government in case of a catastrophic event.
	Prohibit desecration of the U.S. flag.

SOURCES: The U.S. Constitution Online: Some Proposed Amendments, www.usconstitution.net/constamprop.html (accessed 3/22/12); http://thomas.loc.gov (accessed 12/6/13).

stated in the Constitution. Alexander Hamilton defended the presidential power to make such a proclamation as implied in both the executive powers clause and the president's explicitly granted powers in the area of foreign policy (receiving ambassadors, negotiating treaties, and serving as commander in chief). Thomas Jefferson, in contrast, thought it was a terrible idea for presidents to have that kind of power. He preferred that such general policy statements be left to Congress.

The Supreme Court made its mark on the notion of implied powers in a landmark case involving the creation of a national bank. In *McCulloch v. Maryland* (1819), the Court ruled that the federal government had the power to create a national bank and denied the state of Maryland the right to tax a branch of that bank. The Court said it was not necessary for the Constitution to expressly grant Congress the power to create the bank; rather, it was implied in Congress's power over financial matters and from the necessary and proper clause of the Constitution.

Congress got into the act with an early debate over the president's implied power to remove appointed officials. The Constitution clearly gives the president the power to make appointments to cabinet positions and other top executive branch offices, but it is silent on how these people can be removed. This was one of the most difficult issues in the first Congress, and members spent more than a month debating the topic.

The record of the debate is the most thorough examination of implied powers ever conducted in Congress. However, Congress ended up not taking any action on the issue, which left the president's removal power implicit in the Constitution.

Issues concerning implied powers continue to surface. The president's appointment powers have recently evolved as the Senate has played a much more aggressive role in providing its "advice and consent" on presidential nominations to the federal courts. As we explore in Chapter 14, in the past 20 years, the Senate has blocked court appointments at a significantly higher rate than it did in the first half of the twentieth century. The relevant language in the Constitution is the same, yet the Senate's understanding of its role in this important process has changed.

Public opinion and social norms also influence the prevailing interpretation of the Constitution, as is evident in the evolving meanings of capital punishment (the death penalty) and freedom of speech. When the Constitution was written, capital punishment was broadly accepted, even for horse thieves. The framers were only concerned that people not be "deprived of life, liberty, or property without the due process of law." Therefore, the prohibition in the Eighth Amendment against "cruel and unusual punishment" certainly did not mean to the framers that the death penalty was unconstitutional. However, in 1972, the Supreme Court struck down capital punishment as unconstitutional because it was being applied arbitrarily.[23] Subsequently, after procedural changes were made, the Court once again upheld the practice. However, the Court has since decided that capital punishment for a mentally retarded man constituted cruel and unusual punishment—a decision that reflects modern sensibilities but not the thinking of the framers. Similarly, the text of the First Amendment protections for freedom of speech has never changed, but the Supreme Court has been willing to uphold significant limitations on free speech, especially in wartime. When external threats are less severe, the Court has been more tolerant of controversial speech.

The line between a new interpretation of the Constitution and constitutional change is difficult to define. Clearly, not every new direction taken by the Court or new interpretation of the constitutional roles of the president or Congress is comparable to a constitutional amendment. In one respect, a constitutional amendment is much more permanent than a new interpretation by the Court. For example, the Supreme Court could not unilaterally decide that 18- to 20-year-olds, women, and African Americans no longer have the right to vote. Constitutional amendments expanded the right to vote to include these groups, and only further amendments could either expand or restrict the right to vote. However, gradual changes in constitutional interpretation are probably just as important as the amending process in explaining the Constitution's ability to keep pace with the times. For example, although the Civil War amendments produced lasting and significant changes in the Constitution, during the New Deal, shifts in constitutional interpretation helped establish a huge growth in national power without changing a single word of the document.

THE EIGHTH AMENDMENT'S BAN ON "cruel and unusual punishment" is generally viewed as excluding capital punishment, but the execution of juveniles and the mentally retarded has been found unconstitutional. This picture shows the electric chair in the Southern Ohio Correctional Facility in Lucasville, Ohio.

CONCLUSION

The debate between Tea Party supporters and opponents outlined in the introduction illustrates many of the themes of this chapter: the conflictual nature of politics established by the Constitution, multiple interpreters, and ambiguous language.

The separation of powers and the system of checks and balances in our political system divide power to protect against majority tyranny. To Tea Party supporters, we have strayed too far from the limited government roots of the Founding. Their opponents claim that the Constitution centralized power in the national government while moving away from the state-centered Articles of Confederation. Well, which side is right? The rather unsatisfying answer is that both are correct. The Founders *did* create a system of limited government that was intended to protect individual liberty from government tyranny, but at the same time, the Founders wanted a strong and effective government that could overcome the limitations of state-centered government. So clearly, a return to founding principles does not mean a return to states' rights; that would be a return to the principles of the Articles of Confederation. But equally clear is that the Founders were concerned about unchecked government power.

Congress, the president, and the Supreme Court all must interpret the Constitution in the normal course of fulfilling their institutional roles. But as the Tea Party debate shows, members of the public can differ in their interpretation of the Constitution as well. It is refreshing to see the Constitution thrust to the fore in congressional and presidential candidate debates. Maybe with enough attention, those public-opinion polls showing that Americans are more familiar with the Three Stooges than with the three branches of government can be reversed. If Americans are more informed about the Constitution, they can become even more significant interpreters of the Constitution.

Finally, the general and ambiguous language of the Constitution means that both supporters and opponents of the Tea Party can stake a claim to having views that are informed by the Constitution. When a Tea Party advocate claims that the Federal Reserve is unconstitutional because it is not specifically mentioned in the document, the other side can point out that if that logic is used, then the Air Force is certainly unconstitutional as well (the Constitution mentions Congress's power to support the Army and Navy, but obviously not the Air Force). Furthermore, Tea Party opponents would say the commerce clause and the necessary and proper clause give Congress all the power it needs.

A leading constitutional scholar, Walter Murphy, addressed the relevance issue this way: "The ideals it enshrines, the processes it prescribes, and the actions it legitimizes must either help to change its citizenry or at a minimum reflect their current values. If a constitution does not articulate, at least in general terms, the ideals that form or will re-form its people and express the political character they have . . . , it will soon be replaced or atrophy."[24] The Constitution's ability to change with the times and reflect its citizens' values has enabled it to remain relevant and important today. Its flexibility and general language means that there will never be definitive answers to the conflict over its meaning, but it ensures that these debates will be enduring and meaningful.

THE HISTORICAL CONTEXT OF THE CONSTITUTION

▶ *Describe the historical circumstances that led to the Constitutional Convention of 1787.* **(Pages 31–37)**

SUMMARY

The U.S. Constitution was shaped by historical events preceding its creation, particularly the period of British rule over the colonies, the Revolutionary War, and the states' experience under the Articles of Confederation. Under British rule, the colonies were relatively independent of one another, and the framers sought to create a strong nation while still maintaining the autonomy of the states in the system. The framers based the Constitution on three key principles: the rejection of a monarchy, popular control of the government, and a limited government that protected against tyranny.

KEY TERMS

Articles of Confederation (p. 32)
limited government (p. 32)
monarchy (p. 35)
republicanism (p.35)
"consent of the governed" (p. 35)
natural rights (p. 35)
Federalists (p. 37)
Antifederalists (p. 37)

CRITICAL THINKING AND DISCUSSION

What evidence from the founding period supports the Tea Party's view of the Constitution, and what evidence would counter their position? Do you think Tea Party supporters are closer to the Federalist or Antifederalist view of the Constitution?

PRACTICE QUIZ QUESTIONS

1. How were members of Congress selected under the Articles of Confederation?

   A by the state governor
   B by the state legislature
   C by the state supreme court
   D by popular election
   E by random lot

2. What power did the president have under the Articles of Confederation?

   A power to raise an army
   B power to veto congressional legislation
   C power to negotiate foreign agreements
   D power to nominate federal judges
   E There was no president under the Articles of Confederation.

3. Who is the philosopher who argued that without government, life would be "nasty, brutish and short"?

   A Thomas Hobbes
   B John Locke
   C Baron de Montesquieu
   D Thomas Paine
   E Thomas Jefferson

4. At the American Founding, what is the best way to describe the economic inequality among classes, and the economic diversity among regions?

   A high inequality/ high diversity
   B high inequality/ low diversity
   C low inequality/ high diversity
   D low inequality/ low diversity

THE POLITICS OF COMPROMISE AT THE CONSTITUTIONAL CONVENTION

▶ *Analyze the major issues debated by the framers of the Constitution.* **(Pages 37–45)**

SUMMARY

Although the framers of the Constitution agreed that the Articles of Confederation needed to be changed, there was little consensus otherwise. The Federalists and Antifederalists clashed on several issues, though the most important were (1) balancing majority rule with minority rights, (2) allocating power between large and small states, (3) allocating power between the legislature and executive, (4) allocating power between the national government and the states, and (5) determining how to handle slavery.

KEY TERMS

pluralism (p. 39)
Virginia Plan (p. 40)
New Jersey Plan (p. 40)
Great Compromise (p. 40)
parliamentary system (p. 41)
reserved powers (p. 42)
national supremacy clause (p. 43)
Three-Fifths Compromise (p. 44)

CRITICAL THINKING AND DISCUSSION

If you had been at the Constitutional Convention, which part of the document would you have worked to change? How would you have negotiated a compromise to make that change possible?

5. Madison argued that the best way to prevent the tyranny of factions was to _____.
   A outlaw political parties
   B establish a strong national government
   C have various groups compete against each other in the government
   D establish strong local governments
   E try to ensure that all people were equal

6. The Great Compromise provided solutions to which issue?
   A balancing majority rule with minority rights
   B allocating power between big and small states
   C allocating power between the legislature and executive
   D allocating power between national and state governments
   E determining how to handle slavery

7. How are executives chosen in most other established democracies?
   A by popular election
   B by electoral college
   C through selection by the judiciary
   D through selection by the legislature
   E by the United Nations

8. The outcome of the Three-Fifths Compromise was that slaves counted for three-fifths of a person for the purposes of _____ and _____.
   A voting; taxation
   B congressional representation; taxation
   C voting; congressional representation
   D taxation; congressional appropriations
   E congressional representation; agricultural subsidies

RATIFICATION

▶ Contrast the arguments of the Federalists with those of the Antifederalists. **(Pages 45–48)**

SUMMARY

After the Constitution was written and approved at the Constitutional Convention, it still needed to be ratified by nine states. The Constitution was primarily criticized by the Antifederalists, which gave way to a lengthy public debate over the merits of the proposed framework. Ultimately, to win over the necessary support in the states, the framers had to include the Bill of Rights, which was tailored to protect the rights of states and individuals from the national government.

KEY TERM

Bill of Rights (p. 48)

CRITICAL THINKING AND DISCUSSION

In the push for ratification of the Constitution, why did the Federalists agree to add the Bill of Rights?

9. What group was concerned about the Constitution's provisions for the strength of the president and the lack of specific guarantees of civil liberties?
   A Tories
   B Unionists
   C Federalists
   D Antifederalists
   E Free Soilers

10. A series of arguments originally published in New York newspapers supported the Constitution and outlined the political theory behind it. What are these assembled works called?
    A *Pickwick Papers*
    B *Federalist Papers*
    C *Antifederalist Papers*
    D *Common Sense*
    E *The Second Treatise of Government*

THE CONSTITUTION: A FRAMEWORK FOR GOVERNMENT

▶ Outline the major provisions of the Constitution. **(Pages 48–55)**

SUMMARY

The defining feature of the Constitution is its separation of powers while still maintaining flexibility for leadership in times of crisis. The system of checks and balances gives each branch of the federal government some explicit powers, some shared powers, and some ability to limit the power of the other two branches of government.

KEY TERMS

necessary and proper clause (p. 51)
impeachment (p. 53)
power of the purse (p. 53)
judicial review (p. 54)

CRITICAL THINKING AND DISCUSSION

The president has clearly dominated the decision to go to war in the past century, despite the Founders' view that war powers are a shared power. How would a Tea Partier respond to this change? What other areas of the Constitution have evolved as a framework for government?

11. The "necessary and proper clause" gives flexibility to which part of government?

   Ⓐ the president

   Ⓑ the Supreme Court

   Ⓒ the bureaucracy

   Ⓓ the Congress

   Ⓔ interest groups

12. Which branch has the fewest explicit powers?

   Ⓐ the president

   Ⓑ the Supreme Court

   Ⓒ the bureaucracy

   Ⓓ the Congress

   Ⓔ the people

13. Which of the following negative powers does the president enjoy?

   Ⓐ the power to veto legislation

   Ⓑ the power to freeze judicial salaries

   Ⓒ the power to review the constitutionality of a law

   Ⓓ the power to impeach federal justices

   Ⓔ the power to dissolve Congress and call new elections

IS THE CONSTITUTION A "LIVING" DOCUMENT?

▶ *Explore how the meaning of the Constitution has evolved.*
(Pages 55–61)

SUMMARY

The Constitution is more than 200 years old, yet it still provides a blueprint for modern governance. It has maintained its relevance due to its ambiguity on several key passages, its ability to be amended rather than entirely rewritten, and its designation of multiple interpreters of the Constitution.

KEY TERMS

executive powers clause (p. 57)

commerce clause (p. 57)

enumerated powers (p. 57)

implied powers (p. 59)

CRITICAL THINKING AND DISCUSSION

Should the Constitution be a "living document" that evolves with the values and norms of our society, or should interpretation of the Constitution follow more closely the original intentions of the framers?

14. Which of the following clauses, central to congressional activity, has been interpreted differently over time though the wording has stayed the same?

   Ⓐ establishment clause

   Ⓑ commerce clause

   Ⓒ enumerated powers clause

   Ⓓ executive powers clause

   Ⓔ prerogative powers clause

15. Which part of government often defines the boundaries of implied powers?

   Ⓐ the president

   Ⓑ the Supreme Court

   Ⓒ the bureaucracy

   Ⓓ the Congress

   Ⓔ the people

SUGGESTED READING

Amar, Akhil Reed, *America's Unwritten Constitution: The Precedents and Principles We Live By.* New York: Basic Books, 2012.

Balkin, Jack M., ed. *The Constitution in 2020.* New York: Oxford University Press, 2009.

Currie, David P. *The Constitution of the United States: A Primer for the People,* 2nd ed. Chicago: University of Chicago Press, 2000.

Dahl, Robert A. *How Democratic Is the American Constitution?* New Haven, CT: Yale University Press, 2001.

Davis, Sue. *Corwin and Peltason's Understanding the Constitution,* 17th ed. Boston: Wadsworth, 2007.

Hamilton, Alexander, James Madison, and John Jay. *The Federalist Papers.* 1788. Reprint, 2nd ed., edited by Roy P. Fairfield. Baltimore, MD: Johns Hopkins University Press, 1981.

Ketcham, Ralph. *The Anti-Federalist Papers and the Constitutional Convention Debates.* New York: Signet Classics, 2003.

Kurland, Philip B., and Ralph Lerner, eds. *The Founders' Constitution.* Chicago: University of Chicago Press, 1987.

Rossiter, Clinton. *1787: The Grand Convention.* New York: MacMillan, 1966.

Strauss, David. *The Living Constitution.* New York: Oxford University Press, 2010.

Sunstein, Cass R. *Designing Democracy: What Constitutions Do.* New York: Oxford University Press, 2001.

Wood, Gordon S. *The Creation of the American Republic.* New York: W. W. Norton, 1969.

3

Federalism

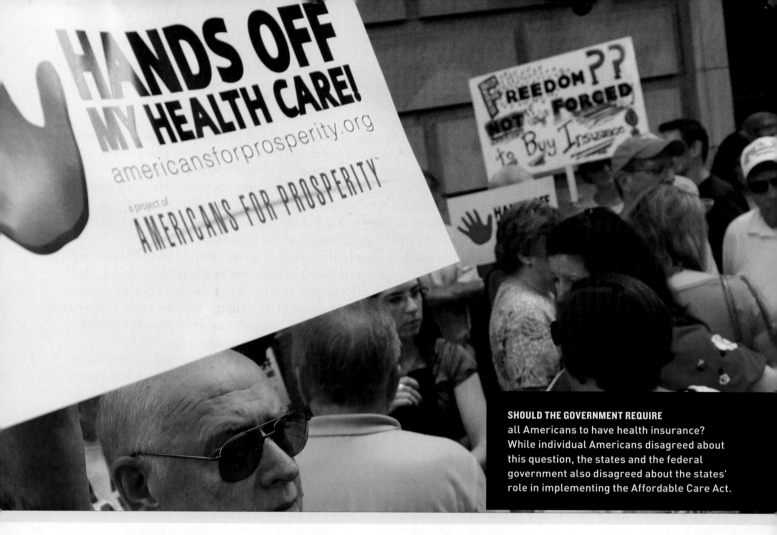

SHOULD THE GOVERNMENT REQUIRE all Americans to have health insurance? While individual Americans disagreed about this question, the states and the federal government also disagreed about the states' role in implementing the Affordable Care Act.

FOLLOWING THE PASSAGE OF THE 2010 AFFORDABLE Care Act (ACA), which is often referred to as "Obamacare,"[1] 26 states sued the national government over the new law. Intended to provide health care coverage to more than 30 million Americans who were uninsured, the law was viewed by the attorneys general from these states as an unconstitutional overreach of federal power. David Rivkin, one of the attorneys who filed the suit on behalf of the states, said, "This is one of the most important Constitutional challenges in history. . . . The states' sovereign authority is being trammeled upon by the federal government."[2] Michael Boldin, executive director of the Tenth Amendment Center, argued that the lawsuit showed ". . . that state level resistance to federal power is not just an old idea relegated to history books. It's something that's alive and well right now."[3]

In their lawsuit against the federal government, the states opposed to the law alleged three instances of constitutional overreach in the ACA: "the individual mandate exceeds Congress's enumerated powers, the Medicaid expansions are unconstitutionally coercive, and the employer mandates impermissibly interfere with state sovereignty."[4] Supporters of the law argued that standardizing these provisions across all 50 states was crucial to ensuring health care for all Americans because without a national law, millions of Americans would be unable to get health insurance. Some states do an excellent job of providing access to health care (such as Massachusetts, which

CONFLICT & COMPROMISE
in American Politics

CHAPTER *goals*

Define federalism and explain its significance.
► PAGES 69–71

Explain what the Constitution says about federalism.
► PAGES 71–74

Trace the major shifts in state and federal government power over time.
► PAGES 74–83

Describe the major trends and debates in federalism today.
► PAGES 83–95

Analyze the arguments for and against a strong federal government.
► PAGES 95–100

has only 5 percent of its residents uninsured), whereas others (such as Texas, which has 26 percent of its residents uninsured) do not do as well.[5] Supporters of the ACA insist that access to health care is a basic right that should not depend on which state you live in.

The Supreme Court largely upheld the ACA in 2012, but the Court agreed with the states on one important point: it ruled that the expansion of Medicaid, which would provide health care for an additional 17 million low-income Americans, was unconstitutionally coercive in requiring states to expand Medicaid or lose all their federal funding for the existing Medicaid program. States could still choose to accept the federal funding to expand Medicaid, but they would not lose their other Medicaid funding if they opted out of the expansion.[6]

However, the battle between the national government and the states did not end with the Court's ruling. Twenty-three states decided not to accept the federal incentives to expand Medicaid, leaving 5 to 6 million poor Americans without health insurance.[7] Twenty-nine states supported two suits challenging the mandate to include contraception as part of business-provided health care on the grounds that it violates religious freedom protected by the First Amendment.[8] Twenty-six states opted not to run the health insurance exchanges, requiring the federal government to do it for them. A few states have actively tried to obstruct implementation of the law by forbidding state employees to do anything to help that is not specifically required by the law.[9]

The conflict triggered by the ACA is a great example of the tensions that exist over how power is distributed between the states and the national government. What are the responsibilities of the states and what is the domain of the national government? What happens when levels of government disagree on a policy? Can the national government simply force the states to do something? How do the states and national government cooperate when they possess shared responsibilities? Why did the Founders give us such a complicated form of government?

THE RELATIONSHIP BETWEEN THE national government and the states also involves cooperation. After Hurricane Sandy hit the East Coast in 2012, President Obama and federal agencies worked with the states to provide emergency relief funds and services. Here, President Obama tours Brigantine, New Jersey, with Governor Chris Christie to view the damage caused by the superstorm.

WHAT IS FEDERALISM AND WHY DOES IT MATTER?

Federalism is a form of government that divides sovereign power across at least two political units. Dividing **sovereign power** simply means that each unit of government (in the U.S. context, the national and state governments) has some degree of authority and autonomy. As discussed in Chapter 2, this division of power across levels of government is central to the system of separated powers in the United States. Dividing power across levels of government seems a simple concept, but as we will see later in this chapter, the political battles over *how* that power is divided have been intense.

In practical terms, federalism is about intergovernmental relations: How do the different levels of government interact and how is power divided? But even that may seem a little abstract. Why does federalism matter? On a broad range of issues, the level of government that dictates policy can make a real difference. The conflict over health care reform is an obvious current example, but other policies include whether the national government should be able to compel states to integrate schools, make the drinking age 21, ban guns within or around public schools, or have a uniform speed limit on federal highways. More recent issues include whether the national government can prevent states from allowing marijuana use for medical and recreational purposes, from allowing "aid in dying" (or what opponents to the practice label "assisted suicides"), or from discriminating against employees based on age or disability. Same-sex marriage is currently determined by the states, but that could change if the Supreme Court applies the equal protection clause of the Fourteenth Amendment to same-sex couples. These questions involve defining the disputed boundaries between what the states and national government are allowed to do. Much of U.S. history has been rooted in this struggle to define American federalism.

federalism The division of power across the local, state, and national governments.

sovereign power The supreme power of an independent state to regulate its internal affairs without foreign interference.

LEVELS OF GOVERNMENT AND THEIR DEGREES OF AUTONOMY

A distinguishing feature of federalism is that each level of government has some degree of autonomy from the other levels—that is, each level can carry out some policies without interference from the others. In the United States, this means that the national and state governments have distinct powers and responsibilities (see Nuts & Bolts 3.1). The national government, for example, is responsible for national defense and foreign policy. State and local governments have primary responsibility for conducting elections and promoting public safety, or **police powers**. In other areas, such as transportation, the different levels of government have **concurrent powers**—that is, they share responsibilities. The national government has also taken on additional responsibilities through implied powers that are inferred from the powers explicitly granted in the Constitution (see Chapter 2 and the later discussion in this chapter).

Local governments—cities, towns, school districts, and counties—are not autonomous units of government. They are creatures of the state government. Thus, state governments create local governments and control the types of

police powers The power to enforce laws and provide for public safety.

concurrent powers Responsibilities for particular policy areas, such as transportation, that are shared by federal, state, and local governments.

NATIONAL AND STATE RESPONSIBILITIES

National Government Powers	State Government Powers	Concurrent Powers
Print money	Issue licenses	Collect taxes
Regulate interstate commerce and international trade	Regulate intrastate (within the state) businesses	Build roads
Make treaties and conduct foreign policy	Conduct elections	Borrow money
Declare war	Establish local governments	Establish courts
Provide an army and navy	Ratify amendments to the Constitution	Make and enforce laws
Establish post offices	Promote public health and safety	Charter banks and corporations
Make laws necessary and proper to carry out these powers	May exert powers the Constitution does not delegate to the national government or does not prohibit the states from using	Spend money for the general welfare; take private property for public purposes, with just compensation

Powers Denied to the National Government	Powers Denied to State Governments	
May not violate the Bill of Rights	May not enter into treaties with other countries	
May not impose export taxes among states	May not print money	
May not use money from the Treasury without an appropriation from Congress	May not tax imports or exports	
May not change state boundaries	May not interfere with contracts	
	May not suspend a person's rights without due process	

SOURCE: GPO Access: Guide to the U.S. Government, http://bensguide.gpo.gov/3-5/government/federalism.html (accessed 12/5/11).

activities they can engage in by specifying in the state charter either what local governments *can* do or only what they *cannot* do (which would allow them to do anything not specifically prohibited in the charter). Despite this lack of autonomy, local governments play an important role in providing public education, police and fire departments, and land use policies. They also raise money through property taxes, user fees, and in some cases, local sales taxes. But, overall, because of their lack of autonomy, local governments do not directly share power within our federal system with the state and national governments.

A COMPARATIVE PERSPECTIVE

It is useful to compare U.S. federalism to forms of government in other countries. Just because a nation is composed of states does not mean that it is a federal system. The key factor is the autonomy of the political subunits. The United Kingdom, for example, is made up of England, Scotland, Wales, and Northern Ireland. In 1998, the British Parliament created a new Scottish government and gave it authority in a broad range of areas. However, Parliament retained the right to unilaterally dissolve the Scottish government; therefore, the subunit (Scotland) is not autonomous (a September 2014 referendum rejected independence for Scotland by a 55–45 margin). This type of government in which power is centralized within the national government is a **unitary government**. Unitary governments are the most common in the modern world (about 80 percent); other examples include Israel, Italy, France, Japan, and Sweden. Although federalism is not as common, Australia, Austria, Canada, Germany, and Switzerland, among others, share this form of government with the United States.

At the opposite end of the spectrum is a **confederal government**, in which the states have most of the power and often can even veto the actions of the central government. This was the first type of government in the United States under the Articles of Confederation. Because so many problems are associated with having such a weak national government (see Chapter 2), few modern examples exist. The Commonwealth of Independent States (CIS), which formed in 1991 after the breakup of the former Soviet Union, has had some success in coordinating the economic activity and security needs of 12 independent states.[10] Over time, however, rifts among the member states have created problems, and today the CIS is viewed as largely ineffective.

Although true confederations are rare, **intergovernmental organizations** have proliferated in recent decades. Member nations have created over 1,200 multilateral organizations in an effort to coordinate their policies on, for example, economic activity, security, or environmental protection. The United Nations (UN), the International Monetary Fund (IMF), and the North Atlantic Treaty Organization (NATO) are important examples. The European Union (EU) is an intergovernmental organization that began as a loose confederation, but it is becoming more federalist in its decision-making process and structure. The EU's relative success, compared to the failure of the CIS, can be explained in part by this move toward a more federal structure, whereas the CIS maintained its confederal status.

unitary government A system in which the national, centralized government holds ultimate authority. It is the most common form of government in the world.

confederal government A form of government in which states hold power over a limited national government.

intergovernmental organizations Organizations that seek to coordinate policy across member nations.

BALANCING NATIONAL AND STATE POWER IN THE CONSTITUTION

> EXPLAIN WHAT THE CONSTITUTION SAYS ABOUT FEDERALISM

Although the Founders wanted a national government that was stronger than it had been under the Articles of Confederation, they also wanted to preserve states' autonomy. These goals are reflected in different parts of the Constitution, which provides ample evidence for advocates of both state-centered and nation-centered federalism. This nation-centered position appears in the document's preamble, which begins, "We the People of the United States," whereas the Articles of Confederation began with the words, "We the undersigned delegates of the States." The Constitution's phrasing emphasizes the nation as a whole over the separate states. The competing perspectives of nation- and state-centered federalism is a lens through which we can examine the evolving conceptions of federalism and the current conflict over intergovernmental power.

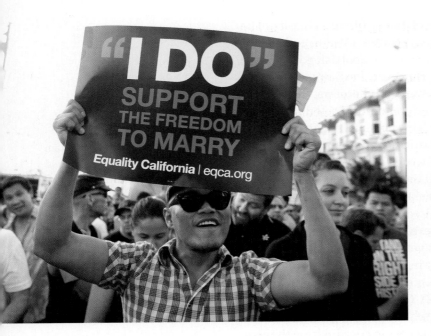

A STRONG NATIONAL GOVERNMENT

The Founders wanted a strong national government to provide national security and a healthy and efficient economy, and so they included various powers in the Constitution that supported the nation-centered perspective. In terms of national security, as we saw in Chapter 2, Congress was granted the power to raise and support armies, declare war, and "suppress Insurrections and repel Invasion," while the president, as commander in chief of the armed forces, would oversee the conduct of war. Congress's power to regulate interstate commerce promoted economic efficiency and centralized an important economic power at the national level, and many restrictions on state power had similar effects. States were *prohibited* from entering into "any Treaty, Alliance, or Confederation" or keeping troops or "Ships of War" during peacetime. They also could not coin money or impose duties on imports or exports (see Article I, Section 10). These provisions in the Constitution ensured that states would not interfere with the smooth operation of interstate commerce or create problems for national defense. Imagine, for example, what would happen if Oklahoma had the power to tax oil produced in other states, or if California decided to create its own army. This would create inefficiencies and potential dangers for the rest of the country.

The necessary and proper clause (Article I, Section 8) was another broad grant of power to the national government: it gave Congress the power "To make all Laws which shall be necessary and proper for carrying into Execution the foregoing Powers." Similarly, the national supremacy clause (Article VI) says that the Constitution and all laws and treaties that are made under the Constitution shall be the "supreme Law of the Land" and that "the Judges in every State shall be bound thereby, any Thing in the Constitution or Laws of any State to the Contrary notwithstanding." This is perhaps the clearest statement of the nation-centered focus of the Constitution. If any state law or constitution conflicts with national law or the Constitution, the national perspective wins. Thus, the laws passed by states to limit implementation of the Affordable Care Act will have no effect now that the Supreme Court has upheld the central parts of the national law.

STATE POWERS AND LIMITS ON NATIONAL POWER

Despite the Founders' nation-centered bias, many parts of the Constitution also address state powers and limits on national power. Article II gives the states the power to choose electors for the Electoral College, and Article V grants the states a central role in the process of amending the Constitution. Three-fourths of the states must ratify any constitutional amendment (either through conventions or their state legislatures, as specified by Congress), but the states can also bypass Congress in proposing amendments if two-thirds of the states call for a

SUPPORTERS OF SAME-SEX marriage celebrated in San Francisco after the Supreme Court ruled that California's Prop 8 ban on same-sex marriage and the federal Defense of Marriage Act (DOMA) were unconstitutional.

Constitutional Convention. This latter route to amending the Constitution has never been used, but the Founders clearly wanted to provide an additional check on national power.

There are also limitations on Congress's authority to regulate interstate commerce. For example, it cannot favor one state over another in regulating commerce, and it cannot impose a tax on any good that is shipped from one state to another. Also, Congress could not prohibit slavery until 1808, but it was allowed to impose a duty of up to $10 per slave.

While Article I of the Constitution enumerates many specific powers for Congress, the list of state powers is much shorter. One could interpret this as more evidence for the nation-centered perspective, but at the time of the Founding, the default position was to keep most power at the state level. Therefore, the federal powers that were exceptions to this rule had to be clearly specified, and state governments received authority over all other matters. The Tenth Amendment supports this view: "The powers not delegated to the United States by the Constitution, nor prohibited by it to the states, are reserved to the states respectively, or to the people."

The Eleventh Amendment, the first one passed after the Bill of Rights, was another important affirmation of state sovereignty. Antifederalists were concerned that the part of Article III that gave the Supreme Court authority over cases involving a "State and Citizens of another State" would undermine state sovereignty by giving the Court too much power over state laws. Federalists assured them this would not happen, but the Supreme Court ruled in *Chisholm v. Georgia* (1793) that citizens of one state could sue the government of another state. The majority opinion ridiculed the "haughty notions of state independence, state sovereignty, and state supremacy." The states struck back by adopting the Eleventh Amendment, which made such lawsuits unconstitutional. Although the Supreme Court lost this skirmish over state power, it continued to serve as the umpire in disputes between the national and state governments.

CLAUSES THAT FAVOR BOTH PERSPECTIVES

Article IV of the Constitution has elements that favor both the state-centered and the nation-centered perspectives. For example, its **full faith and credit clause** specifies that states must respect one another's laws, granting citizens the "Full Faith and Credit" of their home state's laws if they go to another state. At the same time, however, the article's **privileges and immunities clause** says that citizens of each state are "entitled to all Privileges and Immunities" of citizens in the other states, which means that states must treat visitors from other states the same as their own residents. This part of the Constitution favors a nation-centered perspective because it was intended to promote free travel and economic activity among the states.

There are many examples of the full faith and credit clause at work today. If you have a New York driver's license and are traveling to California, you do not need to stop at every state line to get a new license; each state will honor your New York license. Similarly, a legal marriage in one state must be honored by another state. Article IV has also fueled the ongoing controversy over same-sex marriage. In 1996, after courts in Hawaii gave couples in same-sex marriages most of the same legal rights as those in marriages between a man and a woman, many states passed laws saying they would not have to honor same-sex marriages. Congress passed the Defense of Marriage Act in 1996, which said that states would not have to recognize same-sex marriages. But in 2013, the Supreme Court struck down

full faith and credit clause Part of Article IV of the Constitution requiring that each state's laws be honored by the other states. For example, a legal marriage in one state must be recognized across state lines.

privileges and immunities clause Part of Article IV of the Constitution requiring that states must treat nonstate residents within their borders as they would treat their own residents. This was meant to promote commerce and travel between states.

part of this law that denied federal benefits to same-sex couples[11] (see Chapter 5 for a discussion of this important case). As of November 2014, the District of Columbia and 35 states allowed same-sex marriage.[12] In 2012, voters in Maine, Maryland, and Washington approved statewide referendums allowing same-sex marriage. This was the first time that voters, rather than courts or legislatures, had legalized same-sex marriage. In addition, two states recognized civil unions between homosexual partners. Nonetheless, current law holds that the full faith and credit clause does not apply to same-sex marriage because of the "policy exception."[13]

We can also cite examples of the privileges and immunities clause at work in a modern context. For example, Michigan cannot charge the owner of a lakeside cabin different property taxes based on whether she lives in Michigan or in another state. Also, states may not deny welfare benefits to new residents or deny police protection to visitors even though they do not pay state taxes. For example, a 1992 law in California limited the cash welfare benefit for new residents to the same level of benefits that they had been receiving in the state from which they moved. The law was intended to save California's government some money and also to discourage people from moving to California simply to get the higher benefit—this was particularly an issue because California's cash benefit for a mother and one child was $456 a month in 1992, but in the neighboring state of Arizona it was only $275.[14] The Supreme Court ruled that the California state law violated the privileges and immunities clause and the right to travel freely between the states.

But states are allowed to make some distinctions between residents and non-residents. For example, states do not have to permit nonresidents to vote in state elections, and public colleges and universities may charge out-of-state residents higher tuition than in-state residents. Therefore, the privileges and immunities clause cuts both ways on the question of the balance of power: it allows the states to determine and uphold these laws autonomously, but it also emphasizes that national citizenship is more important than state citizenship.

The Constitution sets the boundaries for the battles over federalism. For example, no state can decide to print its own currency and the U.S. government cannot take over the public schools. But within those broad boundaries, the balance between national and state power at any given point in history is a political decision, the product of choices made by elected leaders and the courts. The continuing struggle over implementing the Affordable Care Act is a perfect example: the national government passed the law, the Supreme Court upheld most of it and struck down part of it, and the states are implementing the law with varying levels of cooperation and resistance. Our federal system of government guarantees that there will be conflict between the national and state governments, but which level of government gains the upper hand has evolved in the past two centuries.

TRACE THE MAJOR SHIFTS IN STATE AND FEDERAL GOVERNMENT POWER OVER TIME

THE EVOLVING CONCEPT OF FEDERALISM

The nature of federalism has changed as the relative positions of the national and state governments have evolved. In the first century of our nation's history, the national government played a relatively limited role and the boundaries between the levels of government were distinct. As the national government took on more power in the twentieth century, intergovernmental relations became more cooperative and the boundaries less distinct. Even within this more cooperative framework, federalism remains a source of conflict within our political system as the levels of government share lawmaking authority.

THE EARLY YEARS

As the United States gained its footing, clashes between the advocates of state-centered and nation-centered federalism turned into a partisan struggle. The Federalists, the party of George Washington, John Adams, and Alexander Hamilton, controlled the new government for its first 12 years and favored strong national power. Their opponents, the Democratic-Republicans, led by Thomas Jefferson and James Madison, favored state power.

ESTABLISHING NATIONAL SUPREMACY The first confrontation came when the Federalists established a national bank in 1791, over Jefferson's objections. This controversy did not come to a head until Congress chartered the second national bank in 1816. At that time, the state of Maryland, which was controlled by the Democratic-Republicans, tried to tax the National Bank's Baltimore branch out of existence, but the head cashier of the bank refused to pay the tax and the case eventually ended up at the Supreme Court. The Court had to decide whether Congress had the power to create the bank, and if it did, whether Maryland had the right to tax the bank.

In the landmark decision *McCulloch v. Maryland* (1819), the Court ruled in favor of the national government on both counts. In deciding whether Congress could create the bank, the Court held that even though the word "bank" does not appear in the Constitution, Congress's power to create one is implied through its relevant enumerated powers—such as the power to coin money, levy taxes, and

IN THE EARLY 1800S, THE SUPREME Court confirmed the national government's right to regulate commerce between the states. The state of New York granted a monopoly to a ferry company serving ports in New York and New Jersey, but this was found to interfere with interstate commerce and was therefore subject to federal intervention.

borrow money. The Court also ruled that Maryland did not have the right to tax the bank because of the Constitution's national supremacy clause. Both the concept of implied powers and the validation of national supremacy were critical for establishing the centrality of the national government.

A few years later, the Supreme Court decided another case that cemented Congress's power to act based on the commerce clause in the Constitution. In *Gibbons v. Ogden* (1824), the Supreme Court held that Congress has broad power to regulate interstate commerce and struck down a New York law that had granted a monopoly to a private company operating steamboats on the Hudson River between New York and New Jersey. By granting this monopoly, the ruling stated, New York was interfering with interstate commerce.

TENSION OVER THE SEDITION ACT Another early clash over federalism concerned the Sedition Act of 1798, which was passed by a majority-Federalist Congress.[15] The act banned "any false, scandalous writing against the government of the United States." It was a reaction to the rejection of authority and mass political movements that were sweeping through France at that time; the stated purpose of the law was to prevent these from taking hold in the United States. But Jeffersonians argued, rightly, that the law was an attempt to silence dissent and criticism of the government and was a clear violation of the First Amendment protection of freedom of speech. Indeed, under this law, 10 Democratic-Republican newspaper editors were arrested, fined, and jailed. The issue was important in the 1800 presidential campaign, and when Jefferson was elected he pardoned everyone who had been convicted under the law.

The Sedition Act is important for our purposes here in light of a political tactic that Jefferson devised to try to overturn the law before he became president. His opponents controlled Congress and the Supreme Court, so he had little hope of using the normal political channels to change the law. Thus, Jefferson and Madison circumvented the national government by working through the states: they convinced the Kentucky and Virginia legislatures to pass resolutions challenging the national government's power to pass the Sedition Act through an idea they called the **doctrine of interposition**. Under this doctrine, if the national government passes an unconstitutional law, the people of the states can interpose—or insert—themselves between the law and the national government and declare the law void. This doctrine views the Constitution as a compact among the states. Although the tension over the Sedition Act was defused when Jefferson was elected president, the approach to federalism he had devised to overthrow the Sedition Act had important implications for national power.[16]

The idea of interposition soon regained significance as the basis for the southern states' push for broader **states' rights** on issues such as tariffs and slavery. John Calhoun, a South Carolina senator, used the term "nullification" to refer to the same principle, urging South Carolina to ignore a tariff law passed by Congress in 1832. The states' rights perspective was at the center of the dispute between southern and northern states over slavery, and it ultimately led to the secession of the Confederate states and subsequently to the Civil War. The stakes were enormous in the battles over federalism: about 528,000 people died in that bloodiest of American wars.[17] As Abraham Lincoln forcefully argued, concepts such as nullification and states' rights, when taken to their logical extremes, were too divisive to be allowed to stand. If states could ignore national laws, the basis of the United States would fall apart.

doctrine of interposition The idea that if the national government passes an unconstitutional law, the people of the states (through their state legislatures) can declare the law void. This idea provided the basis for southern secession and the Civil War.

states' rights The idea that states are entitled to a certain amount of self-government, free of federal government intervention. This became a central issue in the period leading up to the Civil War.

DUAL FEDERALISM

The ideas of states' rights and nullification did not produce the Civil War by themselves. The Supreme Court's infamous *Dred Scott* decision lent fuel to the fire, but before explaining the significance of that case, we will look at some key players in the evolution of the Court's approach to federalism. In this section, we will discuss the system of dual federalism, which defined intergovernmental relations for nearly the first 150 years of our nation's history. The Supreme Court's narrow interpretation of the Fourteenth Amendment and the commerce clause greatly limited the power of the national government in this period (see Table 3.1).

THE MARSHALL COURT VERSUS THE TANEY COURT The early to mid-nineteenth century saw incredible stability in the leadership of the Court, because only two chief justices served during this time—John Marshall from 1801 to 1835, and Roger Taney from 1835 to 1864. However, these men had very different ideas about federalism. Marshall was a Federalist who opposed states' rights, whereas Taney was a supporter of states' rights. A series of decisions under Marshall's leadership secured the place of the national government within our federal system. But in the years that followed, Taney was able to limit the reach of the national government through his vision of federalism, which is known as dual federalism.

TABLE » 3.1

EARLY LANDMARK SUPREME COURT DECISIONS ON FEDERALISM

CASE	HOLDING AND SIGNIFICANCE FOR STATES' RIGHTS	DIRECTION OF THE DECISION
Chisholm v. Georgia (1793)	Held that citizens of one state could sue another state; led to the Eleventh Amendment, which prohibited such lawsuits.	Less state power
McCulloch v. Maryland (1819)	Upheld the national government's right to create a bank and reaffirmed the idea of "national supremacy."	Less state power
Gibbons v. Ogden (1824)	Held that Congress, rather than the states, has broad power to regulate interstate commerce.	Less state power
Barron v. Baltimore (1833)	Endorsed a notion of "dual federalism" in which the rights of a U.S. citizen under the Bill of Rights did not apply to that same person under state law.	More state power
Dred Scott v. Sandford (1857)	Sided with southern states' view that slaves were property and ruled that the Missouri Compromise violated the Fifth Amendment, because making slavery illegal in some states deprived slave owners of property. Contributed to the start of the Civil War.	More state power
National Labor Relations Board v. Jones & Laughlin Steel Corporation (1937)	Upheld the National Labor Relations Act of 1935 as consistent with Congress's commerce clause powers, reversing the Court's more narrow interpretation of that clause.	Less state power

dual federalism The form of federalism favored by Chief Justice Roger Taney in which national and state governments are seen as distinct entities providing separate services. This model limits the power of the national government.

Under **dual federalism,** the national and state governments were viewed as distinct, with little overlap in their activities or the services they provided. In this view, the national government's activities are confined to powers strictly enumerated in the Constitution, despite the necessary and proper clause and the implied powers endorsed in *McCulloch v. Maryland.* Although Taney fully developed the idea of dual federalism, one decision toward the end of Marshall's tenure endorsed a notion of "dual citizenship" in which an individual's rights as a U.S. citizen under the Bill of Rights did not apply to the same person under state law. That decision, *Barron v. Baltimore* (1833), held that a man whose wharf in the Baltimore harbor had been ruined by the city's dumping of sand and gravel could not sue the city for violating the Fifth Amendment's prohibition of taking property without due process. The Court ruled that the Fifth Amendment applied only to the U.S. Congress and not to state and local governments, which is a core principle of dual federalism.

Within this framework of distinct national and state powers, the Taney Court expanded the power of the states over commerce in ways that would not be accepted today. For example, this Court gave the mayor of New York City the right to control immigration by requiring shipmasters to post bonds for foreign passengers who might later go on welfare[18] and it allowed the city of Philadelphia to require ships to use local captains when entering the that city's harbor.[19] Today, these areas of commerce would be regulated by Congress, not local governments.

DRED SCOTT AND CIVIL WAR The state-centered views of the Taney Court also produced a tragic decision, *Dred Scott v. Sandford* (1857). Dred Scott was a slave who had lived for many years with his owner in the free Wisconsin Territory but was living in Missouri, a slave state, when his master died. Scott petitioned for his freedom under the Missouri Compromise, which said that slavery was illegal in any free state. The majority decision held that slaves were not citizens but private property, and that therefore the Missouri Compromise violated the Fifth Amendment because it deprived people (slave owners) of property without the due process of law. This unfortunate decision contributed to the Civil War, which started four years later, because it indicated that there could not be a political solution to the problem of slavery.

The Civil War ended the dispute over slavery, but it did not resolve basic questions about the balance of power between the national and state governments. At the end of the Civil War, the Constitution was amended to ensure that the Union's views on states' rights were the law of the land. The Civil War Amendments banned slavery (Thirteenth Amendment), prohibited states from denying citizens due process or equal protection of the laws (Fourteenth Amendment), and gave newly freed male slaves the right to vote (Fifteenth Amendment). The Fourteenth Amendment was the most important in terms of federalism because it was the constitutional basis for many of the civil rights laws passed by Congress during Reconstruction.

THE SUPREME COURT AND LIMITED NATIONAL GOVERNMENT The assertion of power by Congress during Reconstruction was short-lived, as the Supreme Court soon stepped in again to limit the power of the national government. In 1873, the Court reinforced the notion of dual federalism, ruling that the Fourteenth Amendment did not change the balance of power between the national and state governments despite its clear language aimed at state action. Endorsing the notion of dual citizenship, the Court ruled that the Fourteenth Amendment right to due process and equal treatment under the law applied to individuals' rights only as citizens of the United States, not to their state citizenship.[20] By extension, freedom of speech, freedom of the press, and the other liberties protected in the Bill of Rights applied only to laws passed by Congress, not to state laws. This distinction between state and national citizenship sounds odd today, partly because the Fourteenth Amendment has long been viewed as the basis for ensuring that states do not violate basic rights.

In 1883, the Court overturned the 1875 Civil Rights Act, which had guaranteed equal treatment in public accommodations. The Court argued that the Fourteenth Amendment did not give Congress the power to regulate private conduct, such as whether a white restaurant owner had to serve a black customer; it affected only the conduct of state governments.[21] This narrow view of the Fourteenth Amendment left the national government powerless to prevent southern states from implementing state and local laws that led to complete segregation of blacks and whites in the South (called Jim Crow laws) and the denial of many basic rights to blacks after northern troops left the South at the end of Reconstruction.

The other area in which the Supreme Court limited the reach of the national government concerned Congress's authority to regulate the economy through its commerce clause powers. In a series of cases in the late nineteenth and early twentieth centuries, the Supreme Court endorsed a view of laissez-faire capitalism— French for "leave alone"—aimed at protecting business from regulation by the national government. To this end, the Court defined clear boundaries between *inter*state and *intra*state commerce, ruling that Congress could not regulate any economic activity that occurred *within* a state (intrastate). The Supreme Court allowed some national legislation that was connected to interstate commerce, such as limiting monopolies through the Sherman Antitrust Act (1890). However, when the national government tried to use this act to break up a cartel of four sugar companies that controlled 98 percent of the nation's sugar production, the Court ruled that Congress did not have this power.

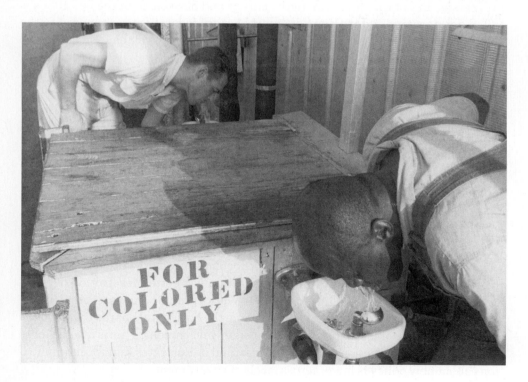

AFTER THE SUPREME COURT STRUCK down the 1875 Civil Rights Act, southern states were free to impose Jim Crow laws. These state and local laws led to complete racial segregation, even for public drinking fountains.

FRANKLIN DELANO ROOSEVELT'S
New Deal shifted more power than ever to the national government. Through major new programs to address the Great Depression, the federal government expanded its reach, and spent more to pay for these programs.

cooperative federalism A form of federalism in which national and state governments work together to provide services efficiently. This form emerged in the late 1930s, representing a profound shift toward less concrete boundaries of responsibility in national–state relations.

picket fence federalism A more refined and realistic form of cooperative federalism in which policy makers within a particular policy area work together across the levels of government.

According to the Court's decision, the commerce clause dealt with the transportation of goods, not their manufacture, and the sugar in question was made within a single state. Even if the sugar was sold throughout the country, this was "incidental" to its manufacture.[22] On the same grounds, the Court struck down attempts by Congress to regulate child labor.[23] In some instances, the Court's laissez-faire perspective led the justices to strike down state laws, as in a case that ruled unconstitutional a New York law limiting the working hours of bakers to no more than 60 hours a week or 10 hours a day.[24] Therefore, the limits that the Court placed on Congress during this antiregulation phase did not necessarily tip the balance to the state governments. Rather, big business was the winner over both national and state governments.

COOPERATIVE FEDERALISM

From the early years of the twentieth century through the 1930s, a new era of American federalism emerged. The national government became much more involved in activities that were formerly reserved for the states, such as education, transportation, civil rights, agriculture, social welfare, and management–labor relations. At first, the Supreme Court resisted this broader reach of national power, clinging to its nineteenth-century conception of dual federalism.[25] But as commerce became more national, the distinction between interstate and intrastate commerce, and between manufacture and transportation, became increasingly difficult to sustain. Starting in 1937 with the landmark ruling *National Labor Relations Board v. Jones and Laughlin Steel,* the Supreme Court largely discarded these distinctions and gave Congress far more latitude in shaping economic and social policy for the nation.[26]

SHIFTING NATIONAL–STATE RELATIONS The type of federalism that emerged in the Progressive Era of the early twentieth century and blossomed in the late 1930s is called **cooperative federalism**, or "marble cake" federalism, as opposed to the "layer cake" model of dual federalism.[27] As the image of a marble cake suggests, the boundaries of state and national responsibilities are less well defined than they are under dual federalism. With the increasing industrialization and urbanization of the late 1930s and 1940s, more complex problems arose that could not be solved at one level of government. Cooperative federalism adopted a more practical focus on intergovernmental relations and how to efficiently provide services. State and local governments maintained a level of influence as the implementers of national programs, but the national government played an enhanced role as the initiator of key policies.

Cooperative federalism accurately describes this important shift in national–state relations in the first half of the twentieth century, but it does not begin to capture the complexity of modern federalism. The marble cake metaphor falls short in one important way: the lines of authority and patterns of cooperation are not as messy as implied by the gooey flow of chocolate through white cake. Instead, the 1960s metaphor of **picket fence federalism** is a better description of cooperative federalism in action. As the How It Works graphic shows, each picket of the fence represents a different policy area, and the horizontal boards that hold the pickets together represent the different levels of government. This is a much more orderly image than the marble cake provides, and it illustrates important implications about how policy is made across levels of government.

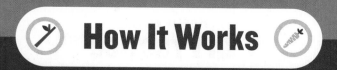

VERSIONS OF FEDERALISM

LAYER CAKE FEDERALISM
1789–1937

No interactions between the levels of government.

NATIONAL

STATE

LOCAL

MARBLE CAKE FEDERALISM
1937–today

Interactions between the levels of government are common.

NATIONAL

STATE

LOCAL

PICKET FENCE FEDERALISM
1960s–today

Horizontal boards represent different levels of government, and the pickets are policy areas within which coordination happens across those levels.

NATIONAL

STATE

LOCAL

AGRICULTURE · ENVIRONMENT · HIGHWAYS · HOUSING · EDUCATION · MEDICAL CARE · TAX POLICY

COERCIVE FEDERALISM
1970s–today

National government uses regulations, mandates, and conditions to pressure states to fall into line with national policy goals.

NATIONAL GOVERNMENT PROVIDES RULES (STICKS)

STATE & LOCAL

NATIONAL GOVERNMENT PERSUADES WITH INCENTIVES (CARROTS)

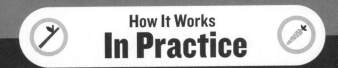

How It Works
In Practice

FEDERALISM AND ENVIRONMENTAL POLICY

Environmental policy shows contemporary federalism in action. As you can see below, all levels of government combine to affect environmental policy (exemplifying picket fence federalism). Also, the national government provides both rules and incentives for state and local governments to change their environmental policies (exemplifying coercive federalism).

 NATIONAL: Environmental Protection Agency, Department of the Interior, Department of Energy

 STATE: State Department of Natural Resources, State Park Service, State Environmental Protection Agencies

 LOCAL: City park system, city and county oversight boards for land use policy, zoning

ENVIRONMENTAL POLICY

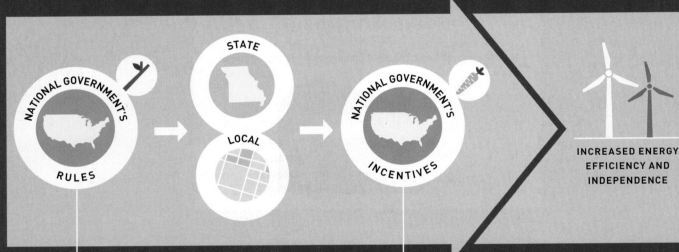

NATIONAL GOVERNMENT'S RULES

STATE

LOCAL

NATIONAL GOVERNMENT'S INCENTIVES

INCREASED ENERGY EFFICIENCY AND INDEPENDENCE

Over the last several decades, Congress has passed the Coastal Zone Management Act, the Clean Water Act, the Endangered Species Act, and the Clean Air Act. These have all provided states and localities with federal regulations and mandates. In 2011, the Environmental Protection Agency enacted the Cross-State Air Pollution Rule, which slashed emissions from power plants.

The federal government provides incentives designed to preserve the environment. These include tax credits for electric cars, biodiesel and hydrogen fuel cells, and home improvements that increase energy efficiency. With $3.2 billion from the stimulus package passed by Congress in 2009, the federal government funded the Energy Efficiency and Conservation Block Grant Program, which provides incentives for states and localities to reduce fossil fuel emissions, reduce energy use overall, and improve the energy efficiency of public transportation.

POP QUIZ

1 Which of the following is no longer practiced today?

a coercive federalism

b layer cake federalism

c marble cake federalism

d picket fence federalism

e fiscal federalism

2 The federal government provides rules and incentives designed to help the environment. This is an example of

a layer cake federalism.

b the New Deal.

c the commerce clause.

d coercive federalism.

e picket fence federalism.

The most important point to be drawn from this analogy is that activity within the cooperative federal system occurs *within* pickets of the fence—that is, within policy areas. Policy makers within a given policy area will have more in common with others in that area (even if they are at different levels of government) than they do with people who work in different areas (even if they are at the same level of government). For example, someone working in a state's Department of Natural Resources will have more contact with people working in local park programs and the national Department of Interior than with people who also work at the state level but who focus on, say, transportation policy.

Cooperative federalism, then, is likely to emerge within policy areas rather than across them. This may create problems for the chief executives who are trying to run the show (mayors, governors, the president), as rivalries develop among policy areas competing for funds. Also, contact within policy areas is not always cooperative. (Think of detective shows in which the FBI arrives to investigate a local crime and pulls rank on the town sheriff, provoking resentment from local law enforcement officials.) This is the inefficient side of picket fence federalism in action. But overall, this version of federalism provides great opportunities for coordination and the development of expertise within policy areas.

FEDERALISM TODAY

DESCRIBE THE MAJOR TRENDS AND DEBATES IN FEDERALISM TODAY

Federalism today is a complex mix of all the elements our nation's political system has experienced in the past. Our current system is predominantly characterized by cooperative federalism, but it has retained strong elements of national supremacy, dual federalism, and states' rights. Therefore, rather than categorizing types of federalism into neat time periods, the following discussion characterizes the dominant tendency within each period, keeping in mind that competing versions of federalism have always been just below the surface (see Nuts & Bolts 3.2). In the past 20 years, the competing versions are so evident that this period could be considered the "era of balanced federalism."[28]

COOPERATIVE FEDERALISM LIVES ON: FISCAL FEDERALISM

The cooperative relationship between the national and state governments is rooted in the system of transfer payments, or grants, from the national government to lower levels of government. This is called **fiscal federalism**. However, just because money flows from Washington, D.C., does not mean that cooperation by the recipients follows. Depending on how the money is transferred, the national government can either help local and state governments achieve their own goals or use its fiscal power to impose its will. This may sound familiar. When your parents let you use the car or lent you $50, did they expect something in return—such as your help with yard work—or was it "no strings attached"? Even in the era of dual federalism this type of issue arose between different levels of government, but it happened far less frequently then because the national government provided very little aid to the states.

fiscal federalism A form of federalism in which federal funds are allocated to the lower levels of government through transfer payments or grants.

THE EVOLUTION OF FEDERALISM

Type of Federalism	Period	Characteristics
Dual federalism (layer cake)	1789–1937	The national and state governments were viewed as very distinct with little overlap in their activities or the services they provided. Within this period, federalism could have been state-centered or nation-centered, but relations between levels of government were limited.
Cooperative federalism (marble cake)	1937–present	This indicates greater cooperation and collaboration between the levels of government.
Picket fence federalism	1961–present	This version of cooperative federalism emphasizes that policy makers within a given policy area have more in common with others in their area at different levels of government than with people at the same level of government who work on different issues.
Fiscal federalism	1937–present	This system of transfer payments or grants from the national government to lower-level governments involves varying degrees of national control over how the money is spent: categorical grants give the national government a great deal of control whereas block grants involve less national control.
New Federalism	1969–present	New Federalism attempts to shift power to the states by consolidating categorical grants into block grants and giving the states authority over programs such as welfare.
Coercive federalism	1970s–present	This involves federal preemptions of state and local authority and unfunded mandates on state and local governments to force the states to change their policies to match national goals or policies established by Congress.

categorical grants Federal aid to state or local governments that is provided for a specific purpose, such as a mass-transit program within the transportation budget or a school lunch program within the education budget.

block grants Federal aid provided to a state government to be spent within a certain policy area, but the state can decide how to spend the money within that area.

general revenue sharing (GRS) A type of grant used in the 1970s and 1980s in which the federal government provided state governments with funds to be spent at each state's discretion. These grants gave states more control over programs.

GRANTS IN AID Today, most aid to the states comes in one of two forms. **Categorical grants** are for specific purposes—they have strings attached—and therefore we discuss them in the section on coercive federalism. **Block grants** are financial aid to states for use within a specific policy area, but within that area the states have discretion on how to spend the money.

A third type of grant, **general revenue sharing (GRS)**, was tried briefly in the 1970s and 1980s and was popular with the states because it came with *no* strings attached. President Nixon started GRS in 1972 as part of his New Federalism program to return more control over programs to the states. At its peak in 1979, the federal government granted $6.8 billion to the states through this program, which would be more than $25 billion in today's budget. However, beginning in 1980, the state component of the program was phased out and was ended in 1986 during a period of large national budget deficits. The political support for GRS was difficult to sustain because of opposition by conservatives who wanted a smaller national government and from liberals who preferred more targeted spending.[29]

Instead, advocates of cooperative federalism promoted block grants as the best way for the levels of government to work together to solve problems: the national government identified problem areas and then provided money to the states to

FIGURE » 3.1

FEDERAL AND STATE/LOCAL GOVERNMENT SPENDING (INCLUDING GRANTS), 1946–2013

Since the early 1950s, federal spending as a percentage of the overall size of the economy has been flat, whereas the share of state and local spending has nearly tripled. What does this say about the debates between nation-centered and state-centered federalism?

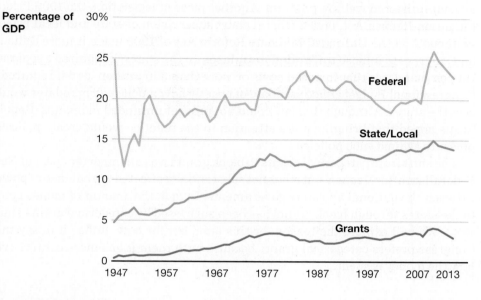

SOURCE: 2012 Statistical Abstract of the United States, Table 4.31, and the Bureau of Economic Analysis, "Government Current Receipts and Expenditures" (accessed 6/19/14).

help solve them. Between 1966, when the first block grant was created, and 1994, 23 block grants were established.[30] For example, Community Development Block Grants were started in 1974 to help state and local governments revitalize their communities; such grants may support ongoing programs or help with large capital expenditures, such as building a waste treatment plant or a highway. Since the 1970s, grants to the states as a proportion of the size of the national economy (gross domestic product, or GDP) have been relatively constant, whereas the rate of state and local spending has continued to inch up (see Figure 3.1). Even including those that were part of the 2009 stimulus package, grants to the states were only 4 percent of GDP in 2009.

NEW FEDERALISM Richard Nixon's New Federalism seemed to be a short-lived experiment in state-centered fiscal federalism, but then it was revived during Ronald Reagan's presidency in the 1980s. In his 1981 inaugural address, Reagan emphasized, "All of us need to be reminded that the federal government did not create the states. The states created the federal government." This classic statement of the states' rights position is similar to the Antifederalists' position at the Constitutional Convention.

Reagan's goal of returning more power to the states involved consolidating 77 categorical grants into 9 general block grants that gave local politicians more control over how money was spent. This change reflected the belief that because state and local politicians were closer to the people, they would know better how to spend the money. Nonetheless, the increase in state control came with a 25 percent cut in the amount of federal money granted to the states.

The next phase of New Federalism came when Republicans won control of Congress in 1994. Working with President Clinton, a moderate Democrat, the Republican-controlled Congress passed several pieces of significant legislation that shifted power toward the states. In 1996, the Personal Responsibility and Work Opportunity Act reformed welfare by creating a block grant to the states, Temporary Assistance to Needy Families (TANF), to replace the largest nationally administered welfare program. Another piece of legislation, the 1996 Prison Litigation Reform Act, ended federal court supervision of state and local prison systems. And the Unfunded Mandate Reform Act of 1995 made it more difficult for Congress to impose **unfunded mandates** on the states; it required a separate vote on mandates that imposed costs of more than $50 million, and it required a Congressional Budget Office estimate of exactly how much such mandates would cost the states. Although this law could not prevent unfunded mandates, Republicans hoped that bringing more attention to the practice would create political pressure against such policies.

The shift from categorical grants to block grants was an important part of New Federalism after Reagan, but it has not substantially affected the balance of power between the national and state governments. In fact, the amount of money going to the states through block grants has been surpassed by categorical grants since 1982. We will explore the reason for this later, but for now, suffice it to say that Congress prefers categorical grants because with them it has more control over how the money is spent.

unfunded mandates Federal laws that require the states to do certain things but do not provide state governments with funding to implement these policies.

THE RISE OF COERCIVE FEDERALISM

Despite the overall shift toward cooperative federalism, strong overtones of national government supremacy remain. Three important characteristics of American politics in the past 60 years have reinforced the role of the national government: (1) reliance on the national government in times of crisis and war; (2) the "rights revolution" of the 1950s and 1960s, as well as the Great Society programs of the 1960s; and (3) the rise of coercive federalism.

CRISIS AND WAR The first point, mentioned above, has always been a characteristic of American politics. Even in the 1800s, during the period of dual federalism and strong state power, the national government's strong actions were needed during the Civil War to hold the nation together. More recently, following the terrorist attacks on September 11, 2001, most Americans expected the national government to improve national security and retaliate for the attacks. Even Republicans, who normally oppose increasing the size of government, largely supported President Bush's proposal to create a cabinet-level Department of Homeland Security. The other major crises of the twentieth century—the Great Depression's New Deal policies, the massive mobilization for World War II, and the response to the banking meltdown of 2008–2009—also dramatically shifted the balance of power toward Washington.

THE "RIGHTS REVOLUTION" AND GREAT SOCIETY PROGRAMS The "rights revolution" created by the Supreme Court, as well as Lyndon Johnson's Great Society programs, contributed to increased national control over state policies. Landmark

Court decisions thrust the national government into policy areas that had typically been reserved to the states. In the school desegregation and busing cases of the 1950s and 1960s, for example, the Court upheld the national goal of promoting racial equality and fighting discrimination over the earlier norm of local control of school districts.[31] The "one person, one vote" decisions, which required that the populations of legislative districts be equalized when district lines were redrawn, put the federal courts at the center of another policy area that had always been left to the states.[32] The rights revolution also applied to police powers, another area of traditional state control, including protection against self-incrimination and preventing illegally obtained evidence from being used in a criminal trial.[33]

These Court actions were paralleled by a burst of legislation that tackled civil rights, education, the environment, medical care for the poor, and housing. These so-called Great Society policies gave the national government much more leverage over policy areas previously controlled by state and local governments. For example, after passage of the 1965 Voting Rights Act, federal marshals were sent to the South to make sure that African Americans were allowed to vote. Another part of this act required some state and local governments to submit changes in their electoral practices, including the boundaries of voting districts, to the Justice Department to make sure they did not have a discriminatory impact. But in 2013, the Court effectively overturned this part of the law by striking down the formula that determined which state and local governments were covered by the act.[34]

During this period, the national government also expanded its reach through a large increase in categorical grants, which the states sorely needed even though the monies came with strings attached. For example, the 1964 Civil Rights Act required nondiscrimination as a condition for receiving any kind of federal grants. The Elementary and Secondary Education Act of 1965 gave the federal government heightened control over public education by attaching certain conditions to federal grant money.

OTHER SHIFTS TOWARD NATIONAL SUPREMACY Categorical grants aimed at a broad national goal have also reinforced national supremacy in recent decades—for

WITH THE NO CHILD LEFT BEHIND Act, the Bush administration increased the national government's power over education. States are required to test students and meet goals determined by the federal government in order to receive federal funding.

example, requiring a state to set the legal drinking age to 21 before granting it federal highway funds. This policy direction from Washington is part of a trend known as **coercive federalism**. This practice involves the use of federal regulations, mandates, or conditions to force or entice the states to change their policies to match national goals or policies established by Congress. The Clean Air and Clean Water Acts, the Americans with Disabilities Act (which promotes making public buildings and commercial facilities more accessible to those with disabilities), and the "Motor Voter Act" (which requires states to provide voter registration services at motor vehicle departments) are all laws that forced states to change their policies. The laws most objectionable to the states are unfunded mandates, which require states to do certain things but carry no federal money to pay for them.

Along with these mandates, federal preemption is another method of coercive federalism. Derived from the Constitution's national supremacy clause, **federal preemptions** impose national priorities on the states. Many preemptions also include unfunded mandates, making the state and local governments pick up the tab for policies that the national government wants them to implement. The U.S. Conference of Mayors has identified 10 federal mandates that consume 11 percent of city budgets, and the National Association of Counties estimates that 12 mandates account for 12 percent of county budgets.[35] Many of the most expensive mandates are environmental laws aimed at goals that a majority of Americans share. However, state and local governments complain that they should not have to shoulder so much of the burden.[36] These are among the most controversial assertions of national power because they impose such high costs on state and local governments.

The presidency of George W. Bush provided strong evidence of this shift toward national power. Beyond the apparent centralization of power associated with fighting terrorism, Bush pushed the national government into areas that previously had been dominated by the states—for example, imposing significant mandates and preemptions in education testing, sales tax collection, emergency management, infrastructure, and election administration. This is particularly noteworthy

THE AMERICANS WITH DISABILITIES Act of 1990 requires that public accommodations and commercial facilities be accessible, but recent Supreme Court rulings have held that the law does not apply to most state and local government buildings. Activists for the disabled community are shown in front of the White House lobbying for stronger legislation.

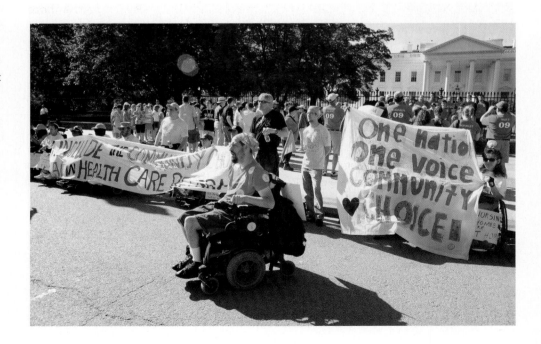

because it happened at a time when Republicans, who have traditionally supported states' rights, largely controlled the presidency and Congress.[37]

President Obama continued the shift toward national power with one of the most active domestic policy agendas since the New Deal of the 1930s. A $787 billion economic stimulus package of tax cuts and spending designed to address the financial collapse of 2008–2009, a $938 billion health care reform law, efforts to prop up and stimulate the battered housing industry, strengthened regulations of finance and banking, and an expanded jobs program were all on the agenda in Obama's first term. His objectives for the second term are more modest given the persistence of budget deficits and split-party control of government. But Obama is still pushing for comprehensive immigration reform, action on climate change, and job creation. Health care reform has been especially controversial, as many state governments see the law as an unwarranted expansion of federal power. This view was supported by the Supreme Court's ruling that states could not be coerced by the federal government into expanding their Medicaid coverage. This Court decision means that there are limits on the scope of coercive federalism. Although the overall impact of national health care reform has centralized more power at the national level, states remain very important in this period of "balanced federalism," as the next section will demonstrate.

THE STATES FIGHT BACK

Most Americans support the national policies that have been imposed on the states: racial equality, clean air and water, a fair legal process, safer highways, and equal access to the voting booth. At the same time, there has always been strong support for state and local governments. In fact, in most national surveys, Americans typically say that they trust state and local governments more than the national government, and they believe their tax dollars are spent more efficiently at the lower levels of government. Indeed, the shift in public opinion toward favoring national power after the 9/11 terrorist attacks was temporary, and it appears that state and local governments quickly reasserted their position as the more trusted level of government. For example, a Gallup poll taken late in 2013 showed that 71 percent of Americans trust their local government "a great deal or a fair amount" to "handle local problems," compared to 62 percent who trust their state government to handle state problems, and 42 percent who trust the national government to handle domestic problems.[38]

States appear to be reversing their traditional role of resisting change and protecting the status quo. In recent years, states have taken the lead on environmental policy, refusing to accept national pollution standards that are too lenient or the lack of national action on issues such as global warming. Many policies to address climate change—including the development of renewable energy sources, carbon emissions limits, and carbon cap-and-trade programs—have been advocated at the state level. States have been out in front on fighting electronic waste, mercury emissions, and air pollution more generally.[39] States have also taken a lead role on health care policy, immigration, same-sex marriage, and stem cell research.

Nonetheless, the willingness of the states to fight back in recent years has not always been for progressive causes. Indeed, with the Republican gains in the 2010 elections and the influence of the Tea Party, many states have been attempting to curb national power and protect their more conservative policies in a broad range of areas, including land use, gun control, immigration, same-sex marriage, and health care. For example, Utah enacted a law that asserted local police powers over federal authority, even on federal lands.[40] Kansas and Montana passed laws holding that federal gun laws do not apply to guns that are manufactured in their states (and make it a felony to try to enforce those laws).[41] Eight states have refused to enforce the Defense Department's order giving military personnel equal spousal and family benefits regardless of sexual orientation. Some soldiers have been forced to drive several hours to an army base to process their applications for benefits for same-sex couples because they are being refused service at their National Guard units.[42] "There's a tsunami of interest in states' rights and resistance to an overbearing federal government; that's what all these measures indicate," said Gary Marbut, a states' rights activist from Montana.[43] Many of these state laws will not stand up in federal court. Indeed, the Montana gun law and the Utah police power law have already been struck down. But the laws are clearly a reflection of state frustration with assertions of federal power.

States have one important advantage over the national government when it comes to experimenting with new policies: their numbers. There are 50 states potentially trying a mix of different policies—another reason that advocates of state-centered federalism see the states as the proper repository of government power. In this view, such a mix of policies produces **competitive federalism**—competition among states to provide the best policies to attract businesses, create jobs, and maintain a healthy social fabric. Supporters point out that competitive federalism is also a check on tyranny because people will "vote with their feet"—that is, move to a different state—if they do not like a given state's policies. One advocate of this view argues that it "disciplines government and forces the states to compete for the citizens' business, talents, and assets," which makes government act more like a free market.[44]

But competitive federalism can also create a "race to the bottom" as states compete in a negative way. Cass Sunstein, of Harvard Law School, points out that when states compete for businesses and jobs, they may do so by eliminating more environmental or occupational regulations than would be desirable. Likewise, a priority to keep taxes low may lead to cuts in benefits to those who can least afford it, such as welfare or Medicaid recipients.[45]

There is no doubt that competition among states provides citizens with a broad range of choices about the type of government they prefer. Choices by different state leaders about tax policies, levels of support for public schools and parks, and regulation of business all provide a range of options for businesses in deciding where to locate or expand, and to citizens considering a move. Because different citizens prefer different policies, this is generally viewed as an overall advantage to American democracy.

FIGHTING FOR STATES' RIGHTS: THE ROLE OF THE MODERN SUPREME COURT

Just as the Supreme Court played a central role in defining the boundaries of dual federalism in the nineteenth and early twentieth centuries and in opening the door to a more nation-centered cooperative federalism in the late 1930s, today's Court is once again reshaping federalism. But this time the move is decidedly in the direction of state power.

competitive federalism
A form of federalism in which states compete to attract businesses and jobs through the policies they adopt.

THE TENTH AMENDMENT On paper, it seems that the Tenth Amendment would be at the center of any resurgence of state power because it ensures that all powers not delegated to the national government are reserved to the states or to the people. In practice, however, the amendment has had little significance except during the early 1930s and quite recently.

Thirty-five years ago, a leading text on the Constitution said that the Tenth Amendment "does not alter the distribution of power between the national and state governments. It adds nothing to the Constitution."[46] To understand why, consider the following example. State and local governments have always controlled their own public schools. Thus, public education is a power reserved to the states under the Tenth Amendment. However, a state law concerning public education is void if it conflicts with the Constitution—as racial segregation conflicted with the equal protection clause of the Fourteenth Amendment—or with a national law that is based on an enumerated power. For example, a state could not compel an 18-year-old to attend school if the student had been drafted to serve in the army. Under the Tenth Amendment, the constitutionally enumerated national power to "raise and support armies" would trump the reserved state power to support public education.

This view was validated as recently as 1985 when the Court ruled that Congress had the power to impose a national minimum wage law on state governments, even if this was an area of traditional state power.[47] How times change! With the appointment of three conservative justices between 1986 and 1991 who favored a stronger role for the states, the Court started to limit Congress's reach. One technique was to require that Congress provide an unambiguous statement of its intent to overrule state authority. For example, the Court ruled that the Missouri constitution, which requires state judges to retire by age 70, did not violate the Age Discrimination in Employment Act because Congress did not make its intentions "unmistakably clear in the language of the statute."[48] In another case showing that the Tenth Amendment still had some life, the Court ruled that Congress may not "commandeer" state regulatory processes by ordering states to dispose of low-level radioactive waste (under the Low-Level Radioactive Waste Policy Act).[49] The Court also ruled that Congress cannot require local law enforcement officers to perform background checks on prospective handgun purchasers, thus striking down part of the 1993 Brady Handgun Violence Prevention Act (known as the Brady Bill).[50]

A potentially far-reaching decision in 2011 said that individuals, not just states, have the right to challenge the constitutionality of a federal law under the Tenth Amendment. The case involved a woman who was trying to hurt her husband's lover with dangerous chemicals; she was prosecuted under a federal law aimed at limiting the spread of chemical weapons. In the majority opinion, Justice Kennedy harkened back to Madison's "double security" in soaring language touting the virtues of federalism in protecting liberty: "Federalism is more than an exercise in setting the boundary between different institutions of government for their own integrity. State sovereignty is not just an end in itself: 'Rather, federalism secures to citizens the liberties that derive from the diffusion of sovereign power.'"[51] That is, federalism is more than some theoretical debate about dividing power between the levels of government; it is about providing citizens with freedom. In 2014, the Court unanimously ruled in the retrial of this case that federal prosecutors overreached in applying the chemical weapons treaty to the woman because Congress did not explicitly express its intent to apply the treaty in this context."[52] The ultimate significance of this ruling remains to be seen (because it isn't clear how many individuals will use the Tenth Amendment to challenge federal law), but it does allow for more challenges to the federal government's power over the states.

THE FOURTEENTH AMENDMENT The Fourteenth Amendment was intended to give the national government broad control over the potentially discriminatory laws of southern states after the Civil War. Section 1 guarantees that no state shall make or enforce any law depriving any person of "life, liberty, or property, without due process of law," or denying any person the "equal protection of the laws," and Section 5 empowers Congress "to enforce" those guarantees by "appropriate legislation."

The Supreme Court narrowly interpreted the Fourteenth Amendment in the late nineteenth century, severely limiting Congress's ability to affect state policy. However, throughout most of the twentieth century, the Court interpreted Section 5 to give Congress broad discretion to pass legislation to remedy bad state laws. For example, discriminatory application of literacy tests prevented millions of African Americans from voting in the South before the Voting Rights Act was passed in 1965. As part of the federalism revolution of the 1990s, the Court started to chip away at Congress's Fourteenth Amendment powers.

In one important case in 1997, the Supreme Court struck down the Religious Freedom Restoration Act as an overly broad attempt to curtail state-sponsored harassment based on religion. This case established a new standard to justify **remedial legislation**—that is, national legislation that fixes discriminatory state law—under Section 5, saying, "There must be a congruence and proportionality between the injury to be prevented or remedied and the means adopted to that end."[53] Two applications of this logic also applied to the Eleventh Amendment, which originally was interpreted to mean that residents of any state could not sue other (non-home-state) state governments. More recently, the Supreme Court has expanded the reach of the Eleventh Amendment through the concept of **states' sovereign immunity**. States are now immune from a much broader range of lawsuits in state and federal court (see Table 3.2 for some examples). In one application of the new standard for remedial legislation, the Court ruled that the Age Discrimination in Employment Act of 1967 could not be applied to state employees because it was not "appropriate legislation."[54] The Supreme Court also struck down the portion of the Americans with Disabilities Act (ADA) that applied to the states. Passed in 1990 with nearly unanimous support to protect the 45 million Americans who have some type of disability, the ADA required employers, including state agencies, to make "reasonable accommodations" for a "qualified individual with a disability." However, the majority opinion said that states could refuse to hire people in wheelchairs, or deaf or blind people, as "States are not required . . . to make special accommodations for the disabled."[55] Three years later, the Court made a narrow exception to this ruling, saying that states did need to provide the disabled with access to courthouses.[56]

In another exception to the federalism revolution, the Court upheld Congress's power to apply the 1993 Family Leave Act to state employees as "appropriate legislation" under Section 5 of the Fourteenth Amendment.[57] The key difference between this case and the age or disability cases is that, in passing the Family Leave Act, Congress explicitly recognized the gender inequality of family care. That is, when a family member gets sick, the mother or wife typically bears the burden. Constitutional protections for discrimination based on age or disability are much weaker than discrimination based on gender or race. However, in 2013 the Court demonstrated that it would uphold states' rights even when the issue concerned race. In striking down an important part of the Voting Rights Act, the Court established a new principle of "equal sovereignty" in saying that Congress had placed an unfair burden on the states.[58]

---

remedial legislation National laws that address discriminatory state laws. Authority for such legislation comes from Section 5 of the Fourteenth Amendment.

states' sovereign immunity Based on the Eleventh Amendment, immunity that prevents state governments from being sued by private parties in federal court unless the state consents to the suit.

TABLE » 3.2

RECENT IMPORTANT SUPREME COURT DECISIONS ON FEDERALISM

CASE	HOLDING AND SIGNIFICANCE FOR STATES RIGHTS	DIRECTION OF THE DECISION
Gregory v. Ashcroft (1991)	The Missouri constitution's requirement that state judges retire by age 70 did not violate the Age Discrimination in Employment Act.	More state power
United States v. Lopez (1995)	Carrying a gun in a school did not fall within "interstate commerce," thus Congress could not prohibit the possession of guns on school property.	More state power
Seminole Tribe v. Florida (1996)	The Court used the Eleventh Amendment to strengthen states' sovereign immunity, ruling that Congress could not compel a state to negotiate with Indian tribes about gaming and casinos.	More state power
Printz v. United States (1997)	The Court struck down part of the Brady Handgun Violence Prevention Act, saying that Congress cannot require local law enforcement officers to perform background checks on prospective handgun purchasers.	More state power
City of Boerne v. Flores (1997)	The Court struck down the Religious Freedom Restoration Act as an overly broad attempt to curtail the state-sponsored harassment of religion, saying that national legislation aimed at remedying states' discrimination must be "congruent and proportional" to the harm.	More state power
Alden v. Maine (1999)	State employees could not sue the state of Maine for violating the overtime pay provisions of the federal Fair Labor Standards Act.	More state power
United States v. Morrison (2000)	The Court struck down part of the Violence Against Women Act, saying that Congress did not have the power under the commerce clause to provide a national remedy for gender-based crimes.	More state power
Kimel et al. v. Florida Board of Regents (2000)	The Court said that the Age Discrimination in Employment Act of 1967 could not be applied to state employees because it was not considered "appropriate legislation" under Section 5 of the Fourteenth Amendment.	More state power
Alabama v. Garrett (2001)	The Court struck down the portion of the Americans with Disabilities Act that applied to the states, saying that state governments are not required to make special accommodations for the disabled.	More state power
Nevada Department of Human Resources v. Hibbs (2003)	The Court upheld Congress's power to apply the 1993 Family Leave Act to state employees as "appropriate legislation" under Section 5 of the Fourteenth Amendment.	Less state power
United States v. Bond (2011)	The Court upheld an individual's right to challenge the constitutionality of a federal law under the Tenth Amendment.	More state power
National Federation of Independent Business v. Sebelius (2012)	The Court upheld most provisions of the Affordable Care Act, but struck down the expansion of Medicaid as an unconstitutional use of coercive federalism (states could voluntarily take the additional funding to cover the expansion, but they would not lose existing funds if they opted out).	Mixed
United States v. Windsor (2013)	The Court held that Section 3 of the Defense of Marriage Act was unconstitutional because it denied federal benefits to same-sex couples who were legally married under state law.	More state power
Shelby County v. Holder (2013)	The Court struck down Section 4 of the Voting Rights Act on the grounds that it violated the "equal sovereignty" of the states.	More state power

THE COMMERCE CLAUSE Another category of cases leading to more state power concerns the commerce clause of the Constitution. The first Court case to limit Congress's commerce powers since the New Deal of the 1930s came in 1995. The case involved the Gun-Free School Zones Act of 1990, which Congress passed in response to the increase in school shootings around the nation. The law made it a federal offense to have a gun within 1,000 feet of a school. Congress assumed that it had the power to pass this legislation, given the Court's expansive interpretation of the commerce clause over the previous 55 years, even though it concerned a traditional area of state power. Although it was a stretch to claim that carrying a gun in or around a school was related to interstate commerce, Congress might have been able to demonstrate the point by showing that most guns are made in one state and sold in another (thus commercially crossing state lines), that crime affects the economy and commerce, and that the quality of education, which is also crucial to the economy, is harmed if students and teachers are worrying about guns in their schools. However, members of Congress did not present this evidence because they did not think it was necessary.

Alfonso Lopez, a senior at Edison High School in San Antonio, Texas, was arrested for carrying a concealed .38 caliber handgun with five bullets in it. Attorneys for Lopez moved to dismiss the charges, arguing that the law was unconstitutional because carrying a gun in a school could not be regulated as "interstate commerce." The Court agreed in *United States v. Lopez*,[59] and the ruling was widely viewed as a warning shot over Congress's bow. If Congress wanted to encroach on the states' turf in the future, it would have to demonstrate that the law in question was a legitimate exercise of the commerce clause powers.

Congress learned its lesson. The next time it passed legislation that affected law enforcement at the state level, it was careful to document the impact on interstate commerce. The Violence Against Women Act was passed in 1994 with strong bipartisan support after weeks of testimony and thousands of pages of evidence were entered into the record showing the links between violence against women and commerce. Despite the evidence Congress presented, the Supreme Court ruled that Congress did not have the power under the commerce clause to make a national law that gave victims of gender-motivated violence the right to sue their attackers in federal court (the Court struck down only that part of the law, however; the program funding remained unaffected and was reauthorized in 2013).[60]

The significance of this line of federalism cases is enormous. Not only has the Supreme Court set new limits on Congress's ability to address national problems (the "congruence and proportionality" test), but it has also clearly stated that the Court alone will determine which rights warrant protection by Congress. The cases have also shown how polarized the Court has become on some of these contentious issues. Nearly all of the cases mentioned here were decided by 5–4 margins, with

THE LOPEZ DECISION STRUCK DOWN the 1990 Gun-Free School Zones Act, ruling that Congress did not have the power to forbid people to carry guns near schools. After the shooting of 12 students and 1 teacher at Columbine High School in Jefferson County, Colorado, on April 20, 1999, there were renewed calls nationwide for strengthening gun control laws.

intense and persistent dissents. In many instances, the dissenters took the unusual step of reading their opinions from the bench.

Many constitutional experts see these rulings as an important shift of power from the national government to the states. However, it is important to recognize that the Court does not consistently rule against Congress; it often rules against the states because of broader constitutional principles or general public consensus behind a specific issue. For example, the Court struck down Arkansas's three-term limit for members of Congress, ruling that states could not impose any additional limits on the qualifications for being a member of Congress beyond those in the Constitution.[61] The Court has also struck down state laws limiting gay rights as a violation of the equal protection clause of the Fourteenth Amendment,[62] it ruled that the death penalty for those younger than 18 and the "mentally retarded" is "cruel and unusual punishment" and thus prohibited by the Eighth Amendment,[63] it upheld Congress's power to regulate marijuana over state laws that had allowed its medical use,[64] and although the Court rejected the commerce clause as the constitutional justification for national health care reform, it did uphold the ACA based on Congress's taxing power. [65]

Based on these cases, some would argue that the shift in power toward the states has been relatively marginal. Furthermore, the national government still has the upper hand in the balance of power and has many tools at its disposal to blunt the impact of a Court decision. First, Congress can pass new laws to clarify its legislative intent and overturn any of the Court cases that involved statutory interpretation. Second, Congress can use its financial power to impose its will on the states, as it did with raising the drinking age. So, for example, Congress could pass a law saying that before a state could receive money from the federal government related to the relevant law, it had to agree to abide by the Americans with Disabilities Act or the Age Discrimination in Employment Act. However, as noted earlier, there are new limits on budgetary coercion. In the health care reform case, the Court ruled that the threat to withhold Medicaid funds was a "gun to the head" of states,[66] meaning states did not have a real choice. This was the first time the Court limited Congress's coercive budgetary power over the states, and the boundaries of the new limits will have to be decided in future cases.

ASSESSING FEDERALISM

ANALYZE THE ARGUMENTS FOR AND AGAINST A STRONG FEDERAL GOVERNMENT

From Madison's "double security," which protects individual liberty, to states as the "laboratories of democracy" in policy innovation, there is much to recommend federalism as a cornerstone of our political system. However, there are disadvantages as well, such as inefficiency in the policy process and inequality in policy outcomes. This section will assess the advantages, disadvantages, and ideological complexities of federalism.

IDEOLOGICAL COMPLEXITIES

Issues concerning federalism often seem to break down along traditional liberal and conservative lines. Liberals generally favor strong national power to fight discrimination against women, minorities, disabled people, gay men and lesbians, and the elderly, and they push for progressive national policies on issues such as protecting the environment, providing national health care, and supporting the poor. Conservatives, in contrast, tend to favor limited intrusion from the national government and allowing the states to decide their own mix of social welfare and regulatory policies, including how aggressively they will protect various groups from discrimination.

However, assessing federalism is not so simple. In recent years the tables have turned, and in many cases liberals are suddenly arguing for states' rights while conservatives are advocating the virtues of uniform national laws. On a broad range of new issues, such as medical use of marijuana, same-sex marriage, cloning, and aid in dying, state governments are passing socially liberal legislation.[67] And the Court's earlier, state-centered rulings give it little precedent for striking down these laws. The Court's conservative majority will have to either continue applying its state-centered federalism and uphold these liberal state laws, or strike them down on ideological grounds, which would undermine the Court's credibility. Recognizing this conundrum, the Court recently struck down a law passed by Congress—the Defense of Marriage Act—on the grounds that it usurped an area of traditional state power and undermined the states' ability to treat their citizens equally, regardless of their sexual orientation.[68]

One potential solution, from a socially conservative perspective, involves passing congressional legislation that bans, for example, cloning. This approach would also be difficult for the Court to sustain, however, given its earlier, narrow definition of "economic activity" under the commerce clause. The most interesting of these cases, in many ways, pertains to the medical use of marijuana and assisted suicide (see the You Decide feature). In these cases, political ideology and policy views about the drug laws and the right to die were apparently more important for most of the justices than was consistency on questions of federalism.

ADVANTAGES OF A STRONG ROLE FOR THE STATES

WHAT DO POLITICAL SCIENTISTS DO?

To find out more about how political scientists study the spread of policies from state to state, visit **wwnpag.es/wdpsd**

In addition to pointing out the ideological complexities of federalism, any assessment of federalism today must consider the advantages and disadvantages for our political system. The advantages of a strong role for the states can be summarized in four main points: (1) states can be laboratories of democracy, (2) state and local government is closer to the people, (3) states provide more access to the political system, and (4) states provide an important check on national power.

The first point refers to the role that states play as the source of policy diversity and innovation. If many states are trying to solve problems creatively, their efforts can complement those of the national government. Successful policies first adopted at the state level often percolate up to the national level. Consider welfare reform. Many states had great success in helping people get off welfare by providing worker training, education assistance, health benefits, and child care. The national government decided that states were doing a better job than the federal government was and, through the TANF block grant mentioned earlier, devolved welfare funding and responsibility to the states. Health care and environmental policy, especially on climate change, are other areas in which states have innovated.

Second, government that is closer to the people encourages participation in the political process. Local politicians know better what their constituents want than further-removed national politicians do. If the voters want higher taxes to pay for

MEDICAL MARIJUANA AND AID IN DYING

The debate over the balance of state and national power has grown increasingly complicated in the past several years. The courts have played a larger but inconsistent role, and issues of states' rights have increasingly cut across normal ideological and partisan divisions. Since the mid-1990s, the Supreme Court has played a central role in the shift of power to the states, but two recent cases involving medical marijuana (*Gonzales v. Raich*, 2005) and aid in dying—or "assisted suicide" as it was called at the time of the decision—(*Gonzales v. Oregon*, 2006) show how the typical debate between national and state power can change when a moral dimension is introduced.

In both cases, state voters supported liberal policies. In 1996, California voters passed the Compassionate Use Act, by 56 to 44 percent. This law allowed seriously ill Californians, typically AIDS and cancer patients, to use marijuana as part of their medical treatment with the permission of a doctor. Oregon voters approved the Death with Dignity Act in 1994 by a margin of 51 to 49 percent. This law allows physicians to prescribe a lethal drug dosage for terminally ill patients who wish to end their lives. A court order delayed implementation of the law until 1997, the same year that the matter was put before the voters again, but they rejected repealing the law by a margin of 60 to 40 percent. Both of these states' laws were challenged in federal court in classic confrontations between the states' rights and national power perspectives. Surprisingly, the Supreme Court ruled against medical marijuana and in favor of assisted suicide. (This summary oversimplifies the legal arguments, but these were the bottom-line outcomes.)

Should Congress be able to tell a state that it cannot allow the use of medical marijuana? Can the U.S. attorney general interpret a congressional law as a prohibition of assisted suicide? Unlike many of the cases discussed in this chapter, the states' rights position in these cases represented the liberal perspective, rather than the conservative position typically associated with state-centered federalism. Social liberals tended to support both the medical marijuana law and the assisted suicide law, whereas social conservatives tended to oppose them both. However, if you examine these cases in terms of the question of federal versus state power, the traditional liberal and conservative perspectives both look more complex. That is, a national-power liberal and a social conservative would agree that the national government should regulate medical marijuana and assisted suicide. Likewise, states' rights conservatives and social liberals would share the view that the states should decide these issues on their own.

Somewhat surprisingly, there was almost no consistency among the eight justices who voted on both cases (William Rehnquist was replaced as chief justice by John Roberts during the time between the two cases). Only Justice Sandra Day O'Connor supported the states' rights position in both cases, while Justice Antonin Scalia voted as a moral conservative against both laws—and counter to his previously

Federal drug enforcement agents raid a medical club.

articulated views on national power and federalism. The other six justices mixed their views, voting to uphold one of the laws and to strike down the other. The resulting rulings were inconsistent on the question of federalism as well. In the medical marijuana case, the Court upheld Congress's power to regulate the medical use of marijuana under the Controlled Substances Act. But in the assisted suicide case, the Court said that under that same congressional law, the U.S. attorney general did not have the power to limit the drugs that doctors in Oregon could prescribe for use in an assisted suicide.

Despite the Court's endorsement of Congress's power to regulate medical marijuana, the actual situation is more complex because of the Obama administration's evolving position on enforcing the law. Initially, the Obama administration said it would not enforce the federal law in 19 states that had legalized or decriminalized medical marijuana. But then in 2011 and 2012, the Justice Department shifted course, cracking down on large medical marijuana dispensaries in California, saying that the drug had become widely available for recreational use, not just medical use. More recently, the Justice Department decided not to contest Washington's and Colorado's legalization of marijuana. (Alaska and Oregon also legalized marijuana in 2014.) The struggle between the national and state governments is likely to continue on this issue in the foreseeable future.

CRITICAL THINKING QUESTIONS

1. As a matter of policy, should doctors be able to prescribe marijuana to alleviate pain? Should they be able to prescribe lethal drugs to terminally ill patients?

2. Do you tend to support a state-centered or nation-centered perspective on federalism? Now revisit your answers to question 1. Are your positions more consistent with your views on federalism or with your policy concerns?

more public benefits, such as public parks and better schools, they can enact these changes at the state and local levels. On the other hand, if they prefer lower taxes and fewer services, local politicians can be responsive to those desires. Also, local government provides a broad range of opportunities for direct involvement in politics, from working on local political campaigns to attending school board or city council meetings. When citizens are able to directly affect policies, they are more likely to get involved in the political process.

Third, our federalist system provides more potential paths to address problems. For example, the court system allows citizens to pursue complaints under state or federal law. Likewise, cooperative federalism can draw on the strengths of different levels of government to solve problems. A local government may recognize a need and respond to it more quickly than the national government, but if additional resources are needed to address the problem, the municipality may be able to turn to the state or national government for help.

Finally, federalism can provide a check on national tyranny. Competitive federalism ensures that Americans have a broad range of social policies, levels of taxation and regulation, and public services to choose from (see Figure 3.2). When people "vote with their feet" by deciding whether to move and where to live, they encourage healthy competition among states that would be impossible under a unitary government.

DISADVANTAGES OF TOO MUCH STATE POWER

IN THE DEBATE OVER HEALTH CARE reform and the Affordable Care Act, supporters of nationalized health care argued the federal government could do a better job than the patchwork of state policies to ensure that all Americans receive sufficient care.

A balanced assessment of state and national power must acknowledge that there are problems with a federalist system that gives too much power to the states. The disadvantages include unequal distribution of resources across the states, unequal protection for civil rights, and competitive federalism that produces a "race to the bottom." Also, one puzzle (which we will explore in other chapters) is that more people vote in national elections than in state and local elections. Turnout at the local level is often ridiculously low. If people support local government so strongly, why aren't they more interested?

The resource problem becomes more acute when dealing with national-level problems that are intractable at the local or state level. For example, pollution spills across state lines, and the deteriorating public infrastructure, like the highway system, crosses state boundaries. In fact, one study estimated that 26 percent of U.S. bridges are structurally deficient or obsolete, 15 percent of highways are in need of repair, and 25 percent of mass transit needs to be updated. Solving these and other infrastructure problems will cost $2.2 trillion, vastly outstripping the resources of state and local governments.[69]

The second problem, unequal civil rights protection, is evident in various federalism cases that have passed before the Supreme Court. These clearly show that states are not uniformly willing to protect the civil liberties and civil rights of their citizens. This was critically important during the 1950s and 1960s when the national government forced southern states to end segregation and passed laws outlawing discrimination in housing, employment, transportation, and voting. More recently, some states are providing equal rights based on sexual orientation, but other states are not. Without national laws, there will be large differences in the levels of protection against discrimination based on age, disability, and sexual orientation.

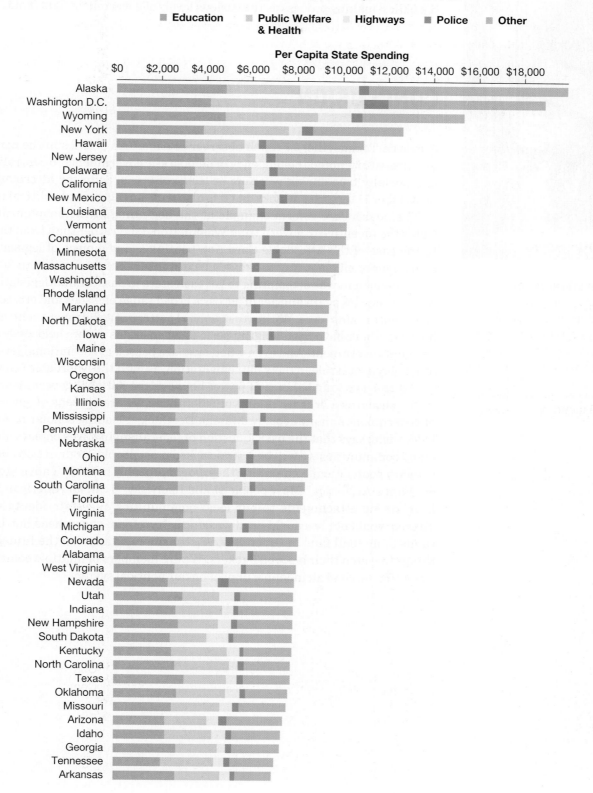

TYPES OF SPENDING PER CAPITA BY STATE

Spending per capita varies dramatically by state. What are some of the advantages and disadvantages of living in a low-spending state or in a high-spending state? What type of state would you rather live in?

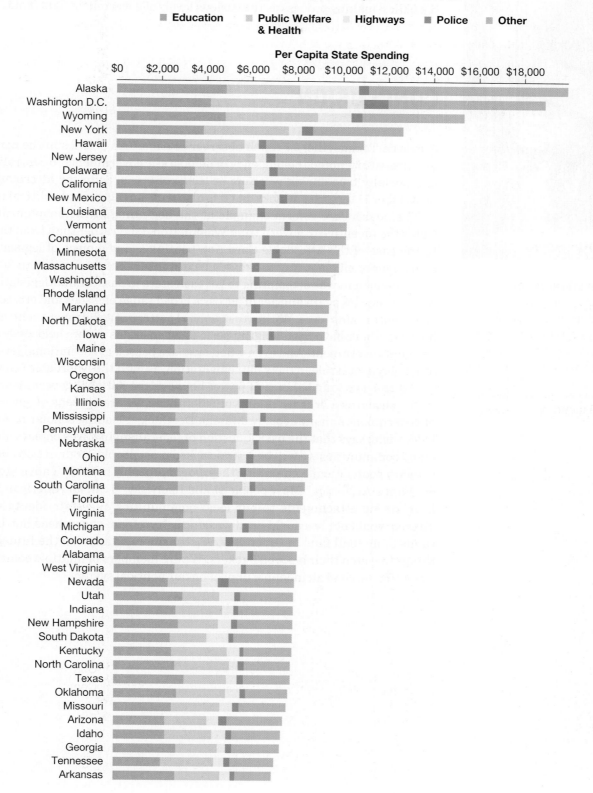

SOURCE: State and Local Government Finance Data Query System, http://slfdqs.taxpolicycenter.org (accessed 6/19/14).

And last, competitive federalism can create a "race to the bottom" as states attempt to lure businesses by keeping taxes and social spending low. This can place an unfair burden on states that take a more generous position toward the poor. Thus, overall, there is no clear "winner" in determining the appropriate balance of national and state power. The advantages and disadvantages of our federal system ensure that federalism will always remain a central source of conflict in the policy-making process as the various levels of government fight it out.

CONCLUSION

Alexis de Tocqueville, a French observer of American politics in the early nineteenth century, noted the tendency of democratic governments to centralize. This is especially true during wartime or times of crisis, as in the aftermath of the September 11 terrorist attacks, but it is also true during normal political times.

The health care reform example at the beginning of the chapter also illustrates the incentive to govern from Washington, D.C., rather than from the states. In the case of the Affordable Care Act, passing a single piece of legislation was a much more efficient way to provide health insurance for more than 30 million Americans than was attempting to get each state to pass similar legislation. This scenario occurs again and again across a broad range of issues and creates a powerful centralizing force. Within that general pattern of government centralization, however, there have been lengthy periods when states' rights held sway over the national government. And even when laws are passed at the national level, states often play a vital role in their implementation, as with the Affordable Care Act.

But this evolving balance of power between the national government and the states obscures a broader reality of federalism: we are citizens of several levels of government simultaneously. Martha Derthick, a leading scholar of American federalism, says that the basic question of federalism involves choices about how many communities we will be.[70] If you asked most people in our nation about their primary geopolitical community, they would probably not say, "I am a Montanan" or "I am a Arizonan." Most people would likely say, "I am an American." Yet, we have strong attachments to our local communities and state identities. Most Texans would not be caught dead wearing a Styrofoam cheesehead hat, but thousands of football fans in Green Bay, Wisconsin, regularly don the funny-looking things to watch their beloved Packers. We are members of multiple communities, a fact that has had an indelible impact on our political system.

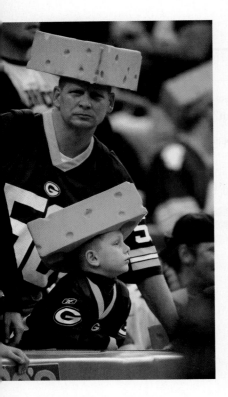

ONE OF THE STRENGTHS OF federalism is that it allows regional diversity to flourish. Green Bay Packers fans proudly wear their cheesehead hats at Lambeau Field, showing that what passes for normal behavior in one part of the country would be viewed differently in other areas.

WHAT IS FEDERALISM AND WHY DOES IT MATTER?

▶ *Define federalism and explain its significance.* **(Pages 69–71)**

SUMMARY

A federal system simultaneously allocates power to both the state and federal government, whereas a confederal system gives power only to the states, and a unitary government gives power only to the federal government.

KEY TERMS

federalism (p. 69)
sovereign power (p. 69)
police powers (p. 69)
concurrent powers (p. 69)
unitary government (p. 71)
confederal government (p. 71)
intergovernmental organizations (p. 71)

CRITICAL THINKING AND DISCUSSION

Are there any responsibilities that are currently at one level of government that might be better to be done at a different level of government? Are there any primary responsibilities that should be concurrent powers?

PRACTICE QUIZ QUESTIONS

1. What system of government did the Articles of Confederation establish?

    A unitary

    B federal

    C confederal

    D monarchy

    E dictatorship

2. Which is an example of a concurrent power?

    A printing money

    B building roads

    C conducting elections

    D declaring war

    E establishing post offices

BALANCING NATIONAL AND STATE POWER IN THE CONSTITUTION

▶ *Explain what the Constitution says about federalism.* **(Pages 71–74)**

SUMMARY

Although the state governments have considerable power in our system, the Founders disproportionately favored the federal government in the Constitution, so that the federal government's interests superseded those of the states in the event of a conflict.

KEY TERMS

full faith and credit clause (p. 73)
privileges and immunities clause (p. 73)

CRITICAL THINKING AND DISCUSSION

Which do you think has the stronger basis in the Constitution: nation-centered or state-centered federalism?

PRACTICE QUIZ QUESTIONS

3. States' rights are protected in which of the following constitutional provisions?

    A the Ninth Amendment

    B the Tenth Amendment

    C Article I of the Constitution

    D Article III of the Constitution

    E the First Amendment

4. Contemporary conflict over same-sex marriage falls under which constitutional provision?

    A privileges and immunities clause

    B exclusionary clause

    C national supremacy clause

    D full faith and credit clause

    E establishment clause

THE EVOLVING CONCEPT OF FEDERALISM

▶ *Trace the major shifts in state and federal government power over time.* **(Pages 74–83)**

SUMMARY

The relationship between the state and federal governments has changed dramatically over time. Whereas the federal and state governments traditionally operated with little interaction under the era of dual federalism, the trend over the past 80 years has been one of increasing federal interaction with state governments to address particular policy areas.

PRACTICE QUIZ QUESTIONS

5. Which analogy best describes the federalism arrangement today?

- Ⓐ layer cake federalism
- Ⓑ marble cake federalism
- Ⓒ picket fence federalism
- Ⓓ gumbo federalism
- Ⓔ dual federalism

6. Which case bolstered the federal government's power over the states?

- Ⓐ *Barron v. Baltimore*
- Ⓑ *McCulloch v. Maryland*
- Ⓒ *Dred Scott v. Sanford*
- Ⓓ *Mapp v. Ohio*
- Ⓔ *Shelby County v. Holder*

7. When did the federal government begin cooperating with the states on policy goals?

- Ⓐ 1890s
- Ⓑ 1930s
- Ⓒ 1950s
- Ⓓ 1970s
- Ⓔ 1990s

FEDERALISM TODAY

▶ *Describe the major trends and debates in federalism today.* **(Pages 83–95)**

SUMMARY

Today's federal structure offers a complex mix of all previous components of federalism: some elements of national supremacy combine with states' rights for a varied federal landscape. Although the federal and state governments still exercise cooperative federalism to achieve joint policy goals, the federal government has also utilized coercive federalism to impose federal priorities on the states without offering compensation.

PRACTICE QUIZ QUESTIONS

8. Which form of revenue sharing is given to the states by the federal government with explicit conditions on how it is to be allocated?

- Ⓐ block grants
- Ⓑ categorical grants
- Ⓒ general revenue sharing
- Ⓓ federal mandates
- Ⓔ tax refunds

9. Richard Nixon's plans to increase states' rights led to the increase in _____.

- Ⓐ block grants
- Ⓑ categorical grants
- Ⓒ general revenue sharing
- Ⓓ federal mandates
- Ⓔ state taxes

10. The imposition of national priorities on the states through congressional legislation and imposition of the national supremacy clause is called _____.

- Ⓐ cooperative federalism
- Ⓑ dual federalism
- Ⓒ competitive federalism
- Ⓓ federal preemption
- Ⓔ remedial legislation

11. A state would usually challenge the constitutionality of a federal law under which of the amendments listed below?

- Ⓐ Eighth Amendment
- Ⓑ Tenth Amendment
- Ⓒ Thirteenth Amendment
- Ⓓ Fourteenth Amendment
- Ⓔ First Amendment

12. The Eleventh Amendment's protections of state sovereign immunity guarantee that _____.

- A residents of one state cannot sue the government of another state
- B state governments cannot commit a legal wrong
- C ambassadors from foreign countries cannot be detained by state governments
- D state governments can sue the federal government
- E state governments cannot be sued by anybody

13. The Court has recently overturned a number of congressional laws rooted in the _____.

- A national supremacy clause
- B reserve clause
- C establishment clause
- D commerce clause
- E free exercise clause

ASSESSING FEDERALISM

▶ *Analyze the arguments for and against a strong federal government.* **(Pages 95–100)**

SUMMARY

Although conservatives have traditionally advocated for states' rights and liberals generally prefer a stronger national government, contemporary issues do not always fit neatly in this scheme. There are several reasons that strong state governments are beneficial for our country, such as the proximity of state and local governments to the citizens; however, there are also some drawbacks to the federal system, such as the vastly disproportionate distribution of resources across states.

CRITICAL THINKING AND DISCUSSION

How would our country be different if it were a unitary system? Do you think we would be better or worse off?

PRACTICE QUIZ QUESTIONS

14. Conservatives favor strong _____ rights on same-sex marriage, and strong _____ rights on providing health care.

- A states'; states'
- B states'; federal government
- C federal government; states'
- D federal government; federal government
- E individual; federal government

15. Which of the following is a drawback to strong state power?

- A State governments are often innovators on policy solutions.
- B State governments give citizens more access to politicians than does the national government.
- C State governments give citizens several paths to pursue policy reform.
- D State governments give different civil rights protections to their citizens.
- E States have an equal distribution of resources.

SUGGESTED READING

Banks, Christopher P. , and John C. Blakeman. *The U.S. Supreme Court and New Federalism: From the Rehnquist to the Roberts Court.* Lanhan, MD: Rowman & Littlefield, 2012.

Beer, Samuel. *To Make a Nation: The Rediscovery of American Federalism.* Cambridge, MA: Harvard University Press, 1993.

Conlan, Timothy. *From New Federalism to Devolution: Twenty-Five Years of Intergovernmental Reform.* Washington, D.C.: Brookings Institution, 1998.

Derthick, Martha. *Keeping the Compound Republic: Essays on American Federalism.* Washington, D.C.: Brookings Institution, 2001.

Elkins, Stanley, and Eric McKitrick. *The Age of Federalism: The Early American Republic, 1788–1800.* New York: Oxford University Press, 1993.

Grodzins, Martin. *The American System: A New View of Government in the United States.* Chicago: Rand McNally, 1966.

LaCroix, Alison L. *The Ideological Origins of American Federalism.* Cambridge, MA: Harvard University Press, 2010.

Manna, Paul. *School's In: Federalism and the National Education Agenda.* Washington, D.C.: Georgetown University Press, 2006.

McDonald, Forrest. *States' Rights and the Union: Imperium in Imperio, 1776–1876.* Lawrence, KS: University Press of Kansas, 2000.

Nagel, Robert F. *The Implosion of American Federalism.* New York: Oxford University Press, 2001.

Peterson, Paul E. *The Price of Federalism.* Washington, D.C.: Brookings Institution, 1995.

Posner, Paul L. *The Politics of Unfunded Mandates: Whither Federalism?* Washington, D.C.: Georgetown University Press, 1998.

Scheberle, Denise. *Federalism and Environmental Policy: Trust and the Politics of Implementation*, 2nd ed. Washington, D.C.: Georgetown University Press, 2004.

Civil Liberties

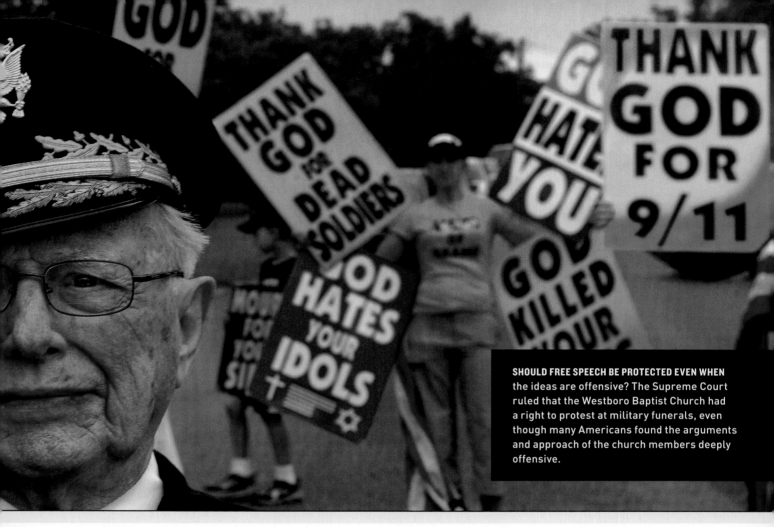

SINCE 2005, MEMBERS OF THE WESTBORO BAPTIST CHURCH (WBC) have protested at hundreds of funerals of members of the armed services who were killed in Iraq and Afghanistan. However, these are not typical antiwar protests. Instead, the protesters claimed that the troops' deaths were God's punishment for "the homosexual lifestyle of soul-damning, nation-destroying filth."[1]

**CONFLICT &
COMPROMISE**
in American Politics

The church and its members have drawn strong reactions and counterprotests for their confrontational approach at the military funerals, including their use of signs that say "God Hates Fags," "Thank God for Dead Soldiers," "God Killed Your Sons," and "God Hates America." Critics, including many veterans groups and attorneys general from 48 states, argue that the protests should not be considered protected speech under the First Amendment. The Veterans of Foreign Wars issued a statement saying, "In a time of profound grief and emotional vulnerability, these personal attacks are an affront of the most egregious kind." While recognizing that the First Amendment protects offensive speech, they argued it does not allow "personal attacks targeted at private individuals during a time of mourning."[2] A group of veterans called the Patriot Guard Riders have gathered at the funerals to serve as a buffer for the grieving families by riding motorcycles along the funeral route and singing patriotic songs or revving their engines to drown out the hateful speech.

State legislatures and Congress have also attempted to limit the disruption caused by the WBC. Forty-three states have passed laws limiting protests at military funerals to a certain distance from the actual services. In 2006,

CHAPTER *goals*

Define what we mean by civil liberties.
▶ PAGES 106–09

Explain why the Bill of Rights was added to the Constitution, and how it came to apply to the states.
▶ PAGES 109–12

Describe the First Amendment rights related to freedom of religion.
▶ PAGES 112–19

Describe the major First Amendment rights related to freedom of speech.
▶ PAGES 119–30

Explore why the Second Amendment's meaning on gun rights is often debated.
▶ PAGES 130–32

Describe the protections provided for people accused of a crime.
▶ PAGES 132–42

Explain why the rights associated with privacy are often controversial.
▶ PAGES 142–45

Congress passed the "Respect for Fallen American Heroes Act" that prohibited protests within 300 feet of a federal cemetery one hour before or after a funeral.

When the WBC protested at the funeral of Marine Lance Corporal Matthew Snyder, his father, Albert Snyder, sued the church for defamation, intentional infliction of emotional distress, and invasion of privacy. The district federal court ruled in Snyder's favor, awarding $5 million in damages. But the appeals court reversed the ruling, setting up an appeal to the Supreme Court. The case drew extensive attention with 48 states, 42 U.S. senators, and many veterans groups, including the American Legion and Veterans of Foreign Wars, filing briefs on behalf of Snyder, while more than 20 national news organizations filed briefs arguing that the WBC's protests should be protected by the First Amendment.

In their 2011 decision, the Supreme Court ruled 8–1 that the WBC's protests were protected speech. The majority opinion said, "Speech is powerful. It can stir people to action, move them to tears of both joy and sorrow, and—as it did here—inflict great pain. On the facts before us, we cannot react to that pain by punishing the speaker. As a nation we have chosen a different course—to protect even hurtful speech on public issues to ensure that we do not stifle public debate."[3] They said that the speech was not defamation because most of the WBC's signs were related to political issues, such as American involvement in wars and the service of gays in the military. They also argued that the Snyder family's privacy rights were not violated because the protesters were 1,000 feet from the funeral. Indeed, the family could only see the tops of the signs on the way to the funeral and did not learn about their content until reading about the protests after the funeral. Justice Samuel Alito, the only dissenter, disagreed: "Our profound national commitment to free and open debate is not a license for the vicious verbal assault that occurred in this case. . . . In order to have a society in which public issues can be openly and vigorously debated, it is not necessary to allow the brutalization of innocent victims."[4]

The Court's strong reaffirmation of the First Amendment's protection of hurtful and unpopular speech is an excellent illustration of our central theme that politics is conflictual. It is difficult to imagine speech that is more conflictual than the WBC's protests. Indeed, the entire purpose of the speech is to generate conflict. But the case also shows that, even in such a difficult case, compromise is possible. The "time, manner, and place" restrictions that limit the protests to areas away from the funeral maintain the privacy rights of the families, at least to some extent, while protecting the First Amendment rights of the protesters. Although the plaintiffs and their supporters were not happy with this compromise, it represents a resolution of conflict through the legislative and judicial process.

DEFINE WHAT WE MEAN BY CIVIL LIBERTIES ▶

DEFINING CIVIL LIBERTIES

civil liberties Basic political freedoms that protect citizens from governmental abuses of power.

The terms "civil rights" and "civil liberties" are often used interchangeably, but there are some important differences (see Nuts & Bolts 4.1). To oversimplify a bit, **civil liberties** are about freedom and civil rights are about equality. Given that civil liberties are rooted in the Bill of Rights, it might have been less confusing if it had been called the "Bill of Liberties." (This distinction is discussed further in Chapter 5.)

DISTINGUISHING CIVIL LIBERTIES FROM CIVIL RIGHTS

Civil Liberties	Civil Rights
Basic freedoms and liberties	Protection from discrimination
Rooted in the Bill of Rights and the "due process" protection of the Fourteenth Amendment	Rooted in laws and the "equal protection" clause of the Fourteenth Amendment
Primarily restrict what the government can do to you ("*Congress* shall make no law . . . abridging the freedom of speech")	Protects you from discrimination both by the government and by individuals

Civil liberties are deeply rooted in our key idea that politics is conflictual and involves trade-offs. When the Supreme Court rules on civil liberties cases, it must balance an individual's freedom with government interests and the public good. In some cases, the Court must not only balance these interests but also "draw a line" between permissible and illegal conduct concerning a specific liberty.

BALANCING INTERESTS

Civil liberties must be balanced against competing interests because when it comes to our freedoms, there are no absolutes. The trade-off between civil liberties and national security in the "war on terrorism" illustrates this point. Many Americans were concerned that our civil liberties were being eroded upon discovering that the government was conducting surveillance of U.S. citizens without court orders, including collecting data from millions of phone calls and e-mail messages; had condoned the abuse of Iraqi prisoners; and was applying a process called "extraordinary rendition" in which suspected terrorists were arrested in the United States and taken to a foreign country that is less protective of civil liberties, such as Egypt, Syria, Jordan, or Morocco, to be interrogated through torture.[5] Despite these concerns, even the strongest critic of state-sponsored torture would have to admit that, in some instances, it might be justified. For example, if a nuclear device were set to detonate in Manhattan in three hours, few would insist on protecting the civil liberties of someone who knew where the bomb was hidden. Once we recognize that our freedoms are not absolute, it becomes a question of how they are balanced against other interests, such as national security.

Other interests that compete with civil liberties include public safety and public health. For example, members of some Christian fundamentalist churches regularly handle dangerous snakes in their services, but many states and cities have laws against "the handling of poisonous reptiles in such manner as to endanger the public health, safety, and welfare." These conflicting interests collided in a 1947 case in which members of a church in North Carolina were each fined $50 for handling a poisonous copperhead snake in a church service. They appealed all the way to the North Carolina Supreme Court, arguing that the local ordinance "impinges on the freedom of religious worship." The court rejected this view, saying that "public safety is superior to religious practice."[6] In 2013, Tennessee

Wildlife Resource Agency officials cited a minister for keeping 53 poisonous snakes and using them in services (an estimated 125 churches still handle snakes, despite the laws). But Reverend Andrew Hamblin, co-star of the National Geographic Channel reality show *Snake Salvation,* was acquitted by a grand jury and will not be indicted. A couple of months later, his co-star Reverend Jamie Coots died after being bitten by a rattlesnake in his church and refusing treatment.[7] Similarly, in some states, the Amish are forced to place reflective "slow-moving vehicle" triangles on their horse-drawn carriages, even if it violates their religious beliefs, because of the paramount concern for public safety (see the How It Works graphic in this chapter).[8] Yet, the Amish are not forced to send their children to public schools despite a state law requiring all children to attend school through age 16. The Court said this law presented "a very real threat of undermining the Amish community and religious practice as it exists today."[9] Similarly, the Court ruled that a Florida town could not prevent animal sacrifice by practitioners of the Santeria religion because the local ordinance was neither neutral nor generally applicable and was targeted at that religion.[10]

These decisions show that balancing interests is never a simple process but involves deciding whether a specific civil liberty or some competing public interest is more compelling in a specific case.

DRAWING LINES

Along with balancing competing interests, court rulings draw the lines defining the limits of permissible conduct by the government or an individual in the context of a specific civil liberty. For example, despite the First Amendment protection of freedom of speech, it is obvious that some speech cannot be permitted; the classic example is falsely yelling "fire!" in a crowded theater. Therefore, the courts must interpret the law to draw the line between protected speech and impermissible speech.

HOW CAN CONFLICTS BE RESOLVED between civil liberties and other legitimate interests, such as public safety and public health? Sometimes freedom is forced to give way. Courts have upheld bans on the religious practice of snake handling and laws requiring the Amish to display reflective triangles when driving slow-moving buggies on public roads, despite religious objections to doing so.

The same applies to other civil liberties, such as the establishment of religion, freedom of the press, freedom from illegal searches, or other due process rights. For example, the First Amendment prohibits the government from establishing an official religion, which the Court has carefully interpreted over the years to avoid "excessive entanglement" between any religion and the government. On these grounds, government-sponsored prayer in public schools has been banned since the early 1960s. But sometimes it is difficult to draw the line between acceptable and impermissible government involvement concerning religion in schools. One such ruling allowed taxpayer subsidies to fund parochial schools for buying books but not maps. This odd hair-splitting led the late senator Daniel Patrick Moynihan to quip, "What about atlases?"[11] Another difficult issue is the Fourth Amendment prohibition against "unreasonable searches and seizures" and the role of drug-sniffing dogs. Here the line drawing involves deciding whether a sniff is a search, and if so, under what circumstances it is reasonable (see the You Decide feature in this chapter). Search and seizure cases also involve balancing interests: in this case, the individual freedoms of the target of police action and the broader interests in public order and security.

THE ORIGINS OF CIVIL LIBERTIES

EXPLAIN WHY THE BILL OF RIGHTS WAS ADDED TO THE CONSTITUTION, AND HOW IT CAME TO APPLY TO THE STATES

Courts define the boundaries of civil liberties, but the other branches of government and the public often get involved as well. The earliest debates during the American Founding illustrate the broad public involvement concerning the basic questions of how our civil liberties would be defined: Should government be limited by an explicit statement of individual liberties? Would these limitations apply to the state governments or just the national government? How should these freedoms evolve as our society changes?

ORIGINS OF THE BILL OF RIGHTS

The original Constitution provided only limited protection of civil liberties: a guarantee of habeas corpus rights (a protection against illegal incarceration), a prohibition of bills of attainder (legislation punishing someone for a crime without the benefit of a trial), and ex post facto laws (laws that retroactively change the legal consequences of some behavior). There were a few attempts to include a broader statement of civil liberties, including one by George Mason and Elbridge Gerry five days before the Constitutional Convention adjourned. But their motion to appoint a committee to draft a bill of rights was rejected. Charles Pinckney and Gerry also tried to add a provision to protect the freedom of the press, but that too was rejected.[12]

Mason and Gerry opposed ratification of the Constitution, partly because it did not include a bill of rights, and many Antifederalists echoed this view. In a letter to James Madison, Thomas Jefferson predicted that four states would withhold ratification until a bill of rights was added.[13] Some states ratified the Constitution but urged Congress to draft specific protections for individuals' and states' rights from federal action (they believed protection of civil liberties from state actions

THE BILL OF RIGHTS: A STATEMENT OF OUR CIVIL LIBERTIES

First Amendment	Freedom of religion, speech, press, and assembly; the separation of church and state; and the right to petition the government.
Second Amendment	Right to bear arms.
Third Amendment	Protection against the forced quartering of troops in one's home.
Fourth Amendment	Protection from unreasonable searches and seizures; requirement of "probable cause" for search warrants.
Fifth Amendment	Protection from forced self-incrimination or double jeopardy (being tried twice for the same crime); no person can be deprived of life, liberty, or property without due process of law; private property cannot be taken for public use without just compensation; and no person can be tried for a serious crime without the indictment of a grand jury.
Sixth Amendment	Right of the accused to a speedy and public trial by an impartial jury, to an attorney, to confront witnesses, to a compulsory process for obtaining witnesses in his or her favor, and to counsel in all felony cases.
Seventh Amendment	Right to a trial by jury in civil cases involving common law.
Eighth Amendment	Protection from excessive bail, excessive fines, and cruel and unusual punishment.
Ninth Amendment	The enumeration of specific rights in the Constitution shall not be construed to deny other rights retained by the people. This has been interpreted to include a general right to privacy and other fundamental rights.
Tenth Amendment	Powers not delegated by the Constitution to the national government, nor prohibited by it to the states, are reserved to the states or to the people.

should reside in state constitutions). In other states, the Antifederalists who lost the ratification battle continued making their case to the public and Congress. One of the most famous arguments came from the Antifederalists of Pennsylvania, who claimed that a bill of rights was needed to "fundamentally establish those unalienable and personal rights of men, without the full, free, and secure enjoyment of which there can be no liberty, and over which it is not necessary for a good government to have the control."[14] Their statement went on to outline many of those civil liberties that ultimately became the basis for the Bill of Rights.

Madison and other supporters of the Constitution agreed that the first Congress would take up the issue. State conventions submitted 124 amendments for consideration. That list was whittled down to 17 by the House and then to 12 by the Senate. This even dozen was approved by the House and sent to the states, which in 1791 ratified the 10 amendments that became the Bill of Rights (see Nuts & Bolts 4.2).[15]

Despite the profound significance of the Bill of Rights, one point limited its reach: it applied only to the national government and not the states. For example, the First Amendment says that *Congress* shall make no law" infringing on freedom of religion, speech, and the press, among others. Madison submitted another amendment, which he characterized as "the most valuable of the whole list," requiring states to protect some civil liberties: "The equal rights of conscience, the freedom of speech or of the press, and the right of trial by jury in criminal cases shall not be infringed by any State."[16] But Antifederalists feared another power grab by the Federalists in limiting states' rights, so the proposed amendment was voted down in Congress. This decision proved consequential because the national government was quite weak for the first half of our nation's history. Given that states exercised as much or more power over people's lives than did the national government, it would have been more important for the Bill of Rights to limit the reach of the state governments rather than that of the federal government, but this did not occur. Thus, the Bill of Rights played a surprisingly small role for more than a century. The Supreme Court used it only once before 1866 to invalidate a federal action—in the infamous *Dred Scott* case that contributed to the Civil War.

SELECTIVE INCORPORATION AND THE FOURTEENTH AMENDMENT

The significance of the Bill of Rights increased somewhat with the ratification of the Fourteenth Amendment in 1868. It was one of the three **Civil War Amendments** that attempted to guarantee equal rights to the newly freed slaves. (The other two Civil War Amendments were the Thirteenth, which abolished slavery, and the Fifteenth, which gave male former slaves the right to vote.) Northern politicians were concerned that southerners would deny basic rights to the former slaves, so the sweeping language of the Fourteenth Amendment was adopted.

Section 1 of the Fourteenth Amendment says:

> *All persons born or naturalized in the United States, and subject to the jurisdiction thereof, are citizens of the United States and of the State wherein they reside. No State shall make or enforce any law which shall abridge the privileges or immunities of citizens of the United States; nor shall any State deprive any person of life, liberty, or property, without due process of law; nor deny to any person within its jurisdiction the equal protection of the laws.*

This language was intended to make sure that states would not deny newly freed slaves the full protection of the law.[17] The **due process clause**, which forbids any state from denying "life, liberty, or property, without due process of law," led to an especially important expansion of civil liberties because the similar clause of the Fifth Amendment had previously been interpreted by the Court to apply only to the federal government.

EVOLVING INTERPRETATIONS BY THE SUPREME COURT Despite the clear language of the amendment saying that "no State shall make or enforce any law," in its first opportunity to interpret the Fourteenth Amendment in 1873, the Court continued to rule in favor of protection from national government actions only, embracing the "dual citizenship" idea set forth in *Barron v. Baltimore* (the 1833 case ruling that the Fifth Amendment's protection of property from being taken by the government without compensation only applied to the federal government, not to state governments).[18] Over the next 50 years, a minority of justices tried mightily to strengthen the power of the Fourteenth Amendment and use it to protect civil liberties against state government action. The first step was an 1897 case in which the Court ruled that the Fourteenth Amendment's due process clause forbade the state of Illinois from taking private property without just compensation. However, the decision did not specifically mention the Fifth Amendment's compensation clause.[19]

Civil War Amendments
The Thirteenth, Fourteenth, and Fifteenth Amendments to the Constitution, which abolished slavery and granted civil liberties and voting rights to freed slaves after the Civil War.

due process clause Part of the Fourteenth Amendment that forbids states from denying "life, liberty, or property" to any person without due process of law. (A nearly identical clause in the Fifth Amendment applies only to the national government.)

The next step came in a self-incrimination case in which a state judge gave the jury instructions that included references to the fact that the accused did not take the stand in his defense. The Supreme Court upheld his conviction but said, "It is possible that some of the personal rights safeguarded in the first eight amendments against National action may also be safeguarded against state action, because a denial of them would be a denial of the due process of law."[20] Thus, in both the property and self-incrimination cases, the Supreme Court started to use the Fourteenth Amendment to prohibit state governments from violating individual rights—but without specific reference to the Bill of Rights.

This progression culminated in the 1925 case *Gitlow v. New York*. Here the Court said for the first time that the Fourteenth Amendment incorporated one of the amendments in the Bill of Rights (provisions protecting freedom of speech and freedom of the press) and applied it to the states. The case involved Benjamin Gitlow, a radical socialist convicted under New York's Criminal Anarchy Act of 1902 for advocating the overthrow of the government. The Court upheld his conviction, arguing that his writings were the "language of direct incitement," but also warned state governments that there were limits on such suppression of speech.[21]

APPLYING CIVIL LIBERTIES TO THE STATES Slowly over the next 50 years, most civil liberties covered in the Bill of Rights were applied to the states on a case-by-case basis through the Fourteenth Amendment (see Table 4.1). However, this process of **selective incorporation** was not smooth and incremental; rather it progressed in surges. The first flurry of activity came in the 1930s when most of the First Amendment was incorporated, requiring the states to allow a free press, the right to assemble, free exercise of religion, and the right to petition. The next flurry came in the 1960s with a series of cases dealing with criminal defendants' rights and due process. After another 38-year gap, the incorporation of the Second Amendment's right to bear arms in 2010 meant that all the significant amendments now apply not only to the national government but also to state and local governments. As a result, the Bill of Rights has evolved from only protecting people against national government actions during the early nineteenth century to a robust set of protections for freedom and liberty that limit national, state, and local government actions today.

selective incorporation The process through which the civil liberties granted in the Bill of Rights were applied to the states on a case-by-case basis through the Fourteenth Amendment.

FREEDOM OF RELIGION

The First Amendment's ringing words are the most famous statement of personal freedoms in the Constitution: "Congress shall make no law respecting an establishment of religion, or prohibiting the free exercise thereof; or abridging the freedom of speech, or of the press; or the right of the people peaceably to assemble, and to petition the Government for a redress of grievances." (The How It Works feature illustrates how much is packed into this one amendment.)

The First Amendment has two parts that deal with religion: the **establishment clause**, which says that Congress cannot sponsor or endorse any particular religion, and the **free exercise clause**, which states that Congress cannot interfere with the practice of religion. To simplify only slightly, the former says that Congress should not help religion and the latter that it should not hurt religion. The establishment clause is primarily concerned with drawing lines; for example,

establishment clause Part of the First Amendment that states "Congress shall make no law respecting an establishment of religion," which has been interpreted to mean that Congress cannot sponsor or favor any religion.

free exercise clause Part of the First Amendment that states that Congress cannot prohibit or interfere with the practice of religion.

TABLE » 4.1

SELECTIVE INCORPORATION

The process of applying the Bill of Rights to the states progressed in two stages. The first, coming in the 1920s and 1930s, applied the First Amendment to the states; the second came a few decades later and involved criminal defendants' rights.

AMENDMENT	ISSUE	CASE
First Amendment	Freedom of speech	*Gitlow v. New York* (1925)
	Freedom of the press	*Near v. Minnesota* (1931)
	Freedom of assembly	*De Jonge v. Oregon* (1937)
	Right to petition the government	*Hague v. CIO* (1939)
	Free exercise of religion	*Hamilton v. Regents of the University of California* (1934); *Cantwell v. Connecticut* (1940)
	Separation of church and state	*Everson v. Board of Education of Ewing Township* (1947)
Second Amendment	Right to bear arms	*McDonald v. Chicago* (2010)
Fourth Amendment	Protection from unreasonable search and seizure	*Wolf v. Colorado* (1949); *Mapp v. Ohio* (1961)[a]
Fifth Amendment	Protection from forced self-incrimination	*Malloy v. Hogan* (1964)
	Protection from double jeopardy	*Benton v. Maryland* (1969)
Sixth Amendment	Right to a public trial	*In re Oliver 333 U.S. 257* (1948)
	Right to a fair trial and an attorney in death-penalty cases	*Powell v. Alabama* (1932)
	Right to an attorney in all felony cases	*Gideon v. Wainwright* (1963)
	Right to an attorney in cases involving jail time	*Argersinger v. Hamlin* (1972)
	Right to a jury trial in a criminal case	*Duncan v. Louisiana* (1968)
	Right to cross-examine a witness	*Pointer v. Texas* (1965)
	Right to compel witnesses to testify who are vital for the defendant's case	*Washington v. Texas* (1967)
Eighth Amendment	Protection from cruel and unusual punishment	*Robinson v. California* (1962)[b]
	Protection from excessive bail	*Schilb v. Kuebel* (1971)[c]
Ninth Amendment	Right to privacy and other nonenumerated, fundamental rights	*Griswold v. Connecticut* (1965)[d]

NOT INCORPORATED

Third Amendment	Prohibition against the quartering of troops in private homes	
Fifth Amendment	Right to indictment by a grand jury	
Seventh Amendment	Right to a jury trial in a civil case	
Eighth Amendment	Prohibition against excessive fines	

[a]*Wolf v. Colorado* applied the Fourth Amendment to the states (which meant that states could not engage in unreasonable searches and seizures); *Mapp v. Ohio* applied the exclusionary rule to the states (which excludes the use in a trial of illegally obtained evidence).

[b]Some sources list *Louisiana ex rel. Francis v. Resweber* (1947) as the first case that incorporated the Eighth Amendment. While the decision mentioned the Fifth and Eighth Amendments in the context of the due process clause of the Fourteenth Amendment, this argument was not included in the majority opinion that upheld as constitutional the bizarre double-electrocution of prisoner Willie Francis (the electric chair malfunctioned on the first attempt but was successful on the second attempt; see Abraham and Perry, *Freedom and the Court*, pp. 71–72).

[c]Justice Blackmun "assumed" in this case that "the Eighth Amendment's proscription of excessive bail [applies] to the states through the Fourteenth Amendment," but later decisions did not seem to share this view. However, Justices Stevens and O'Connor agreed with Blackmun's view in *Browning-Ferris v. Kelco Disposal* (1989). Some sources argue that the excessive bail clause of the Eighth Amendment is unincorporated.

[d]Justice Goldberg argued for explicit incorporation of the Ninth Amendment in a concurring opinion joined by Justices Warren and Brennan. The opinion of the Court referred more generally to a privacy right rooted in five amendments, including the Ninth, but did not explicitly argue for incorporation.

does a prayer at a public high school football game or a nativity scene on government property constitute state sponsorship of religion? The free exercise clause has more to do with balancing interests; recall the earlier examples of balancing public safety concerns against snake handling in religious services and the use of Amish buggies on highways.

The combination of the establishment and free exercise clauses results in a general policy of noninterference and government neutrality toward religion. As Thomas Jefferson put it in 1802, the First Amendment provides a "wall of eternal separation between church and state." This language continues to be cited in Court cases in which religion and politics intersect.[22] Since both areas carry great moral weight and emotional charge, it's no wonder that vehement debates continue over the appropriateness of the saying "In God We Trust" on our currency, of the White House Christmas tree, and of whether evolution and "intelligent design" should be taught in the public schools. Since politics is everywhere, the boundaries of religious expression remain difficult to draw, as the case of the Westboro Baptist Church protests at military funerals demonstrated.

THE ESTABLISHMENT CLAUSE AND SEPARATION OF CHURCH AND STATE

Determining the boundaries between church and state—the central issue of the establishment clause—is very difficult. As a leading text on civil liberties puts it, the words of the establishment clause—"Congress shall make no law respecting an establishment of religion"—are commanding and clear, but their meaning is entirely unclear. What does the clause allow or forbid?[23] We know that the Founders did not want an official state religion and did not want the government to favor one religion over another, but beyond that, it's hard to say. Jefferson's "eternal wall of separation" comment has been used in Court decisions that prohibit state aid for religious activities, but lately the Court has been moving toward a more "accommodationist" perspective that sometimes allows religious activity in public institutions.

SCHOOL PRAYER The prohibition of prayer in public schools has become the most controversial establishment clause issue. It exploded onto the political scene in 1962 when the Court ruled in *Engle v. Vitale*[24] that the following prayer, written by the New York Board of State Regents and read every day in the state's public schools, violated the separation of church and state: "Almighty God, we acknowledge our dependence upon Thee, and we beg Thy blessing upon us, our parents, our teachers, and our country." Banning the prayer caused a huge public outcry protesting the perceived attack on religion.

Over the next 50 years, Congress repeatedly tried, unsuccessfully, to amend the Constitution to allow school prayer. Meanwhile, the Court continued to take a hard line on school-sponsored prayer. In 1985, the Court struck down the practice of observing a one-minute moment of silence for "meditation or voluntary prayer" in the Alabama public schools.[25] More recently, the Court said that benedictions or prayers at public school graduations and a school policy that allowed an elected student representative to lead a prayer at a high school football game also

CAN A CROSS BE DISPLAYED ON federal land? The Supreme Court has ruled that religious displays on government property must be part of larger, secular displays. This cross on federal land in the Mojave Desert was covered up after it became controversial. Now it looks like a sign.

violated the establishment clause.[26] Yet, the Court has upheld the practice of opening every session of Congress with a prayer, has let stand without comment a lower-court ruling that allowed a prayer that was planned and led by students (rather than being school policy) at a high school graduation, and most recently in 2014 upheld prayers by voluntary chaplains for town board meetings in Greece, New York.[27] The latter case was especially significant because the town meetings included residents, unlike the previously approved legislative prayers that were intended for the elected leaders.

AID TO RELIGIOUS ORGANIZATIONS The Court has had an even more difficult time coming up with principles to govern aid to religious organizations, either directly, through tax dollars, or indirectly, through the use of public space. One early attempt was known as the ***Lemon* test**, after one of the parties in a 1971 case involving government support for religious schools (*Lemon v. Kurtzman*). This case said that a practice violated the establishment clause if it (1) did not have a "secular legislative purpose," (2) either advanced or inhibited religion, or (3) fostered "an excessive government entanglement with religion."[28] The third part of the test was later found open to interpretation by lower courts and therefore led to conflicting rulings.

The Court started to move away from the *Lemon* test in a 1984 case involving a crèche owned by the city of Pawtucket, Rhode Island, and displayed in a park owned by a nonprofit corporation. The Court allowed the nativity display, saying, "The Constitution does not require complete separation of church and state; it affirmatively mandates accommodation, not merely tolerance, of all religions, and forbids hostility toward any."[29] This "endorsement test" simply says that government action is unconstitutional if a "reasonable observer" would think that the action either endorses or disapproves of religion. Later rulings upheld similar religious displays, especially if they conformed to what observers have labeled the "three plastic animals rule"—if the baby Jesus is surrounded by Rudolph the red-nosed reindeer and other secular symbols, the overall display is considered sufficiently nonreligious to pass constitutional muster.[30] This picture became more muddled in 2005 when the Court said that the Ten Commandments could not be posted in two Kentucky courthouses but could be displayed on a monument outside the capitol in Austin, Texas. However, there was some consistency between the seemingly contradictory rulings on the commandments and the "three plastic animals rule." Justice Breyer noted that Austin's monument was one of 40 on the capitol grounds, so the display served a "mixed but primarily nonreligious purpose," whereas the Kentucky courthouses' displays were clearly religious.[31]

The Court has also applied the accommodationist perspective to funding for religious schools by looking more favorably on providing tax dollars to students' families to subsidize tuition costs rather than funding the parochial schools directly. For example, a 2002 case upheld an Ohio school voucher program that distributed scholarships to needy students so they could attend the Cleveland school of their choice, including private, religious schools. The Court said the program did not violate the establishment clause because it allowed students and their families "to exercise genuine choice among options public and private, secular and religious."[32] Critics of the decision pointed out that 96 percent of the students participating in the scholarship program were enrolled in religiously affiliated schools, which amounted to state sponsorship of religious education, something that the Court had not previously allowed. In 2011, the Court expanded taxpayer support for religious education when it upheld an Arizona law that provides state tax credits for contributions to organizations that provide tuition for religious schools.[33] The Court has also ruled that it is acceptable

Lemon **test** The Supreme Court uses this test, established in *Lemon v. Kurtzman*, to determine whether a practice violates the First Amendment's establishment clause.

to use federal funds to buy computers and other educational equipment to be used in public and private schools for "secular, neutral, and nonideological programs"[34] and tax dollars for a sign language interpreter for a deaf student who attended a parochial school.[35]

THE FREE EXERCISE CLAUSE

While the freedom of belief is absolute, freedom of religious conduct cannot be unrestricted. That is, you can believe whatever you want without government interference, but if you *act* on those beliefs, the government may regulate your behavior. And while the government has restricted religious conduct in dozens of cases, the freedom of religion has been among the most consistently protected civil liberties.

There is one prominent example of the Court restricting the free exercise of religion but then quickly correcting its error. This 1940 case concerned the children in a Jehovah's Witness family who were kicked out of a public school in Minersville, Pennsylvania, for refusing to recite the Pledge of Allegiance.[36] The children cited Exodus 20:3, "you shall have no other Gods before Me," in explaining why they refused to recite the pledge and salute the flag. The Court surprised the experts by siding with the school—until, three years later, the justices reversed course and ruled that the school could not force anyone to say the pledge, especially when it served no important government interest, such as protecting public safety.[37]

Hundreds of cases have come before the Court in the area of the free exercise of religion.[38] Here are some examples of the questions they addressed: May Amish parents be forced to send their children to schools beyond the eighth grade? (No.) May religion serve as the basis for attaining "conscientious objector" status and avoiding the draft? (Generally yes, but with many qualifications.) Is animal sacrifice as part of a religious ceremony protected by the First Amendment? (Generally yes.) May Mormons have multiple wives? (No.) May people be forced to work on Friday night and Saturday if those are their days of worship? (No.) May a city levy licensing fees that target the selling of religious books? (No.) Does the First Amendment protect distributing religious leaflets on public streets? And religious meetings in public parks?

LAWYERS FOR TOM GREEN ARGUED that laws against bigamy and polygamy infringed on his religious freedom. Green belonged to a fundamentalist sect of Mormonism that teaches plural marriage. When this photo was taken in 2000, he had 5 wives and at least 29 children.

THE FIRST AMENDMENT

Political speech and symbolic speech

FREEDOM OF THE PRESS

Less protected forms of speech

FREE EXERCISE
The government cannot prevent people from practicing their religion.

FREEDOM OF SPEECH

FREEDOM TO PETITION THE GOVERNMENT

ESTABLISHMENT
The government cannot establish an official state religion or favor one religion over others.

FREEDOM OF ASSEMBLY

FREEDOM OF RELIGION

FREEDOM OF EXPRESSION

FIRST AMENDMENT

Congress shall make no law respecting an establishment of religion, or prohibiting the free exercise thereof; or abridging the freedom of speech, or of the press; or the right of the people peaceably to assemble, and to petition the government for a redress of grievances.

BALANCING INTERESTS AND DRAWING LINES: GOVERNMENT AND RELIGION

While the different branches of the First Amendment on the previous page are an accurate representation of the various aspects of our religious and expressive freedoms, in practice, the implementation of these civil liberties is more complicated.

Religious freedom | Public safety

FREE EXERCISE

The Supreme Court often must balance religious freedom against other state interests, such as public safety. The Court has ruled that the state may require the Amish to have slow-moving-vehicle signs on their buggies.

School-sponsored prayer | Vouchers for religious schools

Excessive government entanglement with religion | Government neutrality toward religion

ESTABLISHMENT

The establishment clause often involves drawing lines between what type of religious conduct is allowed and what would be considered an "excessive entanglement" between church and state.

POP QUIZ

1 Which type of speech is strongly protected under the First Amendment?

- **a** political speech
- **b** commercial speech
- **c** obscenity
- **d** libel
- **e** fighting words

2 The First Amendment's "establishment clause" says that the government cannot

- **a** establish categories of speech.
- **b** prevent people from practicing their religion.
- **c** ban offensive speech.
- **d** create an official state religion.
- **e** prevent people from peaceably assembling.

(Yes, for both, but the latter is subject to "time, manner, and place" restrictions.) May religious dress be regulated? (Generally not, but in some contexts, such as the military, yes.) Are all prison inmates entitled to hold religious services? (Apparently yes, but this is still an open question.) Are religious organizations subject to child labor laws? (Yes.) Whew! Keep in mind that this list is by no means exhaustive.

One case had broad implications that defined the general basis for government restrictions of religious expression. The Court ruled that the state of Oregon had not violated the free exercise clause in denying unemployment benefits to the plaintiffs who were fired for using peyote as part of a religious ceremony. The broader significance of the ruling came with the Court's announcement of a new interpretation of the free exercise clause: the government does not need a "compelling interest" in regulating a particular behavior to justify a law that limits a religious practice.[39] In other words, after this decision, it would be easier for the government to limit the exercise of religion because the Court would no longer require a "compelling" reason for the restrictions, just a good one.

Congress responded by passing the Religious Freedom Restoration Act (RFRA) in 1993, reinstating the need to demonstrate a "compelling state interest" before limiting religious freedoms; the act also specified exceptions to the Controlled Substances Act to allow the use of peyote in religious ceremonies. The Court replied in a 1997 decision that Congress could not usurp its power to define the constitutional protections for religion and that the 1993 law did not apply to the states.[40] Congress retaliated in 2000 by passing a more narrowly written law, and the Court backed off, first in a case involving the religious freedoms of prison inmates in Ohio[41] and then in another case allowing a small religion in New Mexico to use a hallucinogenic tea in its services even though the tea is considered a controlled substance by the federal government. The Court ruled that the government had not demonstrated a compelling interest in barring the sacramental use of the tea, indicating a shift back toward the stricter standard favored by Congress for justifying limits on religious practices.[42] The Court relied on the compelling interest standard required in the RFRA in a controversial 2014 case involving the family-owned Hobby Lobby stores. In this case the Court ruled that "closely held" corporations could not be forced to provide contraceptives under the Affordable Care Act to their employees because it violated their free exercise of religion. Critics of the case argued that corporations should not have First Amendment religious protections and worried that the case could allow other corporations to ignore federal laws they disagreed with.[43]

The struggle between Congress and the Court in defining civil liberties illustrates the importance of the political process. When Congress decides to tackle an important civil liberty such as religious freedom, it can influence outcomes in an area that is usually dominated by the courts.

FREEDOM OF SPEECH, ASSEMBLY, AND THE PRESS

> DESCRIBE THE MAJOR FIRST AMENDMENT RIGHTS RELATED TO FREEDOM OF SPEECH

As we noted earlier, defining the scope of our civil liberties depends on balancing interests and drawing lines. This is especially true of the First Amendment's freedom of speech, which can be envisioned on a continuum from most to least protected types of speech based on the Supreme Court cases that have tested their limits.

GENERALLY PROTECTED EXPRESSION

Any time you attend a religious service or a political rally, write an article for your student paper, or express a political idea, you are being protected by the First Amendment. However, the nature of this protection is continually evolving due to political forces and shifting constitutional interpretations. For much of our nation's history, freedom of speech and the press were not strongly protected. Only recently have the courts developed a complex continuum ranging from strongly protected political speech to less protected speech.

strict scrutiny The highest level of scrutiny the courts can use when determining whether a law is constitutional. To meet this standard, the law or policy must be shown to serve a "compelling state interest" or goal, it must be narrrowly tailored to achieve that goal, and it must be the least restrictive means of achieving that goal.

intermediate scrutiny The middle level of scrutiny the courts can use when determining whether a law is constitutional. To meet this standard, the law or policy must be "content neutral," must further an important government interest in a way that is "substantially related" to that interest, and must use means that are a close fit to the government's goal and not substantially broader than is necessary to accomplish that goal.

STANDARDS FOR PROTECTION The basis for the continuum of protected speech is rooted in the content of the speech. The Supreme Court has interpreted the law to mean that content-based regulation of speech is not permissible (unless it falls into one of the categories of exceptions we outline later). For example, the Court struck down a local ordinance that banned picketing outside of schools except for labor picketing.[44] This ordinance was content-based regulation because it favored one form of speech (from labor unions) over others. Such regulation is subject to the **strict scrutiny** standard of judicial review, which means the regulation must be narrowly tailored so that it is the least restrictive on an individual's fundamental right to free speech and the government must demonstrate a compelling state interest to curtail the speech. In most cases, such strict scrutiny by the courts means that the speech will be protected and the regulation will be struck down. If a regulation is content neutral and does not favor any given viewpoint over another, then it is subject to the less demanding **intermediate scrutiny** standard. This means that the government must only demonstrate a substantial interest in curtailing the speech, the interest must be unrelated to the content of the speech, and there must be alternative opportunities for communication.[45]

POLITICAL SPEECH Freedom of speech got off to a rocky start when Congress passed the Alien and Sedition Acts in 1798. The controversial Sedition Act made it a crime to "write, print, utter or publish . . . any false, scandalous and malicious writing or writings against the government of the United States." Supporters of the four acts claimed they were necessary to strengthen the national government in response to the French Revolution, but in reality they were an attempt by the governing Federalist Party to neutralize the opposition Democratic-Republican Party. As many as 25 people, mostly newspaper editors, were tried under the law and 10 were jailed, including Benjamin Franklin's grandson. The outcry against the laws helped Thomas Jefferson to win the presidential election in 1800. Jefferson pardoned the convicted editors, Congress repealed one of the acts in 1802, and the other acts were allowed to expire before the Supreme Court had a chance to rule that they were unconstitutional.

World War I prompted the harshest crackdowns on free speech since the Sedition Act of 1798. The most important case from this period involved the general secretary of the Socialist Party, Charles Schenck, who opposed U.S. involvement in the war. He had printed a leaflet urging young men to resist the draft. Schenck was arrested under the Espionage Act of 1917, which prohibited "interfering with military or naval operations," including the draft. He appealed all the way to the Supreme Court, arguing that the First Amendment permitted him to protest the war and to urge others to resist the draft, but the Court sustained his conviction, noting that free speech is not an absolute right:

> The most stringent protection of free speech would not protect a man in falsely shouting fire in a theatre and causing a panic. . . . The question in every case is whether the words used are used in such circumstances and are of such a nature as to create a clear and present danger that they will bring about the substantive evils that Congress has a right to prevent.[46]

This **clear and present danger test** meant that the government could suppress speech it deemed dangerous (in this instance, preventing the government from fighting the war). However, critics of the decision argue that Schenck's actions were not dangerous for the country.[47]

While Schenck's actions would have been legal under the current standard for protecting speech, things got worse for supporters of the First Amendment before they got better. Eugene V. Debs, a union leader and the Socialist presidential candidate five times between 1900 and 1920, was also arrested and sentenced to federal prison for making a speech that condemned U.S. involvement in World War I. Moreover, two newspaper publishers were jailed for publishing articles critical of the war. Both high-profile convictions were sustained by the Court.[48] Then Congress passed the more restrictive Sedition Act of 1918, which outlawed any "disloyal, profane, scurrilous, or abusive language about the form of government, the Constitution, soldiers and sailors, flag or uniform of the armed forces" and any words that favored the cause of the German empire or opposed the cause of the United States. In the first test case for the new law, the Court upheld the conviction of six anarchists who supported the cause of the Bolsheviks in Russia and urged the "workers of the world" to strike.

Justice Oliver Wendell Holmes, author of the *Schenck* decision and the clear and present danger test, had had enough. He dissented in the anarchists' case, arguing that the "surreptitious publishing of a silly leaflet by an unknown man" posed no danger to the country. In one of the most famous statements of the importance of

clear and present danger test Established in *Schenck v. United States*, this test allows the government to restrict certain types of speech deemed dangerous.

MANY AMERICAN SOCIALISTS opposed U.S. involvement in World War I. Eugene Debs, pictured here delivering an antiwar speech at a Socialist meeting in Canton, Ohio, on June 16, 1918 (about a year after the United States entered the war), was jailed merely for speaking out against the war.

the freedom of speech, he touted the "free trade in ideas" saying, "The best test of truth is the power of the thought to get itself accepted in the competition of the market.... [W]e should be eternally vigilant against attempts to check the expression of opinion that we loathe and believe to be fraught with death."[49] This notion of the marketplace of ideas in which good ideas triumph over bad is still central to modern defenses of the First Amendment.

Over the next several decades, the Court struggled to draw the line between dangerous speech and words that were simply unpopular. During the Red Scare of the late 1940s and early 1950s, the Court had many opportunities to defend unpopular speech, but for the most part it declined to do so. For example, in 1951, the Court upheld the conviction of 11 members of the Communist Party under the Smith Act, which banned the advocacy of force or violence against the United States.[50]

In 1969, the Court established a strong protection for free speech that still holds today. This case involved a leader of the Ku Klux Klan who made a threatening speech at a cross-burning rally that was subsequently shown on television. Twelve hooded figures were shown, many with weapons. The speech said that "revengence" [sic] might be taken if "our president, our Congress, our Supreme Court continues to suppress the white, Caucasian race." He continued, "We are marching on Congress July the Fourth, four hundred thousand strong." The Klan leader was convicted under the Ohio law banning "sabotage, violence, or unlawful methods of terrorism as a means of accomplishing industrial or political reform," but the Court unanimously reversed his conviction, arguing that threatening speech could not be suppressed just because it sounded dangerous. Specifically, the **direct incitement test** holds that speech is protected "except where such advocacy is directed to inciting or producing imminent lawless action and is likely to incite or produce such action."[51] Under this standard, most, if not all, of the sedition convictions during World War I and the Red Scare would have been overturned.

However, direct incitement is not the only basis for limiting speech that could be viewed as political. One example involved a high school student from Juneau, Alaska, who was suspended from school for unfurling a banner on a public sidewalk that said "Bong Hits 4 Jesus." The incident occurred as the Olympic torch relay passed through Juneau on its way to the 2002 Winter Games in Utah. The student sued the school, claiming his First Amendment rights had been violated, but the Supreme Court agreed with the school, saying, "It was reasonable for [the principal] to conclude that the banner promoted illegal drug use—and that failing to act would send a powerful message to the students in her charge." Dissenters lamented the invention of "a special First Amendment rule permitting the censorship of any student speech that mentions drugs," based on "a silly, nonsensical banner."[52]

SYMBOLIC SPEECH The use of signs, symbols, or other unspoken acts or methods to communicate in a political manner—**symbolic speech**—enjoys many of the same protections as regular speech. For example, during the Vietnam War, the Court protected the First Amendment right of a war protester to wear an American flag patch sewn on the seat of his pants,[53] high school students' right to wear an armband to protest the war,[54] and an individual's right to tape a peace symbol on the flag and fly it upside-down outside an apartment window.[55] Lower courts had convicted these protesters under state laws that protected the American flag, or under a school policy that prohibited wearing armbands to protest the Vietnam War. In the flag desecration case involving the peace symbol, the Court stated that protected "speech" need not be verbal: "there can be little doubt that appellant communicated through the use of symbols."[56]

---

direct incitement test Established in *Brandenburg v. Ohio*, this test protects threatening speech under the First Amendment unless that speech aims to and is likely to cause imminent "lawless action."

symbolic speech Nonverbal expression, such as the use of signs or symbols. It benefits from many of the same constitutional protections as verbal speech.

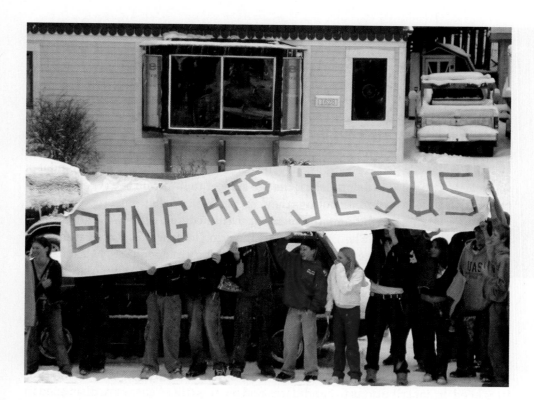

IN 2002, A STUDENT IN JUNEAU, Alaska, was suspended for holding up a banner across from his school that proclaimed "Bong Hits 4 Jesus" when the Olympic torch was passing through Juneau. The student sued the principal of the school, and the case ultimately went to the Supreme Court. The Court ruled in favor of the principal, saying that the student's right to free speech could be curtailed because it was promoting illegal drug use.

A 1989 case provided the strongest protection for symbolic speech yet. The case involved a man who burned a flag outside the 1984 Republican national convention in Texas, chanting along with other protesters, "America the red, white, and blue, we spit on you. You stand for plunder, you will go under." The Court refrained from critiquing the jingle, but its 5–4 decision overturned the man's conviction under Texas's flag desecration law on the grounds that symbolic political speech is protected by the First Amendment.[57] In response to this unpopular decision, Congress passed the Flag Protection Act of 1989, which the Court also struck down as an unconstitutional infringement on political expression.[58] Congress then attempted to pass a constitutional amendment to overturn the Court decision; the House passed the amendment six times between 1995 and 2005 with the necessary two-thirds vote, but each time the measure failed by a narrow margin in the Senate (by just one vote in 2006).

Although the Court has protected flag burning and other forms of symbolic speech, there are limits, especially when the symbolic speech conflicts with another substantial governmental interest. Here the critical test is whether the action can be regulated for important reasons unrelated to ideas. If so, then the "intermediate scrutiny" standard will apply. For example, Vietnam War protesters who burned their draft cards were not protected by the First Amendment because their actions interfered with Congress's constitutional authority to "raise and support" armies and the purpose of the draft was not to suppress speech.[59]

Spending money in political campaigns may also be protected by the First Amendment since it provides the means for more-conventional types of political speech. Here the central question is whether the government can control campaign contributions and spending for a broader public purpose such as controlling corruption, or whether such laws violate the First Amendment rights of candidates or their supporters. You probably have heard the old saying "Money talks," which implies that money is speech. Given the importance of advertising in modern campaigns,

THE AMERICAN FLAG IS A POPULAR target for protesters: it has been spat upon, shredded, turned into underwear, and burned, as it was during this protest on July 14, 2013, after the jury acquitted George Zimmerman of the second-degree murder of Trayvon Martin. Zimmerman (who claimed self-defense) fatally shot the unarmed 17-year-old while on a neighborhood watch.

limitations on raising and spending money could limit the ability of candidates and groups to reach voters with their message. The Court has walked a tightrope on this one, balancing the public interest in honest and ethical elections and the First Amendment rights of candidates and their advocates. The Court has upheld individual candidates' right to spend their own money in federal elections, but presidential candidates give up that right if they accept federal campaign funds (taxpayers' money) in a presidential election. Also, candidates in federal elections are subject to limits on the types and size of contributions they can receive, and they must report all contributions and spending to the Federal Election Commission.[60]

The Bipartisan Campaign Reform Act, which went into effect for the 2004 elections, included a "Millionaires' Amendment" that lifted restrictions on campaign contributions for candidates whose opponents spent more than $350,000 of their own money in the election. This attempt to level the campaign finance playing field was struck down by the Supreme Court in 2008 as a violation of wealthy candidates' First Amendment rights.[61] In 2010, the Court also extended First Amendment rights to corporations and labor unions that want to spend money on campaign ads, and in 2014 it struck down the aggregate (collective) limits placed on contributions to candidates and parties (these cases are discussed in more detail in Chapter 9). In 2014, the Court struck down aggregate limits placed on individual contributions.[62] However, the Court upheld a ban on unlimited "soft money" contributions because they were seen by the Court as the type of contribution with the most potential for corruption.[63]

Student fees as a form of symbolic speech came up in a case in 2000 involving student activity fees at the University of Wisconsin. A group of students argued that they should not have to pay fees to fund groups whose activities they opposed, including a student environmental group, a gay and bisexual student center, a community legal office, an AIDS support network, a campus women's center, and the Wisconsin Student Public Interest Research Group. The Court ruled that mandatory student fees could continue to support the full range of groups as long as the process for allocating money was "viewpoint neutral." The Court also said that student referendums that could add or cut money for specific groups violated viewpoint neutrality. The potential for the majority to censor unpopular views was unacceptable to the Court, since "the whole theory of viewpoint neutrality is that minority views are treated with the same respect as are majority views."[64]

hate speech Expression that is offensive or abusive, particularly in terms of race, gender, or sexual orientation. It is currently protected under the First Amendment.

HATE SPEECH Whether or not freedom of speech should apply to **hate speech** has been a controversial issue both on college campuses and in society generally. Do people have a right to say things that are offensive or abusive, especially in terms of race, gender, and sexual orientation? By the mid-1990s, more than 350 public colleges and universities said no by regulating some forms of hate speech.[65] One example was a speech code adopted at the University of Michigan that prohibited "any behavior, verbal or physical, that stigmatizes or victimizes an individual on the basis of race, ethnicity, religion, sex, sexual orientation, creed, national origin, ancestry, age, marital status, handicap, or Vietnam veteran status," and "creates an intimidating, hostile, or demeaning environment for educational pursuits, employment or participation in University-sponsored extra-curricular activities."[66]

The Supreme Court has yet to rule on this issue, but lower courts struck down the University of Michigan's speech code as well as similar rules at several other universities. If the Court took up any of these cases, it would be likely to strike down the speech codes because they are not "content neutral" regulations and they do not meet the direct incitement test of targeting only expressions that would spur imminent violence.

Another significant issue combines the topics of symbolic speech and hate speech. Can a person who burned a cross on a black family's lawn be convicted under a city ordinance that prohibited conduct "arous[ing] anger, alarm, or resentment in others on the basis of race, color, creed, religion, or gender"? Or is the ordinance an unconstitutional limit on First Amendment rights? The Court said the cross burner could be punished for arson, terrorism, trespassing, or other violations of the law, but he could not be convicted under this St. Paul, Minnesota, ordinance because it was overly broad and vague. The Court said, "Let there be no mistake about our belief that burning a cross in someone's front yard is reprehensible. But St. Paul has sufficient means at its disposal to prevent such behavior without adding the First Amendment to the fire."[67] The city ordinance was unconstitutional because it took selective aim at a disfavored message; it constituted "viewpoint discrimination." However, the Court has since upheld more carefully worded bans of cross burning. Eleven years after the St. Paul case, the Court ruled that Virginia could prohibit cross burning if there was intent to intimidate. The Court also noted that the law was content neutral because it did not engage in viewpoint discrimination: any burning of a cross in a threatening context was illegal.[68]

Internet hate speech has become increasingly controversial in recent years. Cyberbullying, some of which was done on social media like Myspace, Twitter, and Facebook, precipitated several suicides. In 2013, Facebook cracked down on offensive content that glorified violence against women, such as pages with headlines like "Violently Raping Your Friend Just for Laughs."[69] Facebook's "community standards" have a more restrictive definition of hate speech than is allowed by the direct incitement test. While Facebook makes a distinction between humor and serious speech, they "do not permit individuals or groups to attack others based on their race, ethnicity, national origin, religion, sex, gender, sexual orientation, disability or medical condition."[70] This led law professor Jeffrey Rosen to conclude, "today, lawyers at Google, YouTube, Facebook, and Twitter have more power over who can speak and who can be heard than any president, judge, or monarch."[71] This may sound like hyperbole, but he is right: corporations are not restricted by the First Amendment (which, after all, says "*Congress* shall make no law . . ."). So if Facebook and other social media want to restrict hate speech, they can. Although free speech advocates are concerned about restrictions on Internet hate speech, civil rights groups such as the Anti-Defamation League, Leadership Conference on Civil Rights, and the National Organization for Women all support the move. Early in 2014, a bill was proposed by 13 House Democrats that would mandate a study of how the Internet, cell phones, television, and radio are used to advocate and encourage violent acts and the commission of crimes of hate.[72]

FREEDOM OF ASSEMBLY The right to assemble peaceably has been consistently protected by the Supreme Court.[73] Perhaps the most famous freedom of assembly case involved a neo-Nazi group that wanted to march in Skokie, a suburb of Chicago that had 70,000 residents, nearly 60 percent of whom were Jewish, including many Holocaust survivors. The village passed ordinances that effectively banned

ARE LAWS BANNING HATE SPEECH constitutional? Sometimes yes, but the threshold is relatively high. These Ku Klux Klan members are free to hold rallies, preach racism and xenophobia, and burn crosses, as long as they do not directly incite violence or display an "intent to intimidate."

the group from marching, arguing that residents would be so upset by the Nazi marchers that they might become violent. But the lower courts did not accept this argument, ruling that if "the audience is so offended by the ideas being expressed that it becomes disorderly and attempts to silence the speaker, it is the duty of the police to attempt to protect the speaker, not to silence his speech."[74] Otherwise, the right to assemble would be restricted by a "heckler's veto." The Court elaborated on this responsibility to protect expressions of unpopular views by striking down another town's ordinance that allowed them to charge a higher permit fee to groups whose march would likely require more police protection.[75]

While broad protection is provided for peaceable assemblies, governments may regulate the time, manner, and place of expression as long as the regulation does not favor certain groups or messages over others. For example, antiabortion protesters were not allowed to picket a doctor's home in Brookfield, Wisconsin. The Court ruled that the ordinance banning all residential picketing was content neutral and that there was a government interest in preserving the "sanctity of the home, the one retreat to which men and women can repair to escape from the tribulations of their daily pursuits."[76] "Time, manner, and place" restrictions also may be invoked for practical reasons. If the Ku Klux Klan planned to hold a march around a football stadium on the day of a game, the city council could deny them a permit and could suggest that they choose another day that would not interfere with game day activities. The legal standard for these regulations is that they are "reasonable." For example, in 2014 the Court ruled that a Massachusetts state law creating a 35-foot buffer zone around entrances to abortion clinics violated the First Amendment. While the buffer zone was content neutral, it was unreasonable because it was more restrictive than necessary to allow access to the clinics. While the "reasonableness" standard is vague, it allows the courts to balance the right to assemble against other practical considerations.

FREEDOM OF THE PRESS The task of balancing interests is central to many First Amendment cases involving freedom of the press. Which is more important, the First Amendment freedom of the press to disclose details about current events or the Sixth Amendment right to a fair trial, which may require keeping important information out of the public eye? When do national security concerns prevail over journalists' right to keep citizens informed? The general issue here is **prior restraint**, the government's right to prevent the media from publishing something.

prior restraint A limit on freedom of the press that allows the government to prohibit the media from publishing certain materials.

Prior restraint has never been clearly defined by the Court, but several landmark cases have set a very high bar for applying it. The first involved a Minnesota law that banned "obscene, lewd and lascivious" publications or "malicious, scandalous and defamatory" content. Under this law, the state shut down a racist, bigoted publication that railed against many groups of people. In 1931, the Court subsequently struck down the law in *Near v. Minnesota*, saying, "The fact that the liberty of the press may be abused by miscreant purveyors of scandal does not make any less necessary the immunity of the press from previous restraint."[77] However, the Court did not specify when prior restraint would be acceptable.

In 1971, the Pentagon Papers case involved disclosure of parts of the top-secret report on internal planning for the Vietnam War. This incredibly divided case had nine separate written opinions! In a 6–3 decision, the Court said that the government could not prevent the publication of the Pentagon Papers, but at least five justices supported the view that, under some circumstances, the government could use prior restraint—although they could not agree on the standard.[78] For some of the justices, a crucial consideration was the Pentagon Papers' revelation that the U.S. government had lied about its involvement in and the progress of the Vietnam War. Justice Hugo Black noted the importance of this point saying, "Only a free and unrestrained press can effectively expose deception in government."[79]

Prior restraint has taken on new significance in the war on terror. The media, especially the *New York Times*, skirmished with the Bush administration over publishing stories on various classified programs, including extraordinary rendition of suspected terrorists, domestic surveillance, and the Terrorist Finance Tracking Program, which monitors all large financial transactions in the international banking system. The debate over restraining the media heated up again in 2010, when WikiLeaks released a classified video of an airstrike in Baghdad showing U.S. pilots mistakenly firing on two Reuters reporters and more than 91,000 classified battlefield incident reports from Iraq and Afghanistan and U.S. State Department cables. All of these documents had been leaked to them by U.S. Army Private First Class Bradley Manning (see Chapter 7). This sensational leaking ratcheted up the stakes, and some members of Congress called the leaks "treason" and urged for prosecution (Manning was tried and convicted in a military court for violations of the Espionage Act and for copying and releasing classified information). Similar arguments were made in 2013 when Edward Snowden (see Chapter 7) revealed classified information about the NSA's "big data" surveillance program that collected information from millions of phone calls, e-mails, and business transactions within the United States (in Snowden's case, the debate is over whether federal "whistleblower" laws should apply, although freedom of the press to publish Snowden's revelations is involved as well).

The forms of expression discussed in this section—speech, assembly, and press—all have strong protections based on the First Amendment. The strongest protections are for content-based expression—that is, if a regulation is trying to limit *what* can be said, the Court applies the strict scrutiny standard and usually strikes down the regulation. However, there are exceptions, such as speech that directly incites an imminent danger. If the regulation is content neutral and does not favor one viewpoint over another, then it is easier to uphold. But even then, the government must have a substantial reason for limiting expression.

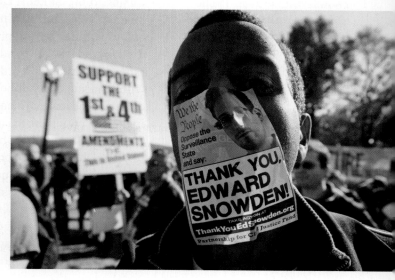

THE PUBLICATION OF THOUSANDS of government documents, including some sensitive reports and communications, raised new questions about press freedom and national security. Here, demonstrators protest government surveillance and thank Edward Snowden for his revelations.

LESS PROTECTED SPEECH AND PUBLICATIONS

Some forms of speech do not warrant the same level of protection as political speech because they do not contribute to public debate or express ideas that have important social value. Four categories of speech may be more easily regulated by the government than political speech: fighting words, slander and libel, commercial speech, and obscenity.

fighting words Forms of expression that "by their very utterance" can incite violence. These can be regulated by the government but are often difficult to define.

FIGHTING WORDS Governments may regulate **fighting words**, "which by their very utterance inflict injury or tend to incite an immediate breach of the peace."[80] Such laws must be narrowly written; it is not acceptable to ban all foul language, and the prohibited speech must target a single person rather than a group. Moreover, the question of whether certain words provoke a backlash depends on the reaction of the targeted person. Inflammatory words directed at Archbishop Emeritus Desmond Tutu would not be fighting words because he would turn the other cheek, whereas the same words yelled at musician Kanye West or actor Alec Baldwin *would* be fighting words because they would probably deck you. The Court has further clarified the test, based on "what persons of common intelligence would understand to be words likely to cause an average addressee to fight."[81] While this is a more objective test than the previous subjective standard, the fighting words doctrine has still been difficult to apply.

slander Spoken false statements that damage a person's reputation. They can be regulated by the government but are often difficult to distinguish from permissible speech.

libel Written false statements that damage a person's reputation. They can be regulated by the government but are often difficult to distinguish from permissible speech.

SLANDER AND LIBEL A more extensive line of cases prohibiting speech concerns **slander**, spoken false statements that damage someone's reputation, and **libel**, written statements that do the same thing. As in many areas of First Amendment law, it is difficult to draw the line between permissible speech and slander or libel. The current legal standard distinguishes between speech about a public figure, such as a politician or celebrity, and about a regular person. In short, public figures must have much thicker skin than the average person because it is much more difficult for them to prove libel. A public figure has to demonstrate that the defamatory statement was made with "actual malice" and "with knowledge that it was false or with reckless disregard of whether it was false or not."[82]

One of the most famous libel cases was brought against *Hustler* magazine by the Reverend Jerry Falwell, a famous televangelist and political activist. Falwell sued *Hustler* for libel and emotional distress after the magazine published a parody of a liquor advertisement depicting him in a "drunken incestuous rendezvous with his mother in an outhouse" (this quote is from the Supreme Court case).[83] The lower court said that the parody wasn't believable, so *Hustler* couldn't be sued for libel, but they awarded Falwell damages for emotional distress. The Court overturned this decision, saying that public figures and public officials have to put up with such things and compared the parody to outrageous political cartoons, which have always been protected by the First Amendment.

commercial speech Public expression with the aim of making a profit. It has received greater protection under the First Amendment in recent years but remains less protected than political speech.

COMMERCIAL SPEECH **Commercial speech**, which mostly refers to advertising, has evolved from having almost no protection under the First Amendment to enjoying quite strong protection. One early case involved a business owner who distributed leaflets to advertise rides on his submarine, which was docked in New York City. Under city ordinances, leafleting was permitted only if it was devoted to "information or a public protest," but not for a commercial purpose. The plaintiff changed the leaflet to have his advertisement on one side and a statement protesting a city policy on the other side (clever guy!). He was arrested anyway, and the Supreme Court upheld his conviction, saying that the city council had the right to regulate the distribution of leaflets.[84]

The Court became much more sympathetic to commercial speech in the 1970s when it struck down a law against advertising prescription drug prices and a law prohibiting placing newspaper racks on city streets to distribute commercial publications such as real estate guides.[85] The key decision in 1980 established a test that is still central today. The Court ruled that the government may regulate commercial speech if it concerns an illegal activity, if the advertisement is misleading, or if regulating speech directly advances a substantial government interest and the regulation is not excessive. In practice, this test means that commercial speech can be regulated but that the government has to have a very good reason to do it. Even public health concerns have not been allowed to override commercial speech rights. For example, the Court struck down a Massachusetts regulation that limited the content of advertisements aimed at children (the ban on R. J. Reynolds's Joe Camel character is the classic example) in a manner that was more restrictive than federal law.[86]

OBSCENITY One area in which the press has never experienced complete freedom involves the publication of pornography and material considered obscene. The difficulty arises in deciding where to draw the line. Nearly everyone would agree that child pornography should not be published[87] and that pornography should not be available to minors. However, beyond these points there is not much consensus. For example, some people are offended by nude paintings in art museums, while others enjoy watching hard-core X-rated movies.

JOE CAMEL PEDDLES HIS WARES on a New York City billboard. Commercial speech, as a general category, is not as strongly protected by the First Amendment as political speech, but advertising can be limited by the government only in specific circumstances.

Defining obscenity has proven difficult for the courts. In an often-quoted moment of frustration, Justice Potter Stewart wrote that he could not define obscenity, but "I know it when I see it."[88] In its first attempt, the Court ruled that a particular publication could be banned if an "average person, applying contemporary community standards" would find that the material appeals to prurient interests and is "utterly without redeeming social importance."[89] This standard proved unworkable because lower courts differed in their interpretation. The Court took another stab at it in 1973 in a case that gave rise to the **Miller test**, which is still applied today.[90] The test has three standards that must all be met in order for material to be banned as obscene: (1) it appeals to prurient interests, (2) it is "patently offensive," and (3) the work as a whole lacks serious literary, artistic, political, or scientific value. The Court also clarified that *local* community standards were to apply rather than a single national standard, reasoning that what passes for obscenity in Sioux City, Iowa, probably would be considered pretty tame in Las Vegas.

Miller **test** Established in *Miller v. California*, the Supreme Court uses this three-part test to determine whether speech meets the criteria for obscenity. If so, it can be restricted by the government.

Congress and the president also have tried to control the dissemination of what they consider to be obscene. In general, they take a more conservative approach: they seek legislation to limit obscenity. In contrast, the Court focuses on whether certain speech is protected. Furthermore, the Court tends to rein in Congress and the president when they try to limit obscene speech.

Recent efforts have focused on the Internet as a pornography medium. Congress passed the Communications Decency Act in 1996, which criminalized the use of any computer network to display "indecent" material, unless the provider could offer an effective way of screening out potential users under age 18. The Court struck down the law in 1997 because it was overly vague and because limiting access to websites based on age is technically impossible. This ruling gives the Internet the same free speech protection as print.[91] But Congress wasn't going to give up without a fight. In 1998, it enacted the Child Online Protection Act, which prohibited commercial websites from distributing material that is "harmful to minors," using the language of the *Miller* test to specify what this means. The law bounced around in the federal courts for six years, twice making it to the Supreme Court, which ultimately struck it down.[92]

In 2009, the Supreme Court addressed an area of the law that it had not touched for more than 30 years: regulating vulgar language that does not rise to the level of obscenity on broadcast television and radio (but not on cable or other paid-subscription services, which are not regulated as to language). In 1978, the Court had ruled that the Federal Communications Commission (FCC) had the power to regulate indecent language, but the FCC had always interpreted that power to only cover repeated use of vulgar words.[93] After the use of vulgar words by Bono during the 2003 Golden Globe Awards and by Cher and Nicole Richie during the 2002 and 2003 Billboard Music Awards, the FCC announced that it would no longer tolerate even "isolated uses of sexual and excretory words."

Fox Television challenged this new rule, but in 2009 the Supreme Court upheld the ban on "fleeting expletives" as "entirely rational" under existing law, while taking a swipe at the "foul-mouthed glitteratae from Hollywood."[94] The Court also ruled the following week that the FCC had not acted capriciously in fining CBS $550,000 for Janet Jackson's infamous "wardrobe malfunction" at the 2004 Super Bowl.[95] However, after sending the cases back to the lower courts and another round of appeals, the Supreme Court ruled that television networks had not been given "fair notice" about the changed policy on fleeting expletives, and therefore the regulations were unconstitutionally vague and the networks could not be fined. The Court also let stand a lower-court ruling that voided the fine against CBS on similar grounds.[96] But the Court did not address the broader constitutional questions, holding open the possibility of stronger First Amendment protections for broadcast radio and television in the future.

Two more-recent cases made clear that violence in published material could not be regulated in the same way as sexual content. In 2010, the Court struck down a federal law that criminalized depictions "in which a living animal is intentionally maimed, mutilated, tortured, wounded, or killed." The law focused on "crush videos," which show the torture and killing of helpless animals, but also included dog fighting and other forms of animal cruelty. In striking down the law, the Court said the First Amendment protected such depictions, even if the underlying behavior itself could be illegal.[97] In 2011, the Court struck down a California law that banned the sale of violent video games to children, saying, "Like the protected books, plays and movies that preceded them, video games communicate ideas—and even social messages—through many familiar literary devices (such as characters, dialogue, plot and music) and through features distinctive to the medium (such as the player's interaction with the virtual world). That suffices to confer First Amendment protection."[98]

EXPLORE WHY THE SECOND AMENDMENT'S MEANING ON GUN RIGHTS IS OFTEN DEBATED

THE RIGHT TO BEAR ARMS

Until recently, the right to bear arms was the only civil liberty that the Supreme Court had played a relatively minor role in defining. Between 1791 and 2007, the Court issued only four rulings directly pertaining to the Second Amendment. The federal courts had always interpreted the Second Amendment's awkward phrasing—"A well regulated Militia, being necessary to the security of a free State, the right of the people to keep and bear Arms, shall not be infringed"—as a right to bear arms within the context of serving in a militia, rather than as an individual right to own a gun.

Although legal conflict over gun ownership has intensified only recently, battles over guns have always been intense in the broader political realm.[99] Interest groups such as the National Rifle Association have long asserted that the Second Amendment guarantees an individual right to bear arms. Critics of this view emphasize the first clause of the amendment and point to the frequent mention of state militias in congressional debates at the time the Bill of Rights was adopted. They argue that the Second Amendment was adopted to reassure Antifederalist advocates of states' rights that state militias, not a national standing army, would provide national security. In this view, the national armed forces and the National Guard have made the Second Amendment obsolete.

Before the Court's recent entry into this debate, Congress and state and local lawmakers had largely defined gun ownership and gun carrying rights, creating significant variation among the states. Wyoming and Montana have virtually no restrictions on gun ownership, for example, whereas California and Connecticut have many. At the national level, Congress tends to respond to crime waves or high-profile assassinations by passing new gun control laws. The broadest one, the Gun Control Act of 1968, was passed in the wake of the assassinations of Robert F. Kennedy and Martin Luther King, Jr. The law sets standards for gun dealers, bans the sale of weapons through the mail, and restricts the sale of new machine guns, among other provisions.

Following the assassination attempt on President Reagan in 1981, the push for stronger gun control laws intensified. Spearheading this effort was Sarah Brady, whose husband, James Brady (Reagan's press secretary) was shot and disabled in the assassination attempt. It took nearly 13 years for the campaign to bear fruit, but in 1993 Congress passed and President Clinton signed the Brady Bill, which mandates a background check and a five-day waiting period for any handgun purchase.

But not all gun tragedies lead to more gun control. In December 2012, a lone gunman killed 20 young children and 6 staff members at the Sandy Hook Elementary School in Newtown, Connecticut. President Obama made a strong push for restrictions on sales at gun shows, stronger background checks, and limitations on assault weapons. But Congress failed to pass any legislation. A year after the shootings at Sandy Hook, eight states had passed gun control laws, including background

WHILE THE CONSTITUTION guarantees the individual right to bear arms (as shown by the woman taking target practice), the shootings at Sandy Hook Elementary School in Newtown, Connecticut, shocked the nation and led to sympathy for the victims and their survivors. President Obama is shown here comforting the father of one of the victims at a ceremony marking the anniversary of the shooting.

checks, but twenty-seven states passed 93 laws that strengthened individuals' gun rights (the most common of these laws were concealed carry laws).[100]

In 2008, a landmark ruling recognized for the first time an individual right to bear arms for self-defense and hunting.[101] The decision struck down the District of Columbia's ban on handguns, while noting that state and local governments could enforce ownership restrictions, such as preventing felons or the mentally impaired from buying guns. The Court did not apply the Second Amendment to the states in this decision but it did so two years later in striking down a gun control ordinance in Chicago, while reaffirming the ownership restrictions noted in the Washington, D.C., case.[102] The dissenters in both strongly divided 5–4 decisions lamented the Court's activism in reopening a legal question considered settled for 70 years (in 32 instances since a 1939 Court ruling, appeals courts had affirmed the focus on a collective right—in the context of a militia—rather than an individual right to bear arms, and recognized an individual right only twice).[103]

Given the strong public support for gun ownership—there are about 300 million privately owned guns in the United States—and the Supreme Court's endorsement of an individual right to bear arms, stronger gun control at the national level is highly unlikely (especially given the unsuccessful push after the shootings at Sandy Hook Elementary School). However, extensive litigation will be necessary to define the acceptable boundaries of gun control and which state and local restrictions will be allowed to stand. To this point, the verdicts have been mixed, with some lower courts upholding limitations on gun ownership (such as prohibiting felons from owning guns), while other lower courts have struck them down. Almost all challenges to gun laws in criminal cases, however, have been unsuccessful.[104]

LAW, ORDER, AND THE RIGHTS OF CRIMINAL DEFENDANTS

> DESCRIBE THE PROTECTIONS PROVIDED FOR PEOPLE ACCUSED OF A CRIME

due process rights The idea that laws and legal proceedings must be fair. The Constitution guarantees that the government cannot take away a person's "life, liberty, or property, without due process of law." Other specific due process rights are found in the Fourth, Fifth, Sixth, and Eighth Amendments, such as protection from self-incrimination and freedom from illegal searches.

Every advanced democracy protects the rights of people who have been accused of a crime. In the United States, the **due process rights** of the Fourth, Fifth, Sixth, and Eighth Amendments include the right to a fair trial, the right to consult a lawyer, freedom from self-incrimination, knowing what crime you are accused of, the right to confront the accuser in court, and freedom from unreasonable police searches.

It is difficult to apply the abstract principles of due process to concrete situations in a way that protects civil liberties without jeopardizing order. The Fifth and Fourteenth Amendments specify that life, liberty, and property may not be denied "without due process of law." In general, this language refers to *procedural* restrictions on what government can do and is based on the idea of fairness and justice. The difficulty comes in defining what is fair or just.

The difference between abstract principles of due process and their specific application also raises difficult *political* questions. Most people endorse the principle of "due process of law" and general ideas such as requiring that police legally obtain any evidence used in court. However, when the Supreme Court applies these principles to protect the rights of criminal defendants, there is a public outcry that too many suspects are going free on "legal technicalities," such as having to inform a suspect of his right to talk to an attorney before being questioned by the police.

Elected politicians are very vulnerable to such public pressure and have a strong incentive to be "tough on crime," while the courts are left to decide whether a specific case involves a legal technicality or a fundamental civil liberty. The first aspect of due process, discussed next, is a perfect example of the political and legal difficulty of defining and applying due process rights: the Fourth Amendment protection against *unreasonable* searches and seizures.

THE FOURTH AMENDMENT: UNREASONABLE SEARCHES AND SEIZURES

The Fourth Amendment says, "The right of the people to be secure in their persons, houses, papers, and effects, against unreasonable searches and seizures, shall not be violated." Given the abusive practices of the British governors in the colonies, the Founders had strong opinions about this issue, but defining "unreasonable" puts us back in the familiar position of drawing lines and balancing interests.

Over the years, the Supreme Court has provided strong protections against searches within a person's physical space, typically defined as his or her home. With the introduction of new technology—first telephones and wiretapping, then more sophisticated listening and searching devices—the Court had to confront a broad array of complicated questions. It has attempted to achieve a balance between privacy and security by requiring the courts to approve search warrants, yet continuing to carve out limited exceptions to this general rule.

SEARCHES AND WARRANTS Under most circumstances, a law enforcement official seeking a search warrant must provide the court with "personal knowledge" of a "probable cause" of specific criminal activity and must outline the evidence that is the target of the search. Broad, general "fishing expeditions" for evidence are not allowed.

School officials must also balance the constitutional rights of students against the need to maintain discipline. But school searches may be permitted with a weaker "reasonable suspicion"; this is because the courts have viewed the schools as "in loco parentis" (that is, as playing the role of surrogate parents for the students). In 1985, the Court found in favor of a school official who discovered two girls smoking in a school bathroom and, in searching the purse of one of the girls for cigarettes, found marijuana, a pipe, rolling papers, plastic bags, and enough cash to suggest that the girl was selling marijuana. Yet, in other cases, the Court ruled that there are limits to searches by school officials and that students have the right to privacy. For example, in 2003, school administrators in Safford, Arizona, responding to a tip that a student was in possession of prescription-strength ibuprofen pills, subjected 13-year-old Savana Redding to a strip search. After searching her backpack and outer clothing and finding nothing, the police told Savana "to pull her bra out and to the side and shake it, and to pull out the elastic on her underpants, thus exposing her breasts and pelvic area to some degree." The Court ruled that this search violated her Fourth Amendment rights because "the content of the suspicion failed to match the degree of intrusion."[105]

Police searches inherently involve a clash between public safety and an individual's private freedom from government intrusions. These issues came to the fore with the passage of the Patriot Act of 2001 after the terrorist attacks of September 11. (The official name of this law is the USA PATRIOT Act, which is an acronym for "Uniting and Strengthening America by Providing Appropriate Tools Required to Intercept and Obstruct Terrorism.") Several of the most controversial parts of the act strengthen police surveillance powers; make it easier to conduct "sneak and peek" searches (the police enter a home with a warrant, look for evidence, and do not inform the suspect that they searched his home until months later); broaden Internet surveillance; increase the government's access to individuals' library, banking, and medical records; and permit roving wiretaps for suspected terrorists.

Suspects often consent to a warrantless search by police (and the officers are not required to tell suspects that they may say "no" or request a warrant). Here are examples of other instances in which the Court will allow a warrantless search:

- ▶ Conducting a search at the time of a legal arrest that "is confined to the immediate vicinity of the arrest."
- ▶ Collecting evidence that was not included in the search warrant but is out in the open and in plain view.
- ▶ Using a police roadblock to search for information about a crime, to check for illegal immigrants or contraband at borders, or to conduct sobriety checks (but not for random drug searches or license checks), as long as the roadblock stops all drivers.
- ▶ Searching containers in cars if the officer has probable cause to suspect criminal activity.
- ▶ Searching passengers and the passenger area of a car if the driver has been stopped for a traffic offense (because people in automobiles do not have the same Fourth Amendment protections as people do in their homes).
- ▶ Searching an area where the officer thinks there is either a crime in progress or an "armed and dangerous" suspect.
- ▶ Searching school lockers, with probable cause.
- ▶ Searching for weapons and/or to prevent the destruction of evidence.[106]

Strip searches after an arrest and before the suspect is put in jail were upheld in 2012 by the Supreme Court even when there was no suspicion of illegal substances. The dissenting justices argued that "the humiliation of a visual strip-search" after being "arrested for driving with a noisy muffler, failing to use a turn signal and riding a bicycle without an audible bell" should not be allowed under the Fourth Amendment.[107]

In 2013, the Court ruled that a DNA swab of an arrested suspect is simply for identification and therefore is no more intrusive than a photograph or fingerprint. Justice Scalia, a strong defender of privacy rights, wrote in his dissent, "I doubt that the proud men who wrote the charter of our liberties would have been so eager to open their mouths for royal inspection."[108] Scalia argued that DNA evidence could be used to identify the arrestee as a suspect in an unrelated crime and therefore a swab should be taken only if there is probable cause that another crime has also been committed.

The Court has generally made it easier for law enforcement officials to conduct searches without warrants, but two important decisions in the other direction were a 2014 case that required a warrant to search cell phones of people who had been arrested[109] and a 2012 case that required a warrant to place a GPS tracking device on a vehicle. In the latter case, the FBI suspected Antoine Jones of selling cocaine, so agents placed a tracking device on his vehicle without a warrant, monitored his movements for four weeks, and then used the evidence to convict him.

DRUG-SNIFFING DOGS AND THE FREEDOM FROM ILLEGAL SEARCHES

The Supreme Court has ruled that police do not need a search warrant to have drug-sniffing dogs search luggage at an airport or a car that has been stopped for a traffic violation unrelated to drugs. Lower courts have also ruled that sniffs are not considered searches in a hotel hallway, school locker, outside a passenger train's sleeper compartments, or outside an apartment door. However, lower courts have been split on whether drug-sniffing dogs may be used outside a home without a warrant, due, in part, to a Supreme Court precedent giving homes stronger Fourth Amendment protection than cars, lockers, or other areas. For example, in 2001, the Court ruled that police needed a warrant to use a thermal-imaging device outside a home when trying to detect marijuana that was believed to be growing under heat lamps inside.

The Supreme Court resolved the lower-court conflict in a 2013 ruling that drug-sniffing dogs are not allowed outside a home without a warrant. The case started with an anonymous tip that Joelis Jardines was growing marijuana inside his Miami home. Police went to the home with a trained drug-detection dog. On the front porch, the dog gave a positive signal indicating the presence of drugs. The police returned with a search warrant, found a marijuana-growing operation, and arrested Jardines. However, the Florida Supreme Court threw out the evidence, arguing it was an illegal search. The U.S. Supreme Court agreed, saying that there is a general expectation that anyone may come onto a front porch as long as the uninvited person simply knocks and then leaves if there is no answer. The majority opinion wryly noted, "Complying with the terms of that traditional invitation does not require fine-grained legal knowledge; it is generally managed without incident by the Nation's Girl Scouts and trick-or-treaters." But, they continued, "introducing a trained police dog to explore the area around the home in hopes of discovering incriminating evidence is something else. There is no customary invitation to do *that*."[a]

At the opposite end of the technological spectrum from drug-sniffing dogs are the new surveillance technologies that are available to law enforcement. Video surveillance in public places, cell phones with tracking chips, collection of Wi-Fi data, E-ZPass highway toll collection systems, roadside assistance devices, and Web traffic data kept by online merchants and social networking sites could be used by law enforcement officials. Other technologies that are becoming more common or will be used soon include RFIDs (radio frequency identifications), which are the size of a grain of rice and transmit information wirelessly through radio waves; facial recognition software and iris scanners; "smart dust devices"—tiny wireless micromechanical sensors—that can

Federal agents use a drug-sniffing dog to inspect a car.

detect light and movement; and drones, which have primarily been used for military purposes but also have vast potential for tracking suspects in any situation.

In the context of rapidly changing technology, what is the public's "reasonable expectation" for privacy? Justice Alito raised this question in oral arguments in a Supreme Court case involving a GPS tracking device (we discuss the case later in the chapter). He said, "Technology is changing people's expectations of privacy. . . . Maybe 10 years from now 90 percent of the population will be using social networking sites and they will have on average 500 friends and they will have allowed their friends to monitor their location 24 hours a day, 365 days a year, through the use of their cell phones. Then—what would the expectation of privacy be then?"[b]

CRITICAL THINKING QUESTIONS

1. If you had to decide the case of the drug-sniffing dog, how would you have ruled? Do you think that homes should have stronger privacy expectations than cars? Even when it concerns illegal drugs?

2. How would you answer Justice Alito's question about the expectation of privacy in an era of rapidly changing technology? When should law enforcement officials have to get a warrant to monitor our behavior?

Jones was sentenced to life in prison. While the Court required a warrant in this specific case, the basis for the majority's decision was fairly narrow: the placement of the device was a "physical trespass," and the lengthy monitoring of his movement constituted an illegal search.[110] Remote tracking without physical trespass or shorter-term monitoring with a GPS device without a warrant may be acceptable to the Court. Additional cases will be required to sort this out.

A second set of cases determines what to do if the police obtain evidence illegally. Here the need to balance security and privacy becomes concrete. Either the evidence is excluded from a criminal trial to protect privacy rights, or it is allowed to support the conviction of the suspect.

THE EXCLUSIONARY RULE In 1961, the Fourth Amendment was incorporated (applied to the states through the Fourteenth Amendment) in a case, *Mapp v. Ohio,* that established for all courts the **exclusionary rule**, which states that illegally or unconstitutionally obtained evidence cannot be used in a criminal trial. Previously, the rule had applied only at the national level.[111]

In the landmark case, police broke into Dollree Mapp's residence without a warrant looking for a suspect thought to be hiding in the house. The officers did not find him, but they did find illegal pornographic material, and Mapp was convicted of possessing it. Her lawyer tried to defend her on First Amendment grounds, claiming she had the right to own the pornography, but instead the Court used the opportunity to apply the Fourth Amendment to the states. The Court threw out Mapp's conviction because the police did not have a search warrant, arguing that applying the Fourth Amendment only to the national government and not the states didn't make any sense: Why should a state's attorney be able to use illegally obtained evidence while a federal prosecutor could not? The justices ruled that for the exclusionary rule to deter illegal searches and seizures, it must apply to law enforcement at both state and national levels.

Subsequently, the Supreme Court began weakening the exclusionary rule. For example, the Court established a "good faith exception" to the exclusionary rule, allowing evidence to be used as long as the officer believed that he or she had conducted a legal search. In the specific case, the officer had a warrant that turned out to have errors on it, such as the wrong address.[112] Yet another case established an exception allowing the use of evidence that was initially obtained in an illegal search but subsequently acquired with a valid warrant.[113] The bottom line is that the exclusionary rule remains in effect, but in the last several decades, the courts have eased the conditions in which prosecutors can use evidence obtained under questionable circumstances.

DRUG TESTING Another area of Fourth Amendment law concerns drug testing. The clause granting people the right "to be secure in their persons" certainly seems to cover drug testing. However, the courts have long recognized the right of private companies to test their employees for illegal drugs. Moreover, in professional sports, testing for performance-enhancing drugs is increasingly common. Tour de France winner Floyd Landis was stripped of his title in 2006 after testing positive for artificially elevated testosterone levels, Lance Armstrong was stripped of his seven Tour de France titles after admitting

exclusionary rule The principle that illegally or unconstitutionally acquired evidence cannot be used in a criminal trial.

CAN THE POLICE SEARCH YOUR HOME without a warrant? After Dollree Mapp was arrested for possession of pornographic material, the case made its way to the Supreme Court and the search was ruled unconstitutional. This case established the exclusionary rule for evidence that is obtained without a warrant.

in 2013 to doping, and Major League Baseball has struggled to rein in steroid and human growth hormone use by many of its players, including stars such as Ryan Braun, Miguel Tejada, and Alex Rodriguez, who was banned from the entire 2014 season for his use of performance-enhancing drugs.

What about drug testing by the state? The Court has upheld random drug testing for high school athletes and mandatory drug testing for any junior high or high school students involved in extracurricular activities.[114] In the case of athletes, proponents of the policy asserted that safety concerns should preclude a 260-pound lineman or a pitcher with a 90-mile-per-hour fastball from using drugs. However, the same arguments could not be made for members of the choir, band, debate club, social dance, or the chess club, so this decision to include all extracurricular activities was a particularly strong endorsement of schools' antidrug policies.

Federal employees became subject to drug testing in 1986, when President Reagan issued an executive order requiring all employees to refrain from using illegal drugs as a condition of federal employment, and directed each agency to implement drug testing for sensitive positions. Two years later, Congress passed the Drug-Free Workplace Act to apply the same rule to all executive agencies, the uniformed services, and any service providers under contract with the federal government. Despite these prohibitions, drug testing of federal employees is actually limited to people who hold security clearances, carry firearms, or work in public safety or national security. Some employees are subject to random tests; others are tested only when they apply for a job, are involved in a workplace accident, or show signs of drug use. Many states have similar drug-testing policies,[115] and the Court has upheld drug testing of public employees, with one exception. It struck down a Georgia law that would have required all candidates for state office to pass a drug test within 30 days of announcing a run for office because candidates are not public employees.[116] Rather than appealing to the courts, former senator Ernest Hollings of South Carolina had a different approach to avoid drug testing. When his opponent, Representative Tommy Hartnett, challenged him to take a drug test, the senator shot back, "I'll take a drug test if you take an I.Q. test."

THE POST–SEPTEMBER 11 POLITICS OF DOMESTIC SURVEILLANCE The debate over the trade-off between civil liberties and security intensified in 2005 when a White House–approved domestic surveillance program was revealed. At the center of this controversy is the National Security Agency (NSA), which was created during the Korean War in 1952 by President Harry Truman. The agency was initially kept so secret that for many years the government even denied its existence. Insiders joked that the NSA stood for "No Such Agency." Today, the NSA is responsible for surveillance to protect national security (whereas the FBI is in charge of spying related to criminal activity, and the CIA oversees foreign intelligence gathering).

Since the terrorist attacks of September 11, 2001, the NSA has been monitoring the phone calls and Internet usage of many U.S. citizens who have had contact with suspected terrorists overseas. These calls were intercepted without the approval of the Foreign Intelligence Surveillance Court (FISC), which was created by Congress in 1978 under the Foreign Intelligence Surveillance Act (FISA) specifically for approving requests for the interception of calls. The NSA was also found to be creating a database of every phone call made within the borders of the United States. Phone companies AT&T, Verizon, and BellSouth reportedly turned over records of millions of customers' phone calls to the government.[117] In 2013, classified information revealed by Edward Snowden showed that the NSA had been monitoring the phone calls of German chancellor Angela Merkel and other

WHAT DO POLITICAL SCIENTISTS DO?

For more about how political scientists study the trade-offs between security and liberty, visit **wwnpag.es/wdpsd**

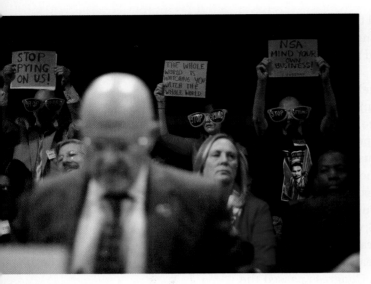

IN 2013, THE DIRECTOR OF NATIONAL Intelligence testified at a congressional hearing on possible changes to the Foreign Intelligence Surveillance Act (FISA) as protesters in the background called for an end to government surveillance.

leaders of allied countries. Outrage over these practices prompted President Obama to outline important changes to how information would be gathered and stored.

Critics warn that phone surveillance may be the tip of the iceberg because the government may be monitoring travel, credit card, and banking records more widely than we think. Government agencies have previously skirted the restrictions in the Privacy Act of 1974 and the Fourth Amendment by purchasing this information from businesses, since the Privacy Act requires disclosure of how the government is using personal information only when the government itself collects the data. The Justice Department spent $19 million in 2005 to purchase commercially gathered data about American citizens, according to a report by the Government Accountability Office. These data are then used to search for suspicious patterns of behavior in a process known as data mining.[118]

The debate over domestic surveillance has generated intense disagreement. At one extreme, critics conjure up images of George Orwell's classic novel *1984* in which Big Brother, a reclusive totalitarian ruler, watches the characters' every move. Critics see the surveillance as a threat to civil liberties and to our system of checks and balances and separation of powers. They believe that when the executive branch refuses to obtain warrants through the FISA court to conduct surveillance, it is taking on too much power without consulting the other branches of government. But supporters of the program argue that getting a court order may take too long, jeopardizing the surveillance necessary to protect the country. Congress tried to strike a balance between these two positions when it enacted the FISA Amendments Act of 2008. This law continued the ban on monitoring the purely domestic communications of Americans without a court order, gave the government authority to intercept international communications, and provided legal immunity to the telecommunications companies that had cooperated in the original wiretapping program. However, the *New York Times* revealed that the NSA had still been engaged in "overcollection" of domestic communication between Americans under the new law, including an attempt to wiretap a member of Congress without a court order. Although the Obama administration has vowed to stop purely domestic surveillance without a court order, technical problems make it difficult to distinguish between communications made within the United States and overseas.[119]

THE FIFTH AMENDMENT: SELF-INCRIMINATION

The familiar phrase "I plead the Fifth" has been part of our criminal justice system since the Bill of Rights was ratified, ensuring that a suspect cannot be compelled to provide court testimony that would cause him or her to be prosecuted for a crime. However, what about outside a court of law? If a police officer coerces a confession out of a suspect, does that amount to self-incrimination?

Such police interrogations were allowed until a landmark case in 1966. Ernesto Miranda had been convicted in an Arizona court of kidnapping and rape, on the basis of a confession extracted after two hours of questioning in which he was not read his rights. The Court overturned the conviction, saying that a police interrogation "is inherently intimidating" and in these circumstances, "no statement obtained from the defendant can truly be the product of his free choice."[120] To make sure a confession is truly a free choice, the Court came up with the well-known **Miranda rights** shown here. If police do not read a suspect these rights, nothing the suspect says can be used in court.

The Court has carved out exceptions to the *Miranda* rights requirement because the public has viewed the practice as "coddling criminals" and letting too many people go free on legal technicalities. In one case, police failed to read a suspect his *Miranda* rights until after frisking him, finding an empty holster, and asking him where his gun was. The suspect led police to a gun. The lower court dismissed the charges because the gun had been used as incriminating evidence in the trial, but the Supreme Court reinstated the conviction because "concern for public safety must be paramount to adherence to the literal language of the *Miranda* rule."[121] In 2010, the Court ruled that once a suspect has invoked his or her *Miranda* rights, the prohibition on police questioning is not "eternal." Instead, if the suspect voluntarily has a change of mind, police may resume questioning 14 days after the suspect's release from custody.[122] In another case that same year, a murder suspect in Michigan was read his *Miranda* rights and then remained silent for nearly three hours of police interrogation. Finally, when asked if he believed in God, he said "yes." When asked, "Do you pray to God to forgive you for shooting that boy down?" he also said "yes" and he was convicted based on that confession. The Court ruled that a suspect must explictly invoke the right to remain silent. The dissenters complained that the decision "turned Miranda upside down.... Criminal suspects must now unambiguously invoke their right to remain silent, which, counterintuitively, requires them to speak."[123]

Although the Court has been willing to carve out limited exceptions to the *Miranda* rule, in 2000 the Court rejected Congress's attempt to overturn *Miranda* by designating all voluntary confessions as legally admissible evidence. The Court ruled that it, and not Congress, has the power to determine constitutional protections for criminal defendants. The justices also affirmed their intent to protect the *Miranda* rule, saying, "*Miranda* has become embedded in routine police practice to the point where the warnings have become part of our national culture."[124]

Another Fifth Amendment right for defendants is protection against being tried more than once for a particular crime. This is known as **double jeopardy** because the suspect is "twice put in jeopardy of life or limb" for a single offense. This prohibition was extended to the states in 1969.[125] But prosecutors can exploit two loopholes in this civil liberty: (1) a suspect may be tried in federal court and state court for the same crime, and (2) if a suspect is found innocent of one set of *criminal* charges brought by the state, he or she may still be found guilty of the same or closely related offenses based on *civil* charges brought by a private individual.

Usually these loopholes are exploited only in high-profile cases in which there is public or political pressure to get a conviction. For example, in 1992, four Los Angeles police officers were acquitted of beating Rodney King, a driver they had chased for speeding. Before the trial, a bystander's video of the beating had been widely broadcast; subsequently, at news of the police officers' acquittal, massive

DEFENDANT	LOCATION

SPECIFIC WARNING REGARDING INTERROGATIONS

1. You have the right to remain silent.

2. Anything you say can and will be used against you in a court of law.

3. You have the right to talk to a lawyer and have him present with you while you are being questioned.

4. If you cannot afford to hire a lawyer one will be appointed to represent you before any questioning, if you wish one.

SIGNATURE OF DEFENDANT	DATE
WITNESS	TIME

☐ REFUSED SIGNATURE   SAN FRANCISCO POLICE DEPARTMENT   PR.9.

THIS IS A TYPICAL EXAMPLE OF THE *Miranda* warning card that police officers carry with them and read to every suspect after an arrest.

Miranda **rights** The list of civil liberties described in the Fifth Amendment that must be read to a suspect before anything the suspect says can be used in a trial.

double jeopardy Being tried twice for the same crime. This is prevented by the Fifth Amendment.

and destructive riots broke out that lasted three days. Responding to political pressure, President George H. W. Bush urged federal prosecutors to retry the officers not for the *criminal* use of excessive force but for violating Rodney King's *civil* rights. (Two were ultimately found guilty, and two were acquitted.)

The final part of the Fifth Amendment is at the heart of a hot legal debate over property rights; the clause says, "nor shall private property be taken for public use, without just compensation." For most of American history, this civil liberty has been noncontroversial. When the government needs private property for a public use such as building a highway or a park, it may force a property owner to sell at a fair market value.

A new, controversial interpretation of the Fifth Amendment's "takings" clause, however, has attempted to expand the principle of just compensation to cover not only "physical takings," but also "regulatory takings." For example, if the Endangered Species Act protects an animal whose habitat is on your land, you would not be able to develop that property. Thus, its market value would probably be lower than if the endangered species did not live on your land. Therefore, the argument goes, because of this law the government has "taken" some of the value of your land by legally protecting the species, so it should compensate you for your loss.

One key Court case decided that if a regulation "deprives a property owner of all beneficial use of his property," the owner must receive compensation. This case involved a man who bought two residential lots on the Isle of Palms, a South Carolina barrier island. His plan was to build single-family homes on the lots, but shortly after his purchase the state legislature enacted a law banning "permanent habitable structures" on this part of the barrier islands to prevent further erosion and destruction of the vulnerable land. The owner sued in state court and won a large monetary judgment, and the Supreme Court upheld this ruling.[126]

This issue became even more controversial after a case involving a development project in New London, Connecticut. A working-class neighborhood was sold to a private developer to build a waterfront hotel, office space, and higher-end housing, but a home owner sued the city to stop the development. The Court supported the local government, saying that "promoting economic development is a traditional and long accepted function of government" so a "plausible public use" is satisfied. Justice O'Connor wrote a strong dissent, saying that the "specter of condemnation hangs over all property. Nothing is to prevent the State from replacing any Motel 6 with a Ritz-Carlton, any home with a shopping mall, or any farm with a factory."[127] In reaction to this decision, between 2005 and 2011, legislation or constitutional amendments have been passed in 42 states restricting the use of eminent domain for economic development.[128]

THE SIXTH AMENDMENT: THE RIGHT TO LEGAL COUNSEL AND A JURY TRIAL

When it comes to criminal law, the right to an attorney is one of the key civil liberties, because the legal system is too complicated for a layperson to navigate. However, at one time, poor people accused of a felony were forced to defend themselves in court because they could not afford a lawyer (except in cases involving the death penalty, for which the state would provide a lawyer).[129] This changed in 1963 with the celebrated case of *Gideon v. Wainwright*. Clarence Gideon was accused of breaking into a pool hall and stealing beer, wine, and money. He could not afford an attorney, so he tried to defend himself. He did a pretty good job—calling witnesses, cross-examining the prosecutor's witnesses, and providing a good summary argument. However, he was convicted and sentenced to five years in jail, based largely on the testimony of the person who turned out to be the guilty party. The Court unanimously overturned his conviction, saying, "In our adversary system of criminal justice, any person hauled into court who is too poor to hire a lawyer cannot be assured a fair trial unless counsel is provided for him."[130]

Unlike the exclusionary rule and the protection against self-incrimination, the right to an attorney has been strengthened over time, through both legislation and subsequent Court rulings. One year after *Gideon*, Congress passed the Criminal Justice Act, which provided better legal representation for criminal defendants in federal court; within two years, 23 states had taken similar action. The Court has defined a general right to *effective* counsel (although the bar is set considerably low in terms of defining "effective"), and more recently mandated that defense attorneys must conduct any reasonable investigation into possible lines of defense when presenting evidence that could help the defendant.[131]

The Sixth Amendment also protects an individual's right to a speedy and public trial by an impartial jury in criminal cases. The Court affirmed the right to a speedy trial in 1967,[132] and today under the Federal Speedy Trial Act a trial must begin within 70 days of the defendant's arrest or first appearance in court. This law was strengthened by a 2006 Court decision stating that a defendant may not waive the right to a speedy trial.[133] The most important legal disputes over the "impartial jury" issue concern the process of jury selection and peremptory challenges, in which lawyers from each side may eliminate certain people from the jury pool without providing any reason. The Court has ruled that race and gender may not be the basis for a peremptory challenge.[134]

THE FIGHT AGAINST TERRORISM HAS raised controversial questions about due process rights. After the United States killed Anwar al-Awlaki—an Al Qaeda leader living in Yemen, and a U.S. citizen—critics argued that his due process rights, such as the right to a fair trial, had been violated.

THE EIGHTH AMENDMENT: CRUEL AND UNUSUAL PUNISHMENT

The Founders would be surprised by the intense debates over whether the Eighth Amendment prohibition against "cruel and unusual punishment" applies to the death penalty. Clearly, the death penalty was accepted in their time (even stealing a horse was a capital offense!), and the language of the Constitution reflects that. Both the Fifth and Fourteenth Amendments say that a person may not be deprived of "life, liberty, or property, without due process of law," which implies that someone *could* be deprived of life as long as the state follows due process. The death penalty continues to be supported by many people in the United States, with 32 states allowing capital punishment. However, there is a clear overall trend away from the death penalty. Six U.S. states have abolished the death penalty since 2007 and dozens of other countries have done so in recent years. There were 39 executions in the United States in 2013, which is the second-lowest number since 1995 and well below the peak of 98 in 1999.[135] A botched execution in Oklahoma in 2014, in which Clayton Lockett writhed and gasped for nearly 30 minutes when one of the lines filled with the lethal drugs failed, led to renewed calls for abolishing the death penality.[136]

SUPREME COURT RULINGS ON THE DEATH PENALTY The Supreme Court remained silent on the issue of the death penalty for nearly two centuries. But in 1972, the Court ruled that the death penalty was unconstitutional because the process of applying it was too inconsistent. Congress and 35 states rushed to make their laws compliant with the Court decision. The typical fix was to say more explicitly which crimes were punishable by death and to make capital sentencing a two-step process: first the determination of guilt or innocence, and then a sentencing phase if the suspect was found guilty. Four years later, the Court approved these changes and allowed states to bring back the death penalty.[137]

While never again challenging the constitutionality of the death penalty, the Supreme Court has been chipping away at its edges for two decades. The Court has struck down state laws that mandated the death penalty in murder cases and a law requiring a death sentence for rape. It has also prohibited the execution of insane prisoners and abolished the death penalty for the "mentally retarded" (2002)—although the Court left it to the states to define who is "mentally retarded" and struck down Florida's strict IQ cutoff as too rigid in defining mental stability (2014). The Court has also prohibited the death penalty for juveniles under the age of 18 (2005) and for child rapists (2008).[138]

These death penalty cases have shown that the Court responds to public opinion and political change (this is sometimes called the "living Constitution" perspective, as discussed in Chapters 2 and 14). In his opinion in the juvenile death penalty case, Justice Anthony Kennedy noted that 30 states forbid the death penalty for offenders younger than age 18, which was an increase of 5 states from 1989, when the Court had upheld the juvenile death penalty. Similarly, the number of states banning the death penalty for the mentally retarded grew from 14 in 1989 (when the practice was upheld) to 25 in 2002 (when it was struck down).

EXPLAIN WHY THE RIGHTS ASSOCIATED WITH PRIVACY ARE OFTEN CONTROVERSIAL

PRIVACY RIGHTS

privacy rights Liberties protected by several amendments in the Bill of Rights that shield certain personal aspects of citizens' lives from governmental interference, such as the Fourth Amendment's protection against unreasonable searches and seizures.

You may be surprised to learn that the word "privacy" does not appear in the Constitution. **Privacy rights** were first developed in a 1965 case that questioned the constitutionality of an 1879 Connecticut law against using birth control. Estelle Griswold, the director of Planned Parenthood in Connecticut, was arrested nine days after opening a clinic that dispensed contraceptives. She was fined $100 and appealed her conviction. Although she lost in state court, she appealed all the way to the Supreme Court, which overturned her conviction.[139]

In a very fractured decision (there were six different opinions), the Court agreed that the law was outdated, but the justices agreed on little else. Even the justices who based their opinions on an implied constitutional right to privacy cited various constitutional roots. Justice William O. Douglas found privacy implicit in the First Amendment right of association, the Third Amendment's protection against the quartering of troops, the Fourth Amendment's prohibition against unreasonable searches and seizures, the Fifth Amendment's protection against self-incrimination, and the Ninth Amendment's catchall statement, "The enumeration in the Constitution, of certain rights, shall not be construed to deny or disparage others retained by the people." These all seem like reasonable grounds for implicit privacy rights except the First Amendment right of association—since the Founders clearly meant political association, not an association with your spouse in bed.

The *Griswold* case was significant for establishing the constitutional basis for a right to privacy, but the dissenters in the case were concerned about where this right would lead. Justice Black warned that privacy "is a broad, abstract and ambiguous concept" that can be shrunk or expanded in subsequent decisions. He said that Douglas's argument required judges to determine what is or is not constitutional on the basis of their own appraisal of what laws are unwise or unnecessary. The power to make such decisions belongs of course to a legislative body. Surely it has to be admitted that no provision of the Constitution specifically gives courts blanket power to exercise such a supervisory veto over the wisdom and value of legislative policies and to hold unconstitutional those laws the courts believe to be unwise or dangerous.[140]

ABORTION RIGHTS

Justice Black's prediction came true eight years later in *Roe v. Wade*, the landmark ruling that struck down laws in 46 states that limited abortion. Twelve of those states allowed abortions for pregnancies due to rape or incest, to protect the life of the mother, and in cases of severe fetal handicap. The much-criticized trimester analysis in the *Roe* ruling said that states could not limit abortions in the first trimester; in the second trimester, states could regulate abortions in the interests of the health of the mother; and in the third trimester, states could forbid all abortions except those necessary to protect the health or life of the mother. The justices cited a constitutional basis for abortion rights in the general right to privacy outlined in *Griswold*; the concept of "personal liberty" in the Fourteenth Amendment's due process clause; and the "rights reserved to the people" in the Ninth Amendment.[141]

Subsequent decisions have upheld *Roe* but endorsed state restrictions on abortion, such as requiring parental consent, a waiting period, or counseling sessions aimed at convincing the woman not to have an abortion (see Figure 4.1 for more on restrictions currently in effect). Most significantly, *Roe*'s trimester analysis has been replaced by a focus on the viability of the fetus. When the fetus would be viable (generally at 22 or 23 weeks), states can ban abortions "except where it is necessary, in appropriate medical judgment, for the preservation of the life or health of the mother."[142] Laws passed in 2013 by Arkansas and North Dakota limiting abortions as soon as a fetal heartbeat can be detected (as early as 6 weeks) were struck down by federal courts, but laws in nine states now ban abortions at 20 weeks, in apparent contradiction with *Roe v. Wade.*

Since *Roe*, most political action concerning abortion has been in the courts, but that could change if the Supreme Court overturns the decision. Opponents of abortion are hoping that *Roe* will be overturned, which would shift the politics of abortion back to state legislatures and make it an even more contested political issue. One effort to challenge *Roe* was a "personhood amendment" to the Mississippi constitution that defined life beginning at conception. But the amendment was soundly defeated in a statewide vote in 2011.[143] The pace of state restrictions on abortions accelerated from 2011 to 2013, with more than 200 limitations on abortion services. In 2013, 22 states enacted 70 new restrictions, including a requirement that abortion doctors have admitting privileges at local hospitals—which would close up to one-third of abortion clinics in affected states.[144] Many of these laws have been struck down in federal court, but the Supreme Court will almost certainly have to rule on these restrictions.

FIGURE » 4.1

MAP OF U.S. PARENTAL CONSENT LAWS FOR ABORTIONS FOR MINORS

Despite the liberties outlined by the Court's decision in *Roe v. Wade*, severe restrictions on abortion rights still exist. For example, most states require minors receiving an abortion to first notify their parents or obtain their formal consent, and many states mandate a waiting period before the procedure can be carried out.

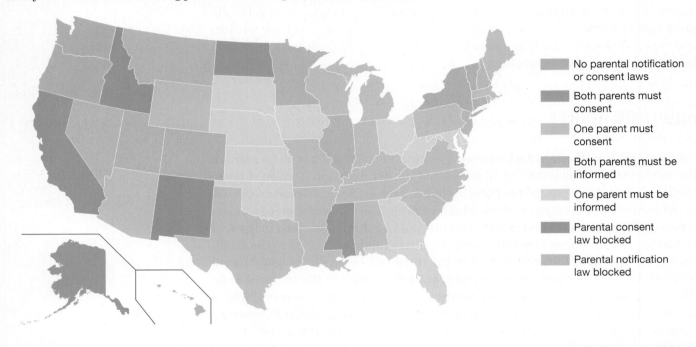

- No parental notification or consent laws
- Both parents must consent
- One parent must consent
- Both parents must be informed
- One parent must be informed
- Parental consent law blocked
- Parental notification law blocked

MAP OF U.S. PRE-ABORTION MANDATORY WAITING PERIOD LAWS

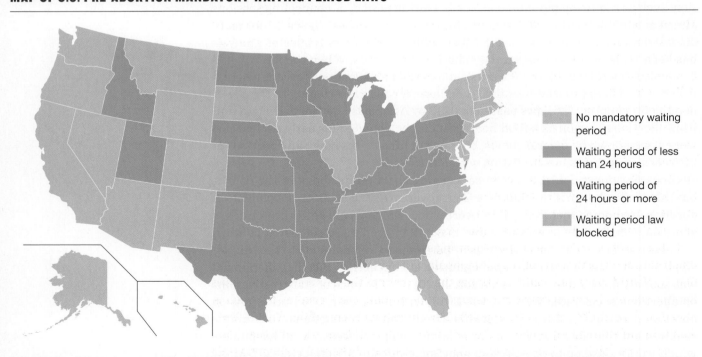

- No mandatory waiting period
- Waiting period of less than 24 hours
- Waiting period of 24 hours or more
- Waiting period law blocked

SOURCES: "Map of U.S. Mandatory Waiting Period Laws" by Lokal_Profil and Kyd, http://commons.wikimedia.org/wiki/File:Map_of_US_mandatory_waiting_period_laws.svg (accessed 8/20/14), licensed under CC BY-SA 2.5, http://creativecommons.org/licenses/by-sa/2.5/legalcode (accessed 8/20/14); "Map of U.S. Minor Abortion Laws" by Lokal_Profil and Kyd, http://commons.wikimedia .org/wiki/File:Map_of_US_minor_abortion_laws.svg (accessed 8/20/14), licensed under CC BY-SA 2.5, http://creativecommons.org/licenses/by-sa/2.5/legalcode (accessed 8/20/14). Both maps have been recolored from the originals.

GAY RIGHTS

Gay rights have typically been thought of more as a civil right (that is, freedom from discrimination) than a civil liberty. In 1986, the Court had ruled in *Bowers v. Hardwick* that that there was no privacy protection or fundamental right for consenting adults to engage in homosexual sodomy.[145] But in 2003, in *Lawrence v. Texas*, the Court established very broad privacy rights for sexual behavior. The case involved two Houston men, John Geddes Lawrence and Tyron Garner, who were prosecuted for same-sex sodomy after police entered Lawrence's apartment—upon receiving a false tip about an armed man—and found the two having sex. Under Texas law, sodomy was illegal for gays but not for heterosexuals. In a landmark 6–3 ruling, the Supreme Court said that the liberty guaranteed by the Fourteenth Amendment's due process clause allows homosexuals to have sexual relations. "Freedom presumes an autonomy of self that includes freedom of thought, belief, expression, and certain intimate conduct."[146] The decision explicitly overturned *Bowers v. Hardwick*, and the majority opinion had harsh words for that earlier decision, saying it "was not correct when it was decided, and it is not correct today." Five members of the majority signed onto the broad "due process" reasoning of the decision, while Justice O'Connor wrote a concurring opinion in which she agreed that the Texas law was unconstitutional but on narrower grounds. With the broader due process logic, a total of 13 state laws that banned sodomy were struck down.

TYRON GARNER AND JOHN GEDDES
Lawrence after the Supreme Court decision in *Lawrence v. Texas* in 2003 established broad privacy rights for sexual behavior (including homosexual behavior).

CONCLUSION

You exercise your civil liberties every day, whether speaking in public, going to church, being searched at an airport, participating in a political demonstration, writing or reading an article in your school newspaper, or being free from illegal police searches in your home. Because civil liberties are defined as those things the government *cannot* do to you, defining civil liberties is a political process. Often this process is confined to the courts, but for many issues—including free speech, freedom of the press, pornography, criminal rights, abortion, and gun control—it takes place in the broader political world, where defining civil liberties involves balancing competing ideals and interests and drawing lines by interpreting and applying the law. For example, debates over how to balance national security and civil liberties—whether newspapers should publish stories about classified government programs that may threaten civil liberties, or if government surveillance powers should be strengthened to fight terrorism—will rage for years.

Other cases, such as the chapter-opening story of protests at military funerals, illustrate how difficult and politically unpopular it can be to protect our freedoms and liberty. Nearly everyone would agree that the behavior of the members of Westboro Baptist Church is completely outrageous. But protecting the freedom of speech is easy if you agree with what is being spoken. It becomes much more difficult if the freedom is manifest in filth directed at the families of fallen soldiers, protects the rights of Nazis to march in Skokie, or defends a person accused of a heinous crime. As with all political questions, the evolving nature of our civil liberties is sure to generate more political conflict. But that process affirms the essence of our political system.

STUDY*guide*

DEFINING CIVIL LIBERTIES

▶ *Define what we mean by civil liberties.* **(Pages 106–09)**

SUMMARY

Civil liberties are the protections that individuals receive from the government. These are not absolute rights, however, as individual freedoms can become at odds with the public good and government interests. The courts often play the deciding role in determining where to draw the line between individual rights and public safety.

KEY TERM	**CRITICAL THINKING AND DISCUSSION**
civil liberties (p. 106)	What is the proper balance between national security and civil liberties? Is it appropriate to restrict civil liberties during a time of war? If so, how much? And if not, why?

PRACTICE QUIZ QUESTIONS

1. Civil liberties are rooted in what document?
   - A the Declaration of Independence
   - B the *Federalist Papers*
   - C the Magna Carta
   - D the Bill of Rights
   - E Article I of the Constitution

2. Why are civil liberties not absolute?
   - A Equality for a group under the law is hard to define.
   - B Individual freedoms may conflict with the public good.
   - C Laws are often outdated and don't characterize modern society.
   - D The Bill of Rights protections were intentionally weakened by Antifederalists.
   - E The Supreme Court generally decides not to hear cases concerning civil liberties.

THE ORIGINS OF CIVIL LIBERTIES

▶ *Explain why the Bill of Rights was added to the Constitution, and how it came to apply to the states.* **(Pages 109–12)**

SUMMARY

The Bill of Rights, which lists individual protections from the federal government, was included in the Constitution in response to demands from the Antifederalists, who feared a strong national government. For most of the nineteenth century, these individual freedoms were only guaranteed from the *federal* government and did not extend to protections from *state* governments. With the ratification of the Fourteenth Amendment and the process of selective incorporation, federal freedoms have been gradually extended to the state level.

KEY TERMS	**CRITICAL THINKING AND DISCUSSION**
Civil War Amendments (p. 111) due process clause (p. 111) selective incorporation (p. 112)	How does the process of selective incorporation apply the Bill of Rights to the states? How would your freedoms be limited if the states did not have to follow the Bill of Rights?

PRACTICE QUIZ QUESTIONS

3. The inclusion of the Bill of Rights in the Constitution reflects the _____ concerns that the federal government would be too _____.
   - A Antifederalists'; strong
   - B Antifederalists'; weak
   - C Federalists'; strong
   - D Federalists'; weak
   - E president's; strong

4. The Bill of Rights originally protected individuals from which level of government?
   - A all levels of American government
   - B state governments
   - C local governments
   - D federal government
   - E the bureaucracy

5. Which amendment has been used as the basis for selective incorporation?
   - A the Eighth Amendment
   - B the Fourteenth Amendment
   - C the Tenth Amendment
   - D the Nineteenth Amendment
   - E the Fifth Amendment

FREEDOM OF RELIGION

▶ *Describe the First Amendment rights related to freedom of religion.* **(Pages 112–19)**

SUMMARY

Religious freedoms are defined by two clauses in the First Amendment: the establishment clause and the free exercise clause. Together, they do not allow the government to do anything to benefit any particular religion, nor do they allow the government to do anything to hinder religious practice. As is often the case, the Court has struggled to define exactly what constitutes "excessive government entanglement" in religion.

KEY TERMS

establishment clause (p. 112)
free exercise clause (p. 112)
Lemon **test** (p. 115)

CRITICAL THINKING AND DISCUSSION

Has the Supreme Court balanced protection for the free exercise of religion without allowing the state establishment of religion, or has it swung too far in one direction? Which rulings support your conclusion?

PRACTICE QUIZ QUESTIONS

6. The establishment clause is invoked under which of the following circumstances?

   Ⓐ allowing "conscientious objectors" to avoid the military draft
   Ⓑ outlawing polygamy
   Ⓒ allowing prayer in public schools
   Ⓓ allowing the Amish to keep children home from school after the eighth grade
   Ⓔ banning the handling of snakes in church services

7. Which test does the Supreme Court use to establish whether there has been "excessive government entanglement in religion"?

   Ⓐ *Lemon* test
   Ⓑ *Kreutz* test
   Ⓒ *Miller* test
   Ⓓ *Meyer* test
   Ⓔ *Brandenburg* test

FREEDOM OF SPEECH, ASSEMBLY, AND THE PRESS

▶ *Describe the major First Amendment rights related to freedom of speech.* **(Pages 119–30)**

SUMMARY

The Supreme Court's attempt to balance individual freedoms and public good is reflected in the scope of protections guaranteed by the First Amendment. The Court generally prioritizes protecting individual rights to political speech, hate speech, symbolic speech, the freedom to assemble, and the freedom of the press unless under extreme circumstances (such as speech that directly incites violence). By contrast, the Court regularly places a lower priority on, and affords less protection to, fighting words, slander, libel, and commercial speech.

KEY TERMS

strict scrutiny (p. 120)
intermediate scrutiny (p. 120)
clear and present danger test (p. 121)
direct incitement test (p. 122)
symbolic speech (p. 122)
hate speech (p. 124)
prior restraint (p. 126)
fighting words (p. 128)
slander (p. 128)
libel (p. 128)
commercial speech (p. 128)
Miller **test** (p. 129)

CRITICAL THINKING AND DISCUSSION

Do you support complete freedom of speech for the most despicable group you can think of? When should speech be limited, if at all?

PRACTICE QUIZ QUESTIONS

8. Which test does the Court use to determine if speech is considered dangerous and should not be legally protected?

   Ⓐ *Lemon* test
   Ⓑ clear and present danger test
   Ⓒ *Miller* test
   Ⓓ direct incitement test
   Ⓔ the balancing test

9. Flag burning is an example of _____ that is currently _____ under the First Amendment.

   Ⓐ symbolic speech; protected
   Ⓑ symbolic speech; not protected
   Ⓒ hate speech; protected
   Ⓓ hate speech; not protected
   Ⓔ offensive slander; not protected

THE RIGHT TO BEAR ARMS

▶ *Explore why the Second Amendment's meaning on gun rights is often debated.* **(Pages 130–32)**

SUMMARY

The Supreme Court has done little to define what freedoms are established in the Second Amendment, largely preferring to allow the national, state, and local governments to make their own laws.

The majority of public sentiment appears in favor of continued gun ownership, and limitations on Second Amendment rights appear unlikely.

PRACTICE QUIZ QUESTION

10. Until 2008, the Supreme Court had been _____ in defining Second Amendment laws, and its decisions generally _____ gun rights.

   A passive; limited

   B passive; supported

   C active; limited

   D active; supported

   E uninvolved; ignored

LAW, ORDER, AND THE RIGHTS OF CRIMINAL DEFENDANTS

▶ *Describe the protections provided for people accused of a crime.* **(Pages 132–42)**

SUMMARY

The Fourth, Fifth, Sixth, and Eighth Amendments provide protections to individuals accused of a crime, known as due process rights. Interpreting these general due process rights in specific cases is difficult, however, because specific standards of fairness and justice are very hard to define.

KEY TERMS	**CRITICAL THINKING AND DISCUSSION**
due process rights (p. 132) exclusionary rule (p. 136) *Miranda* rights (p. 139) double jeopardy (p. 139)	Do you support due process rights for defendants in criminal cases, even if it means that some potentially guilty people go free? If so, why? If not, are you concerned about convicting innocent people?

PRACTICE QUIZ QUESTIONS

11. Protections from unreasonable searches and seizures are guaranteed by which constitutional amendment?

   A the Third Amendment

   B the Fourth Amendment

   C the Fifth Amendment

   D the Seventh Amendment

   E the Eighth Amendment

12. The *Miranda* rights are protections that fall under which constitutional amendment?

   A the Third Amendment

   B the Fourth Amendment

   C the Fifth Amendment

   D the Seventh Amendment

   E the Eighth Amendment

13. In 1972, the Supreme Court banned the death penalty for what reason?

   A It deprived individuals of their rights to "life, liberty, or property."

   B It was cruel and unusual.

   C It was being inconsistently applied.

   D It was racially biased.

   E It was inconsistent with international law.

PRIVACY RIGHTS

▶ *Explain why the rights associated with privacy are often controversial.* **(Pages 142–45)**

SUMMARY

The term "privacy rights" is not found in the Constitution—rather, it was established in a 1965 Supreme Court case—but it may be implied in several amendments in the Bill of Rights. The right to privacy is controversial because of the lack of explicit language in the Constitution, and the lack of consensus on exactly what the right to privacy means.

KEY TERM	**CRITICAL THINKING AND DISCUSSION**
privacy rights (p. 142)	What are the main sources of privacy rights in the Constitution? Do you think the Court has gone too far in extending privacy rights, or should it do even more in these areas to protect our freedom?

PRACTICE QUIZ QUESTIONS

14. Which of the following freedoms guaranteed in the Bill of Rights is thought to imply a right to privacy?

   A right to bear arms

   B right to refuse to quarter soldiers

   C right to secure legal counsel

   D right to request a jury trial

   E freedom of speech

15. In what case did the Supreme Court establish the right to privacy?

Ⓐ *Roe v. Wade*

Ⓑ *Lawrence v. Texas*

Ⓒ *Griswold v. Connecticut*

Ⓓ *Gonzales v. Oregon*

Ⓔ *Lemon v. Kurtzman*

SUGGESTED READING

Abraham, Henry J., and Barbara A. Perry. *Freedom and the Court: Civil Rights and Liberties in the United States*, 8th ed. Lawrence: University Press of Kansas, 2003.

Amar, Akhil Reed. *The Bill of Rights*. New Haven, CT: Yale University Press, 1998.

Bondenhamer, David J., and James W. Ely, eds. *The Bill of Rights in Modern America*. Bloomington: Indiana University Press, 2008.

Lewis, Anthony. *Gideon's Trumpet*. New York: Random House, 1964.

Moynihan, Daniel Patrick. *Secrecy: The American Experience*. New Haven, CT: Yale University Press, 1998.

Posner, Richard A. *Not a Suicide Pact: The Constitution in a Time of National Emergency*. New York: Oxford University Press, 2006.

Pritchett, C. Herman. *Constitutional Civil Liberties*. Englewood Cliffs, NJ: Prentice Hall, 1984.

Schweber, Howard. *Speech, Conduct, and the First Amendment*. New York: Peter Lang, 2003.

Walker, Samuel. *Presidents and Civil Liberties from Wilson to Obama: A Story of Poor Custodians*. New York: Cambridge University Press, 2014.

5

Civil Rights

JOE ARPAIO, SHERIFF OF MARICOPA COUNTY
(Which includes Phoenix), Arizona, argued that strong measures were necessary to discourage illegal immigration. Here he answers questions concerning the two lawsuits that were brought against him for abusing his powers.

JOE ARPAIO OF PHOENIX, ARIZONA, is the self-described "toughest sheriff in America." He was also the target of a four-year investigation by the U.S. Justice Department of discriminatory practices in the enforcement of immigration laws. He is either a hero or villain, depending on one's views concerning illegal immigration. His supporters see him as a courageous and tireless fighter who is enforcing the law that the federal government seems incapable or unwilling to do. His critics see him as a bigoted publicity hound who abuses the civil rights of people who are nonwhite and live in Maricopa County.

In a lawsuit brought by the Justice Department, the brief concluded that, "As a result of the pattern or practice of unlawful discrimination, Latinos in Maricopa County are systematically denied their constitutional rights."[1] The expert who conducted the analysis noted that Latino drivers were 4 to 9 times more likely to be stopped than non-Latino drivers, calling this practice "the most egregious racial profiling he had ever seen."[2] Sheriff's deputies would use minor traffic violations, such as failure to signal a lane change, to pull over Latinos and ask for their documents. One incident that drew international attention was a neighborhood sweep of a town of about 6,000 Yaqui Indians and Latinos outside of Phoenix. Over a period of two days, more than 100 deputies conducted hundreds of searches, netting nine undocumented immigrants. Residents have sued the county, and one critical report said, "The community was so scarred by the event that families are still terrified to leave their homes when they see the sheriff's patrol cars."[3] This case was still in the federal courts in 2014 and, in a

CONFLICT & COMPROMISE
in American Politics

151

CHAPTER *goals*

Describe the historical struggles groups have faced in winning civil rights.
► PAGES 153–61

Analyze inequality among racial, ethnic, and social groups today.
► PAGES 162–65

Explain the approaches used to bring about change in civil rights policies.
► PAGES 166–86

Examine affirmative action and other ongoing civil rights issues.
► PAGES 187–93

separate federal case, District Court Judge Murray Snow issued two injunctions barring the sheriff's office from continuing the pattern of discrimination and establishing an elaborate system of monitoring and reporting to make sure the abuse did not continue.[4]

Sheriff Arpaio defended his office, saying, "We don't racially profile, I don't care what everybody says," while his deputy called the court order "ludicrous crap."[5] Arpaio was upset that the Justice Department would no longer provide the immigration status of suspects held in his custody (given the report's findings of discrimination), saying that the move "was tantamount to setting up a neon welcome sign for illegal immigrants."[6]

Enforcing immigration law is an extremely conflictual issue. Hard-liners on immigration, such as Sheriff Arpaio, see illegal immigrants as a threat to the country and want to make securing our borders the top priority of immigration policy (while deporting all illegal immigrants). The alternative perspective emphasizes controlling illegal immigration, while protecting the civil rights of citizens and legal residents, and providing a path to citizenship for illegal residents who are productive and law-abiding. It would seem that such a conflictual issue would not be very amenable to compromise. Indeed, both President Bush and President Obama tried and failed to enact comprehensive immigration reform. Frustrated with Congress's inactivity on the DREAM Act, which would have given legal status to young immigrants who came to the United States as children, Obama took steps in June 2012 to halt the deportation of "dreamers," and then in April 2014 he issued an executive order aimed at curbing deportations.[7] Then, in the summer of 2014, another crisis brewed on the border as tens of thousands of unaccompanied children entered the United States. Many were reunited with family in the U.S., but thousands remained in limbo in detention facilities that were not suited to handle the crush of children. Nearly everyone agrees that the current immigration system is broken, and Obama is still working with Congress to pass comprehensive reform. Nonetheless, gridlock in Washington is making that look unlikely. Any reform that secures our borders while protecting the civil rights of law-abiding people will involve compromise.

The concept of civil rights encompasses much more than immigration policy. Indeed, it is one of the best examples of the idea that politics is everywhere: policies concerning discrimination in the workplace and in housing, and against women, minorities, gays, and the disabled affect millions of Americans every day. To see how civil rights may affect you, consider the following scenarios.

► Scenario 1: You are driving home one night with a few of your friends after a party. It is late at night, but you have not had anything to drink and you are following all traffic laws. Your heart sinks as you see the flashing lights of a squad car signaling you to pull over. As the police officer approaches your car, you wonder if you have been pulled over because you and your friends are African Americans driving in an all-white neighborhood. Have your civil rights been violated? Change the scene to a car full of white teenagers with all the other facts the same. Can an officer pull you over just because he thinks that teenagers are more likely to be engaging in criminal activity than older people?

► Scenario 2: You are a 21-year-old Asian-American woman applying for your first job out of college. After being turned down for a job at an engineering firm, you suspect that you didn't get the job because you are a woman and because management thought that you would not fit in with the "good ol' boy" atmosphere of the firm. Have your civil rights been violated?

▶ Scenario 3: You and your gay partner are told that "your kind" are not welcome in the apartment complex that you wanted to live in. Should you call a lawyer?

▶ Scenario 4: You are a white male graduating from high school. You have just received a letter of rejection from the college that was first on your list. You are very disappointed, but then you get angry when a friend tells you that one of your classmates got into the same school even though he had virtually the same grades as you and his SAT scores were a bit lower. Your friend says that it is probably because of the school's affirmative action policy—the classmate who was accepted is Latino. Are you a victim of "reverse discrimination"? Have your civil rights been violated?

All of these scenarios would seem to be civil rights violations. However, some are, some are not, and some depend on additional considerations (we will return to these examples in the chapter's conclusion).

A BLACK TEENAGER IS ARRESTED by police for riding his bike on a sidewalk. When is a police stop legitimate? How do we know if it might be a violation of civil rights?

THE CONTEXT OF CIVIL RIGHTS

DESCRIBE THE HISTORICAL STRUGGLES GROUPS HAVE FACED IN WINNING CIVIL RIGHTS

In general, **civil rights** are rights that guarantee individuals freedom from discrimination. In the United States, individuals' civil rights are monitored by the U.S. Commission on Civil Rights, a bipartisan, independent, federal commission that was established by the 1957 Civil Rights Act.[8] The commission's mission is to "appraise federal laws and policies," investigate complaints, and collect information with regard to citizens who are "being deprived of their right to vote" or who are being discriminated against or denied the "equal protection of the laws under the Constitution because of race, color, religion, sex, age, disability, or national origin." It investigates government actions, such as allegations of racial discrimination in elections, and discriminatory actions of individuals in the workplace, commerce, housing, and education.

This definition seems straightforward enough, but confusion may arise when comparing the terms "civil rights" and "civil liberties." They are often used interchangeably, but there are important differences. Civil liberties refer to the freedoms guaranteed in the Bill of Rights, such as the freedom of speech, religious expression, and the press, as well as the due process protection of the Fourteenth Amendment. In contrast, civil rights protect all persons from discrimination and are rooted in laws and the equal protection clause of the Fourteenth Amendment. Moreover, civil liberties primarily limit what the government can do to you (*"Congress* shall make no law . . . abridging the freedom of speech"), whereas civil rights protect you from discrimination both by the government and by individuals. To oversimplify, civil liberties are about freedom, and civil rights are about equality.

Neither civil liberties nor civil rights figured prominently at the Constitutional Convention. Equality is not even mentioned in the Constitution or the Bill of Rights. The Bill of Rights is centrally concerned with freedom, but it was not added to the Constitution until the Antifederalists made it a condition for ratification, as

civil rights Rights that guarantee individuals freedom from discrimination. These rights are generally grounded in the equal protection clause of the Fourteenth Amendment and more specifically laid out in laws passed by Congress, such as the 1964 Civil Rights Act.

discussed in Chapter 2. However, equality was very much on the Founders' minds, as is evident in this ringing passage from the Declaration of Independence: "We hold these truths to be self evident, that all men are created equal, that they are endowed by the Creator with certain unalienable rights, that among these are life, liberty, and the pursuit of happiness." Despite the broad language, this was a limited conception of equality. The reference to "men" was intentional: women had no political or economic rights in the late eighteenth century. Similarly, equality did not apply to slaves or to Native Americans. Even propertyless white men did not have full political rights until several decades after the Constitution was ratified. Equality and civil rights in the United States have been a continually evolving work in progress.

AFRICAN AMERICANS

From the early nineteenth century and the movement for the abolition of slavery, until the mid-twentieth century and the civil rights movement, the central focus of civil rights was on the experiences of African Americans. Other groups received attention more gradually. Starting in the mid-nineteenth century, women began their fight for equal rights, and over the next century the civil rights movement expanded to include other groups such as Native Americans, Latinos, and Asian Americans. Most recently, attention has turned to the elderly, the disabled, and LGBTs (lesbian, gay, bisexual, and transgender people). The most divisive civil rights issue with the greatest long-term impact, however, has been slavery and its legacy.

Slavery was part of the American economy from nearly the beginning of the nation's history. Dutch traders brought 20 slaves to Jamestown, Virginia, in 1619, a year before the Puritans landed at Plymouth Rock. It is impossible to overstate the importance of slaves to the southern economy. The 1860 census shows that there were 2.3 million slaves in the Deep South, constituting 47 percent of its population, and there were nearly 4 million slaves in the South overall. The economic benefits of slavery for the owners were clear. By 1860, the per capita income for whites in the South was $3,978; in the North, it was $2,040. The South had only 30 percent of the nation's free population, but it had 60 percent of the wealthiest men.[9]

Abolitionists worked to rid the nation of slavery as its importance to the South grew, setting the nation on a collision course that would not be resolved until the Civil War. The Founders largely ducked the issue (see Chapter 2), and subsequent legislatures and courts did not come any closer to resolving the impasse between the North and South over slavery. The Missouri Compromise of 1820, which limited the expansion of slavery and kept the overall balance between slave states and free states, eased tensions for a while, but the issue persisted. Slave owners became increasingly frustrated with the success of the Underground Railroad, which helped some slaves escape to the North. The debate over admitting California as a free state or a slave state (or making it half free and half slave) threatened to split

SLAVERY WAS PART OF THE AMERICAN economy from the 1600s until the Civil War in 1861. The system of slavery in the South created a highly unequal society in which African Americans were denied virtually all rights.

the nation once again. Southern states agreed to admit California as a free state, but only if Congress passed the Fugitive Slave Act, which required northern states to treat escaped slaves as property and return them to their owners. Soon after, Congress enacted the Compromise of 1850, which overturned the Missouri Compromise and allowed each new state to decide for itself whether to be a slave state or a free state.

All possibility of further compromise on the issue ended with the misguided *Dred Scott v. Sandford* decision in 1857. The Supreme Court ruled that states could not be prevented from allowing slavery. It also held that slaves were property rather than citizens and, as such, had no legal rights. But believing that slavery was in jeopardy when Abraham Lincoln won the presidency in 1860, the southern states seceded from the Union and formed the Confederacy.

The outcome of the Civil War restored national unity and ended slavery, but the price was very high. About 528,000 Americans died in the war, with an astonishingly high casualty rate of 25 percent among combatants.[10] After the war, Republicans moved quickly to ensure that the changes accomplished by the war could not easily be undone: they promptly adopted the Civil War Amendments to the Constitution. The Thirteenth Amendment banned slavery, the Fourteenth guaranteed that states could not deny newly freed slaves the equal protection of the laws and provided citizenship to anyone born in the United States, and the Fifteenth gave African-American men the right to vote. These amendments were ratified within five years of the war, although southern states resisted giving freed slaves and their descendants "equal protection of the laws" over the next 100 years.

During Reconstruction (1866–1877), blacks in the South gained political power through institutions such as the Freedmen's Bureau and the Union League. With the protection of the occupying northern army, blacks were able to vote and even hold public office. When federal troops withdrew and the Republican Party abandoned the South, however, blacks were almost completely **disenfranchised** (denied the right to vote) through the imposition of residency requirements, poll taxes, literacy tests, the **grandfather clause** (which permitted those who had voted before the war and their descendants to vote even if they did not meet current voting requirements), physical intimidation, and other forms of disqualification. Later, the practice known as the "white primary" allowed only whites to vote in Democratic primary elections, and given that the Republican Party did not exist in most southern states, blacks were effectively disenfranchised. Although most of these provisions claimed to be race neutral, their impact fell disproportionately on black voters. For example, the grandfather clause enabled illiterate whites (but not illiterate blacks) to avoid the literacy test.[11] Many states also had "understanding" or "good character" exceptions to the literacy tests, which gave election officials substantial discretion over who would be allowed to vote.

The collective impact of these obstacles virtually eliminated black voting. For example, only 6 percent of blacks were registered to vote in Mississippi in 1890, and only 2 percent were registered in Alabama in 1906. After the last post-Reconstruction black congressman left the House in 1901, seventy-two years passed before another black represented a southern district in Congress. In Mississippi, one county in 1947 had 13,000 blacks who were eligible to vote, but only 6 were actually registered. Despite the constitutional guarantees of the Fourteenth and Fifteenth Amendments, blacks had little access to the political system in the South, and they had little success in winning office at any level in the rest of the nation.[12]

disenfranchised To have been denied the ability to exercise a right, such as the right to vote.

grandfather clause A type of law enacted in several southern states to allow those who were permitted to vote before the Civil War, and their descendants, to bypass literacy tests and other obstacles to voting, thereby exempting whites from these tests while continuing to disenfranchise African Americans and other people of color.

Jim Crow laws State and local laws that mandated racial segregation in all public facilities in the South, many border states, and some northern communities between 1876 and 1964.

The social and economic position of blacks in the South followed a path similar to their political fortunes. Soon after the Civil War ended, sympathetic Republicans passed the Civil Rights Acts of 1866 and 1875, which aimed to outlaw segregation and provide equal opportunity for blacks. However, there were no enforcement provisions, and when Reconstruction ended in 1877, the southern states enacted "black codes," or **Jim Crow laws,** that led to complete segregation of the races. Then in 1883, the Supreme Court ruled that the 1875 Civil Rights Act was unconstitutional because Congress did not have the power to forbid racial discrimination in private businesses. Southern states interpreted this decision as a signal that the national government was unconcerned about protecting the rights of blacks.

Jim Crow laws forbade interracial marriage and mandated the complete separation of the races in neighborhoods, hotels, apartments, hospitals, schools, restrooms, drinking fountains, restaurants, elevators, and even cemetery plots. In cases where it would have been inconvenient to completely separate the races, as in public transportation, blacks had to sit in the back of the bus or in separate cars on the train and give up their seats to whites if asked. The Supreme Court validated these practices in *Plessy v. Ferguson* (1896) in establishing the **separate but equal doctrine**, officially permitting segregation as long as blacks had equal facilities.

separate but equal doctrine The idea that racial segregation was acceptable as long as the separate facilities were of equal quality; supported by *Plessy v. Ferguson* and struck down by *Brown v. Board of Education.*

In the first several decades after Reconstruction, the rest of the nation mostly ignored the status of blacks because 90 percent of all African Americans lived in the South. But blacks' northward migration to urban areas throughout the first half of the twentieth century transformed the nation's demographic profile and its racial politics. America's "race problem" was no longer a southern problem. Although conditions for blacks were generally better outside the South, they still faced discrimination and lived largely segregated lives throughout the nation. In World Wars I and II, black soldiers fought and died for their country in segregated units. Professional sports teams were segregated, and black musicians and artists could not perform in many of the nation's leading theaters. Moreover, blacks largely were hired for the lowest-paying menial jobs.

Progress began in the 1940s. The Supreme Court struck down the white primary in 1944, Jackie Robinson broke the color line in Major League Baseball in 1947, and President Harry Truman issued an executive order integrating the U.S. armed services in 1948. Then came the landmark decision *Brown v. Board of Education* (1954), which rejected the separate but equal doctrine, followed by *Brown II* (1955), which ordered that public schools be desegregated "with all deliberate speed." These events set the stage for the growing success of the civil rights movement, discussed later in this chapter.

NATIVE AMERICANS, LATINOS, AND ASIAN AMERICANS

The legacy of slavery and racial segregation in the South has been the dominant focus of U.S. civil rights policies, but many other groups have also fought for equal rights. For example, discrimination was evident in the eradication and removal of Native Americans from huge parts of the East and Midwest, in battles with and prejudice against Mexicans in the Southwest, and in the poor treatment of Asian Americans on the West Coast and the internment of Japanese Americans during World War II. This historical review is necessary to understand today's civil rights policies, which were created, at least in part, in response to historical events and current conditions.

Native Americans were the first group to come in contact with the European immigrants. Although initial relations between the Native Americans and the European settlers were good in many places, the settlers' appetite for more land and their insensitivity to Native American culture soon led to continual conflict. The Native Americans were systematically pushed from their land and placed on reservations. The most infamous example was the removal of 46,000 members of the "Five Civilized Tribes" from the southeastern United States following the enactment of the Indian Removal Act in 1830. Thousands of Native Americans died on the Trail of Tears on their way to reservations in Oklahoma.[13] Native Americans had no political rights; indeed, through much of the nineteenth century, the U.S. government considered them "savages" to be eliminated. They did not gain the universal right to vote until 1924, just after women and well after black men. Although the U.S. government signed treaties with Native American tribes that recognized them as sovereign nations (not as foreign nations but as "domestic dependent nations"),[14] in practice the government ignored most of the agreements. Only in recent decades has the government started to uphold its obligations, although compliance remains spotty. Native Americans have struggled to maintain their cultural history and autonomy in the face of widespread poverty and unemployment.

Latinos have also struggled for political and economic equality. The early history of Latinos in the United States is rooted in the Mexican-American War (1846–1848) and the conquest by the United States of the territory that today makes up most of the southwestern states. Since that time, Mexicans have resided in large numbers in the Southwest. Although Latinos had long experienced prejudice and discrimination, one of their first major political successes was Cesar Chavez's effort to organize farmworkers in the 1960s and 1970s. He established the United Farm Workers Union and forced growers to bargain with 50,000 mostly Mexican-American fieldworkers in California and Florida. Although many Mexican Americans have roots that go back hundreds of years, a majority of Latinos have been in the United States for less than two generations. Consequently, they have become a political force only recently, despite the fact that they now are the nation's largest minority.

Latinos' relative lack of political clout when compared to that of African Americans can be explained by two factors: (1) Latinos vote at a much lower rate than African Americans because many have language barriers and about one-third of Latinos are not U.S. citizens and therefore cannot vote in national elections, and (2) unlike African Americans, Latinos are a relatively diverse group politically. They include Mexican Americans, Cuban Americans, Puerto Ricans, Dominicans, and people from many other Latin American nations. Most Latino voters are loyal to the Democratic Party, but a majority of Cuban Americans are strong Republicans. Although this diversity means that Latino voters do not speak with one voice, it brings opportunity for increased political clout in the future. The diversity of partisan attachments among Latinos and their relatively low levels of political involvement mean that both parties are eager to attract them as new voters.

IN THE 1960S AND 1970S, CESAR Chavez and the United Farm Workers Union successfully organized mostly Mexican-American farm workers, first in California and then in other parts of the country. Here, Chavez speaks to a group in Texas.

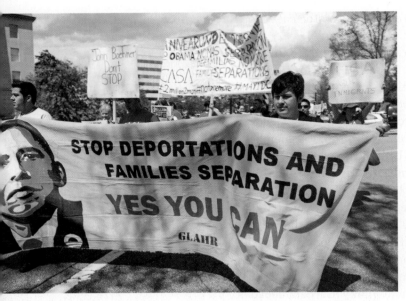

Asian Americans experienced discrimination beginning with their arrival in the United States in the nineteenth century. The first wave of Chinese immigrants came with the 1848 California gold rush. Initially foreign miners, including the Chinese, were able to stake out their claims along with Americans. But by 1850, when the easy-to-find gold was gone, Americans tried to drive out the Chinese through violence and the Foreign Miners Tax. Subsequently, Chinese immigrants played a crucial role in building the intercontinental railroad between 1865 and 1869. Yet, because they were given the most dangerous jobs, many lost their lives. After the railroad was completed, Chinese workers returned to the West Coast, where they experienced increasing discrimination and violence. Following several race riots, Congress passed the Chinese Exclusion Act of 1882, which prevented Chinese already in the United States from becoming U.S. citizens—although the Supreme Court later granted their American-born children automatic citizenship under the Fourteenth Amendment.[15] The Chinese Exclusion Act also barred virtually all immigration from China—the first time in U.S. history that a specific ethnic group was singled out in this way. In recent decades, a much broader range of Asians has emigrated to the United States, including Koreans, Filipinos, Hmong, Vietnamese, and Asian Indians. This variation in national heritage, culture, and language means that Asian Americans are quite diverse in their political views, partisan affiliation, and voting patterns.

THROUGHOUT AMERICAN HISTORY, immigrant groups have been crucial to the nation's growth, but they have often faced discrimination and deportation if they are found to be undocumented and not legally in this country. Today, debates over the rights of immigrants continue.

WOMEN AND CIVIL RIGHTS

When John Adams attended the Constitutional Convention in 1787, his wife, Abigail, advised him not to "put such unlimited power in the hands of the husbands. Remember, all men would be tyrants if they could. . . . If particular care and attention is not paid to the ladies, we . . . will not hold ourselves bound by any laws in which we have no voice or representation."[16] John Adams did not listen to his wife. The Constitution did not give women the right to vote, and they were not guaranteed that civil right until the Nineteenth Amendment was ratified in 1920—although 16 states had allowed women to vote before then. Until the early twentieth century, women in most parts of the country could not hold office, serve on juries, bring lawsuits in their own name, own property, or serve as legal guardians for their children. A woman's identity was so closely tied to her husband that if she married a noncitizen, she automatically gave up her citizenship!

protectionism The idea under which some people have tried to rationalize discriminatory policies by claiming that some groups, like women or African Americans, should be denied certain rights for their own safety or well-being.

The rationale for these policies was called **protectionism**. The argument was that women were too frail to compete in the business world and that they needed to be protected by men. This reasoning served in many court cases to deny women equal rights. For example, in 1869, Myra Bradwell requested admission to the Illinois bar to practice law. She was the first woman to graduate from law school in Illinois, the editor of *Chicago Legal News*, and held all the qualifications to be a lawyer in the state except for one—she was a woman. Her request was denied, and she sued all the way to the Supreme Court. In 1873, the Court ruled that the prohibition against women lawyers did not violate the Fourteenth Amendment's privileges and immunities clause because there was no constitutional right to be an attorney. If the Court had stopped there, the decision would have been unremarkable for its time. But Justice Joseph Bradley went on to provide a classic example of protectionism:

> The civil law as well as nature itself has always recognized a wide difference in the respective spheres and destinies to man and woman. Man is, or should be, women's protector and defender. The natural and proper timidity and delicacy which belongs to the female sex evidently unfits it for many of the occupations of civil life. The constitution of the family organization which is founded in the divine ordinance, as well as the nature of things, indicates the domestic sphere as that which properly belongs to the domains and functions of womanhood.[17]

While protectionist sentiment on the Court had waned by the mid-twentieth century, as recently as 1961 a court upheld a Florida law that automatically exempted women, but not men, from compulsory jury duty. The case involved a woman who killed her husband with a baseball bat after he admitted that he was having an affair and wanted to end the marriage. The woman argued that her conviction by an all-male jury violated her Fourteenth Amendment guarantee of "equal protection of the laws" and that a jury panel containing some women would have been more sympathetic to her "temporary insanity" defense. The court rejected this argument, ruling that the Florida law excluding women from jury duty was reasonable because "despite the enlightened emancipation of women from the restrictions and protections of bygone years, and their entry into many parts of community life formerly considered to be reserved to men, woman still is regarded as the center of home and family life."[18] Apparently it was unthinkable to the all-male court that a man might have to stay home from work and take care of the kids while his wife served on a jury. Later in this chapter, we will describe how the Supreme Court has moved away from this discriminatory position and rejected protectionist thinking.

THE PROTECTIONIST VIEW THAT women are weaker and unfit for some occupations was one reason women were excluded from the military for most of the nation's history. In 2008, Specialist Monica Brown became the second woman to receive the Silver Star medal for valor in the face of the enemy.

GAYS AND LESBIANS

The most recent group in the struggle for civil rights is the LGBT (lesbian, gay, bisexual, and transgender) community. For most of American history, gays and lesbians lived secret lives and were subject to abuse and discrimination if they openly acknowledged their sexual preferences. The critical moment that spurred the gay rights movement occurred on June 28, 1969, during a routine police raid on the Stonewall Inn in New York City.[19] (Police often raided gay bars to harass patrons and selectively enforce liquor laws.) This time, rather than submitting to the arrests, the customers fought back, throwing stones and beer bottles, breaking windows, and starting small fires. A crowd of several hundred people gathered, and the fighting raged for three nights. The Stonewall Rebellion galvanized the gay community by demonstrating the power of collective action.

Since Stonewall, the gay rights movement has made steady progress through a combination of political mobilization and protest, legislative action, and legal action. Public support for gay rights has increased dramatically in recent years. Between two-thirds and three-fourths of Americans (depending on the poll) agree with the new national policy that gays may openly serve in the military, whereas a majority of Americans opposed this policy when it was first proposed by President Clinton in 1993. Between 54 and 59 percent of Americans support same-sex marriage in recent polls, whereas only 35 to 40 percent held that view in 2009. More than 60 percent believe that same-sex couples should be able to adopt children, 81 percent think that businesses should not be able to discriminate against gays and lesbians, and 63 percent believe that same-sex couples should be entitled to the same benefits as heterosexual couples (whereas only 32 percent think they should not).[20] In May 2012, President Obama endorsed same-sex marriage for the first time, completing his gradual evolution on the issue. As of November 2014, the District of Columbia and 35 states now recognize same-sex marriage and two more have legalized civil unions for same-sex couples (we will discuss this and other issues concerning gay and lesbian rights later in the chapter).

A COLOR-BLIND SOCIETY?

Why does this history matter for politics today? There are two main responses. First, the effects of slavery and Jim Crow laws are still quite evident: legal racial segregation ended 50 years ago, but its legacy—especially evident in the difference that exists in the relative quality of education available to most whites and blacks—remains. Second, active discrimination based on race, gender, and sexual orientation is still evident in our society. Given the importance of race in the everyday lives of millions of Americans and in gaining an understanding of American politics, a grasp of the history that got us to where we are today is an important starting point (this section will focus on race, but the struggle for civil rights applies to the other groups discussed in this chapter as well).

Martin Luther King Jr. presented the vision for a color-blind society in his "I Have a Dream" speech, which he delivered before 250,000 people at the March on Washington in August 1963. He said, "I have a dream that my four little children will one day live in a nation where they will not be judged by the color of their skin but by the content of their character." Most Americans share this dream, but there are differences of opinion about how close we are to that goal. Those who feel that we must "move beyond race" argue that we already have achieved a level playing field on which all people have equal opportunities to succeed. Furthermore, they argue, efforts to make up for past discrimination or to create additional opportunities for racial minorities through affirmative action perpetuate discrimination by classifying people based on race. Others feel that discrimination is still an all-too-real part of life for racial minorities.

To see if you think we have reached King's color-blind ideal, consider what you notice when you meet people for

CIVIL RIGHTS LEADER MARTIN Luther King Jr. waves to supporters from the steps of the Lincoln Memorial on August 28, 1963, in Washington, D.C. The March on Washington drew an estimated 250,000 people who heard King deliver his famous "I Have a Dream" speech.

the first time. Do you notice their hair color, height, body type, or whether they wear glasses? Do you notice their skin color? If you have met a person once or twice, you may not remember her hair color or whether she wears glasses. But you probably do remember her skin color as a defining feature. In a truly color-blind society, race will be as unimportant for forming an opinion about someone as whether he wears glasses or, say, has a beard. That is, awareness of race will not affect our opinions or our actions. However, considerable research shows that awareness of race still influences many people's opinions and behavior. Some people engage in racial stereotyping without even being aware of it.[21] Others intentionally discriminate based on race.

In addition to research data, personal anecdotes can be informative. Let's consider two examples from a liberal, northern midwestern city that prides itself on being tolerant. The first example represents unintentional stereotyping; the second, racial discrimination. One morning one of the authors was at the checkout line at a local grocery store, and the cashier was giving the lady ahead of him a hard time. The woman had a large basket of groceries, and her bill was well over $100. She wanted to pay for some of the groceries with food stamps and the rest with a personal check. The cashier wanted to see a driver's license or two other forms of photo ID, and the lady did not have them. The author couldn't see exactly what was going on, but the woman had some type of ID that was not adequate. After calling over the store manager and a lot of hemming and hawing, the cashier finally accepted her check. Then the author unloaded his similarly sized cart of groceries and paid by check, which the cashier accepted without hesitation—and with no identification. In fact, he has never been asked for identification when paying by check in that store, despite not being personally known by any of the cashiers. It was hard not to conclude that the woman and the author were treated differently because she was black and using food stamps and he was white.

The second example involves a former graduate student in our department who is white and whose wife is black. The couple wanted to rent a bigger apartment, so they searched the want ads and made appointments to see some apartments. One landlord told them to meet him in front of the apartment at a specific time. They waited where they were told, but the landlord didn't show up. Later, they remembered seeing a car that slowed down and almost stopped but then sped away. They wondered if this was a case of a "drive-by landlord"—one who checks out potential tenants' race from a distance; if they are not white, he or she skips the appointment and tells them it is rented if they ask. This is exactly what happened. They called the landlord, asked what had happened, and were told that the apartment was already rented. To check their suspicions, they had some friends ask about the apartment, and the friends were told it was available. Their friends (both white) made an appointment to meet the landlord, and this time the same car pulled up and stopped. The landlord showed them the apartment and was very friendly. The next day, the graduate student filed a racial discrimination lawsuit.

These kinds of stories, ranging from irritating and demeaning to a serious violation of the law, are familiar to nearly every racial minority, woman, and gay person in the United States. Consider the well-dressed businessman who cannot get a cab in a major city because he is black, the woman who is sexually harassed by her boss but hesitates to say anything for fear of losing her job, the teenage Latino who is shadowed in the music store by a clerk, the Arab American who endures taunts about her head covering, or the lesbian couple who cannot find an apartment. Such anecdotal evidence as well as research data indicates continuing discrimination and that we have not yet achieved a color-blind (or gender- and sexual orientation–neutral) society.

WHAT DO POLITICAL SCIENTISTS DO?

To find out more about how political scientists measure racial bias, visit **wwnpag.es/wdpsd**

THE RACIAL DIVIDE TODAY

In addition to the unequal treatment of racial minorities, women, gays, and lesbians, a gulf remains between the objective condition of minorities and that of whites as well as between the political views that they hold. Although substantial progress has been made in bridging that gulf, inequalities in political, social, and economic conditions remain.

DIFFERENCES IN VOTING ACCESS

The United States has a long history of discriminating against racial and ethnic minorities in the election process. Although African Americans now vote at a rate that is equal to or slightly higher than that of whites in presidential elections (but still somewhat lower than that of whites in midterm elections), other racial and ethnic minorities have lower turnouts (see Figure 5.1). Much of the difference in voter turnout can be accounted for by education and income, but there still are practices and institutions that specifically depress minority-voter turnout. And many of these deterrents are intentional. The NAACP, the U.S. Commission on Civil Rights, and the Brennan Center for Justice have all documented such practices in elections going back to 2000, including moving and reducing the number of polling places in areas with predominantly minority voters, changing from district-based to at-large elections (city-wide or county-wide elections in which there is often a mix of minority and white voters), using voter challenges to target minority voters, redistricting to dilute minority voting power, withholding information about registration and voting procedures from blacks, and "causing or taking advantage of Election Day irregularities."[22]

FIGURE » 5.1

PERCENT VOTING IN PRESIDENTIAL ELECTIONS BY RACE AND HISPANIC ORIGIN: 1996–2012

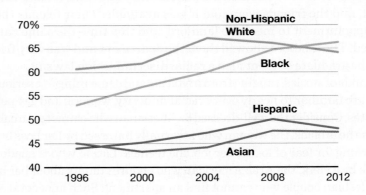

SOURCE: The Diversifying Electorate—Voting Rates by Race and Hispanic Origin in 2012 (and Other Recent Elections), from Current Population Survey, www.census.gov/newsroom/releases/pdf/cb13-84_figure.pdf (accessed 5/19/14).

There are other state practices that are not specifically aimed at minority voters but that have a disproportionate impact on them. For example, in the 2008 election, three states removed voters' names from the voting rolls if there wasn't an identical match between the name the voter used when registering to vote and the name as it appeared in another state database (often the database of driver's license information). Seven states purged the names of people who had committed felonies from the voting registration lists, which often produced false matches to people with the same names who had not committed a crime. Fourteen states engaged in voter intimidation and deceptive practices. Moreover, several states used technical barriers to voter registration and voting, limited access to voter registration services at social services offices (even though such access was required by federal law), and used poorly designed ballots that were especially confusing to less educated or older voters.[23]

In the buildup to the 2014 midterm elections, there were 30 changes in state laws that restricted access to voting, including requiring a photo ID to vote (which has a disproportionate impact on minorities because they are less likely to have a photo ID), proof of citizenship before being allowed to vote, cutbacks in early voting days and times, and making it more difficult to register people to vote. In addition, as we will discuss later, in 2013 the Supreme Court struck down an important part of the Voting Rights Act, making it easier for the nine states that had been covered by this provision of the law to implement discriminatory practices.[24]

DESPITE THE REMOVAL OF MOST formal barriers to voting, Latinos are less likely to vote and participate in politics than whites, blacks, and Asian Americans. Groups like Voto Latino (represented here by Rosario Dawson and John Leguizamo) have tried to mobilize Latino voters in recent elections.

SOCIOECONOMIC INDICATORS

The racial divide is also evident in social and economic terms. Nearly three times as many black families are below the poverty line as white families: 27.2 percent compared to 9.6 percent in 2013. The poverty rate of 23.5 percent for Hispanic families in 2013 was similar to that of black families. While white median household income (that is, income from wages, salaries, interest, and disability and unemployment payments) was $55,257 in 2013, black median household income was $34,598 (62.6 percent of white family income) and Hispanic median household income was $40,963 (74.1 percent of white family income).[25] Moreover, the gap in overall wealth is much more dramatic. The average white household has more than six times the assets of the typical nonwhite family. In 2013, the median household net worth (that is, the sum of all assets, including houses, cars, and stock) was $140,200 for whites and $18,100 for nonwhites.[26] Poverty is not distributed equally throughout the United States but rather is concentrated in areas where the minority population is the highest (see Figure 5.2).

Other indicators show similar patterns. The rate of black adult male unemployment has been about twice as high as that of white adult male unemployment for the past 45 years. In October 2014, the unemployment rate among blacks was 10.9 percent, compared to 4.8 percent for whites and 6.8 percent for Latinos.[27] Moreover, slightly more than 41 percent of black children lived in two-parent households in 2013, compared to 73.7 percent of white children and 65.1 percent of Latino children.[28] Also, blacks are significantly more likely than whites to be victimized by crime. African Americans are nearly seven times as likely to be murdered as whites.[29]

FIGURE » 5.2

PERCENTAGE OF PEOPLE IN POVERTY AND PERCENTAGE OF THE POPULATION THAT IS WHITE, 2010

Together, these maps show that the poverty rate in the United States is closely related to the minority population. How do you think these patterns might affect the politics of civil rights policies that are aimed at reducing discrimination in the workplace or housing?

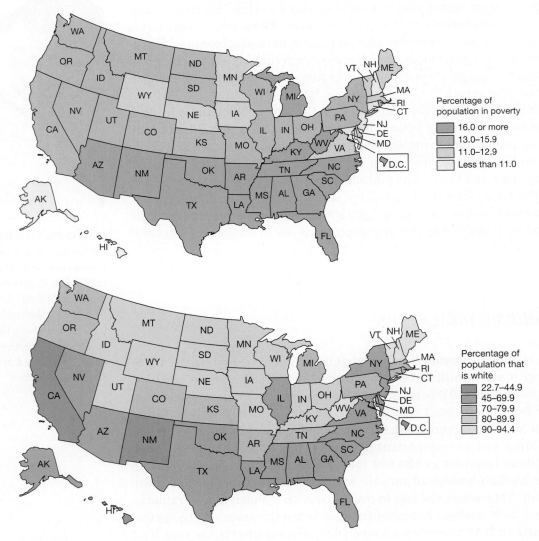

SOURCE: Poverty data from U.S. Census Bureau, "Poverty: 2010 and 2011 American Community Surveys," September 2010, www.census.gov/acs; race data from U.S. Census Bureau, *2012 Statistical Abstract*, Population Table 18, "Resident Population by Hispanic Origin and State: 2010," www.census.gov/compendia/statab/2012/tables/12s0018.pdf (accessed 11/3/12).

On every measure of health—life expectancy, infectious diseases, infant mortality, cancer rates, heart disease, and strokes—the gaps between whites and blacks are large and, in some cases, increasing. For example, life expectancy for blacks is about four years shorter than for whites (74.5 years for blacks compared with 78.8 years for whites), the infant mortality rate is more than double for blacks (13.31 deaths per 1,000 live births compared with 5.62 deaths per 1,000 live births for whites), and maternal mortality is more than triple (35.6 deaths per 100,000 births for black women compared with 11.7 deaths per 100,000 births for white women). Similar gaps also exist for incidences of cancer, diabetes, strokes, and heart attacks in blacks and whites.[30]

The greatest disparity between racial minorities and whites may be in the criminal justice system. Racial profiling subjects many innocent blacks to intrusive searches. Nick Cannon, the rapper and host of *America's Got Talent*, has complained about constantly being stopped for "driving while black." He said, "Now in L.A. I get pulled over like once a week. Honestly, I think it's because I'm a black man in a nice car."[31] Studies have shown that blacks are not only more likely than whites to be convicted for the same crimes, but blacks are also more likely to serve longer sentences.[32] In many large American cities, tensions between police departments and minority communities periodically boil over. The largest race riots since the 1960s were in Los Angeles in 1992 following the acquittal of four white police officers who had been videotaped brutally beating a black man, Rodney King. The riots left 54 people dead and more than 2,000 injured, and caused more than $1 billion in damage. Nearly every year there is a major incident involving the police shooting unarmed African Americans and Latinos. Moreover, urban minorities often complain of profiling by police. In 2013, a federal district court ruled that New York City's "stop-and-frisk" policy, which disproportionately targeted minorities, was unconstitutional. Early in 2014, Bill de Blasio, the newly elected mayor of New York City, said he would change the police department's practices.[33]

African Americans and other minorities are also subjected to hate crimes much more frequently than whites. A murder that received national attention in 1998 involved a black man, James Byrd Jr., who was chained to the back of a pickup truck by three white men and dragged to his death. Two of the murderers were sentenced to death, and the other received life in prison. In 2012, an unarmed 17-year-old African American, Trayvon Martin, was shot by a neighborhood watch member, George Zimmerman, in Sanford, Florida. This incident raised concerns about racism, both about Zimmerman's conduct and about how the local police department, which did not immediately arrest Zimmerman, had handled the case. Zimmerman was later acquitted.[34]

According to the FBI's hate-crime statistics, of the 5,796 hate crimes in 2012, 48.3 percent were race related. These figures show nearly 66.1 percent were "anti-black" and only 22.4 percent were "anti-white." This means that the rate of anti-black hate crimes is nearly five times what would be expected based on the percentage of African Americans in the United States, while the rate of anti-white hate crimes is about one-third as high as would be expected.[35]

This backdrop of racial inequality, discrimination, and violence drives civil rights activists to push their agenda in the three branches of government: legislative, executive, and judicial. In some instances, activists work in several arenas simultaneously; in others, they seek redress in one arena after exhausting alternatives in the others. The civil rights movement, which was crucial in early policy successes, also continues to mobilize from the grass roots.

HATE CRIMES AGAINST AFRICAN Americans have not totally disappeared from America. In 1998, James Byrd Jr. was murdered in Jasper, Texas, by three white supremacists who chained him to a pickup truck and dragged him down a road until he was decapitated. According to FBI statistics, in 2012 nearly two-thirds of race-related hate crimes in the United States were "anti-black." The 2012 shooting of Trayvon Martin, an unarmed 17-year-old African-American man, by a neighborhood watch member also raised concerns about racism.

KEY PLAYERS IN THE CONFLICT OVER CIVIL RIGHTS

Our civil rights policies are produced by several key players. First, the public becomes involved through social movements to put pressure on the political system to change. But Congress, the president, and the courts all also exert their own influence on policies that define civil rights.

SOCIAL MOVEMENTS From the early women's rights movement and abolitionists of the nineteenth century to the gay rights and civil rights movements of the mid-twentieth century, activists have pressured the political system to change civil rights policies. Through collective action, these social movements have made sure that such controversial issues remained on the policy agenda.

CIVIL RIGHTS TIMELINE

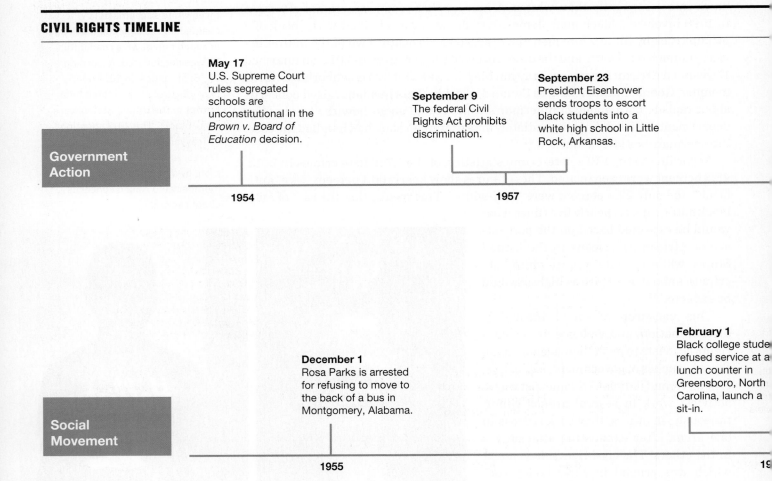

Government Action

May 17
U.S. Supreme Court rules segregated schools are unconstitutional in the *Brown v. Board of Education* decision.

1954

September 9
The federal Civil Rights Act prohibits discrimination.

September 23
President Eisenhower sends troops to escort black students into a white high school in Little Rock, Arkansas.

1957

Social Movement

December 1
Rosa Parks is arrested for refusing to move to the back of a bus in Montgomery, Alabama.

1955

February 1
Black college stude refused service at a lunch counter in Greensboro, North Carolina, launch a sit-in.

19

SOURCE: Adapted from "Key Moments in Civil Rights History," *Ann Arbor News*, January 11, 2004, www.mlive.com/news/aanews/index.ssf?/base/features-0/1073819921106320.xml.

Women started to push for the right to vote at a convention in 1848 at Seneca Falls, New York. Subsequently, a constitutional amendment to give women the right to vote was regularly introduced in Congress between 1878 and 1913 but never was passed, despite the efforts of women such as Susan B. Anthony and Elizabeth Cady Stanton. After a parallel movement at the state level had some success, the Nineteenth Amendment giving women the right to vote was finally passed in 1919 and was ratified in 1920.

The civil rights movement of the 1950s and 1960s, aimed at ending segregation and guaranteeing equal political and social rights for blacks, is the most famous example of a successful social movement (see Figure 5.3). Although the *Brown v. Board of Education* decision, which struck down segregation in public schools, gave the movement a boost, most southern blacks saw little change in their daily lives. As white school boards and local governments resisted integration, black leaders became convinced that the courts would not effect change because of resistance to their decisions. The only way to change the laws was to get the public, both black and white, to demand change.

The spark came on December 1, 1955, in Montgomery, Alabama, when a woman named Rosa Parks refused to give up her seat on a bus to a white person, as she was required to do by law. Parks is often described as a seamstress who was tired after a

FIGURE » 5.3

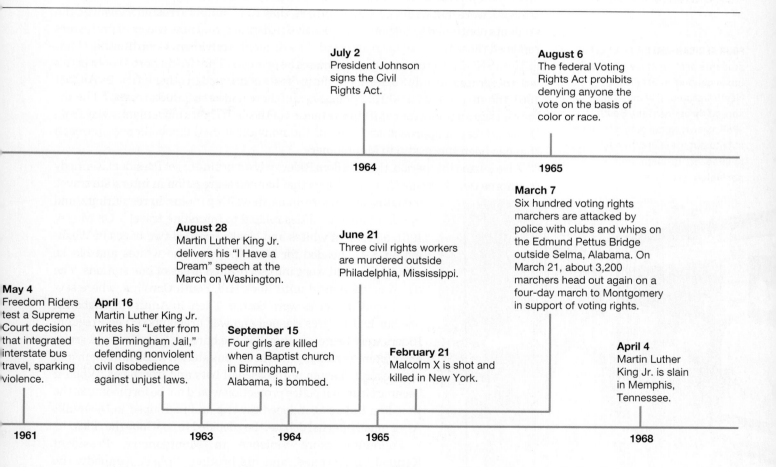

July 2
President Johnson signs the Civil Rights Act.

August 6
The federal Voting Rights Act prohibits denying anyone the vote on the basis of color or race.

1964

1965

March 7
Six hundred voting rights marchers are attacked by police with clubs and whips on the Edmund Pettus Bridge outside Selma, Alabama. On March 21, about 3,200 marchers head out again on a four-day march to Montgomery in support of voting rights.

August 28
Martin Luther King Jr. delivers his "I Have a Dream" speech at the March on Washington.

June 21
Three civil rights workers are murdered outside Philadelphia, Mississippi.

May 4
Freedom Riders test a Supreme Court decision that integrated interstate bus travel, sparking violence.

April 16
Martin Luther King Jr. writes his "Letter from the Birmingham Jail," defending nonviolent civil disobedience against unjust laws.

September 15
Four girls are killed when a Baptist church in Birmingham, Alabama, is bombed.

February 21
Malcolm X is shot and killed in New York.

April 4
Martin Luther King Jr. is slain in Memphis, Tennessee.

1961

1963

1964

1965

1968

long day's work and simply did not want to give up her seat. That is true, but there is more to the story. Local civil rights leaders had been waiting for years for an opportunity to boycott the local bus company because of its segregation policy. They needed a perfect test case—someone who would help draw attention to the cause.

Rosa Parks was just that person. She was a well-educated, law-abiding citizen who had been active in local civil rights organizations. In her book, *My Story*, Parks says, "I was . . . no more tired than I usually was at the end of a working day. . . . No, the only tired I was, was tired of giving in."[36] When she was arrested for refusing to give up her seat, local civil rights leaders organized a boycott of the bus company that lasted more than a year. Whites in Montgomery tried to stop the boycott. The police arrested and fined blacks who had arranged a car pool system to get to work: people waiting for a car to pick them up were arrested for loitering, and car pool drivers were arrested for lacking appropriate insurance or having too many people in their car. Martin Luther King Jr. was elected leader of the bus boycott, and he was subjected to harassment and violence—his house was firebombed, and he was arrested several times. Finally, a federal district court ruled that Montgomery's segregation policy was unconstitutional, and the Supreme Court upheld the ruling.

NONVIOLENT PROTEST On February 1, 1960, four black students in Greensboro, North Carolina, went to a segregated lunch counter at a local Woolworth's and asked to be served. They sat there for an hour without being served and had to leave when the store closed. When 20 students returned the next day, national wire services picked up the story. Within two weeks, the sit-ins had spread to 11 cities. In some cases, the students were met with violence; in others, they were simply arrested. However, the students continued to respond with passive resistance, and new waves of protesters replaced those who had been arrested. The Student Nonviolent Coordinating Committee (SNCC) was created to coordinate the protests. The Greensboro Woolworth's was integrated on July 26, 1961, but the protests continued in other cities. By August 1961, the sit-ins had 70,000 participants and there had been 3,000 arrests.[37] The sit-ins marked an important shift in the tactics of the civil rights movement: away from the court-based approach and toward the nonviolent civil disobedience approach that had been successful in Montgomery.

Also during this period, the Freedom Riders were working to get President Kennedy to enforce two Supreme Court decisions that banned segregation in interstate travel, including at bus terminals, in waiting rooms, in restaurants, and in other public facilities related to interstate travel.[38] On May 4, 1961, a group of whites and blacks boarded two buses in Washington, D.C., headed for New Orleans. The whites and blacks sat together and went into segregated areas of bus stations. The trip was uneventful until Rock Hill, South Carolina, where several Freedom Riders were beaten. Then, in Anniston, Alabama, one bus had its tires slashed and was firebombed. The Freedom Riders were beaten as they fled the burning bus. A second group encountered an angry mob at the bus station in Birmingham and was severely beaten with baseball bats and iron pipes. When it became clear that police protection would not be forthcoming, the Freedom Riders abandoned the trip and regrouped in Nashville. After much internal debate, they decided to continue the rides.

Following more violence in Montgomery, President Kennedy intervened, and his brother, Robert Kennedy, the attorney general, worked out a deal: the Freedom Riders would

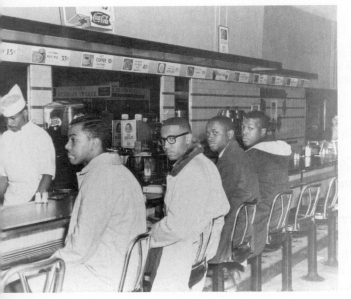

FOUR AFRICAN-AMERICAN COLLEGE students protest at a whites-only lunch counter in Greensboro, North Carolina. These sit-ins spread throughout the South in 1960 as civil rights activists were able to put pressure on businesses to integrate through their nonviolent protests.

receive police protection, federal troops would not intervene, and they would face the local courts upon their arrest for "disturbing the peace." The Freedom Rides continued throughout the summer. They successfully drew national attention to the continuing resistance in the South to desegregation rulings, forced the Kennedy administration to take a stand on this issue, and led to a stronger Interstate Commerce Commission ruling banning segregation in interstate travel.[39]

THE LETTER FROM THE BIRMINGHAM JAIL The next significant events occurred in Birmingham, Alabama, in 1963. Birmingham had more racial violence than any southern city, with 18 unsolved bombings of black churches and homes in a six-year period. The city had closed its parks and golf courses rather than integrate them, and there was no progress on integrating the local schools. A leading supporter of integration had been castrated to intimidate other blacks who might advocate integration. The city's police chief, "Bull" Connor, was a strong segregationist who had allowed the attacks on the Freedom Riders. During a peaceful protest in April 1963, Martin Luther King Jr. and many others were arrested. While in solitary confinement, King wrote his now-famous "Letter from the Birmingham Jail," an eloquent statement of the principles of nonviolent civil disobedience.

The letter was a response to white religious leaders who had told King in a newspaper ad that his actions were "unwise and untimely" and that "when rights are consistently denied, a cause should be pressed in the courts and in negotiations among local leaders, and not in the streets." King responded with a justification for civil disobedience, writing that everyone had an obligation to follow just laws but an equal obligation to break unjust laws.

King also laid out the four steps of nonviolent campaigns: (1) collection of the facts to determine whether injustices are alive; (2) negotiation with white leaders to change the injustices; (3) self-purification, which involved training to make sure that the civil rights protesters would be able to endure the abuse that they would receive; and (4) direct action (for example, sit-ins and marches) to create the environment in which change could occur, but always in a nonviolent manner. By following these steps, civil rights protesters ensured that their social movement would draw attention to their cause while turning public opinion against their opponents' violent tactics.

Following King's release from jail, the situation escalated. The protest leaders decided to use children in the next round of demonstrations. After more than 1,000 children were arrested and the jails were overflowing, the police turned fire hoses and police dogs on children who were trying to continue their march. Media coverage of the incident turned the tide of public opinion in favor of the marchers as the country expressed outrage over the violence in Birmingham. Similar protests occurred throughout the South, with more than 1,000 actions in over 100 different southern cities and more than 20,000 people arrested throughout the summer.

Mass protest became the preferred tool of many other social movements for civil rights and other causes. Vietnam War protesters marched on Washington by the hundreds of thousands in the late 1960s and early 1970s. The women's rights, gay rights, and environmental movements have staged many mass demonstrations in Washington and other major cities. Most recently, large-scale demonstrations against Wall Street and international organizations, such as the International Monetary Fund and the World Trade

A 15-YEAR-OLD CIVIL RIGHTS demonstrator, defying an anti-parade ordinance, is attacked by a police dog in Birmingham, Alabama, on May 3, 1963. The next day, during a meeting at the White House, President Kennedy discussed this photo, which had appeared on the front page of the *New York Times*. Reaction against this police brutality helped spur Congress and the president to enact civil rights legislation.

Organization, have swept the nation. The Occupy Wall Street movement, which started in September 2011, spread to more than 1,500 cities in 82 nations. Rooted in the nonviolent protests of the civil rights era, protesters occupied public spaces to make their views known. The Occupy movement's slogan, "We are the 99%," drew attention to income inequality and helped set the tone for the 2012 presidential election. Conservative activists, such as those in the pro-life movement, have also used nonviolent protests, sit-ins, and mass demonstrations. Protests against President Obama's policies early in 2009 evolved into the Tea Party movement (evoking the Boston Tea Party of the American Revolution). Rooted in opposition to high taxes and activist government, the Tea Party movement organized protests on Tax Day (April 15, 2009) that drew more than 300,000 people in 346 cities.[40] The legacy of the civil rights movement has been not only to help change unjust laws but also to provide a new tool for political action across a broad range of policy areas.

THE COURTS

The Supreme Court has played an important role in defining civil rights. In the mid-twentieth century, the justices moved away from the separate but equal doctrine, required the desegregation of public schools, and upheld landmark civil rights legislation passed by Congress. More recently, they have expanded civil rights for women and LGBTs, but they also have endorsed a color-blind position that some see as a movement away from protecting civil rights.

CHALLENGING SEPARATE BUT EQUAL IN EDUCATION In the 1930s, the National Association for the Advancement of Colored People (NAACP), which was established to fight for equal rights for black people (and more recently for equal rights for all racial and ethnic minorities and LGBT), started a concerted effort to nibble away at the separate but equal doctrine. Rather than tackling segregation head-on, the NAACP challenged an aspect of segregation that would be familiar to the Supreme Court justices: the ways in which states kept blacks out of all-white law schools. Another strategy was to challenge admission practices in law schools outside the Deep South to demonstrate that segregation was not just a "southern problem" and to raise the chances for compliance with favorable Court decisions. A young NAACP attorney named Thurgood Marshall (who later became the first African-American Supreme Court justice) argued that the University of Maryland's practice of sending black students to out-of-state law schools rather than admitting them to the university's all-white law school violated the black students' civil rights. (The state gave black students a $200 scholarship, which did not cover the costs of tuition and travel and was not available to all black students who wanted to attend law school.) The circuit court and subsequently the Maryland appeals court in 1936 rejected this arrangement and ordered that black students be admitted to the University of Maryland law school.[41]

Over the next 15 years, a series of successful lawsuits slowly chipped away at the idea of separate but equal. After these victories, there was a debate within the NAACP whether to continue the case-by-case approach against the separate but equal doctrine or to directly challenge the principle itself. The latter approach was risky because it was unclear if the Court was ready to take this bold step and because defeat in the Court would set back the movement. However, the signals increasingly indicated that the Supreme Court was ready to strike down the separate but equal doctrine. In addition to the law school cases, in 1948 the Court ruled that "restrictive covenants"—clauses in real estate contracts that prevented a property owner from selling to an African American— could not be enforced by state or local courts because of the Fourteenth Amendment's prohibition against a state denying blacks the "equal protection of the laws."

This application of the Fourteenth Amendment was expanded in the landmark ruling *Brown v. Board of Education*. The case arrived on the Court's docket in 1951, was postponed for argument until after the 1952 election, and then was reargued in December 1953. The ruling was postponed for so long because the Court was keenly aware of the firestorm that would ensue. In its unanimous decision, the Court ruled, "In the field of public education, the doctrine of separate but equal has no place. Separate educational facilities are inherently unequal, depriving the plaintiffs of the equal protection of the laws. Segregated facilities may generate in black children a feeling of inferiority that may affect their hearts and minds in a way unlikely ever to be undone."[42] The case was significant not only because it required all public schools in the United States to desegregate but also because it used the equal protection clause of the Fourteenth Amendment in a way that had potentially far-reaching consequences.

Nonetheless, the decision was limited by focusing on segregation in schools rather than segregation more generally, and by focusing on the psychological damage done to black schoolchildren because of segregation rather than on the broader claim that racial classification itself was not allowed by the Constitution. Chief Justice Earl Warren wanted a unanimous vote and knew that two justices would not support a broader ruling that would overturn *Plessy v. Ferguson* and rule segregation unconstitutional in all contexts. Even if segregation in other public places still was legal, the *Brown* ruling provided an important boost to the civil rights movement.

BUSING STUDENTS FROM ONE school district to another in the interest of desegregation has been controversial since the 1960s. In 2007, the Supreme Court invalidated voluntary desegregation plans in Louisville and Seattle school districts.

THE PUSH TO DESEGREGATE SCHOOLS In 1955, *Brown v. Board of Education II* addressed the implementation of desegregation and required the states to "desegregate with all deliberate speed."[43] The odd choice of words, "all deliberate speed," was read as a signal by southerners that they could take their time with desegregation. The phrase does seem to be contradictory: being deliberate does not usually involve being speedy. Southern states engaged in "massive resistance" to the desegregation order, as articulated by Harry F. Byrd, the segregationist senator from Virginia. In some cases, they even closed public schools rather than integrate them—and then reopened the schools as "private" segregated schools for which the white students received government vouchers. However, Maryland, Kentucky, Tennessee, Missouri, and the District of Columbia desegregated their schools within two years.

Eight years after *Brown I*, little had changed in the Deep South: fewer than 1 percent of black children attended school with white children.[44] The Supreme Court became frustrated with the lack of progress in desegregating the schools, saying there was "too much deliberation and not enough speed."[45] Through the 1960s, the courts had to battle against continued resistance. In 1971, the Court shifted its focus from **de jure** segregation (segregation mandated by law) to **de facto** segregation

de jure Relating to actions or circumstances that occur "by law," such as the legally enforced segregation of schools in the American South before the 1960s.

de facto Relating to actions or circumstances that occur outside the law or "by fact," such as the segregation of schools that resulted from housing patterns and other factors rather than from laws.

(segregation that existed because of segregated housing patterns) and approved school busing as a tool to integrate schools.[46] This approach was extremely controversial. The Court almost immediately limited the application of busing by ruling in a Detroit case that busing could not go beyond the boundaries of a city's school district—that is, students did not have to be bused from suburbs to cities unless it could be shown that the school district's lines were drawn in an intentionally discriminatory way.[47] This rule encouraged "white flight" from the cities to the suburbs in response to court-ordered busing.

In 2007, in perhaps the most important decision on race in education since *Brown*, the Court invalidated voluntary desegregation plans implemented by public school districts in Seattle and Louisville. Both districts set goals for racial diversity and denied assignment requests if they tipped the racial balance above or below certain thresholds. In a ringing endorsement of the color-blind approach, the majority opinion said, "The way to stop discrimination on the basis of race is to stop discriminating on the basis of race." In this case, the discrimination was against white students who wanted to be in schools with few minority students rather than black students who wanted to be in integrated schools. However, it was not immediately clear how race would factor into school desegregation plans in the future, because only four justices signed on to the strict color-blind view. Justice Anthony Kennedy articulated a position between the conservatives' view, that race may not be used to classify students, and the liberals' view, that racial considerations are necessary to achieve integrated schools.[48]

EXPANDING CIVIL RIGHTS Other significant rulings in the 1960s struck down state laws that forbade interracial marriages (16 states had such laws), upheld all significant parts of the Civil Rights Act, and upheld and expanded the scope of the Voting Rights Act. In central cases, the justices ruled that Congress had the power to eliminate segregation in public places, such as restaurants and hotels, under the commerce clause of the Constitution.

The first case involved a hotel in Atlanta that was close to an interstate highway, advertised extensively on the highway, and had a clientele that was about 75 percent from out of state. The Court ruled that this establishment was clearly engaging in interstate commerce, so Congress had the right to regulate it.[49] Ironically, the white hotel owner objected that his Thirteenth Amendment rights had been violated when Congress forced him to serve black people (he claimed to have been forced into "involuntary servitude"), but the Court rejected that argument. In the second case, "almost all, if not all" of the patrons of Ollie's Barbeque in Birmingham, Alabama, were local. However, the Court pointed out that meat purchased for the restaurant came from out of state, and this constituted 46 percent of the total amount spent on supplies. Therefore, the practice of segregation would place significant burdens on "the interstate flow of food and upon the movement on products generally."[50]

The next important area of cases was in employment law. In 1971, the Court ruled that employment tests, such as written exams or general aptitude tests, that are not related to job performance and that discriminate against blacks violate the 1964 Civil Rights Act.[51] This **disparate impact standard** of discrimination meant that if the employment practice had a bad *effect* on a racial group, it didn't matter whether or not the discrimination was *intended*. The Supreme Court and Congress have gone back and forth in defining this concept, but it is still important in workplace discrimination suits. (See Nuts & Bolts 5.1 for the legal definition of race-based workplace discrimination.)

disparate impact standard
The idea that discrimination exists if a practice has a negative effect on a specific group, whether or not this effect was intentional.

RACE-RELATED DISCRIMINATION AS DEFINED BY THE EQUAL EMPLOYMENT OPPORTUNITY COMMISSION

Below are excerpts from the U.S. Equal Employment Opportunity Commission's publication defining race/color discrimination.

Race/Color Discrimination

Race discrimination involves treating someone (an applicant or employee) unfavorably because he/she is of a certain race or because of personal characteristics associated with race (such as hair texture, skin color, or certain facial features). Color discrimination involves treating someone unfavorably because of skin color complexion. . . . Discrimination can occur when the victim and the person who inflicted the discrimination are the same race or color.

Race/Color Discrimination and Work Situations

The law forbids discrimination when it comes to any aspect of employment, including hiring, firing, pay, job assignments, promotions, layoff, training, fringe benefits, and any other term or condition of employment.

Race/Color Discrimination and Harassment

It is unlawful to harass a person because of that person's race or color. Harassment can include, for example, racial slurs, offensive or derogatory remarks about a person's race or color, or the display of racially offensive symbols. Although the law doesn't prohibit simple teasing, offhand comments, or isolated incidents that are not very serious, harassment is illegal when it is so frequent or severe that it creates a hostile or offensive work environment or when it results in an adverse employment decision (such as the victim being fired or demoted). The harasser can be the victim's supervisor, a supervisor in another area, a coworker, or someone who is not an employee of the employer, such as a client or customer.

Race/Color Discrimination and Employment Policies/Practices

An employment policy or practice that applies to everyone, regardless of race or color, can be illegal if it has a negative impact on the employment of people of a particular race or color and is not job-related and necessary to the operation of the business.

SOURCE: U.S. Equal Employment Opportunity Commission, "Race/Color Discrimination," www.eeoc.gov/laws/types/race_color.cfm (accessed 10/4/12).

THE COLOR-BLIND COURT AND JUDICIAL ACTIVISM The Roberts and Rehnquist Courts of the past two decades have been gradually imposing a "color-blind jurisprudence" over a range of issues. One significant area was the 1992 racial redistricting in which 15 new U.S. House districts were drawn to help elect African Americans and 10 new districts were drawn to help elect Latino members. The resulting dramatic change in the number of minorities in Congress (an increase greater than 50 percent) was rooted in the 1982 amendments to the Voting Rights Act. Instead of mandating a fair *process*, this law and subsequent interpretation by the Supreme Court mandated that minorities be able to "elect representatives of their choice" when their numbers and configuration permit. As a result, the legislative redistricting process now had to avoid discriminatory *results* rather than being concerned only with discriminatory *intent*.

However, in a series of decisions starting with the 1993 landmark case *Shaw v. Reno*, the Supreme Court's adherence to a color-blind jurisprudence has thrown the constitutionality of black-majority districts into doubt. The Court has ruled that black-majority districts are legal as long as they are "done right,"[52] but it has consistently held that if race is the predominant factor in drawing district lines, the districts are unconstitutional because they violate the equal protection clause of the Fourteenth Amendment. Based on this reasoning, black-majority districts in North Carolina, Georgia, Louisiana, Virginia, Texas, and Florida were found to be unconstitutional. In the most recent case, in 2001, the Court upheld the redrawn 12th District in North Carolina, which no longer was a black-majority district, arguing that when race and partisanship are so intertwined—as they are when 90 percent of African Americans vote for a Democratic candidate—plaintiffs cannot assume that African Americans were placed together for racial reasons. This ruling opens the door for a greater consideration of race than had been allowed in the previous cases. However, racial redistricting remains an unsettled area of the law.[53]

The Court also struck down an important part of the 1965 Voting Rights Act in a 2013 ruling. This case concerned the "coverage formula" that determines which states have to get approval from the Justice Department before implementing changes in an election law or practice (such as redistricting or moving the location of a polling place). This "preclearance" provision of the law was viewed as one of the best ways to stop discriminatory voting practices because it could prevent them before they were implemented, rather than having to wait until they went into effect. The Court ruled that the coverage formula was an unconstitutional burden on the covered states and was a violation of the Tenth Amendment.[54]

The racial redistricting and voting rights cases illustrate that the Supreme Court is increasingly activist in civil rights. It is generally unwilling to defer to any other branch of government that disagrees with its view of discrimination and equal protection (see Chapter 14 for a discussion of judicial activism). In some periods, judicial activism may serve to further civil rights, as in the 1950s and 1960s, or to limit them, as in the recent period.

WOMEN'S RIGHTS The Supreme Court has also been central in shaping women's civil rights. Until relatively recently, the Court did not apply the Constitution to women, despite the Fourteenth Amendment's language that states may not deny any *person* the equal protection of the laws. Apparently, women were not regarded as people when it came to political and economic rights in the nineteenth and early twentieth centuries. These protectionist notions were finally rejected in three cases between 1971 and 1976, when the Court made it much more difficult for states to treat men and women differently.

The first case involved an Idaho state law that gave a man priority over a woman when they were otherwise equally entitled to execute a person's estate. This law was justified on the "reasonable" grounds that it reduced the state courts' workload by having an automatic rule that would limit challenges. But the Court ruled that the law was arbitrary, did not meet the "reasonableness" test, and therefore violated the woman's equal protection rights under the Fourteenth Amendment.[55] The second case involved a female Air Force officer who wanted to count her husband as a dependent for purposes of health and housing benefits. Under the law at the time, a military man could automatically count his wife as a dependent, but a woman could claim her husband only if she brought in more than half the family income. The Court struck down this practice, saying protectionist laws "in practical effect, put women not on a pedestal, but in a cage."[56]

rational basis test The use of evidence to suggest that differences in the behavior of two groups can rationalize unequal treatment of these groups.

These two cases relied on the **rational basis test** for discrimination between men and women. Along with the strict scrutiny test (see Chapter 4), it allowed the Fourteenth Amendment to be applied differently to particular categories of people. Under the rational basis test, states could discriminate against a group of people as long as there was a "rational basis" for that state law. Today, for example, states can pass drinking laws that only allow those who are 21 and older to drink on the grounds that traffic fatalities will be lower with that drinking age rather than a law that allows 18-year-olds to drink.

The strict scrutiny test gave racial minorities the strongest protection as the "suspect classification" under the Fourteenth Amendment. This test stipulated that there must be a "compelling state interest" to discriminate among people if race is involved. The suspect classification was first used in a case involving the internment of Japanese Americans during World War II. It is one of the few instances in which racial classification has survived strict scrutiny. In a controversial ruling, the Court said that the internment camps were justified on national security grounds.[57]

In 1976, the Court established a third test, the intermediate scrutiny test (see Chapter 4), in a case involving the drinking age. In the early 1970s, some states had a lower drinking age for women than for men on the "rational basis" that 18- to 20-year-old women are more mature than men of that age (states argued that women were less likely to be drunk drivers and less likely to abuse alcohol than men). The new intermediate scrutiny standard meant that the government's policy must be "substantially related" to an "important government objective" to justify the unequal treatment of men and women, so the law was struck down.[58]

The intermediate scrutiny test gives women stronger protections than the reasonable basis test, but it is not as strong as strict scrutiny (see How It Works: Civil Rights). To use the legal jargon, the gender distinction would have to serve an "important government objective," but not a "compelling state interest," in order to withstand intermediate scrutiny. Some distinctions between men and women are still allowed. For example, in 1981, the Supreme Court said that gender differences influence combat roles and military needs and therefore justify male-only draft registration. This issue has not been relevant recently because of the all-volunteer armed services, but it would become relevant again if the draft were reinstated.[59]

In many instances, as with the Idaho case, the rights of women were strengthened by the new standard of equal protection. However, in other instances, women may actually be more restricted by being treated the same as men. For example, in the drinking age case, instead of dropping the drinking age for men to 18, states raised the age for women to 21. Similarly, the Court struck down an Alabama divorce law in which husbands but not wives could be ordered to pay alimony.[60] Arguably, women would have been better off in these two specific instances under the old discriminatory laws (because they could drink at 18 instead of 21 and did not have to pay alimony in some states). However, the more aggressive application of the Fourteenth Amendment for women was an important step in providing them with the equal protection of the laws, as clearly shown in a Court decision that struck down the Virginia Military Institute's (VMI) male-only admission policy. The majority opinion stated that VMI violated the Fourteenth Amendment's equal protection clause because it failed to show an "exceedingly persuasive justification" for its sex-biased admissions policy.[61]

Two other areas where the Supreme Court helped advance women's rights were affirmative action and protection against sexual harassment. In 1987, the Court approved affirmative action in a case involving a woman who was promoted over a man despite the fact that he had scored slightly higher than she did on a test. The Court ruled that this was acceptable to make up for past discrimination.[62] And in 1993, the Court made it easier to sue employers for sexual harassment, saying that a woman did not have to reach the point of a nervous breakdown before claiming that she was being harassed; it was enough to demonstrate a pattern of "repeated

FIGURE » 5.4

WOMEN'S EARNINGS AS A PERCENTAGE OF MEN'S EARNINGS, 2012

There is a substantial difference between women's and men's earnings in the United States. What could account for this variation? How much do you think it has to do with levels of discrimination and how much with differences in the nature of the jobs that men and women hold?

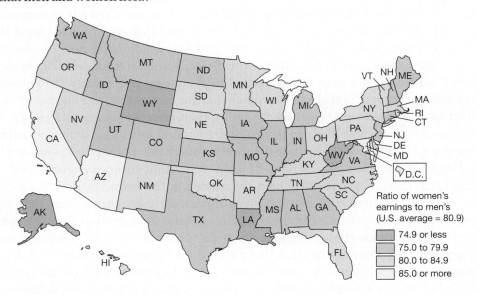

Ratio of women's earnings to men's (U.S. average = 80.9)

- 74.9 or less
- 75.0 to 79.9
- 80.0 to 84.9
- 85.0 or more

SOURCES: Data from "Highlight of Women's Earnings in 2012," *BLA Reports*, U.S. Bureau of Labor Statistics, October 2013, Table 3, p. 37, www.bls.gov/cps/cpswom2012.pdf (accessed 4/8/14); map taken from U.S. Bureau of Labor Statistics, "Women's Earnings in Washington—2012," Chart 3, www.bls.gov/ro9/wawomen.htm (accessed 4/15/14).

and unwanted" behavior that created a "hostile workplace environment."[63] Later rulings stated that if a single act is flagrant, the conduct did not have to be repeated to create a hostile environment.

More recently, Lilly Ledbetter sued Goodyear Tire and Rubber Company for having received lower pay than men doing the same work over a 20-year period, which she claimed was gender discrimination. However, the Court rejected her claim, saying that she did not meet the time limit required by the law, as the discrimination must have occurred within 180 days of the claim (this overturned the long-standing policy of the EEOC—the Equal Employment Opportunity Commission—which held that each new paycheck restarted the 180-day clock as a new act of discrimination).[64] Dissenters pointed out that pay discrimination usually occurs in small increments over long periods, so it would be impossible to recognize unequal pay within 180 days of an initial paycheck. Furthermore, workers do not have access to information about fellow workers' pay, so it would be almost impossible to meet the standard set by the Court. Congress restored the old standard in January 2009 by passing the Lilly Ledbetter Fair Pay Act. But as Figure 5.4 shows, significant pay disparities between men and women remain throughout much of the United States.

More-recent verdicts won by the EEOC include a $19 million settlement that Outback Steakhouse agreed to pay in a sex discrimination and "glass ceiling" lawsuit. Thousands of female employees at hundreds of restaurants alleged they were denied equal opportunities for advancement. The EEOC has also won large settlements for sexual harassment and pay discrimination in recent years against FedEx, Jack in the Box, Dunkin' Donuts, Ruby Tuesday, IHOP, and dozens of other corporations.[65]

CIVIL RIGHTS

CASES INVOLVING "SUSPECT CLASSIFICATION" (race, ethnicity, creed, or national origin)

STRICT SCRUTINY TEST

1. Is unequal treatment justified by a "compelling state interest"?

2. Is unequal treatment the "least restrictive" option?

YES If yes to both, discrimination is legal. However, very few cases meet this standard.

NO If not, discrimination is illegal.

CASES INVOLVING SEX OR GENDER EQUALITY

INTERMEDIATE SCRUTINY TEST

1. Is the discriminatory policy "substantially related" to an "important government objective"?

2. Is the discrimination "no greater than necessary" to achieve this objective?

YES If yes to both, discrimination is legal. Some discrimination based on gender is permitted, but this test is harder to pass than the rational basis test applied to gender cases in the past.

NO If not, discrimination is illegal.

CASES INVOLVING AGE, ECONOMIC STATUS, OR OTHER CRITERIA

RATIONAL BASIS TEST

1. Is the law rationally related to furthering a legitimate government interest?

2. Does the policy avoid "arbitrary, capricious, or deliberate" discrimination?

YES If yes to both, discrimination is legal. This is the easiest hurdle for a law or policy to pass.

NO If not, discrimination is illegal.

How It Works
In Practice

EVALUATING DISCRIMINATION CASES

Several Supreme Court cases illustrate the various tests applied to discrimination cases.

CLASSIFICATIONS BASED ON RACE

STRICT SCRUTINY TEST

1. Is unequal treatment justified by a "compelling state interest"?

2. Is unequal treatment the "least restrictive" option?

 YES

In *Grutter v. Bollinger* (2003), the Court ruled that the state's interest in racial diversity in higher education was compelling and that the University of Michigan law school's admissions policy (promoting diversity) was narrowly tailored.

NO

In *Gratz v. Bollinger* (2003), the Court struck down Michigan's undergraduate admissions policy for not being narrowly tailored.

CLASSIFICATIONS BASED ON GENDER

INTERMEDIATE SCRUTINY TEST

1. Is the discriminatory policy "substantially related" to an "important government objective"?

2. Is the discrimination "no greater than necessary" to achieve this objective?

 YES

In *Michael M. v. Superior Court* (1981), the Court upheld a California state law that men but not women could be guilty of statutory rape. The Court found that the state had a strong interest in preventing illegitimate pregnancy and in punishing only the participant who, by nature, suffers few of the consequences of his conduct.

NO

In *United States v. Virginia* (1996), the Court struck down Virginia Military Institute's male-only admissions policy as a violation of the equal protection clause of the Fourteenth Amendment.

CLASSIFICATIONS BASED ON AGE

RATIONAL BASIS TEST

1. Is the law rationally related to furthering a legitimate government interest?

2. Does the policy avoid "arbitrary, capricious, or deliberate" discrimination?

YES

Various state supreme courts have upheld the 21-year-old drinking age that applies equally to men and women on the rational basis that the law may help prevent drunk driving among 18- to 20-year-olds.

NO

In *Craig v. Boren* (1976), the Court struck down an Oklahoma law that allowed 18- to 20-year-old women but not 18- to 20-year-old men to buy 3.2% beer, rejecting the rational basis that Oklahoma had claimed and instead applying intermediate scrutiny.

POP QUIZ

1 Unequal treatment based on race is typically subject to

a strict scrutiny by the courts.

b intermediate scrutiny by the courts.

c rational basis test by the courts.

d First Amendment protections.

e majority preferences.

2 An example of unequal treatment that would pass the rational basis test is

a affirmative action programs.

b hiring whites only.

c banning Jews from certain government positions.

d preventing people under 21 years of age from drinking alcohol.

e systematically paying men more than women.

Answers: 1.a; 2.d

The largest sexual discrimination lawsuit in the nation's history was filed in 2001 against Walmart on behalf of 1.5 million women who had worked at Walmart since 1998. Among other things, the plaintiffs alleged the following:

► Over objections from a female executive, senior management regularly referred to female store employees as "little Janie Qs" and "girls."

► A Sam's Club [Walmart's warehouse retail chain] manager in California told another woman that she should "doll-up" to get promoted.

► Managers have repeatedly told female employees that men "need to be paid more than women because they have families to support."

► A male manager in South Carolina told a female employee that "God made Adam first, so women would always be second to men."

► A female personnel manager in Florida was told by her manager that men were paid more than women because "men are here to make a career and women aren't. Retail is for housewives who just need to earn extra money."[66]

But in 2011, the Court ruled that the class action lawsuit was not valid because there was no "convincing proof of a companywide discriminatory pay and promotion policy." That is, women would have to prove discrimination individually, not as a group. Civil rights experts said this was the "death knell" for class action lawsuits seeking monetary damages for discrimination.[67]

GAY RIGHTS The Supreme Court has a similarly mixed record on gay rights. The Court's decisions in the early cases were not supportive of gay rights. One of the first cases concerned Georgia's law banning sodomy. As we have discussed in Chapter 4, the Supreme Court ruled in *Bowers v. Hardwick* (1986) that homosexual behavior was not protected by the Constitution and that state laws banning it could be justified under the most lenient reasonable basis test.[68] In other cases, the Supreme Court sidestepped the controversial issue of gay rights, choosing alternative constitutional grounds to reach its decisions. For example, in 1995, the Court ruled that the South Boston Allied War Veterans Council did not have to let the Irish-American Gay, Lesbian, and Bisexual Group of Boston

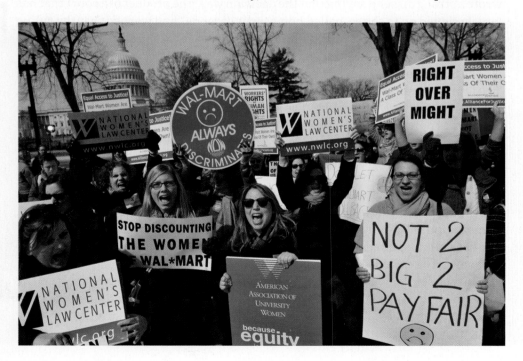

DEMONSTRATORS RALLIED IN support of the female workers who had filed a sexual discrimination lawsuit against Walmart. Betty Dukes (the lead plaintiff in the case) and a class of 1.6 million women who worked for Walmart filed a class-action suit against Walmart, claiming that Walmart paid men more than women and favored men over women when deciding on promotions. In 2011, the Supreme Court ruled in favor of Walmart, saying that women would have to prove discrimination individually rather than in a class-action lawsuit.

march in its St. Patrick's Day parade because of the veterans' First Amendment rights of free expression, thus ignoring the alternative "equal protection" claim made by the gay group.[69] A similar ruling held that the Boy Scouts of America did not have to admit an "avowed homosexual" as an assistant scoutmaster and found that New Jersey's public accommodations law did not require them to do so because of the Boy Scouts' First Amendment right of expressive association.[70]

In the first endorsement of civil rights for gays, the Court struck down in 1996 an amendment to the Colorado state constitution that would have prevented gays from suing for discrimination in employment or housing. The Court said that the state amendment violated gays' equal protection rights because it "withdrew from homosexuals, but no others, specific legal protection from the injuries caused by discrimination."[71] The Court rejected the state's "reasonable basis" arguments and came close to putting gays in the "suspect classification" that has been restricted to racial and ethnic minorities.

A more important ruling came in 2003 in a case involving two Houston men. As we have discussed in Chapter 4, John Geddes Lawrence and Tyron Garner were prosecuted for same-sex sodomy (which was illegal in Texas) after police found them having sex in Lawrence's apartment. The Supreme Court ruled in an historic 6–3 decision that the due process clause of the Fourteenth Amendment not only guarantees freedom of thought, belief, and expression, but also certain intimate conduct (including homosexual relations). This reasoning is rooted in the **substantive due process doctrine** that underlies constitutional protections for birth control, abortion, and decisions about how to raise one's children.

The decision overturned *Bowers v. Hardwick*, and the majority opinion had harsh words for that decision, saying it "was not correct when it was decided, and it is not correct today." Five members of the majority signed on to the broad "due process" reasoning of the decision, rather than the narrower reasoning in Justice O'Connor's concurring opinion, in which she said that the decision should apply only to the four states that treated homosexuals differently (that is, banning sodomy for homosexuals but not for heterosexuals). With the broader due process logic, a total of 13 state laws that banned sodomy were struck down. Justice Scalia wrote a strong dissent, saying that the decision was "the product of a court that has largely signed on to the so-called homosexual agenda" and warned that the ruling "will have far-reaching implications beyond this case." He predicted that the ruling would serve as the basis for constitutional protections for same-sex marriage.[72]

The Supreme Court issued two important rulings on same-sex marriage in 2013. The first case was a narrow ruling that reinstated same-sex marriage in California, but did not affect any other state. The second case was a more far-reaching decision that struck down part of the Defense of Marriage Act (DOMA) as a violation of the Fifth Amendment's due process clause. The majority opinion said that the federal government cannot deny benefits to same-sex couples who are legally married under state law (for more on the Supreme Court's ruling in this case, see How It Works: The Court System in Chapter 14). Through the end of 2014, 40 federal court opinions in more than 25 states have decided that same-sex marriages are not barred by the U.S. Constitution while only one appeals court has upheld a ban on same-sex marriage. The case was also cited by the 9th Circuit Court in a case saying that gays and lesbians may not be excluded from juries based on their sexual orientation.[73]

This section demonstrates that the courts can be both a strong advocate of and an impediment to civil rights. In general, however, the courts have a limited *independent* impact on policy. That is, as the school desegregation cases clearly demonstrate, the courts must rely on the other branches of government to carry out their decisions.

substantive due process doctrine One interpretation of the due process clause of the Fourteenth Amendment; in this view the Supreme Court has the power to overturn laws that infringe on individual liberties.

CONGRESS

Congress has provided the basis for today's protection of civil rights through a series of laws that were enacted starting in the 1960s. Applying to racial and ethnic minorities and to women, these laws attempted to ensure that there is a "level playing field" of equal opportunity.

KEY EARLY LEGISLATION The bedrock of equal protection that exists today stems from landmark legislation passed by Congress in the 1960s—the 1964 Civil Rights Act, the 1965 Voting Rights Act, and the 1968 Fair Housing Act. President Kennedy was slow to seek civil rights legislation for fear of alienating southern Democrats. The events in Birmingham prompted him to act, but he was assassinated before the legislation was passed. President Lyndon Johnson, a former segregationist, helped push through the Civil Rights Act when he became president. The act barred discrimination in employment based on race, sex, religion, or national origin; banned segregation in public places; and established the EEOC as the enforcement agency for the legislation. One of the southern opponents of the legislation inserted the language referring to sex, thinking that it would defeat the bill (assuming, perhaps, that there would be a majority coalition of male chauvinists and segregationists), but it became law anyway.

The Voting Rights Act of 1965 (VRA) eliminated direct obstacles to minority voting in the South, such as discriminatory literacy tests and other voter registration tests, and also provided the means to enforce the law: federal marshals were charged with overseeing elections in the South. After its passage, President Johnson hailed the VRA as a "triumph for freedom as huge as any ever won on any battlefield."[74] The VRA, which is often cited as one of the most significant pieces of civil rights legislation in our nation's history,[75] precipitated an explosion in black political participation in the South. The most dramatic gains came in Mississippi, where black registration increased from 6.7 percent before the VRA to 59.8 percent in 1967. As one political scientist noted, "The act simply overwhelmed the major bulwarks of the disenfranchising system. In the seven states originally covered, black registration increased from 29.3 percent in March, 1965, to 56.6 percent in 1971–1972; the gap between black and white registration rates narrowed from 44.1 percentage points to 11.2."[76]

The last piece of landmark legislation, the Fair Housing Act of 1968, barred discrimination in the rental or sale of a home based on race, sex, religion, and national origin. Important amendments to the law enacted in 1988 added disability and familial status (having children under age 18), provided new administrative enforcement mechanisms, and expanded Justice Department jurisdiction to bring suit on behalf of victims in federal district courts.[77]

There have been many other amendments to civil rights laws since the 1960s. Most important were the 1975 amendments to the VRA that extended coverage of many of the law's provisions to language minorities (that is, guaranteeing that registration and voting materials would be made available to voters in their native language in certain districts with large numbers of citizens who are not proficient in English); the 1982 VRA amendments, which extended important provisions of the law for 25 years and made it easier to bring a lawsuit under the act; the 1991 Civil Rights Act; and the 2006 extension of the VRA for another 25 years. The 1991 law overruled or altered parts of 12 Supreme Court decisions that had eroded the intent of Congress when it passed the civil rights legislation. It expanded earlier legislation and increased the costs to employers for intentional, illegal discrimination.

One central debate concerned the standard that had to be met in discrimination cases. Democrats in Congress pushed for a relatively tough standard that discrimination had to be "essential to business practice" in order to be permitted. For example, if a university required all assistant professors to have a PhD, and if it could be shown that more white applicants had PhDs than minority applicants, the university would have the burden of proof to demonstrate that the PhD was essential for doing the job. Although President George H. W. Bush wanted a less stringent standard of "legitimate business objectives," Congress ended up adopting language that was somewhere in between: the employer must show that the practice is "job related for the position in question and consistent with business necessity."

PROTECTIONS FOR WOMEN Women have also received extensive protection through legislation. As noted, Title VII of the Civil Rights Act, which barred discrimination based on gender, was almost an accidental part of the bill (it was included by an opponent to the legislation). Indeed, the first executive director of the EEOC would not enforce the gender part of the law because it was a "fluke." In 1966, the National Organization for Women (NOW) was formed to push for enforcement of the law. Its members convinced President Johnson to sign an executive order that eliminated sex discrimination in federal agencies and among federal contractors, but it was difficult to enforce. Finally, in 1970, the EEOC started enforcing the law. Before long, one-third of all civil rights cases involved sex discrimination, and those numbers have remained high in recent years (see Figure 5.5).

Congress passed the next piece of important legislation for women in 1972: Title IX of the Higher Education Act, which prohibits sex discrimination in institutions that receive federal funds. The law has had the greatest impact in women's

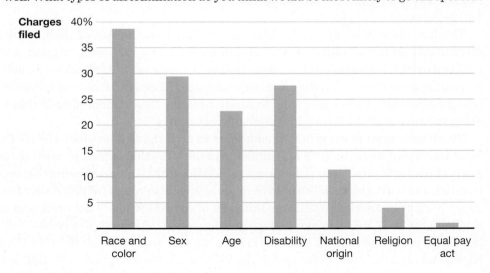

FIGURE » 5.5

DISCRIMINATION CASES IN THE EQUAL EMPLOYMENT OPPORTUNITY COMMISSION, 2013

Discrimination based on race and on sex are the two types that are most frequently reported, but there is a significant amount of discrimination based on age and disability as well. What types of discrimination do you think would be most likely to go unreported?

Note: Percentages do not sum to 100 because complaints may be filed in more than one category.

SOURCE: U.S. Equal Employment Opportunity Commission, "Charge Statistics," http://eeoc.gov/eeoc/statistics/enforcement/charges.cfm (accessed 4/15/14).

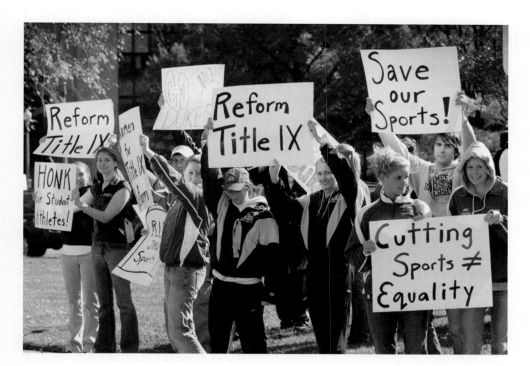

IN NOVEMBER 2006, STUDENTS from James Madison University rallied outside the Department of Education in Washington, D.C., to protest the university's plan to cut 10 of its men's athletic teams. The cuts were made to bring the school into compliance with the federal law requiring equity in men's and women's sports.

sports. In the 1960s and 1970s, opportunities for women to play sports in college or high school were extremely limited. Very few women's scholarships were available at the college level, and budgets for women's sports were tiny compared with the budgets for men's sports. Although it took nearly 30 years to reach parity between men and women, most universities are now in compliance with Title IX. Nonetheless, the law has its critics. Many men's sports, such as baseball, tennis, wrestling, and gymnastics, were cut at universities that had to bring the number of male and female student athletes into rough parity. Critics argued that such cuts were unfair, especially given that the interest in women's sports was not as high. Defenders of the law argue that the gap in interest in women's and men's sports will not change until there is equal opportunity. There is some evidence to support that claim, as interest is increasing in professional women's soccer with the NWSL (National Women's Soccer League) and professional women's basketball with the WNBA (Women's National Basketball Association), as well as in well-established women's professional sports such as golf and tennis.

Another significant effort during this period was the failed Equal Rights Amendment. The amendment was approved by Congress in 1972 and was sent to the states for ratification. Its wording was simple: "Equality of rights under the law shall not be denied or abridged by the United States or any state on account of sex." Many states passed it within months, but the process lost momentum, and after seven years (the deadline set by Congress for ratification by the states), the amendment fell three states short of the required 38 states required for adoption. The amendment received a three-year extension from Congress, but it still did not get the additional three states.

In 1994, Congress passed the Violence against Women Act, which allowed women who were the victims of physical abuse and violence to sue in federal court, and provided funding for investigating and prosecuting violent crimes against women, for helping the victims of such crimes, and for prevention programs. In 2000, part of the law was overturned by the Supreme Court, which ruled that Congress had exceeded its powers under the commerce clause.[78] Nonetheless, the funding provisions of the act were reauthorized and expanded by Congress in 2000, 2005, and then in 2013.

PROTECTIONS FOR THE DISABLED AND FOR GAY RIGHTS Yet another important piece of civil rights legislation was the 1990 Americans with Disabilities Act, which provided strong federal protections for the 45 million disabled Americans to prevent workplace discrimination and to provide access to public facilities. This law produced curb-cuts in sidewalks, access for wheelchairs on public buses and trains, special seating in sports stadiums, and many other changes that make the daily lives of the disabled a little easier and that provide them with an equal opportunity to participate more fully in society. In 2001, the Supreme Court narrowed the law's scope when it ruled that the law did not apply to state employees.[79]

Congress's track record in protecting gay rights has not been as strong. In fact, most of the steps taken by Congress have been to restrict rather than expand gay rights. In 1996, Congress passed the Defense of Marriage Act to avert the possibility that some liberal states such as Hawaii would allow gay marriage. This act defined marriage as only between a man and woman and barred couples in same-sex marriages from receiving federal insurance and Social Security spousal benefits and from filing joint federal tax returns. Nonetheless, as we have noted, the part of the law depriving same-sex spouses of federal benefits was struck down by the Supreme Court in 2013.

In what may represent a change of course, in October 2009, Congress passed the Matthew Shepard and James Byrd, Jr., Hate Crimes Prevention Act. This legislation expanded the previous hate-crimes laws based on race, color, religion, or national origin to include attacks based on a victim's sexual orientation, gender identity, or mental or physical disability. The law also lifted a requirement that a victim had to be attacked while engaged in a federally protected activity, such as attending school, for it to be a federal hate crime. In signing the bill, President Obama said, "After more than a decade of opposition and delay, we've passed inclusive hate-crimes legislation to help protect our citizens from violence based on what they look like, who they love, how they pray or who they are."[80] The law commemorates the horrific murders of James Byrd, Jr. (mentioned earlier), and Matthew Shepard, a gay teenager who in 1998 was beaten by two men, tied to a fence, and left to die. Also, the Employment Non-Discrimination Act, which would prohibit discrimination in employment based on sexual orientation, has been proposed in nearly every Congress since 1994. A version of the bill passed the House in 2007 but died in the Senate. President Obama supports the bill, but today it is unlikely to pass the Republican-controlled House.

THE PRESIDENT

The civil rights movement has benefited greatly from presidential action, such as President Truman's integration of the armed services in 1948 and President Eisenhower's use of the National Guard to enforce a court order to integrate Central High School in Little Rock, Arkansas, in 1957. Executive orders by President Kennedy in 1961 and President Johnson in 1965 established affirmative action, and in 1969 Richard Nixon expanded the "goals and numerical ranges" for hiring minorities in the federal government.

The most significant unilateral action taken by a president in the area of civil rights for gays was President Clinton's effort to end the ban on gays in the military. Clinton was surprised by the strength of the opposition to his plan, so he ended up crafting a compromise policy of "don't ask, don't tell," which pleased no one. Under

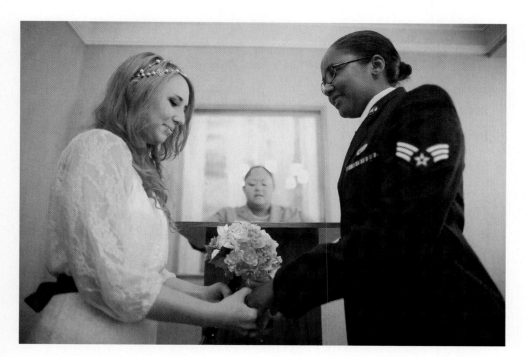

this policy, the military would stop actively searching for and discharging gays from the military ranks, and recruits would not need to reveal their sexual orientation. But if the military did find out (without conducting an investigation) that a person was gay, he or she still could be disciplined or discharged.

During the 2008 campaign, President Obama promised to repeal "don't ask, don't tell." Several attempts to change the policy toward gays in the military were stopped by Republican filibusters in 2010, but Congress finally passed the "Don't Ask, Don't Tell" Repeal Act of 2010 in December. The repeal would not go into effect, however, until 60 days after the Joint Chiefs of Staff and the president had filed a report indicating that the change in policy would not harm "military readiness and effectiveness, unit cohesion, and military recruiting and retention." That report was filed in July 2011, and the repeal went into effect on September 20, 2011. Minutes after the new policy was in place, Navy Lieutenant Gary Ross and his long-time partner were married in Vermont, and Ross became the first openly gay married person in the military.[81]

The low priority that recent presidential candidates have given to civil rights policy more generally means that it is less likely that significant and dramatic change will come from unilateral action by the president. Instead, attention to civil rights concerns in the executive branch has primarily been in two areas since 1993: racial diversity in presidential appointments and use of the bully pulpit to promote racial concerns and interests.

President Clinton was active in both areas. In 1992, as a candidate, Clinton promised a government that "looks like America." His cabinet, subcabinet, and judicial appointments achieved the greatest gender and racial balance of any in history. Fourteen percent of Clinton's first-year presidential appointments were African American (compared with 12 percent of the country's population in 1992), 6 percent were Hispanic (compared with 9.5 percent of the country's population), and the percentages of Asian Americans and Native Americans who were appointed were identical to their proportions in the population. Clinton delivered an administration that "looked like us." And even though the proportion of women appointees—27 percent—was well short of the proportion of women in the population, it still was

PRESIDENT OBAMA HAS HAD A diverse Cabinet in terms of race and gender since the beginning of his presidency, exemplified by his first-term Cabinet, shown here.

a record high. Clinton also used the bully pulpit to advocate a civil rights agenda. Most significant was his effort to promote a "National Conversation on Race," which helped focus national attention on many of the problems faced by minorities.

President George W. Bush did not achieve the same level of diversity in his appointments as had Clinton, but his administration was more diverse than the administrations of other Republican presidents had been. His initial 19 cabinet and cabinet-rank appointments included 15 men and 4 women, of whom 6 were members of racial minorities. The rhetoric that surrounded these appointments, however, was not couched in terms of affirmative action, but rather merit. Critics argued that gender and race played a central role in these decisions, just as they had with Clinton, even if the rhetoric had a different tone. Despite the different approach, Bush made serious overtures to minorities, especially Latinos, in his effort to expand the Republican party base.

Although it is too early to know the impact of the Obama presidency on the civil rights movement, the historical significance of his successful campaign as a minority candidate is clear. At the 2008 Democratic National Convention, some African-American delegates openly wept as Obama accepted the party's nomination. Many delegates had not expected that they would live to see an African American become a strong contender for the presidency. Obama's nominations for his cabinet and cabinet-level offices consisted of a diverse group of 14 men and 7 women, with 7 of them members of racial minorities. Eric Holder was the first African American to serve as attorney general, and Sonia Sotomayor is the first Latina on the Supreme Court. Obama also nominated Elena Kagan to the Supreme Court, putting three women on the Court for the first time. Obama's second-term team was similar, consisting of 14 men, 8 women, 6 of them racial minorities. In general, Obama tried to downplay race and diversity concerns. Indeed, some observers argue that Obama's victory signals the beginning of a "post-racial politics" that places less emphasis on race and devotes more attention to issues that concern all Americans, such as the economy, education, and health care. However, Obama himself rejects this view. In Obama's second term, he is attempting to use the bully pulpit to draw more attention to women's issues, such as rape on college campuses.

CIVIL RIGHTS ISSUES TODAY

EXAMINE AFFIRMATIVE ACTION AND OTHER ONGOING CIVIL RIGHTS ISSUES

There is vigorous debate over the likely direction of the civil rights movement in the twenty-first century. There are three main perspectives. The first group, whose views are articulated by such scholars as Stephan Thernstrom of Harvard University and Abigail Thernstrom of the Manhattan Institute, has suggested that our nation must "move beyond race." This group argues that on many social and economic indicators, the gap between blacks and whites has narrowed and that public opposition to race-based policies indicates the need for a new approach. The Supreme Court has largely endorsed this view by implementing a color-blind jurisprudence over a broad range of issues. The second group is represented by traditional civil rights activists and groups such as the Congressional Black Caucus and the NAACP; it argues that the civil rights movement must continue to fight for equal opportunity by enforcing existing law and pushing for equality of outcomes by protecting and expanding affirmative action programs and other policies that address racial inequality. These first two groups share the goal of racial equality and integration but differ on how much progress we have made and how to make further progress. A final group does not support the goal of integration; instead, activists such as Louis Farrakhan and the Nation of Islam argue for African-American self-sufficiency and separation. They believe that African Americans can never gain equality within what they see as the repressive, white-dominated economic and political system.

Most civil rights advocates endorse the second view. They argue that it would be a mistake to conclude that the work of the civil rights movement is complete. They point to the resegregation of public schools, persistent gaps between whites and racial minorities in health and economic status, racial profiling, hate crimes, a backlash against immigrant groups, and continuing discrimination in employment and housing. At the same time, this group rejects calls for racial separation as short-sighted and self-defeating.

The other two groups would argue that, although the traditional civil rights agenda made important contributions to racial equality, further progress will require a different approach. Advocates of the color-blind approach prefer to stop making distinctions between people based on race. They want to use government policies to make sure there is no overt discrimination and to provide equal opportunity for all, and then let merit decide outcomes. The segregationists have given up on the civil rights agenda and believe that minorities can achieve success only on their own. Debates among advocates of these three views play out over a broad range of issues, several of which are outlined in the last section of the chapter.

AFFIRMATIVE ACTION

The Civil Rights Act of 1964 ensured that, at least on paper, all Americans would enjoy equality of opportunity. But even after the act was passed, blacks continued to lag behind whites in socioeconomic status; there was still a substantial gap between the equality of opportunity and the equality of outcomes. In an important speech at Howard University in 1965, President Johnson outlined his argument for affirmative action, saying, "This is the next and the more profound stage of the battle for civil rights. . . . We seek not just legal equity but human ability, not just equality as a right and a theory but equality as a fact and equality as a result. . . . To this end equal opportunity is essential, but not enough, not enough."[82] Later that year, Johnson attempted to move closer to equality of outcomes by issuing an executive order requiring all federal agencies and government contractors to submit written proposals to provide an equal opportunity for employment of blacks, women, Asian Americans, and Native Americans within various job categories and to outline programs to achieve those goals. The policy was expanded under President Nixon, and, throughout the 1970s and 1980s, affirmative action programs grew in the private sector, higher education, and government contracting. Through such programs, employers and universities gave special opportunities to minorities and women, either to make up for past discrimination or to pursue the general goals of diversity.

Affirmative action takes many forms. The most passive type involves extra effort to recruit women and minorities for employment or college admission by placing ads in newspapers and magazines, visiting inner-city schools, or sending out targeted mailings. A more active form involves including race or gender as a "plus factor" in the admissions or hiring decisions. That is, from a pool of qualified candidates, a minority applicant may receive an advantage over white applicants. (Women generally do not receive special consideration in admissions decisions, but gender may be a "plus factor" in some employment decisions; in fact, many selective schools have been quietly applying affirmative action for men because more highly qualified women apply than men.) The strongest form of affirmative action is the use of quotas—strict numerical targets to hire or admit a specific number of applicants from underrepresented groups.

Affirmative action has been a controversial policy. Many whites view it as "preferential treatment" and "reverse discrimination." Polls indicate that minorities are much more supportive of the practice than are whites. A majority of whites support passive forms of affirmative action, such as "education programs to assist minorities in competing for college admissions," but draw the line at preferences, even when they are intended to make up for past discrimination.[83] This backlash has spilled over into state politics. California passed Proposition 209 in 1996, which banned the use of "race, sex, color, ethnicity or national origin as a criterion for either discriminating against, or granting preferential treatment to, any individual or group in the operation of the State's system of public employment, public education, or public contracting."[84] Voters in Washington State passed a similar resolution in 1998, Florida banned the use of race in college admission decisions in that year, and Michigan passed a broad ban on affirmative action in 2006. Several other state legislatures have considered taking up the issue, but the state and local decisions have been mixed. Voters in Houston, Texas, voted to continue affirmative action in their city in November 1997. The different results in various states may result from differences in the wording of the resolutions. The wording of Proposition 209 in California mentioned the hot-button term "preferential treatment," whereas the Houston resolution simply asked voters if they wanted to retain the city's affirmative action program.[85] Fifty-five percent of voters in California and 58 percent in Michigan voted to eliminate "preferential treatment," while 55 percent of Houston's voters supported keeping the city's affirmative action program.

The Supreme Court has helped define the boundaries of this policy debate. The earliest cases concerning affirmative action in employment upheld preferential treatment and rigid quotas when the policies were necessary to make up for past discrimination. The cases involved a worker training program that set aside 50 percent of the positions for blacks, a labor union that was required to hire enough minorities to get its nonwhite membership to 29.23 percent, and a state police force that was required to promote one black officer for every white even if there was a smaller pool of blacks who were eligible for promotion.[86] In each instance, there had been a previous pattern of discrimination and exclusion.

The Court moved in a more color-blind direction in an important reverse-discrimination employment case in 2009. In that case, 17 white firefighters and 1 Hispanic firefighter sued the city of New Haven, Connecticut, for throwing out the results of a test that would have been used to promote them. The city tried to ignore the results of the test because no African-American firefighters would have qualified for promotion and the city feared a "disparate impact" lawsuit. However, the Court ruled that the exam did appear to be "job related and consistent with business necessity" (as required by Section VII of the Civil Rights Act) and that unless the city could provide a "strong basis in evidence" that it would have been sued, it had to consider the results of the exam.[87]

The landmark decision for affirmative action in higher education was *University of California Regents v. Bakke* (1978).[88] Allan Bakke, a white student, sued when he was denied admission to medical school at the University of California, Davis, in successive years. Bakke's test scores and GPA were significantly higher than those of some minority students who were admitted under the school's affirmative action program. Under that program, 16 of the 100 slots in the entering class were reserved for minority or disadvantaged students. The Supreme Court agreed with Bakke that rigid racial quotas were unconstitutional but allowed race to be used in admissions decisions as a "plus factor" to promote diversity in the student body. This standard was largely unquestioned until 1996, when the 5th Circuit Court of Appeals held that it was unconstitutional to consider race in law school admissions at the University of Texas. In 2000, the 9th Circuit Court of Appeals in Seattle, however, reached the opposite conclusion and ruled that race could be considered in admissions to promote educational diversity.[89]

ABIGAIL FISHER SUED THE University of Texas over their affirmative action policy. She is shown talking to reporters outside the Supreme Court after the case was heard in 2012. The Court sent the case back to be reconsidered by the appeals court in Texas.

In two conflicting cases from the University of Michigan, a district court held that race-conscious undergraduate admissions were acceptable, but a decision a few months later in the same court held that considering race in law school admissions was not constitutional. An appeals court reversed the law school decision, leaving the Supreme Court to issue a definitive ruling in 2003. The Court's rulings were consistent with *Bakke*, saying that the law school's "holistic approach" that considered race as one of the factors in the admission decision was acceptable but that the more rigid approach for undergraduate admissions, which automatically gave minority students 20 of the 100 points needed to guarantee admission, was unacceptable.[90] Although these two decisions affirmed *Bakke*, it was the first time that a majority of the Court clearly stated that "student body diversity is a compelling state interest that can justify the use of race in university admissions."[91] In 2006, voters in Michigan passed Proposal 2, an initiative to make it illegal for state bodies to consider race in admissions and hiring decisions. Opponents initiated a lawsuit against the ban, and in 2014, the Supreme Court upheld the ban against affirmative action in public-college admissions in Michigan.[92] This means that states will be able to decide whether to consider affirmative action in higher education because the policy is neither prohibited nor required by the Constitution.

In 2008, the University of Texas at Austin was sued by a white student who claimed she was a victim of reverse discrimination. Texas had achieved a racially diverse student body by giving admission to the top 10 percent of every graduating high school class (in recent years, this policy was changed to the top 7 percent). This approach worked since most high schools in Texas were still segregated. In 2013, the Court affirmed that diversity could be a legitimate goal for the state but that the appeals court that upheld the admissions policy had failed to apply the strict scrutiny standard. The case was therefore sent back to the appeals court, which upheld Texas's affirmative action policy in July 2014. As of fall 2014, the case is being appealed to the full 5th Circuit.[93] For more on affirmative action in college admissions, see the You Decide feature.

MULTICULTURAL ISSUES

A host of issues involving the multicultural, multiracial nature of American society will become more important as whites cease to constitute the majority of the population by mid-century. Two key issues are English as the country's official language and immigration reform.

Decisions to establish English as the official language in many states have had wide-reaching consequences. For example, the Supreme Court upheld an Alabama state law requiring that the state driver's license test be conducted only in English. A Mexican immigrant, Martha Sandoval, sued under Title VI of the 1964 Civil Rights Act, claiming that the Alabama law had had a disparate impact on non-English-speaking residents. However, the Court held in *Alexander v. Sandoval* (2001) that individuals may not sue federally funded state agencies over policies that have a discriminatory effect on minorities under Title VI. This decision has had far-reaching consequences for the use of the Civil Rights Act to fight patterns of discrimination. Two areas that have been affected are education policy (for example, civil rights advocates have challenged the use of standardized testing because of its disparate impact on minorities) and environmental policy (lawsuits brought under Title VI have alleged "environmental racism" in decisions to place hazardous waste dumps in predominantly minority areas).

AFFIRMATIVE ACTION IN COLLEGE ADMISSIONS

The Court cases involving affirmative action at the University of Michigan posed some difficult questions. In the undergraduate case, Jennifer Gratz had a high school GPA of 3.76 and an ACT score of 25 (eighty-third percentile), and Patrick Hamacher had a GPA of 3.37 and an ACT of 28 (eighty-ninth percentile), but they were denied admission to the University of Michigan. The student in the law school case, Barbara Grutter, was a 43-year-old returning student who had an undergraduate GPA of 3.81 at Michigan State University and a 161 on the LSAT. All three students showed that they had higher scores than some of the minority students who were admitted under the university's affirmative action program. The legal question that the Court had to decide was whether the university's affirmative action program violated the equal protection clause of the Fourteenth Amendment and civil rights laws barring discrimination on the basis of race, or if the program could be justified as serving a "compelling state interest" under the strict scrutiny standard.

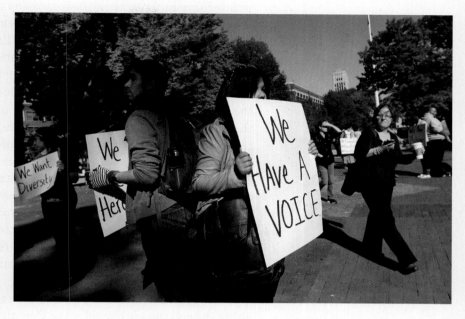

University of Michigan students demonstrate in a rally to promote diversity at the university in 2013; the Supreme Court later upheld the state's ban on affirmative action in higher education in 2014.

The crucial point of contention in the debate over the use of race in college admissions decisions is "viewpoint diversity"—that is, the claim that affirmative action produces a diverse student body. Advocates of affirmative action argue that viewpoint diversity is essential to learning and that having racial diversity in the student body is likely to produce more viewpoint diversity in classroom discussions than would occur with an all-white student body. Furthermore, proponents argue, the courts are not the proper place to decide these issues. Instead, as with the complex and highly charged topic of racial redistricting, the political branches of government are where these decisions should be made. Advocates also make a very pragmatic argument that getting rid of affirmative action would almost certainly lead to a system that is *less* rooted in merit-based admissions than the current system. This outcome is possible because states that get rid of race as a factor in admissions often adopt a "10 percent solution," which says that the top 10 percent of any graduating high school class can be admitted to the state university. Therefore, a student who may be in the top 20 percent of an excellent school might not be admitted even if she had better test scores and grades than a student who was in the top 10 percent of a high school that was not as good.

Opponents reply that supporters of affirmative action have not provided convincing evidence that racial diversity in colleges has any beneficial effects. They also argue that "viewpoint diversity" arguments assume that members of all racial minorities think alike, drawing a comparison to racial profiling in law enforcement. It is just as offensive, they say, that an admissions committee thinks that one black student has the same views as another black student as it is that a police officer may pull over a black teenage male just because he fits a certain criminal profile. Opponents also argue that affirmative action amounts to "reverse discrimination" and that any racial classification is harmful.

The Supreme Court may choose to revisit these questions; at this point, affirmative action is neither constitutionally required nor prohibited, so the states get to decide. How would you decide?

CRITICAL THINKING QUESTIONS

1. To what extent should race be used as a "plus factor" to promote racial diversity and viewpoint diversity, if at all? Is the "top 10 percent" plan in Texas a better approach?

2. Think of your own experiences in high school and college. Has racial diversity contributed to viewpoint diversity?

The second key issue, immigration, regained center stage in the wake of the September 11 terrorist attacks. At that time, some people saw immigration as a threat that must be curtailed. The government made it clear that it would not engage in racial profiling of Arab Americans—for example, subjecting them to stricter screening at airports—but many commentators argued that such profiling would be justified, and there was at least anecdotal evidence of an increase in discrimination against people of Middle Eastern descent.

Over the past two decades, immigration has been central in many political debates. The intensity of that debate increased in 2010 when Arizona enacted an anti-immigration law that requires local law enforcement officials to check the immigration status of a person in a "lawful stop, detention, or arrest" if there is a "reasonable suspicion" that the person is an illegal alien. The law also requires immigrants to always carry papers verifying their immigration status and bans people without proper documents from seeking work in public places. States with similar laws include South Carolina, Alabama, Utah, Georgia, and Indiana. Arizona governor Jan Brewer said, "Decades of federal inaction and misguided policy have created a dangerous and unacceptable situation, and states deserve clarity from the court in terms of what role they have in fighting illegal immigration."[94] Opponents of the law argue that it requires illegal racial profiling and that the federal government has the sole responsibility for deciding immigration law.

The Supreme Court struck down three of the four main provisions of the law, citing the supremacy clause of the Constitution (see Chapter 14 for details on this case). This decision meant that Congress, not the states, determines immigration law when the two laws conflict. The Court upheld the controversial "show me your papers" part of the law, saying that the state was simply enforcing the federal law. However, the Court indicated that the law must be applied in a race-neutral way and could be struck down if there was clear evidence of racial profiling.[95] Several months later, a federal district court judge cleared the way for implementation of the "show me your papers" law, saying that the Supreme Court wanted to see actual evidence of discrimination rather than speculation that the law could have a discriminatory effect.[96]

As noted in the introduction, the immigration system is widely viewed as broken and in need of reform. However, neither President Bush nor President Obama were able to get Congress to approve their proposals to provide a "path to citizenship" for undocumented immigrants. Americans are in favor of reform, but their level of support varies depending on the wording of the question. In 2014, a CBS News poll showed that 56 percent of those surveyed said that illegal immigrants "should be allowed to stay in their jobs and to eventually apply for U.S. citizenship," another 12 percent said they should be able to stay without applying for citizenship, while only 29 percent said they should have to leave the United States. When a CNN poll taken also taken in 2014 stipulated that illegal immigrants should be allowed to become citizens "if they hold a job, speak English, and are willing to pay back taxes" (which were conditions in both the Bush and Obama proposals), support for the path to citizenship increased to 81 percent (with only 17 percent saying they should be sent back to their home country).[97]

The debates over affirmative action, English as the country's official language, and immigration reform clearly illustrate the conflictual nature of civil rights policy. However, history has shown that when public opinion strongly supports a given application of civil rights—for example, the integration of African Americans in the South in the 1960s and, more recently, allowing gays to openly serve in the

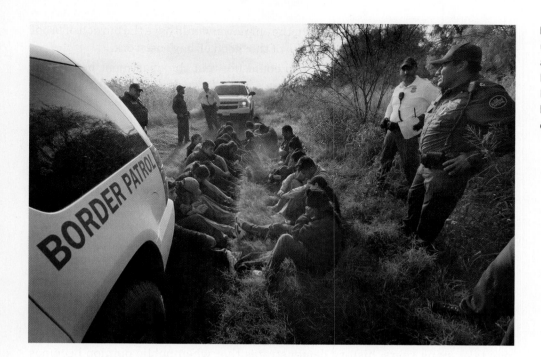

military and recognizing same-sex marriage in many states—public policy soon reflects those views. Although it is impossible to say how soon same-sex marriage will be nationally recognized or when there will be comprehensive immigration reform that includes a path to citizenship, policy appears to be headed in that direction, given the trends in public opinion.

CONCLUSION

Enforcing civil rights means providing equal protection of the law to individuals and groups that are discriminated against, which may include noncitizens and illegal immigrants. Figuring out exactly when an individual's civil rights have been violated can be tricky. When does a routine traffic stop by a police officer turn into racial profiling?

To help figure that out, we now can answer the questions about possible civil rights violations that introduced this chapter.

▶ Scenario 1: The African-American teenagers who were pulled over by the police may or may not have had their civil rights violated, depending on the laws in their state. In Massachusetts, for example, it is prohibited to consider the "race, gender, national or ethnic origin of members of the public in deciding to detain a person or stop a motor vehicle" except in "suspect specific incidents."[98] On the other hand, in the scenario in which the police pulled over white teenagers, the traffic stop would have been acceptable as long as there had been "probable cause" to justify the stop.

▶ Scenario 2: The Asian-American woman who did not get the job could certainly talk to a lawyer about filing a "disparate impact" discrimination suit.

Under the 1991 Civil Rights Act, the employer would have the burden of proof to show that she was not a victim of the "good ol' boy" network.

▶ Scenario 3: The gay couple who could not rent the apartment because of their sexual orientation might have a basis for a civil rights lawsuit based on the Fourteenth Amendment. But this would depend on where they lived, given that there is no federal protection against discrimination against gay men and lesbians (and the Supreme Court has not applied the Fourteenth Amendment in this context).

▶ Scenario 4: Court decisions concerning affirmative action at the University of Michigan show that the white student who was not admitted to the university of his choice would just have to take his lumps, as long as the affirmative action program considered race as a general "plus factor" rather than assigning more or fewer points for it (and the practice was allowed by her state).

This review of civil rights in the United States has highlighted only some of the most important issues, but a significant agenda remains. The civil rights movement will continue to use the multiple avenues of the legislative, executive, and judicial branches to secure equal rights for all Americans. Although this process may take many years, history demonstrates that when public opinion becomes more supportive of diversity and stronger civil rights, our political institutions support the views of the people.

THE CONTEXT OF CIVIL RIGHTS

▶ *Describe the historical struggles groups have faced in winning civil rights.* **(Pages 153–61)**

SUMMARY

Civil rights are protections from discrimination both by the government and by individuals and are rooted in laws and the equal protection clause of the Fourteenth Amendment. The concept of equality has evolved over time, with protections now for women, African Americans, Native Americans, Asian Americans, and Latinos. Despite our attempts to live in a color-blind society, awareness of race still influences many people's opinions and behavior.

KEY TERMS

civil rights (p. 153)
disenfranchised (p. 155)
grandfather clause (p. 155)
Jim Crow laws (p. 156)
separate but equal doctrine (p. 156)
protectionism (p. 158)

CRITICAL THINKING AND DISCUSSION

If you have ever experienced discrimination, was it overt or more subtle? How can discrimination best be addressed by the government? How was a "protectionist" policy for women justified by its proponents?

PRACTICE QUIZ QUESTIONS

1. The distinction between civil rights and civil liberties is that civil rights _____ while civil liberties _____.

   A protect against discrimination; are guaranteed in the Bill of Rights

   B are guaranteed in the Bill of Rights; protect against discrimination

   C are guaranteed in the Bill of Rights; limit what the government can do to you

   D limit what the government can do to you; protect against discrimination

   E limit what the government can do to you; are guaranteed in the Bill of Rights

2. The Missouri Compromise _____.

   A ruled that people held as slaves are not protected by the Constitution

   B established that three-fifths of the slaves could count in a state's population

   C limited the expansion of slavery while maintaining the balance of slave states

   D gave slaves the right to vote

   E ended slavery in the South

3. *Plessy v. Ferguson* established _____.

   A the legitimacy of poll taxes

   B the separate but equal doctrine

   C that Jim Crow laws were illegal

   D the process of desegregation in the South

   E the legality of slavery

4. The principle of _____ was used in many court cases to deny women equal rights.

   A matriarchy

   B separate but equal

   C sectionalism

   D misandry

   E protectionism

THE RACIAL DIVIDE TODAY

▶ *Analyze inequality among racial, ethnic, and social groups today.* **(Pages 162–65)**

SUMMARY

Beyond the unequal treatment of racial minorities, women, and LGBT individuals, inequalities in political, social, and economic conditions also persist. Whites are able to participate in politics at a higher rate, enjoy a better standard of living, and avoid prejudice in the criminal justice system.

CRITICAL THINKING AND DISCUSSION

Have you ever faced discrimination based on your race, gender, or sexual orientation? If so, what did you learn in this chapter about whether your civil rights were violated?

PRACTICE QUIZ QUESTIONS

5. *Most* of the differences in voter turnout among whites relative to racial minorities can be accounted for by _____.

   A contemporary Jim Crow laws

   B voter purge lists

   C voter ID laws

   D poll taxes

   E education and income

6. The gaps between whites and blacks on health measures are _____ and in many cases _____.

 A large; decreasing

 B large; increasing

 C small; decreasing

 D small; increasing

 E small; staying the same

7. In economic terms, the average Hispanic family is _____.

 A better off than the average white family from the same area

 B likely to have more assets than the average white family

 C roughly equal with the average white family

 D worse off than the average white family

 E more likely than any other group to be poor

....

KEY PLAYERS IN THE CONFLICT OVER CIVIL RIGHTS

▶ *Explain the approaches used to bring about change in civil rights policies.* **(Pages 166–86)**

SUMMARY

Depending on the political context, each branch of government has played a role in the expansion of civil rights. Moreover, federalism has played a role in this process. Although the state governments often lagged behind the federal government in African-Americans' civil rights, they have been on the forefront in protecting the rights of gays and lesbians.

KEY TERMS	CRITICAL THINKING AND DISCUSSION
de jure (p. 171) **de facto** (p. 171) **disparate impact standard** (p. 172) **rational basis test** (p. 174) **substantive due process doctrine** (p.180)	Which policy-making institution has historically played the most important role in protecting the civil rights of Americans? Does that institution still play that role today?

PRACTICE QUIZ QUESTIONS

8. Early in the nation's history, civil rights activism was focused on _____.

 A women

 B gays and lesbians

 C African Americans

 D Latinos

 E Native Americans

9. Early in the civil rights movement, which branch provided most of the successes?

 A state governments

 B Congress

 C the presidency

 D the bureaucracy

 E the Supreme Court

10. The difference between de facto segregation and de jure segregation is that de facto segregation _____, while de jure segregation _____.

 A is the result of circumstances; is mandated by law

 B is mandated by law; is the result of circumstances

 C applies to racial minorities; applies to women

 D applies to women; applies to racial minorities

 E applies to all groups; applies to racial minorities

11. The strongest protection as the "suspect classification" applies which test?

 A rational basis

 B strict scrutiny

 C intermediate scrutiny

 D privileged interest

 E disparate impact

12. The Voting Rights Act of 1965 _____.

 A established "majority-minority" districts

 B established compulsory voter registration for African Americans

 C eliminated direct obstacles to minority voting in the South

 D barred discrimination in the rental or sale of a home

 E reduced participation by African Americans in the South

13. Relative to the protection of individuals with disabilities, Congress's track record in protecting gay rights is _____.

 A stronger

 B about the same

 C weaker

 D nonexistent

 E more focused on job discrimination

....

CIVIL RIGHTS ISSUES TODAY

▶ *Examine affirmative action and other ongoing civil rights issues.* **(Pages 187–93)**

SUMMARY

The public is divided on the appropriateness of civil rights policies, with some groups preferring a "color-blind" and some groups preferring a "color-conscious" approach. Furthermore, the debates over issues such as affirmative action, immigration reform, and establishing English as the official language in many states indicate the level of conflict over civil rights policy. Nonetheless, when public opinion does strongly support the application of civil rights in a particular arena, policy makers generally respond to these views.

CRITICAL THINKING AND DISCUSSION

Should government attempt to provide a level playing field by making sure that there is no discrimination, or should it go beyond providing equality of opportunity to also be concerned with the equality of outcomes?

PRACTICE QUIZ QUESTIONS

14. The Supreme Court's implementation of "color-blind jurisprudence" fits the agenda of those who argue
_____.

   Ⓐ that the gap between blacks and whites has narrowed

   Ⓑ that the civil rights movement needs to continue to fight for equal opportunity

   Ⓒ that African Americans need to be separate and fully self-sufficient

   Ⓓ that equality of outcomes is important

   Ⓔ that the gap between blacks and whites has widened

15. What did the case *University of California Regents v. Bakke* establish?

   Ⓐ that race could play no role in the college admissions process

   Ⓑ that gender could play no role in the college admissions process

   Ⓒ that strict racial quotas in the admissions process were legal

   Ⓓ that race could be used as a "plus factor" in the admissions process

   Ⓔ that gender could be used as a "plus factor" in the admissions process

SUGGESTED READING

Canon, David T. *Race, Redistricting, and Representation: The Unintended Consequences of Black-Majority Districts*. Chicago: University of Chicago Press, 1999.

Dawson, Michael C. *Behind the Mule: Race and Class in African-American Politics*. Princeton, NJ: Princeton University Press, 1994.

Gross, Ariela J. *What Blood Won't Tell: A History of Race on Trial in America*. Cambridge, MA: Harvard University Press, 2008.

Hochschild, Jennifer L., Vesla M. Weaver, and Traci R. Burch. *Creating a New Racial Order: How Immigration, Multiracialism, Genomics, and the Young Can Remake Race in America*. Princeton, NJ: Princeton University Press, 2012.

Katznelson, Ira. *When Affirmative Action Was White: An Untold History of Racial Inequality in Twentieth-Century America*. New York: W. W. Norton, 2005.

Kluger, Richard. *Simple Justice: The History of Brown v. Board of Education and Black America's Struggle for Equality*. New York: Vintage, 2004.

Kousser, J. Morgan. *Colorblind Injustice: Minority Voting Rights and the Undoing of the Second Reconstruction*. Chapel Hill: University of North Carolina Press, 1999.

Lublin, David. *The Paradox of Representation: Racial Gerrymandering and Minority Interests in Congress*. Princeton, NJ: Princeton University Press, 1997.

Tate, Katherine. *Black Lawmaking in the U.S. Congress from Carter to Obama*. Ann Arbor, MI: University of Michigan Press, 2014.

Thernstrom, Stephan, and Abigail Thernstrom. *America in Black and White: One Nation, Indivisible—Race in Modern America*. New York: Simon and Schuster, 1997.

6

Public Opinion

WHY HAS APPARENT PUBLIC SUPPORT FOR GUN CONTROL NOT RESULTED IN NEW legislation? Even though polls taken after the 2012 Newtown, Connecticut, school shootings indicated broad public support for tightening restrictions on guns, understanding the nature of public opinion and the difficulty of measuring it can help us understand why gun control legislation stalled in Congress. Pictured here are teddy bears with the names and ages of the children who were shot and killed at Sandy Hook Elementary School in Newtown.

A T FIRST GLANCE, IT SEEMS CLEAR THAT AMERICANS demand stricter controls on gun ownership. In a January 2013 poll, taken soon after 20 children were killed by a mentally ill shooter in a Newtown, Connecticut, elementary school, 91 percent of respondents favored criminal background checks for gun sales, 82 percent favored increased mental health spending, 79 percent favored programs to train police and teachers how to respond to school shootings, and 73 percent favored criminal penalties for anyone who sold a gun to someone who had not passed a background check.[1] Despite apparently strong public support, none of these measures came up for a vote in Congress. This suggested to some that House members and Senators feared that a vote for gun control would prompt the National Rifle Association to run campaign ads against them. If so, wasn't this a case of politicians not listening to the people and instead giving in to the pressure of a well-funded special interest group?

Before we blame elected officials, we need to examine public opinion itself. What does it mean when someone expresses a political opinion—for example, support for a gun control proposal, or disapproval of the president's performance? Where do these sentiments come from? Are they long held or fleeting? Are these sentiments real, in the sense that they reflect judgments that shape a person's behavior, or are they just something that a person says without really believing it? Candidates, political parties, journalists, and political

CONFLICT & COMPROMISE
in American Politics

199

CHAPTER *goals*

Define public opinion and explain why it matters in American politics.

▶ PAGES 200–06

Explain how people form political attitudes and opinions.

▶ PAGES 206–11

Describe basic survey methods and potential issues affecting accuracy.

▶ PAGES 212–19

Present findings on what Americans think about major political issues.

▶ PAGES 219–29

Evaluate the relationship between public opinion and what government does.

▶ PAGES 229–31

ARE AMERICANS POORLY INFORMED ABOUT POLITICS? One survey found that more Americans could identify characters on *The Simpsons* than could list which liberties the Bill of Rights guarantees, and another found most respondents unable to name any Supreme Court justices.

scientists take thousands of polls to determine who is likely to vote; what sorts of arguments, slogans, and platforms would appeal to these voters; and which policies are in demand by the electorate. Yet, some evidence suggests that most Americans make up answers or provide random responses to poll questions. Some research indicates that the public often has no firm opinions about government policy, and that people are easily swayed by candidates, advocacy groups, or the media, and may respond inconsistently to questions that ask the same thing but are worded differently. If such studies are correct, how can we have any confidence that surveys reveal what people really think—in the sense that their stated opinions are based in reality and shape their choice? How much weight should government officials ascribe to public opinion when they tackle controversial issues like gun control?

WHAT IS PUBLIC OPINION?

DEFINE PUBLIC OPINION AND EXPLAIN WHY IT MATTERS IN AMERICAN POLITICS

public opinion Citizens' views on politics and government actions.

Public opinion describes what the population thinks about politics and government—what government should be doing, evaluations of what government *is* doing, and judgments about elected officials and others who participate in the political process, as well as the wider set of beliefs that shape these opinions.

Public opinion matters for three reasons. First, citizens' political actions—including voting, contributing to campaigns, writing letters to senators, and other kinds of activism—are driven by their opinions.[2] For example, as we discuss in more detail in Chapter 8, party identification shapes voting decisions. A voter who thinks of herself as a Democrat is more likely to vote for Democratic candidates than a voter who identifies as a Republican.[3] Therefore, if we want to understand an individual's behavior or analyze broader political outcomes, such as who wins an election or the fate of a legislative proposal, we need good data on public opinion.

Second, examining public opinion helps explain the behavior of candidates, political parties, and other political actors. Later chapters (particularly Chapter 9 and Chapter 11) show a strong link between citizens' opinions and candidates' campaign strategies and their actions in office. Politicians look to public opinion to determine what citizens want them to do and how satisfied citizens are with their behavior in office. For example, in Chapter 11, we see how congressional representatives are

POLITICIANS READ PUBLIC OPINION polls closely to gauge whether their behavior will anger or please constituents. Few politicians always follow survey results—but virtually none would agree with Calvin's father that polls should be ignored entirely.

reluctant to cast votes that are inconsistent with their constituents' preferences, especially on issues that constituents consider important. Therefore, to explain a legislator's votes, you need to begin with data on constituents' opinions.

Third, because public opinion is a key to understanding what motivates both citizens and political officials, it can shed light on the reasons for specific policy outcomes. For example, changes in the policy mood—the public's demand for new policies—are linked to changes in government spending.[4] When people want government to do more, spending increases more rapidly; when people want government to do less, spending goes down (or increases more slowly).

EARLY THEORIES OF PUBLIC OPINION

Though it may sound strange, early studies of public opinion, based on surveys conducted during the 1950s, found little evidence that the public's political opinions existed at all.[5] The surveys revealed significant inconsistency: many people expressed liberal responses to some questions and conservative responses to others. Responses also varied across time: many people who said in one survey that they favored an activist government switched to favoring a limited government when asked two years later. Few respondents could say why they liked a particular candidate or why they identified as conservative, liberal, or moderate. Americans also had low levels of factual information, such as knowing which party held majorities in the House and Senate. One author estimated that up to 70 percent of survey respondents either were making up their responses—answering more or less at random—or were unable to say anything meaningful. As he put it, "Large portions of the electorate do not have meaningful beliefs, even on issues that have formed the basis for intense political controversy among elites for substantial periods of time."[6] Only a small fraction of the electorate, perhaps 5 percent or less, was categorized as having consistent, stable beliefs—for example, an individual who was conservative across issues, favoring higher defense spending and lower spending on social programs, and expressed the same preferences when asked about them years later.

Some more recent research seems to support these claims. For example, a 2011 study found that 29 percent of Americans did not know who the vice president was—and 73 percent could not explain what the Cold War was about. If these early studies and more recent examples were the last word, there would be little need to study public opinion, because most people would have little to say, many others would make up their responses, and, most important, what little public opinion you might discern would have minimal impact on individual behavior or government actions.

CONTEMPORARY THEORY OF PUBLIC OPINION

Many of these early claims about public opinion were found to be false, the product of badly worded survey questions and the fact that since relatively few Americans monitor political events or talk about politics every day, they may have trouble expressing their opinions when asked. The bigger problem was that to capture public opinion accurately, scholars needed to expand their picture of what public opinion might look like. Early surveys sought evidence that citizens' beliefs were internally consistent, stable, and based on a rationale that citizens could explain. In contrast, the new work began with the premise that none of these conditions were necessary and that earlier scholars had failed to find evidence of public opinion because they were looking for the wrong thing, rather than because it didn't exist.[7]

DESCRIBING PUBLIC OPINION Modern theories of public opinion distinguish between two types of opinions: opinions that are pre-formed as well as opinions that are formed on the spot as needed. The first kind of opinions are broad expressions, such as how a person thinks about politics, what a citizen wants from government, or principles that apply across a range of issues. These kinds of beliefs typically form early in life and remain stable over time. Some of these beliefs are obviously political, such as party identification, **liberal or conservative ideology**, and judgments about whether elected officials lose touch with citizens. Others, such as beliefs about homosexuality or religion, may seem irrelevant to politics, but their presence on the questionnaire illustrates an important finding: Americans' political opinions are shaped by a wide range of beliefs and ideas, including some that are not inherently political.

Some of these broad beliefs are formed early in life and are relatively stable. Liberal or conservative ideology is a good example of a stable opinion: the best way to predict an American's ideology at age 40 is to assume it will match his ideology at age 20. The same is true for party identification. However, even these typically stable opinions sometimes change in response to events. In a later section, we will look more closely at how such opinions form and why they change.

MANY OPINIONS ARE LATENT The most important thing to understand about public opinion is that although ideology and party identification are largely consistent over time, they are exceptions to the rule.[8] The average person does not maintain a set of fully formed opinions on all political topics, such as evaluations of all the candidates for state or local office or assessments of the entire range of government programs. Instead, most Americans' political

liberal or conservative ideology A way of describing political beliefs in terms of a position on the spectrum running from liberal to moderate to conservative.

A PERSON'S IDEOLOGICAL perspective is relatively stable over time. People who have a conservative ideology generally oppose increasing government spending and taxes.

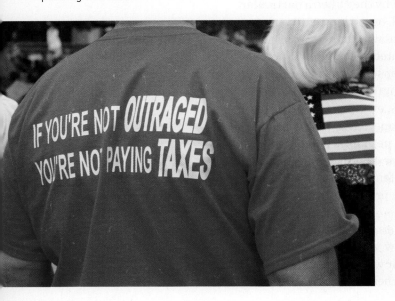

judgments are **latent opinions**: they are constructed only as needed, such as when answering a survey question or deciding just before Election Day how to vote. For example, when an individual is first asked about his opinions on global warming, he will probably not have a specific response in mind. He simply will not have thought much about the question. He might have, at best, some vague ideas about the subject. His opinions on global warming become more concrete only when he is asked to describe them.

People who follow politics closely have more pre-formed opinions than the average American, whose interest in politics is relatively low. But very few people are so well informed that they have ready opinions on a wide range of political questions. Moreover, even when people do form opinions in advance, they may not remember every factor that influenced their opinions. Thus, an individual may identify as a liberal or a conservative, or as a supporter of a particular party but may be unable to explain the reasons behind these ideological leanings.[9]

latent opinion An opinion formed on the spot, when it is needed (as distinct from a deeply held opinion that is stable over time).

HOW PEOPLE FORM OPINIONS

When people form opinions on the spot, they are based on *considerations*, the pieces of relevant information—such as ideology, party identification, religious beliefs, recent events, and personal circumstances—that come to mind when the opinion is requested.[10] The process of forming an opinion usually is not thorough or systematic, since most people don't take into account everything they know about the issue.[11] Rather, they only use considerations that come to mind immediately.[12] Highly informed people who follow politics use this process, as do those with low levels of political interest and knowledge.[13]

Consider how people decide whether they approve of the job the president is doing. Surveys on this topic typically ask respondents whether they approve or disapprove of the president's performance, although the questions' wording can vary. Figure 6.1 shows approval and disapproval percentages for President Obama through 2014. The data show a pattern that is typical for new presidents: initially high approval percentages, then a gradual decline during the first year or two in office. Generally, when a new president takes office, many voters hold high expectations about what will be accomplished during the first term. In the case of Obama, many Americans expected a speedy economic recovery and enactment of many new programs, from health care reform to climate change legislation and an expansion of LGBT individuals' rights, such as the right to marry. Others opposed these initiatives from the beginning, so they never approved of Obama's performance. The downward trend in approval for Obama reflects the fact that some voters switched their positive responses during 2009 as they became disillusioned either with Obama's failure to satisfy their policy demands or the weak state of the American economy. Obama's approval rating increased somewhat in the run-up to the 2012 election as the economy began to improve, and gradually declined in 2013 and 2014 due to continued economic weakness, various scandals including revelations about NSA surveillance and citizens' overall negative feelings about the state of the nation.

Many studies of public opinion support the idea that most people form opinions on the spot using a wide range of considerations. Consider the following findings: Attitudes about immigration are shaped by evaluations of the state of the economy.[14] People judge government spending proposals differently depending on whether a Republican or a Democrat made the proposal, using their own party identification

FIGURE » 6.1

APPROVAL RATINGS FOR PRESIDENT BARACK OBAMA

President Barack Obama had high approval ratings (around 80 percent approval) in October 2009, but his approval ratings tended to level off in February 2010 (with about 45 percent approval and 45 percent disapproval), remaining fairly level through the presidential election in November 2012. After the election, however, his approval ratings fell due to a lackluster economy, various minor scandals, and high levels of dissatisfaction with the federal government.

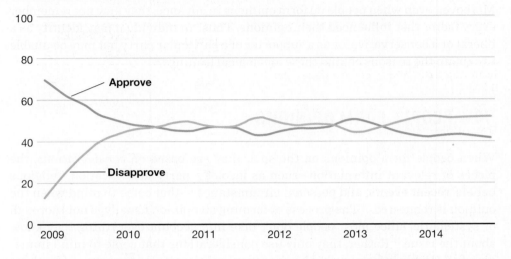

SOURCE: "President Barack Obama Job Approval," elections.huffingtonpost.com/pollster/obama-job-approval (accessed 10/15/14).

as a consideration.[15] Evaluations of affirmative action programs vary depending on whether the survey question reminds respondents that their own personal economic well-being may be hurt by these programs.[16] Voters' party identification and ideology influence their evaluations of candidates.[17] Individuals' willingness to allow protests and other expressions of opinions they disagree with depends on their belief in tolerance.[18] And if people feel obligated to help others in need, they are more likely to support government programs that benefit the poor.[19]

Sometimes competing or contradictory considerations influence the opinion-formation process. In the case of abortion laws, many people believe in protecting human life but also in allowing women to make their own medical decisions.[20] When a survey asks someone who holds both beliefs for her opinion about abortion laws, her response will depend on which consideration comes to mind and seems most relevant when she is answering the question. Opinions about other morally complex issues such as right-to-die legislation, or about race-related issues such as affirmative action, also often involve competing considerations.[21]

Events can influence considerations. Following the attacks of September 11, 2001, the Pew Research Center began surveying Americans about their fears of another terrorist attack. As Table 6.1 shows, almost every time a terrorist attack occurred during the next few years—regardless of its location—the percentage of Americans answering that they were "very worried" about a future attack rose significantly. After the July 2005 bombings in London, the "very worried" segment of the U.S. population increased from 17 to 26 percent, a jump of almost 50 percent.

TABLE » 6.1

FEARS OF TERRORIST ATTACK

In this chapter, we argue that opinions are often sensitive to new information or events. Is this true of worries about future terrorist attacks? Besides assessing whether respondents had followed the events very closely, the survey asked if respondents were very worried that there would be another terrorist attack on the United States. "Before" percentages are from the closest available survey prior to the incident and "after" percentages are from the closest survey following the incident.

	FOLLOWED VERY CLOSELY	VERY WORRIED	
		BEFORE	AFTER
Terrorist attacks in New York and Washington, D.C. (9/01)	74%	—	28%
Failed shoe bombing on Paris flight (1/02)	20	13%	20
Arrest of alleged "dirty bomber" (6/02)	30	20	32
Terrorist bombings in Kenya (12/02)	21	20	31
Terrorist bombings in Madrid (3/04)	34	13	20
Terrorist bombings in London (7/05)	48	17	26
Thwarted British terrorist plot (8/06)	54	17	25
U.S. Special Forces kill Osama bin Laden (5/11)	50	—	22
Bombing at the Boston Marathon (4/13)	63	21	23

SOURCES: Pew Research Center, "American Attitudes Hold Steady in Face of Foreign Crises," August 16, 2006, www.people-press.org/reports/display.php3?ReportID=285; Pew Research Center, "More Optimism about Afghanistan but No Boost in Support for Troop Presence," May 3, 2011, www.people-press.org/2011/05/03/more-optimism-about-afghanistan-but-no-boost-in-support-for-troop-presence/ (accessed 4/18/12); Pew Research Center, "Most Expect 'Occasional Acts of Terrorism' in the Future." April 23, 2013, www.people-press.org/2013/04/23/most-expect-occasional-acts-of-terrorism-in-the-future/ (accessed 11/25/13).

PERSONAL KNOWLEDGE AND CONSIDERATIONS

Most Americans form legitimate, meaningful opinions when they are needed. Though they don't usually seek out new information or take account of everything they know, their opinions reflect at least some of their knowledge of politics, as well as their bedrock ideological beliefs and their ideas about what they want from government.

One of the most appealing features of this description of public opinions about politics is that it resembles the way most people think about other aspects of their lives. Do you prefer blue or black jeans? Coke or Pepsi? Jon Stewart or Stephen Colbert? Regular coffee, decaffeinated coffee, or tea? These decisions are probably easy because you face them every day and, as a result, you are likely to have highly accessible opinions about which option you prefer. You don't have to think much to form your opinion. Now consider a different question: What kind of house would you like to own? If you are in your late teens or early twenties, you probably have not thought much about this. New or old? Ranch, split-level, colonial, bungalow, Victorian, or contemporary? Granite counters, slate, Formica, or Corian? Oil, gas, or electric heat—or solar? How do you feel about walkout basements, decks, wall color, floor coverings, and appliances? The list is virtually endless.

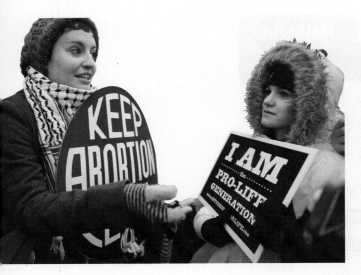

IMAGES OF CONFRONTATION
between pro-choice and pro-life protesters may conceal the more nuanced considerations that underlie most Americans' opinions about abortion. A majority of Americans believe that the decision to have an abortion should be left up to the woman but are uncomfortable allowing unrestricted access to the procedure.

If today someone asked you to describe your preferred house, it is likely that you could only begin to answer the question. You would probably base your response on a relatively small set of ideas, using a few mental snapshots of your image of the perfect house and relying on your impressions of the houses you have lived in. You would probably say something very different if you had a longer time to think about it, were asked the same question on a different day, or were asked at a time when you were actually in the market for a house—or after you already owned one.

This strategy is exactly how most Americans form their opinions about politics. When someone is asked for an opinion on a political question she knows little about, she bases her response on a few general, simple considerations. A question about gun control may call to mind a recent school shooting, the respondent's love for hunting (or her dislike of venison), an armed robbery of a nearby store, or even her views on the president's recent performance. These considerations may not lead to the most well-thought-out answer, but they may be all that many people use to form their opinions.

This description of how most people think about politics explains some of the poll data cited at the beginning of this chapter. Strong support for gun control after the Newtown shooting was to some extent a response to the tragedy. Over time, as the debate in Washington over gun control split along party lines, support for all of these measures began to decline, probably reflecting the increased use of partisan considerations to form opinions. In fact, by November 2013, overall support for gun control had returned to pre-shooting levels, with Americans evenly split on the need for additional laws.[22] Given these opinions, it is not surprising that no new laws were passed.

Thinking about opinions in terms of considerations implies that it is impossible to measure public opinion once and for all. Even if nothing major happens—no big events, new proposals, or other high-profile political activity—opinions may change as people call up different considerations. Such variation does not mean that people are indecisive or that they do not understand what they are being asked. Rather, it reflects how the average person thinks and develops opinions.

EXPLAIN HOW PEOPLE FORM POLITICAL ATTITUDES AND OPINIONS

WHERE DO OPINIONS COME FROM?

This section describes the sources of public opinion. Some influences come from early life experiences, such as exposure to the beliefs of parents, relatives, or teachers; others result from later life events. Politicians also play a critical role in the opinion-formation process.

SOCIALIZATION: FAMILIES AND COMMUNITIES

political socialization The process by which an individual's political opinions are shaped by other people and the surrounding culture.

Theories of **political socialization** show that many people's political opinions start with what they learned from their parents. These principles include a liberal or conservative ideology, level of trust in others, class identity, and ethnic identity.[23] There is also a high correlation between both the party identification and the liberal or conservative ideology of parents and those of their children.[24] These principles are not necessarily permanent; in fact, people sometimes respond to events by modifying their opinions, even those developed early in life. Even so, for many people, ideas learned during childhood continue to shape their political opinions throughout their lives.[25]

There is also some emerging evidence that biological factors such as genes and personality traits shape how we think about politics. For example, there is some evidence that genes may drive socialization—we think about politics as our parents do both because we learned from them and because we have the same genetic makeup, and these genes shape our political thinking.[26] Other research appears to show a relationship between genes and voter turnout in elections.[27] Similarly, some political psychologists believe that the "Big Five" personality traits—agreeableness, openness, conscientiousness, extraversion, and neuroticism—influence behavior, and political scientists have indeed found that these traits correlate with political activity.[28] People with high agreeableness, for example, are more likely to favor economic policies that help the disadvantaged, and they are more likely to participate in local politics. However, these findings are on the very frontier of political science research, and much more work will be needed to establish how genes and personality shape public opinion and political behavior.

Beyond these influences, research finds broader aspects of socialization that shape political opinions. People are socialized by their communities, the people they interact with while growing up, such as neighbors, teachers, clergy, and others.[29] Support for democracy as a system of government and for American political institutions is higher for individuals who take a civics class in high school.[30] Growing up in a homogeneous community, one where many people share the same cultural, ethnic, or political beliefs, increases an adult's sense of civic duty—his belief that voting or other forms of political participation are important social obligations.[31] Volunteering in community organizations as a child also shapes political beliefs and participation in later life.[32] Engaging in political activity as a teenager, such as volunteering in a presidential campaign, generates higher levels of political interest as an adult; it also strengthens the belief that people should care about politics and participate in political activities.[33]

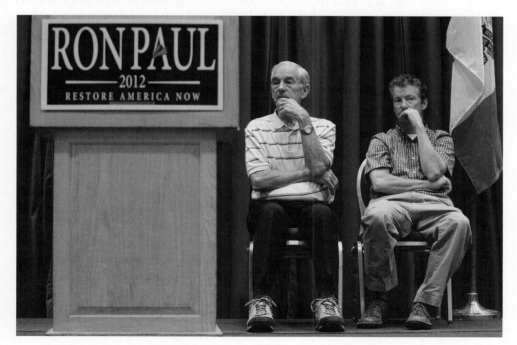

CHILDREN TEND TO ADOPT THEIR parents' ideology and party affiliation. Senator Rand Paul (right) and his father, the presidential candidate and House member Ron Paul, are both Republicans and share a libertarian ideology.

EVENTS

Although socialization often influences individuals' fairly stable core beliefs, public opinion is not fixed. All kinds of events—from everyday interactions to traumatic, life-changing disasters—can capture a person's attention and force her to revise her understanding of politics and the role of government. For example, though an individual's initial partisan affiliation likely reflects her parents' leanings, this starting point will change in response to subsequent events such as who runs for office, what platforms they campaign on, and their performance in office.[34]

Some events that shape beliefs are specific, individual experiences. For example, someone who believes that he managed to get a college degree only because of government grants and guaranteed student loans might favor a large, activist government that provides a range of benefits to its citizens. Other events shape the beliefs of large numbers of people in similar ways. Political realignments are a good example. A realignment is a nationwide shift in which many people move from identifying with one political party to identifying with another (see Chapter 8). Beginning in the early 1960s, large numbers of white southerners shifted their party identification from Democratic to Republican. This gradual change was driven by national events, including support of civil rights and voting rights legislation by many Democratic elected officials in Washington.[35]

Recent events have also shaped beliefs. Scholars have shown that after the 9/11 terrorist attacks, many citizens became more willing to restrict civil liberties to reduce the chances of future attacks.[36] Support for restrictions increased soon after the 9/11 attacks and remained elevated even 10 years later, suggesting a long-term change in public opinion, although these opinions may be further revised in light of revelations in 2013 about governmental surveillance of Americans' cell phone calls. Similarly, many Americans responded to the financial crisis of 2008 by reducing their expectations about future income and changing their spending patterns, becoming less willing to incur debt for new homes, cars, and vacations.[37]

Events hold a similar sway over other opinions, such as presidential approval, which is driven by factors such as changes in the economy. Presidents are more likely to have high approval ratings when economic growth is high and inflation and unemployment are low, whereas their approval ratings fall when growth is negative and unemployment and inflation are high. Many of these factors shape attachments to political parties.[38]

Some events have a greater impact on public opinion than others, and some people are more likely than others to change their views. Political scientist John Zaller has shown that opinion changes generated by an event or some other new information are more likely when an individual considers the event or information to be important and when it is unfamiliar; in such cases, the individual does not have a set of preexisting principles or other considerations with which to interpret the event or information. Changes in opinions are also more likely for people who do not have strong beliefs than they are for people who hold strong opinions.[39]

Because events matter in shaping opinion, political scientists often find *generational effects,* differences in opinions that vary with respondents' age. For example, the percentage of Americans aged 50 and over who believed luck to be the major reason there had not been a major attack since 9/11 was almost double (42 percent versus 22 percent) the percentage of Americans aged 18 to 29 who expressed the same belief.

Finally, as we discuss in Chapter 7, the news media serve both as a source of information and as a delivery mechanism for many of the other ways people get socialized. For example, the reaction to events depends on how political

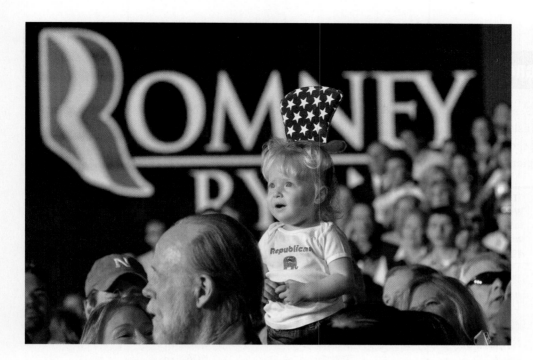

ALTHOUGH EVENTS SUCH AS WARS, economic upheavals, and major policy changes certainly influence public opinion, research shows that most Americans acquire some political opinions early in life from parents, friends, teachers, and others in their community.

information is delivered to people. A study of public opinion on the death penalty found that opposition to the death penalty increased as media coverage of death penalty cases began to deemphasize moral arguments and put more emphasis on the possibility that innocent people were being mistakenly executed.[40] We discuss this phenomenon, known as framing, in the next chapter.

GROUP IDENTITY

Individuals' opinions are also influenced by social categories or groups, such as gender, race, income, and education level. Political scientists refer to these differences in opinion as *cohort effects*. These characteristics might shape opinions in three ways. First, people learn about politics from the people around them. Therefore, those who live in the same region or who were born in the same era might have common beliefs because they experienced the same historical events at similar points in their lives or learned political viewpoints from one another. In the United States, opinions on many issues are highly correlated with the state or region where a person grew up. For example, until the 1970s, relatively few native white southerners identified with the Republican Party.[41] Even today, native white southerners tend to have distinctly different attitudes about many issues (such as less support for affirmative action policies) and hold different attitudes (such as lower support for government involvement in creating racial equality) when compared to people of color and people from other regions of the country.[42]

Individuals also may rely on others who "look like" them as a source of opinions. Political scientists Donald Green, Bradley Palmquist, and Eric Schickler, for example, argue that group identities shape partisanship: when someone is trying to decide between being a Republican or a Democrat, she thinks about which demographic groups are associated with each party and picks the party that has more members from the groups she thinks she is a part of.[43]

One reason for looking at group variations in public opinion is that candidates and political consultants often formulate their campaign strategies in terms of

TABLE » 6.2

THE IMPORTANCE OF GROUPS

The General Social Survey (GSS) has been conducted since 1972 to assess the opinions of Americans on certain key issues. Those who take the surveys are asked to indicate if they agree or disagree with statements such as those shown in the table. The percentages indicate those who agree with the statements. Group differences based on such factors as gender, age, race, family income, and region of the country have been shown to affect the answers given by the respondents.

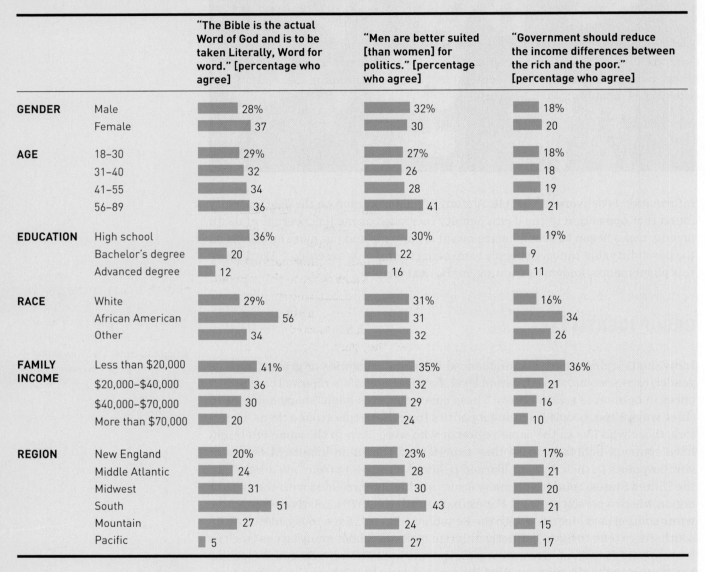

		"The Bible is the actual Word of God and is to be taken Literally, Word for word." [percentage who agree]	"Men are better suited [than women] for politics." [percentage who agree]	"Government should reduce the income differences between the rich and the poor." [percentage who agree]
GENDER	Male	28%	32%	18%
	Female	37	30	20
AGE	18–30	29%	27%	18%
	31–40	32	26	18
	41–55	34	28	19
	56–89	36	41	21
EDUCATION	High school	36%	30%	19%
	Bachelor's degree	20	22	9
	Advanced degree	12	16	11
RACE	White	29%	31%	16%
	African American	56	31	34
	Other	34	32	26
FAMILY INCOME	Less than $20,000	41%	35%	36%
	$20,000–$40,000	36	32	21
	$40,000–$70,000	30	29	16
	More than $70,000	20	24	10
REGION	New England	20%	23%	17%
	Middle Atlantic	24	28	21
	Midwest	31	30	20
	South	51	43	21
	Mountain	27	24	15
	Pacific	5	27	17

SOURCE: Data from General Social Survey 1972–2012, Cumulative Datafile, Survey Documentation and Analysis (SDA) at UC Berkeley, http://sda.berkeley.edu/archive.htm (accessed 3/24/14).

groups. For example, analyses of the 2012 election argued that Obama's presidential win was driven by high levels of support from young Americans, African Americans, Hispanics, and women.[44]

Table 6.2 reports data on the variation in opinions across different groups of Americans, as measured in the General Social Survey. The table shows group differences on three broad questions: an individual's feelings about the Bible, the role of women in politics, and whether government should redistribute income (that is, tax some people and give the money to others as credits or benefits). There are sharp differences among groups on some questions. For example, people of different education levels tend to respond very differently to a question about whether the Bible is the actual word of God: of respondents with a high school education, about 35 percent agree with the statement shown in the table, compared with only 12 percent of respondents with an advanced degree. However, the data also show a great deal of consensus. There is little variation between men and women on the role of women in politics, although relatively sharp regional and educational differences are apparent.

These data indicate that group characteristics can be important predictors of some of an individual's opinions, but they are not the whole story.[45] Americans' opinions are also a product of their socialization and life experiences. A person's group characteristics may tell us something about his opinions on some issues but reveal little about his thoughts on other issues.

POLITICIANS AND OTHER POLITICAL ACTORS

Opinions and changes in opinion are also subject to influence by politicians and other political actors. The latter group includes political parties and party leaders; interest groups; and leaders of religious, civic, and other large organizations. In part, this link exists because Americans look to these individuals for information based on their presumed expertise. For example, if you do not know what to think about immigration reform or Obamacare, you might seek out someone who knows more about the issues than you do; if that person's opinions seem reasonable, you might adopt them as your own.[46] Of course, people do not search haphazardly for advice; they only take account of an expert's opinions when they generally agree with the expert, perhaps because they are both conservatives, or Democrats, or because the individual has some other basis for thinking their preferences are alike.

Politicians and other political actors also work to shape public opinion. Political scientists Lawrence Jacobs and Robert Shapiro argue that politicians describe proposals through arguments and images designed to tap the public's strong opinions, with the goal of winning support for these proposals.[47] Although President Obama and his staff expended much time and effort to promote health care reform, giving dozens of public speeches, holding rallies, and briefing legislators, opponents of the proposal were able to shape the opinions of many Americans by making dire pronouncements about what the proposal might do. While health care reform was eventually passed into law in April 2010, these opposition efforts turned majority public support into a dead heat at the time of enactment, and likely contributed to the strong opposition that continues to this day.

In sum, public opinion at the individual level is driven by many factors, most notably life experiences, including current events as we perceive them. In the case of gun control, for example, beliefs are likely to depend on an individual's background—whether he owns a gun, hunts, or knows someone who does; his political beliefs, including how tolerant he is of government regulation of individual behavior; as well as horrific events involving guns. Thus, although public opinion may shift somewhat in response to events like the Newtown shooting, such events are only one factor that shapes opinion. As a result, even though an event may be momentous, the shift in opinion may be quite small.

POLITICIANS ON BOTH SIDES OF THE debate tried to influence public opinion about health care reform. While Obama and the Democrats sought to convince Americans that the new plan was necessary, opponents played up the possible disadvantages, with references to "death panels" and other dangers.

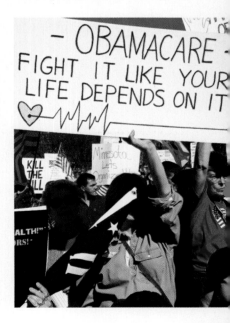

MEASURING PUBLIC OPINION

mass survey A way to measure public opinion by interviewing a large sample of the population.

population The group of people that a researcher or pollster wants to study, such as evangelicals, senior citizens, or Americans.

sample Within a population, the group of people surveyed in order to gauge the whole population's opinion. Researchers use samples because it would be impossible to interview the entire population.

For the most part, information about public opinion comes from **mass surveys**— in-person or phone interviews with hundreds or thousands of individuals. The aim of a mass survey is to measure the attitudes of a particular **population**, or group of people, such as the residents of a particular congressional district, evangelicals, senior citizens, or even the entire adult population in America (see How It Works: Measuring What A Nation of 320 Million Thinks: A Checklist). For large groups such as these, it would be impossible to survey everyone. So, surveys typically involve **samples** of between a few hundred and several thousand individuals. One of the principal attractions of mass surveys is that they can, in theory, provide very accurate estimates of public opinion for a large population (such as a state, or even the entire United States) using relatively small samples. This property of surveys is detailed in Nuts & Bolts 6.1. For example, although polls taken early in a presidential campaign (such as a year in advance of the election) are poor predictors of the ultimate outcome on Election Day, polls taken at the beginning of the official presidential race, when both party's nominees are known, can provide very good predictions of who will win the election and how many votes they will receive.[48]

An alternate technique for measuring public opinion uses focus groups, which are small groups of people interviewed in a group setting. Focus groups allow respondents to answer questions in their own words rather than being restricted to a few options in a survey question, and they can provide deep insights into why people hold the opinions they do. Candidates sometimes use focus groups to test campaign appeals or fine-tune their messages. However, because of their small size, focus groups cannot be used to draw conclusions about public opinion across the entire country.

Large-scale surveys such as the American National Election Study (ANES), which is conducted every election year (typically both before and after the general election), use various types of questions to measure citizens' opinions. In presidential election years, participants in the ANES are first asked whether they voted for president. If they say they did, they are asked which candidate they voted for: a major party candidate (Barack Obama or Mitt Romney in 2012), an independent candidate, or some other candidate.

Another kind of survey question measures people's preferences using an *issue scale*. For a range of topics, two opposing statements are given, and respondents are asked to agree with the one that comes closest to their views, including options in the middle of the two extremes. As we discuss later, on questions such as these, most Americans pick positions in the middle of these scales.

A typical survey will ask about a hundred questions related to issues and candidates, along with additional questions that elicit personal information such as a respondent's age, education, marital status, and other factors. Some surveys conducted by candidates or political parties are shorter, focusing on voter evaluations of the candidates and the reasons for these evaluations. In the main, the length of a survey reflects the fact that interviewing people is expensive, so there is a trade-off between learning more about each respondent's opinions and maximizing the number of individuals included in the survey—the fewer the number of questions that are asked, the higher the number of people who can be interviewed, given the time and cost constraints.

SAMPLING ERROR IN MASS SURVEYS

The **sampling error** in a survey (the predicted difference between the average opinion expressed by survey respondents and the average opinion in the population, sometimes called the margin of error) using a random sample depends on the sample size. Sampling error is large for small samples of around 200 or less, but decreases rapidly as sample size increases.

The graph shows how the sampling for a random sample decreases as sample size increases. For example, in surveys with 1,000 respondents, the sampling error is 3 percent, meaning that 95 percent of the time, the results of a 1,000-person survey will fall within the range of 3 percentage points above or below the actual percentage in the population that holds a particular opinion surveyed. If the sample size was increased to 5,000 people, the sampling error would decline to 1.4 percent.

Sampling errors need to be taken into account in interpreting what a poll says about public opinion. For example, a November 2013 Rasmussen poll of 1,500 Americans found that 46 percent approved of President Obama's performance in office, whereas 55 percent disapproved. Because the difference in support (9 points) exceeds the sampling error (about 2.5 points), it is reasonable to conclude that more Americans disapprove of Obama's performance than approve.

In contrast, suppose the poll found a narrow 51 to 49 percent split slightly favoring approval. Because the difference in support is smaller than the sampling error, it would be a mistake to conclude that the majority of

Americans approve of Obama. Even though more people in the sample express this opinion, there is a good chance that the opposite is true in the overall population.

You don't need to calculate sampling errors to make sense of political polls—just keep two things in mind. First, large samples (1,000 or more) are much more likely to provide accurate information about population opinions compared with small ones (less than 500). Second, be cautious when you read about small differences in survey responses, as these patterns are unlikely to hold true in the entire population.

An important development in recent years is the use of techniques to combine different surveys into a more powerful measure of public opinion. One technique is to simply average survey results—that is, if two surveys ask about support for candidates A and B, with one reporting a 60–40 split and the other a 50–50 dead heat, the two surveys will be averaged and a 55–45 split will be shown. More sophisticated techniques, such as those used by Nate Silver at FiveThirtyEight.com and by political scientist Simon Jackman at pollster.com, weight data from different polls based on their accuracy in previous elections. Silver's and Jackman's techniques also combine state- and national-level results to generate predictions—thus, if a poll finds that candidate A is ahead in state 1, and polls have found that the winner in state 1 will also win state 2, then the results from state 1 will be used to predict the result in state 2. These techniques generate powerful predictions of election returns—for example, Silver was able to correctly predict the winner of 49 out of 50 states in the 2008 and 2012 presidential elections.

sampling error A calculation that describes what percentage of the people surveyed may not accurately represent the population being studied. Increasing the number of respondents lowers the sampling error.

PROBLEMS IN MEASURING PUBLIC OPINION

Although measuring public opinion might seem an easy task—just find some people and ask them questions!—it is actually very complicated. The problems begin with determining and gathering an appropriate, representative sample of subjects. These difficulties are compounded by issues pertaining to the wording of the questions, and further complicated by the very nature of public opinion itself. Consequently, survey results must be read carefully, taking into account who is being surveyed, when they are being surveyed, what opinions people are being asked about, and what mechanism is used to ask survey questions.

random sample A subsection of a population chosen to participate in a survey through a selection process in which every member of the population has an equal chance of being chosen. This kind of sampling improves the accuracy of public opinion data.

ISSUES WITH SURVEY METHODS Building a **random sample** of individuals is not an easy task. One standard tactic is to choose households at random from census data and to send interviewers out for face-to-face meetings, or to contact people by telephone using random digit dialing, which allows surveyors to find people who have unlisted phone numbers or who only use a cell phone. In theory, each of these techniques produces a random sample, but in practice, they both may deviate from this ideal. For example, face-to-face interviews of people in their homes during work hours won't include adults who work during the day and are not home.

To keep costs down, many organizations use other strategies. These may include Internet polling, in which volunteer respondents log on to a website to participate in a survey, or robo-polls, in which a computer program phones people and interviews them. Although these techniques are less expensive, there are serious doubts about the randomness of the samples they produce.[49] (*Push polls*, in which a campaign uses biased survey questions as a way of driving support away from an opponent, are not legitimate polls because they are not designed to measure opinion—they are designed to shape it and are a form of negative campaigning; see Chapter 9.)

The wording of questions can also influence survey results. Figure 6.2 shows four different questions asked during summer 2013 to measure opinions about government surveillance of e-mails and cell phone calls. As you can see, support for greater government surveillance depends on whether a question mentions that surveillance has been ordered by a court, that the motivation is to deter terrorists, what kind of data is collected, and what method of collection is used.

UNRELIABLE RESPONDENTS Another problem with surveys is that people are sometimes reluctant to reveal their opinions. Rather than speaking truthfully, they often give socially acceptable answers or answers that they believe the interviewers want to hear. In the case of voter turnout in elections, up to one-fourth of respondents who say they voted when surveyed actually did not vote at all.[50] Political scientists refer to this behavior as the social desirability bias, meaning that people answering survey questions were less willing admit to actions or express opinions, such as racial prejudice, which they believed their neighbors or society at large would disapprove of.[51]

Pollsters use various techniques to address this problem. One approach is to verify answers whenever possible, such as checking with County Boards of Election to see if respondents who said they voted had actually gone to the polls. When there is concern that respondents will try to hide their prejudices, pollsters sometimes frame a question in terms of the entire country rather than the respondent's own beliefs. For example, during the 2012 presidential primaries, rather than asking respondents whether they were willing to vote for a Mormon candidate (such as Republicans Mitt Romney or John Huntsman), some pollsters posed the

MEASURING WHAT A NATION OF 320 MILLION THINKS: A CHECKLIST

A RANDOM SAMPLE

Were the people who participated in the survey selected randomly, such that any member of the population had an equal chance of being selected?

SAMPLE SIZE

How many people do researchers need to survey to know what 320 million Americans think? Major national surveys usually use a sample of 1,000–2,000 respondents.

SAMPLING ERROR

As Nuts & Bolts 6.1 explains, for a group of any size (even 320 million), 95 percent of the time a survey of 1,000 randomly selected respondents will measure the average opinion in a population within 2 percentage points. Reputable surveys will usually give the sampling error (sometimes also called "margin of error").

QUESTION WORDING

Did the way the question was worded influence the results? Scientific surveys try to phrase questions in a neutral way, but even in reputable polls, differences in question wording can influence answers.

RELIABLE RESPONDENTS

Respondents often give socially acceptable answers rather than truthful ones—or invent opinions on the spot. Is there a reason to think people may not have answered a survey honestly and thoughtfully?

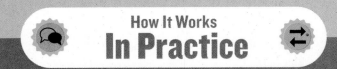

How It Works
In Practice

SURVEYING THE 2012 ELECTIONS: TWO APPROACHES

To illustrate how these requirements for good survey design play out in real life, we examine how two well-known polling organizations, the Pew Research Center and Rasmussen Reports, designed polls to measure presidential preference during the 2012 campaign.

	RASMUSSEN REPORTS[1]	PEW RESEARCH CENTER[2]	OUTCOME
A RANDOM SAMPLE	Use a land-line only sample.	Generate a random sample of Americans, including people who only have cell phones.	Rasmussen misses people who only use cell phones (many of whom are younger and are Democrats).
SAMPLE SIZE	Survey the first person who answers the phone.	When you call a residence, only talk to the person who's in your sample.	Rasmussen is biased toward people likely to answer the phone. These people tend to be older and include more men than average.
SAMPLING ERROR	If there are more Democrats in your sample than you expect, adjust your results to reduce support for Obama.	If the partisan divide in the sample is not what you expect, treat it as a finding—people may be changing their party ID.	Adjusting for partisanship assumes that no changes in party ID have occurred since the last election.
RELIABLE RESPONDENTS	Use a computer script, and only call once. Do the survey in a short time period (hours).	Use a live interviewer, and call back people you miss the first time. Implement the survey over several days.	Rasmussen tactic lowers response rate. Rasmussen tactic makes poll results sensitive to short-term events.

Pew's results were generally regarded as more reliable than Rasmussen's—and ultimately made better predictions about the 2012 results. Furthermore, Rasmussen kept its data largely private, while Pew released its questionnaire. This made Pew's survey verifiable and provided an opportunity for further analysis.

[1] Rasmussen Reports, "Election 2012: Ohio President," November 5, 2012, www.rasmussenreports.com/public_content/politics/ elections/election_2012/election_2012_presidential_election/ohio/election_2012_ohio_president (accessed 9/10/14).

[2] Pew Research Center, "Obama Gains Edge in Campaign's Final Days," November 4, 2013, www.people-press.org/2012/11/04/obama-gains-edge-in-campaigns-final-days/ (accessed 9/10/14).

POP QUIZ

1 To measure public opinion, most reputable national surveys use a sample of

  a 320 million people.
  b 2–5 percent of the population.
  c at least 10,000 people.
  d 1,000–2,000 people.
  e none of the above

2 Which of the following means that each individual in the population has an equal chance of being selected?

  a random sample
  b reliable respondents
  c sampling error
  d sample size
  e none of the above

Answers: 1.d, 2.a

FIGURE » 6.2

THE IMPACT OF QUESTION WORDING ON OPINIONS

How questions are worded can affect survey results. In this 2013 survey on the surveillance of phone records and digital metadata by the National Security Agency (NSA), support or opposition to the NSA surveillance changed based on whether the questions mentioned court approval or the terrorist threat and based on the types and source of data. In light of how the responses to survey questions are shaped by the precise wording of these questions, what sort of question would you ask if your goal was to show that Americans favored increased surveillance? What if you wanted to show high levels of opposition?

		Favor	Oppose	Don't know
Mention of courts	Court approval mentioned	37%	56%	7%
	No mention of court approval	25	67	8
	Difference	+12	−11	
Mention of terrorism	Anti-terrorism efforts mentioned	35%	57%	8%
	No mention of anti-terrorism efforts	26	67	7
	Difference	+9	−10	
Type of data collected	Metadata	34%	59%	7%
	Recordings and text	28	64	7
	Difference	+6	−5	
Source of data	Phone calls	31%	60%	9%
	E-mail communications	31	63	6
	Difference	0	−3	

SOURCE: Pew Research Center, "Government Surveillance: A Question Wording Experiment," July 26, 2013, www.people-press.org/2013/07/26/government-surveillance-a-question-wording-experiment (accessed 11/26/13).

question indirectly, asking whether a respondent believed that the country was ready for a Mormon president.

THE ACCURACY OF PUBLIC OPINION As previously noted, early theories of public opinion held that the average American's views about politics were incomplete at best and wildly inaccurate at worst. Modern theories have revised these conclusions. It is true that many Americans have significant gaps in factual information, such as which party controls the House or the Senate.[52] Americans also routinely overestimate the amount of federal money spent on government programs such as foreign aid. However, rather than reflecting ignorance, these misperceptions often result from poor survey design or participants' misinterpretation of survey questions.

In some cases, inaccurate or outlandish survey returns result because some respondents don't take surveys seriously. They agree to participate but are not interested in explaining their beliefs to a stranger. Faced with a long list of questions, they give quick, thoughtless responses so as to end the interview as quickly as possible. Misperceptions may also result when respondents form opinions on the basis of whatever considerations come to mind. This strategy causes many respondents to exclude important pieces of information from their opinion-formation process.

Consider claims about health care reform. In a 2009 survey, the Pew Research Center found that 86 percent of respondents had heard that reform legislation would create so-called death panels. (The question asked about "government organizations that will make decisions about who will and will not receive health services when they are critically ill.")[53] Moreover, 30 percent of these respondents believed these claims, even though no such provision was included in any of the proposals offered by President Obama or members of Congress.

How can these findings be squared with our earlier statement that Americans generally hold opinions that have some basis in reality? For one thing, many respondents probably had not thought about these questions in detail—and it's likely that only a very few had read through all the health care reform proposals, which were hundreds of pages long. When asked for an opinion as part of a survey, respondents had no time to do research or think things through, so they guessed. Thus, it's no surprise that a significant percentage of respondents said that death panels were part of the bill: some people who guess an answer say yes, and some say no.

Incomplete or inaccurate responses to survey questions may also reflect respondents' unwillingness to admit they don't know about something. There is good evidence that survey participants sometimes make up responses to avoid appearing ill informed.[54] Thus, when asked about death panels and health care reform, respondents might affirm that a link existed even if they know little or nothing about the situation. In the main, people are more likely to express sensible, thoughtful, and accurate opinions when an issue or topic is *salient*, or important to them.

Moreover, opinions about health care proposals are subject to influence by politicians and others. While health care was under debate, some Republican politicians claimed that death panels *were* part of reform proposals or that reform might lead to future death panels. Thus, when survey respondents mention death panels, their response might reflect opinions formed after hearing these public figures. (The fact that Republican respondents were more likely to say that claims about death panels were true supports this conclusion—after all, Republican legislators were the more vocal proponents of this claim.)

Finally, many supposed facts are actually "contested truths," meaning that it is reasonable for individuals to hold a range of views.[55] In the case of death panels, respondents might have known that the proposals did not contain this provision but, nevertheless, they may have answered in the affirmative because they thought that the reforms might lead to such panels at some future time. Since it is impossible to be sure either way, we cannot say that such respondents were mistaken in their beliefs.

Such problems do not arise in all areas of public opinion. Studies show that respondents' ability to express specific opinions, as well as the accuracy of their opinions, rises if the survey questions have something to do with their everyday life.[56] Thus, the average American would be more likely to have an accurate sense of the state of the economy or their personal economic condition than of the military situation in Afghanistan. Everyday life gives us information about the economy; we learn about Afghanistan only if we take time to gather information. These effects are magnified insofar as the respondent considers the economy the more salient issue of the two.

HOW USEFUL ARE SURVEYS?

Survey results are most likely to be accurate when they are based on a simple, easily understood question about a topic familiar to most Americans—such as their evaluation of the president—and when the survey designers have worked to construct a random sample of their target population. You can be even more confident if multiple surveys addressing the same topic in different ways and at different times produce similar findings. If a single survey asks about a complex, unfamiliar topic—replacing the income tax with a national sales tax, for example—then the results may not provide much insight into public opinion.

Surveys taken after an event—for example, a survey on gun control taken immediately after the Newtown shooting—are generally not a good guide to public opinion. The problem is not that people are being insincere or thoughtless; rather, it is because respondents' opinions are colored by the recent tragedy—but only in the short-term. Over the next days, weeks, or months, opinions are likely to return to what they were before the event. Thus, polls taken in the wake of a powerful event may not be a good guide to what people might demand from government in light of what has happened, nor may they reflect how people might react a year later given government inaction.

CHARACTERISTICS OF AMERICAN PUBLIC OPINION

PRESENT FINDINGS ON WHAT AMERICANS THINK ABOUT MAJOR POLITICAL ISSUES

In this section, we describe American public opinion in detail, including peoples' ideological beliefs, what they think of the federal government, and their positions on public policy questions such as abortion rights and global warming. These opinions drive public demands for government action, and range from spending to regulation and to other types of policy. So, to understand what America's national government does and why, we have to determine what Americans ask of it. The other priority is to describe the differences of opinion that divide Americans, from specific questions of policy to general statements of belief.

IDEOLOGICAL POLARIZATION

We begin by examining liberal and conservative ideology and party identification to see whether historical data show evidence of polarization. Are there fewer moderates and more strong liberals and conservatives today than a generation ago? Figure 6.3 shows data from the General Social Survey (GSS) on Americans' ideological opinions from 1970 to 2012. The group of liberals in the figure combines people who said they were either "extremely liberal" or "liberal." Similarly, the group of conservatives includes respondents calling themselves either "extremely conservative" or "conservative." Moderates said they were either "moderate," "slightly liberal," or "slightly conservative."

The plots in Figure 6.3 show no evidence of **ideological polarization**—that is, there is no indication of a culture war expressed in Americans' ideology. Over the last several decades, a strong majority of Americans have continued to say they are moderates, with fewer than 40 percent saying they are liberal or conservative. There is also no evidence that ideological polarization has increased; in fact, the percentage of liberals and of conservatives has remained relatively constant.[57]

Figure 6.4 shows data about how citizens describe their party identification. Here, again, there is little evidence of polarization.

ideological polarization The effect on public opinion when many citizens move away from moderate positions and toward either end of the political spectrum, identifying themselves as either liberals or conservatives.

FIGURE » 6.3

LIBERAL OR CONSERVATIVE IDEOLOGY IN AMERICA

Many commentators describe politics in America as highly conflictual, with most Americans holding either liberal or conservative points of view and very few people in between. Do opinion data confirm or disprove this description?

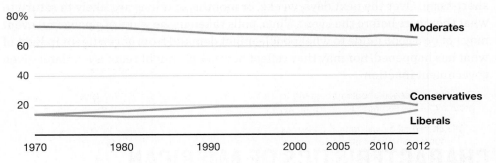

SOURCE: Data from General Social Survey 1972–2012, Cumulative Datafile, Survey Documentation and Analysis (SDA) at UC Berkeley, http://sda.berkeley.edu/archive.htm (accessed 9/5/12).

FIGURE » 6.4

PARTY IDENTIFICATION IN AMERICA, 2012

Party identification is another place to look for evidence of an increasingly polarized America. Do these data show evidence of polarization?

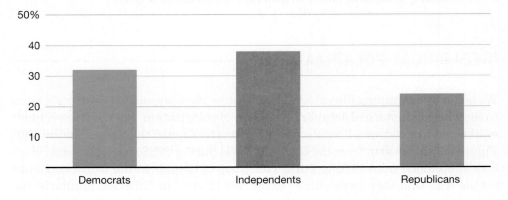

SOURCE: Pew Research Center, "Trends in American Values: 1987–2012," June 4, 2012, www.people-press.org/files/legacy-pdf/06-04-12%20 Values 7.20 Release.pdf (accessed 8/28/14).

Looking more closely at opinion polarization, Figure 6.5 shows responses to questions that tap important principles. These range from foreign policy to domestic issues, civil liberties, and morality. Principles such as these form the basis for opinions that people express in surveys or act on when they vote or engage in other political behavior. Although the responses show considerable disagreement, supporting the idea that a culture war really exists in America,

FIGURE » 6.5

MEASURING AMERICAN PUBLIC OPINION: EXAMPLES OF PRINCIPLES

If polarization is evident in ideological or party identification, perhaps it can be found in responses to specific questions about principles. The bars represent the percentage of people who either "totally agree" or "totally disagree" with the statements (because some people don't agree at all or don't know if they agree, the percentages do not add up to 100). Do responses to these questions show consistent evidence of polarization? Why might opinion surveys overstate the amount of polarization in the population?

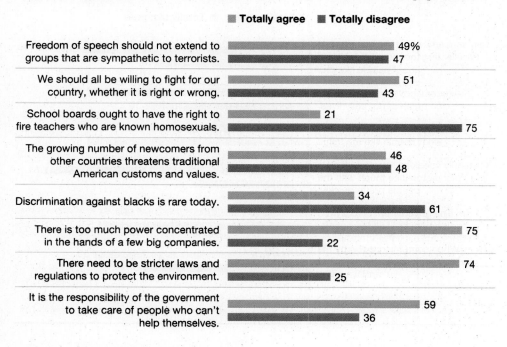

SOURCE: Pew Research Center, "2012 American Values Survey" June 4, 2012, www.people-press.org/values-questions/ (accessed 3/24/14).

it is important to point out that this particular survey was *designed* to divide people into categories based on what they believe and what they want from government. All the questions tapped subjects of impassioned debate during recent political campaigns.

EVALUATIONS OF GOVERNMENT AND OFFICEHOLDERS

Another set of opinions that are important in American politics addresses how people view their government: How well or poorly do they think the government is doing? Do they trust the government? How do they evaluate individual politicians, notably their own representatives in Congress? These opinions matter for several reasons. A citizen's judgments about the government's overall performance may shape his evaluations of specific policies, especially if he does not know much about them.[58] Evaluations of specific policies may also be shaped by how much a citizen trusts the government; more trust brings higher evaluations.[59] Trust in government

FIGURE » 6.6

MEASURING AMERICAN PUBLIC OPINION: BELIEFS ABOUT GOVERNMENT

Surveys show that Americans generally like their elected representatives in Congress. Presidents are sometimes extremely popular. Do Americans have positive feelings about government itself? The bars represent the percentage of people who either "totally agree" or "totally disagree" with the statements (because some people only partially agree or disagree or don't know if they agree, the percentages do not add up to 100).

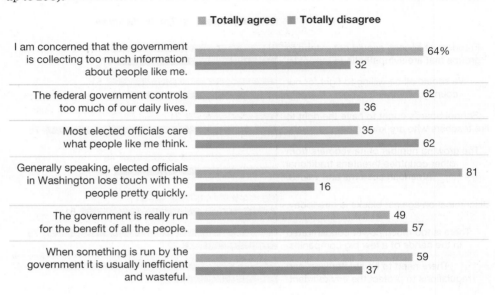

■ Totally agree   ■ Totally disagree

I am concerned that the government is collecting too much information about people like me. — 64% / 32

The federal government controls too much of our daily lives. — 62 / 36

Most elected officials care what people like me think. — 35 / 62

Generally speaking, elected officials in Washington lose touch with the people pretty quickly. — 81 / 16

The government is really run for the benefit of all the people. — 49 / 57

When something is run by the government it is usually inefficient and wasteful. — 59 / 37

SOURCE: Pew Research Center "2012 American Values Survey" June 4, 2012, www.people-press.org/values-questions/ (accessed 3/24/14).

and overall evaluations might also influence a citizen's willingness to vote for incumbent congressional representatives or for a president seeking reelection.[60]

Figure 6.6 reveals that the average American is fairly disenchanted with the government. A majority believes that elected officials lose touch with the people and don't care what average people think, and that corporations have too much power. A near-majority believes that government is almost always wasteful and inefficient. These evaluations are nothing new; many surveys over the last two generations show similar responses.[61]

This impression of a disenchanted and disapproving public is illustrated in Figure 6.7, which shows declining levels of trust in government since the 1960s. Trust reached an all-time low in the mid-1970s during the Watergate scandal, in which high-level government officials, going all the way up the president himself, were implicated in the cover-up of the break-in at Democratic National Committee headquarters at the Watergate Hotel in Washington, D.C., prior to the 1972 presidential election. The Senate hearings brought to light the illegal activities and abuse of power by Nixon and his aides and would have led to the impeachment and conviction of Nixon, had he not resigned the presidency on August 9, 1974. Trust in government was later also eroded in the early 1990s during an economic downturn as well as during the financial crisis that began in 2008. As noted earlier, many scholars have argued that low levels of trust make it harder for elected officials to enact new policies, especially those that require large expenditures.[62]

FIGURE » 6.7

TRUST IN GOVERNMENT

In America, trust in government varies widely over time. What factors drive these changes? The curve represents the percentage of people who say that they trust the federal government to do what is right "just about always" or "most of the time."

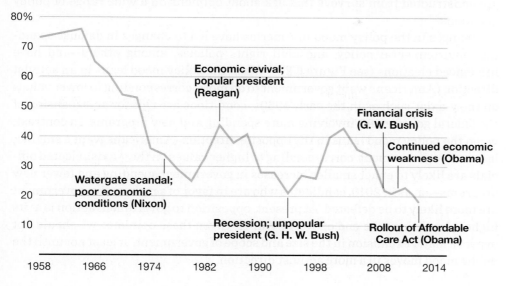

SOURCES: Pew Research Center, "Obama Leadership Image Takes a Hit, GOP Ratings Decline," August 25, 2011, www.people-press.org/files/legacy-pdf/8-25-11%20Political%20Release.pdf (accessed 9/5/12). Pew Research Center, "Public Trust in Government, 1978–2013," October 26, 2013, www.people-press.org/2013/10/18/trust-in-government-interactive/ (accessed 11/25/13).

On a more profound level, some scholars argue that low levels of trust raise questions about the future of democracy in America.[63] How can we say that American democracy is a good or popular form of government when so many people are unhappy with the performance of elected officials and bureaucrats?

One important response is that although Americans don't like the government in general, they tend to be far more satisfied with their own representatives in Washington (see Chapter 11). One possibility is that putting a human face on government by asking about specific individuals in office improves respondents' opinions because it calls to mind different considerations. Asking about "the government" may call to mind a vast room of bureaucrats pushing paperwork from one desk to another, whereas asking about "your representative" may lead people to think of someone working on their behalf.

In addition, members of Congress work hard to convince their constituents that they are doing everything possible to satisfy constituents' demands. Sometimes members blame the institution of Congress and the government bureaucracy for shortcomings, portraying themselves as standing between their constituents and an inept, inefficient government. As one scholar put it, "House members run for Congress by running against Congress."[64] In fact, members who deviate from this strategy while running for reelection by trying to convince their constituents that Congress does a good job are more likely to be defeated—not because they do a worse job than their colleagues, but because their statements call to mind unfavorable impressions of government that constituents consider when deciding how to vote.[65]

TRUST IN GOVERNMENT REACHED a low point during the mid-1970s. The decline partly reflected the economic downturn and conflict over the Vietnam War, but opinions were also shaped by the discovery that President Richard Nixon lied about the Watergate scandal. Here, Nixon resigns from office to avoid impeachment.

POLICY PREFERENCES

policy mood The level of public support for expanding the government's role in society; whether the public wants government action on a specific issue.

In a diverse country of more than 320 million, people care about a wide range of government policies. One useful measure of Americans' policy preferences is the **policy mood**, mentioned earlier, which captures the public's collective demands for government action on domestic policies.[66] Policy mood measures are constructed from surveys that ask about opinions on a wide range of policy questions.[67]

Changes in the policy mood in America have led to changes in defense spending, environmental policy, and civil rights policies, among others—and have influenced elections (see Figure 6.8).[68] When the policy mood leans in an activist direction (Americans want government to do more, corresponding to lower values on the y-axis), such as in the early 1960s, conditions are ripe for an expansion of the federal government involving more spending and new programs. In contrast, when the policy mood leans in the opposite direction (Americans want a smaller, less-active government, corresponding to higher values on the y-axis), elected officials are likely to enact smaller increases in government spending and fewer new programs—or, as in 2010, candidates who are in favor of a more active government are more likely to be defeated. At present, opposition to government action is at its highest level since the end of World War II. Given these opinions, we should not expect a major expansion in the size and scope of government, at least not until the public mood moves in a more activist direction.

FIGURE » 6.8

POLICY MOOD

Surveys assess the public's policy mood by asking questions about specific policy questions such as levels of taxation and government spending and the role of government. The level of conservatism (for example, support for smaller, less-active government) was at a high in 1952 and 1980 and 2008. Could you have used the policy mood prior to the election to predict the outcomes of the 2012 presidential and 2012 and 2014 congressional elections?

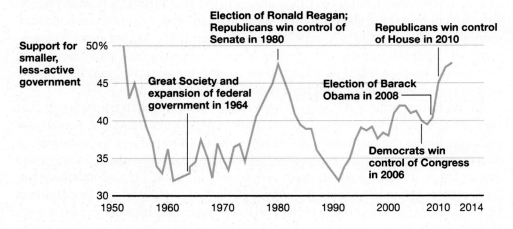

SOURCE: Larry Bartels, "Americans Are More Conservative Than They Have Been in Decades," *The Monkey Cage*, September 30, 2013, www.washingtonpost.com/blogs/monkey-cage/wp/2013/09/30/americans-are-more-conservative-than-they-have-been-in-decades/ (accessed 3/18/14).

The remainder of this section presents opinion data on some important policy questions: economic conditions, health care, immigration, and same-sex marriage. In some cases, people's attitudes toward an issue vary greatly, sometimes leading to significant levels of conflict over what a policy should be. In other cases, either most people hold similar opinions or the level of conflict depends on how the question is asked, meaning that most people's opinions are not very strong.

ECONOMIC CONDITIONS It is no exaggeration to say that Americans are always worried about the economy. Even when other pressing issues, such as terrorism, surpass the economy as the most important problem to Americans, the economy is typically listed second or third. In general, as the state of the economy declines, more and more people rate the economy as their greatest concern. Moreover, the percentage of people who make reference to their personal economic concerns—for example, unemployment or worries about retirement—also increases. These patterns make sense, given what we know about the opinion-formation process. Most Americans base their judgments about the economy on whatever considerations come to mind when the survey takes place; these considerations may be personal circumstances, long-held values, or information from a recent news broadcast. Since individual considerations vary, so do people's judgments about the economy and their diagnoses of the problems. These differences in opinion have an important policy implication: policies designed to improve economic conditions may prove widely unpopular if they do not address the considerations that lead individuals to worry.

HEALTH CARE Health care is another important concern for Americans. In recent years, many surveys showed that Americans were worried about losing their health insurance coverage and complained about the high cost of health care. This raises a puzzling question: If a majority of Americans were unhappy with the health care system, why was it so difficult to enact health care reform, and why has Obamacare remained so controversial several years after it was passed into law?[69] Part of the answer is that fears about health care do not translate into strong support for specific reforms. For example, a 2009 Pew Research Center poll found that only about a third of Americans expected that President Obama's health care proposal would improve their access to care if they had a preexisting condition or if they lost their job.[70] A much lower percentage expected Obama's proposal to lower the cost of medical care or increase their access. Given these perceptions, it is no surprise that Obama's proposal was controversial at the time it was enacted.

Our earlier discussion of considerations provides additional insights into opinions about health care. Respondents might have believed that the reform proposals included other provisions, such as the "death panels" mentioned earlier. Regardless of whether these claims were true, they certainly were prominent in much media coverage. In later polls, such as the 2013 Pew Research Center survey shown in Table 6.3, evaluations of the proposal are highly correlated with partisanship.

The table shows approval and disapproval percentages for the Affordable Health Care Act (Obamacare) among Republicans and Democrats, with Republicans split between those who described themselves as Tea Party supporters and those who did not. The strong support for Obamacare among Democrats (nearly three-fourths) is matched by even stronger opposition among Republicans and nearly universal opposition among Tea Party members. The partisan split in Washington over Obamacare may have driven these perceptions.

WHAT DO POLITICAL SCIENTISTS DO?

For more on how the economy affects public opinion, visit **wwnpag.es/wdpsd**

TABLE » 6.3

ATTITUDES ABOUT HEALTH CARE

The Affordable Care Act was passed by Congress in 2010, but as implementation of the new law got underway, opposition to the law persisted, leading to efforts to undermine or even repeal the law. The table shows the percentage of Republican/Republican leaning (both Tea Party and Not Tea Party) and Democrat/Democrat leaning who approve or disapprove of Obamacare. Given the strong relationship between partisanship and evaluations of Obamacare, how do you think people with different party identifications reacted to the widespread difficulties with enrollment during the first months of the program?

| | Total | Republican/Republican leaning | | Democrat/Democrat leaning |
		Tea Party	Not Tea Party	
Approve	42%	5%	17%	73%
Disapprove	53	94	80	23

SOURCE: Pew Research Center, "As Health Care Law Proceeds, Opposition and Uncertainty Persist," September 16, 2013, www.people-press.org/2013/09/16/as-health-care-law-proceeds-opposition-and-uncertainty-persist/ (accessed 11/26/13).

In any case, these data explain the difficulties that Democrats faced in 2009 and 2010 when trying to build support for health care reform as well as the persistent calls for repeal thereafter. Perceptions of Obamacare are likely to change only after most Americans have some experience with the program—whether it affects their costs and access to care, and how they interpret these changes.

IMMIGRATION Like gun control, immigration is an issue where apparent public consensus breaks down once people are asked about the details (see the You Decide feature). Consider Figure 6.9, which reports data from a 2013 Pew Research Center poll. The pie chart on the left shows strong support for changing America's immigration policies (74 percent of the respondents said that immigration policy should be either totally revamped or changed considerably). But the bar graph on the right shows where the consensus breaks down. Although more than 70 percent of respondents favor allowing illegal immigrants to stay in the country through some sort of process that would give them legal status, the country is split on whether these reforms should await increased border security. This additional requirement could postpone the legalization process indefinitely.

These data provide a strong explanation for Congress's failure to enact immigration reform. The problem is not that Americans favor the current policy. Rather, they disagree on a fundamental piece of any reform proposal—whether border security and legalization would happen simultaneously, or one after the other. Without a consensus on the issue, the current policy stays in place.

SAME-SEX MARRIAGE Social issues such as abortion rights and same-sex marriage are among the most divisive in American politics. Typically, matters such as these involve the question of whether the government should restrict an individual's behavior to fall into line with a particular moral code. But as attitudes change, governmental policy generally changes with it. Changes in attitudes about same-sex

RESPONDING TO PUBLIC OPINION ON IMMIGRATION

As we discuss in Chapter 11, elected officials in America work hard to cast votes and take other actions that their constituents will like. At first glance, this behavior seems easy. All a politician needs to do is take a poll, measure public opinion in her state or district, and comply with the demands expressed in the survey responses.

Actually, it is not easy for a representative to find out what her constituents want, because public opinion is hard to measure. Everything you have learned in this chapter suggests that taking a poll doesn't necessarily tell the whole story. Poll results need interpretation and may not provide clear guidance to elected officials.

Consider public opinion on immigration. Suppose a member of the House represents a district where public opinion on this issue mirrors the results of (current) national averages: a majority supports allowing individuals here illegally to stay if they meet certain requirements, and a majority supports making changes at the border to make it harder for illegal immigrants to enter the country in the first place. Suppose this representative wants to mirror district opinion to gain political support and stay in office. What sort of guide does this data provide to the representative?

The problem is that these data provide different guidance depending on which question the representative looks at. As we discuss throughout this chapter, the way in which a question is asked can produce large changes in responses. At first glance, these data would lead the politician to strongly support reform packages that combined some form of legalization procedure combined with increased border controls. However, that would be a very dangerous strategy for the politician to follow, as it ignores the question of what the "certain requirements" for legalization would be. Pay a large fine? Learn English? A requirement to travel back to their country of origin and reenter legally? The pollsters probably asked the question this way to determine how many people might support legalization in general, letting the respondent "fill in the blank" on what proper conditions for legalization might be. This strategy is a sensible way to measure public opinion but does not give our representative clear guidance about what to do.

The second danger for the representative comes in determining what should come first, legalization or border controls? The majority's preference for legalization may be based on the assumption that these changes would happen only after border controls were tightened. As a result, a representative who supported legalization first could easily find him or herself on the wrong side of district opinion.

This example illustrates that an issue which appears to be noncontroversial, where a large percentage of Americans agree on what to do, can turn out to be highly controversial

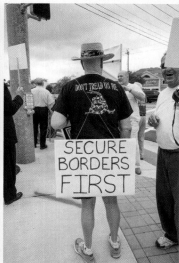

Americans in both parties agree on the need for immigration reform but differ as to what they think the new immigration policies should be. (Left) These Democrats are demonstrating in support of citizenship for illegal immigrants, while (right) these Tea Party Republicans are rallying for border security and against the Senate's proposed immigration reform bill.

once the details come into play. In the case of immigration policy, Americans want changes, but disagree on what change should look like.

These data also explain the failure of immigration reform in recent congresses. While there may be good reasons to change America's immigration policies, elected officials face a situation that virtually every reform they might consider will offend large portions of their constituencies. Under these conditions, the politically astute choice may be to avoid taking any votes at all, and keep the existing policies in place—which is exactly what has happened.

CRITICAL THINKING QUESTIONS

1. Suppose you are a politician who feels that changes in immigration policy are needed but are faced with the quandary described above. Would you do nothing, so as to avoid alienating your constituency, or would you force a policy change and accept the political consequence—possible removal from office?

2. What poll questions would you use to get a clearer picture of public opinion on immigration?

FIGURE » 6.9

ATTITUDES ABOUT IMMIGRATION

Although most people indicate strong support for immigration reform (as shown in the pie chart), there is not a consensus on how to implement reform (as shown in the bar graph). In light of Americans' opinions about immigration reform, how is it that a strong majority favors changes, but none of the proposals offered by elected officials or interest groups have attracted much support?

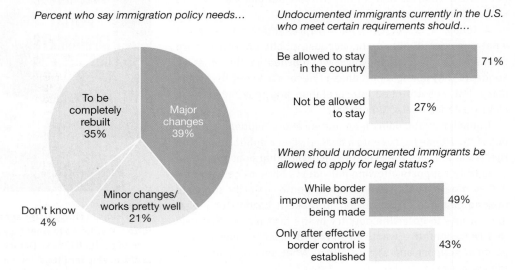

Percent who say immigration policy needs...

To be completely rebuilt 35%

Major changes 39%

Don't know 4%

Minor changes/ works pretty well 21%

Undocumented immigrants currently in the U.S. who meet certain requirements should...

Be allowed to stay in the country — 71%

Not be allowed to stay — 27%

When should undocumented immigrants be allowed to apply for legal status?

While border improvements are being made — 49%

Only after effective border control is established — 43%

SOURCE: Pew Research Center, "Immigration: Key Data Points from Pew Research," September 23, 2013, www.pewresearch.org/key-data -points/immigration-tip-sheet-on-u-s-public-opinion/ (accessed 3/18/14).

marriage over the last decade provide a rare example of sharp shifts in public opinion, as shown in Figure 6.10. The figure shows that support for allowing gay and lesbian couples to marry (or allowing civil unions) has doubled in the last decade. Moreover, although younger Americans are more likely to express support than are older Americans, opinions have shifted in all age cohorts. Additional questions reveal that one of the critical factors in the opinion shift is the increased likelihood that Americans know someone who is gay or a lesbian. This finding is consistent with our discussion of how opinions are formed—one of the prime considerations used to form attitudes about gay marriage is personal contact with people who have different sexual orientations.

These examples show conflict in American politics. In fact, it is hard to find an issue where nearly everyone agrees about what should be done. Of course, in a country that is as large and diverse as the United States, this is no surprise. What is surprising is the potential for policy compromise in these data—a finding that argues against describing American politics in terms of a culture war. Questions that ask about ideology or party identification find that most Americans are moderates. And with regard to specific issues, while there is considerable disagreement on health care and immigration reform, the trend in attitudes regarding same-sex marriage is toward a consensus that gays and lesbians should have the same access to marriage and civil unions that everyone else does.

FIGURE » 6.10

ATTITUDES ABOUT SAME-SEX MARRIAGE

There is growing support for same-sex marriage, as indicated by the graph on the left, which shows the change in attitudes toward same-sex marriage from 2003 until 2013 among all adults. The graph on the right further breaks down support for same-sex marriage by cohorts: the silent generation (those born between 1928 and 1945), the baby-boom generation (those born between 1946 and 1964), Gen X (those born between 1965 and 1980), and the Millennials (those born after 1980).

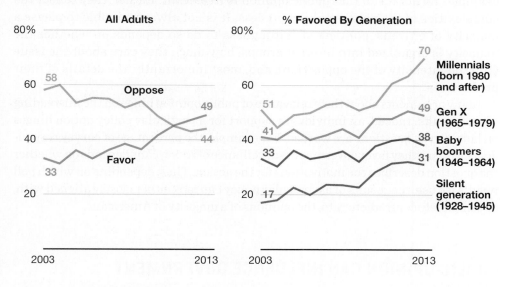

SOURCE: Pew Research Center, "Growing Support for Same-Sex Marriage," March 13–17, 2013, www.people-press.org/2013/03/20/growing-support-for-gay-marriage-changed-minds-and-changing-demographics/ (accessed 3/18/14).

Attitudes toward gun control, however, are more like attitudes toward health care and immigration than attitudes toward same-sex marriage. While polls taken around the time of the Newtown shooting revealed strong support for various gun control measures, this support waned in the following months, leaving the nation essentially split on most gun control measures. These preferences are also highly correlated with party, with Democrats generally favoring reform and Republicans generally opposed. It is this split that explains why on the one hand, gun control remains on the legislative agenda, but on the other hand, reform proposals never come up for a vote. The problem is not that representatives are ignoring public demands, rather it is that they are reflecting them all too well.

DOES PUBLIC OPINION MATTER?

EVALUATE THE RELATIONSHIP BETWEEN PUBLIC OPINION AND WHAT GOVERNMENT DOES

As we mentioned earlier, some observers of American politics argue that most Americans have no real opinions about candidates, policies, or anything else. Others claim that these opinions exist but that government officials ignore them. Having described what political scientists know about American public opinion, we can now analyze these claims.

PUBLIC OPINION IS RELEVANT

We can say with confidence that public opinion remains highly relevant in American politics today. One key piece of evidence is the amount of time and effort politicians, journalists, and political scientists spend trying to find out what Americans think. Of course, it is easy to find examples in which the political process appears to ignore public opinion in cases in which policy has stayed the same despite a majority supporting change. In other cases, new policies have been enacted even though a majority preferred the status quo. But these examples do not mean that public opinion is irrelevant. Rather, they reflect the complexities of the policy-making process. It is not always possible to please a majority of citizens; politicians' willingness to do so depends on whether the majority is organized into interest groups, how much they care about the issue (and the intensity of the opposition), and, most importantly, the details of their preferences.

Many arguments about the irrelevance of public opinion hinge on the misreading of poll results. Indeed, an individual's support for a particular policy option hinges on how survey questions are worded. For example, the percentage of survey respondents who say they favor government surveillance of Americans depends on whether the question describes the motivations for the action. Thus, depending on which poll results we use, the results of a particular policy can look either closely aligned with, or completely contradictory to, the opinions of a majority of Americans.

PUBLIC OPINION INFLUENCES government at election time, when voters' opinions about incumbent politicians and the party in power influence voters' decisions at the polls. In 2014, voters' evaluations of President Obama were an important influence on the election outcome.

PUBLIC OPINION CAN INFLUENCE GOVERNMENT

Despite all the difficulties described, public opinion exerts a conspicuous influence in widespread areas of government. We mention this broad influence repeatedly throughout this book. For example, our preceding discussion noted that significant policy mood changes have often been followed by changes in government policy. In Chapter 11, we describe how legislators endeavor to determine what their constituents want and how their constituents will respond to different actions. In Chapter 9, we see how voters use retrospective evaluations to form opinions about whom to vote for and how candidates incorporate the public's views into campaign platforms that will attract widespread support. And in Chapter 8, we discuss how voters use candidates' party affiliations like brand names to determine how candidates will behave if elected.

Many political scientists have found evidence that congressional outcomes and government policy reflect public opinion. Scholars have found that congressional actions on a wide range of issues, from votes on defense policy to the confirmation of Supreme Court nominees, are shaped by constituent opinion.[71] Moreover, careful analysis of the connection between opinions and actions shows that this linkage does not exist because politicians are able to shape public opinion in line with what they want to do;

rather, politicians behave in line with their constituents' opinions because to do otherwise would place the politicians in jeopardy of losing the next election.[71]

Of course, all politicians, particularly those with a national audience such as the president, work to shape public opinion. In the main, however, these efforts serve to publicize opinions that people already hold, as a way of influencing the behavior of other elected officials, rather than changing what citizens believe.[72]

Recent events also speak to the influence of public opinion. Think about the failure of elected officials in 2013 to modify Obamacare, enact immigration reform, or pass new limits on the ownership of handguns and assault rifles. In all of these cases, a significant portion of Americans wanted policy change, but a substantial percentage were opposed, and even the supporters disagreed on what kinds of changes were best. Congressional inaction on these measures does not reflect a willful ignorance of public opinion. Rather it reflects the lack of a public consensus about what government should do. Inaction on these issues is exactly what we should expect if public opinion is real and relevant to what happens in politics.

CONCLUSION

Public opinion is real, and it matters. Americans have ideas about what they want government to do, and they use these ideas to guide their political choices. While Americans disagree about many issues, they also do agree about some issues— which provides areas in which compromise is possible. In a country as large and diverse as the United States, disagreement over government policy is inevitable. However, as we have shown in this chapter, disagreement does not make compromise impossible—and it does not support the idea that Americans are engaged in a culture war. In many areas, people disagree, but their opinions reflect a willingness to accept compromise.

The role of public opinion in shaping the policy response to the 2008 financial crisis, the budget deficit, or any of the policy questions we have discussed in this chapter are all examples of how much public opinion matters in American politics. The average American is not an expert on government policies and knows relatively little about possible alternatives. But even a small amount of information is enough to inform beliefs about what policies should be enacted. Moreover, politicians generally take care to behave in accordance with these demands, which may even make them backtrack on positions or votes they have previously taken if they believe the public mood has changed. And the changes in the last few years in government policy, politicians' statements, and election outcomes all reflect such changes in the policy mood.

Likewise, very few Americans are experts about gay rights, health care reform, or immigration reform. Their responses to questions about these issues may vary from day to day, but most Americans know enough to decide what they want government to do about these problems—and to act on these opinions. Politicians, in turn, take public opinion very seriously, as it provides the yardstick that measures citizens' judgments of their behavior in office.

Gun control is an example of all of these phenomena. Absent events like the Newtown shootings, Americans are divided on the need for making it harder to own or carry a handgun and on whether ownership of assault weapons should be banned. While most gun control questions are marked by strong conflict, there is consensus on some issues, such as regulating gun ownership by people judged to be mentally ill—although even here, there is disagreement as to how an individual's mental health would be evaluated. In light of all of these factors, Congress's inability to enact gun control legislation makes sense. The problem is not that legislators are ignoring Americans' opinions. Rather, the problem is that different groups are demanding different things. It is true that support for reform increased after the Newtown shootings, but this shift was short-lived, and therefore not something that moved elected officials to act.

WHAT IS PUBLIC OPINION?

▶ *Define public opinion and explain why it matters in American politics.* **(Pages 200–06)**

SUMMARY

What the population thinks about politics and government matters for three reasons: people's political actions are driven by their opinions; there is a strong linkage between people's opinions and political actors' behavior; and public opinion helps us understand how specific policy outcomes are achieved. Although early research was skeptical that people held meaningful opinions, current research shows that people do have real and meaningful policy positions.

KEY TERMS

public opinion (p. 200)
liberal or conservative ideology (p. 202)
latent opinion (p. 203)

CRITICAL THINKING AND DISCUSSION

Given that many Americans cannot answer basic political questions and many of the opinions they express vary from day to day without anything changing in the political world, how can we say that public opinion exists?

PRACTICE QUIZ QUESTIONS

1. What does it mean that most political judgments are latent opinions?

   Ⓐ Most Americans have pre-formed opinions.

   Ⓑ Most Americans have well-thought-out reasons for preferring a policy.

   Ⓒ Most Americans do not have any meaningful political attitudes.

   Ⓓ Most Americans form their opinions only as needed.

   Ⓔ Most opinions are not accurate.

2. Which of the following is *not* true regarding considerations?

   Ⓐ Well-informed and poorly informed people use them in forming opinions.

   Ⓑ Opinions on morally complex issues do not involve considerations.

   Ⓒ Political events can become considerations.

   Ⓓ They may be contradictory.

   Ⓔ Party identification is often used in considerations.

WHERE DO OPINIONS COME FROM?

▶ *Explain how people form political attitudes and opinions.* **(Pages 206–11)**

SUMMARY

Political opinions are influenced by a number of factors. The belief systems of parents and relatives influence our opinions early on, and our social groups influence our perspectives later in life. Personal events such as attending college or moving to a new city may also influence how we think about politics, as do national events such as the attacks on September 11, 2001, or the decision to go to war. Even debates among political elites and party leaders shape our political attitudes.

KEY TERM

political socialization (p. 206)

CRITICAL THINKING AND DISCUSSION

When competing against forces as strong as political socialization and feelings of group identification, to what degree can politicians meaningfully influence individuals' opinions?

PRACTICE QUIZ QUESTIONS

3. The theory of political socialization says that people's opinions are influenced first by _____.

   Ⓐ what they learned from their parents

   Ⓑ the way political parties change over time

   Ⓒ genetic and biological factors

   Ⓓ their personality traits

   Ⓔ politicians

4. An event or some other new information is most likely to change an individual's opinion when _____.

   Ⓐ the individual is highly informed about the issue

   Ⓑ the individual holds strong opinions

   Ⓒ the individual is strongly partisan

   Ⓓ the individual does not have a set of preexisting principles with which to interpret the event

   Ⓔ the individual does not watch the news

5. The idea that individuals will rely on others who "look like" them for opinions relates to _____.

   Ⓐ party identification

   Ⓑ political socialization

   Ⓒ group identity

   Ⓓ political events

   Ⓔ generational effects

6. Which phrase best completes the following statement regarding the sources of public opinion? "Politicians and other political actors work to _____ public opinion."

   A respond to

   B ignore

   C disregard

   D stabilize

   E shape

MEASURING PUBLIC OPINION

▶ *Describe basic survey methods and potential issues affecting accuracy.* **(Pages 212–19)**

SUMMARY

While most information on public opinion comes from mass surveys where thousands of people respond, some information comes from focus groups where small groups of people are interviewed together. Despite a number of limitations, most research on public opinion focuses on mass surveys, as they can be used to draw broad conclusions about the country.

KEY TERMS	CRITICAL THINKING AND DISCUSSION
mass survey (p. 212) **population** (p. 212) **sample** (p. 212) **sampling error** (p. 213) **random sample** (p. 214)	In light of the many problems with measuring public opinion, how should you read survey results?

PRACTICE QUIZ QUESTIONS

7. Why are focus groups helpful in understanding public opinion?

   A They provide deep insights into why people hold the views that they do.

   B They provide a representative sample of the population.

   C They use a small number of respondents to draw conclusions about the country.

   D It is impossible to understand someone's partisanship based on a survey.

   E They restrict respondents to a few answer choices.

8. Which of the following is *not* a random sampling technique?

   A random digit dialing

   B face-to-face interviewing

   C Internet polling

   D push polls

   E robo-polling

9. Why is it important to get a large random survey sample?

   A to keep costs down

   B to provide deep insights into why people hold their opinions

   C to help candidates fine-tune their campaign messages

   D to be able to generalize about the broad population

   E to prevent question wording from biasing survey results

10. Suppose a survey of Americans' attitudes about NSA surveillance of cell phone records reveals that the level of opposition to surveillance varies with how the question is phrased. What is the best explanation for this variation?

   A People don't take surveys seriously.

   B People are afraid to express truthful opinions on surveys.

   C Changes in the wording of questions call to mind different considerations.

   D Changes in in the wording of questions make people suspicious.

   E Few people can respond in a rational way to survey questions.

CHARACTERISTICS OF AMERICAN PUBLIC OPINION

▶ *Present findings on what Americans think about major political issues.* **(Pages 219–29)**

SUMMARY

As a whole, the American electorate is ideologically moderate, with relatively little ideological polarization. Moreover, there is considerable agreement on the most important problems in the country and potential for compromise on most policy areas. Paradoxically, although trust in the government has declined steadily since the 1960s, people are still generally happy with their own representatives in Washington, D.C.

KEY TERMS	CRITICAL THINKING AND DISCUSSION
ideological polarization (p. 219) **policy mood** (p. 224)	How much conflict is there in American public opinion?

PRACTICE QUIZ QUESTIONS

11. In the 1970s, the majority of Americans identified themselves as ideologically _____; in the 2000s, most Americans identified themselves as _____.

   A moderate; conservative

   B moderate; moderate

   C moderate; liberal

   D conservative; moderate

   E conservative; conservative

12. What is policy mood?

   [A] public support for Congress

   [B] presidential approval rating

   [C] trust in government

   [D] public demand for government action on domestic policies

   [E] public demand for government action on international policies

13. Which policy area is always near the top of Americans' concerns?

   [A] economic conditions

   [B] health care

   [C] same-sex marriage

   [D] immigration

   [E] the environment

14. Americans generally _____ of the government and generally _____ of their own representatives.

   [A] approve; approve

   [B] approve; disapprove

   [C] disapprove; approve

   [D] disapprove; disapprove

DOES PUBLIC OPINION MATTER?

▶ *Evaluate the relationship between public opinion and what government does.* **(Pages 229–31)**

SUMMARY

While it can be difficult to determine exactly what the American public wants, public opinion is still quite relevant in American politics. Government policy and congressional outcomes are responsive to changes in public mood, and most policy decisions reflect the demands of a majority of Americans.

CRITICAL THINKING AND DISCUSSION

Is public opinion more powerful during the election process or during the policy-making process?

PRACTICE QUIZ QUESTION

15. When the government enacts policies even though a majority of Americans prefer the status quo, it serves as evidence that _____.

   [A] public opinion is irrelevant

   [B] the policy-making process is complex

   [C] politicians don't listen to what their constituents want

   [D] the government is not trustworthy

   [E] public opinion is stable

SUGGESTED READING

Alvarez, R. Michael, and John Brehm. *Hard Choices, Easy Answers.* Princeton, NJ: Princeton University Press, 2002.

Baum, Matthew A., and Tim J. Groeling. *War Stories: The Causes and Consequences of Public Views of War.* Princeton, NJ: Princeton University Press, 2009.

Campbell, David. *Why We Vote: How Schools and Communities Shape Our Civic Life.* Princeton, NJ: Princeton University Press, 2006.

Carmines, Edward G., and James A. Stimson. *Issue Evolution: Race and the Transformation of American Politics.* Princeton, NJ: Princeton University Press, 1990.

Converse, Phillip E. "The Nature of Belief Systems in Mass Publics." In *Ideology and Discontent*, edited by David E. Apter (pp. 206–61). Glencoe, IL: Free Press of Glencoe, 1964.

Delli Carpini, Michael X., and Scott Keeter. *What Americans Know about Politics and Why It Matters.* New Haven, CT: Yale University Press, 1997.

Green, Donald P., Bradley Palmquist, and Eric Schickler. *Partisan Hearts and Minds.* New Haven, CT: Yale University Press, 2002.

Hibbing, John R., and Elizabeth Theiss-Morse. *Congress as Public Enemy: Public Attitudes toward American Political Institutions.* New York: Cambridge University Press, 1995.

Jacobs, Lawrence R., and Robert Y. Shapiro. *Politicians Don't Pander: Political Manipulation and the Loss of Democratic Responsiveness.* Chicago: University of Chicago Press, 2000.

Marcus, George E., John L. Sullivan, Elizabeth Theiss-Morse, and Sandra L. Wood. *With Malice toward Some: How People Make Civil Liberties Judgments.* New York: Cambridge University Press, 1995.

Peffley, Mark, and Jon Hurwitz. *Justice in America: The Separate Realities of Blacks and Whites.* New York: Cambridge University Press, 2010.

Zaller, John. *The Nature and Origins of Mass Opinion.* New York: Cambridge University Press, 1992.

7

The Media

MEDIA COVERAGE OF POLITICS OFTEN SEEMS LIKE THE PLAY-BY-PLAY at a sports event. Like sportscasters who scrutinize every pass, pitch, or dunk, dissecting the action one frame at a time, the political media sometimes seem to focus solely on polls, scandals, and verbal gaffes—the daily drama and conflict in Washington. Of course, some people (your authors included) are hard-core political junkies who would like to see congressional proceedings covered by the media as thoroughly and enthusiastically as they cover the Super Bowl. But although political junkies like the attention paid to politics, they often question the media's choice of content: the focus on winning and losing, the tendency to make snap judgments, and the obsession with reporting on scandals instead of concentrating on policy.

Think about the media's coverage of President Obama in his second term. One month, the journalists are writing about how he is going to build on his reelection to enact immigration reform, fix the budget deficit, and establish a new Democratic majority that will control the national government for the next generation. The next month, the media are describing Obama as a lame duck who is certain to cave under Republican pressure, allowing his signature health care legislation to be undone. And the month after that, the newscasts are saying that Obama is once again the master of Washington, D.C., and the Republicans will surely be cowed into accepting his stance on the debt ceiling. But wait—after another month, the pundits contend that Obama is a failed president who is enmeshed in scandal, from

CONFLICT & COMPROMISE
in American Politics

237

Trace how the American mass media have evolved over time, and describe the major types of news sources today.

▶ PAGES 238–47

Describe where reporters and others in the news media get political information.

▶ PAGES 247–51

Analyze who uses which news sources and whether it matters.

▶ PAGES 251–54

Explain the ways in which the media may influence politics.

▶ PAGES 254–57

Assess whether the media fulfill their role in American democracy.

▶ PAGES 258–63

the National Security Administration's monitoring of Americans' cell phone records, to the poorly operating Healthcare.gov website, to the selfie that he and British Prime Minister David Cameron and Danish Prime Minister Helle Thorning-Schmidt posed for at Nelson's Mandela's memorial service, to the poor Democratic showing in the 2014 elections.

Are the events focused on by the media always important enough to warrant a political play-by-play? Will they have long-term consequences for President Obama or for the country? In retrospect, the media spend a lot of time on events that seem trivial, and ignore many other events that turn out to be crucial.

This misplaced emphasis is especially important because media coverage is a primary mechanism through which Americans are informed about politics and public policy, and studies indicate that Americans learn a great deal from media coverage.[1] For democracy to work, citizens need to have a sense of which candidates and policy options are consistent with their own goals. Not everyone has to be an expert, but people have to meet a minimum standard of knowing which direction they would like government policy to go and which candidates would work toward this goal if elected.

Many critics blame the media for gaps in Americans' political knowledge, low levels of civic engagement, and distrust of the federal government.[2] These observers want media coverage that gives Americans a detailed appreciation of the policy questions facing elected officials and that holds elected officials accountable for their campaign promises and behavior in office; they desire sound, substantiated coverage and are not interested in access to what seems to be a steady stream of scandals, failures, and poll results.[3] Why do the media fail to fulfill this important role in American politics?

Not only does the content of many news stories influence politics, but political processes and outcomes also influence the news industry. Coverage is shaped by federal regulations that affect what journalists can print or broadcast, as well as by the structure and ownership of media corporations, most of which need to make a profit to survive. These political influences on the media can, in turn, affect how Americans view officeholders, candidates, and events.

In this chapter, our discussion of the news media addresses these arguments about the nature of and forces behind media coverage of American politics. Who are the media, and how do they cover politics? Who decides which stories make the news and how they are reported? Is media coverage politically biased? Where do people get their political information? How has the Internet's evolution into a major source of political information changed both the traditional media business and what Americans know about politics?

TRACE HOW THE AMERICAN MASS MEDIA HAVE EVOLVED OVER TIME, AND DESCRIBE THE MAJOR TYPES OF NEWS SOURCES TODAY

THE NEWS MEDIA IN AMERICA

mass media Sources that provide information to the average citizen, such as newspapers, television networks, radio stations, podcasts, and websites.

This section describes the **mass media**, the many sources of political information, including newspapers, television networks, radio stations, podcasts, and websites, available to Americans. It also describes the dramatic changes occurring in new forms of media and the way these changes affect not only the amount of political information available and how it is delivered, but also how people use this information.

HISTORICAL OVERVIEW

The role of the media as an information source and the controversy over how the media report about politics are nothing new. Since the Founding, politicians have understood that Americans learn about politics largely from the media, and they have complained about coverage and sought to influence both the media's selection of stories and the way they report on them.

THE EARLY DAYS Long before there was a United States, the news media were active in colonial America. Ben Franklin published one of the earliest newspapers, the *Pennsylvania Gazette*, beginning in 1729. For the most part, newspapers had relatively low circulations, due partly to their cost and partly because they were available only in major cities.[4] During the Revolutionary War and afterward, many newspapers chronicled the conflict and became a venue for debates over the proposed federal government.[5]

Despite the guarantee of freedom of the press included in the First Amendment of the Constitution, in 1798, Congress and President John Adams enacted the Alien and Sedition Acts, which made it a crime to criticize the president or Congress.[6] While these press restrictions were later repealed or allowed to expire, they serve as a reminder that the American media have never been free of government regulation, both in terms of what is published and who can own a newspaper or other media source.

THE PENNY PRESS, YELLOW JOURNALISM, AND MUCKRAKERS Beginning in the 1830s, a combination of new technologies, entrepreneurs, and political ambition transformed the news media. In 1833, the *New York Sun* began selling papers for a penny a copy rather than the standard price of six cents. The price reduction, which was facilitated by cheaper, faster printing presses, made the newspaper available to the mass public for the first time, and this increase in circulation made it possible, even with the lower price, to hire larger staffs of reporters.[7] The development of the telegraph also aided newspapers by enabling reporters on assignment throughout the country to quickly send stories back home for publication. The Associated Press, the first **wire service**, was formed in the 1840s by a group of newspaper owners to share the benefits and costs of this new technology.[8]

Other inexpensive newspapers soon appeared. Many were unabashedly partisan, using their coverage of events to support a particular political party or position. Some were even published by party organizations. For example, the *New York Tribune* was strongly antislavery. By 1860, the *Tribune*'s circulation was larger than that of any other newspaper in the world, and its articles "helped to add fuel to the fires of slavery and sectionalism that divided North and South."[9]

The period after the Civil War saw the beginning of **yellow journalism**. This new type of newspaper reporting appealed to a wider audience by using bold headlines, illustrations, and sensational stories (the name came from the yellow paper they were printed on). The best example was the *New York Journal*, published by William Randolph Hearst. During the months before the Spanish-American War, Hearst's reporter in Cuba cabled that there were no signs of war and asked whether he should return home. Hearst cabled back, "Please remain. You furnish the pictures and I'll furnish the war."[10] Of course, America did not fight the Spanish-American War just because of the articles in Hearst's newspaper—but it appears that the paper had a significant impact

wire service An organization that gathers news and sells it to other media outlets. The invention of the telegraph in the early 1800s made this type of service possible.

yellow journalism A style of newspaper popular in the late 1800s that featured sensationalized stories, bold headlines, and illustrations to increase readership.

on public opinion toward this country's involvement in that conflict.

At the same time, other authors and reporters used newspapers and books to call for reforms to federal, state, and local governments. These **investigative journalists**, known as muckrakers, included Lincoln Steffens, who criticized corruption in municipal governments, and Upton Sinclair, who raised concerns about food safety and public health.[11] Another new group of newspapers attracted audiences because they moved away from promoting partisan or ideological goals to providing complete, unbiased, accurate coverage of events. This motivation was exemplified by Adolph Ochs, who transformed a small New York paper into a nonpartisan paper with the goals of journalistic impartiality, accuracy, and complete coverage of events. He gave the *New York Times* a new motto: "All the News That's Fit to Print."[12] This emphasis on objectively reporting events became the dominant model of news sources, which continues to this day.[13]

WITH THE DEVELOPMENT OF national radio networks in the 1920s and 1930s, Americans throughout the nation could hear coverage of important events as they occurred.

investigative journalists Reporters who dig deeply into a particular topic of public concern, often targeting government failures and inefficiencies.

Federal Communications Commission (FCC) A government agency created in 1934 to regulate American radio stations and later expanded to regulate television, wireless communications technologies, and other broadcast media.

broadcast media Communications technologies, such as television and radio, that transmit information over airwaves.

fairness doctrine An FCC regulation requiring broadcast media to present several points of view to ensure balanced coverage. It was created in the late 1940s and eliminated in 1987.

NEW TECHNOLOGIES AND FEDERAL REGULATION After World War I, new communications technology made it possible to broadcast programs over radio—and for many Americans to buy radios to hear these programs.[14] During the 1920s, hundreds of small, local stations appeared, along with some larger stations that could broadcast nationwide, eventually leading to the development of networks, groups of local radio (and later, TV) stations owned by one company that broadcast a common set of programs.

The Communications Act of 1934 authorized the **Federal Communications Commission (FCC)** to regulate **broadcast media**, which at the time meant radio stations and subsequently included television stations, cable TV, and other communications technologies. FCC regulations reflected the assumption that the airways were public property, so no one had an inherent right to operate a radio or TV station. Rather, station owners were expected to serve the public interest, as defined by the FCC.

A central concern of the FCC was that one company or organization might buy enough stations to dominate the airwaves in an area, so that only one set of programs or point of view would be available. Over the next two generations, the FCC developed regulations to limit the number of radio and TV stations a company could own in a community and the total nationwide audience that a company's TV stations could reach.[15]

The 1940s saw the rise of TV as Americans' primary news source. Television made it possible to report on stories using instantly accessible visual footage rather than printed words—a crucial distinction, given that many citizens are not highly motivated to learn about political events and issues. In fact, a frequent argument made about public opinion during the Vietnam War was that declining public support for the war arose at the first time in American history that stories depicting the war's horror firsthand were a staple on nightly news broadcasts.[16] Such images were not new (previous wars had produced graphic photos in magazines and many newsreels), but they became commonplace with the advent of television.

In the late 1940s, the FCC also developed the **fairness doctrine**. It required TV and radio stations to offer a variety of political views in their programming.[17]

As a result of this rule, stations offered debates and presentations supporting different political positions as part of their news programs, as well as talk shows and interviews featuring a wide range of political figures. The FCC also created the **equal time provision**, which states that if a radio or television station gives airtime to a candidate outside its news coverage—such as during an entertainment show or a cooking program—it has to give equal time to other candidates running for the same office. TV satirist Stephen Colbert's brief (and mock-serious) presidential candidacy in 2007 raised the question of whether *The Colbert Report* was subject to the equal time provision, since news and interview shows are normally exempted but comedy shows are not. The issue became moot when Colbert withdrew from the race.

DEREGULATION The FCC's limits on ownership and content assumed that radio and TV stations were public trustees with a responsibility to provide full, fair, and unbiased coverage of political events. This assumption changed with the development of new communications technologies such as cable TV, satellite TV, and the Internet. After all, with so many sources of information, if one broadcaster ignored a candidate, an issue, or a viewpoint, citizens could still find out what they wanted to know from another source. Pressure for deregulation also came from the owners of media companies, who wanted to buy more TV, radio, and cable stations, as well as from book and magazine publishers, Internet service providers, and newspapers, in order to increase efficiencies and profits.[18] After much debate, Congress passed the Telecommunications Act of 1996, which gave the FCC the power to revise all ownership and content restrictions enacted over the last two generations; since then, the FCC has abolished most ownership restrictions. (The equal time provision is still in place, but the fairness doctrine was eliminated in 1987.)[19]

These regulatory changes accelerated two trends in American news media. The first is concentration, which involves one company owning more than one media source in a town or community. For example, Clear Channel Communications owns multiple AM and FM radio stations in more than 30 cities. The second trend is cross-ownership, which involves one company owning several different kinds of media outlets, often in the same community. The Tribune Company in Chicago owns the WGN radio station, the WGN TV station, and the *Chicago Tribune* daily newspaper. These trends have given rise to **media conglomerates**, companies that control a wide range of news sources.[20]

Today, all four major television networks (ABC, CBS, NBC, and Fox) are part of larger companies that each own many other broadcast and cable stations, movie production and distribution companies, radio stations, newspapers, and other media outlets. Nuts & Bolts 7.1 shows the diverse holdings of one such company, the News Corporation.

One FCC commissioner argued for deregulation, saying, "Democracy and civic discourse were not dead in America when there were only three to four stations in most markets in the 1960s and 1970s, and they will surely not be dead in this century when there are, at a minimum, four to six independent broadcasters in most markets, plus hundreds of cable channels and unlimited Internet voices."[21]

UNDER THE FCC'S EQUAL TIME regulations, if comedian Stephen Colbert had campaigned for president while remaining host of *The Colbert Report*, other presidential candidates could have forced the Comedy Central cable channel to give them free airtime.

equal time provision An FCC regulation requiring broadcast media to provide equal airtime on any non-news programming to all candidates running for an office.

media conglomerates Companies that control a large number of media sources across several types of media outlets.

HOLDINGS OF NEWSCORP/21ST CENTURY FOX

NewsCorp/21st Century* is an example of a media conglomerate, a company that controls a variety of media outlets throughout the world. It owns cable television networks, TV and radio stations, newspapers, movie-production companies, magazines, and even sports teams. This structure allows the company to rebroadcast or reprint stories in different outlets, and thus operate more efficiently, but opponents are concerned that conglomerates might expand to control most—or even all—of the sources that are available to the average citizen, making it impossible to access alternate points of view.

Fox Television Stations	Film Companies	Books and Magazines
27 U.S. stations	21st Century Fox	45 book publishers (including HarperCollins) worldwide
	Fox Searchlight Pictures	
	Fox Television Studios	3 magazines
	Blue Sky Studios	
	11 other film companies	

Satellite and Cable Holdings	Newspapers	Other Holdings
Fox News Channel	*New York Post*	AmericanIdol.com
17 other cable channels in U.S.	*Wall Street Journal*	Hulu.com (32 percent ownership)
47 other cable channels outside U.S.		
6 satellite TV channels	3 U.K. newspapers	16 news and entertainment websites
	19 Australian newspapers	Many other businesses
	24 local U.S. newspapers	

These two companies were created in 2013 by dividing the operations of the News Corporation. However, the founder of the News Corporation, Rupert Murdoch, is the chairman and CEO of 21st Century Fox and the executive chairman of NewsCorp, and his family trust still holds a controlling interest in both corporations.

Other commissioners disagreed, arguing that concentration would limit citizens' choices and force programming to become increasingly homogenized. As one commissioner put it, "As big media companies get bigger, they're likely to broadcast even more homogenized programming that increasingly appeals to the lowest common denominator. If [television] is [like] the toaster with pictures, soon only Wonder Bread will pop out."[22] As of now, it is not clear which viewpoint is most valid, although, as we show later, there is no sign that the increased number of sources is leading to a better-informed population—or that media concentration in some markets is having the opposite effect.

MEDIA SOURCES

There are many sources of political information, ranging from mainstream media such as newspapers, TV and radio stations, books, and magazines, to countless Internet-based sources. Of course, all print and broadcast media sources are not the same: the looks, sound, and content across available sources can vary widely. They may differ in the frequency of publication, the breadth of coverage, or the amount of time or space they choose to devote to a story. There is also a discrepancy among the different media sources as to the amount and kinds of resources they can direct toward reporting the news. These differences mean that media sources are not interchangeable—and as a news consumer it is important to realize that what you learn about politics depends on where you look.

NEWSPAPERS AND MAGAZINES National newspapers, such as the *New York Times*, *Washington Post, Los Angeles Times,* and *Wall Street Journal,* cover American politics using a large worldwide staff. Foreign publications, such as the United Kingdom's *Financial Times,* also cover American politics. Smaller regional and local papers serve medium- to large-sized cities and smaller towns. The main drawback of newspapers as an information source is timeliness—they are prisoners of the news cycle because they publish only once per day, although many update their websites and mobile apps as events warrant.

Recent years have seen significant declines in newspaper readership. Companies that once owned newspapers in Chicago, Philadelphia, and Minneapolis have gone bankrupt, and one major U.S. city, Seattle, now has no hometown daily newspaper that appears in print form. It is too early to say that newspapers are "dead," but decreases in both circulation and advertising revenues are forcing many newspapers to cut foreign bureaus, reduce the number of local reporters, and thin the amount of news in every edition.[23]

Of the many magazines that cover politics, national weeklies such as *Time* often feature political events as front-page news. A small number of magazines offer extensive coverage of political events; these include the *National Journal,* the *New Republic,* the *Nation,* and the *National Review.*

TELEVISION The four major national TV networks (ABC, CBS, Fox, and NBC) and many cable channels, such as CNN, offer nightly news as well as prime-time news programs. Some cable stations offer news coverage throughout the day and night, creating the 24-hour **news cycle**. Local TV stations also cover some local political

news cycle The time between the release of information and its publication, such as the 24 hours between issues of a daily newspaper.

AS THESE STARK IMAGES FROM Vietnam and Iraq illustrate, photos and televised images of war have the potential to capture attention and shape public opinion.

events in addition to running the national networks' programming. News coverage varies from the "talking head" format of a person behind a desk reading copy to the camera, to investigative reporting that involves reporters and camera crews gathering information in the field and assembling it for broadcast, to talk shows that air interviews with political figures. Some programs combine these formats; one example is *The O'Reilly Factor,* a nightly show on the Fox News Network hosted by conservative commentator Bill O'Reilly. In a typical episode, O'Reilly reports news stories; offers political commentary; and interviews elected officials, party officials, journalists, and other prominent people in the news.

The main drawback of TV news coverage of politics is its lack of breadth. Nightly news programs on the major networks have only 30 minutes to deliver their report (23 minutes excluding commercials). As a result, even an important political event like the president's State of the Union address receives only a brief discussion. Cable news channels, such as MSNBC or the Fox News Channel, have more time, but politics is only one of the topics those networks must cover on any one day.

RADIO The major radio networks, such as ABC, CBS, and Clear Channel Communications, offer brief news programs throughout the day, but most political content on the radio consists of talk radio programs that include a host discussing politics with listeners who phone in. The major nationwide talk radio shows, such as *The Rush Limbaugh Show,* generally offer a politically conservative point of view—and openly advertise this orientation.[24] Liberal talk radio programs also are broadcast, but their audience is a small fraction of the size of conservative programs' audience. Other political programs air on National Public Radio, an organization funded by the government and private donations. Overall, there are more than 13,000 radio stations in America. Just as with other media sources, only a fraction of these focus on delivering news or political coverage.

THE INTERNET Over the last two decades, the Internet has become a major and often dominant information source for information about American politics. Most U.S. newspapers, magazines, television networks, radio stations, and cable

COVERAGE OF IMPORTANT EVENTS today becomes instantaneously available through Internet sources like Twitter feeds and blogs. Here we see a screenshot of the National Review Online Twitter feed (@nro) from October 2014.

stations offer free or (increasingly) paid access to all of their content via websites and mobile apps. And most of these sources use Twitter feeds to announce new articles or photos, especially about emerging or time-critical events.

As this description suggests, much of the reporting on politics that is found on the Internet is simply a different (sometimes more elaborate) version of stories that are also available elsewhere.[25] Along with these sources, there are many Internet-only sites, most with small audiences, that offer a combination of rumor, inside information, and deep analysis of American politics. For example, Politico's Playbook offers collections of links to daily national political coverage and provides a political rundown of people and events inside Washington.[26] SCOTUSblog (Supreme Court of the United States blog) analyzes Supreme Court decisions, judicial nominations, and other legal questions.[27] And many blogs, such as The Monkey Cage and the Mischiefs of Faction, use political science research to explain contemporary American politics.[28]

The evolution of the Internet has also made new kinds of political information available to the average citizen. For example, The Center for Responsive Politics offers a searchable database of contributions to candidates and political organizations.[29] Pollster.com collects and analyzes public opinion surveys, including presidential election polls, and offers interpretations of the results as well as discussions of possible sources of bias.[30] Other websites offer less useful but entertaining political information. For example, when then Congressman Anthony Weiner resigned in 2011 after sending lewd photos to a supporter via Twitter, various websites promptly found the photos and put them online.

Twenty years after the first Web pages went online, it is clear that the Internet also has fundamentally lowered the barriers to publication. A generation ago, it was all but impossible for average citizens to report on what they knew or to present their analyses to the general public.[31] The Internet has created more opportunities for homegrown media, allowing a would-be political reporter to easily set up a website, Facebook page, YouTube channel, or some other way to present information. Such reporting has the potential to shape elections, or at least to distract politicians from their desired message. During the 2012 presidential campaign, for example, Republican Mitt Romney spent several days explaining his comments at a fundraiser about the "47 percent" of Americans

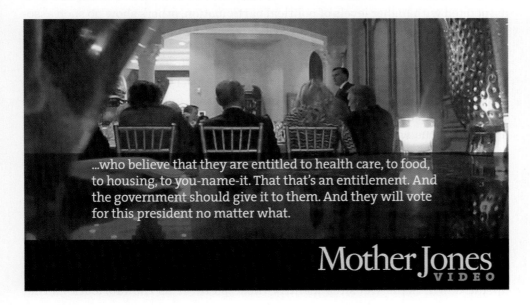

...who believe that they are entitled to health care, to food, to housing, to you-name-it. That that's an entitlement. And the government should give it to them. And they will vote for this president no matter what.

Mother Jones VIDEO

MOTHER JONES, A LIBERAL MEDIA organization, released video footage from a Republican fundraiser in May 2012 in which Republican presidential candidate Mitt Romney remarked that 47 percent of the people "believe that they are entitled to health care, to food, to housing, to you-name-it. . . . These are people who pay no income tax. . . . And so my job is not to worry about these people—I'll never convince them that they should take personal responsibility and care for their lives."

THE INTERNET MAKES IT EASY FOR ORDINARY citizens to share political information and report on political events as they happen. In one example, the founders of a local Tea Party group in Massachusetts keep up with the group's activity by checking its Facebook page (left). In another, photos of police arresting mostly peaceful Occupy Wall Street protesters (right) circulated widely after activists posted the images on Twitter.

whom he said did not pay income taxes and therefore expected government to take care of them. The video had been taken by someone working for the company catering the event, who then posted it online during the campaign. Politicians must now assume that anything they say or do (good or bad) will be instantly publicized using these technologies.

The Internet creates new opportunities for interaction between citizens, reporters, and government officials. Many reporters respond to comments posted by readers or host live online chat sessions, allowing people to ask follow-up questions about published stories.[32] Politicians do the same: aides in the Obama administration, for example, have used a variety of social media sites, including Facebook, Twitter, reddit, and live Skype events, to answer questions from citizens—and they respond to Twitter questions with the hashtag #AskTheWhiteHouse.

There is little evidence that the rise of the Internet has led to a better-informed, more politically active citizenry.[33] While some studies show that Internet usage is associated with higher levels of political participation, others show no such association.[34] Moreover, there is no clear evidence that surfing the Web makes people more politically informed.[35]

Why hasn't the Internet created a more-informed citizenry? Although the percentage of people who routinely use the Internet is very high, access is only the first step in becoming informed. One problem is that finding information on the Internet still requires doing your own research. Despite search engines, it is not always obvious where to look for political information. Suppose you wanted to learn more about the conflict in Afghanistan. A Google search in late 2013 of the terms "America," "Afghanistan," and "war" returned over 100 million Web pages, ranging from reports on America's military strategy to pictures of Afghan civilian casualties. Thus, the problem is not in finding information, but in deciding which of the millions of pages available will help you learn about the conflict.[36]

Second, some of the vast quantity of information on the Internet is of questionable reliability. For example, it is easy to find fake photographs showing President Barack Obama talking on the phone while holding the receiver upside down. Some websites identify these pictures as the fabrications that they are, but others do not. In a world where websites come and go, and where citizens often do not take the time to investigate what they see or read, false information may easily be accepted as true.

Another problem is that most people do not consult a wide range of media sources; instead they tend to focus on sites with views on political events that are compatible with their own—thus, Democrats look for sites that favor Democratic policies, conservatives look for websites run by conservative individuals or organizations, and so on.[37] The use of information supplied by political blogs shows the same pattern.[38]

In short, despite the Internet's wealth of information, there is no guarantee that people will sit down, search for what they want or need to know, distinguish truth from falsehood, and assemble their findings into coherent conclusions. In fact, rather than creating a uniformly well-informed citizenry, the availability of information on the Internet may exacerbate the "knowledge gap" we saw in Chapter 6, where a small percentage of Americans are extremely well informed about politics because they have the time, interest, and resources to think through and reconcile different sources of information, whereas the vast majority of the public may simply throw up their hands and make no attempt to become better informed.[39]

One of the most important things to take away from this section's discussion of the media is that there are many ways to learn about American politics, and each source offers information packaged and presented in different ways. However, virtually all media sources have the goal of maintaining or increasing their audience, whether as a means to sell more advertising or as a way to increase their reputation and influence. As we will see later in the chapter, this drive to maximize audience is one of the reasons the media focus so much on winners, losers, drama, and scandal in the coverage of American politics.

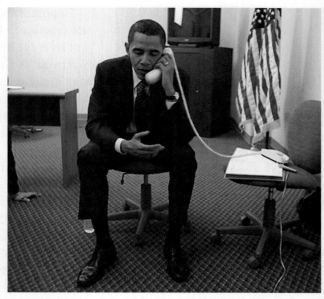

THIS FABRICATED PHOTO SHOWS President Obama apparently talking into a telephone he is holding upside down. The easy availability of doctored photos of many elected officials on the Internet highlights the dangers of relying on unvetted websites as a primary source of political information.

POLITICAL REPORTING: SOURCES, LEAKS, AND SHIELD LAWS

DESCRIBE WHERE REPORTERS AND OTHERS IN THE NEWS MEDIA GET POLITICAL INFORMATION

As we have seen, media coverage of politics influences both what citizens believe and how they vote. Media reports often shape the public's evaluations of government programs as well as the demands they place on elected officials or bureaucrats. The reality of reporting on politics is that many people involved in the political process don't want the public to be apprised of everything their elected officials are doing—or want only their own version of events to be publicized. Politicians want media coverage that highlights their achievements, which ideally will build public support and secure their election (or reelection). Bureaucrats want favorable attention for their programs, and interest groups want publicity to further their causes. Thus, coverage of American politics reflects trade-offs between reporters who want complete, accurate information and sources who want favorable coverage.

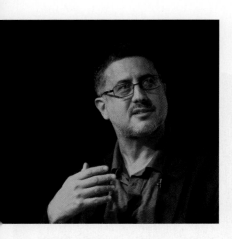

BARTON GELLMAN, PICTURED HERE, is leading the *Washington Post*'s coverage of Edward Snowden's release of classified documents on the NSA's surveillance activities to the media.

Reporters also face legal hurdles as they research stories. Notwithstanding the freedom of the press guaranteed in the Bill of Rights, reporters are subject to legal limitations, including the clear and present danger test and prior restraint. If the government can convince a judge that publication of a particular story would lead to immediate harm to a person or persons, a judge can halt publication; this action is called prior restraint. But the clear and present danger test sets the bar extremely high for stopping publication of a story. As we discussed in Chapter 4, most attempts to prevent publication have been unsuccessful.

To appreciate the issues surrounding classified information and prior restraint, consider the case of Edward Snowden, who while working as a contractor for America's National Security Agency downloaded a collection of files that documented the NSA's surveillance activities, including the collection of data on American's phone calls overseas and the monitoring of foreign politicians' cell phones. In 2012, Snowden approached several major publications across the world, including the *Washington Post*, to offer access to these documents. After several months of negotiation, the *Post* would not agree to all of Snowden's conditions— among other things, he wanted certain documents to be published in their entirety, while the *Post* wanted to hold back some classified information.[40] Snowden then came to an agreement with a British newspaper, the *Guardian*, which has gradually made the documents public, although he also allowed the *Post* to publish some of the documents.

The *Post*'s refusal to accept Snowden's demands was the product of several months of discussions with the U.S. government over what information could be released without harming national security or placing confidential sources in jeopardy. Although some government officials mentioned the possibility of invoking the prior restraint prohibition, no attempts were made to do so. In any case, even if the *Post* could be deterred from publication, the information would soon appear in stories published by other outlets.

The Snowden episode illustrates how government officials work to deter leaks or influence the media's coverage of a story without resorting to prior restraint. First, there are laws prohibiting the disclosure of classified information. The Obama administration, in particular, has worked to prosecute government employees who leak classified information to reporters (see the You Decide feature).[41] Thus, if Snowden ever returns to the United States, he will face a trial for leaking classified information, with a likely conviction and a long prison sentence. The *Post* sat on the Snowden documents for several months, publishing only when it was rumored that the *Guardian* planned to release its own story. Moreover, *Post* reporters and editors agreed to keep certain information out of their stories.

Why do reporters and publishers restrain their stories? Sometimes they agree with the government that keeping secrets is in the national interest. For example, for several years, mainstream media voluntarily decided not to run stories about secret American bases in Saudi Arabia from which drone missions were being flown over Iran and other countries. But ultimately the information was revealed in a *Wired* magazine story.[42] Other times, reporters are rewarded for cooperating— they may get information about another government policy or be promised future access to officials. Alternately, reporters may be coerced to back down from a story through the threat of losing future access to people in government or of even going to jail.

PRIOR RESTRAINT OF SECRET INFORMATION

The conflict between reporters and government officials is particularly sharp in the case of confidential information. Consider the diplomatic cables that were released to the public by the online source WikiLeaks in 2010 and 2011 (WikiLeaks had been given the information by a U.S. Army communications technician, Bradley Manning). Some of the information was simply embarrassing—such as reports of a foreign leader's mistress. But other information contained in these documents was more serious, such as the identities of confidential informants. As Porter Goss, former director of the CIA, argued, if a U.S. citizen living abroad is found to be an employee of the CIA, that person's ability to gather information will surely be compromised; in some places, the person's life might be in danger.[a]

Publishing confidential analyses is still a problem even if sources are removed. The leaked reports revealed, for example, that the United States had little confidence that the Afghan government could win support from its citizens, suggesting that if the Taliban forces could hold out until U.S. forces left the country, they could topple the government and return to power.

These concerns speak to the need for prior restraint, which gives the government the power to keep the details of secret operations and the names of covert operatives out of the newspapers and other media sources. But as we discussed in Chapter 4, attempts to invoke prior restraint are almost never successful. In this case, the U.S. government could not stop WikiLeaks from releasing the information because that organization is located outside the country. But the government could have gone to court to prevent American sources from publishing analyses based on the WikiLeaks information. Even if the information would eventually be released, restraining Americans from publishing might have helped to minimize the damage. Why isn't the decision to restrain or not to restrain secret information an easy call?

The problem is accountability. If the media are restrained from publication, then there is a risk that government officials will be able to do whatever they want, because the public and most elected officials will not find out. Put another way, without media watchdogs, the small number of unelected bureaucrats who make decisions about secret operations would never have to answer to the public or to elected representatives for those decisions. Moreover, these same bureaucrats would have decided which operations would be considered secret in the first place. In some cases, the ability to keep operations secret has allowed intelligence agencies to carry out programs that might have been prohibited had they been publicized from the start, such as the network of CIA prisons in Eastern Europe that was revealed in 2005.

The situation is somewhat different for individuals who leak classified information to the press. Bradley Manning, the source for WikiLeaks, violated a series of criminal statutes and army regulations that prohibit the unauthorized release of

Bradley Manning (center), whose job in the U.S. military gave him access to classified information, downloaded thousands of classified videos, diplomatic cables, reports, and other information and gave them to the website WikiLeaks.

classified information; he was convicted in 2013 and is serving a long prison sentence. The Manning case is notable because of the size of the leak and because Manning was caught. Often, the source of a leak is never identified. Even if a lead can be traced back to an individual, in many cases criminal charges are not brought, although a leaker may be fired, face disciplinary proceedings, or have no chance of being promoted—threats that are in place to discourage people from leaking information in the first place. Of course, without leaks, many government failures and embarrassing incidents will not come to light, which further weakens accountability.

In sum, decisions about prior restraint are difficult, precisely because they involve balancing two important goals: allowing the government to carry out covert operations and informing the public about government actions so that citizens can evaluate and respond to them.

CRITICAL THINKING QUESTIONS

1. If you had to evaluate an intelligence agency's request for prior restraint, what criteria would you use to decide whether to grant the request?

2. Should individuals such as Bradley Manning or Edward Snowden who leak classified information to the press be punished or praised for their actions? What circumstances or specifics would lead you to decide one way or the other?

STAGING THE NEWS

People inside the federal government, from the president to the large numbers of bureaucrats, work to shape media coverage to suit their personal goals. President Reagan's press secretary had a sign in his office that said, "You don't tell us how to stage the news, and we won't tell you how to cover it."

Politicians and others in government try to influence coverage by providing select information to reporters. Sometimes they hold press conferences where they take questions from the media. Other times, they speak to single reporters or to a group **on background** or **off the record**, meaning that the reporter can use the information but cannot attribute it to the politician by name. Another strategy is to hold events aimed at securing favorable press coverage.

Some scholars argue that elected officials use the media to shape public opinion, doling out information to reward reporters who write stories that support the officials' points of view.[43] To some extent this argument is true: much of the information reporters use to write their stories comes from political appointees, bureaucrats, elected officials, and party leaders.[44] Reporters who are known to be writing stories that are critical of a government program or a political leader may find that some people refuse to talk to them. However, while there is no doubt that elected officials would like to receive sympathetic media coverage and are sometimes successful, news reports on American politics reflect a multitude of sources and information. If nothing else, the fact that conflict is endemic to American politics means that one official's attempt to shape coverage by talking or remaining silent may be negated by another's efforts to promote a different point of view. The result is that different sources cover the same events differently; if you are interested in different points of view, they are generally not hard to find.

on background or **off the record** Comments a politician makes to the press on the condition that they can be reported only if they are not attributed to that politician.

REVEALING SOURCES

Reporters covering important or controversial stories often promise their sources that they will remain anonymous in any coverage based on the information they provide. These assurances are an important factor in the decision to leak information, especially classified information. However, these assurances are not absolute. Reporters and their editors can, under certain circumstances, be compelled by a court to reveal the sources for their stories. Although some states have shield laws that allow reporters to refuse to name their sources, there is no such law at the federal level. As a result, federal prosecutors can ask a judge to force journalists to name their sources, on the grounds that the source's identity is fundamental to their case. If the judge agrees, the reporter can be jailed for contempt for an indefinite period unless he or she provides the information. For example, in 2005, *Times* reporter Judith Miller was jailed for refusing to name the Bush administration official who gave her the identity of a clandestine CIA employee whose husband had written a report discrediting the administration's claim that Iraq was developing nuclear weapons. After three months in prison, Miller's source agreed to let her release his name: I. Lewis "Scooter" Libby, who at the time was Vice President Dick Cheney's deputy chief of staff. Libby was later convicted of lying to a grand jury about his actions.

The complex relationship between reporters and their sources highlights three important influences on media coverage of politics. A reporter's desire to tell the whole story about a political event may be trumped by (1) his or her concerns over jeopardizing national security, (2) his or her equally strong concern with maintaining good relationships with government sources, or (3) the possibility that the political event itself has been shaped by the goal of generating favorable press coverage.

Thus, the shaping of the news can also affect the way that the media report about politics. Insofar as elected officials see politics as a contest or battle to determine public policy, they will try to shape media coverage in ways that show them winning and their opponents losing, and to depict their opponents as ill-advised and scandal-ridden. Given the multitude of media sources, it is not hard for a politician to find a reporter who is willing to write exactly what that politician wants, either because the reporter believes the information is true or because he wants to attract an audience or to gain the politician's trust.

HOW DO AMERICANS USE THE MEDIA TO LEARN ABOUT POLITICS?

> ANALYZE WHO USES WHICH NEWS SOURCES AND WHETHER IT MATTERS

Americans now have more ways to learn about politics than they did a generation or two ago. Imagine yourself in the late 1940s. Suppose you wanted to learn about President Truman's State of the Union address. If you couldn't go to Washington to hear it in person, where could you have gotten information about the speech? If you lived in a big city, the speech would probably be covered in the next day's newspaper. If you lived in a small town, your local paper might or might not run the story, and if it didn't, you would need a subscription to either a big-city paper (which would arrive a week after the fact) or to a weekly or monthly news magazine, or you would need to have access to a radio that could pick up a station broadcasting the speech.

Now consider the modern era in which major political events saturate the media. You can tune in to one of the four major television networks, numerous cable news channels, public TV stations, or radio stations, or listen to live streaming of the speech or clips of important moments. Most TV stations will feature pundits' commentaries on the speech and will interview prominent politicians and commentators about what the president said. Jimmy Fallon and Stephen Colbert will make jokes about the speech in their opening monologues on late-night TV, and Jon Stewart and John Oliver will skewer it on their shows. Tomorrow the speech will be front-page news, and larger papers will publish the full text. Countless Internet sites will offer information and analyses. And you will be able to watch a video of the speech on YouTube and many other sites.

The fact that there are many sources of political information in the modern era does not imply that the average American uses most of them. For the most part, Americans learn about politics in the same way they become aware of other things, through a process explained using the **by-product theory**.[45] This theory posits that many Americans acquire political information accidentally. They read a newspaper's sports pages and glance at front-page stories along the way. They watch the *Daily Show* and learn about politics while laughing

by-product theory The idea that many Americans acquire political information unintentionally rather than by seeking it out.

FIGURE » 7.1

MAIN SOURCE OF NATIONAL AND INTERNATIONAL NEWS

A survey was conducted from 1991 until 2012 to determine where participants had learned about the news on the previous day. Participants could give multiple responses if they got the news from multiple sources. Most people continued to get the news from television, but fewer were reading newspapers or listening to the radio to get news and many more people were getting their news from the Internet or from mobile alerts.

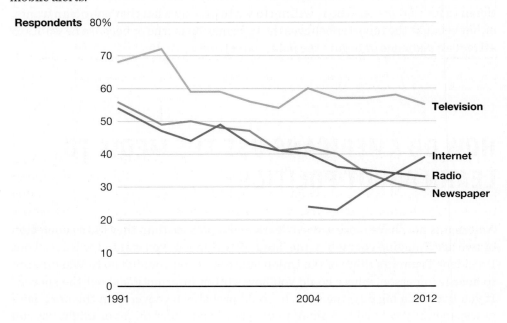

SOURCE: Pew Research Center, "In Changing News Landscape, Even Television Is Vulnerable," September 27, 2012, www.people-press .org/2012/09/27/in-changing-news-landscape-even-television-is-vulnerable/ (accessed 12/24/13).

at Jon Stewart's reports. They read a story on a political blog or Internet news site because the title catches their eye as they're looking for something else. Thus, while Edward Snowden's stolen NSA documents were published by the *Guardian,* a British newspaper that very few Americans read, most people found out about the revelations from the many other news sources that picked up the story.

After encountering new information, it depends on the individual's level of interest as to whether she remembers that information later or uses it to modify her thoughts about politicians or policies. John Zaller's research on information processing shows that highly interested people are unlikely to change their minds when they learn something new, as they have already decided what they think. Other people who are uninterested in politics are less likely to encounter new political information in the first place. Thus, media coverage is most likely to affect the beliefs of people who take a moderate interest in politics.[46]

There are many news sources, but there is no one source that suits everyone. Figure 7.1 highlights some important trends in media usage.[47] The percentage of people who read newspapers declined by almost a third over the last decade;

TABLE » 7.1

TRADITIONAL NEWS SOURCES FACE STIFF COMPETITION

Older Americans grew up without cable channels, the Internet, or even color TV. Are there generational differences in the use of different media sources?

	Age 18–29	30–49	50–64	65+
Watched TV news	52%	63%	71%	79%
Read a newspaper	21	22	38	47
Listened to radio news	15	19	34	13
Got news online	65	48	15	14

SOURCE: Pew Research Center, "Internet Gains on Television as Public's Main News Source," January 4, 2011, www.people-press .org/2011/01/04/internet-gains-on-television-as-publics-main-news-source/(accessed 8/28/12).

the percentage of people watching TV news has also declined. Use of online sources, including blogs and social media, has tripled and will likely continue to increase. Table 7.1, which shows data on respondents' main news source, indicates that all age groups use Internet-based sources, but that usage is most prevalent among younger Americans, as is the decline in traditional news sources such as newspapers.

DOES THE SOURCE MATTER?

People acquire different kinds of information in different formats from each type of media source. A newspaper can report on a Taliban attack in Afghanistan in a fair amount of detail and may include a few pictures, whereas a TV news show may include footage of the attack and the aftermath while providing a less detailed story. Do people who rely on different kinds of media sources learn different things about politics? And do most people tend to accumulate broad, general political knowledge, or are they apt to gather information only about specific topics?

In 2012, the Pew Research Center used a series of questions to determine if respondents were relatively well informed about politics, then asked which media outlets they used as information sources. Using this data, Figure 7.2 shows how much of the audience for different news programs are rated as well informed. For example, 38 percent of the audience for the *Rachel Maddow Show* (a left-leaning program on MSNBC) are well informed, versus 4 percent of individuals who get information from daytime television talk shows.

One way to look at these data is to say that some sources provide better, more accurate information than others, thus producing a better-informed audience. But we know that people generally consult a variety of news sources, so we can't attribute their knowledge or ignorance to only one source. What is more likely is that different sources tailor their programming to their particular audience. In other words, if the writers on the *Daily Show* know that a relatively high percentage of their audience is well informed about politics, they will offer different

FIGURE » 7.2

POLITICAL KNOWLEDGE BY PREFERRED MEDIA SOURCE

One of the most important questions about media usage is whether people who know a lot about politics get their information from different sources than the news sources used by people who don't know as much. Does this figure show differences between high information and low information?

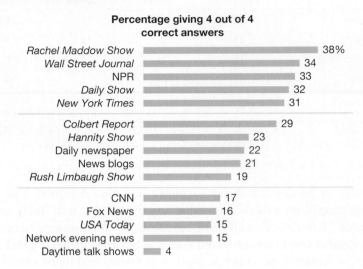

Percentage giving 4 out of 4 correct answers

Rachel Maddow Show	38%
Wall Street Journal	34
NPR	33
Daily Show	32
New York Times	31
Colbert Report	29
Hannity Show	23
Daily newspaper	22
News blogs	21
Rush Limbaugh Show	19
CNN	17
Fox News	16
USA Today	15
Network evening news	15
Daytime talk shows	4

SOURCE: Pew Research Center, "In Changing News Landscape, Even Television Is Vulnerable," September 27, 2012, www.people-press .org/2012/09/27/in-changing-news-landscape-even-television-is-vulnerable/ (accessed 12/24/13).

(probably more-detailed, more-complex) stories about political events compared to the stories presented on daytime TV talk shows.

These findings about media usage reinforce the argument made earlier about the media's coverage of American politics: although there are many different sources of political information available, very few Americans undertake a systematic search to gain a full and accurate understanding of American politics, no matter if the topic concerns presidential performance—or anything else. Most people learn about politics as a by-product of consulting the media for other reasons. As a result, the biggest problem for the media is to gain the attention of a disinterested, distracted audience.

> EXPLAIN THE WAYS IN WHICH THE MEDIA MAY INFLUENCE POLITICS

MEDIA EFFECTS ON AMERICAN CITIZENS AND GOVERNMENT POLICY

media effects The influence of media coverage on average citizens' opinions and actions.

The study of **media effects** explores whether exposure to media coverage of politics changes what people think or do. There is considerable evidence that media coverage influences its audience. However, much of the impact stems not from what such stories contain but from what they leave out, how they present information, or even whether a story is reported at all. Political scientists label these mechanisms priming, filtering (also called agenda-setting), slant, and framing.[48]

THEORIES OF MEDIA INFLUENCE

Theories of media influence distinguish various ways in which coverage can affect media consumers' beliefs. The most obvious mechanism is the use of the media as a forum for persuasion, in which an overt effort seeks to persuade people to change their minds about a candidate or an issue. However, people are not always conscious of the ways media reports shape their beliefs. Theorists describe four media effects that work largely without consumers' awareness:

▶ **Filtering** (also called agenda-setting) results from journalists' and editors' decisions about which of many potential news stories to report.

▶ **Slant** in a story gives favorable coverage to one candidate or policy without providing "balanced" favorable coverage of other sides.

▶ **Priming** occurs when media coverage of a story affects the importance people place on the issues or events mentioned in the coverage.

▶ **Framing** refers to how the description or presentation of a story, including the details, explanations, and context, changes the reaction people have to the information.

The existence of these media effects does not imply that reporters or editors try to mislead the public or sway public opinion to conform to their own ideas (see How It Works: How News Makes It to the Public). If you read an article about a particular issue and decide to change your position, this doesn't suggest that the story was inaccurate or biased. Your decision may well be justified by the facts of the situation. Similarly, when slanted campaign coverage praises one candidate

filtering The influence on public opinion that results from journalists' and editors' decisions about which of many potential news stories to report.

slant The imbalance in a story that covers one candidate or policy favorably without providing similar coverage of the other side.

priming The influence on the public's general impressions caused by positive or negative coverage of a candidate or an issue.

framing The influence on public opinion caused by the way a story is presented or covered, including the details, explanations, and context offered in the report.

THE WAY A STORY IS REPORTED—which information is included in an article or which images are used—makes a big difference in what people learn from it. A story about the Palestinian-Israeli conflict, for example, might emphasize the hardships faced by poor Palestinians (left) or suicide bombings by Palestinians in Israel (right).

and dismisses another as unqualified, you might conclude that the author agrees with the first candidate's positions and wrote the story to help that candidate get elected. But what if the first candidate is actually the most qualified? If so, then slanted coverage of the campaign might be objective.

The same is true for other media effects. Space limitations mean that some filtering is inevitable as reporters and editors decide which stories to cover. Similar decisions about what to report and how to present the information lead to priming and framing effects. Even if everyone in the political media adhered to the highest standards of accuracy, these influences would still exist.

James Druckman and Michael Parkin's 2005 study of a Senate race in Minnesota exemplifies the modern conception of media effects. The researchers found that different newspapers covered the candidates differently, both in the amount of coverage for each candidate and in the percentage of positive versus negative stories that they published. Druckman and Parkin showed that a given paper's slant in coverage was correlated with endorsements, such that papers gave more coverage and more positive coverage to the candidates they endorsed. Voters who were regular readers of a paper that endorsed a particular candidate were more likely to hold a positive opinion of that candidate and more likely to vote for him.[49]

A study of priming by Jon Krosnick and Laura Brannon found that exposure to press coverage of the Persian Gulf War in 1990 and 1991 moved citizens to evaluate President George H. W. Bush on the basis of his effectiveness in managing the war rather than on other factors such as the state of the economy.[50] Such priming is more likely when citizens are politically knowledgeable about the issues being discussed and trust the authors of the related news stories.[51]

The concept of filtering is illustrated by Project Censored's annual list of Top Censored Stories.[52] The group's list for 2013 included stories about increased cancer rates in Iraq after the U.S. invasion and occupation, the growing income inequality in America, and the possibility of worldwide food shortages in the near future. The group's point is not that the government forces reporters to keep quiet; it claims that reporters and their editors decide against covering these stories, sometimes for self-serving reasons, such as beliefs about what their audience wants to see or read. Of course, everyone can think of stories that they believe deserve more attention. However, because no media source can report on everything—due to lack of space, time, and staff—some events or problems fall through the cracks, receiving little or no attention despite their significance.

An example of framing comes from the work of Thomas Nelson, Rosalee Clawson, and Zoe Oxley, who recruited a group of people who live in Columbus, Ohio, divided them randomly into two groups, and had the members of each group watch one of two versions of a news story that had run on two different local TV stations. Both versions of the story described a rally that a local chapter of the Ku Klux Klan planned to hold in a nearby town. The different frames for these stories are shown in Table 7.2. The first version of the story emphasized the threat to public order and safety posed by the rally—that members of the Klan might incite others to violence, or that there might be fights between Klan members and counterprotesters. The second version of the story was almost identical, except it omitted public order and safety concerns, focusing instead on the free speech and assembly issues raised by the rally—that constitutional rights of freedom of speech and assembly allow the expression of beliefs and attitudes that a majority finds hateful and distasteful.

TABLE » 7.2

MEASURING FRAMING EFFECTS

Researchers studied whether the framing of a story affected participants' attitudes. To do so, they (1) measured participants' political beliefs before exposing them to a television story about a rally that was being planned by the Ku Klux Klan, (2) had the participants watch one of two versions of the story (one with a public-order frame and one with a free-speech frame), and (3) measured the participants' political beliefs based on their answers to a questionnaire after they watched the story. The participants' mean tolerance scores after viewing one of the two versions of the story are shown below, with higher numbers indicating greater tolerance.

	PUBLIC-ORDER FRAME	FREE-SPEECH FRAME
Tolerance for rallies	3.31	3.96
Tolerance for speeches	3.54	4.17
Importance of free speech	5.25	5.49
Importance of public order	5.43	4.75

SOURCE: Thomas E. Nelson, Rosalee A. Clawson, and Zoe M. Oxley, "Media Framing of a Civil Liberties Conflict and Its Effects on Tolerance," *American Political Science Review* 91 (1997): 567–83.

After watching one of the two versions of the story, people answered a series of questions that measured their tolerance for the rally, as well as how important they considered free speech and public order. The results for the two groups, shown in Table 7.2, provided clear evidence of framing. The group that saw the version of the story that emphasized free speech had a far greater tolerance for the rally and speeches than the people who saw the safety-focused version of the story did; they also placed a higher importance on free speech and a lower importance on public order.

As this section illustrates, reporters move beyond "just the facts" for many different reasons, one of which is that much of what happens in American politics requires interpretation. They must choose what to report because so many things happen every day, and they must decide how to report staged news, whether to reveal secrets, and which sources to rely on. Thus, filtering and framing of the news are inevitable. You may disagree with the decisions of a particular reporter or publication, but there is no such thing as completely objective journalism; your preferred coverage would just involve a different frame, a different filter, and different kinds of priming. Moreover, one of the biggest determinants of how stories are filtered and framed is the desire to attract an audience. The central finding of the political science literature on media influence is that, in the main, reporting on politics is not biased ideologically. The principal concern is with standing out and making stories simple and dramatic in order to catch the attention of a distracted audience. By this logic, stories that say "nothing much happened today to President Obama," or "today's events have no long-term implications for the Obama presidency," will lose out to reporting that casts the day's events in life-and-death terms.

WHAT DO POLITICAL SCIENTISTS DO?

For more on how political scientists study media framing, visit **wwnpag.es/wdpsd**

ASSESSING MEDIA COVERAGE OF AMERICAN POLITICS

In a democracy, the media's job is to provide citizens with information about politicians, government actions, and policy debates. Here we examine some of the arguments about how the media fall short, why journalists and editors make the choices they do, and what the impact of those decisions is on coverage and on what Americans know.

MEDIA BIAS

Surveys of the American electorate routinely find that Democrats generally think the media favor Republicans, whereas Republicans have the opposite belief.[53] Conservative critics point to surveys that show that most reporters identify themselves as liberals; liberal critics respond that most pundits, especially on radio and TV, offer conservative points of view—and many media sources are owned by large corporations, which leads to underreporting of some stories, such as those offering a favorable portrayal of labor unions.[54] The common thread is that media coverage of American politics falls short of some ideal of objective, full coverage.

In the main, most Americans, regardless of their party affiliation, do not have great confidence in the mainstream media, as Figure 7.3 illustrates, with

FIGURE » 7.3

PARTISANSHIP AND NEWS SOURCE CREDIBILITY

Do Americans consider all media sources equally reliable for learning about politics? Are there partisan differences in the sources people choose? When questioned about whether they believed all or most of what news sources said, Republicans and Democrats varied in which sources they thought were credible. The percentages are based on those who could rate each source.

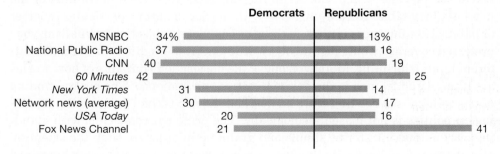

SOURCE: Pew Research Center, "Americans Spending More Time Following the News," September 12, 2010, www.people-press .org/2010/09/12/americans-spending-more-time-following-the-news/ (accessed 8/29/12).

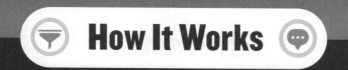

How It Works

HOW NEWS MAKES IT TO THE PUBLIC

The content of media coverage of political events often reflects conscious or unconscious efforts to frame, filter, and prime. Here we show the steps that lead to publication of a story, and where these media effects enter into the reporting process.

EDITOR ASSIGNS REPORTER TO COVER A PARTICULAR STORY OR EVENT

Filtering

Editor decides which stories are important and will attract an audience.

REPORTER GATHERS INFORMATION AND PREPARES A STORY

Framing

Reporter's story includes the overall argument and other information that shapes what the audience learns.

Priming

By describing events using some words or phrases and omitting others, the reporter has additional influence over what the audience learns.

EDITOR REVISES STORY, DECIDES ON LENGTH, CONTENT, AND PLACEMENT

Decision about where, when, and how to carry the story gives an additional opportunity for filtering.

In addition, the editor can make changes to a story that involve framing, priming, and filtering.

How It Works
In Practice

THE MEDIA'S COVERAGE OF A NATIONAL SECURITY LEAK

Edward Snowden, a programmer who was employed by a consulting firm that did work for the National Security Agency in Hawaii, had access to highly classified NSA documents, which he leaked to the press in June 2013. The way the media covered this situation shows framing, filtering, and priming in action.

Filtering

Snowden initially contacted several newspapers, including the *Washington Post*, but only a British newspaper, the *Guardian*, agreed to his confidentiality and publication requirements.

Framing

Some news stories focused on Snowden's flight from Hawaii to Hong Kong and then to Russia to avoid prosecution, while others, such as the *Nation*, a left-leaning weekly, focused on Snowden's revelations of NSA surveillance of cell phone conversations.

Priming

Some stories identified Snowden as a whistleblower, while others called him a leaker or a traitor.

Filtering   **Framing**   **Priming**

After Snowden accepted asylum in Russia, most major news outlets ended or deemphasized coverage, while others, such as *Mother Jones* magazine and many Internet sites, continued to give the story top billing.

POP QUIZ

1 When an editor tells a reporter to cover the council passing a new noise ordinance but not to cover the protests outside, this is an example of

  a filtering.

  b priming.

  c media consolidation.

  d framing.

  e equal time rule.

2 Regarding the Snowden story, which of the following illustrates the concept of framing?

  a The *Guardian* not revealing Snowden's name.

  b The *Nation* focusing on NSA surveillance activities and not just Snowden's actions.

  c Various papers calling Snowden a whistle-blower and others calling him a traitor.

  d Russia granting Snowden asylum.

  e *Mother Jones* continuing to put the Snowden story on the front page months after the initial revelations.

Republicans showing lower levels of confidence for all sources except Fox News. However, while people do not have a great deal of confidence in the media as a group, they have more confidence in the sources they regularly consult for information—and most people can find several sources that they consider reliable.[55]

It is easy to find examples of suspicious decisions by reporters and their editors that suggest some sort of overt bias in coverage. In fall 2013, a host on the Saturday edition of the Fox News program *Fox & Friends* discussed the closure of the World War II Memorial in Washington, D.C., due to a government shutdown, reporting that President Obama had done nothing to keep the memorial open but stating that at the same time Obama donated some of his own money to support a museum of Muslim culture. In fact, the story about Obama's donation came from a satirical website and was completely false. Fox retracted the story, saying they had made an honest mistake, but critics charged that the story reflected an anti-Obama bias by Fox reporters and editors.[56]

Many journalists and commentators admit that they take an ideological or partisan perspective. The talk show host Rush Limbaugh, for example, describes himself as a strong conservative. And many commentators on the Fox News Channel make no secret of their conservative viewpoint. Similarly, the political news magazine the *Nation* describes itself as "a weekly journal of left/liberal opinion, covering national and international affairs as well as the arts."[57] These journalists' and organizations' points of view are well known and easy to identify. Some people might even find the bias useful. A liberal, for example, could use the *Nation*'s endorsements as a guide as to which candidates to support, and a conservative might listen to Rush Limbaugh to get similar information.

Leaving aside these obvious gaffes and clear statements of points of view, claims about overt media bias make strong assumptions about what fair coverage would look like. For example, during 2005 and 2006, many media critics argued that reports on the Iraq War overemphasized negative events and failed to report on positive developments. However, during this time, thousands of American troops and large numbers of civilians were killed or wounded; there were thousands of bombings, kidnappings, and other attacks by insurgent forces; and most economic indicators revealed a country in deep crisis.[58] In other words, if the expectation was that the media should give an accurate picture of what was happening in Iraq, it is not clear that optimism was appropriate in 2005 and 2006. Also, as the situation improved in Iraq during 2007 and 2008, media coverage changed in a more positive direction.

It is hard to find a scholarly study that presents strong evidence of systematic media bias in a liberal or conservative direction. Part of the problem is that it is hard to measure media bias. For example, one study found that when the Fox News Network began broadcasting in a community, voting for Republican candidates in the next election increased significantly.[59] Does this mean that some viewers became pro-Republican after listening to allegedly pro-Republican broadcasts on Fox News? Perhaps, but the study did not directly measure the behavior of individuals in these communities, so there was no way to be sure that new Republican supporters were actually Fox News viewers. Even if they were, it may be that watching Fox News had no effect on voting, but that Fox News executives were looking for communities that were trending Republican when deciding which new markets to enter. Untangling these effects is a complex task.

WHERE ELSE DOES MEDIA COVERAGE FALL SHORT?

Even if media coverage is not openly biased in one direction or another, there are many ways in which it fails to provide essential information about politics to the American public. As political scientist and journalism professor Andrew Cline puts it, there are many ways in which media coverage of politics is biased—meaning influenced—in one direction or another by various forces.[60] Various aspects of content and slant affect the media's performance in covering politics. For example, scholars such as Thomas Patterson have documented the rise of **attack journalism**, where journalists focus on scandal, government failures, and politicians' personal failings.[61] Other researchers have argued that campaign coverage overemphasizes the **horse race** aspects, such as which candidates are ahead and which are falling behind, rather than offering a complete description of each candidate's promises and an analysis of how they are likely to behave in office.[62] Similarly, coverage of debates over public policy often focuses on personalities and predictions about who is likely to achieve his or her goals. In all of these cases, coverage of how these events might shape government policy often gets ignored until after the scandal, election, or policy debate is over.[63] Such practices virtually guarantee incomplete coverage of any news story, particularly at the time when people are actually paying attention.

Media coverage of politics also emphasizes **soft news** (stories that are sensational or entertaining) over **hard news** (stories that focus on important issues and emphasize facts and figures).[64] At the same time, talk shows and shows focused on entertainment have increased their political coverage mainly by reporting on scandals, personalities, and other topics that attract an audience rather than presenting hard facts.[65]

Moreover, citizens' perceptions of government may mirror press coverage. Many authors have suggested that citizens' low level of trust in government, as

attack journalism A type of increasingly popular media coverage focused on political scandals and controversies, which causes a negative public opinion of political figures.

horse race A description of the type of election coverage that focuses more on poll results and speculation about a likely winner than on substantive differences between the candidates.

soft news Media coverage that aims to entertain or shock, often through sensationalized reporting or by focusing on a candidate or politician's personality.

hard news Media coverage focused on facts and important issues surrounding a campaign.

well as high levels of disapproval and dissatisfaction, may have more to do with how the media report on American politics than with how government actually works.[66] The lack of hard information in much political coverage also fails to address the profound ignorance that many Americans have about the structure of the federal government, particular government policies, and decision-making processes.

THE EFFECT OF MARKET FORCES

A deeper question about the American media's coverage of politics is *why* there is so much attack journalism, soft news, sensationalism, and scandal. If journalists are aware of the problem, why don't they take their role as political watchdogs for the public interest more seriously? One response is that journalists may feel the need to demonstrate their independence from politicians and government interests, and perhaps counter or prevent claims of media bias. The result can be overly aggressive questioning of elected officials and cynical stories about the political process.[67]

The more significant explanation for the soft, sensationalistic nature of much political coverage is that reporters and their editors are in a competitive business to attract a paying audience.[68] Describing the media as an information source for citizens makes sense in terms of how American politics works, but this description does not capture the sometimes contradictory incentives that journalists face. Most American media outlets are for-profit enterprises. Because they need to produce coverage that attracts an audience, they often seek to create stories that consumers want and that are consistent with how members of their target audience think about politics. For example, many Americans hold dismal evaluations of the Republican and Democratic parties, of Congress, and of the American political system in general. Given these perceptions, the prevalence of attack journalism is no surprise; journalists provide coverage that fits the public's preconceptions. Americans are not changing what they think in response to attack stories and soft news. Rather, the way journalists cover politics reflects the tone of American public opinion.[69]

Even if reporters tried to explain how our democratic government works, especially the need for compromise, it is unlikely that citizens would respond favorably. As researchers John Hibbing and Elizabeth Theiss-Morse discovered, "Citizens... dislike being exposed to processes endemic to democratic government. People do not wish to see uncertainty, conflicting options, long debate, competing interests, confusion, bargaining, and compromised, imperfect solutions."[70] In other words, coverage that offers exclusively hard news, policy details, and sober analysis rather than at least some soft news, cynicism, scandals, and attack journalism would probably not find much of an audience.

Thus, complaints about how the media covers American politics are to a large extent misdirected. The media give Americans the coverage they want. If the average citizen wants to become an expert on politics and public policy, the necessary information is surely available. But few people are interested in seeking that degree of understanding. For most of us, the media's coverage of politics as a sports event is enough to keep us satisfied, even as we complain about a lack of details and an emphasis on scandal.

CONCLUSION

News media are the primary source of public information about American politics and policy. The considerable controversy about how well the media fulfill this role reflects both the importance of the task and the interest many people have in the shaping of political coverage. The news media landscape is undergoing a massive transition, as the Internet supports an ever-growing variety of new information sources and fewer people rely on newspapers or television for news. Even so, these traditional news sources remain important. While these sources differ radically in resources, timeliness, and other factors, and while coverage of politics is nowhere near perfect, their failure to offer a full and complete picture of American politics generally does not result from a concerted effort by reporters and editors to color coverage with biased views.

Stories about Barack Obama's presidency illustrate the causes and consequences of media coverage. In running story after story about Obama's certain triumph or sure defeat, media sources are largely responding to public demand for dramatic coverage. Americans might be better informed if the media ignored sensational stories and focused on the details of public policy, but lurid stories help attract and keep the audience that media companies need to stay in business. Americans will get different media coverage when they alter how they search for information and value sources that emphasize details and complexity over scandals and drama.

The average American consults only a tiny fraction of the information provided by the media. Americans tend to learn about politics as a by-product of other activities and focus on exciting stories regardless of their importance. This process can lead people to some peculiar conclusions, even about well-reported events. Such shortcomings do not constitute an indictment of the news media or of the average American. For most policy questions, for example, even a small amount of research using different sources would produce a detailed understanding about the pros and cons of different options and the political forces aligning for and against change. We cannot blame people for refusing to become well informed, but at the same time, we cannot blame the media for citizens' refusal to consider what is placed before them.

THE NEWS MEDIA IN AMERICA

▶ *Trace how the American mass media have evolved over time, and describe the major types of news sources today.* **(Pages 238–47)**

SUMMARY

The media have been the primary sources of political information in America since the Founding, though the forms of media have changed considerably over time. In the early days, media sources were very partisan and sensationalistic, but journalistic integrity standards became commonplace in the twentieth century. While the term "media" traditionally referred only to print sources, technological advances allowed political information to be spread through radio, TV, and now the Internet.

KEY TERMS

mass media (p. 238)

wire service (p. 239)

yellow journalism (p.239)

investigative journalists (p. 240)

Federal Communications Commission (FCC) (p. 240)

broadcast media (p. 240)

fairness doctrine (p. 240)

equal time provision (p. 241)

media conglomerates (p. 241)

news cycle (p. 243)

CRITICAL THINKING AND DISCUSSION

One argument against deregulating the media is that consolidation and the formation of media conglomerates would reduce the number of independent sources of information available to the average American. Based on the media sources that you and your friends use, do you agree or disagree with this argument? Why?

PRACTICE QUIZ QUESTIONS

1. What is the fairness doctrine?
   - A TV and radio stations must offer a variety of political views in programs.
   - B TV and radio stations must give equal time to candidates running advertisements.
   - C News anchors cannot slander political candidates.
   - D Radio station owners cannot also own TV and print media outlets.
   - E Journalists must investigate challengers as well as incumbents.

2. The deregulation of the media has resulted in _____.
   - A increasing enforcement of the equal time provision
   - B increasing enforcement of the fairness doctrine
   - C increasing use of the Internet
   - D increasing scrutiny of media concentration
   - E increasing frequency of cross-ownership

3. Which is the result of the decreased barriers to publication on the Internet?
   - A Few opportunities exist for citizens to interact with reporters or government officials.
   - B People with no official connection to candidates can have a significant influence on elections.
   - C The accuracy of political information has improved.
   - D Few average citizens report on events as they happen.
   - E Like-minded political supporters have difficulty organizing and staying informed on issues.

4. Why hasn't the Internet increased citizens' political knowledge?
   - A It can be hard to find political news on the Internet.
   - B Most people do not have access to the Internet.
   - C Most people read content from a wide range of balanced media sources.
   - D Most people focus only on websites that reinforce their own views.
   - E Search engines don't include political topics.

POLITICAL REPORTING: SOURCES, LEAKS, AND SHIELD LAWS

▶ *Describe where reporters and others in the news media get political information.* **(Pages 247–51)**

SUMMARY

Coverage of politics requires that the reporter make a trade-off between cultivating sources with favorable stories and providing complete and accurate information. One of the best ways reporters can cover political events is to get information "off the record." To maintain this information resource, the confidentiality of sources must be protected, although reporters can be compelled to reveal them in court.

KEY TERMS

on background or **off the record** (p. 250)

CRITICAL THINKING AND DISCUSSION

Under what circumstances would it be beneficial for a journalist to publish confidential information? When would it be harmful?

5. "Staging the news" refers to _____.

   A the media's attempts to frame public opinion

   B sources' attempts to remain confidential

   C newspaper editors determining which story to put on the front page

   D politicians attempting to influence coverage by providing select information

   E reporters' choices to delay a story

6. Shield laws _____.

   A allow editors to protect their reporters from vengeful politicians

   B allow politicians to protect reporters who provide favorable coverage

   C protect politicians from slander

   D allow reporters to protect confidential sources

   E protect reporters from being sued for slander

HOW DO AMERICANS USE THE MEDIA TO LEARN ABOUT POLITICS?

▶ *Analyze who uses which news sources and whether it matters.* **(Pages 251–54)**

SUMMARY

Whereas most Americans in the 1940s would learn about political events from a small subset of media sources, today we have a variety of ways to stay informed about politics. However, research shows that the average American does not utilize many of these resources, and learns about politics indirectly. Studies find that the more sources individuals rely on for their news, the better informed they are.

KEY TERM

by-product theory (p. 251)

CRITICAL THINKING AND DISCUSSION

What advice would you give to someone who wants to learn about American politics? What types of media sources should they seek out, which ones should they avoid, and why?

PRACTICE QUIZ QUESTIONS

7. What is the by-product theory of political information?

   A Local media sources often rely on major sources for their national news coverage.

   B Most Americans learn about politics accidentally.

   C Reporters often learn about a political story while working on a different story.

   D Bloggers typically do not produce news; rather, they comment on news gathered secondhand.

   E News coverage often influences policy decisions.

8. Which news source has the greatest proportion of high-knowledge viewers?

   A NPR

   B Fox News Channel

   C a network evening news show

   D The *Rachel Maddow Show*

   E The *New York Times*

MEDIA EFFECTS ON AMERICAN CITIZENS AND GOVERNMENT POLICY

▶ *Explain the ways in which the media may influence politics.* **(Pages 254–57)**

SUMMARY

Nearly all modern research finds that the media have significant effects on both government policy and American citizens. By determining which stories to cover, how a story is written, or how many stories to write on a given topic, media sources influence the way that citizens think about politics.

KEY TERMS

media effects (p. 254)
filtering (p. 255)
slant (p. 255)
priming (p. 255)
framing (p. 255)

CRITICAL THINKING AND DISCUSSION

Which of these media effects do you think has the most significant impact on the way you interpret a news story: filtering, slant, priming, or framing?

PRACTICE QUIZ QUESTIONS

9. What is priming?

   A a journalist's decision about which story to report on, and which story to skip

   B a journalist's decision to give favorable coverage to one candidate without providing balanced coverage of the opponent

   C the effect of a journalist's story on the importance people place on the issue being covered

   D the particular way that a journalist decides to present and describe a story

   E the decision to prioritize one story over another

10. Space limitations mean that some _____ is inevitable.

    A filtering

    B slant

    C priming

    D framing

    E soft news

11. Why do reporters move beyond "just the facts" reporting?

    A Politicians are corrupt, and people need to know about it.

    B Americans don't realize the media are not always objective.

    C Readers have already interpreted the news themselves.

    D Politics is complicated and often requires some interpretation.

    E Reporters have a strong personal bias and can't write strictly factual stories.

13. Which is an example of "soft news"?

    A CNN's coverage of a White House press conference

    B ABC's coverage of the president's State of the Union address

    C NPR's report on the details of the debt-ceiling debate

    D CBS's coverage of election results

    E CNN's story about a member of Congress posting risqué photos of himself to his Twitter account

14. Which of the following statements best characterizes soft news?

    A Soft news stories sell far better than hard news stories.

    B Journalists aren't interested in writing hard news, and would prefer to write soft news pieces.

    C Hard news and policy analysis articles tend to sell better than soft news.

    D Most citizens have several sources of hard news, and they have to search to find soft news stories.

    E Soft news was popular in the past but is now declining.

ASSESSING MEDIA COVERAGE OF AMERICAN POLITICS

▶ *Assess whether the media fulfill their role in American democracy.* **(Pages 258–63)**

SUMMARY

In a democracy, the media's job is to provide citizens with information about politicians, government action, and policy debates. Although the media often fall short of this ideal, there are many reasons for this failure. In particular, the effects of filtering and framing are simply unavoidable given limited resources.

KEY TERMS

attack journalism (p. 262)
horse race (p. 262)
soft news (p. 262)
hard news (p. 262)

CRITICAL THINKING AND DISCUSSION

To what extent are journalists, editors, and the owners of media businesses to blame for the fact that the average American is often uninformed about and uninterested in politics?

PRACTICE QUIZ QUESTIONS

12. What is one problem with research on media bias?

    A Few scholars are interested in studying media bias.

    B It is difficult to measure bias.

    C No journalist will admit that bias exists.

    D There's little chance that media sources are biased.

    E There are not enough media sources to create a sample.

SUGGESTED READING

Baum, Matthew A. *Soft News Goes to War: Public Opinion and American Foreign Policy in the New Media Age*. Princeton, NJ: Princeton University Press, 2003.

Bennett, W. Lance, and Shanto Iyengar. "A New Era of Minimal Effects? The Changing Foundations of Political Communication." *Journal of Communication* 58 (2008):707–31.

Brader, Ted. *Campaigning for Hearts and Minds: How Emotional Appeals in Political Ads Work*. Chicago: University of Chicago Press, 2006.

Cappella, J. N., and K. H. Jamieson. *Spiral of Cynicism: The Press and the Public Good*. New York: Oxford University Press, 1997.

Davenport, Christian. *Media Bias, Perspective, and State Repression: The Black Panther Party*. New York: Cambridge University Press, 2010.

Kuklinski, James H., and Lee Sigelman. "When Objectivity Is Not Objective." *Journal of Politics* 54:3 (1992): 810–33.

Mutz, Diana. "Effects of 'In Your Face' Television Discourse on Perceptions of a Legitimate Opposition." *American Political Science Review* 101 (2007): 621–36.

Norris, Pippa. *A Virtuous Circle? Political Communications in Post-Industrial Democracies*. New York: Cambridge University Press, 2000.

Patterson, Thomas. *Out of Order*. New York: Knopf, 1993.

Prior, Markus. *Post-Broadcast Democracy: How Media Choice Increases Inequality in Political Involvement and Polarizes Elections*. New York: Cambridge University Press, 2007.

8

Political Parties

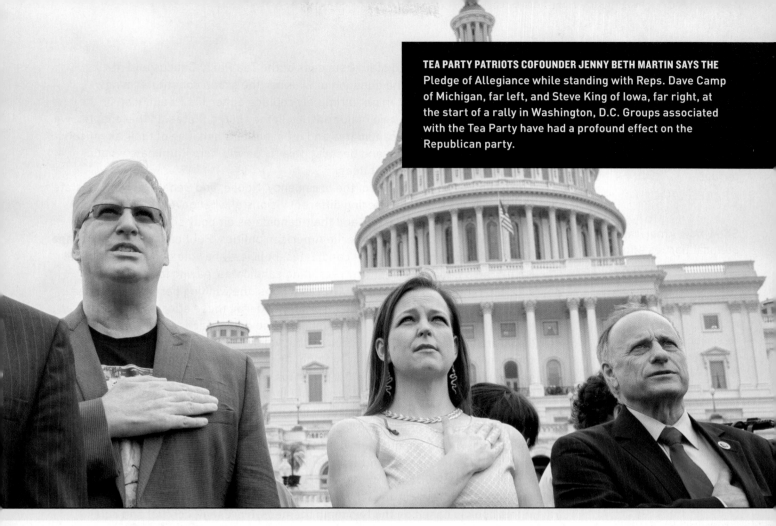

BEGINNING IN 2009, GROUPS THAT MAKE UP the Tea Party movement began encouraging candidates sympathetic to their goals to run for office. Their recruitment efforts bore fruit in the 2010 midterm elections, when nearly 150 candidates ran for Congress with the endorsement of one or more Tea Party groups. About a third were elected, and there were additional winners in 2012. By 2013, the Congressional Tea Party Caucus included over 80 Republican House and Senate members. Two of the senators, Rand Paul and Ted Cruz, are likely to run for the Republican presidential nomination in 2016. Those in the Tea Party Caucus were among the most vocal members of Congress demanding cuts in federal spending. They often disagreed with the legislative strategies of Republican Party leaders in areas such as immigration reform, gun control, and raising the federal debt limit. Though the Tea Party Caucus was unsuccessful in 2013 in pressing its demands for policy change, and Tea Party candidates had limited success in winning elections in the 2014 midterms, Caucus members remain key players in the House and Senate.

The rise of the Tea Party movement highlights the enduring conflict in American politics over the proper role of government in society. While Tea Party groups differ on the specifics, in the main they are unified around the goal of significantly reducing the size of the federal government and its regulations. While some congressional Republicans share these goals, Tea Party members generally hold more extreme views and are less willing to compromise, even with other Republicans.

**CONFLICT &
COMPROMISE**

in American Politics

CHAPTER *goals*

Define political parties and identify the three major aspects of American parties.

▸ PAGES 270–71

Show how American political parties and party systems have evolved over time.

▸ PAGES 271–75

Describe the main characteristics of American parties as organizations, in the government, and in the electorate.

▸ PAGES 275–84

Explain the important functions parties perform in the political system.

▸ PAGES 285–94

Consider the role of minor parties in a system dominated by two major parties.

▸ PAGES 295–96

Evaluate the benefits and possible problems of the American party system.

▸ PAGES 297–300

DEFINE POLITICAL PARTIES AND IDENTIFY THE THREE MAJOR ASPECTS OF AMERICAN PARTIES

The electoral and legislative success of the Tea Party Caucus and its members also raises the question of whether the group constitutes a new political party, one that might ultimately replace either the Republican or the Democratic Party—the two major parties in the United States. In this chapter, we will focus on Tea Party candidates and officeholders because of their significance in contemporary politics, and because this focus will help illuminate what a political party is and what it does.

By competing for control of the presidency, House, and Senate, as well as state and local offices, and by offering different visions of what government should do, American political parties and their candidates embody some of the most fundamental conflicts that underlie American politics. Political parties help shape the way Americans think about candidates, policies, and vote decisions. Political parties also impact elections by recruiting candidates, paying for campaign ads, and mobilizing supporters. After elections, the winning party's candidates implement their vision, while the losers try to derail these efforts and develop an alternative vision that will attract support. In so doing, parties unify and mobilize disparate groups, simplify the choices that voters face, and bring efficiency and coherence to government policy making. As you will see, although the politicians and activists who make up Tea Party groups do some of these things, they have not even begun to undertake others. Until they do, the Tea "Party" is unlikely to supplant one of the major political parties in American politics.

The emergence of the Tea Party movement illustrates that there is not an obvious answer to the question political scientists ask: "Why parties?"[1] Although American political parties often have an impact on elections and policy, the same organizations can sometimes seem inept, irrelevant, and paralyzed by conflict. A good answer to "Why parties?" must explain this variation. Our answer in this book is based on the two main themes we present, conflict and rules. While American political parties are the product of disagreements about what government should do, these differences can sometimes split politicians and activists within an established party organization. Nonetheless, the way parties are organized and the constitutional provisions and laws that regulate their behavior shape what parties can and cannot do in American politics.

WHAT ARE POLITICAL PARTIES?

Political parties are organizations that run candidates for political office and coordinate the actions of officials elected under the party banner. Looking around the world, we find many different kinds of parties. In many western European countries, the major political parties have millions of dues-paying members, and party leaders control what their elected officials do. In contrast, in many new democracies, candidates run as representatives of a party, but party leaders have no control over what candidates say during the campaign or how they act in office. America's major political parties, the Republican Party and the Democratic Party, lie somewhere between these extremes. Many Americans have a deep, enduring connection to one of these parties, and these organizations' actions affect both election returns and policy outcomes.

Rather than being unified organizations with party leaders at the top, candidates and party workers in the middle, and citizen-members at the bottom,

American political parties are decentralized, each one a loose network of organizations, groups, and individuals who share a party label but are under no obligation to work together.[2] For example, the Speaker of the House of Representatives, John Boehner, is the leader of Republican House members, but he works independently of the party's national organization, the Republican National Committee (RNC); neither one is in charge of the other. Boehner is also not in charge of other Republican groups in Congress, such as the Tea Party Caucus—and although Caucus members may listen to Boehner's arguments, they are under no obligation to do what he asks. Similarly, the RNC cannot command state and local Republican Party organizations to take some actions and not others. Moreover, while many Americans think of themselves as members of a political party, neither the Republican Party nor the Democratic Party have formal membership. Thus, someone who identifies with the Republican Party is not obligated to work for or give money to the party or to vote for its candidates.

In light of this defining characteristic of American political parties, scholars describe these organizations as comprising three separate and largely independent pieces.[3] The **party organization** involves the structure of national, state, and local parties, including party leaders and workers. The **party in government** is made up of the politicians who were elected as candidates of the party. And the **party in the electorate** includes all the citizens who identify with the party. As you will see, organization matters: the fact that American political parties are split into three parts has important implications for what they do and for their impact on the nation's politics.

party organization A specific political party's leaders and workers at the national, state, and local levels.

party in government The group of officeholders who belong to a specific political party and were elected as candidates of that party.

party in the electorate The group of citizens who identify with a specific political party.

HISTORY OF AMERICAN POLITICAL PARTIES

SHOW HOW AMERICAN POLITICAL PARTIES AND PARTY SYSTEMS HAVE EVOLVED OVER TIME

The Republican and Democratic parties have existed for a long time—the Republicans since 1854 and the Democrats since the early 1800s. This section shows that, at different points in history, American political parties have looked and acted very differently from the way they do today, and that the contemporary parties do not resemble their historical counterparts.

AMERICAN POLITICAL PARTIES have three largely separate components: the party organization, represented here by Debbie Wasserman Schultz (D-FL), chair of the Democratic National Committee; the party in government, represented by House minority leader Nancy Pelosi (D-CA) and House minority whip Steny Hoyer (D-MD); and the party in the electorate, exemplified by the crowd at a rally for Barack Obama.

TABLE » 8.1

AMERICAN PARTY SYSTEMS

There have been six party systems in the United States since 1789.

PARTY SYSTEM	MAJOR PARTIES (DOMINANT PARTY IN BOLDFACE)	KEY ISSUES
First (1789–1828)	Federalists, Democratic-Republicans (neither party was dominant)	Location of the capital, financial issues (e.g., national bank)
Second (1829–1856)	**Democrats**, Whigs	Tariffs (farmers vs. merchants), slavery
Third (1857–1896)	Democrats, **Republicans**	Slavery (pre–Civil War), Reconstruction (post–Civil War), industrialization
Fourth (1897–1932)	Democrats, Republicans (neither party was dominant)	Industrialization, immigration
Fifth (1933–1968)	**Democrats**, Republicans	Size and scope of the federal government
Sixth (1969–present)	Democrats, Republicans (neither party is dominant)	Size and scope of the federal government, civil rights, social issues, foreign policy

party system Periods in which the names of the major political parties, their supporters, and the issues dividing them have remained relatively stable.

Political scientists use the term **party system** to describe periods of time in which the major parties' names, their groups of supporters, and the issues dividing them have all been constant. As Table 8.1 shows, there have been six party systems in America.[4] For each party system, the table gives the names of the two major parties, indicates which party dominated (won the most presidential elections or controlled Congress), and describes the principal issues dividing the parties.

THE EVOLUTION OF AMERICAN POLITICAL PARTIES

Political parties formed soon after the Founding of the United States. The first American parties, the Federalists and the Democratic-Republicans, were primarily parties in government. As political scientist John Aldrich put it, members of Congress had ideas about what the new government should look like and what it should do, but they needed votes to translate these ideas into concrete policies.[5] The first parties consisted of like-minded legislators: Federalists wanted a strong central government and a national bank, and they favored assumption of state war debts by the national government; Democratic-Republicans took the opposite positions based on their preference for concentrating power at the state level. These political parties were quite different from their modern counterparts. In particular, there were no national party organizations, few citizens thought of themselves as party members, and candidates for office did not campaign as representatives of a party.

For two decades, the two parties were more or less evenly matched in Congress, although the Federalists did not win a presidential contest after 1800. However, during the 1814 elections, the Federalist Party lost most of its congressional seats because many Federalist legislators had opposed the War of 1812 or supported a politically unpopular pay raise for members of Congress.[6]

These defeats led to the demise of the Federalist Party and the start of the Era of Good Feelings, when there was only one political party, the Democratic-Republican Party. Following the election of President Andrew Jackson in 1828, this party became known as the Democratic Party. At the same time, another new party, the Whig Party, was formed, and the second party system came into existence.

The new Democratic Party cultivated electoral support by building organizations to mobilize citizens and bind them to the party. The party also implemented the **party principle**, the idea that a party is not just a group of elected officials but an organization that exists apart from its candidates, and the **spoils system**, whereby party workers were rewarded with benefits such as federal jobs.[7]

In the 1840s, the issue of slavery split the second party system. Most Democratic politicians either supported slavery outright or wanted to avoid debating the issue.[8] The Whig Party was split between politicians who agreed with the Democrats and the abolitionists who wanted to end slavery. Ultimately, antislavery Whigs left the party and formed the Republican Party, which also attracted antislavery Democrats, and the Whig Party soon ceased to exist. These changes initiated the third party system, in which the country was divided into a largely Republican Northeast, a largely Democratic South, and politically split midwestern and border states.[9]

These developments illustrate that political parties exist only because elites, politicians, party leaders, and activists want them to. The Republican Party was created by people who wanted to abolish slavery, but many other politicians subsequently joined the party because of ambition: these politicians believed that their chances of winning political office were higher as Republicans than as Whigs or Democrats.

After the Civil War, the Republicans and Democrats remained the two prominent national parties. They were divided over the size and scope of the federal government, questioning whether the federal government should help farmers and rural residents or inhabitants of rapidly expanding cities, and whether it should regulate America's rapidly growing industrial base. Democrats built a coalition of rural and urban voters by proposing a larger, more active federal government, as well as other policies that would help both groups. These strategies demonstrate how American political parties change and subsequently reflect the basic divisions in society over what government should do.

During this period, especially in the late 1800s when the fourth party system came into existence, political machines were common in cities and towns. A **political machine** is a party organization built around the goal of gaining political power to enrich party leaders, party workers, and citizen supporters.[10] Political machines give government services to citizens, government jobs to party workers, and government contracts to higher-level party officials and contributors. In return, the recipients of these benefits are expected to help by campaigning and voting for the machine's candidates, as well as by contributing to the party. One classic example was the Tammany Hall political machine, an organization of Democratic Party politicians in New York City who were especially powerful during the late 1800s and early 1900s.[11] However, civil

THE TAMMANY HALL POLITICAL Machine, depicted here as a rotund version of one of its leaders, William "Boss" Tweed, controlled New York City politics for most of the nineteenth and early twentieth centuries. Its strategy was "honest graft," rewarding party workers, contributors, and voters for their efforts to keep the machine's candidates in office.

"THAT'S WHAT'S THE MATTER."

Boss Tweed. "As long as I count the Votes, what are you going to do about it?"

service legislation in the 1890s and other reforms brought about a decline in party machines.

The fifth party system was born out of the Great Depression, the worldwide economic collapse that led to the unemployment of millions of people, and grappled with the question of what the federal government should do to get the economy moving again. Many Republicans argued that conditions would improve over time and that government intervention would do little good, whereas Democrats proposed new programs that would help people in need and spur economic growth. The Democratic landslide in the 1932 election led to the New Deal, a series of federal programs proposed by President Franklin Delano Roosevelt and enacted by Congress to stimulate the national economy, help needy people, and impose a variety of new regulations. Debate over the New Deal brought together the New Deal Coalition of African Americans, Catholics, Jews, union members, and white southerners, who became strong supporters of Democratic candidates over the next generation.[12] This transformation established the basic division between the parties that exists to the present day: Democrats generally favor a large federal government that takes an active role in managing the economy and regulating behavior, and Republicans believe that many such programs should be provided by state and local governments or not done at all.

The move from the fifth to the sixth party system was marked by issue expansion: the introduction of new political questions and debates that divided the parties.[13] Beginning in the late 1940s, many Democratic candidates and party leaders, particularly outside the South, came out against the "separate but equal" system of racial discrimination in southern states and in favor of programs designed to ensure equal opportunity for minority citizens. Then, during the 1960s, many Democratic politicians, particularly President Lyndon Johnson, argued for expanding the role of the federal government in health care, antipoverty programs, and education. There were Republican politicians who supported some of these initiatives, but there was considerable Republican opposition to expanding the role of government in society.

This division on civil rights and the size and scope of government produced a gradual but significant shift in the groups that identified with each party beginning in 1969 and up to the present. White southerners and some Catholics moved to the Republican Party, and minorities, particularly African Americans, started identifying more strongly as Democrats. By the late 1980s, all three elements of the Republican and Democratic parties (organization, government, and electorate) were much more like-minded than they had been a generation earlier.

The sixth party system also brought changes in party organizations. Both the Republican and Democratic parties became "parties in service," increasing their involvement in recruiting, training, conducting fund-raising, and campaigning for their party's congressional and presidential candidates.[14] Just as in the first party system, the parties in government became much more involved in elections in an effort to elect like-minded colleagues who would vote with them to enact their preferred policies. At the same time, disagreements between congressional Republicans and Democrats increased, making it harder to find common ground in many policy areas. (The rise of the Tea Party Caucus is one indicator of this change.)

DEBATE OVER ROOSEVELT'S NEW
Deal programs established the basic divide between Democrats and Republicans that continues to this day: Democrats favor a strong federal government that takes an active role in the economy; Republicans prefer a smaller federal government and fewer programs and regulations.

REALIGNMENTS

Each party system is separated from the next by a **realignment**, a change in one or more of the factors that define a party system, including the issues that divide the parties, the nature and function of the party organizations, the composition of the party coalitions, and the specifics of government policy.

In some cases, a realignment begins with the emergence of a new question or issue debate that captures the attention of large numbers of ordinary citizens, activists, and politicians.[15] To spur a realignment, the issue has to be *cross-cutting*, meaning that within each party coalition, there are people who disagree on what government should do.

A realignment between the fifth party system (1933–1968) and the sixth (1969–present) produced the division between modern-day Republicans and Democrats.[16] Parties in the fifth party system were primarily divided by their positions on the appropriate size of the federal government. In the sixth party system, new issues such as civil rights emerged to divide the parties and their supporters. By the 1980s, the changes in party coalitions and election outcomes were apparent, with control of Congress and the presidency divided between the two parties. Republicans gained House and Senate seats in southern states, and Democrats gained seats in the Northeast, West, and Southwest.[17] After the 2014 elections, Republicans controlled only two Senate seats in the Northeast.

realignment A change in the size or composition of the party coalitions or in the nature of the issues that divide the parties. Realignments typically occur within an election cycle or two, but they can also occur gradually over the course of a decade or longer.

MODERN AMERICAN POLITICAL PARTIES

DESCRIBE THE MAIN CHARACTERISTICS OF AMERICAN PARTIES AS ORGANIZATIONS, IN THE GOVERNMENT, AND IN THE ELECTORATE

We've seen that, from the beginning, political parties have been a central feature of American politics. The next steps are to examine the different aspects (the party organization, the party in government, and the party in the electorate) of American political parties, describe the role they play in elections and in government, and compare their behavior in practice to the job description presented earlier in the chapter.

THE PARTY ORGANIZATION

The principal body in each party organization is the **national committee**, which consists of representatives from state party organizations, usually one man and one woman per state. The state party organizations in turn are made up of professional staff plus thousands of party organizations at the county, city, and town levels. The job of these organizations is to run the party's day-to-day operations, recruit candidates and supporters, raise money for future campaigns, and work to build a consensus on major issues. (Of course, other groups in the party, as well as individual politicians, carry out similar tasks at the same time and not always in agreement with the national or state committees.)

Both parties also include a number of *constituency groups* (the Democrats' term) or *teams* (the Republicans' term). These organizations within the party work to attract the support of demographic groups—such as African Americans,

national committee An American political party's principal organization, comprising party representatives from each state.

PARTY ORGANIZATIONS AT THE LOCAL level coordinate support for the party's candidates, but they don't necessarily have to follow the lead of the national party organization. Here, Charlie Christ, Democratic candidate for governor of Florida, speaks at a local campaign office.

political action committee (PAC) An interest group or a division of an interest group that can raise money to contribute to campaigns or to spend on ads in support of candidates. The amount a PAC can receive from each of its donors and the amount it can spend on federal electioneering are strictly limited.

527 organization A tax-exempt group formed primarily to influence elections through voter mobilization efforts and issue ads that do not directly endorse or oppose a candidate. Unlike political action committees, they are not subject to contribution limits and spending caps.

Hispanics, people with strong religious beliefs, senior citizens, women, and many others—who are considered likely to share the party's issue concerns and to assist in fund-raising.[18] In some cases, they also attempt to win over groups typically identified with the other party. For example, African Americans have long been strong supporters of Democratic candidates. Accordingly, the Democratic Party has a constituency group that informs African Americans about the party's candidates and works to convince these citizens to vote on Election Day. The Republican Party's corresponding constituency team works toward the opposite goal, trying to convince African Americans that Republican policies and candidates would better serve their interests.

Each party organization also includes groups designed to build support for, or coordinate the efforts of, particular individuals or politicians. These groups include the Democratic and the Republican Governors' Associations, the Young Democrats, the Young Republicans, and more specialized groups such as the Republican Lawyers' Organization or the Democratic Leadership Council (DLC), an organization of moderate Democratic politicians.[19] The parties use their college and youth organizations to motivate politically minded students to work for the party and its candidates. Groups such as the Governors' Associations and the DLC hold meetings where elected officials discuss solutions to common problems and try to formulate joint strategies. People who work for a party organization perform a wide range of tasks, from recruiting candidates and formulating political strategies to mobilizing citizens, conducting fund-raising, filling out campaign finance reports, researching opposing candidates and parties, and developing websites for the party and its candidates.

Many other groups, such as **political action committees (PACs)** or **527 organizations**, labor unions, and other interest groups and organizations, are loosely affiliated with one of the major parties. For example, the organization MoveOn.org typically supports Democratic candidates. Similar organizations on the Republican side include the Club for Growth, Americans for Prosperity, Crossroads GPS, and many evangelical groups. Many of these organizations take advantage of a loophole in a provision of the IRS code to legally solicit large, anonymous donations from corporate and individual contributors. Although these groups often favor one party over the other, they are not part of the party organization and do not always agree with the party's positions or support its candidates—in fact, many have to operate independently of the parties and their candidates to preserve their tax-exempt status. (For more details on campaign finance, see Chapter 9 and Chapter 10.)

As this description suggests, the party organization has a fluid structure rather than a rigid hierarchy.[20] Individuals and groups work with a party's leaders and candidates when they share the same goals, but unless they are paid party employees, they are under no obligation to do so (even paid party workers can, of course, quit rather than work for a candidate or a cause they oppose).

While the Tea Party organizations use the word "party" in their name, in function and appearance they more closely resemble the more loosely affiliated political action committees and interest groups. The Tea Party organizations do not run candidates on their own; rather, they endorse and give contributions to candidates (almost always Republicans) who are running for a major party nomination. As of 2014, there is no unified national organization with the Tea Party

FIGURE » 8.1

REPUBLICAN AND DEMOCRATIC BRAND NAMES

When asked about the ideologies of the Republican and Democratic parties, Americans have consistently rated the Republican Party as the more conservative of the two and the Democratic Party as more liberal. How might these perceptions shape candidates' decisions about which party to join and how to campaign?

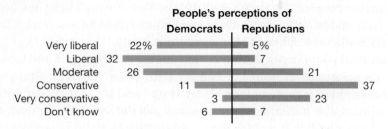

SOURCE: Pew Research Center, "More Now See GOP as Very Conservative," September 12, 2011, www.people-press.org/2011/09/12/more-now-see-gop-as-very-conservative/ (accessed 1/10/14).

label—rather, there are a large number of groups of varying size and activity that share a common name and some policy preferences, but that generally do not work together to elect candidates or shape government policy.

PARTY BRAND NAMES The Republican and Democratic Party organizations have well-established "brand names." Because the parties stand for different things, both in terms of their preferred government policies and their ideological leanings, the party names themselves become a shorthand way of providing information to voters about the parties' candidates.[21] Hearing the term "Democrat" or "Republican" calls to mind ideas about what kinds of positions the members of each party support, what kinds of candidates each party runs, and how these candidates will probably vote if they are elected to office. Citizens can use these brand names as a cue to decide whom to vote for in an election. (See Chapter 9 for more information on voting cues.)

Figure 8.1 provides a general guide to the Democratic and Republican brand names. The figure reports voters' impressions of the two parties, measured on a five-category liberal–conservative scale. The average American sees significant differences between the parties, placing the Democratic Party toward the liberal end of the ideological spectrum and the Republican Party toward the conservative end. Although this bar graph refers to the contemporary parties, the differences seen here have been in place for over two generations. Moreover, as we show later, these differences in brand names reflect actual differences between Democratic and Republican politicians.

THE LIMITS OF THE PARTY ORGANIZATION The critical thing to understand about the Democratic and Republican party organizations is that they are not hierarchies. No one person or group in charge determines what either organization does. Because the Republican National Committee (RNC) and Democratic National

Committee (DNC) are organized in the same way, we can consider the example of Debbie Wasserman Schultz (D-FL), the current chair of the DNC. She has some influence over who works at the DNC. However, the party organization's issue positions are set not by Wasserman Schultz's employees but by DNC members from all 50 states. The individual committee members are appointed by their state party organizations, so they do not owe their jobs to Wasserman Schultz—in fact, they can remove *her* from office if they like. If Wasserman Schultz and the committee disagree, she can't force the committee members to do what she wants. In cases such as health care reform in 2009–2010, the Democratic Party has been internally divided, and party leaders have been unable to force a consensus. The Republican Party is likewise subject to the same limitations.

The national party organization is also unable to force state and local parties to share its positions on issues or comply with other requests. State and local parties make their own decisions about state- and local-level candidates and issue positions. The national committee can ask nicely, cajole, or even threaten to withhold funds. But if a state party organization, an independent group, or even an individual candidate disagrees with the national committee, there's little the national committee can do to force compliance. For example, Republican leaders could not prevent Tea Party candidates from running in 2014 primaries against two incumbent senators, Pat Roberts of Kansas and Thad Cochran of Mississippi.

An example of friction between the national committees and their respective state party organizations occurred during 2011 and 2012. At that time, some state parties moved their states' presidential primaries and caucuses to dates earlier in the primary season, such that one month into the five-month primary season, most states' delegates to the parties' presidential nominating conventions would already be committed to a candidate.[22] The Republican and Democratic national committees preferred a drawn-out process, in which many populous states with large numbers of delegates would not hold their primary or caucus until May or June. Both national party committees could penalize states that held their primaries early without authorization by halving their convention delegations. But if the threats of the national committees were ignored by the state organizations, there was nothing else the national party committees could do to prevent the changes.

THE PARTY IN GOVERNMENT

The party in government consists of elected officials holding national, state, and local offices who took office as candidates of a particular party. They are the public face of the party, somewhat like the players on a sports team. Although players are only one part of a sports franchise—along with owners, coaches, trainers, and support staff—the players' identities are what most people call to mind when they think of the team. Because the party in government is made up of officeholders, it has a direct impact on government policy. Members of the party organization can recruit candidates, write platforms, and pay for campaign ads, but only those who win elections—the party in government—serve as members of Congress or as executive officials and actually propose, debate, vote on, and sign the legislation that determines what government does.

CAUCUSES AND CONFERENCES In the House and Senate, the Democratic and Republican parties are organized around working groups called a **caucus** (Democrats) or a **conference** (Republicans). The party caucus or conference serves as a forum for debate, compromise, and strategizing among a party's elected officials. For example, throughout 2013 and 2014, members of the Senate Democratic Caucus held numerous meetings to decide their group's position on issues such as deficit reduction and the repeal of Obamacare. These discussions helped senators coordinate their actions around a common bargaining strategy, which helped them to minimize budget cuts and preserve Obamacare.

Each party's caucus or conference meets to decide legislative committee assignments, leadership positions on committees, and leadership positions within the caucus or conference.[23] Caucus or conference leaders also serve as spokespeople for their respective parties, particularly when the president is from the other party. The party in government also contains groups that recruit and support candidates for political office, the Democratic Congressional Campaign Committee (DCCC), the Democratic Senatorial Campaign Committee (DSCC), the National Republican Congressional Committee (NRCC), and the National Republican Senatorial Committee (NRSC).

caucus (congressional) The organization of Democrats within the House and Senate that meets to discuss and debate the party's positions on various issues in order to reach a consensus and to assign leadership positions.

conference The organization of Republicans within the House and Senate that meets to discuss and debate the party's positions on various issues in order to reach a consensus and to assign leadership positions.

POLARIZATION AND HETEROGENEITY The modern Congress is polarized: in both the House and the Senate, Republicans and Democrats hold different views on government policy. Figure 8.2 compares legislators on the basis of their ideology,

FIGURE » 8.2

IDEOLOGY OF THE PARTIES IN GOVERNMENT: 83RD HOUSE AND 113TH HOUSE

Over the last several decades, ideological differences between Democrats and Republicans in Congress have increased significantly. However, even in the 113th House, both parties still included a wide range of views. In light of these data, would you expect more or less partisan conflict in the modern Congress than there was in the early 1950s? According to these data, would you expect House members in each party to agree on what policies to pursue?

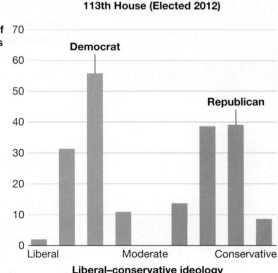

SOURCE: Calculated from Royce Carroll, Jeff Lewis, James Lo, Nolan McCarty, Keith Poole, and Howard Rosenthal, "DW-NOMINATE scores with Bootstrapped Standard Errors," January 23, 2009, www.voteview.com/dwnomin.htm (accessed 4/14/14).

or their general feelings about government policy, as measured by a liberal–conservative scale. The data reflect two House sessions: the 83rd House of 60 years ago (elected in 1952) and the contemporary 113th House (elected in 2012).

These graphs tell us two things. First, over the last 60 years, the magnitude of ideological differences between the parties in Congress has increased. In the 83rd House, there was some overlap between the positions of Democrats and Republicans, but it had disappeared by the 113th House.[24] Of course, because Democrats and Republicans in Congress often disagree does not mean that compromise is impossible—just that the differences that must be bridged are that much wider.

Second, Figure 8.2 reveals that both parties in government include a heterogeneous mixture of ideologies, not a homogeneous or uniform consensus opinion. In the graph depicting the 83rd House, for example, Democrats vary from the relatively liberal left end of the axis to the moderate (middle) and even somewhat conservative right end. Democrats in the 113th House were, on average, more liberal than their colleagues were in the 83rd, but a range of ideologies was still represented in the Democratic Caucus. The same is true for Republicans, who leaned in the conservative direction in both the 83th and the 113th Houses.

The heterogeneity of the party in government can create situations where a caucus or conference is divided on a policy question. Compromise within a party caucus is not inevitable—even though legislators share a party label, they may not be able to find common ground. In the last few years, congressional Democrats have been divided on issues such as immigration reform and limits on domestic surveillance. On the Republican side, divisions arose on issues of immigration policy as well as spending levels and the federal debt limit.[25]

While there is a Tea Party Caucus in Congress, its activities and powers fall far short of the Republican and Democratic caucuses and conferences. As we discuss here and in Chapter 11, the major parties are active in organizing Congress, recruiting and supporting candidates, and building legislative coalitions. Members of the Tea Party Caucus meet to discuss legislation, but they appear to have had little direct influence on the legislative process. Even in the 2013 fight over the government shutdown and federal debt limit, the negotiations that produced a compromise proposal were conducted by Republican and Democratic party leaders in Congress—members of the Tea Party Caucus voted on the deal, but they had no role in producing it. In the main, the Tea Party Caucus and its members are defined more in terms of their opposition to existing policies than in terms of a coherent agenda of policy proposals.

THE PARTY IN THE ELECTORATE

The party in the electorate consists of citizens who identify with a particular political party. Most Americans say they are either Democrats or Republicans, although the percentage has declined over the last two generations. Party identification is a critical variable in understanding votes and other forms of political participation.

PARTY IDENTIFICATION **Party identification (party ID)** is different from formal membership in a political party. Although the Republicans and the Democrats have websites where people can sign up to receive e-mail alerts and to contribute

? WHAT DO POLITICAL SCIENTISTS DO?

To learn more about how political scientists study party polarization, visit **wwnpag.es/wdpsd**

party identification (party ID) A citizen's loyalty to a specific political party.

online to party causes, joining a party does not give a citizen any direct influence over what the party does. Rather, the party leaders and the candidates themselves make the day-to-day decisions. These individuals often heed citizens' demands, but there is no requirement that they do so. Real participation in party operations is open to citizens who become activists by working for a party organization or one of its candidates. Activists' contributions vary from stuffing envelopes to helping out with a phone bank, being a delegate to a party convention, attending campaign rallies, or campaigning door-to-door. As a percentage of the population, relatively few Americans are activists.

Early theories of party identification described it as a deep attachment to a party that was acquired early in life from parents, friends, and political events and was generally unaffected by subsequent events.[26] Further work showed that party ID does not necessarily remain the same, but rather involves continuing evaluation that takes account of new information.[27] Thus, when someone says he identifies with the Republican Party, he is saying that, based on what he has seen in American politics, he prefers the positions suggested by the Republicans' brand name and how Republicans behave in office. New information tends to reinforce existing loyalties, which is why party identification is generally stable (see Chapter 6). But citizens can revise their party identification when circumstances warrant.

Figure 8.3 gives data on party identification in America over the last 60 years. The first segment of the graph shows that the Democratic Party had a

ACTIVIST VOLUNTEERS UNDERTAKE most of the one-on-one efforts to mobilize support for a party and its candidates.

FIGURE » 8.3

PARTY IDENTIFICATION TRENDS AMONG AMERICAN VOTERS

In terms of party identification, the parties have moved from rough parity in the late 1930s and 1940s, to a period of Democratic advantage that lasted from the 1950s to the 1980s. Beginning in 2003, Democrats appeared to be opening up another advantage, although this change has eroded in recent years. What events might have caused these changes in party identification?

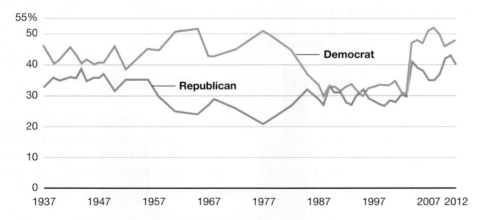

SOURCE: Pew Research Center, "Trends in American Values: 1987–2012," June 4, 2012, www.people-press.org/files/legacy-pdf/06-04-12%20Values%20Release.pdf (accessed 1/16/14).

considerable advantage in terms of the number of citizens identifying with the party from the late 1930s until the late 1980s. During the 1970s, nearly half of adults identified with the Democratic Party, and only about 20 percent identified with the Republicans. During the 1990s, the percentage of Democratic identifiers decreased significantly and the percentage of Republican identifiers increased slightly, to the point that in 2002 the parties had roughly the same percentage of identifiers.[28] But beginning in 2003, the Democrats again opened up a significant advantage in terms of identifiers, although the difference has largely disappeared in recent years. The two lines in Figure 8.3 do not add up to 100 percent, and the difference represents the percentage of independent voters who do not identify with either party. Just like the percentages of Republican and Democratic identifiers, the percentage of Independents fluctuates over time.

Here again, the Tea Party falls short of being a formal party organization. Although some Americans express sympathy for the issue stands taken by various Tea Party organizations, they don't say they belong to the Tea Party when asked about their party affiliation. Rather, they either affiliate with the Republicans, the Democrats, or, occasionally, with a minor party. While some members of the Tea Party Caucus, most notably Senators Rand Paul and Ted Cruz, attract support across the nation, there is no sign that Americans are moving toward a lasting connection with the Tea Party itself.

INDEPENDENTS Some early analyses concluded that Independents were unaffiliated with a party because they were in the process of shifting their identification from one party to the other.[29] Others saw Independents as evidence that more and more people regard the parties as irrelevant to their view of politics and their voting decisions.[30] The rise in the number of Independents was also seen as an indication that Americans were becoming more politically savvy—learning more about candidates and not always blindly voting for the same party.[31]

FIGURE » 8.4

THE IMPACT OF PARTY IDENTIFICATION ON VOTING DECISIONS IN THE 2012 PRESIDENTIAL ELECTION

Americans are much more likely to vote for candidates who share their party affiliation. What does this relationship tell us about the impact of campaign events (including speeches, debates, and gaffes) on voting decisions?

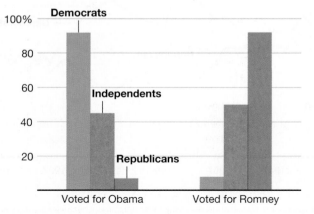

SOURCE: Data compiled from CNN Exit Poll, www.cnn.com/election/2012/results/race/president#exit-polls (accessed 11/7/12).

More-recent work has modified these findings. The percentage of independent voters has remained relatively constant over the last 20 years, and many Independents actually have some weak attachment to one of the major political parties.[32] Although some Independents are angry about or alienated from politics, most of them simply do not find the parties attractive enough to identify with either of them.[33] In any case, Independents are not necessarily better informed about candidates, parties, or government policy than party identifiers. Rather, Independents' voting decisions are more sensitive to things that happen during political campaigns than are the voting decisions of party identifiers.[34]

With a closer look at voting decisions, Figure 8.4 shows how Democrats, Republicans, and Independents voted in the 2012 presidential election. Almost all Democrats voted for Barack Obama, the Democratic nominee, and almost all Republicans voted for Mitt Romney, the Republican nominee. Independent voters slightly favored Romney, but Obama won because Democrats are the largest group in the electorate. Simply put, if you are trying to predict how someone will vote, the most important thing to know is his or her party identification.[35] Party ID also influences other kinds of political behavior. For example, people whose identification is strong are more likely to work for the party or to make a contribution than are people with weak party identification.[36]

PARTY COALITIONS Data on party identifications enable scholars to study **party coalitions**—that is, groups of citizens who identify with each party. Figure 8.5

party coalitions The groups that identify with a political party, usually described in demographic terms such as African-American Democrats or evangelical Republicans.

FIGURE » 8.5

THE PARTY COALITIONS

Many groups, such as African Americans and white evangelicals, are much more likely to affiliate with one party than the other. What are the implications of these differences for the positions taken by each party's candidates?

		Democratic	Republican
Gender	Male	27%	25%
	Female	37	24
Birth Year	1981–1994	31%	18%
	1965–1980	29	24
	1946–1964	34	27
	1945 and earlier	34	34
Race	White non-Hispanic	26%	32%
	African American	69	5
	Hispanic	32	11
Religion	White evangelical	17%	49%
	White mainline Protestant	26	38
	White Catholic	28	30
	Unaffiliated	32	12

SOURCE: Pew Research Center, "Partisan Polarization Surges in Bush, Obama Years," June 4, 2012, www.people-press.org/2012/06/04/partisan-polarization-surges-in-bush-obama-years/ (accessed 4/24/14).

FIGURE » 8.6

ISSUE DIFFERENCES BETWEEN THE REPUBLICAN AND DEMOCRATIC PARTIES IN THE ELECTORATE

The Republican and Democratic Party coalitions have different priorities on many issues, ranging from environmental protection to deficit reduction—and on a few issues their differences are small, such as reforming the tax system and reducing the influence of lobbyists. Do these differences make sense in light of each party's "brand name"?

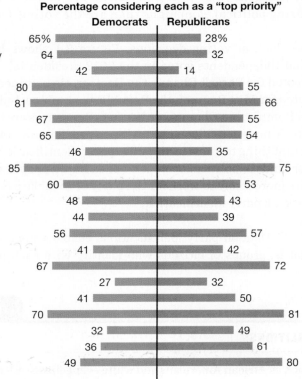

Percentage considering each as a "top priority"

Issue	Democrats	Republicans
Protecting the environment	65%	28%
Dealing with problems of the poor and needy	64	32
Dealing with global warming	42	14
Improving the educational system	80	55
Improving the job situation	81	66
Reducing health care costs	67	55
Making Medicare system sound	65	54
Improving roads, bridges, and transit	46	35
Strengthening the nation's economy	85	75
Reducing crime	60	53
Dealing with the nation's energy problem	48	43
Dealing with the issue of immigration	44	39
Reforming the nation's tax system	56	57
Reducing the influence of lobbyists	41	42
Making Social Security system sound	67	72
Dealing with global trade issues	27	32
Dealing with illegal immigration	41	50
Defending the country from terrorism	70	81
Dealing with moral breakdown	32	49
Strengthening the U.S. military	36	61
Reducing the budget deficit	49	80

SOURCE: Pew Research Center, "Deficit Reduction Declines as Policy Priority," January 27, 2014, www.people-press.org/2014/01/27/deficit-reduction-declines-as-policy-priority/ (accessed 4/24/14).

shows the contemporary Democratic and Republican party coalitions. As you can see, some groups are disproportionately likely to identify as Democrats (African Americans), some are disproportionately likely to identify as Republicans (white evangelicals), and other groups have no clear party favorite (people born in 1945 and earlier).

The Republican and Democratic party coalitions differ systematically in terms of their policy preferences—what they want government to do—as shown in Figure 8.6. This indicates the extent to which they disagree about the relative importance of issues like providing health insurance to the uninsured, dealing with global warming, and strengthening the military. On only a few issues—for example, reducing the budget deficit—are the percentages of those in both parties who consider the matter a priority nearly the same. These data demonstrate that party labels are meaningful: if you know someone is a Republican (or a Democrat), this information tells you something about what that person probably wants government to do, and how he or she will likely vote in the next election.

THE ROLE OF POLITICAL PARTIES IN AMERICAN POLITICS

EXPLAIN THE IMPORTANT FUNCTIONS PARTIES PERFORM IN THE POLITICAL SYSTEM

Political parties play an important role in American politics, from helping to organize elections to building consensus across branches of government. But these activities are not necessarily coordinated. Candidates and groups at different levels of a party organization may work together, refuse to cooperate, or even actively oppose one another's efforts.

ORGANIZING ELECTIONS

In modern American politics, virtually everyone elected to a state or national political office is either a Republican or a Democrat. In the 113th Congress, elected in 2012, there were only two independent senators and no independent House members. As of 2014, the governors of 49 states were either Democrats or Republicans (Alaska has an independent governor), and of more than 7,300 state legislators, very few were Independents or minor-party candidates, including those elected with Tea Party support.

RECRUITING AND NOMINATING CANDIDATES Historically, the recruitment of candidates was left up to local party organizations. But the process has become much more systematic, with national party leaders playing a central role in recruiting candidates—and often promising those candidates help in assembling a staff, organizing a campaign, and raising money.[37]

After the 2008 election, for example, Republican leaders believed that the party could win seats in the 2010 midterms by running candidates, particularly political outsiders with business experience, minorities, and women, who would take strong positions against many of President Obama's policy priorities. They began a two-year process of persuading these individuals to run, and training them in the art of campaigning.[38] Their efforts were one reason that Republican congressional candidates did so well in the 2010 midterms. Republican leaders made similar efforts in 2014. For example, they encouraged Rep. Cory Gardner (R-CO) to run against incumbent Mark Udall and discouraged Tea Party challengers from running against Republican incumbents.

For all of these efforts, however, parties do not control who runs in House or Senate races (see the You Decide feature). In most states, candidates for these offices are selected in a **primary election** or a **caucus,** in which they compete for a particular party's spot on the ballot. (About two-thirds of the states use some type of primary election while the rest use caucuses to select candidates; see Nuts & Bolts 8.1 for a further explanation of the different ways that the parties select candidates.)

Running as a party's nominee is almost always the easiest way to get on the general election ballot. Some states give the Republican and Democratic nominees an automatic spot on the ballot. Even in states that don't automatically allocate ballot slots this way, the requirements for the major parties to get a candidate on the ballot are much less onerous than those for minor parties and Independents. For example, in California, a party and its candidates automatically qualify for a position on the ballot if any of the party's candidates for statewide office received

primary election A ballot vote in which citizens select a party's nominee for the general election.

caucus (electoral) A local meeting in which party members select a party's nominee for the general election.

TYPES OF PRIMARIES AND CAUCUSES

PRIMARY ELECTION	An election in which voters choose the major party nominees for political office, who subsequently compete in a general election.
Closed primary	A primary election system in which only registered party members can vote in their party's primary.
Nonpartisan primary	A primary election system in which candidates from both parties are listed on the same primary ballot. Following a nonpartisan primary, the two candidates who receive the most votes in the primary compete in the general election, even if they are from the same party.
Open ("crossover") primary	A primary election system in which any registered voter can participate in either party's primary, regardless of the voter's party affiliation.
Semi-closed primary	A primary election system where voters registered as party members must vote in their party's primary, but registered Independents can vote in either party's primary.
CAUCUS ELECTION	A series of local meetings at which registered voters select a particular candidate's supporters as delegates who will vote for the candidate in a later, state-level convention. (In national elections, the state-convention delegates select delegates to the national convention.) Caucuses are used in some states to select delegates to the major parties' presidential nominating conventions. Some states' caucuses are open to members of any party, while others are closed.

more than 2 percent of the vote in the previous election. In contrast, independent candidates need to file petitions with more than 150,000 signatures to get on the ballot without a major-party label—an expensive, time-consuming task.[39] These advantages help explain why virtually all prominent candidates for Congress and the presidency run as Democrats or Republicans—including many congressional candidates who ran with Tea Party support in 2010, 2012, and 2014.

National parties also manage the nomination process for presidential candidates. This process involves a series of primaries and caucuses held over a six-month period beginning in January of a presidential election year. The type of election (primary or caucus) and its date are determined by state legislatures, although national party committees can limit the allowable dates, using their control over seating delegates at the party conventions to motivate compliance. Voters in these primaries and caucuses don't directly select the parties' nominees. Instead, citizens' votes are used to determine how many of each candidate's supporters become delegates to the party's national **nominating convention**, where delegates vote to choose the party's presidential and vice-presidential nominees. The national party organizations determine how many delegates each state sends to the convention based on factors such as state population, the number of votes the party's candidate received in each state in the last presidential election, and the number of House members and senators from the party that each state elected (see How It Works: Nominating Presidential Candidates).

nominating convention
A meeting held by each party every four years at which states' delegates select the party's presidential and vice-presidential nominees and approve the party platform.

CAMPAIGN ASSISTANCE One of the most visible ways that the political parties support candidates is by contributing to and spending money on campaign activities. By and large, federal law mandates that these funds be spent by the organization that raised them—the national party, for example, is limited in the amount of money it can contribute to congressional and presidential candidates or to state

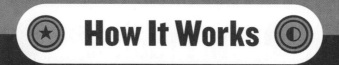

NOMINATING PRESIDENTIAL CANDIDATES

OPEN PRIMARIES

Open to voters from any political party and Independents

CLOSED PRIMARIES

Only voters registered with party vote

CAUCUS OR LOCAL CONVENTION

Party members meet in groups to select delegates

SELECT DELEGATES TO NATIONAL CONVENTION

Republican Party
States can divide delegates between candidates or give all to the winning candidate.

Democratic Party
The state's delegates are divided proportionally.

NATIONAL NOMINATING CONVENTIONS

Delegates from all states attend the national convention, where they vote for the party's presidential and vice-presidential nominees, based on the primary and caucus results. Superdelegates—important party leaders—also vote at the convention.

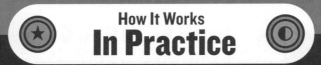
THE NOMINATION OF MITT ROMNEY FOR PRESIDENT, 2012

Multiple challengers tried to steal the Republican nomination for president from Mitt Romney in 2012, yet rules around the allocation of delegates made it too challenging for less well-financed candidates. Through "Super Tuesday" (March 6), Romney won all but one state that held winner-take-all primaries. This gave Romney a strong lead in the delegate count, which he never relinquished.

			ROMNEY	PAUL	GINGRICH	SANTORUM
	PRIMARY ■ CAUCUS/CONVENTION ◑ PROPORTIONAL ○ WINNER-TAKE-ALL ★ WINNER (1) NUMBER OF DELEGATES ALLOCATED TO EACH CANDIDATE					
JAN. 10	◑	NEW HAMPSHIRE	★ 39% (8)	23% (3)	9% (0)	9% (0)
JAN. 21	○	SOUTH CAROLINA	28% (2)	13% (0)	★ 40% (23)	17% (0)
JAN. 31	○	FLORIDA	★ 46% (50)	7% (0)	32% (0)	13% (0)
FEB. 4	◑	NEVADA	★ 50% (20)	19% (8)	21% (0)	10% (0)
FEB. 28	○	ARIZONA	★ 47% (29)	9% (0)	16% (0)	27% (0)
	◑	MICHIGAN	★ 41% (16)	12% (0)	7% (0)	38% (14)
MARCH 6 "SUPER TUESDAY"	◑	ALASKA	★ 32% (8)	24% (6)	13% (2)	30% (8)
	◑	GEORGIA	26% (21)	7% (0)	★ 47% (52)	20% (3)
	○	IDAHO	★ 62% (32)	18% (0)	2% (0)	18% (0)
	○	MASSACHUSETTS	★ 72% (38)	10% (0)	5% (0)	12% (0)
	◑	NORTH DAKOTA	24% (7)	28% (8)	8% (2)	★ 40% (11)
	◑	OHIO	★ 38% (38)	9% (0)	15% (0)	37% (25)
	◑	OKLAHOMA	28% (13)	10% (0)	27% (13)	★ 34% (14)
	◑	TENNESSEE	28% (17)	9% (0)	24% (9)	★ 37% (29)
	◑	VERMONT	★ 39% (9)	25% (4)	8% (0)	24% (4)
	○	VIRGINIA	★ 60% (43)	40% (3)		
	◑	KANSAS	21% (7)	13% (0)	14% (0)	★ 51% (33)
		TOTAL DELEGATES	**(358)**	**(32)**	**(101)**	**(141)**

Source: Constructed from data at http://www.cnn.com/ELECTION/2012/primaries.html (accessed 11/19/13).

POP QUIZ

1 In presidential nominating contests, _____ candidates are generally at an advantage in terms of delegate counts in winner-take-all primary and caucus rules, while _____ candidates are at a disadvantage.

a also-ran, front-running

b extreme, moderate

c front-running, also-ran

d moderate, extreme

e none of the above; these rules do not affect the number of delegates that candidates receive

2 In the 2012 Republican nominating primary contests shown above, in which states did Mitt Romney win the contest and get a disproportionate share of delegates?

a Florida, Arizona, Massachusetts, and Virginia

b Virginia

c New Hampshire, Florida, Nevada, Arizona, Idaho, Massachusetts, and Virginia

d South Carolina, Georgia, and North Dakota

e Michigan, Arizona, Massachusetts, and Virginia

party organizations. As we will discuss in Chapter 9, however, party organizations that raise campaign funds can use them to help candidates get elected through independent expenditures—running their own ads in a candidate's district or state.

Figure 8.7 shows the amount of money raised by the top groups within the Republican and Democratic parties for the 2014 election (through November 4). The final figures show that the parties and their various committees raised over a billion dollars. The Democratic and Republican National Committees (DNC and RNC) raised the most money, but the congressional campaign committees also raised significant sums. Congressional Democratic committees outraised their Republican counterparts. State and local party committees also raised large sums in the 2014 elections.[40]

Along with supplying campaign funds, party organizations give candidates other assistance, ranging from offering campaign advice (including which issues to emphasize, how to deal with the press, and the like) to conducting polls. Party organizations at all levels also undertake get-out-the-vote activities, encouraging supporters to get to the polls. During the last few elections, the Republican Party has organized a "72-Hour Task Force" of volunteers to spend the days just before the election staffing phone banks and going door-to-door campaigning for candidates in close races.

FIGURE »8.7

DEMOCRATIC AND REPUBLICAN FUND-RAISING IN THE 2013–2014 ELECTION CYCLE

In the 2013–2014 election cycle, party committees raised more than one billion dollars in campaign funds. Although most of this money was raised by the national committees, the state, local, and candidate committees also raised significant sums. To what extent might these funds allow the national committees to force candidates to run on the party platform?

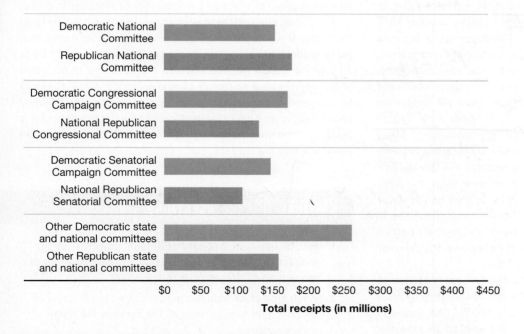

SOURCE: Calculated by authors from data at "Political Parties," www.opensecrets.org/parties/ (accessed 11/4/14).

SHOULD PARTIES CHOOSE THEIR CANDIDATES?

One of the facts of life for the leaders of the Democratic and Republican parties is that they cannot determine who runs as their party's candidate for political office. They can encourage some candidates to run and attempt to discourage others by endorsing their favorites and funneling money, staff support, and other forms of assistance to the candidates they prefer. But in the end, congressional candidates get on the ballot by winning a primary or a vote at a state party convention; presidential candidates compete in a series of primaries and caucuses.

Political parties don't always get the nominees their leaders want. In the 2012 election cycle, for example, Tea Party candidates Richard Mourdock in Indiana and Todd Akin in Missouri captured their party's nominations for U.S. Senate seats. In Indiana, Mourdock defeated incumbent Richard Lugar; in Missouri, Akin won a primary against several other candidates. After their primary victories, both candidates struggled to justify extreme positions they had taken in the past and during the primary campaign. These problems came as no surprise to Indiana and Missouri Republican state party leaders, virtually all of whom had favored the losing candidates based on the calculation that they were more likely to win in the general election. The expectations of the state party leaders proved correct, as both candidates lost their races in November. A similar outcome almost occurred in the 2014 primaries in Kansas and Mississippi, but incumbent Republican senators in both states (barely) defeated their Tea Party challengers.

Party leaders cannot force candidates out of a race. In March 2012, many Republican Party leaders wanted Rick Santorum to end his presidential candidacy as it became increasingly clear that Mitt Romney would win the nomination. Nonetheless, Santorum stayed in the race until mid-April, forcing Romney to campaign aggressively, spend additional campaign funds, and respond to attacks from the Santorum campaign.

Why not let party leaders pick their candidates? Many scholars have argued that doing so would increase the chances of getting experienced, talented candidates on the ballot.[a] After all, party leaders probably know more than the average primary voter about who would make a good candidate or elected official. Plus, party leaders have a strong incentive to find good candidates and convince them to run—their party's influence over government policy increases with the number of people they can elect to political office.

Why, then, do voters in America get to pick party nominees in primaries? Direct primaries were introduced in American politics during the late 1800s and early 1900s.[b] The goal was explicit: reform-minded party activists wanted to take the choice of nominees out of the hands of party leaders and

In 2012, some Republicans worried that the fierce fight in the primary elections had turned off voters, divided the party, and depleted campaign funds that would have been better spent campaigning against President Obama in the general election.

to give it to the electorate, with the assumption that voters should be able to influence the choice of candidates for the general election. Moreover, reformers believed that this goal outweighed the expertise held by party leaders.

Here is the trade-off: if party leaders select nominees, they would likely choose electable candidates who share the policy goals held by party leaders. If voters choose nominees, they can pick whomever they want, using whatever criteria they like—but there is no guarantee that these candidates will be skilled general-election campaigners or effective in office.

Of course, our system of primary elections is unlikely to go away. But it would be possible to increase the influence that party leaders have over the process. One option would be to change campaign finance laws to increase the importance of the parties as a source of campaign funds. Another would be to create a mechanism such as a state- or district-level convention where party leaders could select candidates for a primary—and thus make it harder for candidates to get on the ballot without the leaders' endorsement.

CRITICAL THINKING QUESTIONS

1. Would a system that gave additional power to party leaders to select nominees generally help incumbents more than challengers or the reverse?

2. What kind of nomination procedure would be favored by insurgent groups such as the various Tea Party organizations?

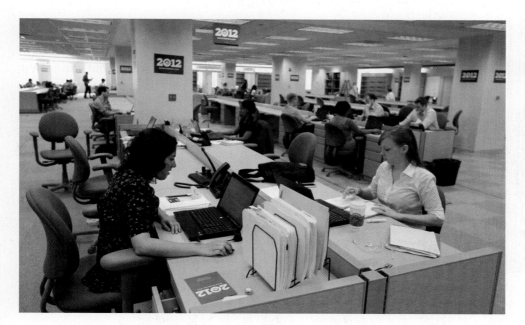

PARTY PLATFORMS The **party platform** is a set of promises explaining what candidates from the party will do if elected. The most visible party platform is the one approved at each party's presidential nominating convention, but the party organizations in the House and Senate also release platforms, as do other groups in the major parties. Party platforms generally reflect the brand name differences between the parties discussed earlier. For example, in the case of abortion rights, the 2012 Republican presidential platform favored a total ban on abortions, while the Democratic presidential platform expressed support for a woman's right to choose, meaning that abortion would be legal under a wider range of conditions.

In theory, party platforms describe differences between the major parties, capture each party's diagnosis of the problems facing the country, and give the party's plan for solving those problems. In this way, party platforms give citizens an easy way to evaluate candidates. However, candidates are not obligated to support their party's platform, and many take divergent stances on some issues. For example, notwithstanding the consistently strong pro-choice position on abortion in the Democratic Party's presidential platforms over the last generation, some Democratic congressional candidates, such as Pennsylvania senator Robert Casey, promised to vote to restrict abortions—a position closer to the Republican platform.[41] For some of these candidates, this position reflected personal or religious beliefs; for others, it was driven by the desire to reflect the opinion of voters in their district or state.

Despite these exceptions, party platforms are important documents. To the extent that there is conflict in American politics, it is likely to be revealed in differences between the platforms of the major parties. Moreover, political scientist John Geering's research shows that platforms provide a general guide for voters about the issues and issue positions that separate the major parties. Platforms indicate what sorts of policies winning candidates are likely to vote for if elected— and while some candidates may ignore or run against their party's platform, most candidates will support the platform because they agree with it, or because they believe it is popular with their constituents.[42]

party platform A set of objectives outlining the party's issue positions and priorities. Candidates are not required to support their party's platform.

WITHIN THE GOVERNMENT, politicians from the same party work together to develop an agenda and try to get it enacted. Here, President Obama meets with Democratic leaders from the Senate.

COOPERATION IN GOVERNMENT

The theory of conditional party government states that as policy differences between the parties in government increase in number and intensity, the parties in government will become increasingly active as a forum for like-minded legislators to develop policy plans and as a source for legislative strategies to enact these proposals. This theory explains what has happened in Congress over the last 50 years. Although conditional party government has led to the enactment of many important proposals, there is no guarantee that party members will cooperate. Party leaders in the modern Congress work to find agreements that are attractive to their members, but in many recent instances these efforts have failed. And if the party in government can't reach agreement, it will stay on the sidelines.

AGENDA SETTING Throughout the year, the parties in government meet to devise strategies for legislative action—that is, to set agendas. What proposals should they offer, and in what order should they be considered? Should they try to make a deal with the president or with legislators from the other party? For example, after the 2008 election, Democratic congressional leaders met with president-elect Barack Obama and his staff to discuss priorities for the 2009–2010 legislative term, including climate change legislation, health care reform, and an economic stimulus package. Some of these efforts were highly successful. Less than a month after Obama took office, Congress passed a $787 billion stimulus plan, which Democrats passed with no Republican support in the House and only three Republican votes in the Senate. Congress enacted landmark health care reform legislation with no Republican votes a year later.

Similarly, when Republicans gained control of the House after the 2010 midterms, the House Republican Conference used its control of the chamber to shape negotiations with President Obama over deficit reduction. Their efforts ensured that the package enacted in April 2011 to increase in the federal debt limit contained no tax increases and established a congressional "Supercommittee" to recommend additional reductions.

Yet, the party in government can act collectively this way only when its members can agree on what they want. Such agreement is not always possible or may require extensive negotiation and compromise. For example, health care legislation was enacted only after protracted negotiations with Democratic senators and the granting of concessions in return for their support. And during the fight over raising the federal debt limit and enacting a budget, Republican leaders struggled to convince members of the Tea Party Caucus to allow a compromise proposal to be voted on by the entire House. In the Senate, Republican leaders were unable to stop freshman Senator Ted Cruz from conducting a 23-hour filibuster that prevented the Senate from accomplishing any other business. The Republican conferences in both houses were also divided on other issues, including immigration reform and limits on domestic surveillance.

COORDINATION Political parties play an important role in coordinating the actions taken in different branches of government. Such coordination is extremely important for enacting new laws, because unless supporters in Congress can amass a two-thirds majority to override a veto, they need the president's support. Similarly, the president needs congressional support to enact the proposals he favors. To these ends, the president routinely meets with congressional leaders from his party and occasionally meets with the entire caucus or conference. Various members of the president's staff also meet with House and Senate members to present the president's proposals and to hear what members of Congress from both parties want to enact.

During 2009, President Obama held many meetings with Democratic members of Congress to lobby them to support his proposals for health care reform. Although many congressional Democrats supported Obama's proposals, enactment was nearly derailed by several Democratic representatives and senators who demanded amendments to restrict government payment for abortions. The president opposed these efforts but was powerless to stop them. In fact, getting the last few votes needed for enactment required Obama to promise to issue an executive order that had essentially the same effect as the proposed amendments.

Coordination can also occur between caucuses or conferences in the House and Senate. At the same time that President Obama and Democrats in Congress were negotiating over health care reform, congressional Republicans were devising strategies for delaying and defeating these proposals. Although Republican efforts did not prevent the enactment of reform legislation, the strong opposition of the Republicans required the president and congressional leaders to accept many changes favored by moderate and conservative Democrats in order to enact the legislation without Republican support.

Such coordination efforts require real work and compromise since party leaders in the House and the Senate do not have authority over each other or over the elected members of their party. Nor can the president order a House member or senator to do anything, even if the legislator is from the president's own party. In 2010, for example, President Obama and congressional leaders needed the votes of several anti-abortion Democrats, including Congressman Bart Stupak, to pass health care legislation through the House of Representatives. The congressional leaders and the president held repeated meetings with Stupak and his allies, offering various promises and enticements to secure their votes. Ultimately, these legislators voted for the proposal, but neither the president nor party leaders could have forced them to support it.

ACCOUNTABILITY One of the most important functions political parties play in a democracy is to give citizens identifiable groups to reward or punish for government action or inaction. Using the ballot box, voters will reward and punish elected officials, often based on their party affiliation and on the behavior of that party's members in office. In this way, the electorate uses the party system to hold officials accountable for outcomes such as the state of the economy or America's relations with other nations.

During periods of **unified government**, when one party holds majorities in both the House and the Senate *and* controls the presidency, that party has enough votes to enact policies in Congress and a good chance of having them signed into law by the president. During times of **divided government**, when one party controls Congress but not the presidency, or when different parties control the House and Senate, the president's party is considered the party in power.

Focusing on parties makes it easy for a citizen to issue rewards and punishments. Thus, for example, if the economy is doing well, people can reward the party in power by voting for its candidates. But if the economy is doing poorly, or if people feel that government is wasting tax money or enacting bad policies, they can punish the party in power by voting for candidates from the party that is currently out of power. When citizens behave this way, they strengthen the incentive for elected officials from the party in power to work together to develop policies that address voters' concerns—on the premise that if they do, voters will reward them with another term in office. Consider the 2010 midterm elections, when many Americans voted against Democratic candidates because of poor economic conditions. Although Democrats lost seats in both the House and the Senate, most Democratic incumbents were still returned to office. Why? Some were elected from states or districts dominated by Democratic identifiers. But many others were reelected because they campaigned on a platform of changing policy or because of their efforts to help local businesses, saying in effect, "Instead of punishing me for my party affiliation, reward me for working on your behalf."

The three-part structure of contemporary American parties complicates decisions about accountability. Suppose, for example, a legislator from the party in power opposed the policies enacted by her party. If so, it may not make sense for a voter to reward this legislator for good outcomes of those policies or to punish her for bad outcomes. Even though she is from the party in power, she did not cause the outcomes that the voter cares about. What should a voter do in this case?

In the end, reelecting members of the party in power despite a poor economy or other troubles makes sense given how American political parties are organized and their lack of control over individual officeholders. Of course, insofar as incumbent members of the party in power present themselves as loyal party members and cast votes in accordance with the wishes of party leaders, they will increase the chances that their constituents will take account of their party label when casting their votes—which will help them get reelected in good times, but will increase the chances of defeat when conditions turn against their party.

unified government A situation in which one party holds a majority of seats in the House and Senate and the president is a member of that same party.

divided government A situation in which the House, Senate, and presidency are not controlled by the same party—for example, when Democrats hold the majority of House and Senate seats, and the president is a Republican.

MINOR PARTIES

CONSIDER THE ROLE OF MINOR PARTIES IN A SYSTEM DOMINATED BY TWO MAJOR PARTIES

So far, this chapter has focused on the major American political parties, the Republicans and the Democrats, and paid less attention to other party organizations. The reason is that minor political parties in America are *so* minor that they are generally not significant players on the political stage. Many such parties exist, but few run candidates in more than a handful of races, and very few minor-party candidates win political office. Few Americans identify with minor parties, and most of these parties exist for only a relatively short period.

Even so, you may think we are giving minor parties too little attention. Consider Ralph Nader, who ran as the Green Party nominee for president in 2000, winning almost 5 percent of the vote. In some states, the number of votes Nader received exceeded the margin separating Democrat Al Gore from Republican George Bush. In particular, in Florida, where Bush won by only a few hundred votes after a disputed recount, Nader received almost 100,000 votes—enough to swing the state, and the election, to Gore.

However, the outcome of Nader's 2000 presidential campaign doesn't so much highlight the importance of minor parties as it illustrates the closeness of the 2000 presidential election. If Nader had not run, Gore might have received enough additional support to win. But given that Bush's margin of victory in Florida was so small, any number of seemingly minor events (a polling station closing early, or rain in some areas and sunshine in others) could have changed the outcome.

EFFECTS ON ELECTION OUTCOMES

Minor parties did not play a decisive role in the 2012 presidential election, but in several swing states they received more votes than the margin of difference between Barack Obama and Mitt Romney. The most successful were the Green Party (469,000 votes) and the Libertarian Party (1.2 million votes). In all, minor parties won about 1.9 million votes in the 2012 presidential race, about 1.6 percent of the total.

Even in terms of lower offices, minor-party candidates typically attract only meager support. The Libertarian Party claimed to have 15 officeholders as of 2014. However, many of these officials held unelected positions such as seats on county planning boards or ran unopposed for relatively minor offices such as justice of the peace.[43]

Looking back in history, some minor-party candidates for president have attracted a substantial percentage of citizens' votes. George Wallace ran as the candidate of the American Independent Party in 1968, receiving about 13 percent of the popular vote nationwide. Ross Perot, the Reform Party candidate for president in 1996, won 8.4 percent of the popular vote. Perot also ran as an Independent in 1992, winning 18.2 percent of the popular vote.

As we have already discussed, as of 2014, the Tea Party still does not qualify as a minor party because of the lack of an organization or a position on the ballot. It may be that, over time, the organizations that make up the Tea Party will unite and work together to formulate a joint platform, get their candidates on the ballot, and,

MINOR PARTY PRESIDENTIAL candidates, such as Ralph Nader in 2000, sometimes attract considerable press attention because of their distinctive, often extreme policy preferences—but they rarely affect election outcomes. Nader ran again, as an Independent, in 2004 and 2008.

ultimately, win elections to state and national offices—although this development is looking increasingly unlikely. But if this scenario does happen, the new organization would likely look like one of the minor parties discussed here, unless and until it manages to elect a significant number of its candidates.

UNIQUE ISSUES FACING MINOR PARTIES

The differences between major and minor political parties in contemporary American politics grow even more substantial when considered in terms other than election outcomes. For most minor parties, the party in government does not exist, as few of their candidates win office. Many minor parties have virtually no organization beyond a small party headquarters and a website. Some minor parties, such as the Green Party, the Libertarian Party, and the Reform Party, have local chapters that meet on a regular basis. But these modest efforts pale in comparison to the nationwide network of offices, thousands of workers, and millions of dollars deployed by Republican and Democratic party organizations.

Research shows that people vote for minor-party candidates because they find these candidates' positions more attractive than those of the major parties and also because they believe that neither major party can govern effectively.[44] In 2012, for example, Libertarian presidential candidate Gary Johnson advocated an immediate withdrawal of American troops from Afghanistan, as well as deep cuts in defense spending. To vote for Johnson, a citizen would have had to like Johnson's positions on issues and believe that neither of the major parties could effectively address these problems.

The issues and issue positions taken by minor parties and their candidates are almost always very different from those espoused by the major parties. The Constitution Party, for example, advocates an end to government civil service regulations; a ban on compulsory school attendance laws; withdrawal of the United States from the United Nations and all international trade agreements; abolishing foreign aid, the income tax, the Internal Revenue Service, and all federal welfare programs; and repealing all campaign finance legislation, the Endangered Species Act, and federal firearms regulations. These positions are extreme, not in the sense of being silly or dangerous, but in the sense that relatively few Americans agree with them.

The basic structure of the American political system also works against minor political parties. This principle is summed up by **Duverger's law**, which states that in a democracy that has **single-member districts** and **plurality voting**, there will be only two political parties that are able to elect a significant number of candidates to political office, which is the case in contemporary America. Given these electoral institutions (see Chapter 9), many people consider a vote for a minor-party candidate to be a wasted vote, as there is no chance that the candidate will win office. As a result, well-qualified candidates are driven to affiliate with one of the major political parties because they know that running as a minor-party nominee will put them at a considerable disadvantage. These decisions reinforce citizens' expectations that minor-party candidates have no chance of winning elections and that a vote for them is a wasted vote. Although there is no evidence that the Founders wanted to choose electoral institutions that made it hard for minor parties and their candidates, there is no doubt that the rules of the American electoral game have these effects.

Duverger's law The principle that in a democracy with single-member districts and plurality voting, only two parties' candidates will have a realistic chance of winning political office, as in the United States.

single-member districts An electoral system in which every elected official represents a geographically defined area, such as a state or congressional district, and each area elects one representative.

plurality voting A voting system in which the candidate who receives the most votes within a geographic area wins the election, regardless of whether that candidate wins a majority (more than half) of the votes.

WHAT KIND OF DEMOCRACY DO AMERICAN POLITICAL PARTIES CREATE?

Parties help political activists, party leaders, and citizens who identify with the party to pursue their policy goals by focusing collective efforts on electing people who share their priorities. For politicians, parties provide ballot access, a brand name, campaign assistance, and a group of like-minded colleagues with whom they can coordinate, compromise, and strategize. For citizens, political parties provide information and a means of holding specific individuals accountable for what government does.

The question of whether political parties are good or bad for democracy depends on how individual party members and officials carry out these tasks. Political parties can help democracy by filling the ballot with well-qualified candidates, helping them get elected, offering citizens clear choices about government policies, informing citizens about platforms and candidates, motivating citizens to vote, and helping elected officials enact the party platform. The problem is that the people who make up American political parties are not primarily interested in democracy; they are interested in their own careers, policy goals, and winning political office. These goals often lead them away from actions that would improve American democracy.

RECRUITING GOOD CANDIDATES

One of the most important things the Republican and Democratic parties can do for democracy is to recruit candidates for national political offices who can run effective campaigns and responsibly uphold their elected positions. After all, a citizen's choices as a voter are limited to the people on the ballot. If good candidates decide against running or are prevented from doing so, citizens will be dissatisfied no matter who wins the election.

As we discussed, the Republican and Democratic parties work to find good candidates and to persuade them to run. However, the potential candidates have to decide for themselves whether their chances of winning justify the enormous investment of time and money needed to run a campaign. When a party is unpopular, the best potential candidates may decide to wait until the next election to run, leaving the already disadvantaged party with a less competitive set of candidates.[45] And even when a party does not face economic or other headwinds, state- or district-level factors may deter good candidates from running under the party's banner. As a result, insofar as conditions favor one party's candidates over those from the other party, the disadvantaged party may find it difficult to offer citizens a compelling candidate to vote for on Election Day.

WORKING TOGETHER IN CAMPAIGNS

Parties can also work to simplify voters' choices by trying to get candidates to emphasize the same issues or to take similar issue positions. That way, citizens know that when they vote for, say, a Democrat, they are getting someone whose policy positions are likely to differ from those held by a Republican. The problem is that members of the party organization and the party in government do not always agree. Sometimes the differences within the parties reflect genuine differences of opinion. Other times, candidates are trying to match the preferences of citizens in their state or district. Either way, the simple fact is that political parties in America generally speak with many voices, not one.

Why don't party leaders simply order their candidates to support the party platform or to work together in campaigns? As we have discussed, party leaders actually have very little power over candidates.[46] They can't kick a candidate off the ballot because candidates win the nomination in a primary election or caucus, not through party appointment. Even though parties have a lot of campaign money to dispense, their contributions typically make up only a fraction of what a candidate spends on a campaign. And incumbent candidates, who generally hold an advantage over challengers when seeking reelection, are even less beholden to party leaders. Even if party leaders could somehow prevent an incumbent from running for reelection, they would have to find another candidate to take the incumbent's place, which would mean losing the incumbent's popularity and reputation and reducing the party's chances of holding the seat.

WORKING TOGETHER IN OFFICE

Because candidates are not required to support their party's platform, there is no guarantee that they will be able to work together with other members of the party in office. Sometimes, as with the Democrats and the economic stimulus plan, the members of a party can compromise to resolve their differences. However, there are also many examples of issues that can split a party wide open, such as health care reform (for the Democrats) or immigration reform (for the Republicans). Sometimes party members can compromise their differences, as in the case of Democrats' positions on health care reform, but sometimes compromise may be impossible, as in the case of Republicans' immigration proposals. And of course, even if the members of a party can find common ground, they may fail at building the bipartisan coalitions that are often necessary to enact major legislation, such as in the case of deficit-reduction proposals.

The fact that American political parties are heterogeneous means that elected members of the party may not agree on spending, policy, or anything else. In that sense, voters can't expect that putting one party in power will result in specific policy changes. Instead, policy outcomes depend on how (and whether) individual officeholders from the party can resolve their differences. Institutions such as the party caucuses or conferences provide a forum in which elected officials can meet and seek common ground, but there is no guarantee that they will find acceptable compromises.

Moreover, concerted action by members of a party in government may be aimed at political rather than policy goals. For example, during the last several years, Republicans in the House and Senate uniformly opposed many Democratic initiatives. Moreover, legislators from both parties failed to find common ground around proposals to cut the deficit, enact new controls on firearms, reform immigration law, or make changes to the Affordable Care Act. For many legislators, opposition was based on policy concerns. But for others, their opposition reflected a political calculation—that this strategy was their party's best bet for gaining seats in the 2014 elections. In this way, American political parties can work against the enactment of effective responses to public problems and increase, rather than decrease, the amount of conflict in American politics.

PROVIDING ACCOUNTABILITY

As we discussed earlier, a party serves as an accountability mechanism that gives citizens an identifiable group to reward when policies work well and to punish when policies fail. However, individual legislators also work to build a reputation with voters that is independent of their party label. They are happy to emphasize their party affiliation when it brings them support, but they choose not to mention it when the party is associated with unpopular policies or outcomes. Republican legislators, for example, highlighted their party identification in the 2002 and 2004 elections, as many voters held the party in high regard.[47] However, by 2006, with voter evaluations of the party and President Bush at all-time lows, many Republican candidates deemphasized their connection to the party.[48] The same was true for many Democratic candidates in 2010 and 2012: given the unpopularity of many of President Obama's policies and low voter evaluations of the party in power, these candidates' best bet for reelection was to emphasize their efforts to respond to district concerns and downplay their party affiliation or past support for the president.

When politicians work to secure their own political future in this way, they make it harder for voters to use party labels to decide who should be rewarded and who should be punished for government performance. The result is that legislators are held accountable for their own performance in office, such as how they voted—but no one in Congress is accountable for large-scale outcomes such as the state of the economy or for foreign policy. Of course, some voters hold legislators accountable based on whether they are members of the party in power, which is why Republicans lost House and Senate seats in 2006 and 2008 and Democrats lost seats in 2010. Even so, most Republicans and Democrats in Congress managed to survive these elections, suggesting that party-based accountability is rather weak in contemporary American politics.

VOTERS MAY PUNISH THE PARTY in power if they are unhappy with its policies. In 2010, frustration with many of President Obama's policies worked against Democrats and helped Republicans. Senator Marco Rubio of Florida was one of the new Republican members elected to Congress that year.

CITIZENS' BEHAVIOR

As we have seen, most Americans identify as either Republican or Democrat, and many citizens use party labels to cue their voting decisions. However, citizens are under no obligation to give money or time to the party they identify with or to any of its candidates. They don't have to vote for its candidates or even vote at all. All these actions would strengthen party organizations, but citizens do not have to take them even if they strongly identify with a party.

Here again, citizens are free to choose how to participate in American politics, including the option of not participating. But many of the things citizens do—such as not contributing to campaigns or party organizations, splitting their votes between candidates from different parties in the general election, or ignoring party affiliation in their retrospective evaluations—weaken party organizations and make it harder for them to operate as a team to enact policies and oversee the bureaucracy.

CONCLUSION

American political parties help organize elections, unify disparate social groups, simplify the choices facing voters, and build compromises around party members' shared concerns—all with the goals of winning elections and setting government policy. A close look at how parties operate demonstrates that the various Tea Party groups and candidates, for all their electoral success and press attention, fall far short of what it takes to make a political party. There is no unified Tea Party organization that exists apart from its candidates, and no evidence that Americans are abandoning the Republican and Democratic parties in favor of long-term attachment to Tea Party groups or their candidates. These differences are not just definitional—the lack of an organization and a core of loyal voters severely limit the political power of Tea Party officeholders, as the 2013 government shutdown illustrated.

The 2013 government shutdown also indicates that the success of political parties depends on whether individual party members—candidates, citizens, and party leaders—are willing to take the actions necessary to achieve electoral and policy goals. In recent years, congressional Republicans have campaigned on a platform of making substantial changes in the size and scope of the federal government. However, their apparent consensus disappeared once they were in office, as legislators disagreed on which programs should be cut, constituents demanded that their favorite programs be saved, and party leaders worried that taking a hard line would lead to electoral defeat. In the case of the shutdown (and the larger debate about the size of government), Republican House members and senators ultimately realized that the only thing they could agree on was that there was no consensus within the party about what to do. Though the Republicans gained control of the Senate and strengthened their House majority in the 2014 midterm elections, the election of additional conservatives may only serve to increase conflict within the party.

Of course, these difficulties do not reflect a problem with the Republican Party per se. The Democrats' success at enacting Obamacare and other significant proposals in 2009–2010 masked significant differences of opinion among the Democratic party's elected officials, activists, and citizen supporters. As we have seen, parties try to find a way to bridge such differences in order for members to act together to accomplish common goals. However, parties' ability to bring people together is not absolute. Individual party members respond to constituents, party leaders, and public opinion in many ways, sometimes taking actions in line with party goals and other times acting in ways that help themselves and that defy the party.

WHAT ARE POLITICAL PARTIES?

▶ *Define political parties and identify the three major aspects of American parties.* **(Pages 270–71)**

SUMMARY

Political parties are organizations that run candidates for political office and coordinate the actions of officials elected under the party banner. Here in the United States, parties are relatively decentralized, putting forth a loose configuration of candidates who share a party label but don't necessarily work together. The parties are composed of three semiautonomous units: the party organization, the party in government, and the party in electorate.

KEY TERMS

party organization (p. 271)
party in government (p. 271)
party in the electorate (p. 271)

CRITICAL THINKING AND DISCUSSION

Who controls political parties: leaders in government, party organizations, or the people?

PRACTICE QUIZ QUESTION

1. Which statement best characterizes the American political parties?

   A Parties in the electorate pay dues to the party organization; leaders in the party organization tell elected officials what to do.

   B Candidates run as representatives of the party; leaders have no influence on how candidates campaign or govern.

   C Candidates are generally autonomous of the party organization, although they do receive support from the party organization.

   D Parties help candidates only after they are elected.

   E Parties handle 90 percent of fund-raising for candidates.

HISTORY OF AMERICAN POLITICAL PARTIES

▶ *Show how American political parties and party systems have evolved over time.* **(Pages 271–75)**

SUMMARY

Political parties are a central feature of American politics, although they look and act very differently today than they have over time.

Political scientists use the term "party system" to refer to a period of party stability; in all, there have been six different party systems in the country's history. Party systems are broken up by realignments, which occur when some of the defining factors of the party system are changed or specified, and rifts in the group develop because of these changes.

KEY TERMS

party system (p. 272)
party principle (p. 273)
spoils system (p. 273)
political machine (p. 273)
realignment (p. 275)

CRITICAL THINKING AND DISCUSSION

Is the spoils system a good idea or a bad idea? Why?

PRACTICE QUIZ QUESTIONS

2. Which were the first well-known parties in the United States?

   A Federalists and Democratic-Republicans

   B Democrats and Republicans

   C Whigs and Federalists

   D Democrats and Whigs

   E Whigs and Republicans

3. The idea that a party is not just a group, but an organization that exists apart from its candidate, is called the _____.

   A party system

   B spoils system

   C conditional party government

   D party identification

   E party principle

MODERN AMERICAN POLITICAL PARTIES

▶ *Describe the main characteristics of American parties as organizations, in the government, and in the electorate.* **(Pages 275–84)**

SUMMARY

The modern party is composed of three parts. The party organization is a loosely defined group of individuals and organizations that are focused on supporting political candidates when they share the same policy goals. The party in the government consists of elected officials who are the members of a particular party. The party in the electorate consists of citizens who identify with a particular political party.

KEY TERMS

national committee (p. 275)
political action committee (PAC) (p. 276)
527 organization (p. 276)
caucus (congressional) (p. 279)
conference (p. 279)
party identification (party ID) (p. 280)
party coalitions (p. 283)

CRITICAL THINKING AND DISCUSSION

How would we know that a realignment is taking place in American politics?

PRACTICE QUIZ QUESTIONS

4. The Democratic and Republican party organizations _____ hierarchical; they are _____ to force state and local parties to share their positions on issues.

    A are not; able

    B are not; unable

    C are; able

    D are; unable

    E are; sometimes able

5. A group of elected officials of the same party who come together to organize and strategize is called a _____.

    A cabal

    B conditional party government

    C primary

    D political action committee

    E caucus

6. The modern Congress is _____; the distance between the parties has _____ over the past 60 years.

    A polarized; increased

    B polarized; stayed the same

    C not polarized; decreased

    D not polarized; stayed the same

    E not polarized; increased

7. What has recent analysis of political Independents concluded?

    A They are in the process of changing parties.

    B More and more people regard parties as irrelevant.

    C Americans are politically savvy and do not blindly follow party lines.

    D The number of Independents has grown substantially in the past 20 years.

    E Independents are not better informed on candidates, parties, or policy.

THE ROLE OF POLITICAL PARTIES IN AMERICAN POLITICS

▶ *Explain the important functions parties perform in the political system.* **(Pages 285–94)**

SUMMARY

Political parties serve two major roles in the political system. First, they contest elections by recruiting and nominating candidates and supporting candidate campaigns. Second, they facilitate cooperation in government by providing a framework for agenda setting, coordination, and accountability among members of the same party.

KEY TERMS

primary election (p. 285)
caucus (electoral) (p. 285)
nominating convention (p. 286)
party platform (p. 291)
unified government (p. 294)
divided government (p. 294)

CRITICAL THINKING AND DISCUSSION

Suppose you are the leader of your party's caucus or conference in the House of Representatives. Why would you want to convince your party's elected officials to support the party's position on an issue? Why might you want to let them vote as they think best?

PRACTICE QUIZ QUESTIONS

8. Which is *not* one of the ways political party organizations support candidates?

    A by controlling who runs in House and Senate races

    B by contributing money to campaign activities

    C by offering advice on how to deal with the press

    D by organizing get-out-the-vote activities

    E by offering advice on which issues to emphasize

9. Why do most candidates support their party platforms?

    A because candidates are required to support the platforms

    B because all candidates vote on the platforms that are written

    C because candidates get kicked out of the party for not doing so

    D because both major parties' platforms are essentially the same

    E because most candidates and their constituents generally agree with the platform

10. Which of the following options best defines the theory of conditional party government?

    "As policy differences between the parties in government _____, the parties in government will be _____ important in helping legislators develop policy plans and strategies."

    A increase; less

    B increase; more

C decrease; less

D decrease; more

E decrease; equally

11. When the president, House, and Senate are controlled by the same party, this is called:

A party in government

B responsible party government

C unified government

D divided government

E conditional party government

MINOR PARTIES

▶ *Consider the role of minor parties in a system dominated by two major parties.* **(Pages 295–96)**

SUMMARY

There are many different minor political parties, and while they rarely make a significant impact on the political stage, they do occasionally influence election outcomes. The two big issues facing minor parties are that their platforms do not appeal to a large portion of Americans, and that the electoral system makes it hard for minor parties to win elections.

KEY TERMS

Duverger's law (p. 296)
single-member districts (p. 296)
plurality voting (p. 296)

CRITICAL THINKING AND DISCUSSION

Even though minor parties have little to no influence on policy outcomes in American politics, why might a citizen nevertheless decide to vote for a minor party candidate?

PRACTICE QUIZ QUESTION

12. The principle that single-member districts and plurality voting will support only two political parties is _____.

A Condorcet's theorem

B Pascal's paradox

C Duverger's law

D Fermat's theorem

E conditional party government

WHAT KIND OF DEMOCRACY DO AMERICAN POLITICAL PARTIES CREATE?

▶ *Evaluate the benefits and possible problems of the American party system.* **(Pages 297–300)**

SUMMARY

Political parties do a number of things that are important to facilitate good democracy: they generally recruit good candidates, simplify voters' choices, encourage candidates to work together in office, and provide a mechanism for holding politicians accountable. Nonetheless, there are limits to the extent to which parties are able to achieve these goals, partially due to the fact that the people who make up the parties are primarily interested in their own careers.

CRITICAL THINKING AND DISCUSSION

Are party organizations ultimately more useful for politicians or for the electorate? Why?

PRACTICE QUIZ QUESTION

13. Which feature of political parties is undermined by legislators who build a reputation with voters independent of the party label?

A the recruitment of good candidates

B the provision of ballot access

C the simplification of voter choices

D the encouragement of policy cooperation

E the provision of electoral accountability

SUGGESTED READING

Aldrich, John. *Why Parties?* Chicago: University of Chicago Press, 1995.

Bartels, Larry M. *Unequal Democracy: The Political Economy of the New Gilded Age.* New York: Russell Sage Foundation, 2008.

Carmines, Edward G., and James A. Stimson. *Issue Evolution: Race and the Transformation of American Politics.* Princeton, NJ: Princeton University Press, 1989.

Cohen, Marty, David Karol, Hans Noel, and John Zaller. *The Party Decides: Presidential Nominations before and after Reform.* Chicago: University of Chicago Press, 2008.

Cox, Gary, and Mathew McCubbins. *Setting the Agenda: Party Government in the U.S. House of Representatives.* New York: Cambridge University Press, 2005.

Fiorina, Morris. *Retrospective Voting in American National Elections.* New Haven, CT: Yale University Press, 1981.

Green, Donald, Bradley Palmquist, and Eric Schickler. *Partisan Hearts and Minds.* New Haven, CT: Yale University Press, 2004.

Polsby, Nelson. *Consequences of Party Reform.* New York: Oxford University Press, 1983.

Rohde, David. *Parties and Leaders in the Post-Reform House.* Chicago: University of Chicago Press, 1991.

Schattschneider, E. E. *Party Government.* New York: McGraw-Hill, 1942.

Sundquist, James L. *Dynamics of the Party System.* Rev. ed. Washington, D.C.: Brookings Institution, 1983.

9

Elections

IN THE 2014 MIDTERM ELECTIONS, THE REPUBLICAN PARTY rode a wave of voter discontent over gridlock in Washington and the performance of President Obama to secure majority control in the Senate. One of the key Senate races was in Arkansas, where incumbent Mark Pryor (pictured here) lost to challenger Tom Cotton. What will the Republicans do with their newfound power in the Senate? And what does that mean for the last two years of Obama's presidency?

EVERY TWO YEARS, AMERICANS ELECT 435 HOUSE MEMBERS and 33 or so senators; every four years, we elect a president. Out of these many separate contests, a few races attract disproportionate interest because they provide insights into what voters are thinking, reveal the usefulness of different campaign strategies, and highlight the consequences of elections. In the 2014 election, the focus was on control of the Senate, and especially on two Democratic incumbents, Mark Pryor of Arkansas and Jeanne Shaheen of New Hampshire.

In Pryor's case, the question was whether a once-popular incumbent, who had no Republican opponent in 2008 and whose votes often broke with the Democratic Caucus, could overcome discontent with his party's president (in 2012, President Obama received less than 37 percent of the vote in Arkansas). It also raised the question of whether Pryor could be defeated by a well-funded conservative Republican challenger, Representative Tom Cotton, who highlighted Pryor's support for Obama's economic stimulus and health care legislation.

Shaheen's race attracted attention because of increasing Democratic strength in her state—and the fact that she was opposed by a popular former senator from Massachusetts, moderate Scott Brown. Given two experienced, well-qualified ideological moderates, would voters in New Hampshire vote for the party or the person? Would they think of Brown as a carpetbagger (someone who is running for office in an area where he hasn't lived very long and/or doesn't have deep ties) or accept his argument that Shaheen's support for President Obama's proposals was out of step with her constituents' wishes?

CONFLICT &
COMPROMISE
in American Politics

CHAPTER *goals*

Present the major
rules and procedures of
American elections.
► PAGES 306–18

Describe the features and
strategies of campaigns for
federal office.
► PAGES 318–32

Explain the key factors that
influence voters' choices.
► PAGES 332–40

Analyze the issues and
outcomes in the 2014
election.
► PAGES 340–46

As these examples illustrate, American national elections are about conflict. They are contests in which candidates compete for political office, offering voters a choice between different backgrounds, records, and promises. Candidates from different parties generally offer their electorates distinct, competing visions of what the federal government should do—from what the tax code should look like, to how the government should spend the tax money it collects, to what regulations the government should impose on individuals and corporations.

The fact that candidates hold different visions confirms another of the central themes of this chapter—that political process (in this case, elections) matters. Ultimately, Shaheen defeated Brown in New Hampshire but Pryor lost to Cotton in Arkansas. In both cases, the winners' behavior in office on a wide range of issues from health care to Supreme Court nominees will be sharply different from what the losers would have done. Moreover, the fact that Republicans captured eight Senate seats and majority control of the chamber in 2014 has important policy consequences, such as what kinds of proposals will be debated and voted on in the next two years, the outcomes of these votes, and the prospects for enacting treaties and approving President Obama's nominations to the federal judiciary and bureaucracy.

Candidates in American elections are elected for different periods of time to represent districts, states, or the entire nation—places that vary tremendously in terms of what constituents want from government. A variety of rules determines who can run, who can vote, and how candidates can campaign. Even ballot layouts and how votes are cast and counted vary across states. Elections also differ in the amount of media coverage they receive, the level of involvement of political parties and other organizations, and how much attention citizens pay to the contests. All these aspects of the election process—who runs, how candidates campaign, and how voters respond—shape outcomes.

Our goal in this chapter is to explain how American elections work. By making the election process more comprehensible and by focusing on the promises candidates make in campaigns, we aim to demonstrate how and why elections matter. We show that there are real differences between candidates and that these differences have profound implications for public policy. We show that the actions candidates take during campaigns shape citizens' perceptions and their voting decisions. We show that despite Americans' general detachment from politics, their votes reflect both their policy preferences and their insight into candidates' promises and performance. Finally, we show how all of these factors influence who wins and who loses in American elections, as well as the policy consequences of these contests.

HOW DO AMERICAN ELECTIONS WORK?

The American political system is a representative democracy: Americans do not make policy choices themselves, but they vote for individuals who make these choices on their behalf. This section describes the rules and procedures that define American national elections.

FUNCTIONS OF ELECTIONS

Our working assumption for explaining the rules and processes of elections as well as the behavior of candidates and voters is that they are tied directly to what elections do: selecting representatives, giving citizens the ability to influence the direction of government policy, and providing citizens with the opportunity to reward and punish officeholders seeking reelection. We will discuss each of these functions in turn.

SELECTING REPRESENTATIVES The most visible function of American national elections is the selection of officeholders: members of the House and Senate, and the president and vice president. Candidates can be **incumbents** or challengers. America has a representative democracy, which means that by voting in elections, Americans have an indirect effect on government policy. Although citizens do not make policy choices themselves, they determine which individuals get to make these choices. In this way, elections are supposed to connect citizen preferences and government actions.

incumbent A politician running for reelection to the office he or she currently holds.

SHAPING POLICY The fundamental choice in an election is between two or more candidates running for some political office—a seat in the House or the Senate, or the presidency. But elections also involve a choice between candidates' policy platforms, the set of things they promise to do if elected. By investigating candidates' platforms, citizens learn about the range of options for government policy. Moreover, their voting decisions determine who gets to make choices about future government policy, and thereby shape government policy itself. This description is particularly true for the 2014 Senate elections, where the outcome of these contests gave Republicans majority control of the chamber.

PROMOTING ACCOUNTABILITY The election process also creates a way to hold incumbents accountable. When citizens choose between voting for an incumbent or a challenger, they can make a retrospective evaluation. They consider the incumbent's performance, asking, "Has she done a good job on the issues I care about?"[1] Citizens who answer yes typically vote for the incumbent, and those who answer no typically vote for the challenger.

Retrospective evaluations are significant because they make incumbents responsive to their constituents' demands.[2] If an elected official anticipates that some constituents will make retrospective evaluations, he will try to take actions that these constituents will like. If an incumbent ignores the possibility of voters' retrospective evaluations, he may be removed from office in the next election. Retrospective evaluations can also form the basis for prospective judgments—voters' beliefs about how the country will fare if different candidates win. This provides an additional reason for incumbents to be responsive to citizens' demands.

In the case of the 2014 Senate elections, voters judged incumbents such as Mark Pryor or Jeanne Shaheen based on their voting behavior as senators, including their support for President Obama and for programs such as Obamacare. Particularly in Arkansas, where Obama and his policies were very unpopular, retrospective evaluations appear to have provided a significant boost to the Republican challenger, Tom Cotton.

AMANDA RENTERIA, A DEMOCRATIC candidate for Congress at a rally in California. Although Renteria's campaign argued that incumbent Republican David Valadao was not serving his district effectively. However, she lost to Valadao by a significant margin.

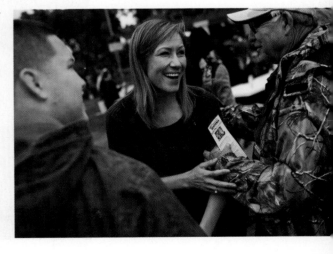

House and Senate candidates running for office face a two-step procedure. First, if the prospective candidate wants to run on behalf of a political party, she must win the party's nomination in a primary election. If the would-be candidate wants to run as an Independent, she needs to gather signatures on a petition to secure a spot on the ballot. Different states hold either **open primaries** or **closed primaries**, and state law sets the timing of these elections. A few states hold single primaries, where there is one election involving candidates from both parties, with the top two finalists (regardless of party) receiving nominations to the general election.

The second step in the election process is the **general election**, which is held throughout the nation on the first Tuesday after the first Monday in November. Federal law designates this day as Election Day. General elections determine who wins elected positions in government. The offices at stake vary depending on the year. Presidential elections occur every four years (2008, 2012, 2016, . . .). In a presidential election year, Americans elect the entire House of Representatives, one-third of the Senate, and a president and vice president. During midterm elections (2006, 2010, 2014, . . .), there is no presidential contest, but the entire House and a third of the Senate are up for election.

The Constitution limits voting rights to American citizens who are at least 18 years old. There are also numerous restrictions on voter eligibility that vary across states, including residency requirements (usually 30 days) and whether people convicted of a major crime can vote. A new development in American elections is an increase in the practice of no-excuse absentee voting as well as early voting, or casting a general election vote prior to Election Day.[3] Voters in Oregon vote entirely by mail, and over 98 percent of voters in Washington State vote by mail. Although many Americans vote early (about a third of votes cast in recent elections), and some candidates have distributed absentee ballots as part of their mobilization efforts, it is unclear whether these developments have changed

open primary A primary election in which any registered voter can participate in the contest, regardless of party affiliation.

closed primary A primary election in which only registered members of a particular political party can vote.

general election The election in which voters cast ballots for House members, senators, and (every four years) a president and vice president.

AMERICANS VOTE IN ALL SORTS OF places—even private homes. Here, people vote in a garage in Stockton, California, during the 2008 general election.

election outcomes.[4] If enough people vote early in future elections, it could have a significant impact on campaign tactics; for example, candidates would have to begin campaign advertising earlier to ensure that early voters see these appeals.

CONSTITUENCIES: WHO CHOOSES REPRESENTATIVES?

Another critical feature of American elections is that officeholders are elected in single-member districts in which only the winner of the most votes takes office. (Although each state's senators both represent the whole state, they are elected separately, usually in different years.) Senate candidates compete throughout the state; House candidates compete in congressional districts. In most states, congressional district lines are drawn by state legislatures. In a few states, nonpartisan commissions or committees of judges perform this function. Redistricting can happen at any time, but in general, district lines are revised after each census to make sure the boundary lines reflect shifts in population across and within states. (For details on redistricting, see Chapter 11.)

Because members of the House and Senate are elected from specific geographic areas, they often represent very different kinds of people. Their constituents differ in terms of age, race, income level, occupation, and political leaning, including party affiliation and ideology. Therefore, legislators from different areas of the country face highly diverse demands from their constituents, which often leads them to pursue very dissimilar kinds of policies.

For example, Democratic senator Elizabeth Warren, who is one of the senators from Massachusetts, represents a liberal state where same-sex marriage is legal, while Republican senator Mike Crapo is one of the senators from the conservative state of Idaho, where most voters have long opposed same-sex marriage. Suppose the Senate votes on a constitutional amendment to allow same-sex marriage nationwide. Warren knows that most of her constituents would probably want her to vote for the proposal, and Crapo knows that most of his constituents would probably want him to vote against it. This example illustrates that congressional conflicts over policy often reflect differences in constituents' demands. Warren and Crapo themselves may hold different views on a same-sex marriage ban, but even if they agreed, their constituents' distinct demands would make it likely that as legislators they would vote differently.

DETERMINING WHO WINS Most House and Senate contests involve **plurality voting**: the candidate who gets the most votes wins. However, some states use **majority voting**, meaning that a candidate needs a majority (more than 50 percent of the vote) to win. If no candidate has a majority, a **runoff election** takes place between the top two finishers. Some candidates have lost runoff elections even though they received the most votes in the first contest.

The two-step process of primary and general elections can have a similar effect on the election's outcome. Sometimes the winner of a primary is not a party's best candidate for the general election. For example, in the 2012 Indiana Republican primary, a very conservative Tea Party candidate, Richard Mourdock, defeated a less conservative, longtime incumbent, Richard Lugar. In the general election, Mourdock was defeated by the Democratic nominee, Congressman Joe Donnelly. Yet, it was not inevitable that Donnelly would win the general election. If Lugar had won the Republican primary, he might well have gone on—given his voting record, reputation, and less conservative views—to defeat Donnelly in the general election.

plurality voting A voting system in which the candidate who receives the most votes within a geographic area wins the election, regardless of whether that candidate wins a majority (more than half) of the votes.

majority voting A voting system in which a candidate must win more than 50 percent of votes to win the election. If no candidate wins enough votes to take office, a runoff election is held between the top two vote-getters.

runoff election Under a majority voting system, a second election held only if no candidate wins a majority of the votes in the first general election. Only the top two vote-getters in the first election compete in the runoff.

Americans vote using a wide range of machines and ballots based on where they live and vote.[5] Some counties use paper keypunch ballots, on which voters use a stylus to punch out holes next to the names of their preferred candidates on a ballot card. These ballots are then scanned, although they can also be hand-counted. Other counties use mechanical voting machines that require voters to pull a lever next to the name of their preferred candidates. A few localities still use paper ballots on which voters mark their preferred candidate with an "X." Touch-screen voting machines are becoming increasingly popular, but this type of voting is controversial because of its cost, the potential for delays on Election Day (since voters often take longer to cast their votes using this technology), and concerns that machines could be manipulated to change election outcomes.[6] One increasingly common solution is to have optical machines generate a paper receipt that citizens can inspect after they vote and then put into a secure box, or paper ballots that are scanned electronically. Of course, earlier technologies aren't perfect either; vote totals in lever machines can also be manipulated, and paper ballots can be lost or altered. Moreover, the widespread use of touch screens in recent elections has occurred without major problems.[7]

Different voting methods show different rates of undervotes. Such undervotes can happen when a voter casts an unmarked ballot, votes in some races on the ballot but not others, or casts a ballot that cannot be counted for some reason. The confusion that surrounded the 2000 presidential election outcome in Palm Beach County, Florida, showed what a difference the ballot structure can make. Palm Beach County residents marked their votes on a "butterfly ballot." This type of ballot lists the candidates on both sides of a center column, and voters indicate their preference by pressing down with a stylus on the circle in the center column that corresponds to the name of their preferred candidate. A punch card inserted underneath the ballot records the stylus marks, and votes are counted by tallying holes in the punch cards.

While punch-card ballots are generally regarded as a good technique—the technology is relatively cheap, and it is easy to manually recount ballots if needed—the butterfly ballot structure appears to have caused some supporters of Al Gore in Palm Beach County to mistakenly vote for Pat Buchanan. As the photo shows, Gore's name and Buchanan's were on facing pages at about the same level, so it would be easy for a voter to press down on the wrong circle. Analyses suggested that the butterfly ballot cost Gore several thousand Palm Beach County votes—enough to change the results of the election in Florida, and thus the outcome of the 2000 presidential election.[8] We don't know whether ballots used in other counties

MANY DIFFERENT MECHANISMS are used to record votes in American elections, including paper keypunch ballots and computerized, electronic machines (left). The design of the infamous butterfly ballot (right), which was used in the 2000 presidential election to vote in Palm Beach County, Florida, inadvertently led some people who intended to vote for Democrat Al Gore to select Reform Party candidate Patrick Buchanan.

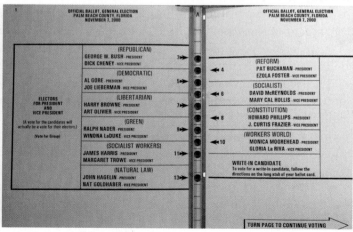

and states favored Gore or some other candidates. But it is clear that choices about how ballots are structured can affect who wins elections.

Ballot counting adds more complexities. Most states have laws that allow vote recounts if a race is sufficiently close (typically within 1 percent or less). Even when a recount occurs, it may be impossible to definitively determine who won a particular election, as the rules that determine which ballots are valid are often open to interpretation. More significant is that when an election is close, the question of which candidate wins may depend on how ballots are structured and votes are counted. The problem is not that election officials are dishonest; rather, close elections inherently tend to produce ambiguous outcomes.

Claims are often made that officials manipulate election rules to guarantee wins for their favored candidates. In some states, Republican state and local officials have enacted laws that require voters to verify their identity by showing polling officials an official form of identification such as a driver's license or a passport. The purported goal of these laws is to prevent voter fraud—one person voting under another's name. However, there is almost no evidence of voter fraud in American elections. Moreover, voter ID laws would create barriers to voting for individuals who lack an official ID—these individuals are generally poor and nonwhite, and they disproportionately vote Democratic. While some supporters of voter ID laws may be sincerely concerned about preventing fraud, there is little doubt that enacting these laws hurts Democratic candidates.

PRESIDENTIAL ELECTIONS

Many of the rules governing elections, such as who is eligible to vote, are the same for both presidential and congressional elections. But presidential contests have several unique rules regarding how nominees are determined and how votes are counted. Moreover, the constitutional requirements for presidential candidates are also somewhat stricter than those for congressional candidates (see Nuts & Bolts 9.1).

primary A ballot vote in which citizens select a party's nominee for the general election.

THE NOMINATION: PRIMARIES AND CAUCUSES Presidential nominees from the Democratic and Republican parties are determined by state-level **primaries** and **caucuses** over a five-month period beginning in January of an election year.[9] Voters in these elections select delegates to attend the nominating conventions

caucus A local meeting in which party members select a party's nominee for the general election.

9.1 **NUTS** *& bolts*

CONSTITUTIONAL REQUIREMENTS FOR CANDIDATES

Office	Minimum Age	Residency Requirement	Term of Office
President	35	Born in the United States	4 years
Senator	30	Resident of state; U.S. citizen for at least 9 years	6 years
Representative	25	Resident of state; U.S. citizen for at least 7 years	2 years

that take place during the summer. There, the delegates cast the votes that determine their party's presidential and vice-presidential nominees. The format of these elections, including their timing and the number of delegates selected per state, is determined on a state-by-state basis by the state and national party organizations.[10] In some states, each candidate preselects a list of delegates who will attend the convention if the candidate wins sufficient votes in the primary or caucus. In other states, candidates select delegates from a list developed by party leaders. In both cases, a candidate's principal goal is to win as many delegates as possible—and to select delegates who will be reliable supporters at the convention. Surprisingly, neither party requires delegates to support the candidates who selected them, but there is an expectation that the delegates will do so.

The details of translating primary and caucus votes into convention delegates vary from state to state, but some general rules apply. All Democratic primaries and caucuses use **proportional allocation** to divide each state's delegate seats among the candidates; thus, if a candidate receives 40 percent of the votes in a state's primary, the candidate gets roughly 40 percent of the convention delegates from that state. Some Republican contests use proportional allocation, but others use **winner-take-all**. In these, the candidate who receives the most votes gets all of the state's convention delegates. These rules can have a significant effect on candidates' campaign strategies and the outcome of the nomination process (see How It Works: Nominating Presidential Candidates in Chapter 8).

The order in which the primaries and caucuses in different states take place is important because many candidacies do not survive beyond the early contests.[11] Most presidential candidates pour everything they have into the first few elections. Candidates who do well attract financial contributions, campaign workers, endorsements, and additional media coverage, all of which enable them to move on to subsequent primaries or caucuses. But for candidates who do poorly in the first contests, contributions and coverage dry up, and these candidates usually drop out. Thus, the candidate who leads after the first several primaries and caucuses generally wins the nomination.[12] However, when the first few contests do not yield a clear favorite, the race can continue until the last states have voted, or even until the convention.

If a sitting president runs for reelection, as Barack Obama did in 2012, he typically faces little opposition for his party's general-election nomination—not because challengers defer to the president, but because most presidents are popular enough among their own party's faithful supporters that they can win the nomination without too much trouble. Only presidents with particularly low approval ratings have faced serious opposition in their nomination bids.

Among the states, the presidential nomination process is always changing.[13] In 2012, many states in particular regions of the country elected delegates on the same day (a trend known as regional primaries), and some states moved up their primaries to take place earlier in the primary process (a trend known as frontloading). For many years, Iowa and New Hampshire held the first presidential nomination contests, with the Iowa caucus held a week before the New Hampshire primary in January. These states' position at the beginning of the process is largely a historical accident, but it is often controversial. State party officials from other states often complain about the media attention given to these contests and their disproportionate influence in winnowing the candidate pool, but there is no consensus around an alternate schedule. As a result,

proportional allocation
During the presidential primaries, the practice of determining the number of convention delegates allotted to each candidate based on the percentage of the popular vote cast for each candidate. All Democratic primaries and caucuses use this system, as do some states' Republican primaries and caucuses.

winner-take-all During the presidential primaries, the practice of assigning all of a given state's delegates to the candidate who receives the most popular votes. Some states' Republican primaries and caucuses use this system.

the 2012 nomination process was roughly the same as in previous years, with Iowa and New Hampshire holding the initial contests, in early January 2012, followed by primaries in South Carolina and Florida later in the month, and the remaining contests beginning in February and continuing to June.

One rule that distinguishes the parties' candidate selection process is that about one-fifth of the delegates to the Democratic Convention are not supporters of a particular candidate nor have they been chosen to attend the convention based on primary and caucus results. Rather, they are elected officials and party officials whom their colleagues select to serve as superdelegates. Most are automatically seated at the convention regardless of primary and caucus results, and they are free to support any candidate for the nomination. By forcing candidates to court support from superdelegates, the party aims to ensure that the nominee is someone these officials believe can win the general election and whom they can work with if he or she is elected.[14]

DURING THE 2012 PRESIDENTIAL campaign, the media extensively covered the candidates and their wives and families during both the primaries and the general election. Here, Diane Sawyer of ABC News interviews Michelle Obama during the Democratic National Convention.

THE NATIONAL CONVENTION Presidential nominating conventions happen late in the summer of an election year. Their main task is to select the party's presidential nominee, although usually the vote at the convention is a formality; in all recent contests, one candidate has emerged from the nomination process going into the convention with a clear majority of delegates and is able to win the nomination on the first ballot.[15] To get the nomination, a candidate needs the support of a majority of the delegates. If no candidate receives a majority after the first round of voting at the convention, the voting continues until someone does.

After the convention delegates nominate a presidential candidate, they select a vice-presidential nominee. The presidential nominee gets to choose his or her running mate (generally before the convention), and the delegates almost always ratify this choice without much debate. Delegates also vote on the party platform, which describes what the party stands for and what kinds of policies its candidates will supposedly seek to enact if they are elected.

The final purpose of a convention is to attract public attention to the party and its nominees. Public figures give speeches during the evening sessions when all major television networks have live coverage. At some recent conventions, both parties have drawn press attention by recruiting speakers who support their political goals despite being associated with the opposing party.

Once presidential candidates are nominated, the general election campaign officially begins—although it often unofficially starts much earlier, as soon as the presumptive nominees are known. We say more about presidential campaigns in a later section.

COUNTING PRESIDENTIAL VOTES Even though in the voting booth you choose between the candidates by name, you actually don't vote directly for a presidential candidate. Rather, when you select your preferred candidate's name, you are choosing that person's slate of pledged supporters from your state to serve as electors, who will then vote to elect the president.

The number of electors for each state equals the state's number of House members (which varies by state population) plus the state's number of senators (two per state). Altogether, the electors chosen by the citizens of each state

electoral college The body that votes to select America's president and vice president based on the popular vote in each state. Each candidate nominates a slate of electors who are selected to attend the meeting of the college if their candidate wins the most votes in a state or district.

constitute the **electoral college**, the body that formally selects the president. Small-population states, therefore, have few electoral votes—Delaware and Montana each have only 3—while the highest-population state, California, has 55 (see How It Works: The Electoral College). In most states, electoral votes are allocated on a winner-take-all basis: the candidate who receives the most votes from a given state's citizens gets all of that state's electoral votes. But two states, Maine and Nebraska, allocate most of their electoral votes at the congressional district level: in those states, the candidate who wins the most votes in each congressional district wins that district's single electoral vote. Then, the remaining 2 electoral votes go to the candidate who gets the most votes statewide.[16]

The winner-take-all method of allocating most states' electoral votes makes candidates focus their attention on two kinds of states: high-population states with lots of electoral votes, and so-called swing states where the contest is relatively close. It's better for a candidate to spend a day campaigning in California (55 electoral votes) than in Montana (3 electoral votes). However, if one candidate is sure to win a particular state, both candidates will direct their efforts elsewhere. For example, in the last days of the 2012 campaign, Mitt Romney's campaign bought additional TV time in Pennsylvania and Ohio, but not in Nevada and Iowa, believing that the first two states might be winnable but that the other two were probably out of reach. The Obama campaign responded with additional advertising in Ohio and Pennsylvania and in Florida. The result: Obama won all three of the contested states (see How It Works In Practice: Obama's Electoral College Strategies, 2012).

Nuts & Bolts 9.2 divides states based on their electoral vote and whether they are swing states—defined as a state that each party won at least once in 2000,

9.2 NUTS & bolts

ELECTORAL VOTES AND SWING STATES

Presidential campaigns focus their attention on states with high electoral votes and swing states, those where each candidate has a good chance of winning. In this box, we group states into categories based on their number of electoral votes, and on whether one party always won the state in recent presidential elections.

| | Number of Electoral Votes | One Party Dominates in Recent Elections | |
		Yes	No
Electoral Votes (2012 Election)	3–5	D.C., Delaware, Alaska, Montana, North Dakota, South Dakota, Vermont, Wyoming, Hawaii, Maine, Rhode Island, Idaho, Nebraska, West Virginia	New Hampshire, New Mexico
	6–10	Arkansas, Kansas, Utah, Connecticut, Oregon, Oklahoma, Kentucky, Louisiana, Alabama, South Carolina, Wisconsin, Maryland, Mississippi, Missouri, Minnesota	Iowa, Nevada, Colorado
	More than 10	Massachusetts, Arizona, Tennessee, Washington, New Jersey, Michigan, Georgia, Illinois, Pennsylvania, New York, Texas, California	Indiana, Virginia, North Carolina, Ohio, Florida

THE ELECTORAL COLLEGE

538
TOTAL ELECTORS

ELECTORAL VOTES PER STATE

The number of electors from each state equals the state's number of House members (which varies based on state population) plus the number of senators (two per state). Each elector has one vote in the electoral college.

A   B

WHO ARE THE ELECTORS?

Candidates to be electors are nominated by their political parties. They pledge to support a certain candidate if they are elected to the electoral college. When you cast your vote for a presidential candidate, you are in fact voting for the slate of potential electors who support that candidate.

37%

100%
OF ELECTORAL VOTES
GO TO WINNER

61%

WINNING A STATE

Most states give all of their electoral college votes to the candidate who wins the most votes from citizens in the state. So, even if a candidate only gets 51 percent of the vote in the state, his or her entire slate of electors is elected, and he or she gets all of the state's votes in the electoral college.

How It Works
In Practice

OBAMA'S ELECTORAL COLLEGE STRATEGIES, 2012

To gain the 270 electoral votes that would be needed to win the 2012 election, Obama's staff had four possible strategies that involved concentrating resources in states in which neither Obama nor Romney had an insurmountable lead.

Obama's campaign started with the states Democratic candidate John Kerry won in 2004. The Obama team felt that all of these states would remain solidly in the Democratic column. They then targeted the following combinations of states that would get them from 246—the total electoral votes represented by the states Kerry won—to the 270 votes needed for victory.

JOHN KERRY MAP

MN 10	CA 55	NY 29	MA 11	NJ 14
HI 4	WI 10	PA 20	ME 4	DE 3
WA 12	IL 20	VT 3	RI 4	MD 10
OR 7	MI 16	NH 4	CT 7	D.C. 3

TOTAL VOTES
246

THE WESTERN STRATEGY

NV 6
CO 9
AZ 11
NM 5

246 + 31
277

THE MIDWESTERN STRATEGY

IA 6   OH 18

246 + 24
270

THE FLORIDA STRATEGY

FL 29

246 + 29
275

THE "NEW SOUTH" STRATEGY

VA 13
NC 15

246 + 28
274

2012 RESULTS

Ultimately, a combination of the four strategies led the Obama campaign to victory.

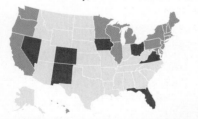

OBAMA'S FINAL WINNING ELECTORAL COLLEGE MAP

MN 10	CA 55	NY 29	MA 11	NJ 14	NV 6	OH 18
HI 4	WI 10	PA 20	ME 4	DE 3	CO 9	FL 29
WA 12	IL 20	VT 3	RI 4	MD 10	NM 5	VA 13
OR 7	MI 16	NH 4	CT 7	D.C. 3	IA 6	

TOTAL VOTES
332

Source: Adapted from Jim Messina: "Paths to 270 Electoral Votes," YouTube video, 3:22, posted by Obama for America, December 29, 2011, http://youtube/_7Y-Q9ZY5Ao (accessed 11/18/13).

POP QUIZ

1 The number of electors that each state has in the electoral college is based on

a   voter turnout in the previous election.

b   an equal number for all states.

c   the number of parties in the state.

d   the date the state joined the Union.

e   population.

2 In most states, if 51 percent of the citizens vote for a candidate in a presidential election, what happens?

a   The candidate receives all of the electors from that state.

b   The candidate receives 51 percent of the electors from that state.

c   The candidate receives 51 electoral votes from that state.

Answers: 1.e, 2.a

2004, and 2008. The table explains why both campaigns in 2012 spent so much time and campaign funds on states such as Virginia, Ohio, and Florida (swing states with a large number of electoral votes)—and why they largely ignored the District of Columbia and other states in the small-state, one-party-dominates category.

After citizens' votes are counted in each state, the slates of electors meet following the general election in December in the state capitals. At their meetings, the electors almost always vote for the presidential candidate they have pledged to support. After the votes are certified by a joint session of Congress, the candidate who wins a majority of the nation's electoral votes (at least 270) is the new president. One peculiarity of the electoral college is that in most states it is legal for an elector to either (1) vote for a candidate he or she is not pledged to support, or (2) abstain from voting.[17] Such events are uncommon for the simple reason that electors are selected by the presidential candidates with an eye toward reliable support.

If no candidate receives a majority of the electoral college votes, the members of the House of Representatives choose the winner. They follow a procedure in which the members from each state decide which candidate to support and then cast one collective vote per state, with the winner needing a majority of these state-level votes to win. This procedure has not been used since 1824, although it might be required if a third-party candidate wins a significant number of electoral votes or if a state's electors refuse to cast their votes.[18]

A presidential candidate can win the electoral college vote, and thus the election, without receiving a majority of the votes cast by citizens—one way this can happen is if a third-party candidate for president receives a substantial number of votes. Bill Clinton, for example, won a substantial electoral college majority in 1992, while receiving only 43 percent of the **popular vote**. This was because Ross Perot, running as a third-party candidate, received almost 19 percent of the national popular vote but not enough support in any one state to win **electoral votes**. Even in a race where no third-party candidate wins a significant percentage of the vote, the electoral college magnifies the winning candidate's vote percentage.

Yet, because of the way popular votes translate into electoral votes, even when there are only two candidates, a candidate can receive a majority of the electoral votes even though another candidate wins more popular votes (see Figure 9.1). In 2000, George Bush received about 540,000 fewer votes than his main rival, Al Gore, but Bush still won the electoral college vote, and the election. Other presidents who won the electoral college vote but lost the popular vote were John Quincy Adams in 1824, Rutherford B. Hayes in 1876, and Benjamin Harrison in 1888.

IN THE 2000 PRESIDENTIAL ELECTION, the popular vote was so close in Florida that individual ballots were examined to make sure every last vote was counted accurately before Florida's electoral votes were all given to the winner. In the end, all of Florida's electoral votes went to George W. Bush, giving him the additional electoral votes he needed to win the presidency.

popular vote The votes cast by citizens in an election.

electoral votes Votes cast by members of the electoral college; after a presidential candidate wins the popular vote in a given state, that candidate's slate of electors casts electoral votes for the candidate on behalf of that state.

FIGURE » 9.1

POPULAR VOTE VERSUS ELECTORAL VOTE, 2000–2012

Political scientists argue that the electoral college system tends to magnify the winning candidate's margin of victory. Do the data presented here support this view?

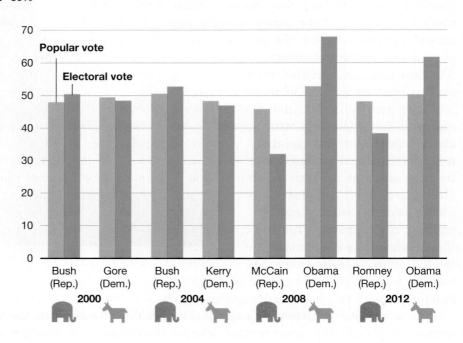

SOURCE: U.S. National Archives and Records Administration, www.archives.gov/federal-register/electoral-college/historical.html (accessed 11/12/12).

DESCRIBE THE FEATURES AND STRATEGIES OF CAMPAIGNS FOR FEDERAL OFFICE

ELECTORAL CAMPAIGNS

This section explores the campaign process and what candidates do to convince people to vote for them on Election Day. Our emphasis is on things that candidates do regardless of the office they are running for, across the entire **election cycle**, the two-year period between general elections.

SETTING THE STAGE

election cycle The two-year period between general elections.

On the day after an election, candidates, party officials, and interest groups all start thinking about the next election cycle. They consider who won and who lost the election, which incumbents look like safe bets for reelection and which ones might be vulnerable, who might retire soon or run for another office in the next election, and whether the election returns reveal new information about what kinds of campaigns or issues might increase voter turnout or support.

These calculations also reflect the costs of running for office. Challengers for House and Senate seats know that a campaign will consume at least a year of their time and deplete their financial resources. Presidential campaigns require even more money and effort. If a potential challenger already holds elected office, such as a state legislator running for the House or a House member running for the Senate, that person may have to give up his or her current office to run for a new one.[19]

Party organizations and interest groups face similar constraints both in recruiting candidates and in discouraging some people from running. They do not have the funds to offer significant support to candidates in all 435 congressional districts, in 33 or 34 Senate races, and in a presidential contest.[20] So which races draw their attention? The answer depends on many factors, including how well incumbents did in the last election, how much money those who won have available for the next election, whether party affiliation in the state or district favors Republicans or Democrats (and by how much), and whether the newly elected officeholders are likely to run for reelection.

In the year before the 2014 election, many reports noted the poor reelection prospects of many Democratic senators, including Senators Pryor and Shaheen discussed at the beginning of the chapter. Given their circumstances, it was no surprise that highly regarded, experienced challengers were recruited to run against them—an incumbent House member against Pryor, and a former Senator against Shaheen—and that both incumbents and challengers received party support.

Party committees and candidates also consider the likelihood that incumbents might retire, thereby creating an **open seat**. In the run-up to the 2014 election, some elderly legislators such as Harry Waxman (D-CA, 74 years old) announced their retirement, as well as younger incumbents such as Tom Latham (R-IA) who were frustrated with congressional gridlock. Open seats are of special interest to potential candidates and other political actors because incumbents generally hold an election advantage.[21] So, when a seat opens up, candidates from the party that does not control the seat know that they may have a better chance to win because they will not have to run against an incumbent. Consequently, the incumbent's party leaders have to recruit an especially strong candidate in order to hold the seat. Interest groups watch all these decisions with an eye toward deciding whom to endorse or support with campaign donations and advertisements.

Presidential campaigns work the same way. Virtually all first-term presidents run for reelection. Potential challengers in the opposing party study the results of the last election to see how many votes the president received and how this support was distributed across the states to determine their own chances of winning against the incumbent. Candidates in the president's party make the same calculations, although no sitting president in the twentieth century was denied renomination. Nonetheless, some presidents (Harry Truman in 1952, Lyndon Johnson in 1968) retired because their chances of being renominated were not good, while others (Gerald Ford in 1976, Jimmy Carter in 1980) faced tough primary contests.[22]

BEFORE THE CAMPAIGN

Most incumbent House members, senators, and presidents work throughout the election cycle to secure their reelection. Political scientists label this activity

open seat An elected position for which there is no incumbent.

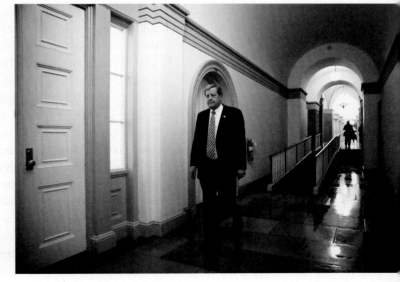

FRUSTRATED WITH GRIDLOCK IN Congress, moderate Republican Tom Latham (IA) decided not to seek reelection to his seat in the House in 2014. Latham had served in Congress since 1995 and was on the House Appropriations Committee.

the permanent campaign.[23] To stay in office, incumbents have to do two things: keep their constituents happy, and raise money for their campaign. As we will see in Chapter 11, congressional incumbents try to keep their constituents happy by taking actions that ensure the voters can identify something good that the incumbent has done. This, in turn, boosts voters' retrospective evaluations at election time.[24]

Incumbent presidents make the same kinds of calculations. During Barack Obama's first months in office, many of his advisers argued that he had to offer an economic stimulus plan in light of polls showing the economy was an overriding concern to most Americans. Obama did so—a decision driven by political as well as policy concerns. Of course, many presidential actions are taken in response to events rather than being initiated to gain voter support. Particularly in the case of wars and other conflicts, it is far-fetched to say that presidents initiate hostilities for political gain. Even so, presidents, just like other politicians, are keenly aware of the political consequences of their actions and the need to build a record they can run on in the next election.

Presidents can also use the federal bureaucracy to their own advantage and to help members of their party. For example, some scholars have argued that presidents try to increase economic growth in the months prior to elections, with the aim of increasing support for themselves (if they are eligible to run for reelection) and for their party's candidates.[25] Given the size and complexity of the U.S. economy, and the fact that the independent Federal Reserve System controls monetary policy, it is unlikely that such efforts could have much success. Even so, out of a desire to stay in office and help their party's candidates, it seems clear that presidents would want to be seen as having a positive impact on the economy.

Candidates for all offices, incumbents and challengers alike, also devote considerable time before the campaign to raising campaign funds. Fund-raising helps an incumbent in two ways.[26] First, it ensures that if the incumbent faces a strong opponent, she or he will have enough money to run an aggressive campaign. Second, successful fund-raising deters opposition. Potential challengers are less likely to run against an incumbent if that individual is well funded with a sizable campaign war chest.[27]

The other thing candidates do before the campaign is build their campaign organization.[28] Just like fund-raising, the success or failure of these efforts is a signal of a candidate's prospects. If experienced, well-respected people agree to work in a candidate's campaign, observers conclude that the candidate's prospects for being elected are probably good.

Skilled campaign consultants are among the most sought-after campaign staff. These consultants plan strategies, run public opinion polls, assemble ads and buy television time, and talk with members of the media on the candidate's behalf, among other things. For many consultants, electioneering is a full-time, year-round position. Many concentrate on electing candidates from one party, although some work for whoever will hire them.

Almost all campaigns have paid and volunteer staff, ranging from the dozen or so people who work for a typical House candidate to the thousands needed to run a major-party candidate's presidential campaign. Some campaign staff work full-time for an incumbent's campaign committee or are on the incumbent's congressional or presidential staff. With some exceptions for senior presidential staff, federal law prohibits government employees from engaging in campaign activities during work hours or with congressional resources.[29] As a result, many congressional staffers take a leave of absence from their government jobs to work on their bosses' reelection campaigns during the last few months of the election cycle, then return to working for the government after the election—assuming the incumbent is reelected.

It's hard to separate what candidates do at election time from what they do between elections—incumbents are *always* campaigning, which is part of the reason they are so likely to win reelection. In many cases, incumbent House members and senators wind up running against poorly funded, inexperienced candidates because stronger challengers—seeing that the incumbent has been working hard to solidify a hold on the constituency—decide to wait until the incumbent retires, when they can run for the open seat. Thus, incumbents are not automatically favored for reelection, but they often win by large margins because of all the things they do while holding office in between elections.[30]

MOST OFFICEHOLDERS ARE ALWAYS campaigning—traveling around their states or districts, talking with constituents, and explaining their actions in office—all in the hope of winning and keeping support for the next election. Here, Representative Beto O'Rourke (D-TX) meets with local veterans at an event at El Paso Community College.

THE GENERAL ELECTION CAMPAIGN

General election campaigns begin in early September. By then, both parties have chosen their presidential nominees and their congressional candidates. Interest groups, candidates, and party committees have raised most of the funds they will use or donate in the campaign. The race is on.

Having made numerous trips to the first primary and caucus states, presidential campaigns shift focus once voting actually begins and delegates are selected. Now the campaigns emphasize wholesale politics, in which candidates contact voters indirectly, such as through media coverage and campaign advertising. At this point, presidential campaign events generally involve large numbers of citizens, or if they are smaller events or one-on-one encounters, they are designed to generate media coverage and thereby reach a larger audience. In contrast, some campaigns for the House and even a few Senate races are more likely to stress direct contact with voters, a practice known as retail politics. At the same time,

CANDIDATES MAY GAIN MEDIA attention and name recognition by hosting campaign events alongside well-known "surrogates." Here, former presidential candidate Mitt Romney (right) attends a news conference in support of Tom Cotton (left), the Republican challenger for Arkansas' Senate seat in 2014.

GOTV ("get out the vote") or the **ground game** A campaign's efforts to "get out the vote" or make sure their supporters vote on Election Day.

average citizens start to pay more attention to the various campaigns. This combination of increased voter attention and a shift in campaign tactics means that preelection polls can show sharp shifts in support for different candidates as the campaign gets under way.

BASIC CAMPAIGN STRATEGIES One of the most fundamental campaign strategies, particularly in congressional campaigns, is to build name recognition. Since many citizens tend not to be well informed about congressional candidates, efforts to increase a candidate's name recognition in these races can deliver a few extra percentage points of support—enough to turn a close defeat into a victory. (Practically all voters can identify the major party presidential candidates, so name recognition efforts are not as central to these elections.)

A second basic strategy is mobilization. Turnout is not automatic: just because a citizen supports a candidate does not mean that he or she will actually vote. Candidates have to make sure that their supporters go to the polls and vote. Moreover, focusing on getting supporters to the polls is a relatively efficient use of candidates' resources. Given that most people don't pay much attention to politics, it's much easier to get a supporter to go to the polls than it is to convert an opponent into a supporter.

Campaign professionals refer to voter mobilization efforts as **GOTV ("get out the vote")** or the **ground game**.[31] Most campaigns for Congress or the presidency use extensive door-to-door canvassing, as well as phone banks and e-mail. Both Republican and Democratic campaigns use sophisticated databases, combining voter registration data with demographics and even purchasing data to determine who their potential supporters are and how best to reach them.[32] There is clear evidence that these efforts boost a candidate's electoral support.[33]

Sometimes candidates also try to decrease support and turnout for their opponent. One tactic is push polling, in which a candidate or a group that supports a candidate conducts a voter "survey," typically by phone, that isn't actually designed to measure opinions so much as to influence them. Campaigns use these so-called polls to spread false or misleading information about another candidate by including this (mis)information in questions posed to large numbers of citizens.[34]

The availability of the Internet and social media sites has important implications for how campaigns are run. In part, these technologies help candidates do things that they always have done, such as recruiting supporters and informing them about a candidate's appearances and issue positions. A generation ago, this information might have been disseminated using a phone bank, flyers, or volunteers going door-to-door. Now, candidates get the word out using e-mail, Twitter, Facebook, Instagram photos, and more. Social media are especially useful for organizing large numbers of volunteers. In 2012, for example, Barack Obama's campaign ran extensive GOTV operations during the general election by using the Internet as the primary point of contact between the campaign and the volunteers, and by developing databases that enabled them to target certain groups, such as likely Obama supporters who were unlikely to vote without being contacted. Given Obama's success, other candidates adopted these methods in 2014, and they will likely become part of regular campaign strategy.

The Internet also allows candidates to do things that were impossible a generation ago. For example, many candidates prepare Internet-only campaign ads, counting on media attention to spread the word about the ad's content. Particularly for campaigns with low budgets, this strategy can be a useful form of advertising.

However, just as we saw in the Chapter 7 discussion of how the Internet has changed what voters know about politics, it is hard to say how the Internet has changed the essentials of campaigning for political office in contemporary America. The essential goals of a campaign are to convince people to support a candidate and to motivate them to vote on Election Day. The Internet provides new ways to contact supporters and potential supporters, and creates some new strategies for campaign advertising, but the problems candidates face in winning office remain largely unchanged.

PROMISES AND PLATFORMS Another set of campaign decisions involves the candidate's campaign platform, which includes stances on issues and promises about how the candidate will act in office. Given that few voters are well informed about public policy or inclined to learn, candidates do not win elections by trying to educate the electorate or making complex promises. What works is making promises and taking positions that are simple and consistent with what the average voter believes, even if these beliefs are inconsistent with reality. For example, many people believe that interest groups have too much power in Washington, although their influence is far less powerful than most Americans believe (see Chapter 10). Even so, many candidates accuse their opponents of being beholden to interest groups. These claims may be far-fetched, but they work well politically because they play to citizens' perceptions.

In writing their platform, candidates may be constrained by positions they have taken in the past or by their party affiliation. Chapter 8 showed that the parties have strong brand identities that lead many citizens to associate Democrats with liberal policies and Republicans with conservative ones. Candidates often find it difficult to make campaign promises that contradict these perceptions. In 2014, many Democratic candidates, including the senators mentioned earlier, tried to avoid talking about Obamacare, even though their opponents emphasized the issue. Why avoid the topic? Because these incumbents had voted for the program, so voters would not see opposition as credible. Better to say nothing (or as little as possible) than to be attacked for trying to dodge past behavior.

A candidate's positions are also influenced by demands from potential supporters. In a state or district with many conservative or Republican voters, opposition to Obamacare or to amnesty for undocumented immigrants might be a winning electoral strategy—just as support for these proposals would generally be helpful for candidates running in states or districts where most voters are moderate to liberal or Democrats.

The two-step electoral process in American elections also influences candidate positions. To win office, candidates have to campaign twice, first in a primary and then in a general election. Voters in primary elections generally hold more-extreme views than the average voter in a general election. As a result, in the typical congressional district, Republican candidates win primaries by taking conservative positions, while Democratic candidates win primaries by upholding liberal views. However, a position or promise that attracts votes in a primary election might not work so well in the general election, or vice versa. For example, during debates before the 2012 Iowa caucuses, some Republican presidential candidates cited their religious beliefs as an influence on their personal lives and political stands—a useful strategy given the large number of religious conservatives expected to attend the Iowa caucuses, but a less useful strategy given the lower proportion of such voters across the entire nation.

For all these reasons, different parties' candidates for the same office often make some similar campaign promises even though they disagree on other matters. During the 2012 open-seat Maine Senate race, the three candidates in the race (Republican Charles Summers, Democrat Cynthia Hill, and Independent former Republican Governor Angus King) held roughly similar positions on most important issues. As a result, the race turned on other factors, such as favorable impressions of King's performance as governor.

Table 9.1 lists part of the campaign platforms of the 2012 presidential candidates and shows the similarities and differences in six issue areas that received considerable attention during the campaign. In all of these areas, Romney and Obama offered sharply different ideas of what government should do. However,

TABLE » 9.1

PRESIDENTIAL CANDIDATES' ISSUE POSITIONS (SELECTED), 2012

The table indicates where Barack Obama and Mitt Romney stood on six key issues in 2012 as the presidential election approached in November: abortion rights, same-sex marriage, Medicare, Social Security, defense spending, and the economy and taxes.

ISSUE	BARACK OBAMA	MITT ROMNEY
ABORTION RIGHTS	Supports *Roe v. Wade* and a woman's right to make decisions regarding pregnancy	Believes unborn children have a right to life that cannot be infringed
SAME-SEX MARRIAGE	Supports marriage equality and equal treatment under the law for same-sex couples	Supports a constitutional amendment that defines marriage as between one man and one woman
MEDICARE	Opposes privatization or voucher program	Favors transition to a voucher program
SOCIAL SECURITY	Opposes changes that would eliminate guaranteed benefits	Favors changes to give Americans more control over how their contributions are invested
DEFENSE SPENDING	Favors reduction in defense spending as part of deficit reduction	Opposes automatic cuts in defense spending
ECONOMY AND TAXES	Favors raising taxes on high-income Americans to reduce the deficit and maintain government programs	Does not favor tax increases; supports reducing federal spending to balance the budget and increase economic growth

there were some similarities between the two candidates' platforms. In the case of energy policy, for example, their positions were essentially identical, differing only in the details of their proposals.

Issues matter in American elections. A candidate's issue positions help to mobilize supporters and attract volunteers, activists, interest-group endorsements, and contributions. Issue positions also define what government will do differently depending on who gets elected. And as we see later in this chapter, some citizens vote based on candidates' issue positions. Even so, there is considerable evidence that many voters do not know much about candidates' issue positions, particularly for House and Senate races. As a result, when a candidate wins a race or a party wins seats across the country, it is risky to read the outcome as a sign that the winners had the most popular set of issue positions.

CONFRONTING OTHER CANDIDATES Candidates often contrast their own records or positions with those of opposing candidates or make claims designed to lower citizens' opinions of their opponents. Sometimes these interactions occur during a formal debate. Most congressional campaigns involve debates in front of an audience of likely voters, a group of reporters, or the editorial board of a local newspaper. Typically candidates take questions from reporters, although sometimes candidates question each other or answer questions from the audience.

Presidential campaigns involve multiple debates during the primary and caucus season. During the months before the first primaries and caucuses, each party's candidates gather for many single-party debates using a variety of formats. During the general election, the Republican and Democratic nominees meet for several debates. (The number and format are negotiated by the campaigns and the Commission on Presidential Debates, an organization that coordinates the debates.)[35] The 2012 presidential campaign featured three debates between the presidential nominees and one between the vice-presidential nominees.

The debates not only give candidates a chance to present themselves to the electorate, but they also offer valuable free exposure. Given a relatively uninterested electorate, candidates must figure out how to present themselves to voters in a way that captures their attention and gains their support. Thus, in the 2012 presidential elections, Republican Mitt Romney positioned himself as a successful businessman who could manage the economy—a good fit to Romney's career as a venture capitalist, a good match to voters' concerns about the economy, and a way to turn his personal wealth into a campaign asset.

Candidates also attempt to win support by emphasizing their understanding of citizens' concerns and their willingness to address them. In fact, many campaign events are designed to reinforce the impression that candidates share voters' concerns and values. Ideally, they have reporters watching in order to gain wide coverage. For example, on St. Patrick's Day in 2012, President Obama visited an Irish bar in Washington, D.C., the Dubliner, wearing a green jacket. He drank Guinness beer while surrounded by surprised patrons and the White House Press Corps. Although these efforts don't always work as intended, there is no doubt about what candidates are trying to do: convince voters that they are "just like them."

Candidates also try to raise doubts about their opponents by citing politically damaging statements or unpopular past behavior. In conducting opposition research, candidates and interest groups dig into an opponent's past for embarrassing incidents or personal indiscretions, either by the candidate or by a

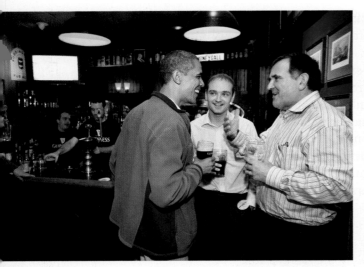

DURING CAMPAIGNS, CANDIDATES often seek to strengthen the perception that they share (or at least are sympathetic to) average Americans' beliefs and interests. Here, Barack Obama enjoys a Guinness on St. Patrick's Day with patrons at an Irish bar in Washington, D.C., during the 2012 presidential campaign.

member of the candidate's family or staff. Campaigns may then leak this information to the media or release it on their own. For example, during the 2014 Texas gubernatorial race, various sources released information about Democrat Wendy Davis's messy divorce—including (untrue) allegations that she had abandoned her children as part of the divorce agreement. The aim, presumably, was to paint Davis as an unfit mother, and therefore not worthy of political office.[36]

The Internet also facilitates efforts to popularize damaging information. For example, early in the 2012 presidential campaign, Mitt Romney was speaking at a private meeting with some large donors and made comments about the difficulty of winning the election given that he would never receive support from the "47 percent" of Americans who receive benefits from the government without paying taxes.[37] The speech was videotaped by an employee of the company that catered the event, and it was released during the general election campaign. While the comments were damaging enough, the fact that the video was widely available on the Internet—that people could see Romney actually saying the words—made the situation even worse for Romney.

Candidates who are behind in the polls (or the organizations that support them) sometimes resort to attack ads, campaign ads that criticize the opponent. Many such ads stretch the truth (or break it outright), trying to get voters to stop and think—or to get the opposing candidate to spend time and money denying the ads' claims. For example, one ad in 2014 cited the Ebola virus, the ISIL terrorist organization, "insecure borders," Iranian nuclear weapons, Russia, and China to argue that "the world is a dangerous place" and to encourage people to "vote this year as if your life depended on it."[38]

CAMPAIGN ADVERTISING: GETTING THE WORD OUT

One of the realities of modern American electoral campaigns is that they are, for the most part, conducted indirectly—through social media, through news coverage of events, and (most importantly) through paid campaign advertising. Candidates, party committees, and interest groups spend more than several billion dollars during each election cycle on campaign-related activities by all candidates for federal office. Most of that money is spent on 30-second television spots. Campaign advertising is critical because, as we discussed in Chapter 7, candidates cannot assume that citizens will take the time to learn from other sources about the candidates, their qualifications, and their issue positions.

WHAT DO THE ADS INVOLVE? Campaign advertising has evolved considerably over the last generation.[39] During the early years of television, many campaign ads consisted of speeches by candidates or endorsements from supporters, and they ran several minutes in length. In the 1964 presidential race, Lyndon Johnson's campaign ran a five-minute ad titled "Confessions of a Republican" that featured an actor talking about why he didn't want to vote for Republican presidential candidate Barry Goldwater.[40] Johnson's campaign also ran a one-minute ad titled

"Peace Little Girl" (nicknamed "Daisy"), which featured a child holding a daisy and pulling its petals off as she counted them aloud one by one. In the background, a voice provided a parallel countdown to the detonation of a nuclear bomb. The ad ended as the TV screen filled with the image of the nuclear mushroom cloud produced by the nuclear explosion.[41] The implication was that electing Goldwater would increase the chances of a future conflict involving nuclear weapons. The ad remains one of the most iconic pieces of campaign advertising.

Much like the "Daisy" ad, modern campaign ads are short, with arresting images that often use photo montages and bold text to engage a distracted citizenry. Content varies depending on who is running the ads. Table 9.2 gives data from the 2012 presidential general election campaign, showing that the overwhelming percentage of campaign ads from candidates, parties, and interest groups (the top three from each side are listed) are negative—and positive ads, if they are aired at all, come from the candidate's own campaign organization. Moreover, the parties are a minor source of campaign advertising compared with the candidates and outside groups as sources of advertising. In 2012, Obama's funding advantage over Romney was counterbalanced by increased spending by outside groups on the Republican side.

The other finding in Table 9.2 is that most ads are placed by only a few organizations, and that the other organizations running campaign ads place far fewer ads and spend far less than the amounts listed in the table. For example, the

THE "DAISY" AD FROM THE
1964 presidential campaign interspersed images of a child in a field of flowers and footage of a nuclear detonation. It was broadcast only once but caused much controversy—and helped to crystallize doubts about Republican candidate Barry Goldwater.

TABLE » 9.2

CAMPAIGN ADVERTISING BY MAJOR SPENDERS IN THE 2012 PRESIDENTIAL ELECTION

The table shows total spending and the total number of ads, as well as the percentage of negative ads, as paid for directly by the candidates, their parties, and Republican PACs and Democratic PACs.

	ORGANIZATION	SPENDING (MILLIONS)	NUMBER OF ADS	NEGATIVE ADS (%)
Candidates	Obama Campaign	$333	562,664	82
	Romney Campaign	147	223,584	91
Parties	Republican National Committee	30	34,233	100
	Democratic National Committee	23	10,572	100
Republican Groups	American Crossroads	128	162,307	97
	Restore Our Future	77	81,013	81
	Americans for Prosperity	35	45,373	100
Democratic Groups	Priorities USA Action	39	63,719	100
	Planned Parenthood Fund	3	3,164	100
	Service Employees Union	2	1,770	73

SOURCE: "Mad Money: TV Ads in the 2012 Presidential Campaign," *Washington Post*, www.washingtonpost.com/wp-srv/special/politics/track-presidential-campaign-ads-2012/whos-buying-ads/, last updated November 14, 2012 (accessed 3/17/14).

SO WHERE DID THE OBAMA STIMULUS MONEY GO?

IN THE 2012 PRESIDENTIAL RACE, many of the ads aired by the Romney campaign and Republican groups criticized President Obama, blaming him for the nation's ongoing economic problems.

pro-Republican NRA Victory fund spent $4 million on presidential campaign ads in 2012; the pro-Democratic MoveOn .org spent less than $500,000.

DO CAMPAIGN ADS WORK? One critical question about campaign advertising is whether the ads work—whether they shape what people know or influence their voting decisions or other forms of participation. Some observers have complained that campaign ads depress voter turnout and reinforce citizens' negative perceptions of government.[42] Many of these arguments focus on attack ads or negative campaigning. For example, during the 2010 campaign, one candidate's ad showed the opponent as an evil blimp hovering over Washington.[43] Such ads seek to catch voters' attention, to get them to focus on a race long enough to consider the candidates and their real messages.

Insofar as ads matter and Americans pay attention to politics, studies of campaign advertising suggest that Americans are reasonably thoughtful when assessing campaign ads. Evidence suggests that campaign advertising has several beneficial effects. Researchers have found that people who are exposed to campaign ads tend to be more interested in the campaign and to know more about the candidates.[44] Moreover, many campaign ads highlight real differences between the candidates and the parties.[45] Nonetheless, average citizens know that they cannot believe everything they see on television, so campaign advertising, if it does anything at all, captures their attention without necessarily changing their minds.[46]

With regard to negative campaigning, evidence suggests that attack ads often do not help the candidates who run them.[47] In fact, negative ads run by a candidate's campaign can backfire, driving away supporters and depressing turnout. As a result, candidates often rely on party committees and interest groups to run negative ads. Then the candidates themselves can run more positive ads (recall Table 9.2) and can try to disassociate themselves from the negative ads run by others.

In the end, despite all the money and effort poured into campaign advertising, these messages must be designed to capture the attention of citizens whose interest in politics is minimal, delivering a message that can be understood without too much interpretation. In this way, campaign advertising reflects an old political belief, that most things candidates do in campaigns are wasted efforts that have little impact on the election. The problem is that candidates don't know which of their actions will amount to wasted efforts and which will help them win, so they try them all.

Federal Election Commission
The government agency that enforces and regulates election laws; made up of six presidential appointees, of whom no more than three can be members of the same party.

CAMPAIGN FINANCE

Campaign finance refers to money collected for and spent on campaigns and elections by candidates, political parties, and other organizations and individuals. The **Federal Election Commission** is in charge of administering election laws, including the complex regulations pertaining to how campaigns can spend money. Changes in campaign finance rules, which were passed as the Bipartisan Campaign Reform Act (BCRA), took effect after the 2002 elections and have been modified by subsequent Supreme Court decisions, most notably *Citizens United v. Federal Election Commission* (2010) and *McCutcheon v. Federal Election Commission* (2013), which we describe below.

TYPES OF FUNDING ORGANIZATIONS The limits on campaign contributions in the BCRA—also known as the McCain-Feingold Act—vary depending on whether contributions are made by an individual or a group, and by the type of group, as shown in Table 9.3. For example, during the 2014 elections, individuals could contribute up to $2,600 to a candidate per election; $32,400 to a national party committee; $10,000 combined to a state, district, and local party committee; and $5,000 to a PAC. But in a 5–4 ruling in *McCutcheon v. Federal Election Commission* in April 2014, the Supreme Court struck down limits on overall campaign contributions to candidates and political action committees, which meant that donors could contribute to as many candidates and PACS as they liked. These contributions are called **hard money**, meaning funds that can be used to help elect or defeat a specific candidate (donations to primaries and general elections count separately).

Contributions that are not used to help a specific candidate are called **soft money** and are not subject to the limits imposed on hard money. A 527 organization (the number refers to a provision in IRS regulations) can raise unlimited so-called soft money from individuals or corporations for voter mobilization and for issue advocacy, but these expenditures must not be coordinated with a candidate or a party. Ads by 527s cannot advocate the election or defeat of a particular candidate

hard money Donations that are used to help elect or defeat a specific candidate.

soft money Contributions that can be used for voter mobilization or to promote a policy proposal or point of view as long as these efforts are not tied to supporting or opposing a particular candidate.

TABLE » 9.3

CONTRIBUTION LIMITS IN THE 2014 ELECTIONS

The Bipartisan Campaign Reform Act of 2002 put into effect limits on what individuals, organizations, and corporations could contribute to candidates' campaigns. The limits were changed based on Supreme Court decisions in 2010 and 2014. At present, although there are still limits on contributions that individuals and PACs can make to each individual candidate, there are no limits on total overall contributions to multiple candidates by individuals and PACs.

	INDIVIDUAL CANDIDATES	NATIONAL PARTY COMMITTEE	STATE, DISTRICT, AND LOCAL PARTIES	POLITICAL ACTION COMMITTEE	LIMIT ON TOTAL CONTRIBUTIONS
Individuals	$2,600	$32,400	$10,000 (combined limit)	$5,000	No limit
Political action committees	$5,000	$15,000	$5,000 (combined limit)	$5,000	No limit
National party committee	$5,000	No limit	No limit	$5,000	$45,400 to Senate candidate per campaign
State, district, and local party committees	$5,000 (combined limit)	No limit	No limit	$5,000 (combined limit)	No limit

SOURCE: Federal Election Commission, "Contribution Limits for 2013–2014," www.fec.gov/pages/brochures/contriblimits.shtml (accessed 5/13/14).

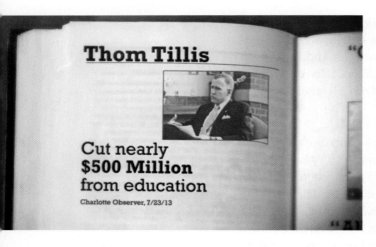

Thom Tillis

Cut nearly
$500 Million
from education

Charlotte Observer, 7/23/13

PACS OFTEN USE THEIR UNLIMITED money to produce ads attacking opponents of their preferred candidate. In 2014, an ad produced by Senate Majority PAC accused Thom Tillis, the Republican challenger for North Carolina's Senate seat, of cutting education funding when he was a North Carolina state representative.

or political party.[48] Another type of organization, again described using the IRS code as a 501(c)(4), has been active in recent elections. The principal difference between 527s and 501(c)(4)s is that the latter type of organization does not have to disclose the names of its contributors. Chapter 10 looks more closely at PACs, 527s, and 501(c)(4)s.

Political action committees (PACs) are groups that aim to elect or defeat particular candidates or political parties. A company or an organization can form a PAC and solicit contributions from employees or group members. As Table 9.3 shows, the amount PACs can give to each candidate in an election is limited, but these limits pertain only to hard money. PACs can also form a 527, which can then accept unlimited amounts of soft money.

As discussed in Chapter 8, political party committees are entities within the Republican and Democratic parties. Both major parties have a national committee and a campaign committee in each house of Congress. Party committees are limited in the amount of hard money they can give to a candidate's campaign and in the amount they can spend on behalf of the candidate as a coordinated expenditure. But a party committee (and, after *Citizens United*, corporations and labor unions) can spend an unlimited amount in independent expenditures to elect a candidate or candidates. To be considered independent (not coordinated), expenditures must not be controlled, directed, or approved by any candidate's campaign. Independent expenditures can pay for campaign advertising, either to promote a party's candidate or to attack an opponent, but the candidate or candidates cannot be consulted on the specific messages.

Presidential campaigns have different financing rules. During the primary process, the federal government provides matching funds to candidates who raise $5,000 in each of at least 20 states in individual contributions of $250 or less, showing a broad base of public support for the candidate. Once a candidate passes this fund-raising threshold, the government matches the first $250 of each subsequent contribution by each individual. To receive these funds, candidates must agree to an overall cap on the amount they will spend during the primaries ($45.6 million in 2012), and to spending caps for each primary or caucus of 67 cents per voting-age person in the state. If candidates forgo the federal matching funds, they can ignore these spending caps—a strategy followed by all of the major presidential candidates in 2012.

During the general election, presidential candidates can receive federal funding for their campaigns, amounting to $91.2 million in 2012. Candidates do not have to accept this funding, although every major party nominee did so between 1976 (when the law took effect) and 2008, when Democrat Barack Obama became the first candidate to opt out—he also did so in 2012, as did his challenger, Mitt Romney. Funds are also given to minor political parties if their candidate received more than 5 percent of the vote in the previous election.

These federal funds are generated, in part, by money that taxpayers voluntarily allocate out of the taxes they pay to the federal government by checking off a particular box on their federal tax return form. In recent years, the amount of money an individual taxpayer can choose to put to this use is $3. When this voluntary check-off procedure has not allocated sufficient funds to pay for candidates' public funding, the rest has been taken from general government revenues.

These complex campaign finance regulations reflect two simple truths. First, any limits on campaign activities involve balancing the right to free speech about candidates and issues with the idea that rich people or well-funded organizations should not be allowed to dominate what voters hear during the campaign. Second, an enormous amount of money is spent on American elections. Table 9.4 shows the amount raised by candidates, political parties, and others in 2008, 2010, 2012, and 2014. More than $5 billion was raised for the 2008 election, nearly $3 billion in 2010, over $6 billion in 2012, and over $3 billion in 2014. The amount of midterm election independent expenditures (other spending besides that by candidates and party groups) increased sharply from about $286 million in 2008 to over $977 million in 2014. Moreover, campaign spending is concentrated among a relatively small number of organizations with sizable electioneering budgets. In each of the last several election cycles, the largest organizations have spent more than $100 million.

The principal concern about all this campaign cash is that the amount of money spent on candidates' campaigns might matter more than the candidates' qualifications or issue positions. That is, candidates—in particular, wealthy candidates who could self-fund their campaigns—could get elected regardless of how good a job they would do, simply because they had more money than competing candidates to pay for campaign ads, polls, a large staff, and mobilization efforts. Another concern is that individuals and organizations or corporations that can afford to make large

TABLE » 9.4

CANDIDATE, PARTY, AND INTEREST-GROUP ELECTION FUND-RAISING, 2008–2014

Candidates and political parties raise and spend a great deal of money in their campaigns. Do these numbers help to explain the high reelection rates for members of Congress?

	2008	2010	2012	2014
PRESIDENTIAL CANDIDATES*				
Republican	(McCain) $360,000,000	—	(Romney) $989,652,023	—
Democrat	(Obama) $639,000,000	—	(Obama) $928,497,835	—
CONGRESSIONAL CANDIDATES				
House incumbents	$539,879,135	$481,226,815	$631,553,983	$614,461,886
House challengers	$193,381,140	$256,639,703	$198,720,761	$154,056,805
House open-seat candidates	$150,938,532	$141,773,031	$163,615,546	$188,948,198
Senate incumbents	$361,183,002	$186,563,786	$282,484,082	$330,229,985
Senate challengers	$100,188,001	$129,210,379	$162,483,481	$144,176,116
Senate open-seat candidates	$59,328,470	$320,664,118	$265,825,062	$140,150,238
POLITICAL PARTIES				
Republicans	$1,228,025,068	$497,570,243	$906,957,839	$574,483,784
Democrats	$1,210,831,060	$559,585,362	$859,745,655	$731,318,780
INDEPENDENT EXPENDITURES	$286,459,718	$294,379,276	$977,495,372	$781,690,240
TOTALS	$5,268,316,289	$2,867,612,713	$6,367,026,932	$3,659,516,032

*Presidential spending includes federal matching funds for the general election.

SOURCE: Calculated by authors from data at www.opensecrets.org (accessed 11/5/14).

contributions (or to fund their own electioneering efforts) might be able to dictate election outcomes or, by funding campaigns, garner a disproportionate amount of influence over the subsequent behavior of elected officials. In the main, these concerns affect soft money contributions and independent expenditures because the current law places no limits on how much soft money a party can collect, or on the size of a group's independent expenditures (see the You Decide feature).

MAKING SENSE OF CAMPAIGN FINANCE Campaign finance records are amazingly transparent. In general, it is easy to find which individuals or organizations gave money to a candidate, political party, or other organization.[49] Thus, if you are worried that a particular organization is using campaign contributions to influence elected officials, you can learn which officeholders have received the group's donations. In fact, campaign finance records are so readily available that it is generally easy to identify fraudulent organizations.

When you look at campaign finance data, the first thing you will see is that a lot of money is spent trying to win elections. However, the raw data do not always tell the whole story. For example, the total amount spent on electioneering represents the sum of all funding for the 435 House contests, 33 or 34 Senate races, and a presidential election. Moreover, consider the cost of television advertising. Nearly 80 percent of campaign expenditures are for television time. In major media markets, a 30-second ad on a major television network can cost tens or hundreds of thousands of dollars.[50] Given that even House campaigns may run hundreds of ads, and presidential campaigns generally run tens of thousands of ads, it is easy to see why campaign costs pile up so quickly.

There is little evidence that campaign contributions alter legislators' behavior, or that contributors are rewarded with votes supporting their causes or favorable policies. Research suggests that most contributions are intended to help elect politicians whom contributors already like, with no expectation that these officials will do anything differently because they received a contribution.[51] But contributions may help contributors gain access, getting the contributor an appointment to present arguments to a politician or her staff. And yet, people and organizations that generally contribute are already friendly with the politicians they support, and so the politicians would likely hear their arguments in any case.

In sum, although money helps shape elections, claims about the power of large contributors and big spenders are typically overstated. Much of the campaign spending in American elections is funded by average Americans making small donations. Moreover, no candidate, political organization, or corporation has the ability to dominate the airwaves and crowd out other voices. In the end, citizens are exposed to campaign advertising from a variety of sources, and they must decide which arguments to take seriously—just as they do with all the other information they receive during the campaign.

EXPLAIN THE KEY FACTORS THAT INFLUENCE VOTERS' CHOICES

HOW DO VOTERS DECIDE?

All the electoral activities we have considered so far are directed at citizens: making sure they are registered to vote, influencing their voting decisions, and getting them to the polls. In this section, we examine how citizens respond to these influences. The first thing to understand is that the high level of attention,

CAMPAIGN FINANCE REGULATIONS

Campaign finance regulations place restrictions on what Americans can do to influence election outcomes. Suppose you are a wealthy person or the head of a corporation with deep pockets. Under current law, you and your corporation can only donate about $15,000 to a candidate's campaign; corporations have to form a political action committee to do so and cannot pay for the contribution with business revenues. You can also form an organization called a 527 that can run campaign ads designed to help elect your preferred candidates or donate to an existing 527. You can make unlimited independent expenditures to help a particular candidate, as long as the candidate or campaign has no control over these expenditures. But if your goal is to help your favorite candidate directly, whether by a cash contribution or an ad linked to the campaign, you face serious limits.

These limits on campaign spending arguably conflict with fundamental tenets of American democracy. The Bill of Rights states that Congress cannot abridge "freedom of speech, or of the press; or the right of the people peaceably to assemble, and to petition the Government for a redress of grievances." One interpretation of the First Amendment that has shaped recent Supreme Court decisions on campaign finance is that people should be free to spend whatever they want on contesting elections—excluding bribes, threats, and other illegal actions, of course. Thus, ending limits on campaign contributions would support free speech rights, although in practice it would affect only a small number of individuals: those who have large sums of money to spend.

The principal argument for restricting campaign contributions is that money conveys political power. That is, if we let rich people spend as much as they want on electioneering, they could control election outcomes by giving their favored candidates enough money to win regardless of who ran against them. This argument implies that removing contribution restrictions would result in election outcomes driven purely by campaign spending rather than by voters' preferences. (Of course, the lack of limits on independent expenditures works against this logic.)

However, even with unlimited funds, it is hard to get voters' attention—and harder still to change their minds. There are many examples of candidates who lost despite outspending their opponents. Similarly, there is no evidence in the corporate world that a company that spends enough on advertising can dominate its market and put its competitors out of business.

Even so, because money for ads is a necessary component of a political campaign, the possibility remains that a rich donor could change election outcomes by giving large sums to challengers in congressional elections. Although most poorly funded challengers would stand no chance of beating their incumbent opponents even with an unlimited advertising budget, some might. And in close races, giving a candidate extra funds to increase his or her get-out-the-vote

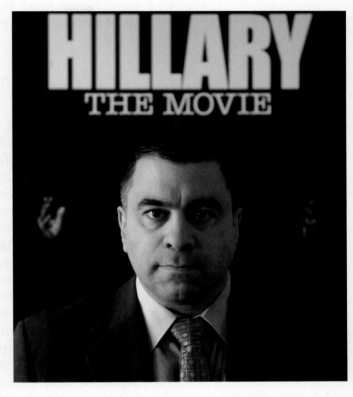

In a 2010 decision, the Supreme Court ruled that the Citizens United group (whose leader David Bossie is shown here) should have been allowed to release the film *Hillary: The Movie* during the 2008 presidential campaigns. This decision opened the door to more campaign spending by groups and corporations.

efforts or to run additional campaign ads might be enough to change the outcome. Does the risk of allowing rich donors disproportionate power over elections outweigh the dangers associated with restricting their speech rights? You decide.

CRITICAL THINKING QUESTIONS

1. Limits on individual campaign contributions guard against allowing wealthy people to dominate elections. What are some of the possible drawbacks of such regulations?

2. Since the *Citizens United* decision in 2010, corporations and unions (not just individuals) are allowed unlimited political expenditures as long as they are independent of a candidate's campaign organization. Why do you think independent expenditures are less regulated than direct contributions to campaigns?

commitment, and energy exhibited by candidates and other campaign actors is not matched by ordinary citizens. We have seen throughout this chapter and others that politics is everywhere, and we have described elections as the primary mechanism citizens have to control the federal government. Even so, only a minority of citizens report high levels of interest in campaigns, many people know little about the candidates or the issues, and many people do not vote.[52]

THE DECISION TO VOTE

Politics is everywhere, but getting involved is your choice; voting and other forms of political participation are optional. Surprisingly, even a strong preference between two candidates may not drive a citizen to the polls because each citizen's vote is just one of many.[53] The only time a vote "counts," in the sense that it changes the outcome, is when the other votes are split evenly so that one vote breaks the tie. Moreover, voting involves costs. Even if you don't learn about the candidates but vote anyway, you still have to get to the polls on Election Day. Thus, the **paradox of voting** is this: Why does anyone vote, given that voting is costly and the chances of affecting the outcome are small?

Figure 9.2 shows that, among Americans, the percentage of registered voters who actually voted has been, in recent presidential elections, around 60 percent, although the turnout has been close to 50 percent. (Voter turnout is calculated based on the whole voting age population, including people who didn't vote because they opted not to register or were ineligible to register because of a felony conviction or other factors.)[54] As the figure shows, turnout is significantly higher in presidential elections than in midterm elections. Turnout is even lower in primaries and caucuses: in the 2012 presidential primaries, some states reported turnout exceeding 30 percent, which was regarded as unusually high. For caucuses, which require individuals to spend several hours voting, turnout is generally only a few percentage points.

In the main, turnout is higher for whites than for nonwhites, for older Americans than for younger Americans, and for college graduates than for people with a high school education or less. Men and women, however, say they vote at roughly the same rate. Many factors explain variation in turnout. People who vote regularly

paradox of voting The question of why citizens vote even though their individual votes stand little chance of changing the election outcome.

VOTING IS COSTLY IN TERMS OF TIME and effort. After registering and informing themselves about the election, voters have to take the time to go to the polls and possibly wait in line.

FIGURE » 9.2

TURNOUT IN PRESIDENTIAL AND MIDTERM ELECTIONS, 1992–2014

The figure shows how turnout varies both over time and between presidential and midterm elections. What factors drive this variation?

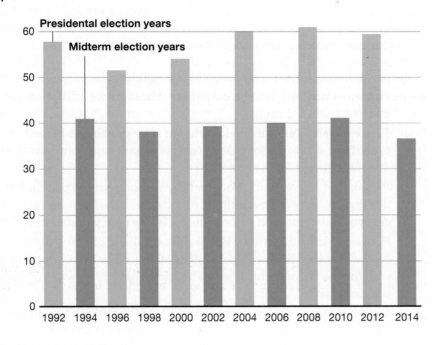

Turnout of population

Presidental election years
Midterm election years

70%
60
50
40
30
20
10
0

1992 1994 1996 1998 2000 2002 2004 2006 2008 2010 2012 2014

SOURCE: United States Election Project, http://elections.gmu.edu/voter_turnout.htm (accessed 11/5/14).

are more likely to consider going to the polls as an obligation of citizenship, to feel guilty when they do not vote, and to think that the elections matter. In contrast, turnout is much lower among those who are angry with the government, think that government actions do not affect them, or think that voting will have no impact on government policy. Citizens who hold these beliefs are unlikely to care about the outcome of the election, are unlikely to feel guilty for abstaining, and are unlikely to see voting as an obligation.[55]

These findings demonstrate the importance of mobilization in elections. As we discussed earlier, many candidates for political office spend at least as much time trying to convince their supporters to vote as they do attempting to persuade others to become supporters in the first place. Because many Americans either do not vote or vote only sporadically, mobilization is a vital strategy for winning elections.

HOW DO PEOPLE VOTE?

Some people are highly interested in politics, collect all the information they can about the candidates, and vote based on this information; they are known as **issue voters**.[56] But most citizens are not interested enough in politics to spend their

issue voters People who are well informed about their own policy preferences and knowledgeable about the candidates, and who use all of this information when they decide how to vote.

time that way, and they don't care enough about the details of politics to find out which candidates come closest to their preferences. Reliable information about candidates is also often difficult to find. Although candidates, parties, and other organizations produce a blizzard of endorsements, reports, and press releases throughout the campaign, much of this information may be difficult to interpret. It is a daunting task, even for the rare, highly motivated voter.

This combination of a lack of interest and the relatively complex task of seeking information leads the majority of American voters to base their voting decision on easily interpretable pieces of information, or **voting cues**.[57] Voters in American national elections use many kinds of cues to decide how to vote, including the following cues, which often lead to these voting decisions:

voting cues Pieces of information about a candidate that are readily available, easy to interpret, and lead a citizen to decide to vote for a particular candidate.

- ▶ *Incumbency:* Vote for the incumbent candidate.[58]
- ▶ *Partisanship:* Vote for the candidate whose party affiliation matches your own.[59]
- ▶ *Personal vote:* Vote for the incumbent if he or she has helped you get assistance from a government agency or has helped your community benefit from desirable government projects.[60]
- ▶ *Personal characteristics:* Vote for the candidate whose personal characteristics (age, race, gender, ethnicity, or religious beliefs) match your own or suggest you have common values, ideologies, or policy preferences.[61]
- ▶ *Retrospective evaluations:* Focus on a small set of votes the incumbent has cast while in office or other duties of the office that you care about, and vote for the incumbent if he or she has behaved the way you want in these circumstances.[62]
- ▶ *For (or against) the party in power:* Vote for a candidate based on a comparison of that candidate's party with an assessment of the party in power (the party that controls the presidency and has majorities in the House and Senate).[63]

WHAT DO POLITICAL SCIENTISTS DO?

To find out more about how party identification affects voters' choices, visit **wwnpag.es/wdpsd**

Cues give people a low-cost way to cast what political scientist and campaign consultant Samuel Popkin called a reasonable vote—a vote that, more likely than not, is consistent with the voter's true preference among candidates.[64] Studies have found that citizens who use cues and are politically well informed are more likely to cast a reasonable vote than those who use cues but are otherwise relatively politically ignorant. In essence, information helps people to select the right cue.[65]

A candidate's personal characteristics also play a crucial role in voting decisions. As we saw in Chapter 6, information about race, ethnicity, gender, religion, or age provides a fairly solid basis for predictions about some of a person's ideological beliefs. For example, in the 2012 presidential election, a Mormon voter was more likely to vote for fellow Mormon Mitt Romney. Thus, when voters choose a candidate who "looks like them," they are not necessarily behaving irrationally. Rather, they may be using a cue that suggests they share the candidate's priorities.

Table 9.5 is based on surveys of voters in congressional elections and shows how incumbent-based cues shape voting decisions. People were more likely to vote for a House or a Senate incumbent if they felt that the incumbent had done a good job keeping in touch with constituents, had responded well to constituents' requests for assistance, and had voted (or would vote) in line with the respondent's preferences.

TABLE » 9.5

VOTING DECISIONS IN CONGRESSIONAL ELECTIONS: CANDIDATE CUES

Americans are much more likely to vote for candidates who keep in touch, respond to contacts, vote as their constituents prefer, and would do a good job on important problems. Of those who think that the incumbent is doing a very good job, a large percentage (but not all) actually vote for the incumbent. If you were a member of Congress who wanted to stay in office, what sorts of actions would you take to secure reelection?

QUESTION	RESPONSE	PERCENTAGE VOTING FOR INCUMBENT
How good a job does the incumbent do keeping in touch with people?	Very good	88%
	Very poor	24
Level of satisfaction with incumbent's response to voter-initiated contact?	Very satisfied	90
	Not at all satisfied	13
Agreed or disagreed with incumbent's vote on particular bill?	Agreed	93
	Disagreed	43
Which candidate would do a better job on the most important problem?	Incumbent	97
	Challenger	11

SOURCE: Gary Jacobson, *The Politics of Congressional Elections*, 6th ed. (New York: Pearson Longman, 2004), Table 5.11.

Some Americans also look to the candidates' background and life experiences when deciding how to vote. Table 9.6 offers some details on what these voters are looking for. For example, many voters consider a candidate's military service, experience as a governor, or business experience as assets. On the other hand, Americans tend not to vote for a candidate who is a known atheist, has had an extramarital affair, or is homosexual. These data are a reminder that even though the average American spends little effort to learn about the candidates in congressional or presidential elections, information about the candidates still matters. If voters happen to learn about a candidate's life experiences or beliefs from media coverage or an opponent's ads, this information can have an enormous impact on their willingness to support the candidate.

VOTING IN NORMAL AND NATIONALIZED ELECTIONS

All the strategies discussed so far are used to some extent in every election. However, in normal elections, when congressional reelection rates are high and the seat shift between the parties is small, voters generally use cues that focus on the candidates themselves, such as incumbency, partisanship, a personal connection to a candidate, the candidate's personal characteristics, or retrospective evaluations. This behavior is consistent with what Tip O'Neill, Speaker of the House from 1977 to 1987, meant when he said that "all politics is local": many congressional elections are independent, local contests in which a candidate's

TABLE » 9.6

CANDIDATE TRAITS AND VOTER CHOICE

Many Americans cast votes based on candidates' personal characteristics and background. What sorts of candidates are advantaged by this practice—and what sorts are disadvantaged?

LIKELIHOOD OF SUPPORTING A CANDIDATE WHO . . .	MORE LIKELY	LESS LIKELY	WOULDN'T MATTER
Has served in the military	49%	4%	47%
Has been a governor	37	5	55
Has been a business executive	35	14	49
Has been an elected official in Washington for many years	26	25	46
Is a woman	14	7	77
Is Hispanic	8	11	80
Is black	7	3	89
Is Mormon	5	25	68
Does not believe in God	5	61	33
Has used marijuana in the past	5	24	69
Has been divorced	3	11	85
Is homosexual	3	33	62
Had an extramarital affair in the past	2	46	49

SOURCE: Pew Research Center, "Republican Candidates Stir Little Enthusiasm," June 2, 2011, www.people-press.org/2011/06/02/republican-candidates-stir-little-enthusiasm/ (accessed 9/5/12).

coattails The idea that a popular president can generate additional support for candidates affiliated with his party. Coattails are weak or nonexistent in most American elections.

split ticket A ballot on which a voter selects candidates from more than one political party.

straight ticket A ballot on which a voter selects candidates from only one political party.

chances of winning depend on what voters think of the candidate in particular—not the president, Congress, or national issues. It also explains why electoral **coattails** are typically very weak in American elections, and why so many Americans cast **split tickets** rather than **straight tickets**. In the main, voting decisions in presidential and congressional elections are made independently of each other.

Nationalized or "wave" elections generally occur when a large number of voters switch to using the anti-party-in-power cue, which leads them to vote against candidates from the president's party. Typically this kind of shift happens when many voters become highly concerned about a national issue such as the state of the economy or an international conflict. In 1994, economic concerns were salient, along with disapproval of President Clinton. In 2006, many voters rated the war in Iraq as the most important issue, and generally disapproved of how the war was being conducted.[66] And in 2010, economic concerns again returned to the fore, with many voters disapproving of economic conditions in general, as well as corporate bailouts, economic stimulus legislation, and health care reform.

National-level concerns such as these cause citizens to lower their evaluations of the president and of Congress, and to use different cues to guide their voting decisions.[67] Specifically, many voters look for someone to blame, focusing on members of Congress from the party in power. They then vote against these members, either as a protest vote, because they disapprove of their performance,

FIGURE » 9.3

PERCENT OF INCUMBENTS REELECTED

The figure shows that, despite public dissatisfaction with Congress, incumbents still tend to be reelected in their respective districts.

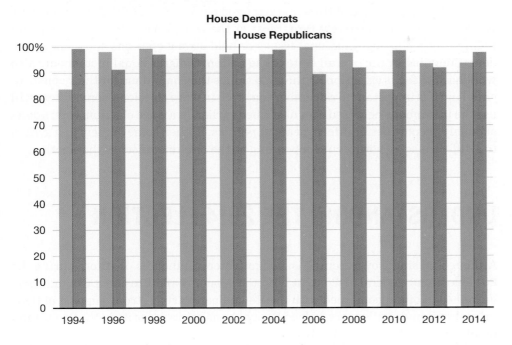

SOURCE: Calculated by authors from election results.

or because they want to put different individuals in charge in the hope that new members will bring about improved conditions. Whether viewed in terms of voting against one party's incumbents or for the other party's challengers, these motivations lead to the same voting behavior; the difference is a matter of voters' attitudes and emphases.

Even in nationalized elections, reelection rates for members of Congress (the percentage of incumbents who successfully ran for reelection) are generally high, as Figure 9.3 shows. Over the last generation, neither party has had a House reelection rate less than 80 percent—even in 2006, when 100 percent of Democratic House incumbents running for reelection won, the reelection rate for House Republican incumbents was almost 90 percent. In nationalized elections such as those in 2006 and 2010, one party's House reelection rate is significantly higher than that of the other party's; in normal elections such as the ones in 2000 and 2002, the House reelection rates are similar and approach 100 percent. Reelection rates for Senate incumbents are somewhat lower but show the same patterns.

Reelection rates for members of Congress are so high because the members work to insulate themselves from electoral challenges through tactics we discussed in this chapter and will discuss further in Chapter 11. They raise large sums of campaign cash well in advance of upcoming elections, use redistricting to give themselves a safe district populated by supporters, and enact pork-barrel legislation that provides government benefits and programs to their constituents.

Even so, congressional incumbents are not necessarily safe from electoral defeat. Rather, their high reelection rates result from the actions they take every day, which are calculated to win favor with their constituents. In normal elections, these strategies are generally enough to ensure reelection. In nationalized elections, however, they are not enough to guarantee reelection for some legislators from the disadvantaged party, such as Democrats in 2010.

Despite the sequence of three nationalized elections in 2006, 2008, and 2010, wave elections are relatively rare. Most of the time, relatively few citizens are highly concerned about national issues or hold strong opinions about the president, Congress, or the overall state of the nation. Congressional incumbents also work hard to focus attention on the good things they have done for their constituents. And it is important to remember that even in wave elections, some voters still use the incumbent-centered cues described earlier. In a wave election, voters don't suddenly become better informed about politics. Rather, some of them just switch to a different set of voting cues depending on the circumstances of the election.

ANALYZE THE ISSUES AND OUTCOMES IN THE 2014 ELECTION

UNDERSTANDING THE 2014 ELECTION

Although no single overarching issue motivated candidates or voters during the 2014 elections, general discontent with the economy and President Obama's performance in office, combined with the Republican Party's strong support of their incumbents and challengers, helped Republicans gain a majority in the Senate and maintain their majority in the House.

THE PATH TO 2014: THE 2010 AND 2012 ELECTIONS

The 2010 and 2012 elections were very different contests. Though Republicans won control of the House in 2010, in 2012 Democrats gained seats in both chambers of Congress and retained control of the presidency. The two elections illustrate that Americans are sharply divided on many issues and that short-term factors such as the state of the economy can produce large changes from election to election. However, no issue in either election gave Republican or Democratic candidates a solid advantage. Rather, success seemed to hinge on candidates' personal characteristics, their campaign promises, and, for incumbents, their record in office.

THE 2010 MIDTERM ELECTION In the two years following the 2008 election, Democrats managed to enact significant portions of the party's policy agenda, most notably, the Affordable Care Act. However, debate over these policies exposed deep divisions within the House and Senate Democratic caucuses, as well as strong differences of opinion among voters. More important, Republicans regained the initiative, offering proposals for sharp changes in government policy, and many voters who had supported Democratic candidates in 2008 switched to become equally strong supporters of Republican candidates in 2010.

The explanation for Republican successes in 2010 lies in two of our central themes. First, politics is conflictual. The first two years of Obama's presidency had shown what a president with united congressional majorities can accomplish. But they also reminded Americans of their policy disagreements and, in doing so, gave Republicans a ready-made constituency of people who opposed some or all of

TABLE » 9.7

ISSUES AND VOTING IN THE 2012 ELECTION

In the 2012 election, many Americans appear to have based their vote on their feelings about tax increases, the state of the economy, evaluations of health care legislation enacted in 2010, and evaluations of President Obama. How can you explain the sharp divisions in the table given the relatively high reelection rates for incumbents in 2012?

		VOTE IN HOUSE RACE	
ISSUE	OPINION	DEMOCRAT	REPUBLICAN
Should taxes be raised to cut the deficit	Yes	74%	23%
	No	38	60
Condition of the U.S. economy	Excellent or good	89	10
	Not so good or poor	39	58
Health care law	Expand	88	9
	No change	78	21
	Repeal	19	81
President Barack Obama	Approve	86	12
	Disapprove	7	91

SOURCE: http://elections.msnbc.msn.com/ns/politics/2012/all/house (accessed 11/7/12).

Obama's achievements or who favored the Democratic Party's overall goals but disagreed with their implementation. Moreover, process matters: Democratic gains in the 2006 and 2008 House and Senate elections meant that a significant number of incumbent Democrats were vulnerable to defeat because they were running in pro-Republican constituencies.

THE 2012 PRESIDENTIAL AND CONGRESSIONAL ELECTIONS The economy was the central issue in the 2012 campaign (see Table 9.7). Unemployment remained relatively high throughout the primary and general election contests, dipping below 8 percent nationally only in the final month before the general election. Economic growth was relatively low as well, holding steady at about 1.5 percent per year.

At first glance, the economic data appeared to pose a serious threat to President Obama's reelection chances—historically, a poor economy dooms a president's chance of reelection. But in Obama's case, many Americans seemed to hold him only partially responsible for the economy, believing that he had inherited many of the problems from the previous administration. The result was that at the national level, Obama's economic policies, including the economic stimulus legislation, did not hinder his chances of reelection, although they did not help him much either.

One difference between the 2012 election and the previous few elections was that international conflicts were not central issues in the campaign, both because of the withdrawal of American ground forces from Iraq and the gradual drawdown of forces from Afghanistan and because of the Obama administration's successes in the war on terror and the NATO operation in Libya. Differences between Republicans and Democrats centered on details, such as whether the United States

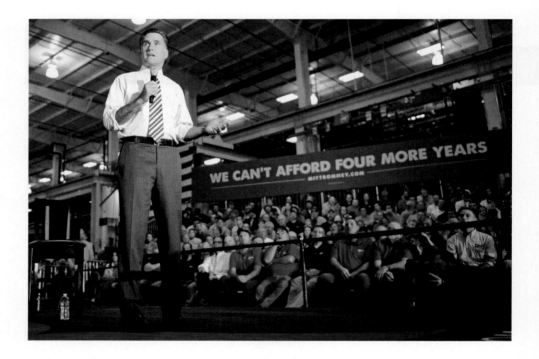

ROMNEY AND THE REPUBLICANS criticized President Obama's handling of the economy, arguing that voters should not give Obama another four years. But many Americans seemed to hold Obama only partly responsible for the country's economic problems.

should firmly commit to a withdrawal from Afghanistan by 2014 (the Obama policy) or use this date simply as a goal (the position of many Republicans, including presidential nominee Mitt Romney). Republicans also criticized the Obama administration for its handling of an attack by militants on an American consulate in Libya and the trade deficit with China. In the end, however, these issues did not move many voters.

In the presidential race, Mitt Romney was the front-runner on the Republican side from the beginning to the end of the nomination process, although he faced serious opposition for most of the primary season from several candidates. Nonetheless, it was not a surprise when Romney clinched the Republican nomination. He was an experienced candidate who had run for president in 2008 and had served as governor of Massachusetts from 2003 until 2007. His record as a businessman appealed to voters who thought that government should be run more efficiently. He was conservative but had not taken many controversial stands. For example, he did not call for a total ban on abortion, although he did say that he would sign such a measure if Congress enacted it. So, while Romney was not a perfect candidate—some voters disliked him because of his Mormon faith and his personal fortune, which together suggested to some that he was unfamiliar with the conditions facing average Americans—he was well positioned to win the Republican nomination. Doubts about whether he was sufficiently conservative were muted after he selected conservative representative Paul Ryan of Wisconsin as his vice-presidential running mate. In contrast to Romney and the Republicans, President Obama won renomination with no significant opposition, as is usual for incumbent presidents. His team spent the primary campaign raising money and developing an extensive network of field offices and volunteers.

Early in the general election campaign, Obama appeared to be opening up a significant lead over Romney, after a Democratic convention that was perceived to have made an effective case for his reelection. With most states squarely in one candidate's camp or the other, attention focused on nine swing states where neither candidate was significantly ahead: North Carolina, Ohio, Virginia, Florida, New Hampshire, Nevada, Wisconsin, Colorado, and Iowa.

Although both candidates refused federal funding and spent over a billion dollars each on the campaign (along with an equal amount spent by outside groups), there is little evidence that spending had much impact on the outcome. Part of the problem was that most Americans had largely made up their minds fairly early in the campaign, and few were open to persuasion. Under these conditions, voter mobilization played a crucial role, and Obama's campaign was much better organized to get people to the polls, both for early voting and on Election Day.

Obama also gained an unexpected advantage in the last week of the campaign as the Northeast was hit by an extremely large storm, Hurricane Sandy. Effective relief efforts by the Federal Emergency Management Agency (FEMA) as well as Obama's well-publicized tour of storm-damaged coastal towns with Republican New Jersey governor Chris Christie (and Christie's enthusiastic thank you to Obama) countered Romney's closing arguments that bipartisanship was lacking under Obama and that government under Obama was ineffective. In the end, Obama's record and campaign organization were just enough: he defeated Romney by a slight margin in the popular vote and by a somewhat larger margin in the electoral college. Figure 9.4 displays the state-by-state electoral college results, showing Obama's strength in the Northeast, Midwest, and West Coast states, and Romney's dominance in the West and South.

FIGURE » 9.4

THE 2012 PRESIDENTIAL ELECTION: STATE-BY-STATE

SENATOR CLAIRE MCCASKILL OF
Missouri—shown here canvassing for votes in the state—was one of several Democratic incumbents considered vulnerable in 2012. However, McCaskill prevailed after her opponent Todd Akin's remarks about rape drew wide criticism.

At the congressional level, many Republican candidates ran on platforms emphasizing the need to reduce government spending and regulations, generally saying that they would make the repeal of President Obama's health care reforms a central priority if they were elected or reelected. Most Democrats either championed the health care reforms or, in swing districts and states, talked about them as little as possible. In the main, Democratic candidates, including President Obama, supported immigration reform that gave undocumented immigrants a path to residency status, while Republicans generally opposed such measures.

At the beginning of the 2012 campaigns, given the public's dissatisfaction with the economy and with the gridlock in Congress, many political scientists and pundits believed that the Democrats would lose seats in both the House and the Senate. But surprisingly, Democrats won one additional Senate seat (counting two Independents who were expected to caucus with the Democrats) and eight House seats. Their success was due to two factors: (1) There were not that many vulnerable Democratic House incumbents in 2012 because many such candidates had already been defeated or had retired in 2010. Conversely, Republicans faced the problem of securing their gains from the 2010 election. (2) Although there were vulnerable Democratic senators in 2012, some Republican senators were vulnerable as well, most notably Scott Brown of Massachusetts, who had won a special election in 2009 in a state that typically sends Democrats to Congress. And the seat held by Maine's Senator Olympia Snowe, a liberal Republican, also was up for grabs when she decided to retire unexpectedly. Moreover, the election of Tea Party candidates in Republican primaries in Indiana and Missouri also translated into Democratic gains, as both Tea Party candidates proved to be too conservative to win their general election contests.

ANALYZING THE 2014 ELECTIONS

ELECTIONS MATTER, ESPECIALLY
when they determine who controls the congressional agenda. Republican gains in the Senate in 2014 led to Mitch McConnell (R-KY) taking over as Senate majority leader. It remains to be seen if he will be able to unify his party and work productively with President Obama.

On one level, the 2014 midterm election was among the least exciting in recent years. Various Tea Party organizations remained active, but had limited success in electing their preferred candidates. No single overarching issue, such as fears of an economic collapse or the costs of a protracted war in Iraq, informed voters' choices or debates between candidates. The president's party ended up losing seats in the House (at least 10) and the Senate (at least 9), with several seats undecided at the end of November 2014, but these losses were modest compared to those of past presidents in their sixth year in office. Just as in other midterm elections, however, a great deal was at stake in 2014, most notably majority control of the Senate and, consequently, the Senate's power to approve treaties, executive branch appointments, and Supreme Court nominees.

As in the 2010 midterm elections, national conditions in 2014 favored the Republican Party and its candidates. Few voters gave President Obama and the Democrats much credit for the economic recovery. (See Figure 9.5 for a more detailed look at the kinds of voters who supported each party.) Moreover, President Obama's approval rating had declined steadily since his reelection, enough so that he did not campaign with many Democratic candidates to avoid hurting their election efforts. These factors, combined with fears about Ebola and the ISIL terrorist organization, contributed to a small but discernible advantage for Republican candidates in most areas of the country.

FIGURE » 9.5

GROUPS AND VOTES IN THE 2014 CONGRESSIONAL ELECTION

This figure shows variation in group support for Democrats and Republicans in the 2014 elections. How did the positions and issues emphasized by candidates in the two parties create or strengthen these differences?

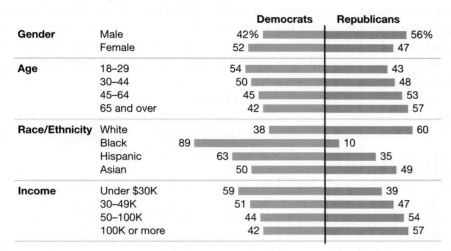

		Democrats	Republicans
Gender	Male	42%	56%
	Female	52	47
Age	18–29	54	43
	30–44	50	48
	45–64	45	53
	65 and over	42	57
Race/Ethnicity	White	38	60
	Black	89	10
	Hispanic	63	35
	Asian	50	49
Income	Under $30K	59	39
	30–49K	51	47
	50–100K	44	54
	100K or more	42	57

SOURCE: Exit poll data at www.elections.nytimes.com (accessed 11/6/14).

Democrats were also disadvantaged because they had more Senate seats to defend: of the 35 seats being contested, Democrats controlled 21 and Republicans only 15. More important, many of the Democratic seats were in states where the party was weak—for example, in incumbent Mark Pryor's Arkansas, Republican Mitt Romney won more than 60 percent of the popular vote in the 2012 presidential election, compared to less than 37 percent for Democrat Barack Obama. These conditions, coupled with the Republican Party's success in helping their incumbents and strong challengers to win primaries and caucuses, meant that, even before the general election campaign began, Republicans stood an excellent chance to gain control of the Senate. Control of the House was not at stake, as the 2010 and 2012 elections had left relatively few vulnerable Democratic or Republican incumbents.

One notable feature of the 2014 election was the significant role played by independent candidates in some Senate elections. In South Dakota, the candidacy of independent and former Senator Larry Pressler turned what was assumed to be an easy Republican victory into a hard-fought contest. In Kansas, the Democratic candidate withdrew in favor of independent Greg Orman after a series of polls showed that Orman stood a good chance of defeating incumbent Republican Pat Roberts. (Roberts, however, ultimately won.)

Many stories about the campaigns described 2014 as "an election about nothing," meaning that the issues motivating voters varied somewhat from state to state. These differences can be seen across the two elections we have discussed throughout this chapter: Jeanne Shaheen versus Scott Brown in New Hampshire and Mark Pryor versus Tom Cotton in Arkansas. Though both Republican challengers highlighted their opponent's support of the president and his health care reforms, in the end the races turned on the question of how good a job the incumbents, Shaheen and Pryor, had done in responding to their constituents' demands. Ultimately, Shaheen was able to make her case well enough to gain a narrow victory (aided by a near-even split between Republican and Democratic voters in her state), while Pryor, running in deep-red Arkansas, could not do so.

In the end, the narrow Republican advantage translated into modest gains for the party in both the House and the Senate, with the most significant change being the switch to Republican control of the Senate. However, Democrats still control the presidency, and the basic differences between the parties remain. Though these conflicts do not preclude compromise on issues such as tariffs or tax reform, the most likely outcome for the 113th Congress is continued gridlock on most issues.

CONCLUSION

Candidates in American national elections compete for different offices using a variety of rules that determine who can run for office, who can vote, and how ballots are counted and winners determined. Election outcomes are shaped by who runs for office and how they campaign, who decides to vote, and how they decide whom to support, but also by the rules that govern electoral competition. By taking these factors into account, we can explain why Barack Obama defeated Mitt Romney in 2012, why Jeanne Shaheen won over Scott Brown (but Tom Cotton defeated Mark Pryor), or why Republicans captured the Senate in 2014.

It is easy to complain about American elections. Citizens are not experts about public policy. They often know little about the candidates running for office. Candidates sensationalize, attack, and dissemble rather than giving details about what they would do if elected. Even so, there are clear, systematic differences between Democratic and Republican candidates that translate into different government policies depending on who holds office. It matters that Obama was reelected in 2012, and that Democrats lost their Senate majority in 2014. Moreover, the criteria that average Americans use to make voting decisions reflect these differences.

In addition, many examples of seemingly strange behavior in American elections make more sense once you examine them. It is understandable that so few Americans are issue voters and that many people decide to abstain. It also makes sense that candidates seeking the attention of distracted voters tend to emphasize sensationalism over sober discussion of policies, or that attack ads often succeed. The outcome of every election is the result of all these individual-level choices added together. In that sense, election outcomes reflect the preferences of the American people.

HOW DO AMERICAN ELECTIONS WORK?

▶ *Present the major rules and procedures of American elections.* **(Pages 306–18)**

SUMMARY

Elections in America generally have two steps. Primary elections select candidates for each party, and general elections determine who wins the office. Some of the rules for presidential elections differ from other elections; notably, the electoral college system determines the winner of the general election.

KEY TERMS

incumbent (p. 307)
open primary (p. 308)
closed primary (p. 308)
general election (p. 308)
plurality voting (p. 309)
majority voting (p. 309)
runoff election (p. 309)
primary (p. 311)
caucus (p. 311)
proportional allocation (p. 312)
winner-take-all (p. 312)
electoral college (p. 314)
popular vote (p. 317)
electoral votes (p. 317)

CRITICAL THINKING AND DISCUSSION

If the electoral college were eliminated, how would presidential candidates' campaign strategies change? How would third-party candidates be affected?

PRACTICE QUIZ QUESTIONS

1. Runoff elections occur only in states that use _____.

   Ⓐ majority voting

   Ⓑ primary elections

   Ⓒ plurality voting

   Ⓓ absentee ballots

   Ⓔ proportional allocation

2. The recent trend in the presidential nomination process has been to _____.

   Ⓐ schedule primary elections later in the process

   Ⓑ schedule primary elections earlier in the process

   Ⓒ replace primaries with caucuses

   Ⓓ break up primaries so that they are not held in the same region at the same time

   Ⓔ limit the influence of third-party candidates

3. The winner-take-all method of allocating most states' electoral votes results in candidates focusing on _____ states and _____ states.

   Ⓐ low population; safe

   Ⓑ high population; safe

   Ⓒ low population; swing

   Ⓓ high population; swing

   Ⓔ safe; swing

ELECTORAL CAMPAIGNS

▶ *Describe the features and strategies of campaigns for federal office.* **(Pages 318–32)**

SUMMARY

Party organizations and candidates begin preparing for the next election the day after the last election ends. They focus on fundraising and determining which races are likely to be competitive. Incumbents work throughout the election cycle to maintain their good standing among the voters and secure their reelection bids. During a campaign, candidates work hard, particularly through the use of advertisements, to increase their name recognition and mobilize their supporters.

KEY TERMS

election cycle (p. 318)
open seat (p. 319)
GOTV ("get out the vote") or the **ground game** (p. 322)
Federal Election Commission (p. 328)
hard money (p. 329)
soft money (p. 329)

CRITICAL THINKING AND DISCUSSION

What kinds of candidates are helped by limits on campaign contributions by individuals and organizations such as PACs? What kinds of candidates do these restrictions hurt? Why do such limits affect these types of candidates differently?

PRACTICE QUIZ QUESTIONS

4. An open-seat election is one where _____.

   Ⓐ there is no challenger in the race

   Ⓑ there is no incumbent in the race

   Ⓒ an incumbent loses his/her seat due to redistricting

   Ⓓ an incumbent faces a challenger in his/her own primary

   Ⓔ an incumbent faces a challenger in the general election

5. What effect does fund-raising have for incumbents?

A It ensures the potential for an aggressive campaign, but it has no effect on opposition.

B It ensures the potential for an aggressive campaign, and it deters opposition.

C It ensures the potential for an aggressive campaign, and it encourages opposition.

D It has no effect on the potential for an aggressive campaign, but it does deter opposition.

E It has no effect on the potential for an aggressive campaign, nor does it deter opposition.

6. GOTV and "ground game" refer to a candidate's attempts to _____.

A boost name recognition

B mobilize supporters

C increase fund-raising

D deter opposition

E win endorsements

7. Research shows that modern campaign ads are likely to _____.

A change voters' minds

B feature speeches by the candidate

C have beneficial effects, such as informing voters

D run several minutes in length

E increase turnout

8. What is soft money?

A money that can be given directly to a candidate

B money that is given by members of the opposing party

C money that can be spent to mobilize voters for a specific candidate

D money that candidates spend to boost the party's reputation

E money that is not tied to a specific candidate

HOW DO VOTERS DECIDE?

▶ *Explain the key factors that influence voters' choices.*
(Pages 332–40)

SUMMARY

Despite the fact that politics is everywhere, ordinary voters don't pay much attention to politics. Turnout rates are modest, and people know relatively little about the candidates and their positions. While some voters are highly interested in politics and collect all the information they can about the candidates, most voters make their decision based on voting cues. Most elections are determined by local-level politics, but occasionally national issues come to the fore.

KEY TERMS

paradox of voting (p. 334)
issue voters (p. 335)
voting cues (p. 336)
coattails (p. 338)
split ticket (p. 338)
straight ticket (p. 338)

CRITICAL THINKING AND DISCUSSION

Using cues to make voting decisions lowers the cost of voting, in terms of the time and effort involved in a voter's decision. Under what conditions will cues help a voter make the right choice in an election, defined as the same choice that would result from having complete information about the candidates? Under what conditions will cues lead a voter to make the wrong choice?

PRACTICE QUIZ QUESTIONS

9. What is the paradox of voting?

A Voting is costly, and the chances of affecting the election outcome are small.

B Voting is costly, and approval for government is high.

C Voting is easy, and the chances of affecting the election outcome are large.

D Voting is easy, but informing yourself about the candidates takes time.

E Approval for government is low, but voter turnout rates are high.

10. Voters who rely on voting cues to determine their voting choice are _____.

A likely to cast a reasonable vote, regardless of their information level

B unlikely to cast a reasonable vote, regardless of their information level

C likely to cast a reasonable vote, and more so if they are informed

D unlikely to cast a reasonable vote, and less so if they are informed

E neither more nor less likely to cast a reasonable vote than voters who ignore cues

11. Weak coattails and split tickets serve as indicators that _____.

A most voters don't know anything about the candidates

B most elections are determined by local issues

C most elections are determined by national issues

D most voters use political parties as their dominant voting cue

E most voters use incumbency as their dominant voting cue

UNDERSTANDING THE 2014 ELECTION

▶ *Analyze the issues and outcomes in the 2014 election.*
(Pages 340–46)

SUMMARY

The 2014 elections produced a modest victory for Republicans, as they captured the Senate and gained seats in the House. These victories were the result of several factors, including an electoral map that favored Republican candidates, President Obama's relatively low approval ratings, and Republican success in nominating candidates that appealed to the general electorate. Even so, Republican gains may not translate into policy change given the disagreements within the Republican ranks and Democratic control of the presidency at least until the 2016 elections.

CRITICAL THINKING AND DISCUSSION

Do you think the now-unified Congress will be more productive in passing legislation than the previous divided Congress? Why or why not? How do you think the types of laws passed by Congress will be affected by the new Republican majority?

PRACTICE QUIZ QUESTIONS

12. What is the most accurate statement about the role of economic conditions in the 2012 election?

Ⓐ Looking across the entire nation, economic conditions did not strongly favor either candidate.

Ⓑ The Obama campaign's mobilization efforts offset the loss of support from a weak economy.

Ⓒ Mitt Romney's campaign avoided talking about the economy.

Ⓓ Economic conditions did not matter because most Americans based their vote on other issues.

Ⓔ The Obama campaign convinced voters that Republican Senate leaders were to blame for the poor economy.

13. How did the electoral map favor Republican candidates in 2014?

Ⓐ Republican efforts at redistricting gave them a sharp advantage in Senate contests.

Ⓑ Economic growth was uneven across the states, particularly in House seats controlled by the Democrats.

Ⓒ Democrats had to defend a disproportionate number of Senate seats, and many of these seats were in states where Republicans outnumbered Democrats.

Ⓓ Independent candidates drew votes away from Democratic candidates.

Ⓔ States where a majority of voters supported President Obama in 2012 were more likely to defeat Democratic incumbents in 2014.

14. What is the most important factor that explains Jeanne Shaheen's victory in Hew Hampshire's Senate race compared to Mark Pryor's defeat in Arkansas?

Ⓐ Pryor's strong opposition to President Obama's policies compared to Shaheen's frequent support.

Ⓑ Pryor's opponent used attack ads while Shaheen's opponent did not.

Ⓒ President Obama's efforts to campaign on behalf of Shaheen but not Pryor.

Ⓓ The proportion of Democrats in New Hampshire is much higher than in Arkansas.

Ⓔ Shaheen's decision to advocate for repeal of Obamacare.

SUGGESTED READING

Abramson, Paul, John Aldrich, and David Rohde. *Change and Continuity in the 2004 and 2006 Elections*. Washington, D.C:. CQ Press, 2007.

Bartels, Larry. *Presidential Primaries and the Dynamics of Public Choice*. Princeton, NJ: Princeton University Press, 1988.

Cramer, Richard Ben. *What It Takes: The Way to the White House*. New York: Vintage, 1993.

Donovan, Todd, and Shaun Bowler. *Reforming the Republic: Democratic Institutions for the New America*. New York: Pearson, 2007.

Fiorina, Morris P. *Retrospective Voting in American National Elections*. New Haven, CT: Yale University Press, 1981.

Hellemann, John, and Mark Halpern. *Game Change: Obama and the Clintons, McCain and Palin, and the Race of a Lifetime*. New York: Random House, 2009.

Jacobson, Gary. *The Politics of Congressional Elections*, 6th ed. New York: Pearson Longman, 2004.

Key, V. O. *The Responsible Electorate*. New York: Vintage, 1966.

Museum of the Moving Image, "The Living Room Candidate: Presidential Campaign Commercials, 1952–2004," online exhibit at http://livingroomcandidate.movingimage.us.

Niemi, Richard G., and Herbert F. Weisberg. *Controversies in Voting Behavior*, 4th ed. Washington, D.C.: CQ Press, 2001.

Popkin, Samuel. *The Reasoning Voter*. Chicago: University of Chicago Press, 1991.

10

Interest Groups

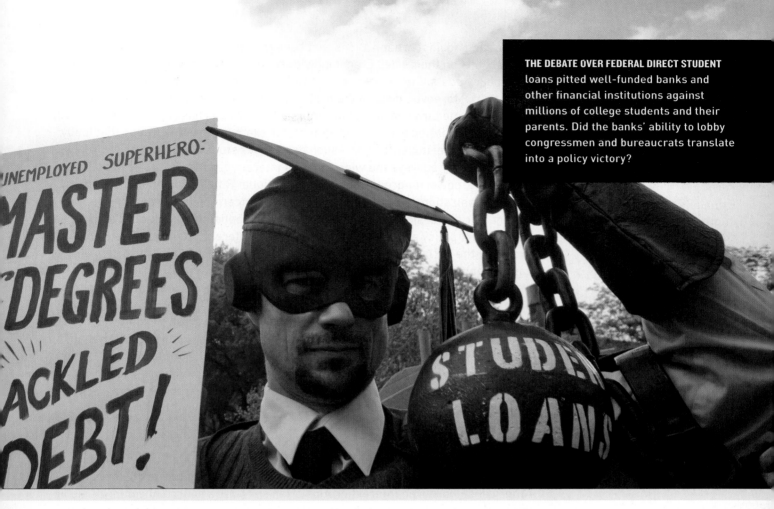

THERE ARE NEARLY 20 MILLION COLLEGE STUDENTS in America today. Many of these students (or their parents) take on large student loans to fund their education. Over the last 20 years, there have been several proposals to change how these loans are made. These policy suggestions range from a system whereby banks and other financial institutions provide the money, to a plan that has the federal government making the loans directly to students and their parents. Either of these proposals would reduce borrowing costs and free up billions of dollars for Pell grants and other programs benefiting college students.

At first glance, reducing the cost of student loans would be an easy sell—who would oppose making college more affordable? The answer is the companies and institutions that make money originating and managing these loans—financial institutions like Sallie Mae, Citibank, and others. If the country were to move to direct loans, these financial institutions would lose a lucrative source of income. To avert this kind of legislation, these institutions spend millions on lobbyists to make their case before the public and Congress, emphasizing that a move to direct loans would put thousands of their employees out of work (and reminding politicians that many of those who work for the financial institutions live and vote in political swing states like Florida and Pennsylvania).

For most Americans, this story looks all too common: organized, well-funded groups lobbying against changes that would benefit broader segments of the population. How can individuals have a voice in the policy process when they

CONFLICT & COMPROMISE
in American Politics

352–359
363–376

Define interest groups and describe the characteristics of different types of groups.

▸ PAGES 352–62

Explain how successful interest groups overcome collective action problems.

▸ PAGES 363–65

Explore the ways interest groups try to influence government policies.

▸ PAGES 365–76

Evaluate interest group influence.

▸ PAGES 376–81

interest group An organization of people who share common political interests and aim to influence public policy by electioneering and lobbying.

lobbying Efforts to influence public policy through contact with public officials on behalf of an interest group.

are fighting against organizations that have millions of dollars and extensive connections on their side? Even if individuals try to form new groups to advance their policy goals, their battle against well-entrenched groups does not seem like a fair fight. Moreover, despite the proliferation of interest groups and lobbyists in America, some large groups of like-minded Americans have no identifiable group fighting for their policy concerns. Where, for example, are the groups that lobby for what college students want—such as cheaper student loans?

This chapter surveys the wide range of interest groups in American politics—from large, powerful groups such as the National Rifle Association (NRA) to small organizations that lobby on issues that concern only a few Americans. In part, our discussion will confirm the common belief that conflicts over government policy are the driving force behind interest group activities. For example, the NRA fights to maintain and extend Americans' ability to own and carry firearms, while other groups, such as Handgun Control, work to impose restrictions on these rights. Government policy reflects, at least in part, the actions taken by these groups.

Nonetheless, interest groups serve the rich and powerful. Virtually all Americans belong to interest groups or have groups that lobby on their behalf. And many of the clubs, groups, and organizations to which Americans belong have extensive (even if little known) lobbying arms. Policy victories do not always go to the organization that spends the most money or has hired the most expensive talent. Interest groups can succeed by mobilizing their members, forming alliances with other interest groups, becoming sources of political or policy expertise, or using the courts to fight policy battles. Thus, although people are correct to understand interest groups in terms of conflict, they are wrong in thinking that these groups invariably work against the interests of average Americans. Moreover, interest groups often serve as a source of compromise in the policy process, either in the proposals they offer or in their efforts to work together with other groups.

You will also see that many of the claims about the vast influence of interest groups are not supported by evidence. In the case of student loans, for example, advocates of direct loans ultimately succeeded in enacting legislation in 2011—although their victory occurred nearly two decades after the proposal was first made. In many other policy areas, interest groups on one side of an issue are matched by equally organized and well-funded groups on the other side. And lobbying victories often do not go to the side that spends the most on lobbying.

Taken together, our description of how interest groups operate highlights how America's political institutions provide many opportunities for policy influence. While it is surely wrong to say that interest groups are irrelevant—in many cases, their efforts have an important impact on public policy—it is equally wrong to say that they are the dominant force in the policy process.

DEFINE INTEREST GROUPS AND DESCRIBE THE CHARACTERISTICS OF DIFFERENT TYPES OF GROUPS ▸

THE INTEREST GROUP UNIVERSE

Interest groups are organizations that seek to influence government policy by helping to elect candidates who support their policy goals and by lobbying elected officials and bureaucrats. In its most basic form, **lobbying** involves persuasion—using reports, protests, informal meetings, or other techniques to convince an elected official or bureaucrat to help enact a law, craft a regulation, or do something else that a group wants. The members of an interest group can be individual citizens, local governments, businesses, foundations or nonprofit organizations, churches, or virtually any other entity. An interest group's employees or members may lobby on the group's behalf, or a group may hire a lobbyist or lobbying firm to do the work for it. Groups may lobby on their own or work with other groups to enact compromise proposals. (See Nuts & Bolts 10.1 for some examples of the types of interest groups found in contemporary American politics.)

Lobbying deals with policy changes that are intended to help only a small fraction of the population at the expense of everyone else. To some extent, this characteristic of lobbying is inevitable—policy changes that benefit majorities are likely to be enacted without the need for lobbying since they already have strong public support. Yet, where lobbying by interest groups does occur, does it benefit all Americans, or are some people left out, either because no interest group exists to fight for what they want, or because lobbying efforts on their behalf were unsuccessful? In the case of student loans, one explanation for why it took so long to move to direct loans is that the banks and loan providers had strong lobbying operations, whereas ordinary citizens had no one fighting on their behalf.

Interest groups and political parties both hope to change what government does, but there are three critical differences between these organizations. First, political parties focus on running candidates for office and coordinating the activities of elected officials. Some interest groups do these things, but they do not have an official position on electoral ballots to offer their candidates. Moreover, many interest groups do not get involved in elections at all. Second, the major political parties hold certain legal advantages over even the largest interest groups when it comes to influencing policy (one such advantage is having guaranteed positions on electoral ballots). Third, the elected members of political parties have a direct influence over government activity: they propose, debate, and vote on policies. In contrast, interest groups have, at best, an indirect influence: they must either persuade elected officials to support their point of view or help to elect candidates who already share their goals.

Sometimes interest groups are primarily political organizations. One such group is Public Citizen, which conducts research projects, lobbies legislators and bureaucrats, and tries to rally public opinion on a range of environmental, health, and energy issues. In some cases, lobbying is only one part of what an organization does. The NRA, for example, endorses candidates, contributes to campaigns, and lobbies elected officials. But it also runs gun-safety classes, holds competitions, and sells gun accessories to its members. In other cases, interest group activity is almost hidden within an organization. For example, most drivers know that the AAA (formerly the Automobile Association of America) provides emergency roadside service and maps, but many people are not aware that AAA is also an interest group that lobbies for increased funding for highways and for less funding for mass transit.

As these descriptions suggest, interest groups and lobbying are ubiquitous in American politics. Many organizations have lobbying operations or hire lobbyists to work on their behalf. You may think that you don't belong to a group that lobbies the federal government, but the odds are that you do.

MORE THAN 4 MILLION INDIVIDUALS belong to the National Rifle Association, one of the most powerful interest groups in America. At their national convention, shown here, members can attend a gun show and meetings where they debate the group's goals and select leaders.

TYPES OF INTEREST GROUPS

Scholars often divide interest groups into categories based on who their members are or the number or kinds of things they lobby for. While it's important to not take these categories too literally—very few groups, for example, lobby on only one issue—the categories explain what kinds of interest groups exist and what they lobby for.

▶ *Economic groups* include corporations, trade associations, labor groups, and professional organizations. Economic interest groups aim to influence policy in ways that will bring their members economic—that is, monetary—benefits. Many corporations such as Google, Exxon, Boeing, or Facebook have lobbying operations that petition government for contracts or favorable regulations of their firm or industry. And as we discussed at the beginning of the chapter, financial firms like Citibank and Sallie Mae have extensive lobbying operations—in the case of direct loans, one of the groups opposing them was the National Association of Student Financial Aid Administrators.

▶ *Labor organizations* are another kind of interest group. The American Federation of Labor and Congress of Industrial Organizations (AFL-CIO) lobbies

for regulations that make it easy for workers to form labor unions, as well as for a range of other policies.

▶ Another interest group category is *citizen groups*, or public interest groups. This category captures a range of organizations, from those with mass membership (such as the Sierra Club) to those that have no members but claim to speak for large segments of the population. One such group is the Family Research Council (FRC), which describes itself as "promoting the Judeo-Christian worldview as the basis for a just, free, and stable society." FRC Action (the lobbying arm of the organization) promotes a range of policies, from legislation that defines marriage as between a man and a woman to legislation that would eliminate estate taxes.

▶ *Single-issue groups* make up another category of interest groups. These groups focus on a narrow range of topics or a single government program or piece of legislation. Examples include the National Right to Life Committee, which lobbies for restrictions on abortion rights, and NumbersUSA, which lobbies against guest worker programs for noncitizens.

---

interest group state
A government in which most policy decisions are determined by the influence of interest groups.

In fact, one important view of American politics, *pluralism*, identifies interest groups as America's fundamental political actors.[1] Pluralists argue that most Americans participate in politics through their membership in interest groups like Public Citizen, the NRA, or even AAA. These groups lobby, try to elect candidates who share their views, and negotiate among themselves to encourage legislators to pursue policies that benefit their members. Others describe America as an **interest group state**, meaning that these groups are involved whenever policy is made.[2]

THE BUSINESS OF LOBBYING

Interest group lobbying is heavily regulated.[3] Lobbying firms must file annual reports identifying their clients and specifying how much each client paid. Similarly, interest groups and corporations must file reports listing staff members who spent more than 20 percent of their time lobbying Congress, and detailing expenditures to lobbying firms. Also, most executive or legislative branch employees who take lobbying jobs are legally required to refrain from lobbying people in

FIGURE » 10.1

GROWTH IN SPENDING ON LOBBYING AND FEDERAL SPENDING, 2000–2013

These data show that in recent years, interest groups have spent several billion dollars lobbying the federal government. Does this amount seem surprisingly large or surprisingly small, given what lobbyists do and given the total federal outlays of money?

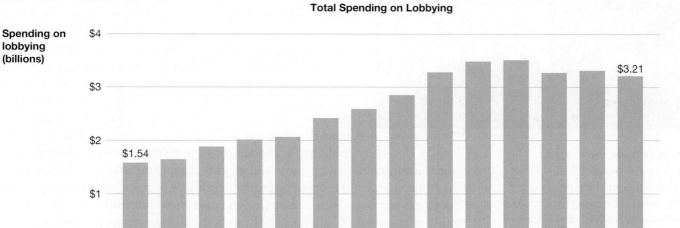

Total Spending on Lobbying

Spending on lobbying (billions)

$1.54 ... $3.21

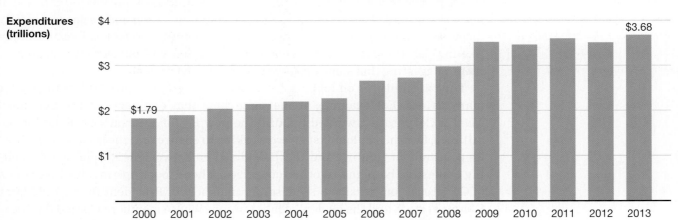

Total Federal Outlays

Expenditures (trillions)

$1.79 ... $3.68

SOURCES: Data available at Center for Responsive Politics, "Lobbying Database," www.opensecrets.org/lobby/index.php (accessed 1/31/14); Office of Management and Budget, Table 1.1, www.whitehouse.gov/omb/budget/historicals (accessed 2/1/14).

their former office or agency for one year; elected officials who become lobbyists must wait two years.

Today, lobbying involves billions of dollars a year. Figure 10.1 presents annual lobbying expenditures for 2000 through 2013. As the figure shows, a total of $3.21 billion was spent on lobbying in 2013. The amount spent as well as the number of groups lobbying government has increased significantly over the last decade, although it has declined slightly in the last few years.

Why are there so many interest groups and registered lobbyists, and why are their numbers increasing? Figure 10.1 suggests that this proliferation is related

THIS CARTOON SUMMARIZES public assumptions about lobbying and its impact on members of Congress. Although the public often believes that lobbyists are giving gifts and making campaign contributions to buy influence, such conduct is the exception rather than the rule among lobbyists.

to the large size and widespread influence of the federal government. Corporations lobby to get a government contract, or they want a new regulation to favor their business sector. Individuals lobby to limit what citizens can do or to get the government to relax restrictions on behavior—or to change corporate behavior. Simply put, the federal government does so many things and spends so much money that many individuals, organizations, and corporations have strong incentives for lobbying. Studies of Washington-based lobbying operations confirm this: interest groups are more likely to form around issues that have high levels of government involvement, or when new programs or changes in government policy are likely.[4] Moreover, as groups form on one side of a policy question and start to lobby, people who oppose them may form their own interest groups and start lobbying as well, either separately or in concert.[5] The pressure of lobbying is especially strong when new policies are under consideration, such as in the proposed move to direct student loans. Firms such as Sallie Mae had always lobbied elected officials and bureaucrats, but the prospect of losing lucrative student-loan operations gave these institutions a strong incentive to increase their efforts. In fact, the data show that over the last 15 years, Sallie Mae spent over $40 million on direct lobbying, and even more was spent by associations and other groups that the firm was a member of.

Changes in communication technology may also contribute to the increasing number of interest groups and lobbyists.[6] Television and the Internet make it easier for people to discover their common interests, and cell phones, e-mail, social networking, and other forms of electronic communication enable geographically dispersed groups to organize and implement lobbying strategies. Even so, many like-minded groups in America remain unorganized, without a group to represent them, suggesting that some people still opt not to participate.

The expenditures on lobbying, which are shown in Figure 10.1 (top), pay for many things. For example, at the same time that engineers at the Lockheed Martin Corporation worked to build the new F-35 fighter-attack plane for the military, Lockheed's lobbyists were working to ensure that the program retained its government funding and that Lockheed had government approval for selling copies of the plane to other countries. These meetings involved members of Congress, congressional staff, senior members of President Bush's (and later Obama's) staff, and the leaders of labor unions whose members worked for Lockheed.[7] Lockheed also ran ads in newspapers in Washington, D.C., promoting its new warplane. Thus, to support its goal of F-35 sales, Lockheed paid the salaries of its employees who planned and executed the lobbying effort, paid for outside lobbyists and their meetings on Capitol Hill, and spent money on broader publicity efforts.

The data in Table 10.1 reveal the top ten spenders on lobbying from 1998 to 2013. Dominating the list are business groups such as the U.S. Chamber of Commerce and corporations like General Electric (GE). Big spenders outside the corporate world are the American Medical Association and AARP (formerly the American Association of Retired Persons). General Electric spent over $302 million on lobbying between 1998 and 2013. And of the nearly $18.3 million it spent on lobbying in 2013, about 80 percent was spent on GE employees engaged in lobbying, with the rest used to hire a number of lobbying firms.[8]

TABLE » 10.1

TOP 10 SPENDERS ON LOBBYING, 1998–2013

U.S. Chamber of Commerce	$1,041,425,680
General Electric	$302,180,000
American Medical Association	$299,442,500
National Association of Realtors	$258,402,003
American Hospital Association	$254,470,343
Pharmaceutical Research & Manufacturers of America	$250,466,420
AARP	$232,432,064
Blue Cross/Blue Shield	$226,390,332
Northrop Grumman	$210,075,253
Exxon Mobil	$195,812,742

SOURCE: "Top Spenders," www.opensecrets.org/lobby/top.php?indexType=s (accessed 1/31/14).

Most interest groups or corporations spend much less on lobbying efforts. The Sierra Club, for example, spent less than $350,000 on lobbying in 2013.[9] All of these funds helped pay the salaries of Sierra Club employees whose jobs include lobbying. Many other groups spend even less, barely scraping together enough cash to send someone to plead their case in Washington.

Other companies lobby through their membership in **trade associations**. Consider the National Beer Wholesalers Association (NBWA), a nationwide group of local businesses that buy beer from brewers and resell it to stores and restaurants. The NBWA's principal lobbying goal is to ensure that laws remain in place requiring intermediaries between beer producers and the stores, bars, and restaurants that sell beer to consumers. If the rules change to allow beer producers to deal with the end-sellers directly, then the NBWA's members would likely lose business.

Although the amount of money spent on lobbying by interest groups may seem like a lot (and often leads to calls for restrictions on lobbying, as discussed in the You Decide feature), it is small compared to how much is at stake.[10] The federal government now spends more than $3 trillion every year. In recent years, spending by interest groups and by the lobbying arms of organizations and corporations amounts to $3 billion every year. That's a lot of money, but it's still only about 1 percent of total federal spending. This difference raises a critical question: If interest groups could control policy choices by spending money on lobbying, why aren't they spending more?

ORGANIZATIONAL STRUCTURES

There are two main models of interest group structure. Most large, well-known organizations like AARP and the NRA are **centralized groups**. These national organizations typically have headquarters in Washington, D.C., field offices in

trade association An interest group composed of companies in the same business or industry (the same "trade") that lobbies for policies that benefit members of the group.

centralized groups Interest groups that have a headquarters, usually in Washington, D.C., as well as members and field offices throughout the country. In general, these groups' lobbying decisions are made at headquarters by the group leaders.

RESTRICTIONS ON INTEREST GROUP LOBBYING

Under current congressional rules, members of Congress and their staffs are severely limited in the size of gifts they can receive from lobbyists—similar restrictions had existed for decades, but were tightened in the mid-2000s after it was revealed that a former congressional staffer-turned-lobbyist, Jack Abramoff, had used "golf junkets, free meals at the restaurant he owned, seats at sporting events, and, in some cases, old-fashioned cash" to lobby members of Congress.[a] The current restrictions limit members and their staffs to accepting gifts only if they are valued at less than $50—moreover, the total worth of the gifts that any lobbyist can give to a particular member of Congress or staffer is limited to $100 per year.

These regulations are based on a sensible intuition that laws are needed to prevent well-funded, unscrupulous lobbyists from offering money and other inducements to members of Congress and their staffs in return for policy change. As we have discussed, interest group lobbying often involves cases where resources favor one side. If nothing else, these resources can buy access—lobbyists can offer lunch at a fancy restaurant in return for listening to their concerns or a trip to a resort to hear from experts who support the lobbyist's positions. Regardless of how restrictions are fashioned, there will always be loopholes that can be exploited. As a result, many reform proposals would go further, preventing lobbyists from giving anything to a member of Congress, legislative staff, or bureaucrat—not even a cup of coffee.

While making it impossible for lobbyists to tempt policy makers may seem like a no-brainer, these restrictions have significant costs. The current rules create a lot of paperwork for members and their staffs, who have to file reports on just about anything they receive from a lobbyist, even if that individual is a former colleague, neighbor, or friend. There is also a complicated process for making exceptions to the limits in cases, such as when a staffer is getting married and is inviting guests who happen to be lobbyists, or when a bureaucrat inherits something from a relative who once worked as a lobbyist.

A deeper and more significant problem is that it is difficult to tell whether such a ban on gifts would accomplish its intended goal. As discussed in this chapter, interest groups are already highly regulated in terms of who can lobby, how they can lobby, and what kinds of gifts and assistance they can offer to government officials. Giving legislators, staffers, or bureaucrats gifts in return for policy changes is already against the law, and if those laws aren't working, it is hard to see how new, similar laws will solve the problem. Put another way, if Jack Abramoff had faced the new gift restrictions, he probably would have found some other way to deliver benefits to members of Congress—and the recipients of these gifts would have done their best to circumvent the reporting requirements.

When scandals surrounding Jack Abramoff came to light in 2005, many Americans considered him a typical lobbyist who used gifts, bribes, and favors to get advantageous policy decisions from elected officials and bureaucrats. Abramoff's actions were illegal, but the question remains: Are his tactics common in Washington, or was he a rare exception?

Finally, this chapter shows that these lobbying reforms are, to some extent, based on a misunderstanding of how interest groups operate. The case of Jack Abramoff is interesting precisely *because* it is a glaring exception. Most interest groups are small and have such limited resources that they couldn't offer gifts or threaten to withhold large campaign donations even if they wanted to. Moreover, interest groups tend to focus on offering advice and information to people in government who already support their goals. Reform proposals would be unlikely to change anything about these practices, except to add some additional reporting requirements and to further limit their (already restricted) ability to hire people who used to work in government.

CRITICAL THINKING QUESTIONS

1. To what extent do you think current congressional rules limiting the size of gifts that members of Congress and their staffers can receive from lobbyists have curbed illegal behavior by interest groups?

2. Are these rules aimed at exceptional cases or average interest groups?

large state capitals, and members nationwide. Their defining feature is that the organization's leadership is concentrated in its headquarters. These leaders have the responsibility to determine the group's lobbying goals and tactics. The other structural model is a **confederation**, which is comprised of largely independent, local organizations. For example, the National Independent Automobile Dealers Association (NIADA) is made up of 50 state-level organizations that provide most of the membership benefits to car dealers who join the organization and that raise much of the money that NIADA contributes to candidates running for political office (several million dollars in recent elections).

Both organizational structures have advantages and disadvantages. A centralized organization controls all of the group's resources and can deploy them efficiently, but it can be challenging for these groups to find out what their members want. Confederations have the advantage of maintaining independent chapters at the state and local levels, so it is easier for the national headquarters to learn what their members want—all they have to do is contact their local groups. But this strength is closely related to a weakness. State and local chapters mostly function independently of the national headquarters, since they attract members and raise money largely on their own. The national headquarters depends on the local organizations for funds to pay its staff and make campaign contributions. Thus, in most confederated organizations, when local chapters send money to headquarters to be used for campaign contributions, they also specify which candidates they want to receive it.[11] As a result, confederated groups often are beset with conflict, as different local chapters may disagree over what to lobby for and which candidates to support.

Some organizations are hard to categorize, such as the Tea Party movement discussed in Chapter 8. The organizations that make up this movement are very diverse. Some hold meetings or public protests, some endorse candidates, and some simply consist of a website run by one or two people. The issues that motivate each Tea Party organization also vary widely, from opposition to President Obama to calls for radical changes in government. Virtually all lack formal dues-paying members, a headquarters, or a formal organizational structure, and few engage in the wide range of lobbying activities that we describe later in this chapter. Moreover, it is unclear whether many of these organizations will survive more than a few months or years. For all these reasons, very few of the organizations that identify themselves as part of the Tea Party are interest groups as we describe them here, although some may evolve into formal interest groups in the future.

confederations Interest groups made up of several independent, local organizations that provide much of their funding and hold most of the power.

CENTRALIZED INTEREST GROUPS in America often have an office in Washington, D.C., which helps them to stay in touch with members of Congress, bureaucrats, and the president and his staff. It also provides a venue for attracting press coverage of the group's concerns. This 2009 town hall meeting on health care held at the Washington headquarters of AARP was attended by President Obama.

STAFF

Interest group staff fall into two categories: experts on the group's main policy areas, and people with useful government connections and knowledge of procedures. The first group includes scientists, engineers, and others with advanced degrees; the second is dominated by people who have worked inside government as elected officials, bureaucrats, or legislative staff.[12] Sometimes these former members of government are also policy experts, but their unique contribution is their knowledge of how government works and their relationships with officeholders and other former coworkers.

The practice of moving from a government position to a job with an interest group or lobbying firm, or of transitioning from a lobbyist to an officeholder, is often called the **revolving door**.[13] A 2012 study found that 44 percent of all registered lobbyists had worked in government at some point in their careers.[14] The concern is that past government employees might capitalize on personal ties with their former colleagues—or that someone working in government may favor a corporation that might hire them as a lobbyist in the future. These concerns were behind President Obama's policy to bar people who had served in his administration from lobbying the government after they left their position, and to prevent registered lobbyists who were appointed to government positions from administering policies or agencies that they once had lobbied.[15]

The Obama policy highlights the dilemma of the revolving door. On the one hand, people who have worked in industry or as lobbyists know a particular field and the relevant laws, making them well qualified to work in this area of the executive branch. Similarly, former officeholders, congressional staff, and bureaucrats are attractive to lobbying firms, as they have firsthand knowledge of how policies are made and enjoy established relationships with people in government. Thus, although Obama's policy was well intentioned, it may lead to a shortage of experienced candidates for government positions. On the other hand, the problem with the revolving door is that people in government may try to help particular firms and interest groups in return for a well-paid position after they leave government service. Or, when the influence works in the opposite direction, lobbyists-turned-lawmakers may favor the firms and organizations that once employed them. It is very hard to craft restrictions that avoid these problems.

MEMBERSHIP

Interest groups can also be distinguished by the size of their membership and the members' role in the group's activities. Some are **mass associations** with many dues-paying members. One example is the Sierra Club, which has over 2 million members who each pay annual dues of about $30. Besides keeping its members informed about the implementation of environmental policy in Washington, D.C., the Sierra Club endorses judicial nominees and candidates for elected positions, files lawsuits to increase environmental protection on government projects, and works with members of Congress to develop legislative proposals. The group's members elect the organization's board of directors.

Yet, not all mass associations give members a say in selecting their leaders or determining their mission. To join AARP, which has more than 40 million members, you have to be at least 50 years old and pay dues of about $16 per year. Members get discounts on insurance, car rentals, and hotels, as well as driver safety courses and help doing their taxes. AARP claims to lobby for policies its members favor, but members actually have no control over which legislative causes the group chooses. Moreover, AARP does not poll members to determine its issue positions, nor do members pick AARP leadership.

Peak associations have a different type of membership,[16] exemplified by the Business–Industry Political Action Committee (BIPAC). This association of several hundred businesses and trade associations aims to elect "pro-business individuals" to Congress.[17] Individuals cannot join peak associations—they may work for member companies or organizations, but they cannot become dues-paying

revolving door The movement of individuals from government positions to jobs with interest groups or lobbying firms, and vice versa.

mass associations Interest groups that have a large number of dues-paying individuals as members.

peak associations Interest groups whose members are businesses or other organizations rather than individuals.

members on their own. The umbrella organization that led efforts to enact direct funding for student loans, the Student Aid Alliance, was another such peak association.

RESOURCES

The resources that interest groups use to support their lobbying efforts are people, money, and expertise. We examine interest group strategies in a later section; here we emphasize that a group's resources influence its available lobbying strategies. Some large groups have sufficient funding and staff to pursue a wide range of strategies, whereas some smaller groups with fewer resources have only a few lobbying options.

PEOPLE A crucial resource for most interest groups is the membership. Group members can write to or meet with elected officials, travel to Washington for demonstrations, and even offer expertise or advice to their leaders. When the "members" of a group are corporations, as is the case with trade associations, CEOs and other corporate staff can help with the group's lobbying efforts.

Many mass organizations try to get their members involved in the lobbying process. MoveOn.org, for example, has a Web page that helps people send letters to the editors of various national and local newspapers. MoveOn.org hopes to bring public attention to its political priorities by getting these Web-generated letters printed. Using the organization's site, you provide your address, choose from a list of papers to contact, and compose a message—using MoveOn.org's "talking points," which cover a wide range of issues—if you so choose. The page automatically imports your message into correctly addressed e-mails to your selected newspapers.[18] Other groups have similar pages that send e-mails to members of Congress or to the president.

Interest groups' ability to use people as a resource faces two major challenges. First, it requires having members, and recruiting new members can be difficult and expensive. The second challenge is motivating members to participate. As we discuss later, although some interest groups have managed to change government policy by persuading their members to write to and visit elected officials, the more common situation is that interest groups ask for members' help but receive little response.[19]

MONEY Virtually everything interest groups do, from meeting with elected officials to fighting for what they want in court, can be purchased as services. Money can also go toward campaign contributions or developing and running campaign ads. And, of course, money is necessary to fund interest groups' everyday operations.

Well-funded interest groups have a considerable advantage in the lobbying process. If they need an expert, a lobbyist, or a lawyer, they can hire one. They can pay for campaign ads and make campaign contributions, whereas groups with less cash cannot use these strategies. The importance of money for interest group operations is evident in their funding appeals to members. For example, the donations page from the Sierra Club's website shows that supporters can give a membership as a gift, join as a life member, or pay dues monthly. They can make commemorative or memorial gifts, set up a planned giving scheme, or donate stock. The group even

MANY INTEREST GROUPS SPEAK for large numbers of Americans, but some lobby for changes that would benefit only a few people or a single corporation. The Coalition for Luggage Security, for example, has only one member: a company that specializes in shipping travelers' baggage, which would gain considerable business if the coalition's lobbying efforts succeeded.

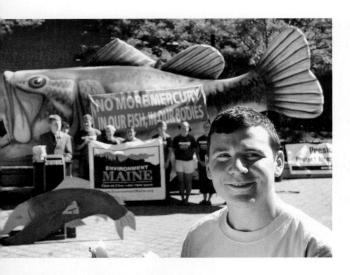

INTEREST GROUPS USE A VARIETY of tactics to draw attention to their concerns, including events designed to generate media coverage. Jon Davids, a Public Interest Research Group staffer, traveled nearly 20,000 miles across America with an 18-foot inflatable largemouth bass named Freddie to publicize the dangers of mercury pollution in lakes and streams.

offers gift-giving plans for non-U.S. residents and a Spanish-language version of its donations page.

For many groups, spending on lobbying is sensitive to economic conditions. For example, many banking and financial firms slashed lobbying expenditures during early 2009, even though they faced government proposals to limit top executives' pay and to impose restrictions on many transactions. Because these firms were facing huge losses and declining revenues, they cut expenses across the board, including amounts spent on lobbying. As these companies' balance sheets improved in later years, their lobbying expenses increased to previous levels.

Still, groups can be effective without spending much. They can rely on members to lobby for them, hire staff willing to work for low pay because they share the group's goals, or cite published research rather than funding their own studies to bolster their case for policy change. Moreover, the fact that a group has lots of money is no guarantee that its lobbying efforts will succeed. As we discussed earlier, even though Sallie Mae spent a considerable sum on lobbying against direct student loans, it was unable to prevent this policy change.

EXPERTISE Expertise takes many forms. Some interest group leaders know a lot about their members' preferences or about what people in a community, congressional district, or state want.[20] Other groups can offer information to elected officials and bureaucrats that ranges from reports on policy questions to concrete legislative proposals. Group leaders can use this information to negotiate with officials or bureaucrats as part of a trade to get what the group wants. For example, during the debate over student loans, the Student Aid Alliance could have one of its member organizations, the National Association of Student Financial Aid Administrators, write a report detailing how the move to direct loans would save money but not impose any additional burdens on students.

Expertise can also involve knowledge of political factors, such as what kinds of policies party caucuses or individual legislators support, or information about the constitutionality of proposed laws. Lobbying firms that employ former members of Congress and bureaucrats are a good source of such information.

Consider AARP, whose website offers a vast array of research and analyses, including information about seniors' part-time employment, how people invest their 401(k) retirement accounts, and a comparison of long-term care policies in Europe and the United States.[21] AARP's lobbyists use this research when arguing for policy changes in their public testimony and in private meetings with members of Congress and congressional staff.

Not all interest groups have such expertise. Some groups focus on mobilizing people outside government. However, particularly for groups headquartered in Washington, D.C., or state capitals, expertise often comes naturally. In the course of their jobs, most interest group staff become well versed in the details of current policies and policy options. When they talk with members of Congress and government bureaucrats on a daily basis, they learn who their friends are—and how to convert enemies into friends. Expertise can also help a group gain access to congressional or bureaucratic offices—getting in the door does not ensure that the group will get what it wants, but will at least allow its staff an opportunity to present its arguments.

GETTING ORGANIZED

EXPLAIN HOW SUCCESSFUL INTEREST GROUPS OVERCOME COLLECTIVE ACTION PROBLEMS

A new interest group's first priority is to get organized, which involves raising the money needed to hire staff, renting an office, setting up a website, and formulating policy goals and a lobbying strategy. In some cases, a lobbying firm is hired to perform these jobs. Once organized, the group must continue to attract funds for ongoing operations. These tasks are not easy. Even if a group of people (or corporations) shares the same goals, the challenge is to persuade them to donate time or money to the lobbying operation.

THE LOGIC OF COLLECTIVE ACTION

Research has found that a problem arises when a group of individuals (or corporations) has an opportunity to make itself better off through the provision of public goods. (For interest groups, the public good would be a change in government policy desired by group members.) Scholars refer to these situations as involving collective action. Even when all members of a group agree on the desirability of a public good and the costs of producing the good are negligible, cooperation is neither easy nor automatic (see Nuts & Bolts 10.2). Scholars refer to this situation as a **collective action problem**.

collective action problem
A situation in which the members of a group would benefit by working together to produce some outcome, but each individual is better off refusing to cooperate and reaping benefits from those who do the work.

10.2 NUTS & bolts

COLLECTIVE ACTION PROBLEMS

Collective action refers to situations in which a group of individuals can work together to provide themselves with public goods. For example, changes in government policy (such as those lobbied for by interest groups) are public goods: if the government changes policy, such as increasing the size of college tuition grants, everyone who is eligible for the grants benefits from the increase. These circumstances make it hard to motivate people to contribute to collective efforts, because each would-be member can see that his contribution would be only a minuscule portion of what the group needs to succeed. This is known as a collective action problem. Regardless of how many other people join, an individual is better off free riding—refusing to join but still being able to enjoy the benefits of any successes the group might have. But if everyone acts on this calculation, no one will join the group and the organization will be unable to lobby for tuition grants or anything else.

One class of real-world collective action problems involves situations where people can exploit a renewable natural resource, such as a forest or fishery. The problem is that each participant can maximize her profits by taking as much as she can from the resource area without worrying about whether the area can sustain this activity. However, if everyone behaves this way, the common resource will be destroyed—all the fish will be caught or all the trees will be cut down.

The same kinds of problems arise in everyday life. As a college student, you may live in some sort of group housing situation, either a dormitory or an off-campus apartment or house. Anyone who has ever lived in such a situation knows that one constant problem is sharing the responsibility for common living spaces. Everyone typically agrees that these areas should be kept clean, but each resident sees an opportunity for free riding by leaving his mess for someone else to take care of. But if every resident follows this incentive, common living spaces will remain messy, if not uninhabitable.

The logic of collective action provides insights into how interest groups are organized and how they make lobbying decisions. First, the logic of collective action tells us that group formation is not automatic. Even when a number of citizens want the same things from government, their common interest may not lead them to organize. Some groups remain latent and are not able to organize, which explains why certain debates in Washington feature well-organized groups on one side of the issue but few on the other. Unless people can easily see benefits from participating, which does not happen often, group leaders must worry about finding the right strategies to get people to join. Thus, given the logic of collective action, attracting members is just as important for a group's success as its lobbying strategy.

Society is full of groups of like-minded people (such as college students) who do not organize to lobby or who choose to engage in **free riding** and so enjoy the benefits of organizations without participating. Most organizations develop mechanisms to promote cooperation in such situations. These solutions fall into three categories: benefits from participation, coercion, and selective incentives.

Studies of political parties and interest groups find that some individuals volunteer out of a sense of duty or because they enjoy working together toward a common goal. Scholars refer to these benefits of participation as either **solidary benefits**, which come from working with like-minded people, or **purposive benefits**, which come from working to achieve a desired policy goal.[22] If most people were spurred to political action because of participation benefits, the free rider problem wouldn't exist. However, when these benefits are not enough, groups try other measures in order to organize.

A second way to solve the free rider problem is through **coercion**, or requiring participation. Consider labor unions. They provide public goods to workers by negotiating with management on behalf of worker-members over pay and work requirements. Why don't union members free ride? Because in many cases, they have to join the union: union shop laws require them to pay union dues as a condition of their employment. These laws are critical to unions; states with laws that make union membership optional typically have weak unions—if any.

Finally, **selective incentives** are benefits given only to the members of an interest group. These incentives are not public goods; an individual can receive a selective incentive only by joining the group. Thus, interest groups offer selective

free riding The result of relying on others to contribute to a collective effort while failing to participate on one's own behalf, yet still benefiting from the group's successes.

solidary benefits Satisfaction derived from the experience of working with like-minded people, even if the group's efforts do not achieve the desired impact.

purposive benefits Satisfaction derived from the experience of working toward a desired policy goal, even if the goal is not achieved.

coercion A method of eliminating nonparticipation or free riding by potential group members by requiring participation, as in many labor unions.

selective incentives Benefits that can motivate participation in a group effort because they are available only to those who participate, such as member services offered by interest groups.

AAA (FORMERLY THE AUTOMOBILE Association of America) is a well-known provider of emergency road service, yet few people are aware of its role as an interest group that lobbies for a wide range of policy changes and builds awareness of key transportation issues.

DUI
IT COSTS MORE THAN YOU THINK!

ESTIMATED COSTS FOR A FIRST DUI CONVICTION:

Fine (minimum)	$390
Penalties	$1,245
Vehicle Tow/Storage	$350
Alcohol Education Class	$575
Victim Restitution Fund	$140
DMV License Re-Issue	$125
Booking	$170
Insurance Increase	$10,154
Legal Fees	$2,500
TOTAL COST	**$15,649**

incentives in the hope of providing a new reason to participate. One of the most interesting cases of selective incentives provided by an interest group involves AAA. Members with car trouble can call AAA at any time for emergency service. AAA also provides annotated maps and travel guides to its members, a travel agency, a car-buying service, discounts at hotels and restaurants, and other benefits. These services mask the interest group role of AAA. For example, its Foundation for Traffic Safety delivers research reports to legislators on topics ranging from lowering the blood alcohol level threshold that legally defines drunk driving to increasing the restrictions on driving by senior citizens.[23] It's unlikely that many AAA members—who join for the selective incentives—are aware of the organization's lobbying efforts. The inducements drive membership, which funds the organization's lobbying operation.

INTEREST GROUP STRATEGIES

EXPLORE THE WAYS INTEREST GROUPS TRY TO INFLUENCE GOVERNMENT POLICIES

Once a group has organized and determined its goals, the next step is to decide how to lobby. There are two types of possible tactics: **inside strategies**, which are actions taken in Washington, D.C., and **outside strategies**, which involve actions taken outside Washington, D.C. (see How It Works: Lobbying the Federal Government).[24] Generally, these strategies involve a single group that is working on its own, sometimes in opposition to another group or groups. However, as we discuss later, interest groups sometimes work together toward common legislative goals.

inside strategies The tactics employed within Washington, D.C., by interest groups seeking to achieve their policy goals.

outside strategies The tactics employed outside Washington, D.C., by interest groups seeking to achieve their policy goals.

INSIDE STRATEGIES

Inside strategies involve some form of contact with elected officials or bureaucrats. Thus, inside strategies require a group to establish an office in Washington, D.C., or to hire a lobbying firm to act on its behalf.

DIRECT LOBBYING When interest group staff meet with officeholders or bureaucrats, they plead their case through **direct lobbying**, asking government officials to change policy in line with the group's goals.[25] Such contacts are very common—on any given day, each congressional or administrative office gets phone calls, visits, or e-mails from dozens of lobbyists.

direct lobbying Attempts by interest group staff to influence policy by speaking with elected officials or bureaucrats.

Direct lobbying is generally aimed at officials and bureaucrats who are sympathetic to the group's goals.[26] In their efforts, interest groups and their representatives do not try to convert opponents into supporters; rather, they help like-minded legislators secure policy changes that they both want. Their help can range from sharing information about proposed changes, to providing lists of legislators who might be persuadable, to drafting legislative proposals or regulations.

These efforts usually do not involve a trade in which the group expects legislative action in return for its help. Rather, the group's efforts are a way of helping a legislator to enact policies that she prefers—and that the group prefers as well.[27] The legislator knows that a like-minded group has no reason to misrepresent its policy information. In fact, the legislator and her staff will be happy to meet with the group's representatives, as their information may be vital to the legislator's efforts to enact legislation, manage the bureaucracy, or keep the support of constituents back home in the district.[28] For example, corporations that stood to lose business if the government moved to direct student loans lobbied legislators whose districts included the companies' call centers and headquarters. For these legislators, helping these companies might be good public policy, but it was also a way of preserving their constituents' jobs.

Interest groups also contact legislators who disagree with their goals as well as fence sitters (legislators who are not supporters or opponents), with the goal of converting them into supporters. These efforts are less extensive than the lobbying of supporters, however, because opponents are unlikely to change their minds unless a group can provide new information that causes them to rethink their position. But lobbying opponents may be useful if it forces opposing interest groups to use some of their limited resources in lobbying their own supporters to make sure that they do not change their position.[29]

As these descriptions indicate, interest groups place a high priority on maintaining access to their lobbying targets and being able to present their arguments, regardless of whether they expect to get what they want. Of course, interest groups want to achieve their policy goals, but access is the necessary first step that makes persuasion possible. Therefore, many interest groups try to keep their efforts low-key, providing information to friends and opponents alike, avoiding threats or harsh words, in the hope that they will leave a favorable impression and be able to gain access the next time they want to lobby them. After all, people who are opposed to a group's current priorities one day may agree with them on some future issue.

Who do these groups contact for direct lobbying? Analysis of lobbyists' annual disclosure forms shows that they contact people throughout the federal government: elected officials, members of the president's staff, and bureaucrats in the executive branch. They seek this wide range of contacts because different officials play distinct roles in the policy-making process and thus have various types of influence. Members of Congress shape legislation and budgets; members of the president's staff influence the formation of new policies and obtain presidential consent for new laws; and executive branch bureaucrats change the ways regulations are written and policies are implemented.

DRAFTING LEGISLATION AND REGULATIONS Interest groups sometimes draft legislative proposals and regulations, which they deliver to legislators and bureaucrats as part of their lobbying efforts.[30] Surveys of interest groups found that more than three-quarters reported drafting proposals for members of Congress.[31] In the case of direct student loans, for example, the antireform forces developed a plan that would cut fees and lower interest rates for student loans, but preserve the existing system.

Interest groups do not give proposals to just anyone. As with direct lobbying, they seek out legislators who already support their cause and who have significant influence within Congress. A lobbying effort aimed at cutting interest rates on student loans would target supporters of this change who are also members of the congressional committee with jurisdiction over student loan programs—preferably someone who chairs the committee or one of its subcommittees.[32] Interest groups also lobby bureaucrats to influence the details of new regulations.[33] If the types of regulations involved can go into effect without congressional approval, then lobbying can give groups what they want directly. But even if new regulations require approval by Congress or White House staff, interest groups can increase their chances of success by getting involved in the initial drafting.

RESEARCH Interest groups often prepare research reports on topics of interest to the group. For example, Public Citizen recently featured on its website a series of research reports on topics such as medical malpractice, the house building industry, toy safety, and international trade.[34] Such reports serve multiple purposes. They may sway public opinion or help persuade elected officials or bureaucrats, and they are another way for lobbyists to directly influence an industry. They also help interest group staff claim expertise on some aspect of public policy. Members of Congress are more likely to accept a group's legislative proposal if they think that the group's staff have research to back up their claims. Journalists are also more likely to respond to an interest group's requests for publicity if they think that the group's staff have evidence supporting their claims.

HEARINGS Interest group staff often testify before congressional committees. In part, this activity is aimed at informing members of Congress about issues that matter to the interest group. For example, the NRA's website shows that its staff have testified in favor of "right to carry" laws as well as laws that would grant immunity to gun manufacturers for harm committed with weapons they produced.[35]

LITIGATION Another inside strategy involves taking the government to court. In bringing their case, interest groups can argue that the government's actions are not consistent with the Constitution or that the government has misinterpreted the existing law.[36] Interest groups can bring these actions via lawyers on their staff, a hired law firm, or lawyers who will work for no fees. Interest groups can also become involved in an existing case by filing amicus curiae ("friend of the court") briefs, documents that offer judges the group's rationale for how the case should be decided. The drawback of litigation is that it is costly and time-consuming—cases can take years to work through the federal court system. At a minimum, groups that use the litigation strategy generally combine it with direct lobbying or other strategies.

WORKING TOGETHER To increase their chances for success, interest groups can work together in their lobbying efforts, formulating a common strategy and future plans. Generally these collaborations are short-term efforts focused on achieving a specific outcome, like supporting or opposing the confirmation of judicial and cabinet nominees.[37] The fight against direct student loans, for example, involved corporations like Citibank and Sallie Mae, along with the U.S. Chamber of Commerce. Support for change came from the Student Aid Alliance, a group of colleges, think tanks, and associations of law schools and other professional schools. This group had formed in 1999 to lobby for increases in student aid, then stayed together to lobby on other issues.

Why do groups work together? The most obvious reason lies in the power of large numbers: legislators are more likely to respond, or at least provide access, when many groups with large or diverse memberships are all asking for the same thing.[38]

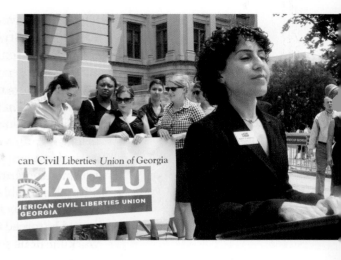

THE AMERICAN CIVIL LIBERTIES Union is an interest group that often uses litigation strategies in its efforts to change government policy. Here, an ACLU attorney speaks at a news conference to describe the group's legal challenge to Georgia's new state immigration law.

The groups involved may also have different kinds of resources to contribute. The Alliance for Student Aid, for example, can send college presidents to lobby their members of Congress or to testify at hearings, while staff at affiliated think tanks can write op-ed pieces in newspapers, and members of the organization can work on direct lobbying of bureaucrats and congressional staff.

The problem with working together is that groups may agree on general goals but disagree on specifics, thereby requiring negotiation. If differences cannot be bridged, groups may undertake separate and possibly conflicting lobbying efforts or decide against lobbying entirely. For example, although there are many groups pressing for climate change legislation, they have not developed a unified lobbying effort. The problem? The groups disagree on which policies should be implemented, who should pay for them, and whether the government should aid companies that would be forced to purchase new antipollution equipment. Without an agreement, working alone seems a better strategy.[39]

OUTSIDE STRATEGIES

Outside strategies involve things that groups do across the country rather than in Washington. Again, these activities can be orchestrated by the group or be organized by a firm hired by the group.

GRASSROOTS LOBBYING Directly involving interest group members in lobbying efforts is called **grassroots lobbying**. Members may send letters, make telephone calls, participate in a protest, or express their demands in other ways. Many groups encourage grassroots lobbying. For example, AARP's website has a page where members can find contact information for their representatives in Congress.[40] Other links allow members to e-mail or to fax their representatives letters that are prewritten by AARP to express the group's positions on various proposals, such as pension protection legislation and proposals to curb identity theft. AARP also organizes district meetings with elected officials and encourages its members to attend.

Mass protests are another form of grassroots lobbying. In addition to trying to capture the attention of government officials, mass protests also seek to draw media attention, with the idea of publicizing the group's goals and perhaps gaining new members or financial support. During the 2013 debate over gun control, groups such as "Moms Demand Action for Gun Sense in America" held many such rallies—although their efforts were overshadowed in some communities by counterprotests in which gun owners took advantage of open-carry laws to attend rallies while brandishing assault rifles and shotguns.[41]

Grassroots strategies are useful because elected officials are loath to act against a large group of citizens who care enough about an issue to express their position.[42] These officials may not agree with the group's goals, but they are likely to at least arrange a meeting with its staff, so that they appear willing to learn about their constituents' demands.[43] However, these member-based strategies work only for a small set of interest groups. To take advantage of these strategies, groups first need a large number of members. Legislators begin to pay attention to a letter-writing campaign only when they receive several thousand pieces of mail. (Remember,

MASS PROTESTS, SUCH AS THIS
April 4, 2009, Tea Party rally in California, attract media attention and demonstrate the depth of public support for a group's goals.

congressional districts contain roughly 700,000 citizens.) And, as the gun control rallies illustrate, protests may generate counterprotests that help the other side make its case.

In addition, for grassroots lobbying to be effective, the letters or other efforts have to come from a Congress member's own constituents. For example, a representative who opposes increases in student aid is not going to worry about a letter-writing campaign if most of the letters come from people outside his district. The effectiveness of grassroots lobbying also depends on perceptions of how much a group has done to motivate participation. Suppose a representative gets 10,000 e-mails demanding an increase in student aid. However, virtually all the messages contain the same appeal because they were generated and sent from a group's website. People in Washington sometimes refer to these efforts as **astroturf lobbying**.[44] Given the similarity of the letters, the representative may discount the effort, believing that it says more about the group's ability to make campaign participation accessible than it does about the number of district residents who strongly support an increase in student aid. Even so, politicians are sometimes reluctant to completely dismiss astroturf efforts—the fact that so many people participated, even with facilitation by an interest group, means that their demands must at least be considered.

The evolution of the Internet has important implications for grassroots lobbying. As noted earlier, one argument is that technological developments such as blogs and e-mail make grassroots lobbying easier: they lower the costs of encouraging the members and would-be members of an interest group to get involved by writing a letter, sending an e-mail, making a phone call, or showing up for a protest. Certainly the Internet makes it easier to contact people and lowers the cost of getting involved in some kinds of lobbying efforts. However, if Internet-driven grassroots lobbying looks like astroturf lobbying, it may be less likely to achieve its goal of influencing elected officials and bureaucrats.

MOBILIZING PUBLIC OPINION One strategy related to grassroots lobbying involves trying to change what the public thinks about an issue. The goal is not to get citizens to do anything, but to influence public opinion in the hope that elected officials will see this change and respond by enacting (or opposing) new laws or regulations to keep their constituents happy. Virtually all groups try to influence opinion. Most maintain a Web page that presents their message, and they write press releases to get media coverage. Any contact with citizens, whether to encourage them to join the group, contribute money, or engage in grassroots lobbying, also involves elements of persuasion—trying to transform citizens into supporters, and supporters into true believers and even activists. In the case of gun control, for example, the National Rifle Association has an aggressive campaign to make it easier for members to contact their elected officials and to express their opinions. Moreover, local NRA chapters and individual members organize and publicize counterprotests such as those described earlier.

A focused mobilization effort involves contacting large numbers of potential supporters through e-mail, phone calls, direct mail, television advertising, print media, social media, and websites. In order to get legislators to respond, a group has to persuade large numbers of people to get involved. One example of mobilization occurs during congressional hearings on nominees to the Supreme Court or other federal judgeships. One study found that about one-third of the groups that lobbied for or against these nominees also deployed direct mail and leaflets, and ran phone banks as a way to influence public opinion.[45]

astroturf lobbying Any lobbying method initiated by an interest group that is designed to look like the spontaneous, independent participation of many individuals.

501(c)(3) organization A tax code classification that applies to most interest groups; this designation makes donations to the group tax deductible but limits the group's political activities.

political action committee (PAC) An interest group or a division of an interest group that can raise money to contribute to campaigns or to spend on ads in support of candidates. The amount a PAC can receive from each of its donors and the amount it can spend on federal campaigning are strictly limited.

527 organization A tax-exempt group formed primarily to influence elections through voter mobilization efforts and issue ads that do not directly endorse or oppose a candidate. Unlike political action committees, 527s are not subject to contribution limits and spending caps.

ELECTIONEERING Interest groups get involved in elections by making contributions to candidates, mobilizing people (including their staff) to help in a campaign, endorsing candidates, funding campaign ads, or mobilizing a candidate's or party's supporters. All these efforts seek to influence who gets elected, with the expectation that changing who gets elected will affect what government does.

Federal laws limit groups' electioneering and lobbying efforts. (See Nuts & Bolts 10.3.) For example, most private organizations and associations in America are organized as **501(c)(3) organizations**, a designation based on their Internal Revenue Service classification, which means that donations to the group are tax deductible. However, 501(c)(3) organizations are not allowed to engage in any political activities or lobbying (other than certain voter-education programs or voter-registration drives that are conducted in a nonpartisan manner), although some groups are always looking for loopholes in these restrictions. Groups that want to engage in lobbying or electioneering without looking for exceptions can incorporate under other IRS designations and operate as a **political action committee (PAC)**, a **527 organization**, or a 501(c)(4). Although contributions to these organizations are not tax deductible, such organizations have fewer restrictions on the size of the contributions they can make and on how their money is spent—for example, 527 organizations have no contribution or spending limits.

10.3 NUTS & bolts

INTEREST GROUPS AND ELECTIONEERING: TYPES OF ORGANIZATIONS

An interest group's ability to engage in electioneering depends on how it is organized—specifically, what section of the IRS code applies to the organization. The following table gives details on four common organizations: 501(c) organizations, 527 organizations, political action committees (PACs), and so-called Super PACs.

Therefore, many choose to contribute money to nonprofits organized as 501(c)(4) groups, which can lobby and engage in electioneering as long as their "primary activity" (at least half of their overall activity) is not political.

Type of Organization	Advantages	Disadvantages
501(c)(3)	Contributions tax-deductible	Cannot engage in political activities or lobbying, only voter education and mobilization
527	Can spend unlimited amounts on issue advocacy and voter mobilization	Cannot make contributions to candidates or coordinate efforts with candidates or parties
501(c)(4)	Can spend unlimited amounts on electioneering; do not have to disclose contributors	At least half of their activities must be nonpolitical; cannot coordinate efforts with candidates or parties
PACs	Can contribute directly to candidates and parties	Strict limits on direct contributions
Super PACs	Can spend unlimited amounts on electioneering; can support or oppose specific candidates	Cannot make contributions to candidates or coordinate efforts with candidates or parties

How It Works

LOBBYING THE FEDERAL GOVERNMENT:
INSIDE AND OUTSIDE STRATEGIES

INSIDE STRATEGIES

*Groups lobby government officials
directly in Washington, D.C.*

Examples: meeting with lawmakers,
drafting legislation, providing research and
testimony, taking the government to court.

OUTSIDE STRATEGIES

*Groups use public pressure, elections,
and the media to influence government.*

Examples: grassroots e-mail, letter, or phone
campaigns; contributing to election campaigns;
getting media coverage of their cause.

How It Works
In Practice

THE NATIONAL RIFLE ASSOCIATION'S LOBBYING STRATEGIES IN THE FIGHT FOR GUN CONTROL

After a shooting at Sandy Hook Elementary School in Connecticut, in which 20 students and 6 staff members were killed, many people inside and outside the government called for stricter gun control laws. The National Rifle Association (NRA) disagreed and an intense debate ensued. Using their size and high level of funding, the NRA engaged in a diverse set of lobbying activities, and gun legislation stalled in Congress.

- **INSIDE STRATEGIES**
- **OUTSIDE STRATEGIES**
- **EVENTS AND GOVERNMENT ACTION**

DEC. 14, 2012 — 20 students and 6 teachers and staff shot at Sandy Hook Elementary School, reigniting debate about gun control legislation.

DEC. 2012 — NRA holds press conference to propose arming schoolteachers and staff.

JAN. 2013 — NRA announces opposition to bans on assault weapons proposed by House Democrats and Senate Democrats.

JAN. 2013 — Head of NRA testifies before Senate hearing on gun control legislation.

JAN.–APR. 2013 — NRA issues series of "Grassroots Alerts" encouraging NRA members to write senators and House members opposing universal background checks and assault weapons ban.

FEB. 2013 — NRA launches an ad campaign against universal background checks for gun ownership.

MAR. 2013 — NRA announces support for Republican proposal for limited background check system designed to ensure that mentally ill individuals cannot purchase firearms.

APR. 10, 2013 — Senators Joe Manchin (D-WV) and Pat Toomey (R-PA) propose bill to mandate universal background checks of potential gun buyers.

APR. 2013 — NRA lobbies senators against passage of Manchin-Toomey gun control compromise.

APR. 17, 2013 — The Manchin-Toomey bill, as well as other restrictions on gun sales, fails in the Senate.

POP QUIZ

1 Which of the following is an example of outside lobbying?

- **a** providing research to lawmakers
- **b** suing the government
- **c** working with bureaucrats
- **d** making campaign contributions
- **e** meeting with lawmakers

2 Suppose you represent an interest group that has a small membership but employs a well-respected group of policy researchers and lawyers. What combination of lobbying strategies would give you the best chance of success?

- **a** grassroots lobbying and mass protests
- **b** drafting legislation and going to court
- **c** electioneering and encouraging media coverage
- **d** meeting with elected officials and their staff
- **e** all of the above

Answers: 1.d; 2.b

TABLE » 10.2

BIG SPENDERS IN THE 2014 ELECTION: 527 ORGANIZATIONS

This table shows the amount of money spent on electioneering by the top ten 527 organizations. Does this information support claims of interest groups having a disproportionate influence over election outcomes, especially in light of the high costs of campaigning described in Chapter 9?

ORGANIZATION	GENERALLY SUPPORTS	TOTAL EXPENDITURES
ActBlue	Democrats	$14,626,209
College Republican National Committee	Republicans	$14,156,096
Service Employees International Union	Democrats	$10,872,872
EMILY's List	Democrats	$9,894,653
Citizens United	Republicans	$9,305,909
Gay & Lesbian Victory Fund	Democrats	$7,175,540
International Brotherhood of Electrical Workers	Democrats	$6,768,467
Plumbers/Pipefitters Union	Democrats	$5,796,679
RightChange.com	Republicans	$5,206,186
GOPAC	Republicans	$4,482,304

SOURCE: Calculated by author from data at www.opensecrets.org/pacs/ (accessed 11/4/14).

In 2014, federally focused 527 organizations spent more than $100 million on electioneering, and PACs spent nearly $400 million.[46] Table 10.2 reports campaign spending for the top ten 527 organizations. The top-spending 527, ActBlue, spent over $14 million in 2014, and even the tenth-ranked organization, GOPAC, spent over $4 million, which was more than the largest PAC. The table also shows that most of the large 527 organizations are strongly tied to one of the major parties. Indeed, the literature from these organizations leaves no doubt about their partisan leanings. Although some 527s spend a lot on electioneering, the average amount is lower than you might think. In the 2014 election, the 210 active 527 organizations that participated in the campaign spent an average of about $483,000 each. In other words, although some 527 organizations run substantial national ad campaigns, the average 527 gets involved in only a few races.

The data on the top ten political action committees in 2014 are shown in Table 10.3. The largest PAC contributed just over $3 million to candidates in the 2014 election, and the tenth largest contributed slightly more than $2 million. The donation of millions of dollars by these PACs, however, is not typical; rather, in the 2014 election, the average PAC gave only $100,000 in contributions. Part of the reason for this lower spending is that PACs' direct contributions to candidates are capped at $5,000 per candidate, and their contributions to party committees are also strictly limited.

Two new options for electioneering by interest groups emerged in recent elections: "Super PACs" and 501(c)(4) organizations. The former was a consequence

TABLE » 10.3

BIG SPENDERS IN THE 2014 ELECTION: POLITICAL ACTION COMMITTEES

Do the largest PACs disproportionately support Republican or Democratic candidates, or is there no clear pattern?

ORGANIZATION	GENERALLY SUPPORTS	TOTAL CONTRIBUTIONS
National Association of Realtors	Mixed	$3,374,705
National Beer Wholesalers Association	Mixed	$3,125,800
Honeywell International	Republicans	$2,701,956
Operating Engineers Union	Democrats	$2,577,492
National Auto Dealers Association	Republicans	$2,541,100
Lockheed Martin	Mixed	$2,484,500
American Bankers Association	Republicans	$2,448,973
Credit Union National Association	Mixed	$2,431,000
AT&T, Inc.	Republicans	$2,406,650
Northrop Grumman	Republicans	$2,395,250
International Brotherhood of Electrical Workers	Democrats	$2,365,964

Note: Support is mixed if fewer than 60 percent of contributions are given to one party.

SOURCE: Calculated by author from data at www.opensecrets.org/pacs/(accessed 11/4/14).

WHAT DO POLITICAL SCIENTISTS DO?

To find out more about how money affects politics, visit **wwnpag.es/wdpsd**

of the *Citizens United* Supreme Court decision that authorized unlimited independent spending by corporations and labor unions in federal elections.[47] Many groups set up new political action committees to take advantage of these latest rules—the "super" label reflects the fact that these groups take in and spend much more money than the typical PAC. For example, President George W. Bush's former political strategist Karl Rove set up the Super PAC American Crossroads, which helped elect Republicans in 2012 and 2014. However, many businesses preferred that their contributions remain secret because they were afraid of angering shareholders and customers who might disagree with their political spending. Rove also established a 501(c)(4), Crossroads GPS, for businesses that did not want to have their contributions disclosed. Rove's two groups spent more than $50 million in the 2014 elections. Overall, there were over a thousand Super PACs active in the 2014 election, and they spent almost $600 million during the campaign. However, here again, most of these organizations are small, with the average spending about $500,000 in 2014.

These data highlight a sharp difference in electioneering strategies between the very few large, well-funded interest groups and everyone else. A few 527s, Super PACs, 501(c)(4)s, and PACs have the money to deploy massive advertising and mobilizing efforts for a candidate or issue they like or against those they don't like. There are also some very large associations that can persuade large numbers of members to work for and vote for candidates that the group supports or against candidates that the group wants to defeat. And just a few rich individuals can make outsized contributions to a candidate they favor—this is especially true now after the Supreme Court struck down aggregate limits on campaign contributions in the 2014 *McCutcheon v. FEC* case (see Chapter 9). But these strategies are not available to the vast majority of interest groups, which simply don't have the resources. For the most part, they hope to give modest help to a few candidates who are sympathetic to the group's goals. These contributions are generally made in the hope that, once elected, the officeholder will remember their contribution when the group asks for a meeting. Some groups give money to both candidates in a race (as long as neither candidate actively opposes the group's position), figuring that regardless of who wins, they will be able to meet with the winner.[48] A few groups wait until after the election to make their contribution to the winning candidate.

It is important to remember that electioneering is only one strategy available to interest groups. Some groups do not do any electioneering at all, possibly because they lack sufficient funds, because they want to avoid making enemies based on whom they support or don't support, or because other strategies are more promising given the resources that are available to them. Many groups opt for quiet lobbying efforts that use their expertise, or they undertake grassroots efforts to build public support for their policy goals. Massive electioneering operations by interest groups are relatively rare.

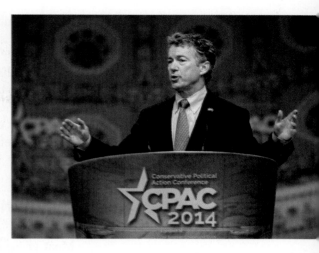

SUPER PACS, SUCH AS THE Conservative Political Action Committee (CPAC), have been influential in recent elections. Here, Rand Paul (R-KY) speaks at the 2014 annual meeting of CPAC, which serves as a forum for bringing together possible conservative candidates and leaders from around the country.

CULTIVATING MEDIA CONTACTS Media coverage helps a group publicize its concerns without spending any money. Thus, most interest group leaders talk often with journalists to suggest news stories that pertain to the group's issues and to pursue favorable coverage. Such attention may mobilize public opinion indirectly, by getting people to join the group, contribute money, or demand that elected officials support the group's agenda. Favorable media coverage also helps a group's leaders assure members that they are actively working on members' concerns.

Journalists listen when interest groups call if they feel that the group's story will catch their readers' attention or address their concerns. Smart interest group leaders make it easy for journalists to cover their cause, holding events that produce intriguing news stories. These stories may not change anyone's mind, but the media coverage provides free publicity for the groups' policy agendas.

BYPASSING GOVERNMENT: THE INITIATIVE PROCESS A final outside strategy for interest groups bypasses government entirely: a group can work to get its proposed policy change voted on by the public in a general election through an initiative or a referendum. Referenda and initiatives allow citizens to vote on specific proposed changes in policy. The difference between these procedures lies in the source of the proposal. In a **referendum**, the legislature or another government body proposes the question that is put to a vote, whereas an **initiative** allows citizens to put questions on the ballot, typically after gathering signatures of registered voters on a petition.

Initiatives can occur only in states and municipalities that have the appropriate procedures in place; there is no mechanism for a nationwide vote on an interest group's proposal. So if a group wants to use this process to effect national change, it has to get its measure on the ballot in one state at a time. Moreover, only some states allow initiatives, and some permit this kind of vote only on a narrow range of issues. The champion state for initiatives is California, whose citizens often vote on dozens of initiatives in each general election, ranging from funding for stem cell research to limits on taxation and spending.[49]

There are many examples of groups using the initiative process to change government policy. Most notably, advocates of term limits for state legislators have

referendum A direct vote by citizens on a policy change proposed by a legislature or another government body. Referenda are common in state and local elections, but there is no mechanism for a national-level referendum.

initiative A direct vote by citizens on a policy change proposed by fellow citizens or organized groups outside government. Getting a question on the ballot typically requires collecting a set number of signatures from registered voters in support of the proposal. There is no mechanism for a national-level initiative.

used the initiative process to establish such limits in 21 states, although the limits in some states have since been overturned by legislative action or subsequent initiatives.[50]

One of the principal concerns about the initiative process is that it favors well-funded groups that can advertise heavily in support of their proposals and can mobilize their supporters to vote on Election Day.[51] But spending a lot of money often is not enough: even groups with substantial resources have sometimes been unable to reform policy through the initiative process.[52]

CHOOSING STRATEGIES

Most groups give testimony, do research, contact elected officials and bureaucrats, talk with journalists, and develop legislative and regulatory proposals.[53] A particular group's decisions about which strategies to use depend partly on its resources and partly on what approach the group believes will be most effective in promoting its particular issues. Some strategies that work well for one group's agenda might not be appropriate for another's. The Humane Society of the United States is an organization that lobbies to prevent the abuse and neglect of animals. It had over 11 million members and a $125 million annual budget in 2012, but only a small Washington office. This is because the group focuses on investigations and grassroots lobbying. During 2013, the Humane Society organized investigations of horse trainers, laboratories that used chimpanzees for research, and the use of so-called gestation crates to immobilize livestock.[54]

Other interest groups have few members and not much money, but they can use other resources to attract attention to their cause. For example, during the 2011–2012 congressional debate over the Stop Online Piracy Act (SOPA), many Internet firms and websites organized viral campaigns to get users to contact their representatives and tell them to oppose the proposals.[55] Several sites, including Wikipedia, even went offline on January 18, 2012, to emphasize the seriousness of their concerns. While SOPA had already attracted opposition, these protests attracted considerable media attention and were one factor that led to modification of the proposals.

EVALUATE INTEREST GROUP INFLUENCE

HOW MUCH POWER DO INTEREST GROUPS HAVE?

Whether from the left or the right, it is easy to find claims about how interest groups dominate in the making of public policy:

> *Evidence abounds that the U.S. political system is increasingly dominated by wealthy interests, and strong majorities of the public believe—rightly—that the deck is stacked against ordinary voters. . . . As private interests have come to wield more influence over public policy, with ever larger sums of money shaping elections and the policymaking process, our political system has become less responsive to those looking for a fair shot to improve their lives and move upward.*[56]

Other critics echo these arguments. For example, the website of the Alliance for Retired Americans includes detailed critiques of the Medicare Prescription Drug Benefit, arguing that key elements of the program, including the ban on importing cheaper prescription drugs from abroad, resulted from health care industry lobbying. As the Alliance sees it, drug companies got what they wanted; the rest of us did not. Interest groups are also thought to have enormous influence over the actions of unelected bureaucrats. Their claims are an example of the theory of bureaucratic capture, which posits that agencies are vulnerable to being "captured," or having their policy goals displaced by the aims of the individuals and corporations they are supposed to regulate. When this happens, bureaucrats become more interested in catering to interest groups than in implementing policies that are good for the general population.[57] (See Chapter 13 for further discussion of bureaucratic capture.)

The evidence on interest group influence does not support these claims. In fact, most studies of actual lobbying efforts show that interest groups often have very little influence.[58] Some interest groups get what they want from government some of the time, but that success can prove elusive even for groups with many members and large budgets. More important, there is no correlation between the amount of money spent on lobbying and a group's success at achieving its policy goals.[59] Even in the case of lobbying against direct federal student loans, the groups working against change were ultimately unsuccessful, despite having large lobbying operations and essentially unlimited budgets.

This outcome, and what it implies about the limited power of interest groups, makes sense in light of four facts about interest group influence. First, interest groups lobby their friends in government rather than their enemies and usually moderate their demands in the face of resistance. A high success rate for an interest group's efforts may reflect these kinds of calculations rather than supporting the case that they are extremely powerful. For example, the NRA leadership would probably favor a new federal law that made it legal to carry a concealed handgun throughout the nation, since the NRA has lobbied for these laws at the state level and sent its representatives to testify at congressional hearings.[60] Why doesn't the NRA demand federal legislation? Because there is no sign that Congress would enact this proposal. A proposal that would force states to honor concealed carry permits issued by other states has been introduced in Congress several times but never brought up for debate or a vote.[61] Thus, the NRA's decision to forgo lobbying for a federal concealed carry law shows the limits of the organization's power.

Second, some complaints about the power of interest groups come from the losing side in the political process. Consider the Alliance for Retired Americans and its claims about the Medicare Prescription Drug Benefit just mentioned. The Alliance lobbied against the Medicare legislation just as the drug companies lobbied for it. However, the Alliance was on the losing side, and many of the provisions the group favored were not enacted, making it more prone to complain about the influence of "special interests."

Third, many interest groups claim responsibility for policies and election outcomes regardless of whether their lobbying made the difference. Consider former senator Kay Hagan (D-NC), who was defeated in her 2014 reelection bid. Many interest groups funded ads criticizing Hagan or contributed to her opponent's campaign. The ads may have helped defeat Hagan, but she was also hurt by having a well-funded, experienced opponent, Thom Tillis; President Obama's unpopularity; and the nearly even ratio of Democrats to Republicans in the state. Yet, the leaders of interest groups have a considerable incentive to

WHILE MANY OBSERVERS CREDIT lobbying by the pharmaceutical industry for policies such as the Medicare Prescription Drug Benefit (and its ban on importing medicines), favorable public opinion, the efforts of AARP, and bureaucrats' independent judgments probably had greater influence on passing the Drug Benefit Act.

make strong claims about their group's influence and impact, as these claims help them attract members and keep their jobs.[62] But much of what groups do—issuing reports, testifying, sending out appeals, talking with journalists—has little direct impact on policy. Publicizing these activities may reflect a leader's desire to build support for himself, but they say little about the group's influence.

Fourth, arguments about the impact of interest groups on election outcomes, such as Hagan's defeat in 2014, ignore the fact that interest groups are almost always active on both sides of an election campaign. Although Hagan was the target of attack ads funded by interest groups, and although many groups gave contributions to his opponent, Hagan also received support from interest groups in the form of campaign contributions and independent ads. Thus, it doesn't make sense to attribute Hagan's defeat to actions taken by one set of groups without asking why similar efforts on Hagan's behalf had no effect. You can't conclude that interest groups are all-powerful without explaining why Hagan's supporters were unable to save her seat.

After discussing these four facts, we can return to the case of federal student loans. In this case, it's important to remember that the coalition of groups opposed to reforming federal student loans actually lost—legislation establishing a direct loan program was enacted in 2011 and is in place today. While the antireform groups had considerable resources, and were able to delay a change in policy for over a decade, in the end they could not defeat the president's proposal. The message is simple: rather that explaining why groups are so powerful, we should focus instead on identifying the conditions that lead to interest group influence, and the conditions that mitigate against such influence.

WHAT DETERMINES WHEN INTEREST GROUPS SUCCEED?

When are interest groups powerful? Two related factors determine the success of lobbying efforts. The first is salience: How many Americans care about what a group is trying to do? The second is conflict: To what extent do other groups or the public oppose the policy change?

SALIENCE Interest groups are more likely to succeed when their request has low **salience**, or attracts little public attention.[63] When the average voter does not know or care about a group's request, legislators and bureaucrats do not have to worry about the political consequences of giving the group what it wants—there is no cost to allowing access or complying with a group's demands. The only question is whether the officials themselves favor the request or can be convinced that the group's desired change is worthwhile. In contrast, when salience is high, a legislator's response to lobbying will hinge on her judgment of constituent opinion: Do voters favor what the group wants? After all, the average legislator has a strong interest in reelection and is unlikely to act against her constituents' wishes. As a result, lobbying may count for nothing in the face of public opposition or be superfluous when the group's position already has public support.[64]

Many policies that are the focus of lobbying efforts are not at all salient. Consider the National Turkey Federation, an association of turkey farmers and processors. The federation sponsors the annual ritual of presenting the president with a live Thanksgiving turkey, which is officially "pardoned" by the president and sent to a local petting zoo. In 2002, the federation persuaded federal bureaucrats

salience The level of familiarity with an interest group's goals among the general population.

to change federally funded school lunch program regulations in a way that increased the allowable amount of turkey in various entrees. The policy change resulting from the federation's lobbying efforts attracted no publicity, which is precisely the point. When few people know or care about a policy change, interest groups are able to dominate the policy-making process.

Low-salience issues are surprisingly common. The idea of interest group lobbying probably brings to mind titanic struggles on controversial issues, such as gun control, abortion rights, or judicial nominations, over which groups try to capture public attention as a way of pressuring people in government. And, in fact, many groups are active for or against these issues. However, the typical issue attracts much less activity. One analysis of lobbying disclosure forms found that 5 percent of issues attracted more than 50 percent of lobbying activity, and 50 percent of issues attracted less than 3 percent.[65] Thus, the typical issue debated by members of Congress may involve relatively little interest group activity, and a group's request may generate little or no opposition from other groups. On these noncontroversial issues, getting access to legislators is probably easy to obtain, and all a group needs to do is persuade the legislator that its demands have merit.

CONFLICT Lobbying is subject to two kinds of conflict. One involves disagreements between interest groups: some prefer spending more on a given program, some less. The other involves differences between what a particular interest group wants and the preferences of the general public. Both kinds of conflict can exist over the same issue, and both work against the success of a lobbying effort.[66]

In the case of the National Turkey Federation, for example, virtually no one in the general public knew about its proposal, and no interest group lobbied against it. In essence, bureaucrats heard one group asking for something and, hearing no opposition, decided the policy change was worth making. The situation might have been very different if another group—perhaps the American Pork Producers or the American Cattlemen—had lobbied against the Turkey Federation. If so, satisfying one group would have required displeasing at least one other group. Faced with this no-win situation, bureaucrats or legislators would be less likely to give the group what it wanted. At a minimum, they would have had to measure the Turkey Federation's arguments against those made by the other groups.

As the analysis mentioned earlier suggests, many cases of interest group influence look a lot like the Turkey Federation's request: a group asks for something, there is relatively little opposition, and Congress or the bureaucracy responds with appropriate policy changes. These cases are examples of true interest group influence, because a group asks for something and gets it. However, one of the primary reasons for the group's success is that its efforts are essentially unopposed. In contrast, as we have discussed here, the forces aligned against student loan reform in 2011 were matched in number, if not in monetary resources, by groups pressing for change. Under these conditions, the antireform groups were not the only voices heard by members of Congress and bureaucrats.

But if conflict is fundamental to politics, shouldn't there be at least one group opposing every lobbying effort? The answer is, not necessarily. Potential opponents may remain latent (unorganized) or decide against lobbying to concentrate their efforts on other matters. Many policy questions are just not that important to many people. Thus, the obstacles to a group's goals may not be the other groups

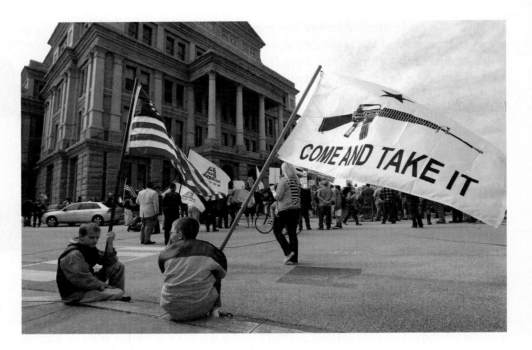

CONGRESS HAS CONSIDERED VARIOUS forms of gun control legislation in recent years, but the NRA continues to lobby for laws that would benefit them, such as the right to carry concealed weapons. Members of the NRA and other gun rights supporters are gathered here in the Texas state capitol to rally against stricter limits on firearms.

that oppose its request; rather, the obstacles may be the groups that are asking for something completely different, because members of Congress and bureaucrats have time to make only so many policy changes in any year.

Interest group influence is much less apparent on conflictual issues—those over which public opinion is split and groups are typically active on both sides of the question. Consider a high-salience issue such as gun control. The 2013 debate over gun control attracted many well-funded interest groups and coalitions, which supported different versions of gun control or wanted no change at all. There was no consensus either among members of Congress, interest groups, or the American public about which policy changes were needed. Under these conditions, access doesn't count for very much—legislators have a keen sense of the political costs of accommodating a group's demands. Under these conditions, stalemate is the likely result. If policy change occurs at all, it is likely to reflect a complex process of bargaining and compromise, with no groups getting exactly what they want. In such cases, it is hard to say whether a particular group won or lost, or to attribute any aspect of the final bargain to a particular group's efforts.

The case of gun control illustrates that being large or well funded often does not help an interest group convince government officials to comply with its requests. As mentioned earlier, many people worry that well-funded interest groups will use their financial resources to dominate the policy-making process, even if public opinion is against them, but these fears are largely unfounded. The conditions that are ripe for well-funded interest groups to become involved in a policy debate typically ensure that there will be well-funded groups on all sides of a question. Under these conditions, no group is likely to get everything it wants, and no group's lobbying efforts are likely to be decisive. Some groups may not get anything.

HOW GROUPS SUCCEED

Even when issues are highly salient, interest groups can still be influential. Research and testimony may help members of Congress develop legislative proposals and give them arguments to use in the bargaining process. Grassroots and media efforts may mobilize public opinion, pressuring members to vote for options favored by their constituents. If a particular group decided against doing these things, and no other group took its place, then groups on the other side of the debate might be more likely to carry the day. But interest group leaders are well aware of the potentially dire consequences of not getting involved and are unlikely to be inactive on questions that matter to them and the members of their group—even if a full-fledged lobbying effort is unlikely to produce many identifiable benefits, given the opposition by other groups.

Even on high-salience issues, lobbying efforts may produce identifiable benefits when they are focused on relatively small details of a policy change. However, groups are successful in these efforts precisely because they seek relatively modest policy changes, which are important to their members but generate minimal opposition. Particularly when policy questions are complex, groups may focus their attention on achieving seemingly minor policy changes that have large benefits for their members.

Another measure of the limits of lobbying on conflictual questions is evident in groups' decisions about which issues to refrain from lobbying on. Think about one of the most powerful interest groups, the NRA, and its advocacy of concealed carry laws. There is little doubt that the NRA's leaders and most of its members favor the passage of such laws nationwide, but its efforts are unlikely to be successful at the national level given public opinion and well-funded opposition. As a result, the NRA chooses to lobby on other matters—policy questions with which it might succeed or where its efforts are necessary to prevent other groups from succeeding in changing policies in ways that the NRA opposes.

Thus, being large or well funded often does not help an interest group convince government officials to comply with its requests. It all depends on what the group is asking for and, in particular, whether there is significant opposition in the form of opposing groups or public opinion. As mentioned earlier, many Americans worry that well-funded interest groups will use their financial resources to dominate the policy-making process, even if public opinion is against them. It would be a considerable overstatement to say that interest groups have no power and lobbying makes no difference, because, if nothing else, groups may lobby to prevent the policy changes that would occur if they stayed inactive. And interest groups often succeed in efforts to change low-salience policies or small details of salient proposals. But when large, powerful groups seek controversial changes, their resources are matched by the difficulty of the task. These groups can send staff to lobby officeholders, commission research reports, testify, bring lawsuits, and encourage grassroots activity, but such tactics are unlikely to prevail in the face of public opposition or counteractive lobbying by other groups.

CONCLUSION

Many Americans think that interest groups are powerful manipulators of the American policy process, and that they are able to get what they want regardless of the impact on everyone else. Federal direct student loans are seemingly a perfect example: a small number of well-funded lobbyists worked to defeat a policy change that would lower the cost of attending college for most students.

As you have seen, the truth is much more complex. Interest groups represent many different Americans, many of whom are unaware that lobbying occurs on their behalf. Moreover, for many groups, the challenge is to get organized in the first place or to scrape together enough resources to start lobbying. These efforts don't always succeed. Interest groups are more likely to get what they want when their demands attract little public attention and no opposition from other groups. When a group asks for a large or controversial policy change, it stands little chance of success, even if the group has many members, a large lobbying budget, or an influential leader directing its operation.

The debate over direct student loans exemplifies all of these findings. Although the corporations that stood to lose from the direct loan proposal had significant lobbying operations, the proposal was relatively high-salience and controversial. Consequently, legislators' voting decisions were less likely to be affected by lobbying or other interest group strategies such as electioneering. These lobbying efforts may have helped to inform members of Congress about the details of the proposal or the impact that the change would have on employment in their districts, but there is no evidence that support for these proposals was shaped by lobbying. And although these lobbying efforts delayed the move to direct loans, they did not prevent it.

In sum, while individual lobbying efforts often reflect the efforts of small groups to achieve favored policy outcomes at the expense of the majority, looking across the entire range of interest group activities, a different picture emerges: in the main, interest groups reflect the conflictual nature of American politics and the resulting drive of individuals, groups, and corporations to shape American public policy in line with their policy goals. The average citizen benefits as well as loses from lobbying activities.

THE INTEREST GROUP UNIVERSE

▶ *Define interest groups and describe the characteristics of different types of groups.* **(Pages 352–62)**

SUMMARY

Interest groups are organizations that seek to influence government policy by helping elect candidates who support their policy goals, and by lobbying elected officials and bureaucrats. Although they are generally viewed with disdain, interest groups are ubiquitous—most organizations have lobbyists working on their behalf—and under the theory of pluralism, are regarded as fundamental actors in American politics.

KEY TERMS

interest group (p. 352)
lobbying (p. 352)
interest group state (p. 354)
trade association (p. 357)
centralized groups (p. 357)
confederations (p.359)
revolving door (p. 360)
mass associations (p. 360)
peak associations (p. 360)

CRITICAL THINKING AND DISCUSSION

Why do you think that Americans' opinions of lobbyists are generally unfavorable, despite the fact that nearly all Americans either belong to an interest group or have groups that lobby for policy positions that they agree with?

PRACTICE QUIZ QUESTIONS

1. In contrast to political parties, interest groups
   _____

   A run candidates for office

   B coordinate the activities of elected officials

   C guarantee that certain candidates appear on electoral ballots

   D directly influence government activity

   E indirectly influence government activity

2. Why is the number of lobbyists increasing?

   A The federal government is growing in size and influence.

   B Lobbying is not closely regulated.

   C Citizens are now more supportive of special interests.

   D Politicians can concurrently serve their terms and work as lobbyists.

   E Interest groups have more money to spend.

3. In contrast to a confederation, a centralized interest group _____

   A maintains lots of independent chapters

   B often has local chapters competing over resources

   C deploys the group's resources more efficiently

   D is able to find out what its members want

   E has no weaknesses

4. The practice of moving from government positions to working for interest groups is called _____.

   A interest-group capture

   B the revolving door

   C an iron triangle

   D escalator politics

   E the spoils system

GETTING ORGANIZED

▶ *Explain how successful interest groups overcome collective action problems.* **(Pages 363–65)**

SUMMARY

A primary challenge in operating an interest group is getting members to coordinate with one another. Interest groups have a number of different ways of overcoming the problem of collective action, with varying degrees of success.

KEY TERMS

collective action problem (p. 363)
free riding (p. 364)
solidary benefits (p. 364)
purposive benefits (p. 364)
coercion (p. 364)
selective incentives (p. 364)

CRITICAL THINKING AND DISCUSSION

As described in this chapter, college students are an unorganized group in American politics. Based on the logic of collective action, what would an interest group entrepreneur have to do to organize this group?

PRACTICE QUIZ QUESTIONS

5. The logic of collective action says that when people _____ on policy priorities, and the costs are _____, cooperation is not easy.

   A agree; high

   B agree; covered by one person

   C agree; low

   D disagree; high

   E disagree; low

6. Purposive benefits come from _____, while solidary benefits come from _____.

   Ⓐ working with like-minded people; working to achieve a desired policy goal

   Ⓑ receiving material goods; working with like-minded people

   Ⓒ receiving material goods; working to achieve a desired policy goal

   Ⓓ working to achieve a desired policy goal; receiving material goods

   Ⓔ working to achieve a desired policy goal; working with like-minded people

7. Labor unions are generally able to overcome the collective action problem through the use of _____.

   Ⓐ solidary benefits

   Ⓑ purposive benefits

   Ⓒ coercion

   Ⓓ selective incentives

   Ⓔ recruitment

INTEREST GROUP STRATEGIES

▶ *Explore the ways interest groups try to influence government policies.* **(Pages 365–76)**

SUMMARY

Interest groups have two types of tactics for lobbying elected officials. They can attempt to influence politics by taking action in Washington, or they can take action elsewhere. The decision to pursue an inside or outside strategy comes down to the interest group's resources and which strategy members think will be most effective.

KEY TERMS

inside strategies (p. 365)
outside strategies (p. 365)
direct lobbying (p. 365)
grassroots lobbying (p. 368)
astroturf lobbying (p. 369)
501(c)(3) organization (p. 370)
political action committee (PAC) (p. 370)
527 organization (p. 370)
referendum (p. 375)
initiative (p. 375)

CRITICAL THINKING AND DISCUSSION

The chapter describes the last few decades' significant increases in the number of interest groups and lobby-ists, and in the amount spent on lobbying. What factors could cause this increase to level off or even reverse?

PRACTICE QUIZ QUESTIONS

8. Asking government officials to change policy in line with the group's goals is _____.

   Ⓐ revolving door lobbying

   Ⓑ astroturf lobbying

   Ⓒ direct lobbying

   Ⓓ indirect lobbying

   Ⓔ outside lobbying

9. Interest groups generally _____ draft legislation; they generally _____ provide testimony before committees.

   Ⓐ do; do

   Ⓑ do not; do

   Ⓒ do; do not

   Ⓓ do not; do not

10. Directly involving interest group members in lobbying efforts is called _____.

   Ⓐ astroturf lobbying

   Ⓑ grassroots lobbying

   Ⓒ democratic lobbying

   Ⓓ lobbying through referendum

   Ⓔ inside lobbying

11. For indirect lobbying to be effective, _____.

   Ⓐ only a few pieces of mail are necessary

   Ⓑ mail must come from all over the country

   Ⓒ all messages have to have exactly the same appeal

   Ⓓ letters have to come from constituents

   Ⓔ letters have to come from prominent officials

12. Interest groups who want to maximize the amount of access they receive in return for a campaign contribution will sometimes _____.

   Ⓐ contribute to weak candidates who need the money

   Ⓑ contribute to candidates who oppose the group's goals

   Ⓒ wait until the general election to make a contribution

   Ⓓ wait until after an election to make a contribution to the winning candidate

   Ⓔ avoid electioneering efforts altogether

HOW MUCH POWER DO INTEREST GROUPS HAVE?

▶ *Evaluate interest group influence.* **(Pages 376–81)**

SUMMARY

It is commonly argued that elected officials are letting interest groups define their agenda. However, the evidence on interest groups does not support these claims: there is no correlation between the amount of money spent on lobbying and a group's suc-cess, nor is there conclusive evidence that group lobbying influences policy. Groups are generally most influential when the issues attract little public attention and when an issue does not have organized opposition.

KEY TERM

salience (p. 378)

CRITICAL THINKING AND DISCUSSION

A friend complains to you about the enormous power of organized interests in American politics, citing a group's recent victory in getting members of Congress to approve its policy proposal. Present three other possible explanations for this victory that do not involve the political power of the interest group.

PRACTICE QUIZ QUESTIONS

13. Interest groups generally lobby _____ in government.

    A their opponents

    B their friends

    C the undecided

    D the newly elected

    E the less informed

14. Interest groups are more likely to succeed when their request has _____ salience, and when it has _____ conflict.

    A low; little

    B high; little

    C low; high

    D high; high

    E high; zero

SUGGESTED READING

Ainsworth, Scott. *Analyzing Interest Groups: Group Influence on People and Policies.* New York: W. W. Norton, 2002.

Baumgartner, Frank, Jeffrey M. Berry, Marie Hojnacki, David C. Kimball, and Beth L. Leech. *Lobbying and Policy Change: Who Wins, Who Loses, and Why.* Chicago: University of Chicago Press, 2009.

Carpenter, Daniel. *The Forging of Bureaucratic Autonomy: Reputations, Networks, and Policy Innovation in Executive Agencies, 1862–1928.* Princeton, NJ: Princeton University Press, 2002.

Gilens, Martin, and Benjamin Page. *Testing Theories of American Politics: Elites, Interest Groups, and Average Citizens.* Princeton, NJ: Princeton University Press, 2014.

Kollman, Kenneth. *Outside Lobbying: Public Opinion and Interest Group Strategies.* Princeton, NJ: Princeton University Press, 1998.

Lowi, Theodore. *The End of Liberalism: The Second Republic of the United States.* New York: W. W. Norton, 1979.

Olson, Mancur. *The Logic of Collective Action,* 2nd ed. Cambridge, MA: Harvard University Press, 1971.

Schattschneider, E. E. *The Semi-Sovereign People.* New York: Harper and Row, 1959.

Schlozman, Kay Lehman, and John Tierney. *Organized Interests and American Democracy.* New York: HarperCollins, 1986.

Stigerwalt, Amy. *The Battle over the Bench: Senators, Interest Groups, and Lower Court Confirmations.* Charlottesville: University of Virginia Press, 2010.

Verba, Sidney, Kay Lehman Schlozman, and Henry Brady. *Voice and Equality: Civic Participation in America.* Cambridge, MA: Harvard University Press, 1995.

11

Congress

THE CASUAL OBSERVER READING THE HEADLINE early in March 2014, "Senate Approves McCaskill Sexual Assault Bill in 97–0 Vote," may have reasonably assumed that there was massive bipartisan agreement on this important issue.[1] However, digging past the headline would have revealed bruising partisan (and intraparty) conflict. Despite the unanimous support for the compromise bill in the Senate, the House declined to take up the bill, with Speaker John Boehner saying he wanted to see how previous reforms worked out: "I don't frankly see any reason at this point for any further action to be taken."[2]

A 2013 Pentagon report showed that 26,000 troops had "unwanted sexual contact" in 2012, comprising 6.1 percent of active-duty women and 1.2 percent of active-duty men. This was a 37 percent increase in incidents of unwanted sexual contact compared with such incidents in 2010 and more than eight times the 3,374 sexual assaults reported in 2010.[3] The report led to an outcry in Congress, with two senators, Claire McCaskill (D-MO) and Kirsten Gillibrand (D-NY), providing alternative plans. Both bills provided much stronger protections for victims of sexual assaults by removing the "good soldier" defense (a defense that takes an accused soldier's good military record into account, even if it is unrelated to the alleged crime) and strengthening prosecutors' role in advising commanders on whether to go to court martial. But Senator Gillibrand pushed for an even stronger overhaul that would have removed prosecutions for sexual assaults from the military chain of command, while Senator McCaskill did not. This difference led to a protracted battle that lasted nearly a year and isolated

CONFLICT & COMPROMISE
in American Politics

387

CHAPTER goals

Describe how the Founders envisioned Congress's role.
▶ PAGES 389–90

Explain how members of Congress represent their constituents and how elections hold members accountable.
▶ PAGES 390–403

Analyze the factors that help members of Congress get reelected.
▶ PAGES 403–07

Examine how parties, the committee system, and staffers enable Congress to function.
▶ PAGES 407–17

Trace the steps in the legislative process.
▶ PAGES 417–25

Describe how Congress ensures that the bureaucracy implements policies correctly.
▶ PAGES 425–26

Evaluate arguments for making Congress more accountable.
▶ PAGES 427–28

McCaskill as the only one of the 16 Democratic women senators to vote against Gillibrand's bill.[4] Nonetheless, as we noted above, McCaskill's version of the bill was the one that passed by a unanimous vote in the Senate. While supporters of the stronger reforms were disappointed, this case shows that even on a deeply conflictual issue such as how to address the problem of sexual assaults in the military, it is possible to find common ground and a compromise that can win the support of a majority in the Senate and, perhaps at some point, the House. As of this writing, the House has not taken up the bill.

The essential nature of conflict and compromise in the legislative process is not very well understood by the general public. Americans often view the type of wheeling and dealing that is necessary to reach compromises as improper and wonder why there is so much conflict. A typical sentiment is, "Why does there have to be so much partisan bickering? Can't they just implement the best solutions to our problems?" Many don't even attempt to understand the legislative process and the nature of conflict and compromise because it seems hopelessly complex. Anyone who has watched congressional debates on C-SPAN knows that legislative maneuvers can make your head spin, and the discussions can seem mind-numbing.

In this chapter, we show that the basic characteristics of Congress are straightforward and that the motivations that guide members' behavior and the way that Congress works are transparent. This chapter argues that members' behavior is driven by their desire to respond to constituent interests (and the closely related goal of reelection) and constrained by the institutional structures within which they operate (such as the committee system, parties, and leadership). At the same time, members try to be responsible for broader national interests, which are often at odds with their constituents' interests and, subsequently, the goal of reelection.

This tension between being responsible and responsive is a source of conflict and requires members of Congress to make tough decisions, often involving political trade-offs and compromises. Should a House member vote for dairy price supports for her local farmers even if it means higher milk prices for families around the nation? Should a senator vote to subsidize the production of tobacco, the biggest cash crop in his state, despite the tremendous health costs it imposes on millions of Americans? Should a member vote to close a military base, as requested by the Pentagon, even if it means the loss of thousands of jobs back home? These are difficult questions. On a complex issue, such as how best to deal with sexual assaults in the military, there is no obvious "responsible" solution, and fair-minded people can disagree. These disagreements take on a partisan edge, as most Republicans favor maintaining the chain of command, while most Democrats do not, which obviously leads to conflict.

This chapter begins by examining the constitutional underpinnings of the representational tensions Congress must address. After exploring different ways of understanding representation, we describe Congress's image problem, the incumbency advantage, and Congress's central institutional features. We conclude by considering some potential reforms that might make Congress work better. How can members of Congress best serve the collective interests of the nation while also representing their local constituents? How do the institutions of Congress, such as committees and political parties, help members pursue their goals? What did the Founders envision as the proper role for Congress within our political system?

CONGRESS'S PLACE IN OUR CONSTITUTIONAL SYSTEM

DESCRIBE HOW THE FOUNDERS ENVISIONED CONGRESS'S ROLE

Congress was the "first branch" in the early decades of our nation's history. The Constitution specified for Congress a vast array of enumerated powers, including regulating commerce, coining money, raising and supporting armies, creating the courts, establishing post offices and roads, declaring war, and levying taxes (see Article I, Section 8, of the Constitution in the Appendix). In contrast, the president was given few explicit powers and played a much less prominent role early in our history. Furthermore, many of Congress's extensive powers came from its implicit powers, which were rooted in the elastic clause of Article I of the Constitution, which gives Congress the power "to make all Laws which shall be necessary and proper for carrying into Execution the foregoing Powers."

As noted in Chapter 2, the compromises that gave rise to Congress's initial structure reflected an attempt to reconcile the competing interests of the day (large versus small states, northern versus southern interests, and proponents of strong national power versus state power). These compromises included establishing a system of **bicameralism**—that is, a bicameral (two-chambered) institution made up of a popularly elected House and a Senate chosen by state legislatures—allowing slaves to count as three-fifths of a person for purposes of apportionment for the House, and setting longer terms for senators (six years) than for House members (two years). But these compromises also laid the foundation for the split loyalties that members of Congress have between their local constituencies and the nation's interests. Although the Founders hoped that Congress would pass legislation that emphasized the national good over local interests, they also recognized the importance of local constituencies. Thus, the two-year House term was intended to tie legislators to public sentiment.

At the same time, the *Federalist Papers* made it clear that the new government was by no means a direct democracy that would put all policy questions to the public. In *Federalist 57*, Madison asserted that "the aim of every political constitution is, or ought to be, first to obtain for rulers men who possess most wisdom to discern, and most virtue to pursue, the common good of the society." This common good may often conflict with local concerns, such that members are expected to both "refine and enlarge the debate" to encompass the common good *and* represent their local constituents.

In general, the Founders viewed the Senate as the more likely institution to enlarge the debate and speak for the national interests; it was intended to check the more responsive and passionate House. Because senators were indirectly elected and served longer terms than House members, the Senate was more insulated from the people. A famous (although perhaps fictional) story that points out the differences between the House and Senate involves an argument between George Washington and Thomas Jefferson. Jefferson did not think the Senate was necessary, while Washington supported having

bicameralism The system of having two chambers within one legislative body, like the House and Senate in the U.S. Congress.

THE FOUNDERS VIEWED THE HOUSE as more passionate than the Senate, or as the "hot coffee" that needed to be cooled in the "saucer" of the Senate. This perception probably did not include coming to blows over differences in policy as Congressmen Albert G. Brown and John A. Wilcox did in 1851 about whether Mississippi should secede from the Union.

A ROW IN CONGRESS.

two chambers. During the argument, Jefferson poured some coffee he was drinking into his saucer. Washington asked him why he had done so. "To cool it," replied Jefferson. "Even so," said Washington, "we pour legislation into the senatorial saucer to cool it."

This idea of a more responsible Senate survived well into the twentieth century, even after the Seventeenth Amendment in 1913 allowed the direct, popular election of senators. Today, the Senate is still more insulated than the House. Because of the six-year terms of senators, only one-third of the 100 Senate seats are contested in each election, while all 435 House members are elected every two years. However, differences between the representational roles of the House and the Senate have become muted as senators seem to campaign for reelection 365 days a year, every year, just like House members.[5] This "permanent campaign" means that senators are less insulated from electoral forces than they were earlier.

The relationship between the president and Congress has also evolved significantly. Congress's roots in geographic constituencies made it well suited for the politics of the nineteenth century. Early in U.S. history, several great presidents left their mark on national politics (George Washington, Andrew Jackson, and Abraham Lincoln, among others), but Congress dominated much of the day-to-day politics, which revolved around issues such as the tariff (taxes on imported or exported goods), slavery, and internal improvements such as building roads and canals. Given the tendency to address these issues with patronage and the **pork barrel**—that is, jobs and policies targeted to benefit specific constituents—Congress was better suited for the task than the president was.

Beginning around the turn of the twentieth century and accelerating with the New Deal of the 1930s (which established modern social welfare and regulatory policies), the scope of national policy expanded and politics became more centered in Washington. With this nationalization of politics and the increasing importance of national security issues during World War II, the Cold War, the wars in Korea, Vietnam, and Iraq, and the war on terror, the president has assumed a more central policy-making role. Nonetheless, the central tensions between representing local versus national interests remain essential in understanding the legislative process and the relationship between members of Congress and their constituents.

pork barrel Legislative appropriations that benefit specific constituents, created with the aim of helping local representatives win reelection.

CONGRESS AND THE PEOPLE

Americans have a love-hate relationship with Congress; that is, we love our own member of Congress, but we hate Congress as a whole. Well, "hate" is a strong word, but as we show later in this section, members of Congress routinely have approval ratings 30 to 40 points higher than the institution's. Before explaining that puzzling pattern and Congress's more general image problem, we'll explore the nature of representation in Congress. What are the linkages between members of Congress and their constituents? How are congressional districts formed? And what do we really think about our members of Congress?

REPRESENTATION AND THE CONSTITUENCY

TYPES OF REPRESENTATION Let's examine the two basic relationships between constituents and their member of Congress: descriptive representation and substantive representation. The former is rooted in the politician's side of the relationship. Does the member of Congress "look like" the constituents in demographic terms—for example, African American, Latino, or white; male or female; Catholic, Protestant, or some other religion? Many people believe that such **descriptive representation** is a distinct value in itself. Having positive role models for various demographic groups helps create greater trust in the system. Moreover, there are benefits in being represented by someone who shares something as basic as skin color with constituents.

Descriptive representation is also related to the perceived responsiveness of a member of Congress. In general, constituents report higher levels of satisfaction with representatives who are of the same racial or ethnic background as the constituents themselves. Thus, descriptively represented constituents are more likely to assume that their interests are being represented than those who are not.[6] If you doubt that descriptive representation makes a difference, ask yourself whether it would be fair if all 435 House members and 100 senators were white male Protestants. Although the demographics of Congress are considerably more diverse than this, the legislature does not come close to "looking like us" on a nationwide scale (see Figure 11.1). This is especially true in the Senate, where only five African Americans and nine Latinos have been elected in the history of the institution (two African Americans and three Latinos currently are in the Senate as of 2015).[7]

Although descriptive representation is important, it goes only so far. More important than a member's race, gender, or religion, many argue, is the *substance* of what that person does. Merely because a representative shares some characteristics with you does not necessarily mean that he or she will represent your interests. **Substantive representation** moves beyond appearances to specify how the member serves constituents' interests. Two long-standing models of representation are (1) the **trustee**, who represents the interests of constituents from a distance, weighing numerous national, collective, local, and moral concerns; and (2) the **delegate**, who carries out the direct desires of the voters. In a sense, trustees are more concerned with being responsible and delegates are more interested in being responsive.

One of the most famous examples of a representative acting as a trustee was Marjorie Margolies-Mezvinsky (D-PA) in a crucial 1993 vote on President Clinton's budget, which included controversial tax increases and spending cuts to balance the budget. Hours before the vote, she told reporters that she would vote against the budget, in accordance with her constituents' wishes. But she had also promised Clinton she would support the bill if her vote was needed. As she cast the critical vote in the 218–216 cliffhanger (in which she fulfilled her promise to the president), she did what she thought was in the best long-term interests of her constituents and the nation, even though it meant voting against their wishes, which led to her defeat in the next election. More recently, bipartisan majorities in the House and Senate voted for the hugely unpopular Troubled Asset Relief Program (TARP, or as its critics called it, "the Wall Street bailout") because President Bush and congressional leaders convinced them it was necessary to prevent a complete economic meltdown.

descriptive representation When a member of Congress shares the characteristics (such as gender, race, religion, or ethnicity) of his or her constituents.

substantive representation When a member of Congress represents constituents' interests and policy concerns.

trustee A member of Congress who represents constituents' interests while also taking into account national, collective, and moral concerns that sometimes cause the member to vote against the preference of a majority of constituents.

delegate A member of Congress who loyally represents constituents' direct interests.

FIGURE » 11.1

WOMEN AND MINORITIES IN CONGRESS, 1933–2015

Although Congress still does not have gender parity, there have been substantial gains in recent years (with the exception of 2011, when the number of women in the House dropped for the first time in 30 years). How could having more women in Congress affect legislation and policy decisions? Hispanics now make up the largest ethnic minority in the United States, yet they still lag behind African Americans in terms of representation in the House. What do you think explains this difference? How might it affect policy?

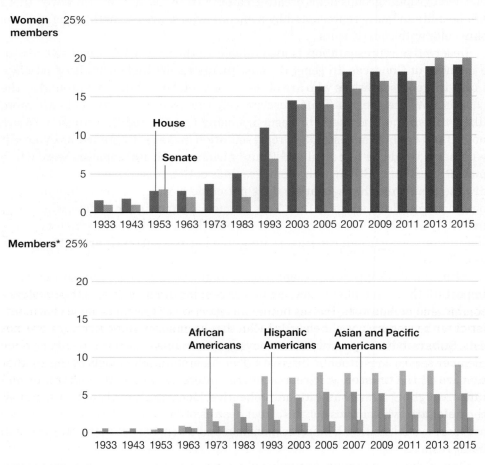

* Numbers refer to both the House and Senate.

SOURCES: Jennifer E. Manning and Ida A. Brudnick, "Women in the United States Congress 1917–2014: Biographical and Committee Assignment Information, and Listings by State and Congress," Congressional Research Service Report RL30261, February 18, 2014, www.senate .gov/CRSReports/crs-publish.cfm?pid='0E%2C*PLS%3D%22%40%20%20%0A (accessed 4/23/14); Compiled from Jennifer E. Manning and Colleen J. Shogan, "African American Members of the United States Congress: 1870–2012," Congressional Research Service Report RL30378, November 26, 2012; Government Printing Office, *Hispanic Americans in Congress, 1822–1995*, www.loc.gov/rr/hispanic/congress/chron.html; Lorraine H. Tong, "Asian Pacific Americans in the United States Congress," Congressional Research Service Report, June 12, 2013; and Jennifer E. Manning, "Membership of the 113th Congress: A Profile," Congressional Research Service Report R42964, March 14, 2014 (accessed 4/23/14). Data from the 2014 elections from various sources.

politico A member of Congress who acts as a delegate on issues that constituents care about (such as immigration reform) and as a trustee on more-complex or less-salient issues (such as some foreign policy or regulatory matters).

In contrast, a delegate does not have to worry about angering voters because he or she simply does what voters want. Examples are so numerous it is pointless to single out one member for attention: when it comes to tax cuts, agricultural subsidies, increases in Medicare payments, or new highway projects, hundreds of representatives act as delegates for their districts' interests.

Truth be told, nearly all members act like trustees in some circumstances and like delegates in others. The third model of representation is the **politico**, who is more likely to act as a delegate on issues that are highly salient to his or her

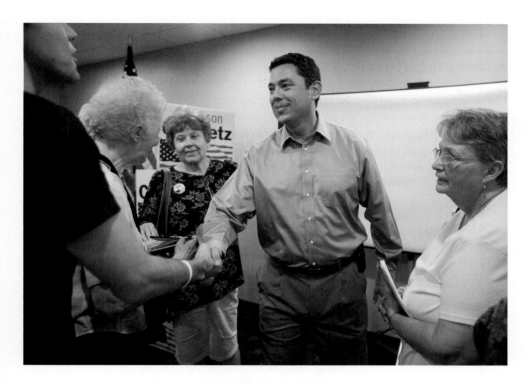

constituency (such as immigration reform), but as a trustee on less salient or very complex issues (such as some foreign policies). Therefore, the crucial component of representation is the nature of the constituency and how the member of Congress attempts to balance and represent constituents' conflicting needs and desires.

THE ROLE OF THE CONSTITUENCY Our characterization of the representative–constituency relationship raises numerous questions. How much do voters monitor their representatives' behavior? Can representation work if voters are not paying attention? The most demanding theory of representation, known as policy responsiveness, requires that voters express their basic policy preferences, that representatives then respond to those preferences, and that voters monitor and assess the politicians' behavior. Yet, those conditions rarely play out because most constituents do not closely follow congressional politics.

Despite this lack of attention, representational links remain strong through indirect mechanisms. Members of Congress behave as if voters were paying attention, even when constituents are inattentive. Incumbents know that at election time, challengers may raise issues that become salient after the public thinks about them, so they try to deter challengers by anticipating what the constituents would want *if they were fully informed*.[8] For example, the public didn't know much about NSA surveillance of phone records until June 2013, when Edward Snowden leaked confidential NSA documents to the media, and it became an issue in the 2014 midterm elections. Savvy incumbents would have tried to preempt vulnerability on that issue *before* a strong challenger raised the issue in a campaign by staking out a position consistent with what the voters would want once they knew more about the issue. Richard Fenno, one of the leading congressional scholars of the twentieth century, points out that some segments of the constituency are more attentive and more important for a member's reelection than others (see Figure 11.2).[9]

Another way to examine the representative–constituency relationship is to look at differences across districts. How do districts vary? First, they differ in size: Senate "districts" (that is, states) vary in terms of area and population. House

FIGURE » 11.2

FENNO'S CONCENTRIC CIRCLES

The concentric circles of a congressional constituency illustrate the various parts of a district that a member represents: personal (advisers, friends, and family), primary (strongest supporters), reelection (those who vote for the member), and geographic (the entire district). Can you think of an issue on which a House member would be more responsive to her reelection constituency than to her geographic constituency?

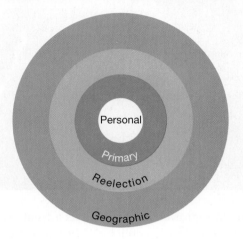

SOURCE: Based on Richard F. Fenno, *Home Style: House Members in Their Districts* (Boston: Little, Brown, 1978).

districts all have about 730,000 people, but they vary tremendously in geographic size. Districts also differ in terms of who lives there and what they want from government. Some districts are located in poor city neighborhoods, where voters' concerns are economic development, crime control, antipoverty programs, and looser immigration regulations. Some are wealthy and urban, where citizens are more supportive of foreign aid and higher taxes. Some are suburban, where funding for education and transportation are critical. Some are conservative and rural, where agricultural policies, gun rights, and support for tax cuts dominate. Districts vary from the religious to the secular, from domination by one industry to a diversified corporate base to no industry at all. Some consider government a force for good, while others argue that government should get off people's backs. And some districts are a mixture of all these things.

Because districts are so multifaceted, the legislators they elect differ from one another as well. Regardless of the office, most voters want to elect someone whose policy positions are close to theirs. As a result, legislators tend to reflect the central tendencies of their districts. At one level, electing a legislature that "thinks like America" sounds good: if legislators act and think like their districts, then the legislature will contain a good mixture of the interests representing the country or state. But finding an acceptable compromise is not easy. We elect legislators to get things done, but they may be unable to agree on anything because their disagreements are too fundamental to bridge. Consider abortion rights. The country is sharply divided on this issue, as are the House, the Senate, and most state legislatures. The fact that legislators have not come to a decision on this issue is no surprise: just as citizens disagree, so do their elected representatives.

FIGURE » 11.3

THE JOB OF A MEMBER OF CONGRESS

The members of Congress are often criticized for being out of touch with their constituents. Based on this recent *USA Today* poll,* Americans seem to clearly want their congressional members to vote in line with their constituents' views, to work across party lines, and to spend more time in the district rather than Washington, D.C. But what happens if these goals conflict: What if the member represents a very partisan district where the majority does not want her to work with the other party? Also, is there no room for a trustee who follows her conscience and sticks to her principles?

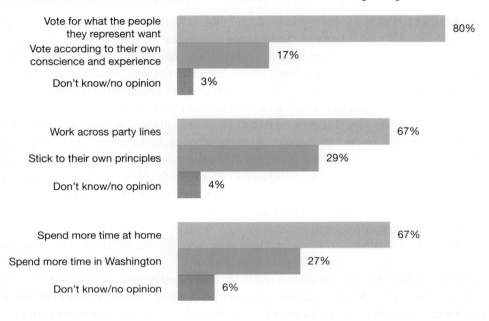

Vote for what the people they represent want — 80%
Vote according to their own conscience and experience — 17%
Don't know/no opinion — 3%

Work across party lines — 67%
Stick to their own principles — 29%
Don't know/no opinion — 4%

Spend more time at home — 67%
Spend more time in Washington — 27%
Don't know/no opinion — 6%

* Poll taken March 3–6, 2014.
SOURCE: *USA Today,* www.usatoday.com/story/news/politics/2014/03/23/congress-divided-poll/6792585/ (accessed 4/11/14).

Despite the vast differences between congressional constituencies, voters want many of the same things: a healthy economy, a safe country (in terms of national defense and local crime), good schools, and effective health care. Figure 11.3 reports responses to a survey about how citizens feel that legislators should do their jobs. The survey showed strong support for our recurring theme concerning tensions between being a delegate and a trustee. Citizens clearly want their elected officials to do **casework** for the district—that is, helping their constituents to solve bureaucratic problems or specific concerns related to government. But respondents showed little interest in having the representatives "spend more time in Washington" and would rather have them spend more time at home. Thus, responsibilities for national interests may be more difficult for members of Congress to explain to their constituents.

casework Assistance provided by members of Congress to their constituents in solving problems with the federal bureaucracy or addressing other specific concerns.

THE ELECTORAL CONNECTION

Members' relationship to their constituents also must be understood within the context of their desire to be reelected. Political scientist David Mayhew argues in

Congress: The Electoral Connection that reelection must come first.[10] Members certainly hold multiple goals, including making good policy, but if they cannot maintain their seats, then they cannot attain other goals in office.

After assuming that reelection is central, Mayhew asks this question: "Members of Congress may be electorally motivated, but are they in a position to do anything about it?"[11] Although individual members of Congress cannot do much to alter national economic or political forces, they can control their own activities in the House or Senate. The importance of the **electoral connection** in explaining the behavior of members of Congress seems especially clear for marginal incumbents who are constantly trying to shore up their electoral base. But for those from safe districts, why should they worry?

electoral connection The idea that congressional behavior is centrally motivated by members' desire for reelection.

INCUMBENTS WORK TOWARD REELECTION Objectively, it looks as though about 90 percent of House members (and a large proportion of senators) are absolutely safe, but incumbents realize that this security is not guaranteed. Even in elections with relatively low turnover, many incumbents are "running scared"; in every election, a few supposedly safe incumbents are unexpectedly defeated, and members tend to think that it could happen to them the next time around. Mayhew warns, "When we say 'Congressman Smith is unbeatable,' we do not mean that there is nothing he could do that would lose him his seat." As we noted in Chapter 9, this actually means, "Congressman Smith is unbeatable as long as he continues to do the things that he is doing."[12] Members recognize that becoming inattentive to their district, being on the wrong side of a key string of votes, or failing to bring home the district's share of pork could cost them their seats. A potential challenger is always waiting in the wings.

Mayhew outlines three ways that members promote their chances for reelection: through advertising, credit claiming, and position taking. Each approach shapes the way members relate to their constituents. Advertising in this context refers to appeals or appearances without issue content that get the member's name in front of the public in a favorable way. Advertising includes activities associated with "working the district," such as attending town meetings; appearing in a parade; going to a local Rotary Club lunch; or sending letters of congratulation for graduations, birthdays, or anniversaries. Members of Congress also spend a fair amount of time meeting with their constituents in Washington, D.C., including seeing school groups, tourists, and interest groups from their districts.

With credit claiming, the member of Congress takes credit for something of value to the voter—most commonly, pork-barrel policies targeted to benefit specific constituents or the district as a whole. The goods must be specific and small enough in scale that the member of Congress may believably claim credit. In other words, it is far less credible to take credit for a national drop in violent crime or an increase in SAT scores than for the renovations at a local veterans' hospital or a highway improvement grant. The other main source of credit claiming is casework for individual constituents who request help with tasks such as tracking down a lost Social Security check or expediting the processing of a passport. This activity, like advertising, has both district-based and Washington-based components.

Position taking refers to any public statement—such as a roll call vote, speech, editorial, or position paper—about a topic of interest to constituents or interest groups. This may be the toughest aspect of a member's job because, on many issues, the member is likely to alienate a certain segment of the population no matter what position she takes. Members try to appeal to specific audiences within their district. For example, while speaking to the Veterans of Foreign Wars, a member might emphasize his support for a particular new weapons program, but in a meeting with college students, he might highlight his opposition to the National Security Agency's collection of millions of phone records.

The focus on reelection has some costs. We'll identify five common ones here. (1) There is a perception that Congress has granted itself too many special privileges aimed at securing reelection (such as funding for large staffs and sending mail at no cost). (2) Evidence suggests that some voters question the value of pork-barrel spending, even when it is targeted to their district.[13] (3) Members' desire to please means that Congress has a difficult time refusing any group's demands, which may lead to passage of contradictory policies. (4) Given that most members are experts at getting reelected, they achieve a certain level of independence from the party leadership—that is, they do not depend on party leaders for their reelection. This fact contributes to the fragmentation of Congress and creates difficulties for congressional leaders as they attempt to shepherd policies through the legislative maze. (5) Time spent actively campaigning takes time away from the responsibilities of enacting laws and overseeing their implementation.

NATIONAL FORCES IN CONGRESSIONAL ELECTIONS There is also another consequence of the electoral connection. Because congressional politics tends to be local, voters generally are not strongly influenced by the president or the national parties. Because most incumbents can insulate themselves from national forces, it is more difficult to hold the government accountable. For example, in the 2014 midterms, 63 percent of the people believed the nation was "on the wrong track." Yet, 95 percent of House incumbents won reelection.

Many House and Senate candidates distance themselves from the national party. For example, in the 2010 West Virginia Senate race, Democratic candidate Joe Manchin made his opposition to the Democratic Party's energy policy very clear with an ad in which he shot a mock version of the bill with a rifle. However, there are nationalized "wave" elections in which national issues can overwhelm incumbents' attempts to insulate themselves. In 2006, many House Republicans tried to distance themselves from President Bush and the unpopular war in Iraq, but more than 20 Republicans were defeated, and Democrats regained control of the House. In the 2010 midterms, the same thing happened to moderate Democrats who were ousted by voters who believed the government had gone too far in its response to the recession and health care. These national forces led the Democrats to lose 63 House seats (and 6 Senate seats), with the result that the Republicans regained control of the House.

National forces in congressional elections also may be evident in presidential years. In 2008, Republicans faced a backlash against Bush, whose approval ratings had hit record lows. Republican members of Congress avoided being seen with him, and Democrats highlighted their opponents' earlier support for the president. In 2012, the congressional elections ratified the status quo; despite Obama's solid win, the Republicans retained control of the House and the Democrats increased their majority in the Senate only slightly. Overall, the localized nature of congressional elections and the incumbency advantage promote congressional stability in the face of presidential change. This has

BECAUSE OF THE MAKEUP OF THEIR state or district, candidates sometimes have to distance themselves from their party in order to win reelection. For example, Mary Landrieu (D-LA) criticized President Obama for his lack of support for the building of the Keystone Pipeline.

profound implications for governance because they increase the likelihood that different parties will control the presidency and Congress. This kind of divided government complicates accountability because the president and Congress have become adept at blaming each other when things go wrong.

REDISTRICTING

To understand the context of legislative constituencies, we also must consider their physical boundaries. District boundaries determine who is eligible to vote in any given congressional race, and these boundaries are redrawn every 10 years, after each national census. **Redistricting** is the task of state legislatures. Its official purpose is to ensure that districts are roughly equal in population, which in turn ensures that every vote counts equally in determining the composition of the legislature.

District populations vary over time as people move from state to state or from one part of a state to another. At the national level, states gain or lose legislative seats after each census through **apportionment**, which is the process of dividing the fixed number of House seats (435) among the states based on increases and decreases in state populations. Thus, states growing the fastest gain seats, and states that are not growing as fast or that are losing population lose seats. The one legislature in America that is not redistricted is the U.S. Senate, which has two legislators elected per state, thus giving voters in small states more influence in the Senate than voters in large states.

REDISTRICTING PRINCIPLES In theory, redistricting proceeds from a set of principles that define what districts should look like. One criterion is that districts should be roughly equal in population. They should also capture "communities of interest," grouping like-minded voters into the same district. There are also technical criteria, including compactness (districts should not have extremely bizarre shapes) and contiguity (one part of a district cannot be completely separated from the rest of the district). Mapmakers also try to respect traditional natural boundaries, avoid splitting municipalities, preserve existing districts, and avoid diluting the voting power of racial minorities.

PARTISAN REDISTRICTING Although the principles above are important, they are not the driving force in the redistricting process. Suppose a Democrat holds a state assembly seat from an urban district populated mainly by citizens with strong Democratic Party ties. After a census, the Republican-dominated state legislature develops a new plan that extends the representative's district into the suburbs, claiming that the change counteracts population declines within the city by adding suburban voters. However, these suburban voters will likely be Republicans, increasing the chance that the Democrat will face strong opposition in future elections and maybe lose her seat. Such changes have an important impact on voters as well. Voters who are "shifted" to a new district by a change in boundaries may be unable to vote for the incumbent they have supported for years, and may instead get a representative who doesn't share their views.

In congressional redistricting, a reduction in the number of seats allocated to a state can lead to districting plans that put two incumbents in the same district, forcing them to run against each other. Incumbents from one party use these

redistricting Redrawing the geographic boundaries of legislative districts. This happens every 10 years to ensure that districts remain roughly equal in population.

apportionment The process of assigning the 435 seats in the House to the states based on increases or decreases in state population.

TYPES OF GERRYMANDERS

▶ **Partisan gerrymanders:** Elected officials from one party draw district lines that benefit candidates from their party and hurt candidates from other parties. This usually occurs when one party has majorities in both houses of the state legislature and occupies the governorship, and can therefore enact redistricting legislation without input from the minority party.

▶ **Incumbent gerrymanders:** Lines are drawn to benefit the current group of incumbents. This usually occurs when control of state government is divided between parties and support from both parties is required to enact a districting plan, or when plans must be approved by judges or bipartisan panels.

▶ **Racial gerrymanders:** Redistricting is used to help or hurt the chances of minority legislative candidates. The Voting Rights Act (VRA) of 1965 mandated that districting plans for many parts of the South be approved by the U.S. Department of Justice or a Washington, D.C., district court. Subsequent interpretations of the 1982 VRA amendments and Supreme Court decisions led to the creation of districts in which racial minorities are in the majority. The original aim of these majority-minority districts was to raise the percentage of African-American and Latino elected officials. However, Republicans in some southern states have used this requirement to enact plans that elect minorities (who tend to be Democrats) in some districts but favor Republicans in adjoining districts. In 2013, the Supreme Court struck down the part of the Voting Rights Act that identified the "covered states"—that is, the states for which preapproval of redistricting plans had been required by the original act in 1965.

▶ **Candidate gerrymanders:** District plans are devised that favor certain individuals, particularly state legislators planning to run for the U.S. House. For example, a Republican state legislator would want to construct a congressional district with a high percentage of Republican voters and as many of her current constituents as possible.

opportunities to defeat incumbents from the other party. Both parties use this technique and other tools of creative cartography to gain partisan advantage. In the 2012 redistricting cycle, Illinois drew a very partisan map in favor of Democrats, including one district in Chicago that looks like a pair of earmuffs, while Pennsylvania drew a "group of Rorschach-inkblot districts" that turned a state that normally tilts Democratic to one in which 12 of 18 districts lean Republican.[14] The most dramatic recent example of redistricting for partisan purposes was in Texas. Deviating from the standard practice of redrawing district lines only once every decade, Republicans decided to change the district boundaries that had been in effect for only one election. Democratic legislators were outraged by the partisan power grab and fled the state (they hid out in Oklahoma) to prevent the special session of the legislature from convening. Eventually Republicans were able to implement their plan and gain five House seats in the 2004 elections. The U.S. Supreme Court upheld the Texas plan, saying that even when partisan advantage is the only motivation for redistricting, this does not make the resulting plan unconstitutional.[15]

These attempts to use the redistricting process for political advantage are called **gerrymandering**. The term is named after Elbridge Gerry, a Massachusetts House member and governor, vice president under James Madison, and author of one of the original partisan redistricting plans (including a district with a thin, winding shape resembling a salamander). In addition to the partisan gerrymanders discussed here, see Nuts & Bolts 11.1 for descriptions of several other types.

gerrymandering Attempting to use the process of redrawing district boundaries to benefit a political party, protect incumbents, or change the proportion of minority voters in a district.

FIGURE » 11.4

NORTH CAROLINA REDISTRICTING, 1992

This set of House districts was the subject of the landmark Supreme Court ruling *Shaw v. Reno* (1993), in which the Court said that "appearances matter" when drawing district lines. Do you agree? Should other factors such as race, party, and competitiveness play a greater role than district shape?

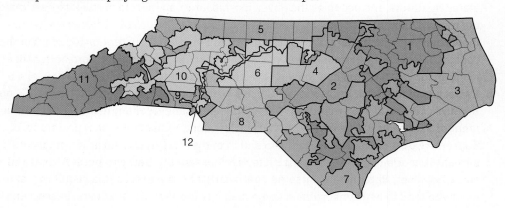

SOURCE: North Carolina General Assembly, 1992 Congressional Base Plan No. 10, http://ncga.state.nc.us/gis/download/referenced -ocs/2011/nc%20congressional%20districts%20-%20historical%20plans%20-%201941-1992.pdf (accessed 10/26/12).

RACIAL REDISTRICTING Redistricting may yield boundaries that look highly unusual. During the 1992 redistricting in North Carolina, the Justice Department told state legislators that they needed to create two districts with majority populations of minority voters (called majority-minority districts). Figure 11.4 shows the plan they enacted, in which the district boundaries look like a pattern of spider webs and ink blots. Moreover, one of the districts had parts that ended up being only as wide as interstate I-85, following the highway off an exit ramp, over a bridge, and down the entrance ramp on the other side. This move prevented the I-85 district from bisecting the district it was traveling through, which would have violated the state law requiring contiguous districts.

The North Carolina example shows how convoluted redistricting plans can become. Part of the complexity is due to the availability of census databases that allow line-drawers to divide voters as closely as they want, moving neighborhood by neighborhood, even house by house. Why bother with this level of detail? Because redistricting influences who gets elected; it is active politicking in its most fundamental form. The North Carolina plan was ultimately declared unconstitutional by the U.S. Supreme Court—a ruling that opened the door for dozens of lawsuits about racial redistricting (see discussion in Chapter 5 of the Voting Rights Act of 1965 and the more-recent Supreme Court rulings on racial redistricting, especially the 2013 case in which the Court struck down the part of the law that had identified states that needed to have their redistricting plans preapproved by the Justice Department[16]). The current legal standard is that race cannot be the predominant factor in drawing congressional district lines, but it can be one of the factors. Nonetheless, there is still plenty of room to create districts that will be composed of voters who will vote in ways that will have profound political consequences. The obvious political implications of redistricting often lead to demands that district plans be prepared or approved by nonpartisan committees or by panels of judges who are theoretically immune from political pressure. Such a process, as in Iowa, often produces more competitive districts.

CONGRESS'S IMAGE PROBLEM

Despite members' strong links to their constituents, efforts to secure reelection, and districts that are designed in their favor, public approval of Congress is generally very low. Bashing Congress has long been a favorite national pastime. Mark Twain said, "It could probably be shown by facts and figures that there is no distinctly native criminal class except Congress." He also said, "Assume you are a fool. Now assume you are a member of Congress . . . but I repeat myself."

Many Americans seem to agree with Twain. Approval of Congress rarely tops 50 percent (one exception was following the terrorist attacks of September 11, 2001). Through most of 2014, approval for Congress hovered in the low teens and was only 12 percent before Election Day in November. And the public's cynical view of Congress runs deep. Eighty-five percent of Americans said that Congress is "more interested in serving special interest groups" than "the people they represent" (8 percent held the more positive view).[17]

A poll conducted by ABC News found that 77 percent of Americans thought that Republicans in Congress were "more interested in doing what was best for themselves politically" and only 20 percent thought that Republicans were more interested in "what was best for the country." The poll found that 63 percent of Americans believed that Democrats were self-interested compared with 30 percent who thought they were more publicly minded.[18] Another poll found that members of Congress landed fifth from the bottom in a ranking of 26 professions in terms of perceived honesty and ethical standards.[19] A more whimsical poll by Public Policy Polling asked respondents questions like, "What do you have a higher opinion of, Congress or root canals?" Root canals won handily, 56 to 32 percent. Congress was also less popular than head lice, traffic jams, cockroaches, and Donald Trump, but narrowly beat out Lindsay Lohan, and had a comfortable margin over the Ebola virus, the Kardashians, and meth labs.[20]

Why does Congress have such an image problem? Some of the abuse heaped on Congress is self-inflicted. Although political corruption for personal gain is rare in Congress (only four members have been indicted on bribery charges since 1981), there are periodic scandals such as the "check bouncing" incident involving members' accounts at the House bank and the misuse of House post office funds in the early 1990s.[21] Several members of Congress, Democrats and Republicans alike, were implicated in the scandal surrounding lobbyist Jack Abramoff (see Chapter 10). Mark Foley (R-FL) brought more shame on the House when his steamy e-mails to 16-year-old House pages were revealed. Foley quickly resigned when his inappropriate behavior was exposed. Other sex scandals involved Senator Larry Craig (R-ID), who pleaded guilty to a "disorderly conduct" charge for an apparent attempt to solicit sex in a men's bathroom in the Minneapolis airport; and Representative Anthony Weiner (D-NY), who resigned after sending lewd pictures of himself to women on Twitter. The two most serious recent cases involved bribery and fraud. In one, Representative William Jefferson (D-LA) was found guilty of soliciting bribes, money laundering, and using his office as a racketeering enterprise. Jefferson was infamous for being caught with

UNFORTUNATELY, MEMBERS OF CONGRESS do include some of the "criminal class" noted by Mark Twain. Former representatives Randy "Duke" Cunningham (R-CA), shown with his wife Nancy, and William Jefferson (D-LA) were both indicted and sent to federal prison on charges of corruption. Cunningham has since been released, but Jefferson is still serving time. The photo on the right shows cash found in Jefferson's freezer.

$90,000 in marked bills hidden in his freezer that the FBI said were to be used to bribe Nigerian officials. In the other, Michael Grimm (R-NY) was indicted on 20 counts of tax evasion, fraud, and perjury related to the business he ran before he was elected (this case went to trial in December 2014).[22] Yet, despite such scandals, most members of Congress are dedicated public servants who work hard for their constituents.

MEDIA INFLUENCES Although politicians traditionally blame the media for their poor standing in the polls, in the case of Congress there is some basis for the complaints. One study examined stories on Congress in various national newspapers and magazines over a 46-year period and concluded that coverage of Congress has always been somewhat superficial and negative: "press coverage of Congress focuses on scandal, partisan rivalry, and interbranch conflict rather than the more complex subjects such as policy, process, and institutional concerns."[23]

From this perspective, the professional context of journalism, with its short news cycle and the need to produce a salable product, creates pressure for superficial coverage that perpetuates Congress's image problem. Burdett Loomis, a congressional scholar, bets his students every year that they cannot find a post-1970 political cartoon that depicts Congress in an unambiguously positive light. In more than 10 years, no student has been able to collect on the bet.[24] However, a recent study using more than 8,000 newspaper stories on members of Congress over a two-year period found that 70 percent of news stories were neutral, and of the 30 percent that had some spin, positive stories outnumbered negative stories five to one. Letters to the editor and editorials or opinion pieces were evenly balanced between negative and positive viewpoints.[25]

THE RESPONSIBILITY–RESPONSIVENESS DILEMMA Congress's image problem isn't simply a matter of negative media coverage or a cynical public. It is rooted in the basic representational conflicts that arise from Congress's dual roles: responsibility for national policy making and responsiveness to local constituencies.[26] This duality may make members of Congress appear to be simultaneously small-minded seekers of meaningless symbolic legislation and great leaders who debate important issues. Indeed, the range of issues that Congress must address is vast, from taxes and health care reform to overseeing the classification of black-eyed peas, from authorizing the war with Afghanistan and expanding free trade to declaring a National Cholesterol

Education Month. Part of the national frustration with Congress arises because we want our representatives to be responsible *and* responsive; we want them to be great national leaders *and* to take care of our local and, at times, personal concerns.

Difficult choices have to be made between being responsive or responsible. Rather than understanding these issues as being inherent in the legislative process, we often accuse members of **gridlock** and partisan bickering when our conflicting demands are not met. For example, public opinion polls routinely show that the public wants lower taxes; more spending in education, the environment, and health care; and balanced budgets. But those three things cannot happen simultaneously. We often expect the impossible from Congress and then are frustrated when it doesn't happen.

The responsibility–responsiveness dilemma brings us back to the puzzle we posed at the beginning of this section: Why is there a persistent 30 to 40 percent gap between approval ratings for individual members and for the institution? As Richard Fenno put it, "If Congress is the 'broken branch,' how come we love our congressman so much?"[27] The answer may simply be that members of Congress tend to respond more to their constituents' demands than to solving national problems. And when Congress becomes embroiled in debates about constituencies' conflicting demands, the institution may appear ineffectual. But as long as members keep the "folks back home" happy, their individual popularity will remain high. The next section describes how members use this and other techniques to cultivate an incumbency advantage.

MEMBERS OF CONGRESS TRY TO KEEP the "folks back home" happy with projects like this groundbreaking ceremony in New Jersey for an $8.7 billion tunnel. (The project was later canceled.)

gridlock An inability to enact legislation because of partisan conflict within Congress or between Congress and the president.

THE INCUMBENCY ADVANTAGE AND ITS SOURCES

ANALYZE THE FACTORS THAT HELP MEMBERS OF CONGRESS GET REELECTED

The desire to be reelected influences House members' and senators' behavior both in their districts and in Congress. Consider the early career of Senator Tammy Baldwin (D-WI), who served as the representative of Wisconsin's 2nd congressional district from 1999 to 2013. Initially elected in 1998, she was Wisconsin's first female representative and the first openly gay person ever elected to a freshman term in Congress.[28] In her first two elections, she won with the overwhelming support of liberal voters in Madison, but she lost the surrounding rural areas and suburbs, narrowly winning districtwide. Baldwin recognized that she needed to shore up support outside Madison, and she spent time over the next several years meeting with constituents in the rural and suburban parts of her district. She also explored issues important to these voters, such as the dairy price-support program and the problem of chronic wasting disease in Wisconsin deer. Having built up her electoral base (and having benefited from favorable redistricting in 2002), she cruised to victories in her next two elections, winning nearly two-thirds of the vote. After winning reelection to the House four more times, she became the first lesbian elected to the Senate in 2012.

Members' success at pleasing constituents produces large election rewards. As Figure 11.5 shows, very few members are defeated in their reelection races. One way that political scientists have documented the growth of **incumbency advantage**

incumbency advantage The relative infrequency with which members of Congress are defeated in their attempts for reelection.

FIGURE » 11.5

HOUSE AND SENATE REELECTION RATES, 1948–2014

The whole House is up for reelection every two years, so the line showing the reelection of House members in a given election year represents the percentage of the entire House. Since senators are up for reelection every six years, only one-third of the members are seeking reelection every two years. The line for the Senate represents the percentage of those who won who were up for reelection in that election year.

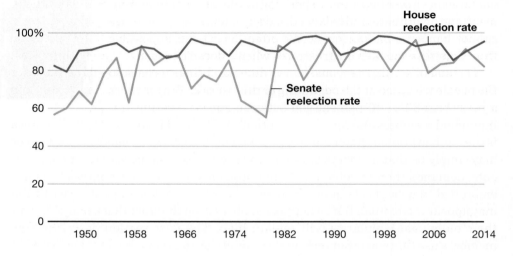

SOURCES: The 1948–2012 percentages were compiled from Norman J. Ornstein, Thomas E. Mann, Michael J. Malbin, and Andrew Rugg, "Vital Statistics on Congress," www.brookings.edu/vitalstats, pages 49–50 (accessed 4/18/14); 2014 percentages calculated from election results.

is to examine the electoral margins in House elections. If a member is elected with less than 55 percent of the vote, he or she is said to hold a marginal seat. Since the late 1960s, the number of marginal districts has been declining. Having fewer marginal districts does not necessarily translate into fewer incumbent defeats, but in the past two decades, incumbent reelection rates have been near record-high levels, with 95 to 98 percent of House incumbents winning in many years.[29]

In 2008, in an election that many called "transformational," 95 percent of House incumbents were reelected. Although the Democrats picked up some seats in the Senate, reelection remained the norm there as well. Even in the "tsunami" election of 2010, in which Republicans made the largest gains in the House since 1948, picking up 63 seats, 86 percent of incumbents were reelected. Why are incumbents so successful? Scholars have offered several reasons for this increase in incumbency advantage.

IN THE DISTRICT: HOME STYLE

One explanation for increasing incumbency advantage is rooted in the diversity of congressional districts and states. Members typically respond to the diversity in their districts by developing an appropriate home style: a way of relating to the district.[30] A home style shapes the way members allocate resources, the way incumbents present themselves to their district, and the way they explain their policy positions.

Given the variation among districts, members' home styles vary as well. In some rural districts it is important for representatives to have local roots, and voters expect extensive contact with members. Urban districts expect a different kind of style. They have a more mobile population, so it is not crucial to be home-grown. Voters expect less direct contact and place more emphasis on how members explain their policy positions. Incumbency advantage may be explained in part by the skill with which members have cultivated their individual home styles in the last two decades. Members are spending more time at home and less time in Washington than was true a generation ago. This familiarity with the voters has helped them remain in office.

Table 11.1 shows how one member, Senator Tammy Baldwin, spent her time in Washington and in her district as a House member. In general, a legislator's workday in the Capitol is split between committee meetings, briefings, staff meetings, meetings with constituents, and various dinners and fund-raisers with interest groups and other organizations, punctuated by dashes to the floor of the House or Senate to vote. Days in the district are spent meeting with constituents to explain what is happening in Washington and to listen to voters' concerns.

CAMPAIGN FUND-RAISING

Raising money is also key to staying in office. Incumbents need money to pay for campaign staff, travel, and advertising. It takes at least $1 million to make a credible challenge to an incumbent in most districts, and in many areas with expensive media markets the minimum price tag is $2 million or more. Few challengers can raise that much money. The gap between incumbent and challenger spending has grown dramatically in the past decade, and incumbents now spend about three times as much, on average, as challengers. Incumbents have far greater potential to raise vast sums of money, in part because political action committees (PACs) are unwilling to risk alienating an incumbent by donating to challengers. (For more on campaign finance, see Chapters 9 and 10.)

Money also functions as a deterrent to potential challengers. A sizable reelection fund signals that an incumbent knows how to raise money and will run a strong campaign. The aim is to convince would-be challengers that they have a slim chance of beating the incumbent—and to convince contributors and party organizations that there's no point in trying to find or support a challenger.

This last point is crucial in explaining incumbency advantage because it is nearly impossible to beat an incumbent with a weak challenger. Consider that only 10 to 15 percent of challengers in a typical election year have any previous elective experience; when such a high proportion of challengers are amateurs, it is not surprising that so many incumbents win.

CONSTITUENCY SERVICE

Another thing incumbents do to get reelected is "work their districts," taking every opportunity to meet with constituents, listen to their concerns, and perform casework (helping constituents interact with government programs or agencies). Most legislators travel around their districts or states with several staffers whose job is to talk to people who meet the incumbent and to write down contact information and what the incumbent has promised to do. High levels

TABLE » 11.1

TYPICAL WORK DAYS FOR A CONGRESSIONAL REPRESENTATIVE

Members of Congress are generally busy from morning until late at night, both in Washington, D.C., and in their districts, attending meetings and events. This is the actual schedule from Tammy Baldwin when she represented Wisconsin's 2nd congressional district in the House.

IN WASHINGTON, D.C.   (votes scheduled throughout the day)

9:15–9:45	Office time
9:45–10:00	Caucus, Democratic members, Subcommittee on Energy and Environment on markup legislation
10:00–12:00	Markup H.R. 3276, H.R. 3258, H.R. 2868, Subcommittee on Energy and Environment
11:30–11:45	Step outside markup to meet with constituents on specifics of health care reform legislation
12:00–12:15	Travel to Department of Justice
12:15–1:15	Lunch with Attorney General Eric Holder
1:30–1:45	Meet with health care CEO on specifics of health care reform legislation
2:00–3:00	Meet with members who support single-payer health care amendment
3:00–4:30	Markup H.R. 3792, Subcommittee on Health
4:30–5:30	Office time
5:30–6:00	Caucus, Democratic members, Energy and Commerce Committee on financial services bill
6:00–6:30	Meet with legislative staff
6:30–7:00	Meet with chief of staff
7:00–7:50	Office time
8:00–10:00	Dinner with chief of staff and political adviser

IN THE DISTRICT

7:00 ET–8:00 CT	Fly from Washington, D.C., to Madison, WI
8:15–10:30	Free time at home
10:30–10:40	Phone interview with area radio station on constituent survey, health care reform, and upcoming listening session
12:15–12:25	Travel to office
12:25–1:00	Office time, edit/sign correspondence
1:00–1:20	Travel to Madison West High School
1:30–1:55	Remarks at school plaza dedication ceremony
2:00–2:30	Travel to Stoughton, WI
2:45–5:00	Listening session (originally scheduled for one hour but continued until all present could speak)
5:00–5:40	Travel home
5:15–5:20	Phone interview with University of Wisconsin student radio station
6:15–6:45	Travel to Middleton, WI
7:00–8:00	Attend and give brief remarks at NAACP annual banquet
8:05–8:25	Travel home

NOTE: The authors would like to thank (then) Representative Tammy Baldwin and her press secretary, Jerilyn Goodman, for sharing this information. Ms. Goodman emphasized that there really isn't a "typical day" for a member but said that these two days illustrate the work load. Baldwin was elected to the U.S. Senate in 2012.

of constituency service may help explain why some incumbents have become electorally secure.

Members of Congress love doing constituency service because it is an easy way to make voters happy. If a member can help a constituent solve a problem, that person will be more likely to support the member in the future.[31] Many voters might give the incumbent some credit simply for being willing to listen. Therefore, most members devote a significant portion of their staff to constituency service, publish newsletters that tout their good deeds on behalf of constituents, and solicit citizens' requests for help through their newsletters and websites. Most House members have a "How can I help?" type of link on their home page that connects to information on government agencies, grants, internships, service academies, and visiting Washington, D.C.

CONGRESSMAN PAUL RYAN (R-WI) with his constituents at a "listening session" in Kenosha, Wisconsin.

Most House members work their districts to an extreme; they are said to be in the "Tuesday to Thursday Club," meaning they are in Washington only during the middle of the week, spending the rest of their time at home in their districts. These members go to diners and coffee shops on Saturday mornings to chat, spend the day at public events in their "Meet Your Representative" RV, then hit the bowling alleys at night to meet a few more people. One member has even joked that his wife has given up sending him out for groceries because he spends three hours talking with people while getting a loaf of bread.

This combination of factors gives incumbents substantial advantages over candidates who might run against them. By virtue of their position, they can help constituents who have problems with an agency or a program. They attract media attention because of their actions in office; small local newspapers will even reprint members' press releases verbatim because they do not have the resources to do their own reporting. Members can use the money and other resources associated with their position for casework and contact with voters (trips home to their district and the salaries of their staffers who do constituency service are taxpayer funded). And they use their official position as a platform for raising campaign cash. A contributor who donates as a way to gain access to the policy-making process will be inclined to give to someone already in office. Finally, most incumbents represent states or districts whose partisan balance (the number of likely supporters of their party versus the number likely to prefer the other party) is skewed in their favor—if it wasn't, they probably wouldn't have won the seat in the first place.

THE STRUCTURE OF CONGRESS

EXAMINE HOW PARTIES, THE COMMITTEE SYSTEM, AND STAFFERS ENABLE CONGRESS TO FUNCTION

As we have seen, the goal of getting reelected greatly influences the behavior of members of Congress. The reelection goal also has a strong influence on the way that Congress is structured, both formally (staff, the committee system, parties, and the leadership) and informally (norms). Despite the importance of the electoral connection, the goal of being reelected cannot explain everything about members' behavior and the congressional structure. This section examines some other explanations for the way Congress is set up: the policy motivations of members, the partisan basis for congressional institutions, and the informational advantages of the committee system.

INFORMAL STRUCTURES

Various norms provide an informal structure for the way Congress works. Universalism is a norm stating that when benefits are being divided up, they should be awarded to as many districts and states as possible. Thus, when it comes to handing out federal highway dollars or expenditures for the Pentagon's weapons programs, the benefits are broadly distributed across the entire country, which means that votes in support of these bills tend to be very lopsided. For example, the $662 billion 2012 defense appropriations bill contained some spending in every part of the country and passed by an 86–13 vote in the Senate and a 286–136 margin in the House.[32]

logrolling A form of reciprocity in which members of Congress support bills that they otherwise might not vote for in exchange for other members' votes on bills that are very important to them.

Another norm, reciprocity or **logrolling**, reinforces universalism with the idea that "if you scratch my back, I'll scratch yours." This norm leads members of Congress to support bills that they otherwise might not vote for in exchange for other members' votes on bills that are very important to them. For example, a House member from a dairy state might vote for tobacco price supports even if his state had no tobacco farmers, and in return he would expect a member from the tobacco state to vote for the dairy-price support bill. This norm can produce wasteful pork-barrel spending. For example, in the 2011 budget, a $1.1 trillion omnibus appropriations bill contained more than 6,488 **earmarks** worth $8.3 billion, so nearly everyone gained something by passing it. The 2014 omnibus appropriations bill did not include any traditional earmarks, following the ban on formal earmarks in both the House and Senate in 2011, but there were still billions of dollars in targeted spending as members of Congress found ways to secure funding for their district or state.[33] The You Decide feature describes some of the debates in Congress and among political commentators about the merits of this type of spending.[34]

earmarks Federally funded local projects attached to bills passed through Congress.

The norm of specialization is also important, both for the efficient operation of Congress and for members' reelection. By specializing and becoming expert on a given issue, members provide valuable information to the institution as a whole and also create a basis for credit claiming. This norm is stronger in the House, where members often develop a few areas of expertise, whereas senators tend to be policy generalists. For example, Representative John Lewis (D-GA) has dedicated much of his decades-long House career to the issue of civil rights, while Senator John McCain (R-AZ) has had his hand in a variety of issues, including campaign finance and lobbying reform, tax policy, telecommunications and aviation issues, national defense, foreign policy, and immigration policy.

seniority The informal congressional norm of choosing the member who has served the longest on a particular committee to be the committee chair.

The **seniority** norm also serves individual and institutional purposes. This norm holds that the member with the longest service on a committee will chair the committee. Although there have been numerous violations of the norm in the past 30 years, whereby the most senior member has been passed over for someone whom the party leaders favored instead, the norm benefits the institution by ensuring orderly succession in committee leadership.[35] The norm also benefits members by providing a tangible reason that voters should return them to Congress year after year. Many members of Congress make this point when campaigning, and the issue is more than just posturing. Committee chairs *are* better able to "bring home the bacon" than a junior member who is still learning the ropes. For example, Don Young, the former Transportation Committee chair in the House, was able to secure funding for the infamous "bridge to nowhere," a $435 million project to connect Ketchikan, Alaska, with a barely inhabited island. (The project was canceled after it became a symbol of pork-barrel spending.)

THE POLITICS OF PORK

The infamous "bridge to nowhere" in Ketchikan, Alaska, mentioned earlier in this chapter, is one of the most publicized recent examples of wasteful pork-barrel spending, but it is unusual only in its scale rather than its kind. It is also unusual because the outcry over the bridge prompted Alaska to pull the plug on the project, whereas most pork-barrel spending survives. Pork traditionally took the form of earmarked funding for a specific project that is not subject to standard, neutral spending formulas or a competitive process. However, since 2011, the House and Senate have banned formal earmarks so members have created new ways to make sure that the benefits continue to flow to their constituents.

One common tactic previously used by legislators to win approval for pork was to insert earmarks into emergency spending bills that were expected to pass, such as disaster relief for flood and hurricane victims, spending for national security after the September 11 attacks, or funding for the wars in Iraq and Afghanistan. For example, the $636.3 billion defense appropriations bill in 2010 included $128.3 billion for the wars in Iraq and Afghanistan and was also stuffed with 1,719 earmarks worth $7.6 billion.[a] Even without specific earmarks, House members and senators were still claiming credit for plenty of pork in the 2014 omnibus spending bill: $404 million for a national Bio- and Agro-Defense facility in Kansas, $310 million for six Coast Guard Fast Response Cutters to be built at Bollinger Shipyards in Louisiana, and $90 million for Abrams tanks to be built in Ohio.[b] As one reporter explained, "[T]he truth is that earmarks haven't really vanished; they've merely changed shape. . . . Call it the era of vegan pork."[c] Members may simply be taking credit for something that was going to pass anyway or they may secure the project through "letter-marking"—writing a letter to the relevant agency to ask for the funding to be directed to their district. This type of "asking nicely" for pork (sometimes referred to as "stealth pork") can be effective because agencies know that their funding depends on keeping members of Congress happy.

Some broader definitions of pork include any benefit targeted to a particular political constituency (typically an important business in a member's district), even if the benefit is part of a stand-alone bill. Examples of this type of targeted federal largesse include the bill that provided federal support to the airlines after the September 11 attacks, which sailed through Congress without much debate, and the lucrative contracts to rebuild Iraq that were awarded to politically well-connected businesses.

Pork has plenty of critics. Citizens Against Government Waste, one of the most outspoken groups to tackle pork-barrel spending, compiles each year's federal pork-barrel projects into their annual *Congressional Pig Book* to draw attention to pork. The ban on earmarks has helped a great

President Obama signs the omnibus spending bill in Washington, D.C., in January 2014. This bill funds a broad range of military and discretionary programs.

deal, but committee and informal earmarks are still pervasive. The arguments against pork are especially urgent during a time of massive budget deficits. According to this view, the national interest in a balanced budget should take priority over localized projects.

Nonetheless, some argue that pork is the "glue of legislating," because these small side payments secure the passage of larger bills. If it takes a little pork for the home district or state in order to get important legislation through Congress, so be it. The motives of budget reform groups that call for greater fiscal discipline in Congress may also be questioned, since many of these groups oppose government spending in general—not just on pork. In some cases, policies they identify as pork have significant national implications: military readiness, road improvements to support economic infrastructure, or the development of new agricultural and food products. National interests can be served, in other words, by allowing local interests to take a dip into the pork barrel. Put another way, "pork is in the eye of the beholder," or one person's pork is another person's essential spending. Finally, defenders of pork point out that even according to the critics' own definition, pork spending constitutes about one-half of 1 percent of the total federal budget.

CRITICAL THINKING QUESTIONS

1. If you were a member of Congress, would you work hard to deliver pork to your district or work to eliminate as much pork as you could from the budget?

2. Why is it so difficult to eliminate pork even in the face of massive budget deficits?

FORMAL STRUCTURES

Formal structures also shape members' behavior in Congress. Political parties, party leadership, the committee system, and staff provide the context within which members of Congress make policy and represent their constituents.

PARTIES AND PARTY LEADERS Political parties are important for allocating power in Congress. Party leaders are always elected on straight party-line votes, with the majority party determining committee leadership, the division of seats on committees, and the allocation of committee resources. Parties in Congress also become more important when opposing parties control the two chambers. This was the case between 1981 and 1986, when Republicans controlled the Senate and Democrats controlled the House, and in part of 2001 and 2002 and 2011–2014 when the opposite was true.

A leading theory of congressional organization points to the importance of parties in solving collective action problems in Congress. Without parties, the legislative process would be much more fractured and decentralized because members would be autonomous agents in battle with each other. Parties provide a team framework that allows members to work together for broadly beneficial goals. Just think how difficult it would be for a member of Congress to get a bill passed if she had to build a coalition from scratch every time. Instead, parties provide a solid base from which coalition building may begin. As discussed in Chapter 8, political parties provide brand-name recognition for members.

The top party leader in the House—and the only House leader mentioned in the Constitution—is the **Speaker of the House**, who is the head of the majority party and influences the legislative agenda, committee assignments, scheduling, and overall party strategy. The Democratic Party made history in January 2007 when its representatives elected Nancy Pelosi as the first woman to serve as Speaker. John Boehner was elected Speaker in 2011 after Republicans regained control of the House in the 2010 midterm elections. The Speaker is aided by the **majority leader**, the majority whip, and the caucus chair (in addition to many others in lower-level party positions). The majority leader is one of the national spokespersons for the party and also helps with the day-to-day operation of the legislative process. The majority whip oversees the extensive **whip system**, which has three functions: information gathering, information dissemination, and coalition building. The whips meet regularly to discuss legislative strategy and scheduling. The whips then pass along this information to colleagues in their respective parties and indicate the party's position on a given bill. Whips also take a head count of party members in the House on specific votes and communicate this information to the party leaders.

If a vote looks close, whips try to persuade members to support the party's position ("whip" comes from the fox-hunting term "whipper-in," meaning the person who keeps the hounds from wandering too far from the pack; similarly, party whips try to ensure that members do not stray too far from party positions). The conference chair for the Republicans (or caucus chair for the Democrats) runs the party meetings to elect floor leaders, to make committee assignments, and to set legislative agendas. The minority party in the House has a parallel

PARTY LEADERSHIP IS CENTRAL IN the legislative process. The House and Senate leadership (from left to right), Speaker of the House John Boehner (R-OH), House minority leader Nancy Pelosi (D-CA), Senate majority leader Mitch McConnell (R-KY), and Senate minority leader Harry Reid (D-NV), spoke to reporters after meeting with the president at the White House.

Speaker of the House
The elected leader of the House of Representatives.

majority leader The elected head of the party holding the majority of seats in the House or Senate.

whip system An organization of House leaders who work to disseminate information and promote party unity in voting on legislation.

structure: its leader is the **minority leader**, and the second in command is the minority whip.

The Senate leadership does not have as much power as the leadership of the House, mostly because individual senators have more power than individual House members due to the Senate's rule of unlimited debate. The majority leader and minority leader are the leaders of their respective parties, and second in command to them are the assistant majority and minority leaders. The Senate also has a whip system, but it is not as developed as the House system. Republicans have a separate position for the conference chair, while the Democratic leader also serves as the conference chair. Officially, the country's vice president is also the president of the Senate, but he appears in the chamber only when needed to cast a tie-breaking vote. The Constitution also mentions the **president pro tempore** of the Senate, whose formal duties involve presiding over the Senate when the vice president is not there. This is typically the most senior member of the majority party, and the position does not have any real power. (In fact, the actual president pro tempore rarely presides over the Senate, and the task is typically given to a more junior senator.)

THE ROLE OF PARTIES AND CONDITIONAL PARTY GOVERNMENT Political parties in Congress also reflect the individualism of the institution. Compared to parliamentary systems, U.S. congressional parties are very weak. They do not impose a party line or penalize members who vote against the party. Indeed, they have virtually no ability to impose electoral restrictions (such as denying the party's nomination) on renegade members. Thus, from the perspective of a member seeking reelection, parties are more useful for what they are not—they do not force members to vote with the party—than for what they are. Although there are significant party differences on many issues, on about half of all **roll call votes**, majorities of both parties are on the same side.

Although still weaker than their overseas counterparts, parties in Congress have greatly strengthened since the 1960s (see Figure 11.6). Partisanship—evident when party members stick together in opposition to the other party—reached its highest levels in the post–World War II era in the mid-1990s. About 70 percent of all roll call votes were **party votes**, a measure created by the *Congressional Quarterly* in 1953, in which a majority of one party opposed a majority of the other party. The proportion of party votes fell to between 50 and 60 percent between 1996 and 2008 but recently has hit new highs. The highest proportion in the Senate was 72 percent in 2009 and 75.8 percent in the House in 2011; the numbers were down a bit in 2012 and 2013, but they remained around 70 percent. **Party unity**, the percentage of party members voting together on party votes, soared during this period as well, especially in the House.

The Democratic Party has become much more cohesive as southern Democrats have started to vote more like their northern counterparts, partly because of the increasing importance of African-American voters who tend to vote for Democrats in the South. Moreover, increasing Republican strength in the South means that the remaining Democratic districts are more liberal because Republicans defeat the more moderate Democrats. Similarly, there are fewer moderates within the Republican Party, as most regions of the country that used to elect moderate Republicans are now electing Democrats.[36] Another way to examine these developments is to examine the ideological distribution of members of Congress (see Figure 11.7). The parties in Congress are now more polarized than at any point in U.S. history (the figure shows the distance between the two parties based on roll call votes). In the 1970s, there was considerable overlap between the Democratic

minority leader The elected head of the party holding the minority of seats in the House or Senate.

president pro tempore A largely symbolic position usually held by the most senior member of the majority party in the Senate.

roll call vote A recorded vote on legislation; members may vote yes, no, abstain, or present.

party vote A vote in which the majority of one party opposes the position of the majority of the other party.

party unity The extent to which members of Congress in the same party vote together on party votes.

FIGURE » 11.6

PARTY VOTES AND UNITY IN CONGRESS, 1962–2013

(A) Party votes are said to occur when a majority of one party opposes a majority of the other party, and **(B)** party unity is the percentage of the party members who vote together on party votes. These two graphs make two important points. First, partisanship has increased in the last two decades, both in terms of the proportion of party votes and the level of party unity. Second, despite these increased levels of partisanship, only about two-thirds of all votes in the House and Senate divide the two parties. Given these potentially conflicting observations, how would you assess the argument that partisanship in Congress is far too intense?

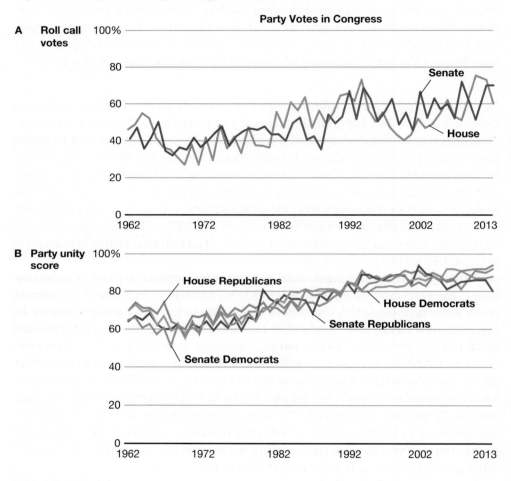

SOURCE: "CQ Roll Call's Vote Studies–2013 in Review," "Party Unity," and "Average Unity Scores," http://media.cq.com/votestudies/ (accessed 4/16/14).

and Republican parties. But in the most recent Congress, the two parties are almost completely separated—that is, only a few Democrats are more conservative than the most liberal Republican. At the same time, the parties are growing further apart, which makes it even harder for the Republicans and the Democrats to work together and compromise to pass legislation.

This greater cohesiveness within parties and separation across parties means that conditional party government (see Chapter 8) may be in play—that is, strong party leadership is possible in Congress, but it is conditional on the consent of party members.[37] That consent is more likely if there are strong differences between the parties

WHAT DO POLITICAL SCIENTISTS DO?

For more on polarization in Congress, visit **wwnpag.es/wdpsd**

FIGURE » 11.7

IDEOLOGICAL POLARIZATION IN CONGRESS, 1879–2013

Although party polarization in Congress has been high in the past, it lessened in the early twentieth century. Polarization has increased steadily in the last 70 years, and today's Congress is more polarized than ever. What do you think causes this extreme polarization?

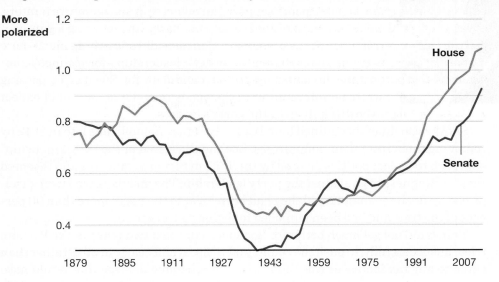

More polarized

SOURCE: "An Update on Polarization through the First Year of the 113th Congress (Part I)," Voteview blog, January 21, 2014, http://voteview.com/blog/?p=990 (accessed 4/16/14).

---

but unity within parties. Leaders' chief responsibility is to get their party's legislative agenda through Congress, but they primarily have to rely on persuasion and control over the timing of when bills come up for a vote rather than telling members what to do. Leaders' success largely depends on personal skills, communicative abilities, and trust. Some of the most successful leaders, such as Lyndon Johnson (D-TX), majority leader of the Senate from 1955 to 1961, and Sam Rayburn (D-TX), Speaker of the House for more than 17 years, kept in touch with key members on a daily basis.

Leaders also must have the ability to bargain and compromise. One observer noted, "To Senator Johnson, public policy evidently was an inexhaustibly bargainable product."[38] Such leaders find solutions where none appear possible. Leaders also do favors for members (such as making campaign appearances, helping with fund-raising, contributing to campaigns, helping them get desired committee assignments, or guiding pet projects through the legislative process) to engender a feeling of personal obligation to the leadership when it needs a key vote.

The party's most powerful positive incentives are in the area of campaign finance. In recent years the congressional campaign committees of both parties and the national party organizations have been supplying candidates with money and resources in an attempt to gain more influence in the electoral process. Party leaders may also help arrange a campaign stop or a fund-raiser for a candidate with party leaders or the president. For example, President Obama held dozens

PRESIDENT OBAMA WORKED tirelessly as his party's chief fund-raiser and campaigner in the 2014 midterm elections. He is shown here accompanied by Rep. Gary Peters (D-MI) and talking with Zingerman's Deli employee Andrea Byl during their visit to Ann Arbor, Michigan.

SPEAKER OF THE HOUSE JOHN Boehner (R-OH) had reached a deal with Democratic leaders on the budget, but he was unable to persuade conservative Republicans (especially Tea Party Republicans) to vote to approve the budget, leading to a 16-day shutdown of the federal government.

of fund-raisers for Democrats in 2014, earning him the label of "Fundraiser-in-Chief" from CNN.[39] Such events typically raise $500,000 to more than $1 million.

Despite these positive reinforcements, members' desire for reelection always comes before party concerns, and leadership rarely tries to force a member to vote against his or her constituents' interests. For example, Democrats from rural areas, where most constituents support gun ownership and many are hunters, would not be expected to vote the party line favoring a gun-control bill. But if a member of Congress did something much more extreme that crossed the party's leadership—for example, supporting the opposing party's candidate for Speaker or passing strategic information to the opposition—he or she could expect to be disciplined by the party's leaders.

Speaker Boehner disciplined four Tea Party House Republicans late in 2012 by removing them from their committees. Boehner had tired of the "brinkmanship" approach to budget politics favored by the Tea Party representatives and resented their willingness to go against the party leadership. The members who were disciplined by Boehner complained they had been loyal to the party more than 90 percent of the time and had been punished for being conservative.

Things did not get much better for Boehner in the next two years as Tea Partiers tried, unsuccessfully, to push the country off a "fiscal cliff" early in 2013 rather than agree to any tax increases (the "cliff" was the economic damage that would have been caused by automatic spending cuts and tax increases that were due to kick in). Boehner then was unable to prevent a government shutdown in the fall of 2013. Earlier in the summer, Boehner had reached a deal with Democratic leaders on a budget that would have kept the government running, but it was voted down by House Republicans who wanted deeper spending cuts and to defund Obamacare. Senate Democrats refused those demands, so the government was shut down from October 1 to 16, 2013 (for all nonessential government services). Eventually a new budget and an extension of the debt ceiling were passed early in 2014 with mostly Democratic votes (indeed, on the debt ceiling vote there were fewer Republicans voting in favor than for any majority party in the House on any winning roll call vote since 1991).[40]

THE COMMITTEE SYSTEM The committee system in the House and Senate is another crucial part of the legislative structure (see Table 11.2). There are four types of committees: standing, select, joint, and conference. **Standing committees**, which have ongoing membership and jurisdictions, are where most of Congress's work gets done. These committees draft legislation and oversee the implementation of the laws they pass. For example, the Agriculture Committee in the House and the one in the Senate have jurisdiction over farm programs such as commodity price supports, crop insurance, and soil conservation. But they also create and oversee policy for rural electrification and development; the food stamp and nutrition programs; and the inspection of livestock, poultry, seafood, and meat products. Many committees share jurisdiction on policy—for example, the House Natural Resources committee oversees the National Forest Service and forests on federally owned lands and the Agriculture Committee oversees policy for forests on privately owned lands.

Select committees typically address a specific topic for one or two terms, such as the Select Committee on Energy Independence and Global Warming that operated from 2007 to 2010. These committees do not have the same legislative authority as standing committees; rather, they mostly serve to collect information, provide policy

standing committees Committees that are a permanent part of the House or Senate structure, holding more importance and authority than other committees.

select committees Committees in the House or Senate created to address a specific issue for one or two terms.

TABLE » 11.2

CONGRESSIONAL COMMITTEES

There are equivalent committees in the House and Senate (and some joint committees) that work on similar problems and craft similar bills whose differences must be reconciled before a final bill becomes law. Equivalent or similar committees in both chambers are listed across from each other.

HOUSE COMMITTEES	SENATE COMMITTEES	JOINT COMMITTEES
Agriculture	Agriculture, Nutrition, and Forestry	Joint Economic Committee
Appropriations	Appropriations	Joint Committee on the Library
Armed Services	Armed Services	Joint Committee on Printing
Budget	Budget	Joint Committee on Taxation
Education and Workforce	Health, Education, Labor, and Pensions	
Energy and Commerce	Commerce, Science, and Transportation	
Ethics	Select Committee on Ethics	
Financial Services	Banking, Housing, and Urban Affairs	
Foreign Affairs	Foreign Relations	
Homeland Security	Homeland Security and Governmental Affairs	
House Administration	Rules and Administration	
Judiciary	Judiciary	
Natural Resources	Energy and Natural Resources	
Select Committee on Intelligence	Select Committee on Intelligence	
Small Business	Small Business and Entrepreneurship	
Transportation and Infrastructure	Environment and Public Works	
Veterans' Affairs	Veterans Affairs	
Ways and Means	Finance	
The committees below are specific to the House.	**The committees below are specific to the Senate.**	
Oversight and Government Reform	Special Committee on Aging	
Rules	Indian Affairs	
Science, Space, and Technology		

options, and draw attention to a given issue. **Joint committees** are made up of members of both the House and the Senate, and they rarely have legislative authority. The Joint Committee on Taxation, for example, does not have authority to send legislation concerning tax policy to the floor of the House or Senate. Instead, it gathers information and provides estimates of the consequences of proposed tax legislation. Joint committees may also be temporary, such as the "Supercommittee" (officially the Joint Select Committee on Deficit Reduction) that was formed in 2011. **Conference committees** are formed to resolve specific differences between House and Senate versions of legislation that are passed in each chamber. These committees mostly comprise standing committee members from each chamber who worked on the bill.

The committee system creates a division of labor that helps members get reelected by supporting their specialization and credit claiming. For example, a chair of the Agriculture Committee or of a key agricultural subcommittee

joint committees Committees that contain members of both the House and Senate but have limited authority.

conference committees Temporary committees created to negotiate differences between the House and Senate versions of a piece of legislation that has passed through both chambers.

may reasonably take credit for passing an important bill for the farmers back home, such as the Cottonseed Payment Program that provides assistance to cottonseed farmers who lost crops due to hurricanes. The number of members who could make these credible claims expanded dramatically in the 1970s with the proliferation of subcommittees (there are 104 in the House and 70 in the Senate). One observer of Congress suggested, with some exaggeration for the House, that if you ever forget a member's name, you can simply refer to him or her as "Mr. or Ms. Chairman" and you will be right about half the time. This view of congressional committees is based on the **distributive theory**, which is rooted in the norm of reciprocity and the incentive to provide benefits for the district. The theory holds that members will seek committee assignments to best serve their district's interests, the leadership will accommodate those requests, and the floor will respect the views of the committees in a big institution-level logroll—that is, committee members will support each other's legislation. This means that members tend to have an interest in and to support the policies produced by the committees they serve on. For example, members from farm states would want to serve on the Agriculture Committee and members with a lot of military bases or defense contractors in their districts would want to be on the Armed Services Committee.

Nonetheless, the committee system does not exist simply to further members' electoral goals. According to **informational theory**, it also provides collective benefits to the rest of the members through committee members' expertise on policy, which helps reduce uncertainty about policy outcomes.[41] By deferring to expert committees, members are able to achieve beneficial outcomes while using their time more efficiently. This informational theory is also consistent with the argument made by Richard Fenno 40 years ago that members will serve on committees for reasons other than simply trying to achieve reelection (which is implied by the distributive theory). Fenno argued that members also were interested in achieving power within the institution and in making good policy.[42] Others argue that goals vary from bill to bill, and all members pursue reelection advantage, institutional power, and effective policy in different circumstances.[43] Thus, the committee system does not exist only to further members' electoral goals, but it often serves that purpose.

Committees also serve the policy needs of the majority party, largely because it controls a majority of seats on every committee. The party ratios on each committee generally reflect the partisan distribution in the overall chamber, but the majority party gives itself somewhat larger majorities on the important committees such as Ways and Means (which controls tax policy), Appropriations, and Rules. This is especially true for the Rules Committee (in which the majority party controls 9 of the 13 seats). The Rules Committee is important to the majority party because it structures the nature of debate in the House by setting the length of debate and the type and number of amendments to a bill that will be allowed. These decisions are called "rules" and must be approved by a majority of the House members. The Rules Committee has become an arm of the majority party leadership, and in many instances it provides rules that support the party's policy agenda or that protect its members from having to take controversial positions. For example, the Rules Committee prevented many amendments on the 2010 health care reform bill; if the amendments had come to a vote, they would have divided the Democratic Party. Majority members are expected to support their party on votes on rules, even if they end up voting against the related legislation.

distributive theory The idea that members of Congress will join committees that best serve the interests of their district and that committee members will support each other's legislation.

informational theory The idea that having committees in Congress made up of experts on specific policy areas helps to ensure well-informed policy decisions.

CONGRESSIONAL STAFF The final component of the formal structure of Congress is congressional staff. The size of personal and committee staff exploded in the 1970s and 1980s and has since leveled off. The total number of congressional staff is more than four times as large as it was 50 years ago. Part of the motivation for this growth was to reduce the gap between the policy-making capability of Congress and the president, especially with regard to fiscal policy. The other primary motivation was electoral. By increasing the size of their personal staff, members were able to open multiple district offices and expand the opportunities for helping constituents. When the Republicans took control of Congress in 1994, they vowed to cut the waste in the internal operation of the institution, in part by cutting committee staff. However, although they reduced committee staff by nearly a third, they made no cuts in personal staff.

The structure of Congress generally serves its members' needs. The norms of the institution and its formal structure facilitate members' electoral and policy goals. If any aspect of this structure were to hinder Congress's goals, it is within members' power to change that aspect of the institution.

HOW A BILL BECOMES A LAW

> TRACE THE STEPS IN THE LEGISLATIVE PROCESS

Every introductory textbook on American politics has an obligatory section, including a neat little diagram that describes how a bill becomes a law (see How It Works: Passing Legislation). But we provide an important truth-in-advertising disclosure: many important laws do not follow this orderly path. In fact, Barbara Sinclair's book *Unorthodox Lawmaking* argues that "the legislative process for major legislation is now less likely to conform to the textbook model than to unorthodox lawmaking."[44] After presenting the standard view, we describe the most important deviations from that path.

THE CONVENTIONAL PROCESS

The details of the legislative process can be incredibly complex, but its basic aspects are fairly simple. The most important thing to understand about the process is that before a piece of legislation can become a law it must be passed *in identical form* by both the House and the Senate and signed by the president. If the president vetoes the bill, it can still be passed with a two-thirds vote in each chamber. Here are the basic steps of the process (but see Nuts & Bolts 11.2 for a description of different types of legislation):

1. A member of Congress introduces the bill.
2. A subcommittee and committee craft the bill.
3. Floor action on the bill takes place in the first chamber (House or Senate).
4. Committee and floor action takes place in the second chamber.
5. The conference committee works out any differences between the House and Senate versions of the bill. (If the two chambers pass the same version, steps 5 and 6 are not necessary.)

NUTS & *bolts*

TYPES OF LEGISLATION

▶ **Bill:** A legislative proposal that becomes law if it is passed by both the House and the Senate in identical form and approved by the president. Each is assigned a bill number, with "H.R." indicating bills that originated in the House and "S." denoting bills that originated in the Senate. Private bills are concerned with a specific individual or organization and often address immigration or naturalization issues. Public bills affect the general public if enacted into law.

▶ **Simple resolution:** Legislation used to express the sense of the House or Senate, designated by "H.Res." or "S.Res." Simple resolutions affect only the chamber passing the resolution, are not signed by the president, and cannot become public law. Resolutions are often used for symbolic legislation, such as congratulating sports teams or naming a post office after a famous person (see Figure 11.8).

▶ **Concurrent resolution:** Legislation used to express the position of both chambers on a nonlegislative matter to set the annual budget or to fix adjournment dates, designated by "H.Con.Res" or "S.Con.Res." Concurrent resolutions are not signed by the president and therefore do not carry the weight of law.

▶ **Joint resolution:** Legislation that has few practical differences from a bill (passes both chambers in identical form, signed by the president) unless it proposes a constitutional amendment. In that case, a two-thirds majority of those present and voting in both the House and the Senate, and ratification by three-fourths of the states, are required for the amendment to be adopted and it does not require the president's signature.

6. The conference committee version is given final approval on the floor of each chamber.

7. The president either signs or vetoes the final version.

8. If the bill is vetoed, both chambers can attempt to override the veto with a two-thirds vote in both chambers.

The first part of the process, unchanged from the earliest Congresses, is the introduction of the bill. Only members of Congress can introduce the bill, either by dropping it into the "hopper," a wooden box at the front of the chamber in the House, or by presenting it to one of the clerks at the presiding officer's desk in the Senate. Even the president would need to have a House member or senator introduce his bill. Each bill has one or more sponsors and often many co-sponsors. Members may introduce bills on any topic they choose, but often the bills are related to a specific constituency interest. For example, Senator Maria Cantwell (D-WA) introduced Senate Resolution 358 "Commending the Seattle Seahawks for winning Super Bowl XLVIII"(see Figure 11.8). Obviously, most legislation is more substantive, but members of Congress are always attentive to issues their constituents care about.

The next step is to send the bill to the relevant committee. House and Senate rules specify committee jurisdictions (there are more than 200 categories), and the bill is matched with the committee that best fits its subject matter. In the House, major legislation may be sent to more than one committee in a practice known as multiple referral, but one of the committees is designated the primary committee, and the bill is reviewed by the other committees sequentially or in parts. The practice is less common in the Senate, partly because senators have more opportunities to amend legislation on the floor. However, there were three committees in the House and two in the Senate that simultaneously worked on health care reform in 2009.

How It Works

PASSING LEGISLATION: THE CONVENTIONAL METHOD

SPEAKER OF HOUSE RECEIVES BILL

COMMITTEE*†

SUBCOMMITTEE*†

RULES COMMITTEE*†

HOUSE FLOOR*†

HOUSE AMENDS SENATE BILL*†

HOUSE FLOOR†

HOUSE BILL

SENATE BILL

PRESIDENT OF SENATE RECEIVES BILL

COMMITTEE*†

SUBCOMMITTEE*†

MAJORITY LEADER

SENATE FLOOR*†

SENATE AMENDS HOUSE BILL*†

SENATE FLOOR†

CONFERENCE COMMITTEE*†

CONFERENCE REPORT*†

HOUSE APPROVES SENATE AMENDMENT†

ADOPTION BY BOTH HOUSES†

SENATE APPROVES HOUSE AMENDMENT†

WHITE HOUSE†

VETO

APPROVE

HOUSE AND SENATE FLOOR†

VETO OVERRIDE

LAW

*Points at which a bill can be amended. †Points at which a bill can die.

How It Works
In Practice

DEVIATIONS FROM THE CONVENTIONAL METHOD: PASSING THE AFFORDABLE CARE ACT ("OBAMACARE")

CONVENTIONAL STEPS after a bill is introduced. (See the preceding page.)

THE 2010 AFFORDABLE CARE ACT (ACA) provides an example of how passing legislation often deviates from the conventional method.

A committee and a subcommittee revise the bill.

In the House, **3 committees** crafted the bill.

5 committees worked on the Senate version.

Speaker Nancy Pelosi assumed a central role in shaping the final bill, adding things that weren't in the committee version.

After a deadlock between two committees, Majority Leader Harry Reid pushed through a merged version of the bill, adding things that weren't in the committee version.

President Obama was intensely involved. The White House held daily meetings with the committees.

Floor action

Floor action

Floor action

Conference committee reconciles House and Senate versions.

No conference committee. Instead, committee leaders, White House staff, and party leadership negotiated the details of the bill.

Adoption of final bill by both House and Senate

The Senate version of the bill was passed by the House, but then the House also passed a separate reconciliation bill that included many amendments to the Senate version.

That reconciliation bill was then passed by the Senate.

President signs bill into law.

President Obama signed the ACA into law.

POP QUIZ

1 A conference committee's job is to
  a draft an original bill.
  b determine whether a bill should be considered by Congress.
  c determine whether a bill is constitutional.
  d reconcile differences between the House and Senate versions of a bill.
  e convince the president to sign the bill.

2 One way the passage of the ACA differed from the conventional process is that
  a committees were not involved.
  b President Obama and party leaders were directly involved in shaping the bill.
  c no floor action took place.
  d only one house voted on the bill.
  e the president signed it into law.

FIGURE » 11.8

TAKING CARE OF THE FANS

The congratulatory resolution below is symbolic and commends the Seattle Seahawks for winning the Super Bowl in 2014.

S. RES. 358
IN THE SENATE OF THE UNITED STATES
February 12, 2014

Commending the Seattle Seahawks for winning Super Bowl XLVIII and the 12th Man for their critical support.

Whereas on February 2, 2014, the Seattle Seahawks won Super Bowl XLVIII with a commanding 43–8 victory over the Denver Broncos;

Whereas Super Bowl XLVIII is the first Super Bowl Championship won by the Seahawks franchise; [. . .]

Whereas in December 1984, the Seahawks retired the number 12 in honor of their fan base, who are among the loudest, proudest, and most impactful group of fans in sports, which is known as "the 12th Man";

Whereas the 12th Man is critical to the home field advantage of the Seahawks at CenturyLink Field, holds a world record for crowd noise at 137.6 decibels, and has twice triggered measurable earthquakes on the Richter Scale;

Whereas the Seahawks have the top-ranked defense in the NFL, led by an unstoppable defensive line and cornerback Richard Sherman and the "Legion of Boom" secondary; [. . .]

Whereas on February 5, 2014, 700,000 fans packed the streets of Seattle to celebrate the Seahawks victory: Now, therefore, be it

Resolved, That the Senate congratulates the Seattle Seahawks for their victory in Super Bowl XLVIII, the first National Football League championship brought home to the Pacific Northwest.

SOURCE: Congress.gov, http://beta.congress.gov/bill/113th-congress/senate-resolution/358/text?q={%22search%22%3A[%22super+bowl%22]} (accessed 6/6/14).

Once the bill goes to a committee, the chair refers it to the relevant subcommittee where much of the legislative work is done. The subcommittee holds hearings, calls witnesses, and gathers the information necessary to rewrite, amend, and edit the bill. The final language of the bill is determined in a collaborative process known as the **markup**. During this meeting, members debate aspects of the issue and offer amendments to change the language or content of the bill. After all amendments have been considered, a final vote is taken on whether to send the bill to the full committee. If it is sent, the full committee then considers whether to pass it along to the floor. This committee also has the option of amending the bill, passing it as is, or tabling it (which kills the bill). Every bill sent to the floor by a committee is accompanied by a report and full documentation of all the hearings. These documents constitute the bill's legislative history, which the courts, executive departments, and the public use to determine the purpose and meaning of the law.

markup One of the steps through which a bill becomes a law, in which the final wording of the bill is determined.

When the bill makes it to the floor, it is placed on one of the various legislative calendars. Bills are removed from the calendar to be considered by the floor under a broad range of possible rules. When the bill reaches the floor, the majority party and minority party each designate a bill manager who is responsible for guiding the debate on the floor. In the House, debate proceeds according to tight time limits and rules governing the nature of amendments. Senate debate is much more open and unlimited in most circumstances (unless all the senators agree to a limit).

If you have ever watched C-SPAN, you know that often there are very few people on the floor during debates. Typically only the small number of people who are most interested in the bill (usually members of the committee that produced it) actively participate and offer amendments.

When debate is completed and all amendments have been considered, the presiding officer calls for a voice vote, with those in favor saying "aye," and those opposed "no." If it is unclear which side has won, any member may call for a "division vote," which requires members on each side to stand and be counted. At that point, any member may call for a recorded vote (there is no way of recording members' positions on voice votes and division votes). If at least 25 members agree that a recorded vote is desired, buzzers go off in the office buildings and committee rooms, calling members to the floor for the vote. Once they reach the floor, members vote by an electronic system in which they insert ATM-like cards into slots and each vote is recorded on a big board at the front of the House or Senate chamber.

If the bill passes the House and the Senate in different forms, the discrepancies have to be resolved. On many minor bills, one chamber may simply accept the other chamber's version to solve the problem. On other minor bills and some major bills, differences are resolved through a process known as amendments between the chambers. In this case, one chamber modifies a bill passed by the other chamber and sends it back. These modifications can go back and forth several times before both houses agree on an identical bill. A complicated version of this approach was used to pass health care reform in 2010.

The most common way to resolve differences on major legislation is through a conference committee made up of key players in the House and the Senate. A majority of major bills go to a conference committee, but only 3 percent of all bills go this route.[45] Sometimes the conferees split the difference between the House and Senate versions, but at other times the House and Senate approaches are so different that one must be chosen—an especially tricky prospect when different parties control the two chambers. Sometimes the conference cannot resolve differences and the bill dies. If the conference committee can agree on changes, each chamber must pass the final version, the conference report, by a majority vote and neither chamber is allowed to amend it.

The bill is then sent to the president. If he approves and signs the measure within 10 days (not counting Sundays), it becomes law. If he objects to the bill, he may **veto** it within 10 days, sending it back to the chamber where it originated, along with a statement of objections. Unless both the House and the Senate vote to override the veto by a two-thirds majority, the bill dies. If the president does not act within 10 days and Congress is in session, the bill becomes law without the president's approval. If Congress is not in session, the measure dies through what is known as a **pocket veto**.

One final point on how a bill becomes a law is important: any bill that appropriates money must pass through the two-step process of authorization and appropriation. In the authorization process, members debate the merits of the bill, determine its language, and limit the amount that can be spent on the bill. The appropriations process involves the Budget Committees in both the House and the Senate, which set the overall guidelines for the national budget, and the Appropriations Committees in the two chambers, which determine the actual amounts of money that will be spent. In recent years, Congress has been unable to pass its appropriations bills in time for the start of the new fiscal year, so it ends up having to pass "continuing resolutions" that spend money at the last year's levels in order to keep the government open. Congress passed four continuing resolutions for the 2012 fiscal year and several more in 2013. That may sound like a lot, but the record is 21 for the 2001 fiscal year.[46]

veto The president's rejection of a bill that has been passed by Congress. A veto can be overridden by a two-thirds vote in both the House and Senate.

pocket veto The automatic death of a bill passed by the House and Senate when the president fails to sign the bill in the last 10 days of a legislative session.

DEVIATIONS FROM THE CONVENTIONAL PROCESS

There are many ways in which legislation may not follow the typical path. First, in some Congresses, up to 20 percent of *major* bills bypass the committee system. This may be done by a discharge petition, in which a majority of the members force a bill out of its assigned committee, or by a special rule in the House. In some cases, a bill may go to the relevant committee, but then party leadership may impose its version of the bill later in the process. For example, in the wake of the terrorist attacks of 9/11, the House Judiciary Committee after hard bipartisan work quickly approved a version of the Patriot Act to be considered by the full House to give the government stronger surveillance powers. But a few days later, according to committee member Representative Jerrold Nadler (D-NY), "Then the bill just disappeared. And we had a new several hundred page bill revealed from the Rules Committee" that had to be voted on the next day. Most members of Congress did not have a chance to read it.[47] The Affordable Care Act also deviated from the standard path (see How It Works In Practice, earlier in this chapter.)

Second, about one-third of major bills are adjusted post-committee and before the legislation reaches the floor by supporters of the bill to increase the chances of passage. Sometimes the bill goes back to the committee after these changes, and sometimes it does not. Thus, although most of the legislative work is accomplished in committees, a significant amount of legislation bypasses committee review.

Third, summit meetings between the president and congressional leaders may bypass or jump-start the normal legislative process. For example, rather than going through the Budget Committees to set budgetary targets, the president may meet with top leaders from both parties and hammer out a compromise that is presented to Congress as a done deal. This technique is especially important on delicate budget negotiations or when the president is threatening to use the veto. Often the congressional rank-and-file go along with the end product of the summit meeting, but occasionally they reject it—as happened in February 2014, when all but 28 House Republicans voted against their leadership on the extension of the debt ceiling that had been agreed to by President Obama and House and Senate leaders.

Fourth, **omnibus legislation**—massive bills that run hundreds of pages long and cover many different subjects and programs—often requires creative approaches by the leadership to guide the bill through the legislative maze. Leadership task forces may be used in place of committees, and alternatives to the conference committee may be devised to resolve differences between the two chambers. In addition, the massive legislation often carries riders—extraneous legislation attached to the "must pass" bill to secure approval for pet projects that would otherwise fail. This is a form of pork-barrel legislation and another mechanism used in the quest for reelection.

omnibus legislation Large bills that often cover several topics and may contain extraneous, or pork-barrel, projects.

DIFFERENCES IN THE HOUSE AND SENATE LEGISLATIVE PROCESSES

There are three central differences in the legislative processes of the House and the Senate: (1) the continuity of the membership and the impact this has on the rules, (2) the way in which bills get to the floor, and (3) the structure of the floor process, including debate and amendments. First, as discussed earlier, the Senate is a continuing body, with two-thirds of its members returning to the next session without facing reelection (because of the six-year term), whereas all House members are up for reelection every two years. This has an important impact on the rules of the two chambers: there has been much greater stability in the rules of the Senate than the House. Whereas the House adopts its rules anew at the start of each new session (sometimes with major changes, sometimes with only minor modifications), the Senate has not had a general reaffirmation of its rules since 1789. However, the Senate rules can be changed at the beginning of a session to meet the needs of the new members.

The floor process is much simpler and less structured in the Senate than in the House. In part, this is due to the relative size of the two chambers: the House with its 435 members needs to have more rules than the Senate with its 100 members. Ironically, however, the floor process is actually much easier to navigate in the House because of its structure. Since the adoption of Reed's Rules in 1890, the House is a very majoritarian body—that is, a majority of House members can almost always have their way. Named after Speaker Thomas Reed, the rules were an implementation of his view that "the best system is to have one party govern and the other party watch."[48] In contrast, the Senate has always been a much more individualistic body. Former majority leader Howard Baker compared leading the Senate to "herding cats," saying it was difficult "trying to make ninety-nine independent souls act in concert under rules that encourage polite anarchy and embolden people who find majority rule a dubious proposition at best."[49] Part of this difficulty is rooted in the Senate's unlimited debate and very open amendment process. Unless restricted by a unanimous consent agreement, senators can speak as long as they want and offer any amendment to a bill, even if it isn't directly related to the underlying bill. Debate may be cut off only if a supermajority of 60 senators agrees in a process known as invoking **cloture**. Therefore, one senator can stop any bill by threatening to talk the bill to death if 40 of his or her colleagues agree. This practice is known as a **filibuster**.

The filibuster strengthens the hand of the minority party in the Senate, giving it veto power over legislation unless the majority party has 60 senators who unanimously support a bill. The filibuster has played a critical role in congressional policy making in recent years, especially after Massachusetts Republican Scott Brown won Democrat Ted Kennedy's seat in a special election held in January 2010 after Kennedy died (which gave the Republicans 41 seats). Republicans filibustered the health care reform bill, which could have killed it if Democratic leaders had not used the reconciliation process to pass the legislation (reconciliation is used in the budget process, typically as a budget-cutting device, and is not subject to the filibuster).

Before the 1960s, senators really did hold the floor for hours by reading from the phone book or reciting recipes. The late Strom Thurmond, the senator from South Carolina who was the longest serving and oldest senator until his retirement in January 2003 (at 100 years old and after 48 years in the Senate), holds the record of 24 hours and 18 minutes of continuous talking. Today it is rare for a filibuster to tie up Senate business, since a senator's threat to filibuster a bill is often enough to take the bill off the legislative agenda. If the bill is actually filibustered, it goes on a separate legislative track so that it does not bring the rest of the business of the Senate to a halt.

cloture A procedure through which the Senate can limit the amount of time spent debating a bill (cutting off a filibuster) if a supermajority of 60 senators agree.

filibuster A tactic used by senators to block a bill by continuing to hold the floor and speak—under the Senate rule of unlimited debate—until the bill's supporters back down.

SENATOR TED CRUZ (R-TX) HELD FORTH on the Senate floor for more than 21 hours, expressing his opposition to the Affordable Care Act in September 2013.

Alternatively, if supporters of the bill think they have enough votes, they can invoke cloture to stop the filibuster and bring the bill to the floor for a vote. Frustrated over repeated Republican filibusters on President Obama's nominations to federal courts and agencies, in November 2013 Senate Democrats removed the filibuster for all presidential nominations, except those to the Supreme Court.[50]

Because of the practice of unlimited debate in the Senate, much of its business is conducted under unanimous consent agreements by which senators agree to adhere to time limits on debate and amendments. However, because these are literally *unanimous* agreements, a single senator can obstruct the business of the chamber by issuing a **hold** on the bill or presidential nomination. This practice is often a bargaining tool to extract concessions from the bill's supporters, but sometimes, especially late in a session when time gets tight, a hold can actually kill a bill by removing it from the active agenda.

hold An objection to considering a measure on the Senate floor.

In contrast, the House is a more orderly, if complex, institution. The Rules Committee exerts great control over the legislative process, especially on major legislation, through special rules that govern the nature of debate on a bill. There are three general types of rules: **closed rules** do not allow any amendments to the bill, **open rules** allow any germane amendments, and **modified rules** allow some specific amendments but not others. Once a special rule is adopted and the Committee of the Whole convenes, general debate is tightly controlled by the floor managers. All amendments are considered under a five-minute rule, but this rule is routinely bent as members offer phantom "pro forma" amendments to, for example, "strike the last word" or "strike the requisite number of words." This means that the member is not really offering an amendment but is simply going through the formal procedure of offering one in order to get an additional five minutes to talk about the amendment.

closed rules Conditions placed on a legislative debate by the House Rules Committee prohibiting amendments to a bill.

open rules Conditions placed on a legislative debate by the House Rules Committee allowing relevant amendments to a bill.

modified rules Conditions placed on a legislative debate by the House Rules Committee allowing certain amendments to a bill while barring others.

These descriptions of the two chambers show that, although the Senate is formally committed to unlimited debate, senators often voluntarily place limits on themselves through unanimous consent, which makes them operate much more like the House. Similarly, although the House has very strict rules concerning debate and amendments, there are ways of bending those rules to make the House operate a bit more like the potentially freewheeling Senate.

OVERSIGHT

DESCRIBE HOW CONGRESS ENSURES THAT THE BUREAUCRACY IMPLEMENTS POLICIES CORRECTLY

Once a bill becomes a law, Congress plays another crucial role by overseeing the implementation of the law to make sure the bureaucracy interprets it as Congress intended. Other motivations drive the oversight process as well, such as the desire to gain publicity that may help in the reelection quest or to embarrass the president if he is of the opposite party. For example, in President Bush's last two years, Democrats investigated fraud and cost overruns in Defense Department contracts to rebuild Iraq that went to corporations with close Republican Party ties. In 2011, Republicans used their oversight powers to call attention to policy failures in the Obama administration such as "Operation Fast and Furious." This was a Justice Department program to sell guns to drug dealers that could then be tracked to Mexican drug lords. The program went horribly awry when hundreds of the guns could not be tracked and two of the guns were found where a Border Patrol agent was killed.[51] Nonetheless, the basic motivation for oversight is to ensure that laws are implemented properly.

There are several mechanisms that Congress may use to accomplish this goal (see also Chapter 13). First, the bluntest instrument is the power of the purse. If members of Congress think an agency is not properly implementing their programs, they can simply cut off the funds to that agency. However, this approach to punishment is rarely used because it often eliminates good aspects of the agency along with the bad.

Second, Congress can hold hearings and investigations. By summoning administration officials and agency heads to a public hearing, Congress can use the media spotlight to focus attention on problems within the bureaucracy or on issues that have been overlooked. For example, House Republicans called former Health and Human Services Secretary Kathleen Sebelius to testify several times in 2013 and 2014 about the rocky rollout of the healthcare.gov website for Obamacare. National security issues continue to produce oversight hearings on a broad range of topics as well. Director of National Intelligence James Clapper and CIA Director John Brennan testified in 2014 before House and Senate Intelligence Committees about the National Security Agency's collection of data on phone records. This type of oversight is known as fire alarm oversight—that is, members wait until there is a crisis before they spring to action.[52] This is in contrast to "police patrol" oversight, which involves constant vigilance in overseeing the bureaucracy. For example, the House Veterans Affairs Committee recently investigated extremely long waits for medical appointments at VA hospitals and the falsification of records to cover up how long veterans had to wait to be seen by doctors, which eventually led to General Eric Shinseki's resignation as the Secretary of Veterans Affairs.[53] Of the two, fire alarm oversight is far more common because Congress does not have the resources to constantly monitor the entire bureaucracy.

Finally, the Senate exercises specific control over other executive functions through its constitutional responsibilities to provide "advice and consent" on presidential appointments and approval of treaties. The Senate typically defers to the president on these matters, but it may assert its power, especially when constituent interests are involved. One current example would be the Senate's increasing skepticism about free trade agreements negotiated by the president's trade representatives and holds on presidential nominations.

The ultimate in congressional oversight is the process of removing the president, vice president, other civil officers, or federal judges through impeachment. The House and Senate share this power: the House issues articles of impeachment, which outline the charges against the official, and the Senate conducts the trial of the impeached officials. Two presidents have been impeached: Andrew Johnson in the controversy over Reconstruction after the Civil War, and Bill Clinton over the scandal involving White House intern Monica Lewinsky. However, neither president was convicted and removed by the Senate.

HEARINGS AND INVESTIGATIONS ARE powerful means of oversight for Congress. Here, James Clapper, Director of National Intelligence, and John Brennan, Director of the CIA, are shown testifying in January 2014 before the Senate Intelligence Committee on national security threats against the United States.

DIR. CLAPPER

DIR. BRENNAN

CONGRESSIONAL REFORM

EVALUATE ARGUMENTS FOR MAKING CONGRESS MORE ACCOUNTABLE

The pork-laden 2014 omnibus spending bill mentioned earlier is a good example of why many Americans are convinced that the entire political system is dysfunctional. This deep cynicism is rooted in the perception that government is not serving the public interest. Attempts to reform Congress address either (1) Congress's external image, or (2) the internal "quality of life" for members of Congress. The former agenda, which attempts to tackle the absence of institutional leadership and accountability, is difficult to address through congressional reforms. The only way to achieve complete accountability is when the same party controls Congress and the presidency, but even then this is an elusive goal (the conditions for accountability through strong parties is called "responsible party government" and is discussed in Chapter 8).

Specific reform proposals seeking to improve Congress's external image try to promote collective responsibility so as to end the perceived gridlock that often prevents legislation from being passed by Congress. Many proposals aim to bring more control to the majority party. Suggested reforms include giving the Speaker more power over committee assignments, strengthening the role of the party caucus, reforming the filibuster in the Senate to give the majority party more control, and requiring the leadership to play a larger role in agenda setting. However, most Americans see strong parties as part of the problem rather than the solution, so these reforms are likely to be unpopular.

The other reform agenda, which aims to improve the quality of life of members of Congress, seeks to expand the time available to members for legislative work and to reduce some of the external pressures that are on them. Specific proposals include closing more of the committee hearings to the general public to insulate members from interest group pressure, having fewer recorded votes, reducing the number of committee and subcommittee assignments, and providing public funding of congressional elections. But unfortunately, this reform agenda is often at odds with the agenda that would enhance Congress's transparency and accountability.

The one exception to the trade-off between improving the quality of life of members of Congress and improving Congress's image is campaign finance reform, which would both free up time for members (if public financing is adopted) and enhance Congress's image (if the public accepts it as true reform). After a decade-long battle, in 2002, Congress passed the Bipartisan Campaign Reform Act, also called the McCain-Feingold Act after two of its main sponsors, John McCain (R-AZ) and Russell Feingold (D-WI). The law banned so-called soft money and limited issue ads. However, in 2010, the Supreme Court struck down part of the law, so now corporations and unions may spend directly on issue ads and other political ads without limitations. In 2014, the Court removed aggregate limits that people can make to national candidates and parties. (See Chapter 9 for a discussion of these cases and campaign finance more generally.)

There have been incremental congressional reforms in other areas besides campaign finance reform. When Democrats regained majority control of the House and the Senate in 2007, they implemented several important reforms, including bans on gifts and meals paid for by lobbyists, restrictions on travel paid for by lobbyists, strong disclosure rules on earmarks, and a two-year "revolving door" ban on lawmakers becoming lobbyists after leaving Congress. The House established a new independent Office of Congressional Ethics (which nonetheless fell short of the hopes of reformers because it does not have subpoena power). House Republicans implemented a complete ban on earmarks when they took control of the House in 2011. While this ban has not been entirely effective (as noted, there are still ways that members can get specific funding for their districts), spending on pork is down substantially since its peak.

One other topic that continues to receive attention from congressional critics and reformers is term limits. Critics complain that incumbents are too entrenched and that there is not enough turnover. They note that more than 95 percent of the House incumbents who ran for reelection between 1984 and 2014 were returned to office (only 86 percent were reelected in 2010). As a reaction to incumbency advantage, a grassroots movement to limit terms started in 1990 and reached a fever pitch in 1992, as voters in 10 states passed term limits for state legislators. Currently 15 states limit terms for state legislators, but the movement appears to have lost steam. Twenty states had passed congressional term limits before the 5–4 Supreme Court decision in *U.S. Term Limits v. Thornton* (1995) ruled that term limits on members of Congress could be accomplished only by constitutional amendment. Then, in 1999, Mississippi voters rejected a state referendum that would have imposed term limits for their state legislature. Four state supreme courts have struck down term limits. In 2002, Idaho became the first state to have its legislature repeal term limits, and Utah followed suit in 2003.

There are two interesting ironies associated with the term limits movement. First, the Founders feared that the House would be an unstable body with excessive turnover and a lack of professionalism. Technically, it *is* possible that 435 new members of Congress could be elected every two years, but obviously the opposite has happened. Second, as noted earlier, although the public is critical of Congress as an institution, most voters do not feel this way about their own individual representative. One bumper sticker opposing term limits succinctly captures this irony: "Stop me before I vote again." Thus, while many people claim to support term limits, they don't want to vote out their own members of Congress.

CONCLUSION

Although the details of the legislative process and the institutions of Congress can be complicated, the basic explanations for members' behavior are quite straightforward when viewed in terms of the trade-off between responsiveness and responsibility. Members of Congress want to be reelected, so they are generally quite responsive to constituents' interests. They spend considerable time on casework—meeting with people in their district and delivering benefits for their district. At the same time, members are motivated to be responsible—to rise above local interests and attend to the nation's best interests. The conflict between these two impulses can create contradictory policies that contribute to Congress's image problem. For example, we subsidize tobacco farming at the same time that we spend billions of dollars to treat the health problems that tobacco use creates. We have laws on water rights that encourage farmers to irrigate the desert at the same time that we pay farmers to leave parts of their land unplanted in areas of the country that are well suited for agriculture. These policies, and others, can be explained both by the desire to serve local interests and by the norms of reciprocity and universalism.

Considering members' motivations is crucial to understanding how Congress functions, but their behavior is also constrained by the institutions in which they operate. The committee system is an important source of expertise and information, and it provides a platform from which members can take positions and claim credit. Parties in Congress provide coherence to the legislative agenda and help structure voting patterns on bills. Rules and norms constrain the nature of debate and the legislative process. Although these institutions shape members' behavior, it is important to remember that members can also change those rules and institutions. Therefore, Congress has the ability to evolve with changing national conditions and demands from voters, groups, and the president.

MEMBERS OF CONGRESS WANT to be reelected, and this goal explains much of their behavior. In 2014, Congressman (and House majority leader) Kevin McCarthy (R-CA) won reelection. Given his leadership position within the party, McCarthy must be especially careful to balance local interests with the good of the nation as a whole.

In this context, much of what Congress does can be understood in terms of the conflicts inherent in politics. How can members act responsibly without sacrificing responsiveness? Can Congress be structured in a way that allows members to be responsive (and therefore have a better chance of getting reelected) without losing the ability to make unpopular decisions when needed, like cutting budget deficits? The example discussed in the chapter introduction concerning sexual assaults in the military demonstrates that, even on issues that nearly everyone would agree are problems (nobody is in favor of sexual assaults), there are important differences of opinion about what actions should be taken. The compromise position that passed with nearly universal support in the Senate was not ideal for those who wanted stronger reforms, but compromise means that many people will not be completely satisfied with the final version.

This chapter also sheds light on some of the ways that political process matters. With a clearer understanding of how Congress operates, you are better able to assess the outputs of government. For example, this chapter provided a closer look at party leaders and pork-barrel spending: party leaders in Congress help members solve their collective action problems rather than causing gridlock and policy failure, as is commonly assumed. Some pork may be wasteful, but in other cases it is important for the districts that receive the benefits and may serve broader collective interests as well. Congress does not always live up to the expectations of being the "first branch" of government, but it often does an admirable job of balancing the conflicting pressures it faces.

STUDY *guide*

CONGRESS'S PLACE IN OUR CONSTITUTIONAL SYSTEM

▶ *Describe how the Founders envisioned Congress's role.* **(Pages 389–90)**

SUMMARY

The Constitution gave Congress vast enumerated powers, making it the "first branch" of government. The bicameral structure represented a number of compromises between competing interests among the Founders—notably the differences in constituency size, election mechanisms, and length of terms. While Congress has long dominated day-to-day politics, the president has become considerably more powerful over time.

KEY TERMS

bicameralism (p. 389)
pork barrel (p. 390)

CRITICAL THINKING AND DISCUSSION

How do you think the Founders would respond to the current institutional balance of power between the president and Congress? Would they think the president is too strong? Why or why not?

PRACTICE QUIZ QUESTIONS

1. What did the Seventeenth Amendment do?
   - A repealed Prohibition
   - B granted women's suffrage
   - C gave senators six-year terms
   - D allowed for direct election of senators
   - E lowered the voting age to 18

2. Why do senators have longer terms than members of the House of Representatives?
   - A to reduce the number of candidates in each election
   - B to make sure that senators were tied to public sentiment
   - C to provide more opportunities for pork-barrel legislation
   - D to make elections easier to administer
   - E to make sure that senators were somewhat insulated from the people

CONGRESS AND THE PEOPLE

▶ *Explain how members of Congress represent their constituents and how elections hold members accountable.* **(Pages 390–403)**

SUMMARY

Despite the low approval ratings for Congress itself, most voters like their members of Congress. Members of Congress work hard to strike a balance between responding to what constituents want, and what is in the constituency's best interest. In the balance, however, they prioritize district interests over national policy.

KEY TERMS

descriptive representation (p. 391)
substantive representation (p. 391)
trustee (p. 391)
delegate (p. 391)
politico (p. 392)
casework (p. 395)
electoral connection (p. 396)
redistricting (p. 398)
apportionment (p. 398)
gerrymandering (p. 399)
gridlock (p. 403)

CRITICAL THINKING AND DISCUSSION

Why do you think Congress is so unpopular? What type of representative would you want—a delegate or a trustee? Would the nation be better off if we had more trustees?

PRACTICE QUIZ QUESTIONS

3. What is the most common style of representatives in Congress?
   - A trustee
   - B politico
   - C delegate
   - D consulate
   - E adviser

4. Most constituents are _____; most members of Congress act as if the constituency _____ paying attention.
   - A inattentive; is not
   - B inattentive; is
   - C attentive; is not
   - D attentive; is
   - E selectively attentive; is not

5. Members of Congress generally hold multiple goals. Which goal comes first?

  A getting reelected

  B passing good policy

  C serving their political party

  D blocking the opposing party

  E serving special interests

6. What is apportionment?

  A determining presidential primary election winners

  B determining whether the state legislature or courts will redraw district lines

  C determining which states win/lose seats in the Senate

  D determining which states win/lose seats in the House

  E determining how many seats a party has in Congress

THE INCUMBENCY ADVANTAGE AND ITS SOURCES

▶ *Analyze the factors that help members of Congress get reelected.* **(Pages 403–07)**

SUMMARY

Very few members of Congress are defeated in their reelection bids. Incumbents are successful because they are able to relate to their constituents well, because they are generally successful in raising money for their political campaigns, and because they perform lots of constituency service.

KEY TERM

incumbency advantage (p. 403)

CRITICAL THINKING AND DISCUSSION

What types of activities do members of Congress undertake to work toward reelection? How do they structure the institutions of Congress to help themselves achieve this goal?

PRACTICE QUIZ QUESTIONS

7. A home style shapes the way members of Congress _____.

  A work with party leaders

  B vote in Congress

  C write legislation in committees

  D present themselves to their district

  E spend campaign money

8. On average, incumbents spend _____ times as much as challengers.

  A one and half

  B three

  C five

  D ten

  E twenty

THE STRUCTURE OF CONGRESS

▶ *Examine how parties, the committee system, and staffers enable Congress to function.* **(Pages 407–17)**

SUMMARY

Many aspects of Congress are set up to meet the needs of its members. The norms of universalism and reciprocity still dominate, meaning that members of Congress share resources more broadly than partisan politics would dictate.

KEY TERMS

logrolling (p. 408)
earmarks (p. 408)
seniority (p. 408)
Speaker of the House (p. 410)
majority leader (p. 410)
whip system (p. 410)
minority leader (p. 411)
president pro tempore (p. 411)
roll call vote (p. 411)
party vote (p. 411)
party unity (p. 411)
standing committees (p. 414)
select committees (p. 414)
joint committees (p. 415)
conference committees (p. 415)
distributive theory (p. 416)
informational theory (p. 416)

CRITICAL THINKING AND DISCUSSION

If you were in charge of the Commission on Congressional Reform, what proposals would you make to change how Congress operates? Would your proposals have a chance of being implemented?

PRACTICE QUIZ QUESTIONS

9. The norm of _____ says that federal highway dollars are likely to be divided up so that many districts benefit.

  A reciprocity

  B seniority

  C party unity

  D universalism

  E specialization

10. Committee leadership, division of seats on committee, and allocation of committee resources are determined by _____.

A the majority party

B the size of the election margin

C unanimous consent

D seniority

E the president pro tempore

11. The Senate leadership is _____ the House leadership.

A more powerful than

B as powerful as

C less powerful than

D irrelevant to

12. Party leaders have the power to _____.

A force members of Congress to vote a particular way

B keep a member of Congress off the ballot in the next election

C force their members to share their campaign money

D exclude a member from a roll call vote

E help their members get favorable committee assignments

HOW A BILL BECOMES A LAW

▶ *Trace the steps in the legislative process.* **(Pages 417–25)**

SUMMARY

Most bills become law in a conventional manner, but major pieces of legislation generally deviate considerably from this path. The legislative process differs for the House and Senate, sometimes making it difficult to reconcile differences between bills.

KEY TERMS

markup (p. 421)
veto (p. 422)
pocket veto (p. 422)
omnibus legislation (p. 423)
cloture (p. 424)
filibuster (p. 424)
hold (p. 425)
closed rules (p. 425)
open rules (p. 425)
modified rules (p. 425)

CRITICAL THINKING AND DISCUSSION

What are the main ways the conventional lawmaking process is not followed? Why would congressional leaders want a bill to deviate from the conventional path?

PRACTICE QUIZ QUESTION

13. Compared to the Senate, the floor process in the House is very _____ and _____.

A unstructured; majoritarian

B structured; majoritarian

C unstructured; individualistic

D structured; individualistic

E individualistic; majoritarian

OVERSIGHT

▶ *Describe how Congress ensures that the bureaucracy implements policies correctly.* **(Pages 425–26)**

SUMMARY

After passing bills into law, Congress oversees the bureaucracy in its implementation of the law, making sure it fits Congress's intentions. Although controlling funding is the most powerful mechanism for this, Congress has a number of other mechanisms for achieving bureaucratic fidelity. Generally, Congress does not actively patrol the bureaucracy, but waits to act until a crisis emerges.

CRITICAL THINKING AND DISCUSSION

If you had to choose between having a responsive or responsible member of Congress, which would you choose and why? Would your answer depend on how other members of Congress were behaving?

PRACTICE QUIZ QUESTION

14. Waiting for a crisis to emerge before taking action is called _____.

A police patrol oversight

B fire alarm oversight

C emergency room oversight

D reactionary oversight

E bureaucratic oversight

CONGRESSIONAL REFORM

▶ *Evaluate arguments for making Congress more accountable.* **(Pages 427–28)**

SUMMARY

Despite the general perception that the government does not serve the public interest, congressional reforms are relatively rare. Generally, reform attempts either address Congress's external image or internally improve the efficiency of lawmaking, and a trade-off exists between the external and internal concerns.

PRACTICE QUIZ QUESTION

15. The McCain-Feingold Act is an example of a reform that _____ Congress's image and _____ the internal efficiency.

A improved; improved

B improved; reduced

C reduced; improved

D reduced; reduced

E reduced; had no effect on

SUGGESTED READING

Adler, Scott E., and John D. Wilkerson. *Congress and the Politics of Problem Solving.* New York: Cambridge University Press, 2013.

Bianco, William T. *Trust: Representatives and Constituents.* Ann Arbor, MI: University of Michigan Press, 1994.

Canon, David T. *Race, Redistricting and Representation: The Unintended Consequences of Black Majority Districts.* Chicago: University of Chicago Press, 1999.

Fenno, Richard F. *Congressmen in Committees.* Boston: Little, Brown, 1973.

Hall, Richard L. *Participation in Congress.* New Haven, CT: Yale University Press, 1996.

Jacobson, Gary C. *The Politics of Congressional Elections,* 5th ed. New York: Addison-Wesley, 2001.

Lapinski, John S. *The Substance of Representation: Congress, American Political Development, and Lawmaking.* Princeton, NJ: Princeton University Press, 2013.

Mayhew, David R. *Congress: The Electoral Connection.* New Haven, CT: Yale University Press, 1974.

Theriault, Sean. *Party Polarization in Congress.* New York: Cambridge University Press, 2008.

12

The Presidency

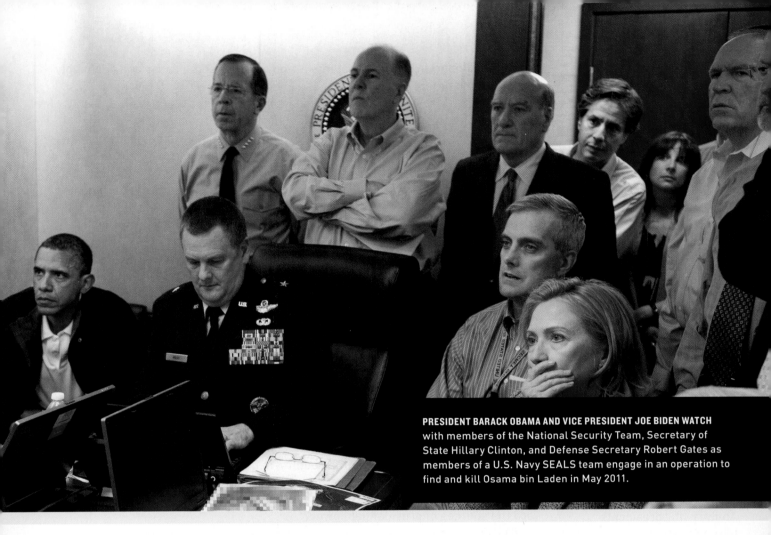

PRESIDENT BARACK OBAMA AND VICE PRESIDENT JOE BIDEN WATCH with members of the National Security Team, Secretary of State Hillary Clinton, and Defense Secretary Robert Gates as members of a U.S. Navy SEALS team engage in an operation to find and kill Osama bin Laden in May 2011.

OMETIMES PRESIDENTS DO THINGS THAT MAKE THEM look like the most powerful person in the world. In 2011, for example, Barack Obama ordered U.S. Special Forces to attack a compound in Pakistan and to kill or capture Al Qaeda leader Osama bin Laden. The Obama administration also directed a series of drone attacks in countries such as Afghanistan, Yemen, and Pakistan that decimated Al Qaeda's leadership and inflicted significant casualties on lower-level fighters.

Yet, other times, presidents look almost like bit players in American politics. Contrary to his successes in the war on terror, President Obama has achieved very few of his second-term domestic policy goals. The House and Senate did not even vote on Obama's gun control and immigration reform proposals. And to increase the minimum wage and mandate equal pay for men and women working the same jobs, Obama had to bypass Congress by using executive orders. Moreover, these latter policies could apply only to companies that did business with the federal government. In foreign policy, Obama was unable to end the civil war in Syria, reverse Russia's annexation of Crimea from Ukraine, or prevent civil war in Iraq.

These examples illustrate both the extent and the limits of presidential power. America's presidents possess considerable power over U.S. foreign and domestic policy, and they have used this power to make changes in government policy that have significantly affected the lives of ordinary Americans. Even so, presidents are often driven to compromise or are forced to abandon deeply held policy goals in the face of opposition from Congress, bureaucrats, judges, or the

**CONFLICT &
COMPROMISE**
in American Politics

CHAPTER *goals*

Trace the evolution of presidential power over time.

▶ PAGES 436–40

Describe the constitutional and statutory powers of the president today.

▶ PAGES 440–54

Explain how the Executive Office of the President, the vice president, and the Cabinet help the president.

▶ PAGES 455–58

Explain how Americans evaluate presidents.

▶ PAGES 458–62

Analyze why presidents have become much more powerful since the Founding.

▶ PAGES 462–67

American public. Why are presidents all-powerful in some cases and seemingly powerless in others?

This chapter shows that U.S. presidents face decisions that are often highly conflictual, with many people holding strong opinions on both sides of the question. Moreover, although presidents can change policy unilaterally in some circumstances, at other times, they require cooperation or consent from other players in American politics. As a result, presidential success is not automatic. Presidents may face obstacles in their efforts to achieve their own policy goals, yet at the same time they must attempt to satisfy the demands of supporters and opponents—while trying to avoid alienating people who disagree with presidential decisions.

To put it another way, although presidents are powerful, they are not kings or dictators. In most cases, their actions either require congressional consent to take effect or can be undone by subsequent congressional action. Presidents must also cultivate public opinion in order to get reelected or to help members of their party to be elected or reelected to office. Moreover, presidents and their staff must monitor the bureaucracy to make sure that presidential decisions are faithfully implemented. And sometimes, as with health care reform for Obama, presidents must decide whether to scale back on a proposal to make it more likely to pass Congress or to risk complete failure by holding firm to the original goal.

With these considerations in mind, we ask these fundamental questions in this chapter: What are the limits of presidential power? When are presidents able to prevail in the face of conflict in the country, in Congress, or in the bureaucracy? Has presidential power grown over time? How does conflict affect the decisions that presidents make and the ways they try to implement their policy goals? What are the sources of presidential power?

The answers to these questions lie in the idea that political process matters. In some situations, the powers allocated in the Constitution enable the president to change government policy unilaterally. However, there are limits on this power. Congress and the Supreme Court can and at times do overturn presidential actions. Moreover, many policy changes require explicit congressional approval. This chapter shows that all presidents face opportunities and constraints, and their success in office depends on the particular challenges that arise, their personal policy goals, and their skill at using the power of the presidency.

PRESIDENTIAL POWER: YESTERDAY AND TODAY

As we consider the history of America's 44 presidents, four facts stand out. (1) Presidents matter. Their actions have had profound consequences for the nation, in both domestic and foreign policy. (2) Presidents get their power from a variety of sources, from provisions of the Constitution to their management of and the actions taken by the executive branch of government. (3) Presidential power has increased over time, not because of changes in the

Constitution, but because of America's growth as a nation, its emergence as a dominant actor in international politics, the expansion of the federal government, and various acts of legislation that have given new authority to the president. (4) There are sharp limits to presidential power. Presidents are often forced to compromise or abandon their plans in the face of public, congressional, or foreign opposition.

EARLY YEARS THROUGH WORLD WAR I

Since the early years of the Republic, presidents' actions have had profound consequences for the nation. Presidents George Washington, John Adams, and Thomas Jefferson forged compromises on issues such as choosing a permanent location for the nation's capital, establishing the federal courts, and devising a system for financing the government.[1] Presidents Andrew Jackson and Martin Van Buren were instrumental in forming the Democratic Party and its local party organizations.

Early presidents also made important foreign policy decisions. For example, the Monroe Doctrine issued by President James Monroe in 1823 stated that America would remain neutral in wars involving European nations and that these nations must cease attempts to colonize or occupy areas in North and South America.[2] Presidents John Tyler and James Polk oversaw the admission of the huge territory of Texas into the Union following the Mexican-American War, as well as the acquisition of land that later became Oregon, Washington, Idaho, and parts of Montana and Wyoming.[3]

Presidents also played key roles in the conflict over slavery in America. President Millard Fillmore's support helped to enact the Compromise of 1850, which limited slavery in California, and Franklin Pierce supported the Kansas-Nebraska Act, which regulated slavery in those territories. And, of course, Abraham Lincoln, who helped form the Republican Party in the 1850s, played a transformative role in setting policy as president during the Civil War. His orders raised the huge Union Army, and as commander in chief he directed the conduct of the bloody war that ultimately brought the southern states back into the Union. Moreover, he issued the Emancipation Proclamation, which freed the slaves in the South.[4]

During the late 1800s and early 1900s, presidents were instrumental in federal responses to the nation's rapid expansion and industrialization.[5] The country's growing size and economy generated conflict over which services the federal government should provide to citizens and the extent to which the government should regulate individual and corporate behavior.[6] Various acts of legislation created new federal agencies and, in doing so, also created new presidential powers and responsibilities. For example, Republican president Theodore Roosevelt used the Sherman Antitrust Act to break up the Northern Securities Company, a mammoth nationwide railroad trust. Roosevelt also increased the power of the Interstate Commerce Commission to regulate businesses and expanded federal conservation programs. Democratic president Woodrow Wilson further increased the government's role in managing the economy through his support of the Clayton Antitrust Act, the Federal Reserve Act, the first federal income tax, and legislation banning child labor.[7]

As these examples illustrate, presidential power has grown over time as the president and members of the executive branch have obtained new regulatory

GEORGE WASHINGTON REMAINS, FOR many Americans, the presidential ideal—a leader whose crucial domestic and foreign policy decisions shaped the growth of America's democracy.

powers over corporations and individual Americans, and as presidents have responded to shifts in public opinion by proposing new policies. Moreover, the power of the presidency grew during this era due to the actions of presidents, particularly Roosevelt and Wilson, who firmly believed that the presidency was the most important federal office.

Yet, Wilson's foreign policy initiatives illustrate the limits of presidential power. Although he campaigned in the 1916 election on a promise to keep America out of World War I, Wilson ultimately ordered American troops to fight on the side of the Allies. After the war, Wilson offered a peace plan that proposed reshaping the borders of European countries in order to mitigate future conflicts; creating an international organization, the League of Nations, to prevent future conflicts; and taking other measures to encourage free trade and democracy.[8] However, America's allies rejected most of Wilson's proposals, and the Senate refused to allow American participation in the League of Nations.

THE GREAT DEPRESSION THROUGH THE PRESENT

Presidential actions defined the government's response to the Great Depression—the worldwide economic collapse in the late 1920s and 1930s marked by high unemployment, huge stock market declines, and bank failures. After winning the 1932 election, Democrat Franklin Roosevelt and his staff began reshaping American government. Roosevelt's New Deal reforms created many federal agencies that helped individual Americans and imposed many new corporate regulations.[9] This expansion continued under Roosevelt's successors. Even Republican Dwight Eisenhower, whose party had initially opposed many New Deal reforms, presided over the creation of new agencies and the building of the interstate highway system.[10]

PRESIDENT FRANKLIN DELANO Roosevelt called on the public to support his New Deal programs and other policies. Here, he delivers one of his "fireside chat" radio broadcasts, designed to communicate his arguments to the American people and to win their support.

Presidents were instrumental in the civil rights reforms and expansion of the federal government in the 1960s. With congressional approval, President Lyndon Johnson's administration created a wide range of domestic programs, such as the Department of Housing and Urban Development, Medicare, Medicaid, and federal funding for schools. The job of enacting voting rights and civil rights legislation also took place during LBJ's presidency.

Both Johnson and his successor, Richard Nixon, directed America's involvement in the Vietnam War, with the goal of forcing the North Vietnamese to abandon their plans to unify North and South Vietnam. But presidential efforts in Vietnam did not meet with success. Despite enormous deployments of American forces and more than 58,000 American soldiers killed, Nixon eventually signed an agreement that allowed American troops to leave but did not end the conflict, which concluded only after a North Vietnamese victory in 1975.

The two presidents after Nixon, Republican Gerald Ford and Democrat Jimmy Carter, faced the worst economic conditions since the Great Depression, largely due to increased energy prices. Both presidents offered plans to reduce unemployment and inflation, restore economic growth, and enhance domestic energy sources. But their efforts were largely unsuccessful, which became a critical factor in their failed reelection bids.

In the last generation, the political and policy importance of presidential actions has continued to increase. This trend continued during the presidency of Republican Ronald Reagan despite his platform of tax cuts, fewer regulations, and smaller government. Reagan and his staff also negotiated important arms control agreements with the Soviet Union. And Reagan's successor, Republican George H. W. Bush, led American and international participation in the Persian Gulf War during 1990 and 1991, which succeeded in removing Iraqi forces from Kuwait with minimal American casualties.

Democrat Bill Clinton's presidency was marked by passage of the North American Free Trade Agreement, welfare reform, arms control agreements, and successful peacekeeping efforts by U.S. troops in Haiti and the Balkans. His presidency also was distinguished by having one of the longest periods of economic growth in U.S. history and the first balanced budgets since the 1960s. However, despite efforts to drum up public support for health care reform, congressional and public opposition doomed Clinton's proposals in this area. The same factors delayed peacekeeping efforts in Bosnia and Kosovo and deterred American efforts to stop the massive genocide from civil war in Rwanda. President George W. Bush won congressional approval of his tax cuts and education reforms, but he is remembered for managing America's response to the September 11 attacks, including the wars in Iraq and Afghanistan.

Through six years in office, President Obama has secured several notable changes in domestic and foreign policy, including the enactment of health care reform, economic stimulus legislation, new financial regulations, and the appointment of two Supreme Court justices. However, he has had to compromise in enacting many of the new policies, and in areas such as immigration reform, he has been completely unsuccessful in achieving his policy goals.

Taken together, the history of presidential successes and failures highlights how presidents are often constrained by circumstances. Even today, although America's president leads the most powerful nation in the world, whoever sits in the Oval Office can face problems for which there are no easy (or even feasible) solutions. Consider Russia's 2014 annexation of Crimea from Ukraine. Aside from

THE PRESIDENT PLAYS A predominant role in American foreign policy. In the 1980s, President Ronald Reagan negotiated numerous arms agreements with the Soviet Union. Here, Reagan and Soviet leader Mikhail Gorbachev sign a treaty eliminating certain types of nuclear missiles.

economic sanctions and diplomatic pressure, the only option open to the Obama administration was some form of military intervention, ranging from sending arms to the Ukrainians to committing American forces to the conflict. Such actions would run the risk of open war with Russia, over an issue that few Americans care deeply about. Put this way, it is at least understandable why the Obama administration stopped short of military action. The problem was not a lack of insight or courage on the part of President Obama and his aides, but the fact that there was no way to reverse Russia's actions without incurring unacceptably high costs.

DESCRIBE THE CONSTITUTIONAL AND STATUTORY POWERS OF THE PRESIDENT TODAY

THE PRESIDENT'S JOB DESCRIPTION

constitutional authority
Powers derived from the provisions of the Constitution that outline the president's role in government.

statutory authority (presidential) Powers derived from laws enacted by Congress that add to the powers given to the president in the Constitution.

This section describes both the president's **constitutional authority** (the powers derived from the provisions of the Constitution that describe the president's governmental role) and presidential **statutory authority** (the powers that come from laws giving the president additional responsibilities). These powers are summarized in Nuts & Bolts 12.1. As the box indicates, some presidential powers arise from one source, such as the Constitution, and others derive from a combination of constitutional and statutory authority. Our aim is to show how these provisions operate in modern-day American politics: what kinds of opportunities and constraints they create for the current president and future holders of the office.

12.1 NUTS & bolts

PRESIDENTIAL POWERS

Power	Source of Power
Head of Government, Head of State (Vesting Clause)	Constitutional authority
Implementation of Laws ("Faithful Execution")	Constitutional and statutory authority
Executive Orders and Similar Directives (Rare)	Constitutional and statutory authority
Administration of Executive Branch	Constitutional authority
Nominations and Appointments to Executive Branch and Judiciary	Constitutional and statutory authority
Commander in Chief of Armed Forces	Constitutional authority
Negotiation of Treaties and Executive Agreements	Constitutional and statutory authority
Veto of Congressional Actions	Constitutional authority
Presidential Pardons	Constitutional authority
Other Ceremonial Powers	Constitutional authority
Executive Privilege	Other
Recommendation of Spending Levels and Other Legislative Initiatives	Other

HEAD OF THE EXECUTIVE BRANCH

A president's responsibilities and the source of presidential power begin with the constitutional responsibilities of the office. The Constitution's **vesting clause**, "The executive Power shall be vested in a President of the United States of America," makes the president the **head of government**, granting authority over the executive branch, as well as **head of state**, or the symbolic and political representative of the country. The precise meaning of the vesting clause has been debated for more than 200 years. Presidents and their supporters argue for an expansive meaning; their opponents counter that the clause is so vague as to be meaningless. These debates are an important clue that a president's power is only partially due to the specific constitutional grants of power—some of it comes from how each president interprets less concrete statements such as the vesting clause.

The Constitution also places the president in charge of the implementation of laws, saying, "he shall take Care that the Laws be faithfully executed." Sometimes the implementation of a law is nearly automatic, as was the case with a 2014 law that raised the cost of federal flood insurance for homeowners who lived in flood-prone areas. In that case, all the president needed to do to implement the law was to ensure that bureaucrats in the Federal Emergency Management Agency collected the higher premiums from policyholders.

More commonly, the president's authority to implement the law requires using judgment to translate legislative goals into programs, budgets, and regulations. For example, the Affordable Care Act of 2010 gave the president and his appointees in the Department of Health and Human Services the authority to modify provisions of the new program, including the deadlines for people to purchase health insurance through the new federal and state exchanges. Although critics charged that congressional consent was required, the Affordable Care Act was typical of major legislation in that it gave the administration significant leeway as it implemented the policy changes mandated by the law's passage.[11]

Finally, the president's control of the executive branch allows him to issue orders to government agencies that make significant policy changes. For example, in April 2014, President Obama signed an order barring federal contractors from retaliating against employees who disclose their salaries as a measure to help close the pay gap between women and men.[12] Although Congress could overturn this order, the president's ability to act unilaterally conveys significant power—unless opponents in Congress can organize, write legislation, shepherd it through the House and Senate, and override a presidential veto, the president's decision will prevail. In this sense, the ability to act unilaterally allows the president to impose outcomes and avoid the need to compromise with opponents in Congress.

APPOINTMENTS The president appoints ambassadors, senior bureaucrats, and members of the federal judiciary, including Supreme Court justices.[13] As the head of the executive branch, the president controls about 8,000 positions, ranging from high-profile jobs such as secretary of state to mundane administrative and secretarial positions. About 1,200 of these appointments—generally high-level positions such as cabinet secretaries—require Senate confirmation. In the main, the Senate approves the majority of the president's nominees without much debate or controversy, with exceptions concentrated in defense, intelligence, and justice positions.

vesting clause Article II, Section 1, of the Constitution, which states "The executive Power shall be vested in a President of the United States of America," making the president both the head of government and the head of state.

head of government One role of the president, through which he or she has authority over the executive branch.

head of state One role of the president, through which he or she represents the country symbolically and politically.

AFTER CONGRESS FAILED TO PASS the DREAM (Development, Relief, and Education for Alien Minors) Act, President Obama issued an executive order to stop the deportation of some young illegal immigrants in 2012. People under age 30 who came to the United States as children, who had been successful students or served in the military, and who posed no security threat were given the chance to earn legal resident status after only two years.

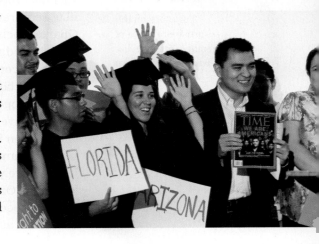

In addition, presidents make nominations to the federal courts; Presidents Bill Clinton and George W. Bush each appointed more than 400 judges. Because federal judgeships are lifetime appointments, they enable the president to put people into positions of power who will remain after he leaves office. For example, President Obama's two Supreme Court appointments, Sonia Sotomayor and Elena Kagan, emerged as influential voices on such issues as health care and the rights of criminal defendants. The full effects of these and other judicial appointments by Obama will not be fully apparent for years to come.

The need for Senate confirmation of the president's appointments fundamentally limits this presidential power. Rather than demanding that the Senate vote on every nomination, presidents have often compromised and withdrawn the most controversial names and found other candidates who were more satisfactory to the Senate. For example, Debo Adegbile, President Obama's 2014 nominee to head the Civil Rights Division in the Justice Department, was rejected by the Senate because of his past work as a criminal defense attorney.[14]

recess appointment Selection by the president of a person to be an ambassador or the head of a department while the Senate is not in session, thereby bypassing Senate approval. Unless approved by a subsequent Senate vote, recess appointees serve only to the end of the congressional term.

One way the president can temporarily dodge the need for Senate approval is to make a **recess appointment** during a period that Congress is not in session. These appointments, however, are temporary, lasting only for the rest of the legislative term. By making recess appointments, the president can fill vacant ambassadorships or designate heads of cabinet departments without waiting for a Senate vote. This provision was included in the Constitution because it was expected Congress would not be in session much of the year; but in the modern era, when Congress is in session almost continuously, recess appointments are sometimes used to bypass the confirmation process for controversial nominees. President Obama used this strategy in January 2012 to appoint Richard Cordray to head the Consumer Financial Protection Bureau—although Cordray could have served until late 2014 under the recess appointment, he was later confirmed by the Senate to a five-year term.

executive orders Proclamations made by the president that change government policy without congressional approval.

EXECUTIVE ORDERS Presidents have the power to issue **executive orders**—that is, proclamations that unilaterally change government policy without subsequent congressional consent[15]—as well as other kinds of orders that change policy, such as National Security Presidential Directives and Presidential Findings. Responding to the December 2012 mass shooting of schoolchildren at Sandy Hook Elementary School in Newtown, Connecticut, President Obama signed 23 executive orders relating to gun control in January 2013.[16] Many of these orders were relatively modest, such as releasing an analysis of how many lost or stolen guns are used in subsequent crimes. Other orders had more significant effects, such as ordering the Consumer Product Safety Commission (CPSC) to develop new requirements for gun locks. More significant policy changes proposed by Obama, such as banning the possession of armor-piercing bullets, limiting the size of handgun ammunition magazines, and increasing federal funding for local police officers, were part of a gun control package sent to Congress at the same time that the executive orders were signed. But as noted earlier, none of these legislative proposals were enacted.

Executive orders may appear to give the president authority to do whatever he wants, even in the face of strong opposition from Congress. However, as the gun control example illustrates, a president's power to issue executive orders is limited to purely administrative matters (such as releasing the study of lost and stolen guns). Or the president may be able to issue an executive order on a specific question because Congress passed a law giving him specific authority in this case (such as the ability to direct the CPSC to develop new gun-lock regulations).

WHAT DO POLITICAL SCIENTISTS DO?

For more on the president's use of executive orders, visit **wwnpag.es/wdpsd**

Moreover, regardless of the authority used to issue an order, if members of Congress had objected to the policy changes or new regulations, they could have passed a law overturning any such executive orders, or they could have denied funding to implement them—although they would have needed support from two-thirds of both houses to override the expected presidential veto. In light of congressional opposition to Obama's gun control legislation, if the president had tried to implement these changes through executive orders, he would surely have faced either legislative or judicial action to overturn the orders.

COMMANDER IN CHIEF The Constitution makes the president the commander in chief of America's military forces but gives Congress the power to declare war. These provisions are potentially contradictory, and the Constitution leaves open the broader question of who controls the military.[17] In practice, however, the president controls day-to-day military operations through the Department of Defense and has the power to order troops into action without explicit congressional approval. For example, in spring 2011, the Obama administration joined over a dozen other nations in using ships and aircraft to help the opposition in Libya to overthrow the country's dictator, Muammar al-Gaddafi. Members of Congress did not approve this action—in fact, the House of Representatives passed a resolution calling for a cutoff of funding. Similarly, the 2011 attack on Osama bin Laden's compound was carried out without prior congressional approval, although some congressional leaders were notified in advance.

Congress has the power to declare war, but this power by itself does not constrain the president. In fact, even though the United States has been involved in hundreds of military conflicts since the Founding, there have been only five declarations of war: the War of 1812, the Mexican-American War (1846), the Spanish-American War (1898), World War I (1917), and World War II (1941).

As a way of restraining presidential war-making power, Congress enacted the War Powers Resolution in 1973 (see Nuts & Bolts 12.2). However, a 2004 report by the Congressional Research Service found that between 1975 and 2003, despite dozens of U.S. military actions—ranging from embassy evacuations to large-scale operations, including the 1991 Persian Gulf War and the invasions of Iraq and Afghanistan—the War Powers Resolution has been invoked only once.[18]

12.2 NUTS *& bolts*

THE WAR POWERS RESOLUTION OF 1973

1. The president is required to report to Congress any introduction of U.S. forces into hostilities or imminent hostilities.

2. The use of force must be terminated within 60 days unless Congress approves of the deployment. The time limit can be extended to 90 days if the president certifies that additional time is needed to safely withdraw American forces.

3. The president is required whenever possible to consult with Congress before introducing American forces into hostilities or imminent hostilities.

4. Any congressional resolution authorizing the continued deployment of American forces will be considered under expedited procedures.

SOURCE: Richard F. Grimmett, "The War Powers Resolution: After Thirty Years," Congressional Research Service Report RL32267, March 11, 2004.

Moreover, despite being in effect for nearly 40 years, it has never faced Supreme Court review. Some scholars have even argued that the resolution actually expands presidential power because it gives the president essentially unlimited control for the first 90 days of a military operation—and in many cases, such as the killing of bin Laden and the Libyan operation, 90 days is more than enough time to complete military action without getting Congress involved.[19]

Despite its limitations, the War Powers Resolution has forced presidents to gain congressional approval, in the form of congressional resolutions, or at least consultation with congressional leaders, for large-scale military actions such as the invasion of Iraq, as well as for lesser operations such as air strikes against ISIL forces in Syria and Iraq in 2014. Members of Congress can also curb a president's war-making powers through budget restrictions, legislative prohibitions, and, ultimately, impeachment.[20]

TREATY MAKING AND FOREIGN POLICY Treaty-making power is shared between Congress and the president: presidents and their staff negotiate treaties, which are then sent to the Senate for approval with the support of a two-thirds majority. In the case of treaties negotiated under **fast-track authority**, both the House and Senate vote on the treaty, with majority support in each chamber required for approval. However, the president has a first-mover advantage in the treaty-making process. Congress considers treaties only after negotiations have ended; there is no way for members of Congress to force the president to negotiate a treaty. However, the need for congressional approval often leads presidents to take account of senators' preferences when negotiating treaties, leading again to significant compromise between the two branches.

Presidents have two strategies for avoiding a congressional treaty vote. One is to announce that the United States will voluntarily abide by a treaty without ratifying it. President Clinton used this tactic to implement the 1997 Kyoto Protocol, an agreement that set limits on carbon emissions by industrialized nations.[21] It is also possible to structure a deal as an **executive agreement** between the executive branch and a foreign government, which does not require Senate approval. Relative to a ratified treaty, which remains in force after the president who negotiated it leaves office, both voluntary compliance and executive agreements have the disadvantage that a subsequent president can simply undo the action, as President George W. Bush did in the case of compliance with the Kyoto Protocol.

The president also serves as the principal representative of the United States in foreign affairs other than treaty negotiations. Presidential duties include communicating with foreign leaders, nongovernmental organizations, and even ordinary citizens to persuade them to act in ways that the president believes are in the best interest of the United States. For example, in April 2014, President Barack Obama made a two-week trip to Asia, where he signed defense agreements with the governments of the Philippines and South Korea, tried to persuade Japanese leaders there was a need for a new trade agreement, and gave public support to Japan in a territorial dispute with China.[22]

The amount of time the administration devotes to forein policy is subject to domestic and world events and therefore not entirely under presidential control. Barack Obama campaigned on a pledge to reduce American military operations abroad and, six years into his time in office, America no longer had combat operations in

fast-track authority An expedited system for passing treaties under which support from a simple majority, rather than a two-thirds majority, is needed in both the House and Senate, and no amendments are allowed.

executive agreement An agreement between the executive branch and a foreign government, which acts as a treaty but does not require Senate approval.

AS HEAD OF STATE, THE PRESIDENT often negotiates agreements with other countries. In 2014, President Obama visited Saudi Arabia to meet with King Abdullah and to reassure him that the United States would remain committed to the security of Saudi Arabia.

Iraq and Afghanistan. But Obama expanded drone and Special Forces attacks on members of terrorist organizations, promoted American participation in NATO operations against the Libyan government, and sent American forces to Eastern Europe in response to Russia's annexation of Crimea. Obama and his aides also spent considerable time coordinating the global response to the financial crisis of 2008–2009, as well as natural disasters such as the 2010 earthquake in Haiti.

Looking at presidential actions since World War II, some scholars have argued that there are "two presidencies," one dealing with domestic policy, the other foreign policy. This theory contrasts high levels of citizen, interest group, and legislator interest in domestic concerns such as taxation, spending, or regulation of industries, with low levels of interest in many foreign policy questions, such as minor treaties or outcomes that affect only people in other countries.[23] As a result, these scholars have argued, presidents may prefer to focus on foreign policy because they can often act without congressional consent or public scrutiny. Although this thesis still makes some sense, the increasing connection between domestic and foreign policy in areas such as trade or environmental protection, or disagreements about the necessity of military operations abroad (such as the ongoing war on terror), means that more often, presidential actions are inherently conflictual regardless of whether they fall into the category of domestic policy, foreign policy, or something in between.

LEGISLATIVE POWER The Constitution establishes lawmaking as a shared power between the president and Congress, and compromise between the two branches is fundamental to passing laws that satisfy both the president and Congress.[24] The president can recommend policies to Congress, notably in the annual **State of the Union** address. The president and staff also work with members of Congress to develop legislative proposals, and although the president cannot formally introduce legislation, it is typically easy to find a member of Congress willing to sponsor a presidential proposal.[25] Presidents and their legislative staff also spend considerable time lobbying members of Congress to support their proposals and negotiating with legislative leaders over policy details.

The president's legislative power also stems from the ability to veto legislation (see Chapter 11). Once both chambers of Congress have passed a bill by simple majority, the president must decide within two weeks of congressional action whether to sign it or issue a veto. Signed bills become law, but vetoed bills return to the House and Senate for a vote to override the veto. If both chambers enact the bill again with at least two-thirds majorities, the bill becomes law; otherwise, it is defeated. If Congress adjourns before the president has made a decision, the president can pocket veto the proposal by not responding to it. Pocket vetoes cannot be overridden, but congressional leaders can avoid them by keeping Congress in session for two weeks after a bill is enacted, thereby forcing the president either to sign the bill or to veto it.

Presidential vetoes can have significant policy consequences. President Bill Clinton vetoed several bills that would have banned some types of late-term abortion. Supporters of these measures made up a majority in both houses of Congress, but they could not amass the two-thirds majority required to override Clinton's veto.[26] After President Bush took office, however, the ban was approved by the House and Senate and signed into law.

Studies show that vetoes are most likely to occur under divided government, when a president from one party faces a House and Senate controlled by the other party.[27] Under these conditions, the veto allows the president to block proposals

State of the Union An annual speech in which the president addresses Congress to report on the condition of the country and to recommend policies.

supported by legislators from the other party, producing gridlock.[28] Vetoes are much less likely under unified government, when one party controls both Congress and the presidency, because the chances are much higher that the president and legislators from his party hold similar policy priorities. By vetoing legislation, presidents gain raw power over the legislative process and can stop a proposal dead in its tracks unless it has strong support in both houses of Congress.

In general, presidents who face a divided government issue more vetoes than those who hold office under a unified government. Democratic president Bill Clinton faced divided government, working with a Republican-controlled Congress for all but the first two years of his eight years in office, and he issued 40 vetoes in all. In contrast, Republican George W. Bush had divided government with Democratic control of the Senate during most of his first two years, unified government for the middle four years, and divided government once again when the Democrats took control of Congress in the 2006 midterms, and he issued a total of 11 vetoes in eight years. As of late 2014, President Obama had vetoed only two pieces of legislation, reflecting unified government during his first two years in office, and the fact that relatively little legislation was passed by Congress after the 2010 Republican takeover of the House.

A president's threats to veto legislation provide an additional source of power: they allow the president to specify what kinds of proposals he is willing or unwilling to accept from Congress. Legislators then know that they need to write a proposal that attracts two-thirds support in both houses or accede to a president's demands. For example, during the 2012–2013 debate over raising the federal debt limit, President Obama said he would veto any legislation that included a repeal of his health care legislation, even if a veto led to a government shutdown. Whether Obama was willing to follow through with his threat is unclear, but the threat worked. In this sense, the veto power can facilitate compromise between presidents and members of Congress—compromises that favor the president's point of view.

Although the veto is useful to block legislation or issue a threat that encourages legislators to negotiate before casting their votes, it cannot force members of Congress to enact a proposal they oppose.[29] For example, President Obama could not use a veto threat to force Congress to take up gun control or immigration legislation. The president and staff bargain with legislators, trying to craft proposals that a majority will support and sometimes offering inducements to individual lawmakers, such as presidential support for other favored policies. House members and senators from the president's party may feel obligated to help, but as congressional inaction on gun control and immigration illustrates, it is very hard for a president to win over opponents in Congress, especially if helping the president will anger a legislator's constituents. Under these conditions, compromises are likely to favor congressional preferences.

In sum, by using a combination of their proposal power, lobbying, issuing vetoes and veto threats, and the other powers discussed in this section, presidents have considerable—but not unlimited—influence over legislative outcomes (see How It Works: The President's Role in the Legislative Process).

OTHER DUTIES AND POWERS The Constitution gives the president several additional powers, including the authority to pardon people convicted of federal crimes or to commute their sentences. The only limit on this power is that a president cannot pardon anyone who has been impeached and convicted by Congress. (Thus, if a president is removed from office via impeachment, he can neither pardon himself nor be pardoned when the vice president assumes the presidency.)

How It Works

THE PRESIDENT'S ROLE IN THE LEGISLATIVE PROCESS

The Constitution describes the president's influence over new policy initiatives in terms of the power to sign or veto acts of Congress. However, the president's staff, ties to the party in government, public profile, and position as head of the executive branch give him or her substantial additional power to shape public policy.

PRESIDENT

President directs staff to gather information and develop proposals—they talk to the public, members of Congress, interest groups, union and corporation heads, party leaders, and others. Some of these groups initiate contact and submit their own ideas or even fully drafted proposals.

THE WHITE HOUSE STAFF

PRESIDENT

Negotiations between the president and Congress produce compromise proposals.

CONGRESS

PRESIDENT AND HIS STAFF

President and his staff lobby members of Congress and propose modifications of proposals to gain support.

CONGRESS

PRESIDENTIAL APPOINTEES

Presidential appointees in federal agencies administer implementation of the new laws.

How It Works
In Practice

THE PRESIDENT'S ROLE IN ECONOMIC STIMULUS LEGISLATION

The passage and implementation of the American Recovery and Reinvestment Act (ARRA) illustrates the president's influence on policy. ARRA was enacted in the early days of the Obama administration and provided over $700 billion in tax credits and government expenditures to stimulate the economy after the 2008 financial crisis.

PRESIDENT AND HIS STAFF

Development of ARRA began soon after Obama's election in 2008 as part of the presidential transition process.

At the same time, Democrats in the House and Senate were preparing their own proposals.

CONGRESS

PRESIDENT AND HIS STAFF

January 26, 2009: after some negotiations, revised proposal was introduced in Congress. The proposal included funding for infrastructure projects, tax credits for purchasers of "green" energy technologies, and help for areas with high unemployment.

CONGRESS

PRESIDENT AND HIS STAFF

The proposal passed the House on a party-line vote on January 29, 2009. Obama and his aides negotiated changes in the Senate in an attempt to gain Republican support. In the end, the Senate passed the bill on February 10, 2009, on a party-line vote.

CONGRESS

YEA VOTES		
	REPUBLICANS	DEMOCRATS
HOUSE	0	244
SENATE	3	57

PRESIDENTIAL APPOINTEES AND BUREAUCRATS

Implementation requires bureaucrats to decide which infrastructure projects should be funded, what energy hardware qualifies for the tax credit, and the level of unemployment that entitles a community to get federal funds.

POP QUIZ

1 The president has direct control over the cabinet departments, but his control of _____ is more limited.

a the White House staff
b the Executive Office of the President
c the bureaucracy
d the independent agencies
e the vice president

2 Who developed the early proposals for an economic stimulus bill?

a the president and his staff and Congress
b bureaucrats and presidential appointees
c the president and his staff only
d Congress only
e interest groups

Answers: 1.d; 2.a

Although most presidential pardons attract little attention, some have been extremely controversial. Presidents have pardoned their own appointees for crimes committed while serving in their administrations, as well as pardoning campaign contributors and personal friends. For example, in July 2007, President Bush commuted a 30-month jail term given to Lewis "Scooter" Libby, Vice President Dick Cheney's former aide. Libby had been convicted of lying to a grand jury about his role in leaking the name of Valerie Plame, a covert CIA agent, to several journalists. Yet, in the main, most pardons attract little attention. For example, President Obama had pardoned about 50 individuals (as of late 2014) who had been convicted of a wide range of crimes, from embezzlement to drug distribution, but none of these pardons made front-page news.

EXECUTIVE PRIVILEGE Finally, although this power is not formally set out in the Constitution or a statute, all presidents have claimed to hold the power of **executive privilege**. This refers to the ability to shield themselves and their subordinates from revealing White House discussions, decisions, or documents (including e-mails) to members of the legislative or judicial branches of government.[30] The nature of executive privilege—exactly what it protects versus what Congress can force the president to release—is an unsettled question. Some constitutional scholars even argue that, in legal terms, executive privilege doesn't exist.[31]

Although claims of executive privilege have been made since the ratification of the Constitution in 1789, it is still not clear exactly what falls under the privilege and what does not. In the 1974 case *United States v. Nixon*, a special prosecutor appointed by the Justice Department to investigate the Watergate scandal challenged President Nixon's claims of executive privilege to force him to hand over tapes of potentially incriminating Oval Office conversations involving Nixon and his senior aides. The Supreme Court ruled unanimously that executive privilege does exist, but that the privilege is not absolute. The Court's decision required Nixon to release the tapes, which proved his involvement with attempts to cover up the scandal—but the ruling did not clearly state the conditions under which a future president could withhold such information.[32]

After he had been in office for six years, President Obama's only claim of executive privilege came in response to a congressional demand for documents related to a Justice Department sting operation involving the sale of illegal firearms at the U.S.-Mexico border, Operation Fast and Furious.[33] (Congressional Republicans alleged that the operation was bungled and that the firearms were later used to kill American border agents.) In response to the refusal, the House Committee on Oversight held Obama's Attorney General, Eric Holder, in contempt of Congress, although to this point no further action has been taken against Holder and the executive privilege claim has held up.

Claims of executive privilege present a dilemma. On the one hand, members of Congress need to know what is happening in the executive branch. In the case of President

executive privilege The right of the president to keep executive branch conversations and correspondence confidential from the legislative and judicial branches.

CONGRESSIONAL INVESTIGATIONS of the Justice Department's failed attempt to prevent illegal arms shipments into the United States (the operation was code-named "Fast and Furious") were stymied by President Obama's use of executive privilege to limit testimony by his appointees.

Nixon and the Watergate scandal, claims of executive privilege allowed the Watergate cover-up to continue for more than a year and would have kept this information secret permanently if the Supreme Court had ruled in Nixon's favor.[34] Exercising executive privilege can also weaken accountability to the public, as restricting information may leave the average voter unaware of what an administration is doing. On the other hand, the president and his staff need to be able to communicate freely, discussing alternative strategies and hypothetical situations or national security secrets without fearing that they will be forced to reveal conversations that could become politically embarrassing or costly. (Suppose the discussions included political strategies for the next election or a sarcastic remark about jailing their opponents.) Moreover, allowing aides to testify before Congress is enormously time-consuming and can be costly for the aides if they need to hire lawyers.

Even when executive privilege does not apply (for example, if Congress has not issued a subpoena), presidents can and sometimes do refuse to provide information to the media, Congress, or the general public. For example, despite President Obama's promises to increase the transparency of government, his administration has refused some requests from Congress, such as demands for documents related to the IRS's investigation of the tax-exempt status of organizations that air campaign advertising. Republicans had charged that conservative groups had been targeted by the IRS, although the evidence to date indicates that the IRS investigated a wide range of groups and did not focus on conservatives. Even so, the details of the investigation, and debate over how to go about it, might prove politically embarrassing. (See the You Decide feature.)

THE PRESIDENT AS POLITICIAN

As the head of the executive branch, the president has considerable influence over policy. However, much of what presidents do (or want to do) requires support from legislators, bureaucrats, and average citizens. As a result, the presidency is an inherently political office. The president has to take into account the political consequences of his decisions—both for their effect on his own reelection prospects and for the reelection of legislators from his party. A president must also contend with the reality that achieving policy goals often requires bargaining and compromising with others, both inside and outside government.

Presidents try to deliver on their campaign promises not only because they believe in them but also because fulfilling them is politically advantageous. For example, one of President Obama's central campaign promises was to restore economic growth, a promise partly fulfilled by the enactment of economic stimulus legislation in February 2010. Although these measures did not restore robust economic growth by the 2012 elections, Obama gained support from voters who believed that the measures had prevented a more extreme economic downturn. Obama also benefited from the positive impact of the stimulus in swing states such as Ohio.

presidential approval rating
The percentage of Americans who think that the president is doing a good job in office.

The president also typically keeps a close eye on the **presidential approval rating**, a survey-based measurement of the percentage of the public who thinks the president is doing a good job in office. Particularly during the first term, one of the president's primary concerns is to build a record that will ensure reelection, and keeping approval levels as high as possible is a crucial part of this strategy.

THE LIMITS OF EXECUTIVE PRIVILEGE

Deciding what information a president can be compelled to release to the public or to other branches of government and what information can be kept confidential requires confronting fundamentally political questions. There are no right answers, and the limits of executive privilege remain unclear. On the one hand, members of Congress need facts, predictions, and estimates from the executive branch to make good public policy. More important, members need to be able to weigh the pros and cons of a range of policy alternatives.

Consider the controversy over the Obama administration's grant of federal loan guarantees to the Solyndra Corporation.[a] These loan guarantees were supposed to allow Solyndra to bring less expensive, more efficient solar power panels to market. However, the company's efforts were unsuccessful, and it declared bankruptcy in August 2011, which cost the government more than $500 million. Republican critics in Congress charged that a high-level Obama appointee in the Department of Energy whose wife did legal work for Solyndra had pushed for the loans and that the Obama administration had ignored warnings about the company because it wanted to claim credit for a "green energy" program. There were several congressional investigations during 2011 and 2012, and numerous congressional subpoenas for documents—some of which were challenged by the Obama administration on grounds of executive privilege.

The Solyndra case may seem like a situation in which executive privilege does not apply. Shouldn't the American people know the reasons the loan guarantees were made? If the Department of Energy staff did nothing wrong, why wouldn't the Obama administration comply with congressional subpoenas and make presidential staff available for congressional hearings?

The problem is that testifying before Congress, or even releasing documents in response to a congressional request, is enormously time-consuming and can be surprisingly expensive. Presidential appointees who have testified before Congress have faced personal legal bills of $100,000 or more. If members of Congress could require information and testimony of executive branch employees whenever they wanted, it would be hard for the executive bureaucracy to get anything done—and hard to convince anyone to work there.

Of course, there are two sides to this story. Republicans opposed the loan guarantees on policy grounds, believing that the free market rather than the government should decide which new companies got funded. And, of course, the investigations did help to publicize the fact that the Obama administration's decision to lend money to Solyndra was, at least in retrospect, a mistake. But even leaving these concerns aside, it is not surprising that the administration invoked executive privilege, as the costs of complying with the subpoenas in terms of time, effort, and a loss of confidentiality were substantial.

Brian Harrison
ent & CEO, Solyndra

Mr. W.G. Stover,
Senior Vice President & CEO, S

The Obama Administration refused to have some Energy Department staffers testify before Congress about loans to the Solyndra Corporation, claiming executive privilege.

In sum, although being able to get information from a president can help members of Congress make better policy choices, there are situations in which confidentiality helps the president and his staff make good choices as well. Nonetheless, executive privilege can also be used to hide crimes or questionable political tactics, or to prevent members of Congress from embarrassing the president by publicizing his mistakes or private comments. Should presidents have an executive privilege? What limits should apply to congressional requests for information and testimony? You decide.

CRITICAL **THINKING** QUESTIONS

1. Decisions about executive privilege involve a trade-off between informing the public and members of Congress about executive branch deliberations, and facilitating the free exchange of information between a president and his or her aides. What criteria or decision rules should determine whether claims of executive privilege are upheld or dismissed?

2. In the case of the Solyndra program, would you allow President Obama to claim executive privilege or force him to release all of the information requested by members of Congress? Would your answer be different if Obama were a Republican?

FIGURE » 12.1

PRESIDENTIAL POPULARITY AND REELECTION

This figure shows the preelection year average approval ratings for recent presidents who ran for reelection. It shows that a president's chances of winning reelection are related to his popularity. At what level of approval would you say that an incumbent president is likely to be reelected?

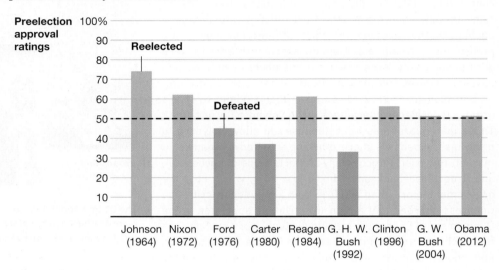

SOURCE: Approval data from the Roper Center for Public Opinion Research, University of Connecticut, "Data Access: Presidential Approval," http://webapps.ropercenter.uconn.edu/CFIDE/roper/presidential/webroot/presidential_rating.cfm (accessed 10/26/12).

Figure 12.1, which shows the presidential approval ratings for the last six presidents who ran for reelection, reveals that first-term presidents with less than 50 percent approval are in real trouble. No recent president has been reelected with less than a 50 percent approval rating. We will say more about presidential approval later in this chapter.

THE PRESIDENT AS PARTY LEADER The president is the unofficial head of his political party and generally picks the party's day-to-day leadership, or at least has considerable influence over the selection. This process begins when a presidential candidate captures the party's nomination. For example, in 2008, soon after Barack Obama became the presumptive Democratic Party nominee, some of his senior aides and advisers took on leadership positions in the Democratic Party organization.[35] During the 2012 campaign, some of these individuals returned to help Obama get reelected, such as Deputy Campaign Manager Jennifer O'Malley Dillon, who had served as the Executive Director of the Democratic National Committee.

The president's connection to the party reflects intertwining interests. The president needs support from members of his party in Congress to enact legislation, and the party and its candidates need the president to compile a record of policy achievements that reflect well on the organization and to help raise the funds needed for the next election. Therefore, party leaders generally defer to a presidential candidate's (or a president's) staffing requests, and most presidents and presidential candidates take time to meet with national party leaders and the congressional leadership from their party to plan legislative strategies, make joint campaign appearances, and raise funds for the party's candidates.

When presidential approval ratings drop to low levels, most members of Congress see no political advantage to campaigning with the president or supporting White House proposals, and they may become increasingly reluctant to comply with the president's requests. In the 2002 and 2004 elections, Republican legislators stressed their connection to President Bush and gladly accepted offers of joint campaign appearances. In 2006 and 2008, however, many Republican candidates deemphasized their connection to Bush and did not ask him to campaign with them.[36] A similar phenomenon arose in the 2010 and (to a lesser extent) 2014 midterms for Democratic candidates and President Obama: in many districts, incumbents believed that campaigning with Obama would reduce their chances of reelection, as it would remind voters of unpopular proposals championed by Obama, such as health care reform.

GOING PUBLIC The president would appear to be in an excellent position to communicate with the American people because of his prominent role and the extensive media coverage devoted to anything he says to the nation. Broadcast and cable networks even give the president prime time slots for the State of the Union speech and other major addresses. The media attention that comes with the presidency provides the president with a unique strategy for shaping government policy: the ability to **go public**, or to appeal directly to American citizens.[37] Presidential appeals are partly designed to persuade, but they also serve to bring an issue that the president considers important to the attention of citizens who already share his views, in the hope that they will pressure members of the House and Senate to support the president's requests. However, there is no guarantee that these efforts will succeed. For example, although President Obama made several nationally televised speeches calling for new gun control legislation, including a major push in the 2013 State of the Union address, no reforms were brought to a vote in Congress. And, as with gun control, there is no sign that Obama's speeches on immigration reform have had much of an effect on public opinion.

The problem for most presidents is that going public is often counterproductive. Although it may energize supporters, it may also have a similar effect on opponents.[38] Thus, rather than facilitating compromise (or a wholesale presidential victory), publicizing an issue may deepen existing conflicts. Presidents are often better off keeping quiet and focusing on trying to negotiate a compromise with opponents in Congress. More generally, studies suggest that most Americans ignore or reject a president's attempts to go public. Thus, although presidents may want to shape public opinion in this way, in general they find it hard to do so.[39] Going public is also politically risky—although it may force members of Congress to agree with the president without the benefit of the usual bargaining and negotiations, it may also alienate members of Congress, as it represents an attempt to go over their heads to reach the American people directly.[40]

PRESIDENTIAL SUCCESSION

Under the Constitution, presidents are limited to two full terms in office. A vice president who becomes president in between elections can, if reelected, serve two more full terms if he or she takes over during the first half of the predecessor's

THE PRESIDENT IS THE UNOFFICIAL head of his party and works with fellow party members in government. Here, President Obama meets with Vice President Joe Biden and Democratic House leaders, clockwise from the bottom left, Steve Israel (D-NY), Chris Van Hollen (D-MD), Steny Hoyer (D-MD), House minority leader Nancy Pelosi (D-CA), James Clyburn (D-SC), Xavier Becerra (D-CA), and Joseph Crowley (D-NY).

go public A president's use of speeches and other public communications to appeal directly to citizens about issues the president would like the House and Senate to act on.

TABLE » 12.1

PRESIDENTIAL SUCCESSION

The order of presidential succession is set out in the Constitution. Why do you think the Founders put the vice president first, congressional leaders second, and cabinet secretaries third?

1. **The Vice President**
2. **Legislative Branch Leaders**

   The Speaker of the House

   The President Pro Tempore of the Senate
3. **Cabinet Secretaries (in the order of their department's creation)**

   Secretary of State

   Secretary of the Treasury

   Secretary of Defense

   Attorney General

   Secretary of the Interior

   Secretary of Agriculture

   Secretary of Commerce

   Secretary of Labor

   Secretary of Health and Human Services

   Secretary of Housing and Urban Development

   Secretary of Transportation

   Secretary of Energy

   Secretary of Education

   Secretary of Veterans Affairs

   Secretary of Homeland Security

term; otherwise, this individual can serve only one additional term. Under the Twenty-Fifth Amendment, a vice president can also temporarily take over as president, a procedure used in 2007 when President George W. Bush had a medical procedure requiring anesthesia.[41]

If both the president and the vice president were to die or become incapacitated, the Speaker of the House of Representatives would become president. Next in line is the president pro tempore of the Senate, and then a list of cabinet secretaries in the order shown in Table 12.1. Whenever the entire Cabinet and Congress gather in one place, such as at the annual State of the Union address, at least one member of the Cabinet is assigned to be somewhere else, so that in the event of a catastrophe someone in the line of succession would survive to assume the presidency.

In the event that the vice president must be replaced due to resignation, impeachment, or incapacity, the Twenty-Fifth Amendment allows the president to nominate a new vice president, who must be confirmed by majority votes in the House and the Senate. This procedure was used twice in the 1970s, first to make Gerald Ford vice president under Richard Nixon (replacing Spiro Agnew), then, after Nixon's resignation, to make Nelson Rockefeller vice president under Ford.[42]

THE EXECUTIVE BRANCH

EXPLAIN HOW THE EXECUTIVE OFFICE OF THE PRESIDENT, THE VICE PRESIDENT, AND THE CABINET HELP THE PRESIDENT

As head of the executive branch, the president runs a huge, complex organization with hundreds of thousands of employees. This section describes the organizations and staff who help the president exercise his vast responsibilities, from managing disaster-response efforts to implementing policy changes.[43] Among these employees are appointees who hold senior positions in the government. These individuals serve as the president's eyes and ears in the bureaucracy, making sure that bureaucrats are following presidential directives.

Many other executive branch employees work within the Executive Office of the President, which has employed about 1,800 people in recent administrations. About one-third of these employees are concentrated in two offices: the Office of Management and Budget, which develops the president's budget proposals and monitors spending by government agencies, and the Office of the United States Trade Representative, which negotiates trade agreements with other nations.

THE EXECUTIVE OFFICE OF THE PRESIDENT

Nuts & Bolts 12.3 lists the organizations that make up the **Executive Office of the President (EOP)** and one of its main components, the White House Office. Both include offices that have clear policy-related or political missions.

One of the most important duties of EOP staff is helping the president and candidates from his party achieve their policy goals and get reelected. For example, two of President Obama's key political operatives, David Plouffe and

Executive Office of the President (EOP) The group of policy-related offices that serves as support staff to the president.

12.3 NUTS & bolts

THE EXECUTIVE OFFICE OF THE PRESIDENT

Council of Economic Advisers	Office of National AIDS Policy
Council on Environmental Quality	Office of National Drug Control Policy
Domestic Policy Council	Office of Science and Technology Policy
Homeland Security Council	Office of United States Trade Representative
National Economic Council	President's Foreign Intelligence Advisory Board
National Security Council	Privacy and Civil Liberties Oversight Board
Office of Administration	USA Freedom Corps
Office of the First Lady	White House Fellows Office
Office of Faith-Based and Community Initiatives	White House Military Office
Office of Management and Budget	White House Office

THE PRESIDENT'S CLOSEST ADVISERS are chosen for their loyalty to the president and his policy goals. For example, Senior Adviser Valerie Jarrett (left, standing) is one of President Obama's longest-serving and most loyal advisers. Other Obama key advisers pictured here are from left: Alyssa Mastromonaco (seated), Deputy Chief of Staff for Operations; Kathryn Ruemmler, Counsel to the President; Pete Rouse, Counselor to the President; Denis McDonough, Chief of Staff; Rob Nabors, Deputy White House Chief of Staff for Policy; and David Simas, Deputy Senior Adviser for Communications and Strategy.

David Axelrod, served in the EOP as senior advisers. Their job was to link the administration and the reelection campaign—as one article put it, "making sure that the actions of one did not threaten the success of the other."[44]

The most influential EOP staff occupy the offices in the West Wing of the White House. The West Wing contains the president's office, known as the Oval Office, and space for the president's chief aide and personal secretary, as well as senior aides such as the vice president, the president's press secretary, and the chief of staff, who coordinates White House operations. Many recent chiefs of staff have been central in the development of policy proposals and negotiations with members of Congress. However, the chief of staff serves as the agent of the president—what matters is what the president wants, not a chief of staff's policy preferences.

Most EOP staff members are presidential appointees who retain their positions only as long as the president who appointed them remains in office. These individuals are often drawn to government service out of loyalty to the president or because they share the president's policy goals. However, most leave their positions after a year or two to escape the pressures of the job, the long hours, and the relatively low government salaries.[45] Despite the fairly frequent turnover in many EOP positions, some EOP offices—such as the Office of Management and Budget, the Office of the United States Trade Representative, and the National Security Council—also have a significant number of permanent staff analysts and experts.[46]

When appointing people to EOP positions, the president's primary expectation of them is loyalty, rather than a concern for the general public or policy expertise.[47] (Exceptions to the loyalty rule for appointees are individuals who received their jobs because of their expertise, their connections to the president's political party as opposed to the president himself, or their links to an important group outside the government.) Why is loyalty so important? Put yourself in the position of a president whose packed day begins with an intelligence briefing and ends with a state dinner. All the while, crucial decisions about public policy are being made throughout the federal government. You have no time to make these decisions yourself or to supervise those who make them, so you need staff who understand what you want the government to do and who will dedicate themselves to implementing your vision.[48]

The emphasis on loyalty in presidential appointments also has an obvious drawback: appointees may not know much about the jobs they are given, and they may not be very effective at managing the agencies they are supposed to control. For example, Ron Klain, Obama's choice to lead the government's efforts to stem the spread of the Ebola virus, was criticized for his lack of experience in medicine and public health.

THE VICE PRESIDENT

As set out in the Constitution, the vice president's job is to preside over Senate proceedings. This largely ceremonial job is usually delegated to the president pro tempore of the Senate, who in turn typically gives the duty to a more junior member.

The vice president also has the power to cast tie-breaking votes in the Senate. As mentioned earlier, the vice president's other formal responsibility is to become president if the current president dies, becomes incapacitated, resigns, or is impeached. Of the 44 people who have become president, 9 were vice presidents who became president in midterm.

These rather limited official duties of the vice president pale in comparison to the influential role played by recent vice presidents. Vice President Dick Cheney, who served with President George W. Bush, exerted a significant influence over many policy decisions, including the rights of terror suspects, tax and spending policy, environmental decisions, and the writing of new government regulations.[49] Although Cheney's level of influence was unique, other recent vice presidents have also had real power. For example, Vice President Al Gore was an important adviser to President Bill Clinton. And Barack Obama's vice president, Joe Biden, plays an important role, attending all significant meetings and serving as the last person the president talks to before making a decision.

THE PRESIDENT'S CABINET

The president's **Cabinet** is composed of the heads of the 15 executive departments in the federal government, along with other appointees given cabinet rank by the president. Nuts & Bolts 12.4 lists the Cabinet and cabinet-level positions. The cabinet members' principal job is to be the frontline implementers of the president's agenda in their executive departments. As we discuss in Chapter 13, these appointees monitor the actions of the lower-level bureaucrats who retain their jobs regardless of who is president and are not necessarily sympathetic to the president's priorities.

Cabinet The group of 15 executive department heads who implement the president's agenda in their respective positions.

12.4 NUTS & bolts

CABINET AND CABINET-LEVEL POSITIONS

The president's Cabinet is composed of the heads of the 15 executive departments along with other appointees given cabinet rank by the president.

Secretary of Agriculture	Secretary of Transportation
Secretary of Commerce	Secretary of the Treasury
Secretary of Defense	Secretary of Veterans Affairs
Secretary of Education	Vice President
Secretary of Energy	White House Chief of Staff
Secretary of Health and Human Services	Attorney General
Secretary of Homeland Security	Head of the Environmental Protection Agency
Secretary of Housing and Urban Development	Head of the Office of Management and Budget
Secretary of the Interior	Head of the Office of National Drug Control Policy
Secretary of Labor	United States Trade Representative
Secretary of State	

Like other presidential appointees, cabinet members are chosen for a combination of loyalty to the president and expertise. Although serving under a Democratic president, Secretary of Defense Chuck Hagel is a former Republican senator and a Vietnam veteran. And Secretary of Energy Ernest Moniz is a nuclear physicist who served on Obama's Science and Technology Advisory Council prior to his appointment.

EXPLAIN HOW AMERICANS EVALUATE PRESIDENTS ▶

THE AMERICAN PUBLIC AND THE PRESIDENT

As we have described, presidents need to cultivate public support to get reelected and to enact their policy proposals. Thus, to understand the kinds of policy goals presidents set and how they seek to come across to the public, it is important to consider what Americans look for in a president.

What combinations of personal characteristics attract the most support for a candidate? Which characteristics might cost a candidate the election? Table 12.2 shows survey results about the qualities Americans want in a president. Military and business experience are clearly beneficial, while the value of political experience depends on whether a candidate has served in Washington or as a governor. Americans say

TABLE » 12.2

CITIZEN DEMANDS ON THE PRESIDENT

These data show that many Americans want the president to stick to his principles, say what he believes, and be forceful and decisive. Fewer consider political experience and willingness to compromise essential presidential qualities. How might the political necessity for bargaining and compromise affect a president's ability to satisfy citizens' expectations?

ESSENTIAL QUALITIES	1995	1999	2003
Sound judgment	76%	78%	76%
High ethical standards	67	63	67
Compassion	64	63	63
Saying what one believes	59	57	56
Consistent positions	51	50	52
Forcefulness and decisiveness	50	46	49
Willingness to compromise	34	33	38
Experiences in public office	30	38	37
Political savvy	31	—	36
Experience in Washington	21	27	32
Party loyalty	25	33	30
Military experiences	—	—	16

SOURCE: Pew Research Center, "Bush Reelect Margin Narrows to 45%–43%," News Release, September 25, 2003, www.people-press.org/reports/pdf/194.pdf (accessed 9/20/12).

they are willing to forgive divorce or past use of marijuana—but not an extramarital affair—and are generally uninterested in a candidate's race or gender.

The most interesting part of this table is the low value placed on Washington experience. Individuals who have served in Washington "for a long time" are less attractive than those who are political novices (a businessman or someone with military service) or who have only served in state government. This finding is consistent with findings presented in other chapters, such as low levels of trust in the federal government and low approval ratings for Congress. It also gives a partial explanation for why many recent presidents have been either governors (Reagan, Clinton, George W. Bush) or first-term senators (Obama)—and why Washington insiders such as Al Gore, John Kerry, and John McCain have had difficulty convincing voters to support them.

GAUGING PRESIDENTIAL POPULARITY

Various factors shape presidential popularity. In general, any issue that is at the top of the public's list of most-important problems is likely to be reflected in presidential popularity. Presidential approval doesn't arise from voters learning about a president's programs and voicing their support or opposition. Rather, approval is mostly about outcomes: most people look at the world around them, decide whether they like what they see, and express approval or disapproval by voting or not voting for those they hold responsible. In this sense, presidential approval is to some extent out of a president's control. Presidents Carter and Ford had the misfortune to be in office at a time when economic conditions were relatively weak and largely beyond their control, and Carter also had the bad luck to be president during the Iranian hostage crisis, in which 52 Americans were held hostage in Tehran for over a year (and were not released before the 1980 presidential election). In this sense, presidential popularity is to some extent a matter of luck.

PRESIDENTIAL APPROVAL IS influenced by international events that concern Americans, such as the taking of American hostages by militant Iranian students in 1979. President Jimmy Carter initially saw his approval ratings increase, but they declined steadily as the crisis continued into 1980.

In contrast, Bill Clinton enjoyed relatively high approval ratings during most of his eight years in office due to a strong domestic economy, but this economic strength probably had less to do with Clinton's policies and more to do with macroeconomic factors that were well out of Clinton's control. Moreover, President Clinton's affair with a White House intern had only a modest impact on his approval numbers, showing that the public is generally forgiving of scandal. In fact, you would have to go back to the 1970s and the Watergate scandal, which resulted in the resignation of President Nixon (and all-time low approval numbers), to find a scandal that had a sustained impact on a president's popularity.

President Obama's approval rating stayed relatively low during 2009–2010, reflecting the poor state of the American economy. But his approval rating began to increase during mid-2011 as unemployment began to decline and economic growth increased, reaching its peak in late 2012. Nonetheless, the revelation of NSA surveillance of Americans' cell phone calls, the

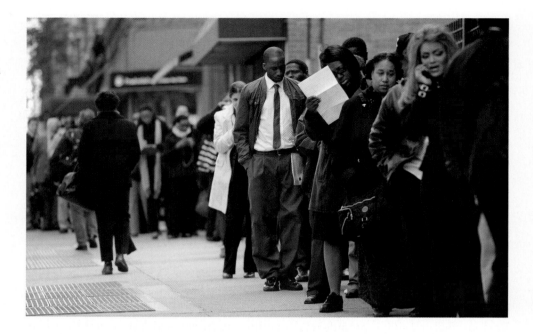

botched rollout of the Affordable Care Act in late 2013, worry over the threats posed by the Ebola virus and the ISIL terrorist organization, and a slow economic recovery caused a measurable decline in Obama's approval ratings.

All presidents have staff and consultants who regularly conduct polls to discern public feelings about the president and to identify what actions might increase approval. These findings influence but do not determine presidential actions. For example, poll results probably played no role in President Obama's decisions to send additional troops to Afghanistan in 2010 or to commence air strikes in 2014 against the ISIL terrorist organization. Although these moves received majority support, Obama likely would have made the same decisions even if he had faced much stronger public opposition. However, some legislators' tepid support for Obama's proposed Affordable Care Act was driven, at least in part, by an absence of public enthusiasm for aspects of the health care reform.

Political considerations matter somewhat less to a second-term president (because running for reelection is not an option), but politics still matters in the second term. Members of Congress are somewhat more likely to support policy initiatives proposed by a popular president, believing that this popularity reflects public support for the president's goals. Obama may have benefited from this effect early in his first term, during passage of economic stimulus legislation. Conversely, an unpopular president, such as Obama in his second term, will often find it much harder to build support for new programs, with immigration reform and gun control legislation as prime examples.

As these examples indicate, presidential popularity is more than just a measure of opinion; it is a resource that presidents can draw on to advance their policy agendas. However, high popularity does not allow presidents to do whatever they want, nor does low popularity make it impossible to do anything.

EXPLAINING PRESIDENTIAL APPROVAL

Mass surveys have asked questions about the public's approval of the president ever since Franklin Roosevelt was president. Figure 12.2 reports presidential

FIGURE » 12.2

PRESIDENTIAL APPROVAL RATINGS FOR RECENT PRESIDENTS

Bill Clinton's approval ratings remained relatively high, despite the scandal over his affair with Monica Lewinsky, probably because the economy remained strong during his presidency. On the other hand, George W. Bush's approval ratings plummeted when the war in Iraq became increasingly unpopular and the economy collapsed. Barack Obama's approval ratings started out high as he enacted a financial stimulus plan, guided passage of health care reform, and withdrew American troops from Iraq, but they started to go down given rising concerns about the economy and the effectiveness of the federal government.

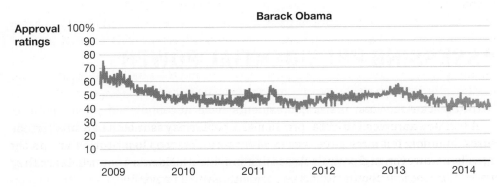

SOURCE: Approval data from the Roper Center for Public Opinion Research, University of Connecticut, "Data Access: Presidential Approval," http://webapps.ropercenter.uconn.edu/CFIDE/roper/presidential/webroot/presidential_rating.cfm (accessed 5/1/14)

approval data for the three most recent presidents: Bill Clinton, George W. Bush, and Barack Obama. The data for Clinton show a relatively rare pattern of steady improvement throughout his time in office. In contrast, George W. Bush's popularity steadily declined following the sharp spike upward after the September 11 attacks. Popularity figures for President Obama show gradual decline during the initial part of his first term, a slight increase in the year before the 2012 elections, and a slight decline in 2013 and 2014.

What explains this variation? Presidential approval generally spikes initially during national crises, such as the Iranian hostage crisis during Jimmy Carter's presidency, the Persian Gulf War during George H. W. Bush's presidency, or the September 11 attacks during the first term of George W. Bush's presidency. This phenomenon has been called the "rally 'round the flag" effect, comparing the electorate to troops gathering around a flag during a battle.[50]

There were no such spikes in the chart for Bill Clinton, reflecting the lack of national crises during his time in office. In such relatively calm times, presidential approval reflects the overall state of the nation, including citizens' perceptions of economic conditions and national security. In Clinton's case, economic conditions steadily improved throughout his presidency, generating the increase in his approval ratings. Even when Clinton was being impeached in 1998 and 1999, his popularity did not suffer. This finding may suggest that even if Americans want an ethical president, they forgive a president's misdeeds if his performance is good on the issues they care about, such as the economy. In contrast, during George W. Bush's two terms in office, he presided over an increasingly unpopular war in Iraq, along with a deteriorating economy, particularly during his last two years in office. Both of these factors contributed to the steady decline in Bush's approval ratings.

Similarly, while President Obama's six years in office have been largely free of major scandal, and Obama has enacted a substantial portion of his first-term campaign agenda, such as economic stimulus, health care reform, withdrawal of American combat forces from Iraq and Afghanistan, and financial industry regulation, his current lackluster poll numbers suggest that most Americans are focused on the mediocre state of the economy, Obama's inability to achieve his domestic policy goals and the perception that government is not responding effectively to crises such as the spread of the Ebola virus. Absent some larger crisis that causes a rally effect, Obama's popularity will increase only if the economy improves significantly.

> **ANALYZE WHY PRESIDENTS HAVE BECOME MUCH MORE POWERFUL SINCE THE FOUNDING**

ASSESSING PRESIDENTIAL POWER

Throughout American history, presidents have accomplished major achievements. They have expanded the territorial boundaries of the United States, fought wars, and enacted large government programs. Yet, the Constitution grants the president only limited powers. Assessing presidential power requires examining this contradiction. Saying that the presidents gained power because of the expansion of the United States or the increased size of the federal budget or bureaucracy tells only part of the story. Why did this power go to presidents rather than to Congress or to bureaucrats?

Debates over the source and extent of presidential powers have a long history. In the 1790s, Alexander Hamilton and James Madison, writing anonymously as Helvidius and Pacificus, argued about whether George Washington needed congressional approval to declare the United States neutral in the war between Britain and France.[51] Even after more than two centuries, many of the limits to presidential powers—including which executive actions require congressional approval and which ones can be reversed by Congress—are not well defined.

These constitutional ambiguities are mirrored by the unwritten nature of many presidential powers. Recall our discussion of the president's ability to influence the legislative process. In the Constitution, the president's powers are limited to advising Congress on the state of the union and to vetoing legislation, subject to congressional override. But presidents often have very real influence at all points in the legislative process. One classic work in presidential studies argues that this influence comes from a president's power to persuade legislators to accept the president's point of view. Presidents can offer a variety of small inducements, such as visits to the Oval Office and campaign assistance, and they can draw on the natural respect that most people (including members of Congress) feel for the presidency regardless of who holds the office, thereby securing compromises that achieve the president's policy goals.[52] The relatively high presidential success scores noted earlier suggest that most presidents have considerable success in their persuasion efforts.

The very ambiguity of the Constitution also creates opportunities for the exercise of presidential power. For example, the Constitution makes the president military commander in chief but gives Congress the power to declare war and to raise and support armies, without specifying which branch of government is in charge of the military. Thus, at least part of presidential authority must be derived or assumed from what the Constitution *does not say*—ways in which it fails to define or delineate presidential power. As a result, presidential power depends in part on how individual presidents interpret these provisions.

PRESIDENTS AND UNILATERAL ACTION

Political scientists Terry Moe and William Howell argue that constitutional ambiguities about presidential power have enabled presidents to take **unilateral action**, changing policy on their own without consulting Congress or anyone else.[53] Although Congress could, in theory, undo unilateral actions through legislation, court proceedings, or impeachment, Moe and Howell maintain that the costs of doing so, in terms of time, effort, and public perceptions, are often prohibitive.

unilateral action (presidential) Any policy decision made and acted upon by the president and presidential staff without the explicit approval or consent of Congress.

THE CONSTITUTION MAKES THE president commander in chief but limits that power by giving Congress the power to raise and support armies. When President Obama ordered a "surge" in the number of American troops in Afghanistan in 2009, he needed Congress to approve the $30 billion it was estimated to cost. The day after announcing the decision, Obama made the case for the "surge" in a speech at West Point.

The result is that presidents can take unilateral action despite congressional opposition, knowing that their actions stand little chance of being reversed. Of course, unilateral action may not lead to policy change—presidents and their staffs have to monitor subsequent actions by bureaucrats to make sure they are implementing the president's decision.

The 2011 debate over U.S. military action in Libya provides a good example of how constitutional ambiguities create opportunities for unilateral action. The Obama administration argued that because American aircraft and ships were not actively engaging Libyan forces (even though they were dropping bombs and launching cruise missiles on Libyan targets), the operation did not trigger the "hostilities or imminent hostilities" provisions of the War Powers Act. Moreover, the Obama team argued that its authority for the operation came from a United Nations Security Council resolution that authorized NATO support of Libyan rebels.[54]

This example is far from the first time that a president has argued that military operations were not subject to congressional review. During the Iraq War, some Democrats in Congress wanted to cut off war funding to force the withdrawal of American forces, but supporters of the Bush administration responded with what they called the **unitary executive theory**. They argued that the Constitution's vesting clause allows the president to issue orders and policy directives that members of Congress cannot undo unless the Constitution explicitly gives them this power. In the case of funding the Iraq War, they maintained that the Constitution's description of the president as commander in chief of America's armed forces meant that, even if Congress refused to appropriate funds for the war, the president could order American forces to stay in Iraq and order the Department of the Treasury to spend any funds necessary to continue operations.

In both cases, the position of the Obama and Bush administrations left members of Congress with a single unattractive option: they could invoke the War Powers Resolution to force the end of combat operations. This option would take time, as it would require building majority support in the House and the Senate for the resolution. It would also trigger Supreme Court review of the War Powers Resolution, which is a significant risk—if the Court were to rule in favor of the president and to hold that the resolution was unconstitutional, it would sharply reduce Congress's control over future military operations. Ultimately, members of Congress did not use the War Powers mechanism, which allowed both operations to continue.

Presidents act unilaterally to make domestic policy as well. For example, in 2014, President Obama unilaterally ordered federal contractors to increase the minimum wage they paid their employees.[55] Obama also ordered the Justice Department to change its deportation policies to focus its efforts on undocumented immigrants with criminal records, a move that reduced the overall number of deportations.[56] And the Obama administration made several important policy changes to smooth the implementation of the Affordable Care Act.

Although some critics argue that Obama's unilateral actions are unprecedented and dangerous, all presidents have behaved similarly. President Bush, for example, authorized wiretaps of Americans' international phone conversations without obtaining warrants from the Foreign Intelligence Surveillance Court, a special federal court created to approve such requests.[57] Moreover, through the nation's history, there have been many other examples of unilateral presidential actions, such as the annexation of Texas, the freeing of slaves in the

unitary executive theory The idea that the vesting clause of the Constitution gives the president the authority to issue orders and policy directives that cannot be undone by Congress.

Emancipation Proclamation, the desegregation of the U.S. military, the initiation of affirmative action programs, and the creation of major agencies such as the Peace Corps.[58]

CONTROL OVER THE INTERPRETATION AND IMPLEMENTATION OF LAWS

Most presidents have tried to control the interpretation and implementation of laws by issuing a **signing statement** when signing a bill into law. These documents, which explain the president's interpretation of the new law, are issued most often when the president disagrees with the interpretation of members of Congress who supported the legislation but still wishes to approve the bill. Presidents issue signing statements so that if the courts have to resolve uncertainties about the bill's intent, judges can take into account not only the views expressed during congressional debates about the bill, but also the president's interpretation of it.[59] The president can also influence the implementation of a law through a signing statement, essentially telling the bureaucracy to follow his interpretation of the law rather than Congress's.

In some cases, presidents have found loopholes in laws that were initially designed to restrict their power. An analysis of legislation designed to curb presidential power found that subsequent presidents actually used these laws to justify unilateral actions—the opposite of what was intended.[60] For example, current law requires the president to give congressional leaders "timely notification" of secret intelligence operations. During the Reagan administration, senior officials did not reveal the existence of ongoing operations for several months. When these operations were eventually discovered, officials claimed they were within the letter of the law because it did not specify a time limit for notification.[61]

signing statement A document issued by the president when signing a bill into law explaining his interpretation of the law, which often differs from the interpretation of Congress, in an attempt to influence how the law will be implemented.

CONGRESS HAS THE POWER TO BLOCK most types of presidential action, if it chooses. For example, in 2009, President Obama ordered the closure of the detention center for terror suspects at Guantánamo Bay, Cuba, but Congress passed legislation preventing the closure until the Obama administration developed detailed plans for relocating the prisoners.

FEDERAL COURTS CAN UNDO unilateral presidential actions. A series of Supreme Court rulings forced the George W. Bush administration to allow terror suspects, such as Salim Hamdan, an Al Qaeda member captured in Afghanistan, to challenge their imprisonment. This courtroom sketch from the U.S. naval base in Guantánamo, Cuba, shows Hamdan (far left) and his legal team.

CONGRESSIONAL RESPONSES TO UNILATERAL ACTION

In theory, members of Congress can undo a president's unilateral action by enacting a law to overturn it, but this is harder than it may sound.[62] Some members of Congress may approve of what the president has done or be indifferent to it, or they may give a higher priority to other policies. Still, reversals do happen: after President Obama announced plans to close the Guantánamo Bay detention center for terrorist suspects, the House and Senate added an amendment to a spending bill stating that the prison could not be closed until the administration released plans explaining where the prisoners would be sent. The facility remains open to this day.

Members of Congress can also write laws in a way that limits the president's authority over their implementation.[63] The problem with this approach is that members of Congress delegate authority to the president or the executive branch bureaucracy for good reasons—either because it is difficult for legislators to predict how a policy should be implemented, or because they cannot agree among themselves on an implementation plan.[64] Members of Congress from the president's party may also want to grant presidential authority because they hold policy goals similar to the president's and would therefore benefit from the exercise of unilateral power.

Even if members of Congress tried to use these strategies to limit the president's authority, it could still be argued—along the lines of the unitary executive theory—that Congress could not overturn the president's actions because the Constitution did not explicitly give the legislature this power. The only option for members of Congress would be to take the president to court (probably all the way to the Supreme Court) to demonstrate that he had overstepped his constitutional authority. In February 2014, Senator Rand Paul (R-KY) filed a lawsuit challenging the Obama administration's decision to allow the National Security Agency to collect Americans' telephone call metadata (the caller, receiver, time and length of call—but not the content of the conversation) without a warrant.[65] While the Obama administration voluntarily ended this data collection soon after Paul filed his lawsuit, in general, lawsuits are not a very practical or expedient option. Aside from the fact that the Court might not side with Congress, these legal proceedings could take years.

Congress also has the power to remove the president or vice president from office through the impeachment process. However, removing a president is much more difficult than passing a law to undo a unilateral action. First, House members must impeach (indict) the president by majority vote, which accuses him of a crime or breach of his sworn duties. Then, senators hold a trial, followed by a vote—in which a two-thirds majority is required to remove the president from office.

These procedures are rarely used. Only two presidents have faced an impeachment vote: Andrew Johnson in 1866 and Bill Clinton in 1999 (a third president, Richard Nixon, resigned from office to prevent an impeachment vote). Johnson was involved in a political dispute over administration of the southern states after the Civil War; Clinton was alleged to have lied under oath in a sexual harassment lawsuit. Although both of these presidents were impeached by the House, they were not convicted by the Senate, so they stayed in office. One reason impeachment is difficult is that members of Congress who are upset about certain presidential actions might nevertheless oppose removing the president from office. They might approve of the president's other initiatives, want to prevent the vice president from becoming president, or have concerns about the political backlash that impeachment could generate against them or their party.

In sum, ambiguities in the Constitution create opportunities for unilateral presidential action. These actions are subject to reversal through legislation, court decisions, and impeachment, but members of Congress face significant costs if they undertake any of these options. As long as the president is careful to limit his exercise of unilateral power to actions that do not generate intense opposition in Congress, he can implement a wide range of policy goals without official congressional consent—provided that bureaucrats go along with the president's wishes, a question we take up in the next chapter.

CONCLUSION

A president's power over government policy is derived from constitutional authority, statutory authority, and ambiguities within these official grants of power that give the president a substantial ability to act unilaterally. Even so, presidential power is limited. The president shares many powers with Congress. Moreover, presidents are politicians who need public support, both to win reelection and to persuade members of Congress to approve their policy initiatives. Public evaluation is based on how the president handles those issues that are considered a priority by many Americans, such as the economy, health care, and national security.

Taken together, these factors explain why President Obama has been successful in some policy areas but not others. Military actions, such as the bin Laden raid or drone attacks on Al Qaeda, do not require congressional assent, at least not in the short term. Obama's legislative successes in his first term, such as the Affordable Care Act and the economic stimulus legislation, were enacted when Democrats controlled both houses of Congress and a majority of House members and senators agreed with Obama's plans.

However, after Democrats lost control of the House in 2010, Obama lost his ability to enact major policy proposals, as doing so required votes from Republican House members who fundamentally disagreed with Obama's proposals in areas such as gun control and immigration reform. Obama's relatively low approval ratings meant that these legislators risked very little by refusing to consider Obama's proposals. The fact that Republicans regained control of the Senate in 2014 is only going to make Obama's job harder.

This is not to say that Obama has been powerless in his second term. As we discussed, he has made significant policy changes using executive orders and his control over the bureaucracy. Moreover, Obama held firm during negotiations over the federal debt limit, allowing public pressure on Republican legislators to grow, which ultimately led to Congress adopting Obama's position with few changes. In this area, as in many others, presidential power depends on whether other actors in American politics are willing (or are forced) to do what the president wants. Without strong public support or like-minded colleagues in Congress, presidential power is fundamentally limited.

PRESIDENTIAL POWER: YESTERDAY AND TODAY

▶ *Trace the evolution of presidential power over time.*
(Pages 436–40)

SUMMARY

Presidential power has increased throughout American history. Even so, there are sharp limits to presidential power, and all presidents must compromise their goals in light of what is politically possible.

CRITICAL THINKING AND DISCUSSION

If presidential power is limited, why have some presidents been so successful at achieving their policy goals while in office?

PRACTICE QUIZ QUESTIONS

1. Presidential power has increased over time for all of the reasons below except:
   - A changes in the Constitution
   - B America's growth as a nation
   - C America's emergence as a dominant actor in international politics
   - D the expansion of the federal government
   - E acts of legislation passed by Congress

2. Which of the following events during Barack Obama's presidency best illustrates the limits of presidential power?
   - A congressional consideration of immigration reforms
   - B Obama's nominees to the Supreme Court
   - C the deployment of U.S. forces in Libya in 2011
   - D the enactment of health care reform legislation
   - E Obama's defeat of Mitt Romney in 2012

THE PRESIDENT'S JOB DESCRIPTION

▶ *Describe the constitutional and statutory powers of the president today.* **(Pages 440–54)**

SUMMARY

The president's formal powers arise from a combination of constitutional provisions and additional laws that give him increased responsibilities. The president has many duties, but the primary responsibilities of the office are to oversee the executive branch and implement laws passed by Congress. Although some presidents might prefer to focus on either domestic or foreign policy, most find that their priorities are determined by domestic and world events.

KEY TERMS

constitutional authority (p. 440)
statutory authority (presidential) (p. 440)
vesting clause (p. 441)
head of government (p. 441)
head of state (p. 441)
recess appointment (p. 442)
executive orders (p. 442)
fast-track authority (p. 444)
executive agreement (p. 444)
State of the Union (p. 445)
executive privilege (p. 449)
presidential approval rating (p. 450)
go public (p. 453)

CRITICAL THINKING AND DISCUSSION

If presidents gain considerable power through legislation passed by Congress, why doesn't divided government (Congress controlled by one party; the presidency by the other) lead to the passage of legislation that repeals these grants of power?

PRACTICE QUIZ QUESTIONS

3. Presidents use recess appointments when they are trying to _____.
   - A fill a judicial vacancy outside the scheduled period
   - B fill a vacant seat in Congress
   - C temporarily dodge the need for Senate approval
   - D temporarily dodge the need for House approval
   - E fill vacancies with a permanent replacement

4. A presidential proclamation that unilaterally changes government policy without congressional consent is called _____.
   - A an executive privilege
   - B a fast-track authority
   - C an executive agreement
   - D an executive order
   - E statutory authority

5. Some scholars argue that the War Powers Resolution has effectively expanded the power of _____.
   - A the president
   - B Congress
   - C the Supreme Court
   - D the Department of Defense
   - E the State Department

6. The first-mover advantage refers to the president's negotiating advantage over _____.
   - A foreign leaders
   - B governors

- C the bureaucracy
- D Congress
- E international organizations

7. For most presidents, the problem with going public is that _____.

- A the public is more focused on Congress
- B the president's speeches are not very persuasive
- C they energize their opponents
- D they generally address unimportant issues
- E they do not reach their target audience

THE EXECUTIVE BRANCH

▶ Explain how the Executive Office of the President, the vice president, and the Cabinet help the president. **(Pages 455–58)**

SUMMARY

The executive branch is a huge, complex organization that helps the president exercise vast responsibilities. Appointees to the branch serve as the president's eyes and ears on the bureaucracy. Almost all appointees are replaced when a new administration begins.

KEY TERMS	**CRITICAL THINKING AND DISCUSSION**
Executive Office of the President (EOP) (p. 455) Cabinet (p. 457)	Why might bureaucrats who are not presidential appointees be more responsive to congressional mandates and demands than to the president's orders, even though the president heads the executive branch?

PRACTICE QUIZ QUESTIONS

8. In most appointments to EOP positions, presidents generally emphasize _____.

- A experience
- B expertise
- C effectiveness
- D public opinion
- E loyalty

9. Recent vice presidents have had _____ official duties, and/but _____ been influential in their role.

- A no; have not
- B limited; have
- C limited; have not
- D extensive; have
- E extensive; have not

THE AMERICAN PUBLIC AND THE PRESIDENT

▶ Explain how Americans evaluate presidents. **(Pages 458–62)**

SUMMARY

Public support is critical for presidents to get reelected and to enact their policy proposals. Nonetheless, presidential popularity itself is affected by factors that may be out of a president's control.

> **CRITICAL THINKING AND DISCUSSION**
>
> Why do you think Americans often hold the president more accountable than Congress for the state of the economy?

PRACTICE QUIZ QUESTIONS

10. Presidential approval is generally based on _____.

- A policy outcomes
- B policy positions
- C presidential actions
- D presidential appointments
- E an absence of scandals

11. Presidential popularity generally _____ over time, and it _____ during national crises.

- A declines; drops
- B increases; drops
- C declines; spikes
- D increases; spikes
- E remains even; spikes

ASSESSING PRESIDENTIAL POWER

▶ Analyze why presidents have become much more powerful since the Founding. **(Pages 462–67)**

SUMMARY

While presidents have gained power over time, the Constitution grants the president rather limited powers. The growth of presidential power is closely related to the fact that most limits on it are not well defined, and presidents have succeeded in taking advantage of these ambiguities.

KEY TERMS	**CRITICAL THINKING AND DISCUSSION**
unilateral action (presidential) (p. 463) unitary executive theory (p. 464) signing statement (p. 465)	What can members of Congress do to stop a president from changing policy unilaterally? Which of these methods seems most effective, and why?

PRACTICE QUIZ QUESTIONS

12. The _____ was used by the George W. Bush administration to argue in favor of the power to station American forces
in Iraq.

    A principal-agent theory

    B unitary executive theory

    C unilateral agreement theory

    D dual presidency theory

    E signing statement power

13. Most presidents use the _____ to control the interpretation and implementation of laws.

    A line item veto

    B recess appointment

    C executive order

    D signing statement

    E pocket veto

14. Congressional challenges to presidential authority are
_____ used and are generally _____
at constraining presidential power.

    A rarely; successful

    B rarely; unsuccessful

    C commonly; successful

    D commonly; unsuccessful

SUGGESTED READING

Alter, Jonathan. *The Promise: President Obama, Year One*. New York: Simon and Schuster, 2010.

Canes-Wrone, Brandice. *Who Leads Whom? Presidents, Policy, and the Public*. Chicago: University of Chicago Press, 2006.

Howell, William G. *Power without Persuasion: The Politics of Direct Presidential Action*. Princeton, NJ: Princeton University Press, 2003.

Katznelson, Ira. *Fear Itself: The New Deal and the Origins of Our Time*. New York: W. W. Norton, 2013.

Lewis, David E. *Presidents and the Politics of Agency Design*. Palo Alto, CA: Stanford University Press, 2003.

Mayer, Kenneth. *With the Stroke of a Pen: Executive Orders and Presidential Power*. Princeton, NJ: Princeton University Press, 2001.

Neustadt, Richard E. *Presidential Power and the Modern Presidents: The Politics of Leadership from Roosevelt to Reagan*. New York: Free Press, 1990.

Rudalevige, Andrew. *Managing the President's Program: Presidential Leadership and Legislative Policy Formation*. Princeton, NJ: Princeton University Press, 2002.

Skowronek, Stephen. *Presidential Leadership in Political Time: Reprise and Reappraisal*. Lawrence, KS: University of Kansas Press, 2008.

13

The Bureaucracy

MILLIONS OF AMERICANS WORK IN THE FEDERAL BUREAUCRACY, doing everything from processing paperwork to driving scientific rovers on Mars. Most of the time, they appear to be dedicated, smart, civil servants who routinely produce near-miracles. NASA's *Opportunity* rover, for example, was built to last only 90 days on Mars—but NASA's scientists have managed to keep it operating for more than a decade after it landed. *Opportunity* and its sister rover *Spirit* (which lasted only nine years before getting trapped in a Martian sand dune) have made many important discoveries about Martian geology, including clues about the presence of water on the surface of Mars and prospects for life on the planet.

On the other hand, bureaucrats can find themselves as poster children for towering governmental waste and inefficiency. Consider the Office of Personnel Management (OPM) and its procedures for determining the pensions of retiring federal workers. Even in 2014, these calculations are done by hand, on paper forms, in a facility located underground in a Pennsylvania cave, where workers spend most of their time walking from file cabinet to file cabinet, as they assemble a retiree's file. Because of this antiquated system, it can take months to process an employee's retirement papers—with a cost that is far higher than in comparable state governments or private corporations.

These two examples illustrate only a tiny part of the federal bureaucracy. Politics is everywhere in America, and so is the federal bureaucracy. Americans encounter the work of government employees every day: when they sort

CONFLICT & COMPROMISE
in American Politics

CHAPTER *goals*

Define bureaucracy and explain its major functions.
▶ PAGES 474–83

Trace the expansion of the federal bureaucracy over time.
▶ PAGES 483–87

Describe the size and structure of the executive branch today.
▶ PAGES 487–92

Describe who bureaucrats are and the regulations that govern their employment.
▶ PAGES 493–97

Explain how Congress and the president oversee the executive branch.
▶ PAGES 497–503

> **DEFINE BUREAUCRACY AND EXPLAIN ITS MAJOR FUNCTIONS**

bureaucracy The system of civil servants and political appointees who implement congressional or presidential decisions; also known as the administrative state.

civil servants Employees of bureaucratic agencies within the government.

political appointees People selected by an elected leader, such as the president, to hold a government position.

through mail delivered by the Postal Service, drive on highways funded by the Department of Transportation, or purchase food inspected by the Food and Drug Administration (FDA). The prices Americans pay to surf the Web, watch television, or use a cell phone are influenced by regulations issued by the Federal Communications Commission (FCC). When people go on vacation, their bags are inspected by the Transportation Security Administration (TSA), the aircraft and pilots are scrutinized by the Federal Aviation Administration (FAA), and many beaches are maintained by the Army Corps of Engineers.

Although many federal bureaucrats work diligently to serve the American public, the comparison of the Mars rover and the federal retirement system illustrates a fundamental fact: the same federal bureaucracy that accomplishes so many big tasks also does things that are inefficient, wasteful, and downright dumb. Do these shortcomings result from inevitable accidents—or are they the consequence of deliberate actions? And if so, why were agencies designed to fail or to do things that look a lot like failure? How does conflict over what government should do translate into bureaucratic successes and failures?

WHAT IS THE FEDERAL BUREAUCRACY?

The federal **bureaucracy** that makes up the government's executive branch is composed of millions of **civil servants**, who work for the government in permanent positions, and thousands of **political appointees**, who hold short-term, usually senior positions, and are appointed by an elected leader, such as the president. Another name for the bureaucracy is the *administrative state*, which refers to the role bureaucrats play in administering government policies.[1] Most constitutional scholars agree that the president is nominally in charge of the bureaucracy—although generally the president shares this power with members of Congress.

WHAT DO BUREAUCRATS DO?

The task of the bureaucracy is to implement policies established by congressional acts or presidential decisions. These tasks are summarized in Nuts & Bolts 13.1. Sometimes the tasks associated with putting these laws and resolutions into effect are very specific. For example, in the appropriations bill for fiscal year 2014, Congress mandated a 1 percent pay increase for military personnel and funds for specific new military equipment. These provisions required no discretion on the part of the bureaucrats who were to implement them. Their tasks were limited to making the administrative changes necessary to raise military pay and following through with the purchase of specified equipment.

More commonly, however, legislation determines only the general guidelines for meeting governmental goals, allowing bureaucrats to develop specific policies and programs. In these cases, bureaucrats' actions determine the essence of government action, deciding "who gets what, when, and how."[2] For example, the

>

1938 Federal Food, Drug, and Cosmetic Act gave the Food and Drug Administration the job of determining which drugs are safe and effective, but it allowed FDA bureaucrats to develop their own procedures for making these determinations.[3] Currently, the FDA requires that drug manufacturers first test new drugs for safety, then conduct further trials to determine their effectiveness. An FDA advisory board of scientists and doctors reviews the results of these tests. Then FDA bureaucrats decide whether to allow the manufacturer to market the drug.

In general, the job of the federal bureaucracy includes a wide range of activities, from regulating the behavior of individuals and corporations to buying everything from pencils to jet fighters. These activities are inherently political and often conflictual: ordinary citizens, elected officials, and bureaucrats themselves often disagree about aspects of these activities, and they work to influence bureaucratic actions to suit their policy goals.

13.1 NUTS & bolts

WHAT DO BUREAUCRATS DO?

The fundamental job of the bureaucracy is to implement executive orders and congressional legislation. To this end, bureaucrats take a variety of actions each day, such as

▶ Develop and enforce regulations that shape choices made by individuals and corporations

▶ Purchase goods and services for the federal government, from office space to pencils and fighter aircraft to Mars rovers

▶ Deliver services to Americans, such as mail delivery and student loans

▶ Do research and development on health care and other scientific questions

▶ Manage contractors who provide services to the government and to individuals

regulation A rule that allows the government to exercise control over individuals and corporations by restricting certain behaviors.

notice-and-comment procedure A step in the rule-making process in which proposed rules are published in the *Federal Register* and made available for debate by the general public.

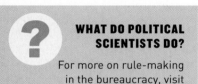

WHAT DO POLITICAL SCIENTISTS DO?

For more on rule-making in the bureaucracy, visit **wwnpag.es/wdpsd**

REGULATIONS A **regulation** is a rule that allows the government to exercise control over individuals and corporations by restricting their behaviors. It does so by either allowing or prohibiting behavior, setting out the conditions under which certain behaviors can occur, or assessing costs or granting benefits based on behavior. For example, in the case of deepwater offshore drilling, which became an issue in 2010 after an explosion at a British Petroleum (BP) oil well in the Gulf of Mexico created a massive oil spill, attention focused on a government agency known as the Minerals Management Service; this agency regulated every aspect of the drilling process—from how many lifeboats should be on a rig to what kinds of hardware should be used to drill and maintain the well site on the ocean floor. Bureaucrats gain the authority to write regulations by the statute that sets up their agency or by a subsequent act of Congress.

Regulations are developed according to the **notice-and-comment procedure**.[4] Before a new regulation can take effect, it must be published in the *Federal Register*, an official publication that includes rules, proposed rules, and other types of government documents. Individuals and companies that will be affected by the regulation can then respond to the agency that proposed it, either supporting or opposing it, and offering different versions for consideration. Those potentially affected can also appeal to members of Congress or to the president's staff for help in getting the proposed rule revised. The agency then issues a final regulation, incorporating changes based on the comments. This final regulation is also published in the *Federal Register* and then put into effect.

The process of devising or modifying regulations is often political. Members of Congress and the president usually have strong opinions about how new regulations should look—and even when they don't, they may still get involved on behalf of a constituent or an interest group. Bureaucrats take account of these pressures from elected officials for two reasons: (1) The bureaucrats' policy-making power may derive from a statute that members of Congress could overturn if they disapproved of bureaucrats' actions. (2) Bureaucrats need congressional support to get larger budgets, to obtain more important tasks for their agency, and to prevent budget cuts. Thus, despite bureaucrats' power to implement policies, their agencies' budgets, appointed leaders, and overall missions are subject to elected officials' oversight (see How It Works: Bureaucracy and Legislation).

Many regulations are issued each year. Lately, the *Federal Register* has contained more than 22,000 pages and about 4,000 new regulations a year.[5] Although nearly all government agencies issue regulations, most come from a few agencies, including the Federal Trade Commission, which regulates commerce; the Federal Communications Commission, which regulates media companies that create content as well as telecommunications companies that transmit information; and the Food and Drug Administration, which regulates drugs, medical products, food, and cosmetics.

Federal regulations affect most aspects of everyday life. They influence the gas mileage of cars sold in the United States, the materials used to build roads, and the price of gasoline. They determine the amounts that doctors can charge senior citizens for medical procedures; the hours that medical residents can work; and the criteria used to determine who gets a heart, lung, or kidney transplant. Regulations set the eligibility criteria for student loans, limit how the military can recruit on college campuses, determine who can get a home mortgage and what their interest rate will be, and describe what constitutes equal funding for men's and women's college sports teams. Regulations also shape contribution limits and spending decisions in political campaigns.

BUREAUCRACY AND LEGISLATION

After Congress passes legislation and the president signs it, a long implementation process begins. Local government officials, interest groups, and others refine the rules around legislation and have a strong influence on how it will affect people "on the ground."

 Congress passes legislation.

 The president signs the bill into law.

 Interest groups provide information and proposals to bureaucrats, and they lobby for their preferred implementation of the legislation.

 Courts respond to challenges to the law, and they can provide guidelines for implementation.

 Bureaucrats interpret the law and design appropriate regulations.

 Other bureaucrats disseminate regulations to state and local governments, corporations, and individuals, and they monitor compliance.

 Regulations can be revised in light of changing circumstances, different political climates, or unanticipated consequences.

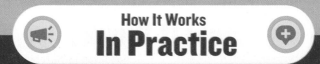

How It Works
In Practice

IMPLEMENTING "OBAMACARE"

In 2009 and 2010, the debate around health care reform raged. After this acrimonious and highly partisan legislative process resulted in the Affordable Care Act (ACA), often called "Obamacare," bureaucrats needed to implement the legislation. This process, which is likely to persist for many years, shows the influence the bureaucracy can have on public policy.

CONGRESSIONAL ACTION November 7, 2009: House approves its version of health care reform bill.
December 24, 2009: Senate approves its version of health care reform bill.
March 21, 2010: House approves the Senate version of the bill with amendments.

PRESIDENTIAL SIGNATURE March 23, 2010: President Obama signs Affordable Care Act.
March 30, 2010: President Obama signs the Health Care and Reconciliation Act.

REQUIRES INSURERS TO ALLOW CHILDREN UNDER AGE 26 TO BE COVERED BY PARENT'S INSURANCE New regulations are issued May 23, 2010.

CHANGES IN MEDICARE PAYMENTS TO HOSPITALS Payment schedule is developed April–October 2010 and implemented October 2010.

EXPANSION OF MEDICARE PRESCRIPTION DRUG COVERAGE New regulations are developed and reviewed March–December 2010 and take effect January 2011. Federal subsidies begin January 1, 2013.

REDUCED MEDICARE REIMBURSEMENTS FOR HOSPITAL READMISSIONS New regulations are developed May–August 2011 and take effect October 2012.

HEALTH INSURANCE EXCHANGES October 2013: Federal and state exchanges go online, and Americans begin to sign up for insurance and federal subsidies.

October–November 2013: Complaints about inability to use exchange websites force "tech surge" to fix problems.

MANDATES February 2014: Deadline for mandate requiring businesses to provide health insurance is postponed.

POP QUIZ

1 Based on this graphic, the bureaucrats have power because

a many are congressional staffers.

b they write regulations needed to implement laws.

c they can appeal to the president for help.

d they usually keep their jobs longer than members of Congress.

e they can appeal to interest groups for help.

2 Which of the following is NOT a way interest groups can influence legislation?

a use the notice-and-comment procedure to critique proposed regulations

b meet with bureaucrats to make their case

c ask the president and his or her staff to intervene in the regulatory process

d ask for a national referendum on the regulations

e go to court to block new regulations

Answers: 1.b; 2.d

Regulations are often controversial because they involve trade-offs between incompatible goals, as well as decisions made under uncertain circumstances. For example, the FDA drug-approval process prioritizes the goal of preventing harmful drugs from coming to market.[6] As a result, patients sometimes cannot get access to experimental treatments because FDA approval has not been granted, even when those treatments are the patients' only remaining option.[7] Advocates for patients have argued that people with dire prognoses should be allowed to use an experimental treatment as a potentially life-saving last resort.[8] However, current FDA regulations prevent them from doing so except under very special circumstances, arguing that unapproved treatments may do more harm than good and that allowing wider access to these drugs may tempt manufacturers to market new drugs without adequate testing.

FEDERAL REGULATIONS INFLUENCE many aspects of everyday life that would not seem likely to be affected by government action. The increase in the number of women's intercollegiate athletic teams is partly due to regulations that require equal funding for men's and women's teams. Pictured here is the University of Connecticut's 2014 NCAA women's basketball championship team.

PROCUREMENT Bureaucrats also handle government purchases. The General Services Administration (GSA) manages 8,600 buildings owned or leased by the government and a fleet of 208,000 vehicles, and provides government agencies with most of their office supplies.[9]

Procurement seems a straightforward task: agencies determine what they need, find out who can supply it, and choose the lowest-cost provider. However, procurement for the federal government can be surprisingly complicated. Consider the purchase of a Mars rover. It's not something that can be bought at a store. Bureaucrats must devise criteria for choosing between designs with very different strengths and weaknesses. Procurement decisions are also shaped by congressional and executive mandates. For example, when the GSA searches for suppliers of a particular product, it often has to give preference to small businesses or firms owned by minorities or veterans. These guidelines are the result of the political process, as elected officials try to shape government actions to suit their own policy goals.

Almost every president has tried to reform the procurement process. President Obama, for example, has proposed an end to cost-plus and no-bid contracts. (Under cost-plus contracts, contractors are paid whatever it costs to provide a service plus a percentage of costs as their profit; under no-bid contracts, contracts are awarded without a competitive bidding process.) Although these practices may seem wasteful, the government may be forced to use them because of the complex and unique goods and services it needs to buy.

PROVIDING SERVICES **Street-level bureaucrats** provide services to help ordinary Americans.[10] These services include certain job-training programs and disaster assistance. In addition, federal employees manage many national tourist attractions—from the National Zoo to the Statue of Liberty to Mount Rushmore. Federal employees also inspect passenger baggage at airports, monitor aircraft maintenance, direct aircraft in flight, and investigate accidents.

street-level bureaucrats Agency employees who directly provide services to the public, such as those who provide job-training services.

RESEARCH AND DEVELOPMENT Government scientists work in areas from medicine to astronomy to agriculture. Sometimes they do basic research, such as working for the National Institutes of Health to discover mechanisms that govern cell reproduction and death. Government scientists also do applied research, from developing new cancer drugs to improving crop-management techniques. Federal funds support university and corporate research that examines similar issues.

MANAGING AND DIRECTING Some bureaucrats supervise actions taken by people outside government. For example, the Department of Defense uses civilian contractors to provide support services in Afghanistan—their roles range from doing laundry to performing maintenance work on planes, trucks, and ships. Many workers at government facilities (such as NASA's Mission Control, which directs manned space missions) and in public works projects are employees of private corporations working on government contracts.

BUREAUCRATIC EXPERTISE AND ITS CONSEQUENCES

AFTER NEWS OF AN $800,000 GSA conference at a Las Vegas resort came to light in 2012, Congress held hearings on the agency's practices. Here, Representative John Mica (R-FL) criticizes the apparent misuse of taxpayer money.

state capacity The knowledge, personnel, and institutions that the government requires to effectively implement policies.

red tape Excessive or unnecessarily complex regulations imposed by the bureaucracy.

standard operating procedures Rules that lower-level bureaucrats must follow when implementing policies.

Bureaucrats are experts. Even compared to most members of Congress or presidential appointees, the average bureaucrat is a specialist in a certain policy area, with a better grasp of his or her agency's mission. For example, people who hold scientific or management positions in the FDA usually know more about the benefits and risks of new drugs than people outside the agency do. Their decision to deny unapproved drugs to seriously ill patients may seem cruel, but it may also reflect a thoughtful balancing of two incompatible goals: preventing harmful drugs from reaching the market, and allowing people who have exhausted all other treatments access to risky, experimental products. A bureaucracy of experts is an important part of what political scientists call **state capacity**—the knowledge, personnel, and institutions needed to effectively implement policies.[11]

RED TAPE AND STANDARD OPERATING PROCEDURES Despite bureaucrats' policy expertise, their decisions often appear to take too much time, rely on arbitrary judgments of what is important, and have unintended consequences—to the point that actions designed to solve one problem may create worse ones. Many critics cite the abundance of **red tape**, which refers to excessive or unnecessarily complex regulations, or **standard operating procedures**, which are the rules that lower-level bureaucrats must follow when implementing policies regardless of whether they are applicable. For example, although the Office of Personnel Management's pension procedures described in the chapter opening certainly seem antiquated and inefficient, the employees carrying out these tasks can hardly be blamed, as they are following long-established procedures that had been approved by OPM managers and (indirectly) members of Congress.

There have been many attempts to make the bureaucracy operate more effectively by mandating that bureaucrats make decisions using specific procedures or criteria. These efforts have added many acronyms to the language of Washington bureaucrats: PPBS, MBO, ZBB, REGO, and PBB.[12] Although each of these efforts can claim modest success, none have fundamentally changed the way the government does business. The lesson seems to be that examples of poor performance by America's bureaucracy have little to do with the bureaucracy itself. Otherwise, one of these reform packages would have solved these problems, resulting in a well-functioning bureaucracy.

Cases of bureaucratic ineptitude and failed reform efforts raise a critical question: How can an organization full of experts develop such dysfunctional ways of doing business? Bureaucrats are neither clueless nor malevolent. What, then, explains red tape and counterproductive standard operating procedures? The answer is the very strength of the American bureaucracy: its expertise.

Because bureaucrats know things that elected officials do not and because bureaucrats have their own policy goals, it is hard for elected officials to evaluate what bureaucrats are doing. For example, building the *Opportunity* and *Spirit* Mars rovers cost considerably more than planned. But did NASA bureaucrats mislead Congress about the difficulty of building the rover, or was the overrun an honest mistake, resulting from factors that could not be anticipated? Of course, given that *Spirit* and *Opportunity* have far outlasted their expected lifetimes, the program is seen as a success and a bargain. But if things had turned out differently (if one or both of the rovers had crash-landed on Mars or had stopped working shortly after landing), members of Congress might easily have thought that NASA had presented the best-case scenario in order to secure funding.

Of course, sometimes bureaucrats simply make mistakes. For example, the FDA has delayed helpful drugs from reaching the market or has approved drugs that were later found to have harmful side effects. However, these decisions may have been justified based on the information available to bureaucrats at the time. Here, again, it is hard to say that bureaucrats are at fault for such decisions.

THE PROBLEM OF CONTROL Political scientists refer to the difficulty that elected officials and their staff face when they try to interpret or influence bureaucratic actions as the **problem of control**.[13] A classic example is the **principal–agent game**. The principal–agent game describes an interaction that involves an individual or a group (an "agent") acting on behalf of another (the "principal"). In the federal government, for example, the president and Congress are principals, and bureaucrats are agents. An agent may not want to work or may prefer outcomes that the principal does not like. Moreover, because the agent is an expert at the task he has been given, he has additional knowledge and experience that is inaccessible to the principal. The conundrum for the principal, then, is this: giving the agent very specific orders prevents the agent from acting based on expertise; but if

problem of control A difficulty faced by elected officials in ensuring that when bureaucrats implement policies, they follow these officials' intentions but still have enough discretion to use their expertise.

principal–agent game The interaction between a principal (such as the president or Congress), who needs something done, and an agent (such as a bureaucrat), who is responsible for carrying out the principal's orders.

the principal gives the agent the freedom to make decisions based on expertise, the principal has less control over the agent's actions.

For example, suppose Congress and the president directed the FDA to shorten its drug-approval process. FDA officials might have mandated a lengthy process based on their expert assessment of the best way to screen out harmful drugs. By giving orders that superseded the FDA officials' screening process, elected officials would be sacrificing the valuable bureaucratic expertise behind the policy and risking the hasty approval of unsafe drugs. On the other hand, if Congress and the president allowed FDA bureaucrats to devise their own procedures and regulations, there would be a chance that the FDA could use this freedom to pursue goals that have nothing to do with drug safety. For example, critics of the FDA's procedures have asserted that a drawn-out approval process is designed to favor large companies that already have drugs on the market over smaller companies trying to get approval for drugs that would compete with existing products.

The principal–agent game can also be framed in terms of citizens. Figure 13.1 shows that a majority of survey respondents agreed that the federal government is typically inefficient and wasteful—although the percentage agreeing with this assessment declined from its peak in 1992 until recent years, where it again increased. Such opinions give citizens a strong motivation to demand that elected officials control the bureaucracy—to reduce the waste and inefficiency that many see as commonplace.

Members of Congress and citizens are sometimes right to question the motives of members of the bureaucracy. Sometimes bureaucratic actions are the result of **regulatory capture**, which occurs when bureaucrats cater to a small group of

regulatory capture A situation in which bureaucrats favor the interests of the groups or corporations they are supposed to regulate at the expense of the general public.

FIGURE » 13.1

HOW AMERICANS VIEW THE FEDERAL BUREAUCRACY

Many Americans believe the bureaucracy is wasteful and inefficient. Note, however, that the magnitude of negative feelings varies over time. Consider the time frame represented on the graph. What happened during these years that might explain the changes in citizens' opinions about the government?

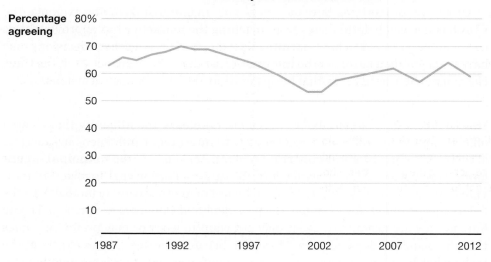

"When something is run by the government, it is usually inefficient and wasteful."

SOURCE: Pew Research Center, "Partisan Polarization Surges in Bush, Obama Years: Trends in American Values: 1987–2012," June 4, 2012, www.people-press.org/2012/06/04/partisan-polarization-surges-in-bush-obama-years/ (accessed 3/28/14).

individuals or corporations, regardless of the impact of these actions on public welfare. In the case of the Minerals Management Service, the government agency that had responsibility for offshore drilling operations, including routine safety inspections on oil rigs such as the BP platform in the Gulf of Mexico that exploded in 2010, press reports documented that agency employees accepted meals, gifts, and sporting trips from companies they were regulating. Several employees even used drugs and had sex with industry employees. More significant, the agency's staff appear to have changed their interpretation of the agency's mission from regulating with an eye on safety to encouraging as much drilling as possible—an ideal scenario for profit-minded energy companies.[14]

You might think that the problem of control isn't too difficult to solve as long as bureaucrats act as impartial experts and set aside their own policy goals. Many studies of bureaucracies, beginning with the work of the early political theorist Max Weber, argue that bureaucrats should provide information and expertise, and avoid taking sides on policy questions or being swayed by elected officials, people outside government, or their own policy goals.[15] However, bureaucrats' behavior doesn't always fit Weber's vision. Many enter the bureaucracy with their own ideas about what government should do, and they make decisions in line with those goals. The typical NASA bureaucrat, for example, probably favors a much larger space program than members of Congress are willing to fund. Bureaucrats may also be tempted to favor interest groups or corporations to secure a better-paying job after they leave government service. However, even if bureaucrats wanted to remain completely dispassionate, they would still face a government in which many other people with their own policy goals would attempt to influence their behavior. Members of Congress or the president sometimes try to use the bureaucracy to implement policies that reflect their personal preferences or reward their political supporters.[16]

The problem of control has existed throughout the history of the federal government. It affects both the kinds of policies that bureaucrats implement and the structure of the federal bureaucracy, including the number of agencies and their missions, staff, and tasks. Moreover, elected officials use a variety of methods to solve the problem of control, including making it easier for people outside government to learn about agency actions before they take effect. However, all these tactics are, at best, partial solutions to the problem of control. The trade-off between expertise and control remains.

WHEN BUREAUCRATS PUT THE interests of a small group of individuals or corporations first, they aren't acting as good agents for the American people or the elected officials in government. Critics of the government's regulation of the financial sector have claimed that government officials are more interested in helping financial firms than the American people.

HOW HAS THE AMERICAN BUREAUCRACY GROWN?

TRACE THE EXPANSION OF THE FEDERAL BUREAUCRACY OVER TIME

The evolution of America's federal bureaucracy was not steady or smooth. Most of its important developments occurred during three short periods: the late 1890s and early 1900s, the 1930s, and the 1960s.[17] In all three periods, the driving force was a combination of demands from citizens for enhanced government services and the desire of people in government to either respond to these demands or to increase the size and scope of the federal government to be more in line with their own policy goals.

THE BEGINNING OF AMERICA'S BUREAUCRACY

From the Founding of the United States until the election of Andrew Jackson in 1828, the staff of the entire federal bureaucracy numbered at most in the low thousands. There were only three executive departments (State, Treasury, and War), along with a postmaster general.[18] The early federal government also performed a narrow range of tasks. It collected taxes on imports and exports and delivered the mail. The national army consisted of a small Corps of Engineers and a few frontier patrols. The attorney general was a private attorney who had the federal government as one of his clients. Members of Congress outnumbered civil servants in Washington, and the president had very little staff at all.[19]

The small size of the federal government during those years reflected Americans' deep suspicion of government, especially unelected officials. In the Declaration of Independence, one of the charges against King George III was that he had "erected a multitude of new offices and sent hither swarms of officers to harass our people and eat out their substance."[20] Executive branch offices were formed only when absolutely necessary. Nonetheless, conflicts soon arose around control of the bureaucracy. The legislation that established the departments of State, Treasury, and War allowed the president to nominate the people in charge of these departments but made these appointments subject to Senate approval. (The same is true today for the heads of all executive departments and many other presidential appointments.)

The election of Andrew Jackson in 1828 brought the first large-scale use of the spoils system, in which people who had worked in Jackson's campaign were rewarded with new positions in the federal government (usually working as local postmasters).[21] The spoils system was extremely useful to party organizations, as it gave them a powerful incentive with which to convince people to work for the party—a particularly important tool for Jackson, as his campaign organization was at that time the largest ever organized.

The challenge facing the spoils system was ensuring that these government employees, who often lacked experience in their new fields, could actually carry out their jobs. The solution was to develop procedures for these employees, so that they knew exactly what to do even if they had little or no experience or training.[22] These instructions became one of the earliest uses of standard operating procedures. They ensured that the government could function even if large numbers of employees had been hired in reward for political work rather than because of their qualifications.[23]

As America expanded in size, so did the federal government, which saw an almost eightfold increase in the bureaucracy between 1816 and the beginning of the Civil War in 1861. This growth did

THIS CARTOON OF A MONUMENT TO President Andrew Jackson riding a pig decries his involvement in the spoils system, which allowed politicians to dole out government service jobs in return for political support.

not reflect a fundamental change in what the government did; in fact, much of the increase came in areas such as the Post Office, which needed to serve a geographically larger nation—and, of course, to provide "spoils" for party workers in the form of government jobs.[24] Even by the end of the Civil War, the federal government still had very little involvement in the lives of ordinary Americans. State and local governments provided services such as education, public works, and welfare benefits, if they were provided at all. The federal government's role in daily life was limited to mail delivery, collecting import and export taxes, and a few other areas.

BUILDING A NEW AMERICAN STATE: THE PROGRESSIVE ERA

Changes in the second half of the nineteenth century transformed America's bureaucracy.[25] This transformation began after the Civil War, but the most significant changes occurred during the Progressive Era, 1890–1920. Many laws and executive actions increased the government's regulatory power during this period, including the Sherman Antitrust Act of 1890, the Pure Food and Drug Act of 1906, the Meat Inspection Act of 1906, expansion of the Interstate Commerce Commission, and various conservation measures.[26] Now the federal government was no longer simply a deliverer of mail and a defender of borders; rather, it had an indirect impact on several aspects of everyday life. When Americans bought food or other products, went to work, or traveled on vacation, the choices available to them were shaped by the actions of federal bureaucrats in Washington and elsewhere.

These developments were matched by a fundamental change in the federal bureaucracy following passage of the 1883 Pendleton Civil Service Act. This measure created the **federal civil service**, in which the merit system (qualifications, not political connections) would be the basis for hiring and promoting bureaucrats.[27] In other words, when a new president took office, he could not replace government workers with his own campaign workers. Initially, only about 13,000 federal jobs acquired civil service protections, but over the next two decades many additional positions were incorporated into the civil service, to the point that in the modern era virtually all full-time, permanent government employees have civil service protection. In some cases, presidents gave civil service protections to people who had been hired under the spoils system to prevent the next president from replacing these bureaucrats with their own loyalists. Over time, these reforms created a bureaucracy in which people were hired for their expertise and allowed to build a career in government without having to fear being fired when a new president or Congress took office.[28]

federal civil service A system created by the 1883 Pendleton Civil Service Act in which bureaucrats are hired on the basis of merit rather than political connections.

THE NEW DEAL, THE GREAT SOCIETY, AND THE REAGAN REVOLUTION

Dramatic expansion of the federal bureaucracy occurred during the New Deal period in the 1930s and during the mid-1960s Great Society era. In both cases, the changes were driven by a combination of citizen demands and the preferences of elected officials who favored an increased role of government in society. This expansion was only marginally curtailed during the Reagan Revolution of the 1980s.

THE NEW DEAL The New Deal refers to the government programs implemented during Franklin Roosevelt's first term as president in the 1930s. At one level, these

"MORE, I PLEASE!"

POWER

REORGANIZATION PROGRAM

CONGRESS

THE EXECUTIVE BRANCH OF THE GOV'T

FRANKLIN ROOSEVELT'S NEW DEAL programs greatly expanded the power of the federal government and the bureaucracy. As this cartoon shows, these changes were controversial, with some seeing them as moving too much power from Congress to the president and bureaucracy.

programs were a response to the Great Depression and the inability of local governments and private charities to provide adequate support to Americans during this economic crisis. Many advocates of the New Deal also favored an expanded role for government in American society, regardless of the immediate need for intervention.[29] Roosevelt's programs included reforms to the financial industry as well as efforts to help people directly, including stimulating employment, economic growth, and the formation of labor unions. The Social Security Act, the first federally funded pension program for all Americans, was also passed as part of the New Deal.[30]

These reforms represented a vast increase in the size, responsibilities, and capacity of the bureaucracy, as well as a large transfer of power to bureaucrats and to the president.[31] While the Progressive Era reforms created an independent bureaucracy and increased its state capacity, the New Deal reforms broadened the range of policy areas in which this capacity could be applied. Before the New Deal, the federal government influenced citizens' choices through activities such as regulating industries and workplace conditions. After the New Deal, the federal government took on the role of directly delivering to individuals a wide range of benefits and services—ranging from jobs to electricity. It also increased the regulation of many industries, including those in the banking and financial sectors.

The expansion of the federal government and the subsequent delegation of power to bureaucrats and to the president were controversial changes, both when they were enacted and as they were implemented in subsequent years.[32] Many Republicans opposed New Deal reforms because they believed that the federal government could not deliver services efficiently and that an expanded federal bureaucracy would create a modern spoils system. Many southerners worried that the federal government's increased involvement in everyday life would endanger the system of racial segregation in southern states.[33] Even so, Democratic supporters of the New Deal, aided by public support, carried the day.

THE GREAT SOCIETY The Great Society was a further expansion in the size, capacity, and activities of the bureaucracy that occurred during Lyndon Johnson's presidency (1963–1969). During these years, Johnson proposed and Congress enacted programs that funded bilingual education, loans and grants for college students, special education, preschools, construction of elementary and secondary schools, mass transit programs in many cities, health care for seniors and poor people, job training and urban renewal, enhanced voting rights and civil rights for minorities, environmental protection, funding for the arts and cultural activities, and space exploration.[34]

Members of Congress frequently attempted to control these new programs, with the goal of delivering valuable benefits to their own constituents. In the case of the Model Cities Program, which was designed to fund efforts to revitalize decaying urban areas, members of Congress demanded expansion of the program from a small set of experimental projects to a nationwide, 150-city effort. In return for congressional support of the agencies associated with the program, bureaucrats were forced by members of Congress to fund lucrative projects in their districts.[35]

The Great Society programs had mixed success. Voting rights and civil rights reforms ended the separate but equal system of social order in southern states and dramatically increased political participation by African Americans.[36] But many antipoverty programs were dismal failures. Poverty rates among most groups remained relatively constant, and other indicators, such as the rate of teen pregnancy, actually increased.[37] In retrospect, the people who designed and implemented these programs did not realize the complexities of the problems they were trying to address.[38] For example, many antipoverty programs were built on the assumption that most people receiving welfare needed job training programs in order to transition from welfare to permanent, paid employment. However, additional data that were available a decade later showed that most people receiving welfare do so for short periods because of medical or family crises—problems that the Great Society programs did not touch.[39] Despite these shortcomings, the expansion of the federal government during the New Deal and Great Society has remained in place well into the twenty-first century.

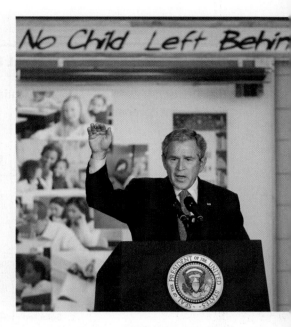

UNDER PRESIDENT GEORGE W. BUSH the federal bureaucracy continued to expand. Programs like No Child Left Behind increased the role of government in society.

THE REAGAN REVOLUTION The election of Ronald Reagan to the presidency in 1980, along with a Republican takeover of the Senate and significant Republican gains in the House of Representatives, created an opportunity for conservatives to roll back the size and scope of the federal government. However, after eight years of Reagan in office followed by four years of George H. W. Bush, and Republican control of Congress during most of Democrat Bill Clinton's presidency as well as during most of the presidency of Republican George W. Bush, the growth of the federal government did not slow. Few programs were eliminated, and the federal budget steadily increased.[40]

Conservative presidents and members of Congress have enacted programs and regulations that increased the impact of government on society. For example, George W. Bush's administration added the No Child Left Behind education reforms, which imposed many new requirements on local schools; the Medicare Prescription Drug Benefit, which at the time was the biggest new health care program since the 1960s; and the Sarbanes–Oxley Act, which increased financial reporting requirements for corporations. The trend toward increased federal regulation continued in the Obama administration, especially as a result of the Obamacare health care reforms and changes mandated by the Dodd–Frank financial industry legislation. President Obama's administration has also issued many new environmental regulations. However, the number of new regulations issued each year by the Obama administration is roughly the same as under his predecessors.[41]

THE MODERN FEDERAL BUREAUCRACY

DESCRIBE THE SIZE AND STRUCTURE OF THE EXECUTIVE BRANCH TODAY

The size and scope of the modern federal bureaucracy reflects the expansion of the federal government over the last half-century and its increased role in the lives of everyday Americans. The structure of the bureaucracy also reflects ongoing attempts by presidents, members of Congress, and others to control bureaucratic actions in line with their policy goals.

FIGURE » 13.2

THE EXECUTIVE BRANCH OF THE FEDERAL GOVERNMENT

The Executive Office of the President includes the 15 cabinet offices, as well as several independent agencies, commissions, and government corporations.

SOURCE: Based on *GPO Access: Guide to the U.S. Government*, http://bensguide.gpo.gov/files/gov_chart.pdf (accessed 9/22/12).

goal
conflict

info
asymmetry

Office of Management and Budget An office within the Executive Office of the President that is responsible for creating the president's annual budget proposal to Congress, reviewing proposed rules, and other budget-related tasks.

THE STRUCTURE OF THE FEDERAL GOVERNMENT

Figure 13.2 shows the structure of the executive branch of the federal government. As discussed in Chapter 12, the Executive Office of the President (EOP) contains organizations that support the president and implement presidential policy initiatives—individuals working in these organizations are part of the administrative presidency that works to ensure that bureaucrats implement the president's policy priorities, bringing the actions of bureaucrats (agents) in line with the president's (principal's) preferences.[42] Among its many offices, the EOP contains the **Office of Management and Budget**, which prepares the president's annual budget proposal to Congress and monitors government spending and the development of new regulations. Below the EOP are the 15 executive departments, from the Department of Agriculture to the Department of Veterans Affairs, which constitute the major divisions within the executive branch. The heads of these 15 organizations make up the president's Cabinet.

Each executive department contains many smaller organizations. Figure 13.3 shows the organizational chart for the Department of Agriculture. As you can see, the Department of Agriculture includes offices that help farmers produce and sell their crops, as well as offices that ensure food safety, but it also houses the Forest Service and offices that manage issues related to housing and utilities in rural areas. The Department of Agriculture also administers the food stamps program, even though the program has no direct connection to farming or food safety.

FIGURE » 13.3

THE STRUCTURE OF THE DEPARTMENT OF AGRICULTURE

The Department of Agriculture is headed by the Secretary of Agriculture and the Deputy Secretary of Agriculture and includes various assistant secretaries and undersecretaries for specific areas such as natural resources and the environment, farm services, rural development, and food safety.

SOURCE: U.S. Department of Agriculture, "USDA Organization Chart," www.usda.gov/documents/AgencyWorkflow.pdf (accessed 4/23/10).

Below the executive departments, but not subordinate to them, are a set of agencies, commissions, and government corporations that are called **independent agencies**, or independent establishments, to highlight that they are not part of an executive department. Most of these carry out specialized functions, such as the Federal Reserve System (which manages the money supply, banking system, and interest rates) and the Federal Deposit Insurance Corporation (which regulates the banking industry and between 2008 and 2010 closed or merged several hundred banks that had lost money as a result of increased mortgage foreclosures). The figure includes only some noteworthy or well-known agencies; there are many more.

There are two important lessons to draw from these charts. First, the federal government handles an enormous range of functions. Second, the division of activities among executive departments and independent agencies does not always have an obvious logic. Why, for example, does the Department of Agriculture administer rural utilities programs and food stamps? Similarly, it is not always clear why certain tasks are handled by an independent agency whereas others fall within the scope of an executive department.[43] Why is the Federal Reserve an independent agency rather than part of the Department of the Treasury?

Organizational decisions like these often reflect elected officials' attempts to shape agency behavior—and the extent to which political process matters. Part of the difference between independent agencies and the organizations contained within executive departments has to do with the president's ability to

independent agencies
Government offices or organizations that provide government services and are not part of an executive department.

control these organizations' activities. Organizations that fall within an executive department, such as the Internal Revenue Service, can be controlled by the president (to some extent) through his appointees.[44] In contrast, independent agencies have more freedom from oversight and control by the president and Congress. For example, the president nominates governors of the Federal Reserve, who (if the Senate confirms them) can serve for 14 years. Outside the nomination and confirmation process, the president and Congress have very little control over the Federal Reserve's policies; the organization is self-financing, and its governors can be removed from office only if Congress takes the extreme step of impeaching them.

These details about the hiring and firing of bureaucrats and the location of agencies in the structure of the federal government matter because they determine the amount of political control that other parts of the government can exercise over an agency, as well as who gets to exercise this power. As political scientist Terry Moe puts it, "The bureaucracy rises out of politics, and its design reflects the interests, strategies, and compromises of those who exercise political power."[45]

THE SIZE OF THE FEDERAL GOVERNMENT

The federal government employs millions of people. Table 13.1 reports the number of employees in each executive department. The Department of Defense is the largest cabinet department, with more than 700,000 civilian personnel. The Department of Education is the smallest, with only 4,300 employees. Many departments

TABLE » 13.1

EMPLOYMENT IN SELECTED CABINET DEPARTMENTS

ORGANIZATION	TOTAL EMPLOYEES
Defense (civilian only)	765,000
Veterans Affairs	319,300
Homeland Security	191,000
Justice	117,700
Treasury	112,700
Agriculture	90,000
Interior	69,800
Health and Human Services	72,600
Transportation	57,600
Commerce	43,000
State	33,200
Labor	17,500
Energy	15,900
Housing and Urban Development	9,200
Education	4,300

SOURCE: "Budget of the United States Government Fiscal Year 2013: Analytical Perspectives, Chapter 11—Improving the Federal Workforce," www.whitehouse.gov/sites/default/files/omb/performance/chapter11-2013.pdf (accessed 3/31/14).

FIGURE » 13.4

THE SIZE OF THE FEDERAL BUDGET

(A) This graph shows that federal spending has increased sharply since the late 1960s. **(B)** This graph shows that, as a percentage of gross domestic product (GDP), which measures the size of the American economy, the increase is much smaller, except for the financial bailout and economic stimulus programs enacted in 2008 and 2009. What might these figures suggest about the increase in government spending?

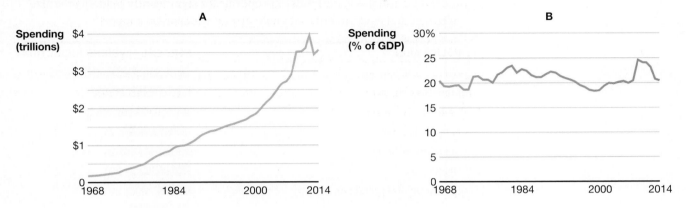

SOURCE: Congressional Budget Office "Budget Projections: February 2014 Baseline," http://www.cbo.gov/publication/45069 (accessed 3/31/14).

are on the small side: four cabinet departments have fewer than 20,000 employees. The same is true for many independent agencies. The General Services Administration, for example, has only about 12,000 employees. Millions of additional people work for the government as members of the armed forces, as employees of the Postal Service, for civilian companies that contract with the government, or as recipients of federal grant money.

Figure 13.4 shows the size of the federal budget since 1968. Clearly, the budget has steadily increased, to the point that annual spending in recent years tops $3 trillion per year. The best explanation for the size of the federal government is the size of America itself—more than 320 million people spread out over an area more than twice the size of the European Union—coupled with America's position as the most powerful nation in the world. However, some observers argue that the real explanation has to do with bureaucrats themselves. This view suggests that the government is so large because bureaucrats are **budget maximizers** who never pass up a chance to increase their own funding, regardless of whether the new spending is worthwhile.[46]

This argument misses some important points. First, the increase in total federal spending masks the fact that many agencies see their budgets shrink.[47] Particularly in recent administrations, one of the principal missions of presidential appointees, both in agencies and in the Executive Office of the President, has been to scrutinize budget requests with an eye to cutting spending as much as possible.[48] And every year, some government agencies are eliminated.[49]

Moreover, public opinion data provide an explanation for the overall growth in government: the American public's demand for services.[50] Despite complaints about the federal bureaucracy, polls find little evidence of demands for less government. When the Pew Research Center asked people in 2013 to decide which two programs should have their spending cut as a way of reducing the budget deficit, a

budget maximizers
Bureaucrats who seek to increase funding for their agency whether or not that additional spending is worthwhile.

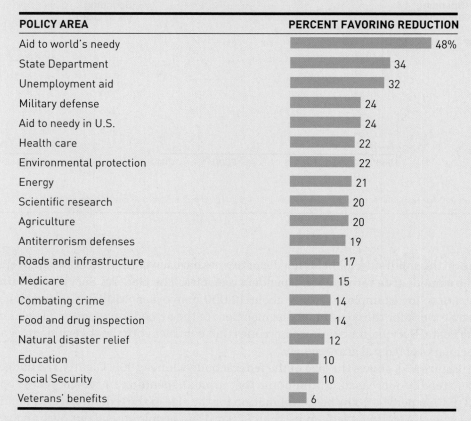

TABLE » 13.2

PUBLIC OPINION ON SPENDING CUTS

Many Americans complain about the size of the federal government. However, their complaints do not translate into support for reductions in policy areas or cuts in specific programs that could significantly reduce spending. Based on these data, are there any kinds of proposals for significantly reducing the size of the federal government that might attract widespread support?

POLICY AREA	PERCENT FAVORING REDUCTION
Aid to world's needy	48%
State Department	34
Unemployment aid	32
Military defense	24
Aid to needy in U.S.	24
Health care	22
Environmental protection	22
Energy	21
Scientific research	20
Agriculture	20
Antiterrorism defenses	19
Roads and infrastructure	17
Medicare	15
Combating crime	14
Food and drug inspection	14
Natural disaster relief	12
Education	10
Social Security	10
Veterans' benefits	6

SOURCE: Pew Research Center, "As Sequester Deadline Looms, Little Support for Cutting Most Programs," February 22, 2013, www.people-press.org/2013/02/22/as-sequester-deadline-looms-little-support-for-cutting-most-programs/ (accessed 3/31/14).

majority favored cutting relatively small programs: 34 percent picked the State Department and 48 percent picked foreign economic aid (see Table 13.2). Far fewer people favored cuts in the programs that account for the overwhelming majority of federal spending: defense, health care spending, and Social Security. In other words, while in the abstract Americans might want a smaller government that is less involved in everyday life, they do not support the large-scale budget cuts that would be necessary to achieve this goal. The public's desire for more government services is often encouraged by elected officials, who create new government programs (and expand existing ones in response to constituent demands) as a way of building support and improving their chances of reelection.

THE HUMAN FACE OF THE BUREAUCRACY

The term "bureaucrat" applies to a wide range of people with different qualifications and job descriptions. Nuts & Bolts 13.2 shows data on the range of jobs that federal workers do. There are a lot of managers (670,000 people) and administrative support staff (253,000), but there are also 723,000 professionals, such as scientists and 7,000 people whose positions involve farming, fishing, and forestry. The federal government includes so many different kinds of jobs because of the vast array of services it provides. This section describes who these people are and the terms of their government employment.

Although complaints are often heard about the efficiency or motivations of federal bureaucrats, surveys show that many employees in these positions have a strong interest in public service or implementing good public policy. In fact, these motivations are often strong enough that scholars such as James Perry have argued against attempts to motivate federal workers with monetary incentives—bureaucrats who work hard because they feel it is the right thing to do may resent incentive schemes that presume they are lazy or only interested in money.[51]

13.2 NUTS & bolts

TYPES OF FEDERAL WORKERS

Occupation	Employees	Percentage of Federal Workforce
Professional and related jobs (e.g., scientists, engineers, computer specialists, lawyers, doctors, nurses)	723,000	36%
Management, business, and financial jobs (e.g., purchasing agents, accountants, tax collectors)	670,000	33
Office and administrative support jobs (e.g., secretaries, record clerks)	253,000	13
Service jobs (e.g., jailers, police officers, detectives)	178,000	9
Installation, maintenance, and repair jobs (e.g., mechanics, electricians)	141,000	7
Transportation and moving jobs (e.g., air traffic controllers, transportation inspectors)	52,000	3
Farming, fishing, and forestry jobs (e.g., agricultural inspectors, farmworkers, loggers)	7,000	0.3

SOURCE: Based on the U.S. Bureau of Labor Statistics, "Occupational Employment Statistics NAICS 999100–Federal Executive Branch," www.bls.gov/oes/current/naics4_999100.htm#00-0000 (accessed 4/3/14).

CIVIL SERVICE REGULATIONS

A key characteristic of most jobs in the federal bureaucracy is that they are subject to the civil service regulations mentioned earlier.[52] The current civil service system sets out a job description and pay ranges for all federal jobs.[53] People with less than a college degree are generally eligible for clerical and low-level technical jobs. As in the private sector, a college degree or an advanced degree and work experience qualify an individual for higher-level positions. Federal salaries are supposed to be comparable to what people earn in similar, private-sector positions, and salaries are increased somewhat for federal employees who work in areas with a high cost of living.

The civil service system also establishes tests that determine who is hired for low-level clerical and secretarial positions. The people who receive the highest scores are hired as vacancies arise. A similar system applies for Postal Service employees and for federal air traffic controllers. Hiring for higher-level jobs involves comparing the qualifications and experience of candidates who meet the educational requirements for the position. Seniority, or the amount of time a person has worked for the government or at a particular type of position, also determines which employees receive promotions.

Civil service regulations provide job security. After three years of satisfactory performance, employees cannot be fired except "for cause," meaning that the firing agency must cite a reason. Civil service regulations set out a multistep procedure for firing someone, beginning with low performance evaluations, then warning letters given to the employee, followed by a lengthy appeals process before a firing takes place. In simple terms, it is very hard to fire someone from the federal bureaucracy as long as he or she shows up for work. One study found that only about 11,000 civil servants are fired in a given year.[54] A subpar performer may be assigned other duties, transferred to another office, or even given nothing to do in the hope that the person will leave voluntarily out of boredom.

Despite the difficulties associated with firing an underperforming bureaucrat, it is possible to reduce the size of the federal workforce through reductions in force (RIF), which occasionally occur when an entire office or program is terminated. Employees who have been laid off due to an RIF can apply for civil service positions in other parts of government. Another strategy for reducing the federal workforce is simply not to replace employees who decide to leave government service, or to hire contractors, who lack civil service protections and can be terminated at will. For example, after the end of the Space Shuttle Program at NASA in 2011, the Mission Operations Directorate ("Mission Control") went from 3,000 employees to only 600 without any layoffs, as all of the departing employees worked for outside firms who lost their NASA contracts after the shuttles stopped flying.[55]

If you think civil service regulations sound extraordinarily cumbersome, you're right.[56] The hiring criteria remove a manager's discretion to hire someone who would do an excellent job but lacks the education or work experience that the regulations specify as necessary for the position. The firing requirements make it extremely difficult to remove poor performers. The salary and promotion restrictions create problems with rewarding excellent performance or promoting the best employees rather than those with the most seniority.

Why do civil service requirements exist? Recall that the aim of these regulations was to separate politics from policy. The mechanism for achieving this goal was a set of rules and requirements that made it hard for elected officials to control the hiring and firing of government employees to further their own political goals. In effect, even though civil service regulations have obvious drawbacks, they also provide this less apparent but very important benefit. For example, without civil service protections, employees in the Office of Personnel Management might be pressured by members of Congress who wanted to increase pensions for retiring federal workers who were their constituents.

Although loyalty to the president is a widely accepted criterion for hiring agency heads and other presidential appointees, professionals with permanent civil service positions are supposed to be hired on the basis of their qualifications, not their political beliefs. In fact, it is illegal to bring politics into these hiring decisions. However, there are well-documented cases in which administrations have made political beliefs a priority in hiring mid-level bureaucrats. For example, during the presidency of George W. Bush, Justice Department officials admitted to screening job applicants based on their ideological leanings. Membership in a liberal organization such as Greenpeace listed on a candidate's resumé reduced the likelihood of the person's being hired, while membership in a conservative organization such as the Federalist Society boosted an applicant's chances.[57] Although this example occurred during the Bush administration, it is likely that other administrations have behaved similarly.

LIMITS ON POLITICAL ACTIVITY

Federal employees are limited in their political activities. The Hatch Act, enacted in 1939 and amended in 1940, prohibited federal employees from engaging in organized political activities.[58] Under the act, employees could vote and contribute to candidates but could not work for candidates or for political parties. These restrictions were modified in the 1993 Federal Employees Political Activities Act, allowing federal employees to undertake a wider range of political activities, including fund-raising and serving as an officer of a political party. Senior members of the president's White House staff and political appointees are exempt from most of these restrictions, although they cannot use government resources for political activities.

While the Hatch Act is often invoked when government employees express controversial views, the key restriction is on activities that directly help a particular political candidate, such as a public endorsement at a mass rally. For example, former NASA scientist James Hansen (he retired in 2013) has written and testified about the dangers of global warming, taking positions that contradict the official statements of NASA leadership as well as those of Presidents Bush and Obama.[59] However, because Hansen limited his comments to the scientific debate over global warming without speaking for or against a candidate, his actions did not fall under the Hatch Act.

Even so, the Hatch Act makes life especially difficult for presidential appointees whose job duties often mix government service with politics, such as helping the president they work for get reelected. In order to comply with Hatch Act restrictions, these officials need to carry separate cell phones to make calls related to their political activities and maintain separate e-mail accounts— usually provided by the party or campaign committee—for their political communications. For example, in 2014, Dave Walker, the former head of the Government Accountability Office (an agency that investigates and audits

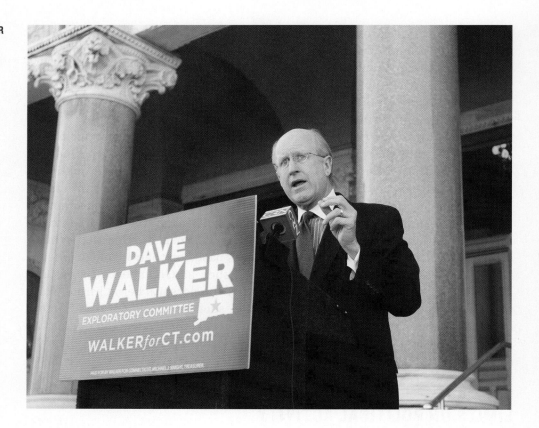

government programs), sent e-mails to his former colleagues telling them about a possible run for lieutenant governor of Connecticut. While it was not a violation of the Hatch Act for Walker to run for office or to contact his colleagues, it was a violation to send the message to government e-mail addresses.[60]

POLITICAL APPOINTEES AND THE SENIOR EXECUTIVE SERVICE

Not every federal employee is a member of the civil service. The president appoints over 7,000 individuals to senior positions in the executive branch that are not subject to civil service regulations, such as the leaders of executive departments and independent agencies like NASA, as well as members of the Executive Office of the President. (In some cases, the Senate must confirm these nominees.) Some of these presidential appointees get their jobs as a reward for working on the campaign staff, contributing substantial funds, or raising money from other donors. These individuals may not be given positions with real decision-making power. Some government agencies have the reputation of being **turkey farms**, places where campaign stalwarts can be appointed without the risk that their lack of experience will lead to bad policy.[61]

turkey farms Agencies to which campaign workers and donors can be appointed in reward for their service because it is unlikely that their lack of qualifications will lead to bad policy.

The majority of a president's appointees act as the president's eyes, ears, and hands throughout the executive branch. They hold positions of power within government agencies, serving as secretaries of executive departments, agency heads, or senior deputies. Their jobs involve finding out what the president wants from their agency and ordering, persuading, or cajoling their subordinates to implement presidential directives.

In many agencies, people in the top positions are members of the Senior Executive Service (SES), who are also exempt from civil service restrictions.[62] As of 2014, there were a few thousand SES members, most of whom were career government employees who held relatively high-level agency positions before moving to the SES. This change of employment status costs them their civil service protections but allows them to apply for senior leadership positions in the bureaucracy. Some political appointees are also given SES positions, although most do not have the experience or expertise held by career bureaucrats who typically move to the SES.

The president's ability to appoint bureaucrats in many different agencies helps him control the bureaucracy. By selecting people who are loyal or like-minded, a president can attempt to control the actions of lower-level bureaucrats and implement his policy agenda. The SES also provides civil servants an incentive to do their jobs well, as good performance in an agency position can help build a career that might allow them to transfer to the SES.

CONTROLLING THE BUREAUCRACY

EXPLAIN HOW CONGRESS AND THE PRESIDENT OVERSEE THE EXECUTIVE BRANCH

As the expert implementers of legislation and presidential directives, bureaucrats hold significant power to influence government policy. This situation creates the problem of political control illustrated by the principal–agent game: elected officials must figure out how to reap the benefits of bureaucratic expertise without simply giving bureaucrats free rein to do whatever they want.

One strategy is to take away discretion entirely and give bureaucrats simple, direct orders. For example, after Russia's annexation in 2014 of a portion of the Ukraine, the Obama administration implemented retaliatory sanctions that, among other things, forced NASA personnel to have no contact with employees of the Russian space program, except for the minimum necessary to operate the International Space Station.[63] This restriction forced NASA to stop work on a wide range of joint activities, from planetary exploration to discussions of how to respond if an asteroid was found to be on a collision course with Earth. However, the order did not leave NASA bureaucrats any discretion to determine which activities could be continued.

The problem with eliminating bureaucrats' discretion is that it limits the positive influence of their expertise. Particularly when new policies are being developed, taking away bureaucratic discretion is costly for legislators or presidential appointees, as it forces them to work out the policy details themselves—and may still produce less effective policies than those constructed by bureaucrats with specialized knowledge.[64] Moreover, preventing bureaucrats from using their judgment makes it impossible for them to craft policies that take into account new developments or unforeseen circumstances.[65] Directives may also make it impossible for bureaucrats to develop and implement policies incrementally, meaning a process where new rules and regulations are developed and put in place over time as opposed to all at once.[66] Incrementalism is a good strategy to follow when policies are complex and no one is sure what the impact of new regulations will be—but directives from elected officials to develop and implement regulations as fast as possible can make this strategy impossible.

For all these reasons, elected officials must find ways to reduce or eliminate **bureaucratic drift**—that is, bureaucrats pursuing their own goals rather than

bureaucratic drift Bureaucrats' tendency to implement policies in a way that favors their own political objectives rather than following the original intentions of the legislation.

their assignments from officeholders or appointees—while still reaping the benefits of bureaucratic expertise. This section describes two common strategies: changing the way agencies are organized and staffed, and using standardized procedures for monitoring agency actions. In both cases, the aim is to set up the agency so that bureaucrats can use their expertise, while making sure their actions are consistent with elected officials' wishes.[67] These measures mitigate—but do not eliminate—the problem of control discussed earlier (see the You Decide feature).

AGENCY ORGANIZATION

Over the last 20 years, political scientists have shown how agencies can be organized to minimize bureaucratic drift.[68] Specifically, when an agency is set up or given new responsibilities, the officials who initiate the change don't simply tell the agency what to do. To make sure that they get the policies they want, they also determine where the agency is located within the federal government structure and who runs it. These efforts may occur solely within Congress, involve both Congress and the president, or be arranged by presidential actions.[69]

For example, one of the Obama administration's responses to the 2008–2009 financial crisis was to form a new agency, the Consumer Financial Protection Bureau, which would help to enforce new bank regulations and investigate consumer complaints about financial firms. In 2011, it was expected that Elizabeth Warren, a Harvard Law professor who had helped to set up the agency, would become the first head of the agency. However, many Republican and some Democratic senators and financial-industry lobbyists opposed Warren's appointment, believing she would encourage her subordinates to be excessively pro-consumer in their investigations. As a result, Obama appointed the former attorney general of Ohio, Richard Cordray, who was more acceptable to more senators.

In the case of the Federal Communications Commission, elected officials were concerned that the organization would adopt regulations on political advertising that favored one political party over the other. To prevent this, the legislation that created the agency mandates that the agency will be run by five commissioners, all of whom are nominated by the president and confirmed by the Senate.[70] However, no more than three of the commissioners can be from the same political party. As a result, if a partisan majority on the commission tries to enact laws that favor one party, opponents need to convince only one supporter to switch positions in order to block the measure. In many cases, during the time they are in office, commissioners are also prohibited from having a business relationship (as a consultant, stockholder, or otherwise) with any company that is subject to their agency's rulings.

MONITORING

One of the most important ways elected officials prevent bureaucratic drift is to know what bureaucrats are doing or planning to do. Information gathering by members of Congress about bureaucratic actions is termed **oversight**.

oversight Congressional efforts to make sure that laws are implemented correctly by the bureaucracy after they have been passed.

KATHLEEN SEBELIUS TESTIFYING IN October 2013 when she was Secretary of Health and Human Services at a congressional hearing about problems with the rollout of the Affordable Care Act.

IS POLITICAL CONTROL OF THE BUREAUCRACY BENEFICIAL?

When working with bureaucrats, elected officials face the problem of political control: Should they allow bureaucrats to exercise judgment when implementing policies or give them specific, narrow directives? Letting bureaucrats set policy allows them to base decisions on their expertise or private information, but it also gives them the freedom to ignore elected officials' policy goals and preferences in favor of their own. While this exercise of expertise sounds like a good idea—shouldn't we let government policy be formulated by the most-knowledgeable people?—in practice it remains a difficult question.

Consider the case of America's involvement in the Libyan civil war in 2011. The United States, along with its allies in NATO, provided the Libyan rebels with weapons and other supplies, and conducted manned and drone air strikes on the government's military bases and infrastructure. After some initial strikes, the U.S. involvement was limited to drone missions, refueling of NATO aircraft, and logistics support. However, by the provisions of the War Powers Act (see Chapter 12), after 60 days the president was obligated to determine whether U.S. involvement constituted "hostilities," and, if it did, to inform members of Congress, who could vote on whether to continue the mission or end it.

While the final decision about whether an operation constitutes hostilities rests with the president, typically, presidents have relied on the judgment of lawyers in the State Department to make this determination. In the case of Libya, these lawyers argued that the Libyan mission constituted hostilities. However, the president ignored this advice and relied on the judgment of his advisers in the Executive Office of the President, who came to the opposite conclusion, meaning that there was no need to ask Congress to pass judgment on the operation.

Many observers criticized President Obama's decision to overrule the judgment of his legal experts. As Speaker of the House, Republican John Boehner, put in, "The White House says there are no hostilities taking place. Yet we've got *drone attacks* under way. We're spending $10 million a day. We're part of an effort to drop bombs on Gaddafi's compounds. It just doesn't pass the straight-face test, in my view, that we're not in the midst of hostilities."[a] Even leaving politics aside—the Libya operation was opposed by many Republicans, including Boehner—the episode raises an important question: If bureaucrats are experts, why shouldn't they make policy decisions, rather than leaving them up to politicians, who may know far less about the decisions they face?

The problem with bureaucratic discretion is that it cuts both ways. Allowing bureaucrats to act as they think best means that they can disregard the stated goals of legislation or the preferences of elected officials and simply implement the policies they favor. Even bureaucrats' public statements can have policy consequences—they may influence public

While legal experts in the State Department said that U.S. involvement in Libya in 2011 constituted "hostilities" and was therefore subject to a possible vote in Congress, the Obama administration chose to ignore the experts and follow its own plan.

opinion and in turn shape government policy. If experts in the bureaucracy sound the alarm, people outside government may listen and even take action in the form of protests, legal action, or other organized attempts to overturn the decision inside government. Even if their efforts are unsuccessful, the president and the people working for him or her may spend considerable time responding to public pressure.

Another downside that comes with bureaucratic discretion is that bureaucrats are unelected, and most are very difficult to fire because of their civil service protections. Moreover, if bureaucrats are given a great deal of leeway to use their judgment in policy making, it becomes very difficult to determine the criteria for judging whether their removal is warranted or not. How much discretion should elected officials allow bureaucrats to use? You decide.

CRITICAL THINKING QUESTIONS

1. It's easy to see why opponents of the president's policies would like to reduce political control of the bureaucracy. However, there are situations where even a president might want to reduce his or her control over bureaucratic actions. Why?

2. The benefits and costs of political control vary across the different agencies and departments that make up the bureaucracy. Where do you think the benefits are high, and where do you think they are low? What about costs?

Congressional committees often hold hearings to question agency heads, secretaries of executive departments, or senior agency staff. Similarly, one of the primary responsibilities of presidential appointees is to monitor how bureaucrats are responding to presidential directives. The problem is that presidential appointees may be unable to fulfill this role. Because they are chosen for their loyalty to the president, they may lack the experience needed to fully understand what bureaucrats in their agency are doing. Moreover, given that appointees typically hold their position for only a year or two, they have little time to learn the details of agency operations.

ADVANCE WARNING Members of Congress, the president, and his staff gain advance knowledge of bureaucratic actions through the notice and comment procedure described earlier in the chapter, which requires bureaucrats to disclose proposed changes before they take effect.[71] This delay gives opponents the opportunity to register complaints with their congressional representatives, and it allows these legislators time either to pressure the agency to revise the regulation or even to enact another law undoing or modifying the agency action.

INVESTIGATIONS: POLICE PATROLS AND FIRE ALARMS Investigations involve Congress, legislative staff, or presidential appointees selecting some government program or office and scrutinizing the organization, its expenditures, and its activities. There are two types of oversight, police patrols and fire alarms. Ideally, every agency would be investigated as often as possible, with agencies that had large budgets or carried out important functions being investigated more frequently. These investigations may involve fact-finding trips to local offices, interviews with senior personnel, audits of agency accounts, and calls to the agency to see how it responds to citizens' requests. This method of investigation is called **police patrol oversight**.[72] Think of a police officer walking her beat, rattling doors to see if they are locked, checking out broken windows, and looking down alleys for suspicious behavior.

The disadvantage of police patrol oversight is that it is costly in terms of money and staff time. Moreover, these investigations often find that agencies are doing what they should. Because of these problems, Congress and the president also look outside government for information on what bureaucrats are doing. Rather than undertaking a series of investigations, they wait until they receive a complaint about bureaucratic actions, then focus investigative efforts on those cases, a practice labeled **fire alarm oversight**.[73] The so-called fire alarm can take many different forms. Representatives and their staff meet frequently with constituents, who may let them know of a problem with the bureaucracy. Similarly, the president and his staff are often contacted by lobbyists, corporate executives, and ordinary citizens with complaints about bureaucratic actions. Newspaper reporters and Internet bloggers also provide information on what bureaucrats are doing—this is how the Office of Personnel Management (OPM) retirement processing system came to light, in a *Washington Post* article. Some agencies have advisory committees that not only help make agency decisions but also serve to keep Congress and the president informed about them.[74]

The case of NASA climate change scientist James Hansen described earlier provides a clear example of fire alarm oversight. At one point, NASA managers required that Hansen submit all his public statements and work for review before publication. But this order soon became known when the *New York Times* and other

police patrol oversight A method of oversight in which members of Congress constantly monitor the bureaucracy to make sure that laws are implemented correctly.

fire alarm oversight A method of oversight in which members of Congress respond to complaints about the bureaucracy or problems of implementation only as they arise rather than exercising constant vigilance.

newspapers reported it. The resulting firestorm of protest from members of Congress forced NASA head Michael Griffin to rescind the order. Similarly, overly long wait times for appointments at Veterans Administration hospitals in Arizona came to light in 2014 only after a retired VA employee gave this information to reporters.

These fire alarms provide exactly the sort of information that Congress and the president often lack about how bureaucrats are implementing laws and directives, including cases when bureaucrats are doing (or planning to do) something that contradicts their mandate. Such communications tell Congress and the president where to focus their efforts to monitor the bureaucracy, drawing their attention to agencies or programs in which problems have been reported, rather than driving them to try to oversee the entire government at once.

CORRECTING VIOLATIONS

When members of Congress or the president find a case of bureaucratic drift, they can take steps to influence the bureaucrats' actions. Many tactics can be used to bring a wayward agency into line. Legislation or an executive order can send a clear directive to an agency or remove its discretion, tasks and programs can be moved to an agency that is more closely aligned with elected officials' goals, political appointees at an agency can be replaced, and agencies can be reorganized. For example, soon after the *Washington Post* reported on the antiquated federal retirement processing system, a bipartisan group of senators sent a letter to the head of the OPM demanding specific reforms—in this case, bipartisan support signals that members of Congress may enact their own reforms if OPM fails to make changes.[75]

One of the most significant difficulties in dealing with bureaucratic drift is disagreement between members of Congress and the president about whether an agency is doing the right thing—regardless of whether the agency is following its original orders. Most of the tactics discussed earlier require joint action by the president and congressional majorities. Without presidential support, members of Congress need a two-thirds majority to impose corrections. Without congressional support, the president can only threaten to cut an agency's proposed budget, change its home within the federal bureaucracy, or set up a new agency to do what the errant agency refuses to do. Actually carrying out these threats requires congressional approval. As a result, disagreements between the president and Congress can give an agency significant freedom, as long as it retains the support of at least one branch of government.

An agency may also be able to fend off elected officials' attempts to take political control if it has a reputation for expertise. For example, one reason that

WHILE SOME PEOPLE ARE FRUSTRATED that bureaucratic agencies don't move more quickly, complex rules and procedures are often necessary. The FDA's careful (and often lengthy) approval process is aimed at avoiding incidents like the Vioxx recall, in which an arthritis drug caused an estimated 27,000 people to suffer heart attacks before it was taken off the market.

attempts to pass legislation forcing the FDA to alter its drug-approval process have had little success is that the FDA's process is thought to have worked mostly as intended, approving new drugs that are safe and effective and keeping ineffective or unsafe drugs off the market. At the same time, the FDA has responded to pressure from Congress and the president to revise some rules on its own.[76]

Finally, agencies can sometimes combat attempts to control their behavior by appealing to groups who benefit from agency actions.[77] For example, since the 1980s, the Occupational Safety and Health Administration (OSHA) has resisted attempts by Republican presidents and Republican members of Congress to eliminate the agency.[78] One element of its strategy has been to build strong ties to labor unions. As a result, OSHA is much more likely to receive complaints about workplace safety from companies with strong unions. The second prong of the strategy has involved building cooperative arrangements with large companies to prevent workplace accidents, an approach that not only protects workers but can save companies a lot of money over the long term. Moreover, when OSHA levies fines against companies that violate safety regulations, the fines are generally much less than would be allowed by law. As a result, when proposals to limit or eliminate OSHA are debated in Congress, members hear from unions as well as many large corporations in support of keeping the agency in place. Over time, this strategy has generated support for the agency from Democrats and Republicans in the House and Senate.

THE CONSEQUENCES OF CONTROL

This discussion of attempts to control what bureaucrats do while at the same time tapping their expertise explains many of the seemingly dysfunctional aspects of the bureaucracy. Part of the problem is the nature of the tasks given to bureaucrats. Even when members of Congress and the president agree on which problems deserve attention, bureaucrats often face the much harder task of translating these officials' lofty problem-solving goals into concrete policies. Given the magnitude of this job, it is no surprise that even the best efforts of government agencies do not always succeed. For example, while it's clear that officials at OPM could have been more aggressive about computerizing their retirement systems, the fact they they've tried several times and failed suggests that calculating pension benefits may be more complicated than it seems, perhaps because of the various rules and regulations that affect pension benefits and the wide range of jobs in the federal bureaucracy.

Most important, the use of standard operating procedures is rooted partly in the complexity of bureaucrats' tasks—but also in the desire of agency heads and elected officials to control the actions of lower-level staff. Some of FEMA's failures after Hurricane Katrina were the product of preset plans and procedures that did not anticipate a disaster of the magnitude faced in New Orleans. Moreover, giving laptops to government employees so they can work while out of the office sounds like a good idea, but it also puts sensitive data at risk because laptops are easily lost or stolen. And while the FDA's drug-approval process succeeds for the most part at preventing harmful drugs from coming to market, the delays imposed by the process do prevent some patients from receiving life-saving treatments. However, in all these cases, the decisions do not reflect incompetence or malice.

Rules and procedures are needed in any organization to ensure that decisions are made fairly and that they reflect the goals of the organization. But it is impossible to find procedures that will work well in all cases, particularly for the kinds of policy decisions made by bureaucrats.

It is also important to remember that many government regulations, even those that are the product of standard operating procedures, work as intended and provide socially beneficial results. For example, regulations restricting pollution have led to dramatic increases in air and water quality throughout the United States.

Dysfunctional bureaucratic behavior can also arise from the problem of political control. While it seems obvious that modernizing the Office of Personnel Management's retirement processing system would save money and reduce the time needed to process a new claim, this would probably only happen after a painful and costly transition period. Thus, congressional mandates to change the system may, in the short run, only make things worse. Someone who retires during this period and has to wait several months for her first pension check may think that OPM is more out of control than ever—even though the agency is doing exactly what Congress told it to do.

In sum, when government agencies do things that seem counterproductive, it would be wrong to immediately conclude that the organizations involved are inept or willfully shirking their responsibilities. Rather, they may be doing the best they can to achieve formidable goals, carrying out procedures that are often—but not always—productive, or responding to directives from elected officials.

CONCLUSION

Bureaucrats implement government policy—often in situations in which the problems as well as potential solutions are vast and poorly understood, and in the face of sharp disagreements about what government should do. On the government's behalf, bureaucrats spend money on everything from pencils to Mars rovers. They formulate regulations that determine what can be created, produced, transported, bought, sold, consumed, and disposed of in America. Elected officials want to control what bureaucrats do while also tapping into their expertise on policy matters. In this way, conflict over public policy often translates into conflicting ideas about what bureaucrats should do, resulting in complex, often contradictory mandates and directions imposed on bureaucrats. In recent years, for example, NASA has had to reconcile congressional mandates to develop new spacecraft and programs for exploring the solar system, while at the same time receiving very small budget increases.

These characteristics of the bureaucracy and the fundamentally political nature of bureaucrats' jobs explain many cases of ineptitude and red tape. Sometimes bureaucrats simply make mistakes, choosing the wrong policy because they—and, in some cases, everyone else—lack full information about the tasks they were given. Bureaucrats may drag their feet when they oppose their tasks on policy grounds. Policies may reflect direct or implicit orders given by elected officials or political appointees. For example, since the Office of Personnel Management's retirement processing center (discussed at the beginning of this chapter) is a major employer in a remote area, local elected officials may not want to implement reforms, because many of their constituents would lose their jobs. Attempts at political control also shape the structure of the bureaucracy, from influencing which agencies function independently and which ones fall within executive departments to determining the qualifications for commissioners and agency heads and the rules they must follow when making decisions.

WHAT IS THE FEDERAL BUREAUCRACY?

▶ *Define bureaucracy and explain its major functions.*
(Pages 474–83)

SUMMARY

The bureaucracy is composed of both civil servants and political appointees and is in charge of interpreting and implementing a wide range of government policies. While bureaucrats are policy experts, most members of Congress are not. Nonetheless, Congress tries to control how the bureaucracy operates, which can result in inefficiencies.

KEY TERMS

bureaucracy (p. 474)
civil servants (p. 474)
political appointees (p. 474)
regulation (p. 476)
notice-and-comment procedure (p. 476)
street-level bureaucrats (p. 479)
state capacity (p. 480)
red tape (p. 480)
standard operating procedures (p. 480)
problem of control (p. 481)
principal–agent game (p. 481)
regulatory capture (p. 482)

CRITICAL THINKING AND DISCUSSION

What kinds of bureaucrats would members of Congress want to give discretion to? What kinds of bureaucrats would they want to control?

PRACTICE QUIZ QUESTIONS

1. A government rule that affects the choices that individuals or corporations make is called _____.

   Ⓐ an initiative

   Ⓑ a referendum

   Ⓒ a regulation

   Ⓓ a procurement

   Ⓔ an appropriation

2. One of the reasons bureaucrats respond to pressure from elected officials is because _____.

   Ⓐ they need congressional support to get larger budgets

   Ⓑ elected officials are experts

   Ⓒ they are all appointed by members of Congress

   Ⓓ their offices are housed in the Congress

   Ⓔ they are required by law to do so

3. In the problem of control, the _____ is the principal and the _____ is the agent.

   Ⓐ bureaucracy; president

   Ⓑ bureaucracy; Congress

   Ⓒ president; Congress

   Ⓓ president; bureaucracy

   Ⓔ Congress; president

4. _____ occurs when bureaucrats cater to a small group of individuals regardless of the impact of these actions on the public welfare.

   Ⓐ Bureaucratic drift

   Ⓑ Regulatory capture

   Ⓒ The revolving door

   Ⓓ An iron triangle

   Ⓔ Neutral competence

HOW HAS THE AMERICAN BUREAUCRACY GROWN?

▶ *Trace the expansion of the federal bureaucracy over time.*
(Pages 483–87)

SUMMARY

The bureaucracy has grown substantially since the turn of the twentieth century, largely in response to citizen demands that the government do more for the people. The federal government had a very limited role in daily life for much of the nineteenth century, but it expanded during the Progressive Era, when regulatory activity increased and the spoils system was replaced by the federal civil service. The bureaucracy expanded again with the New Deal and Great Society programs, which increased the number of services the government provided.

KEY TERM

federal civil service (p. 485)

CRITICAL THINKING AND DISCUSSION

If, as the chapter argues, the growth of the federal bureaucracy in the late nineteenth century was driven by citizen demands, what kinds of demands are being made today, at a time when the bureaucracy is large but not growing?

5. How did the bureaucracy change during the Progressive Era?

    [A] It expanded the delivery of government services directly to individuals.

    [B] The spoils system was first established.

    [C] It created a number of antipoverty and educational programs.

    [D] It reduced the government regulatory activity.

    [E] It increased the government's regulatory activity.

6. The civil service reforms of the Progressive Era _____ the spoils system and _____ the power of party organizations.

    [A] ended; increased

    [B] ended; decreased

    [C] instituted; increased

    [D] instituted; decreased

    [E] expanded; increased

7. What effect did the Reagan Revolution have on bureaucracy?

    [A] The government stopped passing regulatory policies.

    [B] The size of the federal government shrank.

    [C] The size of the federal government increased.

    [D] The civil service reforms were weakened.

    [E] The civil service reforms were strengthened.

THE MODERN FEDERAL BUREAUCRACY

▶ *Describe the size and structure of the executive branch today.* **(Pages 487–92)**

SUMMARY

The modern bureaucracy serves a wide range of functions, but the division of labor within the bureaucracy does not always have an obvious logic. Overlapping or confusing jurisdictions can be the result of elected officials attempting to shape the agency behavior by assigning a task to an executive department rather than an independent agency. The overall size of the bureaucracy reflects the demands of constituents, but also fits the needs of elected officials to improve their chances of reelection.

KEY TERMS

Office of Management and Budget (p. 488)
independent agencies (p. 489)
budget maximizers (p. 491)

CRITICAL THINKING AND DISCUSSION

Suppose you are a member of Congress who must decide whether to give bureaucrats in a particular agency direct orders that allow them little or no input, or to allow them to exercise their own discretion. What factors should you consider when making this decision?

8. What is the job of the Office of Management and Budget?

    [A] to prepare the president's annual budget proposal for the Congress

    [B] to prepare a response to the budget passed by Congress

    [C] to prepare annual budget proposals for the states

    [D] to monitor government spending for the Supreme Court

    [E] to monitor government spending for Congress

9. Independent agencies have _____ freedom from oversight than executive departments do and _____ be controlled by the president through his appointees.

    [A] more; cannot

    [B] more; can

    [C] less; cannot

    [D] less; can

10. The federal budget is growing in size because _____.

    [A] bureaucrats are budget maximizers

    [B] politicians do not scrutinize budget requests

    [C] government agencies are never eliminated

    [D] the public does not support large-scale budget cuts

    [E] a growing percentage of Americans are going into civil service

THE HUMAN FACE OF THE BUREAUCRACY

▶ *Describe who bureaucrats are and the regulations that govern their employment.* **(Pages 493–97)**

SUMMARY

The regulations within the civil service system were established to separate politics from policy. Rather than getting and retaining a job for political reasons, individuals are hired based on merit and are quite difficult to fire. However, the president makes senior-level appointments that are not protected by civil service regulations and are more political in nature. These appointments are instrumental in helping the president control the bureaucracy.

KEY TERM

turkey farms (p. 496)

CRITICAL THINKING AND DISCUSSION

What are the advantages and disadvantages of bureaucrats often having their own preferences about how to implement the policies they administer?

PRACTICE QUIZ QUESTIONS

11. Compared with employees in private business, government employees are motivated _____ by salary and benefits than/as by the chance to make a difference.

   A more

   B just as much

   C less

12. The civil service regulations _____ the flexibility that managers have in their hiring decisions and _____ the influence of elected officials.

   A decrease; decrease

   B increase; increase

   C increase; decrease

   D decrease; increase

   E increase; have no effect on

14. Giving direct orders to bureaucrats _____ the influence of their policy expertise and _____ the potential for incrementalism.

   A limits; reduces

   B increases; reduces

   C limits; increases

   D increases; increases

   E limits; has no effect on

15. While police patrol oversight has the advantage of being _____, it has the drawback of being _____.

   A affordable; unresponsive

   B responsive; costly

   C affordable; generally unnecessary

   D responsive; unpopular

   E affordable; ineffective

CONTROLLING THE BUREAUCRACY

▶ *Explain how Congress and the president oversee the executive branch.* **(Pages 497–503)**

SUMMARY

With their expertise, bureaucrats have the power to significantly influence government policy. This creates a dilemma for elected officials, who want to enjoy the benefits of the expertise while retaining control of the bureaucracy. Lawmakers can generally organize agencies and monitor their behavior to reduce, but not eliminate, bureaucratic drift.

KEY TERMS

bureaucratic drift (p. 497)
oversight (p. 498)
police patrol oversight (p. 500)
fire alarm oversight (p. 500)

CRITICAL THINKING AND DISCUSSION

Why might bureaucrats pay more attention to orders and directives from members of Congress than those from the president or his political appointees?

PRACTICE QUIZ QUESTIONS

13. When bureaucrats pursue their own goals rather than their assignments from officeholders, this is called _____.

   A an iron triangle

   B regulatory capture

   C problem of control

   D turkey farming

   E bureaucratic drift

SUGGESTED READING

Brehm, John, and Scott Gates. *Teaching, Managing Tasks, and Brokering Trust: Functions of the Public Executive.* New York: Russel Sage Foundation, 2008.

Carpenter, Daniel P. *The Forging of Bureaucratic Autonomy: Reputations, Networks, and Policy Innovation in Executive Agencies, 1862–1928.* Princeton, NJ: Princeton University Press, 2001.

Epstein, David, and Sharyn O'Halloran. *Delegating Powers: A Transaction Cost Politics Approach to Policy Making under Separate Powers.* New York: Cambridge University Press, 1999.

Huber, John D., and Charles R. Shipan. *Deliberate Discretion? The Institutional Foundations of Bureaucratic Autonomy.* New York: Cambridge University Press, 2002.

Lewis, David E. *The Politics of Presidential Appointments: Political Control and Bureaucratic Performance.* Princeton, NJ: Princeton University Press, 2010.

Light, Paul. *A Government Well-Executed: Public Service and Public Performance.* Washington, D.C.: Brookings Institution Press, 2003.

McCubbins, Mathew D., Roger G. Noll, and Barry R. Weingast. "Structure and Process as Solutions to the Politician's Principal–Agency Problem," *Virginia Law Review* 74 (1989): 431–82.

Meier, Kenneth, and Lawrence O'Toole. *Bureaucracy in a Democratic State: A Governance Perspective.* Baltimore: Johns Hopkins University Press, 2008.

Miller, Gary. *Managerial Dilemmas: The Political Economy of Hierarchy.* New York: Cambridge University Press, 1987.

Moe, Terry M. "Political Control and the Power of the Agent." *Journal of Law, Economics, and Organization* 22 (2006): 1–21.

Nelson, Michael. "A Short, Ironic History of American National Bureaucracy." *Journal of Politics* 44 (1982): 747–78.

Skowronek, Stephen. *Building a New American State: The Expansion of National Administrative Capacities, 1877–1920.* New York: Cambridge University Press, 1982.

Wilson, James Q. *Bureaucracy: What Government Agencies Do and Why They Do It,* 2nd ed. New York: Basic Books, 2000.

14

The Courts

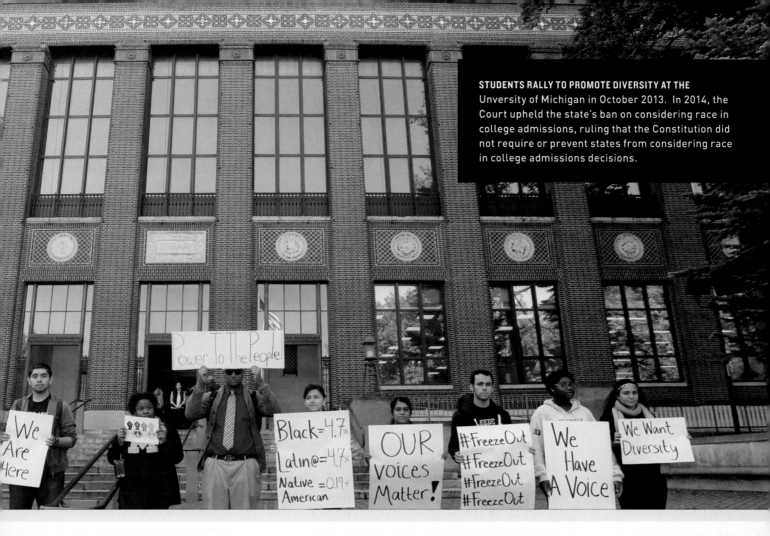

DURING THE OBAMA PRESIDENCY, THE SUPREME COURT has decided an unusual number of cases with important political implications, including cases on affirmative action in higher education, same-sex marriage, voting rights, health care reform, global warming, religious freedom versus reproductive rights, campaign finance, and immigration. Scholars had to reach back to 1936 and the battles between the Court and President Franklin Roosevelt to find a comparable period in which the Court was so involved with the central political debates of the day.

In addition to their formal authority in reviewing cases brought before them, Supreme Court justices display two roles in our political system: either asserting their own policy-making authority or deferring to the decisions of others (Congress, the president, or the people). Two cases from 2014 illustrate these roles. The more active role was evident in a campaign finance case in which the Court struck down limits on the total combined amount of money that individuals can contribute to candidates and national political parties in federal elections (see *McCutcheon v. FEC* in Chapter 9). Congress had imposed these limits in 1974 to curb the perceived corrupting influence of money in elections. But in 2014, the Court ruled that the First Amendment protects the right to contribute money to a broad range of candidates.[1] The Court displayed its second role—deferring to others—in a case about affirmative action. In this case, the Court ruled that the Constitution did not require or prevent states from considering race in college admissions decisions. As Justice Breyer argued in his concurring opinion,

CONFLICT COMPROMISE
in American Politics

CHAPTER *goals*

Explain how the power
of judicial review was
established.
▶ PAGES 511–15

Outline the structure of the
court system.
▶ PAGES 515–28

Describe how cases reach
the Supreme Court.
▶ PAGES 528–34

Describe the Supreme
Court's procedures for
hearing a case.
▶ PAGES 534–38

Analyze the factors that
influence Supreme Court
decisions.
▶ PAGES 538–45

Assess the Supreme
Court's power in the
political system.
▶ PAGES 545–48

"[T]he Constitution foresees the ballot box, not the courts, as the normal instrument for resolving differences and debates about the merits of these programs." When there is not a clear constitutional principle involved, the people or their elected leaders should decide policy rather than the courts.[2]

The Court's decision about which path to take in a given case is often political, involving conflict, trade-offs, and compromise, much like decision making in Congress. That the Supreme Court is a policy-making and political institution may seem inappropriate. After all, the guiding principles of the "rule of law" in the American political system—embodied in the words carved above the entrance to the Supreme Court ("equal justice under the law") and the statue of Justice represented as a blindfolded women holding a set of scales—seem to contradict the view of a political Supreme Court. We normally think of the courts as objectively applying the law and interpreting the Constitution for each case. Indeed, there is often consensus among the justices on how to rule in a given case. But the fractured nature of the affirmative action decision, with four separate opinions and no more than three justices agreeing with any opinion in its entirety, illustrates that politics is an inherent part of the judiciary and a single set of objective standards is not always available for a given case.

Although we certainly expect them to be fair and objective, judges have their own political views and opinions, and these often shape their views of cases, in part *because* there are usually multiple legal justifications for any case. For example, there is no simple or clear-cut way to determine objectively the relative legal merits of Justice Sotomayor's dissenting view that banning affirmative action is "entirely at odds with our idea of equality under the law," or the majority's view that the Constitution allows Michigan voters to pass a state constitutional amendment banning the consideration of race in higher education admissions decisions. To a large extent, these positions depend on the justices' views of how the equal protection clause of the Fourteenth Amendment applies in these contexts.

For those who resist the view that the courts are a policy-making institution, the theme "political process matters" may not seem to apply in this chapter.

DECISIONS BY THE SUPREME COURT affect ordinary Americans in countless ways. However, the Founders left the Court's powers unclear, and debates over its proper role in politics continue to this day.

However, the courts often *do* make policy, and the way they make decisions has an impact on outcomes. To see how political process matters for the courts, it is important to answer the following questions: What are the different roles of the courts? What is the structure of the judicial system? How do court decisions shape policy? In a nutshell, what is the nature of judicial decision making? This chapter also examines the questions suggested by the campaign finance and affirmative action cases: What is the proper place of the courts within our political system? How much power should unelected judges have? Are the courts a necessary check on the other branches of government or a source of unaccountable power that contradicts core principles of democracy? How do the courts interact with the other branches? Before addressing these questions, we discuss how the Founders viewed the judicial system.

THE DEVELOPMENT OF AN INDEPENDENT AND POWERFUL FEDERAL JUDICIARY

> EXPLAIN HOW THE POWER OF JUDICIAL REVIEW WAS ESTABLISHED

The role of the courts in American politics and the Supreme Court's authority as the ultimate interpreter of the Constitution were not definitively established in the Constitution. The powers of the Supreme Court evolved over time, and debates about its proper role continue to this day.

THE FOUNDERS' VIEWS OF THE COURTS: THE WEAKEST BRANCH?

The Federalists and Antifederalists did not see eye to eye on much, and the judiciary was no exception. Alexander Hamilton, writing in *Federalist 78*, said that the Supreme Court would be "beyond comparison the weakest of the three departments of power." In contrast, the author of the *Antifederalist Papers* wrote, "The supreme court under this constitution would be exalted above all other power in the government and subjected to no control."[3] Hmmm, which is it, weakest or strongest? Although the framers could not agree on the likely relative power of the Court, there was surprisingly little debate at the Constitutional Convention about the judiciary. Article III of the Constitution, which concerns the judicial branch of government (see Nuts & Bolts 14.1), created one Supreme Court and gave the courts independence by providing federal judges with lifetime terms (assuming "good behavior").

The main disagreements about the judiciary had to do with how independent the courts should be vis-à-vis the other branches of government and how much power to give to the courts. Some of the framers feared a tyrannical Congress and wanted to create judicial and executive branches that could check this power. Others argued for making the executive and judicial branches more closely related so they would be better able to balance Congress. A central debate was whether to give the judiciary some "revisionary power" over Congress, similar to the president's veto power. This idea of judicial review would have given the Supreme Court

JURISDICTION OF THE FEDERAL COURTS AS DEFINED IN ARTICLE III OF THE CONSTITUTION

JURISDICTION OF LOWER FEDERAL COURTS

▶ Cases involving the U.S. Constitution, federal laws, and treaties.

▶ Controversies between two or more states. (Congress passed a law giving the Supreme Court exclusive jurisdiction over these cases.)

▶ Controversies between citizens of different states.

▶ Controversies between a state and citizens of another state. (The Eleventh Amendment removed federal jurisdiction in these cases.)

▶ Controversies between a state or its citizens and any foreign states, citizens, or subjects.

▶ Cases affecting ambassadors, public ministers, and consuls.

▶ Cases of admiralty and maritime jurisdictions.

▶ Controversies between citizens of the same state claiming lands under grants of different states.

JURISDICTION OF THE SUPREME COURT

Original Jurisdiction*

▶ Cases involving ambassadors, public ministers, and consuls.

▶ Cases to which a state is a party.

Appellate Jurisdiction

▶ Cases falling under the jurisdiction of the lower federal courts, "with such exceptions, and under such Regulations as the Congress shall make."

---

*This does not imply exclusive jurisdiction. For example, the Supreme Court may refer to a district court for a case involving an ambassador (the more likely outcome).

SOURCE: Lee Epstein and Thomas G. Walker, Constitutional Law for a Changing America: Institutional Powers and Constraints, 5th ed. (Washington, D.C.: CQ Press, 2004), p. 65.

---

the power to strike down laws passed by Congress that violated the Constitution. The framers could not agree on judicial review, so the Constitution remained silent on the matter. As the power of judicial review has evolved, it has become a central part of the system of checks and balances (see Chapter 2).

Many details about the Supreme Court were left up to Congress, including its size, the time and place it would meet, and its internal organization. These details, and the system of lower federal courts, were outlined in the **Judiciary Act of 1789**. This law set the number of justices at six (one chief justice and five associates). The number of justices gradually increased to ten by the end of the Civil War and was then restricted to seven under Reconstruction policies. The number was set at nine in 1869, where it has remained ever since.[4] The 1789 Act also created a system of federal courts, which included 13 **district courts** and 3 circuit courts— the intermediate-level courts that heard appeals from the district courts. The district courts each had one judge, while the circuit courts had two Supreme Court justices and one district judge. This odd arrangement for staffing the circuit courts remained in place for more than 100 years, over the objections of the justices who resented having to "ride circuit" in difficult traveling conditions.[5] Today, separate judges are appointed to fill the circuit courts (what we call "appeals courts"). Furthermore, the act defined the jurisdiction of the federal courts. One controversial provision was Section 25, which expanded the Court's **appellate jurisdiction** (cases heard on appeal from lower courts) to include state supreme court cases involving conflicts between state law on one hand and federal law or treaties or the U.S. Constitution on the other.

The Supreme Court had a rough start. Indeed, it seemed determined to prove Alexander Hamilton right that it was the weakest branch. Of the six original

Judiciary Act of 1789 The law in which Congress laid out the organization of the federal judiciary. The law refined and clarified federal court jurisdiction and set the original number of justices at six. It also created the Office of the Attorney General and established the lower federal courts.

district courts Lower-level trial courts of the federal judicial system that handle most U.S. federal cases.

appellate jurisdiction The authority of a court to hear appeals from lower courts and change or uphold the decision.

justices appointed by George Washington, one declined to serve and another never showed up for a formal session. The Court's first sessions lasted only a few days because it did not have much business. In fact, the Court did not decide a single case in 1791 or 1792. When Justice Rutledge resigned in 1791 to take a state court position, two potential appointees turned down the job in order to keep their positions in their state legislatures! Such career decisions would be unimaginable today, when serving on the Supreme Court is considered the pinnacle of a legal career.[6]

JUDICIAL REVIEW AND MARBURY V. MADISON

The Court started to gain more power when John Marshall was appointed chief justice in 1801. Marshall single-handedly transformed the Court into an equal partner in the system of checks and balances. The most important step was the decision *Marbury v. Madison* (1803), which gave the Supreme Court the power of **judicial review**. As noted earlier, the framers were split on the wisdom of giving the Court the power to strike down laws passed by Congress; therefore, the Constitution does not explicitly address the issue. However, historians have established that a majority of the framers, including the most influential ones, favored judicial review. Given that the Constitution did not address the issue of judicial review, Marshall simply asserted that the Supreme Court had the power to determine when a law was unconstitutional.

judicial review The Supreme Court's power to strike down a law or an executive branch action that it finds unconstitutional.

The facts and legal reasoning behind *Marbury* are worth explaining because this is one of the most important court cases in American history. The Federalists had just lost the election of 1800 to Thomas Jefferson and the Democratic-Republicans. In a last-minute power grab, the Federalist-controlled lame-duck Congress gave outgoing President Adams an opportunity to appoint 42 new justices of the peace for the District of Columbia and Alexandria, Virginia. Adams made the appointments, and the Senate confirmed them, but not before time ran out and the new administration took over. The secretary of state, John Marshall (the same Marshall who had just been confirmed as chief justice before President Adams left office), failed to ensure that all the commissions for the new judges were delivered by midnight. When President Jefferson assumed office, he ordered his new secretary of state, James Madison, not to deliver the remaining commissions that had been issued by the outgoing Federalist administration. William Marbury was one of the people who did not receive his commission, and he asked the Supreme Court to issue an order giving him the position.

CHIEF JUSTICE JOHN MARSHALL favored the idea of judicial review and claimed this power for the Court in the *Marbury v. Madison* decision.

As leading figures in opposing parties, Chief Justice Marshall and President Jefferson did not like each other. This put Marshall in a difficult position. He was concerned that if he issued the order that Marbury wanted (giving Marbury his job), Jefferson probably would ignore it (technically, Secretary of State Madison was the other party in the lawsuit, but Jefferson was calling the shots). Given the weakness of the Court, having such an order disregarded by the president could have been a final blow to its position in the national government. However, if the Court did not issue the order, it would be giving in to Jefferson despite the merits of Marbury's case—he really had been cheated out of his job. It appeared that the Court would lose whether it issued the order or not.

To get out of the predicament, Marshall applied the idea of judicial review. Although the idea was not original to Marshall (as noted, the framers debated the issue and Hamilton endorsed it in some detail in *Federalist 78*), the Court had never exercised its authority to rule on the constitutionality of a federal law. Marshall's reasoning was quite clever: the Court's opinion said that Marbury was due his commission, but the Court did not have the power to give him his job because the part of the Judiciary Act of 1789 that gave it that power was unconstitutional! The core issue was Section 13 of the Act, which gave the Court the power to issue orders (writs of mandamus) to anyone holding federal office. This section expanded the **original jurisdiction** of the Supreme Court, and that was where Congress overstepped its bounds, according to Marshall. The original jurisdiction of the Court is clearly specified in the Constitution, so any attempt by Congress to change that jurisdiction through legislation would be unconstitutional; the only way to change original jurisdiction would be through a constitutional amendment.[7] Marshall writes, "It is emphatically the province and duty of the judicial department to say what the law is. . . . If two laws conflict with each other, the courts must decide on the operation of each. So if a law be in opposition to the Constitution . . . the court must determine which of these conflicting rules governs the case. This is of the very essence of judicial duty."[8]

original jurisdiction The authority of a court to handle a case first, as in the Supreme Court's authority to initially hear disputes between two states. However, original jurisdiction for the Supreme Court is not exclusive; it may assign such a case to a lower court.

JUDICIAL REVIEW IN PRACTICE

Chief Justice Marshall lost the battle—poor Mr. Marbury never did get his job, and Jefferson appointed the people he wanted to be justices of the peace—but the Supreme Court won the war. By asserting its power to review the constitutionality of laws passed by Congress, the Court became an equal partner in the institutional balance of power. Although it would be more than 50 years until the Court would use judicial review again to strike down a law passed by Congress (in the unfortunate 1857 *Dred Scott* case, which concerned slavery and effectively led to the Civil War), the reasoning behind *Marbury* has never been challenged by subsequent presidents or Congresses.[9]

Interpreting federal laws may seem like a logical responsibility for the Supreme Court, but what about state laws? Should the Supreme Court have final say over them as well? The Constitution does not answer this question. But the supremacy clause requires that the Constitution and national laws take precedence over state constitutions and state laws when they conflict. The Judiciary Act of 1789 made it clear that the Supreme Court would rule on these matters.

It didn't take long for the Court to assert its power in this area. In 1796, the Court heard a case concerning a British creditor who was trying to collect a debt from the state of Virginia. The state had passed a law canceling all debts owed by Virginians (or the state) to British subjects. However, the Treaty of Paris, which ended the Revolutionary War and recognized American independence, ensured the collection of such debts. This conflict was resolved when the Court struck down the state law and upheld Americans' commitments under the treaty.[10] Advocates of states' rights were not happy with this ruling, but it was crucial for the national government that the Constitution be applied uniformly rather than be subject to different interpretations by every state.

The contours of the relationship between the national government and the states were largely defined by how active the Supreme Court was in asserting judicial review and how willing it was to intervene in matters of state law. For much of the nineteenth century, the Court embraced dual federalism, in which the national government and the states operated on two separate levels (see Chapter 3). Later, the Court involved itself more in state law as it moved toward a more active role for the national government in regulating interstate commerce and using the Fourteenth Amendment to selectively incorporate the amendments that constitute the Bill of Rights (see Chapter 4).

All in all, the Court has struck down more than 180 acts of Congress and about 1,400 state laws. This sounds like a lot, but Congress passed more than 60,000 laws in its first 225 years, so only about one-quarter of 1 percent have been struck down by the Court. The number of state laws passed throughout history is more difficult to measure, but the percentage of state laws that have been struck down is also quite small. Over time, the Court has ruled on state laws in many important areas, including civil liberties, desegregation and civil rights, abortion, privacy, redistricting, labor laws, employment and discrimination, and business and environmental regulation.

When the Supreme Court strikes down a congressional or state law, it engages in **constitutional interpretation**—that is, it determines that the law is unconstitutional. But the Supreme Court also engages in **statutory interpretation**—that is, it applies national and state laws to particular cases (statutes are laws that are passed by legislatures). Often the language of a statute may be unclear, and the Court must interpret how to apply the law. For example, should the protection of endangered species prevent economic development that may destroy the species' habitat? How does one determine if an employer is responsible for sexual harassment in the workplace? How should the voting rights of minorities be protected? In each case, the Court must interpret the relevant statutes to determine what Congress really meant. In addition, the Court is sometimes required to assess the appropriateness of statutory interpretation by federal agencies that are responsible for implementing the laws. Often, this involves the controversial practice of consulting legislative histories—floor debates, congressional hearings, and so on—to determine legislative intent. But Justice Antonin Scalia argues that such searches are inherently subjective and that justices should only interpret the actual statutory text.

Although politicians and other political actors accept judicial review as a central part of the political system, critics are concerned about its antidemocratic nature. Why, for example, do we give nine unelected justices such extraordinary power over our elected representatives? Debates about the proper role for the Court will continue as long as it is involved in controversial decisions. We will take up this question later in the chapter when we address the concepts of judicial activism and judicial restraint.

constitutional interpretation The process of determining whether a piece of legislation or governmental action is supported by the Constitution.

statutory interpretation The various methods and tests used by the courts for determining the meaning of a law and applying it to specific situations. Congress may overturn the courts' interpretation by writing a new law; thus, it also engages in statutory interpretation.

THE AMERICAN LEGAL AND JUDICIAL SYSTEM

OUTLINE THE STRUCTURE OF THE COURT SYSTEM

Two sets of considerations are necessary to understand the overall nature of our judicial system: the fundamentals of the legal system that apply to all courts in the United States, and the structure of the court system within our system of federalism.

COURT FUNDAMENTALS

plaintiff The person or party who brings a case to court.

defendant The person or party against whom a case is brought.

plea bargaining Negotiating an agreement between a plaintiff and a defendant to settle a case before it goes to trial or the verdict is decided. In a civil case, this usually involves an admission of guilt and an agreement on monetary damages; in a criminal case, this often involves an admission of guilt in return for a reduced charge or sentence.

class-action lawsuit A case brought by a group of individuals on behalf of themselves and others in the general public who are in similar circumstances.

O. J. SIMPSON DONS A PAIR of gloves during testimony in his double-murder trial in Los Angeles in June 1995. The jury was not convinced of his guilt "beyond a reasonable doubt" and thus acquitted Simpson in this criminal trial. However, a subsequent civil trial found that a "preponderance of evidence" was against him.

The general characteristics of the court system begin with the people who are in the courtroom. The **plaintiff** brings the case, and the **defendant** is the person or party who is being sued or charged with a crime. If the case is appealed, the petitioner is the person bringing the appeal, and the respondent is on the other side of the case. In a civil case, the plaintiff sues to determine who is right or wrong and to gain something of value, such as monetary damages, the right to vote, or admission to a university. For example, imagine that your neighbor accidentally backs his car into the fence that divides your property, destroying a large section of it. The neighbor does not have adequate insurance to cover the damages and refuses to pay for the repairs. You do not want to pay the $1,000 deductible on your insurance policy, so you (the plaintiff) sue your neighbor (the defendant) to see whether your neighbor has to pay for the repairs. In a criminal case, the plaintiff is the government, and the prosecutor attempts to prove the guilt of the defendant (the person accused of the crime).

Many, but not all, civil and criminal cases are heard before a jury that decides the outcome in the case, which is called the verdict. Often cases get settled before they go to trial (or even in the middle of the trial) in a process known as **plea bargaining**. In a civil case, this would mean that the plaintiff and the defendant agree on a monetary settlement and admission of guilt (or not; in some cases the defendant may agree to pay a fine or damages but not to admit guilt). In a criminal case, the defendant may agree to plead guilty in exchange for receiving a shorter sentence or being charged with a lesser crime. Plea bargaining is an excellent example of how legal conflict between two parties can be resolved through a compromise that is satisfactory to both sides.

DIFFERENCES BETWEEN CIVIL AND CRIMINAL CASES There are important differences between civil and criminal cases. One is the standard of proof that serves to determine the outcome of the case. In civil cases, the jury has to determine whether the "preponderance of evidence"—that is, a majority of the evidence—proves that the plaintiff wins. In criminal cases, a much stiffer burden must be met—the defendant must be found guilty "beyond a reasonable doubt."

Another difference is where the burden of proof lies. In criminal cases, there is a presumption of "innocent until proven guilty"—that is, the state must prove the guilt of the defendant. However, in civil cases, the burden of proof may be on the plaintiff or the defendant, depending on the law that governs the case. Even more complicated, in civil cases, the plaintiff may have to prove certain points and the defendant other points. For example, in certain race-based voting rights cases, the plaintiff would have to prove that race was the predominant motivation for creating a black-majority congressional district. If that point is demonstrated, then the burden of proof shifts to the defendant to show that there was some "compelling state interest" to justify the use of race as a predominant factor.

One type of civil suit is the **class-action lawsuit**, a case brought by a group of individuals on behalf of themselves and others in similar circumstances. The target may be a corporation that produced hazardous or defective products, or that engaged in illegal behavior that harmed a particular group. For example, 1.5 million current and former female Walmart employees sued the retailing giant for sex discrimination in 2011, claiming that the store had paid women less than men for the same work and had promoted fewer women than men.[11] Suits are often filed on behalf of shareholders of companies that have lost value because of fraud committed by corporate leaders. Cases like these are a very important mechanism for providing accountability and justice in our economic system. Federal regulators do not have the ability to ensure the complete safety of food, drugs, and consumer products or to continually monitor all potential business fraud. Therefore, consumers rely on the legal system and class-action lawsuits to ensure that businesses act fairly and produce safe products.

COMMON ELEMENTS OF THE JUDICIAL SYSTEM Several characteristics of the judicial system apply to all cases. First, ours is an adversarial system in which lawyers on both sides have an opportunity to present their case, challenge the testimony of the opposing side, and try to convince the court that their version of the events is true. The process of "discovery," in which both sides share the information that will be presented in court, ensures a fair process and few last-minute surprises. Second, 49 of the 50 states and the federal courts operate under a system of **common law**, which means that legal decisions build from precedent established in previous cases and apply commonly throughout the jurisdiction of the court. The alternative, which is practiced only in Louisiana, is the civil law tradition, which is based on a detailed codification of the law that is applied to each specific case. Common law is the most general way of describing how judges make their decisions, and it includes the three main areas of American law: constitutional, statutory, and administrative. The first two were described earlier, and administrative law refers to court decisions concerning the administrative agencies that implement policy.

The notion of **precedent** (or stare decisis—"let the decision stand") deserves special attention. Precedent is a previously decided case or set of decisions that serves as a guide for future cases on the same topic. Lower courts are bound by Supreme Court decisions when there is a clear precedent that is relevant for a given case. In many cases, following precedent is not clear-cut because several precedents may seem relevant. The lower courts have considerable discretion in sorting out which precedents are the most important. The Supreme Court tries to follow its own precedents. But in the past 50 years, justices have been willing to deviate from earlier decisions when they think that the precedent is flawed. As Table 14.1 shows, the Court has overruled more than twice as many decisions since 1953 than in the previous 164 years. Part of this can be explained by the relatively small number of precedents that *could* have been overturned in the first few decades of our nation's history. But even when accounting for the natural accumulation of more precedents to potentially overturn, recent courts have been much more willing to deviate from precedent than previous courts. For example, in the campaign finance case discussed in the opener, the Court overturned part of a 38-year-old precedent that had upheld aggregate limits on contributions.[12] As this record indicates, precedent is not a rule the Court must follow but a norm that constrains its behavior.

Two more points must be considered before a case is filed. First, the person bringing the case must have **standing** to sue in a civil case, which means that the person has a legitimate basis for bringing the case. This usually means that the individual has suffered some direct and personal harm from the action addressed in the court case. Standing is easy to establish for private parties—as in the previous example, if your neighbor destroys your fence, you have been harmed. However, it gets more interesting when the government is a party. For example, when an environmental group challenged the Interior Department's interpretation of the Endangered Species Act, the Supreme Court ruled that the group did not have

common law Law based on the precedent of previous court rulings rather than on legislation. It is used in all federal courts and 49 of the 50 state courts.

precedent A legal norm established in court cases that is then applied to future cases dealing with the same legal questions.

standing Legitimate justification for bringing a civil case to court.

TABLE » 14.1

SUPREME COURT CASES OVERRULING PRECEDENT AND ACTS OF CONGRESS, 1789–2014

The Supreme Court has overruled precedent in a far higher proportion of cases in the past 60 years than it did during the first 160 years of U.S. history. More acts of Congress have also been struck down in recent years—but even in some earlier periods, the Court has played an activist role. What do these data say about the role of the Supreme Court within our constitutional system?

Court (Chief Justice)	Years	Cases Overruling Precedent	Precedents Overruled	Cases Overruling Acts of Congress	Acts Overruled per Year
Jay Court	1789–1795	0	0	0	0
Rutledge Court	1795	0	0	0	0
Ellsworth Court	1796–1800	0	0	0	0
Marshall Court	1801–1836	1	1	1	0.03
Taney Court	1836–1864	2	3	1	0.03
Chase Court	1864–1874	1	1	8	0.8
Waite Court	1874–1888	9	11	7	0.5
Fuller Court	1888–1910	3	4	13	0.52
White Court	1910–1921	4	4	10	1.1
Taft Court	1921–1930	5	6	13	1.44
Hughes Court	1930–1941	15	22	15	1.36
Stone Court	1941–1946	8	11	1	0.20
Vinson Court	1946–1953	6	11	2	0.28
Warren Court	1953–1969	37	53	23	1.44
Burger Court	1969–1986	46	62	31	1.82
Rehnquist Court	1986–2005	38	44	35	1.84
Roberts Court	2005–present	10	not available	10	1.25

Note: This table includes only cases in which the reversal of precedent is clearly stated in the Court decision. A single case can overrule more than one precedent.

SOURCES: For 1789–2003, David G. Savage, *Guide to the Supreme Court,* 4th ed. (Washington, D.C.: CQ Press, 2004), pp. 320, 1192–1204. For 2004–2011, The Supreme Court Database, Washington University, http://scdb.wustl.edu (accessed 7/8/14).

standing because it did not demonstrate that the government's policy would cause "imminent" injury to the group.[13] Similarly, federal courts ruled that 10 members of Congress did not have standing to challenge American bombing in Libya and that taxpayers do not have standing to sue the government if they disagree with a specific policy.[14] Depending on your politics, you may not want your hard-earned cash going to buy school lunches for poor children or to fund various wars. However, your status as a taxpayer does not give you enough of a personal stake in these policies to challenge them in court, and so you do not have standing. Later, in the section discussing how cases get to the Supreme Court, we will see that justices have some leeway in defining standing.

jurisdiction The sphere of a court's legal authority to hear and decide cases.

The final general characteristic of the legal system is the **jurisdiction** of the court—when bringing a case before the court, you must choose a court that actually has the power to hear your case. For example, if you wanted to contest a speeding ticket, you would not file your case in the state supreme court or in the federal district court; you would file it in your local traffic court. What if you believed you were the victim of discrimination in the workplace? Would you sue in state or federal court? You probably could do either, but the decision would be based on which set of laws would provide you with more protection from discrimination. This varies by state, so the proper jurisdiction for a given case is often a judgment call based on specific legal questions (this practice of seeking the best court for your case is called "venue shopping").

STRUCTURE OF THE COURT AND FEDERALISM

The structure of the court system is like the rest of the political system: it is divided within and across levels of government. Across the levels of government, the court system operates on two parallel tracks within (1) the state and local courts and (2) the federal courts. Within each level of government, both tracks include courts of original jurisdiction, appeals courts, and courts of special jurisdiction. As shown in the How It Works graphic, the state courts are entirely separate from the federal courts, with the exception of the small proportion of cases that are appealed from a state supreme court to the U.S. Supreme Court. There is much variation in the structure of state courts in terms of their names and the number of levels of courts. However, they all follow the same general pattern of trial courts with limited and general original jurisdiction and appeals courts (either one or two levels, depending on the state).

DISTRICT COURTS The Judiciary Act of 1789 created the lower federal courts. Workhorses of the federal system, the district courts handle more than a quarter of a million filings a year. There are 89 districts in the 50 states, with at least one district court for each state. There are also district courts in Puerto Rico, the Virgin Islands, the District of Columbia, Guam, and the Northern Mariana Islands to bring the total to 94 districts with 677 judges.[15] There are two limited jurisdiction district courts: the Court of International Trade, which addresses cases involving international trade and customs issues, and the U.S. Court of Federal Claims, which handles most claims for money damages against the United States, disputes over federal contracts, unlawful "takings" of private property by the federal government, and other claims against the United States.

APPEALS COURTS The **appeals courts** (called "circuit courts" until 1948) are the intermediate courts of appeals, but in practice they are the final court for most federal cases that are appealed from the lower courts. The losing side in a federal case can appeal to the Supreme Court, but given that the highest court in the land hears so few cases, the appeals courts usually get the final word. Appeals courts did not always have this much power; in fact, through much of the nineteenth century they had very limited appellate jurisdiction and did not hear many significant cases.

The number of appeals courts in the nation slowly expanded as the workload of these courts grew, to the current 12 regional courts (the 11 numbered districts shown in Figure 14.1, plus the appeals court for the District of Columbia) and the court of appeals for the Federal Circuit, which handles specialized cases from all over the country. The smallest of the regional appeals courts is the First Circuit, which has 6 judges, and the largest is the Ninth Circuit, which has 29 judges.[16] In 2014, there were 179 appeals court judges and 92 "senior judges" (these numbers include the 12 judges and 5 senior judges of the appeals court for

appeals courts The intermediate level of federal courts that hear appeals from district courts. More generally, an appeals court is any court with appellate jurisdiction.

FIGURE » 14.1

MAP OF THE FEDERAL APPEALS COURTS

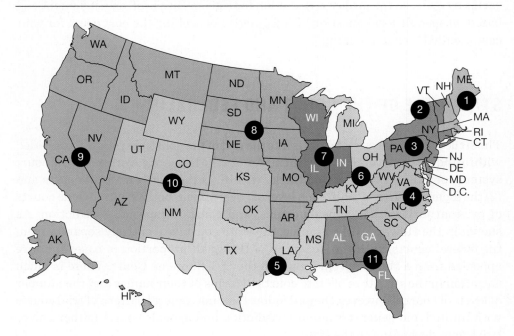

SOURCE: United States Courts, Court Locator, www.uscourts.gov/court_locator.aspx (accessed 4/30/14).

the federal circuit).[17] Senior judges are semi-retired judges who hear certain cases to help out with the overall federal court system workload; they typically handle about 15 percent of the workload for the federal court system.

THE SUPREME COURT The Supreme Court sits at the top of the federal court system. The Supreme Court is the "court of last resort" for cases coming from both the state and the federal courts. One important function of the Court is to ensure that the application and interpretation of the Constitution is consistent nationwide by resolving conflicts between lower courts, or between a state law and a federal law, or between laws in different states. For example, before the Court took up the issue of affirmative action in higher education, there were several conflicting lower court decisions, which meant that affirmative action was legal in certain parts of the country and unconstitutional in other parts. A district court or appeals court ruling is applicable only for the specific region of that court, whereas Supreme Court rulings apply to the entire country. For example, the affirmative action case mentioned in the chapter opener meant that by upholding the ban on affirmative action in Michigan, similar measures in seven other states were also endorsed by the Court.

Although the Supreme Court is the most important interpreter of the Constitution, the president and Congress also interpret the Constitution on a regular basis. This means that the Supreme Court does not always have the final say. For example, if the Court strikes down a federal law for being overly vague, Congress can rewrite the law to clarify the offending passage. When this happens, Congress may have the final word. For example, Congress overturned *Ledbetter v. Goodyear Tire & Rubber* (2007) when it passed the "Lilly Ledbetter Fair Pay Act" in 2009. The law said that the Supreme Court had misinterpreted the 1964 Civil Rights

THE COURT SYSTEM

If federal question

FINAL APPEALS COURTS

State Supreme Courts
About 85,000 cases in 50 courts.

U.S. Supreme Court
Received 7,509 filings for the 2012–2013 term; 77 cases argued; 76 disposed of in 73 signed opinions.*

INTERMEDIATE APPEALS COURTS

Courts of Appeals
300,000 cases in the 38 states with courts of appeals.

U.S. Courts of Appeals
12 regional courts and the U.S. Court of Appeals for the Federal Circuit; decided 56,475 cases in 2012–2013.

TRIAL COURTS

TRIAL COURTS OF LIMITED AND SPECIAL JURISDICTION

Examples: Juvenile Court, Traffic Court, Small Claims Court, Justice of the Peace, Family Court.

TRIAL COURTS OF GENERAL AND ORIGINAL JURISDICTION

District courts, county courts, municipal courts; about 90 million cases filed in state and local courts of original jurisdiction.

TRIAL COURTS OF GENERAL AND ORIGINAL JURISDICTION

94 district courts; decided 284,604 civil cases and 91,266 criminal cases in 2012–2013.

TRIAL COURTS OF LIMITED AND SPECIAL JURISDICTION

Examples: Federal Claims Court, Tax Court, Court of International Trade, Court of Veterans Appeals.

STATE AND LOCAL COURTS

FEDERAL COURTS

*Data on federal courts are from the U.S. Supreme Court. "2013 Year-End Report on the Federal Judiciary." www.supremecourt.gov/publicinfo/year-end/2013year-endreport.pdf (accessed 4/9/14).

How It Works
In Practice

HOW CASES TRAVEL THROUGH THE COURT SYSTEM

Decisions by the Supreme Court bring publicity to cases that often have been in the court system for years. The issue of same-sex marriage has been addressed in dozens of state and federal cases, but was only recently taken up by the Supreme Court. Two landmark decisions, decided on the same day in June 2013, illustrate how cases fraught with challenges make their way through the court system.

■ STATE AND LOCAL COURTS   ■ FEDERAL COURTS

FINAL APPEALS COURTS

1 State Supreme Courts
The first case involved California's Proposition 8, which banned same-sex marriage in that state in 2008. Several lawsuits challenged the constitutionality of the voter-approved ban under the state constitution. Giving the case expedited review, the state supreme court ruled in *Strauss v. Horton* (2009) that Proposition 8 was constitutional, but that existing same-sex marriages would still be valid.

4 U.S. Supreme Court
In *Hollingsworth v. Perry* (2013), the U.S. Supreme Court decided that Prop. 8 supporters did not have legal standing to appeal the case, thus upholding the district court opinion, which enabled same-sex couples to marry in California.

7 U.S. Supreme Court
The judgment was confirmed by the U.S. Supreme Court in *United States v. Windsor* (2013), which declared Section 3 of DOMA to be unconstitutional as a deprivation of liberty under the due process clause of the Fifth Amendment.

INTERMEDIATE APPEALS COURTS

3 U.S. Courts of Appeals
The state of California decided not to appeal the decision, but supporters of Prop. 8 did, and the 9th Circuit Court of Appeals upheld the district court opinion.

6 U.S. Courts of Appeals
The 2nd Circuit Court of Appeals upheld the district court opinion, which had found DOMA unconstitutional and had ordered the federal government to refund the taxes Windsor had paid.

TRIAL COURTS

The state case did not begin in a trial court because in important cases the California state supreme court has original jurisdiction in "proceedings for extraordinary relief."

2 U.S. DISTRICT COURT
Prop. 8 was challenged in federal district court in 2010 under the U.S. Constitution by a different set of petitioners. The district court struck down Proposition 8 as a violation of the due process and equal protection clauses of the Fourteenth Amendment.

5 U.S. DISTRICT COURT
Edith Windsor and Thea Spyer were legally married in Canada and lived in New York City. When Spyer died, she left Windsor her estate. But since the Defense of Marriage Act (DOMA) recognized only heterosexual marriages at the federal level, Windsor did not qualify for the spousal tax exemption and was charged over $350,000 in taxes. The federal district court found DOMA unconstitutional under the due process clause of the Fifth Amendment.

POP QUIZ

1 If you are convicted in a U.S. district court and want to appeal the ruling, with which court would you file an appeal?

a the state supreme court

b the state court of appeals

c the U.S. Court of Appeals for your region

d the U.S. Supreme Court

e none of the above

2 Which of the following is true?

a Same-sex marriage is illegal in California.

b The U.S. Supreme Court upheld lower-court rulings that DOMA was unconstitutional.

c The California supreme court overturned Proposition 8.

d Proposition 8 is currently the law of the land in California.

e The U.S. federal courts upheld Proposition 8.

Act when it ruled that Ledbetter would have had to file her pay discrimination suit within 180 days of being hired.[18]

Even on matters of constitutional interpretation rather than statutory interpretation, Congress can fight back by passing a constitutional amendment. However, this is a difficult and time-consuming process (see Chapter 2). Nevertheless, that option is available as a way of overturning an unpopular Court decision. Perhaps the best example of this is the very first major case ever decided by the Supreme Court—*Chisholm v. Georgia* (1793). This case upheld the right of a citizen of one state to sue another state in federal court. The states were shocked by this challenge to their sovereignty, and a constitutional amendment to overturn the decision quickly made its way through Congress. By 1795, the Eleventh Amendment had been ratified, and citizens could no longer sue a state (in federal court) in which they did not live.[19]

HOW JUDGES ARE SELECTED

There are many mechanisms for placing judges in courts. At the national level, the president makes the appointments with the advice and consent of the Senate. At the state level, various methods are in use.

STATE-LEVEL JUDGES At the state level, there are 130 trial courts (some states have two or three levels), 40 appeals courts, and 50 supreme courts. At the state level, judges can be selected for trial courts in five different ways: appointment by the governor (8 courts), appointment by the state legislature (5 courts), partisan elections (45 courts), nonpartisan elections (39 courts), and the system called the Missouri Plan in which the governor makes appointments from a list compiled by a nonpartisan screening committee (33 courts).[20] With this last method, the appointed judge usually has to run in a retention election within several years of the appointment, making this system a hybrid of the political nomination and popular election routes to the court.

There is some controversy over the wisdom of electing judges, as doing so may undermine the courts' role as the protector of unpopular minority rights. Even in states where judicial elections are officially nonpartisan, it is clear who the liberal and conservative candidates are, so judicial elections can be very partisan. Interest groups often get involved by making endorsements or running their own advertisements for or against the judicial candidates. Electing judges also raises the potential for conflicts of interest if campaign contributors have cases before the court.[21] On the other hand, elected judges will be more responsive to public opinion, especially on salient issues such as the death penalty[22] and abortion.[23] Furthermore, the alternative to elections—appointing judges—has been criticized as elitist by giving power over nominations to lawyers with the claim that the process is "merit-based," which has not been supported by much evidence.[24]

FEDERAL JUDGES The Constitution does not specify requirements for serving on the federal courts, unlike the detailed stipulations for Congress and the president. Federal judges don't even have to have a law degree! (This is probably due to the limited number of law schools at the time of the Founding; when the Constitution was written, someone who wanted to be a lawyer generally would serve as an apprentice in a law office to learn the trade.) The president appoints federal judges with the "advice and consent" of the Senate (the Senate must approve the nominees with a majority vote).

Nomination battles for federal judges can be intense because the stakes are high. As the discussion of judicial review made clear, the Supreme Court plays a central role in the policy process, and because a justice has life tenure, a justice's impact can outlive the president and Senate who put him or her on the Court. The justices often serve for decades, much longer than the people who appoint them.

THE ROLE OF THE PRESIDENT Given the Constitution's silence on the qualification of federal judges, presidents have broad discretion over whom to nominate. Presidents have always tried to influence the direction of the federal courts and especially the Supreme Court by picking people who share their views. Because the Senate often has different ideas about the proper direction for the Court, nomination disputes end up being a combination of debates over the merit of a nominee and partisan battles about the ideological composition of the Court.

Although presidents would *like* to influence the direction of the Court, it is not always possible to predict how judges will behave once they are on the Court. Earl Warren is a good example. He was appointed by Republican president Dwight Eisenhower and had been the Republican governor of California, yet he turned out to be one of the most liberal chief justices of the last century. Eisenhower called Warren's nomination the biggest mistake he ever made.[25] Former justices Brennan, Souter, and Stevens also were nominated by Republican presidents but regularly voted with the liberal bloc on the Court.

Nonetheless, the president can make a good guess about how a justice is likely to vote based on the nominee's party affiliation and the nature of his or her legal writings and decisions (if the nominee has prior judicial experience). Not surprisingly, 102 of 112 justices who have served on the Court have shared the nominating president's party (91 percent). Overall, more than 90 percent of the lower court judges appointed by presidents in the twentieth century have also belonged to the same party as the president.

The most partisan move to influence the Court was President Franklin Delano Roosevelt's infamous plan to pack the Court. FDR was frustrated because the Court had struck down several pieces of important New Deal legislation, so to get a more sympathetic Court he proposed nominating a new justice for every justice who was over 70 years old. Six justices were over 70, so this would have increased the size of the Court to 15 justices. This effort to disguise the partisan power play as a humanitarian gesture (to help the old-timers with their workload) didn't fool anyone. The plan to pack the Court ran into opposition, but in the so-called switch in time that saved nine, the Court started ruling in favor of the New Deal legislation, so the plan was dropped.

In addition to the ideological considerations about whom to nominate, the president also considers the individual's reputation as a legal scholar and his personal relationship to the candidate. Further considerations are the candidate's ethical standards, gender, and race (see Table 14.2 for data on the latter two points).

PRESIDENTS CAN INFLUENCE THE direction of the federal courts by selecting judges who share their views. In his first term, President Obama had the opportunity to nominate two justices to the Supreme Court: Sonia Sotomayor and Elena Kagan (shown here).

TABLE » 14.2

THE DEMOGRAPHICS OF FEDERAL DISTRICT COURTS

All presidents try to appoint qualified candidates to the federal courts; however, there is variation in the types of people they nominate. Identify some characteristics common to most judges and some that vary across presidents. Which traits vary by the president's party?

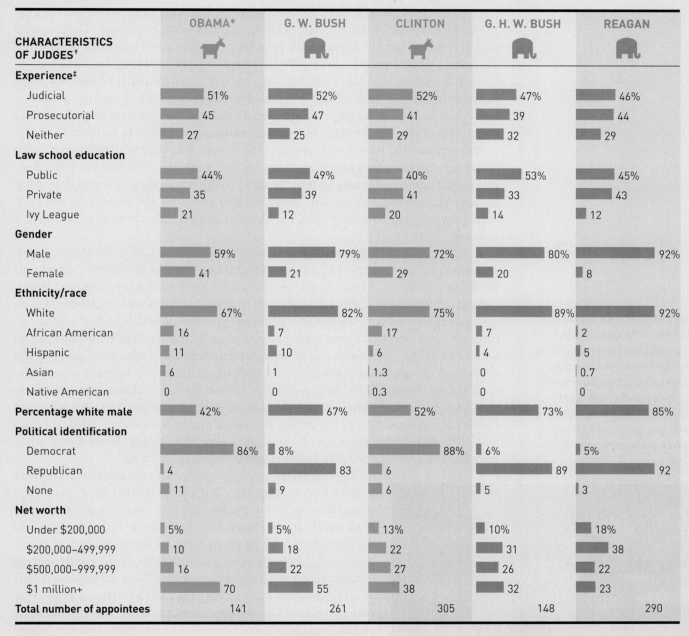

CHARACTERISTICS OF JUDGES[†]	OBAMA*	G. W. BUSH	CLINTON	G. H. W. BUSH	REAGAN
Experience[‡]					
Judicial	51%	52%	52%	47%	46%
Prosecutorial	45	47	41	39	44
Neither	27	25	29	32	29
Law school education					
Public	44%	49%	40%	53%	45%
Private	35	39	41	33	43
Ivy League	21	12	20	14	12
Gender					
Male	59%	79%	72%	80%	92%
Female	41	21	29	20	8
Ethnicity/race					
White	67%	82%	75%	89%	92%
African American	16	7	17	7	2
Hispanic	11	10	6	4	5
Asian	6	1	1.3	0	0.7
Native American	0	0	0.3	0	0
Percentage white male	42%	67%	52%	73%	85%
Political identification					
Democrat	86%	8%	88%	6%	5%
Republican	4	83	6	89	92
None	11	9	6	5	3
Net worth					
Under $200,000	5%	5%	13%	10%	18%
$200,000–499,999	10	18	22	31	38
$500,000–999,999	16	22	27	26	22
$1 million+	70	55	38	32	23
Total number of appointees	141	261	305	148	290

* Through 2012.

† Some percentages sum to more than 100 due to rounding.

‡ Percentages sum to more than 100 because some appointees have both judicial and prosecutorial experience.

SOURCE: Sheldon Goldman, Elliot Slotnick, and Sara Schiavoni, "Obama's First-Term Judiciary," *Judicature* 97:1 (July–August 2013): 7–47.

 = DEMOCRAT   = REPUBLICAN

THE ROLE OF THE SENATE The Senate is the other half of the equation that determines the composition of the federal courts. The Senate has shifted from a very active role in providing "advice and consent" on court appointments to a passive role and then back to an active role. One constant is that the Senate rarely rejects nominees because of their qualifications; rather, it tends to reject them for political reasons. Of 28 Supreme Court nominees rejected by the Senate in the history of the United States, only 2 were turned down because they were seen as unqualified: George Williams in 1873 and G. Harrold Carswell in 1970. Serious questions were also raised about a third justice, Clarence Thomas, who had served for only 18 months as a federal judge before being nominated to the Court. Thomas also was accused of sexual harassment by a former colleague. Nonetheless, Thomas ultimately won confirmation by a 52-to-48 vote, the second narrowest successful margin in history. The other 26 nominees were rejected for political reasons. Most commonly, when a "lame-duck" president makes a nomination and the Senate is controlled by the opposing party, the Senate will kill the nomination, hoping that its party will win the presidency and nominate a justice more to its liking.

Throughout the nineteenth century, the Senate was very willing to turn down Court nominations for political reasons. In fact, between 1793 and 1894, the Senate did not confirm 21 nominees to the Court, which was about a third of the total number nominated. In contrast, between 1894 and 1968, the Senate did not even require nominees to testify, and during that period only three nominees were rejected.

A rethinking of this passive role occurred in the late 1960s. President Nixon vowed to pull the Court back from the "liberal excesses" of the Warren Court, but the Senate stiffened its spine and rejected two nominees in a row: Clement Haynsworth (in 1969) and G. Harrold Carswell (in 1970). With Haynsworth, there were ethical problems involving his participation in cases in which he had a financial interest. Carswell had a mediocre judicial record, and civil rights groups raised questions about his commitment to enforcing antidiscrimination laws. Nixon must have thought that the Senate wouldn't reject his choice twice in a row! The most recent Senate rejection was of Judge Robert Bork, a brilliant, very conservative, and controversial figure. Liberal interest groups mobilized against him, and the Senate rejected him by the widest margin of any nominee since 1846 (the vote was 42 to 58), giving the English language a new verb: to get "borked" means to have your character and record challenged in a very public way.

Yet, not all recent Supreme Court nominations have been controversial. President Bill Clinton's two Supreme Court picks were judicial moderates who were overwhelmingly confirmed—Ruth Bader Ginsburg by a 96-to-3 vote and Stephen Breyer by an 87-to-9 vote. George W. Bush's nominees, John Roberts and Samuel Alito, were confirmed by comfortable margins; the former by a 78-to-22 vote, with half of the Democrats supporting him, and the latter by a 58-to-42 vote. President Obama appointed the first Hispanic to serve on the Supreme Court, Sonia Sotomayor, who was confirmed by a 68-to-31 vote. Elena Kagan's confirmation by a 63-to-37 vote in 2010 meant that three women are serving on the Court for the first time.

The contentious battles between the president and the Senate over nominees to the federal bench and the Supreme Court have recently expanded to include nominees to the

SENATE HEARINGS ON SUPREME
Court nominations have been more conflictual since the 1960s. Although President Obama's nomination of Sonia Sotomayor was confirmed by a 68-to-31 vote in 2009, Senate Republicans challenged her to explain and defend her views on several issues.

FIGURE » 14.2

AVERAGE CONFIRMATION DELAY FOR UNCONTROVERSIAL FEDERAL COURT NOMINATIONS, 1981–2012

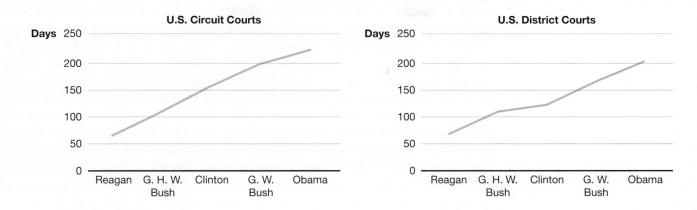

SOURCE: "Length of Time from Nomination to Confirmation for 'Uncontroversial' U.S. Circuit and District Court Nominees: Detailed Analysis," Barry J. McMillion, Congressional Research Service, September 18, 2012, http://fas.org/gsp/crs/misc/R42732.pdf (accessed 6/25/14). "Uncontroversial" nominees are those who were reported from the Judiciary Committee by a voice vote or a unanimous vote and were confirmed by the Senate with a voice vote or no more than 5 votes in opposition.

district and appeals courts. For much of the nation's history, the president did not play a very active role in the nomination process for district courts, instead deferring to the home-state senators of the president's party to suggest candidates—a norm called **senatorial courtesy**. If neither senator from the state was from the president's party, he would consult House members from his party and other high-ranking party members from the state for district court nominees. The president typically has shown more interest in appeals court nominations. The Justice Department plays a key role in screening candidates, but the local senators of the president's party remain active as well through the "blue slip" process: home-state senators record their support or opposition to nominees on blue slips of paper. Some committee chairs have allowed a single home-state senator to use the blue slip to veto a nominee, but others have not followed the process so strictly.

Recently, the process has become much more contentious. While the confirmation rate for federal judges has been relatively stable in the past 35 years (between 80 and 90 percent), the average time to confirm nominees has increased dramatically. The average length of delay from nomination to confirmation has increased from a little over 50 days in the 1980s to over 200 days in recent years (see Figure 14.2 for data on noncontroversial nominations; when all nominations are included, the waits are even longer, especially for George W. Bush's nominees), and the situation has intensified. Democrats blocked 39 of President Bush's nominees between 2001 and 2009,[26] and Republicans have been returning the favor since then, blocking dozens of President Obama's nominees, which included employing a record number of filibusters of lower-court nominees. After the Senate blocked three nominees to the D.C. Court of Appeals, the second most important court in the nation, Democrats responded in November 2013 by eliminating the filibuster on lower-court and executive branch nominations but not Supreme Court nominations (see the You Decide feature).[27] The partisan battle over nominations means that more than 10 percent of all federal judgeships remain vacant, which increases the workload for current judges and creates a growing backlog of cases.

senatorial courtesy A norm in the nomination of district court judges in which the president consults with his party's senators from the relevant state in choosing the nominee.

Although there is no definitive answer as to how active the Senate should be in giving "advice and consent"—especially how much power a minority of 41 senators (the number of senators who, until recently, could block a nomination through agreeing to a filibuster; see Chapter 11) should have—it is clear that the Founders intended the Senate to play an active role. The first draft of the Constitution gave the Senate the sole power to appoint Supreme Court justices. However, the final version made appointment a shared power with the president. It was not expected that the Senate would compete with the president over whom to nominate, but it *was* assumed that the Senate would exercise independent judgment as to the suitability of the president's nominees. Furthermore, the Founders did not expect that the process would be free of politics or that the Senate would be an essentially passive and subordinate player in a nominally joint enterprise. Even George Washington had two of his nominations turned down by the Senate for political reasons. Therefore, politics will continue to play an important role in deciding who serves on the federal bench.

DESCRIBE HOW CASES REACH THE SUPREME COURT

ACCESS TO THE SUPREME COURT

It is extremely difficult to have a case heard by the Supreme Court. Currently the Court hears about 1 percent of the cases submitted (76 of 7,509 cases in the most recent completed term). This section explains how the Court decides which cases to hear. When a case is submitted, the clerk of the Court assigns it a number and places it on the docket, which is the schedule of cases.

THE COURT'S WORKLOAD

Statistics on the Supreme Court's workload initially suggest that the size of the docket has increased dramatically since the 1970s (see Figure 14.3). However, a majority of cases are frivolous and are dismissed after limited review. The Court has become increasingly impatient with these frivolous petitions and has moved to prevent "frequent filers" from harassing the Court. One often-cited case involved Michael Sindram, who asked the Court to order the Maryland courts to remove a $35 traffic ticket from his record. Our favorite example concerned a wealthy drug dealer, Frederick W. Bauer, who was convicted on 10 counts of dealing drugs (7 counts involved a total of 4,100 pounds of marijuana, 2 counts for nearly 250 pounds of cocaine, and 1 count for six gallons of hashish oil and a package of black gum hashish) and repeatedly petitioned the Court. In his initial trial, he applied for a court-appointed attorney (which is supplied for people who cannot afford their own legal counsel) but was turned down because a court hearing revealed that he had "unencumbered assets [that] totaled almost $500,000." The court found the petitioner's testimony that he was poor "ambiguous, evasive and in many respects completely incredible."[28] Bauer petitioned the Court 12 times on various issues, and finally the justices had had enough. They ruled that "Bauer has repeatedly abused this Court's certiorari and extraordinary writ processes" and directed "the Clerk not to accept any further petitions for certiorari or petitions for extraordinary

ADVICE AND CONSENT: DETONATING THE NUCLEAR OPTION

The use of the filibuster to stop presidential nominations to the federal courts has been the source of intense partisan battles in the past 20 years (until recently, 41 senators could stop action on any nomination through a filibuster). However, the positions in those battles are determined by which party controls the Senate and the presidency. Democrats who railed against Republican obstruction when Clinton was president used the same tactics when they were the minority party and George W. Bush was president. The tables were turned again as Republicans filibustered many of Obama's court nominees.

For nearly 10 years, there have been serious discussions about limiting the use of the filibuster for court nominations. When the Democrats blocked many of President George W. Bush's lower-court nominees, the Republican leadership in the Senate considered implementing the "nuclear option," which would have prevented filibusters on judicial nominations. (This plan gets its name because Democrats threatened to essentially shut down the Senate if they lost the use of the filibuster.) This crisis was defused when the "Gang of 14"—seven moderate Republicans and seven moderate Democrats—agreed to a compromise that preserved the Democrats' right to filibuster a nominee, but only in the most extreme cases. The compromise was honored for a while, but then Republicans stepped up the pace by obstructing many of President Obama's nominees. Between 1967 and 2013, there have been 77 attempts to invoke cloture (to stop a filibuster) on a court nomination. More than half of those (41) came during Obama's presidency.[a] The Gang of 14 compromise dissolved when Republicans refused to act on *any* nominee to the D.C. Court of Appeals in 2013, the second most important court in the nation, in an effort to preserve the even partisan balance on that court. When Democrats were unable to stop filibusters on three nominees to that court, they detonated the nuclear option, so a simple majority of the Senate could stop a filibuster.

Let's do a thought experiment to try to strip partisanship from this issue and figure out if you support the principle of filibustering judicial nominations. Put yourself in the place of a Democratic senator on the Judiciary Committee during the Bush years. Suppose that President Bush has nominated a candidate for an appeals court position whom you believe is too ideologically extreme. Should you support a filibuster to stop the nomination even if it means that the Republican leadership might take away the filibuster using the nuclear option? Now put yourself in the place of a Republican senator. You strongly favor President Bush's right to nominate

When they have been the minority party in the Senate, both Democrats and Republicans have been willing to use the filibuster to block judicial nominees.

whom he wants to the federal courts, and you support his policy positions, especially on abortion and the regulation of the free market. However, the Democrats are opposed and threatening to filibuster. You have to decide whether to support the nuclear option to take away the Democrats' right to filibuster the nomination. There are at least 56 votes in favor of the nominee but not the 60 needed to cut off the filibuster. On the one hand, you don't think it is fair that Democrats are obstructing the vote. But on the other hand, you were in the Senate back when the Republicans were in the minority, and you remember how important the filibuster was to protect the views of the minority party. You are worried that supporting the nuclear option would seriously damage the institution that you value and respect as the world's greatest deliberative body. What is the best option? You decide.

CRITICAL THINKING QUESTIONS

1. What would you do in the situation just described? Why?

2. Now to complete the thought experiment, flip the positions of the senators for an Obama nominee to the appeals court. Is your position still the same?

FIGURE » 14.3

THE COURT SEES MORE OPPORTUNITIES . . . BUT HEARS FEWER CASES

The Supreme Court's workload appears to be headed in two directions: the Court is receiving more cases but hearing fewer of them. What are the implications of having the Supreme Court hear fewer cases? Should something be done to try to get the Court to hear more cases?

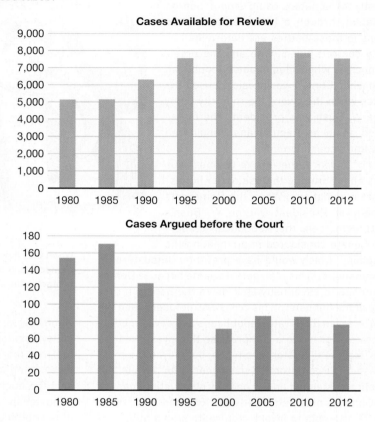

SOURCE: Data compiled from "Chief Justice's Year-End Reports on the Federal Judiciary," www.supremecourt.gov/publicinfo/year-end/2013year-endreport.pdf (accessed 5/6/14).

writs from Bauer in noncriminal matters" unless he paid his docketing fees. They concluded that the order will "allow this Court to devote its limited resources to the claims of petitioners who have not abused our processes."[29]

Although the increase in workload is not as significant as it appears due to the high number of frivolous cases, another change is more important: the number of opinions issued by the Court has fallen by more than half in the past 20 years. The Court heard roughly 150 cases a year through the 1980s, but this number has fallen to only 75 to 85 cases in recent years (see Figure 14.3).[30] The change is even more dramatic when one considers that the Court has reduced the number of "summary decisions" it issues (cases that do not receive a full hearing but on which the Court rules on the merits of the case) from 150 a year in the 1970s to a handful today. The number of summary judgments declined when Congress gave the Court more control over its docket and dramatically reduced the number of cases that it was *required* to hear on appeal. However, there is no good explanation for why the Court issues half as many opinions as it used to, other than that the chief justices have decided that the Court shouldn't issue so many opinions.[31]

RULES OF ACCESS

With the smaller number of cases being heard, it is even more important to understand how the Court decides which cases to consider. There are four paths that a case may take to get to the Supreme Court. First, Article III of the Constitution specifies that the Court has original jurisdiction in cases involving foreign ambassadors, foreign countries, or cases in which a state is a party. As a practical matter, the Court shares jurisdiction with the lower courts on these issues.

In recent years, the Court has invoked original jurisdiction only in cases involving disputes between two or more states over territorial or natural resource issues. For example, New Jersey and New York had a disagreement about which state should control 24 acres of filled land that the federal government had added around Ellis Island. Another case involved a dispute between Kansas and Colorado over which state should have access to water from the Arkansas River (recent disputes often concern water rights).[32] If original jurisdiction is granted and there are factual issues to be resolved, the Court will appoint a "special master" (usually a retired federal judge) to hold a hearing, gather evidence, and make a recommendation to the Court. This process is necessary because the Supreme Court is not a trial court. In the history of our nation, only about 175 cases have made it to the Court through this path, an average of less than one per year, and typically these cases do not have any broader significance beyond the parties involved.[33]

The other three routes to the Court are all on appeal: as a matter of right (usually called "on appeal"), through certification (a process that has been used only five times since 1982), or through a writ of certiorari. Cases on appeal are those that Congress has determined to be so important that the Supreme Court must hear them. Before 1988, these cases constituted a larger share of the Court's docket, and they included (1) cases in which a lower court declared a state or federal law unconstitutional, or (2) cases in which a state court upheld a state law that had been challenged as unconstitutional under the U.S. Constitution. The Court currently has much more discretion on these cases, however; the only ones that the Court is still compelled to take on appeal are some voting rights and redistricting cases.

The third path is the most common: at least 95 percent of the cases in most sessions arrive through a **writ of certiorari** (from the Latin "to be informed"). In these cases, a litigant who lost in lower court can file a petition to the Supreme Court explaining why the Court should hear the case. If four justices agree, the case will get a full hearing (this is called, reasonably enough, the "Rule of Four"). This process may sound simple, but sifting through the 7,500 or so cases that the Court receives every year and deciding which 75 of them will be heard is daunting. Former justice William O. Douglas said that this winnowing process is "in many respects the most important and interesting of all our functions."[34]

THE COURT'S CRITERIA

How does the Court decide which cases to hear? Several factors come into play, including the specific characteristics of the case and the broader politics surrounding it. Although several criteria generally must be met before the Court will hear the case, justices still have leeway in defining the boundaries of these conditions.

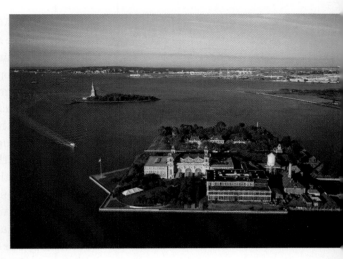

ON RARE OCCASIONS THE SUPREME Court serves as a court of original jurisdiction. One of those unusual times is when there is a dispute between two states, such as when the Court had to settle a disagreement between New York and New Jersey over Ellis Island.

writ of certiorari The most common way for a case to reach the Supreme Court, in which at least four of the nine justices agree to hear a case that has reached them via an appeal from the losing party in a lower court's ruling.

COLLUSION, STANDING, AND MOOTNESS First, there are the constitutional guidelines, which are sparse. The Constitution limits the Court to hearing actual "cases and controversies," which has been interpreted to mean that the Court cannot offer advisory opinions about hypothetical situations but must deal with actual cases. The term "actual controversy" also includes several other concepts that limit whether a case will be heard: collusion, standing, and mootness. Collusion simply means that the litigants in the case cannot want the same outcome and cannot be testing the law without an actual dispute between the two parties.[35]

Standing is the most general criteria; as we noted earlier, it means that the party bringing the case must have a personal stake in the outcome. The Court has discretion in defining standing: it may hear cases that it thinks are important even when the plaintiff may not have standing, as traditionally understood, or it may avoid hearing cases that may be politically sensitive on the grounds that there is no standing. For example, the Court decided several important racial redistricting cases even when the white plaintiffs had not suffered any personal harm by being in the black-majority districts.[36] On the other hand, in a politically sensitive case involving the pledge of allegiance and the First Amendment, the Court decided not to hear the case, saying that the father of the student who brought the case did not have standing because he did not have sufficient custody over his daughter (he was divorced and the mother had primary custody).[37] Clearly, the Court was more eager to voice its views on redistricting than on the pledge of allegiance because it could have just as easily avoided hearing the former case by saying the plaintiffs did not have standing and ruled on the merits of the latter case. This is an important point to consider: the Court may often avoid hearing a controversial case based on a "threshold" issue like standing and not have to decide the merits of the case.

A controversy must still be relevant when the Court hears the case; **mootness** is when it is irrelevant by the time the case is brought before a federal court. Nonetheless, there have to be exceptions to this principle because some types of cases would always be moot by the time they got to the Supreme Court. For example, exceptions have been made for abortion cases because a pregnancy lasts only nine months, and for a case to get from district court to the appeals court to the Supreme Court always takes longer than that. Similarly, in the Michigan affirmative action case discussed in the chapter opener and in Chapter 5, the state constitutional amendment banning consideration of race in state-college admissions was passed in 2006, but the Supreme Court did not rule on the case until 2014. Therefore, any student affected by the amendment when it first went into effect would have graduated long before the Supreme Court ruled on the case (so the case would have been moot). Thus, the state attorney general, Bill Schuette, challenged the constitutionality of the amendment on behalf of all future applicants to public universities and colleges in Michigan.

Thousands of cases every year meet the basic criteria. One very simple guideline eliminates the largest number of cases: if a case does not involve a "substantial federal question," it will not be heard. This essentially means that the Court does not have to hear a case if the justices do not think the case is important enough. Of course, the "federal" part of this standard is also important: if a case is governed by state law rather than federal law, the Court would decline to hear the case unless there are constitutional implications. The "political question doctrine," discussed later, is another basis upon which the Court may decide not to hear a case. This still leaves about 20 to 30 percent of the cases that are winnowed to the final list with the more specific guidance of Rule 10 in the Supreme Court rules (see Nuts & Bolts 14.2). Of the criteria listed in Rule 10, conflict between appeals court decisions is most likely to produce a Supreme Court hearing.

mootness The irrelevance of a case by the time it is received by a federal court, causing the Court to decline to hear the case.

DECIDING TO HEAR A CASE IN THE SUPREME COURT

Rule 10 of the *Rules of the U.S. Supreme Court* says that a case is more likely to be heard when

▶ there is conflict between appeals court opinions,

▶ there is conflict between a federal appeals court and a state supreme court on a substantial federal question,

▶ a lower court decision has "departed from the accepted and usual course of judicial proceedings,"

▶ a state court or appeals court has ruled on a substantial federal question that has not yet been addressed by the Court, or

▶ a state supreme court or appeals court ruling conflicts with Supreme Court precedent.

Rule 10 also states that certiorari is unlikely to be granted when "the asserted error consists of erroneous factual findings or the misapplication of a properly stated rule of law."

SOURCE: U.S. Supreme Court, Rules of the U.S. Supreme Court, *adopted January 27, 2003, effective May 1, 2003, www.supremecourtus.gov/ctrules/rulesofthecourt.pdf (accessed 11/5/12).*

INTERNAL POLITICS

Not much is known about the actual discussions that determine which cases will be heard by the Court. The justices meet in conference with no staff or clerks. Leaks are rare, but a few insider accounts and the papers of retired justices provide some insights to the process. First, since the late 1970s, most justices have used a **cert pool**, whereby their law clerks take a first cut at the cases (law clerks to the justices are top graduates of elite law schools who help justices with background research at several stages of the process). Clerks write joint memos about groups of cases, providing their recommendations about which cases should be heard. The ultimate decisions are up to the justices, but clerks have significant power to help shape the agenda.

Second, the chief justice has an important agenda-setting power: he decides the "discuss list" for a given day. Any justice can add a case to the list, but there is no systematic evidence on how often this happens. Only 20 to 30 percent of the cases are discussed in conference, which means that about three-quarters of the cases that are submitted to the Supreme Court are never even discussed by the Court. In most cases, this is justified because of the high proportion of frivolous suits submitted to the Court.[38]

Many factors outside the legal requirements or internal processes of the Court influence access to the Court and which cases will be heard. Cases that have generated a lot of activity from interest groups or other governmental parties, such as the solicitor general, are more likely to be heard. The **solicitor general** is a presidential appointee who works in the Justice Department and supervises the litigation of the executive branch. In cases in which the federal government is a party, the solicitor general or someone else from that office will represent the government in court. The Court accepts about 70 to 80 percent of cases in which the U.S. government is a party compared with about 1 percent overall.[39]

cert pool A system initiated in the Supreme Court in the 1970s in which law clerks screen cases that come to the Supreme Court and recommend to the justices which cases should be heard.

solicitor general A presidential appointee in the Justice Department who conducts all litigation on behalf of the federal government before the Supreme Court and supervises litigation in the federal appellate courts.

Even with these influences, the Court has a great deal of discretion as to which cases it hears. Well-established practices such as standing and mootness may be ignored (or modified) if the Court wants to hear a specific case. However, one final point is important: although the justices may pick and choose their cases, they cannot set their own agenda. They can select only from the cases that come to them.

DESCRIBE THE SUPREME COURT'S PROCEDURES FOR HEARING A CASE

HEARING CASES BEFORE THE SUPREME COURT

A surprisingly small proportion of the Court's time is actually spent hearing cases—only 39 days in the 2013–2014 term. The Court is in session from the first Monday in October through the end of June. It hears cases on Mondays through Wednesdays in alternating two-week cycles in which it is in session from 10 A.M. to 3 P.M., with a one-hour break for lunch. In the other two weeks of the cycle when it is not in session, justices review briefs, write opinions, and sift through the next batch of petitions. On most Fridays when the Court is in session, the justices meet in conference to discuss cases that have been argued and decide which cases they will hear. Opinions are released throughout the term, but the bulk of them come in May and June.[40]

The Court is in recess from July through September. Justices may take some vacation, but they mostly use the time for study, reading, writing, and preparing for the next term. During the summer, the Court also considers emergency petitions (such as stays of execution) and occasionally hears important cases. For example, on September 9, 2009 (nearly a month before the fall session started), the Court heard a challenge to the Bipartisan Campaign Reform Act, more commonly known as the McCain–Feingold Act after its two principal sponsors. Congress urged the Court to give the law a speedy review, given its importance for the upcoming 2010 elections. In the blockbuster case *Citizens United v. Federal Election Commission*, the Supreme Court decided that independent spending in campaigns by corporations and labor unions is protected by the First Amendment (see Chapter 9).

BRIEFS

During the regular sessions, the Court follows rigidly set routines. The justices prepare for a case by reading the briefs that both parties submit. Because the Supreme Court hears only appeals, it does not call witnesses or gather new evidence. Instead, in structured briefs of no more than 50 pages, the parties present their arguments about why they either support the lower-court decision or believe the case was improperly decided. Interest groups often submit **amicus curiae** ("friend of the court"; plural is amici curiae) briefs that convey their opinions to the Court; in fact, 85 percent of cases before the Supreme Court have at least one amicus brief.[41] The federal government also files amici curiae on important issues such as school busing, school prayer, abortion, reapportionment of legislative districts, job discrimination against women and minorities, and affirmative action in higher education.

amicus curiae Latin for "friend of the court," referring to an interested group or person who shares relevant information about a case to help the Court reach a decision.

It is difficult to determine the impact of amici curiae on the outcome of a case, but those that are filed early in the process increase the chances that the case will be heard. Interestingly, even amici curiae that are filed *against* a case increase the chances that the case will be heard.[42] Given the limited information that justices have about any given case, interest group involvement can be a strong signal about the importance of a case.

ORAL ARGUMENT

Once the briefs are filed and have been reviewed by the justices, cases are scheduled for **oral arguments**. Except in unusual circumstances, each case gets one hour, which is divided evenly between the two parties. In especially important cases, extra time may be granted (for example, the Obamacare case had six hours of oral argument, which was the most since a Voting Rights Act case in 1966).[43] Usually there is only one lawyer for each side who presents the case, but parties who have filed amicus briefs may participate if their arguments "would provide assistance to the Court not otherwise available." Given the tight time pressures, the Court is usually unwilling to extend the allotted time to allow "friends of the court" to testify.[44] The relevant party can share part of its 30 minutes if it wants, but that does not happen often. Therefore, the participation of friends of the court is usually limited to written briefs rather than oral arguments.

The Court is strict about its time limits and uses a system of three lights to show the lawyers how much of their allotted 30 minutes is left. A green light goes on when the speaker's time begins, a white light provides a five-minute warning, and a red light means to stop. Most textbooks cite well-known examples of justices cutting people off in midsentence or walking out of the courtroom as the lawyer drones on. One source implies that these anecdotes are generally revealing of Court procedure, saying, "Anecdotes probably tell as much about the proceeding of the Court during oral argument as does any careful study of the rules and procedures."[45]

However, having a preference for "careful study" over anecdotes, we were curious about how common it was for justices to strictly impose the time limits. Initially, we examined 42 cases from the 2004–2005 term, using the online transcripts on the Court's website.[46] We found that most lawyers did not use all their allotted time, with 62 percent of the cases coming in under 60 minutes, 17 percent at exactly an hour, and 21 percent at over an hour. One-sixth of the lawyers still had at least five minutes left on the clock. We found only two instances in which a justice cut someone off in midsentence after the person had gone over the half-hour limit. We updated the analysis for the Roberts Court, examining all 74 cases argued in the 2009 calendar year. Roberts was not much of a stickler for adhering to the time limits: nearly 60 percent of oral arguments went past their allotted time (most by only a minute or two), 13.5 percent were exactly one hour, and 27 percent were under an hour. Again, only 2 of the 74 oral arguments ended with an attorney being cut off in midsentence by the chief justice. Thus, while the Court tries to encourage attorneys to stay within the time limits, it is not as draconian as some anecdotes imply.

oral arguments Spoken presentations made in person by the lawyers of each party to a judge or an appellate court outlining the legal reasons their side should prevail.

CAMERAS ARE NOT ALLOWED IN the Supreme Court, so artists' sketches are the only images of oral arguments. This sketch shows the full Supreme Court listening to attorney Bobby Burchfield (standing on the right) arguing for then–Senate minority leader Mitch McConnell (R-KY, seated center), who favors eliminating all limits on campaign contributions, as he believes that such limits violate the principle of free speech.

Some lawyers may not use all of their time because their train of thought is interrupted by aggressive questioning. Transcripts reveal that justices jump in with questions almost immediately, and some attorneys never regain their footing. The frequency and pointedness of the questions vary by justice, with Justices Scalia, Breyer, Kagan, and Sotomayor being the most aggressive on the current Court, while Justice Thomas has gone more than eight years without asking a single question.[47] Cameras are not allowed in the courtroom, so most Americans have never seen the Court in action—although a small live audience is admitted every morning the Court is in session. If you are curious about oral arguments, audio recordings of every case since 1995 are available at www.oyez.org.

CONFERENCE

After oral arguments, the justices meet in conference to discuss and then vote on the cases. As with the initial conferences, these meetings are conducted in secret. We know, based on notes in the personal papers of retired justices, that the conferences are orderly and structured but can become quite heated. The justices take turns discussing the cases and outlining the reasons for their positions. Justice Thurgood Marshall described the decision-making process in conference and the need for secrecy as

> *a continuing conversation among nine distinct individuals on dozens of issues simultaneously. The exchanges are serious, sometimes scholarly, occasionally brash and personalized, but generally well-reasoned and most often cast in understated, genteel language. . . . In other cases, a majority of justices start down one path, only to reverse direction. . . . This is the kind of internal debate that the justices have argued should remain confidential, taking the position that only their final opinions have legal authority. They have expressed concern that premature disclosure of their private debates and doubts may undermine the court's credibility and inhibit their exchange of ideas.[48]*

OPINION WRITING

After the justices indicate how they are likely to vote on a case, if the chief justice is in the majority (which is most of the time), he decides who will write the majority opinion. For example, Warren Burger assigned 1,891 of the 2,201 opinions (about 86 percent) when he was chief justice in the 1970s and 1980s.[49] Otherwise, the most senior justice in the majority assigns the opinion. Many considerations determine how a case will be assigned. First, the chief justice will try to ensure the smooth operation of the Court. Along these lines, in 1989, Chief Justice Rehnquist announced a change in how he assigned opinions. In his first three terms, he tried to give each justice the same number of cases, but he recognized that "this policy does not take into consideration the difficulty of the opinion assigned or the amount of work that the 'assignee' may currently have backed up in his chambers. . . . It only makes sense in the assignment of additional work to give some preference to those who are 'current' with respect to past work."[50] A second factor is the justices' individual areas of expertise. For example, Justice Blackmun had developed expertise in medical law when he was in private practice. This experience played a role in Chief Justice Burger's decision to assign Blackmun the majority opinion in the landmark abortion decision *Roe v. Wade* (1973). Likewise, Justice O'Connor developed expertise in racial redistricting cases and authored most of those decisions in the 1990s.

The final set of factors is more strategic: it includes the Court's external relations, internal relations, and the personal policy goals of the opinion assigner. The Court must be sensitive to how others might respond to its decisions because it must rely on the other branches of government to enforce its decisions. One famous example of this consideration in an opinion assignment came in a case from the 1940s that struck down a practice that had prevented African Americans from voting in Democratic primaries.[51] Originally, the opinion was assigned to Justice Felix Frankfurter, but Justice Robert Jackson wrote a memo suggesting that it might be unwise to have a liberal, politically independent Jew from the Northeast write an opinion that was sure to be controversial in the South. Chief Justice Harlan Fiske Stone agreed and reassigned the opinion to Justice Stanley Reed, a Protestant and Democrat from Kentucky.[52] It may not seem that the Court is sensitive to public opinion, but these kinds of considerations happen fairly frequently in important cases. Internal considerations occasionally cause justices to vote strategically—differently from the justice's sincere preference—in order to be in the majority so that the justice can assign the opinion (often to himself or herself) as the most senior justice in the majority.

Justices may also assign opinions to help achieve their personal policy goals. The most obvious strategy is for the chief justice to assign opinions to justices who are closest to his position. Obviously, this practice is constrained by the first point—ensuring the smooth operation of the Court. If the chief justice assigned all the opinions to the justices who are closest to him ideologically, then justices with other ideological leanings would get a chance to write opinions only in the 15 to 20 percent of cases in which the chief is in the minority. That wouldn't work. Charles Hughes, chief justice from 1930 to 1941, sometimes assigned opinions on liberal decisions to conservative justices and cases with conservative outcomes to liberal justices in order to downplay the importance of ideology on the Court.[53]

After the opinions are assigned, the justices work on writing a draft opinion. Law clerks typically help with this process. Some justices insist on writing all of their opinions, whereas others allow a clerk to write the first draft. The drafts are circulated to the other justices for comment and reactions. Some bargaining may occur, in which a justice says he or she will withdraw support unless a provision is changed. Justices may join the majority opinion, may write a separate concurring opinion, or may dissent (see Nuts & Bolts 14.3 for details on the types of opinions).

Two final points about the process of writing and issuing opinions are important. First, until the 1940s, there was a premium placed on unanimous decisions. John Marshall, who was chief justice from 1800 to 1835, started this practice. Through the 1930s, about 80 to 90 percent of decisions were unanimous. This changed dramatically in the 1940s, when most cases had at least one dissent. In recent decades, about two-thirds of cases have a dissent.[54] However, in the 2013–2014 term, two-thirds of the cases were unanimous, the highest proportion since at least 1946.[55]

IF HE OR SHE IS IN THE MAJORITY, THE chief justice decides who will write the majority opinion. Otherwise, the most senior justice in the majority makes the assignment. Since being named chief justice in 2005, John Roberts has spread opinion-writing duties fairly evenly among the justices.

TYPES OF SUPREME COURT DECISIONS

▶ **Majority opinion:** The core decision of the Court that must be agreed upon by at least five justices. The majority opinion presents the legal reasoning for the Court's decision.

▶ **Concurring opinion:** Written by a justice who agrees with the outcome of the case but not with part of the legal reasoning. In a regular concurrence, the justice agrees with the majority but has something extra he or she wants to add. A special concurrence means that the justice agrees with the outcome but disagrees on the rationale. Concurring opinions may be joined by other justices. A justice may sign on to the majority opinion and write a separate concurring opinion.

▶ **Plurality opinion:** Occurs when a majority cannot agree on the legal reasoning in a case. The plurality opinion is the one that has the most agreement (usually three or four justices). Because of the fractured nature of these opinions, they typically are not viewed as having as much clout as majority opinions.

▶ **Dissent:** Submitted by a justice who disagrees with the outcome of the case. Other justices can sign on to a dissent or write their own, so there can be as many as four dissents. Justices can also sign on to part of a dissent but not the entire opinion.

▶ **Per curiam opinion:** (Latin for "by the court") An unsigned opinion of the Court or a decision written by the entire Court. However, this is not the same as a unanimous decision that is signed by the entire Court. Per curiam opinions are usually very short opinions on noncontroversial issues, but not always. For example, *Bush v. Gore*, which decided the outcome of the 2000 presidential election, was a per curiam opinion. Per curiam decisions may also have dissents.

Second, dissents serve an important purpose. Not only do they allow the minority view to be expressed, but they also often provide the basis for reversing a poorly reasoned case. When justices strongly oppose the majority opinion, they may take the unusual step of reading a portion of the dissent from the bench, as did Justice Sotomayor who dissented in the affirmative action case discussed in the chapter opener.

ANALYZE THE FACTORS THAT
INFLUENCE SUPREME COURT
DECISIONS

SUPREME COURT DECISION MAKING

Judicial decision making is influenced by many different factors, but the two main categories are *legal* and *political*. Legal factors include the precedent of earlier cases and norms that justices must follow the language of the Constitution. Political influences include the justices' preferences or ideologies, their stances on whether the Court should take a restrained or activist role with respect to the elected branches, and external factors such as public opinion and interest group involvement. Some scholars argue that all Court behavior is political and that the use of legal factors is just a smoke screen for hiding personal preferences.

LEGAL FACTORS

Those who put forward the legal view usually present their position in normative terms—that is, justices *should* follow precedent and the words of the Constitution.

Advocates of this view recognize that justices often stray from these legal norms, but these critics see the interjection of personal preferences as a harmful politicization of the courts. Our view is that legal factors are often used as justification for political positions on the Court, but they also independently influence judicial decision making on a broad range of cases.

PRECEDENT The most basic legal factor is stare decisis, or precedent, discussed earlier. Precedent does not determine the outcome of any given case, because every case has a range of precedents that can serve to justify a justice's decision. The "easy" cases, in which settled law makes the outcome obvious, are less likely to be heard by the Court because of the justices' desire to focus on the more controversial areas of unsettled law. However, there are areas of the law—such as free speech, the death penalty, and search and seizure—in which precedent is an important explanation for how the justices decide a case.

THE LANGUAGE OF THE CONSTITUTION The various perspectives that emphasize the language of the Constitution all fall under the heading of **strict construction**. The most basic of these is the literalist view of the Constitution. Sometimes this view is called a textualist position because it sees the text of the document as determining the outcome of any given case. Literalists argue that justices need to look no further than the actual words of the Constitution.

Justice Hugo Black was one of the most famous advocates of the literalist position. When the First Amendment says that "Congress shall make no law . . . abridging the freedom of speech," that literally means *no* law. Justice Black said, "My view is, without deviation, without exception, without any ifs, buts, or whereases, that freedom of speech means that government shall not do anything to people . . . either for the views they have or the views they express or the words they speak or write."[56] While that may be clear enough with regard to political speech, how about pornography, Internet speech, or symbolic speech, such as burning an American flag or wearing an armband to protest the Vietnam War? A literal interpretation of the Constitution does not necessarily help determine whether these forms of speech should be restricted. (Indeed, Black was one of the two dissenters in a case that upheld students' right to wear armbands as a form of symbolic speech. Black believed that school officials should be allowed to decide whether a symbolic protest would be too disruptive in the classroom and argued that only spoken and written speech should be afforded the strongest protection of the First Amendment. So much for "without deviation, without exception" concerning restricting expression of the "views [people] have"!)

Critics of strict construction also point out that the Constitution is silent on many important points (such as a right to privacy) and could not have anticipated the many legal implications of changes in technology in the twentieth and twenty-first centuries, such as eavesdropping devices, cloning, and the Internet. Also, although the language of the First Amendment is relatively clear when it comes to political speech, other equally important words of the Constitution such as "necessary and proper," "executive power," "equal protection," and "due process" are open-ended and vague. Some strict constructionists respond by arguing that, if the words of the Constitution are not clear, the justices should be guided by what the Founders *intended,* a perspective called the **original intent** or originalist perspective. Clarence Thomas is the current justice who is most influenced by this view, especially on issues of federalism.

Justice Antonin Scalia has a similar view, arguing that the text of the Constitution should be closely followed and, if the text is ambiguous, justices should

strict construction A way of interpreting the Constitution based on its language alone.

original intent The theory that justices should surmise the intentions of the Founders when the language of the Constitution is unclear.

MARY BETH TINKER AND TWO OTHER students in the Des Moines, Iowa, public schools were suspended for wearing armbands to protest the Vietnam War. The Supreme Court ruled that the First Amendment protected symbolic political speech, even in public schools. Mary Beth is shown here with her mother at the trial.

figure out what the words generally meant to people at the time they were written. This view leads Scalia to some unpopular positions, such as his view that the Sixth Amendment provision that "in all criminal prosecutions the accused shall enjoy the right . . . to be confronted with the witnesses against him" applies even in the case of an accused child molester. The majority of the Court disagreed and held that it was acceptable to have the child testify in front of the prosecutor and defense attorney, with the judge, jury, and the accused viewing from another room over closed-circuit television because of the potential trauma the child would experience by having to confront the defendant face-to-face.[57]

Critics of the strict constructionist view are often described as supporting a **living Constitution** perspective on the document (see Chapter 2). They argue that originalism or other versions of strict construction can "make a nation the prisoner of its past, and reject any constitutional development save constitutional amendment."[58] If the justices are bound to follow the literal words of the Constitution, *with the meaning they had when the document was written*, we certainly could be legally frozen in time. The option of amending the Constitution is a long and difficult process, so that is not always a viable way for the Constitution to reflect changing norms and values. Justice William Brennan, a critic of originalism, also argued it was "arrogance cloaked in humility" to presume to know what the framers intended. According to this view, interpreting the Constitution is always somewhat subjective and it is misleading to claim otherwise.[59]

living Constitution A way of interpreting the Constitution that takes into account evolving national attitudes and circumstances rather than the text alone.

POLITICAL FACTORS

The living Constitution perspective points to the second set of influences on Supreme Court decision making: political factors. Indeed, many people are uncomfortable thinking about the Court in political terms and prefer to think of the image of "blind justice," in which constitutional principles are fairly applied. However, political influences are clearly evident in the Court—maybe less than in Congress or the presidency, but they are certainly present. This means that the courts respond to and shape politics in ways that often involve compromise, both within the courts themselves and in the broader political system.

POLITICAL IDEOLOGY AND ATTITUDES The most important political factor is the justices' ideology or attitudes about various issues (this is often called the **attitudinalist approach** to understanding Supreme Court decision making). Liberal judges are strong defenders of individual civil liberties (including defendants' rights), tend to be pro-choice on abortion, support regulatory policy to protect the environment and workers, support national intervention in the states, and favor race-conscious policies such as affirmative action. Conservative judges favor state regulation of private conduct (especially on moral issues), support prosecutors over defendants, tend to be pro-life on abortion, and support the free market and property rights over the environment and workers, states' rights over national intervention, and a color-blind policy on race.

attitudinalist approach A way of understanding decisions of the Supreme Court based on the political ideologies of the justices.

These are, of course, just general tendencies. However, they do provide a strong basis for explaining patterns of decisions, especially on some types of cases. For example, there were dramatic differences in the chief justices' rulings on civil liberties cases from 1953 to 2001: Earl Warren took the liberal position on 79 percent of the 771 cases he participated in, Warren Burger took the liberal position on

30 percent of 1,429 cases, and William Rehnquist took the liberal position on only 22 percent of his 2,127 cases.[60] If justices were neutrally applying the law, there would not be such dramatic differences.

Proponents of the attitudinalist view also argue that justices who *claim* to be strict constructionists or originalists are really driven by ideology because they selectively use the text of the Constitution. For example, Justice Thomas voted against the University of Michigan's affirmative action program without considering whether the authors of the Fourteenth Amendment supported the practice (the historical record shows that they supported similar policies for the newly freed slaves). Therefore, if Justice Thomas had been true to his originalist perspective, he would have supported affirmative action, but his ideology led him to oppose the policy. The example of Hugo Black's contradictory position on free speech rights cited earlier demonstrates that a liberal textualist view may also be inconsistently applied.

THE STRATEGIC MODEL A strategic approach to understanding Supreme Court decision making focuses on justices' calculations about the preferences of the other justices, the president, and Congress; the choices that other justices are likely to make; and the institutional context within which they operate. After all, justices do not operate alone: at a minimum, they need the votes of four of their colleagues if they want their position to prevail. Therefore, it makes sense to focus on the strategic interactions that take place to build coalitions.

The median voter on the Court—the one in the middle when the justices are arrayed from the most liberal to the most conservative—has an especially influential role in the strategic model. For many years, the median justice was Sandra Day O'Connor; when Samuel Alito replaced her, Anthony Kennedy became the new median justice (see Figure 14.4). The four conservatives to his right (Thomas, Scalia, Roberts, and Alito) and the four liberals to his left (Breyer, Ginsberg, Souter, and Stevens) all wanted to attract his vote. When Justice Sotomayor replaced Justice Souter and when Justice Kagan replaced Justice Stevens, Kennedy remained the median voter on the Court (because Souter, Sotomayor, Stevens, and Kagan are all to his left). Research shows that at least one justice switches his or her vote at some stage in the process (from the initial conference to oral arguments to the final vote) on at least half of the cases, so strategic bargaining appears to be fairly common.[61] Our earlier discussion of opinion assignment and writing opinions to attract the support of a specific justice is more evidence in support of the strategic model.

SEPARATION OF POWERS Another political influence on justices' decision making is their view of the place of the Court with respect to the democratically elected institutions (Congress and the president). Specifically, do they favor an activist or a restrained role for the Court? Advocates of **judicial restraint** argue that judges should defer to the elected branches and not strike down their laws or other actions. In contrast, advocates of **judicial activism** argue that the Court must play an active role in interpreting the Constitution to protect minority rights even if it means overturning the actions of the elected branches. Yet another approach says that these normative arguments about how restraint or activism ought to work don't really matter because the Court usually follows public opinion and rarely plays a lead role in promoting policy change. One scholar found that three-fifths to two-thirds of Supreme Court decisions are consistent with public opinion when the public has a clear preference on an issue.[62] Nonetheless, there

judicial restraint The idea that the Supreme Court should defer to the democratically elected executive and legislative branches of government rather than contradicting existing laws.

judicial activism The idea that the Supreme Court should assert its interpretation of the law even if it overrules the elected executive and legislative branches of government.

FIGURE » 14.4

IDEOLOGY OF SUPREME COURT JUSTICES, 2014

Notice that the estimates of the justices' ideology vary in their precision. What might explain the relatively tight distribution for Breyer or Kennedy, compared with the broad distribution for Thomas?

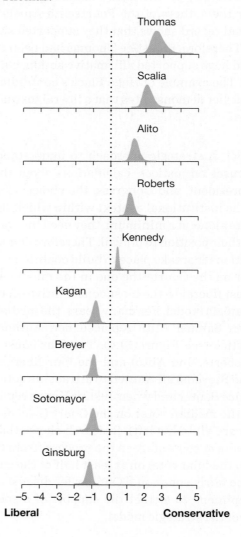

SOURCE: Alexander Tahk and Stephen Jessee, Supreme Court Ideology Project, http://sct.tahk.us/current.html (accessed 7/9/14).

are plenty of examples of when the Court has stood up for unpopular views, such as banning prayer in schools, allowing flag burning, and protecting criminal defendants' rights.

Often, assessments of the Court's role vary with the views of a specific line of cases. A political conservative may favor activist decisions striking down environmental laws or workplace regulations but oppose activist decisions that defend flag burning or defendants' rights. Political liberals may do the opposite—calling for judicial restraint on the first set of cases but for judicial activism to protect civil liberties. Sometimes, the popular media mistakenly assert that liberal justices are more activist than conservative justices. In fact, though, that is not always the case. The current Court is quite conservative, but it is also activist.[63] Two conservative justices, Kennedy and Thomas, have voted to overturn laws passed by Congress 93 percent and 81 percent of the time, respectively, whereas two of the most liberal justices, Breyer and Ginsburg, have taken the activist position in only 42 percent and 48 percent of the cases.[64] The 1930s Court that struck down much of the New Deal legislation was also conservative and activist, but the Warren Court of the late 1950s and early 1960s was liberal and activist (see Table 14.1).

A prominent legal journalist observed that the way the popular media describe activism and restraint typically boils down to ideology: if you like a decision, it is restrained; if you do not like a decision, it is activist. For example, *Bush v. Gore*, the decision that decided the outcome of the 2000 presidential election, shows that "most conservatives tie themselves in knots to defend judicial activism when they like the results and to denounce it when they do not. As the reactions to *Lawrence* [the gay sex case discussed in Chapter 4] and, earlier, *Roe* [the landmark abortion case] have shown, liberals have been no less selective in their outrage at judicial adventurousness."[65] However, there are instances in which restraint reflects more than ideology and preferences. Justice O'Connor, for example, took restrained positions on abortion and affirmative action, despite her personal views against these policies. And in a more recent example of judicial restraint, shown in the health care reform decision, Chief Justice Roberts said that some decisions "are entrusted to our nation's elected leaders, who can be thrown out of office if the people disagree with them." However, despite providing the pivotal vote to uphold central provisions of the law, he made his personal views against the law clear. "It is not our job," he said, "to protect the people from the consequences of their political choices."[66]

It is important to define activism and restraint in terms of the Court's role in our nation's system of separated powers: Does it check the elected branches by overturning their decisions through judicial review? This is the only objective way to define activism and restraint.

OUTSIDE INFLUENCES: INTEREST GROUPS AND PUBLIC OPINION Finally, there are external influences on the Court, such as public opinion and interest groups. We have already talked about the role of interest groups in filing amicus briefs. This is the only avenue of influence open to interest groups; other tactics such as lobbying or fund-raising are either inappropriate or irrelevant (because justices are not elected). The role of public opinion is more complex. Obviously, justices do not consult public opinion polls the way elected officials do. However, the Court expresses the public's preferences in several indirect ways.

The first was most colorfully expressed by Mr. Dooley, a fictional Irish-American bartender whom newspaper satirist Finley Peter Dunne created in 1898. Mr. Dooley offered keen insights on politics and general social criticism, including this gem on the relationship between the Supreme Court and the public: "th' supreme coort always follows th' iliction returns."[67] That is, the public elects the president and the Senate, who nominate and confirm the justices. Therefore, sooner or later, the Court should reflect the views of the public. Subsequent work by political scientists has confirmed this to be largely the case,[68] especially in recent years when Supreme Court nominations have become more political and more important to the public.[69]

The second mechanism through which public opinion may influence the Court is more direct: when the public has a clear position on an issue that is before the Court, the Court tends to agree with the public. One study found that the "public mood" and Court opinions correlated very highly between 1956 and 1981, but that their association was weaker through the rest of the 1980s.[70] More recent work demonstrates that the Court is constrained by public opinion, in part because they may fear resistance to implementing an unpopular decision.[71]

Several high-profile examples support the idea that the Court is sensitive to public opinion: the Court's switch during the New Deal in the 1930s to support Roosevelt's policy agenda after standing in the way for four years, giving in to wartime opinion to support the internment of Japanese Americans during World War II, limiting an accused child molester's right to confront his accuser in a courtroom, and declaring that laws limiting sex between consenting gay adults were unconstitutional. In each of these cases, the justices reflected the current public opinion of the nation rather than a strict reading of the Constitution or the Founders' intent.

Sometimes the Court may shift its views to reflect *international* opinion. The most recent example struck down the death penalty for minors in 12 states. Ruling by a 5-to-4 vote that the execution of 16- or 17-year-olds violated the Eighth Amendment's prohibition against "cruel and unusual punishments," the majority opinion overturned a 1989 case and said that the new decision was necessary to reflect the "evolving standards of decency" concerning the definition of "cruel and unusual punishments." Justice Kennedy, who had voted on the other side of this issue 16 years earlier, wrote, "It is fair to say that the United States now stands alone in a world that has turned its face against the juvenile death penalty." Justice Kennedy said that although the Court was not obligated to follow foreign developments, "it is proper that we acknowledge the overwhelming weight of international opinion" for its "respected and significant confirmation for our own conclusions."[72] This explicit recognition of the role of public opinion firmly placed a majority of the Court on the side of the "living Constitution" perspective on this issue, while rejecting the strict constructionist view of the dissenters.

Another way that the Court may consider the public mood is to shift the timing of a decision. The best example here is the landmark school desegregation case,

Brown v. Board of Education (1954), that the Court sat on for more than two years—until after the 1952 presidential election—because it didn't think the public was ready for its bombshell ruling.[73] Others have argued that the Court rarely *changes* its views to reflect public opinion,[74] but at a minimum the evidence supports the notion that the Court is usually in step with the public.

WHAT DO POLITICAL SCIENTISTS DO?

For more on how the Supreme Court can be an agent of change, visit **wwnpag.es/wdpsd**

THE ROLE OF THE COURT AS A POLICY MAKER

ASSESS THE SUPREME COURT'S POWER IN THE POLITICAL SYSTEM

We conclude with the topic addressed early in the chapter—the place of the Court within the political system. Is the Court the "weakest branch"? As Alexander Hamilton pointed out, the Court has "neither the power of the purse nor the sword." Therefore, it is not clear how it can enforce decisions. In some instances the Court can force its views on the other branches; in other cases it needs their support to enforce its decisions.

COMPLIANCE AND IMPLEMENTATION

To gain compliance with its decisions, the Court can rely only on its reputation and on the actions of Congress and the president to back them up. If the other branches don't support the Court, there isn't much it can do. The Court's lack of enforcement power is especially evident when a ruling applies broadly to millions of people who care deeply about the issue. Consider school prayer, which still exists in hundreds of public schools nationwide despite having been ruled unconstitutional more than 40 years ago. It is impossible to enforce the ban unless someone in a school complains and is willing to bring a lawsuit.

In most cases that involve a broad policy, the Court depends on the president for enforcement. After *Brown v. Board of Education* (1954), the landmark school desegregation case, presidents Eisenhower and Kennedy had to send in federal troops to desegregate public schools and universities. However, presidential foot-dragging can have a big impact on how the law is enforced. President Nixon attempted to lessen the impact of a school busing decision in 1971 that forced the integration of public schools by interpreting it very narrowly. Republican presidents who oppose abortion have limited the scope of *Roe v. Wade*, which legalized abortion in 1973, by denying federal support for abortions for Medicaid recipients, banning abortions on military bases, and preventing doctors from mentioning abortion as an option during pregnancy counseling. The Court must rely on its reputation and prestige to compel the president and Congress not to stray too far from its decisions.

RELATIONS WITH THE OTHER BRANCHES

Relations with the other branches of government may become strained when the Court rules on fundamental questions about institutional power. In some cases, the other branches may fight back; in others, the Court may exercise self-restraint

HIGH SCHOOL STUDENTS IN MAIZE, Kansas, join hands around a flagpole at the annual nationwide event calling Christian youth to pre-class schoolyard prayer at the start of the new school year. Enforcing the prohibition of school prayer and drawing the line between permissible and impermissible prayer have both been difficult for the Court.

THE COURTS HAVE BEEN AN important protector of minority rights, including in the civil rights era. This picture from 1953 shows people waiting in line at the Supreme Court to hear oral arguments in *Brown v. Board of Education*. But at other times, the Court has supported the will of the majority.

and not get involved. The most important question goes back to the topic raised in the chapter opener: Does the Court defer to the elected branches or the people, as in the Michigan affirmative action case, or does it strike down the action of the elected branches, as in the campaign finance case?

RESISTANCE FROM THE OTHER BRANCHES The president and Congress often fight back when they think the Court is exerting too much influence, which can limit the Court's power as a policy-making institution. For the president, this can escalate to open conflict. Examples include the battle between Jackson and Marshall over jurisdiction within the Cherokee Nation; the conflict between Jefferson and Marshall, which included the impeachment of a Supreme Court justice for political reasons (although the Senate acquitted the justice on all charges) and the repeal of the 1801 Judiciary Act; FDR's court-packing scheme, which was his response to the obstructionist New Deal Court; and President Obama's criticism of the Supreme Court in his 2010 State of the Union message for the Court's ruling in *Citizens United v. Federal Election Commission* (2010). When Obama stated in his speech that the decision had opened the floodgates for corporate spending—including foreign corporations—in elections, Justice Alito was caught on camera mouthing the words "not true." Washington was abuzz for days about whether the president's comment or Alito's response was out of line. Chief Justice Roberts added fuel to the fire a few weeks later when he said that he found the president's comment and the partisan atmosphere of the speech "very troubling" and indicated that justices may not attend State of the Union addresses in the future.

The president can counter the Court's influence in a more restrained way by failing to enforce a decision vigorously. Congress can try to control the Court by blocking appointments it disagrees with (however, this often involves a disagreement with the president more than the Court), limiting the jurisdiction of the federal courts, changing the size of the Court, or even impeaching a judge. The latter three options are rarely used, but Congress often threatens to take these drastic steps. The most common way for Congress to respond to a Court decision that it disagrees with is simply to pass legislation that overturns the decision (if the case concerns the interpretation of a law). Sometimes these disputes last for a while, as with the recent flap over sentencing guidelines. Congress wanted the federal courts to get tougher on criminals, so it passed a law telling federal judges the range of sentences that they had to give for specific crimes. Chief Justice Rehnquist was upset that Congress passed the law without input from the judiciary, and the Court struck back by invalidating the sentencing guidelines as an unfair imposition on the judiciary. The Roberts Court is deeply involved in this issue as well: there have been 17 Supreme Court cases on sentencing between 2010 and 2014.[75]

SELF-IMPOSED RESTRAINT In general, the Court avoids stepping on the toes of the other branches unless it is absolutely necessary. The Court often exercises self-imposed restraint and refuses to act on "political questions"—issues that are outside the judicial domain and should be decided by elected officials. The practice dates back to an 1804 dispute over whether a piece of land next to the Mississippi

River belonged to Spain or the United States. The Court observed, "A question like this, respecting the boundaries of nations, is . . . more a political than a legal question, and in its discussion, the courts of every country must respect the pronounced will of the legislature."[76]

A more recent application of the doctrine came when the Washington, D.C., district court dismissed a lawsuit from Rep. Charles Rangel (D-NY) against Speaker John Boehner (R-OH) concerning the House of Representatives' censure of Rangel for tax evasion and other unethical behavior. The district court dismissed the suit, in part on the grounds that this was a political question that should be decided by Congress, not the Court: "The House has wide discretion to discipline its Members under the Discipline Clause, and this Court may not lightly intrude upon that discretion."[77] The Court is generally reluctant to get involved in internal congressional disputes.

Although this self-imposed limitation on judicial power is important, one must also recognize that the Court reserves the right to decide what a political question is. Therefore, one could argue that this is not much of a limit on judicial power after all. For example, for many decades, the Court avoided the topic of legislative redistricting, saying that it did not want to enter that "political thicket." However, it changed its position in the 1960s in a series of cases that imposed the idea of "one person, one vote" on the redistricting process, and it has been intimately involved in redistricting ever since. The Court's ability to define the boundaries of political questions is an important source of its policy-making power.

THE COURT'S MULTIFACETED ROLE This "big picture" question about the relationship of the Court to the other branches boils down to this: Does the judiciary constrain the other branches, or does it defer to their wishes? Given the responsiveness of the elected branches to the will of the people, this question can alternatively be stated: Does the Court operate against the political majority to protect minority interests, or does it defer to the popular will? The evidence on this is mixed.

The judicial branch as a whole contains a basic paradox: it may be simultaneously seen as the least democratic and most democratic branch.[78] The least democratic part is obvious: federal judges and many state and local judges are unelected and are not accountable to the voters (except indirectly through the elected leaders who appoint them). But the judiciary can also be seen as the most democratic branch. Cases that are brought to the courts come from the people and, as long as the legal criteria for bringing a case are met, the courts must hear those cases. Although people have the right to petition "the government for a redress of grievances," there is no guarantee that Congress or the executive branch will listen to them. Of course, only a small fraction of the cases brought to the Supreme Court are heard, so the antidemocratic charge carries more weight at the top. However, the court system as a whole may be seen as providing an important outlet for participation in our political system.

Whether the Supreme Court goes against our elected leaders is also a complicated question to sort out. The Court is activist on many issues, exercising judicial review, but on many other issues it defers to the elected institutions. Sometimes an activist Court defends minority interests on issues such as criminal defendants' rights, school prayer, gay rights, and flag burning, but that is not always the case. Is the Court acting undemocratically when it exercises its power of judicial review (or, as critics would say, "legislates from the bench")? Or is it playing its vital role in our constitutional system as a check on the other branches, as with some of its recent cases concerning the legal rights of enemy combatants in the war on terror?

The answers depend somewhat on one's political views. Conservatives would generally applaud the activism of the Rehnquist and Roberts Courts, while liberals would see it as an unwarranted check on the elected branches. Moreover, the Court's role has varied throughout history: in some instances, it defended unpopular views and strongly protected minority rights; in other cases, it followed majority opinion and declined to play that important role. But clearly, the Court has the *potential* to play an important policy-making role in our system of checks and balances; whether it actually plays that role depends on the political, personal, and legal factors outlined in this chapter.

CONCLUSION

The courts demonstrate that politics is conflictual. Although plenty of unanimous Supreme Court decisions do not involve much conflict among the justices, many landmark cases deeply divide the Court on constitutional interpretation and how to balance those competing interpretations against other values and interests. These conflicts in the Court often reveal deeper fault lines in the broader political system.

It shouldn't be surprising that political process matters in the courts. The rules of courtroom procedures, including discovery and how evidence is presented, can have an important impact on outcomes. Political process is also important for selecting judges and determining which cases the Supreme Court hears.

Politics is indeed everywhere, even in the courts, where you would least expect to see it. Despite the idealized image of Justice as a blindfolded woman holding a set of scales, politics affects everything from the selection of judges to the decisions they make. Some characteristics of the federal courts (the most important of which is judges' lifetime tenure) insulate the system from politics. However, courts are subject to influence by judges' ideologies, interest groups, and the president and Senate, who try to shape the courts' composition through the nomination process.

The chapter opening example demonstrates the important role that the courts play in the political system. Recall that the Supreme Court deferred to the voters of Michigan in the affirmative action case, saying that states should be able to decide this controversial issue, not the Court. In the campaign finance case, however, it struck down part of a law that placed aggregate limits on how much individuals could contribute to federal candidates and parties. Thus, the federal courts can serve as a referee between the other branches of government, and between the national and state governments, by defining the boundaries of permissible conduct.

THE DEVELOPMENT OF AN INDEPENDENT AND POWERFUL FEDERAL JUDICIARY

▶ *Explain how the power of judicial review was established.* **(Pages 511–15)**

SUMMARY

In contrast to other branches of government, the Constitution offers few specifics on the organization of the judiciary. In fact, most of the details on the arrangement of the judiciary do not come from the Constitution at all, but from congressional action. In addition, the Supreme Court's strongest power—judicial review—is not even mentioned in the Constitution, but was established in the *Marbury v. Madison* decision.

KEY TERMS	CRITICAL THINKING AND DISCUSSION
Judiciary Act of 1789 (p. 512) **district courts** (p. 512) **appellate jurisdiction** (p. 512) **judicial review** (p. 513) **original jurisdiction** (p. 514) **constitutional interpretation** (p. 515) **statutory interpretation** (p. 515)	What do recent decisions on immigration and health care reform reveal about the role of the Supreme Court in our political system? Did the Founders approve of the practice of judicial review?

PRACTICE QUIZ QUESTIONS

1. Most of the details about the Supreme Court were established in _____.

   A the Judiciary Act of 1789

   B Article I of the Constitution

   C Article II of the Constitution

   D the *Federalist Papers*

   E *Marbury v. Madison*

2. *Marbury v. Madison* is significant because it _____.

   A established the Supreme Court

   B introduced the process of selective incorporation

   C changed the manner of judicial selection

   D established judicial review

   E gave Supreme Court justices lifetime appointments

3. Judicial review enables the Supreme Court to _____.

   A submit legislation to Congress

   B strike down laws passed by Congress

   C revise laws passed by Congress

   D oversee presidential appointments to the bureaucracy

   E approve judicial appointments to lower courts

4. The Court's application of national and state laws to particular cases is called _____.

   A constitutional interpretation

   B judicial restraint

   C judicial activism

   D original jurisdiction

   E statutory interpretation

THE AMERICAN LEGAL AND JUDICIAL SYSTEM

▶ *Outline the structure of the court system.* **(Pages 515–28)**

SUMMARY

All courts within the United States have a similar set of fundamental attributes, such as the distinction between civil and criminal cases and the reliance on legal precedent. The judicial system is divided between state and federal courts, and within each level of government, there are courts of original jurisdiction and appeals courts.

KEY TERMS	CRITICAL THINKING AND DISCUSSION
plaintiff (p. 516) **defendant** (p. 516) **plea bargaining** (p. 516) **class-action lawsuit** (p. 516) **common law** (p. 517) **precedent** (p. 517) **standing** (p. 517) **jurisdiction** (p. 518) **appeals courts** (p. 519) **senatorial courtesy** (p. 527)	What is the proper role for the Senate in providing "advice and consent" on the selection of federal judges? Should the Senate play the role of an equal partner to the president or simply approve most of the president's choices?

PRACTICE QUIZ QUESTIONS

5. A system of _____ relies on legal decisions that are built from precedent established in previous cases.

   A common law

   B civil law

   C statutory law

   D stare decisis

   E plea bargaining

6. When one has suffered direct and personal harm from the action addressed in a case, it is called _____.

   Ⓐ precedent

   Ⓑ appellant

   Ⓒ plea bargaining

   Ⓓ jurisdiction

   Ⓔ standing

7. The president appoints federal judges with the "advice and consent" of the _____.

   Ⓐ House of Representatives

   Ⓑ Senate

   Ⓒ Supreme Court

   Ⓓ attorney general

   Ⓔ vice president

9. _____ means that the controversy is not relevant when the Court hears the case.

   Ⓐ Mootness

   Ⓑ Amicus

   Ⓒ Collusion

   Ⓓ Standing

   Ⓔ Precedent

10. Most justices _____ in initially deciding which cases should be heard.

   Ⓐ personally review all cases

   Ⓑ personally review a random sample of cases

   Ⓒ follow the recommendations of the chief justice

   Ⓓ use a random selection process

   Ⓔ use a cert pool

ACCESS TO THE SUPREME COURT

▶ *Describe how cases reach the Supreme Court.* **(Pages 528–34)**

SUMMARY

The Supreme Court hears only about 1 percent of the cases that are brought to it. To help decide which cases to hear, the Court generally uses three factors: collusion, standing, and mootness. Ultimately, the justices have a great deal of discretion in deciding to hear a case, but they can only hear cases that come to them.

KEY TERMS

writ of certiorari (p. 531)
mootness (p. 532)
cert pool (p. 533)
solicitor general (p. 533)

CRITICAL THINKING AND DISCUSSION

How do you think the power of the Supreme Court would change if it didn't have to wait for cases to come to it? Would this be a positive change for our system, or would it give the Court too much power? Should the Court have more leeway over the cases it does hear, or does the system seem to work pretty well?

PRACTICE QUIZ QUESTIONS

8. When a litigant who lost in a lower court files a petition, the case reaches the Supreme Court _____.

   Ⓐ as a matter of right

   Ⓑ through a writ of certification

   Ⓒ through a writ of certiorari

   Ⓓ as a matter of original jurisdiction

   Ⓔ through senatorial courtesy

HEARING CASES BEFORE THE SUPREME COURT

▶ *Describe the Supreme Court's procedures for hearing a case.* **(Pages 534–38)**

SUMMARY

When hearing a case, the justices prepare by reading briefs before they hear the oral arguments. After oral arguments, the justices meet in conference to discuss and vote on the cases. The majority opinion explains the rationale for how a decision is reached, although justices can also write dissenting and concurring opinions.

KEY TERMS

amicus curiae (p. 534)
oral arguments (p. 535)

CRITICAL THINKING AND DISCUSSION

Should the discussions among the justices in conference be more open, like on the floor of the U.S. Congress and in most congressional committee meetings, or is it important to keep these discussion secret and off-the-record? Why are dissenting opinions important?

PRACTICE QUIZ QUESTIONS

11. Oral arguments generally last _____, and justices _____ wait until the end of the arguments to ask questions.

   Ⓐ one hour; will

   Ⓑ one hour; do not

   Ⓒ one day; will

D one week; will

E one week; do not

12. Generally, the chief justice or the _____ justice decides who writes the majority opinion; justices' individual areas of expertise _____ a factor in making this assignment.

A most junior; are not

B most junior; are

C most senior; are not

D most senior; are

E dissenting; does not

SUPREME COURT DECISION MAKING

▶ *Analyze the factors that influence Supreme Court decisions.* **(Pages 538–45)**

SUMMARY

The Court makes decisions based on legal factors such as precedent and informal norms, and political factors such as the justices' own ideologies and positions on the role that the Court plays in government. Although the Court does not consider public opinion the way elected officials do, most decisions generally stay in step with the public.

KEY TERMS

strict construction (p. 539)
original intent (p. 539)
living Constitution (p. 540)
attitudinalist approach (p. 540)
judicial restraint (p. 541)
judicial activism (p. 541)

CRITICAL THINKING AND DISCUSSION

Should unelected judges have the ability to overturn laws passed by the elected branches? If so, should there be any mechanism for *political* accountability?

PRACTICE QUIZ QUESTIONS

13. The perspective that when the Constitution is not clear, the justices should be guided by what the Founders wanted is called _____.

A judicial activism

B strict construction

C original intent

D attitudinalist approach

E interpretive statute

14. Advocates of _____ argue that the Court must defer to the elected branches and not strike down their laws.

A judicial restraint

B judicial activism

C judicial limitation

D legal maximization

E the strategic model

THE ROLE OF THE COURT AS A POLICY MAKER

▶ *Assess the Supreme Court's power in the political system.* **(Pages 545–48)**

SUMMARY

Given the constitutional weakness of the Court, it is unclear how it is able to enforce its decisions. Depending on context, the Court is occasionally able to force its views on the elected branches, although more often it requires their support.

CRITICAL THINKING AND DISCUSSION

In a practical sense, is the Supreme Court ultimately more accountable to the citizens or to elected officials? To whom do you think it should be more accountable?

PRACTICE QUIZ QUESTION

15. In general, the Court _____ challenges with the elected branches and often _____ to act on "political questions."

A avoids; agrees

B avoids; refuses

C pursues; agrees

D pursues; refuses

SUGGESTED READING

Baum, Lawrence. *Judges and Their Audiences: A Perspective on Judicial Behavior.* Princeton, NJ: Princeton University Press, 2006.

Black, Ryan C., and Ryan J. Owens, *The Solicitor General and the United States Supreme Court: Executive Influence and Judicial Decisions.* New York: Cambridge University Press, 2012.

Cornell University Law School, Supreme Court Collection, www.law.cornell.edu/supremecourt/text/home

Eisgruber, Christopher L. *Constitutional Self-Government.* Cambridge, MA: Harvard University Press, 2001.

Hansford, Thomas G., and James F. Spriggs II. *The Politics of Precedent on the U.S. Supreme Court.* Princeton, NJ: Princeton University Press, 2006.

Northwestern University, Oyez: Supreme Court Multimedia, www.oyez.org.

O'Brien, David M. *Storm Center: The Supreme Court in American Politics*, 9th ed. New York: W. W. Norton, 2011.

Rosen, Jeffrey. *The Most Democratic Branch: How the Courts Serve America.* New York: Oxford University Press, 2006.

Sunstein, Cass R., David Schkade, Lisa M. Ellman, and Andres Sawicki. *Are Judges Political? An Empirical Analysis of the Federal Judiciary.* Washington, D.C.: Brookings Institution Press, 2006.

Tushnet, Mark. *A Court Divided: The Rehnquist Court and the Future of Constitutional Law.* New York: W. W. Norton, 2006.

U.S. Supreme Court website, www.supremecourt.gov.

15

Economic Policy

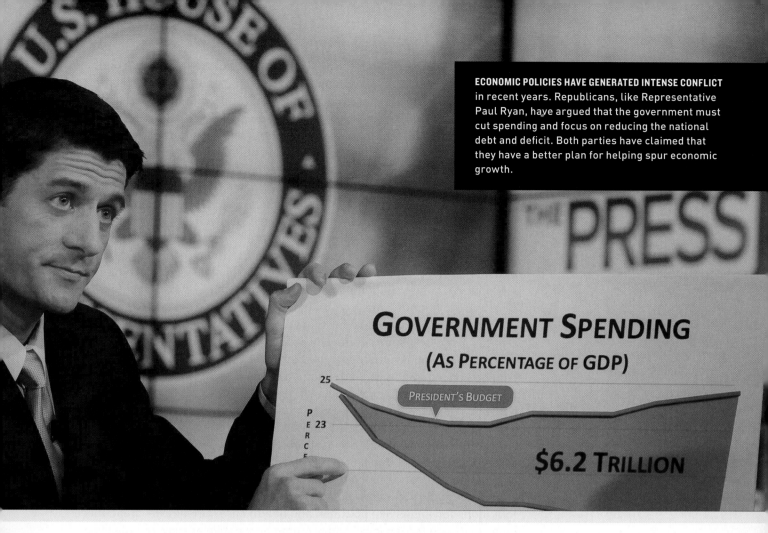

ECONOMIC POLICIES HAVE GENERATED INTENSE CONFLICT in recent years. Republicans, like Representative Paul Ryan, have argued that the government must cut spending and focus on reducing the national debt and deficit. Both parties have claimed that they have a better plan for helping spur economic growth.

GOVERNMENT SPENDING
(AS PERCENTAGE OF GDP)

PRESIDENT'S BUDGET

$6.2 TRILLION

EARLY IN THE 2012 CAMPAIGN, PRESIDENT OBAMA SIGNALED that tax policy and income inequality would be important themes in the election. In a speech in December 2011, he argued, "Today, the wealthiest Americans are paying the lowest taxes in over half a century. . . . Today, thanks to loopholes and shelters, a quarter of all millionaires now pay lower tax rates than millions of you, millions of middle-class families. Some billionaires have a tax rate as low as one percent. One percent. That is the height of unfairness. It is wrong."[1] This argument gained political relevance about a month later when the leading Republican candidate for president, Mitt Romney, revealed that he paid only 13.9 percent in federal taxes on the $21.7 million income he earned in 2010. Many people at that level of income pay 25 percent to 30 percent in federal taxes (for example, President Obama paid 26 percent on $1.8 million in 2010, while Newt Gingrich paid 31.6 percent on $3.2 million).[2]

How is it possible that Romney's tax rate was only 13.9 percent? Romney paid every dollar he owed; his taxes were so low because most of his income came from dividends and capital gains that are taxed at only 15 percent, rather than the top marginal rate of 35 percent. Middle-income people who have a marginal rate of 25 percent and pay 7.65 percent of their income in payroll taxes can easily have a total tax burden higher than 13.9 percent. To address this inequity in the tax code, Obama called for a "millionaire's tax" that would set a minimum rate of 30 percent for incomes that reach that level. Late in 2013 Obama called income inequality "the defining challenge of our time"; he also focused on inequality in

CONFLICT & COMPROMISE
in American Politics

CHAPTER *goals*

Explain the main purposes of government involvement in the economy.

▸ PAGES 555–61

Describe the roles played by each of the branches of government in shaping economic policy.

▸ PAGES 561–72

Examine how fiscal, monetary, regulatory, and trade policies influence the economy.

▸ PAGES 572–89

his 2014 State of the Union message and vowed to make it the focus of that year's policy agenda with a call to increase the hourly minimum wage to $10.10, expand early childhood education, and increase the earned income tax credit (which goes to the working poor).[3]

Republicans rejected Obama's proposals, saying that the minimum wage increase is a "job killer" and that a millionaire's tax is bad policy because the problem is not low taxes on the rich, but rather excessive government spending. They argue that low taxes stimulate job creation and that lower taxes on capital gains and dividends encourage investment.[4]

The recent focus on income inequality necessarily turns attention to the proper level of taxation. Tax policies are inherently conflictual, due to their redistributive nature: when the government takes money from one group and gives it to another, there will be conflict over those decisions. For example, if tax policy is used to help the poor, the wealthy will necessarily pay a larger percentage of their income in taxes than the poor. But even taxes that do not seem obviously redistributive hit some people harder than others. A 5 percent sales tax is more of a burden for the poor than for the non-poor because poorer people spend a higher proportion of their income. The home mortgage interest deduction on income tax benefits homeowners over renters. The 15 percent tax rate on dividends favors people who invest in stocks over bonds (because interest on bonds is taxed as regular income, usually at a much higher rate than 15 percent). In short, tax policies aimed at helping one segment of the economy come at the expense of another part, which creates political conflict.

Conflict over economic policy goes beyond tax policy. Many of America's political debates concern economic policy: Should we run deficits or have balanced budgets? Should we have a largely unregulated, free market—or regulations for things like pollution and health care? Should we spend more money to create "green jobs" and promote alternative energy, or subsidize more offshore drilling and build pipelines to maximize the extraction of oil and natural gas? Democrats tend to favor a more activist government that supports a

JOB SEEKERS LINE UP FOR A JOB FAIR at Columbia-Greene Community College in Hudson, New York. Unemployment remained stubbornly high through 2013, but the employment picture began to improve in 2014.

broader range of redistributive programs and regulates the economy to ensure a range of public goods, such as rebuilding the infrastructure. Republicans tend to favor a more limited approach to government that promotes lower taxes and less regulation and allows the free market to determine more social and economic decisions, such as allowing greater development of domestic energy sources.

As our political leaders debate how best to support a growing economy it becomes increasingly important to understand the economic policy-making process. What are the goals of economic policy, and how can political institutions meet those goals? What is the proper role of the government in a free market economy? How do political players deal with the conflict that is inherent in economic policy making?

GOALS OF ECONOMIC POLICY

EXPLAIN THE MAIN PURPOSES OF GOVERNMENT INVOLVEMENT IN THE ECONOMY

Policy makers have specific goals in mind when they try to influence the economy. Many of these goals seem obvious, such as full employment (obviously, it is better to have more people working than not working), but others may be less clear. Also, it is difficult to pursue all the goals simultaneously because there are trade-offs among some of them.

FULL EMPLOYMENT

Employment seems like a good starting point for a healthy economy. If people have jobs, they pay taxes and do not directly depend on the government for support. Despite this, **full employment** was not an explicit goal of economic policy until 1946, when Congress passed the Employment Act. Leaders were concerned that with millions of returning World War II veterans and the wartime economy gearing down, the nation might slide back into the **economic depression** that had created so much hardship in the 1930s. Although the act was largely symbolic (there was no guaranteed right to employment), it did create the **Council of Economic Advisers**, which provides the president with economic information and advice. A more concrete effort to ensure that returning veterans could find jobs was the Servicemen's Readjustment Act (the GI Bill). Enacted in 1944, it provided low-interest home mortgages for 2.4 million veterans and higher education assistance to 7.8 million veterans by the time the law expired in 1956. Today, the government seeks to support the creation of as many jobs as possible through a strong economy. By early in 2014, the number of American workers finally reached the level of employment before the 2008–2009 recession, but policy makers disagreed whether more government action was necessary to stimulate more job growth.

On a more technical level, "full employment" does not literally mean that everyone is working. There is always a substantial portion of the potential workforce that is not looking for a job. It does not even mean that everyone who is looking for work can get a job, because there is always a certain amount of "frictional unemployment" when people are between jobs. Instead, economists consider a 5 to 5.5 percent unemployment rate to be the level of full employment, or the "natural rate of unemployment."

full employment The theoretical point at which all citizens who want to be employed have a job.

economic depression A deep, widespread downturn in the economy, like the Great Depression of the 1930s.

Council of Economic Advisers A group of economic advisers, created by the Employment Act of 1946, which provides objective data on the state of the economy and makes economic policy recommendations to the president.

STABLE PRICES

inflation The increase in the price of consumer goods over time.

The importance of having stable prices is not as obvious as the need for jobs. Why are rising prices—**inflation**—a problem? This is a common question during periods of low inflation. Especially for workers who have automatic raises (cost of living adjustments, or COLAs) as part of their basic pay package, moderate inflation isn't much of a problem. For example, if your rent goes up 4 percent, the price of groceries goes up 3 percent, and the cost of entertainment goes up 3 percent, and you get a 4 percent raise, you will likely be at least as well off as you were in the previous year. However, from 1979 to 1980, inflation was running at 12 to 14 percent rather than the 2 to 3 percent that has been typical in recent years (Figure 15.1).

Double-digit inflation can have serious effects on the economy. First, the entire economy is not indexed to inflation, so some people experience an erosion of their purchasing power. If your rent goes up 10 percent and groceries are up 15 percent, but your pay goes up by only 4 percent, you are substantially worse off. Second, high inflation penalizes savers and rewards debtors as savings interest rates may be outstripped by inflation (so savings are actually worth *less* over time), but people who go into debt can repay those debts with dollars that are worth less in the future. Finally, long-term economic planning by businesses becomes more difficult when inflation is high, because investors demand high interest rates to compensate for the added risk of future inflation. In 1979 and 1980, short-term interest rates spiked as high as 18 percent. Very few businesses were willing to take on additional debt at that rate of interest as opposed to the more typical 6 to 8 percent, so the economy headed into a recession.

FIGURE » 15.1

INFLATION AND UNEMPLOYMENT, 1960–2014

The Misery Index is the sum of the unemployment rate and the inflation rate. Which periods have had the highest misery rate since 1960? Were there any external explanations for the high misery rate? How did the government respond to the high levels of unemployment and inflation?

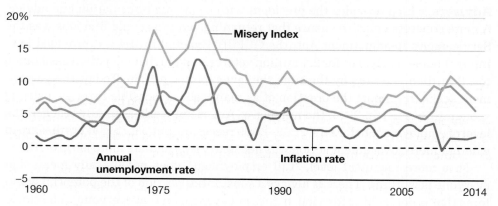

SOURCES: Data from the U.S. Department of Labor, Bureau of Labor Statistics, www.bls.gov/home.htm. Inflation data from http://data.bls.gov/timeseries/CUSR0000SA0?output_view=pct_1mth. Unemployment data from http://data.bls.gov/timeseries/LNS14000000 (accessed 11/7/14).

The period of relatively high unemployment and inflation generated two new economic terms: "stagflation" (a stagnant economy with inflation) and the "Misery Index" (the sum of the inflation rate and the unemployment rate). Typically, unemployment and inflation are not high at the same time, so policy makers were desperate to do something about them. The Misery Index started to creep up in 1970–1971, and President Nixon wanted to halt inflation in its tracks, in part to help his reelection chances in 1972. He announced a 90-day wage freeze in 1971, followed by wage and price controls after his reelection. The experiment was abandoned in 1974 when it became obvious that interfering with market forces in these ways was not working.[5] From that point on, fighting inflation has largely been left to the Federal Reserve, which raises interest rates to cool down the economy. This process is discussed later in the chapter.

PROMOTE THE FREE MARKET AND GROWTH

The American economy is a capitalist system, which means that most economic decisions are voluntarily made between individuals and firms for their mutual benefit. The government generally stays out of most economic activity, except to regulate the market when it produces too much of something that is not in the public's interest, such as pollution or unsafe products. Economists tout the advantage of the free market as promoting the most efficient use of resources. Economic growth is also a central goal. A growing economy provides a better standard of living for each generation.

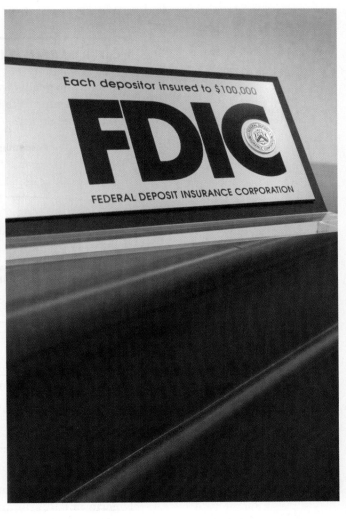

ONE IMPORTANT WAY THAT THE government supports the free market and economic growth is by promoting the stability of the banking system. The Federal Deposit Insurance Corporation (FDIC) bolsters confidence in banks by insuring each account holder's deposits in its member banks up to $250,000.

The government does not get directly involved in most economic transactions, but it can provide the foundation for a strong free market and economic growth. The government protects property rights so that businesses that invest in the growth of their company know that another firm or the government cannot appropriate their property. Property rights also include intellectual property that is protected by patent and copyright laws. If entrepreneurs know that they will benefit from their own discoveries and labor, they are more likely to put in the countless hours required for innovative breakthroughs in science, technology, and medicine. The foundation for the free market is also provided by secure and transparent capital markets through the oversight of the Securities and Exchange Commission and through a secure banking system, as ensured by the Federal Deposit Insurance Corporation and the Federal Reserve System.

Critics of the government's focus on the market and growth claim that the free market often produces inequality and that growth doesn't measure well-being. The "Occupy" movement, with its slogan "we are the 99 percent," has drawn attention to income inequality. But historically, the United States has not focused as much on this economic policy goal as many other Western nations have. As a consequence, the United States ranks 101st in the world (out of 141 nations in the study)

FIGURE » 15.2

WEALTH INEQUALITY IN THE UNITED STATES AND EUROPE: 1810–2010

Economic inequality was higher in Europe than in the United States until the mid-twentieth century. What are the factors that have led to increased economic inequality in the United States?

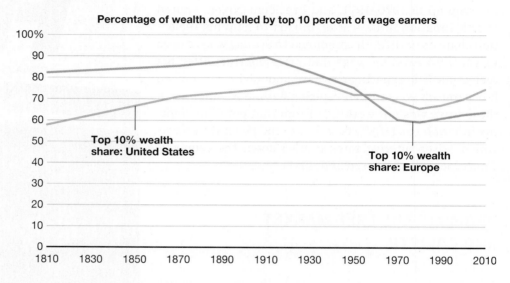

Percentage of wealth controlled by top 10 percent of wage earners

Top 10% wealth share: United States

Top 10% wealth share: Europe

SOURCE: Gabriel Zucman and Thomas Piketty, "Wealth and Inheritance in the Long Run," April 6, 2014, http://gabriel-zucman.eu/files/PikettyZucman2014HID.pdf (accessed 6/10/14).

in income equality, just behind nations such as Cameroon, Guyana, Iran, Uganda, Nigeria, and Russia, and it has become less equal than Europe in the distribution of wealth (see Figure 15.2).[6] Other critics of the focus on growth include environmentalists who advocate a "small is beautiful"[7] approach and point out the environmental costs of economic growth. In addition, there are economists who question the traditional interpretations of economic growth measurements—in particular, the increase in **gross domestic product (GDP)**, a measure of the nation's overall economic output and activity. These critics argue that a significant part of GDP actually captures a decline in well-being. For example, if we have to spend billions of dollars putting alarms in our homes and cars to warn against intruders, this is not an improvement in the standard of living from the time when such alarms were unnecessary. Yet the purchase of such crime-fighting tools adds to GDP. An ideal measure of economic growth would distinguish between positive and negative forms of economic activity.[8]

gross domestic product (GDP) The value of a country's economic output taken as a whole.

BALANCED BUDGETS

balanced budget A spending plan in which the government's expenditures are equal to its revenue.

budget deficit The amount by which a government's spending in a given fiscal year exceeds its revenue.

Maintaining a **balanced budget** has been a central economic goal since the 1980s, when **budget deficits** skyrocketed (see Figure 15.3 and Nuts & Bolts 15.1). Large deficits are a concern for several reasons. First, they take a big bite out of current spending. About $266 billion, or 7 percent, of the 2015 fiscal year budget is for financing the federal debt. These dollars went to people and financial institutions

FIGURE » 15.3

DEFICITS AND DEBT

The federal deficit is the amount by which the government's spending exceeds its revenue in a given year; the federal debt is the accumulation of these annual deficits. Why do the federal deficits and debt matter? Does the answer depend on the state of the economy?

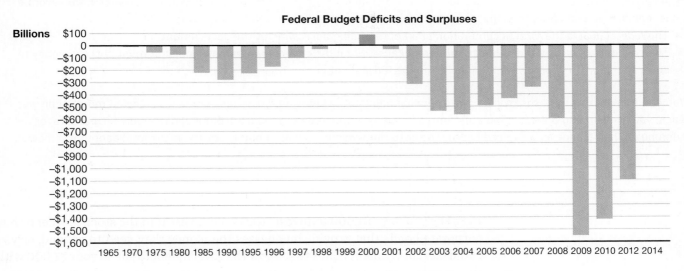

Federal Budget Deficits and Surpluses

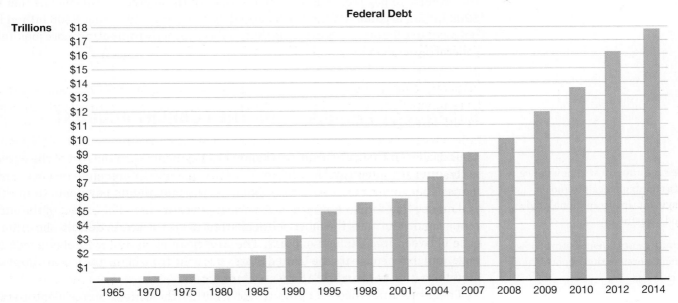

Federal Debt

Note: Totals in Figure 15.3 exclude the Social Security Trust Fund and reflect total public debt, including intragovernmental holdings.

SOURCE: Congressional Budget Office, Budget Projections, April 2014 Baseline, www.cbo.gov/publication/45069 (accessed 6/10/14).

that earn interest on the money that they loaned to the federal government; this money did not buy a single uniform for a soldier, highway exit ramp, or student loan. Second, the total federal debt is a burden on future generations. Each man, woman, and child in the United States in effect carries more than $57,270 of debt (total debt has grown steadily; see Figure 15.3). Third, public borrowing "crowds out" private borrowing because there is a finite pool of dollars that people can invest.

DEFICITS AND DEBT

Budget deficits and the federal debt are related concepts that are easily confused.

▶ A *budget deficit* occurs when tax revenue is not sufficient to cover government spending in a given year. If tax revenue is higher than spending, then there is a budget surplus.

▶ The *federal debt* is the total accumulation of all outstanding borrowing by the government.

▶ The concepts of deficit and debt are related because when the government runs a deficit, it must borrow money to cover the gap. This borrowing then builds up the federal debt.

You can think of this in terms of your own spending habits. Any time you spend more money in a given month than you earn, you are running a deficit. You must borrow money to make up that deficit from a bank, from your parents, or by running up the balance on your credit card. The accumulated sum of your monthly deficits is the total debt that you owe.

Let's say you have $1,000 to invest. You could invest it in the stock market or buy corporate bonds that provide businesses the money they need to expand, or you could buy government bonds that allow the government to spend your $1,000 with the promise to pay it back later with interest. In the aggregate, this means that if $266 billion is going to fund the federal debt every year, then that $266 billion is not available for private borrowing that could go directly to creating more jobs and generating economic growth.

BALANCE OF PAYMENTS, OR THE CURRENT ACCOUNT

current account The balance of a country's receipts and its payments in international trade and investment.

trade deficit A measure of how much more a nation imports than it exports.

The broadest measure of a nation's balance of payments with the rest of the world is the **current account**: the difference between a nation's receipts (exports and money that Americans earn on foreign investments) and its payments (imports and money that foreigners earn on American investments). The aspect of the current account that gets the most political attention is the **trade deficit**, the difference between imports and exports. The American appetite for foreign goods is huge, and in recent years the United States has gone from being the world's largest creditor nation to the world's largest debtor nation.

There are differences of opinion over whether the United States' debtor status is a problem. Most economists agree that if the current account deficit is driven by a surplus in investments (more foreign investment in America than America has invested overseas), there is no great cause for concern. Although some economists worry about having an increasing share of U.S. businesses and real estate owned by foreign investors, overall this is simply evidence of the strength of the U.S. economy—that is, investors think they can get a greater return on their investments in America than in other countries. However, when the current account deficit is driven by the trade deficit, which is based on consumption rather than investment, this creates longer-term potential economic problems that are not sustainable. We discuss this topic more in the section on trade policy.[9]

TRADE-OFFS BETWEEN ECONOMIC GOALS

One challenge facing economic policy makers is that it is difficult to "have it all." The period of economic growth, low unemployment, and low inflation with falling budget deficits (and a surplus by the end of the decade) and a healthy current account that the United States enjoyed through much of the 1990s was relatively unusual. Typically, at least part of the economy is not performing well, and some goals are not being met. For example, if inflation starts to increase, the Federal Reserve will attempt to bring it down by increasing interest rates. When this happens, the economy slows because businesses are less willing to expand when the cost of borrowing increases; as a result, unemployment increases. Therefore, there is a trade-off, at least in the short run, between stable prices and full employment and economic growth.

Steps to address the trade deficit also conflict with other goals. Politicians are often under pressure to protect American jobs and prevent them from going overseas. But if policy makers impose barriers to free trade to protect domestic products and jobs, this action violates the goal of promoting an efficient free market. Policy makers must tread carefully when addressing economic problems to ensure that they are not making some other problem worse. The next section explores who these policy makers are.

THE KEY PLAYERS IN ECONOMIC POLICY MAKING

> DESCRIBE THE ROLES PLAYED BY EACH OF THE BRANCHES OF GOVERNMENT IN SHAPING ECONOMIC POLICY

Now that we know the goals of economic policy, we need to answer these questions: Who are the key policy makers? What role do they play in shaping American economic policy?

CONGRESS

The Constitution places Congress at the center of economic policy making by giving legislators the "power of the purse"—that is, power over the nation's fiscal policy of taxing and spending. In a way, everything Congress does has an impact on the economy, whether it is providing money for an interstate highway or a student loan, regulating the level of air pollutants, or funding the Social Security system. Some committees are more directly related than others to economic policy: budget, appropriations, and tax committees (Ways and Means in the House and Finance in the Senate; see Chapter 11) direct Congress's **fiscal policy**—taxing and spending. The banking committees have a hand in overseeing aspects of the nation's **monetary policy**—controlling the money supply and interest rates. (However, as we discuss later, monetary policy is primarily the domain of the Federal Reserve System, or "the Fed.") The commerce committees, especially in the House, also have their hand in a range of economic policies. Because it is the most important of Congress's economic policy-making responsibilities, we focus our discussion on the budget-making process.

fiscal policy Government decisions about how to influence the economy by taxing and spending.

monetary policy Government decisions about how to influence the economy using control of the money supply and interest rates.

Budget making in Congress was decentralized through much of its history, with various committees and subcommittees serving as the center of the legislative process and no real way to coordinate activity among them. The appropriations committees tried to be the "guardians of the Treasury," but it was difficult to keep the spending requests from other committees in line with overall budgetary expectations because of the two-step process Congress uses to approve any spending: the authorizing committee writes the law that authorizes the spending and then the appropriations committee approves the level of spending.[10] As a result, budgetary power shifted from Congress to the president, starting with the Budget and Accounting Act of 1921. From that point on, presidents have played a central role in the budget process by submitting their budgets to Congress. The president's budget often serves as the starting point for the congressional budget.

Congress revamped the budget process in 1974 with the Budget and Impoundment Control Act. This law created the budget committees in the House and Senate, set up the budget process (see How It Works: The Budget Process), and established the Congressional Budget Office (CBO). This office gave Congress independent expertise and advice on budgetary matters so it did not have to rely on the president's numbers. For the first time, Congress had the institutional capacity on budgetary matters to deal with the president on an equal footing.

However, the new process and institutions did not guarantee smooth sailing. In fact, Congress had a difficult time meeting the various deadlines, and the new process didn't help eliminate the budget deficits. There was a powerful tool in the 1974 Budget Act that was ignored for the first five years: **budget reconciliation** was first used in 1980 to bring spending levels into line with the budget resolution (which obviously requires that there *is* a budget resolution—eight times since 1974 Congress has failed to adopt the overall budget blueprint, most recently with the 2014 fiscal year budget).[11] This process requires committees to meet specific spending targets, and then all the changes are combined into one omnibus reconciliation bill. This procedure has two advantages in terms of adopting budget cuts—which are always difficult because most programs have strong advocates who oppose the cuts. First, having everything in a single huge bill makes it much more difficult for members to vote against it because that would mean turning down the entire package, including elements of the bill that individual members of Congress like as well as those that they oppose. Depending on the timing, failure to pass an omnibus spending bill may mean shutting down the government. Second, the Senate treats reconciliation bills differently from other bills or amendments. Most important, in the Senate these bills cannot be filibustered—and anything unrelated to deficit reduction can be struck down.[12] (This is an important tool in deficit reduction.) Overall, reconciliation has been used in about two-thirds of the budgets since 1980 and has been responsible for cutting hundreds of billions of dollars of spending. As we discuss in Chapter 16, reconciliation was crucial in passing health care reform in 2010 because it allowed Democrats to avoid a Republican filibuster.

Even the powerful tool of reconciliation was inadequate to address the exploding budget deficits of the early to mid-1980s. So, an additional mechanism was employed in 1990 to give Congress more traction in managing the deficits: a zero-sum, pay-as-you-go (PAYGO) process whereby any new tax cut or spending increase had to be paid for by raising another tax or cutting spending in some other program. The PAYGO procedure, along with the tax increases in President Clinton's 1993 budget, put the nation on the path for the first budget surpluses since the 1960s. By 1999, the budget was balanced, and in 2000 there was a substantial surplus ($86.3 billion) for the first time in nearly 50 years.[13]

How It Works

THE BUDGET PROCESS

1ST MONDAY IN FEB.

The president submits budget request to Congress.

FEB. 15

Congressional Budget Office (CBO) issues budget and economic outlook report.

WITHIN SIX WEEKS OF PRESIDENT'S SUBMISSION

Other committees with budgetary responsibilities submit "views and estimates" to budget committees.

EARLY APR.

House Budget Committee creates its budget resolution and the House votes on it.

Senate Budget Committee creates its budget resolution and the Senate votes on it.

Budget Conference Committee reconciles the House and Senate versions of the budget resolution.

BY APR. 15

House votes on conference version.

Senate votes on conference version.

APPROPRIATIONS

After both houses approve the budget resolution, appropriations committees draft legislation authorizing expenditures to the relevant agencies. Each appropriations bill must be passed by both houses and signed into law by the president. If this process is not completed by October 1, and no temporary measure (a "continuing resolution") is in place, the government will shut down.

OCT. 1

Start of the fiscal year.

How It Works
In Practice

THE 2013 BUDGET BATTLE

While there is a "textbook" path politicians try to follow when passing a budget, they almost always deviate wildly from it. Conflicts over the budget in 2013 reveal how Congress and the executive branch constantly strive for more power and how they use— and deviate from—the rules when it serves their interests.

MAR. 13, 2013 — House Budget Committee passes budget resolution.

MAR. 14, 2013 — Senate Budget Committee passes budget resolution.

MAR. 21, 2013 — Senate passes first budget in four years. After the House passes its budget, regular order dictates that both chambers name members of a conference committee to resolve the differences.

MAR. 23, 2013 — House passes budget resolution.

APR. 10, 2013 — President Obama submits his budget to Congress, about nine weeks late (citing uncertainty caused by the "fiscal cliff" and sequester negotiations).

APR.-AUG. 2013 — House and Senate Republicans block efforts to form a conference committee, saying that the two sides are too far apart to meet. Appropriations committees fail to pass any of the appropriations bills.

MID-SEP. 2013 — House Speaker Boehner's deal for a continuing resolution to keep the government open without a new budget (at last year's spending levels) is shot down by the conservative wing of his party, which wants to defund Obamacare as part of any budget.

OCT. 1, 2013 — All nonessential parts of the government are shut down for 16 days.

DEC. 18, 2013 — Congress passes a two-year budget plan that puts the appropriations committees back in their role in the budget process for the first time in several years.

JAN. 16-17, 2014 — Congress passes a $1.1 billion spending bill over the objections of Tea Party Republicans.

FEB. 12-13, 2014 — For the first time since 2009, Congress raises the debt ceiling (through March 2015) with no conditions.

POP QUIZ

1 When does each house of Congress vote on its own version of a budget resolution?

- **a** the first Monday in February
- **b** February 15
- **c** within 6 weeks of receiving the president's budget proposal
- **d** early April
- **e** October 1

2 If the budget process is not completed by October 1 and no temporary measure is in place

- **a** the president withdraws his proposal.
- **b** both houses of Congress vote on the conference version.
- **c** the government shuts down.
- **d** the start of the fiscal year is postponed until January.
- **e** the appropriations committees draft legislatio

The surpluses evaporated, and massive budget deficits returned in 2002 (the deficit hit $317 billion in 2002 and averaged $475 billion over the next five years). One major contribution to this explosion in the deficits was that PAYGO was allowed to lapse for the 2002 budget—in part to enable funding the war in Iraq and the war on terrorism, but also to make it politically easier to pass additional tax cuts. Without the need to pay for tax cuts or spending increases, it has proved too tempting to let the deficits increase to unsustainable levels. When Democrats regained control of Congress in January 2007, they reinstated the PAYGO rule. However, the PAYGO rule has been routinely suspended whenever Congress wants to extend a popular tax cut or pay for emergency spending, such as drought relief or extending unemployment benefits.[14]

Increased partisan polarization in Congress and differences between Democrats and Republicans in their view of taxing and spending policy makes it difficult to pass a budget in a timely fashion. In recent years, Congress has relied on "continuing resolutions," which keep spending at the level of last year's budget, when they cannot agree on a new budget. Even traditionally noncontroversial aspects of fiscal policy, such as increasing the debt ceiling to authorize government borrowing, have become opportunities for partisan politics.

THE PRESIDENT

Once they are in office, presidents quickly realize that the public expects them to promote a healthy economy. Indeed, the state of the economy has a big impact on the public's assessment of presidential performance, and it also influences election outcomes. President Obama focused on the economy in his first months in office, pushing through a massive stimulus bill; later, in the face of major unemployment, Obama also signed legislation aimed at creating more jobs.

As mentioned in Chapter 12, the president is unable to accomplish much single-handedly on the economic front: Congress, the Fed, and broader domestic and international economic forces all exert an equal or greater influence on the health of the economy. However, the president has a large advising structure to help formulate economic policy. The Office of Management and Budget (OMB), the Council of Economic Advisers (CEA), the Office of the **United States Trade Representative (USTR)**, and the **National Economic Council (NEC)** all provide important economic advice to the president.

The department with the longest track record is the Office of Management and Budget. The OMB plays a central role in creating the budget by soliciting spending requests from all federal agencies, suggesting additional cuts, and then coordinating these requests with presidential priorities. It is ultimately responsible for putting together the president's budget, which is then submitted to Congress. The OMB also oversees government reorganization plans and recommends improvements in departmental operations.

The Council of Economic Advisers was created by the Employment Act of 1946. The CEA's central function is to provide the president with objective data on the state of the economy and expert advice on economic policy. The agency is responsible for creating the *Annual Economic Report of the President*, which has a wealth of data on various aspects of the economy and an overview of the president's policies. Presidents have varied in how closely they work with the CEA or the other parts of their economic team. Some prominent CEA members have been

United States Trade Representative (USTR) An agency founded in 1962 to negotiate with foreign governments to create trade agreements, resolve disputes, and participate in global trade policy organizations. Treaties negotiated by the USTR must be ratified by the Senate.

National Economic Council (NEC) A group of economic advisers created in 1993 to work with the president to coordinate economic policy.

THE REMINDER THAT HUNG ON the wall of Bill Clinton's campaign headquarters in 1992 was just as relevant for President Obama in 2009 when he took office during the deepest economic recession since the 1930s.

influential in shaping and promoting the administration's tax policy and jobs program. Others have had a more secondary role.

The United States Trade Representative is responsible for developing and coordinating U.S. international trade, commodity, and direct investment policy, and for overseeing negotiations on trade policy with other countries.[15] With the increasing importance of globalization, international trade, and Congress's deference to the executive branch on trade issues through the fast-track authority, the USTR is an important player in economic policy making.

The National Economic Council was established in 1993 to fulfill a campaign promise by President Clinton to elevate economic policy to the level of national security and foreign policy. The NEC has four principal functions: "to coordinate policy-making for domestic and international economic issues, to coordinate economic policy advice for the President, to ensure that policy decisions and programs are consistent with the President's economic goals, and to monitor implementation of the President's economic policy agenda."[16] The NEC coordinates policy by bringing together cabinet secretaries who work on economic issues, such as the Treasury secretary, budget director, Commerce secretary, CEA chairman, and Labor secretary. The NEC initially appeared to challenge the CEA's advisers' turf, but a division of labor has preserved an important role for each: the NEC is the political arm that coordinates economic policy, and the CEA is the technical arm that provides information about the economy.

These last two sections have described the roles of Congress and the president separately, but obviously the interactions between these government branches are central to understanding economic policy. If the president's party controls Congress, then the president's budget becomes the starting point for congressional negotiations over the budget. If the opposing party controls Congress, then the president's budget is usually considered "dead on arrival" and Congress creates its own document. Of course, the president can use the veto threat to try to move Congress closer to his position, but when the budget is contained in one large package that must be signed or vetoed in its entirety, it is difficult to carry out such threats.[17]

THE BUREAUCRACY

All the departments explained so far could be considered part of the larger bureaucracy, but they are included within the Executive Office of the President and therefore are usually considered in conjunction with the president. We will focus on two bureaucratic agencies that are key in creating monetary policy: the **Federal Reserve System**, an independent agency; and the **Treasury Department**, a cabinet-level department.

THE FEDERAL RESERVE SYSTEM The Federal Reserve Act of 1913 established the Federal Reserve System (commonly known as the Fed) to bring stability and continuity to the nation's banking system. The chair and six other governors serve on the Board of Governors of the Federal Reserve System. The chair has a four-year term, and the others have 14-year overlapping terms. All governors are appointed by the president and approved by the Senate. The board is responsible for establishing monetary policy for the nation, which includes influencing interest rates and the money supply, and regulating the lending activity of member banks (discussed in more detail later in the chapter). There are 12 regional Federal Reserve banks and more than 2,900 member banks out of the approximately 7,800 banks in the nation.[18] We examine the Fed's operations in the section on monetary policy, but briefly, the regional banks lend money to banks, hold reserves for them, supply currency and coins, buy and sell government securities, and report on the state of the economy in their regions.

One crucial characteristic of the Fed is its political independence, which has three primary sources. First, the Fed is an independent agency: its decisions are not subject to presidential or congressional review. Second, the 14-year terms for the six governors and the four-year term for the chair and vice chair purposefully do not overlap with the federal election calendar. One strong indication of the Fed's independence is that presidents typically reappoint chairs who were initially appointed by presidents of the other party. For example, Ben Bernanke was nominated by Bush and renominated by Obama.[19] Unlike other presidential appointees in the bureaucracy, members of the **Federal Reserve Board** can be removed only

Federal Reserve System An independent agency that serves as the central bank of the United States to bring stability to the nation's banking system.

Treasury Department A cabinet-level agency that is responsible for managing the federal government's revenue. It prints currency, collects taxes, and sells government bonds.

Federal Reserve Board The group of seven presidential appointees who govern the Federal Reserve System.

U.S. FEDERAL RESERVE CHAIR JANET Yellen gives her first testimony to Congress during a House Financial Services Committee hearing on February 11, 2014, a week after she became the first woman to lead the Fed.

THE 1970S WITNESSED ECONOMIC stagnation along with high inflation, yielding the term "stagflation." As the economy started to recover after the 2008–2009 financial crisis, rising prices remained a concern and the possibility of stagflation returned.

WHAT DO POLITICAL SCIENTISTS DO?

For more on how the Fed is insulated from politics, visit **wwnpag.es/wdpsd**

"for cause," the precise definition of which has never been tested. This largely insulates the Fed from the political process.

Third, the Fed does not depend on Congress for its operating budget because it can literally create its own money (see later discussion). Congress's control of the bureaucracy is rooted in the power of the purse (see Chapter 13), but because Congress does not provide the Fed's budget, Congress has much less leverage over it. The Fed's primary source of income is interest on the Treasury securities it owns. After paying for all of its expenses, the Fed returned about $88.4 billion to the Treasury in 2012. Overall, in 2013 the Fed employed 18,656 people with total expenditures of $4.7 billion.[20] The employees are not subject to civil service rules or pay grades; thus, the Fed can offer top salaries and hire some of the best people in finance and economics.

Is the Fed's independence a good thing or a bad thing? Supporters point out that the Fed's central goal is shared by nearly all politicians and Americans: a stable economy and slow, steady growth (the Federal Reserve Reform Act of 1977 gives the Fed a dual mandate of pursuing stable prices and maximum employment). Therefore, the argument goes, we should leave the Fed alone, let it do its job, and keep politics out of monetary policy. However, critics argue that the Fed's lack of accountability means that it can do things that hurt the economy—and voters have no recourse. For example, during Janet Yellen's confirmation hearings in 2013, senators grilled the nominee about the impact of the Fed's policies on the economy. Senator Mike Johanns (R-NE) said the Fed's stimulus had artificially inflated housing prices and the stock market, setting the stage for another bubble and downturn; he said, "I think the economy has gotten used to the sugar you've put out there. And I just worry you're on a sugar high."[21] If this is the impact of the Fed's policies—and that point is debatable—voters can do nothing about it.

But the Fed is not immune to political influence. In fact, one line of research argues that the Fed tries to help presidents during reelection years by encouraging a pro-growth economy.[22] Evidence on this point is mixed, but at a minimum, presidents do have the ability to make it clear when they disagree with the Fed's policies. Presidents also have the opportunity to appoint the chair and vice chair of the Fed, but presidents rarely fire them because they do not want to upset the financial markets. Other research has shown that the Fed is at least somewhat sensitive to the preferences of the president and Congress.[23]

The Fed's ultimate accountability is to Congress, because if things really got out of hand—for example, if the Fed decided to increase interest rates to 20 percent without good reason—Congress could amend the Federal Reserve Act and remove the Fed's responsibility or autonomy in specific areas. The Fed must report to Congress annually on its activities and to the banking committees of Congress twice a year on its plans for monetary policy. The Fed's annual report is subject to an outside audit. Fed officials also frequently testify before Congress on a broad range of issues. And Congress may publicly criticize the Fed when it disagrees with the Fed's policies.

THE TREASURY DEPARTMENT The Treasury Department is another part of the bureaucracy that plays an important role in economic policy making. According to its website, the mission of the Treasury "is to promote the conditions for prosperity and stability in the United States and encourage prosperity and stability in the rest of the world." Specifically, the range of its responsibilities related to economic policy making includes:

- managing federal finances;
- collecting taxes, duties, and monies paid to and due to the United States and paying all bills of the United States;
- producing currency and coinage;
- managing government accounts and the public debt;
- supervising national banks and thrift institutions;
- advising on domestic and international financial, monetary, economic, trade, and tax policy;
- enforcing federal finance and tax laws; and
- investigating and prosecuting tax evaders, counterfeiters, and forgers.[24]

Some of these responsibilities overlap with the Fed's, especially supervising banks and managing the public debt. In most instances the responsibilities are complementary rather than competing, such as the management of currency and coins: the Treasury produces currency at the Bureau of Engraving and Printing (about 26 million bills are printed every day) and coins at the United States Mint (which makes between 10 and 12 *billion* coins a year), and the Fed distributes them to member banks.[25] Financing federal debt is another matter. The Treasury generally prefers to have lower interest rates to keep down the cost of financing the debt and to promote economic growth, whereas the Fed is also concerned about keeping rates high enough to avoid inflation. Therefore, the Fed and Treasury must often coordinate their policies to avoid working at cross-purposes.

HOW ECONOMIC POLICY MAKERS INTERACT: THE 2008 ECONOMIC CRISIS

A dramatic example of cooperation between the Fed and Treasury is the 2008 economic crisis. Problems in the subprime, or high-risk, mortgage market; the collapse of housing prices; and the tightening of credit markets had been putting pressure on the economy through the spring and summer. The first sign of serious trouble came in March 2008 when the New York Federal Reserve made a loan of $30 billion to JP Morgan Chase to facilitate the buyout of Bear Stearns, an investment bank that was going bankrupt because of its exposure to mortgage-backed securities. Concerns deepened in September, when the federal government took over the Federal National Mortgage Association and the Federal Home Mortgage Corporation because they were about to go under. These two government-sponsored enterprises, nicknamed "Fannie Mae" and "Freddie Mac," fund most of the home loans in the nation. This federal acquisition, involving a commitment of $200 billion to back up Fannie's and Freddie's assets, was "one of the most sweeping government interventions in private financial markets in decades."[26] The takeover calmed the credit markets for a few days, until it became evident that two Wall Street giants, the investment banks Lehman Brothers and Merrill Lynch, were becoming financially unstable because of subprime mortgage exposure and other bad debt. Lehman Brothers went bankrupt; Merrill Lynch was bought by Bank of America, and the markets panicked.

DURING THE FINANCIAL CRISIS OF 2008–2009, the government had to take unprecedented action to avoid an even deeper crisis. Here, then–Senate majority leader Harry Reid (D-NV) speaks to reporters. He was joined by other congressional leaders and Ben Bernanke (far right), who was Federal Reserve chairman at the time.

The next day, September 16, 2008, brought more bad news: the world's largest insurance company, American International Group (AIG), was also deep in the subprime mess and teetering on the edge of bankruptcy, so the Fed stepped in with an $85 billion loan to save it. Despite these dramatic moves, credit markets seized up, and investors started pulling money out of any institution remotely related to the financial crisis. A few days later, Washington Mutual, the nation's sixth-largest bank, failed. This series of disasters and near-disasters led to around-the-clock meetings of Fed and Treasury leaders who produced a plan for the government to buy mortgage-related assets from banks and other financial institutions. The three-page proposal was a sweeping request for Congress to grant the Treasury secretary unprecedented, unilateral powers to spend taxpayers' money. Congressional leaders embraced the idea of helping financial institutions deal with their bad debt, but they questioned the lack of oversight and accountability in the proposal.

Congressional leaders hammered out a compromise bailout bill and then put it up for a vote, assuming that they had enough votes to pass it. In a stunning rebuke to party leaders and President Bush, the House defeated the $700 billion bailout bill by a vote of 205 to 228, with 133 Republicans and 95 Democrats opposing it. The stock market plummeted by 7 percent in the hours following the bill's failure. Analysis of the House vote showed that two factors were central to the bill's failure to pass: ideology and electoral vulnerability. It was a coalition of the "ends against the middle," with extreme liberals and conservatives voting against it and moderates voting for it. Politically vulnerable members also voted against the unpopular bill, believing their constituents viewed it as an unfair bailout of Wall Street.

Throughout this economic crisis, which was the worst since the Great Depression, Fed Chair Ben Bernanke and Treasury Secretary Henry Paulson worked together to restore confidence in financial institutions.[27] Secretary Paulson said, "The financial security of all Americans—their retirement savings, their home values, their ability to borrow for college and the opportunities for more and higher-paying jobs—depends on our ability to restore our financial institutions to a sound footing."[28] Congressional leaders picked up this theme, emphasizing the benefits of the plan for "Main Street" rather than just for Wall Street. They emphasized that small businesses were having a hard time getting short-term loans to meet their payrolls and that individuals were getting turned down for loans to buy cars or to fund college tuition. Legislators even started calling the plan a "rescue" rather than a "bailout."

The Senate took the lead on retooling the bill, given the House's earlier inability to act. Wanting to ensure a solid majority behind the bill, leaders added sweeteners (such as increasing the amount of savings insured by the federal government from $100,000 to $250,000 per account to help restore confidence in regular savings accounts) and imposed more accountability (by limiting to $350 billion the amount of mortgage-related assets the Treasury secretary could buy without congressional authorization; Congress could approve an additional $350 billion). The Senate passed the bill by a bipartisan 75-to-24 vote.[29] Two days later the House passed the bill by a 263-to-171 vote, with strong support from both parties.[30] President Bush signed the Emergency Economic Stabilization Act into law on October 3, 2008. The Troubled Asset Relief Program (TARP) was established under the Act to buy up to $700 billion in bad assets to help stabilize the banks.

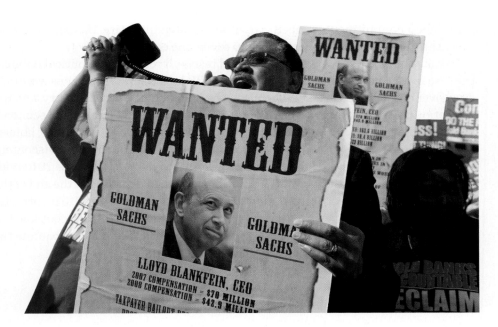

Despite this significant rescue plan, the crisis spiraled out of control in the following weeks. Stock markets plunged worldwide, with the U.S. stock market shedding 35 percent of its value in the two months after the crisis began. Credit markets remained frozen, and it became clear that an alternative approach was needed. The government's purchase of "toxic debt" posed many technical obstacles, and financial markets had no confidence that the plan would work. European leaders swiftly agreed to an approach in which governments would directly invest in banks, providing them with desperately needed capital in return for equity stakes in the banks. The United States followed suit with an initial allocation of $250 billion to directly invest in banks, followed by an announcement that the Treasury would abandon its plan to buy toxic debt and use all the funds to directly invest in banks. By mid-November, the economic panic had eased, but the situation remained fragile.

When President Obama took office in 2009, things were still very grim. Stocks finally bottomed in March 2009 (down 56 percent from their October 2007 high), shortly after Treasury Secretary Timothy Geithner announced the administration's Financial Stability Plan. The plan focused on four problems: frozen credit markets, weakened bank capital, a backlog of troubled mortgage assets on bank balance sheets, and falling home prices. Working with the Fed to stabilize the financial markets, the Treasury had largely resolved three of those four problems one year later. Credit markets were operating, and banks were in much better shape, having raised more than $140 billion in capital and $60 billion in unsecured debt. Banks used these funds to repay the Treasury, which as of June 2014, had shown an 18 percent profit to the government. The Treasury expects to eventually recover all of the TARP expenditures (with 99.4 percent recovered to date).[31] The housing market, though not fully recovered, has also stabilized, with sales up and prices steady in most markets. Troubled mortgage assets remained on the balance sheets of many banks, but with their stronger base of capital and the strengthened housing market, these securities were not as great a concern as they had been a year earlier.[32] In September 2012, the Fed announced a new policy to inject money into the economy, promising to buy $40 billion a month of mortgage-backed securities. Three months later this policy was increased to $85 billion a month. This was an open-ended commitment, dubbed "QE-infinity" (Quantitative Easing), and was seen as the boldest move yet by the Fed to revive the economy.

Despite the broad success of the financial rescue, it remained a political liability. The rescue was widely perceived as a bailout of Wall Street. Many citizens were outraged over corporate salaries and bonuses, the bailout of the auto industry, and the perception that not enough was being done to help average Americans. The economy lost 8.4 million jobs in 2008–2009, millions of Americans were losing their homes, and unemployment remained stuck around 9.5 percent through 2010. Discontent with the bailout contributed to the crushing defeat for Democrats in the 2010 midterm elections, despite the fact that it was a bipartisan plan passed at the end of the Bush administration. Exit polls showed that 47 percent of voters in 2010 incorrectly thought that the bailout was passed under Obama, while only 34 percent knew it was under Bush and 19 percent said they didn't know.[33] The financial rescue and the regulation of Wall Street remained pertinent issues in the 2012 elections.

TOOLS AND THEORIES OF ECONOMIC POLICY

Now that we know the key players in economic policy, and their goals, it is time to examine the tools those policy makers use to accomplish those goals. Policy makers cannot pull levers and push buttons to achieve desired outcomes, nor are they immune from external forces that can sink the economy despite their best efforts. However, there are certain things that leaders can do to move the massive U.S. economy in the right direction.

FISCAL POLICY

Keynesian economics The theory that governments should use economic policy, like taxing and spending, to maintain stability in the economy.

Fiscal policy is the use of the government's taxing and spending power to influence the direction of the economy. Developed by economist John Maynard Keynes in the 1930s, **Keynesian economics** argues that policy makers can soften the effects of a recession by stimulating the economy when overall demand is low—during a recession, when people aren't spending as much—through tax cuts or increased government spending. Tax cuts put more money in people's pockets, allowing them to spend more than they otherwise would, whereas government spending stimulates the economy through the purchase of various goods, such as highways or military equipment, or direct payments to individuals, for example, Social Security checks. From this perspective, it is acceptable to run budget deficits in order to increase employment and national income to give a short-term boost to the economy. Keynes also pointed out that if overall demand is too high, which might result in inflation, policy makers should cool off the economy by cutting spending or raising taxes.[34]

STRATEGIES TO STIMULATE THE ECONOMY Perhaps the best example of a Keynesian tax cut used to stimulate the economy was the Revenue Act of 1964. The politics of getting the bill passed were tricky: in contrast to today's partisan politics, liberal Democrats favored the tax cuts to stimulate the economy, and conservative Republicans opposed them because they were afraid of ballooning deficits. But extensive lobbying by President Johnson eventually led to strong bipartisan support.[35] The tax cut, one of the largest in the twentieth century, helped lay the foundation for unprecedented economic expansion in the 1960s.[36]

A more recent version of fiscal policy was the basis for Ronald Reagan's tax cuts in 1981 and has been the centerpiece of economic policy for many Republicans since then. **Supply-side economics** focuses on the ways that tax policy and regulations affect the labor supply rather than on the impact of these policies on overall demand. The primary focus was on how tax rates affect how much people work rather than how they spend. The idea is based on the relationship between the top **marginal tax rate** and total tax revenue as shown in the Laffer curve, named for economist Arthur Laffer. If tax rates are too high, people will work less because a large percentage of their income is going to the government. The basic shape of the curve is intuitive, and the endpoints are noncontroversial: if the tax rate is zero, there will be no tax revenue; if the tax rate is 100 percent, nobody will work because they won't get to keep any of their money, so total tax revenue at that end of the curve is also zero.[37] Laffer argued that if tax rates are too high (to the right of the peak in the graph; see Figure 15.4), the government should cut taxes in order to raise total government revenue, which is counterintuitive.[38]

It was too good to be true. When taxes were cut, with the top marginal rate going from 70 to 50 percent, revenue fell and the budget deficits exploded. Supporters of the supply-side theory argue that the problem was on the spending side of the equation rather than with tax revenue. That is, deficits went up because the Democratic Congress spent too much, not because of Reagan's tax cuts. However, taxes and spending as a share of the overall economy both fell during the Reagan presidency, which suggests that spending was not the source of the budget deficits in the 1980s.[39] A similar relationship between cutting tax rates and falling revenue could be observed with the Bush tax cuts in 2001.

supply-side economics The theory that lower tax rates will stimulate the economy by encouraging people to save, invest, and produce more goods and services.

marginal tax rate The tax rate paid on income up to some threshold. For example, in 2014 single people paid no income tax on their first $10,150 in income (because of the $6,900 standard deduction and $3,950 personal exemption); after deductions, you would pay 10 percent on the first $9,075, 15 percent on income between $9,075 and $36,900, all the way up to 39.6 percent on income over $406,750.

FIGURE » 15.4

THE LAFFER CURVE

The Laffer curve shows the theoretical relationship between the tax rate and total tax revenue. How did this curve contribute to the budget deficits of the 1980s?

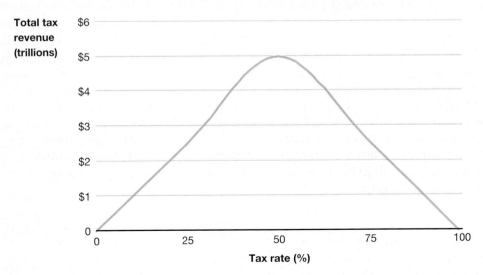

business cycle The normal
pattern of expansion and
contraction of the economy.

Economists continue to debate the extent to which fiscal policy can influence the economy. Two factors have limited the effectiveness of fiscal policy. First, fiscal policies often cannot be implemented quickly enough to have the intended impact on the **business cycle**—the normal expansion and contraction of the economy. This is especially true when one party controls Congress and the other controls the presidency, but it happens even during unified government.

The $787 billion American Recovery and Reinvestment Act of 2009, designed to stimulate the economy and create jobs, ran into problems along these lines. Although the legislation had some immediate impact on the economy, it is impossible to spend that much money (or implement tax cuts) without some time lag. The website that tracks the spending of the stimulus money, Recovery.gov, reports that of the $787 billion, tax cuts comprise $288 billion; contracts, grants, and loans are $275 billion; and entitlements are $224 billion. One year after the recovery bill was enacted, the government reported that nearly 600,000 jobs had been saved but only 34.6 percent of the money had been spent ($272.2 billion). Republicans criticized the Democrats for spending too much money and not enacting policies that would have had a more immediate effect (such as payroll tax cuts), and critics on the left argued that the stimulus wasn't big enough. A payroll tax cut was implemented for 2011–2012 that reduced the rate from 6.2 to 4.2 percent, putting an additional $1,000 in the pocket of the average American household for each of those years.

Second, on the other side of the Keynesian coin, increasing taxes or cutting spending during good economic times is much more difficult to implement than the more politically popular tax cuts or spending increases. Although the latter is limited by the difficulty of timing the fiscal policy to have a maximum economic impact, the former is limited by politics: politicians do not like to raise taxes or cut spending. Furthermore, even if politicians *wanted* to cut spending, this aspect of fiscal policy is becoming increasingly difficult to use because a growing portion of the federal budget is devoted to **mandatory spending**—that is, entitlements such as Social Security, which must be spent by law, and interest on the federal debt, which must be paid (if the United States defaulted on its debt, there would be an international economic meltdown). So reducing the federal deficit by cutting spending is increasingly difficult.

mandatory spending
Expenditures that are required
by law, such as the funding for
Social Security.

With the 2014 deficit at $531 billion, Congress would have to eliminate all nondefense **discretionary spending**—spending that can be cut from the budget without changing the underlying law—which is everything other than defense, entitlements, and interest on the debt ($528 billion), to balance the budget. This would literally mean shutting down the State Department; Homeland Security; the Justice Department, which includes the FBI and all federal law enforcement; and the Interior Department, which includes the National Park Service and the National Forest Service; and eliminating all spending on science, including the National Science Foundation and NASA; transportation; the arts and public broadcasting; student loans; as well as the food stamps and child nutrition programs. The share of the budget allotted to discretionary spending is projected to fall from 67.6 percent of the budget in 1962 to only 31.2 percent by 2015 (see Figure 15.5). This has clear implications for efforts to balance the budget in the future: it cannot be done through cutting discretionary spending alone but will have to include cuts in mandatory spending (such as Social Security and Medicare) and tax increases.

discretionary spending
Expenditures that can be cut from
the budget without changing the
underlying law, which is everything other than defense, entitlements, and interest on the debt.

Given this tenuous relationship between fiscal policy and the state of the economy, critics have suggested an alternative rationale for large budget deficits

FIGURE » 15.5

MANDATORY AND DISCRETIONARY SPENDING, 1962–2015

The percentage of the budget allocated for discretionary spending has been shrinking since the 1960s. What implications does this have for members of Congress and the president as they try to reduce the federal deficits?

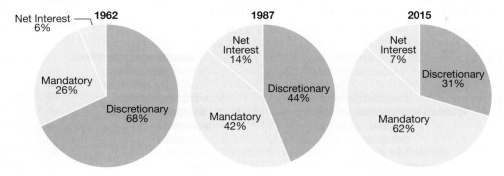

SOURCE: Congressional Budget Office, *An Analysis of the President's 2015 Budget*, April 2014, Table 2, p. 4, www.cbo.gov/sites/default/files/cbofiles/attachments/45230-APB_0.pdf (accessed 7/16/14).

in relatively good economic times. (Recall that a Keynesian account says that the government should run surpluses during good times, and supply-siders argue that tax cuts should produce surpluses rather than deficits.) Instead of being an effort to stimulate the economy, the large tax cuts and budget deficits of the 1980s and early 2000s were, as Reagan's budget director David Stockman called it, an attempt to "starve the beast."[40] That is, large deficits are the only way to cut down the size of government. If there is no money available, liberals will not be able to propose new programs, and conservatives will be more likely to cut existing programs. The only alternative is raising taxes, which is usually politically unpopular, even though our tax bite is relatively small compared to that of other countries (see Figure 15.6). The other possibility, of course, is simply to accept large budget deficits as a permanent part of the economic landscape. Although that may be politically tempting, it is not a sustainable strategy in the long run.

REDISTRIBUTIVE IMPLICATIONS OF FISCAL POLICY Fiscal policy may have a relatively modest impact on the economy, but it determines how the tax burden is distributed and which parts of the economy and policy areas benefit from federal spending. In other words, fiscal policy has *redistributive* implications. There are two ways of thinking about the characteristics of federal taxes: (1) the different types of taxes and (2) their redistributive nature—that is, whether a specific tax is regressive, neutral, or progressive. There are four major types of federal taxes: personal income taxes, corporate taxes, payroll taxes (for Social Security and Medicare), and excise taxes (such as taxes on cigarettes, alcohol, gasoline, air travel, and telephone lines). The pie charts in Figure 15.7 show how the distribution of tax revenue changed between 1962 and 2014. The proportion of personal income taxes held relatively steady, but excise taxes and corporate taxes fell, and payroll taxes more than doubled.

The increasing share of tax revenue that comes from the payroll tax has important implications for the redistributive nature of taxes. Payroll taxes are

FIGURE » 15.6

COMPARING GLOBAL TAX RATES

Tax rates vary considerably around the world. Given the data below, do you feel that taxes in the United States are too low or too high?

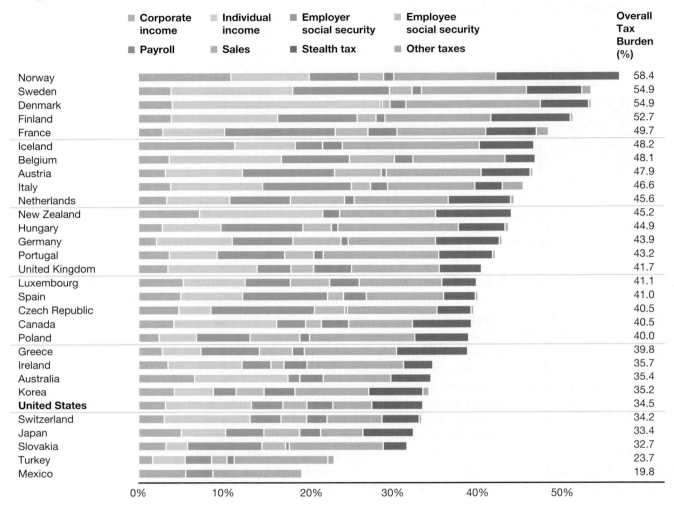

| | Corporate income | Individual income | Employer social security | Employee social security |
| Payroll | Sales | Stealth tax | Other taxes |

Country	Overall Tax Burden (%)
Norway	58.4
Sweden	54.9
Denmark	54.9
Finland	52.7
France	49.7
Iceland	48.2
Belgium	48.1
Austria	47.9
Italy	46.6
Netherlands	45.6
New Zealand	45.2
Hungary	44.9
Germany	43.9
Portugal	43.2
United Kingdom	41.7
Luxembourg	41.1
Spain	41.0
Czech Republic	40.5
Canada	40.5
Poland	40.0
Greece	39.8
Ireland	35.7
Australia	35.4
Korea	35.2
United States	34.5
Switzerland	34.2
Japan	33.4
Slovakia	32.7
Turkey	23.7
Mexico	19.8

SOURCE: Jack Anderson, "Tax Burden and Spending," *Forbes Magazine*, April 3, 2009, www.forbes.com/global/2009/0413/034-tax-burden-spending.html (accessed 5/15/12).

regressive Taxes that take a larger share of poor people's income than wealthy people's income, such as sales taxes and payroll taxes.

regressive because everyone who works pays the same rate of 6.2 percent, up to a certain income level ($117,100 in 2014; in addition, all workers pay an additional 1.45 percent on all income to support Medicare). Thus, someone who earns $117,100 pays the same *amount* of Social Security tax ($7,254) as a wealthy individual such as Bill Gates does, but the tax represents a much larger share of the lesser-paid person's income than it does for Gates's. During the 2008 presidential campaign, Barack Obama proposed lifting the earnings cap on the payroll tax to address this inequality and placing Social Security on a more secure financial foundation, but the proposal has not been widely supported, even among Democrats. Excise taxes are also regressive—poor people spend a larger portion of their income on cigarettes, alcohol, and gas than wealthier people do. Income taxes, in

FIGURE » 15.7

FEDERAL REVENUES AND SPENDING, 1962 AND 2014

A much larger share of tax revenue comes from payroll taxes than was true in the 1960s. What implications does this have for the redistributive nature of federal taxes? What have been the biggest changes since the 1960s in the way the federal tax dollar is spent? Are these trends likely to reverse or continue in the next 30 years?

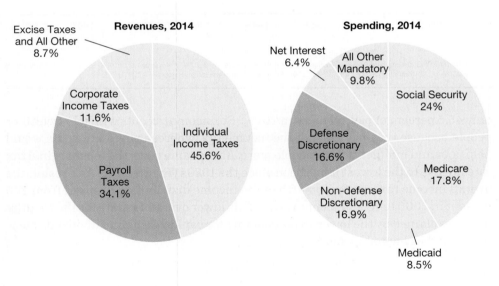

SOURCE: Congressional Budget Office, "Updated Budget Projections: 2014 to 2024," April 2014 Baseline, Tables 1, 2, and 3, April 14, 2014, www.cbo.gov/publication/45069 (accessed 6/12/14).

contrast, are **progressive**: upper-income people pay a larger share of their income in taxes than poorer people.

One criticism of President Bush's tax cuts in 2001 and 2002 was that a disproportionate share of the cuts went to the wealthiest people in the country, making taxes less progressive. This may make sense from one perspective, given that the bottom 40 percent of taxpayers do not pay any personal income tax. However, poor and lower-middle-income people do pay a large share of the total payroll tax. Thus, the top fifth of the income distribution paid 92.9 percent of all income taxes but

progressive Taxes that require upper-income people to pay a higher tax rate than lower-income people, such as income taxes.

FIGURE » 15.8

TOP MARGINAL TAX RATES, 1913–2014

The top marginal tax rate, which is the tax rate paid by the richest Americans on their income above some threshold ($406,750 in 2014 for a single taxpayer), has plummeted in the past 50 years from more than 90 percent to 35 percent in 2012 and then back up to 39.6 percent in 2013 and 2014. What are the arguments for and against increasing the top marginal tax rate?

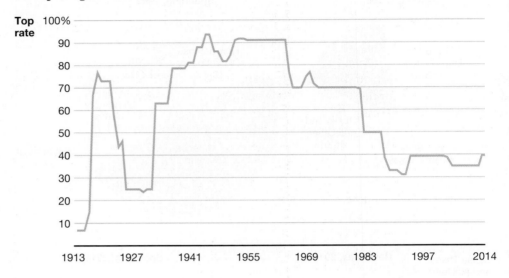

SOURCES: Data from the Internal Revenue Service, "Internal Revenue Bulletin: 2007-45," November 5, 2007, Rev. Proc. 2007-66, www.irs .gov/irb/2007-45_IRB/ar19.html (accessed 5/12/12), 2008–2014 rates from www.irs.gov (accessed 6/12/14).

only 45.5 percent of payroll taxes in 2010.[41] So, income tax cuts will help wealthier people because they pay most of the income tax, whereas payroll tax cuts would help poor and middle-income people more. At the same time, the top marginal tax rate is close to the lowest it has been since the 1920s (Figure 15.8). As a result, the overall income tax rate for top fifth of the income distribution dropped from 17.5 percent in 2000 to 13.8 percent in 2010. This lower overall tax rate for the wealthy is also explained by the lower 15 percent rate for capital gains and dividends mentioned in the chapter opener.[42]

MONETARY POLICY

The starting point of this discussion is to define money. You are probably thinking that you know what the green stuff in your wallet is. You may wish you had more of it, but you know what it is. But if you think about it, money is much more than bills and coins. You probably pay for more things with plastic (debit and credit cards) than with coins and currency. Are those cards "money" as well? Economists categorize debit cards as money because debit cards represent the money you already have in your checking account—which *is* the same as cash. Credit cards are not considered money because when you use a credit card you are, in essence, getting a short-term loan. Broader definitions of money also include savings accounts and certificates of deposit. So far, so good. The tricky part involves understanding where money comes from. The answer may seem simple: the government prints it. But what about the banking part? If you haven't ever thought this through, it can be confusing or even unsettling.

Consider this example: you have just graduated from college and you want to start your own business as a political consultant. You have volunteered on several campaigns and have even run a few statewide campaigns. Two candidates want to hire you for the next election cycle, but you need to rent an office and buy computers, phones, and other office equipment. This will obviously take some money. So, you go to a bank with your business proposal and show them your contracts for the coming election and your plan for repaying the $100,000 loan that you are requesting. To your surprise, the loan officer says yes, and you leave the bank with a checkbook and debit card $100,000 strong! The bank just created $100,000, seemingly out of thin air.[43] How can that be? Doesn't money have to be something more tangible? Doesn't it have to be based on gold or other real assets rather than just a contractual promise to repay the money? No—at least not in this country. In 1933, the United States ended the ability to convert dollars to gold; then in 1971, the country completely abandoned the gold standard. Why doesn't the whole system fall apart? Because it is based on trust and confidence in the banking system. After you receive your loan from the bank, you could go directly to the computer store and purchase $10,000 worth of computers with your new debit card. And because your debit card purchase will be electronically authorized at the cash register, the sales staff will have no reason to ask where your money came from. They would just give you the computers.

Most people rarely think about how the banking system works, simply assuming that their money is safe. But now that we have gotten you thinking about where money comes from, we will provide more details about the banking system by examining the targets and tools of monetary policy.

TARGETS OF MONETARY POLICY The Fed monitors levels of bank lending, the money supply, and interest rates and tries to meet specific targets set at its monthly meetings. Bank lending is important to monitor and regulate because it is the source of most new money in the economy. This is crucial for economic growth because businesses borrow money to expand, and as they grow, they add jobs. If credit is tight and businesses cannot borrow money, economic growth will suffer, as became painfully evident in late 2008 and 2009. Large public corporations can raise money by selling shares of their company in the stock market, but small businesses do not have this option.

The second target of monetary policy, the money supply, is also central to economic growth and directly related to levels of lending activity. The Fed can influence the amount of money in the system by making it easier or harder for banks to lend money. According to the **monetarist theory** of macroeconomic policy, the amount of money in circulation is the most important determinant of economic activity and inflation. If there is too much money chasing too few goods, there could be inflationary pressure on the economy and prices might rise too quickly.[44] In contrast, if there isn't enough money available, a recession could occur.

Perhaps the most obvious targets of monetary policy are interest rates. Changing interest rates affect the economy by making borrowing money either cheaper or more expensive. Businesses and consumers are more likely to borrow if the interest rate is 6 percent than if it is 12 percent. Consumer purchases of big-ticket items, those things that are financed by borrowing rather than being purchased

UNTIL 1971, EACH U.S. DOLLAR WAS backed by a specific amount of gold. In the late 1800s, presidential candidate William Jennings Bryan railed against the burdensome "cross of gold" and argued for a silver-backed currency. But since 1971, the value of the U.S. dollar depends not on gold or silver but on the banking system and international currency markets.

monetarist theory The idea that the amount of money in circulation (the money supply) is the primary influence on economic activity and inflation.

with cash, also increase when interest rates are low. These purchases dry up when interest rates are high. That is why so many appliance stores and car dealers advertise, "Zero dollars down, and zero percent interest until next January!" Entire sectors of the economy, such as housing, construction, consumer durables, and cars, are very sensitive to interest rates.

TOOLS OF MONETARY POLICY What can the Fed do to meet targets it sets on credit availability, the money supply, and interest rates? There are three central tools of monetary policy. The **reserve requirement** is the most obvious and potentially powerful tool for affecting the availability of credit, but it isn't used as often as the other two tools. Banks are required to have a certain amount of money in reserve to make sure they have cash on hand to cover withdrawals. If everyone decided to take all their money out at once, the banking system would collapse, because banks are required to have only 10 percent of all deposits on reserve.

By simply changing the amount of money that banks are required to hold for every deposit, the Fed can have a big impact on the amount of money that banks can lend. For example, requiring banks to hold 15 percent of all deposits in reserve instead of 10 percent would contract the amount of money those institutions could lend, whereas dropping the requirement to 5 percent would have the opposite effect. However, because changing the reserve requirement has such a powerful impact on the economy, the Fed has rarely used this tool.[45]

Interest rates are more difficult to manage than the reserve requirement. With the reserve requirement, the Fed simply announces the change in the rate. With interest rates, there is only one rate—the **discount rate**—that the Fed sets directly. This is the rate that the Fed charges member banks for short-term loans. However, it is far less important as a policy tool than the **federal funds rate (FFR)**, the rate that member banks charge one another on overnight loans, which are the short-term loans that banks use to meet their reserve requirements. Beginning in 1995, the FFR has been the central interest rate target for the Fed.[46] The FFR is set by the demand for overnight loans that are necessary to settle accounts, but the Fed greatly affects those rates.

To make this process clearer, let's go back to our example of the enterprising campaign consultant who got the $100,000 loan. If the bank that gave the loan also had some unexpected withdrawals during that business day, its "vault cash" at the end of the day may have been short of the 10 percent reserve requirement. The bank would have to go to the federal funds market and borrow money from a bank that had excess reserves on that given day. This process of borrowing and lending allows money to flow smoothly throughout the banking system. If reserves are tight all around the country, the price of the short-term loans will be bid up and the FFR will rise. If this happens, the Fed can inject more reserves into the system to keep the FFR at its target (we explain how that happens in the next section). The FFR has a broader impact on the economy because many short-term interest rates track the FFR quite closely.

Despite the Fed's ability to influence short-term interest rates, it has only indirect impact on long-term interest rates, including consumer rates such as mortgages and student loans. These rates are set by the market—specifically by the expectations of the bond market for inflation. If an investor thinks that inflation will increase from 3 percent to 6 percent over the next five years, the investor will demand a higher interest rate for lending his money to the government or a corporation than if he thinks inflation will hold steady at about 3 percent. For example, starting in June 2004, the Fed raised the target FFR 17 times in quarter-point

reserve requirement The minimum amount of money that a bank is required to have on hand to back up its assets.

discount rate The interest rate that a bank must pay on a short-term loan from the Federal Reserve Bank.

federal funds rate (FFR) The interest rate that a bank must pay on an overnight loan from another bank.

increments from 1 percent to 5.25 percent by June 2006. Short-term consumer rates, such as the prime interest rate (the loan rate given to banks' best customers), rose in lockstep with the FFR from 4 percent to 8.25 percent over that period. However, long-term rates, such as the 10-year Treasury note, experienced major fluctuation, actually *falling* from May 2004 to June 2005 by three-fourths of a percentage point at the same time the FFR had *increased* by 2.25 percent, much to the surprise of many financial experts.[47] Clearly the bond market felt confident that long-term inflation was being held in check, because it did not demand higher interest rates for long-term loans. Similarly, when the Fed lowered the FFR in 2008 to fight the recession and credit market freeze, the short-term rates followed. Long-term rates also initially dropped but then increased through much of 2009 as inflation fears picked up, only to fall to record lows in 2012 and to remain low through 2014 as those concerns dissipated.[48]

The last tool that the Fed uses to meet its monetary targets is **open market operations**—the buying and selling of securities. This is the most important tool because it influences the FFR and the level of bank reserves, and thus the money supply. If the Fed wants to increase the money supply and put downward pressure on the FFR, it will purchase securities such as government bonds from a bank. The bank gives the Fed its bond, and the Fed deposits the appropriate amount of money into the bank's account at the Fed. The bank can use this money to support new loans. Where does the Fed gets its money to buy the bond from the bank? Well, the Fed simply creates the money. You probably have heard the claim that if the government wants to, it could just "print money" to pay for its programs and policies. That claim is literally true, but it would be completely irresponsible. Any government that would run the printing presses to pay for its programs, rather than raising the money through taxes, fees, and borrowing, would soon find itself with hyperinflation as experienced in Germany, Poland, Austria, and Hungary after World War I. (The worst inflation ever recorded was in Hungary after World War II: between July 1945 and August 1946, prices rose by a factor of 30,000,000,000,000,000,000,000,000,000!)[49] Our government prints money only to meet the demand for currency from its member banks. However, the Fed's purchase of a government security is like "printing money" and has the same potential inflationary impact, so this powerful tool must be used only when new money is needed in the system. The tool may also be used to contract the money supply or raise interest rates; if this is the desired outcome, the Fed will sell government securities. The member bank will give the Fed money to cover the cost of the bond and therefore take money out of circulation.

In 2008, the supply of new money in the economy was significantly limited, a result of the subprime mortgage market meltdown and related problems in the bond markets. Fed Chair Ben Bernanke responded to this "credit crunch" by "flooding the street with money," just as the famous banker Benjamin Strong had anticipated as the appropriate response to the Great Depression.[50] The Fed increased its balance sheet (its statement of assets and liabilities) from $927 billion on September 10, 2008, to an eye-popping $2.26 trillion by November 11, 2008. About $1.6 trillion of the money injected into the economy came through efforts to stabilize short-term lending, money market funds, and the bailout of AIG (among other things). By October 2012, those loans had been almost entirely repaid as credit markets stabilized. However, overall Fed assets remained at $2.26 trillion, as the securities held by the Fed climbed from

open market operations
The process by which the Federal Reserve System buys and sells securities to influence the money supply.

HYPERINFLATION IN GERMANY, Hungary, and other parts of Europe between the two world wars was so high that some countries' currency became essentially worthless. In Germany in 1923, it was cheaper to burn money than to buy wood, as this woman demonstrates—using several million deutsche marks as kindling.

$514 billion to $2 trillion from February 2009 to September 2010 (including $1.1 trillion in mortgage-backed securities that the Fed purchased from stressed financial institutions).[51] Early in 2013, the Fed continued to expand its injection of money into the economy by purchasing an additional $1.3 trillion in securities; as of mid-2014, the Fed had $2.4 trillion in government securities and $1.6 trillion in mortgage-backed securities.[52] This unprecedented intervention in the financial sector clearly prevented a serious crisis, but as noted, critics argue that the Fed has become a too powerful, unaccountable player in economic policy making.

REGULATORY POLICY

Government regulation has a huge impact on the economy. For example, the federal government regulates the quality of food and water, the safety of workplaces and airspaces, and the integrity of the banking and finance system. In general, regulations address market failures such as monopolies, imperfect information, and negative externalities (explained later). There are two main types of regulation: economic and social. Economic regulation sets prices or conditions on entry of firms into an industry, whereas social regulation addresses issues of quality and safety.[53]

ECONOMIC AND SOCIAL REGULATION A common type of economic regulation concerns price regulation of monopolies. A monopoly occurs when a single firm controls the entire market for a product; thus, it is not subject to competition. In this situation, the firm with the monopoly could charge extremely high prices if the government did not regulate it. Sometimes a "natural monopoly" occurs because getting into a specific business is so costly that it only makes sense to have one company. For example, to have more than one water company in a given town or city would not make sense because it costs so much to install water pipes and other necessary infrastructure. In this instance there is only one company, but the government regulates the prices that the company can charge; alternatively, the water system may be owned by the local government.

When the competitive situation is not a natural monopoly, a large firm may act in a monopolistic way to restrict competition—for example, by slashing prices to drive the competition out of business. As soon as all competitors go out of business, the monopoly is free to raise prices again. Concern about this type of behavior led to the first two significant laws aimed at economic regulation: the Interstate Commerce Act (1887), which created the Interstate Commerce Commission to regulate railroad rates, and the Sherman Antitrust Act (1890), which served to break up Standard Oil in 1910, among other monopolies.

More common than a true monopoly is the situation where a firm that controls most but not all of a market starts acting like a monopoly. For example, in 1998, Microsoft was sued by the Justice Department and 19 states for trying to quash its competition in the rapidly growing area of Internet browsers. Microsoft claimed that Internet Explorer (IE) was an integral part of its Windows operating system, whereas government prosecutors argued that IE was a separate piece of

SOCIAL REGULATIONS HAVE economic effects. For example, although most people want a cleaner environment and less pollution, regulations that reduce pollution impose costs on companies.

software that was being given away for free, putting competitors like Netscape at a huge disadvantage. The district court judge agreed with the Justice Department and ordered that Microsoft be broken up into a Windows-based company and another company that would sell Internet Explorer and other programs. This ruling was overturned on appeal. In the meantime, George W. Bush was elected to his first term as president, and his Justice Department announced that it would not challenge the appeals court ruling. Instead, it proposed a settlement that required Microsoft to share its application programming interfaces with third-party companies.[54] This settlement was challenged by several states but upheld by an appeals court in 2004.

MICROSOFT FOUNDER BILL GATES testifies before Congress. The Justice Department sued Microsoft for antitrust violations.

The Microsoft example offers two lessons. First, regulation affects our daily lives in ways that may not be obvious. The extent to which Microsoft dominates the software industry is determined, in part, by the extent to which the government regulates the company's behavior. Second, politics plays a key role in this process. An important event in the Microsoft case was the election of a president who took a less aggressive stance on regulating potential monopolies than his predecessor had. Recall that Republicans tend to favor a strong role for the free market and advocate a pro-business perspective, which both require a smaller role for government regulation, whereas Democrats generally favor more government regulation to protect the interests of consumers (in the Microsoft case, these interests would have led to a broader range of options for Internet browsers), the environment, and workers.

The most common market failures that lead to social regulation are negative externalities: when the costs of a firm's behavior are not entirely borne by the firm but are passed on to other people. When this happens, the firm produces more of an unwanted good than is socially desirable. The classic example is pollution. In a free market, the owners of a coal-fired power plant do not bear the cost of the pollution spewing out of its smokestacks. The people who live downwind from the plant bear the cost. Therefore, the power plant owners have little incentive to curb pollution unless the government regulates it. Other examples of agencies that set social regulations are those that promote safety, such as the National Highway Traffic Safety Administration, the Consumer Product Safety Commission, and the Occupational Safety and Health Administration. Carbon emissions are another good example of a product (carbon) that will be overproduced by the market if there are no regulations.

THE POLITICS OF REGULATION Regulatory policy also involves interbranch politics between Congress and the bureaucracy. Even when members of Congress agree on some general policy goal—for example, limiting air pollution—they often cannot agree on the precise mechanisms for achieving that goal, so they delegate authority to a regulatory agency. As discussed in Chapter 13, this produces a "principal–agent problem" in which Congress (the principal) cannot be sure that the bureaucracy (the agent) will implement policy according to their legislative goals. A related concern is that the regulatory agency will not be responsive to the wishes of Congress because it has been "captured" by the interests it is supposed to regulate (see Chapter 13). The Food and Drug Administration, the Federal Aviation Administration, and the U.S. Department of Agriculture, among others, have been accused of serving the very industries they are supposed to regulate, rather than protecting American consumers.[55]

Another area in which regulatory policy has generated some political heat concerns the debate about the trade-off between regulation and economic growth. Regulations impose costs on the free market, which may limit job growth. However, in recent years, two developments in the area of environmental regulation have attempted to address that concern. First, economists have long argued for introducing more market incentives and reducing government regulation to achieve environmental goals. Politicians are starting to listen. In the 2008 presidential campaign, both John McCain and Barack Obama endorsed the idea of "cap and trade" policies as a market approach to reducing carbon emissions (more recently McCain reversed his position, but the approach still has some bipartisan support). Under cap and trade, which has been used successfully by many states, the government sets an overall cap on carbon emissions, and then companies buy permits that allow them to emit a certain amount carbon. Companies that reduce their carbon emissions can sell their permits to companies that want to emit more carbon. The benefit of this approach is that it uses market forces to find the best way to reduce carbon emissions rather than regulations. Environmentalists have learned that using market principles can work to their advantage, as shown by the example of grazing rights in the West, discussed in the You Decide feature.

Second, rather than simply regulating old sources of dirtier energy, President Obama has emphasized creating "green jobs." In his 2012 State of the Union message he said, "Transitioning to cleaner sources of energy will enhance our national security, protect the environment and public health, and grow our economy and create new jobs." The White House projects that developing cleaner natural gas to replace other sources of carbon-based energy would create 600,000 jobs over 10 years and tax incentives to promote alternative energy would produce another 100,000 jobs.[56]

So while political debates over regulatory policy may still be quite intense, common ground may be found in pursuing market solutions to regulatory problems. In general, the public interest is often served by regulations that protect the environment, ensure the safety of the food supply, and regulate the dumping of hazardous chemicals, whether it is through traditional economic regulations or more recent market approaches. In each instance, *politics* ends up defining how the public interest is served through regulation.

TRADE POLICY AND THE BALANCE OF PAYMENTS

Many of the factors that shape trade policy are beyond policy makers' control. The strength of the dollar relative to other currencies, consumer tastes, the low cost of labor in developing nations (especially China and India), and economic conditions worldwide all influence the trade balance but are extremely difficult to control. As such, strategies aimed at influencing trade can be considered the most difficult area of economic policy making.

EXCHANGE RATES, CONSUMER TASTES, AND LABOR COSTS The first thing influencing trade and the balance of payment is relative value of currencies. When the dollar is strong, imports are relatively cheap in the United States and U.S. exports are expensive. Therefore, if the United States is running a trade deficit, it would like the value of the dollar to fall. However, there isn't much the government can do

GRAZING RIGHTS AND FREE MARKET ENVIRONMENTALISM

Imagine you are a Republican U.S. House member who represents a western state. You are a firm believer in the free market, capitalism, and limited government. In other words, whenever possible you would like people to make choices in the free market without government interference or regulation. Conveniently, this is a view that is held by a large majority of your constituents. You also are a strong supporter of grazing rights for ranchers in your state. You have often done battle with environmentalists who want to reserve more public lands for recreational uses and conservation than for grazing cattle. On this issue, your constituents are more divided: there is strong support for ranchers, but an increasing proportion of the residents in your district are dependent on tourism.

The scenario that you have to consider here is an actual case that was first publicized in a *New York Times* op-ed piece.[a] The case involves a fifth-generation rancher in southern Utah named Dell LeFevre. He is no friend of environmentalism, saying, "We've got Easterners who don't know the land telling us what to do with it. I am a bitter old cowboy." His bitterness was deepened back in 1991 when he found two dozen of his cows shot to death. He thinks the deed was done by an environmentalist who was trying to get ranchers to leave a scenic part of the Escalante River canyon. So, LeFevre seems to be an unlikely candidate to have sat down with an environmentalist named Bill Hedden to accomplish that very goal of ending ranching in the area. Hedden works for a group called the Grand Canyon Trust (GCT) that, as the *New York Times* article explained, "doesn't use lobbyists or lawsuits (or guns) to drive out ranchers. These environmentalists get land the old-fashioned way. They buy it." GCT spent about $100,000 to buy and retire the grazing rights from LeFevre for this scenic canyon area. The environmentalists are happy because the vegetation is coming back, and LeFevre is happy because he doesn't have to battle the environmentalists anymore and was able to buy grazing rights in a different area that is better for his cattle. Supporters of "free market environmentalism" say this is a perfect example of allowing the market to determine the best use of the land. If an environmentalist is willing to buy a rancher's grazing rights, this means that the market has determined that hiking and conservation have a greater value than grazing for that piece of land.

If the story ended here, there would be no controversy for you to consider. But as you probably guessed, the story does not end here. Local groups, such as the Canyon Country Rural Alliance, which opposed all limitations on ranchers' grazing rights, lobbied Congress and the Interior Department to disallow such arrangements that remove grazing rights from some public lands. Bowing to pressure, the Interior Department decided that "only Congress may permanently exclude lands from grazing use," so GCT had no guarantee that the Bureau of Land Management would not change its mind and allow grazing. The process of resolving this conflict bounced around the Interior Department and the federal courts for nearly 10 years.

Rancher Dell LeFevre and two of his children.

In the meantime, GCT went to plan B from the "if you can't lick 'em, join 'em" school of thought: they decided to become ranchers. If the Interior Department wouldn't grant permanent conservation use permits on land designated for grazing, they would buy some cattle. GCT is now one of the largest ranchers in the Colorado Plateau with 1,000 acres of private land and grazing permits that cover 860,000 acres of federal and state lands, including a large part of the Kaibab National Forest adjacent to the North Rim of the Grand Canyon. They are managing the land in an eco-friendly manner with only 800 head of cattle. Though it may seem odd that an environmental group had to take up ranching to get the policy outcome they wanted, it was a compromise that made all sides of the dispute relatively happy. As one opponent of GCT put it, "We turned them from environmentalists into cowboys. I guess what they can do is get their cows and start losing money like the rest of us."[b]

If you were the member of Congress representing this district, what would you decide to do?

CRITICAL THINKING QUESTIONS

1. Would you support the limitations on permanently removing grazing rights because they are consistent with the desires of many of your constituents? If so, how would you reconcile this with your free market views, and how would you justify the decision to your constituents who support free market environmentalism?

2. Does the compromise position of GCT taking up ranching strike you as a reasonable middle ground? Why or why not?

MANY AMERICAN CONSUMER products, including cars, clothing, and electronics, are made overseas because labor costs are so much less in developing countries. Even people who want to "buy American" have a difficult time, given the increasing globalization of multinational corporations.

about the value of the dollar because that value is determined by international currency markets. How does the value of the dollar affect the trade deficit? Consider the following example. As of June 2014, a euro was worth about $1.35. Therefore, a BMW 335i that would sell for 32,000 euros in Germany would go for about $43,200 in the United States, whereas a Cadillac CTS that would retail in America for $40,000 would sell for about 29,630 euros in Europe—although this example doesn't factor in shipping costs, dealer incentives, higher taxes in Europe, and so on.

Now see what happens if the dollar falls in value so a euro is worth $1.50. It may seem backward to say that the value of the dollar falls when the value of a euro goes from $1.35 to $1.50, but think of it this way: at the new exchange rate, it takes more dollars to buy the same number of euros, so the dollar is worth less. Now that Cadillac could be purchased in Germany for 26,667 euros and the BMW would still cost 32,000 euros, while the BMW would cost an American consumer $48,000 and the Cadillac is still $40,000. Nothing has changed except the value of the dollar, but suddenly the car buyer's choices have changed dramatically. In both countries, the Cadillac has become a much better bargain, and therefore, theoretically, Cadillac sales (and sales of other GM models, as well as those of Chrysler and Ford) should increase and BMW (and Mercedes, Volkswagen, Fiat, MINI Cooper, etc.) sales should fall.

We say "theoretically" because of the second factor—consumer tastes. If consumers are willing to pay an increasing premium for foreign goods, then a weaker dollar may not help the trade deficit. There isn't much policy makers can do about consumer tastes, despite the ongoing campaign urging citizens to "buy American." The low cost of labor is another factor that policy makers cannot do much to influence. If a foreign firm pays its workers a daily wage that is equal to what American workers earn in a single hour for the same job, the foreign firm has a huge competitive advantage. Consequently, the United States has been flooded with cheap consumer goods from nations where labor is very cheap. Low prices are good for American consumers, but they come at the price of large trade deficits and lost American jobs. Furthermore, foreign firms sometimes absorb some currency fluctuations and do not raise the price of their goods in the United States as the dollar falls in value relative to their currency. The final factor—the strength of foreign economies—is also outside the control of American policy makers. If foreign economies are weak, consumers abroad do not have the income to purchase U.S. exports.

TRADE POLICY AND TRADE DEFICITS Although it is difficult to control trade outcomes because exchange rates, consumer tastes, and labor costs in other countries are all largely outside the control of policy makers, Congress and the president still try by altering trade policies. The main target of trade policy is the trade balance, which is defined as the difference between the total value of our exports and imports. In recent years, the balances reached record deficits exceeding $830 billion a year in 2008 before falling back to $490 billion for the 12-month period ending in September 2014 (Figure 15.9). The current account deficit, the broadest measure of the balance of payments including investments, has also been running at record levels. Economists have warned that deficits of this level are not sustainable. There is increasing consensus that something must change—either we need to stop buying as many imports and sell more exports, or the value of the dollar must fall to help make this happen.

FIGURE » 15.9

TRADE DEFICITS, 1974–2013

The trade deficit remains high. Which groups are most likely to support policies aimed at reducing the trade deficit, and which groups would oppose these policies?

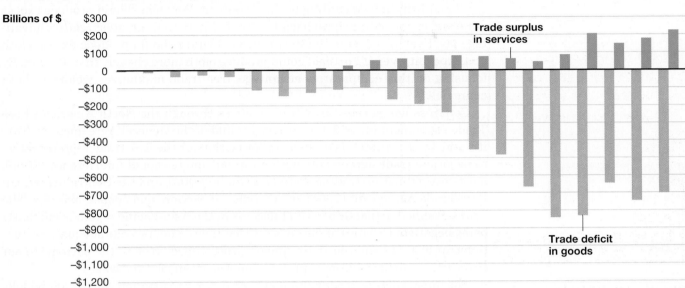

Note: Totals are calculated on a balance of payment basis.

SOURCES: Data from the U.S. Department of Commerce, Bureau of Economic Analysis, International Economic Accounts: Trade in Goods and Services, www.bea.gov/newsreleases/international/trade/2014/pdf/trad0914.pdf (accessed 11/7/14).

The trade deficits have to be financed with borrowing from overseas. In the past, these loans came largely from foreign investment by private individuals who saw greater returns on their investments in the United States than in other countries. The net international investment position in June 2014 was –$5.4 trillion (that is, the value of foreign investments in the United States exceeded the value of U.S. investments abroad).[57] Foreign investors now own about 60 percent of our publicly owned debt, with Japan and China owning 41 percent of that foreign debt. Why does this matter? If these foreign governments decide to stop investing in American assets or to start selling them, interest rates will have to rise, perhaps dramatically, to attract buyers for our debt.

The types of policies that can be used to reduce the trade deficit are protectionist policies such as trade sanctions, tariffs, and quotas, or attempts to reduce the value of the dollar. Advocates for protectionist policies argue that "free trade" is a myth and we are being taken advantage of by nations that engage in unfair trade practices while selling goods in our open markets. Former senator Ernest F. Hollings once said, "We hear those in the national Congress running around saying, 'Free trade, free trade, I am for free trade,' when they know free trade is like dry water. There is no such thing."[58] It is only fair, protectionist proponents argue, that we set up trade barriers or impose quotas to support our own goods and protect American jobs. Although broadly based protectionist policies have been rare in the past couple of decades, U.S. policy makers have applied protection in selected markets. For example, in 1983 Harley Davidson won special trade protection from the Reagan administration that raised tariffs on imported Japanese motorcycles from 4 percent to 49 percent. In September 2009, President Obama imposed a 35 percent tariff on Chinese tires.

In general, Congress and the president have supported free trade much more than protectionism. Economists have long touted the virtues of exploiting "comparative advantage" through free trade. In 1817 David Ricardo was the first to develop this notion with the example of the production of wine and cloth in Portugal and Britain.[59] According to the argument, Portugal should produce excess wine and export it to Britain because that is where their greatest *relative* advantage lay. Even if it seems counterintuitive, Britain should produce excess cloth and export it, even if Portugal could produce cloth more cheaply than Britain. By focusing on this comparative advantage, free trade maximizes wealth in both countries.[60]

Congress has pursued free-trade policies through the North American Free Trade Agreement in 1993, the Uruguay round of the General Agreement on Tariffs and Trade in 1994, fast-track authorization for the U.S. trade representative to negotiate trade agreements with minimal congressional interference (2002), most-favored-nation trading status for China (2000), and the Central American Free Trade Agreement (2005), which reduced barriers and opened markets. The Trans-Pacific Partnership with 11 nations in the Asia-Pacific region is currently being negotiated. Critics of the laws say that they do not provide adequate protections for workers and the environment, promoting a "race to the bottom" to cut costs while putting additional pressure on American jobs and wages.

The impact of free-trade agreements on American jobs and wages vary widely, with estimates ranging from 1 to 4 million jobs lost in the past 20 years.[61] Some of these jobs would have been lost even without the trade agreements, even in areas thought to be our comparative advantage, such as computer programming. When programmers or computer customer support staff in India earn about one-tenth of what they make in the United States, it is difficult for American firms to compete in international markets unless they employ cheaper labor.[62] This downward pressure on wages has also contributed to income inequality in the United States. The same competitive pressures have led to the virtual extinction of some U.S. industries, such as the manufacturing of consumer electronics, textiles, shoes, and, increasingly, clothing. Thus, while free trade generally enhances worldwide economic growth, there can be significant consequences for specific industries.

THE POLITICS OF TRADE POLICY

With stakes this high, it is not surprising that politics often plays a central role in trade policy. There are two main explanations for the nature of political influence on trade policy: constituency and ideology.[63] The constituency explanation sees the two major parties as representing different groups—Democrats and labor, Republicans and capital—which tends to make the Democrats more protectionist and the Republicans more supportive of free trade. Elaborations of this view agree with the central tendency but note divisions within each constituency. For example, auto- and steelworkers' unions are much more protectionist than dockworkers' unions because any industry with strong exports will support free trade, whereas those that have relatively few exports but are vulnerable to cheap imports are more likely to be protectionist. The ideological explanation focuses on the bipartisan consensus on trade that emerged after the Great Depression, which was seen as having been caused in part by the protective tariffs of the 1930 Smoot-Hawley Act.[64] As with the theories of regulation, both perspectives explain part of the truth. Our political leaders largely support a free-trade ideology, but there are divisions along constituency lines on some legislation.

CONCLUSION

There is a common perception that economic policies would work better if we could just take politics out of the economic policy-making process. But that would be like saying "football would be better if we could eliminate the contact," or "poker would be better if we could take out the element of chance." Economic policy making is inherently political. It isn't possible or desirable to have economic policy produced by economists who would deftly push and pull the levers of growth, productivity, and efficiency, implementing their economic theories without interference from politicians. Politics must enter into this process. Economic policy determines who wins and who loses, and elected leaders must be involved in this process if representative democracy is to have any meaning. This is especially true of the budget process because the redistributive implications of taxing and spending are so clear, but as we have discussed, even monetary policy is not insulated from politics. This role for politics is guaranteed by our system of checks and balances: Congress, the president, and to some extent the courts all have a hand in shaping economic policy. The clash between politics and economic theory and the conflicted nature of economic policy making can be illustrated with a few examples.

We discussed earlier the limitation of implementing Keynesian economic theories in fiscal policy. Often, political considerations make it impossible to implement the swift, targeted action called for in the theory. That is because the budget inherently involves debates over some central political questions: How large should the government be? How progressive should the income tax be? Should the millionaires' tax be adopted to reduce income inequality? Should budget deficits be allowed to expand to put pressure on government spending, rather than to stimulate the economy? These are not purely economic questions but also political ones that must be answered through debate and conflict between the opposing parties and branches of government. This is especially true of the debate over tax policy in President Obama's second term. President Obama and congressional Democrats wanted to raise taxes on the wealthiest 2 percent of Americans, whereas congressional Republicans wanted to reduce tax rates. With Republicans controlling Congress and Obama in the White House through 2015–2016, it is likely that fiscal policy will be determined by the politics of compromise more than the purity of economic theory.

Monetary policy is supposed to be more insulated from politics, but even here political pressures are evident. One important example is how fiscal policy (taxing and spending decisions by Congress and the president) can put pressure on monetary policy (the Fed's decisions concerning interest rates and the money supply). With the large budget deficits that the government is currently running, it can become difficult to finance $500 billion a year in new debt. If the demand from private investors, banks, and foreign governments is not sufficient, interest rates may have to rise to attract enough money. This could run counter to Fed policy, which may be concerned that a large increase in long-term interest rates could lead to a recession. However, the alternative would be for the Fed to step in to buy the additional debt, which can create inflationary pressures on the economy. This can put the Fed in a difficult position. The chair of the Fed routinely warns Congress and the president that our budget deficits, debt, and current accounts deficit are not sustainable, but there isn't anything that the chair of the Fed can do to make these entities change their political decisions about what they think are the best economic policies for the country.

Finally, to return to the chapter opener, the politics of income inequality is highly conflictual and demonstrates the clash between economics and politics. Economists have precise measures of income inequality and can track changes in inequality. However, there is substantial disagreement among economists over the impact of policy tools to reduce income inequality. Some economists argue that an increase in the minimum wage to $10.10 would help reduce inequality, whereas others say the main economic consequence of such a raise would be the elimination of many jobs. Even on policies for which there is substantial agreement among economists, such as the effectiveness of estate taxes on reducing wealth inequality, politics may be highly conflictual. When the estate tax was labeled the "death tax," the politics of the policy changed dramatically.

These examples of the budget, financing the debt, and debates over income inequality are not intended to suggest that politics shouldn't enter into the economic policy-making process. Indeed, just the opposite. They are excellent illustrations of the themes that politics is everywhere and politics is conflictual. It shouldn't be surprising when politics enters the economic policy debate. Elected leaders should be responsive to what their constituents think about the central questions concerning the direction of the economy.

GOALS OF ECONOMIC POLICY

▶ *Explain the main purposes of government involvement in the economy.* **(Pages 555–61)**

SUMMARY

Policy makers' pursuit of economic goals—such as full employment, stable prices, or growth—is a complex process. Not only is the government unable to attain these goals on its own, but the pursuit of one goal often comes at the expense of other economic goals.

KEY TERMS

full employment (p. 555)
economic depression (p. 555)
Council of Economic Advisers (p. 555)
inflation (p. 556)
gross domestic product (GDP) (p. 558)
balanced budget (p. 558)
budget deficit (p. 558)
current account (p. 560)
trade deficit (p. 560)

CRITICAL THINKING AND DISCUSSION

Assuming it were politically possible, do you think economic policy should be made by economists and other experts rather than by politicians? Why, or why not?

PRACTICE QUIZ QUESTIONS

1. The Council of Economic Advisors was established _____.

   Ⓐ by the Employment Act of 1946
   Ⓑ by the Balanced Budget Amendment
   Ⓒ in Article I of the Constitution
   Ⓓ in Article III of the Constitution
   Ⓔ by the Federal Reserve Board

2. Technically, full employment means an unemployment level of about _____.

   Ⓐ 0 percent
   Ⓑ 2 percent
   Ⓒ 5 percent
   Ⓓ 8 percent
   Ⓔ 10 percent

3. The responsibility of fighting inflation largely falls on _____.

   Ⓐ the president
   Ⓑ the Office of Management and Budget
   Ⓒ the Congress
   Ⓓ the Federal Reserve
   Ⓔ the private sector

4. When the government attempts to reduce inflation, it typically results in _____.

   Ⓐ businesses growing
   Ⓑ higher interest rates
   Ⓒ lower unemployment
   Ⓓ an increase in GDP
   Ⓔ lower interest rates

THE KEY PLAYERS IN ECONOMIC POLICY MAKING

▶ *Describe the roles played by each of the branches of government in shaping economic policy.* **(Pages 561–72)**

SUMMARY

The primary actors in making economic policy are Congress, through the "power of the purse"; the president, in shaping taxing and spending policy; and the bureaucracy, in implementing the monetary policy. While they all share the same general goal of a healthy economy, coordinating action across these actors can be difficult.

KEY TERMS

fiscal policy (p. 561)
monetary policy (p. 561)
budget making (p. 562)
budget reconciliation (p. 562)
United States Trade Representative (USTR) (p. 565)
National Economic Council (NEC) (p. 565)
Federal Reserve System (p. 567)
Treasury Department (p. 567)
Federal Reserve Board (p. 567)

CRITICAL THINKING AND DISCUSSION

If you were a member of Congress, what would your position be on international trade? Would you support free trade or more protectionist policies? Why?

PRACTICE QUIZ QUESTIONS

5. The difference between fiscal policy and monetary policy is that fiscal policy is concerned with _____, while monetary policy is concerned with _____.

   Ⓐ controlling the money supply and spending; taxing and interest rates

    B taxing and controlling the money supply; spending and interest rates

    C taxing and spending; controlling the money supply and interest rates

    D controlling the money supply and interest rates; taxing and spending

    E taxing and interest rates; spending and controlling the money supply

6. Budget reconciliation has the advantages of _____ and _____.

    A decreasing bipartisanship; preventing a Senate filibuster

    B allowing members to get everything they want; not being subject to a presidential veto

    C making it difficult for members to vote against the bill; preventing a Senate filibuster

    D not being subject to a presidential veto; decreasing bipartisanship

    E making it difficult for members to vote against the bill; not being subject to presidential veto

7. The Federal Reserve Board's actions _____ subject to presidential or congressional review, while the appointment terms of personnel _____ overlap with the federal election calendar.

    A are; do

    B are; do not

    C are sometimes; do

    D are not; do

    E are not; do not

8. The Treasury generally prefers _____ interest rates; the Federal Reserve board generally prefers _____ rates.

    A higher; lower

    B higher; higher

    C lower; lower

    D lower; higher

    E stable; lower

TOOLS AND THEORIES OF ECONOMIC POLICY

▶ *Examine how fiscal, monetary, regulatory, and trade policies influence the economy.* **(Pages 572–89)**

SUMMARY

Policy makers have a variety of tools at their disposal to help push the economy in their desired direction. Although there are different theories on the best approach, the use of fiscal policy, monetary policy, and regulation allows the government to influence the country's economic performance.

KEY TERMS

Keynesian economics (p. 572)
supply-side economics (p. 573)
marginal tax rate (p. 573)
business cycle (p. 574)
mandatory spending (p. 574)
discretionary spending (p. 574)
regressive (p. 576)
progressive (p. 577)
monetarist theory (p. 579)
reserve requirement (p. 580)
discount rate (p. 580)
federal funds rate (FFR) (p. 580)
open market operations (p. 581)

CRITICAL THINKING AND DISCUSSION

Do you support an active role for the government in regulating the economy, or would you prefer the free market to be largely unregulated?

PRACTICE QUIZ QUESTIONS

9. Keynesian economics argues that the effects of an economic recession can be reduced by _____.

    A decreasing government spending

    B increasing government spending

    C increasing income taxes

    D reducing the budget deficit

    E discouraging consumer spending

10. Reducing the federal deficit by cutting spending is difficult because _____.

    A the interest rates are too high

    B a growing portion of the budget is mandatory spending

    C a growing portion of the budget is discretionary spending

    D members of Congress put too much pork in budgetary bills

    E large deficits benefit the economy in the long run

11. Regressive taxes, like the payroll tax, mean that compared to the wealthy, poor people spend _____ of their income on taxes.

    A none

    B much less

    C slightly less

    D an equal amount

    E more

12. What does the "reserve requirement" refer to?

    A the interest rate the Fed charges to member banks

    B the rate member banks charge one another on overnight loans

    C the minimum activity level of the Fed's open market operations

D the lowest price for government bonds

E the minimum level of money banks must always have on hand

13. When the competitive situation is a natural monopoly, the government generally _____.

A regulates prices

B breaks up the monopoly

C stimulates competition

D works to reduce negative externalities

E does not intervene

14. In general, Congress supports _____; the president supports _____.

A protectionism; free trade

B protectionism; protectionism

C free trade; protectionism

D free trade; free trade

E tariffs; protectionism

SUGGESTED READING

Friedman, Milton. *Capitalism and Freedom.* 40th anniversary ed. Chicago: University of Chicago Press, 2002.

Friedman, Thomas L. *The World Is Flat: A Brief History of the Twenty-First Century.* New York: Farrar, Straus and Giroux, 2005.

Hacker, Jacob S., and Paul Pierson. *Winner-Take-All Politics: How Washington Made the Rich Richer—and Turned Its Back on the Middle Class.* New York: Simon and Schuster, 2011.

Keynes, John Maynard. *General Theory of Employment, Interest, and Money.* New York: Macmillan, 2007; originally published in 1936.

Krugman, Paul. *The Great Unraveling: Losing Our Way in the New Century.* New York: W. W. Norton, 2003.

Lewis, Michael. *The Big Short: Inside the Doomsday Machine.* New York: W. W. Norton, 2010.

Phillips, Kevin. *Bad Money: Reckless Finance, Failed Politics, and the Global Crisis of American Capitalism.* New York: Viking, 2008.

Piketty, Thomas. *Capital in the Twenty-First Century.* Cambridge, MA: Belknap Press, 2014.

Soros, George. *The New Paradigm for Financial Markets: The Credit Crash of 2008 and What It Means.* New York: PublicAffairs Books, 2008.

Stiglitz, Joseph E. *The Price of Inequality: How Today's Divided Society Endangers Our Future.* New York: W. W. Norton, 2013.

16

Social Policy

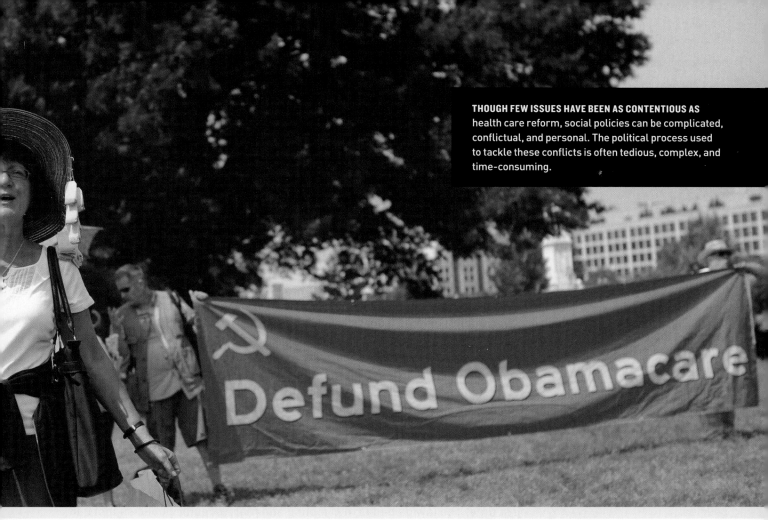

P RESIDENT OBAMA SIGNED THE PATIENT PROTECTION and Affordable Care Act into law on March 30, 2010. This comprehensive and historic health care reform legislation was the culmination of a 15-month partisan struggle in Congress. The $1 trillion law (over 10 years) will make health insurance available to an additional 32 million Americans while preventing health insurance companies from dropping sick policyholders or refusing to cover people with preexisting conditions.

Health care reform was controversial from the start. Democrats controlled the House and Senate in 2009, but there was significant conflict between the chambers on issues such as federal funding of abortion, how illegal immigrants would be excluded from the policy, and how the programs would be funded. For the first six months of the process, Democratic leaders in the Senate tried to reach out to moderate Republicans to create a bipartisan bill, while Speaker Nancy Pelosi pursued a more partisan process in the House. Early in the fall, as public opposition grew, it became clear that the votes for health care reform would have to come from within the Democratic Party. Indeed, the final version of the bill passed without any Republican support. Republicans cried foul because Democratic leaders used the reconciliation process in an unorthodox way to avoid a filibuster in the Senate (the process is typically used for budget-related issues, not for passing substantive policy; see the How It Works graphic in Chapter 11 for a description of the unorthodox process used to pass the act).

CONFLICT COMPROMISE
in American Politics

CHAPTER *goals*

Explain what we mean by social policy, and how the national government's role in social policy has evolved.
▶ PAGES 597–600

Examine the problem of poverty as a target of social policies.
▶ PAGES 600–04

Describe the roles played by each branch of the national government and by the states in making and implementing social policy.
▶ PAGES 604–06

Trace the steps through which problems are addressed by social policies.
▶ PAGES 606–10

Analyze the current major areas of social policy.
▶ PAGES 610–29

The day after the law went into effect, House Republicans introduced a bill to repeal it. Public dissatisfaction with the law grew throughout the summer, especially with the individual mandate that requires everyone to buy insurance through the health insurance exchanges if their employer does not provide it. In the 2010 midterm elections, Republicans rode this discontent to the largest gains for any party in midterm elections since 1938, picking up 63 seats and gaining control of the House while trimming the Democrats majority in the Senate by six seats.[1]

Over the next four years, House Republicans voted 54 times to repeal or change part of Obamacare, including 6 times to repeal the entire law.[2] Of course, Senate Democrats were having none of it and ignored the House's efforts. These conflicting views came to a head in the fall of 2013 when House Republicans tied approval of the annual budget to repealing Obamacare. Democrats viewed this as blackmail and refused to negotiate, while Republicans argued that the public was on their side as polls showed that most Americans did not approve of Obamacare. This disagreement led to a shutdown of all nonessential federal government services from October 1 to 16, 2013. The White House estimated that the shutdown cost the economy about 120,000 jobs and between $2 and $6 billion.[3] While Obamacare remained unpopular, most Americans rejected the confrontational tactics and blamed House Republicans for the shutdown.[4]

Over the first six months of the program, the projected enrollments in Obamacare were lagging behind the original estimates. The rollout of the registration website, Healthcare.gov, was rocky, to say the least. Some people spent hours trying to access information about their insurance options and to sign up—only to have their computer freeze up and all the information they had painstakingly entered be lost. However, by the summer of 2014, nearly 10 million Americans had signed up, many gaining health insurance coverage for the first time. The law gained firmer footing and more popular public support. In Congress, most Republicans shifted from their emphasis on repealing the law to working to make it more consistent with a small-government, market-based approach to health care; and while Democrats weren't quite taking a victory lap, they started embracing the law and working to improve it.

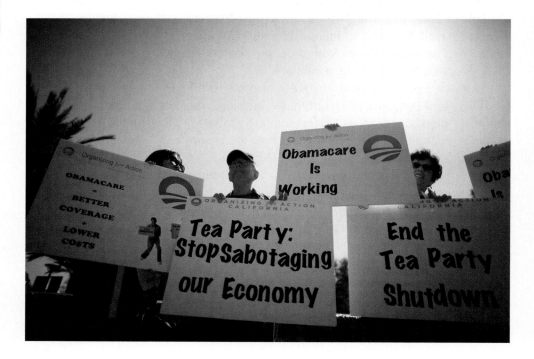

THE CONFLICTS OVER SOCIAL POLICY run deep. Conflicts over Obamacare led to a government shutdown, with Obamacare supporters and detractors each blaming the other side.

Although the level of conflict around Obamacare is unusual in American politics—trade-offs between social policy and other government priorities often produce political conflict. More money for health insurance subsidies, Social Security, Medicare, food stamps, and welfare means less money for building highways, supporting the military, or developing alternative energy. These trade-offs become especially acute as an aging population necessitates an increasing share of federal spending goes to Social Security and Medicare. Resolving these trade-offs must be done through a political process filled with conflict and compromise.

That the political process matters is clearly shown by the importance of the filibuster in the Senate and the reconciliation process that allowed passage of the bill with a majority vote. Also, process matters in that decisions made by individual presidents and members of Congress shape social policy. In each instance, policies and their effect on Americans' daily lives could have been very different if alternative procedures had been used or different proposals had passed.

The politics of social policy is everywhere. Social policy directly affects all Americans at some point in their lives—possibly from the very beginning of life (with programs such as Women, Infants, and Children [WIC] and Head Start), through the middle of life (income support, job training, housing, food stamps, Medicaid, and need-based scholarships), to the end of life (Social Security and Medicare). This chapter discusses the evolution of social policy in the United States, outlines the conditions that create the need for social policies, describes the key players in the social policy-making process, and explains the status of key social policies today and the efforts to reform them. We begin with the historical background of social policy.

THE HISTORY AND BACKGROUND OF SOCIAL POLICY

EXPLAIN WHAT WE MEAN BY SOCIAL POLICY, AND HOW THE NATIONAL GOVERNMENT'S ROLE IN SOCIAL POLICY HAS EVOLVED

Social policy is generally defined in terms of the "social safety net," or **welfare**, which the *American Heritage Dictionary* defines as "regular assistance from the government or a private agency because of need." A broader conception includes government programs aimed at achieving some general social goal, such as support for public education, the income tax deduction for interest paid on home mortgages (to encourage home ownership), or policies aimed at helping job creation and growth. This chapter will address both conceptions of social policies and discuss how some traditional social welfare programs, such as Social Security, are not based on need. This section outlines the evolution of social policy in the United States and describes various types of social policy (see Nuts & Bolts 16.1).

Early in our nation's history, the federal government took little responsibility for social welfare. Private charities, churches, and families largely took care of the poor and disadvantaged. The first significant social policy appeared in the nineteenth century in the form of federal financial support for Civil War veterans and their families. Between 1880 and 1910, the national government spent more than a quarter of its budget on Civil War pensions and support for veterans' widows. Other than interest on the debt, this was a larger share of the budget than any

social policy An area of public policy related to maintaining or enhancing the well-being of individuals.

welfare Financial or other assistance provided to individuals by the government, usually based on need.

TYPES OF SOCIAL POLICY

There are two main types of social policy:

1. *Contributory* (or social insurance) programs include Social Security, Medicare, disability insurance, and unemployment compensation.

   ▶ similar to insurance programs in that people pay a specified amount of money to cover some future benefit (either expected, as with the programs related to retirement, or unexpected, as with disability and unemployment)

   ▶ not means-tested; that is, all people may participate in the program regardless of their income

2. *Noncontributory* (or public-assistance) programs include Medicaid, food stamps, housing assistance, welfare, and school lunches.

   ▶ recipients are not expected to pay for the programs, which are means-tested, meaning that they are aimed at helping poor people

The Affordable Care Act ("Obamacare") has elements of both contributory and noncontributory programs. People who are required to buy health insurance are "contributing" to their own insurance. However, those who cannot afford to pay for their insurance receive government subsidies (and thus are participating in a noncontributory program).

---

other single item and a greater percentage of federal spending than today's expenditure on Social Security. (Today we spend about one-fifth of our budget on Social Security, but, of course, the overall budget was much smaller then.[5]) During the recession of the mid-1890s, populist and progressive reformers sought a national system of unemployment compensation, but such broadscale policies were several decades ahead of their time.

The stock market crash in 1929 and the ensuing Great Depression created a desperate economic situation for millions of Americans. The value of the stock market shrank by 80 percent, the gross national product decreased by 25 percent, and unemployment climbed to at least 25 percent in the depth of the Depression in 1933. Yet, during the presidential campaign of 1932, the Republican incumbent, Herbert Hoover, upheld the administration's policy of limited government intervention in the economy and in social welfare policies. In contrast, the Democratic candidate, Franklin Delano Roosevelt, pledged "a new deal for the American people." FDR won a sweeping victory. Democrats also gained control of both houses of Congress, which provided the platform for enacting FDR's policies.

An immediate concern was to alleviate the suffering caused by unemployment. As FDR argued, "No country, however rich, can afford the waste of its human resources. Demoralization caused by vast unemployment is our greatest extravagance. Morally, it is the greatest menace to our social order."[6] But FDR also wanted to implement a broader "preventative social policy" as outlined by social scientists at the University of Wisconsin, including John R. Commons, who was a significant force in the creation of unemployment compensation policies, and Edwin Witte, the architect of Social Security.[7] The **New Deal** policies enacted between 1933 and 1935 included the following:

New Deal The set of policies proposed by President Franklin Roosevelt and enacted by Congress between 1933 and 1935 to promote economic recovery and social welfare during the Great Depression.

   ▶ the Agricultural Adjustment Administration, which provided farmers with much-needed assistance (farmers were hit hard in the Depression when plummeting commodity prices forced many family farms into bankruptcy);

- the National Recovery Administration and Public Works Administration, which reinvigorated the business sector;
- the Federal Emergency Relief Administration, which provided $500 million in emergency aid for the poor (about $7 billion in today's dollars);
- jobs programs such as the Civil Works Administration and Civilian Conservation Corps, which put more than 2 million people to work, and later the Works Progress Administration, which was a broader program that employed at least one-third of the nation's unemployed;
- Social Security, which included the familiar retirement policy and supported the states for spending on unemployment compensation, disability programs, and support for dependent children of single mothers—the precursor of the central welfare program, Aid to Families with Dependent Children (AFDC), which existed until 1996;
- the National Labor Relations Act, which guaranteed the right to organize a union and set regulations for collective bargaining between management and labor.[8]

The role of the federal government in social policy was forever changed. Although some aspects of the New Deal were never repeated on such a broad scale, such as the jobs programs, most of its other programs became the cornerstone of social policy for subsequent generations.

The next major expansion of social policy came during the **Great Society** of President Lyndon Johnson in the mid-1960s. We discussed part of this social agenda in Chapter 5: the civil rights movement, which culminated with the passage of the Civil Rights Act in 1964 and the Voting Rights Act in 1965. The other important aspect of Johnson's Great Society included the War on Poverty and programs concerning health, education, and housing. Johnson's "unconditional" War on Poverty brought economic development and jobs to depressed areas, especially the inner cities, by creating the Office of Economic Opportunity, the Jobs Corps, the Neighborhood Youth Corps, Volunteers in Service to America (VISTA, a domestic counterpart to the Peace Corps), and the Model Cities program. Other programs focused on helping children, including Head Start, which provided preschool education and enrichment for poor children, the Child Nutrition Act of 1966, and an expanded school lunch program. The Food Stamp program was also greatly expanded; urban renewal expanded public housing; a new cabinet-level department, Housing and Urban Development, was created; and the federal government got more involved in an area that typically had been left to the states in the Elementary and Secondary Education Act of 1965. Perhaps the most significant legislation was in health care, with the creation of Medicare, the national program that funds medical care for the elderly, and Medicaid, which funds health care for the poor.[9]

The mounting costs of the Vietnam War created a trade-off: it wasn't possible to continue funding ambitious social programs and the war without causing inflation. Over the following decades, there was some conservative backlash against the "welfare state," especially during the Reagan years (1981–1989), as spending on social programs was cut and some programs were eliminated. However, with some exceptions, the Great Society programs remain core components of today's social safety net.

Great Society The wide-ranging social agenda promoted by President Lyndon Johnson in the mid-1960s that aimed to improve Americans' quality of life through governmental social programs.

BEFORE THE NEW DEAL PROGRAMS in the 1930s, poverty relief was provided mainly by private charities. Here, future first lady Eleanor Roosevelt serves meals to unemployed women and their children in a New York restaurant.

President George W. Bush continued this general direction for social policy, maintaining most existing programs with some cuts and one major expansion, the addition of a prescription benefit to Medicare. As a "compassionate conservative," Bush attempted to place his stamp on American social policy with the idea of an **ownership society**, in which people take more responsibility for their own social welfare. Bush proposed privatizing part of Social Security and creating private savings accounts to cover more out-of-pocket medical expenses, in combination with more free market forces and a bigger role for private charity. President Obama has favored an approach that emphasizes the market and community, while preserving an important role for government. As the recent recession and natural disasters such as Hurricane Sandy have demonstrated, crises may overwhelm even the most aggressive and sustained community responses. Market forces cannot adequately address the needs of the unemployed and very poor, especially in times of economic recession. Obama's social policies have focused on enacting comprehensive health care reform, while maintaining and expanding the social safety net for those devastated by the recession (for example, with the extension of unemployment benefits to cover the long-term unemployed and providing a record number of people with food stamps).

ownership society The term used to describe the social policy vision of President George W. Bush, in which citizens take responsibility for their own social welfare and the free market plays a greater role in social policy.

EXAMINE THE PROBLEM OF POVERTY AS A TARGET OF SOCIAL POLICIES

POVERTY AND INCOME INEQUALITY

The economic dislocation and poverty of the Great Depression and the desire to eliminate poverty in the 1960s were the two central stimuli for social policy. Although these policies had some success in reducing poverty, the persistence of poverty remains the primary motivator for most social policy. In 2014, the poverty line for a family of four was an annual income of $23,850; for a single person it was $11,670. In 2011, official estimates determined 46.2 million Americans were living in poverty—15 percent of the population. Even the social programs that do not directly help the poor and disadvantaged, such as Social Security and Medicare, impact poverty. As Figure 16.1 shows, the percentage of the elderly population living in poverty plummeted from more than 35 percent in 1959 to 8.7 percent in 2011. Official statistics on poverty were not collected before 1959, but the rate was certainly much higher in the 1930s before Social Security was established.[10] Given that more than half of the elderly rely on Social Security as their primary income—for the bottom quintile, nearly 80 percent of their income in retirement comes from Social Security—the poverty rate for the elderly would be much higher if Social Security and Medicare did not exist.

Another source of concern for some policy advocates is the growing income and wealth inequality in the United States. Indeed, the top income levels in the nation are benefiting disproportionately from income increases. In the economic recovery from 2009 to 2012, 95 percent of the net income gains went to the top 1 percent of the income distribution and from 1992 to 2012, two-thirds of the gains went to the top 1 percent. These trends have produced a growing concentration

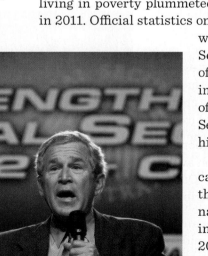

PRESIDENT GEORGE W. BUSH emphasized the idea of an "ownership society." For example, Bush proposed privatizing Social Security to allow people to invest the money collected through payroll taxes.

FIGURE » 16.1

POVERTY RATES BY AGE

Children today are in poverty at nearly twice the rate of the elderly, whereas 45 years ago the poverty rate among the elderly was twice that of children. What changes in social policies in the past 75 years could help explain this change?

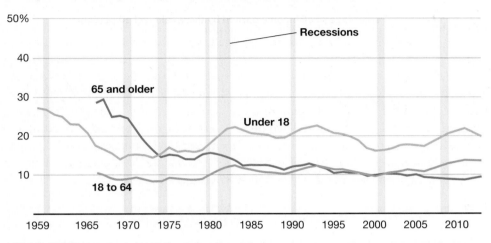

Note: The data points are placed at the midpoints of the respective years. Data for people age 18 and older are not available from 1960 to 1965.

SOURCE: "Income and Poverty in the United States: 2013," Current Population Reports, September 2014, www.census.gov/content/dam/Census/library/publications/2014/demo/p60-249.pdf (accessed 11/6/14)

of income at the top. In 2012, the top 10 percent of households—those earning more than $114,000 a year—earned half of the income, which is the highest proportion since 1917 (see Figure 16.2); and in 2012, the top 1 percent—those earning more than $394,000—earned 21.5 percent of the nation's income.[11]

The wealth gap is far greater. The median (meaning that half are above this level and half are below) net worth of U.S. households in 2013 was $177,900, but the median wealth for the top 10 percent was $1.87 million, and this group held 75.3 percent of the nation's wealth. Even within the top 10 percent, the wealth is concentrated at the top. *Forbes Magazine* publishes a list of the wealthiest Americans every year. Bill Gates topped the 2014 list for the 21st year in a row, with a net worth of $82 billion, and the person at the bottom of the *"Forbes* 400" was worth $1.6 billion. The collective net worth of the nation's wealthiest 400 people grew $270 billion in the past year to reach $2.3 trillion.[12] This is a trillion dollars more than the total wealth held by the bottom 50 percent of the American public ($1.38 trillion held by *61.2 million* households in 2013).[13]

According to a study by the nonpartisan Congressional Budget Office (CBO), despite these patterns of inequality, people who earn more than $100,000 receive more benefits from the federal government ($5,690 on average) than people who earn less than $10,000 ($5,560). The study concludes, "Quite simply, if the federal government wanted to flatten the nation's income distribution, it would do better to mail all its checks to random addresses."[14]

How can that be? Consider one big social welfare program: housing. Poor people receive $20 billion a year from the federal government in direct subsidies for their rent (with another $26.7 billion spent on all housing programs for the poor). However, this number is dwarfed by the $138 billion spent on tax expenditures for housing in 2015, mostly for the mortgage interest deduction, property tax deduction,

FIGURE » 16.2

PERCENTAGE OF ALL INCOME EARNED BY THE WEALTHIEST 10 PERCENT*

Income inequality in the United States today is higher than ever. The wealthiest 10 percent of Americans now receive over 50 percent of all U.S. income. How will this inequality affect the outcomes of social policy?

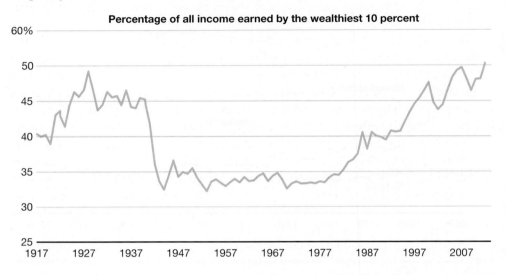

Percentage of all income earned by the wealthiest 10 percent

*Includes capital gains

SOURCE: Emmanuel Saez, "Striking it Richer: The Evolution of Top Incomes in the United States." University of California, Berkeley, September 3, 2013, http://eml.berkeley.edu/~saez/saez-UStopincomes-2012.pdf (accessed 5/31/14).

and capital gains tax exclusions. Most of this money went to relatively wealthy people; for example, 77 percent of the tax savings from deducting mortgage interest goes to people who make more than $100,000 a year.[15] Other government policies that help the wealthy include patent and copyright law, bankruptcy law, bailouts of the financial sector, immigration policy, enforcement of tax law, and monetary policy.[16]

Government programs that help the wealthy not only target individuals but also benefit corporations. These policies, often called "corporate welfare," are defined by the Cato Institute, a libertarian think tank, as "any government spending program that provides unique benefits or advantages to specific companies or industries. That includes programs that provide direct grants to businesses, programs that provide research and other services for industries, and programs that provide subsidized loans or insurance to companies." The Cato Institute estimates that there are more than 100 corporate welfare programs in the federal budget, including crop subsidies to large corporate farmers and tax deductions for oil companies to encourage exploration and drilling, with annual expenditures of more than $100 billion.[17] Liberal groups like Citizens for Tax Justice estimate levels of corporate welfare at nearly 3 times that amount. Clearly, there is much more to welfare policies than programs for the poor.

These statistics generate different reactions among politicians and are a good reminder that politics is conflictual. Republicans look at the statistics on poverty and inequality and at policies that help the wealthy and argue that the best way to address poverty is to create jobs and have a healthy economy through supply-side tax cuts that promote the creation of capital, investment, and jobs (see Chapter 15). From this perspective, income inequality may in fact be a necessary condition for bringing people out of poverty because wealthy people are the only ones who have enough money to invest to create jobs. Indeed, Rick Santorum argued during the 2012 Republican presidential primaries that "There is income inequality in America. There always has been and, hopefully, and I do say that, there always will be."[18] Democrats argue that making the wealthy pay a larger share of their income in taxes could fund programs to help the poor directly rather than waiting for the trickle-down effect of tax cuts for the wealthy. From this perspective, a direct trade-off exists between inequality and reducing poverty, and progressive taxes are needed to help the poor.

Figure 16.3 shows a significant difference between the performance of Democrats and Republicans in reducing poverty. Between 1960 and 2013, Democrats controlled the White House for 25 years and Republicans for 29 years. During Democratic presidencies, the poverty rate fell from the previous year in 19 of those 25 years, and two years remained the same as the previous year. The poverty rate fell during Republican presidencies in only 14 of the 29 years they were in power and remained the same in three years. Overall, the mean change in the poverty rate was –0.40 percent in Democratic years, and it went up by 0.07 percent in Republican years. These differences may not sound like much, but given that each percentage point change in the poverty rate represents more than 3 million people today, the differences are significant. Political scientist Larry Bartels finds that in the past six decades, the inflation-adjusted incomes of working poor families (at the 20th percentile of income) increased 6 times faster under Democratic presidents than under Republican presidents.[19] This makes some sense given the political base of the two parties: Democrats win large percentages of the votes of poor people, and Republicans usually do better among wealthier voters.

Given all the statistics on income inequality and poverty, it is sometimes easy to lose sight of the human face of poverty. Hurricane Katrina, one of our nation's worst natural disasters, serves as a reminder of that human face. The hurricane killed more than 1,800 people, displaced 1.5 million people, and caused more than

WHAT DO POLITICAL SCIENTISTS DO?

For more on income inequality and policy, visit **wwnpag.es/wdpsd**

FIGURE » 16.3

CHANGES IN POVERTY RATES BY PARTY

The poverty rate tends to decrease under Democratic presidents and to go up by about the same margin under Republican presidents. What could explain this difference?

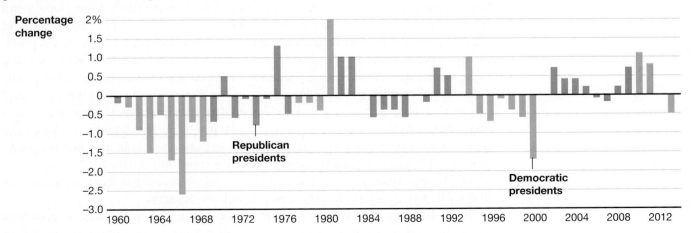

SOURCE: Data from the U.S. Census Bureau, Poverty: Historical Tables, available at www.census.gov/hhes/www/poverty/data/historical/people.html (accessed 11/6/14).

POVERTY AND INCOME INEQUALITY | **603**

$100 billion in damage. Middle-class and wealthier people were able to leave New Orleans as the hurricane approached, but 100,000 city residents did not own cars, and there weren't enough buses to handle all the people. A conservative columnist for the *New York Times* delivered a bitter assessment of the government's response: "The first rule of the social fabric—that in times of crisis you protect the vulnerable—was trampled. Leaving the poor in New Orleans was the moral equivalent of leaving the injured on the battlefield. No wonder confidence in civic institutions is plummeting."[20] The media coverage of Hurricane Katrina was shocking to millions of Americans. Images of bodies floating in the water and people standing outside the Louisiana Superdome with their arms outstretched to passing helicopters served as a stark reminder of the costs of poverty. Many Americans believe that such a thing should not be allowed to happen in our country, and national leaders vowed to address the problems exposed by the hurricane. However, despite $33 billion in public and private aid spent in the seven years after the disaster, large parts of the city have still not been rebuilt. Many of the 800,000 people displaced by the storm never returned: the 2010 census shows that the population of New Orleans is 29 percent smaller than it was in 2000.[21]

THE KEY PLAYERS IN SOCIAL POLICY MAKING

> DESCRIBE THE ROLES PLAYED BY EACH BRANCH OF THE NATIONAL GOVERNMENT AND BY THE STATES IN MAKING AND IMPLEMENTING SOCIAL POLICY

Congress, the president, and bureaucracy all play key roles in shaping social policy. State governments also play a central role in some policy areas such as education and welfare policy, while interest groups are especially important for policies that affect the elderly.

CONGRESS AND THE PRESIDENT

The previous section's argument about differences between Democratic and Republican administrations' performance in lowering the poverty rate ignored one important point: Democratic presidents were more likely than Republican presidents to have a Congress controlled by their party. In 16 of the 26 years of Democratic presidents, Democrats also controlled Congress; Republican presidents enjoyed unified control in only 4 of the 34 years from 1961 through 2014. This means that Democratic presidents had more opportunity to implement their agendas, whereas Republican presidents had to do more negotiating with the other party. You might argue that this divided control only prevented Republican presidents from making even deeper cuts in social programs that could have driven the poverty rate even higher, because Democrats in Congress would have been supporting those policies. Although this is a possibility, especially during the Reagan years, divided control may also have prevented Republican presidents from implementing their alternative vision of the best way to address poverty.

This discussion underlies the more basic point: Congress and the president both play central roles in shaping social policy. In some instances, the president may take the lead, as with FDR and the New Deal or Lyndon Johnson and the Great Society. In other instances, Congress plays a central role, as with health care reform in 2009–2010. In all cases, the president and Congress must find some common ground. This may be especially difficult under divided government, but even when the president and Congress are of the same party, Congress may be obstructionist: in 1993–1994 the Democrat-held Congress shot down President Clinton's health care proposal; in 2005, a Republican-controlled Congress ignored President Bush's effort to partially privatize Social Security; and in 2009–2010 a Democrat-controlled Congress did not follow through on President Obama's comprehensive immigration reform or take action on the administration's initiatives concerning global warming.

THE BUREAUCRACY

It may seem safe to assume that the bureaucracy makes little difference in social policy and that it simply implements the policies that are determined by Congress and the president. For some policies, that is fairly close to what happens. For policies such as Social Security that have levels of benefits determined by law, implementing policy largely involves determining that the proper amount of money is going to the right people and making sure that they receive the money. However, as discussed in Chapter 13, with many social policies, the "on-the-ground" public employees have a great deal of discretion. One study found that welfare agencies that handed out AFDC benefits had a more "hostile and punitive" attitude toward their clients than those who administered the disability program under Social Security. Welfare offices in general tend not to be very welcoming places. People often have to wait for hours, and welfare office workers are sometimes rude and ask their clients personal questions that are not required by law. Some potential welfare recipients are so alienated by the process that they give up.[22] This is not true of all welfare offices, but there are general differences in how recipients are treated in different types of social welfare programs. Sometimes problems of bureaucratic implementation may be at the top, as when problems concerning Veterans Affairs (VA) hospitals came to light in 2014. Thousands of veterans had long waits for services that were covered up by VA hospital administrators. Veterans Affairs Secretary Eric Shinseki was forced to resign for his failure to address the problem.[23]

Bureaucratic discretion may also serve more positive ends, though. Political scientist Daniel Carpenter reported that many bureaucratic agencies in the late nineteenth and early twentieth centuries developed political autonomy and strong reputations that allowed them to analyze and solve problems, create new programs, and plan and administer programs efficiently.[24] Many of the same insights apply to agencies that deliver social policies today, such as the Social Security Administration, which has a very strong base of popular and political support.

THE STATES

Social policy has always been strongly influenced by our system of federalism. As long as welfare has existed in the United States, it has been administered at the state and local level, with varying degrees of national control. The 1996 welfare reform bill, Temporary Assistance to Needy Families, gave more power to the states and eliminated all national guarantees. Medicaid is administered at the state

WELFARE OFFICES CAN BE alienating places in which it is very difficult to navigate through the bureaucracy. Dozens of women and children wait to speak to counselors in this East Los Angeles welfare office.

level (with federal assistance), and education is almost completely controlled by local and state governments. One sticking point with health care reform in 2009–2010 was the extent to which policy would be centered in the states or have a stronger national component. Many Democrats argued for a national "public option," while Republicans favored a more limited approach in which insurance companies would be allowed to compete across state lines. (The stronger national approach failed, but the new law clearly signaled a shift to a more national role in health care.) Education policy is another area where the trend has been toward more involvement of the national government rather than more power returning to the states. But even with the national accountability mechanisms and testing requirements established by President Bush's No Child Left Behind Act, and the incentives provided by President Obama's "Race to the Top" program, education policy remains largely a state and local affair.

INTEREST GROUPS

In general, interest groups that are advocates for social policy are not as influential as groups in other areas, such as business, labor, many other professional associations, or even other public interest groups such as environmental groups or those that focus on specific issues such as gun ownership. A major exception is AARP, one of the most powerful lobbies in the United States (see Chapter 10). AARP has long had a strong voice on behalf of Social Security and Medicare. For example, when President George W. Bush proposed "personal savings accounts" to replace part of the Social Security system, AARP mobilized its significant political muscle to crush the idea before it could receive serious debate in Congress. Similarly, as politicians discussed how to pay for relief efforts following Hurricane Katrina, one proposal was to delay or eliminate the new Medicare prescription drug benefit. AARP was not as vocal on this issue (it is difficult to argue against "everyone chipping in" to pay for hurricane relief), but it worked behind the scenes to make sure that the drug benefit was implemented.

Many interest groups and think tanks work on behalf of the poor, homeless, and other disadvantaged people, but decision makers in Washington, D.C., generally are less responsive to their concerns because these groups and the people they are aligned with are not politically powerful. The poor tend not to vote or donate money to political campaigns. Many politicians in Washington care deeply about issues concerning poverty, homelessness, and other social-policy problems, but the interest groups and think tanks that try to focus politicians' attention on these issues face a particularly difficult task *because of* the relatively disadvantaged position of the people they represent.

TRACE THE STEPS THROUGH WHICH PROBLEMS ARE ADDRESSED BY SOCIAL POLICIES

THE POLICY-MAKING PROCESS

Another way to understand the role of key players in making policy is to examine the various stages of the process. The How It Works graphic shows the stages for Social Security, but all policies go through similar steps. The first stage is to define a problem as an issue that requires the federal government's attention.

How It Works

THE SOCIAL POLICY–MAKING PROCESS

PROBLEM RECOGNITION

Attention is drawn to an existing problem. Often this can be triggered by an event or disaster, such as the emergency response to Hurricane Katrina, the impact of an economic recession on the jobless and the poor, or global warming.

AGENDA SETTING

Public awareness of the problem increases as the media, relevant interest groups, and political leaders talk about the problem. The problem becomes a priority for the government.

IMPLEMENTATION

The relevant bureaucratic agencies put the law into effect, writing specific regulations when needed, distributing benefits, and handling government contracts and procurement.

ENACTMENT

Congress passes the legislation and the president signs it into law.

DELIBERATION AND FORMULATION

Different policy proposals are suggested to address the problem, input is provided by interested parties, relevant executive agencies, and congressional committees.

EVALUATION

Policy analysts, inside and outside government, determine if the policy is working as intended.

POSSIBLE MODIFICATION, EXPANSION, OR TERMINATION OF POLICY

Based on the policy evaluations and public reaction to the policy, political leaders tweak the law to improve it, expand the scope of the law if it is working well, or sometimes repeal the law.

THE ENACTMENT AND EVOLUTION OF SOCIAL SECURITY

Social Security, the federal government's social insurance program to provide financial support to retired people, provides a good example of the various stages of the policy-making process.

A large proportion of elderly living in poverty.

As poverty among elderly worsened during the Great Depression, solving the problem became a priority as part of FDR's New Deal agenda.

The Social Security Administration implements the policy.

Social Security was passed by Congress and signed into law by the president in 1935.

The proposal for Social Security came from FDR's President's Committee on Economic Security.

Social Security has been evaluated at various times, most recently by presidential commissions on reform.

Social Security has been modified and expanded several times, most recently with the 1983 amendments.

POP QUIZ

1 Which stage in the policy process means making the problem or issue a priority for government?

a problem recognition

b agenda setting

c deliberation and formulation

d evaluation

e none of the above

2 In the case of Social Security, how does the implementation step of policy making occur?

a through presidential commissions on refor

b through the 1983 amendments

c through the Social Security Administration

d through the 1935 Social Security Act

e none of the above

Of the thousands of possible issues, Congress acts on only a relatively small number. Consider a social policy like food stamps. Poor and hungry people have been part of American society since the arrival of the first settlers, but this was not seen as a problem requiring government intervention until the twentieth century. What causes a society to change its assumptions about whether and how government should address social problems?

Sometimes there is a triggering event: the assassination of President John F. Kennedy led to the passage of gun control legislation, the energy crisis of the early 1970s led to the first comprehensive discussions of energy policy, and Hurricane Katrina led to a reexamination of our readiness for emergencies and our social safety net. Sometimes redefining an issue can move the policy to the next step of the process. For example, the estate tax has been part of our tax system since 1917, but when Republican leaders in Congress redefined it as the "death tax" in the late 1990s, it transformed the politics of the debate and made it a problem that needed a solution. After all, who could support a tax on dead people? (Of course, dead people don't pay taxes—the estate's heirs do—but that nuance was lost in the redefinition of the problem.)

Recognizing and defining a problem is just the first step; it still needs to come to the attention of political leaders and then get on the **policy agenda**. The basic idea is that when conditions are right, with the appropriate national political mood and participation from key interest groups and government actors, an issue can reach the agenda. Political scientists Frank Baumgartner and Bryan Jones describe a process of more abrupt change in the policy agenda as issues appear suddenly and then disappear almost as quickly after they are addressed, in a process they call "punctuated equilibrium."[25]

policy agenda The set of desired policies that political leaders view as their top priorities.

Once the issue is on the active agenda, alternatives are proposed and debated, and the final version of the policy is formulated in Congress (if it is a bill) or the executive branch (if it is an administrative action). Enactment involves a roll call vote in the House and the Senate and then a signature by the president, or a regulatory decision or administrative action by the bureaucracy, or unilateral action by the president (such as an executive order or agreement).

Many factors affect whether or not the policy is implemented successfully. First, the problem has to be solvable, and the policy must be clear and consistent in its objectives. It wouldn't make sense for Congress to pass a law telling the Department of Health and Human Services to "make sure everyone has health care" because such a law could not indicate how this should be done. Second, the policy must be funded adequately and administered by competent bureaucrats who have the required expertise. Finally, external support from the public and relevant interest groups may be critical to the policy's success. For example, AARP's support is critical for the success of any social policy that affects older people. Its support helped pass the prescription drug benefit that was added to Medicare in 2003 and comprehensive health care reform in 2010, and its opposition to the Catastrophic Coverage Act forced Congress to repeal the program one year after it was passed in 1988.[26]

Implementation of a policy is an ongoing process. To ensure that the desires of Congress and the president are being followed, policy evaluation is a critical stage of the process. (See Chapter 13 for a discussion of attempts by Congress and the president to control the bureaucracy.) Policy evaluation has become an increasingly visible part of the policy-making process in the past decade, following passage of the Government Performance and Results Act of 1993. George W. Bush's administration increasingly used this law, which was largely ignored throughout much of the 1990s, to impose accountability. Under the law, agencies are required to publish strategic plans and performance measures. Though these efforts sound impressive, it is incredibly difficult to assess whether a government program is achieving its aims.

Political scientist James Q. Wilson explains the difference between measuring success in the private and public sectors—specifically, he compares McDonald's to the Department of Motor Vehicles (DMV).[27] It is relatively easy to know whether McDonald's is doing a good job: simply look at the profits being generated and compare them to those of the previous period. If profits are going up at a reasonable pace, the burger flippers and fry cooks are doing their jobs. The DMV's performance is much more difficult to assess because there is no simple measure, such as profit, to look at. Maybe you could review the number of people served per hour or the average length of time people have to wait to get their driver's license. But that would ignore many other considerations, such as how well the DMV serves disadvantaged populations or people for whom English is a second language. We wouldn't expect a DMV office where 50 percent of its applicants don't speak English to be as efficient as one at which all applicants speak English.

Despite these limitations, extensive efforts to evaluate policy do provide decision makers with some basis for deciding whether to modify, expand, or terminate a policy. Programs are notoriously difficult to cut or eliminate. Examples abound, such as wool and mohair subsidies implemented after World War II and the Korean War. More than half of the wool needed to make uniforms during these wars was imported, so the Pentagon wanted to increase domestic production of wool. The National Wool Act in 1954 provided direct subsidies to farmers. By 1994 the program was spending nearly $240 million a year, despite the fact that the Pentagon removed wool from its "strategic materials" list in 1960! The subsidies were finally killed in 1994, but the 2002 Farm Act added wool and mohair to the list of commodities eligible for marketing assistance loans.[28] Some policies are like the zombies in *The Walking Dead*—unless you kill them in just the right way, they keep coming back.

ANALYZE THE CURRENT MAJOR AREAS OF SOCIAL POLICY

SOCIAL POLICY TODAY

In the 2015 fiscal year, Social Security, Medicare, and Medicaid make up nearly half of all federal spending ($1.8 trillion out of $3.8 trillion). With an aging population and health care costs that continue to grow as a percentage of the economy, these policies will take an even greater share of the budget in the future. Given other spending priorities, political pressure is mounting to put spending for social programs on a more sustainable path. This section will explain the nature of these important programs and discuss recent efforts to reform them.

SOCIAL SECURITY

Social Security Security A federal social insurance program that provides cash benefits to retirees based on payroll taxes they have paid over the course of their careers. It is a "pay as you go" program in which working Americans pay taxes to support today's retirees, with a promise that when today's workers retire, their benefits will be paid by the next generation.

Social Security is the most popular social program in the United States. Consequently, it has developed a reputation as the "third rail" of politics—like the dangerous, power-conducting rail on electrified train tracks—because a politician

610   **CHAPTER 16** | SOCIAL POLICY

who dares to touch Social Security risks political death. Despite serious problems concerning its long-term solvency, Social Security has proven remarkably immune to any steps that could be taken to shore up its financial health, such as cutting benefits or raising taxes. The third rail quality of the program has been especially evident to those who would like to privatize part of Social Security. President George W. Bush made a serious push for "personal savings accounts" that would replace some Social Security benefits, but Congress rebuffed him when his appeals fell flat with the American public. Why is Social Security so popular, what long-term challenges does it face, and what are the possible solutions to ensure the program's long-term viability?

One reason that Social Security is so popular is its universal quality—that is, nearly every working American participates in the program, from Donald Trump to the teenager flipping burgers at McDonald's. Once people retire, they are all entitled to Social Security checks without regard to how much income they have from other sources, such as dividends, interest, or other pensions. So, unlike many social programs that develop an "us against them" mentality ("Why should we have to support other people?"), Social Security does not pit citizens from different classes or ethnic groups against each other. Social Security is also popular because it works. It is more efficient than most privately managed pensions, with about 0.8 percent going to administrative expenses, compared with the average mutual fund that spends more than 1 percent. More important, Social Security has accomplished its central goal of helping most Americans have an adequate retirement income: fewer than 10 percent of the elderly are in poverty today, which is a lower rate than for the general public (see Figure 16.2) and significantly lower than the 35 percent of the elderly who were in poverty in 1960. Census data also show that nearly half of the elderly (44 percent) would be in poverty today without their Social Security payments.[29]

SOCIAL SECURITY'S LONG-TERM CHALLENGES Despite its successes and overall popularity, Social Security faces long-term problems. President Bush tried to convince the American public that Social Security was in crisis, but they did not want to hear it. Maybe "crisis" is too strong a word, but unless certain fundamental issues are tackled, the program will be unable to cover its obligations. The longer we wait to address the shortfall, the more difficult solving the problem will be.

The source of the problem is that there are basic changes in the nation's demographic profile. The **baby boom generation**, people born between 1946 and 1964, is just starting to retire, and between 2000 and 2030 the number of Americans over the age of 65 will more than double, whereas the number under 65 will grow by only 18 percent.[30] When this happens, there will be fewer workers to support the retirees. In fact, the number of workers per Social Security recipient has fallen from 15 in 1950 to 2.7 in 2015; by 2035 it will only be 2.1.[31] See Figure 16.4 for evidence of the aging population.

"Wait a minute," you may be saying. "Why does it matter how many workers there are for each retiree? I thought that Social Security was a pension program that you pay into while you're working and then get the benefits when you retire." Not exactly. Social Security is not a self-funded pension, but a "pay-as-you-go" system in which today's workers support today's retirees. Therefore, the huge increase in the number of retirees will strain the system because each worker will have to pay higher taxes to maintain the same level of Social Security benefits for retirees. Of course, benefits could be cut, but the third rail status of the program has prevented that, at least up to now. This problem was exacerbated by the deep

baby boom generation
Americans born between 1946 and 1964, who are retiring in large numbers over the next 20 years.

FIGURE » 16.4

PEOPLE 65 AND OLDER AS A SHARE OF THE U.S. POPULATION

Elderly people will comprise a much larger share of the U.S. population in 2050 than they do today. How might the aging population affect social policy—both in terms of the politics of policy making and in terms of the fiscal implications of this trend?

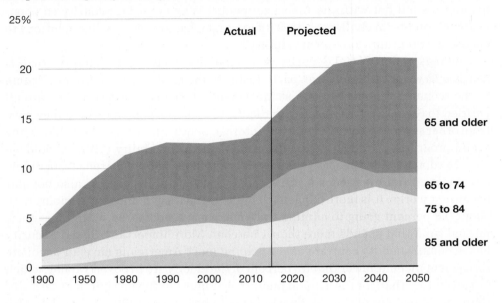

SOURCE: U.S. Census Bureau, 2012 Population Estimates and 2012 National Projections.

recession and prolonged unemployment starting in 2008, which reduced revenue from the payroll tax. Revenue declined even more in 2011–2012 when the payroll tax was cut by 2 percent (about $700 a year for the average worker) to help stimulate the economy.

Another problem with the pay-as-you-go nature of Social Security is the intergenerational transfer of wealth. The flip side of Social Security's success in reducing the poverty rate for seniors is that more children and working poor are in poverty today (21.8 percent of those under 18 are in poverty, compared to only 9.1 percent of those over 65, and 13.7 percent between 18 and 65).[32] Therefore, some critics have wondered if it makes sense, for example, to have a single mother who is working for the minimum wage or a recent college graduate who is just starting to work and paying off student loans pay 6.2 percent of their income in taxes to support the benefits of some people who are living comfortably in retirement. This critique also points out that current retirees will receive far more in benefits than they paid in Social Security taxes, while many current workers won't get back as much as they paid in (if interest on the taxes paid is considered). For example, an average worker who retired in 1990 got back all of his Social Security taxes, plus interest, by 1999. It is difficult to project the rate of return for current workers because we do not know what future benefits or taxes will be.[33] However, it is safe to bet that taxes will be higher and benefits will not keep up the same rate of increase that they have had for the past several decades. Therefore, today's retirees are reaping a windfall that strikes some critics as unfair, especially given that they are better off, on average, than the workers who are currently paying taxes. Now you can start to see why reforming Social Security is so controversial. Debate over Social Security reform exposes highly charged class-based and intergenerational tensions.

THE "PAY-AS-YOU-GO" NATURE of Social Security creates intergenerational inequities. Relatively poor young people working for minimum wage help to fund the Social Security benefits for retired people who are often reasonably well off.

HOW SOCIAL SECURITY WORKS Before we examine the various proposals to change Social Security, it is important to explain how the program works and to describe previous reform efforts. Social Security is funded by a payroll tax of 6.2 percent on income up to $117,000 (in 2014) with an equal 6.2 percent that is paid by employers. (The self-employed have to pay both halves.) The payroll tax also includes 1.45 percent on all income for Medicare (discussed later). This is a regressive tax because poor and middle-income people pay a higher percentage of their income for the Social Security tax than wealthy people pay. The maximum Social Security tax you can pay is $7,254 a year, which is 6.2 percent of $117,000. So a millionaire would pay less than 1 percent of her income in payroll tax (0.72 percent, to be exact) compared to the 6.2 percent that everyone earning less than $117,000 pays. Although the taxes are regressive, the benefits are progressive; that is, poorer people receive back in benefits a larger share of their lifetime payroll taxes than wealthy people receive (see Nuts & Bolts 16.2). One solution to Social Security's long-term fiscal problem is to increase, or even eliminate, the cap on income that is subjected to the payroll tax. This solution is opposed, however, by those who fear that it would undermine Social Security's popularity among wealthier people.

Policy makers have known about the baby boomers since the early 1960s, so why haven't they remedied the boomers' effect on Social Security? Actually, Social Security faced its first real crisis in the early 1980s, well before the boomers started retiring. Benefits had increased faster than payroll taxes throughout the 1970s, and the Social Security Administration estimated that it would not be able to meet its obligations as early as 1983. President Reagan and Congress appointed the National Commission on Social Security Reform to make recommendations regarding the program's short-term crisis and long-term problems. The commission issued its report in January 1983, which served as the basis for the 1983 Social Security Amendments. This law solved Social Security's short-term problems and made many other significant changes in the program.

The 1983 law's most significant changes were a gradual increase in the retirement age from 65 to 67 and increases in the payroll tax that generated surpluses for a trust fund to take care of the boomers' retirement. The first of these changes was relatively straightforward: people born in 1937 or earlier could retire in 2002 at age 65 and receive full benefits. Between 2003 and 2027 the retirement age

SOCIAL SECURITY

How Many People Get Benefits?

Number of Recipients for Old-Age, Survivors, and Disability Insurance

Old-Age Insurance (the basic retirement program)	41,284,000
Survivors Insurance (retirement program for widows, widowers, and the children of deceased primary wage earners)	6,191,000
Disability Insurance (payments for people and their families who cannot work because of a disability and are not yet retired)	10,996,000

How Much Do People Get?

Monthly Retirement Benefits

Individual	Average: $1,252	Maximum: $2,642
Couple	Average: $2,110	Maximum: $3,926
		(if one spouse does not work and the other earns the maximum)

SOURCE: All figures are from the U.S. Social Security Administration Office of Policy, "Monthly Statistical Snapshot, April 2014," available at www.ssa.gov/policy/docs/quickfacts/stat_snapshot/index.html?9s (accessed 6/4/14).

increases gradually to 67 for full benefits. Early retirement at 62 is an option, if the retiree is willing to accept a permanently reduced benefit level.

The second change, concerning the trust fund, is the source of great confusion and controversy. The idea behind the trust fund was sound: build up a surplus while the boomers are working and use that money to pay for their retirement. From 1983 to 2008 payroll taxes generated far more revenue than spending on Social Security. The problem is that the money wasn't really saved but spent on general government spending (for example, the war in Afghanistan, food stamps, school loans, and funding the FBI). In turn, the government gave the Social Security trust fund an IOU in the form of "special public-debt obligation." These IOUs are not tangible assets that can be traded on the open market; rather, their use is more like an internal bookkeeping mechanism. The government will pay off these IOUs, but the only way it can do so is through increasing taxes, cutting spending in other areas, or additional borrowing.

The best way to understand this is to examine the numbers from the Trustees Report on Social Security. In 2013, Old-Age, Survivors, and Disability Insurance had $855 billion in income ($726 billion from payroll taxes, $5 billion from general Treasury funds, $103 billion from interest on the trust fund, and $21 billion from taxation of Social Security benefits) and $823 billion in expenditures. So taxes fell $105 billion short of covering expenses ([$726 + $24] – $855). This means that the shortfall had to be made up with general tax revenue. As Figure 16.5 shows, the present value of the trust fund peaked at $2.7 trillion in 2013 and will move downward when promised benefits exceed payroll tax revenue. The trust fund runs out in 2033, at which point the Social Security system will be able to fund only about 77 percent of its obligations.[34]

FIGURE » 16.5

THE SOCIAL SECURITY TRUST FUND

As of 2015, the cost of the Social Security program exceeds Social Security payroll taxes, so taxes will need to be raised to cover the trust fund's obligations and the program's ongoing expenses. What do you think are the best solutions to address the long-term future of Social Security? What are the politically viable solutions?

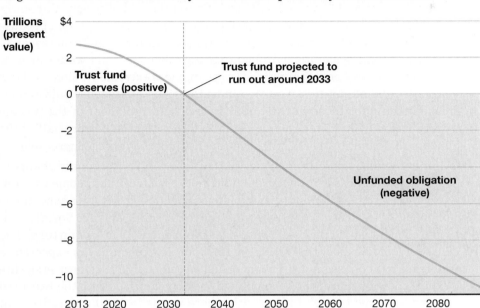

SOURCE: Social Security Administration, 2014 OASDI Trustees Report, Figure II D6, available at www.ssa.gov/OACT/TR/2014/tr2014.pdf (accessed 11/6/14).

Democrats and Republicans alike have misused this issue for political purposes. Democrats criticize Republicans any time they try to reform Social Security, claiming that the program is on strong fiscal ground—while ignoring that the need for $2.7 trillion from general taxes over a 21-year period will further strain the system and that a huge shortfall remains, even after generating that additional money. Republicans note that 2011 is the year in which Social Security started to be in trouble (which is correct) but then use this point to argue that the system is in crisis and that privatization is the only way out. President Bush suggested that Social Security would be "bankrupt" in 2037, which is incorrect given that the system would still be able to pay about 75 percent of its obligations. Although both sides have used the issue as demagoguery, both parties do raise important points. Republicans are correct that the sooner we act, the better. The system may not be in crisis today, but it *will* be if we don't do anything about it soon. Democrats are correct that the problems can be solved with relatively small changes to benefits and taxes, but the required changes won't be small if we wait much longer.

SOCIAL SECURITY REFORM So what is to be done? Dozens of plans to reform Social Security and make it fiscally sound for coming generations have been suggested. There is a surprising amount of agreement among all the serious plans that saving Social Security requires a mixture of benefit cuts and tax increases. The calculations get very complicated in terms of the projected fiscal impact of various reforms, but a mixture of these options would take care of the long-term fiscal problems of Social Security:[35]

▶ Raise payroll taxes by 1 percent and increase the income ceiling that is taxable.

▶ Lower benefits for nonworking spouses. Currently, nonworking spouses receive 50 percent of the benefit of their working spouse. Some proposals would cut that benefit to 33 percent.

▶ Index current and future benefits to inflation instead of wages. Currently, benefit increases are linked to national average wage increases. Because inflation does not increase as fast as wages, linking benefit increases to inflation would generate significant savings. Because this would mean a large reduction of benefits over the long run, a less extreme version has been proposed called progressive price indexing. This approach would reduce benefits only for those in the top 50 percent or 70 percent of the income distribution by indexing them to inflation (those in the bottom half of the income distribution would still have benefits indexed to wage increases).

▶ Gradually raise the retirement age to 70 (by 2030). This proposed change is viewed by many as fair because it adjusts for the fact that people live longer now than they did in the early years of Social Security. Life expectancy of people who turned 65 in 1940 was 78.7 years, so the average Social Security recipient would receive about 14 years of benefits. Those who turned 65 in 2009 could expect to live 18.9 years, and life expectancy is expected to increase by about six months per decade. Therefore, by 2030, the average life expectancy for those who reach 65 will be 85 years. To bring the expected stream of benefits back in line with where it was in 1940, the retirement age would have to be increased to 71.3.[36] Changing the retirement age to 70 would save $620 billion by 2040.

A more controversial proposal is this:

▶ Lower benefits for wealthier recipients. The strongest argument in favor of this approach is that Bill Gates doesn't need the measly couple of thousand dollars he will receive each month from Social Security. In fact, he wouldn't even notice if that money was used to reduce Social Security's deficit. More broadly, if benefits are phased out for those in the top third of income levels, it will save billions of dollars a year. The main argument against this proposal is that it would end the universal nature of Social Security and possibly turn it into another welfare program.

President Obama established a bipartisan commission to examine many of these long-term issues. The commission endorsed many of these ideas in their report with the dramatic title "The Moment of Truth." They favored increasing the retirement age to keep up with longevity, which would mean increasing it about one month every two years (so it would be age 69 by 2075), increasing the amount of income subject to the payroll tax so that 90 percent of all income is taxed, and making benefits more progressive (which would reduce benefits for wealthier people while actually increasing them for poorer people). The commission said that these changes would place Social Security on a secure long-term foundation.[37] However, despite the bipartisan nature of the recommendations, Congress ignored the report.

The most controversial plans concern partial or full **privatization** of Social Security. This is the main issue that divides Democrats and Republicans: Democrats favor maintaining the basic structure of Social Security's public social

privatization The process of transferring the management of a government program (like Social Security) from the public sector to the private sector.

insurance system, and Republicans favor moving part or all of the "pay-as-you-go" system to private accounts. The central argument in favor of private accounts is that over the long term, investing in the stock market has historically provided higher returns than the expected returns from Social Security. Also, with private accounts, all assets in the account are owned by the individual and that person's heirs; whereas with Social Security, when an individual dies, that person's heirs do not receive any additional benefits from his or her lifetime contributions to Social Security (but a surviving spouse continues to receive benefits from those contributions that will vary depending on the couple's work histories). Advocates argue that if everyone were able to take their 6.2 percent payroll tax and put that in a retirement account, they would have a modest nest egg by the time they retired that would almost certainly provide a stream of benefits larger than the Social Security check that they would receive under the current system.

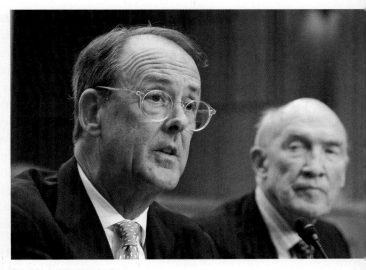

DEBT COMMISSION CHAIRMEN
Erskine Bowles (left) and Alan Simpson made recommendations to Congress and the president about how to fix Social Security. Despite the bipartisan nature of the commission and their recommendations, no reforms were implemented.

Democrats point out the problems with this approach—most important, the transition costs. Because the current system is "pay-as-you-go," if we stopped taking payroll taxes and allowed people to put the money into private accounts, there wouldn't be any money to pay for today's retirees. These transition costs—having to cover the retirement of all current retirees and everyone else who has paid into the system for a substantial number of years—are estimated to be $7 to 8 *trillion*!

A second criticism of privatization is that Social Security should be a part of everyone's retirement plan that they can count on. Investing in the stock market is fine as a supplement to Social Security, but everyone needs that dependable check, and investing in the stock market is too risky (as the collapse of the stock market in 2008–2009 reminded us). Although it is true that the stock market outperforms other investments over the long haul, there have been periods as long as 20 years when stock market returns have been flat. So if you happened to retire at the end of one of those slumps, you could find yourself with a much smaller nest egg than you had counted on. Finally, critics point out that the administrative overhead costs of these private accounts would eat up any additional returns that they might earn. Jack Bogle, the founder of Vanguard Investments and one of the leading proponents of low-fee index funds, points out that $1,000 invested in 1950 in a mutual fund that mirrored the returns of the S&P 500 stocks (with reinvesting dividends) would be worth more than $900,000 in 2014. However, if the mutual fund charged a relatively modest administrative fee of 2 percent a year, the nest egg would be reduced to $250,000![38]

These issues are not likely to be resolved anytime soon, which illustrates that politics is conflictual. Social Security reform can pit one generation against another or wealthy people against poor people. The stakes in Social Security are extremely high because it is the most popular and visible social program, which makes it all the more difficult to handle.

HEALTH CARE

Health care policy seemed as difficult to reform as Social Security. Every president since Theodore Roosevelt who attempted comprehensive reform failed until President Obama's success in 2010 with the Affordable Care Act (ACA). In order to understand the new law, we have to understand how health care is provided in the United States and what factors it addresses: the nation's aging population, health care costs that are rising faster than inflation, and the lack of health insurance among more than 42 million Americans.[39] The United States spends more on health care than any other nation in the world—more than $2.6 trillion, or 17.7 percent of GDP–compared to 9.3 percent for other developed countries (for example, Japan spends 9.6 percent, Germany 11.3 percent, Canada 11.2 percent, and Italy 9.2 percent).[40] All these countries have government-funded universal health care; thus, we spend almost 90 percent more than they do (in relative terms) but leave more than 42 million people without coverage (this number will continue to go down as more people are covered by the ACA). This set up a two-tier system in which those who had access to health care got some of the best care in the world and those without access were much less likely to get the health care they needed.

HOW AMERICA'S HEALTH CARE SYSTEM WORKS How is health care provided in this country, and how will the new law change it? As Figure 16.6 shows, our current system combines government spending (Medicare and Medicaid), private insurance, charity (donated care), and out-of-pocket payments. **Medicare** is the federal health care program for retired people, and Medicaid is the program that covers poor people. Both programs currently are administered by the Department of Health and Human Services.

Medicare has three main parts. Part A automatically applies to retirees when they qualify for Social Security; it covers inpatient care in hospitals and skilled nursing facilities, hospice care, and some home health care. Medicare Part B helps cover doctors' services, outpatient hospital care, and some other medical services

Medicare The federal health care plan created in 1965 that provides coverage for retired Americans for hospital care (Part A), medical care (Part B), and prescription drugs (Part D).

FIGURE » 16.6

THE HEALTH CARE DOLLAR: WHERE IT CAME FROM AND WHERE IT WENT

Funding for our current health care system comes from a variety of sources and is spent on many types of care. In an effort to slow the increases in health care costs, which areas should receive the most attention?

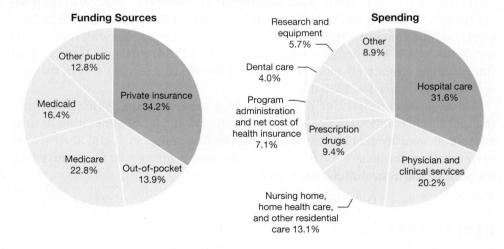

Note: Percentages shown may not add up to 100 percent because of rounding.

SOURCE: Centers for Medicare and Medicaid Services, National Health Expenditures data; spending data from Table 2; funding sources from Table 6, www.cms.gov/Research-Statistics-Data-and-Systems/Statistics-Trends-and-Reports/NationalHealthExpendData/Downloads/tables.pdf (accessed 5/30/14).

that Part A does not cover, such as some physical and occupational therapy, and other types of home health care. In 2003, Congress passed an important new benefit, the Medicare Prescription Drug Improvement and Modernization Act (Part D). The plan covers about 75 percent of the cost of prescription drugs for anyone who is enrolled in Part A or Part B of Medicare, up to a certain level of expenses (see Nuts & Bolts 16.3). The other government health care program is **Medicaid**, which serves poor people who otherwise would have no health care. Medicaid is administered through the states with substantial funding from the federal government. Although Medicaid is an **entitlement**, states have considerable discretion over the program. As the government's website on Medicaid explains, each state

> *(1) establishes its own eligibility standards; (2) determines the type, amount, duration, and scope of services; (3) sets the rate of payment for services; and (4) administers its own program. Medicaid policies for eligibility, services, and payment are complex and vary considerably, even among states of similar size or geographic proximity. Thus, a person who is eligible for Medicaid in one state may not be eligible in another state, and the services provided may differ considerably in amount, duration, or scope.*[41]

This variation in state coverage means that some states cover virtually all poor people, and others cover as few as one-third of those in need. Overall, nearly 71.3 million Americans receive health care through Medicaid at a cost of $544 billion. The federal government reimburses the states for 60 percent of the costs ($328 billion in 2015), but this percentage varies by state income level.[42] The federal government paid 74 percent of the Medicaid costs for the poorest state in 2015, Mississippi, and 50 percent of the costs for the 13 wealthiest states, which is the minimum level set by law.[43] Like Medicare, Medicaid faces growing budgetary pressures in the coming years. An increasing share of Medicaid's costs are for long-term nursing home care for the indigent elderly, which continues to grow as the population ages. Also, Medicaid enrollment is expected to increase by 4 million between 2012 and 2013 and is expected to increase by 8 million when the expansion of the program under Obamacare is fully implemented.[44]

Medicaid An entitlement program funded by the federal and state governments that provides health care coverage for low-income Americans who would otherwise be unable to afford health care.

entitlement Any federal government program that provides benefits to Americans who meet requirements specified by law.

16.3 NUTS & bolts

MEDICARE COVERAGE

Medicare Premiums for 2015

Part A (hospital insurance): Most people do not pay Part A premiums because they or a spouse has 40 or more quarters of Medicare-covered employment.

Part B (medical insurance): $104.90 per month.

Part D (prescription drugs): Varies by plan, $31 average in 2014.

Medicare Deductible and Co-insurance Amounts for 2015

Part A: Medicare pays all covered costs except a deductible of $1,260 during the first 60 days and co-insurance amounts of $315 per day for days 61 through 90 of a hospital stay and $630 per day for up to 60 "lifetime reserve days" that can be used at any time during one's lifetime. No costs beyond 150 days are covered.

Part B: $147 per year and then a 20 percent co-pay after meeting the $147 deductible.

Part D: $310 per year and then a 25 percent co-pay for the first $2,845 of drugs. The beneficiary then pays 50 percent of the next $2,850 of drug costs. After a $4,550 out-of-pocket annual limit is reached, Medicare pays 95 percent of the costs of drugs.

NOTE: Part C, known as Medicare Advantage, is not included here because it is not used nearly as widely as Part A or Part B and its provisions get quite complicated.
SOURCE: Medicare.gov, "Medicare Costs at a Glance," available at www.medicare.gov/your-medicare-costs/costs-at-a-glance/costs-at-glance.html (accessed 11/6/14)

FIGURE » 16.7

PROJECTED NATIONAL SPENDING ON HEALTH CARE (PERCENTAGE OF GDP)

If current spending patterns hold, an increasing percentage of federal spending will be devoted to health care, crowding out other programs. Clearly, such trends are not sustainable. What changes do you support to reduce health care spending in the long run?

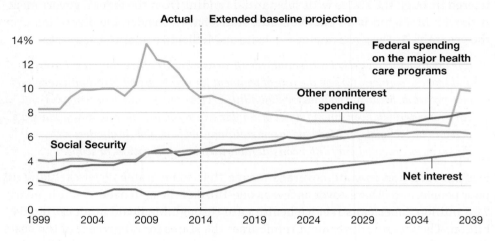

SOURCE: Congressional Budget Office, "The 2014 Long-Term Budget Outlook," July 15, 2014, Summary Figure 1, available at www.cbo.gov/publication/45471 (accessed 10/17/14).

THE AMERICAN HEALTH CARE SYSTEM'S LONG-TERM CHALLENGES The long-term fiscal problems of Medicare and Medicaid are severe. In fact, they dwarf Social Security's problems. The 2014 Medicare Trustees report estimates that Social Security's unfunded liabilities through 2088, or the amount of additional money (beyond the current payroll tax) required to fund all the program's commitments, is $10.6 trillion, and Medicare has unfunded liabilities of $24.7 trillion.[45] Even though such projections depend on assumptions about future economic performance, demographic trends, and other uncertain variables, the *relative* difference between the two programs is significant. Medicare's troubles are more than twice as serious as Social Security's! Although the long-term Medicare deficit is huge, the projected unfunded liabilities were cut in half by the ACA. However, the Trustees noted that their projections assume that cuts in Medicare reimbursements mandated in new health care law will stick. The report expressed skepticism that this would happen.[46]

Another study by the nonpartisan Congressional Budget Office showed that federal spending on health care (including Medicare, Medicaid, and subsidies for the new health insurance exchanges) will continue to grow through 2088 (see Figure 16.7). The CBO estimated that by 2088 federal spending on health care and Social Security would reach about 20.5 percent of GDP. That is, if the size of the federal government stayed around its historic average of 20 percent of GDP, the two major social policy programs would constitute all of noninterest federal spending by 2088. The choices are clear: either everything else must be cut from the budget (defense, education, transportation), health care costs and Social Security must be reined in, or the size of government will grow. There wouldn't be any money for anything else—defense, education—nothing. Clearly, the current trends are not sustainable.

HEALTH CARE REFORM Although comprehensive health care reform had been shot down repeatedly before the passage of the Affordable Care Act in 2010, several incremental reforms added up to substantial change. In 1996 Congress passed the Health Insurance Portability and Accountability Act, which guaranteed that people could not be denied health care coverage when they switched jobs. The new law also protected the privacy of a patient's health information. Medicaid was expanded in 1997 to provide health care for children in families that make too much to qualify for Medicaid but not enough to buy private insurance for their children (incomes that are no more than double the poverty level). By 2012, more than 5.6 million children were enrolled in the program (and 30 million children total are covered by Medicaid).[47] The Bush administration pushed for, and Congress passed, limited tax-free health savings accounts that may be used for paying routine out-of-pocket health care expenses or saving for more substantial, unexpected health care costs. Also, Medicare Part D, the prescription drug plan, went into effect in 2006. Despite these incremental reforms, discontent with the system continued to build.

THE UNFUNDED LIABILITIES FOR Medicare are estimated to be about six times as large as the Social Security shortfall. Yet Congress has a very difficult time acting because any solution involves the politically unpopular combination of tax increases and benefit cuts.

President Obama's primary focus when he took office in January 2009 was to get the economy going. However, he also campaigned on reforming our health care system, and he remained committed to that goal. Initially, Obama stayed out of the legislative fray in an effort to avoid the centralized micromanaging that had doomed President Clinton's attempt at comprehensive reform in 1993–1994. After poll numbers showed the public turning against health care reform, and a series of angry town hall meetings in which members of Congress faced questions about "death panels" and a government takeover of health care, Obama decided he needed to regain control of the debate. In a nationally televised speech before a joint session of Congress, Obama outlined his priorities, answered his critics, and linked the two top priorities of a revitalized economy and health care reform. He vowed to create a health care system

that eases up the pressure on businesses and unleashes the promise of our economy, creating hundreds of thousands of jobs, making take-home wages thousands of dollars higher, and growing our economy by tens of billions more every year. That's how we will stop spending tax dollars to prop up an unsustainable system, and start investing those dollars in innovations and advances that will make our health care system and our economy stronger.[48]

Obama presented several goals: controlling health care costs, providing comprehensive coverage (as close to universal coverage as possible), and paying for the program without adding to the deficit. He then urged Congress to hammer out the details.

In formulating the legislation, Congress sifted through hundreds of options that represent three main types: (1) national single-payer plans, (2) state-regulated health insurance networks combined with public subsidies to help pay for insurance for those who cannot afford it, and (3) market-based solutions based on tax credits and flexible spending accounts. The first of these was quickly rejected by Congress and is never likely to be implemented in the United States, despite being the program of choice for nearly all other Western developed nations. Critics dismiss single-payer plans as "socialized medicine" and point to the rationing of care that often occurs under such programs. Similarly, market-based solutions, which most Republicans supported, were rejected by Democratic leaders who believed the approach would leave too many Americans uninsured. This approach has the greatest potential for addressing the inflation of health care costs, but some health care professionals argued that many people would lack the knowledge base necessary to make the appropriate decisions concerning their own health care, because buying health care is much more difficult than shopping for food, clothing, or other consumer goods.

This left the middle ground between a single-payer plan and market-based approaches. In the introduction to this chapter, we discussed the politics of how reform passed. Here we summarize the main provisions, as it is impossible to discuss all the details of the voluminous, more than 2,000-page law that one reporter described as "twice as long, and half as intelligible, as Tolstoy's masterwork *War and Peace.*"[49]

UNDERSTANDING THE AFFORDABLE CARE ACT ("OBAMACARE") The president's first goal—comprehensive coverage—was essential. The problem had to be tackled as a whole. If the law were to require insurance companies to cover people with preexisting conditions without mandating that everyone obtain insurance, it became obvious that people would avoid personal expense and wait until they were seriously ill before they purchased any health insurance. Comprehensive coverage meant "pooling" healthy people and young people with older and sick people—to spread the costs of expensive care. Two ways this was achieved was by requiring businesses with more than 50 employees to provide coverage, and having all individuals who are not covered by employers to purchase insurance through new state-regulated private health insurance exchanges, which were implemented in 2014. It was determined that businesses and individuals who did not comply with the mandate would face government fines. However, individuals who could not afford to purchase their own insurance would receive federal tax credit subsidies (on a sliding scale—using a complicated formula that would provide the biggest subsidies to the poorest people and some support all the way up to four times the federal poverty rate). The individual mandate was one of the most controversial parts of the bill, but supporters point out that states already require people to purchase auto insurance if they have a car. During the formulation of the law, it was stated that most people who already were pleased with the current health insurance they had through their employer would not have to change anything. However, people with policies that did not meet the minimum standards of the law would be required to get new insurance policies. This became a sticky issue for President Obama once the ACA was rolled out.

Other features of the law included incentives to computerize medical records, seen as a way to improve the quality of care by reducing medical mistakes and facilitating medical evaluations and resultant care. Integration of technology into medical processes and recordkeeping was one of the law's central cost-control mechanisms. In addition, a new nonprofit organization, the Patient-Centered Outcomes Research Institute, would be authorized to engage in "comparative effectiveness research" to identify the best practices in health care. It would research such questions as which health care procedures work to make people healthier, and which are a waste of money, and why some parts of the country spend more than twice as much on treating the same conditions. The ACA would encourage health care providers to adopt identified best practices. The law was designed to also focus more resources on preventive care to keep people healthy rather than to wait until they get sick.

One other goal was that health care had to pay for itself. Obama vowed that the bill would not "add one dime to the deficit." With a price tag of just under $1 trillion over the first 10 years, paying for the bill was a challenge. However, a combination of higher Medicare taxes, a new investment tax for the wealthy, an excise tax on insurers for expensive "Cadillac" health care plans, new fees for drug companies and health insurers, and cuts in Medicare reimbursement meant that the law would actually reduce the federal deficit by $143 billion over the first decade.[50]

Nonetheless, the political battle over health care reform was not over when Obama signed the bill into law. House Republicans repeatedly attempted to repeal the law. As discussed in the chapter opener, although these efforts were not successful—because Democrats still controlled the Senate, and President Obama would have vetoed any bill of that kind that reached his desk—the rollout of the law was very rocky. The national health care insurance exchange, Healthcare .gov, was supposed to be operational on October 1, 2013, but the system repeatedly crashed during the first several months of operation, leading to substantial delays and great frustration for those Americans attempting to enroll. Millions of poor Americans were not able to get coverage when the states they lived in declined the option to expand Medicaid to cover everyone whose income was 138 percent of the poverty line (see Chapter 3 for a discussion of this conflictual issue). Because of the bumpy start, President Obama granted about a dozen extensions of various deadlines, including enrollment deadlines for the individual mandate, the employer mandate to cover all employees for businesses with between 50 and 100 employees (which was extended until the end of 2016), the high-risk pool that was intended to be temporary, and requiring people who had previously been covered by a substandard insurance policy to get insurance on the exchange (this too was extended until the end of 2016).[51] Another fallout included the resignation of Health and Human Services Secretary Kathleen Sebelius, who eventually left her position because of the botched Healthcare.gov rollout, which she described as "terribly flawed."[52]

Despite these substantial problems, the law is likely to survive. First, more than 8 million Americans who previously did not have health insurance have successfully used the exchanges to sign up for insurance, surpassing the original goal of 7 million. Also 4 million are covered through the expansion of Medicaid (a number projected to climb to 8 million enrollees by the end of 2014), and 3 million young adults have been able to remain on their parents' health insurance until age 26.[53] Second, many popular parts of the law have already been in effect for more than two years—and these types of benefits are hard to repeal once the American public recognizes their value. These include a high-risk insurance pool for adults with preexisting conditions (which includes making it against the law for insurers of children under 19 years old with preexisting conditions to be dropped from their parents' policies); a fix for the Medicare prescription drug plan "donut hole" (previously, people who spent above a minimal level on drugs but below a high amount were not covered by the law); and coverage for young adults (up to age 26) on their parents' plan. Other popular parts of the law that went into effect in 2013 prohibit insurers from charging co-payments or deductibles for preventive care on all new insurance plans, and prevent insurers from dropping policyholders when they get sick.

Opponents of the law have argued for "repeal and replace," but the "replace" part is even tougher than the "repeal." No single Republican alternative has universal support within the party, but most Republicans have argued for market-based reforms that would introduce more competition into the system to help keep costs down. One proposal that has received a lot of attention is Representative Paul Ryan's (R-WI) "Roadmap for America's Future." His proposal would change Medicare into a voucher system for everyone who is under 55 years old. Instead of the current Medicare system, people would receive a voucher to buy health insurance in exchanges similar to those that are being set up under Obama's health care reform.[54] Critics of Ryan's plan point out that Medicare is more efficient than private insurance, so this will only drive up the overall cost of health care. However, Ryan is correct that Medicare is currently not on a sustainable path, so some change is necessary.

Despite the uncertainty about the legal challenges and efforts by Republicans in Congress to repeal the legislation, the law will likely survive and be strengthened over the years. The legislation is far from perfect: about 10 to 15 million Americans will remain without health insurance when it is fully implemented in 2018, funding for the policy is shaky, and enforcement of the individual mandate is essentially voluntary (through the federal tax code). But if experience with other social legislation is any guide, the law is likely to be amended and improved as problems become evident. As Senator Tom Harkin put it, health care reform is not a mansion, but a "starter home with a solid foundation, a strong roof, and plenty of room for additions and improvements."[55]

INCOME SUPPORT AND WELFARE

When most people think of social policy aimed at helping the poor, they think of welfare. The earlier section on the history of social policy outlined the evolution of welfare from a limited policy aimed at helping dependent children of single mothers to a broader policy directed more generally to households headed by one person. Welfare is usually thought of as cash support for people who cannot support themselves. However, **income support** can take many forms, including food stamps, unemployment insurance, Supplemental Security Income, and the Earned Income Tax Credit. We will discuss each and then describe the major reform of welfare in 1996.

income support Government programs that provide support to low-income Americans, such as welfare, food stamps, unemployment compensation, and the Earned Income Tax Credit.

The Supplemental Nutrition Assistance Program provides food stamps, which are government-issued coupons that may be used as cash to buy groceries. Anyone who has an income that is less than 130 percent of the poverty level and has resources that do not exceed specific levels may qualify for food stamps. In 2014, the maximum monthly gross income to qualify for food stamps for a family of four was $2,522. As the effects of the economic crisis lingered through 2013, the number of people using food stamps peaked at a record of nearly 47.8 million in June 2013, with an average monthly benefit of $132.88 per person. As the economy improved, by early 2014 the numbers had dropped to just under 46.2 million but with an increase to $214.69 per person.[56]

The Federal-State Unemployment Compensation Program was established in 1935 as part of the Social Security Act. The U.S. Department of Labor oversees the program, but it is administered by the states. The program provides temporary and partial wage replacement for people who have been laid off from their jobs and helps stabilize the economy during recessions. States set a broad range in benefit levels, minimum amount of income earned, and hours worked during the period leading up to unemployment. (For example, you could not qualify for unemployment insurance if you have worked only five hours a week in a minimum wage job.) Also, laid-off workers have to make themselves "available for work." About 97 percent of all workers are covered by unemployment insurance, but only about half of the eligible unemployed make use of the benefit. The regular state programs provide up to 26 weeks of income support, and the Federal-State Extended Benefits Program temporarily provides up to 20 additional weeks in states with relatively high unemployment rates. In the third quarter of 2013, more than 5 million Americans filed claims (with 17.8 million over the previous 12 months), and the average weekly benefit check was $315, which replaced 32.9 percent of the average worker's previous salary. Workers received benefits for an average of 16.8 weeks in 2013.[57]

The Earned Income Tax Credit (EITC) is one of the most successful programs for providing income support for the working poor. Established in 1975, the program aims to help poor people move from welfare to work: it provides tax credits to people who do not earn enough to pay income taxes and are relatively poor. It is intended to offset the burden of Social Security taxes, which all workers pay as part of payroll taxes. In 2014, you could qualify for an EITC if you had two children and earned less than $43,756, one child and earned less than $38,511, or no children and earned less than $14,590; the figures are about $5,200 higher if you are married and filing jointly.[58] The federal government provided $63 billion in EITCs in 2013 to more than 27 million recipients, with an average benefit of $2,300 (a monthly benefit of $192 per recipient);[59] Figure 16.8 shows average monthly figures for other programs. Clearly, nobody is getting rich from this program, but it provides added assistance for the working poor.

FIGURE » 16.8

AVERAGE MONTHLY BENEFITS IN MEANS-TESTED PROGRAMS

Some types of social welfare benefits have increased in the past few decades, whereas others have decreased and some have remained the same. Identify examples from each category and try to provide a political explanation for why those benefits have increased, decreased, or been funded at about the same level.

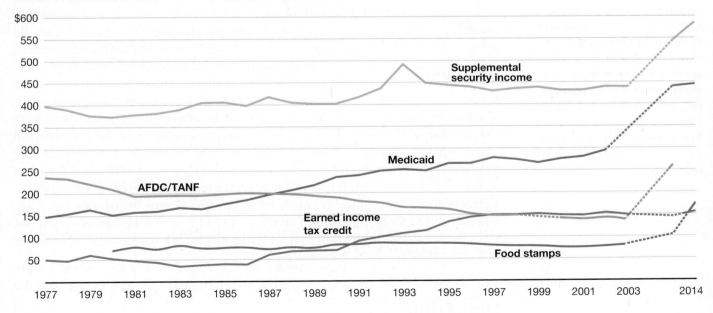

Note: AFDC is Aid to Families with Dependent Children; TANF is Temporary Assistance for Needy Families. Data from AFDC/TANF and the Earned Income Tax Credit cover people of all ages, including the elderly. Data are not available for some programs for certain years, such as TANF in 1999 or 2014. Dotted lines represent gaps in available data.

SOURCE: Congressional Budget Office, Economic and Budget Issue Brief, "Changes in Participation in Means-Tested Programs," April 20, 2005, p. 5, available at www.cbo.gov/ftpdocs/63xx/doc6302/04-20-Means-Tested.pdf, for data through 2003 (accessed 10/9/12). Various sources for 2012 and 2014 (2012 and 2014 figures are reported in 2003 dollars to allow comparison with the previous study).

Another source of income support for poor people is Supplemental Security Income (SSI), a program for aged, blind, and disabled individuals with limited income. The Social Security Administration runs the SSI program, but it is financed through general tax revenues, not Social Security taxes, and it is a means-tested program rather than a contributory program. Many states supplement the maximum monthly federal benefit of $721 for an individual and $1,082 for a couple (in 2014). More than 8.3 million people received SSI benefits in 2012, and 86 percent of those recipients were disabled or blind.[60]

Welfare is straight cash assistance for people who are not working and do not qualify for unemployment compensation. The primary welfare program for the latter half of the twentieth century was **Aid to Families with Dependent Children (AFDC)**. This program became increasingly unpopular through the 1980s, and in 1992 Bill Clinton was the first Democratic presidential nominee to campaign against welfare, promising to "end welfare as we know it."[61] President Clinton did not make this the top priority of his first year in office and instead focused on health care reform and balancing the budget. However, Clinton got the ball rolling on welfare reform in June 1993 by appointing a task force on the issue. Republican leaders offered their own alternatives in the House and Senate late in 1993 and early in 1994. Clinton's commission released its bipartisan plan in January 1994, and the president's plan was submitted to Congress in June.

When the Republicans took over Congress in 1994, the momentum for reform grew. House leaders submitted the Personal Responsibility Act as part of the Republican Contract with America. This bill promised to end welfare as an entitlement, allowing states more flexibility in setting benefit levels and work requirements, creating lifetime limits for the amount of time that people could receive welfare, and attempting to curb out-of-wedlock births by denying benefits. Clinton and Congress haggled over the issue for two years, with the president vetoing three versions of the bill that he believed were too harsh. Finally, in 1996 they agreed on a major reform called **Temporary Assistance for Needy Families (TANF)**. The new law set a five-year lifetime limit on welfare benefits, required single mothers with children above the age of five to find work after two years of receiving benefits, required unmarried mothers who were less than 18 years old to live with an adult and attend school to get full benefits, denied benefits to drug users who were convicted of a felony, and limited people who were not raising children and were between the ages of 18 and 50 to three months of food stamps in any three-year period in which they were not working. Perhaps most important, welfare lost its status as an entitlement and would be administered by the states with the assistance of federal block grants. In February 2006, Congress reauthorized TANF and required that half of a state's caseload participate in work activities for at least 30 hours per week (Congress has not reauthorized TANF since then, but has extended the program through block grants to states). Welfare reform significantly reduced the number of people on welfare, as Figure 16.9 shows, but it has been criticized for being too hard on the people who need government assistance the most. Critics also point out that TANF block grants have not been adjusted for inflation since they were first created in 1996.[62]

EDUCATION

Education policy is largely the domain of state and local governments. For the first century of our nation's history, the national government played virtually

Aid to Families with Dependent Children (AFDC) The federal welfare program in place from 1935 until 1996, when it was replaced by Temporary Assistance for Needy Families (TANF) under President Clinton.

Temporary Assistance for Needy Families (TANF) The welfare program that replaced Aid to Families with Dependent Children (AFDC) in 1996, eliminating the entitlement status of welfare, shifting implementation of the policy to the states, and introducing several new restrictions on receiving aid. These changes led to a significant decrease in the number of welfare recipients.

FIGURE » 16.9

PARTICIPATION IN MEANS-TESTED PROGRAMS

The social policy "safety net" is supposed to protect poor Americans during periods of economic recession. A deep recession happened in the early 1980s, and the other recession during the time frame depicted here was in the early 1990s. To what extent did the safety net accomplish that for which it was intended?

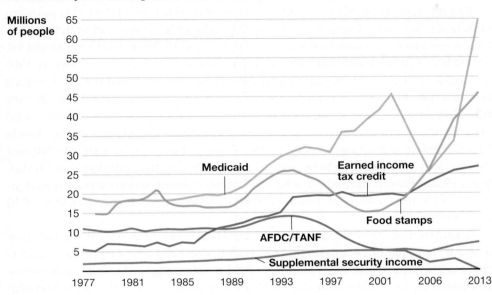

SOURCES: Data for 1977–2003 from Congressional Budget Office, Economic and Budget Issue Brief, "Changes in Participation in Means-Tested Programs," April 20, 2005, p. 3, available at www.cbo.gov/ftpdocs/63xx/ doc6302/04-20-Means Tested.pdf. Data for 2006 and 2009 from "Dynamics of Economic Well-Being: Participation in Government Programs, 2004 to 2007 and 2009—Who Gets Assistance?" www .census.gov/prod/2012pubs/p70-130.pdf (accessed 7/1/14). Most recent data collected by the author from various sources.

no role in education. One important exception was the Morrill Act in 1862, also known as the Land Grant College Act. This law gave land to eligible states to establish colleges that would promote education in the practical professions such as agriculture and mechanical arts. More than 75 colleges and universities today are land grant institutions.

The next major forays by the federal government into education policy came with the GI Bill of Rights in 1944, which provided access to higher education for returning World War II veterans, and the Elementary and Secondary Education Act of 1965, which was part of President Johnson's War on Poverty. The Department of Education was created in 1980, signaling the national government's interest in playing an important role in education policy by

▶ establishing and monitoring policies on federal financial aid for education,

▶ collecting data on America's schools and disseminating research,

▶ focusing national attention on key educational issues, and

▶ prohibiting discrimination and ensuring equal access to education.[63]

A more recent debate concerning the national government's role in education policy has focused on standards-based education reform: Should the national government establish standards and impose accountability as a way to improve public schools? The No Child Left Behind Act of 2001 requires yearly statewide standardized testing in math and reading. If the test results show that a school is not meeting annual academic benchmarks, it is labeled a "failing school," which means that it loses some federal funding and its students may transfer to another public school. Critics argue that standardized test results are a poor measurement of progress, as schools "teach to the test" and manipulate other aspects of the evaluation system. Even with these efforts at imposing a national approach, there is substantial room for variations in state and local implementation of the national law.

The latest example of a national effort to shape education is the Common Core standards that were developed by the National Governors Association in response to concerns that American schools were falling behind. This relatively modest set of standards in math and English was quickly adopted by 44 states between 2010 and 2014, but now is becoming a lightning rod for concern about national control of education. Conservative radio host Glenn Beck said that the standards "are breeding an entire new generation of slaves"; Louisiana Governor Bobby Jindal compared the standards to central planning in the Soviet Union, while Florida State Representative Charles Van Zant said the Common Core's goal is to "attract every one of your children to become as homosexual as they possibly can." So far, the backlash has led Indiana, South Carolina, and Oklahoma to rescind their adoption of the Common Core standards and repeal efforts are under way in at least 10 more states.[64]

President Obama's "Race to the Top" program is taking a "carrot" rather than a "stick" approach to educational innovation, dedicating $4 billion to competitive grants in 2010 and $1.35 billion in 2011 to encourage schools to adopt more challenging standards and better tools of assessment, promote better leadership and methods for assessing and rewarding excellent teaching, create better data systems for tracking students' progress, and obtain stronger commitments for improving the worst-performing schools. These grants were aimed at improving the quality of public education while also improving accountability.[65] Early in 2012 the Obama administration proposed the RESPECT project (Recognizing Educational Success, Professional Excellence and Collaborative Teaching), which is another set of incentive grants aimed at improving education. The grants would encourage school systems to give teachers more autonomy, make teachers' salaries more competitive with those of other professions while tying compensation to performance, improve teacher education programs while making them more selective, create teacher evaluation systems based on multiple measures, and reform the tenure system.[66]

States and local school districts are also experimenting with various policies aimed at introducing more competition for public schools, including public school choice, allowing students to choose which public school they attend, and publicly funded vouchers for attending private schools (see the You Decide feature). Private foundations have also gotten involved in education policy. The Gates Foundation has contributed more than $2 billion to create smaller schools, reduce class sizes, provide scholarships for higher education (most significantly, $1.5 billion to the United Negro College Fund), improve the use of data, and provide access to technology.[67]

UNDER THE NO CHILD LEFT BEHIND Act, schools conduct standardized tests every year. Schools that fail to meet federal goals receive less federal funding. Critics argue that the emphasis on testing distracts from other educational goals.

SCHOOL VOUCHERS

One of the most controversial areas of education policy over the past 15 years has been school vouchers—the practice of providing taxpayers' money directly to families to allow them to send their children to private schools rather than public schools. The vouchers are similar to a scholarship and are used in several states, including Wisconsin, Florida, Ohio, Pennsylvania, and Utah.[a]

Supporters of the program say that it introduces competition into public education, which suffers from the inefficiencies that are typical of monopolies. They argue that many urban school systems have failed to educate their children and that poor minority students deserve a better education than they can get in public schools. They say that students who are given the opportunity to leave public schools often improve their academic performance in private schools. Opponents say that private schools engage in "cherry picking," choosing the more motivated students and leaving the more difficult to educate in the public school classrooms, contributing to a downward spiral in these institutions. Opponents also argue that standardized test scores do not improve for students who participate in voucher programs. Finally, they claim that voucher programs are an unconstitutional violation of the separation between church and state because an overwhelming proportion of the students in these programs attend Catholic parochial schools.

Evidence on voucher opponents' first two points is mixed, but the bulk of the evidence supports their views. The most studied voucher program is the first in the nation, which was established in Milwaukee, Wisconsin, in 1990 using state funding. In the most systematic analysis of that program, John Witte, political scientist and expert on education policy, argues that vouchers should be evaluated on a basic question of values, the clash between freedom of choice and equality of opportunity, rather than specific programmatic outcomes, because the effects are small to nonexistent.[b]

The politics of school vouchers has created an unusual alliance between free market conservatives, who are typically Republicans, and inner-city minorities, who normally are strong Democrats. The former believe that school systems can benefit from introducing competitive market forces, and the latter are desperate for anything that will rescue their children from failing public schools. These supporters of vouchers are opposed by teachers' unions, most Democratic politicians, and those who favor strengthening the public schools by investing more money in them and trying new approaches, such as public magnet schools, charter schools, and public school choice.

The Supreme Court has upheld voucher programs while asserting that they did not violate the separation of church and state. However, in a case upholding Cleveland's voucher program, the Court did not give vouchers a green light beyond the

School vouchers are controversial. Supporters see them as a way to allow poor, inner-city students to escape failing public schools. Critics are concerned that vouchers compound the problems facing public schools, while potentially violating the separation of church and state: most school vouchers go to private, Catholic schools, like the one shown here.

narrow facts of the case. Indeed, that 5–4 decision required a voucher program to, among other things,

- be a part of a much wider program of multiple educational options, such as magnet schools and after-school tutorial assistance;
- offer parents a real choice between religious and nonreligious education, perhaps even providing incentives for nonreligious education; and
- not only address private schools, but ensure that benefits go to schools regardless of whether they are public or private, religious or not.[c]

Meanwhile, the Arizona state supreme court struck down school voucher programs as a violation of the separation of church and state.

CRITICAL THINKING QUESTIONS

1. What do you see as the advantages and disadvantages of providing vouchers to allow students to attend any school they want?

2. Should these programs be expanded, or would they undermine the quality of public schools?

CONCLUSION

The varying successes and failures of efforts to reform Social Security and health care reveal a great deal about the role of key players in the policy-making process. The interaction between the president and Congress is central to both stories. With Social Security reform, the president initiated a serious reform agenda, but Congress killed the proposal by failing to act. With health care reform, Congress and the president worked together to pass significant legislation. In both instances, interest groups played a key role. Doctors, other health care providers, insurance companies, and drug companies largely supported health care reform, which helped Congress pass the historic but controversial legislation. With Social Security reform, opposition from AARP and a tepid response from the public doomed the idea of private savings accounts, at least for now. But the last chapter on reform is yet to be written. Sooner or later, policy makers will have to confront the massive long-term deficits in these programs.

The experiences with social policy reform also illustrate the themes of this book. First, health care reform is a perfect example of the conflictual nature of politics. From initial debates over health coverage for illegal immigrants and abortion to repeated efforts to repeal the law in the House, health care reform ignited many contentious debates. Substantive disagreements about the scope of coverage and how to pay for it also revealed deep fault lines across and within the parties. Despite this conflict, congressional leaders pieced together compromises that created an imperfect but historic law. However, conflict over social policy is far from resolved. The reform of Social Security and Medicare provides fertile ground for intergenerational struggle and class conflict. Clearly, resolving the long-term problems facing social policy in the United States will involve many intense debates.

Social policy, especially the recent legislative struggles over health care reform, demonstrates that political process matters. The filibuster in the Senate played an important role in the first stages of shaping health care reform, and the decision to use the reconciliation process late in the game ensured passage of the law. House Republicans' decision to shut down the government in an effort to repeal the law ended up backfiring, but it is yet another example of how the political process can be used in ways that have substantive impacts: the shutdown cost billions of dollars and slowed economic growth. Politicians' decisions have a key impact on policy outcomes, and the timing and politics of the policy-making process clearly drive the results. Had congressional leaders made different decisions, it is possible that health care reform would have failed. Finally, politics is everywhere. Social policies touch all Americans at some point in their lives, and the struggles over reforming these policies are at the core of contemporary American politics.

THE HISTORY AND BACKGROUND OF SOCIAL POLICY

▶ *Explain what we mean by social policy, and how the national government's role in social policy has evolved.* **(Pages 597–600)**

SUMMARY

"Social policy" is the catch-all term for government programs that are designed to achieve a general social goal. While the early federal government took little responsibility for social welfare, it has gradually expanded its role since the late nineteenth century. Today, the federal government plays a significant part in ensuring the welfare of its people.

KEY TERMS

social policy (p. 597)
welfare (p. 597)
New Deal (p. 598)
Great Society (p. 599)
ownership society (p. 600)

CRITICAL THINKING AND DISCUSSION

What do you think should be the government's responsibilities in the area of social policy? Do you favor more of an "ownership society" or more of a direct role for the government?

PRACTICE QUIZ QUESTIONS

1. The first significant example of federal involvement in social policy is _____.

   Ⓐ the New Deal

   Ⓑ aid to Civil War veterans

   Ⓒ the Great Society

   Ⓓ aid to Mexican-American War veterans

   Ⓔ unemployment compensation in the 1890s

2. Social Security was established under the _____; Medicare was established under the _____.

   Ⓐ New Deal; Great Society

   Ⓑ New Deal; New Deal

   Ⓒ Great Society; Great Society

   Ⓓ Great Society; New Deal

   Ⓔ New Deal; Opportunity Society

3. The principle of the "ownership society" is that _____.

   Ⓐ the government has responsibility for the people's social welfare

   Ⓑ the government has responsibility for the poor's social welfare

   Ⓒ the government has responsibility for health care but not education

   Ⓓ the rich have responsibility for the poor's social welfare

   Ⓔ people have responsibility for their own welfare

POVERTY AND INCOME INEQUALITY

▶ *Examine the problem of poverty as a target of social policies.* **(Pages 600–04)**

SUMMARY

Most social programs have an impact on poverty, either directly or indirectly. There is a growing gap between the top income levels and the incomes at the bottom. Government policies tend to disproportionately favor the wealthy, largely based on the type of social policies the government chooses to implement.

CRITICAL THINKING AND DISCUSSION

Is growing income inequality a problem? If so, what are the most effective social policy programs that can address the inequality?

PRACTICE QUIZ QUESTIONS

4. The primary motivator for social policy is _____.

   Ⓐ economic dislocation

   Ⓑ poverty

   Ⓒ the deficit

   Ⓓ care for the elderly

   Ⓔ gender inequality

5. Under Democratic presidents, the incomes of working poor families _____ than/as under Republican presidents.

   Ⓐ increased faster

   Ⓑ increased slower

   Ⓒ stayed the same

   Ⓓ decreased slower

   Ⓔ decreased faster

THE KEY PLAYERS IN SOCIAL POLICY MAKING

▶ *Describe the roles played by each branch of the national government and by the states in making and implementing social policy.* **(Pages 604–06)**

SUMMARY

At the federal level, social policy is shaped by Congress, the president, and the bureaucracy. Other groups play a role in social policy as well: policy concerning the elderly is particularly affected by interest groups, whereas state governments focus on policy concerning welfare and education.

CRITICAL THINKING AND DISCUSSION

What happens when Congress and the president disagree on the appropriate direction for social policy? How does federalism play a role in shaping social policy?

PRACTICE QUIZ QUESTIONS

6. Bureaucratic discretion _____ agency-to-agency consistency of policy provision; it _____ ability to administer policies efficiently.

   Ⓐ increases; increases

   Ⓑ increases; decreases

   Ⓒ decreases; increases

   Ⓓ decreases; decreases

   Ⓔ decreases; has no effect on

7. States influence policies on _____, but not _____.

   Ⓐ Social Security; education

   Ⓑ Social Security; Medicaid

   Ⓒ education; Medicaid

   Ⓓ Medicaid; education

   Ⓔ Medicaid; Social Security

THE POLICY-MAKING PROCESS

▶ *Trace the steps through which problems are addressed by social policies.* **(Pages 606–10)**

SUMMARY

Once an issue is recognized and defined as a problem, and when the conditions are right, the issue reaches the congressional agenda. Once a policy is in place, its effectiveness and implementation are evaluated in an ongoing process, though very few programs are ultimately terminated.

KEY TERM

policy agenda (p. 609)

CRITICAL THINKING AND DISCUSSION

Which stage of the policy-making process do you think is the most important for having a successful social policy? Why is it so hard to eliminate a policy once it is created?

PRACTICE QUIZ QUESTIONS

8. What is the policy agenda?

   Ⓐ the set of policies political leaders view as priorities

   Ⓑ the set of issues political leaders view as priorities

   Ⓒ the set of issues that issue groups view as priorities

   Ⓓ the set of policies that issue groups view as priorities

   Ⓔ the set of policies issue groups and political leaders view as priorities

9. Relative to the private sector, public sector programs are _____ to evaluate.

   Ⓐ easier

   Ⓑ equally easy

   Ⓒ harder

   Ⓓ equally as hard

   Ⓔ not important

SOCIAL POLICY TODAY

▶ *Analyze the current major areas of social policy.* **(Pages 610–29)**

SUMMARY

The aging population and rising health care costs threaten the future of Social Security and Medicare, which currently make up half the federal budget. Despite the importance of reforming these programs, politicians are reluctant to enact serious policy changes for fear of jeopardizing their own political futures.

KEY TERMS

Social Security (p. 610)
baby boom generation (p. 611)
privatization (p. 616)
Medicare (p. 618)
Medicaid (p. 619)
entitlement (p. 619)
income support (p. 624)
Aid to Families with Dependent Children (AFDC) (p. 626)
Temporary Assistance for Needy Families (TANF) (p. 626)

CRITICAL THINKING AND DISCUSSION

Do you support the health care reform law that was enacted in 2010? Or do you think the law was not ambitious enough, or alternatively, that it was an overreach by the national government?

PRACTICE QUIZ QUESTIONS

10. Which group of working Americans is eligible to receive Social Security benefits?

    Ⓐ those whose income is in the bottom 15 percent

    Ⓑ those whose income is in the bottom 25 percent

    Ⓒ those whose income is in the bottom 50 percent

    Ⓓ income is not a criteria for eligibility

    Ⓔ only the unemployed are eligible

11. The primary reason Social Security will be financially strained in the coming years is because _____.

- A it is a pay-as-you-go program
- B its stipends are indexed to inflation
- C it is transitioning to privately held accounts
- D compensation to nonworking spouses is equal to benefits for the working spouse
- E most Americans don't approve of Social Security

12. State governments _____ have influence on Medicaid; they _____ have influence on Medicare.

- A do; do
- B do; do not
- C do not; do
- D do not; sometimes
- E do not; do not

13. In President Obama's health care plan, why was it essential to guarantee comprehensive coverage?

- A to make sure enough people were paying in to the system
- B to pool risk between sick and healthy people
- C to reduce the risks of fraud
- D to prevent individuals from having only one price to pay
- E to win broad political support

14. The major welfare reform of 1996 instituted the _____ program, which _____ welfare spending relative to its predecessor.

- A Aid for Families with Dependent Children (AFDC); reduced
- B AFDC; increased
- C Temporary Assistance to Needy Families (TANF); reduced
- D TANF; increased
- E Medicaid; reduced

15. The long-term fiscal problems of _____ are most severe.

- A Social Security
- B Medicare/Medicaid
- C welfare
- D federally subsidized student loans
- E education

SUGGESTED READING

Altman, Nancy J. *The Battle for Social Security: From FDR's Vision to Bush's Gamble*. New York: Wiley, 2005.

Bartels, Larry M. *Unequal Democracy: The Political Economy of the New Gilded Age*. Princeton, NJ: Princeton University Press, 2008.

Jacobs, Lawrence R., and Theda Skocpol. *Health Care Reform and American Politics: What Everyone Needs to Know*. New York: Oxford University Press, 2012.

King, Ronald F. *Budgeting Entitlements: The Politics of Food Stamps*. Washington, D.C.: Georgetown University Press, 2000.

Oberlander, Jonathan. *The Political Life of Medicare*. Chicago: University of Chicago Press, 2003.

Piketty, Thomas. *Capital in the Twenty-First Century*. Cambridge, MA: Belknap Press, 2014.

Skocpol, Theda. *Social Policy in the United States: Future Possibilities in Historical Perspective*. Princeton, NJ: Princeton University Press, 1995.

Soss, Joe. *Unwanted Claims: The Politics of Participation in the U.S. Welfare System*. Ann Arbor: University of Michigan Press, 2000.

Weaver, R. Kent. *Ending Welfare as We Know It*. Washington, D.C.: Brookings Institution Press, 2000.

17

Foreign Policy

MANY AMERICANS EXPECT FOREIGN POLICY to be an area of agreement and consensus—believing that as Americans, we hold similar goals and similar ideas of what our country should be doing outside our borders. As a result, many Americans agree with Senator Arthur Vandenberg, who said in 1945, "Politics stops at the water's edge." Americans tend to see disagreement over foreign policy as somehow unpatriotic and motivated by political factors. One of the central goals of this chapter is to demonstrate that simple answers are rare in foreign policy, and that conflict over the means and ends of American foreign policy reflect deep, sincere differences of opinion, among elected officials and the public.

The debate over what to do about the terrorist group ISIL (Islamic State of Iraq and the Levant) is a good example. ISIL, an offshoot of the Al Qaeda group that attacked the U.S. on September 11, 2001, is fighting a bloody conflict with the Syrian and Iraqi governments, with the goal of establishing an Islamic state throughout the Middle East. They have attacked civilians in both states, destroyed civilian neighborhoods and infrastructure, established Sharia law in the areas they control, beheaded Western journalists and aid workers—and released videos of the executions. Millions of refugees have fled the conflict (along with a separate civil war in Syria against the brutal Assad regime) to squalid camps in Turkey and Jordan. Many Western states, along with America's allies in the Middle East, worry that ISIL might launch terrorist attacks throughout the world and move to overthrow other Middle Eastern states, including oil-rich Saudi Arabia and America's ally Israel.

**CONFLICT &
COMPROMISE**
in American Politics

635

Describe the major approaches to understanding foreign policy and trace how America's role in the world has evolved.

▶ PAGES 637–46

Explain how the various branches of government shape foreign policy.

▶ PAGES 646–56

Examine the ways American foreign policy is implemented.

▶ PAGES 657–62

Analyze several major areas of foreign policy and why they are often controversial.

▶ PAGES 662–68

To some elected officials in Washington, D.C., these factors add up to a compelling case for U.S. intervention—that America must take steps by itself or with allies to destroy ISIL and remove the Syrian dictator, Bashir Assad, from power, using air strikes or even by putting "boots on the ground"—that is, sending American soldiers to the region. Though polls show some support for intervention (particularly if ground forces are not involved), some opponents argue that the United States has no responsibility to bear the cost of dealing with these conflicts, while others question whether intervention would have much chance of succeeding. Just as ISIL emerged after Al Qaeda was devastated by a series of U.S.-led attacks, another group might form after ISIL's destruction. And there is no assurance that intervention in the Syrian civil war would lead to a peaceful, democratic Syria.

This example demonstrates that we should expect disagreement over America's foreign policy. And we should not be surprised when these disagreements occur in government, even between civilians and military personnel. Though we will return to the case of ISIL and the Syrian civil war throughout the chapter, we could just as easily focus on the debate over how to deal with the Ebola virus to illustrate the causes and consequences of these conflicts.

This chapter will show that many areas of foreign policy are beset with conflict—and that making and executing policy often requires actors to compromise their differences. This discussion will also highlight how America's foreign and domestic policies are increasingly intertwined. Take the state of America's economy. As discussed in Chapter 15, over the last generation, American politicians have approved a series of treaties that reduced tariffs on imports and exports, generating enormous profits for some American companies. American aircraft manufacturers, for example, prospered under trade liberalization, selling passenger and cargo jets to airlines throughout the world. However, trade liberalization has hurt companies that could not respond to increased foreign competition, such as the financially troubled American auto producers that have required substantial federal aid just to stay in business. Many of their workers have been laid off or have taken incentives to quit their jobs or retire early rather than face an uncertain future of layoffs and wage cuts.

Examples of national unity in foreign policy are actually quite rare. Even after the September 11 attacks, the initial surge of unity and common purpose dissolved into debate over the specifics of America's response—from the initial decisions to invade Afghanistan and Iraq to contemporary debates over how best to fight the ongoing threat of terrorist attacks. Again, this conflict is nothing new. Throughout American history there have been many disagreements over foreign policy issues, from whether and how to use military force or form alliances to questions about foreign trade agreements and human rights policies. Although these debates often have political consequences, with positions sometimes taken for political gain, in the main they reflect sincere differences of opinion; in this sense, foreign policy closely resembles domestic policy.

Finally, the political process matters in foreign policy. The president's central role in the making of foreign policy stems in part from constitutional allocations of executive power, such as the president's leadership of the executive branch and his role as commander in chief of the U.S. armed forces. The president also benefits from his ability to act unilaterally, as discussed in Chapter 12. Even so, presidents do not have complete authority to determine America's foreign policy. Factors such as congressional control over federal spending as well as judicial review exercised by federal judges impose significant limits on presidential power in this area.

WHAT IS FOREIGN POLICY?

DESCRIBE THE MAJOR APPROACHES TO UNDERSTANDING FOREIGN POLICY AND TRACE HOW AMERICA'S ROLE IN THE WORLD HAS EVOLVED

Foreign policy refers to government actions involving countries, groups, and corporations that lie outside America's borders. Foreign policy includes military operations, economic interactions, human rights policies, environmental agreements, foreign aid, democracy assistance, interventions in civil wars and other conflicts, and international efforts to limit weapons of mass destruction, including nuclear weapons.

foreign policy Government actions that affect countries, corporations, groups, or individuals outside America's borders.

FOREIGN POLICY PRINCIPLES AND PERSPECTIVES

Foreign policy actions are often rooted in general principles or rules that guide people in their decision making. These principles and rules capture the decision to act, whether America acts alone or with other nations, and the motivations for actions. (See Nuts & Bolts 17.1 for a summary of these guiding principles.)

SHOULD WE ACT ALONE? Unilateral action occurs when one country does something on its own, without coordinating with other countries. For example, some U.S. antiterrorism operations under both President George W. Bush and President Obama, particularly in Pakistan, have been undertaken without any consultation with or notice to U.S. allies—not even to the Pakistanis.[1]

American foreign policy more commonly involves **multilateral action** by the United States alongside other countries or international organizations such as the United Nations. Since early 2008, more than 20 nations, including the United States, have conducted naval patrols off the Gulf of Aden in an attempt to deter pirate attacks against civilian shipping. The United States, in cooperation with the United Nations and several other nations, has sought to force the

unilateral action (national) Independent acts of foreign policy undertaken by a nation without the assistance or coordination of other nations.

multilateral action Foreign policy carried out by a nation in coordination with other nations or international organizations.

17.1 NUTS & bolts

THEORIES OF FOREIGN POLICY

Realism	Foreign policy is driven by a state's national interest, as defined by its leaders.
Idealism	Foreign policy reflects the ideals held by a state's leaders, such as protection of human rights.
Internationalism	States should, whenever possible, pursue their foreign policy goals by working together with other nations.
Isolationism	States should, whenever possible, work alone to define and implement their foreign policy, working with other nations only when absolutely necessary.
Constructivism	Foreign policy is not determined by objective factors such as national interest, by ideologies such as idealism, or by admonitions about working alone or with other nations, but by how a state's leaders define these factors.

Syrian government to negotiate with rebel forces and end the civil war in Syria peacefully. Along the same lines, the Quartet on the Middle East, a group comprising the United States, Russia, the European Union, and the United Nations, is working to facilitate peace negotiations between Israel and the Palestinians. Similarly, the United States and the European Union worked together to coordinate aid to African nations dealing with the Ebola virus.

SHOULD WE INTERVENE? A second important distinction in foreign policy is between **isolationism** and **internationalism**. Isolationists (including many Libertarians) believe that the United States should avoid making alliances and agreements with other nations, concentrate on defending America's borders, and let the people in other countries work out their problems for themselves. In the case of ISIL, an isolationist might argue that U.S. intervention would be futile or potentially counterproductive, too costly, or simply inappropriate.[2]

An internationalist, however, would argue that the United States should establish many agreements with other nations and intervene in international crises whenever it may be able to help, both because of possible economic and security gains and because intervening in civil wars and helping to solve humanitarian crises is morally right. In the case of ISIL, internationalists would support U.S. efforts to help and protect the local population, either in concert with other nations or alone if other nations are unwilling to intervene.[3]

ARE WE ONLY OUT FOR OURSELVES? The third major distinction in foreign policy making is between **realism** and **idealism**.[4] Realists believe that countries pursue their own interests, seeking to increase their economic and military power and their international influence. In approaching a policy decision, a realist would choose the policy that maximizes American military and economic power relative to other states. Idealists, in contrast, believe that states' concerns extend beyond increasing their power, including principles such as freedom or democracy. For an idealist, upholding these principles should be a primary goal of U.S. foreign policy. **Constructivists** offer an alternative to both positions, arguing that state actions are shaped by past events rather than ideological beliefs.

isolationism The idea that a country should refrain from involvement in international affairs.

internationalism The idea that a country should be involved in the affairs of other nations, out of both self-interest and moral obligation.

realism The idea that a country's foreign policy decisions are motivated by self-interest and the goal of gaining more power.

idealism The idea that a country's foreign policy decisions are based on factors beyond self-interest, including upholding important principles or values.

constructivism The idea that foreign policy is shaped by how a state's leaders define the national interest, ideology, and other factors.

THE QUARTET ON THE MIDDLE EAST is a group of countries and international entities that work together to help the peace process between Israel and Palestine. The quartet is made up of (from left to right) the European Union, represented by E.U. High Representative Catherine Ashton; the United States, represented by U.S. Secretary of State John Kerry; the United Nations, represented by U.N. Secretary-General Ban Ki-moon; and Russia, represented by Russian Federation Minister of Foreign Affairs Sergey Lavrov. Former British Prime Minister Tony Blair (far right) is the Quartet's special envoy.

To illustrate the differences between these explanations, consider the cases made by each side regarding intervention in Syria. Realist John Mearsheimer argued in 2014 that there was no need to intervene. [5] In his view, America had no compelling interest in the outcome of the civil war in Syria. Moreover, intervention would be costly, put American lives at risk, and could produce a wider conflict involving America's allies in the Middle East. In contrast, the idea that America is morally obligated to help Syrian rebels fight against their authoritarian, brutal government is a clear example of idealism, while constructivists would argue that America's unwillingness to intervene in the Syrian civil war (or attack ISIL) was driven by past events, such as the costly wars in Iraq and Afghanistan.

These terms are used often in foreign policy debates because they offer convenient ways to summarize the motivations behind policy decisions. That is how we use them in this chapter, but in reality, none of these terms provides a fully accurate definition of what motivates nations or individuals. No one is a realist or an idealist all the time.

Even President George W. Bush, whom many people have described as an idealist,[6] criticized his opponent, Al Gore, during the 2000 presidential campaign for supporting what Bush called **nation building**—the idea that the United States should intervene to end civil wars in countries such as Bosnia and Kosovo. This criticism is a realist argument; it suggests that because these conflicts did not directly affect the United States, there was no reason to get involved. Yet several years later, when discussing his reasons for going to war in Iraq, Bush said, "I believe we have a duty to free people, to liberate people."[7] Was Bush a realist or an idealist? It depends on the circumstances. His goals motivated him to advocate a realist position in some cases and an idealist one in other situations. The same is true for President Obama. His campaign promise to meet with hostile foreign leaders suggested an idealist perspective, but his increased use of drone aircraft against Al Qaeda in Pakistan and other countries and his decision to assist in NATO operations in Libya but to avoid sending ground troops to fight ISIL are more consistent with realism. For any leader, the realist and idealist labels summarize the motivations behind individual policy decisions and may not necessarily suggest what kinds of policies he or she might prefer in the future.

WHEN THE U.S. ACTS MULTILATERALLY in foreign policy, it often works through organizations such as the United Nations. Here, President Barack Obama addresses a session of the U.N. General Assembly.

nation building The use of a country's resources, including the military, to help create democratic institutions abroad and prevent violence in other countries.

HISTORY OF AMERICAN FOREIGN POLICY

This section reviews the evolution of American foreign policy. Its aim is to illustrate the types of choices American politicians face, how these policy options have changed over time, and the lack of agreement among American politicians about how to resolve these issues.

THE FOUNDING TO WORLD WAR I Until America's entry into World War I in 1917, American foreign policy was largely isolationist. Most presidents and other elected officials behaved in accordance with George Washington's assertion that the United States should "avoid entangling alliances" with other nations.[8] Isolationism made sense during this period for several reasons. America's distance from Europe reduced the potential for international economic interactions, lowered

Monroe Doctrine The
American policy initiated under
President James Monroe in 1823
stating that the United States
would remain neutral in conflicts
between European nations, and
that these nations should stop
colonizing or occupying areas of
North and South America.

the level of military threat, and gave early America room to expand without conflicting with European nations.[9] The **Monroe Doctrine**, established by President James Monroe in 1823, stated that America would remain neutral in wars involving European nations and that the United States expected these nations to stop trying to colonize or occupy areas in North and South America.[10] During this time, America expanded by purchasing land from other countries—adding much of the Midwest through the Louisiana Purchase—and by annexing land after military conflicts, such as the large section of the Southwest acquired from Mexico following the Mexican-American War. All of these actions were controversial at the time they were taken—some members of Congress opposed the Louisiana Purchase, for example, believing that then-President Jefferson had exceeded his authority and that America did not need to expand its territory.

America's foreign policy was never completely isolationist, however, even in the early years. The American navy was deployed on many occasions to protect U.S. ships and citizens, and America had several colonies far beyond its borders. America also built the Panama Canal, leasing land from Panama in the process, and sent troops into conflicts in Nicaragua and other Central American countries. America also maintained significant trading relationships with nations in Europe and elsewhere.

Still, America's involvement in World War I (1914–1918) marked a sharp departure in foreign policy, both in the country's participation in an international alliance and in the president's willingness to continue these activities after the conflict.[11] With the war almost over, President Woodrow Wilson offered a peace plan, the Fourteen Points, which proposed reshaping the borders of European countries to mitigate future conflict, creating measures to encourage free trade and democracy, and establishing an international organization that would prevent wars.[12] American diplomats participated in the negotiations that culminated in the Treaty of Versailles, which officially ended the war.[13] The treaty created the League of Nations, an organization similar to the modern United Nations, but the U.S. Senate rejected the treaty, which meant that the United States never joined the League of Nations.[14] (Again, this example illustrates the conflicts that have marked American foreign policy over the last 200 years.)

THE RISE OF INTERNATIONALISM A great transition in American foreign policy occurred during World War II (1939–1945). The United States became directly involved in the conflict only on December 8, 1941, declaring war on Japan the day after Japanese air attacks on Pearl Harbor in Hawaii and American bases in the Philippines. Germany subsequently declared war on the United States on December 11. However, prior to the United States' official involvement, the U.S. military had been supplying Great Britain and its allies with arms, ships, and other supplies, in return for payments and long-term leases on British military bases throughout the world—actions that only narrowly escaped a congressional veto.

During World War II, the Allied Powers—the United States, Great Britain, the Soviet Union, and other countries—fought as a formal alliance, forming joint plans and sharing military hardware and intelligence. After World War II, American politicians and scholars felt that the United States should be a central actor in world affairs. This new policy was justified by realist arguments, such as the need to deter future conflicts and the desire for economic benefits from trading with other nations.[15] Idealists argued for the same policies on grounds that America had a moral obligation to preserve world peace.[16] However, this shift toward internationalism only increased the amount of conflict in American foreign policy, as actors disagreed on where the United States should get involved; what the goals should be; whether intervention should involve military force, foreign aid, diplomacy, or some other policy tool; and whether the country should act alone or in concert with other nations.

THE COLD WAR Soon after World War II ended, the **Cold War** (1945–1991) began as the victorious Allies disagreed over the reconstruction of Germany and the reformation of Eastern European countries that Germany had occupied during the war. In a 1946 speech, former British prime minister Winston Churchill referred to an "iron curtain" that had split Eastern and Western Europe, leaving the East under Soviet domination with few political freedoms.[17] American diplomat George Kennan argued for **containment**—that America should use diplomatic, economic, and military means to prevent the Soviet Union from expanding the set of countries that it controlled or was allied with.[18] This idea served as a guiding principle for American foreign policy over the next generation.[19]

During this period the United States implemented several measures to build and strengthen alliances against the Soviet threat. The first was the Marshall Plan, a series of aid and development programs enacted in the late 1940s to restore the economies of Western European countries devastated during World War II.[20] The United States was also instrumental in the formation of the World Bank and the International Monetary Fund, as well as international trade agreements such as the General Agreement on Tariffs and Trade, discussed later in the chapter.

The United States also formed alliances with other countries, including the North Atlantic Treaty Organization (NATO) in 1949. The goal of these organizations was collective security, based on the principle that "an attack against one is an attack against all."[21] The aim was to deter Soviet attacks throughout the world by formalizing America's commitment to defend its allies.

Cold War The period of tension and arms competition between the United States and the Soviet Union that lasted from 1945 until 1991.

containment An important feature of American Cold War policy in which the United States used diplomatic, economic, and military strategies in an effort to prevent the Soviet Union from expanding its influence.

THE MARSHALL PLAN, WHICH HELPED European nations rebuild their economies after World War II, was part of America's strategy to build alliances against the Soviet Union.

The Soviets formed their own alliances, most notably the Warsaw Pact, with nations in Eastern Europe.[22]

The United States was also behind the 1945 creation of the United Nations (UN), an international organization with the aim of preventing wars by facilitating negotiations between combatants and, if necessary, sending military forces from member states to stop conflicts. Other aspects of the UN's role have included administering relief efforts for refugees, running development efforts, codifying international law, and publicizing and condemning human rights violations.

Clearly, the goal of containment influenced every aspect of American foreign policy after World War II.[23] The Korean War, in which American troops defended South Korea against invasion by North Korea, was motivated largely by containment—North Korea's efforts had the strong support of the Soviet Union and China.[24] America also supported brutal dictators in other countries, such as the Shah of Iran during the 1970s, and overlooked these governments' dismal human rights records on the grounds that their leaders would be valuable allies against the Soviets.[25]

America also maintained large military forces, beginning its first peacetime draft in the 1950s and building a large store of nuclear weapons. These weapons were intended to deter war with the Soviet Union through the threat of **mutually assured destruction**, the idea that even if the Soviet Union unleashed an all-out nuclear assault on U.S. forces, enough American weapons would remain intact to deliver a similarly devastating counterattack. The United States stationed hundreds of thousands of troops in Western Europe and elsewhere to deter the Soviet threat.

War nearly broke out during the Cuban Missile Crisis, when the Soviets attempted to station nuclear missiles in Cuba—within striking range of the United States. However, the issue was defused by a Soviet withdrawal in the face of an American naval blockade of Cuba and a secret American promise to withdraw similar missiles from Turkey in return.

In the early 1960s America became involved in the conflict in Vietnam, believing that North Vietnam's drive to take over South Vietnam was part of the Soviet Union's plan for world domination.[26] The **domino theory** posited that if the United States did not prevent the fall of South Vietnam, the next step would be a Soviet-backed conflict in the Philippines, Australia, or some other American ally. The Vietnam War demonstrated that the domino theory was fundamentally inaccurate; the conflict between North and South Vietnam was a civil war rather than an international event.[27] Though the North Vietnamese accepted Soviet support, they did not take orders from the Soviets.

Beginning in the early 1970s, President Richard Nixon and his national security adviser, Henry Kissinger, began a process of **détente** with the Soviet Union. It involved a series of negotiations and cultural exchanges designed to reduce tensions and promote cooperation.[28] These efforts culminated in the 1972 Strategic Arms Limitation Treaty (SALT I), which limited the growth of U.S. and Soviet missile forces.[29]

At the same time, the Arab nations' embargo prohibiting oil shipments to Western countries after the 1973 Arab–Israeli war was a reminder that containment of the Soviet Union could not be America's only foreign policy priority. Tensions over oil increased again when the Organization of the Petroleum Exporting Countries (OPEC) raised prices in 1979. Both events contributed to a recession in America and the electoral defeats of two incumbent presidents, Gerald Ford in 1976 and Jimmy Carter in 1980. Carter's defeat was also, in part, the result of the Iran hostage crisis, in which Iranian students, with government backing, held American embassy staff hostage for more than 14 months.[30]

mutually assured destruction The idea that two nations that possess large stores of nuclear weapons—like the United States and the Soviet Union during the Cold War—would both be annihilated in any nuclear exchange, thus making it unlikely that either country would launch a first attack.

domino theory An idea held by American foreign policy makers during the Cold War that the creation of one Soviet-backed communist nation would lead to the spread of communism in that nation's region.

détente An approach to foreign policy in which cultural exchanges and negotiations are used to reduce tensions between rival nations, such as between the United States and the Soviet Union during the 1970s.

Wall, which separated West Berlin from communist East Berlin, provided a powerful symbol of the end of the Cold War. With just one superpower—the United States—left, many predicted that democracy would spread and peace would prevail. However, new foreign policy challenges quickly emerged.

Tensions with the Soviets increased again with their support for the Sandinista rebellion in Nicaragua in the late 1970s and then with their invasion of Afghanistan in 1980.[31] In response to Soviet military actions in Afghanistan, President Carter withdrew the U.S. Olympic team from the 1980 games in Moscow, suspended sales of wheat to the Soviets, and increased defense spending. These increases steepened under Ronald Reagan, who vowed to put communism "on the ash heap of history." Notwithstanding this rhetoric, Reagan also worked to negotiate arms control agreements with the Soviet Union.[32]

The real change in U.S.–Soviet relations began with the selection of Mikhail Gorbachev as leader of the Soviet Union in 1985 and his policies of *glasnost* ("openness") and *perestroika* ("restructuring"). The Warsaw Pact was dissolved in 1991, with most of its former members becoming democracies. The Soviet Union splintered into 15 countries in 1991, effectively ending the Cold War. Scholars still debate the reasons for these changes. Some argue that the costs of responding to America's military buildup bankrupted the Soviet state, while others point to disaffection with the communist ideology and the inability of the Soviet economy to provide goods and services.[33]

Since the end of the Cold War, the United States and Russia have continued to disagree over many policies, including the enlargement of NATO to include most Warsaw Pact countries (Albania, Bulgaria, Czech Republic, Hungary, Poland, and Romania), the U.S. invasion of Iraq in 2003, the Russian invasion of Georgia in 2008, and the 2014 invasion of Ukraine. While tensions have increased in recent years, it is important to remember that only 20 years ago, both countries had enough weapons aimed at each other to destroy the entire world. Today, however, there is little chance of direct conflict between the United States and Russia.

AFTER THE COLD WAR: HUMAN RIGHTS, TRADE, AND TERRORISM The end of the Cold War, along with the growing number of democracies worldwide and the development of democratic peace theories (which argue that democracies will not fight other democracies), suggested to some observers that military conflicts would become much rarer, so that other concerns would more strongly influence America's foreign policy.[34] Events early in the post–Cold War era seemed to

THE AL QAEDA TERRORIST organization headed by Osama bin Laden was the driving force behind many terrorist attacks on Americans, including the 2001 attacks on the World Trade Center and the Pentagon. In 2011, American forces killed bin Laden, but the group, along with newer organizations such as ISIL, remains a significant threat.

support this thesis. Human rights became a more important foreign policy topic.[35] The United States became involved in humanitarian relief and nation-building efforts in Somalia, Bosnia, and Kosovo. A series of agreements, including the North American Free Trade Agreement (NAFTA) in 1994 and the formation of the World Trade Organization (WTO) in 1995, lowered tariffs throughout the world. Technological advances in transportation also lowered the cost of shipping goods worldwide, and the industrialization of many third world countries made them low-cost suppliers of manufactured goods to the United States, causing the closing of many domestic factories.

However, new security threats emerged in the form of terrorist groups, most notably Al Qaeda, led by Osama bin Laden. Al Qaeda organized several attacks on Americans, including the bombing of U.S. embassies in Tanzania and Kenya in 1998 and an attack on an American warship in 2000. Then came the Al Qaeda attacks of September 11, 2001. Some analysts and politicians, including President George W. Bush, described these attacks as part of a worldwide "clash of civilizations" or a global War on Terror, pitting the secular, open West against radical Islam.[36] After the attacks, President George W. Bush announced a new U.S. policy, the **Bush Doctrine**, or the doctrine of preemption, whereby the United States would not wait until after an attack to respond but would use military force to eliminate potential threats before they could be put in motion. This policy was behind the decision to invade Afghanistan in 2002, Iraq in 2003, and the ongoing operations against Al Qaeda, including the attack in August 2011 that resulted in bin Laden's death (see Chapter 12).

Bush Doctrine The foreign policy of President George W. Bush, under which the United States would use military force preemptively against threats to its national security.

In several respects, Barack Obama's presidency represents a sharp reversal of many Bush-era policies. Obama has emphasized improving foreign perceptions of America and Americans and avoiding unilateral action in favor of multilateral coalitions. The U.S.-led intervention against ISIL is typical of this new approach.[37] However, as we describe throughout this chapter, many of Obama's policies in regard to the War on Terror, such as his emphasis on drone attacks (see the You Decide feature in this chapter), are quite similar to those established by the Bush administration.

SHOULD AMERICA CARRY OUT DRONE ATTACKS AGAINST TERRORISTS?

One of the core elements of President Barack Obama's strategy to fight terrorist groups has been the increased use of drones—small, pilotless aircraft that fly into foreign airspace, monitor the activities of terror suspects on the ground, and, once the identities of suspects have been verified and the president's approval received, launch missiles to attack these suspects and their facilities. Over the last six years, drone attacks in countries such as Afghanistan, Yemen, and Pakistan have decimated the leadership and infrastructure of terrorist groups and inflicted significant casualties on lower-level fighters. Drones also played a key role in identifying the safe house in Pakistan where Al Qaeda leader Osama bin Laden was located, making possible the helicopter attack by U.S. Special Operations troops that resulted in bin Laden's death in 2011.

On the one hand, drones allow the United States to attack terrorists and terror organizations throughout the world without putting American troops at risk. Drone attacks are also less expensive than conventional forces. For example, rather than sending a Special Operations unit across the world to attack a target in the Middle East, American crews working at a base in Nevada can remotely control drones launched from a secure base in Saudi Arabia. Because they have no crew, drones can be small, quiet, and stay in the air for long periods of time, making a surprise attack more feasible. Even if an attack is not being planned, drones allow the United States to monitor suspected terrorists to identify their possible link to other individuals and organizations that threaten U.S. security.

Nonetheless, the use of drones by American forces continues to be highly controversial, with critics of the policy found both inside the United States and throughout the world. Some people foresee that the very advantages ascribed to drones—that they are relatively inexpensive and require no human pilots—could likely lead decision makers to use drones more quickly than they might conventional weapons. Opponents also predict that decision makers may be less likely to fully consider the merits and consequences of a drone mission before taking action than they would if contemplating an attack that would put American troops at risk. In a similar vein, there are those who believe that drones remove the personal element from warfare, making it easier to disregard the moral implications of an attack.

Moreover, at least up to now, drone strikes have occurred with little congressional oversight or approval. As we have discussed in Chapter 12, Congress has the power to limit military operations—but doing so in the case of drones would be difficult because most of these operations are carried out in secret. How could members stop an operation they didn't know about until after it occurred?

The use of drones is controversial in the United States and abroad. Here, a protester in Yemen holds a sign denouncing the practice.

Drone strikes also involve the possibility of civilian casualties or damage to the property of people who have nothing to do with terrorism. Of course, collateral damage is possible in any military operation. However, because drone operators view their targets through long-range cameras mounted on the drones, the chances of a mistake are higher compared to Special Forces units who carry out their attacks at short range.

The problem for decision makers is this: prohibiting drone attacks on suspected terrorists does not mean that these individuals and organizations will go scot-free; most of these operations will instead be carried out by American armed forces, with the risk that some of these troops will be wounded, killed, or taken hostage. Should decision makers use drones or send in the Special Forces? You decide.

CRITICAL **THINKING** QUESTIONS

1. The discussion gives several reasons why U.S. leaders might be reluctant to use drones to attack suspected terrorists. Besides the arguments about lower costs and not risking lives, what are the other advantages of utilizing drone attacks?

2. When might civilian and military leaders disagree about the decision to use drones? Why might military leaders be more likely to favor drone attacks?

And in the case of more recent events, such as the Syrian civil war and the ISIL conflict or Russia's conflict with Ukraine, there are no clear differences between the Obama administration's response and policies that would have been chosen by the Bush administration.

The so-called Arab Spring, during which governments in Middle Eastern countries from Tunisia to Yemen were toppled by citizen protests, also creates new challenges for American foreign policy. In some cases, such as Egypt and Libya, early hopes for a peaceful transition to democracy have shifted to criticism of attempts by the government to silence political opposition or the outbreak of open civil war. In other countries, citizens have demanded policies that are contrary to stated American goals, such as U.S. support for the state of Israel. What is clear is that the changes initiated by the Arab Spring raise new concerns for American policy makers.

> **EXPLAIN HOW THE VARIOUS BRANCHES OF GOVERNMENT SHAPE FOREIGN POLICY**

FOREIGN POLICY MAKERS

Who shapes the United States' relations with other nations, and what is the source of their influence? We begin with the president and the executive branch, then consider Congress, the courts, and finally, other groups and individuals outside the government. Nuts & Bolts 17.2 summarizes the foreign policy powers of the two most important actors: the president and Congress.

This discussion focuses on people and organizations in government whose primary job is foreign policy making, but virtually all executive branch departments and agencies have some responsibility for issues with international reach. For example, the Department of Education administers programs that fund undergraduate, graduate, and scholarly study of the politics, history, and culture of other nations, as well as educational exchanges with universities abroad.[38] Similarly, the Department of Agriculture oversees programs that encourage food exports to other nations and that protect Americans against unsafe imports.[39]

17.2 **NUTS** & *bolts*

FOREIGN POLICY POWERS OF THE PRESIDENT AND CONGRESS

President	Congress
Commander in chief of armed forces	Can declare war
Nominates and appoints senior officials in Department of Defense	Senate must approve defense nominees
Negotiates treaties and executive agreements with other nations	Treaties take effect only if approved by Senate
Changes policy with executive orders and findings	Can overturn orders and findings with legislation
Attempts to mobilize public opinion behind foreign policy goals	Makes policy using "Power of the Purse" (annual budget)

THE PRESIDENT AND THE EXECUTIVE BRANCH

The president is the dominant actor in American foreign policy.[40] Working with staff, the president can negotiate treaties or executive agreements with other nations, change policy through executive orders or findings, mobilize public opinion to prompt action by Congress, and shape foreign policy by appointing people to agencies and departments that administer these policies (see Chapter 12). The president also serves as commander in chief of America's armed forces.

Within the Executive Office of the President (EOP), the principal foreign policy agency is the **National Security Council (NSC)**, which develops foreign policy options and presents them to the president. The EOP also includes the Office of the U.S. Trade Representative, which focuses on tariffs and trade disputes; the president's Foreign Intelligence Advisory Board, a group of academics, politicians, and former government officials who advise the president; and the Office of Management and Budget, which prepares the president's annual budget proposals for federal agencies and departments, including those with foreign policy responsibilities.

National Security Council (NSC) Within the Executive Office of the President, an agency that advises the president on matters of foreign policy.

THE DEPARTMENT OF STATE The principal foreign policy department in the executive branch is the Department of State. Its head, the secretary of state, acts as the official spokesperson for the United States in foreign relations and is an important adviser to the president. State Department officials operate U.S. embassies abroad and interact extensively with the leaders of other countries; they also offer expertise on the politics, economics, and cultures of other nations. Aside from senior staff like the secretary of state, who is nominated by the president and confirmed by the Senate, State Department personnel are generally career civil servants who remain in their positions even after a new president takes office. There are many different offices and working groups in the State Department, from people who deal with treaties to coordinators of international aid, arms control, or assistance for refugees. This wide variation highlights the broad range of issues that are considered foreign policy.

SECRETARY OF STATE JOHN KERRY is the official spokesperson for the United States in foreign relations and is often one of the most powerful and influential members of the president's Cabinet.

THE DEPARTMENT OF DEFENSE The Department of Defense carries out military actions as ordered by civilian authorities, ranging from waging full-scale wars such as those in Iraq and Afghanistan, to conducting smaller operations such as the ongoing drone attacks against Al Qaeda forces throughout the Middle East, or sending ships and aircraft to monitor a North Korean attempt to launch a satellite into orbit.

The military's role in foreign policy is not limited to uses of force. Military personnel also deliver humanitarian aid or help American citizens evacuate from areas of conflict. For example, U.S. ships and helicopters delivered medical supplies and evacuated patients from nations in West Africa battling the Ebola virus. The American military advises and trains armed forces in other countries. And military personnel may also play a role in foreign policy making, with senior military officials serving as consultants during policy debates and midlevel officers serving in the NSC and on the staff of some congressional committees.

The overriding principle of America's military is the concept of **civilian control**—the idea that military personnel do not formulate policy but rather implement directives from their civilian leaders in the Executive Branch (the president and senior leaders in the Defense Department) and Congress. Of course, just as in other areas of the executive branch, members of the military are experts who will often know more than their civilian leaders about whether goals are feasible as well as the best ways to achieve them. The question is, what should a president do when military leaders disagree with his or her policy goals? Their disagreement may reflect fundamental problems with the president's plans or simply indicate that military leaders would prefer a different policy. As we discussed in Chapter 13, these dilemmas are inevitable in all areas of the bureaucracy, including the military, given the reality of bureaucratic expertise.

Most of the time, such disagreements are resolved through dialogue, or by the president and other civilian leaders consulting additional sources to either confirm the military's advice or negate it. In general, the norm is that disagreements between the civilians and the military are accepted as long as they are kept private and if military leaders carry out the orders they are ultimately given without hesitation.

THE DEPARTMENT OF HOMELAND SECURITY The Department of Homeland Security was formed after the September 11 attacks by combining the Coast Guard, the Transportation Security Administration, the Border Patrol, and several other agencies. The department's responsibilities are to secure America's borders, prevent future terrorist attacks, and coordinate intelligence gathering. Homeland Security's record is mixed. Although there has not been a major terrorist attack on American soil since September 11, 2001, the department has, to some extent, failed in its secondary mission to facilitate information-sharing and cooperation among various intelligence agencies in government.

INTELLIGENCE AGENCIES Agencies such as the Central Intelligence Agency (CIA) and National Security Agency (NSA) are primarily responsible for government intelligence gathering. Most of their work consists of collecting information from public or semipublic sources, such as data on industrial outputs. The director of national intelligence in the EOP leads and coordinates the activities of the various intelligence agencies.

HOW MUCH FOREIGN POLICY POWER DOES THE PRESIDENT HAVE? Some people argue that the broad powers of the modern presidency have allowed for "imperial presidents" who can implement their preferred foreign policies without the

civilian control The idea that military leaders do not formulate military policy, but rather implement directives from civilian leaders.

consent of Congress, the American people, or anyone else.[41] These complaints reflect a simple truth: presidents dominate the making of American foreign policy. America's initial attacks against ISIL and the Syrian regime, as well as the deployment of forces to aid Ebola victims, were made without explicit congressional authorization. During the 1990s, President Clinton ordered humanitarian aid for Bosnia and Kosovo and sent troops on peacekeeping missions, all despite opposition from Congress.[42] President George W. Bush responded to the September 11 attacks by ordering American forces to invade Afghanistan and Iraq—again with congressional approval given just as forces were getting into position to attack.

IN 2014, PRESIDENT OBAMA MET with Polish President Bronislaw Komorowski during a celebration marking the 25th anniversary of democracy in Poland. In addition to being the United States' chief diplomat, the president also tends to dominate decisions related to war and security.

The explanation for presidents' dominance of foreign policy lies in the theory of unilateral presidential power (see Chapter 12).[43] Although the Constitution grants the president several foreign policy powers, it does not set explicit limits on exactly what the chief executive can and cannot do. This ambiguity has given presidents considerable latitude to make foreign policy as they see fit. Members of Congress who disagree with the president must build veto-proof, two-thirds majorities in the House and Senate to overturn presidential foreign policy actions—an especially daunting task when the president's party holds the majority of seats in one or both chambers.

Nonetheless, presidents sometimes pull back from a new foreign policy if they believe congressional support will not be forthcoming. For example, President Clinton never submitted the Kyoto Protocol, an international treaty on combating climate change, for ratification by the Senate because he felt that if the treaty were put to a vote, it would fail.[44] Similarly, no president has ever submitted the 1996 Nuclear Test Ban Treaty for Senate ratification, although Presidents Clinton, Bush, and Obama have implemented a voluntary moratorium on tests. And congressional opposition was one argument against sending ground forces to fight ISIL.

Clearly, the president dominates foreign policy—but Congress can reverse or thwart presidential initiatives. Thus, in most cases when presidents appear to have acted without constraints, the reality is that members of Congress actually approved of the president's action, were unaware of the action, or were unwilling or unable to organize to overturn the president's policy.

CONGRESS

Several groups within Congress participate in making foreign policy. The Committee on Foreign Affairs in the House and the Foreign Relations Committee in the Senate are responsible for writing legislation that deals with foreign policy, including setting the annual budget for agencies that carry out those policies. These committees also hold hearings in which they pose questions to foreign policy experts from inside and outside government. The hearings not only educate committee members on foreign policy matters but also draw media and public attention to issues important to the committee. For example, during fall 2014, congressional committees held hearings on ISIL, the situation in Syria and Iraq, and America's response to the Ebola crisis.

The House and Senate each have an Intelligence Committee that oversees covert operations and the actions of the CIA, NSA, and similar agencies. Under current law, the president is supposed to give Congress "timely notification" of covert intelligence operations.[45] The intent is to ensure that someone outside the executive branch knows about secret operations and can organize congressional opposition if these actions are deemed illegal, immoral, or unwise.

Congress holds three types of influence over foreign policy, all of which force presidents to compromise with members of Congress when their policy goals are in conflict. The first is the power of the purse. Since members of Congress write annual budgets for every government department and agency, one way for members to shape foreign policy is to forbid expenditures on activities that members want to prevent.

Second, the Senate has the power to approve treaties and confirm the appointments of senior members of the president's foreign policy team, including the secretaries of state and defense, the director of national intelligence, and America's ambassador to the United Nations. Although it is rare for senators to reject a treaty or nominee, sometimes they issue preemptive warnings about what kinds of treaties they will accept or, more commonly, they never put to a vote any treaties that might be voted down.

Third, the Constitution grants Congress the power to declare war on other nations. However, the Constitution does not say that this declaration must occur before hostilities can begin or whether the declaration is necessary at all. In fact, although the United States has been involved in hundreds of military conflicts since the Founding, there have been only five U.S. declarations of war: the War of 1812, the Mexican-American War (declared in 1846), the Spanish-American War (in 1898), and both World Wars (declared in 1917 and 1941, respectively).

In an attempt to codify war-making powers, in 1973 Congress adopted the War Powers Resolution. This legislation was designed to limit the president's war-making powers and to give members of Congress a way to reverse a president's decision to deploy American forces. Although the resolution has been in effect for over 30 years, the question of which branch of the government controls America's armed forces remains controversial. (See the How It Works graphic for more details.)

Of course, members of Congress always have the power to block a president's foreign policy initiatives, but doing so requires enacting a law with enough votes to override a presidential veto, which is often an impossible task. In the debate over funding for the Iraq war, in 2007 the House and Senate passed a funding resolution that included a withdrawal timeline for U.S. troops, but it was approved by a margin of only a few votes in each chamber. After President Bush vetoed the resolution, the two houses passed a new funding resolution without these restrictions. In more recent cases, such as during the debate over U.S. participation in the NATO operations over Libya, resolutions were offered to cut off funding but did not pass either house of Congress.

THE FEDERAL COURTS

The federal courts, including the Supreme Court, weigh in on foreign policy questions through judicial review, determining whether laws, regulations, and presidential actions are consistent with the Constitution. For example, as discussed in Chapter 12, a series of lower court and Supreme Court decisions forced the Bush administration to revise its policies of holding terror suspects indefinitely without charges; the rulings required that the suspects be charged

How It Works

WAR POWERS: WHO CONTROLS THE ARMED FORCES?

THE PRESIDENT

As commander in chief, has the power to deploy troops.

Under the War Powers Resolution, has to notify Congress, and the use of force must be terminated within 60 days if Congress does not approve. However, Congress has never voted to terminate military action, and most presidents have argued that the act is unconstitutional.

Has the power to declare war (but has not used this power since World War II).

Has the power of the purse: can provide or withhold funding for military action.

CONGRESS

ARMED FORCES

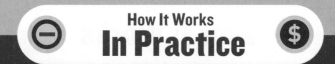

AMERICA'S ROLE IN LIBYA'S CIVIL WAR

America's 2011 intervention in the Libyan civil war illustrates how the constitutional allocation of war powers plays out in practice. Although President Obama had the authority to order American armed forces to participate in the operation, his decision came only after United Nations (UN) action and was subject to congressional control through the power of the purse.

CONGRESS   THE PRESIDENT   KEY EVENT

MAR. 1, 2011
Senate passes nonbinding resolution calling for a no-fly zone over Libya.

American and NATO naval forces move into position off Libyan coast.

MAR. 7–14, 2011
International leaders and organizations call for no-fly zone.

MAR. 17, 2011
UN Security Council passes resolution calling for no-fly zone.

MAR. 18, 2011
President Obama meets with senior members of Congress.

MAY 11, 2011
President Obama calls on Congress to approve American involvement in Libyan operations.

MAR. 28, 2011
President Obama gives speech to nation on Libyan operation.

MAR. 21, 2011
President Obama sends letter to Congressional leaders formally notifying Congress of American involvement in Libyan conflict.

MAR. 19, 2011
U.S. and NATO forces begin air strikes on Libyan ground targets and enforcement of no-fly zone, and send military supplies to Libyan rebels.

JUN. 15, 2011
House Speaker Boehner sends President Obama a letter warning that he would be in violation of War Powers Act unless Congress voted to approve Libyan operations.

JUN. 24, 2011
Approval resolution disapproved in House. Attempts to cut off funds for operations also rejected.

JUN–NOV. 2011
Libyan air strikes, no-fly zone, and shipments continue.

NOV. 1, 2011
Libyan operation ends.

POP QUIZ

1 The Constitution gives _____ the power to declare war.

a the president
b Congress
c the Pentagon
d the State Department
e the ambassador to the target country

2 However, in the past century, almost all military action has been initiated by

a the president.
b Congress.
c the Pentagon.
d the State Department.
e the ambassador to the target country.

with crimes and tried on those charges. Although this example shows how the courts can reverse presidential actions, two points are key. First, the trials did not give the defendants the same rights as those afforded to American citizens in criminal cases, allowing the presentation of evidence gained through coercion. Second, these trials occurred only after several cases spent years proceeding through the judicial system. During that time, the administration's policy remained in place, and the defendants were imprisoned without trial or any way to contest their imprisonment.[46] Even at the end of 2014, dozens of suspects remained imprisoned, years after they were initially detained, with no trial date in sight.

GROUPS OUTSIDE THE FEDERAL GOVERNMENT

A variety of individuals, groups, and forces outside of government influence foreign policy. These may be interest groups; the media; public opinion; as well as inter-governmental, nongovernmental, and international organizations.

INTEREST GROUPS Interest groups are organizations that work to convince elected officials and bureaucrats to implement policy changes in line with the group's goals. A diverse set of groups and organizations lobby government over foreign policy, including some foreign corporations and even foreign governments.[47]

One of the most prominent foreign policy interest groups is the American Israel Public Affairs Committee (AIPAC), which seeks "to help make Israel more secure by ensuring that American support remains strong."[48] AIPAC lobbies for increased military aid to Israel and American sanctions against Iran, among other matters, and the group contributes to the campaigns of congressional candidates who share its goals.[49]

Lobbying efforts can even involve foreign governments. In these cases, lobbying efforts center on economic and military aid, trade deals, and more

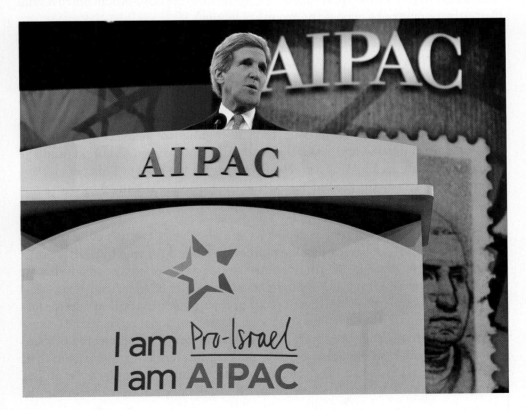

U.S. POLITICIANS AND GOVERNMENT officials regularly speak at American Israel Public Affairs Committee events; Secretary of State John Kerry is shown here addressing the AIPAC's annual convention. However, it would be a mistake to conclude that the attention paid to this or other interest groups automatically translates into U.S. government support for the groups' policy proposals.

general efforts to improve a country's image among members of Congress and the bureaucracy.

Sometimes interest group lobbying pits business interests against other concerns such as national security. For example, the Chinese government and one of its major technology firms, Huawei, have complained that the U.S. government has prevented Huawei from expanding into U.S. markets, even though its prices are lower than those charged by their U.S. rivals such as Cisco Systems.[50] Cisco and other firms argue that Huawei should be kept out of the United States because it sells equipment to the Chinese military that is used for spying and cyber attacks. Although these charges might be true (the evidence is classified, and Huawei may not know what its equipment is used for), it is also the case that U.S. technology firms have lost market share to Huawei in recent years. Raising national security concerns may just be a way to force the federal government to keep Huawei out of the lucrative American market.

Finally, some groups focus on publicizing international events in the hope of prompting citizens to demand government action. For example, the Stop Kony organization created a video to increase global awareness of Joseph Kony, leader of the Lords Resistance Army, and his alleged use of child soldiers in his fight against the governments of Congo, Central African Republic, and South Sudan.

As mentioned in Chapter 10, the impact of these lobbying efforts is hard to determine. Although AIPAC is a powerful interest group, it is likely that America's foreign policy would largely favor Israel regardless of AIPAC's actions, given the continuing strong support for Israel among the American public and elected officials.[51] Similarly, the Kony video, which, by spring 2014, had been viewed over 100 million times on various websites and had attracted considerable press attention, has not resulted in any new international action against Kony. Interest groups' influence over foreign policy depends mainly on the same two factors as their influence over domestic policy: groups hold the most sway when the issue's salience is low (few citizens care about the matter) and the issue is noncontroversial (few citizens or groups oppose the group's objective).

THE MEDIA Television, radio, print media, and the Internet all inform the public about events in America and elsewhere. As discussed in Chapter 7, although media coverage is a prime source of information about domestic and foreign policy for most Americans, one cannot say that evaluations of America's foreign policy are driven solely by the news media's decisions about what to cover and how to report it. In the case of ISIL, there is no doubt that one highlight of media coverage during 2014 was on the costs and risks involved with military intervention, and the dismal prospects for building a stable democracy in the region. This perspective reflected the facts on the ground during that time: a divided insurgency with some extreme elements, and deep tribal and cultural divisions within the population.

PUBLIC OPINION Foreign policy decisions are also sensitive to public opinion. In the case of ISIL, American public opinion in June 2014 was initially against intervention. However, by the time the government was seriously considering air strikes and overt military aid in September, a majority of Americans expressed support for this policy.[52] While these results probably made the military option less costly to administration officials and reduced congressional opposition to these plans, it is unlikely that they were the decisive factor. Though elected officials generally consider public opinion when making foreign policy decisions, their judgments take into account the problems of measuring opinions (see Chapter 6). Thus, as in the case of the Libyan civil war, where public opposition to intervention was almost as strong as it was in the case of Syria, the Obama administration disregarded the majority's opinions and sent in ships, aircraft, and a small number of Special Operations troops.

A second reason that foreign policy does not always mirror public opinion was discussed in Chapter 11. Most politicians have political goals other than winning reelection, including affecting some aspect of American relations with other nations. For example, President Obama's decision to join in NATO's operations in favor of Libyan rebel forces was taken in spite of strong public opposition—Americans opposed the intervention by a nearly 2–1 margin, close to the margin in the ISIL poll mentioned earlier.[53]

The final reason that American public opinion is not decisive is that many Americans know little about other countries. A case in point occurred during the 2014 conflict between Russia and the West over Ukraine: a survey asked Americans to locate Ukraine on a map.[54] The results are shown in Figure 17.1. Although two-thirds of respondents said they were following the situation in Ukraine "very closely," only (16 percent) of respondents were successful in locating Ukraine. Most people knew Ukraine's location only approximately, and a significant percentage were wildly wrong.

Americans are more likely to pay attention to foreign policy news or concerns following an important event. Thus, six months after the September 11 attacks, one poll found that Americans rated preventing future attacks a higher priority than any particular domestic policy, even though domestic policy as a general category took priority over foreign policy.[55] However, as the attacks receded into the past, the intensity of public concern about preventing future attacks

FIGURE » 17.1

WHERE'S UKRAINE?

These data reveal a marked lack of geographic knowledge among Americans. Despite the considerable media attention given to Russia's annexation of a portion of Ukraine, in a 2014 survey, only a small fraction can locate Ukraine on a map (more accurate dots are red, less accurate dots are blue). What might explain this lack of geographical knowledge?

SOURCE: www.washingtonpost.com/blogs/monkey-cage/wp/2014/04/07/the-less-americans-know-about-ukraines-location-the-more -they-want-u-s-to-intervene/ (accessed 8/5/14).

declined somewhat as well, and domestic concerns such as economic growth and unemployment became the paramount concern of most Americans, as noted in Chapter 6. Public opinion regarding ISIL and the Ebola crisis will likely follow a similar pattern in the years to come.

INTERGOVERNMENTAL ORGANIZATIONS, NONGOVERNMENTAL ORGANIZATIONS, AND INTERNATIONAL ORGANIZATIONS America's relationship with the rest of the world is not just about government action. Members of **intergovernmental organizations (IGOs)** and **nongovernmental organizations (NGOs)** provide information and humanitarian assistance and carry out other activities that the U.S. government is unable or unwilling to undertake. IGOs are associations of sovereign states, while NGOs are private organizations. Thousands of IGOs and NGOs operate throughout the world.[56]

A primary goal of NGOs is promoting global economic development and growth. One of the largest IGOs, the **World Bank**, funds economic development projects throughout the world. Another IGO, the **International Monetary Fund (IMF)** helps countries manage budget deficits and control the value of their currencies. Many NGOs, such as the Asia Foundation, focus on development in a particular region or on certain activities, such as microlending, in which banks or other institutions provide small loans to citizens in developing nations as a way of stimulating business growth and reducing poverty.

A second role of NGOs is providing humanitarian relief. In the wake of a disaster such as an earthquake or a flood, or during a famine or a war, organizations such as Oxfam International supply populations in crisis with basic necessities. Other groups such as Doctors without Borders provide medical care to populations threatened by violence, epidemics, or natural disasters. These groups played a key role in the response to Ebola in Africa. Some NGOs also promote human rights. Amnesty International spotlights international cases of people jailed for their political beliefs or held without trial, or the use of cruel punishments such as stoning. Amnesty's campaigns, as well as those of other NGOs, are not always supportive of U.S. policy. In recent years, for example, Amnesty has criticized the rendition of terror suspects by the United States.[57]

Finally, NGOs help to build democracies. The Open Society Institute funds efforts to increase mass political participation, strengthen political organizations, and verify the fairness of elections in new democracies throughout the world. The National Democratic Institute and the International Republican Institute conduct similar activities—both organizations, for example, sent groups in 2011 and 2012 to new democracies in the Middle East to assist with building party organizations and developing election rules in the wake of the so-called Arab Spring.[58]

The United States is also a member of many international organizations. Best known is the **United Nations (UN)**, an assembly of ambassadors representing almost all of the world's nations that addresses issues of worldwide concern. The UN is involved in economic development, environmental protection, humanitarian relief, and peacekeeping efforts. The United Nations has deployed peacekeeping forces to separate warring parties in Africa, the Middle East, and the former Yugoslavia. As of spring 2012, more than 100,000 UN peacekeeping troops, police, and other personnel were deployed in 16 different areas.

Inside the UN, the Security Council, a group of 15 nations (permanent members Britain, China, France, Russia, and the United States, plus 10 rotating nations), makes the most important UN decisions, particularly those involving its military missions. The UN General Assembly, in which each nation has one vote, debates and votes on other concerns.

intergovernmental organizations (IGOs) Organizations that seek to coordinate policy across member nations.

nongovernmental organizations (NGOs) Groups operated by private institutions (rather than governments) to promote growth, economic development, and other agendas throughout the world.

World Bank A nongovernmental organization established in 1944 that provides financial support for economic development projects in developing nations.

International Monetary Fund (IMF) A nongovernmental organization established in 1944 to help stabilize the international monetary system, improve economic growth, and aid developing nations.

United Nations (UN) An international organization made up of representatives from nearly every nation, with a mission to promote peace and cooperation, uphold international law, and provide humanitarian aid.

THE TOOLS OF FOREIGN POLICY

Now that we know the key players in foreign policy making, what are the tools and methods these players use to implement policy?

DIPLOMACY

The process of diplomacy involves using personal contact and negotiations with national leaders and representatives to work out international agreements or persuade other nations to change their behavior. Sometimes these efforts involve the threat of military action or economic sanctions, or incentives such as economic assistance or other forms of aid. The United States may participate directly in such efforts or mediate between the parties in a dispute. When two countries refuse to meet face-to-face, U.S. diplomats may take part in shuttle diplomacy, in which they meet separately with each country's representatives to convey the other country's proposals and counterproposals. For example, over the last generation, one of America's central foreign policy objectives was to help negotiate a peace agreement between Israel and the various groups that represent the Palestinian people. Virtually all of America's Secretaries of State, as well as special representatives appointed by the State Department, have been direct participants in these talks.

Diplomacy has often been a useful but limited foreign policy tool. For example, while America's intervention in the Syrian civil war was limited, the efforts of American and European diplomats were instrumental in forcing the Syrian government to transfer its stockpile of chemical weapons to an international consortium that disassembled and destroyed the weapons. American diplomats are also involved in many behind-the-scenes efforts to help resolve international disputes, such as the ongoing disagreement between Ukraine and Russia over the annexation of Crimea.

TRADE AND ECONOMIC POLICIES

Foreign policy is also aimed at sustaining economic growth in the United States and elsewhere, as well as creating foreign markets for the goods produced by America's domestic industries. Figure 17.2 shows total American trade (imports and exports) with other countries over the last 30 years, expressed as a percentage of U.S. gross domestic product (GDP), which measures the size of the U.S. economy. In recent years, imports and exports have constituted almost 40 percent of GDP. Investment returns (profits from American-owned companies located abroad) are also becoming an ever-larger component of total trade. In dollar terms, the same report estimated that the total value of U.S. trade with other nations was more than $6 trillion per year. Clearly, foreign trade is a critical component of the American economy.

The main tools of trade policy are tariffs and trade agreements. A **tariff** is a tax on the import or export of certain commodities, and a trade agreement sets tariff

tariff A tax levied on imported and exported goods.

FIGURE » 17.2

U.S. IMPORTS AND EXPORTS AS A PERCENTAGE OF GROSS DOMESTIC PRODUCT (GDP)

This figure illustrates the importance of trade to the U.S. economy. In recent years, imports and exports have accounted for almost 40 percent of U.S. economic activity, and the percentage is increasing over time. Based on these data, what arguments would you make for lowering or increasing barriers to trade?

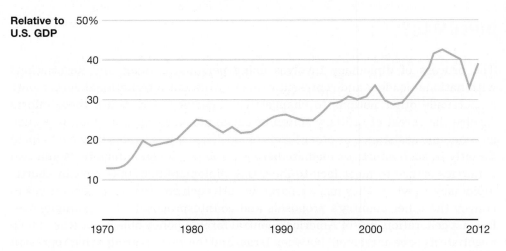

SOURCE: Office of the United States Trade Representative, *2014 Trade Policy Agenda and 2013 Annual Report,* available at www.ustr .gov/about-us/press-office/reports-and-publications/2014-0 (accessed 5/15/14).

levels or limits the quantities of particular items that can be imported or exported. The United States International Trade Commission maintains a list of all tariffs in effect.[59] By adjusting tariff rates, the government can help or hurt domestic industries. High tariffs on imports help American producers charge lower prices than foreign competitors, and low tariffs on exports help American producers sell to overseas markets.

Over the last two generations, the United States and most other nations have been lowering tariffs and establishing free-trade zones, agreements to eliminate tariffs on all imports and exports among specific nations. Examples include the North American Free Trade Agreement (NAFTA), a multilateral agreement involving the United States, Canada, and Mexico; and the Central American Free Trade Agreement (CAFTA) among the United States, five Central American nations, and the Dominican Republic. Other organizations, such as the **World Trade Organization (WTO),** facilitate negotiations over tariffs and provide a mechanism for adjudicating cases when one nation believes that another is using tariffs unfairly. Finally, the United States has granted many other countries **most-favored-nation status**: tariffs on imports to the United States from these nations are set at the lowest rate placed on any other nation.

Trade is an important part of foreign policy. The United States can use free-trade agreements and tariffs to bargain with countries for concessions in other areas. For example, in 2012, the United States and Europe imposed tariffs on solar panels produced in China, on grounds that Chinese firms were selling panels at below their cost of production in order to put American and European producers out of business. Ultimately, these cases were settled and the tariffs removed—partly because the Chinese government promised to limit its exports of solar panels and increase

World Trade Organization (WTO) An international organization created in 1995 to oversee trade agreements between nations by facilitating negotiations and handling disputes.

most-favored-nation status A standing awarded to countries with which the United States has good trade relations, providing the lowest possible tariff rate. World Trade Organization members must give one another this preferred status.

their price, and partly because American and European negotiators believed that China would respond to flexibility on the solar panel issue by eliminating some of its import tariffs and enforcing American and European copyright laws on software, movies, and video games.

Economic policies, which may involve the United States acting alone or with other nations, are also used to threaten or sanction countries as a way of inducing them to change their behavior. As noted earlier, in 2007 the UN Security Council authorized **economic sanctions** against Iran aimed at forcing the nation to stop enriching uranium, a first step in the production of nuclear weapons.[60] These sanctions included freezing bank accounts held by members of Iran's nuclear team and banning arms sales to the country. Additional sanctions imposed in 2012 cut off Iranian banks from international funds transfer networks, making it difficult for Iranian citizens and corporations to do business outside their nation's borders. If Iran agreed to stop its program, it would receive incentives such as civilian nuclear reactor technology and direct talks with the United States over various issues. At the same time, the United States also discouraged Israel from attacking Iranian nuclear facilities. This combination of carrots and sticks led to ongoing negotiations between the Iranians and a group of nations, including the United States and the European Union. However, as of the end of 2014, while the sanctions are clearly doing significant damage to the Iranian economy, no deal had been reached.

FOREIGN AID

Foreign aid is money, products, or services given to other countries or the citizens of these countries. Sometimes aid reflects the desire to provide basic assistance to satisfy fundamental human needs. For example, American military ships and aircraft are often used to deliver food and medical supplies to the victims of earthquakes and other natural disasters. Foreign aid also serves to stimulate economic growth in other nations. For instance, funding from the United States

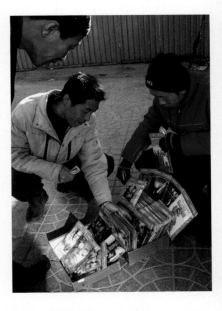

ONE OF THE MOST CONFLICTUAL issues involving international trade is the enforcement of copyrights on movies, music, and computer software. The Chinese government's refusal to enforce American copyrights has been a source of tension between the two nations.

economic sanctions Penalties applied by one country or group of countries on another, usually in the form of tariffs or other trade barriers.

THE AMERICAN MILITARY DELIVERED food and medical supplies to Haiti after a devastating earthquake in 2010.

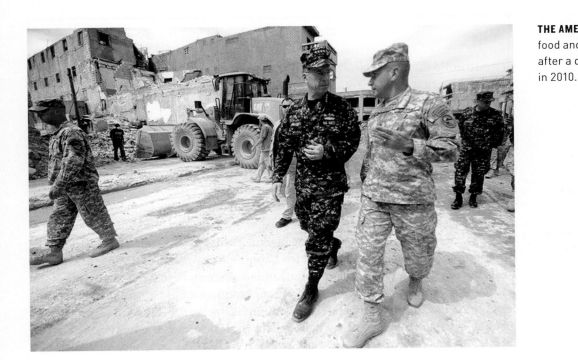

FIGURE » 17.3

U.S. FOREIGN AID IN COMPARATIVE PERSPECTIVE

This figure shows foreign aid contributions expressed as a percentage of gross national income (GNI). Do these data imply that America is less generous than other nations in its willingness to donate aid?

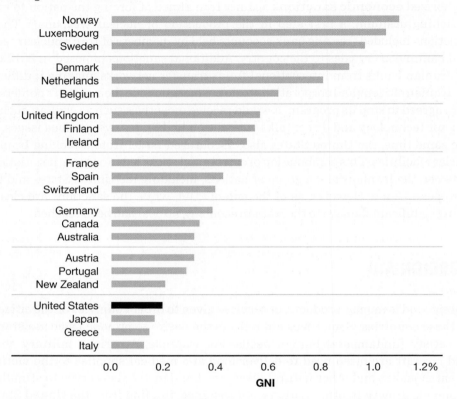

SOURCE: Organization for Economic Cooperation and Development, "Development Cooperation Report 2013," available at www .oecdilibrary.org/development/development-co-operation-report-2013_dcr-2013-en (accessed 5/14/14).

helps to build factories; pays for technical advisers who provide locals training on the construction and operation of water, power, or sewage treatment plants; and buys hardware to support infrastructure such as Internet access or telephone networks. Foreign aid also facilitates international agreements. For example, the peace treaty between Egypt and Israel in 1979 was facilitated by America's agreement to provide substantial military and economic assistance to both countries.[61] Promises of continued American aid to Israel were also one factor in discouraging Israel from attacking Iranian nuclear facilities in 2012.

Figure 17.3 shows the level of American nonmilitary foreign aid in 2012, measured as a percentage of gross national income (GNI, which includes GDP as well as accounting for investment income from other countries), compared to other members of the Organization for Economic Cooperation and Development. Considering the amount of U.S. foreign aid as a percentage of GNI suggests that the United States gives relatively little to other countries. Part of the reason for this perception lies in the size of the U.S. economy: America's foreign aid contributions are the largest of any country when measured in total dollars, but it also has the largest GNI of any country.

ALLIANCES AND TREATIES

A treaty is an agreement between nations to work together on economic or security issues. An alliance is an agreement that commits nations to security guarantees, which are assurances that one country will help another if it is attacked. America is a member of many international alliances, most notably the North Atlantic Treaty Organization (NATO); this alliance was formed by the North Atlantic Treaty after World War II to provide collective security against the Soviet Union and Warsaw Pact countries. The organization's mission shifted after the Cold War to focus on coordinating military force toward common goals, with the organization's air strikes in Libya the first instance of operations outside Europe.[62]

The United States is a party to many treaties, including bilateral agreements between the United States and one other country, and multilateral agreements involving the United States and several countries.[63] Many of these treaties, such as a series of arms control agreements between the United States and Russia (before 1991, the Soviet Union), implemented significant changes in both U.S. and other military forces, from capping the size of nuclear forces, to restricting the numbers of these forces, to banning some kinds of weapons.

Treaties and alliances enable the United States to commit itself to a course of action or signal its intentions to other nations.[64] By joining NATO and stationing troops in Europe, the United States guaranteed that if Warsaw Pact troops invaded the West, U.S. forces would be part of the resistance. More recently, when Russian forces threatened to invade Ukraine in 2014, America and its NATO partners sent aircraft, troops, and ships to countries adjacent to Ukraine to signal their opposition to Russia's plans and their support for the Ukrainian government.

MILITARY FORCE

Military force is a fundamental tool of foreign policy. America's military forces serve throughout the world as a deterrent to conflict. For example, the United States stations more than 28,000 troops in South Korea. Many are deployed at the demilitarized zone that separates North Korea from South Korea. Similarly, until the fall of the Soviet Union in 1991, hundreds of thousands of American troops were stationed in Western Europe (by 2014 only a fraction remained). Military exercises by U.S. troops, aircraft, and ships serve to remind potential adversaries of America's military power. For example, in early 2012, Iran threatened to close the Strait of Hormuz, a narrow passage that must be traveled by tankers carrying Middle Eastern oil exports. The United States responded by sending a carrier battle group to the strait to conduct flight operations—and to demonstrate that America was ready to keep the passage open by using force if necessary.[65]

The United States has also fought wars and lesser conflicts to further its foreign policy goals. Some are all-out military operations, such as the invasion of Iraq. More commonly, these deployments are short-lived operations ranging from the evacuation of American civilians from areas of unrest to the delivery of humanitarian assistance or the use of ship-launched cruise missiles to attack terrorist camps and similar targets.[66]

The size and power of America's military provides numerous options for policy makers. For example, after the September 11 attacks, in an attempt to prevent future terror attacks by Al Qaeda, U.S. forces invaded Afghanistan, which had been used as a base of operations for the organization.[67] It is highly unlikely that any other country could carry out such a large-scale operation so far from home. America's military also provided the majority of international forces in the attacks in Libya and Syria and against ISIL, as well as the aid sent to Ebola victims in Africa.

Nonetheless, military force is not all-powerful. For example, despite over a decade of combat operations in Afghanistan and large amounts of economic and military aid to the Afghan government, the Taliban (a religious-political organization) still controls a significant percentage of the Afghan countryside, and the Afghan government's ability to defeat the Taliban without American help is highly questionable. In the case of Russia's conflict with Ukraine, it is hard to see how American military force could be used productively without risking a much larger conflict.

THE POLITICS OF FOREIGN POLICY TODAY

ANALYZE SEVERAL MAJOR AREAS OF FOREIGN POLICY AND WHY THEY ARE OFTEN CONTROVERSIAL

The making of foreign policy, like everything else in the federal government, is a political act—a contest involving elected officials, bureaucrats, interest groups, and other actors, all of whom have their own goals. In this sense, there are always conflicts over what America's foreign policy should look like, and compromise is fundamental to the making of it. This section describes three of the major foreign policy issues facing America in the contemporary era: trade, terrorism, and nuclear proliferation—and how all of these issues raise human rights concerns. In each case, we will focus on one country: China, Afghanistan, and North Korea. These issues demonstrate the complexity of America's foreign policy choices, and how these decisions are shaped both by conflicts and by political processes.

In addition, this section argues against claims about the decline of American influence throughout the world. Although it is true that other countries such as China and India are increasing their economic and military power and that the United States faces many new and complex issues, it still continues to be an international power, and in many respects is the strongest nation on the globe, with enormous influence over economic, social, and military events worldwide. How the issues described in this section will be resolved remains in question, but there is no doubt that the foreign policy choices of the United States will play a decisive role in their resolution.

MANAGING INTERNATIONAL TRADE: CHINA

For the United States, trade is a necessity. America imports a wide range of resources and manufactured goods from other countries. Increased trade can also enhance economic growth. Many economic analyses describe trade in terms of the theory of comparative advantage, which says that nations export items they can produce cheaply, in return for imports that can be produced more efficiently elsewhere. Similarly, outsourcing jobs to foreign countries with lower labor costs makes American companies more efficient, which raises their profits and allows them to expand operations, which may result in new jobs.

These practices are examples of **globalization**, reflecting the trend toward increasing interaction and connections among individuals, corporations, and nations (see Chapter 15). New technologies have leveled the global playing field, allowing suppliers of goods and services to sell their products throughout the world. Many American companies and their employees profit from this process. Reflecting this development, the last generation of American politics has been marked by international agreements such as NAFTA to reduce or eliminate tariffs among nations, the growth of international organizations such as the WTO to regulate trade and adjudicate trade disputes, and increases in outsourcing of manufacturing jobs and services from developed countries to developing countries.[68]

America's relations with China are a prime example of these developments. Many American companies have factories in China that produce a variety of products that are sold in America. China is also a major producer of rare earth metals that are used to build computer chips. American corporations are also opening stores in China. In recent years, more Kentucky Fried Chicken restaurants have opened in China than in the United States. In all, China is America's second-largest trading partner, with more than $562 billion in combined imports and exports during 2013.[69]

Although these moves toward increased trade with China generate significant benefits for many people, the changes do not make everyone better off. Many American manufacturing jobs have been lost as factories that could not compete with cheaper foreign suppliers have either closed or moved to another country, leaving behind unemployed American workers.[70] Moreover, there have been numerous complaints that Chinese companies have stolen trade secrets from American corporations or violated American copyright laws—in some cases with the apparent support of the Chinese government. In fact, in May 2014, Attorney General Eric Holder made public an indictment that charged that a group within the Chinese armed forces had used computer espionage techniques to obtain information from American companies about nuclear power plant construction and solar panel design.[71]

globalization The increase over the last generation in trade, travel, and the flow of ideas and beliefs between nations.

ONE OF THE EFFECTS OF globalization is outsourcing—moving jobs to different countries usually to take advantage of lower wages and looser restrictions on manufacturing practices. Here, workers in China assemble electronic products for a foreign company.

These developments raise questions for American citizens and elected officials. First, how should America respond to nations that close off their markets, especially given that the same economic and employment pressures exist in America? For example, in recent years the Chinese government has done many things to restrict imports and expand exports. Though these requirements seem arbitrary and unfair to many American exporters, the American government also imposes restrictions on China. Importation limits on Chinese-produced solar panels to the United States are a prime example.

The second question concerns how to help Americans who are hurt by globalization. While there are some federal programs to retrain workers whose jobs are eliminated because of new trade agreements, many workers who have lost their jobs due to globalization (for example, because of outsourcing) are not eligible for these programs, and others are unaware that they exist.[72] Moreover, it is often extremely difficult to retrain people to compete for new jobs that will provide pay and benefits comparable to what they received in their former positions.[73] Lastly, there are no systematic American efforts to help citizens of other countries who are hurt by globalization.

Finally, globalization raises new human rights questions. For example, do U.S. companies such as Apple, which has outsourced the production of iPhones to factories in China, have a responsibility to monitor conditions in these factories and ensure that workers there are paid a fair wage? More generally, should the United States increase its trade with a country like China that restricts the political, religious, and social freedoms of its citizens in ways that most Americans would find objectionable? Or should it push for as much trade as possible, on the grounds that exposure to American commerce and culture will encourage Chinese citizens to press their government for reforms?

Trade is an example of a more general phenomenon: the state of the American economy is increasingly linked to economic conditions throughout the world. For example, China has an enormous trade surplus with America and holds hundreds of billions of dollars in American government bonds. Some observers believe these assets give the Chinese the ability to severely damage the American economy, either by withholding exports or by selling large amounts of American government bonds on international markets, raising the interest rate the United States would have to offer to finance its budget deficit. However, the Chinese economy is equally vulnerable. Eliminating the U.S. market for exports would leave Chinese factories without one of their major buyers. And selling bonds at below-market prices to increase American interest rates would likely damage the Chinese economy even more than the American economy.

In sum, while globalization is a fact of life, America's policy response to these changes is not set in stone. U.S. policy can encourage or discourage trade, outsourcing, and other interactions that cross national borders. Because globalization creates winners and losers, because it touches on other concerns such as human rights, and because other countries have their own concerns that may conflict with America's, the decision to encourage globalization is a real choice, one that is sure to generate high levels of conflict in American politics.

FIGHTING TERRORISM: AFGHANISTAN

There have been no major terrorist attacks on the United States since September 11, 2001, and the worldwide Al Qaeda organization that planned the 9/11 attacks has been decimated by a decade-long series of U.S. counter attacks using drones and special forces troops, and operations by ground forces in Afghanistan. Nevertheless, the potential for terrorism remains, and regional terror groups that are loosely connected to Al Qaeda (such as ISIL) have continued to carry out smaller operations, such as the attack on the U.S. Consulate in Benghazi, Libya, in October 2014 that killed several U.S. citizens including Ambassador Chris Stevens.

It is important to understand that the fight against global terror is different from a conventional war. In a conventional war, there are clear victory criteria: the losing nation's government capitulates. In contrast, terrorism involves multiple organizations with fluid memberships. Eliminating one individual or group (even if that were possible) may not reduce the danger of future attacks, because these victories do not address the factors that drive terrorism, including poverty and a deep-set anger that some individuals have against Western interests.

For example, consider the most visible of America's antiterrorism efforts, the fight against Al Qaeda. Over the last 14 years, the United States has invaded Afghanistan (where the organization was based at the time of the attacks), removed the Afghani Taliban government that supported Al Qaeda, destroyed many camps and other centers in Afghanistan and elsewhere, and captured or killed many operatives and leaders of the organization, including its founder, Osama bin Laden, during an attack in Pakistan in August 2011.

However, while Al Qaeda is far weaker than it was a decade ago, the possibility of an attack on Americans in the United States or abroad by the remnants of Al Qaeda, or another group such as ISIL, remains very real. Moreover, even after over a decade of military action and efforts to build a stable democracy and a growing economy, Afghanistan remains a dangerous, unstable place. Should the United States be responsible for creating a stable, prosperous Afghan nation? What will happen if America withdraws its support? Can the Afghan government control its borders and aid its citizens? Would the Taliban and Al Qaeda return, or would another group emerge?

The fight in Afghanistan, moreover, may only be a distraction from the main problem. Political scientist John Mueller argues that terrorism is hard to deter because its primary purpose is to frighten people; as a result, the set of possible targets is very large.[74] We typically think of terrorists attacking big, visible targets such as the World Trade Center or the U.S. Capitol, but in fact, there are many public places, from malls to urban centers, where an attack could cause high casualties and public panic. This fact makes the job of preventing attacks virtually impossible. And given that the number of actual terrorists is quite small, they are extremely difficult to find, regardless of whether they are in Afghanistan or in America.

Human rights concerns also shape antiterrorism efforts. American attacks against terror groups have the potential to cause civilian casualties—especially in places like Afghanistan, where these groups have tried to hide among civilians to discourage such attacks. Investigating terror groups may involve increased surveillance of Americans and their

ONE OF THE UNITED STATES' strategies to increase stability to Afghanistan is to train the Afghan National Army and police in order to provide the Afghan government a greater level of control over the region.

?

WHAT DO POLITICAL SCIENTISTS DO?

For more about how political scientists view the possibility of preventing terrorism, visit **wwnpag.es/wdpsd**

communications. American decision makers must also decide whether they will overlook problems in other countries to pursue terror suspects. For example, the government of Pakistan is routinely cited for human rights abuses, but Pakistani officials have aided in the capture of Taliban fighters in Afghanistan and have allowed the United States to use Pakistani airspace to deliver supplies to its troops in Afghanistan.

A related human rights concern in the fight against terrorism involves the rights of terror suspects. The Bush administration, while disavowing torture of suspects and prisoners, authorized aggressive interrogation methods that many believe amount to torture, and curtailed suspects' access to lawyers and international observers.[75] (These policies were reversed to some extent by subsequent legislation and by Supreme Court decisions.) The Obama administration has prohibited aggressive interrogation, but the Guantánamo prison for terror suspects remains open because of congressional opposition to its closure, and many individuals have been imprisoned there for many years without any trial (see Chapter 12).

In sum, regardless of whether the United States remains involved in Afghanistan, or whether operations in other countries are successes or failures, the fight against global terrorism will continue for the foreseeable future. It is easy to work backward from this conclusion to a critique of past policies—to conclude, for example, that things would be better if the United States had sent more troops or economic aid to Afghanistan. However, because terror attacks can come from many sources, because the fight against these organizations touches on human rights concerns, and because it is not clear how to eliminate the threat, there is no clear best strategy in the War on Terror. As a result, the threat from terrorism, and the debate over how to respond, will persist.

PREVENTING THE SPREAD OF WEAPONS OF MASS DESTRUCTION: NORTH KOREA

weapons of mass destruction (WMDs) Weapons that have the potential to cause large-scale loss of life, such as nuclear bombs and chemical or biological weapons.

The term **weapons of mass destruction (WMDs)** refers to nuclear bombs, chemical weapons such as nerve gas, and biological weapons such as anthrax. Given the potential for these weapons to inflict mass casualties, the United States has placed a high priority on (1) limiting the number of nations that have these weapons, and (2) preventing terrorist organizations from obtaining or developing them. For example, North Korea's efforts to build a nuclear arsenal raise concerns that they might use the weapons against South Korea or even the United States, or that terrorist organizations could buy or steal the weapons to use themselves.

Until recently, very few countries possessed WMDs. Only five countries admitted to having nuclear weapons: the United States, Russia, China, Great Britain, and France—though a sixth nation, Israel, is generally thought to have them as well. Most nations had signed the Nuclear Non-Proliferation Treaty (NPT), which prohibited the development of nuclear weapons and mandated inspection of civilian nuclear installations by the International Atomic Energy Agency (IAEA). These countries were supposed to have destroyed their stockpiles of biological and chemical weapons after the enactment of the Biological Weapons Convention in 1975 and the Chemical Weapons Convention in 1992.

New efforts to develop nuclear weapons have kept WMDs on the foreign policy agenda. Neither Pakistan nor India signed the NPT; then both countries developed and tested nuclear weapons in the 1990s.[76] North Korea withdrew from the treaty in 2003, banned IAEA inspectors, began reprocessing nuclear reactor fuel into bomb-grade material, and detonated nuclear devices in 2006 and 2009. It has subsequently reneged on several agreements to dismantle its nuclear weapons program and has made numerous threats against the United States, Japan, and South Korea—the latter countries are two of America's strong allies in the region.

The problem for the United States is to determine how to respond to North Korea's nuclear capabilities. Military operations are problematic, as North Korea's weapons and the factories that manufacture them are buried deep underground and may not be destroyed even by a massive attack. An unsuccessful attack might goad the North Korean government to launch its remaining weapons against U.S., Korean, or Japanese targets. Moreover, how should America respond to a WMD attack against its citizens or its allies, particularly if it is unclear which nation or group is responsible for the attack?

In other cases of nuclear proliferation—Iran, for example—the United States and other nations have worked to discourage countries from building nuclear weapons. The approach has emphasized incentives as well as threats. Economic and military sanctions serve to pressure nations that continue to develop weapons, while offers of economic aid and even civilian nuclear reactors serve to persuade nations to give up their weapons programs.[77] These sanctions have worked in Libya and appear to be leading the Iranians to slow down their production of bomb-grade plutonium, although the situation there is far from resolved.

North Korea presents a different problem. Its economy is already in shambles, and it has relatively little trade with other nations. As a result, economic sanctions are not very threatening. The North Korean government has essentially isolated its citizens from the outside world and carried out a widespread program of indoctrination to reinforce beliefs that building nuclear weapons is an appropriate response to threats from the rest of the world. The government also imprisons dissidents and withholds basic resources from the North Korean people, focusing instead on building a strong military.

For all of these reasons, nuclear proliferation in North Korea is a difficult problem to resolve. Economic sanctions are unlikely to work and military operations are problematic. Moreover, given the North Korean government's isolationist policies, promises of economic aid and inclusion in the global

NORTH KOREA HAS ONE OF THE world's least predictable and most isolated political regimes. Their nuclear capabilities and large military make North Korea a threat to the stability of the region. However, because of the poor state of the country's economy, economic sanctions are unlikely to foster changes toward democracy and openness.

economy are not attractive, as these changes would reduce the regime's ability to control and indoctrinate the population.

The difficulty of the problem does not eliminate conflict in American politics over what policy to follow. The disagreement is in part over the potential for success of different tactics. Some believe that North Korea's weapons could be destroyed by a bombing attack, for example. It is also uncertain whether North Korea has the means to send nuclear weapons against American targets. Others see a wider range of motivations, agreeing that North Korea's nuclear capability must be eliminated, but also arguing that it is America's responsibility to free the North Korean people from an oppressive dictatorship.

How this conflict is resolved will drive future policy choices. If human rights concerns dominate, or if the threat is seen as imminent, it is likely that military operations will proceed. On the other hand, if North Korea is seen as making threats it cannot carry out, and if the cost of conflict (including the suffering of the North Korean people) is seen as unacceptably high, then the status quo of diplomacy and the promise of economic aid is likely to continue, even as the threat posed by North Korean weapons remains.

CONCLUSION

Foreign policy matters. National security is a top priority for many Americans. The state of the American economy, from home prices to the unemployment rate, is affected by economic conditions elsewhere. Trade agreements with other nations determine how much American companies are allowed to export and what taxes and fees they must pay to import raw materials and other goods. It is hard to find a domestic issue that does not have a foreign policy component. And some questions, like intervention against ISIL, raise concerns about America's responsibility to protect human rights, even when victims are not American citizens.

Foreign policy is also conflictual. Disagreements among elected officials over what to do against ISIL, or over trade agreements, or any other question of foreign policy are not just attempts to attract political support or get media attention. These differences of opinion reflect real dilemmas over what government should do and how it should do it.

In all these respects, all of the issues discussed in this chapter, including the fight against global terrorism, the Middle East, Ebola, conflicts with China over trade policy, and persuading Iran to curb its nuclear ambitions, are not exceptions to the rule; rather, they epitomize just how close to home foreign policy is. Ordinary Americans are finding their lives increasingly affected by actions taken outside U.S. borders—a trend that is likely to continue over the next generation.

WHAT IS FOREIGN POLICY?

▶ *Describe the major approaches to understanding foreign policy and trace how America's role in the world has evolved.* (Pages 637–46)

SUMMARY

Foreign policy is any government action toward a group outside of America's borders. Foreign policy goals are complex, and debates on what America's goals should be are traditionally framed in terms of general principles. The goals of American foreign policy have changed over time and have become increasingly internationalist.

KEY TERMS

foreign policy (p. 637)
unilateral action (national) (p. 637)
multilateral action (p. 637)
isolationism (p. 638)
internationalism (p. 638)
realism (p. 638)
idealism (p. 638)
constructivism (p. 638)
nation building (p. 639)
Monroe Doctrine (p. 640)
Cold War (p. 641)
containment (p. 641)
mutually assured destruction (p. 642)
domino theory (p. 642)
détente (p. 642)
Bush Doctrine (p. 644)

CRITICAL THINKING AND DISCUSSION

Pick one of the foreign policy problems described in this chapter. What policy choices would a realist make? What choices would an idealist make?

PRACTICE QUIZ QUESTIONS

1. When one country does something on its own without coordinating with other countries, it is _____.
   - A isolationist
   - B internationalist
   - C acting unilaterally
   - D acting multilaterally
   - E nation building

2. _____ believe that countries pursue their own interests.
   - A Realists
   - B Idealists
   - C Constructivists
   - D Internationalists

3. The Monroe Doctrine stated that in European wars, America would _____.
   - A support Britain
   - B support the attacking country
   - C support the attacked country
   - D provide arms but not troops
   - E remain neutral

4. American foreign policy became increasingly internationalist following _____.
   - A the Civil War
   - B World War I
   - C World War II
   - D the Vietnam War
   - E the Cold War

5. The goal of containment influenced the _____ and _____.
   - A war in Iraq; the war in Afghanistan
   - B Korean War; the war in Iraq
   - C Vietnam War; the war in Iraq
   - D Korean War; the Cuban missile crisis
   - E Vietnam War; World War II

FOREIGN POLICY MAKERS

▶ *Explain how the various branches of government shape foreign policy.* (Pages 646–56)

SUMMARY

The major actors in foreign policy are the president and Congress, although the Supreme Court, interest groups, and public opinion all influence foreign policy decisions to a degree. The president's advantage over Congress lies in the ambiguity in the Constitution and the unilateral presidential power.

KEY TERMS

National Security Council (NSC) (p. 647)
civilian control (p. 648)
intergovernmental organizations (IGOs) (p. 656)
nongovernmental organizations (NGOs) (p. 656)
World Bank (p. 656)
International Monetary Fund (IMF) (p. 656)
United Nations (UN) (p. 656)

CRITICAL THINKING AND DISCUSSION

The American president has much more influence over foreign policy than members of Congress do. What are the pros and cons of this allocation of power?

6. The principal foreign policy department in the executive branch is _____ .

   A the Department of Defense

   B the Council on Foreign Relations

   C the Department of International Relations

   D the Department of State

   E the Foreign Intelligence Advisory Board

7. The idea that military personnel do not formulate policy, but rather implement directives from civilians is _____ .

   A military deference

   B civilian control

   C the Geneva system

   D civilian-military alliance

   E the Bush Doctrine

8. Congress holds the _____ and _____ , which both influence foreign policy.

   A power to deploy troops; power of the purse

   B power to approve treaties; power to deploy troops

   C power to declare war; power of the purse

   D power to deploy troops; power to declare war

   E power to approve appointments; power to deploy troops

9. The War Powers Resolution was designed to _____ .

   A limit the president's war-making powers

   B limit the Congress's war-making powers

   C limit the Department of Defense's war-making powers

   D limit the Pentagon's war-making powers

   E limit the State Department's war-making powers

THE TOOLS OF FOREIGN POLICY

▶ *Examine the ways American foreign policy is implemented.* **(Pages 657–62)**

SUMMARY

American foreign policy is implemented using a variety of tools—beyond the use of military force, other tools include the provision of foreign aid or changes to trade policy. Though all tools can be used in pursuit of desired policy outcomes, the specific tool is selected based on careful consideration of context.

KEY TERMS

tariff (p. 657)
World Trade Organization (WTO) (p. 658)
most-favored-nation status (p. 658)
economic sanctions (p. 659)

CRITICAL THINKING AND DISCUSSION

Suppose someone argued that the United States should impose economic sanctions on Russia in response to Russia's annexation of Crimea. Looking across America, which citizens, corporations, or groups might oppose these efforts?

PRACTICE QUIZ QUESTIONS

10. When a country is given "most-favored-nation" status, it means that the United States _____ any other nation.

    A gives the country higher levels of foreign aid than

    B gives the country higher levels of military aid than

    C sets tariffs on imports to the United States to the lowest rate given to

    D sets tariffs on exports from the United States to the lowest rate given to

    E sends that country more troops than

11. The process of _____ involves using personal contact and negotiations with leaders to work out international agreements.

    A nation building

    B diplomacy

    C unilateralism

    D the Bush Doctrine

    E the use of force

12. The North American Free Trade Agreement (NAFTA) is an example of _____ .

    A a bilateral agreement

    B an alliance

    C a tariff

    D a multilateral agreement

    E a sanction

THE POLITICS OF FOREIGN POLICY TODAY

▶ *Analyze several major areas of foreign policy and why they are often controversial.* **(Pages 662–68)**

SUMMARY

Foreign policy is everywhere, and with implications that are real and meaningful to all Americans. Despite the recent economic rise of China and India, America continues to be an international power and, in many cases, is the strongest nation.

KEY TERMS

globalization (p. 663)
weapons of mass destruction (WMDs) (p. 666)

CRITICAL THINKING AND DISCUSSION

Using evidence such as international public opinion data from the Pew Research Center or some other source, argue for or against the theory of a contemporary "clash of civilizations."

PRACTICE QUIZ QUESTIONS

13. What factor limits the American response to potential terrorist threats?

- [A] American public opinion opposes attacks on terrorist organizations.
- [B] The War Powers Act limits military actions to those approved by Congress.
- [C] Other nations would impose economic sanctions on American corporations.
- [D] It is difficult to identify terrorists or determine their plans.
- [E] Addressing terrorism requires a multilateral effort, which is difficult to coordinate.

14. The American government hesitates to pressure Pakistan on human rights violations most likely because _____.

- [A] doing so would threaten economic ties with Pakistan
- [B] attempts to protect human rights may make it harder for the United States to achieve goals in Afghanistan
- [C] evidence of human rights violations in Pakistan is unreliable
- [D] there is little international condemnation for the Pakistani violations of human rights
- [E] Pakistan enforces a Bill of Rights

15. Efforts to eliminate the threat of North Korean WMDs are limited by all of these factors except _____.

- [A] Russian support for the North Korean regime
- [B] the limited impact of economic sanctions
- [C] the possibility that North Korea would respond militarily to an attack
- [D] the isolation of North Korea's population
- [E] the fact that North Korean WMDs are stored in well-protected facilities

SUGGESTED READING

Auerswald, David P., and Stephen Saideman. *NATO in Afghanistan: Fighting Together, Fighting Alone*. Princeton: Princeton University Press, 2014.

Branch, Jordan. *The Cartographic State: Maps, Territory, and the Origins of Sovereignty*. Cambridge: Cambridge University Press, 2014.

Bueno de Mesquita, Bruce. *Principles of International Politics*. Washington, D.C.: CQ Press, 2005.

Fisher, Louis. *Presidential War Power*. Lawrence: University Press of Kansas, 2004.

Friedman, Thomas L. *The World Is Flat 3.0: A Brief History of the Twenty-First Century*. New York: Farrar, Straus and Giroux, 2007.

Huntington, Samuel P. *The Clash of Civilizations and the Remaking of World Order*. New York: Free Press, 2002.

Keohane, Robert O. *After Hegemony: Cooperation and Discord in the International System*. Princeton, NJ: Princeton University Press, 2005 (originally published 1984).

Mearsheimer, John J. *The Tragedy of Great Power Politics*. New York: W. W. Norton, 2001.

Ricks, Thomas. *The Gamble: General David Petraeus and the American Military Adventure in Iraq, 2006–2008*. New York: Penguin Press, 2009.

Sen, Amartya. *Identity and Violence: The Illusion of Destiny*. New York: W. W. Norton, 2007.

Simmons, Beth, Frank Dobbin, and Geoffrey Garrett. *The Global Diffusion of Markets and Democracy*. New York: Cambridge University Press, 2008.

Stiglitz, Joseph E. *Making Globalization Work*. New York: W. W. Norton, 2007.

APPENDIX

The Declaration of Independence

In Congress, July 4, 1776

The unanimous Declaration of the thirteen united States of America,

When in the Course of human events, it becomes necessary for one people to dissolve the political bands which have connected them with another, and to assume among the powers of the earth, the separate and equal station to which the Laws of Nature and of Nature's God entitle them, a decent respect to the opinions of mankind requires that they should declare the causes which impel them to the separation.

We hold these truths to be self-evident, that all men are created equal, that they are endowed by their Creator with certain unalienable Rights, that among these are Life, Liberty and the pursuit of Happiness.— That to secure these rights, Governments are instituted among Men, deriving their just powers from the consent of the governed. —That whenever any Form of Government becomes destructive of these ends, it is the Right of the People to alter or to abolish it, and to institute new Government, laying its foundation on such principles and organizing its powers in such form, as to them shall seem most likely to effect their Safety and Happiness. Prudence, indeed, will dictate that Governments long established should not be changed for light and transient causes; and accordingly all experience hath shewn, that mankind are more disposed to suffer, while evils are sufferable, than to right themselves by abolishing the forms to which they are accustomed. But when a long train of abuses and usurpations, pursuing invariably the same Object evinces a design to reduce them under absolute Despotism, it is their right, it is their duty, to throw off such Government, and to provide new Guards for their future security.—Such has been the patient sufferance of these Colonies; and such is now the necessity which constrains them to alter their former Systems of Government. The history of the present King of Great Britain is a history of repeated injuries and usurpations, all having in direct object the establishment of an absolute Tyranny over these States. To prove this, let Facts be submitted to a candid world.

He has refused his Assent to Laws, the most wholesome and necessary for the public good.

He has forbidden his Governors to pass Laws of immediate and pressing importance, unless suspended in their operation till his Assent should be obtained; and when so suspended, he has utterly neglected to attend to them.

He has refused to pass other Laws for the accommodation of large districts of people, unless those people would relinquish the right of Representation in the Legislature, a right inestimable to them and formidable to tyrants only.

He has called together legislative bodies at places unusual, uncomfortable, and distant from the depository of their public Records, for the sole purpose of fatiguing them into compliance with his measures.

He has dissolved Representative Houses repeatedly, for opposing with manly firmness his invasions on the rights of the people.

He has refused for a long time, after such dissolutions, to cause others to be elected; whereby the Legislative powers, incapable of Annihilation, have returned to the People at large for their exercise; the State remaining in the mean time exposed to all the dangers of invasion from without, and convulsions within.

He has endeavoured to prevent the population of these States; for that purpose obstructing the Laws for Naturalization of Foreigners; refusing to pass others to encourage their migrations hither, and raising the conditions of new Appropriations of Lands.

He has obstructed the Administration of Justice, by refusing his Assent to Laws for establishing Judiciary powers.

He has made Judges dependent on his Will alone, for the tenure of their offices, and the amount and payment of their salaries.

He has erected a multitude of New Offices, and sent hither swarms of Officers to harrass our people, and eat out their substance.

He has kept among us, in times of peace, Standing Armies without the Consent of our legislatures.

He has affected to render the Military independent of and superior to the Civil power.

He has combined with others to subject us to a jurisdiction foreign to our constitution, and unacknowledged by our laws; giving his Assent to their Acts of pretended Legislation:

For Quartering large bodies of armed troops among us:

For protecting them, by a mock Trial, from punishment for any Murders which they should commit on the Inhabitants of these States:

For cutting off our Trade with all parts of the world:

For imposing Taxes on us without our Consent:

For depriving us in many cases, of the benefits of Trial by Jury:

For transporting us beyond Seas to be tried for pretended offences:

For abolishing the free System of English Laws in a neighboring Province, establishing therein an Arbitrary government, and enlarging its Boundaries so as to render it at once an example and fit instrument for introducing the same absolute rule into these Colonies:

For taking away our Charters, abolishing our most valuable Laws, and altering fundamentally the Forms of our Governments:

For suspending our own Legislatures, and declaring themselves invested with power to legislate for us in all cases whatsoever.

He has abdicated Government here, by declaring us out of his Protection and waging War against us.

He has plundered our seas, ravaged our Coasts, burnt our towns, and destroyed the lives of our people.

He is at this time transporting large Armies of foreign Mercenaries to compleat the works of death, desolation and tyranny, already begun with circumstances of Cruelty & perfidy scarcely paralleled in the most barbarous ages, and totally unworthy the Head of a civilized nation.

He has constrained our fellow Citizens taken Captive on the high Seas to bear Arms against their Country, to become the executioners of their friends and Brethren, or to fall themselves by their Hands.

He has excited domestic insurrections amongst us, and has endeavoured to bring on the inhabitants of our frontiers, the merciless Indian Savages, whose known rule of warfare, is an undistinguished destruction of all ages, sexes and conditions.

In every stage of these Oppressions We have Petitioned for Redress in the most humble terms: Our repeated Petitions have been answered only by repeated injury. A Prince whose character is thus marked by every act which may define a Tyrant, is unfit to be the ruler of a free people.

Nor have We been wanting in attentions to our Brittish brethren. We have warned them from time to time of attempts by their legislature to extend an unwarrantable jurisdiction over us. We have reminded them of the circumstances of our emigration and settlement here. We have appealed to their native justice and magnanimity, and we have conjured them by the ties of our common kindred to disavow these usurpations, which, would inevitably interrupt our connections and correspondence. They too have been deaf to the voice of justice and of consanguinity. We must, therefore, acquiesce in the necessity, which denounces our Separation, and hold them, as we hold the rest of mankind, Enemies in War, in Peace Friends.

We, Therefore, the Representatives of the United States of America, in General Congress, Assembled, appealing to the Supreme Judge of the world for the rectitude of our intentions, do, in the Name, and by Authority of the good People of these Colonies, solemnly publish and declare, That these United Colonies are, and of Right ought to be Free and Independent States; that they are Absolved from all Allegiance to the British Crown, and that all political connection between them and the State of Great Britain, is and ought to be totally dissolved; and that as Free and Independent States, they have full Power to levy War, conclude Peace, contract Alliances, establish Commerce, and to do all other Acts and Things which Independent States may of right do. And for the support of this Declaration, with a firm reliance on the protection of divine Providence, we mutually pledge to each other our Lives, our Fortunes and our sacred Honor.

The foregoing Declaration was, by order of Congress, engrossed, and signed by the following members:

John Hancock

NEW HAMPSHIRE
Josiah Bartlett
William Whipple
Matthew Thornton

MASSACHUSETTS BAY
Samuel Adams
John Adams
Robert Treat Paine
Elbridge Gerry

RHODE ISLAND
Stephen Hopkins
William Ellery

CONNECTICUT
Roger Sherman
Samuel Huntington
William Williams
Oliver Wolcott

NEW YORK
William Floyd
Philip Livingston
Francis Lewis
Lewis Morris

NEW JERSEY
Richard Stockton
John Witherspoon
Francis Hopkinson
John Hart
Abraham Clark

PENNSYLVANIA
Robert Morris
Benjamin Rush
Benjamin Franklin
John Morton
George Clymer
James Smith
George Taylor
James Wilson
George Ross

DELAWARE
Caesar Rodney
George Read
Thomas M'Kean

MARYLAND
Samuel Chase
William Paca
Thomas Stone
Charles Carroll, of Carrollton

VIRGINIA
George Wythe
Richard Henry Lee
Thomas Jefferson
Benjamin Harrison
Thomas Nelson, Jr.
Francis Lightfoot Lee
Carter Braxton

NORTH CAROLINA
William Hooper
Joseph Hewes
John Penn

SOUTH CAROLINA
Edward Rutledge
Thomas Heyward, Jr.
Thomas Lynch, Jr.
Arthur Middleton

GEORGIA
Button Gwinnett
Lyman Hall
George Walton

Resolved, That copies of the Declaration be sent to the several assemblies, conventions, and committees, or councils of safety, and to the several commanding officers of the continental troops; that it be proclaimed in each of the United States, at the head of the army.

The Articles of Confederation

Agreed to by Congress November 15, 1777;
ratified and in force March 1, 1781

To all whom these Presents shall come, we the undersigned Delegates of the States affixed to our Names, send greeting. Whereas the Delegates of the United States of America, in Congress assembled, did, on the fifteenth day of November, in the Year of Our Lord One thousand Seven Hundred and Seventy seven, and in the Second Year of the Independence of America, agree to certain articles of Confederation and perpetual Union between the States of Newhampshire, Massachusets-bay, Rhodeisland and Providence Plantations, Connecticut, New-York, New-Jersey, Pennsylvania, Delaware, Maryland, Virginia, North-Carolina, South-Carolina and Georgia in the words following, viz. "Articles of Confederation and perpetual Union between the states of Newhampshire, Massachusettsbay, Rhodeisland and Providence Plantations, Connecticut, New-York, New-Jersey, Pennsylvania, Delaware, Maryland, Virginia, North-Carolina, South-Carolina and Georgia.

Art. I. The Stile of this confederacy shall be "The United States of America."

Art. II. Each state retains its sovereignty, freedom and independence, and every Power, Jurisdiction and right, which is not by this confederation expressly delegated to the United States, in Congress assembled.

Art. III. The said states hereby severally enter into a firm league of friendship with each other, for their common defence, the security of their Liberties, and their mutual and general welfare, binding themselves to assist each other, against all force offered to, or attacks made upon them, or any of them, on account of religion, sovereignty, trade, or any other pretence whatever.

Art. IV. The better to secure and perpetuate mutual friendship and intercourse among the people of the different states in this union, the free inhabitants of each of these states, paupers, vagabonds and fugitives from Justice excepted, shall be entitled to all privileges and immunities of free citizens in the several states; and the people of each state shall have free ingress and regress to and from any other state, and shall enjoy therein all the privileges of trade and commerce, subject to the same duties, impositions and restrictions as the inhabitants thereof respectively, provided that such restriction shall not extend so far as to prevent the removal of property imported into any state, to any other state, of which the Owner is an inhabitant; provided also that no imposition, duties or restriction shall be laid by any state, on the property of the united states, or either of them.

If any Person guilty of, or charged with treason, felony, or other high misdemeanor in any state, shall flee from Justice, and be found in any of the united states, he shall, upon demand of the Governor or executive power, of the state from which he fled, be delivered up and removed to the state having jurisdiction of his offence.

Full faith and credit shall be given in each of these states to the records, acts and judicial proceedings of the courts and magistrates of every other state.

Art. V. For the more convenient management of the general interests of the united states, delegates shall be annually appointed in such manner as the legislature of each state shall direct, to meet in Congress on the first Monday in November, in every year, with a power reserved to each state, to recall its delegates, or any of them, at any time within the year, and to send others in their stead, for the remainder of the Year.

No state shall be represented in Congress by less than two, nor by more than seven Members; and no person shall be capable of being a delegate for more than three years in any term of six years; nor shall any person, being a delegate, be capable of holding any office under the united states, for which he, or another for his benefit receives any salary, fees or emolument of any kind.

Each state shall maintain its own delegates in a meeting of the states, and while they act as members of the committee of the states.

In determining questions in the united states, in Congress assembled, each state shall have one vote.

Freedom of speech and debate in Congress shall not be impeached or questioned in any Court, or place out of Congress, and the members of congress shall be protected in their persons from arrests and imprisonments, during the time of their going to and from, and attendance on congress, except for treason, felony, or breach of the peace.

Art. VI. No state without the Consent of the united states in congress assembled, shall send any embassy to, or receive any embassy from, or enter into any conference, agreement, or alliance or treaty with any King, prince or state; nor shall any person holding any office or profit or trust under the united states, or any of them, accept of any present, emolument, office or title of any kind whatever from any king, prince or foreign state; nor shall the united states in congress assembled, or any of them, grant any title of nobility.

No two or more states shall enter into any treaty, confederation or alliance whatever between them, without the consent of the united states in congress assembled, specifying accurately the purposes for which the same is to be entered into, and how long it shall continue.

No state shall lay any imposts or duties, which may interfere with any stipulations in treaties, entered into by the united states in congress assembled, with any king, prince or state, in pursuance of any treaties already proposed by congress, to the courts of France and Spain.

No vessels of war shall be kept up in time of peace by any state, except such number only, as shall be deemed necessary by the united states in congress assembled, for the defence of such state, or its trade; nor shall any body of forces be kept up by any state, in time of peace, except such number only, as in the judgment of the united states, in congress assembled, shall be deemed requisite to garrison the forts necessary for the defence of such state; but every state shall always keep up a well regulated and disciplined militia, sufficiently armed and accoutred, and shall provide and constantly have ready for use, in public stores, a due number of field pieces and tents, and a proper quantity of arms, ammunition and camp equipage.

No state shall engage in any war without the consent of the united states in congress assembled, unless such state be actually invaded by enemies, or shall have received certain advice of a resolution being formed by some nation of Indians to invade such state, and the danger is so imminent as not to admit of a delay, till the united states in congress asssembled can be consulted; nor shall any state grant commissions to any ships or vessels of war, nor letters of marque or reprisal, except it be after a declaration of war by the united states in congress assembled, and then only against the kingdom or state and the subjects thereof, against which war has been so declared, and under such regulations as shall be established by the united states in congress assembled, unless such state be infested by pirates; in which case vessels of war may be fitted out for that occasion, and kept so long as the danger shall continue, or until the united states in congress assembled shall determine otherwise.

Art. VII. When land-forces are raised by any state for the common defence, all officers of or under the rank of colonel, shall be appointed by the legislature of each state respectively, by whom such forces shall be raised, or in such manner as such state shall direct, and all vacancies shall be filled up by the state which first made the appointment.

Art. VIII. All charges of war, and all other expences that shall be incurred for the common defence or general welfare, and allowed by the united states in congress assembled, shall be defrayed out of a common treasury, which shall be supplied by the several states in proportion to the value of all land within each state, granted to or surveyed for any Person, as such land and the buildings and improvements thereon shall be estimated according to such mode as the united states in congress assembled, shall from time to time direct and appoint.

The taxes for paying that proportion shall be laid and levied by the authority and direction of the legislatures of the several states within the time agreed upon by the united states in congress assembled.

Art. IX. The united states in congress assembled, shall have the sole and exclusive right and power of determining on peace and war, except in the cases mentioned in the sixth article—of sending and receiving ambassadors—entering into treaties and alliances, provided that no treaty of commerce shall be made whereby the legislative power of the respective states shall be restrained from imposing such imposts and duties on foreigners, as their own people are subjected to, or from prohibiting the exportation of any species of goods or commodities whatsoever—of establishing rules for deciding in all cases, what captures on land or water shall be legal, and in what manner prizes taken by land or naval forces in the service of the united states shall be divided or appropriated—of granting letters of marque and reprisal in times of peace—appointing courts for the trial of piracies and felonies committed on the high seas and establishing courts for receiving and determining finally appeals in all cases of captures, provided that no member of congress shall be appointed a judge of any of the said courts.

The united states in congress assembled shall also be the last resort on appeal in all disputes and differences now subsisting or that hereafter may arise between two or more states concerning boundary, jurisdiction or any other cause whatever; which authority shall always be exercised in the manner following. Whenever the legislative or executive authority or lawful agent of any state in controversy with another shall present a petition to congress stating the matter in question and praying for a hearing, notice thereof shall be given by order of congress to the legislative or executive authority of the other state in controversy, and a day assigned for the appearance of the parties by their lawful agents, who shall then be directed to appoint by joint consent, commissioners or judges to constitute a court for hearing and determining the matter in question: but if they cannot agree, congress shall name three persons out of each of the united states, and from the list of such persons each party shall alternately strike out one, the petitioners beginning, until the number shall be reduced to thirteen; and from that number not less than seven, nor more than nine names as congress shall direct, shall in the presence of congress be drawn out by lot, and the persons whose names shall be so drawn or any five of them, shall be commissioners or judges, to hear and finally determine the controversy, so always as a major part of the judges who shall hear the cause shall agree in the determination: and if either party shall neglect to attend at the day appointed, without shewing reasons, which congress shall judge sufficient, or being present shall refuse to strike, the congress shall proceed to nominate three persons out of each state, and the secretary of congress shall strike in behalf of such party absent or refusing; and the judgment and sentence of the court to be appointed, in the manner before prescribed, shall be final and conclusive; and if any of the parties shall refuse to submit to the authority of such court, or to appear to defend their claim or cause, the court shall nevertheless proceed to pronounce sentence, or judgment, which shall in like manner be final and decisive, the judgment or sentence and other proceedings being in either case transmitted to congress, and lodged among the acts of congress for the security of the parties concerned: provided that every commissioner, before he sits in judgment, shall take an oath to be administered by one of the judges of the supreme or superior court of the state, where the cause shall be tried, "well and truly to hear and determine the matter in question, according to the best of his judgment, without favour, affection or hope of reward:" provided also, that no state shall be deprived of territory for the benefit of the united states.

All controversies concerning the private right of soil claimed under different grants of two or more states, whose jurisdictions as they may respect such lands, and the states which passed such grants are adjusted, the said grants or either of them being at the same time claimed to have originated antecedent to such settlement of jurisdiction, shall on the petition of either party to the congress of the united states, be finally determined as near as may be in the same manner as is before prescribed for deciding disputes respecting territorial jurisdiction between different states.

The united states in congress assembled shall also have the sole and exclusive right and power of regulating the alloy and value of coin struck by their own authority, or by that of the respective states—fixing the standard of weights and measures throughout the united states—regulating the trade and managing all affairs with the Indians, not members of any of the states, provided that the legislative right of any state within its own limits be not infringed or violated—establishing and regulating post-offices from one state to another, throughout all the united states, and exacting such postage on the papers passing thro' the same as may be requisite to defray the expences of the said office—appointing all officers of the land forces, in the service of the united states, excepting regimental officers—appointing all the officers of the naval forces, and commissioning all officers whatever in the service of the united states—making rules for the government and regulation of the said land and naval forces, and directing their operations.

The united states in congress assembled shall have authority to appoint a committee, to sit in the recess of congress, to be denominated "A Committee of the States," and to consist of one delegate from each state; and to appoint such other committees and civil officers as may be necessary for managing the general affairs of the united states under their direction—to appoint one of their number to preside, provided that no person be allowed to serve in the office of president more than one year in any term of three years; to ascertain the necessary sums of Money to be raised for the service of the united states, and to appropriate and apply the same for defraying the public expenses—to borrow money, or emit bills on the credit of the united states, transmitting every half year to the respective states an account of the sums of money so borrowed or emitted,—to build and equip a navy—to agree upon the number of land forces, and to make requisitions from each state for its quota, in proportion to the number of white inhabitants in such state; which requisition shall be binding, and thereupon the legislature of each state shall appoint the regimental officers, raise the men and cloath, arm and equip them in a soldier like manner, at the expense of the united states; and the officers and men so cloathed, armed and equipped shall march to the place appointed, and within the time agreed on by the united states in congress assembled: But if the united states in congress assembled shall, on consideration of circumstances judge proper that any state should not raise men, or should raise a smaller number than its quota, and that any other state should raise a greater number of men than the quota thereof, such extra number shall be raised, officered, cloathed, armed and equipped in the same manner as the quota of such state, unless the legislature of such state shall judge that such extra number cannot be safely spared out of the same, in which case they shall raise officer, cloath, arm and equip as many of such extra number as they judge can be safely spared. And the officers and men so cloathed, armed and equipped, shall march to the place appointed, and within the time agreed on by the united states in congress assembled.

The united states in congress assembled shall never engage in a war, nor grant letters of marque and reprisal in time of peace, nor enter into any treaties or alliances, nor coin money, nor regulate the value thereof, nor ascertain the sums and expenses necessary for the defence and welfare of the united states, or any of them, nor emit bills, nor borrow money on the credit of the united states, nor appropriate money, nor agree upon the number of vessels of war, to be built or purchased, or the number of land or sea forces to be raised, nor appoint a commander in chief of the army or navy, unless nine states assent to the same: nor shall a question on any other point, except for adjourning from day to day be determined, unless by the votes of a majority of the united states in congress assembled.

The congress of the united states shall have power to adjourn to any time within the year, and to any place within the united states, so that no period of adjournment be for a longer duration than the space of six Months, and shall publish the Journal of their proceedings monthly, except such parts thereof relating to treaties, alliances or military operations, as in their judgment require secrecy; and the yeas and nays of the delegates of each state on any question shall be entered on the Journal, when it is desired by any delegate; and the delegates of a state, or any of them, at his or their request shall be furnished with a transcript of the said Journal, except such parts as are above excepted, to lay before the legislatures of the several states.

Art. X. The committee of the states, or any nine of them, shall be authorised to execute, in the recess of congress, such of the powers of congress as the united states in congress assembled, by the consent of nine states, shall from time to time think expedient to vest them with; provided that no power be delegated to the said committee, for the exercise of which, by the articles of confederation, the voice of nine states in the congress of the united states assembled is requisite.

Art. XI. Canada acceding to this confederation, and joining in the measures of the united states, shall be admitted into, and entitled to all the advantages of this union: but no other colony shall be admitted into the same, unless such admission be agreed to by nine states.

Art. XII. All bills of credit emitted, monies borrowed and debts contracted by, or under the authority of congress, before the assembling of the united states, in pursuance of the present confederation, shall be deemed and considered as a charge against the united states, for payment and satisfaction whereof the said united states and the public faith are hereby solemnly pledged.

Art. XIII. Every state shall abide by the determinations of the united states in congress assembled, on all questions which by this confederation are submitted to them. And the Articles of this confederation shall be inviolably observed by every state, and the union shall be perpetual; nor shall any alteration at any time hereafter be made in any of them; unless such alteration be agreed to in a congress of the united states, and be afterwards confirmed by the legislatures of every state.

And Whereas it hath pleased the Great Governor of the World to incline the hearts of the legislatures we respectively represent in congress, to approve of, and to authorize us to ratify the said articles of confederation and perpetual union. Know Ye that we the undersigned delegates, by virtue of the power and authority to us given for that purpose, do by these presents, in the name and in behalf of our respective constituents, fully and entirely ratify and confirm each and every of the said articles of confederation and perpetual union, and all and singular the matters and things therein contained: And we do further solemnly plight and engage the faith of our respective constituents, that they shall abide by the determinations of the united states in congress assembled, on all questions, which by the said confederation are submitted to them. And that the articles thereof shall be inviolably observed by the states we respectively represent, and that the union shall be perpetual. In Witness whereof we have hereunto set our hands in Congress. Done at Philadelphia in the state of Pennsylvania the ninth day of July, in the Year of our Lord one Thousand seven Hundred and Seventy-eight, and in the third year of the independence of America.

The Constitution of the United States of America

[PREAMBLE]

We the People of the United States, in Order to form a more perfect Union, establish Justice, insure domestic Tranquility, provide for the common defence, promote the general Welfare, and secure the Blessings of Liberty to ourselves and our Posterity, do ordain and establish this Constitution for the United States of America.

Article I

SECTION 1

[LEGISLATIVE POWERS]

All legislative Powers herein granted shall be vested in a Congress of the United States, which shall consist of a Senate and House of Representatives.

SECTION 2

[HOUSE OF REPRESENTATIVES, HOW CONSTITUTED, POWER OF IMPEACHMENT]

The House of Representatives shall be composed of Members chosen every second Year by the People of the several States, and the Electors in each State shall have the Qualifications requisite for Electors of the most numerous Branch of the State Legislature.

No Person shall be a Representative who shall not have attained to the Age of twenty five Years, and been seven Years a Citizen of the United States, and who shall not, when elected, be an Inhabitant of that State in which he shall be chosen.

Representatives and *direct Taxes*[1] shall be apportioned among the several States which may be included within this Union, according to their respective Numbers, *which shall be determined by adding to the whole Number of free Persons, including those bound to Service for a Term of Years, and excluding Indians not taxed, three fifths of all other Persons.*[2] The actual Enumeration shall be made within three Years after the first Meeting of the Congress of the United States, and within every subsequent Term of ten Years, in such Manner as they shall by Law direct. The Number of Representatives shall not exceed one for every thirty Thousand, but each State shall have at Least one Representative; *and until such enumeration shall be made, the State of New Hampshire shall be entitled to chuse three, Massachusetts eight, Rhode-Island and Providence Plantations one, Connecticut five, New-York six, New Jersey four, Pennsylvania eight, Delaware one, Maryland six, Virginia ten, North Carolina five, South Carolina five, and Georgia three.*[3]

When vacancies happen in the Representation from any State, the Executive Authority thereof shall issue Writs of Election to fill such Vacancies.

The House of Representatives shall chuse their Speaker and other Officers; and shall have the sole Power of Impeachment.

SECTION 3

[THE SENATE, HOW CONSTITUTED, IMPEACHMENT TRIALS]

The Senate of the United States shall be composed of two Senators from each State, *chosen by the Legislature thereof,*[4] for six Years; and each Senator shall have one Vote.

Immediately after they shall be assembled in Consequence of the first Election, they shall be divided as equally as may be into three Classes. The Seats of the Senators of the first Class shall be vacated at the Expiration of the second Year, of the second Class at the Expiration of the fourth Year, and of the third Class at the Expiration of the sixth Year, so that one third may be chosen every second Year; *and if Vacancies happen by Resignation, or otherwise, during the Recess of the Legislature of* *any State, the Executive thereof may make temporary Appointments until the next Meeting of the Legislature, which shall then fill such Vacancies.*[5]

No Person shall be a Senator who shall not have attained to the Age of thirty Years, and been nine Years a Citizen of the United States, and who shall not, when elected, be an Inhabitant of that State for which he shall be chosen.

The Vice President of the United States shall be President of the Senate, but shall have no Vote, unless they be equally divided.

The Senate shall chuse their other Officers, and also a President pro tempore, in the Absence of the Vice President, or when he shall exercise the Office of President of the United States.

The Senate shall have the sole Power to try all Impeachments. When sitting for that Purpose, they shall be on Oath or Affirmation. When the President of the United States is tried, the Chief Justice shall preside: And no Person shall be convicted without the Concurrence of two thirds of the Members present.

Judgment in Cases of Impeachment shall not extend further than to removal from Office, and disqualification to hold and enjoy any Office of honor, Trust or Profit under the United States: but the Party convicted shall nevertheless be liable and subject to Indictment, Trial, Judgment and Punishment, according to Law.

SECTION 4

[ELECTION OF SENATORS AND REPRESENTATIVES]

The Times, Places and Manner of holding Elections for Senators and Representatives, shall be prescribed in each State by the Legislature thereof; but the Congress may at any time by Law make or alter such Regulations, except as to the Places of chusing Senators.

The Congress shall assemble at least once in every Year, and such Meeting shall be on the first Monday in December, unless they shall by Law appoint a different Day.[6]

SECTION 5

[QUORUM, JOURNALS, MEETINGS, ADJOURNMENTS]

Each House shall be the Judge of the Elections, Returns and Qualifications of its own Members, and a Majority of each shall constitute a Quorum to do Business; but a smaller Number may adjourn from day to day, and may be authorized to compel the Attendance of absent Members, in such Manner, and under such Penalties as each House may provide.

Each House may determine the Rules of its Proceedings, punish its Members for disorderly Behaviour, and, with the Concurrence of two thirds, expel a Member.

Each House shall keep a Journal of its Proceedings, and from time to time publish the same, excepting such Parts as may in their Judgment require Secrecy; and the Yeas and Nays of the Members of either House on any questions shall, at the Desire of one fifth of those Present, be entered on the Journal.

Neither House, during the Session of Congress, shall, without the Consent of the other, adjourn for more than three days, nor to any other Place than that in which the two Houses shall be sitting.

---

[1] Modified by Sixteenth Amendment.
[2] Modified by Fourteenth Amendment.
[3] Temporary provision.
[4] Modified by Seventeenth Amendment.
[5] Modified by Seventeenth Amendment.
[6] Modified by Twentieth Amendment.

SECTION 6
[COMPENSATION, PRIVILEGES, DISABILITIES]

The Senators and Representatives shall receive a Compensation for their Services, to be ascertained by Law, and paid out of the Treasury of the United States. They shall in all Cases, except Treason, Felony and Breach of the Peace, be privileged from Arrest during their Attendance at the Session of their respective Houses, and in going to and returning from the same; and for any Speech or Debate in either House, they shall not be questioned in any other Place.

No Senator or Representative shall, during the Time for which he was elected, be appointed to any civil Office under the Authority of the United States, which shall have been created, or the Emoluments whereof shall have been encreased during such time; and no Person holding any Office under the United States, shall be a Member of either House during his Continuance in Office.

SECTION 7
[PROCEDURE IN PASSING BILLS AND RESOLUTIONS]

All Bills for raising Revenue shall originate in the House of Representatives; but the Senate may propose or concur with Amendments as on other Bills.

Every Bill which shall have passed the House of Representatives and the Senate, shall, before it become a Law, be presented to the President of the United States: If he approve he shall sign it, but if not he shall return it, with his Objections to that House in which it shall have originated, who shall enter the Objections at large on their Journal, and proceed to reconsider it. If after such Reconsideration two thirds of that House shall agree to pass the Bill, it shall be sent, together with the Objections, to the other House, by which it shall likewise be reconsidered, and if approved by two thirds of that House, it shall become a Law. But in all such Cases the Votes of both Houses shall be determined by yeas and Nays, and the Names of the Persons voting for and against the Bill shall be entered on the Journal of each House respectively. If any Bill shall not be returned by the President within ten Days (Sundays excepted) after it shall have been presented to him, the Same shall be a Law, in like Manner as if he had signed it, unless the Congress by their Adjournment prevent its Return, in which Case it shall not be a Law.

Every Order, Resolution, or Vote to which the Concurrence of the Senate and House of Representatives may be necessary (except on a question of Adjournment) shall be presented to the President of the United States; and before the Same shall take Effect, shall be approved by him, or being disapproved by him, shall be repassed by two thirds of the Senate and House of Representatives, according to the Rules and Limitations prescribed in the Case of a Bill.

SECTION 8
[POWERS OF CONGRESS]

The Congress shall have Power

To lay and collect Taxes, Duties, Imposts and Excises, to pay the Debts and provide for the common Defence and general Welfare of the United States; but all Duties, Imposts and Excises shall be uniform throughout the United States;

To borrow Money on the credit of the United States;

To regulate Commerce with foreign Nations, and among the several States, and with the Indian Tribes;

To establish an uniform Rule of Naturalization, and uniform Laws on the subject of Bankruptcies throughout the United States;

To coin Money, regulate the Value thereof, and of foreign Coin, and fix the Standard of Weights and Measures;

To provide for the Punishment of counterfeiting the Securities and current Coin of the United States;

To establish Post Offices and post Roads;

To promote the Progress of Science and useful Arts, by securing for limited Times to Authors and Inventors the exclusive Right to their respective Writings and Discoveries;

To constitute Tribunals inferior to the supreme Court;

To define and punish Piracies and Felonies committed on the high Seas, and Offences against the Law of Nations;

To declare War, grant Letters of Marque and Reprisal, and make Rules concerning Captures on Land and Water;

To raise and support Armies, but no Appropriation of Money to that Use shall be for a longer Term than two Years;

To provide and maintain a Navy;

To make Rules for the Government and Regulation of the land and naval Forces;

To provide for calling forth the Militia to execute the Laws of the Union, suppress Insurrections and repel Invasions;

To provide for organizing, arming, and disciplining, the Militia, and for governing such Part of them as may be employed in the Service of the United States, reserving to the States respectively, the Appointment of the Officers, and the Authority of training the Militia according to the discipline prescribed by Congress;

To exercise exclusive Legislation in all Cases whatsoever, over such District (not exceeding ten Miles square) as may, by Cession of particular States, and the Acceptance of Congress, become the Seat of the Government of the United States, and to exercise like Authority over all Places purchased by the Consent of the Legislature of the State in which the Same shall be, for the Erection of Forts, Magazines, Arsenals, dock-Yards, and other needful Buildings;—And

To make all Laws which shall be necessary and proper for carrying into Execution the foregoing Powers, and all other Powers vested by this Constitution in the Government of the United States, or in any Department or Officer thereof.

SECTION 9
[SOME RESTRICTIONS ON FEDERAL POWER]

The Migration or Importation of such Persons as any of the States now existing shall think proper to admit, shall not be prohibited by the Congress prior to the Year one thousand eight hundred and eight, but a Tax or duty may be imposed on such Importation, not exceeding ten dollars for each Person.[7]

The Privilege of the Writ of Habeas Corpus shall not be suspended, unless when in Cases of Rebellion or Invasion the public Safety may require it.

No Bill of Attainder or ex post facto Law shall be passed.

No Capitation, or other direct, Tax shall be laid, unless in Proportion to the Census or Enumeration herein before directed to be taken.[8]

No Tax or Duty shall be laid on Articles exported from any State.

No Preference shall be given by any Regulation of Commerce or Revenue to the Ports of one State over those of another; nor shall Vessels bound to, or from, one State, be obliged to enter, clear, or pay Duties in another.

No Money shall be drawn from the Treasury, but in Consequence of Appropriations made by Law; and a regular Statement and Account of the Receipts and Expenditures of all public Money shall be published from time to time.

No Title of Nobility shall be granted by the United States: And no Person holding any Office of Profit or Trust under them, shall, without the Consent of the Congress, accept of any present, Emolument, Office, or Title, of any kind whatever, from any King, Prince, or foreign State.

---

[7] Temporary provision.
[8] Modified by Sixteenth Amendment.

SECTION 10
[RESTRICTIONS UPON POWERS OF STATES]

No State shall enter into any Treaty, Alliance, or Confederation; grant Letters of Marque and Reprisal; coin Money; emit Bills of Credit; make any Thing but gold and silver Coin a Tender in Payment of Debts; pass any Bill of Attainder, ex post facto Law, or Law impairing the Obligation of Contracts, or grant any Title of Nobility.

No State shall, without the Consent of the Congress, lay any Imposts or Duties on Imports or Exports, except what may be absolutely necessary for executing its inspection Laws: and the net Produce of all Duties and Imposts, laid by any State on Imports or Exports, shall be for the Use of the Treasury of the United States; and all such Laws shall be subject to the Revision and Control of the Congress.

No State shall, without the Consent of Congress, lay any Duty of Tonnage, keep Troops, or Ships of War in time of Peace, enter into any Agreement or Compact with another State, or with a foreign Power, or engage in War, unless actually invaded, or in such imminent Danger as will not admit of delay.

Article II

SECTION I
[EXECUTIVE POWER, ELECTION, QUALIFICATIONS OF THE PRESIDENT]

The executive Power shall be vested in a President of the United States of America. *He shall hold his Office during the Term of four Years, and, together with the Vice President, chosen for the same Term, be elected, as follows*[9]

Each State shall appoint, in such Manner as the Legislature thereof may direct, a Number of Electors, equal to the whole Number of Senators and Representatives to which the State may be entitled in the Congress: but no Senator or Representative, or Person holding an Office of Trust or Profit under the United States, shall be appointed an Elector.

The electors shall meet in their respective States, and vote by ballot for two Persons, of whom one at least shall not be an Inhabitant of the same State with themselves. And they shall make a List of all the Persons voted for, and of the Number of Votes for each; which List they shall sign and certify, and transmit sealed to the Seat of the Government of the United States, directed to the President of the Senate. The President of the Senate shall, in the Presence of the Senate and House of Representatives, open all the Certificates, and the Votes shall then be counted. The Person having the greatest Number of Votes shall be the President, if such Number be a Majority of the whole Number of Electors appointed; and if there be more than one who have such Majority, and have an equal Number of Votes, then the House of Representatives shall immediately chuse by Ballot one of them for President; and if no Person have a Majority, then from the five highest on the List the said House shall in like Manner chuse the President. But in chusing the President, the Votes shall be taken by States, the Representation from each State having one Vote; A quorum for this Purpose shall consist of a Member or Members from two thirds of the States, and a Majority of all the States shall be necessary to a Choice. In every Case, after the Choice of the President, the person having the greatest Number of Votes of the Electors shall be the Vice President. But if there should remain two or more who have equal Votes, the Senate shall chuse from them by Ballot the Vice President.[10]

The Congress may determine the Time of chusing the Electors, and the Day on which they shall give their Votes; which Day shall be the same throughout the United States.

No Person except a natural born Citizen, or a Citizen of the United States, at the time of the Adoption of this Constitution, shall be eligible to the Office of President; neither shall any Person be eligible to that Office who shall not have attained to the Age of thirty five Years, and been fourteen Years a Resident within the United States.

In Case of the Removal of the President from Office, or his Death, Resignation, or Inability to discharge the Powers and Duties of the said Office, the Same shall devolve on the Vice President, and the Congress may by Law provide for the Case of Removal, Death, Resignation or Inability, both of the President and Vice President, declaring what Officer shall then act as President, and such Officer shall act accordingly, until the Disability be removed, or a President shall be elected.

The President shall, at stated Times, receive for his Services, a Compensation, which shall neither be increased nor diminished during the Period for which he shall have been elected, and he shall not receive within that Period any other Emolument from the United States, or any of them.

Before he enter on the Execution of his Office, he shall take the following Oath or Affirmation:—"I do solemnly swear (or affirm) that I will faithfully execute the Office of President of the United States, and will to the best of my Ability, preserve, protect and defend the Constitution of the United States."

SECTION 2
[POWERS OF THE PRESIDENT]

The President shall be Commander in Chief of the Army and Navy of the United States, and of the Militia of the several States, when called into the actual Service of the United States; he may require the Opinion, in writing, of the principal Officer in each of the executive Departments, upon any Subject relating to the Duties of their respective Offices, and he shall have Power to grant Reprieves and Pardons for Offences against the United States, except in Cases of Impeachment.

He shall have Power, by and with the Advice and Consent of the Senate, to make Treaties, provided two thirds of the Senators present concur; and he shall nominate, and by and with the Advice and Consent of the Senate, shall appoint Ambassadors, other public Ministers and Consuls, Judges of the supreme Court, and all other Officers of the United States, whose Appointments are not herein otherwise provided for, and which shall be established by Law: but the Congress may by Law vest the Appointment of such inferior Officers, as they think proper, in the President alone, in the Courts of Law, or in the Heads of Departments.

The President shall have Power to fill up all Vacancies that may happen during the Recess of the Senate, by granting Commissions which shall expire at the End of their next Session.

SECTION 3
[POWERS AND DUTIES OF THE PRESIDENT]

He shall from time to time give to the Congress Information of the State of the Union, and recommend to their Consideration such Measures as he shall judge necessary and expedient; he may, on extraordinary Occasions, convene both Houses, or either of them, and in Case of Disagreement between them, with Respect to the Time of Adjournment, he may adjourn them to such Time as he shall think proper; he shall receive Ambassadors and other public Ministers; he shall take Care that the Laws be faithfully executed, and shall Commission all the Officers of the United States.

SECTION 4
[IMPEACHMENT]

The President, Vice President and all civil Officers of the United States, shall be removed from Office on Impeachment for, and Conviction of, Treason, Bribery, or other high Crimes and Misdemeanors.

---

9 Number of terms limited to two by Twenty-second Amendment.
10 Modified by the Twelfth and Twentieth Amendments.

Article III

SECTION I

The judicial Power of the United States, shall be vested in one supreme Court, and in such inferior Courts as the Congress may from time to time ordain and establish. The Judges, both of the supreme and inferior Courts, shall hold their Offices during good Behaviour, and shall, at stated Times, receive for their Services, a Compensation, which shall not be diminished during their Continuance in Office.

SECTION 2
[JURISDICTION]

The judicial Power shall extend to all Cases, in Law and Equity, arising under this Constitution, the Laws of the United States, and Treaties made, or which shall be made, under their Authority;—to all Cases affecting Ambassadors, other public Ministers and Consuls;—to all Cases of admiralty and maritime Jurisdiction;—to Controversies to which the United States shall be a Party;—to Controversies between two or more States;—*between a State and Citizens of another State;*—between Citizens of different States,—between Citizens of the same State claiming Lands under Grants of different States, *and between a State,* or the Citizens thereof, *and foreign States, Citizens or Subjects.*[11]

In all Cases affecting Ambassadors, other public Ministers and Consuls, and those in which a State shall be Party, the supreme Court shall have original Jurisdiction. In all the other Cases before mentioned, the supreme Court shall have appellate Jurisdiction, both as to Law and Fact, with such Exceptions, and under such Regulations as the Congress shall make.

The Trial of all Crimes, except in Cases of Impeachment, shall be by Jury; and such Trial shall be held in the State where the said Crimes shall have been committed; but when not committed within any State, the Trial shall be at such Place or Places as the Congress may by Law have directed.

SECTION 3
[TREASON, PROOF, AND PUNISHMENT]

Treason against the United States, shall consist only in levying War against them, or in adhering to their Enemies, giving them Aid and Comfort. No Person shall be convicted of Treason unless on the Testimony of two Witnesses to the same overt Act, or on Confession in open Court.

The Congress shall have Power to declare the Punishment of Treason, but no Attainder of Treason shall work Corruption of Blood, or Forfeiture except during the Life of the Person attainted.

Article IV

SECTION I
[FAITH AND CREDIT AMONG STATES]

Full Faith and Credit shall be given in each State to the public Acts, Records, and judicial Proceedings of every other State. And the Congress may by general Laws prescribe the Manner in which such Acts, Records and Proceedings shall be proved, and the Effect thereof.

SECTION 2
[PRIVILEGES AND IMMUNITIES, FUGITIVES]

The Citizens of each State shall be entitled to all Privileges and Immunities of Citizens in the several States.

A Person charged in any State with Treason, Felony or other Crime, who shall flee from Justice, and be found in another State, shall on Demand of the executive Authority of the State from which he fled, be delivered up, to be removed to the State having Jurisdiction of the Crime.

No person held to Service or Labour in one State, under the Laws thereof, escaping into another, shall, in Consequence of any Law or Regulation therein, be discharged from such Service or Labour, but shall be delivered up on Claim of the Party to whom such Service or Labour may be due.[12]

SECTION 3
[ADMISSION OF NEW STATES]

New States may be admitted by the Congress into this Union; but no new State shall be formed or erected within the Jurisdiction of any other State; nor any State be formed by the Junction of two or more States, or Parts of States, without the Consent of the Legislatures of the States concerned as well as of the Congress.

The Congress shall have Power to dispose of and make all needful Rules and Regulations respecting the Territory or other Property belonging to the United States; and nothing in this Constitution shall be so construed as to Prejudice any Claims of the United States, or of any particular State.

SECTION 4
[GUARANTEE OF REPUBLICAN GOVERNMENT]

The United States shall guarantee to every State in this Union a Republican Form of Government, and shall protect each of them against Invasion; and on Application of the Legislature, or of the Executive (when the Legislature cannot be convened), against domestic Violence.

Article V
[AMENDMENT OF THE CONSTITUTION]

The Congress, whenever two thirds of both Houses shall deem it necessary, shall propose Amendments to this Constitution, or, on the Application of the Legislatures of two thirds of the several States, shall call a Convention for proposing Amendments, which, in either Case, shall be valid to all Intents and Purposes, as Part of this Constitution, when ratified by the Legislatures of three fourths of the several States, or by Conventions in three fourths thereof, as the one or the other Mode of Ratification may be proposed by the Congress; *Provided that no Amendment which may be made prior to the Year One thousand eight hundred and eight shall in any Manner affect the first and fourth Clauses in the Ninth Section of the first Article;* and that no State, without its Consent, shall be deprived of its equal Suffrage in the Senate.

Article VI
[DEBTS, SUPREMACY, OATH]

All Debts contracted and Engagements entered into, before the Adoption of this Constitution, shall be as valid against the United States under this Constitution, as under the Confederation.

---

[11] Modified by the Eleventh Amendment.

[12] Repealed by the Thirteenth Amendment.

This Constitution, and the Laws of the United States which shall be made in Pursuance thereof; and all Treaties made, or which shall be made, under the Authority of the United States, shall be the supreme Law of the Land; and the Judges in every State shall be bound thereby, any Thing in the Constitution or Laws of any State to the Contrary notwithstanding.

The Senators and Representatives before mentioned, and the Members of the several State Legislatures, and all executive and judicial Officers, both of the United States and of the several States, shall be bound by Oath or Affirmation, to support this Constitution; but no religious Test shall be required as a Qualification to any Office or public Trust under the United States.

Article VII
[RATIFICATION AND ESTABLISHMENT]

The Ratification of the Conventions of nine States, shall be sufficient for the Establishment of this Constitution between the States so ratifying the Same.

Done in Convention by the Unanimous Consent of the States present the Seventeenth Day of September in the Year of our Lord one thousand seven hundred and Eighty seven and of the Independence of the United States of America the Twelfth. *In Witness* whereof We have hereunto subscribed our Names,

G:⁰ WASHINGTON—
Presidt. and deputy from Virginia

NEW HAMPSHIRE
John Langdon
Nicholas Gilman

MASSACHUSETTS
Nathaniel Gorham
Rufus King

CONNECTICUT
Wm. Saml. Johnson
Roger Sherman

NEW YORK
Alexander Hamilton

NEW JERSEY
Wil: Livingston
David Brearley
Wm. Paterson
Jona: Dayton

PENNSYLVANIA
B Franklin
Thomas Mifflin
Robt. Morris
Geo. Clymer
Thos. FitzSimons
Jared Ingersoll
James Wilson
Gouv Morris

DELAWARE
Geo: Read
Gunning Bedford jun
John Dickinson
Richard Bassett
Jaco: Broom

MARYLAND
James McHenry
Dan of St Thos. Jenifer
Danl. Carroll

VIRGINIA
John Blair—
James Madison Jr.

NORTH CAROLINA
Wm. Blount
Richd. Dobbs Spaight
Hu Williamson

SOUTH CAROLINA
J. Rutledge
Charles Cotesworth
Pinckney
Charles Pinckney
Pierce Butler

GEORGIA
William Few
Abr Baldwin

Amendments to the Constitution

Proposed by Congress and Ratified by the Legislatures of the
Several States, Pursuant to Article V of the Original Constitution.

Amendments I–X, known as the Bill of Rights, were proposed by Congress on September 25, 1789, and ratified on December 15, 1791.

Amendment I
[FREEDOM OF RELIGION, OF SPEECH, AND OF THE PRESS]

Congress shall make no law respecting an establishment of religion, or prohibiting the free exercise thereof; or abridging the freedom of speech, or of the press; or the right of the people peaceably to assemble, and to petition the Government for a redress of grievances.

Amendment II
[RIGHT TO KEEP AND BEAR ARMS]

A well regulated Militia, being necessary to the security of a free State, the right of the people to keep and bear Arms, shall not be infringed.

Amendment III
[QUARTERING OF SOLDIERS]

No Soldier shall, in time of peace be quartered in any house, without the consent of the Owner, nor in time of war, but in a manner to be prescribed by law.

Amendment IV
[SECURITY FROM UNWARRANTABLE SEARCH AND SEIZURE]

The right of the people to be secure in their persons, houses, papers, and effects, against unreasonable searches and seizures, shall not be violated, and no Warrants shall issue, but upon probable cause, supported by Oath or affirmation, and particularly describing the place to be searched, and the persons or things to be seized.

Amendment V
[RIGHTS OF ACCUSED PERSONS IN CRIMINAL PROCEEDINGS]

No person shall be held to answer for a capital, or otherwise infamous crime, unless on a presentment or indictment of a Grand Jury, except in cases arising in the land or naval forces, or in the Militia, when in actual service in time of War or in public danger; nor shall any person be subject for the same offence to be twice put in jeopardy of life or limb; nor shall be compelled in any criminal case to be a witness against himself, nor be deprived of life, liberty, or property, without due process of law; nor shall private property be taken for public use, without just compensation.

Amendment VI
[RIGHT TO SPEEDY TRIAL, WITNESSES, ETC.]

In all criminal prosecutions, the accused shall enjoy the right to a speedy and public trial, by an impartial jury of the State and district wherein the crime shall have been committed, which district shall have been previously ascertained by law, and to be informed of the nature and cause of the accusation; to be confronted with the witnesses against him; to have compulsory process for obtaining witnesses in his favor, and to have the Assistance of Counsel for his defence.

Amendment VII
[TRIAL BY JURY IN CIVIL CASES]

In suits at common law, where the value in controversy shall exceed twenty dollars, the right of trial by jury shall be preserved, and no fact tried by a jury, shall be otherwise reexamined in any Court of the United States, than according to the rules of the common law.

Amendment VIII
[BAILS, FINES, PUNISHMENTS]

Excessive bail shall not be required, nor excessive fines imposed, nor cruel and unusual punishments inflicted.

Amendment IX
[RESERVATION OF RIGHTS OF PEOPLE]

The enumeration in the Constitution, of certain rights, shall not be construed to deny or disparage others retained by the people.

Amendment X
[POWERS RESERVED TO STATES OR PEOPLE]

The powers not delegated to the United States by the Constitution, nor prohibited by it to the States, are reserved to the States respectively, or to the people.

Amendment XI
[*Proposed by Congress on March 4, 1794;
declared ratified on January 8, 1798.*]
[RESTRICTION OF JUDICIAL POWER]

The Judicial power of the United States shall not be construed to extend to any suit in law or equity, commenced or prosecuted against one of the United States by Citizens of another State, or by Citizens or Subjects of any Foreign State.

Amendment XII
[*Proposed by Congress on December 9, 1803;
declared ratified on September 25, 1804.*]
[ELECTION OF PRESIDENT AND VICE PRESIDENT]

The Electors shall meet in their respective states and vote by ballot for President and Vice-President, one of whom, at least, shall not be an inhabitant of the same state with themselves; they shall name in their ballots the person voted for as President, and in distinct ballots the person voted for as Vice-President, and they shall make distinct lists of all persons voted for as President, and of all persons voted for as Vice-President, and of the number of votes for each, which lists they shall sign and certify, and transmit sealed to the seat of the government of the United States, directed to the President of the Senate;—the President of the Senate shall, in presence of the Senate and House of Representatives, open all the certificates and the votes shall then be counted;—The person having the greatest number of votes for President, shall be the President, if such number be a majority of the whole number of Electors appointed; and if no person have such majority, then from the persons having the highest numbers not exceeding three on the list of those voted for as President, the House of Representatives shall choose immediately, by ballot, the President. But in choosing the President, the votes shall be taken by states, the representation from each state having one vote; a quorum for this purpose shall consist of a member or members from two-thirds of the states, and a majority of all the states shall be necessary to a choice. And if the House of Representatives shall not choose a President whenever the right of choice shall devolve upon them, before the fourth day of March next following, then the Vice-President shall act as President, as in the case of the death or other constitutional disability of the President.—The person having the greatest number of votes as Vice-President, shall be the Vice-President, if such number be a majority of the whole number of Electors appointed, and if no person have a majority, then from the two highest numbers on the list, the Senate shall choose the Vice-President; a quorum for the purpose shall consist of two-thirds of the whole number of Senators, and a majority of the whole number shall be necessary to a choice. But no person constitutionally ineligible to the office of President shall be eligible to that of Vice-President of the United States.

Amendment XIII

[*Proposed by Congress on January 31, 1865;
declared ratified on December 18, 1865.*]

SECTION I

[ABOLITION OF SLAVERY]

Neither slavery nor involuntary servitude, except as a punishment for crime whereof the party shall have been duly convicted, shall exist within the United States, or any place subject to their jurisdiction.

SECTION 2

[POWER TO ENFORCE THIS ARTICLE]

Congress shall have power to enforce this article by appropriate legislation.

Amendment XIV

[*Proposed by Congress on June 13, 1866;
declared ratified on July 28, 1868.*]

SECTION I

[CITIZENSHIP RIGHTS NOT TO BE ABRIDGED BY STATES]

All persons born or naturalized in the United States, and subject to the jurisdiction thereof, are citizens of the United States and of the State wherein they reside. No State shall make or enforce any law which shall abridge the privileges or immunities of citizens of the United States; nor shall any State deprive any person of life, liberty, or property, without due process of law; nor deny to any person within its jurisdiction the equal protection of the laws.

SECTION 2

[APPORTIONMENT OF REPRESENTATIVES IN CONGRESS]

Representatives shall be apportioned among the several States according to their respective numbers, counting the whole number of persons in each State, excluding Indians not taxed. But when the right to vote at any election for the choice of electors for President and Vice-President of the United States, Representatives in Congress, the Executive and Judicial officers of a State, or the members of the Legislature thereof, is denied to any of the male inhabitants of such State, being twenty-one years of age, and citizens of the United States, or in any way abridged, except for participation in rebellion, or other crime, the basis of representation therein shall be reduced in the proportion which the number of such male citizens shall bear to the whole number of male citizens twenty-one years of age in such State.

SECTION 3

[PERSONS DISQUALIFIED FROM HOLDING OFFICE]

No person shall be a Senator or Representative in Congress, or elector of President and Vice-President, or hold any office, civil or military, under the United States, or under any State, who, having previously taken an oath, as a member of Congress, or as an officer of the United States, or as a member of any State legislature, or as an executive or judicial officer of any State, to support the Constitution of the United States, shall have engaged in insurrection or rebellion against the same, or given aid or comfort to the enemies thereof. But Congress may by a vote of two-thirds of each House, remove such disability.

SECTION 4

[WHAT PUBLIC DEBTS ARE VALID]

The validity of the public debt of the United States, authorized by law, including debts incurred for payment of pensions and bounties for services in suppressing insurrection or rebellion, shall not be questioned. But neither the United States nor any State shall assume or pay any debt or obligation incurred in aid of insurrection or rebellion against the United States, or any claim for the loss or emancipation of any slave; but all such debts, obligations and claims shall be held illegal and void.

SECTION 5

[POWER TO ENFORCE THIS ARTICLE]

The Congress shall have power to enforce, by appropriate legislation, the provisions of this article.

Amendment XV

[*Proposed by Congress on February 26, 1869;
declared ratified on March 30, 1870.*]

SECTION I

[NEGRO SUFFRAGE]

The right of citizens of the United States to vote shall not be denied or abridged by the United States or by any State on account of race, color, or previous condition of servitude.

SECTION 2

[POWER TO ENFORCE THIS ARTICLE]

The Congress shall have power to enforce this article by appropriate legislation.

Amendment XVI

[*Proposed by Congress on July 2, 1909;
declared ratified on February 25, 1913.*]

[AUTHORIZING INCOME TAXES]

The Congress shall have power to lay and collect taxes on incomes, from whatever source derived, without apportionment among the several States, and without regard to any census or enumeration.

Amendment XVII

[*Proposed by Congress on May 13, 1912;
declared ratified on May 31, 1913.*]

[POPULAR ELECTION OF SENATORS]

The Senate of the United States shall be composed of two Senators from each State, elected by the people thereof, for six years; and each Senator shall have one vote. The electors in each State shall have the qualifications requisite for electors of the most numerous branch of the State legislatures.

When vacancies happen in the representation of any State in the Senate, the executive authority of such State shall issue writs of election to fill such vacancies: *Provided,* That the legislature of any State may empower the executive thereof to make temporary appointments until the people fill the vacancies by election as the legislature may direct.

This amendment shall not be so construed as to affect the election or term of any Senator chosen before it becomes valid as part of the Constitution.

Amendment XVIII

[*Proposed by Congress December 18, 1917;
declared ratified on January 29, 1919.*]

SECTION 1

[NATIONAL LIQUOR PROHIBITION]

After one year from the ratification of this article the manufacture, sale, or transportation of intoxicating liquors within, the importation thereof into, or the exportation thereof from the United States and all territory subject to the jurisdiction thereof for beverage purposes is hereby prohibited.

SECTION 2

[POWER TO ENFORCE THIS ARTICLE]

The Congress and the several States shall have concurrent power to enforce this article by appropriate legislation.

SECTION 3

[RATIFICATION WITHIN SEVEN YEARS]

This article shall be inoperative unless it shall have been ratified as an amendment to the Constitution by the legislatures of the several States, as provided in the Constitution, within seven years from the date of the submission hereof to the States by the Congress.[1]

Amendment XIX

[*Proposed by Congress on June 4, 1919;
declared ratified on August 26, 1920.*]

[WOMAN SUFFRAGE]

The right of citizens of the United States to vote shall not be denied or abridged by the United States or by any State on account of sex.

Congress shall have power to enforce this article by appropriate legislation.

Amendment XX

[*Proposed by Congress on March 2, 1932;
declared ratified on February 6, 1933.*]

SECTION 1

[TERMS OF OFFICE]

The terms of the President and Vice President shall end at noon on the 20th day of January, and the terms of Senators and Representatives at noon on the 3d day of January, of the years in which such terms would have ended if this article had not been ratified; and the terms of their successors shall then begin.

SECTION 2

[TIME OF CONVENING CONGRESS]

The Congress shall assemble at least once in every year, and such meeting shall begin at noon on the 3d day of January, unless they shall by law appoint a different day.

SECTION 3

[DEATH OF PRESIDENT-ELECT]

If, at the time fixed for the beginning of the term of the President, the President elect shall have died, the Vice President elect shall become President. If a President shall not have been chosen before the time fixed for the beginning of his term, or if the President elect shall have failed to qualify, then the Vice President elect shall act as President until a President shall have qualified; and the Congress may by law provide for the case wherein neither a President elect nor a Vice President elect shall have qualified, declaring who shall then act as President, or the manner in which one who is to act shall be selected, and such person shall act accordingly until a President or Vice President shall have qualified.

SECTION 4

[ELECTION OF THE PRESIDENT]

The Congress may by law provide for the case of the death of any of the persons from whom the House of Representatives may choose a President whenever the right of choice shall have devolved upon them, and for the case of the death of any of the persons from whom the Senate may choose a Vice President whenever the right of choice shall have devolved upon them.

SECTION 5

[AMENDMENT TAKES EFFECT]

Sections 1 and 2 shall take effect on the 15th day of October following the ratification of this article.

SECTION 6

[RATIFICATION WITHIN SEVEN YEARS]

This article shall be inoperative unless it shall have been ratified as an amendment to the Constitution by the legislatures of three-fourths of the several States within seven years from the date of its submission.

Amendment XXI

[*Proposed by Congress on February 20, 1933;
declared ratified on December 5, 1933.*]

SECTION 1

[NATIONAL LIQUOR PROHIBITION REPEALED]

The eighteenth article of amendment to the Constitution of the United States is hereby repealed.

SECTION 2

[TRANSPORTATION OF LIQUOR INTO "DRY" STATES]

The transportation or importation into any State, Territory, or Possession of the United States for delivery or use therein of intoxicating liquors, in violation of the laws thereof, is hereby prohibited.

SECTION 3

[RATIFICATION WITHIN SEVEN YEARS]

This article shall be inoperative unless it shall have been ratified as an amendment to the Constitution by conventions in the several States, as provided in the Constitution, within seven years from the date of the submission hereof to the States by the Congress.

Amendment XXII

[*Proposed by Congress on March 21, 1947;
declared ratified on February 27, 1951.*]

SECTION 1

[TENURE OF PRESIDENT LIMITED]

No person shall be elected to the office of President more than twice, and no person who has held the office of President or acted as President, for more than two years of a term to which some other person was elected President shall be elected to the office of the President more than once. But this Article shall not apply to any person holding the office of President when this Article was proposed by the Congress, and shall not prevent any person who may be holding the office of President, or acting as President, during the term within which this Article becomes operative from holding the office of President or acting as President during the remainder of such term.

---

[1]Repealed by the Twenty-first Amendment.

SECTION 2
[RATIFICATION WITHIN SEVEN YEARS]

This article shall be inoperative unless it shall have been ratified as an amendment to the Constitution by the legislatures of three-fourths of the several States within seven years from the date of its submission to the States by the Congress.

Amendment XXIII

[*Proposed by Congress on June 16, 1960; declared ratified on March 29, 1961.*]

SECTION I
[ELECTORAL COLLEGE VOTES FOR THE DISTRICT OF COLUMBIA]

The District constituting the seat of Government of the United States shall appoint in such manner as the Congress may direct:

A number of electors of President and Vice President equal to the whole number of Senators and Representatives in Congress to which the District would be entitled if it were a State, but in no event more than the least populous State; they shall be in addition to those appointed by the States, but they shall be considered, for the purposes of the election of President and Vice President, to be electors appointed by a State; and they shall meet in the District and perform such duties as provided by the twelfth article of amendment.

SECTION 2
[POWER TO ENFORCE THIS ARTICLE]

The Congress shall have power to enforce this article by appropriate legislation.

Amendment XXIV

[*Proposed by Congress on August 27, 1962; declared ratified on January 23, 1964.*]

SECTION I
[ANTI-POLL TAX]

The right of citizens of the United States to vote in any primary or other election for President or Vice President, for electors for President or Vice President, or for Senator or Representative of Congress, shall not be denied or abridged by the United States or any State by reason of failure to pay any poll tax or other tax.

SECTION 2
[POWER TO ENFORCE THIS ARTICLE]

The Congress shall have power to enforce this article by appropriate legislation.

Amendment XXV

[*Proposed by Congress on July 6, 1965; declared ratified on February 10, 1967.*]

SECTION I
[VICE PRESIDENT TO BECOME PRESIDENT]

In case of the removal of the President from office or his death or resignation, the Vice President shall become President.

SECTION 2
[CHOICE OF A NEW VICE PRESIDENT]

Whenever there is a vacancy in the office of the Vice President, the President shall nominate a Vice President who shall take the office upon confirmation by a majority vote of both houses of Congress.

SECTION 3
[PRESIDENT MAY DECLARE OWN DISABILITY]

Whenever the President transmits to the President pro tempore of the Senate and the Speaker of the House of Representatives his written declaration that he is unable to discharge the powers and duties of his office, and until he transmits to them a written declaration to the contrary, such powers and duties shall be discharged by the Vice President as Acting President.

SECTION 4
[ALTERNATE PROCEDURES TO DECLARE AND TO END PRESIDENTIAL DISABILITY]

Whenever the Vice President and a majority of either the principal officers of the executive departments, or of such other body as Congress may by law provide, transmit to the President pro tempore of the Senate and the Speaker of the House of Representatives their written declaration that the President is unable to discharge the powers and duties of his office, the Vice President shall immediately assume the powers and duties of the office as Acting President.

Thereafter, when the President transmits to the President pro tempore of the Senate and the Speaker of the House of Representatives his written declaration that no inability exists, he shall resume the powers and duties of his office unless the Vice President and a majority of either the principal officers of the executive department, or of such other body as Congress may by law provide, transmit within four days to the President pro tempore of the Senate and the Speaker of the House of Representatives their written declaration that the President is unable to discharge the powers and duties of his office. Thereupon Congress shall decide the issue, assembling within forty eight hours for that purpose if not in session. If the Congress, within twenty one days after receipt of the latter written declaration, or, if Congress is not in session, within twenty one days after Congress is required to assemble, determines by two-thirds vote of both Houses that the President is unable to discharge the powers and duties of his office, the Vice President shall continue to discharge the same as Acting President; otherwise, the President shall resume the powers and duties of his office.

Amendment XXVI

[*Proposed by Congress on March 23, 1971; declared ratified on July 1, 1971.*]

SECTION I
[EIGHTEEN-YEAR-OLD VOTE]

The right of citizens of the United States, who are eighteen years of age or older, to vote shall not be denied or abridged by the United States or by any State on account of age.

SECTION 2
[POWER TO ENFORCE THIS ARTICLE]

The Congress shall have power to enforce this article by appropriate legislation.

Amendment XXVII

[*Proposed by Congress on September 25, 1789; declared ratified on May 8, 1992.*]
[CONGRESS CANNOT RAISE ITS OWN PAY]

No law varying the compensation for the services of the Senators and Representatives, shall take effect, until an election of representatives shall have intervened.

The Federalist Papers

No. 10: Madison

Among the numerous advantages promised by a well constructed Union, none deserves to be more accurately developed than its tendency to break and control the violence of faction. The friend of popular governments never finds himself so much alarmed for their character and fate, as when he contemplates their propensity to this dangerous vice. He will not fail therefore to set a due value on any plan which, without violating the principles to which he is attached, provides a proper cure for it. The instability, injustice, and confusion introduced into the public councils have, in truth, been the mortal diseases under which popular governments have everywhere perished, as they continue to be the favorite and fruitful topics from which the adversaries to liberty derive their most specious declamations. The valuable improvements made by the American constitutions on the popular models, both ancient and modern, cannot certainly be too much admired; but it would be an unwarrantable partiality to contend that they have as effectually obviated the danger on this side, as was wished and expected. Complaints are everywhere heard from our most considerate and virtuous citizens, equally the friends of public and private faith and of public and personal liberty, that our governments are too unstable, that the public good is disregarded in the conflicts of rival parties, and that measures are too often decided, not according to the rules of justice and the rights of the minor party, but by the superior force of an interested and overbearing majority. However anxiously we may wish that these complaints had no foundation, the evidence of known facts will not permit us to deny that they are in some degree true. It will be found, indeed, on a candid review of our situation, that some of the distresses under which we labor have been erroneously charged on the operation of our governments; but it will be found, at the same time, that other causes will not alone account for many of our heaviest misfortunes; and, particularly, for that prevailing and increasing distrust of public engagements and alarm for private rights which are echoed from one end of the continent to the other. These must be chiefly, if not wholly, effects of the unsteadiness and injustice with which a factious spirit has tainted our public administration.

By a faction I understand a number of citizens, whether amounting to a majority or minority of the whole, who are united and actuated by some common impulse of passion, or of interest, adverse to the rights of other citizens, or to the permanent and aggregate interests of the community.

There are two methods of curing the mischiefs of faction: the one, by removing its causes; the other, by controlling its effects.

There are again two methods of removing the causes of faction: the one, by destroying the liberty which is essential to its existence; the other, by giving to every citizen the same opinions, the same passions, and the same interests.

It could never be more truly said than of the first remedy, that it is worse than the disease. Liberty is to faction what air is to fire, an aliment without which it instantly expires. But it could not be a less folly to abolish liberty, which is essential to political life, because it nourishes faction, than it would be to wish the annihilation of air, which is essential to animal life, because it imparts to fire its destructive agency.

The second expedient is as impracticable, as the first would be unwise. As long as the reason of man continues fallible, and he is at liberty to exercise it, different opinions will be formed. As long as the connection subsists between his reason and his self-love, his opinions and his passions will have a reciprocal influence on each other; and the former will be objects to which the latter will attach themselves.

The diversity in the faculties of men, from which the rights of property originate, is not less an insuperable obstacle to a uniformity of interests. The protection of these faculties is the first object of Government. From the protection of different and unequal faculties of acquiring property, the possession of different degrees and kinds of property immediately results; and from the influence of these on the sentiments and views of the respective proprietors, ensues a division of the society into different interests and parties.

The latent causes of faction are thus sown in the nature of man; and we see them everywhere brought into different degrees of activity, according to the different circumstances of civil society. A zeal for different opinions concerning religion, concerning Government, and many other points, as well of speculation as of practice; an attachment to different leaders ambitiously contending for pre-eminence and power; or to persons of other descriptions whose fortunes have been interesting to the human passions, have in turn divided mankind into parties, inflamed them with mutual animosity, and rendered them much more disposed to vex and oppress each other, than to co-operate for their common good. So strong is this propensity of mankind to fall into mutual animosities, that where no substantial occasion presents itself, the most frivolous and fanciful distinctions have been sufficient to kindle their unfriendly passions, and excite their most violent conflicts. But the most common and durable source of factions has been the various and unequal distribution of property. Those who hold and those who are without property have ever formed distinct interests in society. Those who are creditors, and those who are debtors, fall under a like discrimination. A landed interest, a manufacturing interest, a mercantile interest, a moneyed interest, with many lesser interests, grow up of necessity in civilized nations, and divide them into different classes, actuated by different sentiments and views. The regulation of these various and interfering interests forms the principal task of modern Legislation, and involves the spirit of party and faction in the necessary and ordinary operations of Government.

No man is allowed to be judge in his own cause, because his interest would certainly bias his judgment and, not improbably, corrupt his integrity. With equal, nay with greater reason, a body of men are unfit to be both judges and parties at the same time; yet what are many of the most important acts of legislation but so many judicial determinations, not indeed concerning the rights of single persons, but concerning the rights of large bodies of citizens; and what are the different classes of legislators but advocates and parties to the causes which they determine? Is a law proposed concerning private debts? It is a question to which the creditors are parties on one side and the debtors on the other. Justice ought to hold the balance between them. Yet the parties are, and must be, themselves the judges; and the most numerous party, or in other words, the most powerful faction must be expected to prevail. Shall domestic manufacturers be encouraged, and in what degree, by restrictions on foreign manufacturers? are questions which would be differently decided by the landed and the manufacturing classes, and probably by neither with a sole regard to justice and the public good. The apportionment of taxes on the various descriptions of property is an act which seems to require the most exact impartiality; yet there is, perhaps, no legislative act in which greater opportunity and temptation are given to a predominant party to trample on the rules of justice. Every shilling with which they overburden the inferior number is a shilling saved to their own pockets.

It is in vain to say that enlightened statesmen will be able to adjust these clashing interests and render them all subservient to the public good. Enlightened statesmen will not always be at the helm. Nor, in many cases, can such an adjustment be made at all without taking into view indirect and remote considerations, which will rarely prevail over the immediate interest which one party may find in disregarding the rights of another or the good of the whole.

The inference to which we are brought is that the *causes* of faction cannot be removed and that relief is only to be sought in the means of controlling its *effects*.

If a faction consists of less than a majority, relief is supplied by the republican principle, which enables the majority to defeat its sinister views by regular vote. It may clog the administration, it may convulse the society; but it will be unable to execute and mask its violence under the forms of the Constitution. When a majority is included in a faction, the form of popular government, on the other hand, enables it to sacrifice to its ruling passion or interest both the public good and the rights of other citizens. To secure the public good and private rights against the danger of such a faction, and at the same time to preserve the spirit and the form of popular government, is then the great object to which our enquiries are directed. Let me add that it is the great desideratum by which alone this form of government can be rescued from the opprobrium under which it has so long labored and be recommended to the esteem and adoption of mankind.

By what means is this object attainable? Evidently by one of two only. Either the existence of the same passion or interest in a majority at the same time must be prevented, or the majority, having such coexistent passion or interest, must be rendered, by their number and local situation, unable to concert and carry into effect schemes of oppression. If the impulse and the opportunity be suffered to coincide, we well know that neither moral nor religious motives can be relied on as an adequate control. They are not found to be such on the injustice and violence of individuals, and lose their efficacy in proportion to the number combined together, that is, in proportion as their efficacy becomes needful.

From this view of the subject it may be concluded that a pure Democracy, by which I mean a Society consisting of a small number of citizens, who assemble and administer the Government in person, can admit of no cure for the mischiefs of faction. A common passion or interest will, in almost every case, be felt by a majority of the whole; a communication and concert results from the form of Government itself; and there is nothing to check the inducements to sacrifice the weaker party or an obnoxious individual. Hence it is that such Democracies have ever been spectacles of turbulence and contention; have ever been found incompatible with personal security or the rights of property; and have in general been as short in their lives as they have been violent in their deaths. Theoretic politicians, who have patronized this species of Government, have erroneously supposed that by reducing mankind to a perfect equality in their political rights, they would at the same time be perfectly equalized and assimilated in their possessions, their opinions, and their passions.

A Republic, by which I mean a Government in which the scheme of representation takes place, opens a different prospect and promises the cure for which we are seeking. Let us examine the points in which it varies from pure Democracy, and we shall comprehend both the nature of the cure and the efficacy which it must derive from the Union.

The two great points of difference between a Democracy and a Republic are: first, the delegation of the Government, in the latter, to a small number of citizens elected by the rest; secondly, the greater number of citizens and greater sphere of country over which the latter may be extended.

The effect of the first difference is, on the one hand, to refine and enlarge the public views by passing them through the medium of a chosen body of citizens, whose wisdom may best discern the true interest of their country and whose patriotism and love of justice will be least likely to sacrifice it to temporary or partial considerations. Under such a regulation it may well happen that the public voice, pronounced by the representatives of the people, will be more consonant to the public good than if pronounced by the people themselves, convened for the purpose. On the other hand, the effect may be inverted. Men of factious tempers, of local prejudices, or of sinister designs, may, by intrigue, by corruption, or by other means, first obtain the suffrages, and then betray the interests of the people. The question resulting is, whether small or extensive Republics are most favorable to the election of proper guardians of the public weal; and it is clearly decided in favor of the latter by two obvious considerations.

In the first place it is to be remarked that however small the Republic may be, the Representatives must be raised to a certain number in order to guard against the cabals of a few; and that however large it may be they must be limited to a certain number in order to guard against the confusion of a multitude. Hence, the number of Representatives in the two cases not being in proportion to that of the Constituents, and being proportionally greatest in the small Republic, it follows that if the proportion of fit characters be not less in the large than in the small Republic, the former will present a greater option, and consequently a greater probability of a fit choice.

In the next place, as each Representative will be chosen by a greater number of citizens in the large than in the small Republic, it will be more difficult for unworthy candidates to practise with success the vicious arts by which elections are too often carried; and the suffrages of the people being more free, will be more likely to centre on men who possess the most attractive merit and the most diffusive and established characters.

It must be confessed that in this, as in most other cases, there is a mean, on both sides of which inconveniencies will be found to lie. By enlarging too much the number of electors, you render the representative too little acquainted with all their local circumstances and lesser interests; as by reducing it too much, you render him unduly attached to these, and too little fit to comprehend and pursue great and national objects. The Federal Constitution forms a happy combination in this respect; the great and aggregate interests being referred to the national, the local and particular to the State legislatures.

The other point of difference is the greater number of citizens and extent of territory which may be brought within the compass of Republican than of Democratic Government; and it is this circumstance principally which renders factious combinations less to be dreaded in the former than in the latter. The smaller the society, the fewer probably will be the distinct parties and interests composing it; the fewer the distinct parties and interests, the more frequently will a majority be found of the same party; and the smaller the number of individuals composing a majority, and the smaller the compass within which they are placed, the more easily will they concert and execute their plans of oppression. Extend the sphere and you take in a greater variety of parties and interests; you make it less probable that a majority of the whole will have a common motive to invade the rights of other citizens; or if such a common motive exists, it will be more difficult for all who feel it to discover their own strength and to act in unison with each other. Besides other impediments, it may be remarked, that where there is a consciousness of unjust or dishonorable purposes, communication is always checked by distrust in proportion to the number whose concurrence is necessary.

Hence, it clearly appears that the same advantage which a Republic has over a Democracy in controlling the effects of faction is enjoyed by a large over a small republic—is enjoyed by the Union over the States composing it. Does this advantage consist in the substitution of representatives whose enlightened views and virtuous sentiments render them superior to local prejudices and to schemes of injustice? It will not be denied that the representation of the Union will be most likely to possess these requisite endowments. Does it consist in the greater security afforded by a greater variety of parties, against the event of any one party being able to outnumber and oppress the rest? In an equal degree does the increased variety of parties comprised within the Union increase this security? Does it, in fine, consist in the greater obstacles opposed to the concert and accomplishment of the secret wishes of an unjust and interested majority? Here again the extent of the Union gives it the most palpable advantage.

The influence of factious leaders may kindle a flame within their particular States but will be unable to spread a general conflagration through the other States: a religious sect may degenerate into a political faction in a part of the Confederacy; but the variety of sects dispersed over the entire face of it must secure the national Councils against any danger from that source: a rage for paper money, for an abolition of debts, for an equal division of property, or for any other improper or wicked project, will be less apt to pervade the whole body of the Union than a particular member of it; in the same proportion as such a malady is more likely to taint a particular county or district than an entire State.

In the extent and proper structure of the Union, therefore, we behold a republican remedy for the diseases most incident to Republican Government. And according to the degree of pleasure and pride we feel in being republicans ought to be our zeal in cherishing the spirit and supporting the character of federalist.

PUBLIUS

No. 51: Madison

To what expedient, then, shall we finally resort, for maintaining in practice the necessary partition of power among the several departments as laid down in the constitution? The only answer that can be given is that as all these exterior provisions are found to be inadequate the defect must be supplied, by so contriving the interior structure of the government as that its several constituent parts may, by their mutual relations, be the means of keeping each other in their proper places. Without presuming to undertake a full development of this important idea I will hazard a few general observations which may perhaps place it in a clearer light, and enable us to form a more correct judgment of the principles and structure of the government planned by the convention.

In order to lay a due foundation for that separate and distinct exercise of the different powers of government, which to a certain extent is admitted on all hands to be essential to the preservation of liberty, it is evident that each department should have a will of its own; and consequently should be so constituted that the members of each should have as little agency as possible in the appointment of the members of the others. Were this principle rigorously adhered to, it would require that all the appointments for the supreme executive, legislative, and judiciary magistracies should be drawn from the same fountain of authority, the people, through channels having no communication whatever with one another. Perhaps such a plan of constructing the several departments would be less difficult in practice than it may in contemplation appear. Some difficulties, however, and some additional expense would attend the execution of it. Some deviations, therefore, from the principle must be admitted. In the constitution of the judiciary department in particular, it might be inexpedient to insist rigorously on the principle: first, because peculiar qualifications being essential in the members, the primary consideration ought to be to select that mode of choice which best secures these qualifications; second, because the permanent tenure by which the appointments are held in that department must soon destroy all sense of dependence on the authority conferring them.

It is equally evident that the members of each department should be as little dependent as possible on those of the others for the emoluments annexed to their offices. Were the executive magistrate, or the judges, not independent of the legislature in this particular, their independence in every other would be merely nominal.

But the great security against a gradual concentration of the several powers in the same department consists in giving to those who administer each department the necessary constitutional means and personal motives to resist encroachments of the others. The provision for defence must in this, as in all other cases, be made commensurate to the danger of attack. Ambition must be made to counteract ambition. The interest of the man must be connected with the constitutional rights of the place. It may be a reflection on human nature that such devices should be necessary to control the abuses of government. But what is government itself but the greatest of all reflections on human nature? If men were angels, no government would be necessary. If angels were to govern men, neither external nor internal controls on government would be necessary. In framing a government which is to be administered by men over men, the great difficulty lies in this: You must first enable the government to control the governed; and in the next place oblige it to control itself. A dependence on the people is, no doubt, the primary control on the government; but experience has taught mankind the necessity of auxiliary precautions.

This policy of supplying, by opposite and rival interests, the defect of better motives, might be traced through the whole system of human affairs, private as well as public. We see it particularly displayed in all the subordinate distributions of power, where the constant aim is to divide and arrange the several offices in such a manner as that each may be a check on the other; that the private interest of every individual may be a sentinel over the public rights. These inventions of prudence cannot be less requisite in the distribution of the supreme powers of the State.

But it is not possible to give to each department an equal power of self-defense. In republican government, the legislative authority necessarily predominates. The remedy for this inconveniency is to divide the legislature into different branches; and to render them, by different modes of election and different principles of action, as little connected with each other as the nature of their common functions and their common dependence on the society will admit. It may even be necessary to guard against dangerous encroachments by still further precautions. As the weight of the legislative authority requires that it should be thus divided, the weakness of the executive may require, on the other hand, that it should be fortified. An absolute negative on the legislature appears, at first view, to be the natural defense with which the executive magistrate should be armed. But perhaps it would be neither altogether safe nor alone sufficient. On ordinary occasions it might not be exerted with the requisite firmness, and on extraordinary occasions it might be perfidiously abused. May not this defect of an absolute negative be supplied by some qualified connection between this weaker branch of the stronger department, by which the latter may be led to support the constitutional rights of the former, without being too much detached from the rights of its own department?

If the principles on which these observations are founded be just, as I persuade myself they are, and they be applied as a criterion to the several State constitutions, and to the federal Constitution, it will be found that if the latter does not perfectly correspond with them, the former are infinitely less able to bear such a test.

There are, moreover, two considerations particularly applicable to the federal system of America, which place that system in a very interesting point of view.

First. In a single republic, all the power surrendered by the people is submitted to the administration of a single government; and usurpations are guarded against by a division of the government into distinct and separate departments. In the compound republic of America, the power surrendered by the people is first divided between two distinct governments, and then the portion allotted to each subdivided among distinct and separate departments. Hence a double security arises to the rights of the people. The different governments will control each other, at the same time that each will be controlled by itself.

Second. It is of great importance in a republic not only to guard the society against the oppression of its rulers, but to guard one part of the society against the injustice of the other part. Different interests necessarily exist in different classes of citizens. If a majority be united by a common interest, the rights of the minority will be insecure. There are but two methods of providing against this evil: The one by creating a will in the community independent of the majority—that is, of the society itself; the other, by comprehending in the society so many separate descriptions of citizens as will render an unjust combination of a majority of the whole very improbable, if not impracticable. The first method prevails in all governments possessing an hereditary or self-appointed authority. This, at best, is but a precarious security; because a power independent of the society may as well espouse the unjust views of the major as the rightful interests of the minor party, and may possibly be turned against both parties. The second method will be exemplified in the federal republic of the United States. Whilst all authority in it will be derived from and dependent on the society, the society itself will be broken into so many parts, interests and classes of citizens, that the rights of individuals, or of the minority, will be in little danger from interested combinations of the majority. In a free government the security for civil rights must be the same as that for religious rights. It consists in the one case in the multiplicity of interests, and in the other in the multiplicity of sects. The degree of security in both cases will depend on the number of interests and sects; and this may be presumed to depend on the extent of country and number of people comprehended under the same government. This view of the subject must particularly recommend a proper federal system to all the sincere and considerate friends of republican government: Since it shows that in exact proportion as the territory of the Union may be formed into more circumscribed Confederacies, or States, oppressive combinations of a majority will be facilitated; the best security, under the republican form, for the rights of every class of citizens, will be diminished; and consequently the stability and independence of some member of the government, the only other security, must be proportionally increased. Justice is the end of government. It is the end of civil society. It ever has been and ever will be pursued until it be obtained, or until liberty be lost in the pursuit. In a society under the forms of which the stronger faction can readily unite and oppress the weaker, anarchy may as truly be said to reign as in a state of nature, where the weaker individual is not secured against the violence of the stronger: And as, in the latter state, even the stronger individuals are prompted, by the uncertainty of their condition, to submit to a government which may protect the weak as well as themselves: So, in the former state, will the more powerful factions or parties be gradually induced, by a like motive, to wish for a government which will protect all parties, the weaker as well as the more powerful. It can be little doubted that if the State of Rhode Island was separated from the Confederacy and left to itself, the insecurity of rights under the popular form of government within such narrow limits would be displayed by such reiterated oppressions of factious majorities that some power altogether independent of the people would soon be called for by the voice of the very factions whose misrule had proved the necessity of it. In the extended republic of the United States, and among the great variety of interests, parties, and sects which it embraces, a coalition of a majority of the whole society could seldom take place on any other principles than those of justice and the general good; and there being thus less danger to a minor from the will of the major party, there must be less pretext, also, to provide for the security of the former, by introducing into the government a will not dependent on the latter, or, in other words, a will independent of the society itself. It is no less certain than it is important, notwithstanding the contrary opinions which have been entertained, that the larger the society, provided it lie within a practicable sphere, the more duly capable it will be of self-government. And happily for the *republican cause*, practicable sphere may be carried to a very great extent by a judicious modification and mixture of the *federal principle*.

PUBLIUS

No. 78: Hamilton

To the People of the State of New York:

we proceed now to an examination of the judiciary department of the proposed government.

In unfolding the defects of the existing Confederation, the utility and necessity of a federal judicature have been clearly pointed out. It is the less necessary to recapitulate the considerations there urged, as the propriety of the institution in the abstract is not disputed; the only questions which have been raised being relative to the manner of constituting it, and to its extent. To these points, therefore, our observations shall be confined.

The manner of constituting it seems to embrace these several objects: 1st. The mode of appointing the judges. 2d. The tenure by which they are to hold their places. 3d. The partition of the judiciary authority between different courts, and their relations to each other.

First. As to the mode of appointing the judges; this is the same with that of appointing the officers of the Union in general, and has been so fully discussed in the two last numbers, that nothing can be said here which would not be useless repetition.

Second. As to the tenure by which the judges are to hold their places; this chiefly concerns their duration in office; the provisions for their support; the precautions for their responsibility.

According to the plan of the convention, all judges who may be appointed by the United States are to hold their offices DURING GOOD BEHAVIOR; which is conformable to the most approved of the State constitutions and among the rest, to that of this State. Its propriety having been drawn into question by the adversaries of that plan, is no light symptom of the rage for objection, which disorders their imaginations and judgments. The standard of good behavior for the continuance in office of the judicial magistracy, is certainly one of the most valuable of the modern improvements in the practice of government. In a monarchy it is an excellent barrier to the despotism of the prince; in a republic it is a no less excellent barrier to the encroachments and oppressions of the representative body. And it is the best expedient which can be devised in any government, to secure a steady, upright, and impartial administration of the laws.

Whoever attentively considers the different departments of power must perceive, that, in a government in which they are separated from each other, the judiciary, from the nature of its functions, will always be the least dangerous to the political rights of the Constitution; because it will be least in a capacity to annoy or injure them. The Executive not only dispenses the honors, but holds the sword of the community. The legislature not only commands the purse, but prescribes the rules by which the duties and rights of every citizen are to be regulated. The judiciary, on the contrary, has no influence over either the sword or the purse; no direction either of the strength or of the wealth of the society; and can take no active resolution whatever. It may truly be said to have neither FORCE nor WILL, but merely judgment; and must ultimately depend upon the aid of the executive arm even for the efficacy of its judgments.

This simple view of the matter suggests several important consequences. It proves incontestably, that the judiciary is beyond comparison the weakest of the three departments of power; that it can never attack with success either of the other two; and that all possible care is requisite to enable it to defend itself against their attacks. It equally proves, that though individual oppression may now and then proceed from the courts of justice, the general liberty of the people can never be endangered from that quarter; I mean so long as the judiciary remains truly distinct from both the legislature and the Executive. For I agree, that "there is no liberty, if the power of judging be not separated from the legislative and executive powers." And it proves, in the last place, that as liberty can have nothing to fear from the judiciary alone, but would have every thing to fear from its union with either of the other departments; that as all the effects of such a union must ensue from a dependence of the former on the latter, notwithstanding a nominal and apparent separation; that as, from the natural feebleness of the judiciary, it is in continual jeopardy of being overpowered, awed, or influenced by its co-ordinate branches; and that as nothing can contribute so much to its firmness and independence as permanency in office, this quality may therefore be justly regarded as an indispensable ingredient in its constitution, and, in a great measure, as the citadel of the public justice and the public security.

The complete independence of the courts of justice is peculiarly essential in a limited Constitution. By a limited Constitution, I understand one which contains certain specified exceptions to the legislative authority; such, for instance, as that it shall pass no bills of attainder, no ex-post-facto laws, and the like. Limitations of this kind can be preserved in practice no other way than through the medium of courts of justice, whose duty it must be to declare all acts contrary to the manifest tenor of the Constitution void. Without this, all the reservations of particular rights or privileges would amount to nothing.

Some perplexity respecting the rights of the courts to pronounce legislative acts void, because contrary to the Constitution, has arisen from an imagination that the doctrine would imply a superiority of the judiciary to the legislative power. It is urged that the authority which can declare the acts of another void, must necessarily be superior to the one whose acts may be declared void. As this doctrine is of great importance in all the American constitutions, a brief discussion of the ground on which it rests cannot be unacceptable.

There is no position which depends on clearer principles, than that every act of a delegated authority, contrary to the tenor of the commission under which it is exercised, is void. No legislative act, therefore, contrary to the Constitution, can be valid. To deny this, would be to affirm, that the deputy is greater than his principal; that the servant is above his master; that the representatives of the people are superior to the people themselves; that men acting by virtue of powers, may do not only what their powers do not authorize, but what they forbid.

If it be said that the legislative body are themselves the constitutional judges of their own powers, and that the construction they put upon them is conclusive upon the other departments, it may be answered, that this cannot be the natural presumption, where it is not to be collected from any particular provisions in the Constitution. It is not otherwise to be supposed, that the Constitution could intend to enable the representatives of the people to substitute their will to that of their constituents. It is far more rational to suppose, that the courts were designed to be an intermediate body between the people and the legislature, in order, among other things, to keep the latter within the limits assigned to their authority. The interpretation of the laws is the proper and peculiar province of the courts. A constitution is, in fact, and must be regarded by the judges, as a fundamental law. It therefore belongs to them to ascertain its meaning, as well as the meaning of any particular act proceeding from the legislative body. If there should happen to be an irreconcilable variance between the two, that which has the superior obligation and validity ought, of course, to be preferred; or, in other words, the Constitution ought to be preferred to the statute, the intention of the people to the intention of their agents.

Nor does this conclusion by any means suppose a superiority of the judicial to the legislative power. It only supposes that the power of the people is superior to both; and that where the will of the legislature, declared in its statutes, stands in opposition to that of the people, declared in the Constitution, the judges ought to be governed by the latter rather than the former. They ought to regulate their decisions by the fundamental laws, rather than by those which are not fundamental.

This exercise of judicial discretion, in determining between two contradictory laws, is exemplified in a familiar instance. It not uncommonly happens, that there are two statutes existing at one time, clashing in whole or in part with each other, and neither of them containing any repealing clause or expression. In such a case, it is the province of the courts to liquidate and fix their meaning and operation. So far as they can, by any fair construction, be reconciled to each other, reason and law conspire to dictate that this should be done; where this is impracticable, it becomes a matter of necessity to give effect to one, in exclusion of the other. The rule which has obtained in the courts for determining their relative validity is, that the last in order of time shall be preferred to the first. But this is a mere rule of construction, not derived from any positive law, but from the nature and reason of the thing. It is a rule not enjoined upon the courts by legislative provision, but adopted by themselves, as consonant to truth and propriety, for the direction of their conduct as interpreters of the law. They thought it reasonable, that between the interfering acts of an equal authority, that which was the last indication of its will should have the preference.

But in regard to the interfering acts of a superior and subordinate authority, of an original and derivative power, the nature and reason of the thing indicate the converse of that rule as proper to be followed. They teach us that the prior act of a superior ought to be preferred to the subsequent act of an inferior and subordinate authority; and that accordingly, whenever a particular statute contravenes the Constitution, it will be the duty of the judicial tribunals to adhere to the latter and disregard the former.

It can be of no weight to say that the courts, on the pretense of a repugnancy, may substitute their own pleasure to the constitutional intentions of the legislature. This might as well happen in the case of two contradictory statutes; or it might as well happen in every adjudication upon any single statute. The courts must declare the sense of the law; and if they should be disposed to exercise WILL instead of judgment, the consequence would equally be the substitution of their pleasure to that of the legislative body. The observation, if it prove any thing, would prove that there ought to be no judges distinct from that body.

If, then, the courts of justice are to be considered as the bulwarks of a limited Constitution against legislative encroachments, this consideration will afford a strong argument for the permanent tenure of judicial offices, since nothing will contribute so much as this to that independent spirit in the judges which must be essential to the faithful performance of so arduous a duty.

This independence of the judges is equally requisite to guard the Constitution and the rights of individuals from the effects of those ill humors, which the arts of designing men, or the influence of particular conjunctures, sometimes disseminate among the people themselves, and which, though they speedily give place to better information, and more deliberate reflection, have a tendency, in the meantime, to occasion dangerous innovations in the government, and serious oppressions of the minor party in the community. Though I trust the friends of the proposed Constitution will never concur with its enemies, in questioning that fundamental principle of republican government, which admits the right of the people to alter or abolish the established Constitution, whenever they find it inconsistent with their happiness, yet it is not to be inferred from this principle, that the representatives of the people, whenever a momentary inclination happens to lay hold of a majority of their constituents, incompatible with the provisions in the existing Constitution, would, on that account, be justifiable in a violation of those provisions; or that the courts would be under a greater obligation to connive at infractions in this shape, than when they had proceeded wholly from the cabals of the representative body. Until the people have, by some solemn and authoritative act, annulled or changed the established form, it is binding upon themselves collectively, as well as individually; and no presumption, or even knowledge, of their sentiments, can warrant their representatives in a departure from it, prior to such an act. But it is easy to see, that it would require an uncommon portion of fortitude in the judges to do their duty as faithful guardians of the Constitution, where legislative invasions of it had been instigated by the major voice of the community.

But it is not with a view to infractions of the Constitution only, that the independence of the judges may be an essential safeguard against the effects of occasional ill humors in the society. These sometimes extend no farther than to the injury of the private rights of particular classes of citizens, by unjust and partial laws. Here also the firmness of the judicial magistracy is of vast importance in mitigating the severity and confining the operation of such laws. It not only serves to moderate the immediate mischiefs of those which may have been passed, but it operates as a check upon the legislative body in passing them; who, perceiving that obstacles to the success of iniquitous intention are to be expected from the scruples of the courts, are in a manner compelled, by the very motives of the injustice they meditate, to qualify their attempts. This is a circumstance calculated to have more influence upon the character of our governments, than but few may be aware of. The benefits of the integrity and moderation of the judiciary have already been felt in more States than one; and though they may have displeased those whose sinister expectations they may have disappointed, they must have commanded the esteem and applause of all the virtuous and disinterested. Considerate men, of every description, ought to prize whatever will tend to beget or fortify that temper in the courts: as no man can be sure that he may not be to-morrow the victim of a spirit of injustice, by which he may be a gainer to-day. And every man must now feel, that the inevitable tendency of such a spirit is to sap the foundations of public and private confidence, and to introduce in its stead universal distrust and distress.

That inflexible and uniform adherence to the rights of the Constitution, and of individuals, which we perceive to be indispensable in the courts of justice, can certainly not be expected from judges who hold their offices by a temporary commission. Periodical appointments, however regulated, or by whomsoever made, would, in some way or other, be fatal to their necessary independence. If the power of making them was committed either to the Executive or legislature, there would be danger of an improper complaisance to the branch which possessed it; if to both, there would be an unwillingness to hazard the displeasure of either; if to the people, or to persons chosen by them for the special purpose, there would be too great a disposition to consult popularity, to justify a reliance that nothing would be consulted but the Constitution and the laws.

There is yet a further and a weightier reason for the permanency of the judicial offices, which is deducible from the nature of the qualifications they require. It has been frequently remarked, with great propriety, that a voluminous code of laws is one of the inconveniences necessarily connected with the advantages of a free government. To avoid an arbitrary discretion in the courts, it is indispensable that they should be bound down by strict rules and precedents, which serve to define and point out their duty in every particular case that comes before them; and it will readily be conceived from the variety of controversies which grow out of the folly and wickedness of mankind, that the records of those precedents must unavoidably swell to a very considerable bulk, and must demand long and laborious study to acquire a competent knowledge of them. Hence it is, that there can be but few men in the society who will have sufficient skill in the laws to qualify them for the stations of judges. And making the proper deductions for the ordinary depravity of human nature, the number must be still smaller of those who unite the requisite integrity with the requisite knowledge. These considerations apprise us, that the government can have no great option between fit character; and that a temporary duration in office, which would naturally discourage such characters from quitting a lucrative line of practice to accept a seat on the bench, would have a tendency to throw the administration of justice into hands less able, and less well qualified, to conduct it with utility and dignity. In the present circumstances of this country, and in those in which it is likely to be for a long time to come, the disadvantages on this score would be greater than they may at first sight appear; but it must be confessed, that they are far inferior to those which present themselves under the other aspects of the subject.

Upon the whole, there can be no room to doubt that the convention acted wisely in copying from the models of those constitutions which have established good behavior as the tenure of their judicial offices, in point of duration; and that so far from being blamable on this account, their plan would have been inexcusably defective, if it had wanted this important feature of good government. The experience of Great Britain affords an illustrious comment on the excellence of the institution.

PUBLIUS

GLOSSARY

501(c)(3) organization A tax code classification that applies to most interest groups; this designation makes donations to the group tax deductible but limits the group's political activities.

527 organization A tax-exempt group formed primarily to influence elections through voter mobilization efforts and issue ads that do not directly endorse or oppose a candidate. Unlike political action committees, they are not subject to contribution limits and spending caps.

Aid to Families with Dependent Children (AFDC) The federal welfare program in place from 1935 until 1996, when it was replaced by Temporary Assistance for Needy Families (TANF) under President Clinton.

amicus curiae Latin for "friend of the court," referring to an interested group or person who shares relevant information about a case to help the Court reach a decision.

Antifederalists Those at the Constitutional Convention who favored strong state governments and feared that a strong national government would be a threat to individual rights.

appeals courts The intermediate level of federal courts that hear appeals from district courts. More generally, an appeals court is any court with appellate jurisdiction.

appellate jurisdiction The authority of a court to hear appeals from lower courts and change or uphold the decision.

apportionment The process of assigning the 435 seats in the House to the states based on increases or decreases in state population.

Articles of Confederation Sent to the states for ratification in 1777, these were the first attempt at a new American government. It was later decided that the Articles restricted national government too much, and they were replaced by the Constitution.

astroturf lobbying Any lobbying method initiated by an interest group that is designed to look like the spontaneous, independent participation of many individuals.

attack journalism A type of increasingly popular media coverage focused on political scandals and controversies, which causes a negative public opinion of political figures.

attitudinalist approach A way of understanding decisions of the Supreme Court based on the political ideologies of the justices.

baby boom generation Americans born between 1946 and 1964, who are retiring in large numbers over the next 20 years.

balanced budget A spending plan in which the government's expenditures are equal to its revenue.

bicameralism The system of having two chambers within one legislative body, like the House and Senate in the U.S. Congress.

Bill of Rights The first 10 amendments to the Constitution; they protect individual rights and liberties.

block grants Federal aid provided to a state government to be spent within a certain policy area, but the state can decide how to spend the money within that area.

broadcast media Communications technologies, such as television and radio, that transmit information over airwaves.

budget deficit The amount by which a government's spending in a given fiscal year exceeds its revenue.

budget making The processes carried out in Congress to determine how government money will be spent and revenue will be raised.

budget maximizers Bureaucrats who seek to increase funding for their agency whether or not that additional spending is worthwhile.

budget reconciliation The process by which congressional committees are held

to the spending targets specified in the budget resolution. During this process, the House and Senate Budget Committees combine the budgetary changes from all the legislative committees into an omnibus reconciliation bill to be approved by Congress.

bureaucracy The system of civil servants and political appointees who implement congressional or presidential decisions; also known as the administrative state.

bureaucratic drift Bureaucrats' tendency to implement policies in a way that favors their own political objectives rather than following the original intentions of the legislation.

Bush Doctrine The foreign policy of President George W. Bush, under which the United States would use military force preemptively against threats to its national security.

business cycle The normal pattern of expansion and contraction of the economy.

by-product theory The idea that many Americans acquire political information unintentionally rather than by seeking it out.

Cabinet The group of 15 executive department heads who implement the president's agenda in their respective positions.

casework Assistance provided by members of Congress to their constituents in solving problems with the federal bureaucracy or addressing other specific concerns.

categorical grants Federal aid to state or local governments that is provided for a specific purpose, such as a mass-transit program within the transportation budget or a school lunch program within the education budget.

caucus (congressional) The organization of Democrats within the House and Senate that meets to discuss and debate the party's positions on various issues in order to reach a consensus and to assign leadership positions.

caucus (electoral) A local meeting in which party members select a party's nominee for the general election.

centralized groups Interest groups that have a headquarters, usually in Washington, D.C., as well as members and field offices throughout the country. In general, these groups' lobbying decisions are made at headquarters by the group leaders.

cert pool A system initiated in the Supreme Court in the 1970s in which law clerks screen cases that come to the Supreme Court and recommend to the justices which cases should be heard.

checks and balances A system in which each branch of government has some power over the others.

civil liberties Basic political freedoms that protect citizens from governmental abuses of power.

civil rights Rights that guarantee individuals freedom from discrimination. These rights are generally grounded in the equal protection clause of the Fourteenth Amendment and more specifically laid out in laws passed by Congress, such as the 1964 Civil Rights Act.

civil servants Employees of bureaucratic agencies within the government.

Civil War Amendments The Thirteenth, Fourteenth, and Fifteenth Amendments to the Constitution, which abolished slavery and granted civil liberties and voting rights to freed slaves after the Civil War.

civilian control The idea that military leaders do not formulate military policy, but rather implement directives from civilian leaders.

class-action lawsuit A case brought by a group of individuals on behalf of themselves and others in the general public who are in similar circumstances.

clear and present danger test Established in *Schenck v. United States*, this test allows the government to restrict certain types of speech deemed dangerous.

closed primary A primary election in which only registered members of a particular political party can vote.

closed rules Conditions placed on a legislative debate by the House Rules Committee prohibiting amendments to a bill.

cloture A procedure through which the Senate can limit the amount of time spent debating a bill (cutting off a filibuster) if a supermajority of 60 senators agree.

coattails The idea that a popular president can generate additional support for candidates affiliated with his party. Coattails are weak or nonexistent in most American elections.

coercion A method of eliminating nonparticipation or free riding by potential group members by requiring participation, as in many labor unions.

coercive federalism A form of federalism in which the federal government pressures the states to change their policies by using regulations, mandates, and conditions (often involving threats to withdraw federal funding).

Cold War The period of tension and arms competition between the United States and the Soviet Union that lasted from 1945 until 1991.

collective action problems Situations in which the members of a group would benefit by working together to produce some outcome, but each individual is better off refusing to cooperate and reaping benefits from those who do the work.

commerce clause Part of Article I, Section 8, of the Constitution that gives Congress "the power to regulate Commerce . . . among the several States." The Supreme Court's interpretation of this clause has varied, but today it serves as the basis for much of Congress's legislation.

commercial speech Public expression with the aim of making a profit. It has received greater protection under the First Amendment in recent years but remains less protected than political speech.

common law Law based on the precedent of previous court rulings rather than on legislation. It is used in all federal courts and 49 of the 50 state courts.

competitive federalism A form of federalism in which states compete to attract businesses and jobs through the policies they adopt.

concurrent powers Responsibilities for particular policy areas, such as transportation, that are shared by federal, state, and local governments.

confederal government A form of government in which states hold power over a limited national government.

confederations Interest groups made up of several independent, local organizations that provide much of their funding and hold most of the power.

conference The organization of Republicans within the House and Senate that meets to discuss and debate the party's positions on various issues in order to reach a consensus and to assign leadership positions.

conference committees Temporary committees created to negotiate differences between the House and Senate versions of a piece of legislation that has passed through both chambers.

"consent of the governed" The idea that government gains its legitimacy through regular elections in which the people living under that government participate to elect their leaders.

conservative One side of the ideological spectrum defined by support for lower taxes, a free market, and a more-limited government; generally associated with Republicans.

constitutional authority Powers derived from the provisions of the Constitution that outline the president's role in government.

constitutional interpretation The process of determining whether a piece of legislation or governmental action is supported by the Constitution.

constructivism The idea that foreign policy is shaped by how a state's leaders define the national interest, ideology, and other factors.

containment An important feature of American Cold War policy in which the United States used diplomatic, economic, and military strategies in an effort to prevent the Soviet Union from expanding its influence.

cooperative federalism A form of federalism in which national and state governments work together to provide services efficiently. This form emerged in the late 1930s, representing a profound shift toward less concrete boundaries of responsibility in national–state relations.

Council of Economic Advisers A group of economic advisers, created by the Employment Act of 1946, which provides objective data on the state of the economy and makes economic policy recommendations to the president.

culture wars Political conflict in the United States between "red-state" Americans, who tend to have strong religious beliefs, and "blue-state" Americans, who tend to be more secular.

current account The balance of a country's receipts and its payments in international trade and investment.

de facto Relating to actions or circumstances that occur outside the law or "by fact," such as the segregation of schools that resulted from housing patterns and other factors rather than from laws.

de jure Relating to actions or circumstances that occur "by law," such as the legally enforced segregation of schools in the American South before the 1960s.

defendant The person or party against whom a case is brought.

delegate A member of Congress who loyally represents constituents' direct interests.

democracy Government by the people. In most contexts, this means representative democracy in which the people elect leaders to enact policies. Democracies must have fair elections with at least two alternatives.

descriptive representation When a member of Congress shares the characteristics (such as gender, race, religion, or ethnicity) of his or her constituents.

détente An approach to foreign policy in which cultural exchanges and negotiations are used to reduce tensions between rival nations, such as between the United States and the Soviet Union during the 1970s.

direct incitement test Established in *Brandenburg v. Ohio*, this test protects threatening speech under the First Amendment unless that speech aims to and is likely to cause imminent "lawless action."

direct lobbying Attempts by interest group staff to influence policy by speaking with elected officials or bureaucrats.

discount rate The interest rate that a bank must pay on a short-term loan from the Federal Reserve Bank.

discretionary spending Expenditures that can be cut from the budget without changing the underlying law, which is everything other than defense, entitlements, and interest on the debt.

disenfranchised To have been denied the ability to exercise a right, such as the right to vote.

disparate impact standard The idea that discrimination exists if a practice has a negative effect on a specific group, whether or not this effect was intentional.

distributive theory The idea that members of Congress will join committees that best serve the interests of their district and that committee members will support each other's legislation.

district courts Lower-level trial courts of the federal judicial system that handle most U.S. federal cases.

divided government A situation in which the House, Senate, and presidency are not controlled by the same party—for example, when Democrats hold the majority of House and Senate seats, and the president is a Republican.

doctrine of interposition The idea that if the national government passes an unconstitutional law, the people of the states (through their state legislatures) can declare the law void. This idea provided the basis for southern secession and the Civil War.

domino theory An idea held by American foreign policy makers during the Cold War that the creation of one Soviet-backed communist nation would lead to the spread of communism in that nation's region.

double jeopardy Being tried twice for the same crime. This is prevented by the Fifth Amendment.

dual federalism The form of federalism favored by Chief Justice Roger Taney in which national and state governments are seen as distinct entities providing separate services. This model limits the power of the national government.

due process clause Part of the Fourteenth Amendment that forbids states from denying "life, liberty, or property" to any person without due process of law. (A nearly identical clause in the Fifth Amendment applies only to the national government.)

due process rights The idea that laws and legal proceedings must be fair. The Constitution guarantees that the government cannot take away a person's "life, liberty, or property, without due process of law." Other specific due process rights are found in the Fourth, Fifth, Sixth, and Eighth Amendments, such as protection from self-incrimination and freedom from illegal searches.

Duverger's law The principle that in a democracy with single-member districts and plurality voting, only two parties' candidates will have a realistic chance of winning political office, as in the United States.

earmarks Federally funded local projects attached to bills passed through Congress.

economic depression A deep, widespread downturn in the economy, like the Great Depression of the 1930s.

economic individualism The autonomy of individuals to manage their own financial decisions without government interference.

economic sanctions Penalties applied by one country or group of countries on another, usually in the form of tariffs or other trade barriers.

election cycle The two-year period between general elections.

electoral college The body that votes to select America's president and vice president based on the popular vote in each state. Each candidate nominates a slate of electors who are selected to attend the meeting of the college if their candidate wins the most votes in a state or district.

electoral connection The idea that congressional behavior is centrally motivated by members' desire for reelection.

electoral votes Votes cast by members of the electoral college; after a presidential candidate wins the popular vote in a given state, that candidate's slate of electors casts electoral votes for the candidate on behalf of that state.

entitlement Any federal government program that provides benefits to Americans who meet requirements specified by law.

enumerated powers Powers explicitly granted to Congress, the president, or the Supreme Court in the first three articles of the Constitution. Examples include Congress's power to "raise and support armies" and the president's power as commander in chief.

equal time provision An FCC regulation requiring broadcast media to provide equal airtime on any non-news programming to all candidates running for an office.

equality In the context of American politics, equality means equality before the law, political equality (one person, one vote), and equality of opportunity (the equal chance for everyone to realize their potential), but not material equality (equal income or wealth).

establishment clause Part of the First Amendment that states "Congress shall make no law respecting an establishment of religion," which has been interpreted to mean that Congress cannot sponsor or favor any religion.

exclusionary rule The principle that illegally or unconstitutionally acquired evidence cannot be used in a criminal trial.

executive agreement An agreement between the executive branch and a foreign government, which acts as a treaty but does not require Senate approval.

Executive Office of the President (EOP) The group of policy-related offices that serves as support staff to the president.

executive orders Proclamations made by the president that change government policy without congressional approval.

executive powers clause Part of Article II, Section 1, of the Constitution that states, "The executive Power shall be vested in a President of the United States of America." This broad statement has been used to justify many assertions of presidential power.

executive privilege The right of the president to keep executive branch conversations and correspondence confidential from the legislative and judicial branches.

factions Groups of like-minded people who try to influence the government. American government is set up to avoid domination by any one of these groups.

fairness doctrine An FCC regulation requiring broadcast media to present several points of view to ensure balanced coverage. It was created in the late 1940s and eliminated in 1987.

fast-track authority An expedited system for passing treaties under which support from a simple majority, rather than a two-thirds majority, is needed in both the House and Senate, and no amendments are allowed.

federal civil service A system created by the 1883 Pendleton Civil Service Act in which bureaucrats are hired on the basis of merit rather than political connections.

Federal Communications Commission (FCC) A government agency created in 1934 to regulate American radio stations and later expanded to regulate television, wireless communications technologies, and other broadcast media.

Federal Election Commission The government agency that enforces and regulates election laws; made up of six presidential appointees, of whom no more than three can be members of the same party.

federal funds rate (FFR) The interest rate that a bank must pay on an overnight loan from another bank.

federal preemptions Impositions of national priorities on the states through national legislation that is based on the Constitution's supremacy clause.

Federal Reserve Board The group of seven presidential appointees who govern the Federal Reserve System.

Federal Reserve System An independent agency that serves as the central bank of the United States to bring stability to the nation's banking system.

federalism The division of power across the local, state, and national levels of government.

Federalists Those at the Constitutional Convention who favored a strong national government and a system of separated powers.

fighting words Forms of expression that "by their very utterance" can incite violence. These can be regulated by the government but are often difficult to define.

filibuster A tactic used by senators to block a bill by continuing to hold the floor and speak—under the Senate rule of unlimited debate—until the bill's supporters back down.

filtering The influence on public opinion that results from journalists' and editors' decisions about which of many potential news stories to report.

fire alarm oversight A method of oversight in which members of Congress respond to complaints about the bureaucracy or problems of implementation only as they arise rather than exercising constant vigilance.

fiscal federalism A form of federalism in which federal funds are allocated to the lower levels of government through transfer payments or grants.

fiscal policy Government decisions about how to influence the economy by taxing and spending.

foreign policy Government actions that affect countries, corporations, groups, or individuals outside America's borders.

framing The influence on public opinion caused by the way a story is presented or covered, including the details, explanations, and context offered in the report.

free exercise clause Part of the First Amendment that states that Congress cannot prohibit or interfere with the practice of religion.

free market An economic system based on competition among businesses without government interference.

free rider problem The incentive to benefit from others' work without making a contribution, which leads individuals in a collective action situation to refuse to work together.

free riding The result of relying on others to contribute to a collective effort while failing to participate on one's own behalf, yet still benefiting from the group's successes.

full employment The theoretical point at which all citizens who want to be employed have a job.

full faith and credit clause Part of Article IV of the Constitution requiring that each state's laws be honored by the other states. For example, a legal marriage in one state must be recognized across state lines.

general election The election in which voters cast ballots for House members, senators, and (every four years) a president and vice president.

general revenue sharing (GRS) A type of grant used in the 1970s and 1980s in which the federal government provided state governments with funds to be spent at each state's discretion. These grants gave states more control over programs.

gerrymandering Attempting to use the process of redrawing district boundaries to benefit a political party, protect incumbents, or change the proportion of minority voters in a district.

globalization The increase over the last generation in trade, travel, and the flow of ideas and beliefs between nations.

go public A president's use of speeches and other public communications to appeal directly to citizens about issues the president would like the House and Senate to act on.

GOTV ("get out the vote") or the **ground game** A campaign's efforts to "get out the vote" or make sure their supporters vote on Election Day.

government The system for implementing decisions made through the political process.

grandfather clause A type of law enacted in several southern states to allow those who were permitted to vote before the Civil War, and their descendants, to bypass literacy tests and other obstacles to voting, thereby exempting whites from these tests while continuing to disenfranchise African Americans and other people of color.

grassroots lobbying A lobbying strategy that relies on participation by group members, such as a protest or a letter-writing campaign.

Great Compromise A compromise between the large and small states, proposed by Connecticut, in which Congress would have two houses: a Senate with two legislators per state and a House of Representatives in which each state's representation would be based on population (also known as the Connecticut Compromise).

Great Society The wide-ranging social agenda promoted by President Lyndon Johnson in the mid-1960s that aimed to improve Americans' quality of life through governmental social programs.

gridlock An inability to enact legislation because of partisan conflict within Congress or between Congress and the president.

gross domestic product (GDP) The value of a country's economic output taken as a whole.

hard money Donations that are used to help elect or defeat a specific candidate.

hard news Media coverage focused on facts and important issues surrounding a campaign.

hate speech Expression that is offensive or abusive, particularly in terms of race, gender, or sexual orientation. It is currently protected under the First Amendment.

head of government One role of the president, through which he or she has authority over the executive branch.

head of state One role of the president, through which he or she represents the country symbolically and politically.

hold An objection to considering a measure on the Senate floor.

horse race A description of the type of election coverage that focuses more on poll results and speculation about a likely winner than on substantive differences between the candidates.

idealism The idea that a country's foreign policy decisions are based on factors beyond self-interest, including upholding important principles or values.

ideological polarization The effect on public opinion when many citizens move away from moderate positions and toward either end of the political spectrum, identifying themselves as either liberals or conservatives.

ideology A cohesive set of ideas and beliefs used to organize and evaluate the political world.

impeachment A negative or checking power over the other branches that allows Congress to remove the president, vice president, or other "officers of the United States" (including federal judges) for abuses of power.

implied powers Powers supported by the Constitution that are not expressly stated in it.

income support Government programs that provide support to low-income Americans, such as welfare, food stamps, unemployment compensation, and the Earned Income Tax Credit.

incumbency advantage The relative infrequency with which members of Congress are defeated in their attempts for reelection.

incumbent A politician running for reelection to the office he or she currently holds.

independent agencies Government offices or organizations that provide government services and are not part of an executive department.

inflation The increase in the price of consumer goods over time.

informational theory The idea that having committees in Congress made up of experts on specific policy areas helps to ensure well-informed policy decisions.

initiative A direct vote by citizens on a policy change proposed by fellow citizens or organized groups outside government. Getting a question on the ballot typically requires collecting a set number of signatures from registered voters in support of the proposal. There is no mechanism for a national-level initiative.

inside strategies The tactics employed within Washington, D.C., by interest groups seeking to achieve their policy goals.

interest group An organization of people who share common political interests and aim to influence public policy by electioneering and lobbying.

interest group state A government in which most policy decisions are determined by the influence of interest groups.

intergovernmental organizations Organizations that seek to coordinate policy across member nations.

intermediate scrutiny The middle level of scrutiny the courts can use when determining whether a law is constitutional. To meet this standard, the law or policy must be "content neutral," must further an important governmental interest in a way that is "substantially related" to that

interest, and must use means that are a close fit to the government's goal and not substantially broader than is necessary to accomplish that goal.

International Monetary Fund (IMF) A nongovernmental organization established in 1944 to help stabilize the international monetary system, improve economic growth, and aid developing nations.

internationalism The idea that a country should be involved in the affairs of other nations, out of both self-interest and moral obligation.

investigative journalists Reporters who dig deeply into a particular topic of public concern, often targeting government failures and inefficiencies.

isolationism The idea that a country should refrain from involvement in international affairs.

issue voters People who are well informed about their own policy preferences and knowledgeable about the candidates, and who use all of this information when they decide how to vote.

Jim Crow laws State and local laws that mandated racial segregation in all public facilities in the South, many border states, and some northern communities between 1876 and 1964.

joint committees Committees that contain members of both the House and Senate but have limited authority.

judicial activism The idea that the Supreme Court should assert its interpretation of the law even if it overrules the elected executive and legislative branches of government.

judicial restraint The idea that the Supreme Court should defer to the democratically elected executive and legislative branches of government rather than contradicting existing laws.

judicial review The Supreme Court's power to strike down a law or executive branch action that it finds unconstitutional.

Judiciary Act of 1789 The law in which Congress laid out the organization of the federal judiciary. The law refined and clarified federal court jurisdiction and set the original number of justices at six. It also created the Office of the Attorney General and established the lower federal courts.

jurisdiction The sphere of a court's legal authority to hear and decide cases.

Keynesian economics The theory that governments should use economic policy, like taxing and spending, to maintain stability in the economy.

latent opinion An opinion formed on the spot, when it is needed (as distinct from a deeply held opinion that is stable over time).

***Lemon* test** The Supreme Court uses this test, established in *Lemon v. Kurtzman*, to determine whether a practice violates the First Amendment's establishment clause.

libel Written false statements that damage a person's reputation. They can be regulated by the government but are often difficult to distinguish from permissible speech.

liberal One side of the ideological spectrum defined by support for stronger government programs and more market regulation; generally associated with Democrats.

liberal or conservative ideology A way of describing political beliefs in terms of a position on the spectrum running from liberal to moderate to conservative.

libertarians Those who prefer very limited government and therefore tend to be conservative on issues such as welfare policy, environmental policy, and public support for education, but liberal on issues of personal liberty such as free speech, abortion, and the legalization of drugs.

liberty Political freedom, such as the freedom of speech, press, assembly, and religion. These and other legal and due process rights protecting individuals from government control are outlined in the Bill of Rights of the U.S. Constitution.

limited government A political system in which the powers of the government are restricted to prevent tyranny by protecting property and individual rights.

living Constitution A way of interpreting the Constitution that takes into account evolving national attitudes and circumstances rather than the text alone.

lobbying Efforts to influence public policy through contact with public officials on behalf of an interest group.

logrolling A form of reciprocity in which members of Congress support bills that they otherwise might not vote for in exchange for other members' votes on bills that are very important to them.

majority leader The elected head of the party holding the majority of seats in the House or Senate.

majority voting A voting system in which a candidate must win more than 50 percent of votes to win the election. If no candidate wins enough votes to take office, a runoff election is held between the top two vote-getters.

mandatory spending Expenditures that are required by law, such as the funding for Social Security.

marginal tax rate The tax rate paid on income up to some threshold. For example, in 2014 single people paid no income tax on their first $10,150 in income (because of the $6,900 standard deduction and $3,950 personal exemption); after deductions, you would pay 10 percent on the first $9,075, 15 percent on income between $9,075 and $36,900, all the way up to 39.6 percent on income over $406,750.

markup One of the steps in which a bill becomes a law, in which the final wording of the bill is determined.

mass associations Interest groups that have a large number of dues-paying individuals as members.

mass media Sources that provide information to the average citizen, such as newspapers, television networks, radio stations, podcasts, and websites.

mass survey A way to measure public opinion by interviewing a large sample of the population.

media conglomerates Companies that control a large number of media sources across several types of media outlets.

media effects The influence of media coverage on average citizens' opinions and actions.

Medicaid An entitlement program funded by the federal and state governments that provides health care coverage for low-income Americans who would otherwise be unable to afford health care.

Medicare The federal health care plan created in 1965 that provides coverage for retired Americans for hospital care (Part A), medical care (Part B), and prescription drugs (Part D).

Miller test Established in *Miller v. California*, the Supreme Court uses this three-part test to determine whether speech meets the criteria for obscenity. If so, it can be restricted by the government.

minority leader The elected head of the party holding the minority of seats in the House or Senate.

Miranda rights The list of civil liberties described in the Fifth Amendment that must be read to a suspect before anything the suspect says can be used in a trial.

modified rules Conditions placed on a legislative debate by the House Rules Committee allowing certain amendments to a bill while barring others.

monarchy A form of government in which power is held by a single person, or monarch, who comes to power through inheritance rather than election.

monetarist theory The idea that the amount of money in circulation (the money supply) is the primary influence on economic activity and inflation.

monetary policy Government decisions about how to influence the economy using control of the money supply and interest rates.

Monroe Doctrine The American policy initiated under President James Monroe in 1823 stating that the United States would remain neutral in conflicts between European nations, and that these nations should stop colonizing or occupying areas of North and South America.

mootness The irrelevance of a case by the time it is received by a federal court, causing the Court to decline to hear the case.

most-favored-nation status A standing awarded to countries with which the United States has good trade relations, providing the lowest possible tariff rate. World Trade Organization members must give one another this preferred status.

multilateral action Foreign policy carried out by a nation in coordination with other nations or international organizations.

mutually assured destruction The idea that two nations that possess large stores of nuclear weapons—like the United States and the Soviet Union during the Cold War—would both be annihilated in any nuclear exchange, thus making it unlikely that either country would launch a first attack.

nation building The use of a country's resources, including the military, to help create democratic institutions abroad and prevent violence in other countries.

national committee An American political party's principal organization, comprising party representatives from each state.

National Economic Council (NEC) A group of economic advisers created in 1993 to work with the president to coordinate economic policy.

National Security Council (NSC) Within the Executive Office of the President, an agency that advises the president on matters of foreign policy.

national supremacy clause Part of Article VI, Section 2, of the Constitution stating that the Constitution and the laws and treaties of the United States are the "supreme Law of the Land," meaning national laws take precedence over state laws if the two conflict.

natural rights Also known as "unalienable rights," the Declaration of Independence defines them as "Life, Liberty, and the pursuit of Happiness." The Founders believed that upholding these rights should be the government's central purpose.

necessary and proper clause Part of Article I, Section 8, of the Constitution that grants Congress the power to pass all

laws related to one of its expressed powers; also known as the elastic clause.

New Deal The set of policies proposed by President Franklin Roosevelt and enacted by Congress between 1933 and 1935 to promote economic recovery and social welfare during the Great Depression.

New Jersey Plan A plan that was in response to the Virginia Plan, in which smaller states at the Constitutional Convention proposed that each state should receive equal representation in the national legislature, regardless of size.

news cycle The time between the release of information and its publication, such as the 24 hours between issues of a daily newspaper.

nominating convention A meeting held by each party every four years at which states' delegates select the party's presidential and vice-presidential nominees and approve the party platform.

nongovernmental organizations (NGOs) Groups operated by private institutions (rather than governments) to promote growth, economic development, and other agendas throughout the world.

notice-and-comment procedure A step in the rule-making process in which proposed rules are published in the *Federal Register* and made available for debate by the general public.

Office of Management and Budget An office within the Executive Office of the President that is responsible for creating the president's annual budget proposal to Congress, reviewing proposed rules, and other budget-related tasks.

omnibus legislation Large bills that often cover several topics and may contain extraneous, or pork-barrel, projects.

on background or **off the record** Comments a politician makes to the press on the condition that they can be reported only if they are not attributed to that politician.

open market operations The process by which the Federal Reserve System buys and sells securities to influence the money supply.

open primary A primary election in which any registered voter can participate in the contest, regardless of party affiliation.

open rules Conditions placed on a legislative debate by the House Rules Committee allowing relevant amendments to a bill.

open seat An elected position for which there is no incumbent.

oral arguments Spoken presentations made in person by the lawyers of each party to a judge or an appellate court outlining the legal reasons their side should prevail.

original intent The theory that justices should surmise the intentions of the Founders when the language of the Constitution is unclear.

original jurisdiction The authority of a court to handle a case first, as in the Supreme Court's authority to initially hear disputes between two states. However, original jurisdiction for the Supreme Court is not exclusive; it may assign such a case to a lower court.

outside strategies The tactics employed outside Washington, D.C., by interest groups seeking to achieve their policy goals.

oversight Congressional efforts to make sure that laws are implemented correctly by the bureaucracy after they have been passed.

ownership society The term used to describe the social policy vision of President George W. Bush, in which citizens take responsibility for their own social welfare and the free market plays a greater role in social policy.

paradox of voting The question of why citizens vote even though their individual votes stand little chance of changing the election outcome.

parliamentary system A system of government in which legislative and executive power are closely joined. The legislature (parliament) selects the chief executive (prime minister) who forms the cabinet from members of the parliament.

party coalitions The groups that identify with a political party, usually described in demographic terms such as African-American Democrats or evangelical Republicans.

party identification (party ID) A citizen's loyalty to a specific political party.

party in government The group of office-holders who belong to a specific political party and were elected as candidates of that party.

party in the electorate The group of citizens who identify with a specific political party.

party organization A specific political party's leaders and workers at the national, state, and local levels.

party platform A set of objectives outlining the party's issue positions and priorities. Candidates are not required to support their party's platform.

party principle The idea that a political party exists as an organization distinct from its elected officials or party leaders.

party system Periods in which the names of the major political parties, their supporters, and the issues dividing them have remained relatively stable.

party unity The extent to which members of Congress in the same party vote together on party votes.

party vote A vote in which the majority of one party opposes the position of the majority of the other party.

peak associations Interest groups whose members are businesses or other organizations rather than individuals.

picket fence federalism A more refined and realistic form of cooperative federalism in which policy makers within a particular policy area work together across the levels of government.

plaintiff The person or party who brings a case to court.

plea bargaining Negotiating an agreement between a plaintiff and a defendant to settle a case before it goes to trial or the verdict is decided. In a civil case, this usually involves an admission of guilt and an agreement on monetary damages; in a criminal case, this often involves an admission of guilt in return for a reduced charge or sentence.

pluralism The idea that having a variety of parties and interests within a government will strengthen the system, ensuring that no group possesses total control.

plurality voting A voting system in which the candidate who receives the most votes within a geographic area wins the election, regardless of whether that candidate wins a majority (more than half) of the votes.

pocket veto The automatic death of a bill passed by the House and Senate when the president fails to sign the bill in the last 10 days of a legislative session.

police patrol oversight A method of oversight in which members of Congress constantly monitor the bureaucracy to make sure that laws are implemented correctly.

police powers The power to enforce laws and provide for public safety.

policy agenda The set of desired policies that political leaders view as their top priorities.

policy mood The level of public support for expanding the government's role in society; whether the public wants government action on a specific issue.

political action committee (PAC) An interest group or a division of an interest group that can raise money to contribute to campaigns or to spend on ads in support of candidates. The amount a PAC can receive from each of its donors and the amount it can spend on federal electioneering are strictly limited.

political appointees People selected by an elected leader, such as the president, to hold a government position.

political machine An unofficial patronage system within a political party that seeks to gain political power and government contracts, jobs, and other benefits for party leaders, workers, and supporters.

political socialization The process by which an individual's political opinions are shaped by other people and the surrounding culture.

politico A member of Congress who acts as a delegate on issues that constituents care about (such as immigration reform) and as a trustee on more-complex or less-salient issues (such as some foreign policy or regulatory matters).

politics The process that determines what government does.

popular vote The votes cast by citizens in an election.

population The group of people that a researcher or pollster wants to study, such as evangelicals, senior citizens, or Americans.

pork barrel Legislative appropriations that benefit specific constituents, created with the aim of helping local representatives win reelection.

power of the purse The constitutional power of Congress to raise and spend money. Congress can use this as a negative or checking power over the other branches by freezing or cutting their funding.

precedent A legal norm established in court cases that is then applied to future cases dealing with the same legal questions.

president pro tempore A largely symbolic position usually held by the most senior member of the majority party in the Senate.

presidential approval rating The percentage of Americans who think that the president is doing a good job in office.

primary election A ballot vote in which citizens select a party's nominee for the general election.

priming The influence on the public's general impressions caused by positive or negative coverage of a candidate or issue.

principal–agent game The interaction between a principal (such as the president or Congress), who needs something done, and an agent (such as a bureaucrat), who is reponsible for carrying out the principal's orders.

prior restraint A limit on freedom of the press that allows the government to prohibit the media from publishing certain materials.

privacy rights Liberties protected by several amendments in the Bill of Rights that shield certain personal aspects of citizens' lives from governmental interference, such as the Fourth Amendment's protection against unreasonable searches and seizures.

privatization The process of transferring the management of a government program (like Social Security) from the public sector to the private sector.

privileges and immunities clause Part of Article IV of the Constitution requiring that states must treat nonstate residents within their borders as they would treat their own residents. This was meant to promote commerce and travel between states.

problem of control A difficulty faced by elected officials in ensuring that when bureaucrats implement policies, they follow these officials' intentions but still have enough discretion to use their expertise.

progressive Taxes that require upper-income people to pay a higher tax rate than lower-income people, such as income taxes.

proportional allocation During the presidential primaries, the practice of determining the number of convention delegates allotted to each candidate based on the percentage of the popular vote cast for each candidate. All Democratic primaries and caucuses use this system, as do some states' Republican primaries and caucuses.

protectionism The idea under which some people have tried to rationalize discriminatory policies by claiming that some groups, like women or African Americans, should be denied certain rights for their own safety or well-being.

public goods Services or actions (such as protecting the environment) that, once provided to one person, become available to everyone. Government is typically needed to provide public goods because they will be underprovided by the free market.

public opinion Citizens' views on politics and government actions.

purposive benefits Satisfaction derived from the experience of working toward a desired policy goal, even if the goal is not achieved.

random sample A subsection of a population chosen to participate in a survey through a selection process in which every member of the population has an equal chance of being chosen. This kind of sampling improves the accuracy of public opinion data.

rational basis test The use of evidence to suggest that differences in the behavior of two groups can rationalize unequal treatment of these groups.

realignment A change in the size or composition of the party coalitions or in the nature of the issues that divide the parties.

Realignments typically occur within an election cycle or two, but they can also occur gradually over the course of a decade or longer.

realism The idea that a country's foreign policy decisions are motivated by self-interest and the goal of gaining more power.

recess appointment Selection by the president of a person to be an ambassador or the head of a department while the Senate is not in session, thereby bypassing Senate approval. Unless approved by a subsequent Senate vote, recess appointees serve only to the end of the congressional term.

red tape Excessive or unnecessarily complex regulations imposed by the bureaucracy.

redistributive tax policies Policies, generally favored by Democratic politicians, that use taxation to attempt to create greater social equality (for example, higher taxation of the rich to provide programs for the poor).

redistricting Redrawing the geographic boundaries of legislative districts. This happens every 10 years to ensure that districts remain roughly equal in population.

referendum A direct vote by citizens on a policy change proposed by a legislature or another government body. Referenda are common in state and local elections, but there is no mechanism for a national-level referendum.

regressive Taxes that take a larger share of poor people's income than wealthy people's income, such as sales taxes and payroll taxes.

regulation A rule that allows the government to exercise control over individuals and corporations by restricting certain behaviors.

regulatory capture A situation in which bureaucrats favor the interests of the groups or corporations they are supposed to regulate at the expense of the general public.

remedial legislation National laws that address discriminatory state laws. Authority for such legislation comes from Section 5 of the Fourteenth Amendment.

republicanism As understood by James Madison and the framers, the belief that a form of government in which the interests of the people are represented through elected leaders is the best form of government. Our form of government is known as a republican democracy.

reserve requirement The minimum amount of money that a bank is required to have on hand to back up its assets.

reserved powers As defined in the Tenth Amendment, powers that are not given to the national government by the Constitution, or not prohibited to the states, are reserved by the states or the people.

revolving door The movement of individuals from government positions to jobs with interest groups or lobbying firms, and vice versa.

roll call vote A recorded vote on legislation; members may vote yes, no, abstain, or present.

runoff election Under a majority voting system, a second election held only if no candidate wins a majority of the votes in the first general election. Only the top two vote-getters in the first election compete in the runoff.

salience The level of familiarity with an interest group's goals among the general population.

sample Within a population, the group of people surveyed in order to gauge the whole population's opinion. Researchers use samples because it would be impossible to interview the entire population.

sampling error A calculation that describes what percentage of the people surveyed may not accurately represent the population being studied. Increasing the number of respondents lowers the sampling error.

select committees Committees in the House or Senate created to address a specific issue for one or two terms.

selective incentives Benefits that can motivate participation in a group effort because they are available only to those who participate, such as member services offered by interest groups.

selective incorporation The process through which the civil liberties granted in the Bill of Rights were applied to the states on a case-by-case basis through the Fourteenth Amendment.

senatorial courtesy A norm in the nomination of district court judges in which the president consults with his party's senators from the relevant state in choosing the nominee.

seniority The informal congressional norm of choosing the member who has served the longest on a particular committee to be the committee chair.

separate but equal doctrine The idea that racial segregation was acceptable as long as the separate facilities were of equal quality; supported by *Plessy v. Ferguson* and struck down by *Brown v. Board of Education*.

separation of powers The division of government power across the judicial, executive, and legislative branches.

signing statement A document issued by the president when signing a bill into law explaining his interpretation of the law, which often differs from the interpretation of Congress, in an attempt to influence how the law will be implemented.

single-member districts An electoral system in which every elected official represents a geographically defined area, such as a state or congressional district, and each area elects one representative.

slander Spoken false statements that damage a person's reputation. They can be regulated by the government but are often difficult to distinguish from permissible speech.

slant The imbalance in a story that covers one candidate or policy favorably without providing similar coverage of the other side.

social policy An area of public policy relating to maintaining or enhancing the well-being of individuals.

Social Security A federal social insurance program that provides cash benefits to retirees based on payroll taxes they have paid over the course of their careers. It is a "pay as you go" program in which working Americans pay taxes to support today's retirees, with a promise that when today's workers retire, their benefits will be paid by the next generation.

soft money Contributions that can be used for voter mobilization or to promote a policy proposal or point of view as long as these efforts are not tied to supporting or opposing a particular candidate.

soft news Media coverage that aims to entertain or shock, often through sensationalized reporting or by focusing on a candidate or politician's personality.

solicitor general A presidential appointee in the Justice Department who conducts all litigation on behalf of the federal government before the Supreme Court and supervises litigation in the federal appellate courts.

solidary benefits Satisfaction derived from the experience of working with like-minded people, even if the group's efforts do not achieve the desired impact.

sovereign power The supreme power of an independent state to regulate its internal affairs without foreign interference.

Speaker of the House The elected leader of the House of Representatives.

split ticket A ballot on which a voter selects candidates from more than one political party.

spoils system The practice of rewarding party supporters with benefits like federal government positions.

standard operating procedures Rules that lower-level bureaucrats must follow when implementing policies.

standing Legitimate justification for bringing a civil case to court.

standing committee Committees that are a permanent part of the House or Senate structure, holding more importance and authority than other committees.

state capacity The knowledge, personnel, and institutions that the government requires to effectively implement policies.

State of the Union An annual speech in which the president addresses Congress to report on the condition of the country and to recommend policies.

states' rights The idea that states are entitled to a certain amount of self-government, free of federal government intervention. This became a central issue in the period leading up to the Civil War.

states' sovereign immunity Based on the Eleventh Amendment, immunity that prevents state governments from being sued by private parties in federal court unless the state consents to the suit.

statutory authority (presidential) Powers derived from laws enacted by Congress that add to the powers given to the president in the Constitution.

statutory interpretation The various methods and tests used by the courts for determining the meaning of a law and applying it to specific situations. Congress may overturn the courts' interpretation by writing a new law; thus, it also engages in statutory interpretation.

straight ticket A ballot on which a voter selects candidates from only one political party.

street-level bureaucrats Agency employees who directly provide services to the public, such as those who provide job-training services.

strict construction A way of interpreting the Constitution based on its language alone.

strict scrutiny The highest level of scrutiny the courts can use when determining whether a law is constitutional. To meet this standard, the law or policy must be shown to serve a "compelling state interest" or goal, it must be narrowly tailored to achieve that goal, and it must be the least restrictive means of achieving that goal.

substantive due process doctrine One interpretation of the due process clause of the Fourteenth Amendment; in this view the Supreme Court has the power to overturn laws that infringe on individual liberties.

substantive representation When a member of Congress represents constituents' interests and policy concerns.

supply-side economics The theory that lower tax rates will stimulate the economy by encouraging people to save, invest, and produce more goods and services.

symbolic speech Nonverbal expression, such as the use of signs or symbols. It benefits from many of the same constitutional protections as verbal speech.

tariff A tax levied on imported and exported goods.

Temporary Assistance for Needy Families (TANF) The welfare program that replaced Aid to Families with Dependent Children (AFDC) in 1996, eliminating the entitlement status of welfare, shifting implementation of the policy to the states, and introducing several new restrictions on receiving aid. These changes led to a significant decrease in the number of welfare recipients.

Three-Fifths Compromise The states' decision during the Constitutional Convention to count each slave as three-fifths of a person in a state's population for the purposes of determining the number of House members and the distribution of taxes.

trade association An interest group composed of companies in the same business or industry (the same "trade") that lobbies for policies that benefit members of the group.

trade deficit A measure of how much more a nation imports than it exports.

Treasury Department A cabinet-level agency that is responsible for managing the federal government's revenue. It prints currency, collects taxes, and sells government bonds.

trustee A member of Congress who represents constituents' interests while also taking into account national, collective, and moral concerns that sometimes cause the member to vote against the preference of a majority of constituents.

turkey farms Agencies to which campaign workers and donors can be appointed in reward for their service because it is unlikely that their lack of qualifications will lead to bad policy.

unfunded mandates Federal laws that require the states to do certain things but do not provide state governments with funding to implement these policies.

unified government A situation in which one party holds a majority of seats in the House and Senate and the president is a member of that same party.

unilateral action (national) Independent acts of foreign policy undertaken by a nation without the assistance or coordination of other nations.

unilateral action (presidential) Any policy decision made and acted upon by the president and presidential staff without the explicit approval or consent of Congress.

unitary executive theory The idea that the vesting clause of the Constitution gives the president the authority to issue orders and policy directives that cannot be undone by Congress.

unitary government A system in which the national, centralized government holds ultimate authority. It is the most common form of government in the world.

United Nations (UN) An international organization made up of representatives from nearly every nation, with a mission to promote peace and cooperation, uphold international law, and provide humanitarian aid.

United States Trade Representative (USTR) An agency founded in 1962 to negotiate with foreign governments to create trade agreements, resolve disputes, and participate in global trade policy organizations. Treaties negotiated by the USTR must be ratified by the Senate.

vesting clause Article II, Section 1, of the Constitution, which states "The executive Power shall be vested in a President of the United States of America," making the president both the head of government and the head of state.

veto The president's rejection of a bill that has been passed by Congress. A veto can be overridden by a two-thirds vote in both the House and Senate.

Virginia Plan A plan proposed by the larger states during the Constitutional Convention that based representation in the national legislature on population. The plan also included a variety of other proposals to strengthen the national government.

voting cues Pieces of information about a candidate that are readily available, easy to interpret, and lead a citizen to decide to vote for a particular candidate.

weapons of mass destruction (WMDs) Weapons that have the potential to cause large-scale loss of life, such as nuclear bombs and chemical or biological weapons.

welfare Financial or other assistance provided to individuals by the government, usually based on need.

whip system An organization of House leaders who work to disseminate information and promote party unity in voting on legislation.

winner-take-all During the presidential primaries, the practice of assigning all of a given state's delegates to the candidate who receives the most popular votes. Some states' Republican primaries and caucuses use this system.

wire service An organization that gathers news and sells it to other media outlets. The invention of the telegraph in the early 1800s made this type of service possible.

World Bank A nongovernmental organization established in 1944 that provides financial support for economic development projects in developing nations.

World Trade Organization (WTO) An international organization created in 1995 to oversee trade agreements between nations by facilitating negotiations and handling disputes.

writ of certiorari The most common way for a case to reach the Supreme Court, in which at least four of the nine justices agree to hear a case that has reached them via an appeal from the losing party in a lower court's ruling.

yellow journalism A style of newspaper popular in the late 1800s that featured sensationalized stories, bold headlines, and illustrations to increase readership.

CHAPTER 1

1. Thomas Hobbes, *Leviathan* (1651; repr. Indianapolis, IN: Bobbs, Merrill, 1958).
2. Alexander Hamilton, James Madison, and John Jay, *The Federalist Papers*, ed. Roy P. Fairfield, 2nd ed. (1788; repr. Baltimore, MD: Johns Hopkins University Press, 1981), p. 160.
3. Hamilton, Madison, and Jay, *The Federalist Papers*, p. 18.
4. Examples include E. E. Schattschneider, *The Semisovereign People: A Realist's View of Democracy in America* (New York: Holt, Rinehart, and Winston, 1960); Larry Bartels, *Unequal Democracy: The Politics of the New Gilded Age* (Princeton, NJ: Princeton University Press, 2008); and Jeffrey A. Segal and Howard Spaeth, *The Supreme Court and the Attitudinal Model Revisited* (New York: Cambridge University Press, 2002).
5. Morris Rosenberg, "Some Determinants of Political Apathy," *Public Opinion Quarterly* 18 (Winter 1954–55): 349–66; Jane Mansbridge, *Beyond Adversary Democracy* (New York: Basic Books, 1980); Nina Eliasoph, *Avoiding Politics: How Americans Produce Apathy in Everyday Life* (New York: Cambridge University Press, 1998); Melanie C. Green, Penny S. Visser, and Philip E. Tetlock, "Coping with Accountability Cross-Pressures: Low-Effort Evasive Tactics and High-Effort Quests for Complex Compromises," *Personality and Social Psychology Bulletin* 26:11 (2000): 1380–91.
6. John R. Hibbing and Elizabeth Theiss-Morse, *Stealth Democracy: Americans' Beliefs about How Government Should Work* (New York: Cambridge University Press, 2002), p. 147. See Diana E. Hess, *Controversy in the Classroom: The Democratic Power of Discussion* (New York: Routledge, 2009), for evidence that diverse viewpoints in the classroom have important effects on discussion.
7. Donald Green, Bradley Palmquist, and Eric Schickler, *Partisan Hearts and Minds* (New Haven, CT: Yale University Press, 2004); Christopher Achen, "Political Socialization and Rational Party Identification," *Political Behavior* 24:2 (2002): 151–70.
8. Robert S. Erikson, Michael B. MacKuen, and James A. Stimson, *The Macro Polity* (New York: Cambridge University Press, 2002).
9. Larry Bartels, "More on Partisan Politics and Economic Perceptions (and Economic Voting)." *The Monkey Cage*, July 26, 2012. http://themonkeycage.org/2012/07/26/more-on-partisan-politics-and-economic-perceptions-and-economic-voting/ (accessed 4/11/14).
10. Congressional Budget Office, "Current Budget Projections," www.cbo.gov/ftpdocs/ 108xx/doc10871/budgetprojections.pdf; The President's Budget for Fiscal Year 2011, "Total Executive Branch Civilian Full-Time Equivalent (FTE) Employees, 1981–2011," Table 17.1, www.whitehouse.gov/omb/budget/Historicals/; Department of Defense, "Military Personnel Active and Reserve Forces," www.whitehouse.gov/omb/budget/fy2011/assets/mil.pdf; Paul Light, "Fact Sheet on the New True Size of Government," Brookings Institution, September 5, 2003, www.brookings.edu/articles/2003/0905politics_light.aspx; *Federal Register*, www.gpoaccess.gov/fr/. (All accessed 7/15/12.)
11. Organization for Economic Co-operation and Development, Divided We Stand: Why Inequality Keeps Rising, OECD 2011, "An Overview of Growing Income Inequalities in OECD Countries: Main Findings." www.oecd.org/els/soc/49499779.pdf (accessed 4/11/14).
12. For details, see Paul R. Abramson, John H. Aldrich, and David W. Rohde, *Change and Continuity in the 2008 and 2010 Elections* (Washington, D.C.: Congressional Quarterly Press, 2011).
13. Charles Taylor, *Multiculturalism: Examining the Politics of Recognition*, ed. Amy Gutmann, with commentary by K. Anthony Appiah, Jürgen Habermas, Steven C. Rockefeller, Michael Walzer, and Susan Wolf (Princeton, NJ: Princeton University Press, 1994); Will Kymlicka, *Multicultural Citizenship: A Liberal Theory of Minority Rights* (New York: Oxford University Press, 1995).
14. Morris P. Fiorina, with Samuel J. Abrams and Jeremy C. Pope, *Culture War: The Myth of a Polarized America*, 2nd ed. (New York: Pearson Longman, 2006), pp. 46–47.

15. Frank M. Bryan, *Real Democracy: The New England Town Meeting and How It Works* (Chicago: University of Chicago Press, 2004).

16. Louis Hartz, *The Liberal Tradition in America: An Interpretation of American Political Thought since the Revolution* (New York: Harcourt, Brace, 1955).

CHAPTER 2

1. Jim DeMint, "Constitution of No," *National Review* Online, June 8, 2010, www.nationalreview.com/articles/229909/constitution-no/jim-demint?pg=2 (accessed 10/16/11).

2. Jennifer Steinhauer, "Constitution Has Its Day (More or Less) in House," *New York Times*, January 6, 2011, www.nytimes.com/2011/01/07/us/politics/07constitution.html (accessed 10/14/11).

3. Mark Trumbull, "On Constitution Day, Tea Party and Foes Duel over Our Founding Document," *Christian Science Monitor*, September 17, 2011, www.csmonitor.com/USA/Politics/2011/0917/On-Constitution-Day-tea-party-and-foes-duel-over-our-founding-document (accessed 10/16/11).

4. For a good overview of the political thought of the American Revolution, see Gordon S. Wood, *The Radicalism of the American Revolution* (New York: Vintage Books, 1993). For an excellent summary of the history, see Wood's *The American Revolution: A History* (New York: Modern Library, 2003).

5. David McCullough, *John Adams* (New York: Simon and Schuster, 2001), p. 90.

6. A classic text on the Founding period is Gordon S. Wood, *The Creation of the American Republic* (New York: W. W. Norton, 1969).

7. J. W. Peltason, *Corwin and Peltason's Understanding the Constitution*, 7th ed. (Hinsdale, IL: Dryden Press, 1976), p. 12.

8. The pamphlet sold 120,000 copies within a few months of publication, a figure that would leave the Harry Potter books in the dust in terms of the proportion of the literate public that purchased the book.

9. Thomas Hobbes, *Leviathan* (1651; repr. Indianapolis, IN: Bobbs, Merrill, 1958); John Locke, *Second Treatise of Government* (1690; repr. Indianapolis, IN: Bobbs, Merrill, 1952).

10. Robert A. Dahl, *How Democratic Is the American Constitution?* (New Haven, CT: Yale University Press, 2001), p. 12.

11. Alexander Hamilton, John Jay, and James Madison, *The Federalist Papers*, ed. Roy P. Fairfield, 2nd ed. (1788; repr. Baltimore, MD: Johns Hopkins University Press, 1981), p. 22.

12. Many delegates probably assumed that the electors would reflect the wishes of the voters in their states, but there is no clear indication of this in Madison's notes. (Hamilton makes this argument in *The Federalist Papers*.) Until the 1820s, many electors were directly chosen by state legislatures rather than by the people. In the first presidential election, George Washington won the unanimous support of the electors, but in only five states were the electors chosen by the people.

13. The actual language of the section avoids the term "slavery." Instead it says, "The Migration or Importation of such Persons as any of the States now existing shall think proper to admit, shall not be prohibited by Congress prior to the Year one thousand eight hundred and eight." The ban on the importation of slaves was implemented on the earliest possible date, January 1, 1808.

14. Patrick Henry, "Shall Liberty or Empire Be Sought?" in *America, 1761–1837*, vol. VIII of *The World's Famous Orations*, ed. William Jennings Bryan (New York: Funk and Wagnalls, 1906), pp. 73, 76.

15. Thomas Jefferson to John Adams, 1787, in *The Writings of Thomas Jefferson*, Memorial Edition, ed. Andrew A. Lipscomb and Albert Ellery Bergh (Washington, D.C.: Thomas Jefferson Memorial Association of the United States, 1903), vol. 6, p. 370.

16. Louis Fisher, *Constitutional Conflicts between Congress and the President* (Lawrence: University Press of Kansas, 1997), p. 244.

17. This ban prompted the White House to seek covert channels through which to support the Contras, which led to the ill-conceived secret arms deal with Iran (a nation that was under a complete U.S. trade embargo at the time) in which the money from the arms sales was funneled to the Contras.

18. Charlie Savage, "Obama's War on Terror May Resemble Bush's in Some Areas," *New York Times*, February 17, 2009, p. A1.

19. Peter M. Shane, *Madison's Nightmare: How Executive Power Threatens American Democracy* (Chicago: University of Chicago Press, 2009).

20. Deroy Murdock, "Ignorance and American Liberty," *National Review Online*, July 3, 2000, www.nationalreview.com (accessed 11/15/07).

21. Thomas Jefferson to James Madison, in *Thomas Jefferson on Democracy*, ed. Saul Padover (New York: Mentor Books, 1953), p. 153.

22. Cass R. Sunstein, "Making Amends," *New Republic*, March 3, 1997, p. 42.

23. *Furman v. Georgia*, 408 U.S. 238 (1972).

24. Walter F. Murphy, "The Nature of the American Constitution," The Edmund Janes James lecture, December 6, 1987 (Department of Political Science, University of Illinois at Urbana-Champaign, 1989), p. 8. http://babel.hathitrust.org/cgi/pt?id=mdp.39015078286518;view=1up;seq=12.

You Decide

a. Clarence Thomas, "How to Read the Constitution," *Wall Street Journal*. October 20, 2008.

b. *State of Missouri v. Holland*, 252 U.S. 416 (1920), 252.

c. William Rehnquist, "The Notion of a Living Constitution," *Harvard Journal of Law and Public Policy* 29 (2006): 402.

d. Rehnquist, "The Notion," p. 405.

e. Thurgood Marshall at the Annual Seminar of the San Francisco Patent and Trademark Law Association, Maui, Hawaii, May 6, 1987, www.thurgoodmarshall.com/speeches/constitutional_speech.htm (accessed 12/20/13).

CHAPTER 3

1. The full title of the law is the Patient Protection and Affordable Care Act (PPACA).

2. Ashby Jones, "Conservative Duo Tests Health Law," *Wall Street Journal,* September 13, 2010, http://online.wsj.com/article/SB10001424052748703897204575487963449135280.html#U301253590305VF (accessed 11/12/11).

3. Tenth Amendment Center, "Ohio Votes to Nullify Insurance Mandates," November 8, 2011, www.tenthamendmentcenter.com/2011/11/08/ohio-votes-to-nullify-insurance-mandates/ (accessed 11/12/11).

4. *State of Florida et al. v. U.S. Department of Health and Human Services et al.,* Petition for Writ of Certiorari to the United States Court of Appeals for the Eleventh Circuit, September 27, 2011, www.azgovernor.gov/dms/upload/PR_092811_Petition.pdf (accessed 10/19/12).

5. State Health Facts.org, Health Care and Coverage, www.statehealthfacts.org/comparecat.jsp?cat=3 (accessed 11/12/11).

6. *National Federation of Independent Business v. Sebelius,* 132 S. Ct. 2566 (2012).

7. Paul Waldman, "The Morning Plum: What the Obamacare Enrollment Numbers Mean," *Washington Post*, March 18, 2014, www.washingtonpost.com/blogs/plum-line/wp/2014/03/18/morning-plum-what-the-obamacare-enrollment-numbers-mean/ (accessed 3/21/14); The Advisory Board, "Where the states stand on Medicaid expansion: 27 states, D.C. expanding Medicaid," Daily Briefing, September 4, 2014, www.advisory.com/daily-briefing/resources/primers/medicaidmap (accessed 9/30/14).

8. Niraj Chokshi, "29 States Want the Supreme Court Weighing In on Another Obamacare Mandate," *Washington Post*, October 24, 2013, www.washingtonpost.com/blogs/govbeat/wp/2013/10/24/almost-30-states-want-the-supreme-court-weighing-in-on-another-obamacare-mandate/. The two cases are *Sebelius v. Hobby Lobby Stores* and *Conestoga Wood Specialties Corp. v. Sebelius.*

9. Robert Pear, "Missouri Citizens Face Obstacles to Coverage," *New York Times*. August 2, 2013, www.nytimes.com/2013/08/03/us/missouri-citizens-face-obstacles-to-coverage.html?_r=1& (accessed 10/22/14).

10. See www.cisstat.com/eng/cis.htm for more information on the Commonwealth of Independent States.

11. *United States v. Windsor*, 570 U.S. ___ (2013).

12. "Same Sex Marriage in the United States," CNN.com, www.cnn.com/interactive/us/map-same-sex-marriage/?iid=article_sidebar (accessed 11/20/14).

13. *Nancy Wilson and Paula Schoenwether v. Richard Lake and John Ashcroft* (2005) No. 8:04-cv-1680-T-30TBM.

14. "The Supreme Court: Excerpts from Court's Welfare Ruling and Rehnquist's Dissent," *New York Times,* May 18, 1999, p. A20.

15. The Sedition Act was passed within a month of three other laws—the Naturalization Act, the Alien Friends Act, and the Alien Enemies Act—which were all aimed at strengthening the hand of the national government in its naval war against France. Collectively, these four laws are often referred to as the Alien and Sedition Acts. But for our purposes here, the relevant law is the Sedition Act.

16. Stanley Elkins and Eric McKitrick, *The Age of Federalism* (New York: Oxford University Press, 1993).

17. John W. Wright, ed., *New York Times 2000 Almanac* (New York: Penguin Reference, 1999), p. 165. Estimates from various online sources are quite a bit higher, averaging about 620,000 deaths.

18. *Mayor of City of New York v. Miln*, 36 U.S. (11 Pet.) 102 (1837).

19. *Cooley v. Board of Wardens of the Port of Philadelphia*, 53 U.S. 229 (1851).

20. Slaughterhouse Cases, 83 U.S. 36 (1873). See Ronald M. Labbe and Jonathan Lurie, *The Slaughterhouse Cases: Regulation, Reconstruction, and the Fourteenth Amendment* (Lawrence: University Press of Kansas, 2003).

21. Civil Rights Cases, 109 U.S. 3 (1883).

22. *United States v. E. C. Knight Co.*, 156 U.S. 1 (1895).

23. *Hammer v. Dagenhart*, 247 U.S. 251 (1918).

24. *Lochner v. New York*, 198 U.S. 45 (1905).

25. *Schechter Poultry Corporation v. United States*, 295 U.S. 495 (1935).

26. Four key cases are *West Coast Hotel Company v. Parrish* (1937), *Wright v. Vinton Branch* (1937), *Virginia Railway Company v. System Federation* (1937), and *National Labor Relations Board v. Jones and Laughlin Steel Corporation* (1937).

27. Martin Grodzins, *The American System* (New York: Rand McNally, 1966).

28. John Shannon, "Middle Class Votes Bring a New Balance to Federalism," February 1, 1997, policy paper 10 from the Urban Institute series "The Future of the Public Sector," www.urban.org/url.cfm?ID=307051 (accessed 1/3/08).

29. Max Sawicky, "An Idea Whose Time Has Returned: Anti-Recession Fiscal Assistance for State and Local Governments," briefing paper (Washington, D.C.: Economic Policy Institute, October, 2001).

30. This number varies depending on which grants are counted. Tim Conlan finds 15 block grants in this period. See his *From New Federalism to Devolution* (Washington, D.C.: Brookings Institution, 1998).

31. *Brown v. Board of Education*, 347 U.S. 483 (1954); *Swann v. Charlotte-Mecklenburg Board of Education*, 402 U.S. 1 (1971).

32. *Baker v. Carr,* 369 U.S. 186 (1962); *Reynolds v. Sims*, 377 U.S. 533 (1964); and *Wesberry v. Sanders*, 376 U.S. 1 (1964). Martha Derthick, *Keeping the Compound Republic: Essays in American Federalism* (Washington, D.C.: Brookings Institution, 2001).

33. *Miranda v. Arizona*, 384 U.S. 436 (1966); *Mapp v. Ohio*, 367 U.S. 643 (1961).

34. *Shelby County v. Holder*, 570 U.S. ___ (2013).

35. "Impact of Unfunded Mandates and Cost Shifts on U.S. Cities," U.S Conference of Mayors, June 2005, www.usmayors.org (accessed 11/13/11).

36. John Kincaid, "Governing the American States," in *Developments in American Politics*, ed. Gillian Peele, Christopher J. Bailey, Bruce Cain, and Guy Peters (Chatham, NJ: Chatham House, 1995), pp. 208–16.

37. Paul Posner, "The Politics of Coercive Federalism in the Bush Era," *Publius* 37:3 (May 2007): 390–412.

38. Gallup Poll, "Trust in Government," September 5–8, 2013, www.gallup.com/poll/5392/trust-government.aspx (accessed 11/15/13).

39. Barry Rabe, "Environmental Policy and the Bush Era: The Collision between the Administrative Presidency and State Experimentation," *Publius* 37:3 (May 2007): 413–31.

40. Robert Gehrke, "Feds Block Utah Law over Police Power on Public Lands and State Rights," *Salt Lake Tribune*, May 13, 2013, www.sltrib.com/sltrib/politics/56303859-90/county-department-employees-federal.html.csp (accessed 11/15/13).

41. Lois Beckett, "Nullification: How States Are Making It a Felony to Enforce Federal Gun Laws," *ProPublica*, May 2, 2013, www.propublica.org/article/nullification-how-states-are-making-it-a-felony-to-enforce-federal-gun-laws (accessed 11/15/13).

42. Richard A. Oppel, Jr., "Texas and 5 Other States Resist Processing Benefits for Gay Couples," *New York Times*, November 10, 2013, www.nytimes.com/2013/11/11/us/texas-and-5-other-states-resist-processing-benefits-for-gay-couples.html (accessed 11/15/13).

43. Kirk Johnson, "States' Rights Is Rallying Cry for Lawmakers," *New York Times*, March 17, 2010, www.nytimes.com/2010/03/17/us/17states.html (accessed 3/21/14). The Supreme Court endorsed this reassertion of state power in an important case concerning immigration policy. In *Chamber of Commerce v. Whiting* 131 S. Ct. 1968 (2011), the Court held that federal immigration law did not preempt an Arizona law that required implementation of federal law in a manner that may have been more aggressive than Congress intended.

44. From a review of Michael S. Greve, *Real Federalism: Why It Matters, How It Could Happen* (Washington, D.C.: American Enterprise Institute Press, 1999), www.federalismproject.org/publications/books (accessed 10/10/07).

45. Cass Sunstein, *Designing Democracy: What Constitutions Do* (New York: Oxford University Press, 2001), p. 107.

46. J. W. Peltason, *Corwin and Peltason's Understanding the Constitution*, 7th ed. (Hinsdale, IL: Dryden Press, 1976), p. 177.

47. *Garcia v. San Antonio Metropolitan Transit Authority*, 469 U.S. 528 (1985).

48. *Gregory v. Ashcroft*, 501 U.S. 452 (1991).

49. *New York v. United States,* 505 U.S. 144 (1992). For a detailed discussion of these issues, see "Constitution of the United States: Analysis and Interpretation" (Washington, D.C.: Government Printing Office, 2006), www.gpo.gov/fdsys/pkg/GPO-CONAN-2006/pdf/GPO-CONAN-2006.pdf (accessed 10/19/12).

50. *Printz v. United States,* 521 U.S. 898 (1997).

51. *Bond v. United States,* 131 S. Ct. 2355 (2011).

52. *Bond v. United States,* 564 U.S. ___ (2014).

53. *City of Boerne v. Flores*, 521 U.S. 507 (1997), 520.

54. *Kimel et al. v. Florida Board of Regents*, 528 U.S. 62 (2000).

55. *Alabama v. Garrett*, 531 U.S. 356 (2001).

56. *Tennessee v. Lane*, 541 U.S. 509 (2004).

57. *Nevada Department of Human Resources v. Hibbs,* 538 U.S. 721 (2003).

58. *Shelby County v. Holder,* 570 U.S. ___ (2013).

59. *United States v. Lopez,* 514 U.S. 549 (1995).

60. *United States v. Morrison,* 529 U.S. 598 (2000). Nia-Malika Henderson, "Obama Signs a Strengthened Violence Against Women Act," *Washington Post,* March 7, 2013, www.washingtonpost.com/politics/obama-signs-a-strengthened-violence-against-women-act/2013/03/07/e50d585e-8740-11e2-98a3-b3db6b9ac586_story.html (accessed 3/21/14).

61. *U.S. Term Limits, Inc. v. Thornton,* 514 U.S. 779 (1995).

62. *Romer v. Evans,* 517 U.S. 620 (1996).

63. *Atkins v. Virginia,* 536 U.S. 304 (2002); *Roper v. Simmons,* 543 U.S. 551 (2005).

64. *Gonzales v. Raich,* 545 U.S. 1 (2005); *Gonzales v. Oregon,* 546 U.S. 243 (2006).

65. *National Federation of Independent Business v. Sebelius,* 132 S. Ct. 2566 (2012).

66. *National Federation of Independent Business v. Sebelius,* 132 S. Ct. 2566 (2012), p. 51.

67. Jonathan Turley, "It's Not the Cannabis, It's the Constitution," *Los Angeles Times,* August 5, 2002, Metro section, part 2, p. 11.

68. *United States v. Windsor,* 570 U.S. ___ (2013).

69. American Society of Civil Engineers, "Report Card for America's Infrastructure: 2009," www .infrastructurereportcard.org/ (accessed 11/ 14/11).

70. Martha Derthick, *Keeping the Compound Republic: Essays in American Federalism* (Washington, D.C.: Brookings Institution, 2001), pp. 9–32.

CHAPTER 4

1. About the Westboro Baptist Church, www.godhatesfags .com/wbcinfo/aboutwbc.html (accessed 12/2/11). The WBC is unaffiliated with the mainstream Baptist Church and has only about 40 members who are mostly relatives of the founder, Fred Phelps. According to the Church's website, the WBC has held more than 47,000 anti-gay demonstrations since 1991.

2. Timothy J. Nieman, Dean H. Dusinberre, and Lawrence M. Maher, "Brief for the Veterans of Foreign Wars as *Amicus Curiae* in Support of Petitioner," U.S. Supreme Court, *Snyder v. Phelps,* May 28, 2010, p. 4.

3. *Snyder v. Phelps,* 131 S. Ct. 1207 (2011).

4. *Snyder v. Phelps,* Alito dissent.

5. *Arar v. Ashcroft et al.,* 2006 WL 346439 (E.D.N.Y.). The case was also dismissed because Arar, a Canadian citizen, did not have standing to sue the U.S. government. Supporters of this decision (and the practice more generally) say that it is an essential part of the war on terror and that the enemy combatants who are arrested have no legal rights. Opponents say that the practice violates international law and our own standards of decency; furthermore, torture almost never produces useful information because people will say anything to get the torture to stop.

6. *State v. Massey et al.,* Supreme Court of North Carolina, 51 S.E.2d 179 (1949). The case was appealed to the Supreme Court, but the Court declined to hear the case, which means that the state decision stands (*Bunn v. North Carolina,* 336 U.S. 942 [1949]).

7. Alan Blinder, "Tennessee Pastor Disputes a Wildlife Possession Charge by State," *New York Times,* November 15, 2013, www.nytimes.com/2013/11/16/us/tennessee -pastor-disputes-wildlife-possession-charge-by-state .html?_r=0 (accessed 1/24/14).

8. *Pennsylvania v. Miller,* Pennsylvania Court of Common Pleas, WL 31426193 (2002). However, supreme courts in Minnesota, Wisconsin, and several other states have decided that requiring the Amish to use orange SMV triangles violates their free exercise of religion.

9. *Wisconsin v. Yoder,* 403 U.S. 205 (1972).

10. *Church of Lukumi Babalu Aye v. City of Hialeah,* 508 U.S. 520 (1993).

11. Jeffrey Rosen, "Lemon Law," *New Republic,* March 29, 1993, p. 17.

12. Max Farrand, ed., *The Records of the Federal Convention of 1787,* rev. ed. (New Haven, CT: Yale University Press, 1937), pp. 587–88, 617–18.

13. *The Papers of Thomas Jefferson,* ed. J. Boyd (Princeton, NJ: Princeton University Press, 1958), pp. 557–83, cited in Lester S. Jayson, ed., *The Constitution of the United States of America: Analysis and Interpretation* (Washington, D.C.: U.S. Government Printing Office, 1973), p. 900.

14. Ralph Ketcham, *The Anti-Federalist Papers and the Constitutional Convention Debates* (New York: Signet Classic, Penguin Putnam, 2003), p. 247.

15. The two that were not ratified by the states were a complicated amendment on congressional apportionment and the pay raise amendment.

16. *Annals of Congress* 755 (August 17, 1789), cited in Lester S. Jayson, ed., *The Constitution of the United States of America* (Washington, D.C.: U.S. Government Printing Office, 1973), p. 898.

17. There is an intense scholarly debate on whether the authors of the Fourteenth Amendment intended for it to apply the Bill of Rights to the states. The strongest argument against this position is Raoul Berger's *The Fourteenth Amendment and the Bill of Rights* (1989), and a good book in support is Amar's *The Bill of Rights* (1998).

18. *Barron v. Baltimore,* 32 U.S. 243 (1833), 250. In this case, John Barron had sued the city of Baltimore when its street-paving project had diverted streams and sent sand and gravel into the harbor area he owned, making it impossible for ships to use his once-valuable wharf. Barron claimed that the city owed him the lost value of his property because the Fifth Amendment says that private property may not be "taken for public use without just compensation." Since the Maryland constitution did not have such a provision, Barron sued under the U.S. Constitution and won in district court but lost on appeal. The Supreme Court agreed with the appeals court, saying that the Bill of Rights applied to actions of the national government but not to those of state and local governments, hence introducing the idea of "dual citizenship."

19. *Chicago, Burlington, and Quincy Railroad v. Chicago*, 166 U.S. 226 (1897).

20. *Twining v. New Jersey*, 211 U.S. 78, 98 (1908).

21. *Gitlow v. New York*, 268 U.S. 652 (1925).

22. James Hudson, "'A Wall of Separation,'" *Library of Congress Information Bulletin* 57:6 (June 1998), www.loc.gov/loc/lcib/9806/danbury.html (accessed 3/3/08).

23. Henry J. Abraham and Barbara A. Perry, *Freedom and the Court: Civil Rights and Civil Liberties in the United States*, 8th ed. (Lawrence: University Press of Kansas, 2003), p. 300.

24. *Engle v. Vitale*, 370 U.S. 421 (1962).

25. *Wallace v. Jaffree*, 482 U.S. 38 (1985).

26. *Lee v. Weisman*, 505 U.S. 577 (1992); *Santa Fe Independent School District v. Doe*, 530 U.S. 290 (2000).

27. *Marsh v. Chambers*, 463 U.S. 783 (1983); *Jones v. Clear Creek Independent School*, 61 LW 3819 (1993); *Town of Greece, N.Y. v. Galloway*, 572 U.S. ___ 2014.

28. *Lemon v. Kurtzman*, 403 U.S. 602 (1971).

29. *Lynch v. Donnelly*, 465 U.S. 668 (1984), 672–73.

30. Jeffrey Rosen, "Big Ten," *New Republic*, March 14, 2004, p. 11.

31. *Van Orden v. Perry*, 03-1500 (2005); *McCreary County et al. v. American Civil Liberties Union of Kentucky*, 03-1693 (2005).

32. *Zelman v. Simmons-Harris*, 536 U.S. 639 (2002).

33. *Arizona Christian School Tuition Organization v. Winn*, U.S. Supreme Court slip. op. 09-987 and 09-991 (2011).

34. *Mitchell v. Helms*, 530 U.S. 793 (2000).

35. *Zobrest v. Catalina School District*, 509 U.S. 1 (1993). A similar decision in 1997 allowed a public school teacher to teach in a special program in a parochial school, *Agostini v. Felton*, 521 U.S. 203 (1997).

36. *Minersville School District v. Gobitis*, 310 U.S. 586 (1940).

37. *West Virginia Board of Education v. Barnette*, 319 U.S. 624 (1943), 642.

38. We will not cite all the cases here. See Abraham and Perry, *Freedom and the Court*, Chapter 6, for a summary of cases on this topic, especially Tables 6.1 and 6.2.

39. *Employment Division, Department of Human Resources of Oregon v. Smith*, 494 U.S. 872 (1990), 878–80. This case is often erroneously reported as having banned the religious use of peyote. In fact, the Court said, "Although it is constitutionally permissible to exempt sacramental peyote use from the operation of drug laws, it is not constitutionally required."

40. *City of Boerne v. Flores*, 521 U.S. 527 (1997).

41. The court case was *Cutter v. Wilkinson*, No. 03-9877 (2005). See Linda Greenhouse, "Supreme Court Rules in Ohio Prison Case," *New York Times*, June 1, 2005, for a discussion of the broader debate.

42. *Gonzales v. O Centro Espirita Beneficente Uniao Do Vegetal (UDV) et al.*, 546 U.S. 418 (2006). The Sherbert test comes from *Sherbert v. Verner*, 374 U.S. 398 (1963).

43. *Burwell v. Hobby Lobby*, 573 U.S. ___ (2014).

44. *Police Department of Chicago v. Mosley*, 408 U.S. 92 (1972).

45. *United States v. O'Brien*, 391 U.S. 367 (1968); *Ladue v. Gilleo*, 512 U.S. 43 (1994).

46. *Schenck v. United States*, 249 U.S. 47 (1919), 52.

47. Alan Dershowitz, *Shouting Fire: Civil Liberties in a Turbulent Age* (New York: Little, Brown, 2002).

48. *Debs v. United States*, 249 U.S. 211 (1919); *Frohwerk v. United States*, 249 U.S. 204 (1919).

49. *Abrams v. United States*, 250 U.S. 616 (1919), 630–31.

50. *Dennis v. United States*, 341 U.S. 494 (1951).

51. *Brandenburg v. Ohio*, 395 U.S. 444 (1969).

52. *Morse v. Frederick*, 551 U.S. 393 (2007).

53. *Smith v. Goguen*, 415 U.S. 566 (1974).

54. *Tinker v. Des Moines School District*, 393 U.S. 503 (1969).

55. *Spence v. Washington*, 418 U.S. 405 (1974).

56. *Spence v. Washington*, 418 U.S. 409–410 (1974).

57. *Texas v. Johnson*, 491 U.S. 397 (1989).

58. *United States v. Eichman*, 496 U.S. 310 (1990).

59. *United States v. O'Brien*, 391 U.S. 367, 376 (1968).

60. *Buckley v. Valeo*, 424 U.S. 1 (1976).

61. *Davis v. Federal Election Commission*, 554 U.S. 724 (2008).

62. *McCutcheon v. Federal Election Commission*, 572 U.S. ___ (2014).

63. *McConnell v. Federal Election Commission*, 540 U.S. 93 (2003).

64. *Board of Regents of the University of Wisconsin System et al., Petitioners v. Scott Harold Southworth et al.*, 529 U.S. 217 (2000).

65. Kermit L. Hall, "Free Speech on Public College Campuses: Overview," www.firstamendmentcenter.org/speech/pubcollege/ overview.aspx (accessed 2/10/08).

66. Carolyn J. Palmer, Sophie W. Penney, Donald D. Gehring, and Jan A. Neiger, "Hate Speech and Hate Crimes: Campus Conduct Codes and Supreme Court Rulings," *National Association of Student Personnel Administrators Journal* 34:2 (1997), http://publications.naspa.org/naspajournal/vol34/iss2/art4 (accessed 12/18/07).

67. *City of St. Paul v. RAV*, 505 U.S. 377 (1992).

68. *Virginia v. Black*, 538 U.S. 343 (2003).

69. The Editorial Board, "Hate Speech on Facebook," *New York Times*, May 30, 2013, www.nytimes.com/2013/05/31/opinion/misogynist-speech-on-facebook.html (accessed 1/28/14).

70. Facebook "community standards" on hate speech, www.facebook.com/communitystandards (accessed 1/28/14).

71. Jeffrey Rosen, "Who Decides? Civility v. Hate Speech on the Internet," *Insights on Law and Society* 13:2 (Winter, 2013), www.americanbar.org/publications/insights_on_law_and_society/13/winter_2013/who_decides_civilityvhatespeechontheinternet.html (accessed 1/29/14).

72. Pete Kasperowicz, "13 House Democrats Offer Bill Demanding Government Study on Internet Hate Speech,"

The Hill, January 16, 2014, www.thehill.com/blogs/floor -action/technology/195647-dems-demand-government -study-on-internet-hate-speech (accessed 1/29/14).

73. *De Jonge v. State of Oregon*, 299 U.S. 353 (1937); *Edwards v. South Carolina*, 372 U.S. 229 (1963).

74. The Supreme Court declined to review the case in *Smith v. Collin*, 439 U.S. 916 (1978), which meant that the lower-court rulings stood (447 F. Supp. 676 [1978], 578 F.2d 1197 [1978]). See Donald A. Downs, *Nazis in Skokie: Freedom, Community and the First Amendment* (Notre Dame, IN: University of Notre Dame Press, 1985), for an excellent analysis of this important case.

75. *Forsyth County v. Nationalist Movement*, 505 U.S. 123 (1992).

76. *Frisby et al. v. Schultz et al.*, 487 U.S. 474 (1988).

77. *Near v. Minnesota*, 283 U.S. 697 (1931), 719–20.

78. *New York Times Co. v. United States*, 403 U.S. 713 (1971).

79. *New York Times v. United States*, 403 U.S. 713 (1971).

80. *Chaplinsky v. State of New Hampshire*, 315 U.S. 568 (1942).

81. *Chaplinsky v. State of New Hampshire*.

82. *New York Times v. Sullivan*, 376 U.S. 254 (1964), cited in Henry J. Abraham and Barbara A. Perry, *Freedom and the Court: Civil Rights and Civil Liberties in the United States,* 8th ed. (Lawrence, KS: University Press of Kansas, 2003), p. 193.

83. *Hustler v. Falwell*, 485 U.S. 46 (1988).

84. *Valentine v. Chrestensen*, 316 U.S. 52 (1942).

85. *Virginia State Board of Pharmacy v. Virginia Citizens Consumer Council, Inc.*, 425 U.S. 748 (1976); *City of Cincinnati v. Discovery Network, Inc. et al.*, 507 U.S. 410 (1993).

86. *Lorillard Tobacco v. Reilly*, 533 U.S. 525 (2001).

87. In 1996, Congress passed the Child Pornography Prevention Act. This law makes the possession, production, or distribution of child pornography a criminal offense punishable with up to 15 years in jail and a fine. However, two parts of the law were struck down by the Court for being "overbroad and unconstitutional." *Ashcroft v. Free Speech Coalition*, 353 U.S. 234 (2002).

88. *Jacobellis v. Ohio*, 378 U.S. 184, 197 (1964).

89. *Roth v. United States*, 354 U.S. 476 (1957).

90. *Miller v. California*, 413 U.S. 15 (1973).

91. *Reno et al. v. American Civil Liberties Union et al.*, 521 U.S. 844 (1997).

92. *Ashcroft v. American Civil Liberties Union*, 535 U.S. 564 (2004).

93. *Federal Communications Commission v. Pacifica Foundation*, 438 U.S. 726 (1978).

94. *Federal Communications Commission et al. v. Fox Television Stations*, 556 U.S. 502 (2009).

95. *Federal Communications Commission and United States v. CBS Corporation*, 556 U.S. 1218 (2009).

96. *Federal Communications Commission v. Fox Television Stations* 567 U.S. ___ (2012), *Federal Communications Commission v. CBS Corporation*, no. 11–1240 (2012), writ of certiorari denied.

97. *United States v. Stevens*, 559 U.S. 460 (2010).

98. *Brown v. Entertainment Merchants Association*, 564 U.S. ___ (2011).

99. Edward Walsh, "U.S. Argues for Wider Gun Rights; Supreme Court Filing Reverses Past Policy," *Washington Post*, May 8, 2002, p. A1. For a lengthy memo from the attorney general that explores the individual rights argument, see www.justice.gov/olc/secondamendment2.pdf (accessed 3/22/12).

100. Karen McVeigh, "Sandy Hook: One Year on, Campaigners Prepare for New Push on Gun Control." *Guardian,* Friday, 13 December 2013, www.theguardian.com/world/2013/ dec/13/sandy-hook-campaigners-push-gun-control (accessed 1/31/14).

101. *District of Columbia v. Heller*, 554 U.S. 290 (2008).

102. *McDonald v. Chicago* 08-1521 (2010).

103. Robert J. Spitzer, *The Politics of Gun Control* (Chatham, NJ: Chatham House, 1995). Also see www.bradycenter. org/cases for a complete list of the cases (accessed 8/21/12). The two cases recognizing the individual right to bear arms were *United States v. Timothy Joe Emerson*, 46 F. Supp. 2d 598 (1999), and the D.C. Circuit Court case that was appealed in the landmark ruling *Parker v. District of Columbia*, 478 F.3d 370 (D.C. Cir. 2007).

104. Legal Community against Violence, "Post *Heller* Litigation Summary," November 8, 2011, www.lcav.org/ content/post-heller_summary.pdf (accessed 12/5/11).

105. *New Jersey v. T. L. O.*, 469 U.S. 325 (1985); *Safford United School District No. 1 et al. v. Redding*, 557 U.S. 364 (2009).

106. See Abraham and Perry, *Freedom and the Court*, Chapter 4, for a discussion of these cases. The most recent case is *Kentucky v. King* 563 U.S. ___ (2011).

107. *Florence v. County of Burlington*, U.S. 10–945 (2012).

108. *Maryland v. King*, 133 S. Ct. 1958 (June 3, 2013).

109. *Riley v. California*, 513 U.S. ___ (2014).

110. *United States v. Jones*, 565 U.S. ___ (2012).

111. *Mapp v. Ohio*, 367 U.S. 643 (1961).

112. *Herring v. United States*, 555 U.S. 135 (2009).

113. *Murray v. United States*, 487 U.S. 533 (1988).

114. *Vernonia School District v. Acton,* 515 U.S. 646 (1995); *Board of Education of Pottawatomie County v. Earls*, 536 U.S. 832 (2002).

115. Sharon L. Larson, Joe Eyerman, Misty S. Foster, and Joseph C. Gfroerer, "Worker Substance Use and Workplace Policies and Programs," June 2007, Substance Abuse and Mental Health Services Administration, www.oas.samhsa.gov/work2k7/work .pdf (accessed 3/3/08).

116. *Chandler v. Miller*, 520 U.S. 305 (1997).

117. Leslie Cauley, "NSA Has Massive Database of Americans' Phone Calls," *USA Today*, May 11, 2006, p. 1.

118. Lorraine Woellert and Dawn Kopecki, "The Snooping Goes beyond Phone Calls," *Business Week*, May 29, 2006, p. 38; "Data Mining: Federal Efforts Cover a Wide Range of Uses," GAO Report 04-548, May 2004, www.gao.gov/assets/250/242241.pdf (accessed 5/13/14).

119. Eric Lichtblau and James Risen, "Officials Say U.S. Wiretaps Exceeded Law," *New York Times*, April 16, 2009.

120. *Miranda v. Arizona*, 384 U.S. 436 (1966).

121. *New York v. Quarles*, 467 U.S. 649 (1984).

122. *Maryland v. Shatzer*, No. 08-680 (2010).

123. *Berghuis v. Thompkins*, 560 U.S. 370 (2010).

124. *Dickerson v. United States*, 530 U.S. 428 (2000).

125. *Benton v. Maryland*, 395 U.S. 784 (1969).

126. *Lucas v. South Carolina Coastal Council*, 505 U.S. 1003 (1992).

127. *Kelo v. City of New London*, 545 U.S. 469 (2005).

128. National Conference of State Legislatures, "Eminent Domain Overview," January 1, 2012, www.ncsl.org/research/environment-and-natural-resources/eminent-domain-overview.aspx (accessed 1/31/14).

129. *Powell v. Alabama*, 287 U.S. 45 (1932).

130. *Gideon v. Wainwright*, 372 U.S. 335 (1963).

131. *Evitts v. Lucy*, 469 U.S. 387 (1985); *Wiggins v. Smith*, 539 U.S. 510 (2003). See Elizabeth Gable and Tyler Green, "*Wiggins v. Smith*: The Ineffective Assistance of Counsel Standard Applied Twenty Years after *Strickland*," *Georgetown Journal of Legal Ethics* (Summer 2004) 755–71, for a discussion of many of these issues.

132. *Klopfer v. North Carolina*, 386 U.S. 213 (1967).

133. The law is 18 U.S.C. § 3161(c)(1) and the ruling is *Zedner v. United States*, 05-5992 (2006).

134. The case concerning African Americans is *Batson v. Kentucky*, 106 S. Ct. 1712 (1986); the case about Latinos is *Hernandez v. New York*, 500 U.S. 352 (1991); and the gender case is *J. E. B. v. Alabama ex rel. T. B.*, 511 U.S. 127 (1994). Two more-recent cases affirming that peremptory challenges could not be used in a racially discriminatory fashion were *Miller-El v. Dretke*, 545 U.S. 231 (2005), and *Snyder v. Louisiana*, 552 U.S. 472 (2008).

135. Pete Yost, "Report: Use of Death Penalty Shows Decline in United States," *Washington Post*, December 22, 2013, www.washingtonpost.com/politics/report-use-of-death-penalty-shows-decline-in-united-states/2013/12/22/261cdf12-68d8-11e3-a0b9-249bbb34602c_story.html (accessed 1/31/14). Also see www.deathpenaltyinfo.org/documents/FactSheet.pdf; *Hall v. Florida*, 572 U.S. ___ (2014).

136. Erik Eckholm, "One Execution Botched, Oklahoma Delays the Next," *New York Times*, April 29, 2014, www.nytimes.com/2014/04/30/us/oklahoma-executions.html (accessed 5/13/14).

137. *Furman v. Georgia*, 408 U.S. 238 (1972); *Gregg v. Georgia*, 428 U.S. 513 (1976).

138. See Abraham and Perry, *Freedom and the Court*, pp. 72–73, for a discussion of the earlier cases, and Charles Lane, "5–4 Supreme Court Abolishes Juvenile Executions," *Washington Post*, March 2, 2005, p. A1, for a discussion of the 2002 and 2005 cases. The cases were *Atkins v. Virginia*, 536 U.S. 304 (2002); *Roper v. Simmons*, 543 U.S. 551 (2005); and *Kennedy v. Louisiana*, 554 U.S. 407 (2008).

139. *Griswold v. Connecticut*, 381 U.S. 479 (1965), 482–86.

140. *Griswold v. Connecticut*, 512–13.

141. *Roe v. Wade*, 410 U.S. 113 (1973), 129.

142. *Planned Parenthood of Southeastern Pennsylvania v. Casey*, 505 U.S. 833 (1992).

143. Katharine Q. Seeyle, "Mississippi Voters Reject Anti-Abortion Measure," *New York Times*, November 8, 2011, www.nytimes.com/2011/11/09/us/politics/votes-across-the-nation-could-serve-as-a-political-barometer.html (accessed 12/5/11).

144. Erik Eckholm, "Access to Abortion Falling as States Pass Restrictions," *New York Times*, January 3, 2014, www.nytimes.com/2014/01/04/us/women-losing-access-to-abortion-as-opponents-gain-ground-in-state-legislatures.html (accessed 1/31/14).

145. *Bowers v. Hardwick*, 478 U.S. 186 (1986)

146. *Lawrence v. Texas*, 539 U.S. 558 (2003).

You Decide

a. *Florida v. Jardines*, 569 U.S. ___ (2013), 6–7.

b. Oral arguments in *U.S. v. Jones* (2012), November 8, 2011, www.supremecourt.gov/oral_arguments/argument_transcripts/10-1259.pdf, p. 44 (accessed 8/20/12).

CHAPTER 5

1. Complaint in *United States v. Maricopa County, Arizona, and Joseph M. Arpaio*, Federal District Court of Arizona, May 10, 2012, www.justice.gov/iso/opa/resources/512012510134311376158.pdf (accessed 4/6/14).

2. Mark Lacey, "U.S. Finds Pervasive Bias against Latinos by Arizona Sheriff," *New York Times*, December 16, 2011, www.nytimes.com/2011/12/16/us/arizona-sheriffs-office-unfairly-targeted-latinos-justice-department-says.html?ref=josephmarpaio (accessed 1/31/12).

3. "The Persistence of Racial and Ethnic Profiling in the United States," American Civil Liberties Union and the Rights Working Group, New York, August, 2009, p.42, www.aclu.org/files/pdfs/humanrights/cerd_finalreport.pdf (accessed 1/31/12).

4. Supplemental Permanent Injunction, *Manuel de Jesus Ortega Melendres v. Joseph M. Arpaio*, Federal District Court of Arizona, October 2, 2013, www.aclu.org/sites/default/files/assets/2013.10.02.606_supplemental_permanent_injunction_judgment_order.pdf (accessed 4/6/14).

5. Fernanda Santos, "Angry Judge Says Sheriff Defied Order on Latinos," *New York Times*, March 24, 2014, www.nytimes.com/2014/03/25/us/judge-says-arpaio-defied-order-on-profiling-latinos.html (accessed 4/6/14).

6. Lacey, "U.S. Finds Pervasive Bias against Latinos."

7. Julia Preston and John H. Cushman, Jr., "Obama to Permit Young Migrants to Remain in U.S.," *New York Times*, June 15, 2012, www.nytimes.com/2012/06/16/us/us-to-stop-deporting-some-illegal-immigrants.html?pagewanted=all (accessed 4/6/14).

8. There are eight commissioners on the U.S. Commission on Civil Rights, four appointed by the president and four by Congress. The commissioners serve six-year terms and do not require Senate confirmation, and no more than four members may be of the same political party.

9. Howard Dodson, "How Slavery Helped Build a World Economy," in *Jubilee: The Emergence of African-American Culture* by the Schomburg Center for Research in Black Culture of the New York Public Library (Washington, D.C.: National Geographic Press, 2003).

10. John W. Wright, ed., *New York Times 2000 Almanac* (New York: Penguin Reference, 1999), p. 165. Estimates from various online sources are quite a bit higher, averaging about 620,000 deaths.

11. V. O. Key, Jr., *Southern Politics in State and Nation* (New York: Knopf, 1949), p. 538. For example, the Louisiana grandfather clause read, "No male person who was on January 1, 1867, or at any date prior thereto, entitled to vote under the Constitution of the United States, wherein he then resided, and no son or grandson of any such person not less than twenty-one years of age at the date of the adoption of this Constitution, . . . shall be denied the right to register and vote in this State by reason of his failure to possess the educational or property qualifications." Grandfather clauses as they applied to voting were ruled unconstitutional in 1915.

12. Chandler Davidson, "The Voting Rights Act: A Brief History," in *Controversies in Minority Voting: The Voting Rights Act in Perspective*, eds. Bernard Grofman and Chandler Davidson (Washington, D.C.: Brookings Institution, 1992), p. 21.

13. "Indian Removal: 1814–1848," Public Broadcasting System, www.pbs.org/wgbh/aia/part4/4p2959.html (accessed 1/26/12).

14. *Cherokee Nation v. Georgia*, 30 U.S. 1 (1831).

15. *United States v. Wong Kim Ark*, 169 U.S. 649 (1898).

16. Institute for Advanced Technology in the Humanities, University of Virginia, Abigail Adams to John Adams, March 31, 1776, www.iath.virginia.edu/seminar/unit1/text/adams.htm (accessed 7/30/08).

17. *Bradwell v. Illinois*, 83 U.S. 130 (1873).

18. *Hoyt v. Florida*, 368 U.S. 57 (1961).

19. Lucian K. Truscott IV, "The Real Mob at Stonewall," *New York Times*, June 25, 2009, A19.

20. ABC News/*Washington Post* poll on gay rights, February 27–March 2, 2014, and various other polls reported on www.pollingreport.com (accessed 4/7/14).

21. There are literally hundreds of books and thousands of articles on the subject of racial discrimination. Two excellent surveys of research are Matthew Desmond and Mustafa Emirbayer, *Racial Domination, Racial Progress: The Sociology of Race in America* (New York: McGraw-Hill, 2010), and Michael K. Brown et al., *Whitewashing Race: The Myth of a Color-Blind Society* (Berkeley, CA: University of California Press, 2003). Several important books on the topic include Tali Mendelberg, *The Race Card: Campaign Strategy, Implicit Messages, and the Norm of Equality* (Princeton, NJ: Princeton University Press, 2001); Paul M. Sniderman and Thomas Piazza, *The Scar of Race* (Cambridge, MA: Belknap Press, 1993); Donald R. Kinder and Lynn M. Sanders, *Divided by Color: Racial Politics and Democratic Ideals* (Chicago: University of Chicago Press, 1996).

22. Davidson, "The Voting Rights Act," p. 22; also see U.S. Department of Justice, Civil Rights Division, "About Section 5 of the Voting Rights Act," www.usdoj.gov/crt/voting/sec_5/obj_activ.htm, for a complete list of cases in which the Justice Department has denied "preclearance" of a change in an electoral practice under Section 5 of the Voting Rights Act. Note that in racially homogeneous single-member districts, minority candidates usually win. But in at-large elections, in which representatives are elected city-wide or county-wide (and thus may contain a mix of minority and white voters from the districts making up the city or county), the majority white voters can outvote the minority voters and elect an all-white city council or school board.

23. "The Long Shadow of Jim Crow: Voter Suppression in America," Special Report, People for the American Way Foundation and NAACP, http://67.192.238.60/sites/default/files/thelongshadowofjimcrow.pdf (accessed 1/23/12). Wendy Weiser and Margaret Chen, "Voter Suppression Incidents, 2008 Analysis," November 3, 2008, www.brennancenter.org/content/resource/voter_suppression_incidents (accessed 1/19/10).

24. "Spreading Suppression: Restrictive Voting Laws across the United States," Fair Elections Legal Network, www.fairelectionsnetwork.com/spreading-suppression-restrictive-voting-laws-across-united-states (accessed 4/7/14). The Court case is *Shelby County v. Holder*, 570 U.S. ___ (2013).

25. Carmen DeNavas-Walt and Bernadette D. Proctor, "Income and Poverty in the United States: 2013," United States Census, Current Population Reports, September 2014. Poverty rates are from Table 3, p.13, income is from Table 1, p.6, www.census.gov/content/dam/Census/library/publications/2014/demo/p60-249.pdf (accessed 11/12/14).

26. Jesse Bricker, et al., "Changes in U.S. Family Finances from 2010 to 2013: Evidence from the Survey of Consumer

Finances," Federal Reserve Bulletin, 100:4, September 2014, Table 2, p.12, www.federalreserve.gov/pubs/bulletin/2014/pdf/scf14.pdf (accessed 9/30/14).

27. Employment Situation Summary, Bureau of Labor Statistics, Tables A2 and A3, November 7, 2014, www.bls.gov/news.release/empsit.nr0.htm (accessed 11/12/14).

28. "America's Families and Living Arrangements: 2013," U.S. Census, Table C3, www.census.gov/hhes/families/data/cps2013C.html (accessed 11/12/14).

29. Federal Bureau of Investigation, "Crime in the United States, 2012, Expanded Homicide Data Tables, Table 2," www.fbi.gov/about-us/cjis/ucr/crime-in-the-u.s/2012/crime-in-the-u.s.-2012/offenses-known-to-law-enforcement/expanded-offense/expandedoffensemain (accessed 9/30/14).

30. Life expectancy data are from Elizabeth Arias, "United States Life Tables, 2009," National Vital Statistics Reports, Centers for Disease Control and Prevention, January 6, 2014, www.cdc.gov/nchs/data/nvsr/nvsr62/nvsr62_07.pdf. Infant mortality numbers are from Marian F. MacDorman, PhD, and T. J. Mathews, "Understanding Racial and Ethnic Disparities in U.S. Infant Mortality Rates," NCHS Data Brief, Centers for Disease Control and Prevention, September 2011, www.cdc.gov/nchs/data/databriefs/db74.pdf. Maternal mortality rates are from "Pregnancy Mortality Surveillance System," March 3, 2014, Centers for Disease Control and Prevention, www.cdc.gov/reproductivehealth/maternalinfanthealth/pmss.html. (All sources accessed 4/7/14.)

31. Evelyn Diaz, "Nick Cannon Accuses L.A. Cops of Racial Profiling," BET News, www.bet.com/news/celebrities/2011/11/18/nick-cannon-accuses-la-cops-of-racial-profiling.html (accessed 1/29/12).

32. Hundreds of studies have examined these patterns, and, not surprisingly, there are divergent findings. However, most have found differences in sentencing based on race. A meta-analysis of 85 studies by Ojmarrh Mitchell and Doris L. MacKenzie funded by the U.S. Department of Justice found, "after taking into account defendant criminal history and current offense seriousness, African-Americans and Latinos were generally sentenced more harshly than whites." See Mitchell and MacKenzie, "The Relationship between Race, Ethnicity, and Sentencing Outcomes: A Meta-Analysis of Sentencing Research," December 2004, www.ncjrs.gov/pdffiles1/nij/grants/208129.pdf. For government studies of racial profiling, see the Justice Department's "A Resource Guide on Racial Profiling Data Collection Systems," November 2000, www.ncjrs.gov/pdffiles1/bja/184768.pdf. For President Bush's statement on racial profiling, see Department of Justice, "Fact Sheet: Racial Profiling," June 17, 2003, www.usdoj.gov/opa/pr/2003/June/racial_profiling_fact_sheet.pdf. For a Government Accountability office Study, see "Racial Profiling: Limited Data on Motorist Stops," March 2000, www.gao.gov/new.items/gg00041.pdf. Government statistics on crime may be found on the Federal Bureau of Investigation site at www.fbi.gov. (All documents accessed 3/21/08.)

33. Benjamin Weiser and Joseph Goldstein, "Mayor Says New York City Will Settle Suits on Stop-and-Frisk Tactics," New York Times, January 30, 2014, www.nytimes.com/2014/01/31/nyregion/de-blasio-stop-and-frisk.html (accessed 4/6/14).

34. "Trayvon Martin, George Zimmerman Case," Orlando Sentinel, www.orlandosentinel.com/news/local/trayvon-martin/ (accessed 4/6/14).

35. Criminal Justice Information Services Division, Federal Bureau of Investigation, 2012 Hate Crime Statistics, www.fbi.gov/about-us/cjis/ucr/hate-crime/2012/topic-pages/incidents-and-offenses/incidentsandoffenses_final (accessed 4/6/14).

36. Rosa Parks with James Haskins, Rosa Parks: My Story (New York: Dial Books, 1992), p. 116.

37. Clayborne Carson, David J. Garrow, Gerald Gill, Vincent Harding, and Darlene Clark Hine, eds., The Eyes on the Prize Civil Rights Reader (New York: Penguin Books, 1997).

38. Boynton v. Virginia, 363 U.S. 454 (1960).

39. David Halberstam, The Children (New York: Ballantine Books, 1999).

40. Nate Silver, "Tea Party Nonpartisan Attendance Estimates: Now 300,000," April 16, 2009, www.fivethirtyeight.com/2009/04/tea-party-nonpartisan-attendance.html (accessed 1/19/10).

41. Pearson v. Murray, 169 Md. 478 (1936).

42. Brown v. Board of Education, 347 U.S. 483 (1954).

43. Brown v. Board of Education (II), 349 U.S. 294 (1955).

44. Paul Brest and Sanford Levinson, Process of Constitutional Decision Making: Cases and Material (Boston: Little, Brown, 1982), pp. 471–80.

45. Griffin et al. v. County School Board of Prince Edward County, 377 U.S. 218 (1964).

46. Swann v. Charlotte-Mecklenberg Board of Education, 402 U.S. 1 (1971).

47. Milliken v. Bradley, 418 U.S. 717 (1974).

48. Parents Involved in Community Schools Inc. v. Seattle School District, 05-98 (2007); Meredith v. Jefferson County (Ky.) Board of Education, 551 U.S. 701 (2007).

49. Heart of Atlanta Motel, Inc. v. United States, 379 U.S. 241 (1964).

50. Katzenbach v. McClung, 379 U.S. 294 (1964).

51. Griggs v. Duke Power, 401 U.S. 424 (1971).

52. Easley v. Cromartie, 532 U.S. 234 (2001), rehearing denied, 532 U.S. 1076 (2001).

53. Easley v. Cromartie, 532 U.S. 1076 (2001).

54. Shelby County v. Holder, 570 U.S. ___ (2013).

55. Reed v. Reed, 404 U.S. 71 (1971).

56. Frontiero v. Richardson, 411 U.S. 677 (1973).

57. Korematsu v. United States, 323 U.S. 214 (1944).

58. Craig v. Boren, 429 U.S. 190 (1976).

59. *Rostker v. Goldberg,* 453 U.S. 57 (1981).

60. *Orr v. Orr,* 440 U.S. 268 (1979).

61. *United States v. Virginia,* 518 U.S. 515 (1996).

62. *Johnson v. Transportation Agency of Santa Clara,* 480 U.S. 616 (1987).

63. *Harris v. Forklift Systems,* 510 U.S. 17 618 (1993).

64. *Ledbetter v. Goodyear Tire & Rubber Co.,* 550 U.S. 618(2007).

65. Equal Employment Opportunity Commission, "Outback Steakhouse to Pay $19 Million for Sex Bias against Women in 'Glass Ceiling' Suit by EEOC," press release, December 29, 2009, www.eeoc.gov/eeoc/newsroom/release/12-29 -09a.cfm (accessed 1/20/10).

66. Women Present Widespread Discrimination at Wal-Mart, press release, April 28, 2003, www.walmartclass.com/ staticdata/press_releases/wmcc.html (accessed 10/4/12).

67. David Savage, "Supreme Court Blocks Huge Class-Action Suit against Wal-Mart," *Los Angeles Times,* June 21, 2011. The case is *Dukes v. Wal-Mart Stores, Inc.* (2011).

68. *Bowers v. Hardwick,* 478 U.S. 186 (1986), rehearing denied, 478 U.S. 1039 (1986).

69. *Hurley v. Irish-American Gay, Lesbian, and Bisexual Group of Boston,* 515 U.S. 557 (1995).

70. *Boy Scouts of America v. Dale,* 530 U.S. 640 (2000).

71. *Romer v. Evans,* 517 U.S. 620 (1996).

72. *Lawrence v. Texas,* 539 U.S. 558 (2003). Because the basis for the decision was the due process clause of the Fourteenth Amendment and not the equal protection clause, this ruling upheld a civil liberty rather than a civil right. As such, it applied to all laws regarding sodomy, not just those that applied to gays. However, the decision has been widely regarded as a landmark civil rights case because it provided equal rights for gays.

73. John Monk, "SC same-sex marriage ban overturned by federal judge," *Charlotte Oberverer,* November 12, 2014, www.charlotteobserver.com/2014/11/12/5309267/sc -same-sex-marriage-ban-overturned.html#.VGPFl8m Vo1w (accessed 11/12/14).

74. Quoted in Voting Rights Act Extension: Report of the Subcommittee of the Constitution of the Committee on the Judiciary, U.S. Senate, 97th Congress, 2nd session, May 25, 1982, S. Rept. 97-417, 4.

75. Drew S. Days III, "Section 5 Enforcement and the Justice Department," in *Controversies in Minority Voting: The Voting Rights Act in Perspective,* eds. Bernard Grofman and Chandler Davidson (Washington, D.C.: Brookings Institution Press, 1992), p. 52; Frank R. Parker, *Black Votes Count* (Chapel Hill, NC: University of North Carolina Press, 1990), p. 1.

76. Davidson, "The Voting Rights Act," p. 21.

77. "Fair Housing: It's Your Right." U.S. Department of Housing and Urban Development, http://portal.hud.gov/hudportal/ HUD?src=/program_offices/fair_housing_equal_opp/ FHLaws/yourrights (accessed 2/2/12).

78. *United States v. Morrison,* 529 U.S. 598 (2000).

79. *Board of Trustees of the University of Alabama v. Garrett,* 531 U.S. 356 (2001). However, in *State of Tennessee v. George Lane and Beverly Jones,* 541 U.S. 509 (2004), the Court ruled that the disabled must have access to courthouses.

80. The White House, "Remarks by the Reception Commemorating the Enactment of the Matthew Shepard and James Byrd Jr. Hate Crimes Prevention Act," October, 28, 2009, www.whitehouse.gov/the-press-office/remarks-president -reception-commemorating-enactment-matthew-shepard -and-James-Byrd (accessed 1/21/10).

81. Tim Mak, "Post 'Don't Ask,' Gay Navy Lt. Marries," *Politico,* September 20, 2011, www.politico.com/news/ stories/0911/63909.html (accessed 1/24/12).

82. *Public Papers of the Presidents of the United States: Lyndon B. Johnson, 1965,* vol. II, entry 301 (Washington, D.C.: Government Printing Office, 1966), pp. 635–40.

83. *New York Times*/CBS poll, December 6–9, 1997. Fifty-nine percent of whites and 82 percent of blacks favored education programs to assist minority students in competing for college admissions, while 57 percent of whites but only 23 percent of blacks opposed preferences in hiring and promotion "to make up for past discrimination."

84. State of California, article 1, section 31.

85. The precise wording of the proposition was, "Shall the charter of the City of Houston be amended to end the use of affirmative action for women and minorities in the operation of City of Houston employment and contracting, including ending the current program and any similar programs in the future?"

86. The training program case was *United Steel Workers of America v. Weber,* 443 U.S. 193 (1979); the labor union case was *Sheet Metal Workers v. EEOC,* 478 U.S. 421 (1986); and the Alabama state police case was *U.S. v. Paradise,* 480 U.S. 149 (1987).

87. *Ricci v. DeStefano,* 557 U.S. ___ (2009).

88. *Regents of University of California v. Bakke,* 438 U.S. 265 (1978).

89. *Smith v. University of Washington,* 233 F.3d 1188 (9th Cir. 2000).

90. *Grutter v. Bollinger,* 539 U.S. 306 (2003), was the law school case and *Gratz v. Bollinger,* 539 U.S. 244 (2003), was the undergraduate admissions case.

91. In *Bakke,* Justice Lewis Powell was the only member of the Court who held this position, even if it became the basis for all affirmative action programs over the next 25 years. Four justices in the *Bakke* decision wanted to get rid of race as a factor in admissions, and another four thought that the "strict scrutiny" standard should not even be applied in this instance.

92. *Schuette v. Coalition to Defend Affirmative Action,* 572 U.S. ___ (2014).

93. *Fisher v. University of Texas, Austin,* U.S. Court of Appeals, 5th Circuit, July 15, 2014, www.ca5.uscourts.gov/

opinions%5Cpub%5C09/09-50822-CV2.pdf (accessed 9/30/14).

94. James Vicini, "Supreme Court to Decide Arizona Immigration Law," Reuters, December 12, 2011, www.reuters.com/article/2011/12/12/us-usa-immigration-arizona-idUSTRE7BB0XJ20111212 (accessed 2/2/12).

95. *Arizona v. United States*, 567 U.S. ___ (2012).

96. Fernanda Santos, "Arizona Immigration Law Survives Ruling," *New York Times*, September 6, 2012, www.nytimes.com/2012/09/07/us/key-element-of-arizona-immigration-law-survives-ruling.html?r=0 (accessed 10/5/12).

97. CBS News poll on immigration, March 20–23, 2014, and CNN/ORC poll from "Immigration," January 31–February 2, 2014, www.pollingreport.com/immigration.htm (accessed 4/9/14).

98. "An Act Providing for the Collection of Data Relative to Traffic Stops," Massachusetts state law, Chapter 228 of the Acts of 2000, www.mass.gov/legis/laws/seslaw00/sl000228.htm (accessed 7/22/08).

CHAPTER 6

1. Gallup Poll, "Americans Back Obama's Proposals to Address Gun Violence," January 23, 2013, www.gallup.com/poll/160085/americans-back-obama-proposals-address-gun-violence.aspx (accessed 11/25/13).

2. For a review, see Arthur Lupia and Mathew D. McCubbins, *The Democratic Dilemma* (New York: Cambridge University Press, 1998).

3. Larry Bartels, "Partisanship and Voting Behavior, 1952–1996," *American Journal of Political Science* 44 (2000): 35–50.

4. Robert S. Erikson, Michael B. MacKuen, and James A. Stimson, *The Macro Polity* (New York: Cambridge University Press, 2002).

5. Angus Campbell, Phillip Converse, Warren Miller, and Donald Stokes, *The American Voter* (New York: Wiley, 1960); Phillip E. Converse, "The Nature of Belief Systems in Mass Publics," in *Ideology and Discontent*, ed. David E. Aptor (Glencoe, IL: Free Press of Glencoe, 1964), pp. 209–61. For more-modern versions of these arguments, see Eric R. A. N. Smith, *The Unchanging American Voter* (Berkeley, CA: University of California Press, 1989); Phillip E. Converse and Gregory Markus, "Plus Ça Change . . . : The New CPS Election Study Panel," *American Political Science Review* 73:1 (March 1979): 32–49.

6. Converse, "The Nature of Belief Systems in Mass Publics," p. 259.

7. For an example focusing on foreign policy opinions, see John Aldrich, John Sullivan, and Eugene Borgida, "Foreign Affairs and Issue Voting: Do Presidential Candidates Waltz before a Blind Audience?" *American Political Science Review* 83 (1989): 125–41.

8. John Zaller, "Coming to Grips with V. O. Key's Concept of Latent Opinion," unpublished paper, University of California, Los Angeles, 1998.

9. Morris Fiorina, *Retrospective Voting in American National Elections* (Cambridge, MA: Harvard University Press, 1981).

10. John Zaller, *The Nature and Origins of Mass Opinion* (New York: Cambridge University Press, 1992).

11. R. Michael Alvarez and John Brehm, *Hard Choices, Easy Answers* (Princeton, NJ: Princeton University Press, 2002).

12. John Zaller and Stanley Feldman, "A Theory of the Survey Response: Revealing Preferences versus Answering Questions," *American Journal of Political Science* 36 (1992): 579–616.

13. Janet M. Box-Steffensmeier and Susan DeBoef, "Macropartisanship and Macroideology in the Sophisticated Electorate," *Journal of Politics* 63:1 (2001): 232–48.

14. Jack Citrin, Donald P. Green, Christopher Muste, and Cara Wong, "Public Opinion toward Immigration Reform: The Role of Economic Motivations," *American Journal of Political Science* 59:3 (1997): 858–82.

15. William G. Jacoby, "Issue Framing and Public Opinion on Government Spending," *American Journal of Political Science* 44:4 (2000): 750–67; L. M. Bartels, "Beyond the Running Tally: Partisan Bias in Political Perceptions," *Political Behavior* 24:2 (2002): 117–50.

16. Donald R. Kinder, "Exploring the Racial Divide: Blacks, Whites, and Opinion on National Policy," *American Journal of Political Science* 45:2 (2001): 439–49; Paul M. Sniderman and Thomas Piazza, *The Scar of Race* (Cambridge, MA: Harvard University Press, 1993).

17. Robert Huckfeldt, Jeffery Levine, William Morgan, and John Sprague, "Accessibility and the Political Utility of Partisan and Ideological Orientations," *American Journal of Political Science* 43:3 (July, 1999): 888–911.

18. George E. Marcus, John L. Sullivan, Elizabeth Theiss-Morse, and Sandra L. Wood, *With Malice toward Some: How People Make Civil Liberties Judgments* (New York: Cambridge University Press, 1995).

19. Stanley Feldman and Marco R. Steenbergen, "The Humanitarian Foundation of Public Support for Social Welfare," *American Journal of Political Science* 45:3 (2001): 658–77.

20. R. Michael Alvarez and John Brehm, "American Ambivalence towards Abortion Policy: Development of a Heteroskedastic Probit Model of Competing Values," *American Journal of Political Science* 39:4 (1995): 1055–82.

21. R. Michael Alvarez and John Brehm, "Are Americans Ambivalent towards Racial Policies?" *American Journal of Political Science* 41 (1997): 345–74.

22. Attitudes on gun control laws returned to pre-Newtown levels by a year after the shooting. See www.gallup.com/poll/1645/guns.aspx (accessed 11/25/13).

23. Virginia Sapiro, "Not Your Parents' Political Socialization: Introduction for a New Generation," *Annual Review of Political Science* 7 (2004): 1–23.

24. Christopher Achen, "Parental Socialization and Rational Party Identification," *Political Behavior* 24 (2002): 151–70.

25. M. Kent Jennings and Richard G. Niemi, *Generations and Politics: A Panel Study of Young Adults and Their Parents* (Princeton, NJ: Princeton University Press, 1981).

26. J. R. Alford, C. L. Funk, and J. R. Hibbing, "Are Political Orientations Genetically Transmitted?"*American Political Science Review* 99:2 (2005): 153–67.

27. James H. Fowler and Christopher Sawes, "Two Genes Predict Voter Turnout," *Journal of Politics* 70:3 (July 2008): 579–94.

28. Alan S. Gerber, Gregory A. Huber, David Doherty, Conor M. Dowling, and Shang E. Ha, "Personality and Political Attitudes: Relationships across Issue Domains and Political Contexts," *American Political Science Review* 104 (February 2010): 111–33.

29. Robert Putnam, *Bowling Alone: The Collapse and Revival of American Community* (New York: Simon and Schuster, 2000).

30. Richard G. Niemi and Mary Hepburn, "The Rebirth of Political Socialization," *Perspectives on Politics* 24 (1995): 7–16.

31. David Campbell, *Why We Vote: How Schools and Communities Shape Our Civic Life* (Princeton, NJ: Princeton University Press, 2006).

32. Sidney Verba, Kay Schlozman, and Henry Brady, *Voice and Equality: Civic Volunteerism in American Politics* (Cambridge, MA: Harvard University Press, 1995).

33. Paul Allen Beck and M. Kent Jennings, "Pathways to Participation," *American Political Science Review* 76 (1982): 94–108.

34. Fiorina, *Retrospective Voting in American National Elections.*

35. Edward G. Carmines and James A. Stimson, *Issue Evolution: Race and the Transformation of American Politics* (Princeton, NJ: Princeton University Press, 1990).

36. Pew Research Center, "United in Remembrance, Divided over Policies: Ten Years after 9/11," September 1, 2011, www.people-press.org/2011/09/01/united-in-remembrance-divided-over-policies/1/ (accessed 9/5/12).

37. Pew Research Center, "Public More Optimistic about the Economy, but Still Reluctant to Spend," June 19, 2009, www.people-press.org/report/523/economy-spending (accessed 11/4/09).

38. Robert S. Erikson, Michael B. Mackuen, and James A. Stimson, "Macro-partisanship," *American Political Science Review* 83 (1989): 1125–42.

39. John Zaller, *The Nature and Origins of Mass Opinion* (New York: Cambridge University Press, 1992).

40. Frank Baumgartner, Suzanna DeBoef, and Amber Bodston, *The Decline of the Death Penalty and the Discovery of Innocence* (New York: Cambridge University Press, 2008).

41. Richard Nadwau et al., "Class, Party, and South-Nonsouth Differences," *American Politics Research* 32 (2004): 52–67.

42. James H. Kuklinski et al., "Racial Prejudice and Attitudes toward Affirmative Action," *American Journal of Political Science* 41 (1997): 402–19.

43. Donald P. Green, Bradley Palmquist, and Eric Schickler, *Partisan Hearts and Minds* (New Haven, CT: Yale University Press, 2002).

44. Pew Research Center, "Young Voters Supported Obama Less, But May Have Mattered More," November 26, 2012, www.people-press.org/2012/11/26/young-voters-supported-obama-less-but-may-have-mattered-more/ (accessed 3/17/14).

45. For elaboration on this point, see William T. Bianco, Richard G. Niemi, and Harold W. Stanley, "Partisanship and Group Support over Time: A Multivariate Analysis," *American Political Science Review* 80 (September, 1986): 969–76.

46. Arthur Lupia and Mathew D. McCubbins, *The Democratic Dilemma* (New York: Cambridge University Press, 1998).

47. Lawrence R. Jacobs and Robert Y. Shapiro, *Politicians Don't Pander: Political Manipulation and the Loss of Democratic Responsiveness* (Chicago: University of Chicago Press, 2000).

48. Christopher Wlezien and Robert S. Erikson, "The Horse Race: What Polls Reveal as the Election Campaign Unfolds," *International Journal of Public Opinion Research* 19:1 (2007): 74–88.

49. Pollster.com, "IVR and Internet: How Reliable?" September 28, 2006, www.pollster.com/mystery_pollster/ivr_internet_how_reliable.php (accessed 2/21/08).

50. For data on reported and actual turnout, see Chapter 9.

51. Anton J. Nederhof, "Methods of Coping with Social Desirability Bias: A Review," *European Journal of Social Psychology* 15:3 (2006): 263–80.

52. James H. Kuklinski et al., "Misinformation and the Currency of Democratic Citizenship," *Journal of Politics* 62:3 (2000): 790–816.

53. Pew Research Center, "Health Care Reform Closely Followed, Much Discussed," www.people-press.org/reports/pdf/537.pdf (accessed 11/5/09).

54. George H. Bishop, *The Illusion of Public Opinion: Fact and Artifact in Public Opinion Polls* (Washington, D.C.: Rowman & Littlefield, 2004).

55. Michael X. Delli Carpini and Scott Keeter, *What Americans Know about Politics and Why It Matters* (New Haven, CT: Yale University Press, 1997).

56. Delli Carpini and Keeter, *What Americans Know about Politics and Why It Matters.*

57. Morris P. Fiorina, Samuel J. Abrams, and Jeremy C. Pope, *Culture War? The Myth of a Polarized America* (New York: Longman, 2002).

58. For a review of the literature on trust in government, see Karen Cook, Russell Hardin, and Margaret Levi, *Cooperation without Trust* (New York: Russell Sage Foundation, 2005), as well as Marc J. Hetherington, *Why Trust Matters:*

Declining Political Trust and the Demise of American Liberalism (Princeton, NJ: Princeton University Press, 2004).

59. William T. Bianco, *Trust: Representatives and Constituents* (Ann Arbor: University of Michigan Press, 1994).

60. Sean M. Theriault, *The Power of the People: Congressional Competition, Public Attention, and Voter Retribution* (Columbus: Ohio State University Press, 2005).

61. John R. Hibbing and Elizabeth Theiss-Morse, *Congress as Public Enemy: Public Attitudes toward American Political Institutions* (New York: Cambridge University Press, 1995).

62. Thomas Rudolph and Jillian Evans, "Political Trust, Ideology, and Public Support for Government Spending," *American Journal of Political Science* 49 (2005): 660–71.

63. Patricia Moy and Michael Pfau, *With Malice toward All? The Media and Public Confidence in Democratic Institutions* (Boulder, CO: Praeger, 2000).

64. Richard Fenno, *Home Style: U.S. House Members in Their Districts* (Boston: Little, Brown, 1978).

65. William T. Bianco, Daniel Lipinski, and Ryan W. Work, "What Happens when House Members 'Run with Congress'? The Electoral Consequences of Institutional Loyalty," *Legislative Studies Quarterly* 26 (2003): 413–27.

66. Robert S. Erikson, Michael B. MacKuen, and James A. Stimson, *The Macro Polity* (New York: Cambridge University Press, 2002).

67. James A. Stimson, *Public Opinion in America: Moods, Swings, and Cycles* (Boulder, CO: Westview Press, 1999).

68. Robert S. Erikson, Michael B. MacKuen, and James A. Stimson, "American Politics: The Model," unpublished paper, Columbia University, 2000.

69. Robert Kuttner, "The American Health Care System," *New England Journal of Medicine* 340 (1999): 163–68.

70. Pew Research Center, "Support for Health Care Principles, Opposition to Package," October 8, 2009, www.people-press.org/reports/pdf/551.pdf (accessed November 11, 2009).

71. Larry Bartels, "Constituency Opinion and Congressional Policy Making: The Reagan Defense Buildup," *American Political Science Review* 85 (June 1991): 457–74; Jonathan Kastellec, Jeffrey R. Lax, and Justin H. Phillips, "Public Opinion and Senate Confirmation of Supreme Court Nominees," *Journal of Politics* 72 (2010): 767–84.

72. Lawrence R. Jacobs and Robert Y. Shapiro, *Politicians Don't Pander: Political Manipulation and the Loss of Democratic Responsiveness* (Chicago: University of Chicago Press, 2000).

73. Brandice Canes-Wrone, *Who Leads Whom: Presidents, Policy, and the Public* (Chicago: University of Chicago Press, 2005).

CHAPTER 7

1. Jason Barabas, and Jennifer Jerit, "Estimating the Causal Effects of Media Coverage on Policy-Specific Knowledge," *American Journal of Political Sciences* 53 (2008): 73–89.

2. Thomas E. Patterson, *Out of Order* (New York: Alfred A. Knopf, 1993); Robert D. Putnam, *Bowling Alone* (New York: Basic Books, 2000).

3. Thomas Patterson, "Bad News, Period," *Political Science and Politics* 29 (1996): 17–20.

4. Charles E. Clark, *The Public Prints: The Newspaper in Anglo-American Culture, 1665–1740* (New York: Oxford University Press, 1994).

5. William H. Riker, *The Strategy of Rhetoric: Campaigning for the American Constitution* (New Haven, CT: Yale University Press, 1996).

6. Geoffrey R. Stone, *Perilous Times: Free Speech in Wartime from the Sedition Act of 1798 to the War on Terrorism* (New York: W. W. Norton, 2004).

7. John D. Stevens, *Sensationalism and the New York Press* (New York: Columbia University Press, 1991).

8. Michael Schudson, *Discovering the News: A Social History of American Newspapers* (New York: Basic Books, 1978).

9. Robert C. Williams, *Horace Greeley: Champion of American Freedom* (New York: New York University Press, 2006).

10. W. Joseph Campbell, *Yellow Journalism: Puncturing the Myths, Defining the Legacies* (Boulder, CO: Praeger, 2003).

11. Lincoln Steffens, *The Shame of the Cities* (New York: McClure, Phillips, 1904); Upton Sinclair, *The Jungle* (New York: Doubleday, Page, 1906).

12. Gay Talese, *The Kingdom and the Power* (New York: Calder and Boyars, 1983).

13. Timothy Cook, *Freeing the Presses: The First Amendment in Action* (Baton Rouge: Louisiana State University Press, 2005).

14. For a detailed history, see United States Early Radio History, www.earlyradiohistory.us (accessed 9/17/12).

15. This discussion draws on the summary "Merging Media: How Relaxing FCC Ownership Rules Has Affected the Media Business," www.pbs.org/newshour/media/conglomeration/fcc2.html (accessed 2/26/08).

16. Peter Braestrup, *Big Story: How the American Press and Television Reported and Interpreted the Crisis of Tet 1968 in Vietnam* (New Haven, CT: Yale University Press, 1983).

17. For an extended discussion of the fairness doctrine and related issues, see "Fairness Doctrine: U.S. Broadcasting Policy," www.museum.tv/eotvsection.php?entrycode=fairnessdoct (accessed 10/17/12).

18. The Project for Excellence in Journalism, "The State of the News Media, 2007: Ownership" (2007), www.stateofthenewsmedia.org/2007/narrative_overview_ownership.asp?cat=5&media=1 (accessed 2/26/08).

19. The FCC website has details of current regulations as well as the agency's strategic goals. See www.fcc.gov (accessed 10/17/12).

20. The *Columbia Journalism Review* maintains a list of holdings for major media companies at Who Owns What, www.cjr.org/tools/owners (accessed 9/17/12).

21. Joanna Glasner, "Tech a Key in Media Rule Change," *Wired*, June 3, 2003, www.wired.com/techbiz/media/news/2003/06/59079 (accessed 2/26/08).

22. Glasner, "Tech a Key in Media Rule Change."

23. See, for example, James J. Cramer, "Newspapers Still Stumble Online," RealMoney.com, May 2, 2005, www.thestreet.com/p/_rms/rmoney/jamesjcramer/10221101.html (accessed 2/26/08).

24. Paul Starr, "Reclaiming the Air," *American Prospect*, March 2004, pp. 57–61.

25. Danny Hayes, "Obama Is Wrong: Traditional Journalism Isn't Dead," *Washington Post* (Wonkblog), August 4, 2013, www.washingtonpost.com/blogs/wonkblog/wp/2013/08/04/obama-is-wrong-traditional-journalism-isnt-dead (accessed 10/27/14).

26. See www.politico.com/playbook/ (accessed 9/17/12).

27. SCOTUSblog, www.scotusblog.com/ (accessed 9/17/12).

28. See www.themonkeycage.org (accessed 9/17/12).

29. The Center for Responsive Politics, www.opensecrets.org (accessed 9/17/12).

30. Pollster, www.pollster.com (accessed 9/17/12).

31. A. J. Liebling, "Do You Belong in Journalism?" *New Yorker*, May 14, 1960, p. 105.

32. The *Washington Post* has an archive of previous online discussions at "Post Politics Hour," www.washingtonpost.com/wp-dyn/content/discussion/2010/04/02/D72010/040202897.html (accessed 4/2/10).

33. For a skeptical introduction to this argument, see the proceedings of "MeetUp, Craigslist, eBay: Has the Web Changed Politics?" a conference at the Harvard School of Law, December 9–11, 2004, http://cyber.law.harvard.edu/is2k4/home (accessed 9/17/12).

34. Bruce Bimber, "Information and Political Engagement in America: The Search for Effects of Information Technology at the Individual Level," *Political Research Quarterly* 54 (2001): 53–67; Caroline J. Tolbert and Ramona S. McNeal, "Unraveling the Effects of the Internet on Political Participation," *Political Research Quarterly* 56 (2003): 175–85.

35. Pew Research Center, "Public Knowledge of Current Affairs Little Changed by News and Information Revolutions," April 15, 2007, www.people-press.org/reports/display.php3?ReportID = 319 (accessed 2/28/08).

36. Matthew Hindman, *The Myth of Digital Democracy* (Princeton, NJ: Princeton University Press, 2008).

37. Shanto Iyengar and Kyu S. Hahn, "Red Media, Blue Media: Evidence of Ideological Selectivity in Media Use," *Journal of Communication* 59 (2009): 19–39.

38. Eric Lawrence, John Sides, and Henry Farrell, "Self-Segregation or Deliberation? Blog Readership, Participation, and Polarization in American Politics," *Perspectives on Politics* 8 (March 2010): 141–57.

39. Markus Prior, *Post-Broadcast Democracy: How Media Choice Increases Inequality in Political Involvement and Polarizes Elections* (New York: Cambridge University Press, 2007).

40. Barton Gellman, "Code Name 'Verax': Snowden, in Exchanges with *Post* Reporter, Made Clear He Knew Risks," *Washington Post*, June 13, 2012, p. A1.

41. Sharon LaFraniere, "Math behind Leak Crackdown: 153 Cases, 4 Years, 0 Indictments," *New York Times*, July 20, 2013, p. A1.

42. Michael Kelly, "Bing Maps Appear to Show the 'Secret' U.S. Drone Base in Saudi Arabia," February 8, 2013, www.businessinsider.com/wired-finds-americas-drone-base-in-saudi-arabia-2013-2.

43. Lance Bennett, *News: The Politics of Illusion* (New York: Pearson, 2012).

44. Danny Hayes and Matthew Guardino, *Influence from Abroad: Foreign Voices, the Media, and U.S. Public Opinion* (New York: Cambridge University Press, 2013).

45. Samuel Popkin, *The Reasoning Voter* (Chicago: University of Chicago Press, 1991).

46. John Zaller, *The Nature and Origins of Mass Opinion* (New York: Cambridge University Press, 1992).

47. S. H. Chaffee, X. Zhao, and G. Leshner, "Political Knowledge and the Campaign Media of 1992," *Communication Research* 21 (1994): 305–24; Jeffrey J. Mondak, *Nothing to Read: Newspapers and Elections in a Social Experiment* (Ann Arbor: University of Michigan Press, 1995).

48. For a discussion of these concepts, see Paul M. Sniderman and Sean M. Theriault, "The Structure of Political Argument and the Logic of Issue Framing," in *Studies in Public Opinion*, ed. William E. Saris and Paul M. Sniderman (Princeton, NJ: Princeton University Press, 2004); Shanto Iyengar and Donald Kinder, *News That Matters* (Chicago: University of Chicago Press, 1987). See also Maxwell McCombs and Donald L. Shaw, "The Agenda-Setting Functions of Mass Media," *Public Opinion Quarterly* 36 (1972): 176–87; and Amos Tversky and Daniel Kahnemann, "The Framing of Decisions and the Psychology of Choice," *Science* 211 (1981): 453–58.

49. James N. Druckman and Michael Parkin, "The Impact of Media Bias: How Editorial Slant Affects Voters," *Journal of Politics* 67:4 (2005): 1030–49; for similar results, see Kim Fridkin Kahn and Patrick J. Kenney, "The Slant of the News," *American Political Science Review* 96 (2002): 381–94.

50. Jon A. Krosnick and Laura Brannon, "The Impact of the Gulf War on the Ingredients of Presidential Evaluations: Multidimensional Effects of Political Involvement," *American Political Science Review* 87 (1993): 963–75.

51. Jon A. Krosnick and Joanne Miller, "News Media Impact on the Ingredients of Presidential Evaluations: Politically Knowledgeable Citizens Are Guided by a Trusted Source," *American Journal of Political Science* 44 (2000): 295–309.

52. For details on the Project Censored annual list of Top Censored Stories, see www.projectcensored.org/ (accessed 12/27/13).

53. Pew Research Center, "Cable and Internet Loom Large in a Fragmented Political Universe," January 11, 2004, www.people-press.org/reports/display.php3?ReportID=200 (accessed 2/26/08).

54. See Eric Alterman, *What Liberal Media?* (New York: Basic Books, 2003), and Bernard Goldberg, *Bias* (New York: Regnery, 2001).

55. Pew Research Center, "Press Widely Criticized, but Trusted More than Other Information Sources," September 22, 2011, www.people-press.org/2011/09/22/press-widely-criticized-but-trusted-more-than-other-institutions/ (accessed 9/17/12).

56. Eric Wemple, "*Fox & Friends* Fails on Obama–Muslim Museum Connection: No Surprise Here," *Washington Post*, October 7, 2013, www.washingtonpost.com/blogs/erik-wemple/wp/2013/10/07/fox-friends-fails-on-obama-muslim-museum-connection-no-surprise-here/ (accessed 12/26/13).

57. This description runs on the editorial masthead of every issue of the *Nation*.

58. For these and other data, see the Brookings Iraq Index, www.brookings.edu/iraqindex (accessed 9/17/12).

59. Stefano DellaVigna and Ethan Kaplan, "The Fox News Effect: Media Bias and Voting," *Quarterly Journal of Economics* 122 (2007): 1187–1234.

60. Andrew Cline, "Media/Political Bias," *Rhetorica*, June 17, 2008, http://rhetorica.net/bias.htm (accessed 11/02/11).

61. Patterson, "Bad News, Period."

62. Shanto Iyengar, Helmut Norpoth, and Kyu Hahn, "Consumer Demand for Election News: The Horserace Sells," *Journal of Politics* 66 (2004): 157–75.

63. Regina G. Lawrence, "Game Framing: Tracking the Strategic Frame in Public Policy News," *Political Communication* 17 (2000): 19–43.

64. Thomas Patterson, "Doing Well and Doing Good: How Soft News and Critical Journalism Are Shrinking the News Audience and Weakening Democracy—and What News Outlets Can Do about It" (Cambridge, MA: Joan Shorenstein Center on the Press, Politics, and Public Policy, Harvard University, 2000), www.ksg.harvard.edu/presspol/research_publications/reports/softnews.pdf (accessed 2/29/08).

65. Matthew A. Baum, *Soft News Goes to War: Public Opinion and American Foreign Policy in the New Media Age* (Princeton, NJ: Princeton University Press, 2005).

66. Thomas J. Mann and Norman Ornstein, *It's Even Worse Than It Looks: How the American Constitutional System Collided with the New Politics of Extremism* (New York: Basic Books, 2012).

67. T. E. Patterson, *The Vanishing Voter* (New York: Knopf, 2002); J. N. Cappella and K. H. Jamieson, *Spiral of Cynicism: The Press and the Public Good* (New York: Oxford University Press, 1997).

68. Robert McChesney *The Problem of the Media: U.S. Communication Politics in the 21st Century* (New York: Monthly Review Press, 2004).

69. Pippa Norria, *A Virtuous Cycle* (New York: Cambridge University Press, 2003).

70. John R. Hibbing and Elizabeth Theiss-Morse, *Congress as Public Enemy* (New York: Cambridge University Press, 1995); see also John R. Hibbing and Elizabeth Theiss-Morse, "The Media's Role in Public Negativity toward Congress: Distinguishing Emotional Reactions and Cognitive Evaluations," *American Journal of Political Science* 42 (April 1998): 475–98.

You Decide

a. Porter Goss, "Loose Lips Sink Spies," *New York Times*, February 10, 2006, p. 25.

CHAPTER 8

1. John Aldrich, *Why Parties?* (Chicago: University of Chicago Press, 2005).

2. Joseph Schlesinger, *Political Parties and the Winning of Office* (Ann Arbor: University of Michigan Press, 1994).

3. The three-part description first appeared in V. O. Key, *Politics, Parties, and Pressure Groups* (New York: Crowell, 1956). For a more recent description, see Paul Allen Beck and Marjorie Hershey, *Party Politics in America* (New York: Longman, 2004).

4. William Nesbit Chambers and Walter Dean Burnham, *The American Party Systems: Stages of Political Development* (Oxford, UK: Oxford University Press, 1966).

5. Aldrich, *Why Parties?*

6. Donald H. Hickey, "Federalist Party Unity and the War of 1812," *Journal of American Studies* 12 (April 1978): 23–39; William T. Bianco, David B. Spence, and John D. Wilkerson, "The Electoral Connection in the Early Congress: The Case of the Compensation Act of 1816," *American Journal of Political Science* 40 (February, 1996): 145–71.

7. Aldrich, *Why Parties?*

8. James MacPherson, *Battle Cry of Freedom: The Civil War Era* (New York: Oxford University Press, 1988).

9. Michael F. Holt, *The Rise and Fall of the Whig Party: Jacksonian Politics and the Onset of the Civil War* (New York: Oxford University Press, 1999).

10. Raymond Wolfinger, "Why Political Machines Have Not Withered Away and Other Revisionist Thoughts," *Journal of Politics* 34:2 (1972): 365–98.

11. For details on Tammany Hall, see William L. Riordon, *Plunkitt of Tammany Hall* (1905; repr. New York: Dutton, 1963), www.marxists.org/reference/archive/plunkett-george/tammany-hall (accessed 9/17/12).

12. Harold W. Stanley, William T. Bianco, and Richard G. Niemi, "Partisanship and Group Support over Time: A Multivariate Analysis," *American Political Science Review* 80 (1986): 969–76.

13. Frank Baumgartner and Bryan D. Jones, *Agendas and Instability in American Politics* (Chicago: University of Chicago Press, 2009).

14. Aldrich, *Why Parties?*

15. James L. Sundquist, *Dynamics of the Party System*, rev. ed. (Washington, D.C.: Brookings Institution, 1983).

16. John H. Aldrich and Richard G. Niemi, "The Sixth American Party System: Electoral Change, 1952–1992," in *Broken Contract: Changing Relationships between Americans and Their Governments*, ed. Steven Craig (Boulder, CO: Westview Press, 1993).

17. Charles S. Bullock III, Donna R. Hoffman, and Ronald Keith Gaddie, "Regional Variations in the Realignment of American Politics, 1944–2004," *Social Science Quarterly* 87:3 (2006): 494–518.

18. The full list of Democratic constituency groups is available at www.democrats.org/people. A list of Republican coalition groups is available at www.gop.com/coalition-support (accessed 10/18/12).

19. Jon F. Hale, "The Making of the New Democrats," *Political Science Quarterly* 110:2 (1995): 207–32.

20. James Monroe, *The Political Party Matrix* (Albany: SUNY Press, 2001).

21. Gary Cox and Mathew McCubbins, *Legislative Leviathan* (Berkeley: University of California Press, 1993); James M. Snyder and Michael M. Ting, "An Informational Rationale for Political Parties," *American Journal of Political Science* 46 (2002): 90–110.

22. Andrew Rudalevige, "Winner Take All?" *The Monkey Cage*, January 24, 2012, http://themonkeycage.org/2012/01/24/winner-take-all/ (accessed 4/24/14).

23. Jason Roberts and Steven Smith, "Procedural Contexts, Party Strategy, and Conditional Party Government," *American Journal of Political Science* 47:2 (2003): 205–317.

24. David Rohde, *Parties and Leaders in the Post-Reform House* (Chicago: University of Chicago Press, 1991); Keith Poole, "An Update on Polarization through the 113th Congress," *Voteview*, September 8, 2013. http://voteview.com/blog/?p=887 (accessed 4/24/14).

25. Catherine Rampell, "Tax Pledge May Scuttle a Deal on Deficit," *New York Times*, November 18, 2011, p. B1.

26. Donald Green, Bradley Palmquist, and Eric Schickler, *Partisan Hearts and Minds* (New Haven: Yale University Press, 2004); Christopher Achen, "Political Socialization and Rational Party Identification," *Political Behavior* 24:2 (2002): 151–70.

27. Morris Fiorina, *Retrospective Voting in American National Elections* (New Haven: Yale University Press, 1981).

28. Michael Meffert, Helmut Norpoth, and Anirudh V. S. Ruhil, "Realignment and Macropartisanship," *American Political Science Review* 95:4 (2001): 953–62.

29. Walter Dean Burnham, "The Reagan Heritage," in *The Election of 1988: Reports and Interpretations*, ed. Gerald M. Pomper et al. (Chatham, NJ: Chatham House, 1989).

30. Martin P. Wattenberg, *The Decline of American Political Parties: 1952–1994* (Cambridge, MA: Harvard University Press, 1996).

31. David S. Broder, *The Party's Over: The Failure of Partisan Politics in America* (New York: Harper and Row, 1971).

32. Donald P. Green and Bradley Palmquist, "Of Artifacts and Partisan Instability," *American Journal of Political Science* 34:3 (August 1990): 872–902.

33. Warren E. Miller and J. Merrill Shanks, *The New American Voter* (Cambridge, MA: Harvard University Press, 1996); Steven J. Rosenstone and John Mark Hansen, *Mobilization, Participation, and Democracy in America* (New York: Macmillan, 1993).

34. D. Sunshine Hillygus and Simon Jackman, "Voter Decision Making in Election 2000: Campaign Effects, Partisan Activation, and the Clinton Legacy," *American Journal of Political Science* 47 (2003): 583–96.

35. Larry M. Bartels, "Partisanship and Voting Behavior, 1952–1996," *American Journal of Political Science* 44:1 (2000): 35–50.

36. Martin P. Wattenberg, *Where Have All the Voters Gone?* (Cambridge, MA: Harvard University Press, 2002).

37. Jill Lawrence, "Party Recruiters Lead Charge for '06 Vote; Choice of Candidates to Run in Fall May Decide Who Controls the House," *USA Today*, May 25, 2006, p. A5.

38. S. A. Miller, "Recruits for 2010 Put Glee in GOP," *Washington Times*, January 6, 2010, p. A1.

39. Compiled from information available at www.ballot-access.org (accessed 12/17/09).

40. See www.opensecrets.org/parties/index.php, based on data released by the Federal Election Commission on 11/2/12 (accessed 11/2/12).

41. Patricia Zapor, "Pro-Life Democrats Describe Lonely Role, but See Improvements," *Catholic News Service*, July 28, 2004, www.catholicnews.com/data/stories/cns/0404122.htm (accessed 3/27/08).

42. John Geering, *Party Ideologies in America, 1828–1996* (New York: Cambridge University Press, 2001).

43. See www.lp.org/our-history (accessed 9/17/12).

44. Steven J. Rosenstone, Roy L. Behr, and Edward Lazarus, *Third Parties in America: Citizen Response to Major Party Failure* (Princeton: Princeton University Press, 1984).

45. Janet Hook and Peter Wallsten, "GOP Feels Sting of Candidates' Rejection," *Los Angeles Times*, October 10, 2005, p. A1.

46. Gary Cox, *Making Votes Count: Strategic Coordination in the World's Electoral Systems* (Cambridge, UK: Cambridge University Press, 1997).

47. Thomas B. Edsall, "GOP Gains Advantage on Key Issues, Polls Say," *Washington Post*, January 27, 2002, p. A4.

48. John D. McKinnon, "Backing Away from Bush; Some Republican Candidates Avoid Ties with Unpopular President," *Wall Street Journal*, May 23, 2006, p. A4.

You Decide

a. Nelson Polsby, *Consequences of Party Reform* (New York: Oxford University Press, 1983).

b. Daniel A. Smith and Caroline J. Tolbert, *Educated by Initiative: The Effects of Direct Democracy on Citizens and Political Organizations in the American States* (Ann Arbor: University of Michigan Press, 2004).

CHAPTER 9

1. Morris P. Fiorina, *Retrospective Voting in American National Elections* (New Haven, CT: Yale University Press, 1981); V. O. Key, *The Responsible Electorate* (New York: Vintage, 1966).

2. David Mayhew, *Congress: The Electoral Connection* (New Haven, CT: Yale University Press, 1973).

3. For details on early voting, see the Early Voting Information Center site at http://earlyvoting.net/ (accessed 10/19/12).

4. Paul Gronke, "Early Voting Reforms and American Elections," paper presented at the 2004 American Political Science Association Annual Meeting, Chicago, IL. For 2006 data, see Pew Research Center, "Public Cheers Democratic Victory," November 16, 2006, www.people-press.org/reports/display.php3?ReportID=296 (accessed 10/19/12).

5. For details, see the Caltech/MIT Voting Technology Project site at www.vote.caltech.edu (accessed 10/19/12).

6. Randall Stross, "The Big Gamble on Electronic Voting," *New York Times*, September 24, 2006, p. 3.

7. An invaluable source for information on election technology, including reports on the use of touch screens in 2006, is the blog Election Updates written by California Institute of Technology professor Michael Alvarez and others at http://electionupdates.caltech.edu/ (accessed 10/19/12).

8. Jonathan N. Wand, Kenneth W. Shotts, Jasjeet S. Sekhon, Walter R. Mebane, Michael C. Herron, and Henry E. Brady, "The Butterfly Ballot Did It: The Aberrant Vote for Buchanan in Palm Beach County, Florida," *American Political Science Review* 95 (2001): 793–809.

9. Minor party candidates are typically selected during party conventions.

10. Barbara Norrander, "Presidential Nomination Politics in the Post-Reform Era," *Political Research Quarterly* 49 (1996): 875–90.

11. Larry Bartels, *Presidential Primaries and the Dynamics of Public Choice* (Princeton, NJ: Princeton University Press, 1988).

12. William G. Mayer, "Forecasting Presidential Nominations or, My Model Worked Just Fine, Thank You," *Political Science and Politics* 36 (2003): 153–59.

13. Marty Cohen, David Karol, Hans Noel, and John Zaller, "Beating Reform: The Resurgence of Parties in Presidential Nominations, 1980 to 2000," paper presented at the 2001 American Political Science Association Annual Meeting, San Francisco, CA.

14. Richard Herrera, "Are 'Superdelegates' Super?" *Political Behavior* 16 (1994): 79–93.

15. For a discussion of the 2004 conventions, see Kennedy School of Government, *Campaigning for President: The Managers Look at 2004* (New York: Rowman & Littlefield, 2005).

16. FairVote, "Maine and Nebraska," www.fairvote.org/e_college/me_ne.htm (accessed 10/19/12).

17. Robert Bennett, "The Problem of the Faithless Elector," *Northwestern University Law Review* 100 (2004): 121–30.

18. James Q. Wilson, "Is the Electoral College Worth Saving?" *Slate*, November 3, 2000, www.slate.com/id/92663 (accessed 10/19/12).

19. Linda Fowler and Robert McClure, *Political Ambition: Who Decides to Run for Congress* (Ann Arbor: University of Michigan Press, 1989).

20. Robin Kolodny, *Pursuing Majorities: Congressional Campaign Committees in American Politics* (Norman, OK: University of Oklahoma Press, 1999).

21. Steven Ansolabehere and Alan Gerber, "Incumbency Advantage and the Persistence of Legislative Majorities," *Legislative Studies Quarterly* 22 (1997): 161–80.

22. For a discussion of Johnson's decision, see Robert A. Caro, *The Path to Power* (New York: Knopf, 1983).

23. Thomas Mann and Norman Ornstein, *The Permanent Campaign and Its Future* (Washington, D.C.: American Enterprise Institute, 2000).

24. David Mayhew, *Congress: The Electoral Connection* (New Haven, CT: Yale University Press, 1973).

25. Henry Chappell and William Keech, "A New Model of Political Accountability for Economic Performance," *American Political Science Review* 79 (1985): 10–19.

26. Jonathan Krasno and Donald P. Green, "The Dynamics of Campaign Fundraising in House Elections," *Journal of Politics* 56 (1991): 459–74.

27. Michael J. Goff, *The Money Primary: The New Politics of the Early Presidential Nomination Process* (New York: Rowman & Littlefield, 2007).

28. Chris Cillizza, "Consulting Firms Face Conflict in 2008," *Roll Call*, June 20, 2005, p. 1.

29. For details, see Committee on Standards of Official Conduct, "Laws, Rules, and Standards of Conduct Governing Campaign Activity," memorandum April 25, 2008, http://ethics.house.gov/sites/ethics.house.gov/files/m_campaign_activity_2008_0.pdf (accessed 11/6/12).

30. Cherie Maestas, Walter Stone, and L. Sandy Maisel, "Quality Counts: Extending the Strategic Politician Model of Incumbent Deterrence," *American Journal of Political Science* 48 (2004): 479–90.

31. Matt Bai, "Turnout Wins Elections," *New York Times Magazine*, December 14, 2003, p. 100.

32. Christopher Drew, "New Telemarketing Ploy Steers Voters on Republican Path," *New York Times*, November 6, 2006.

33. Donald Green and Alan Gerber, "The Effects of Canvassing, Phone Calls, and Direct Mail on Voter Turnout: A Field Experiment," *American Political Science Review* 94 (2000): 653–69; Lynn Vavreck, Constantine J. Spiliotes, and Linda L. Fowler, "The Effect of Retail Politics in the New Hampshire Primary," *American Journal of Political Science* 46 (2002): 595–610.

34. John Dickerson, "Weak Poll," *Slate*, October 30, 2006, www.slate.com/id/2152529 (accessed 10/19/12).

35. For a history of presidential debates, see the Commission on Presidential Debates site at www.debates.org (accessed 10/19/12).

36. For details, see "Was Wendy Davis a Bad Mother Because Her Husband Contributed a Lot of Childcare?" January 28, 2014, www.slate.com/blogs/xx_factor/2014/01/28/was_wendy_davis_a_bad_mother_because_her_husband_contributed_a_lot_of_childcare.html (accessed 3/9/14).

37. Jim Rutenberg and Ashley Parker, "Romney Says Remarks on Voters Help Clarify Position," *New York Times*, September 9, 2012, p. A1.

38. John Arit, "Tea Party Message: Vote or Risk Death," *Bloomberg Politics*, October 26, 2014, www.bloomberg.com/politics/articles/2014-10-26/tea-party-message-vote-or-risk-death (accessed 11/5/14).

39. For a video library of presidential campaign ads, see Museum of the Moving Image, "The Living Room Candidate: Presidential Campaign Commercials 1952–2012," http://livingroomcandidate.org (accessed 10/19/12).

40. Museum of the Moving Image, "The Living Room Candidate: 1964: Johnson vs. Goldwater," http://livingroomcandidate.org/commercials/1964/dowager (accessed 10/19/12).

41. Museum of the Moving Image, "The Living Room Candidate: 1964: Johnson vs. Goldwater."

42. For examples of this argument, see Thomas Patterson, *The Vanishing Voter* (New York: Knopf, 2002), and Jules Witcover, *No Way to Pick a President: How Money and Hired Guns Have Debased American Politics* (London: Routledge, 2001).

43. For examples of these and other campaign ads, see "Most Intriguing Campaign Ads of 2010," ABC News, http://abcnews.go.com/politics/slideshow/intriguing-political-ads-2010-10887147 (accessed 10/19/12).

44. Paul Freeman, Michael Franz, and Kenneth Goldstein, "Campaign Advertising and Democratic Citizenship," *American Journal of Political Science* 48 (2004): 723–41.

45. Constantine J. Spilotes and Lynn Vavreck, "Campaign Advertising: Partisan Convergence or Divergence?" *Journal of Politics* 64 (2002): 249–61.

46. Kathleen Hall Jameson, *Packaging the Presidency: A History and Criticism of Presidential Campaign Advertising* (New York: Oxford University Press, 1996).

47. Steven Ansolabehere and Shanto Iyengar, *Going Negative: How Political Advertisements Shrink and Polarize the Electorate* (New York: Free Press, 1997); Richard Lau, Lee Sigelman, Caroline Heldman, and Paul Babbitt, "The Effects of Negative Political Advertisements: A Meta-Analytic Analysis," *American Political Science Review* 93 (1999): 851–70.

48. Jonathan Krasno and Frank J. Sorauf, "For the Defense," *Political Science and Politics* 37 (2004): 777–80.

49. Contribution and spending data are available from the Center for Responsive Politics at www.opensecrets.org.

50. Brian Stelter, "The Price of 30 Seconds," *New York Times*, October 1, 2007, http://mediadecoder.blogs.nytimes.com/2007/10/01/the-price-of-30-seconds (accessed 10/19/12).

51. For a review of this literature, see Michael Malbin, *The Election after Reform: Money, Politics, and the Bipartisan Campaign Reform Act* (Washington, D.C.: Rowman & Littlefield, 2006).

52. For a discussion, see Patterson, *The Vanishing Voter*, especially Chapter 1, "The Incredible Shrinking Electorate," pp. 3–22.

53. William H. Riker and Peter Ordeshook, "A Theory of the Calculus of Voting," *American Political Science Review* 62 (1968): 25–39.

54. Michael McDonald, The United States Elections Project, http://elections.gmu.edu (accessed 10/19/12).

55. Pew Research Center, "Regular Voters, Intermittent Voters, and Those Who Don't," October 18, 2006, available at www.people-press.org/reports/pdf/292.pdf.

56. For a review of the literature on issue voters, see Jon K. Dalager, "Voters, Issues, and Elections: Are Candidates' Messages Getting Through?" *Journal of Politics* 58 (1996): 486–515.

57. Richard P. Lau and David P. Reslawsk, *How Voters Decide: Information Processing during Electoral Campaigns* (New York: Cambridge University Press, 2006).

58. Gary Cox and Jonathan Katz, "Why Did the Incumbency Advantage in U.S. House Elections Grow?" *American Journal of Political Science* 40 (1996): 478–96.

59. Charles Franklin, "Eschewing Obfuscation: Campaigns and the Perceptions of U.S. Senate Incumbents," *American Political Science Review* 85 (December 1991): 1193–214; Wendy M. Rahn, "The Role of Partisan Stereotypes in Information Processing about Political Candidates," *American Journal of Political Science* 37 (May 1993): 472–96.

60. Bruce Cain, John Ferejohn, and Morris Fiorina, *The Personal Vote* (Cambridge, MA: Harvard University Press, 1985).

61. Jeffrey Koch, "Gender Stereotypes and Citizens' Impressions of House Candidates' Ideological Orientations," *American Journal of Political Science* 46 (2002): 453–62; Monica McDermott, "Candidate Occupations and Voter

Information," *Journal of Politics* 67 (2005): 201–18; Carol Sigelman, Lee Sigelman, Barbara Walkosz, and Michael Nitz, "Black Candidates, White Voters: Understanding Racial Bias in Political Perceptions," *American Journal of Political Science* 39 (February 1995): 243–65.

62. Fiorina, *Retrospective Voting in American National Elections*; Key, *The Responsible Electorate*.

63. Alfred J. Tuchfarber, Stephen E. Bennett, Andrew E. Smith, and Eric W. Rademacher, "The Republican Tidal Wave of 1994: Testing Hypotheses about Realignment, Restructuring, and Rebellion," *Political Science and Politics* 28 (1995): 689–93.

64. Samuel Popkin, *The Reasoning Voter* (Chicago: University of Chicago Press, 1991).

65. Richard R. Lau and David P. Redlawsk, "Advantages and Disadvantages of Cognitive Heuristics in Political Decision Making," *American Journal of Political Science* 45 (2001): 951–71.

66. For 2006 exit poll data, see Pew Research Center, "Public Cheers Democratic Victory," November 16, 2006, www.people-press.org/reports/display.php3?ReportID=296 (accessed 10/19/12).

67. For data on presidential approval and evaluations of Congress in normal and nationalized elections, see Pew Research Center, "Democrats Hold Double-Digit Lead in Competitive Districts," October 6, 2006, www.people-press.org/reports/display.php3?ReportID=293 (accessed 3/31/08).

CHAPTER 10

1. Robert A. Dahl, *A Preface to Democratic Theory* (Chicago: University of Chicago Press, 1951); David Truman, *The Governmental Process* (New York: Harper and Row, 1951).

2. Theodore Lowi, *The End of Liberalism: The Second Republic of the United States* (New York: W. W. Norton, 1979).

3. Lobbying regulations are often changed; the discussion here is just a general guide. Regular reports on past, current, and proposed lobbying regulations can be found on the website of the Congressional Research Service at www.opencrs.com (accessed 9/19/12).

4. Frank Baumgartner and Beth Leech, *Basic Interests: The Importance of Interest Groups in Politics and in Political Science* (Princeton, NJ: Princeton University Press, 1999), p. 109.

5. Beth L. Leech, Frank R. Baumgartner, Timothy M. La Pira, and Nicholas A. Semanko, "Drawing Lobbyists to Washington: Government Activity and the Demand for Advocacy," *Political Research Quarterly* 58: 1 (March 2005): 19–30.

6. Frances Cairncross, *The Death of Distance: How the Communication Revolution Is Changing Our Lives* (Cambridge, MA: Harvard Business School Press, 2001).

7. Roxana Tiron, "Lockheed Martin Leads Expanded Lobbying by US Defense Industry," *Washington Post,* January 26, 2012, www.washingtonpost.com/business/economy/lockheed-martin-leads-expanded-lobbying-by-us-defense-industry/2012/01/26/gIQAlgQtaQ_story.html (accessed 2/4/14).

8. For details, see www.opensecrets.org/lobby/clientsum.php?id=D000000125&year=2013 (accessed 1/31/14).

9. For details, see www.opensecrets.org/lobby/clientsum.php?id=D000000259&year=2013 (accessed 2/4/14.

10. For more on this argument, see Tim Harford, "There's Not Enough Money in Politics," *Slate*, April 1, 2006, www.slate.com/id/2138874 (accessed 4/8/08); Stephen Ansolabehere, John M. de Figueiredo, and James M. Snyder, "Why Is There So Little Money in American Politics?" *Journal of Economic Perspectives* 17 (2003): 105–30.

11. John R. Wright, *Interest Groups and Congress: Lobbying, Contributions, and Influence* (New York: Longman, 1995).

12. Scott Ainsworth, *Analyzing Interest Groups: Group Influence on People and Policies* (New York: W. W. Norton, 2002).

13. Timothy Egan, "For Thirsty Farmers, Old Friends at Interior," *New York Times*, March 3, 2006, p. A1.

14. Lee Drutman and Alexander Furnas, "K Street Pays Top Dollar for Revolving Door Talent," January 21, 2014, http://sunlightfoundation.com/blog/2014/01/21/revolving-door-lobbyists-government-experience/ (accessed 2/4/14).

15. Jacob Weisberg, "A Tale of Two Lobbyists," April 19, 2009, www.slate.com/id/2216433/ (accessed 9/19/12).

16. Robert H. Salisbury, John P. Heinz, Edward O. Laumann, and Robert L. Nelson, "Who Works with Whom? Interest Group Alliances and Opposition," *American Political Science Review* 81 (1987): 1217–34.

17. Business–Industry Political Action Committee, "About BIPAC," www.bipac.org/about/about.asp (accessed 4/8/08).

18. One example campaign is MoveOn.org Political Action Committee, "Letter to the Editor: Tell the Media: We Want to End the War. The President Wants Endless War," http://pol.moveon.org/lte/?lte_campaign_id=72 (accessed 4/8/08).

19. Thomas Holyoke, "Choosing Battlegrounds: Interest Group Lobbying across Multiple Venues," *Political Science Quarterly* 56 (2003): 325–36.

20. Scott Ainsworth, "Regulating Lobbyists and Interest Group Influence," *Journal of Politics* 55 (1993): 41–55.

21 AARP, "Policy and Research for Professionals in Aging," www.aarp.org/research/ppi (accessed 4/8/08).

22. James Q. Wilson, *Political Organizations* (New York: Basic Books, 1974).

23. American Automobile Association, Foundation for Traffic Safety, www.aaafoundation.org/home (accessed 4/8/08).

24. Kenneth Kollman, *Outside Lobbying: Public Opinion and Interest Group Strategies* (Princeton, NJ: Princeton University Press, 1998).

25. Jack Walker, *Mobilizing Interest Groups in America* (Ann Arbor: University of Michigan Press, 1991).

26. John P. Heinz, Edward O. Laumann, and Robert Salisbury, *The Hollow Core: Private Interests in National Policymaking* (Cambridge, MA: Harvard University Press, 1993).

27. Richard L. Hall and Alan V. Deardorff, "Lobbying as Legislative Subsidy," *American Political Science Review* 100 (2006): 69–84.

28. Hall and Deardorff, "Lobbying as Legislative Subsidy."

29. David Austen-Smith and John R. Wright, "Counteractive Lobbying," *American Journal of Political Science* 38:1 (1994): 25–44.

30. Key Lehman Schlozman and John T. Tierney, *Organized Interests and American Democracy* (New York: HarperCollins, 1986).

31. Baumgartner and Leech, *Basic Interests*, p. 152.

32. Christine A. DeGregorio, *Networks of Champions: Leadership, Access, and Advocacy in the U.S. House of Representatives* (Ann Arbor: University of Michigan Press, 1992).

33. Daniel Carpenter, *The Forging of Bureaucratic Autonomy: Reputations, Networks, and Policy Innovation in Executive Agencies, 1862–1928* (Princeton, NJ: Princeton University Press, 2002).

34. Public Citizen Publications, www.citizen.org/publications (accessed 7/25/09).

35. Derived from a search of the NRA Institute for Legislative Action site, www.nraila.org (accessed 9/19/12).

36. Kim Scheppele and Jack L. Walker, "The Litigation Strategies of Interest Groups," in *Mobilizing Interest Groups in America*, ed. Jack Walker (Ann Arbor: University of Michigan Press, 1991).

37. Lauren Cohen Bell, *Warring Factions: Interest Groups, Money, and the New Politics of Senate Confirmation* (Columbus: Ohio State University Press, 2002).

38. Kevin W. Hula, *Lobbying Together: Interest Group Coalitions in Legislative Politics* (Washington, D.C.: Georgetown University Press, 1999).

39. Jeanne Cummings, "Word Games Could Threaten Climate Bill," June 9, 2009, www.politico.com/news/stories/0609/24059.html (accessed 9/19/12).

40. AARP, "Elected Officials," http://capwiz.com/aarp/dbq/officials (accessed 4/8/08).

41. Manny Fernandez, "Gun Sentiments and Guns on Display at Alamo Rally," *New York Times*, October 29, 2013, p. A23.

42. Richard Fenno, *Home Style: U.S. House Members in Their Districts* (Boston: Little, Brown, 1978). See also Brandice Caines-Wrone, David W. Brady, and John F. Cogan, "Out of Step, Out of Office: Electoral Accountability and House Members' Voting," *American Political Science Review* 96 (2002): 127–40.

43. Emily Yoffe, "Am I the Next Jack Abramoff?" April 1, 2006, www.slate.com/id/2137886/ (accessed 8/28/09).

44. Kollman, *Outside Lobbying*.

45. Gregory Calderia, Marie Hojnacki, and John R. Wright, "The Lobbying Activities of Organized Interests in Federal Judicial Nominations," *Journal of Politics* 62 (2000): 51–69.

46. Calculated by author from data at www.opensecrets.org/527s (accessed 11/4/14).

47. *Citizens United v. Federal Election Commission*, 558 U.S. 310 (2010).

48. John R. Wright, "PAC Contributions, Lobbying, and Representation," *Journal of Politics* 51:3 (August 1989): 713–29.

49. John G. Matsusaka, "Direct Democracy and Fiscal Gridlock: Have Voter Initiatives Paralyzed the California Budget?" *State Politics and Policy* 5 (2005): 346–62.

50. Thad Kousser, *Term Limits and the Dismantling of State Legislative Professionalism* (New York: Cambridge University Press, 2004).

51. John G. Matsusaka, *For the Many or the Few: The Initiative, Public Policy, and American Democracy* (Chicago: University of Chicago Press, 2004).

52. Elizabeth R. Gerber, *The Populist Paradox: Interest Group Influence and the Promise of Direct Legislation* (Princeton, NJ: Princeton University Press, 1999).

53. Baumgartner and Leech, *Basic Interests*, Chapter 8, pp. 147–67.

54. Information taken from Humane Society 2012 Annual Report, www.humanesociety.org/about/overview/annual_reports_financial_statements.html#.Uu_SsHddVmk (accessed 2/3/14).

55. Hayley Tsukayama, "Companies Taking a Stand against Piracy Caught in SOPA Crosshairs." *Washington Post*, January 13, 2011, p. B1.

56. For the full text, see www.demos.org/stacked-deck-how-dominance-politics-affluent-business-undermines-economic-mobility-america (accessed 2/3/13).

57. For a review, see Carpenter, *The Forging of Bureaucratic Autonomy*.

58. Marie Hojnacki, David C. Kimball, Frank R. Baumgartner, Jeffrey M. Berry, and Beth L. Leech, "Studying Organizational Advocacy and Influence: Reexamining Interest Group Research," *Annual Review of Political Science* 15 (2012): 379–99.

59. Frank Baumgartner, Jeffrey M. Berry, Marie Hojnacki, David C. Kimball, and Beth L. Leech, *Lobbying and Policy Change: Who Wins, Who Loses, and Why* (Chicago: University of Chicago Press, 2009).

60. National Rifle Association Institute for Legislative Action, "Fact Sheet: Right-to-Carry 2007," www.nraila.org/Issues/FactSheets/Read.aspx?ID=18 (accessed 4/9/08).

61. National Rifle Association Institute for Legislative Action, "Fact Sheet: Right-to-Carry: The Stearns/Boucher Right-to-Carry Reciprocity Bill," www.nraila.org/Issues/FactSheets/Read.aspx?id=189&issue=003 (accessed 4/9/08).

62. David Lowery, "Why Do Organized Interests Lobby? A Multi-Goal, Multi-Context Theory of Lobbying," *Polity* 39 (2007): 29–54.

63. John M. Berry, *The Interest Group Society* (New York: Harper Collins, 1997); Raymond A. Bauer, Ithiel de Sola Pool, and Lewis Dexter, *American Business and Public Policy* (New York: Atherton Press, 1963).

64. Ken Kollman, *Outside Lobbying* (Princeton, NJ: Princeton University Press, 1998).

65. Frank Baumgartner and Beth Leech, "Interest Niches and Policy Bandwagons: Patterns of Interest Group Involvement in National Politics," *Journal of Politics* 63 (2001): 1191–213.

66. Austen-Smith and Wright, "Counteractive Lobbying"; Frank R. Baumgartner and Beth L. Leech, "The Multiple Ambiguities of 'Counteractive Lobbying,'" *American Journal of Political Science* 40 (1996): 521–42.

You Decide

a. Jacob Weisberg, "Three Cities, Three Scandals: What Jack Abramoff, Anthony Pellicano, and Jared Paul Stern Have in Common," *Slate*, April 9, 2006, www.slate.com/id/2140238 (accessed 10/25/12).

CHAPTER 11

1. Ramsey Cox and Jeremy Herb, "Senate Approves McCaskill Sexual Assault Bill in 97-0 Vote," *The Hill*, March 10, 2014, http://thehill.com/blogs/floor-action/senate/200393-senate-votes-97-0-for-military-sexual-assault-bill#ixzz2yaauKflt (accessed 4/9/14).

2. Lisa Mascaro, "Senate Rejects Gillibrand Bill on Sexual Assaults in Military," *Los Angeles Times*, March 6, 2014, http://articles.latimes.com/2014/mar/06/news/la-pn-military-sexual-assualt-20140306 (accessed 6/6/14).

3. "Department of Defense Annual Report on Sexual Assault in the Military, Fiscal Year 2012," Vol. 1, May 3, 2013, www.sapr.mil/public/docs/reports/FY12_DoD_SAPRO_Annual_Report_on_Sexual_Assault-VOLUME_ONE.pdf (accessed 4/9/14).

4. Ed O'Keefe, "How Kirsten Gillibrand Won by Losing," *Washington Post*, March 6, 2014, www.washingtonpost.com/blogs/the-fix/wp/2014/03/06/how-kirsten-gillibrand-won-by-losing/ (accessed 4/9/14).

5. See Paul Gronke, *The Electorate, the Campaign, and the Office: A Unified Approach to Senate and House Elections* (Ann Arbor, MI: University of Michigan Press, 2000), for research showing that the House and Senate elections share many similar characteristics. See Richard F. Fenno, *Senators on the Campaign Trail: The Politics of Representation* (Norman, OK: University of Oklahoma Press, 1996), for a good general discussion of Senate elections.

6. Claudine Gay, "Spirals of Trust? The Effect of Descriptive Representation on the Relationship between Citizens and Their Government," *American Journal of Political Science* 46:4 (October 2002): 717–32; Katherine Tate, *Black Faces in the Mirror: African Americans and Their Representatives in Congress* (Princeton, NJ: Princeton University Press, 2003), Chapter 7. However, Tate shows that African Americans who are represented by African Americans in Congress are not any more likely to vote, be involved in politics, or have higher overall approval rates of Congress than African Americans who are not descriptively represented.

7. In addition to those mentioned in the text, there were two other African Americans who were elected by state legislatures to serve in the Senate during the Reconstruction period. And in more-recent times, there was an African American, Roland Burris (D-IL), who was appointed to serve the remainder of Senator Barack Obama's term.

8. R. Douglas Arnold, *The Logic of Congressional Action* (New Haven, CT: Yale University Press, 1990), pp. 60–71.

9. Richard F. Fenno, *Home Style: House Members in Their Districts* (Boston: Little, Brown, 1978).

10. David R. Mayhew, *Congress: The Electoral Connection* (New Haven, CT: Yale University Press, 1974).

11. Mayhew, *Congress*, p. 17.

12. Mayhew, *Congress*, p. 37.

13. Patrick J. Sellers, "Fiscal Consistency and Federal District Spending in Congressional Elections," *American Journal of Political Science* 41:3 (July 1997): 1024–41.

14. Sean Trende, "In Pennsylvania, the Gerrymander of the Decade? Real Clear Politics, December 14, 2011, www.realclearpolitics.com/articles/2011/12/14/in_pennsylvania_the_gerrymander_of_the_decade_112404.html (accessed 12/20/11); Dennis Byrne, "GOP Can't Catch a Break on Fairness, *Chicago Tribune*, December 20, 2011, www.chicagotribune.com/news/opinion/ct-oped-1220-byrne-20111220,0,7120320.column (accessed 12/20/11).

15. Dan Eggen, "Justice Staff Saw Texas Districting as Illegal: Voting Rights Finding on Map Pushed by DeLay Was Overruled," *Washington Post*, December 2, 2005, p. A1. The case is *League of United Latin American Citizens v. Perry*, 548 U.S. 399 (2006).

16. *Shelby County v. Holder*, 570 U.S. ___ (2013).

17. CBS News/*New York Times* Poll, April 24–28, 2013, www.pollingreport.com/congress.htm#misc (accessed 4/11/14).

18. ABC News/*Washington Post* Poll, October 17–20, 2013, www.pollingreport.com/congress.htm#misc (accessed 4/11/14).

19. All poll data except the poll comparing Congress to other occupations are from PollingReport.com (www.pollingreport.com). The occupations poll was cited in Karlyn Bowman and Everett Carll Ladd, "Public Opinion toward Congress: A Historical Look," in *Congress, the Press, and the Public*, ed. Thomas E. Mann and Norman J. Ornstein (Washington, D.C.: Brookings Institution Press, 1994), p. 50.

20. "Congress Less Popular Than Cockroaches, Traffic Jams," Public Policy Polling, January 8, 2013, www

.publicpolicypolling.com/pdf/2011/PPP_Release_ Natl_010813_.pdf (accessed 4/11/14).

21. "Check bouncing" is in quotes because the checks did not actually bounce. The scandal involved penalty-free overdrafts permitted in members' accounts in the House bank (which allowed some members to abuse the privilege by using the overdrafts as short-term, interest-free loans). Many voters saw this as another unfair benefit to members of Congress, but others considered it a non-scandal because no taxpayers' money was at stake.

22. Wesley Lowery, "We Read the Michael Grimm Indictment So You Don't Have To," *Washington Post*, April 28, 2014, www.washingtonpost.com/blogs/the-fix/wp/2014/04/28/ we-read-the-michael-grimm-indictment-so-you-dont-have -to/ (accessed 6/6/14).

23. Mark J. Rozell, "Press Coverage of Congress, 1946–1992," in *Congress, the Press, and the Public*, ed. Thomas E. Mann and Norman J. Ornstein (Washington, D.C.: Brookings Institution Press, 1994), p. 110.

24. Burdett A. Loomis, *The Contemporary Congress* (Belmont, CA: Wadsworth, 2000), p. 47.

25. R. Douglas Arnold, *Congress, the Press, and Political Accountability* (Princeton, NJ: Princeton University Press, 2004), p. 80.

26. See Kenneth R. Mayer and David T. Canon, *The Dysfunctional Congress: The Individual Roots of an Institutional Dilemma*, 2nd ed. (New York: Columbia University Press, 2011), for an extended discussion of this argument.

27. Richard F. Fenno, "If as Ralph Nader Says, Congress Is the 'Broken Branch,' How Come We Love Our Congressman So Much?" in *Congress in Change: Evolution and Reform*, ed. Norman J. Ornstein (New York: Praeger, 1975), pp. 277–87.

28. David T. Canon, "History in the Making: The 2nd District in Wisconsin," in *The Battle for Congress: Candidates, Consultants, and Voters*, ed. James A. Thurber (Washington, D.C.: Brookings Institution Press, 2001), pp. 199–238.

29. Gary C. Jacobson, *The Politics of Congressional Elections*, 5th ed. (New York: Longman, 2001), pp. 24–30.

30. Fenno, *Home Style*.

31. Morris Fiorina, *Congress: Keystone of the Washington Establishment*, rev. ed. (New Haven, CT: Yale University Press, 1989).

32. Felicia Sonmez and Joby Warrick, "Congress Sends Defense Bill to Obama after Reworking Detainee Provisions," *Washington Post*, December 15, 2011.

33. Paul Blumenthal and Christina Wilke, "Omnibus Budget Proves That Earmarks Will Never Die in Congress," January 15, 2014, Huffington Post, www.huffingtonpost .com/2014/01/15/omnibus-budget-earmarks_n_4603141 .html (accessed 4/16/14).

34. Jonathan Weisman and Jim VandeHei, "Road Bill Reflects the Power of Pork; White House Drops Effort to Rein in Hill," *Washington Post*, August 11, 2005, p. A1.

35. An important qualification to the norm was imposed by Republicans in 1995 when they set a six-year term limit for committee and subcommittee chairs.

36. David W. Rohde, *Parties and Leaders in the Post-reform House* (Chicago: University of Chicago Press, 1991).

37. David Rohde and John Aldrich, "The Transition to Republican Rule in the House: Implications for Theories of Congressional Politics," *Political Science Quarterly* 112:4 (Winter 1997–1998): 541–67.

38. Nelson W. Polsby, *Congress and the Presidency*, 4th ed. (Englewood Cliffs, NJ: Prentice Hall, 1986), p. 111.

39. Paul Steinhauser, "Obama 2014 Campaign Role: Fundraiser-in-Chief," CNN Politics, March 20, 2014, http://politicalticker .blogs.cnn.com/2014/03/20/obama-2014-campaign-role -fundraiser-in-chief/ (accessed 4/16/14).

40. Matt Fuller and Emma Dumain, "Breaking Down the Debt Ceiling Vote, *Roll Call*, February 11, 2014, http://blogs .rollcall.com/218/breaking-down-the-debt-ceiling-vote/ (accessed 4/17/14).

41. Keith Krehbiel, *Information and Legislative Organization* (Ann Arbor, MI: University of Michigan Press, 1992).

42. Richard F. Fenno, *Congressmen in Committees* (Boston: Little, Brown, 1973).

43. Richard L. Hall, *Participation in Congress* (New Haven, CT: Yale University Press, 1996).

44. Barbara Sinclair, *Unorthodox Lawmaking* (Washington, D.C.: CQ Press, 2000), p. xiv.

45. Edward Epstein, "Dusting Off Deliberation," *CQ Weekly*, June 14, 2010, p. 1434–42.

46. Kenneth Chamberlain, "Government Shutdown Scares through the Years," *National Journal*, December 14, 2011, www.nationaljournal.com/congress/government-shutdown -scares-through-the-years-20111214 (accessed 12/19/11).

47. Dafne Eviatar, "Patriot Act Renewal Kicks Off over Party Lines," *Washington Independent*, September 23, 2009, http://washingtonindependent.com/60575/debate-over -patriot-act-renewal-kicks-off-over-party-lines (accessed 12/19/11).

48. Congressional Record, 46th Congress, 2nd session, April 22, 1880, p. 2661.

49. Howard H. Baker, Jr., "Leaders Lecture Series Address to the Senate," July 14, 1998, www.senate.gov/artandhistory/ history/common/generic/Leaders_Lecture_Series_Baker .htm (accessed 5/7/08).

50 Paul Kane, "Reid, Democrats Trigger 'Nuclear' Option; Eliminate Most Filibusters on Nominees," *Washington Post*, November 21, 2013, www.washingtonpost.com/ politics/senate-poised-to-limit-filibusters-in-party-line -vote-that-would-alter-centuries-of-precedent/2013/11/ 21/d065cfe8-52b6-11e3-9fe0-fd2ca728e67c_story .html (accessed 6/6/14).

51. CNN Wire Staff, "Holder to Critics: Have You No Shame?" December 8, 2011, http://articles.cnn.com/2011-12-08/

politics/politics_congress-fast-and-furious_1_operation
-fast-and-furious-darrell-issa-gop-critics?_s=PM:
POLITICS (accessed 12/19/11).

52. Mathew McCubbins and Thomas Schwartz, "Congressional
Oversight Overlooked: Police Patrol versus Fire Alarm,"
American Journal of Political Science 28:1 (February 1984):
165–77.

53. Richard Simon, Christi Parsons, Michael A. Memoli,
"VA Chief and White House Spokesman Resign, Fueling
Unease," *Los Angeles Times*, May 30, 2014, www.latimes
.com/nation/la-na-shinseki-20140531-story.html#page=1
(accessed 6/6/14).

You Decide

a. This figure comes from a report by the Citizens against Government Waste, "Pork Alert: Defense Conference Report
Loaded with Earmarks," www.cagw.org/newroom/releases/
2009/pork-alert-defense.html (accessed 1/6/10). A lower
figure of $4 billion in earmarks was reported in John D.
McKinnon and Brody Mullins, "Defense Bill Earmarks Total
$4 Billion," *Wall Street Journal*, December 23, 2009, p. A1.

b. Blumenthal and Wilke, "Omnibus Budget Proves That
Earmarks Will Never Die in Congress," January 15, 2014,
Huffington Post, www.huffingtonpost.com/2014/01/15/
omnibus-budget-earmarks_n_4603141.html (accessed
4/16/14).

c. Alex Altman, "Congress Feasts on Vegan Pork Despite Ear-
mark Ban," *Time*, January 16, 2014, http://swampland.time
.com/2014/01/16/congress-feasts-on-vegan-pork-despite
-earmark-ban/ (accessed 4/16/14).

CHAPTER 12

1. John Aldrich, *Why Parties?* (Chicago: University of Chicago
Press, 1995).

2. Ernest R. May, *The Making of the Monroe Doctrine* (Cambridge,
MA: Harvard University Press, 1975).

3. Arthur M. Schlesinger Jr., *The Age of Jackson* (Boston:
Little, Brown, 1945).

4. David Greenberg, "Lincoln's Crackdown," *Slate*, November
30, 2001, www.slate.com/id/2059132 (accessed 4/29/08).

5. Steven Skowronek, *Building a New American State: The
Expansion of National Administrative Capacities* (New
York: Cambridge University Press, 1982).

6. Theda Skocpol, *Protecting Soldiers and Mothers: The
Political Origins of Social Policy in the United States*
(Cambridge, MA: Harvard University Press, 1995).

7. Kendrick Clements, *The Presidency of Woodrow Wilson*
(Lawrence, KS: University Press of Kansas, 1992).

8. Thomas J. Knock, *To End All Wars: Woodrow Wilson and
the Quest for a New World Order* (New York: Oxford University Press, 1992).

9. William E. Leuchtenburg, *FDR Years: On Roosevelt and His
Legacy* (New York: Columbia University Press, 1995).

10. Chester Pach and Elmo Richardson, *The Presidency of
Dwight D. Eisenhower* (Lawrence, KS: University Press of
Kansas, 1991).

11. Sarah Kliff, "The White House Keeps Changing Obamacare.
Is That Legal?" *Washington Post*, August 7, 2013, www
.washingtonpost.com/blogs/wonkblog/wp/2013/08/07/
the-white-house-keeps-changing-obamacare-is-that
-legal/ (accessed 4/28/14).

12. Peter Baker, "Obama Signs Measures to Help Close
Gender Gap in Pay," *New York Times*. April 8, 2014, www
.nytimes.com/2014/04/09/us/politics/obama-signs
-measures-to-help-close-gender-gap-in-pay.html?_r=0
(accessed 4/28/14).

13. Thomas J. Weko, *The Politicizing Presidency: The White
House Personnel Office, 1948–1994* (Lawrence, KS: University Press of Kansas, 1995).

14. Wesley Lowery and Ed O'Keefe, "Senate Rejects Obama
Appointment of Debo Adegbile to Top Civil Rights Post,"
Washington Post. March 5, 2014, www.washingtonpost
.com/blogs/post-politics/wp/2014/03/05/senate-rejects
-obama-appointment-of-debo-adegbile-to-top-civil
-rights-post/ (accessed 4/28/14).

15. Kenneth Mayer, *With the Stroke of a Pen: Executive Orders
and Presidential Power* (Princeton, NJ: Princeton University Press, 2001).

16. What's in Obama's Gun Control Proposal?" *New York Times*.
January 16, 2013, www.nytimes.com/interactive/2013/01/16/
us/obama-gun-control-proposal.html (accessed 4/26/14).

17. David G. Adler, "The Constitution and Presidential
Warmaking: An Enduring Debate," *Political Science Quarterly*
103 (1988): 1–36.

18. Richard F. Grimmett, "The War Powers Resolution: After
Thirty Years," Congressional Research Service Report
RL32267, March 11, 2004, www.fas.org/man/crs/RL32267.
html#_1_1 (accessed 6/2/14).

19. Lewis Fisher and David G. Adler, "The War Powers Resolution: Time to Say Goodbye," *Political Science Quarterly*
113:1 (1998): 1–20.

20. William G. Howell and Jon C. Pevehouse, *While Dangers
Gather: Congressional Checks on Presidential War Powers*
(Princeton, NJ: Princeton University Press, 2007).

21. John M. Broder, "The Climate Accord: The Overview;
Clinton Adamant on Third World Role in Climate Accord,"
New York Times, December 12, 1997, pp. A1, A16.

22. "So Long and Thanks for All the Naval Bases." *Economist*,
April 28, 2014, www.economist.com/blogs/banyan/2014/04/
barack-obama-s-asian-tour (accessed 4/30/14).

23. Aaron Wildavsky, "The Two Presidencies," *Trans-Action* 4
(1966): 7–35.

24. Mark A. Peterson, *Legislating Together: The White House
and Capitol Hill from Eisenhower to Reagan* (Cambridge,
MA: Harvard University Press, 1990).

25. Andrew Rudalevige, *Managing the President's Program: Presidential Leadership and Legislative Policy Formation* (Princeton, NJ: Princeton University Press, 2002).

26. "Campaign 2000: Today—Abortion: The Enduring Battle over Choice," *New York Times*, October 11, 2000.

27. Charles Cameron and Nolan M. McCarty, "Models of Vetoes and Veto Bargaining," *Annual Review of Political Science* 7 (2004): 409–35.

28. Keith Krehbiel, *Pivotal Politics: A Theory of U.S. Lawmaking* (Chicago: University of Chicago Press, 1998).

29. Charles Jones, *The Presidency in a Separated System* (Washington, D.C.: Brookings Institution Press, 1994).

30. Mark J. Rozell, "The Law: Executive Privilege: Definition and Standards of Application," *Presidential Studies Quarterly* 29:4 (1999): 918–30.

31. Raoul Berger, *Executive Privilege: A Constitutional Myth* (Cambridge, MA: Harvard University Press, 1974). For commentary, see Saikrisha Prakash, "A Comment on the Constitutionality of Executive Privilege," *Minnesota Law Review* 83:5 (May 1999): 1143–89.

32. See Oyez, *United States v. Nixon*, 418 U.S. 683 (1974), www.oyez.org/cases/1970–1979/1974/1974_73_1766 for a summary of the case (accessed 11/1/12).

33. Sari Horwitz, "A Gunrunning Sting Gone Fatally Wrong," *Washington Post*, July 26, 2011, www.washingtonpost.com/investigations/us-anti-gunrunning-effort-turns-fatally-wrong/2011/07/14/gIQAH5d6YI_story.html (accessed 4/30/14).

34. Mark J. Rozell, *Executive Privilege: The Dilemma of Secrecy and Democratic Accountability* (Baltimore, MD: Johns Hopkins University Press, 1994).

35. Ben Smith and David Paul Kuhn, "Obama Moves Quickly to Reshape DNC," *Politico*, June 13, 2008, www.politico.com/news/stories/0608/11045.html (accessed 7/2/08).

36. John D. McKinnon, "Backing Away from Bush; Some Republican Candidates Avoid Ties with Unpopular President," *Wall Street Journal*, May 23, 2006, p. A4; Carrie Budoff, "Is Bush's Support Worse Than No Support?" *Politico*, July 16, 2007, www.politico.com/news/stories/0707/4960.html (accessed 4/29/08).

37. George C. Edwards III, *The Public Presidency* (New York: St. Martin's Press, 1983); George C. Edwards III, *On Deaf Ears: The Limits of the Bully Pulpit* (New Haven, CT: Yale University Press, 2003).

38. For evidence, see Edwards, *On Deaf Ears.*

39. Edwards, *On Deaf Ears.*

40. Samuel Kernell, *Going Public: New Strategies of Presidential Leadership*, 2nd ed. (Washington, D.C.: Congressional Quarterly Press, 1993).

41. Associated Press, "Bush Regains Power after Colonoscopy," *New York Times*, July 21, 2007, www.nytimes.com/aponline/us/AP-Bush-Colonoscopy.html?hp (accessed 4/29/08).

42. Richard Cohen and Jules Witcover, *A Heartbeat Away: The Investigation and Resignation of Spiro T. Agnew* (New York: Viking, 1974).

43. John Hart, *The Presidential Branch: From Washington to Clinton* (Chatham, NY: Chatham House, 1987).

44. Jackie Calmes, "As Plouffe Departs, a West Wing Job Is Redefined," *New York Times*, January 26, 2013, p. A17, www.nytimes.com/2013/01/27/us/politics/david-plouffe-senior-adviser-leaves-white-house.html?_r=0 (accessed 6/3/14).

45. Kelly Chang, David Lewis, and Nolan McCarthy, "The Tenure of Political Appointees," paper presented at the 2003 Midwest Political Science Association Annual Meeting, Chicago, April 4, 2003.

46. David E. Lewis, "Staffing Alone: Unilateral Action and the Politicization of the Executive Office of the President, 1988–2004," *Presidential Studies Quarterly* 35 (2005): 496–514.

47. Charles E. Walcott and Karen M. Hult, "White House Staff Size: Explanations and Implications," *Presidential Studies Quarterly* 29 (1999): 638–56.

48. Karen M. Hult and Charles E. Walcott, *Empowering the White House: Governance under Nixon, Ford, and Carter* (Lawrence, KS: University Press of Kansas, 2004).

49. For a series of articles detailing Cheney's role, see "Angler: The Cheney Vice Presidency," *Washington Post*, June 24–27, 2007, www.washingtonpost.com/cheney (accessed 4/29/08).

50. John Mueller, *War, Presidents, and Public Opinion* (New York: John Wiley, 1973).

51. Alexander Hamilton and James Madison, *The Pacificus-Helvidius Debates of 1793–1794: Toward the Completion of the American Founding*, ed. Martin J. Frisch (1793; repr. Indianapolis, IN: Liberty Fund, 2007).

52. Richard E. Neustart, *Presidential Power and the Modern Presidents* (New York: Simon and Schuster, 1991).

53. Terry M. Moe and William G. Howell, "The Presidential Power of Unilateral Action," *Journal of Law, Economics, and Organization* 15 (1999): 132–46.

54. Charlie Savage and Mark Landler, "White House Defends Continuing U.S. Role in Libya Operations," *New York Times*, June 15, 2011, p. A1, www.nytimes.com/2011/06/16/us/politics/16powers.html?pagewanted=all (accessed 6/3/14).

55. Eugene Kontorovich, "Obama's Minimum Wage Proposal Has More Statutory Authority Than Prior 'Unilateral' Actions," *Washington Post*, January 29, 2014, www.washingtonpost.com/news/volokh-conspiracy/wp/2014/01/29/obamas-minimum-wage-plan-has-more-statutory-authority-than-prior-unilateral-actions/?tid=pm_national_pop (accessed 5/1/14).

56. Julia Preston, "Report Finds Deportations Focus on Criminal Records," *New York Times*, April 29, 2014, p. A16, www.nytimes.com/2014/04/30/us/report-finds-deportations-focus-on-criminal-records.html?_r=0 (accessed 6/3/14).

57. James Risen and Eric Lichtblau, "Spying Program Snared U.S. Calls," *New York Times*, December 21, 2005, p. A1; David E. Sanger, "After ABM Treaty: New Freedom for U.S. in Different Kind of Arms Control," *New York Times*, December 15, 2001.

58. These examples appear throughout Moe and Howell, "The Presidential Power of Unilateral Action"; see also William G. Howell, "Unilateral Powers: A Brief Overview," *Presidential Studies Quarterly* 35:3 (2005): 417–39.

59. Louis Fisher, *Presidential War Power*, 2nd ed. (Lawrence, KS: University Press of Kansas, 2004); James M. Lindsay, "Deference and Defiance: The Shifting Rhythms of Executive–Legislative Relations in Foreign Policy," *Presidential Studies Quarterly* 33:3 (2003): 530–46; Lawrence Margolis, *Executive Agreements and Presidential Power in Foreign Policy* (New York: Praeger, 1985), 209–32.

60. Phillip Cooper, "George W. Bush, Edgar Allan Poe, and the Use and Abuse of Presidential Signing Statements," *Presidential Studies Quarterly* 35:3 (2005): 515–32.

61. Andrew Rudalevige, *The New Imperial Presidency: Renewing Presidential Power after Watergate* (Ann Arbor, MI: University of Michigan Press, 2005).

62. Christopher Deering and Forrest Maltzman, "The Politics of Executive Orders: Legislative Constraints on Presidential Power," *Political Research Quarterly* 52:4 (1999): 767–83.

63. David E. Lewis, *Presidents and the Politics of Agency Design: Political Insulation in the United States Government Bureaucracy, 1946–1997* (Palo Alto, CA: Stanford University Press, 2003).

64. David Epstein and Sharyn O'Halloran, *Delegating Powers* (Cambridge, UK: Cambridge University Press, 1999).

65. Jamie Fuller, "Rand Paul Files Suit against Obama, NSA Wednesday," *Washington Post*, February 12, 2014, www.washingtonpost.com/blogs/post-politics/wp/2014/02/12/rand-paul-files-suit-against-obama-nsa-today/ (accessed 5/1/14).

You Decide

a. For details on this example, see http://topics.nytimes.com/top/news/business/companies/solyndra/index.html (accessed 4/11/12).

CHAPTER 13

1. Dwight Waldo, *The Administrative State: A Study of the Political Theory of American Public Administration* (1948; repr. Piscataway, NJ: Transaction Publishers, 2006).

2. The original quote is from Robert Dahl and was used in this context in David E. Lewis, *Presidents and the Politics of Agency Design: Political Insulation in the United States Government* (Palo Alto, CA: Stanford University Press, 2003).

3. For a history of the Food and Drug Administration, see John P. Swann, FDA History Office, "History of the FDA," www.fda.gov/oc/history/historyoffda/section2.html (accessed 7/15/08).

4. For details, see Cornelius Kerwin, *Rulemaking: How Government Agencies Write Law and Make Policy* (Washington, D.C.: CQ Press, 1999).

5. Enterprise Risk Management Initiative, "Costs Associated with Regulatory Risks," www.mgt.ncsu.edu/erm/index.php/articles/entry/regulatory-risk-cost/ (accessed 2/3/10).

6. Andrew Pollack, "New Sense of Caution at FDA," *New York Times*, September 29, 2006.

7. There are two exceptions. A patient can enroll in a clinical trial for a new drug during the approval process, but there is a good chance that the patient will get a placebo or a previously approved treatment rather than the drug being tested. The FDA does allow companies to provide some experimental drugs to patients who cannot participate in a trial, but only those drugs that have passed early screening trials.

8. Susan Okie, "Access before Approval—A Right to Take Experimental Drugs?" *New England Journal of Medicine* 355 (2004): 437–40.

9. For details, see the U.S. General Services Administration site at www.gsa.gov.

10. Michael Lipsky, *Street-Level Bureaucracy* (New York: Russell Sage Foundation, 1983).

11. Stephen Skowronek, *Building a New American State: The Expansion of National Administrative Capacities, 1877–1920* (New York: Cambridge University Press, 1982).

12. PPBS was Program Planning Budget System (under the Johnson administration), MBO was Management by Objectives (under the Nixon administration), ZBB was Zero-Based Budgeting (under the Carter administration), REGO was short for Reinventing Government (under the Clinton administration), and PBB (Performance Based Budgeting) was President George W. Bush's effort at bureaucratic reorganization. For details, see Cedilia Ferradino, "New Name, Old Challenges: Performance Budgeting's Continuing Struggle to Succeed in Washington," *Rockefeller College Review* 1:2 (2002): 6–23.

13. Terry Moe, "An Assessment of the Positive Theory of Congressional Dominance," *Legislative Studies Quarterly* 4 (1987): 475–98.

14. Jason DeParle, "Minerals Service Had a Mandate to Produce Results," *New York Times*, August 7, 2010, p. A1.

15. Frances E. Rourke, "Responsiveness and Neutral Competence in American Bureaucracy," *Public Administration Review* 52 (1992): 539–46; Max Weber, *Essays on Sociology* (New York: Oxford University Press, 1958).

16. Terry M. Moe, "Power and Political Institutions," *Perspectives on Politics* 3 (2005): 215–33.

17. Karen Orren and Steven Skowronek, "Regimes and Regime Building in American Government: A Review of the Literature on the 1940s," *Political Science Quarterly* 113 (1998): 689–702.

18. Michael Nelson, "A Short, Ironic History of American National Bureaucracy," *Journal of Politics* 44 (1982): 747–78.

19. Nelson, "A Short, Ironic History of American National Bureaucracy."

20. Nelson, "A Short, Ironic History of American National Bureaucracy."

21. John Aldrich, *Why Parties?* (Chicago: University of Chicago Press, 1995).

22. Nelson, "A Short, Ironic History of American National Bureaucracy."

23. Matthew A. Crenson, *The Federal Machine: Beginnings of Bureaucracy in Jacksonian America* (Baltimore, MD: Johns Hopkins University Press, 1975).

24. James Q. Wilson, "The Rise of the Bureaucratic State," in *The American Commonwealth*, ed. Nathan Glazer and Irving Kristol (New York: Basic Books, 1976).

25. Skowronek, *Building a New American State.*

26. Robert Harrison, *Congress, Progressive Reform, and the New American State* (New York: Cambridge University Press, 2004).

27. The U.S. State Department has an excellent summary of the Pendleton Act at http://usinfo.state.gov/usa/infousa/facts/democrac/28.htm.

28. Lawrence C. Dodd and Richard L. Schott, *Congress and the Administrative State* (New York: John Wiley, 1979).

29. Ira Katznelson and Bruce Pietrykowski, "Rebuilding the American State: Evidence from the 1940s," *Studies in American Political Development* 5:2 (1991) 301–39.

30. David Plotke, *Building a Democratic Political Order: Reshaping American Liberalism in the 1930s and 1940s* (New York: Cambridge University Press, 1996).

31. Theda Skocpol and Kenneth Finegold, "State Capacity and Economic Intervention in the Early New Deal," *Political Science Quarterly* 97 (1999): 255–70.

32. Michael Brown, "State Capacity and Political Choice: Interpreting the Failure of the Third New Deal," *Studies in American Political Development* 9 (1995): 187–212.

33. Ira Katznelson, Kim Geiger, and Daniel Kryder, "Limiting Liberalism: The Southern Veto in Congress, 1933–1950," *Political Science Quarterly* 108 (1993): 283–306.

34. Joseph Califano, "What Was Really Great about the Great Society," *Washington Monthly*, October 1999, www.washingtonmonthly.com/features/1999/9910.califano.html (accessed 7/16/08).

35. Douglas Arnold, *Congress and the Bureaucracy* (New Haven, CT: Yale University Press, 1978).

36. David T. Canon, *Race, Redistricting, and Representation: The Unintended Consequences of Black Majority Districts* (Chicago: University of Chicago Press, 1999).

37. Charles Murray, *Losing Ground: American Social Policy, 1950–1980* (New York: Basic Books, 1984).

38. Henry J. Aaron, *Politics and the Professors: The Great Society in Perspective* (Washington, D.C.: Brookings Institution Press, 1978).

39. Michael B. Katz, *In the Shadow of the Poorhouse: A Social History of Welfare in America* (New York: Basic Books, 1996).

40. Stephen Moore, "How the Budget Revolution Was Lost," Cato Policy Analysis no. 281, September 2, 1997, Cato Institute, www.cato.org/pubs/pas/pa-281.html (accessed 7/21/08).

41. Calculation by the authors from the Government Accountability Office Federal Rules Database, www.gao.gov/legal/congressact/fedrule.html (accessed 3/28/14).

42. Richard P. Nathan, *The Administrative Presidency* (New York: Wiley, 1983).

43. Andrew Rudalevige, "The Structure of Leadership: Presidents, Hierarchies, and Information Flow," *Presidential Studies Quarterly* 35 (2005): 333–60.

44. David E. Lewis, *Presidents and the Policy of Agency Design* (Palo Alto, CA: Stanford University Press, 2003).

45. Terry. M. Moe, "An Assessment of the Positive Theory of Congressional Dominance," *Legislative Studies Quarterly* 4 (1987): 475–98.

46. William A. Niskanen, *Bureaucracy and Public Economics* (Washington, D.C.: Edward Elgar, 1976); Robert Whaples and Jac C. Heckelman, "Public Choice Economics: Where Is There Consensus?" *American Economist* 49 (2005): 66–78.

47. Alan Schick and Felix LoStracco, *The Federal Budget: Politics, Process, Policy* (Washington, D.C.: Brookings Institution Press, 2000).

48. Joel D. Aberbach, "The Political Significance of the George W. Bush Administration," *Social Policy and Administration* 39:2 (2005): 130–49.

49. David E. Lewis, "The Politics of Agency Termination: Confronting the Myth of Agency Immortality," *Journal of Politics* 64 (2002): 89–107.

50. Ronald A. Wirtz, "Put It on My . . . Er, His Tab: Opinion Polls Show a Big Gap between the Public's Desire for Services and Its Willingness to Pay for These Services," *Fedgazette*, January 2004, www.minneapolisfed.org/pubs/fedgaz/04-01/tab.cfm (accessed 7/16/08).

51. James L. Perry and Annie Hondeghem, *Motivation in Public Management: The Call of Public Service* (Oxford, UK: Oxford University Press, 2008).

52. Paul Light, *A Government Well-Executed: Public Service and Public Performance* (Washington, D.C.: Brookings Institution Press, 2003).

53. This discussion of the details of the civil service system is based on Bureau of Labor Statistics, "Career Guide to Industries," March 12, 2008, www.bls.gov/oco/cg/cgs041.htm (accessed 7/16/08).

54. Dennis Cauchon, "Some Federal Workers More Likely to Die Than Lose Jobs," *USA Today,* July 19, 2011, p. A1.

55. Chris Bergin, "MOD Has Hope in a Post-Shuttle Follow on Program Despite Workforce Cull," July 10, 2009, www.nasaspaceflight.com/2009/07/nasas-mod-hope-in-follow-on-program-workforce-cull/ (accessed 4/7/14).

56. Ronald N. Johnson and Gary D. Liebcap, *The Federal Civil Service System and the Problem of Bureaucracy* (Chicago: University of Chicago Press, 1993).

57. Eric Lichtblau, "Report Sees Illegal Hiring Practices at Justice Department," *New York Times*, June 25, 2008, www.nytimes.com/2008/06/25/washington/24cnd-justice.html# (accessed 6/16/14).

58. For the details of the Hatch Act, see Daniel Engber, "Can Karl Rove Plot Campaign Strategy on the Government's Dime?" *Slate*, April 21, 2006, www.slate.com/id/2140418 (accessed 7/16/08).

59. Justin Gillis, "Climate Maverick to Retire From NASA." *New York Times,* April 1, 2013, p. D1.

60. Al Kaman, "Former GAO Head Dave Walker Meets the Hatch Act," *Washington Post*, February 5, 2014, www.washingtonpost.com/blogs/in-the-loop/wp/2014/02/05/former-gao-head-dave-walker-meets-the-hatch-act/ (accessed 4/8/14).

61. Timothy Noah, "Low Morale at Homeland Security," *Slate*, September 14, 2005, www.slate.com/id/2126313 (accessed 7/17/08).

62. For details on the SES, see www.opm.gov/policy-data-oversight/senior-executive-service/ (accessed 4/7/14).

63. Kenneth Chang and Peter Baker, "NASA Breaks Most Contact with Russia," *New York Times.* April 2, 2014, p. A12.

64. John D. Huber and Charles R. Shipan, *Deliberate Discretion? The Institutional Foundations of Bureaucratic Autonomy* (New York: Cambridge University Press, 2002).

65. David Epstein and Sharyn O'Halloran, *Delegating Powers: A Transaction Cost Politics Approach to Policy Making under Separate Powers* (New York: Cambridge University Press, 1999).

66. Charles E. Lindbloom, "The Science of 'Muddling Through,'" *Public Administration Review* 19 (1959): 79–88.

67. Mathew D. McCubbins, Roger G. Noll, and Barry R. Weingast, "Structure and Process as Solutions to the Politician's Principal–Agency Problem," *Virginia Law Review* 74 (1989): 431–82.

68. Barry R. Weingast, "Caught in the Middle: The President, Congress, and the Political-Bureaucratic System," in *Institutions of American Democracy: The Executive Branch*, ed. Joel D. Aberbach and Mark A. Peterson (New York: Oxford University Press, 2006).

69. Keith Whittington and Daniel P. Carpenter, "Executive Power in American Institutional Development," *Perspectives on Politics* 1 (2003): 495–513.

70. Federal Communications Commission, "FCC Commissioners," April 1, 2008, www.fcc.gov/commissioners (accessed 7/17/08).

71. Roger Noll, Mathew McCubbins, and Barry Weingast, "Administrative Procedures as Instruments of Political Control," *Journal of Law, Economics and Organization* 3 (1987): 243–77.

72. Mathew McCubbins and Thomas Schwartz, "Congressional Oversight Overlooked: Fire Alarms vs. Police Patrols," *American Journal of Political Science* 28 (1984): 165–79.

73. McCubbins and Schwartz, "Congressional Oversight Overlooked."

74. Steven J. Balla and John R. Wright, "Interest Groups, Advisory Committees, and Congressional Control of the Bureaucracy," *American Journal of Political Science* 45 (2001): 799–812.

75. Eric Katz, "Senators to OPM: Your Retirement Claims Processing Is So 1977," *Government Executive*, March 28, 2014, www.govexec.com/pay-benefits/2014/03/senators-opm-your-retirement-claims-processing-is-so-1977/81559/ (accessed 4/8/14).

76. Daniel P. Carpenter, "The Gatekeeper: Organizational Reputation and Pharmaceutical Regulation at the FDA" (unpublished paper, Harvard University, 2006).

77. Terry M. Moe, "Political Control and the Power of the Agent," *Journal of Law, Economics, and Organization* 22 (2006): 1–29.

78. See David Weil, "OSHA: Beyond the Politics," *Frontline*, January 9, 2003, www.pbs.org/wgbh/pages/frontline/shows/workplace/osha/weil.html (accessed 7/17/08).

You Decide

a. Charlie Savage, "2 Top Lawyers Lost to Obama in Libya War Policy Debate," *The New York Times,* June 17, 2011, p. A1.

CHAPTER 14

1. *McCutcheon v. Federal Election Commission*, 572 U.S. ___ (2014).

2. *Schuette v. Coalition to Defend Affirmative Action*, 572 U.S. ___ (2014), slip. op., 3.

3. Ralph Ketcham, *The Anti-Federalist Papers and the Constitutional Convention Debates* (New York: Penguin Putnam, 2003), p. 304.

4. Lester S. Jayson, ed., *The Constitution of the United States of America: Analysis and Interpretation* (Washington, D.C.: U.S. Government Printing Office, 1973), p. 585.

5. David G. Savage, *Guide to the U.S. Supreme Court*, 4th ed. (Washington, D.C.: CQ Press, 2004), p. 7.

6. Savage, *Guide to the U.S. Supreme Court*, pp. 5–7.

7. Winfield H. Rose, "*Marbury v. Madison*: How John Marshall Changed History by Misquoting the Constitution," *Political Science and Politics* 36:2 (April 2003): 209–14. Rose argues that in a key quotation in the case, Marshall intentionally left out a clause of the Constitution that suggests that Congress *did* have the power to expand the original jurisdiction of the Court. Other constitutional scholars reject this argument.

8. *Marbury v. Madison*, 5 U.S. 1 Cranch 137 (1803).

9. Revisionist historians, legal scholars, and political scientists have challenged the landmark status of *Marbury v. Madison*. For example, Michael Stokes Paulsen's *Michigan Law Review* article points out that *Marbury* was not cited in subsequent Supreme Court cases as a precedent for judicial review until the late nineteenth century. Legal scholars in the early twentieth century were the first to promote the idea that *Marbury* was a landmark decision. Paulsen also notes that when the opinion was delivered in 1803, it was not controversial. Even the Jeffersonian Democrats, who were at odds with Marshall's Federalists, thought that it was a reasonable decision and not the institutional power grab that is described in modern accounts. Finally, Marshall made a very narrow case for judicial review, arguing that the Supreme Court could declare legislation that was contrary to the Court's interpretation of the Constitution null and void only if it concerned judicial powers. Revisionists argue that what appear to be broad claims of judicial power in *Marbury* (e.g., the Court has the power "to say what the law is") are taken out of the context of a much more narrow claim of power. Michael Stokes Paulsen, "Judging Judicial Review: *Marbury* in the Modern Era: The Irrepressible Myth of *Marbury*," *Michigan Law Review* 101 (August, 2003): 2706–43.

10. *Ware v. Hylton*, 3 U.S. 199 (1796).

11. *Wal-Mart v.* Dukes, 564 U.S. ___ (2011). However, in 2011, the Court struck down any class-action claim unless there was "convincing proof of a companywide discriminatory pay and promotion policy"—statistical evidence of pay disparities would not suffice (David Savage, "Supreme Court Blocks Huge Class-Action Suit against Wal-Mart," *Los Angeles Times*, June 21, 2011).

12. *Buckley v. Valeo*, 424 U.S. 1 (1976) upheld aggregate limits saying that Congress had an interest in preventing the "appearance of corruption." The *McCutcheon* case discussed in the chapter opener limited Congress's interest in corruption to a more narrow "quid pro quo" corruption that is basically bribery (and already prohibited by other laws).

13. *Lujan v. Defenders of Wildlife*, 504 U.S. 555 (1992).

14. The case concerning the bombing in Libya was *Kucinich v. Obama* 821 F. Supp. 2d 110, Dist. of Columbia, 2011. The cases limiting taxpayers' standing to challenge laws they disagree with are *Flast v. Cohen*, 392 U.S. 83 (1968) and *Arizona Christian School Tuition Org. v. Winn*, 131 S. Ct. 1436 (2011).

15. United States Courts, Judges & Judgeships, Federal Judgeships, www.uscourts.gov/JudgesAndJudgeships/FederalJudgeships.aspx (accessed 4/30/14).

16. United States Courts, Federal Judiciary: Frequently Asked Questions, "Federal Judges," www.uscourts.gov/faq.html (accessed 1/17/12).

17. United States Courts, Judges & Judgeships, Federal Judgeships, www.uscourts.gov/JudgesAndJudgeships/FederalJudgeships.aspx (accessed 4/30/14).

18. *Ledbetter v. Goodyear Tire & Rubber Co.*, 550 U.S. 618 (2007).

19. The Eleventh Amendment does not mention lawsuits against a state brought in federal court by citizens of that same state. However, in *Alden v. Maine* (527 U.S. 706 [1999]), the Court extended the logic of sovereign immunity to apply to these cases as well.

20. "Judicial selection in the states," Judgepedia.org, http://judgepedia.org/Judicial_selection_in_the_States:_Trial_Courts_and_General_Jurisdiction (accessed 4/30/14).

21. See, for example, a case involving the West Virginia state supreme court and $3 million in campaign spending by a coal company that had a case pending before the court, *Caperton v. A. T. Massey Coal Co.* 556 U.S. 868 (2009); The Court ruled that the losing party's due process rights under the Fourteenth Amendment had been violated when the justice who benefited from the campaign spending did not recuse himself from the case. Given the disproportionate and significant spending by Massey and the timing of the spending, the majority ruled, "On these extreme facts the probability of actual bias rises to an unconstitutional level."

22. Paul Brace and Brent D. Boyea, "State Public Opinion, the Death Penalty, and the Practice of Electing Judges," *American Journal of Political Science* 52:2 (April 2008): 360–72.

23. Richard P. Caldarone, Brandice Canes-Wrone, and Tom S. Clark, "Partisan Labels and Democratic Accountability: An Analysis of State Supreme Court Abortion Decisions," *Journal of Politics* 71 (2009): 560–73.

24. Stephen Ware, "The Missouri Plan in National Perspective," *Missouri Law Review* 74 (2009): 751–75.

25. Savage, *Guide to the U.S. Supreme Court*, p. 1003.

26. "President Bush Discusses Judicial Accomplishments and Philosophy, Cincinnati, OH, October 6, 2008," georgewbush-whitehouse.archives.gov/news/releases/2008/10/20081006-5.html (accessed 12/14/11).

27. Paul Kane, "Reid, Democrats Trigger 'Nuclear' Option; Eliminate Most Filibusters on Nominees," *Washington Post*, November 21, 2013, www.washingtonpost.com/politics/senate-poised-to-limit-filibusters-in-party-line-vote-that-would-alter-centuries-of-precedent/2013/11/21/d065cfe8-52b6-11e3-9fe0-fd2ca728e67c_story.html (accessed 5/2/14).

28. Supreme Court of the United States *In Re Frederick W. Bauer*, On Petition for a Writ of Mandamus to the United States Court of Appeals for the Seventh Circuit, Brief for the United States in Opposition, No. 90-6351, March 4, 1991, www.usdoj.gov/osg/briefs/1990/sg900418.txt (accessed 7/18/08).

29. Supreme Court of the United States *In Re Frederick W. Bauer*, On Motion for Leave to Proceed in forma pauperis, No. 99-5440, Decided October 18, 1999, per curiam, http://supreme.lp.findlaw.com/supreme_court/decisions/99-5440.html (accessed 7/18/08).

30. John Roberts, U.S. Supreme Court, "2007 Year-End Report on the Federal Judiciary," January 1, 2008, www.supremecourtus.gov/publicinfo/year-end/2007year-endreport.pdf (accessed 3/17/08).

31. For a critical account of the Supreme Court's reduced caseload, which dates back to the Rehnquist Court, see Philip Allen Lacovara, "The Incredible Shrinking Court," *American Lawyer*, December 1, 2003.

32. *New Jersey v. New York*, No. 120 Orig., 118 S. Ct. 1726 (1998), and *Kansas v. Colorado*, No. 105 Orig., 125 S. Ct. 526 (2004).

33. Henry J. Abraham, *The Judiciary: The Supreme Court in the Governmental Process*, Seventh ed. (Boston: Allyn and Bacon, 1987), p. 25, says that original jurisdiction has been invoked "about 150 times." A Lexis search revealed an additional 27 original jurisdiction cases between 1987 and December 2004. See U.S. Department of Justice, Help/Glossary, www.usdoj.gov/osg/briefs/help.html for a basic discussion of the Supreme Court's original jurisdiction.

34. Savage, *Guide to the U.S. Supreme Court*, p. 848.

35. See Thomas G. Walker and Lee Epstein, *The Supreme Court of the United States: An Introduction* (New York: St. Martin's Press, 1993), pp. 80–85, for a more detailed discussion of these concepts and citations to the relevant court cases.

36. *Shaw v. Reno* 509 U.S. 630 (1993).

37. *Elk Grove Unified School District v. Newdow* 542 U.S. 1 (2004).

38. Gregory A. Caldeira and John R. Wright, "The Discuss List: Agenda Building in the Supreme Court," *Law and Society Review* 24 (1990): 813.

39. Walker and Epstein, *Supreme Court*, p. 89; Ryan C. Black and Ryan J. Owens, *The Solicitor General and the United States Supreme Court: Executive Branch Influence and Judicial Decisions* (New York: Cambridge University Press, 2012).

40. U.S. Supreme Court, "The Court and Its Procedures," www.supremecourtus.gov/about/procedures.pdf (accessed 3/17/08).

41. Lee Epstein, Jeffrey A. Segal, Harold J. Spaeth, and Thomas G. Walker, *The Supreme Court Compendium: Data, Decisions, and Developments*, 3rd ed. (Washington, D.C.: CQ Press, 2003), Table 7-25.

42. Gregory A. Caldeira and John R. Wright, "*Amicus Curiae* before the Supreme Court: Who Participates, When, and How Much?" *Journal of Politics* 52 (August 1990): 803.

43. Andrew Christy, "'Obamacare' Will Rank among the Longest Supreme Court Arguments Ever," National Public Radio, November 15, 2011, www.npr.org/blogs/itsallpolitics/2011/11/15/142363047/obamacare-will-rank-among-the-longest-supreme-court-arguments-ever (accessed 5/2/14).

44. U.S. Supreme Court, Rules of the Supreme Court, adopted March 14, 2005, effective May 2, 2005, Rule 28.7, www.supremecourtus.gov/ctrules/rulesofthecourt.pdf (accessed 7/18/08).

45. Savage, *Guide to the U.S. Supreme Court*, p. 852.

46. U.S. Supreme Court, Argument Transcripts, www.supreme courtus.gov/oral_arguments/argument_transcripts (accessed 7/18/08).

47. Adam Liptak, "No Argument: Thomas Keeps Five Year Silence," *New York Times*, February 12, 2011, www.nytimes.com/2011/02/13/us/13thomas.html (accessed 1/18/12); Jeffrey Toobin, "Clarence Thomas's Disgraceful Silence," *New Yorker*, February 21, 2014, www.newyorker.com/online/blogs/comment/2014/02/clarence-thomas-disgraceful-silence.html (accessed 5/2/14).

48. Quoted in Savage, *Guide to the U.S. Supreme Court*, p. 854.

49. Forrest Maltzman, James F. Spriggs II, and Paul J. Wahlbeck, *Crafting Law on the Supreme Court: The Collegial Game* (New York: Cambridge University Press, 2000), p. 33.

50. William H. Rehnquist, "Memorandum to the Conference: Policy Regarding Assignments," November 24, 1989, papers of Justice Thurgood Marshall, Library of Congress Manuscript Division, Washington, D.C., quoted in Maltzman, Spriggs, and Wahlbeck, *Crafting Law*, pp. 30–31.

51. *Smith v. Allwright*, 321 U.S. 649 (1944).

52. Walker and Epstein, *Supreme Court*, p. 110.

53. Savage, *Guide to the U.S. Supreme Court*, p. 854.

54. Lee Epstein, William M. Landes, and Richard A. Posner, "Are Even Unanimous Decisions in the United States Supreme Court Ideological," *Northwestern University Law Review* 106:2 (2012), 702.

55. Adam Liptak, "Compromise at the Court Veils Its Rifts: Roberts Handiwork, Unanimous Rulings," *New York Times*, July 2, 2014, p.A1, A17.

56. Quoted in Lee Epstein and Thomas G. Walker, *Constitutional Law for a Changing America*, 5th ed. (Washington, D.C.: CQ Press, 2004), p. 29.

57. *Maryland v. Craig*, 497 U.S. 836 (1990).

58. Epstein and Walker, *Constitutional Law for a Changing America*, p. 31.

59. Seth Stern and Stephen Wermiel, *Justice Brennan: Liberal Champion* (Boston: Houghton Mifflin Harcourt, 2010).

60. Epstein, Segal, Spaeth, and Walker, *Supreme Court Compendium*, Table 6-2.

61. Forrest Maltzman and Paul J. Wahlbeck, "Strategic Considerations and Vote Fluidity on the Burger Court," *American Journal of Political Science* 90 (1996): 581–92; Maltzman, Spriggs, and Wahlbeck, *Crafting Law*.

62. Thomas R. Marshall, *Public Opinion and the Supreme Court* (Boston: Unwin Hyman, 1989), p. 12; as cited in Epstein and Walker, *Constitutional Law for a Changing America*, p. 92.

63. Thomas M. Keck, *The Most Activist Supreme Court in History: The Road to Modern Judicial Conservatism* (Chicago: University of Chicago Press, 2004).

64. Marshall, *Public Opinion*, Table 6-8.

65. Jeffrey Rosen, "Has the Supreme Court Gone Too Far?" *Commentary* 116:3 (October 2003).

66. *National Federation of Independent Business v. Sebelius*, 567 U.S. ___ (2012).

67. Finley Peter Dunne, Paul Green, and Jacques Barzun, *Mr. Dooley in Peace and in War* (1898; repr. Champaign-Urbana: University of Illinois Press, 2001).

68. Robert Dahl, "Decision-Making in a Democracy: The Supreme Court as a National Policy-Maker," *Journal of Public Law* 6 (1957): 279–95, is the classic work on this topic. More recent work challenged Dahl's methods but largely supports the idea that the Court follows the will of the majority.

69. Jeffrey A. Segal, Richard J. Timpone, and Robert M. Howard, "Buyer Beware? Presidential Success through Supreme Court Appointments," *Political Research Quarterly* 53:3 (September 2000): 557–73; Gregory A. Caldeira and Charles E. Smith Jr., "Campaigning for the Supreme Court: The Dynamics of Public Opinion on the Thomas Nomination," *Political Research Quarterly* 58:3 (August 1996): 655–81.

70. William Mishler and Reginald S. Sheehan, "The Supreme Court as a Countermajoritarian Institution? The Impact of Public Opinion on Supreme Court Decisions," *American Political Science Review* 87:1 (March 1993): 87–101.

71. Matthew E. K. Hall, "The Semiconstrained Court: Public Opinion, the Separation of Powers, and the U.S. Supreme Court's Fear of Nonimplementation," *American Journal of Political Science* 58:2 (April 2014): 352–66; Matthew E. K. Hall, *The Nature of Supreme Court Power* (New York: Cambridge University Press, 2011).

72. *Stanford v. Kentucky,* 492 U.S. 361 (1989); *Roper v. Simmons,* 543 U.S. 551 (2005).

73. David O'Brien, *Storm Center: The Supreme Court in American Politics*, 4th ed. (New York: W. W. Norton, 1996): 276.

74. Helmut Norpoth and Jeffrey A. Segal, "Popular Influence in Supreme Court Decisions," *American Political Science Review* 88 (1994): 711–16.

75. Office of General Counsel of the U.S. Sentencing Commission, *Selected Supreme Court Cases on Sentencing Issues*, January, 2014, www.ussc.gov/sites/default/files/pdf/amendment-process/Supreme_Court_Cases.pdf (accessed 5/2/14).

76. *Foster v. Neilson*, 27 U.S. 253 (1829).

77. *Charles B. Rangel v. John A Boehner,* United States District Court for the District of Columbia, Civil Action No. 13-540, December 11, 2013, p.48, https://ecf.dcd.uscourts.gov/cgi-bin/show_public_doc?2013cv0540-24 (accessed 5/2/14).

78. We thank Dan Smith for raising this point.

You Decide

a. Richard S. Beth, "Cloture Attempts on Nominations: Data and Historical Development," Congressional Research Service Report 7-5700, June 23, 2013, www.senate.gov/CRSReports/crs-publish.cfm?pid=%270E%2C*P%2C%3B%3C%20P%20%20%0A (accessed 5/2/2014); "President Obama's Judicial Nominations," 113th Congress, American Bar Association, www.americanbar.org/content/dam/aba/uncategorized/GAO/2014apr16_obamanomchart.authcheckdam.pdf (accessed 5/2/13).

CHAPTER 15

1. "Remarks by the President on the Economy in Osawatomie, Kansas," Osawatomie High School, Osawatomie, Kansas, December 6, 2011, www.whitehouse.gov/the-press-office/2011/12/06/remarks-president-economy-osawatomie-kansas (accessed 2/10/12).

2. "Tales of the 1040s," *Washington Post*, January 23, 2012, www.washingtonpost.com/politics/tales-of-the-1040s/2012/01/23/gIQA83IRMQ_graphic.html (accessed 2/13/12).

3. Robert Kahn, "Obama's Modest Proposals for Growth," Macro and Markets blog, Council on Foreign Relations, January 29, 2014, http://blogs.cfr.org/kahn/2014/01/29/obamas-modest-proposals-for-growth/ (accessed 6/10/14).

4. John Berlau and Trey Kovacs, "Romney and the Burden of Double Taxation," *Wall Street Journal*, January 24, 2012, online.wsj.com/article/SB10001424052970203718504577178831519223426.html (accessed 2/14/12).

5. Daniel Yergin and Joseph Stanislaw, *The Commanding Heights: The Battle for the World Economy* (New York: Free Press, 2002), pp. 60–64.

6. Central Intelligence Agency, *World Factbook*, "Country Comparison: Distribution of Family Income, Gini Index," www.cia.gov/library/publications/the-world-factbook/rankorder/2172rank.html (accessed 6/10/14).

7. The phrase comes from environmental economist E. F. Schumacher's influential book, *Small Is Beautiful: Economics as if People Mattered* (New York: Harper and Row, 1973).

8. Jonathan Rowe and Judith Silverstein, "The GDP Myth: Why 'Growth' Isn't Always a Good Thing," *Washington Monthly* 31:3 (March 1999).

9. Juann H. Hung, "Recent Shifts in Financing the U.S. Current-Account Deficit," *CBO Economic and Budget Issue Brief* (Washington, D.C.: Congressional Budget Office, July 12, 2005), www.cbo.gov (accessed 3/15/08).

10. The classic work on the appropriations process in the pre-reform era is Richard F. Fenno's *The Power of the Purse: Appropriations Politics in Congress* (Boston: Little, Brown,

1966). D. Roderick Kiewiet and Mathew D. McCubbins reexamine the appropriations process in the post-reform era and find that the appropriations committees have maintained much of their power; see *The Logic of Delegation: Congressional Parties and the Appropriations Process* (Chicago: University of Chicago Press, 1991).

11. Bill Heniff Jr., "Congressional Budget Resolutions: Historical Information," Congressional Research Service, February 7, 2014, www.senate.gov/CRSReports/crs-publish .cfm?pid=%270E%2C*PLS2%23%20%20%20%0A (accessed 6/10/14).

12. The specific provision is paragraph (1)(E) of section 313(b) (1) of the Budget Control Act. James Thurber, "Centralization, Devolution, and Turf Protection in the Congressional Budget Process," in *Congress Reconsidered*, ed. Lawrence C. Dodd and Bruce I. Oppenheimer, 6th ed. (Washington, D.C.: CQ Press, 1997), pp. 325–46.

13. These figures exclude the Social Security surplus. Including Social Security, the government had a small surplus in 1969. See the Congressional Budget Office's historical budget data, www.cbo.gov/showdoc.cfm?index=18/21&sequence=0. For data before 1962, see the 1981 *Economic Report of the President* (Washington, D.C.: Government Printing Office, 1981), p. 316.

14. Lori Montgomery, "House Votes to Revive Pay-as-You-Go Budget Rules," *Washington Post*, February 5, 2010, www.washingtonpost.com/wp-dyn/content/article/ 2010/02/04/AR2010020400354.html (accessed 2/12/10); Eric Pianin, "Congress Adds Payroll Tax Cut to Gov't Credit Card," *Fiscal Times*, February 15, 2012, www.thefiscaltimes .com/Articles/2012/02/15/Congress-Adds-Payroll%20Tax -Cut-to-Govt-Credit-Card.aspx#page1 (accessed 2/16/12).

15. Office of the United States Trade Representative, "About Us," www.ustr.gov/about-us (accessed 6/28/14).

16. National Economic Council, www.whitehouse.gov/ administration/eop/nec (accessed 7/28/14).

17. See Charles M. Cameron, *Veto Bargaining: Presidents and the Politics of Negative Power* (New York: Cambridge University Press, 2000), for a general discussion of the strategic elements of issuing veto threats.

18. Board of Governors of the Federal Reserve System, *The Federal Reserve System: Purposes and Functions*, 9th ed., Washington, D.C., June 2005, www.federalreserve.gov/pf/ pdf/pf_1.pdf, p. 12.

19. William McChesney Martin, who was appointed by Harry Truman, served through the presidencies of Eisenhower, Kennedy, and Johnson, and part of Nixon's first term. Paul Volcker served under Carter and Reagan, while Alan Greenspan's tenure spanned the presidencies of Reagan, Bush, Clinton, and the second Bush. Federal Reserve Board, "Membership of the Board of Governors of the Federal Reserve System, 1914-Present," www.federalreserve.gov/aboutthefed/ bios/board/boardmembership.htm (accessed 7/16/14).

20. Federal Reserve Board, "Annual Report 2013," www .federalreserve.gov/publications/budget-review/files/ 2013-budget.review.pdf (accessed 6/10/14).

21. Steven Russolillo, "Yellen on Stocks: This Isn't a Bubble," Money Beat, *Wall Street Journal*, November 14, 2013, http://blogs.wsj.com/moneybeat/2013/11/14/yellen-on -stocks-this-isnt-a-bubble (accessed 6/10/14).

22. Edward R. Tufte, *Political Control of the Economy* (Princeton, NJ: Princeton University Press, 1978); Douglas Hibbs, "The Partisan Model of Macroeconomic Cycles: More Theory and Evidence for the United States," *Economics and Politics* 6 (1994): 1–23.

23. Jim Granato, "The Effect of Policy-Maker Reputation and Credibility on Public Expectations," *Journal of Theoretical Politics* 8 (1996): 449–70; Irwin L. Morris, *Congress, the President, and the Federal Reserve: The Politics of American Monetary Policy-Making* (Ann Arbor: University of Michigan Press, 2000).

24. U.S. Department of the Treasury, "Duties and Functions," www.treasury.gov/education/duties (accessed 8/5/08).

25. U.S. Department of the Treasury, "FAQs: Currency: Production and Circulation," www.treasury.gov/education/faq/ currency/production.shtml; United States Mint, "Coin Production Figures," www.usmint.gov/about_the_mint/index .cfm?action=ProductionFigures and www.moneyfactory .gov/uscurrency/annualproductionfigures.html (accessed 6/11/14).

26. Zachary A. Goldfarb, David Cho, and Binyamin Appelbaum, "Treasury to Rescue Fannie and Freddie," *Washington Post*, September 7, 2008, p. A1.

27. Peter Baker, "A Professor and a Banker Bury Old Dogma on Markets," *New York Times*, September 21, 2008, p. A1.

28. Renae Merle, "U.S. Stock Markets Soar on Financial Rescue Plan," *Washington Post*, September 19, 2008; Howard Schneider, Neil Irwin, and Binyamin Appelbaum, "Treasury to Temporarily Guarantee Money Market Funds," *Washington Post*, September 19, 2008.

29. Carl Hulse, "Pressure Builds on House after Senate Backs Bailout," *New York Times*, October 1, 2008, p. A1.

30. David M. Herszenhorn, "Bailout Plan Wins Approval; Democrats Vow Tighter Rules," *New York Times*, October 3, 2008, p. A1.

31. U.S. Department of Treasury, "TARP Tracker from September 2008 to Date, www.treasury.gov/initiatives/ financialstability/reports/Pages/TARP-Tracker .aspx#All (accessed 7/16/14).

32. "Department of the Treasury, Financial Stability Plan— One Year Later," February 10, 2010, www.financialstability .gov/latest/pr_02102010.html (accessed 2/12/10).

33. Paula Reid, "Three Laws that Caused Obama Midterm Problems," CBS News, November 3, 2010, www.cbsnews .com/stories/2010/11/03/politics/main7020135.shtml (accessed 11/5/10).

34. John Maynard Keynes, *General Theory of Employment, Interest and Money* (1936; repr. New York: Macmillan, 2007).

35. Robert Dallek, *Flawed Giant: Lyndon Johnson and His Times, 1961–1973* (New York: Oxford University Press, 1998), pp. 71–74.

36. David Shreve, "President John F. Kennedy and the 1964 Tax Cut," Presidential Recordings Project, www.whitehousetapes.org/news/shreve_taxcut_2001.pdf (accessed 4/26/08).

37. In Laffer's original argument, there was only one tax rate. However, to apply the Laffer curve to the real world of tax policy, the theoretical argument must be presented in terms of the top marginal rate, which is the tax rate paid on the last dollars earned (and thus, the rate that influences the marginal decision to work more or fewer hours). The end point of zero tax revenue associated with a 100 percent tax rate would be for Laffer's single tax rate, rather than the top marginal rate (because people would still work as long as they could keep some income in the marginal brackets below the top rate).

38. Arthur B. Laffer, "The Laffer Curve: Past, Present, and Future," Heritage Foundation Backgrounder #1765, June 1, 2004, www.heritage.org/Research/Taxes/bg1765.cfm (accessed 3/27/08).

39. These figures come from the Congressional Budget Office, "Historical Budget Data," www.cbo.gov (accessed 4/18/08). Tax revenue fell from 19.6 percent of GDP in 1981, the last year before the tax cuts went into effect, to 18.1 percent of GDP in 1988, the last year of the Reagan presidency. Individual income tax revenue fell from 9.3 percent to 8 percent of GDP over the same period, so most of the decrease in revenue was due to lower individual income taxes. While overall government spending did increase during the 1982–1983 recession, spending from the beginning of Reagan's term to the end dropped slightly from 22.2 percent to 21.2 percent of GDP.

40. The "starve the beast" line is usually attributed to David Stockman and his book *The Triumph of Politics: The Inside Story of the Reagan Revolution* (New York: Avon Books, 1986). A Web search for "David Stockman" and "starve the beast" produced 566 hits, including a reference in a *National Review* article: Norman B. Ture, "To Cut and To Please," June 10, 2004, www.nationalreview.com/reagan/ture200406101414.asp. However, we have been unable to find the phrase "starve the beast" in Stockman's book. More recently, smaller-government proponents such as conservative political advocate Grover Norquist have embraced the concept.

41. Congressional Budget Office, "The Distribution of Household Income and Federal Taxes, 2010," December 2013, Table 3, p.13, http://cbo.gov/sites/default/files/cbofiles/attachments/44604-AverageTaxRates.pdf (accessed 6/30/14).

42. Congressional Budget Office, "Distribution of Household Income," Table 2, p. 9.

43. The details get a bit more complicated, but this is essentially how money is created. Banks must hold a reserve of 10 percent of all "demand deposits" (which is what economists call checking accounts), so only $90,000 would actually be put into the money stream because the $10,000 reserve would have to come from money that someone deposited in the bank. Also, the money supply would contract as you pay back your loan. The overall effect on the money supply has to take into account the "multiplier effect"—that is, the money you spend from your loan will get spent many times over. The computer store will take your $10,000 and deposit it in its bank, which allows that bank to make more loans, and so on.

44. Milton Friedman, "The Quantity Theory of Money: A Restatement," in *The Optimum Quantity of Money and Other Essays* (Chicago: Aldine, 1969), p. 52.

45. These figures are hypothetical. In reality, under the Monetary Control Act (MCA) of 1980, the reserve requirement can range from 8 percent to 14 percent for all demand deposits greater than $25 million. In the original law, banks with demand deposits under $25 million had to have a reserve of only 3 percent. The amount that is subject to the lower reserve requirement is increased every year to reflect overall money supply and currently is about $71 million. See Board of Governors of the Federal Reserve System "Reserve Requirement," www.federalreserve.gov/monetarypolicy/reservereq.htm#table1 (accessed 2/7/12).

46. In December 2002, the discount rate was effectively discontinued as an active policy tool and was pegged to 1 percent above the targeted FFR (which means that the "discount rate" is oddly named—it really should be called the "premium rate"); see December 2002 *Federal Reserve Bulletin* (pp. 482–83). See also Donald D. Hester, "U.S. Monetary Policy in the Greenspan Era: 1987–2003," unpublished paper, University of Wisconsin, Madison, November 14, 2003, http://ideas.repec.org/p/att/wimass/200323.html (accessed 8/10/08), for an extended discussion of this move.

47. See "Testimony of Chairman Alan Greenspan," Federal Reserve Board's semiannual Monetary Policy Report to the Congress before the Committee on Financial Services, U.S. House of Representatives, July 20, 2005, www.federalreserve.gov/boarddocs/hh/2005/july/testimony.htm (accessed 8/5/08).

48. Between September 2007 and December 2008, the Fed cut the FFR 10 times from 4.75 percent to nearly zero (the official target rate is 0 to .25 percent), and the prime rate fell from 8.25 percent to 3.25 percent. Both the FFR and prime have been unchanged since that time (through 2014). The 10-year Treasury, on the other hand, initially fell by two points during the period FFR cuts, but then increased by nearly a point and a half during the first year and a half of the Obama administration, sunk to record low levels early in May, 2013 (1.66 percent), only to bounce

back to 3 percent at the end of 2013, and then settle at 2.5 percent by the middle of 2014. See Federal Reserve Bank of New York, Federal Funds Data, for historical interest rates, www.newyorkfed.org/markets/omo/dmm/fedfundsdata .cfm (accessed 7/16/2014); see also U.S. Department of the Treasury, Resource Center, Daily Treasury Yield Curve Rates, for the 10-year Treasury rates, www .treasury.gov/resource-center/data-chart-center/interest -rates/Pages/TextView.aspx?data=yield (accessed 7/16/14).

49. Brian W. Cashell, "The Federal Government Debt: Its Size and Economic Significance," Washington, D.C.: Congressional Research Service, Report RL31590, March 1, 2005, p. 9.

50. William Greider, *Secrets of the Temple: How the Federal Reserve Runs the Country* (New York: Simon and Schuster, 1987), pp. 295–98.

51. Board of Governors of the Federal Reserve System, Credit and Liquidity Programs and the Balance Sheet, www .federalreserve.gov/monetarypolicy/bst_recenttrends.htm (accessed 2/16/10).

52. Board of Governors of the Federal Reserve System, Credit and Liquidity Programs and Balance Sheets, Recent Balance Sheet Trends, www.federalreserve.gov/monetarypolicy/ bst_recenttrends.htm (accessed 6/12/14).

53. John B. Taylor, *Economics*, 4th ed. (New York: Houghton Mifflin, 2003), chap. 10. Some economics textbooks also define regulation of externalities, such as pollution, as economic regulation.

54. *United States v. Microsoft*, 87 F. Supp. 2d 30 (D.D.C. 2000). See Alan Reynolds, *Microsoft Antitrust Appeal: Judge Jackson's "Findings of Fact" Revisited* (Washington, D.C.: Hudson Institute, 2002), for a detailed discussion of the case.

55. Daniel Carpenter and David A. Moss, editors, *Preventing Regulatory Capture: Special Interest Influence and How to Limit It.* New York: Cambridge University Press, 2014.

56. Megan Slack, "Everything You Need to Know: President Obama's Blueprint for American-Made Energy," January 26, 2012, www.whitehouse.gov/blog/2012/01/26/everything -you-need-know-president-obamas-blueprint-american -made-energy?tw_p=twt (accessed 2/19/12).

57. U.S. Department of Commerce, Bureau of Economic Analysis, "International Services and International Investment Position Tables," www.bea.gov/iTable/ iTable.cfm?ReqID=62&step=1#reqid=62&step=6&isu ri=1&6210=5&6200=143 (accessed 11/7/14).

58. David E. Rosenbloom, "Free Trade Is Like Dry Water, Y'All," *New York Times*, December 19, 2004, Week in Review.

59. David Ricardo, *The Principles of Political Economy and Taxation* (1817). Robert Torrens actually developed the point first in an 1815 essay on the corn trade, but Ricardo usually gets the credit because he explained it more fully.

60. This argument ignores transportation costs and the costs of shifting labor from one industry to another, but its logic is quite powerful. More intuitive, perhaps, is what happens when one nation has a large *absolute* advantage in the cost of production over another. In these situations, if there is free trade, most production of that good will shift to the country that can produce it more cheaply.

61. Mohammed Aly Sergie, "NAFTA's Economic Impact," Council on Foreign Relations, February 14, 2014, www.cfr.org/trade/naftas-economic-impact/p15790 (accessed 6/13/14).

62. Suketu Mehta, "A Passage from India," *New York Times*, July 12, 2005, p. A21.

63. See Ronald Rogowski, *Commerce and Coalitions* (Princeton, NJ: Princeton University Press, 1986), for the constituency view. James Shoch, *Trading Blows: Party Competition and U.S. Trade Policy in a Globalizing Era* (Chapel Hill: University of North Carolina Press, 2001), pp. 13–19, reviews both explanations.

64. Judith Goldstein, *Ideas, Interests, and American Trade* (Ithaca, NY: Cornell University Press, 1993).

You Decide

a. John Tierney, "The Sagebrush Solution," *New York Times*, July 26, 2005, p. A19. Additional information was drawn from www.highcountrynews.org.

b. A very detailed account of this saga may be found in Raymond B. Wrabley Jr., "Managing the Monument: Cows and Conservation in the Grand-Staircase-Escalante National Monument," *Journal of Land, Resources and Environmental Law* 29:2 (2009): 253–80.

CHAPTER 16

1. Election 2010, *New York Times*, http://elections.nytimes .com/2010/results/house and http://elections.nytimes .com/2010/results/senate (accessed 5/27/14).

2. Ed O'Keefe, "The House Has Voted 54 Times in Four Years on Obamacare," *Washington Post*, March 21, 2014, www .washingtonpost.com/blogs/the-fix/wp/2014/03/21/the -house-has-voted-54-times-in-four-years-on-obamacare -heres-the-full-list/ (accessed 5/27/14).

3. White House, "Impacts and Costs of the October 2013 Federal Government Shutdown," November 2013, www .whitehouse.gov/sites/default/files/omb/reports/impacts -and-costs-of-october-2013-federal-government-shutdown -report.pdf (accessed 5/27/14).

4. Sarah Dutton, Jennifer De Pinto, Anthony Salvanto, and Fred Backus, "Poll: Congress, Tea Party Take Hits from Government Shutdown," CBS News, October 22, 2013, www.cbsnews.com/news/poll-congress-tea-party-take -hits-from-government-shutdown/ (accessed 5/27/14).

5. Theda Skocpol, *Social Policy in the United States: Future Possibilities in Historical Perspective* (Princeton, NJ: Princeton University Press, 1995), p. 37.

6. Franklin D. Roosevelt's second fireside chat on "Government and Modern Capitalism," Washington, D.C., September 30, 1934. For the full text, see "The American Presidency Project," John T. Woolley and Gerhard Peters, University of California, Santa Barbara, www.presidency.ucsb.edu/ws/index.php?pid=14636 (accessed 8/8/08).

7. Skocpol, *Social Policy in the United States*, pp. 145–60.

8. David M. Kennedy, *Freedom from Fear: The American People in Depression and War, 1929–1945* (New York: Oxford University Press, 2001); Byron W. Daynes, William Pederson, and Michael P. Riccards, eds. *The New Deal and Public Policy* (New York: St. Martin's Press, 1998).

9. Robert Dallek, *Flawed Giant: Lyndon Johnson and His Times, 1961–1973* (New York: Oxford University Press, 1998); Irving Bernstein, *Guns or Butter: The Presidency of Lyndon Johnson* (New York: Oxford University Press, 1996).

10. Carmen DeNavas-Walt, Bernadette D. Proctor, and Jessica C. Smith, "Income, Poverty, and Health Insurance Coverage in the United States: 2011," September 2010, www.census.gov/prod/2012pubs/p60-243.pdf, p. 14 (accessed 10/9/12).

11. Emmanuel Saez, "Striking It Richer: The Evolution of Top Incomes in the United States," University of California, Berkeley, September 3, 2013, http://eml.berkeley.edu/~saez/saez-UStopincomes-2012.pdf (accessed 5/29/14).

12. "The Forbes 400: The Richest People in America," Forbes.com, September 19, 2012, www.forbes.com/sites/luisakroll/2012/09/19/the-forbes-400-the-richest-people-in-America/ (accessed 10/9/12). Data for the median net worth and top 10 percent net worth are from "Changes in U.S. Family Finances from 2010 to 2013: Evidence from the Survey of Consumer Finances," *Federal Reserve Bulletin*, September 2014, Figure B, p.10, Table 2, p.12, and Table 3, p.16, www.federalreserve.gov/pubs/bulletin/2014/pdf/scf14.pdf (accessed 11/6/14).

13. Kerry A. Dolan and Luisa Kroll, "Inside the 2014 Forbes 400: Facts And Figures About America's Wealthiest," *Forbes*, www.forbes.com/sites/kerryadolan/2014/09/29/inside-the-2014-forbes-400-facts-and-figures-about-americas-wealthiest/ (accessed 11/6/14).

14. Neil Howe and Philip Longman, "The Next New Deal," *Atlantic Monthly*, April, 1992, pp. 88–99. Somewhat surprisingly, it is difficult to measure accurately how much government money goes to different income groups. The most commonly used census data are notoriously unreliable because wealthy people underreport their income. Tax forms would be useful, but researchers do not have access to them. The only comprehensive analysis to overcome this data problem that we are aware of is this CBO study from the 1990s.

15. The housing expenditure figures are from the President's 2015 Budget, Housing and Urban Development, www.whitehouse.gov/sites/default/files/omb/budget/fy2015/assets/housing.pdf (accessed 5/29/14); the tax expenditure data are from The Joint Committee on Taxation, "Estimates of Federal Tax Expenditures, for Fiscal Years 2012–2017" (Washington, D.C.), February 1, 2013, www.jct.gov/publications.html?func=startdown&id=4503 (accessed 5/29/14).

16. Dean Baker, *The Conservative Nanny State: How the Wealthy Use the Government to Stay Rich and Get Richer*, May 2006, http://deanbaker.net:8080/images/stories/documents/cns.html (accessed 7/23/14).

17. Michael Tanner, "Welfare for the Non-Poor," Cato Institute, August 29, 2013, www.cato.org/publications/commentary/welfare-non-poor (accessed 5/29/14).

18. Charles M. Blow, "Santorum's Gospel of Inequality," *New York Times*, February 17, 2012, www.nytimes.com/2012/02/18/opinion/blow-santorum-exalts-inequality.html (accessed 3/1/12).

19. Larry M. Bartels, *Unequal Democracy: The Political Economy of the New Gilded Age* (Princeton, NJ: Princeton University Press, 2008).

20. David Brooks, "The Bursting Point," *New York Times*, September 4, 2005.

21. Bruce Nolan, "6 Years Later, Hurricane Katrina's Scars Linger alongside Robust Recovery," *Times Picayune*, August 28, 2011, www.nola.com/katrina/index.ssf/2011/08/6_years_later_hurricane_katrin.html (accessed 3/1/12).

22. Joe Soss, *Unwanted Claims: The Politics of Participation in the U.S. Welfare System* (Ann Arbor: University of Michigan Press, 2000).

23. Greg Jaffe and Ed O'Keefe, "Obama Accepts Resignation of VA Secretary Shinseki," May 30, 2014, *Washington Post*, www.washingtonpost.com/politics/shinseki-apologizes-for-va-health-care-scandal/2014/05/30/e605885a-e7f0-11e3-8f90-73e071f3d637_story.html (accessed 7/23/14).

24. Daniel P. Carpenter, *The Forging of Bureaucratic Autonomy: Reputations, Networks, and Policy Innovation in Executive Agencies, 1862–1928* (Princeton, NJ: Princeton University Press, 2001).

25. Frank R. Baumgartner and Bryan D. Jones, *Agendas and Instability in American Politics* (Chicago: University of Chicago Press, 1993).

26. See William T. Bianco, *Trust: Representatives and Constituents* (Ann Arbor: University of Michigan Press, 1994), Chapter 6, for a discussion of the repeal of the Catastrophic Coverage Act.

27. James Q. Wilson, *Bureaucracy: What Government Agencies Do and Why They Do It* (New York: Basic Books, 1989).

28. See U.S. Department of Agriculture, "USDA01: End the Wool and Mohair Subsidy," http://govinfo.library.unt.edu/npr/library/reports/ag01.html, for information on the pre-1994 policy; U.S. Department of Agriculture, "2002 Farm Bill, Title 1: Commodities Programs," www.ers.usda.gov/

Features/farmbill/titles/titleIcommodities.htm, for the current law (accessed 8/10/08).

29. Paul N. Van de Water, Arloc Sherman, and Kathy Ruffing, "Social Security Keeps 22 Million Americans out of Poverty: A State-by-State Analysis," Center on Budget and Policy Priorities, October 25, 2013, www.cbpp.org/cms/?fa=view&id=4037 (accessed 5/29/14).

30. Social Security Administration, Office of Retirement and Disability Policy, and Office of Research, Evaluation, and Statistics, "Fast Facts & Figures about Social Security, 2009," SSA Publication No. 13–11785, July 2009, http://retirement.gov/policy/docs/chartbooks/fast_facts/2009/fast_facts09.pdf (accessed 2/19/10).

31. Social Security Administration, *2013 OASDI Trustees Report*, Table IV.B2—Covered Workers and Beneficiaries, Calendar Years 1945–2090, www.socialsecurity.gov/OACT/TR/2013/IV_B_LRest.html#363526 (accessed 5/30/14).

32. Charles Hokayem and Misty L. Heggeness, "Living in Near Poverty in the United States: 1966–2012," U.S. Census Bureau, May 2014, p.21, www.census.gov/prod/2014pubs/p60-248.pdf (accessed 5/30/14).

33. In general, poorer people get back as much as they paid in plus interest much more quickly than wealthier people because of the progressive nature of the benefits. For a study on projected benefits that retirees will receive, see Dean R. Leimer, "Cohort-Specific Measures of Lifetime Social Security Taxes and Benefits," Social Security Administration, Office of Research, Evaluation, and Statistics, December 2007, www.socialsecurity.gov/policy/docs/workingpapers/wp110.pdf (accessed 8/10/08).

34. Social Security Administration, 2014 OASDI Trustees Report, Tables II B1 and II D6, July 28, 2014, www.ssa.gov/OACT/TR/2014/tr2014.pdf (accessed 11/6/14).

35. See Congressional Budget Office, "Menu of Social Security Options," May 25, 2005, www.cbo.gov/ftpdoc.cfm?index=6377&type=1, for a detailed account of the fiscal impact of the various proposals.

36. The life expectancy numbers provided here are for all people. Women have always lived longer than men: in 1940 the difference was 2 years, and in 2009 the difference was 2.7 years. That is, women's life expectancy at age 65 in 2009 was 85.2 and men's was 82.5. Social Security Administration, Period Life Table, 2009, www.ssa.gov/oact/STATS/table4c6.html (accessed 5/30/14).

37. The National Commission on Fiscal Responsibility and Reform, "The Moment of Truth," White House, Washington, D.C., December, 2010, www.fiscalcommission.gov/sites/fiscalcommission.gov/files/documents/TheMomentofTruth12_1_2010.pdf (accessed 3/13/12).

38. This figure came from a speech by SEC Commissioner Paul R. Carey, "Social Security Privatization," U.S. Securities and Exchange Commission, Washington, D.C., January 31, 2001, www.sec.gov/news/speech/spch459.htm. Calculations

since 2001 by the author based on data and worksheets from www.buyupside.com/calculators/feesdec07.htm and http://dqydj.net/sp-500-return-calculator/ (accessed 5/30/14).

39. The figure of 42 million is the number of Americans without health insurance for all of 2013. That number will continue to fall as the ACA is fully implemented. Jessica C. Smith and Carla Medalia, U.S. Census Bureau, "Health Insurance Coverage in the United States: 2013," September 2014, p.2, www.census.gov/content/dam/Census/library/publications/2014/demo/p60-250.pdf (accessed 9/16/14).

40. Organization for Economic Cooperation and Development, OECD Health Data, "Compare Your Country: Health Profile," www.compareyourcountry.org/health/health-spending-change?cr=oecd&lg=en (accessed 5/30/14).

41. Department of Health and Human Services, Centers for Medicare and Medicaid Services, "Brief Summaries of Medicare and Medicaid," www.cms.hhs.gov/MedicaidGenInfo/03_TechnicalSummary.asp (accessed 8/11/08).

42. Department of Health and Human Services, "2013 Actuarial Report on the Financial Outlook for Medicaid," Table 3, p.24, www.medicaid.gov/Medicaid-CHIP-Program-Information/By-Topics/Financing-and-Reimbursement/Downloads/medicaid-actuarial-report-2013.pdf (accessed 6/2/14).

43. U.S. Department of Health and Human Services, Office of the Assistant Secretary for Planning and Evaluation, ASPE FMAP 2015 Report, February 5, 2014, Table 1, http://aspe.hhs.gov/health/reports/2014/FMAP2015/fmap15.cfm (accessed 6/2/14).

44. U.S. Department of Health and Human Services, ASPE FMAP 2015 Report, Table 1; Carmen DeNavas-Walt, Bernadette D. Proctor, Jessica C. Smith, "Income, Poverty, and Health Insurance Coverage in the United States; 2012," U.S. Census Bureau, September 2013, www.census.gov/prod/2013pubs/p60-245.pdf (accessed 9/16/14).

45. "2014 Medicare Trustees Report," July 28, 2014, p. 229–31, www.cms.gov/Research-Statistics-Data-and-Systems/Statistics-Trends-and-Reports/ReportsTrustFunds/Downloads/TR2014.pdf (accessed 11/6/14).

46. "2014 Medicare Trustees Report," p. 231.

47. Health and Human Services, "2013 Actuarial Report," Table 5 (see note 42).

48. Barack Obama, "Remarks by the President to a Joint Session of Congress on Health Care," U.S. Capitol, Washington, D.C., September 9, 2009, www.whitehouse.gov/the-press-office/remarks-president-a-joint-session-congress-health-care (accessed 5/15/12).

49. Peter Grier, "Health Care Reform Bill 101: Who Must Buy Insurance," *Christian Science Monitor*, March 19, 2010, www.csmonitor.com/USA/Politics/2010/0319/Health-Care-Reform-Bill-101-Who-must-buy-insurance

(accessed 5/14/12). This article provides an excellent over-view of the essential parts of the bill.

50. Congressional Budget Office, "Cost Estimates for H.R. 4872, Reconciliation Act of 2010 (Final Health Care Legislation)," March 20, 2010, www.cbo.gov/doc .cfm?index=11355 (accessed 5/14/12).

51. David Nather and Susan Levine, "A Brief History of Obamacare Delays," Politico.com, March 25, 2014, www.politico.com/story/2014/03/obamacare-affordable -care-act-105036.html#ixzz33QRP8biR (accessed 6/1/14).

52. Charlotte Alter, "Sebelius: Obamacare Rollout Was 'Terribly Flawed'," *Time*, April 14, 2014, http://time .com/61395/kathleen-sebelius-obamacare-rollout/ (accessed 6/1/14).

53. The Editorial Board, "The Vanishing Cry of 'Repeal It'," *New York Times*, June 1, 2014, www.nytimes .com/2014/06/02/opinion/the-vanishing-cry-of-repeal-it .html?ref=opinion&_r=0 (accessed 6/2/14).

54. Congressman Paul Ryan, "A Roadmap for America's Future: Medicare and Medicaid," www.roadmap.republicans.budget .house.gov/Issues/Issue/?IssueID=8520 (accessed 3/14/12).

55. Tom Harkin, "The Senate's 'Starter Home' Health Reform," Huffington Post, December 30, 2009, www .huffingtonpost.com/sentom-harkin/the-senates-starter -home_b_407155.html (accessed 6/18/10).

56. Eligibility information for food stamps may be found at U.S. Department of Agriculture Department, Food and Nutri-tion Services, Supplemental Nutrition Assistance Program (SNAP), "Eligibility," www.fns.usda.gov/snap/eligibility; data on the number of food stamp recipients and average benefits may be found at www.fns.usda.gov/sites/default/ files/pd/34SNAPmonthly.pdf (accessed 6/1/14).

57. U.S. Department of Labor, "Unemployment Insurance Data Summary," http://workforcesecurity.doleta.gov/unemploy/ content/data.asp (accessed 6/1/14).

58. Internal Revenue Service, "Preview of 2014 EITC Income Limits, Maximum Credit Amounts and Tax Law Updates," www.irs.gov/Individuals/Preview-of-2012-EITC-Income -Limits,-Maximum-Credit--Amounts-and-Tax-Law -Updates (accessed 6/1/14).

59. Internal Revenue Service, "EITC Awareness Day: IRS Kicks-Off Tax Season Alerting Low- and Moderate-Income Workers of Significant Tax Benefit," www.irs .gov/uac/Newsroom/EITC-Awareness-Day-IRS-Kicks -Off-Tax-Season-Alerting-Low-and-Moderate-Income -Workers-of-Significant-Tax-Benefit (accessed 6/1/14).

60. Maximum benefits are from Social Security Administra-tion, "SSI Federal Payment Amounts for 2014," www.ssa .gov/oact/cola/SSI.html; average benefits and number of recipients are from Social Security Administration, "Fast Facts & Figures about Social Security, 2013," www.ssa .gov/policy/docs/chartbooks/fast_facts/2013/fast_facts13 .html#page24 (accessed 6/1/14).

61. R. Kent Weaver, *Ending Welfare as We Know It* (Washington, D.C.: Brookings Institution Press, 2000).

62. See the analysis of welfare reform by the Center on Budget and Policy Priorities, www.cbpp.org/pubs/tanf.htm, or by the Urban Institute, www.urban.org/toolkit/issues/ welfarereform.cfm (accessed 8/18/08).

63. U.S. Department of Education, "Department Overview," www .ed.gov/about/landing.jhtml?src=gu (accessed 11/26/08).

64. Trymaine Lee, "Has the World Gone Crazy over Common Core?" MSNBC.com, June 2, 2014, www.msnbc.com/ msnbc/common-core-crazy-reactions-education-teachers (accessed 6/2/14).

65. U.S. Department of Education, Race to the Top Fund, www2 .ed.gov/programs/racetothetop/index.html (accessed 2/23/10).

66. Amanda Paulson, "The Next Race to the Top? Arne Duncan Outlines Vision for Teacher Reform," *Christian Science Monitor*, February 15, 2012, www.csmonitor.com/ USA/Education/2012/0215/The-next-Race-to-the-Top -Arne-Duncan-outlines-vision-for-teacher-reform (accessed 3/14/12).

67. Bill and Melinda Gates Foundation, www.gatesfoundation .org/united-states/Pages/program-overview.aspx (accessed 3/14/12).

You Decide

a. *Milwaukee Journal Sentinel*, "Inside Choice Schools: 15 Years of Vouchers," seven-part series, 2005, www2 .jsonline.com/news/choice.

b. John F. Witte, *The Market Approach to Education: An Anal-ysis of America's First Voucher Program* (Princeton, NJ: Princeton University Press, 2001).

c. *Zelman v. Simmons-Harris*, 536 U.S. 639 (2002).

CHAPTER 17

1. Mark Mazzeti and Eric Schmitt, "C. I. A. Missile Strike May Have Killed Pakistan's Taliban Leader," *New York Times*, August 6, 2009, p. A7.

2. For an example of the isolationist approach, see Justin Raimondo, "Out of Iraq, into Darfur?" *American Conservative*, June 5, 2006. For a longer exposition of isolationism, see Patrick J. Buchanan, *A Republic, Not an Empire*, updated ed. (Washington, D.C.: Regnery Publishing, 2002).

3. Robert O. Keohane, *After Hegemony: Cooperation and Discord in the International System* (1984; repr. Princeton, NJ: Princeton University Press, 2005).

4. The distinction was first made in E. H. Carr, *The Twenty Years' Crisis, 1919–1939: An Introduction to the Study of International Relations* (London, UK: Macmillan, 1939). Realism was elaborated as a general theory in Hans Morgenthau, *Politics among Nations: The Struggle for Power*

and Peace (New York: Knopf, 1948). For a general overview, see Jonathan Haslam, *No Virtue Like Necessity: Realist Thought in International Relations since Machiavelli* (New Haven, CT: Yale University Press, 2002).

5. John Mearsheimer, "America Unhinged," *National Interest*, http://nationalinterest.org/article/america-unhinged -9639, January–February 2014 (accessed 5/5/14).

6. See, for example, Lawrence F. Kaplan, "Regime Change," *New Republic*, 228:8 (March 2003): 21, as well as "Birth of a Bush Doctrine? America's Plans for the Middle East," *Economist*, March 1, 2003, p. 46.

7. Michelle Sun, "Woodward Calls War in Iraq Idealist," *Cornell Daily Sun*, June 21, 2007.

8. Gilbert Felix, *To the Farewell Address: Ideas in Early American Foreign Policy* (Princeton, NJ: Princeton University Press, 1961).

9. A synoptic account of the United States as a world power, which takes the story up to the 2003 invasion of Iraq, is Niall Ferguson, *Colossus: The Price of America's Empire* (New York: Penguin Press, 2004).

10. Samuel Flagg Bemis, *John Quincy Adams and the Foundations of American Foreign Policy* (New York: Knopf, 1949); Ernest R. May, *The Making of the Monroe Doctrine* (Cambridge, MA: Harvard University Press, 1975). The latter stresses domestic political considerations and argues that the Monroe Doctrine was "actually the by-product of an election campaign."

11. Daniel M. Smith, *The Great Departure: The United States and World War I, 1914–1920* (New York: John Wiley, 1965).

12. Thomas J. Knock, *To End All Wars: Woodrow Wilson and the Quest for a New World Order* (New York: Oxford University Press, 1992).

13. Margaret MacMillan, *Paris 1919: Six Months That Changed the World* (New York: Random House, 2001).

14. John M. Cooper, *Breaking the Heart of the World: Woodrow Wilson and the Fight for the League of Nations* (New York: Cambridge University Press, 2001).

15. John Lewis Gaddis, *Strategies of Containment* (New York: Oxford University Press, 2005).

16. Tony Smith, "Making the World Safe for Democracy in the American Century," *Diplomatic History* 23:2 (1999): 173–88.

17. Winston Churchill, "Sinews of Peace (Iron Curtain)," Westminster College, Fulton, MO, March 5, 1946, available from the Churchill Centre at www.winstonchurchill.org/ i4a/pages/index.cfm?pageid=429 (accessed 8/2/08). See also Klaus Larres, *Churchill's Cold War: The Politics of Personal Diplomacy* (New Haven, CT: Yale University Press, 2002).

18. George F. Kennan, "The Sources of Soviet Conduct," *Foreign Affairs* 25:4 (July 1947): 566–82.

19. Robert L. Beisner, *Dean Acheson: A Life in the Cold War* (New York: Oxford University Press, 2006); Dean Acheson, *Present at the Creation* (New York: W. W. Norton, 1969).

20. Michael J. Hogan, *The Marshall Plan: America, Britain, and the Reconstruction of Western Europe* (New York: Cambridge University Press, 1987). See also Martin Schain, ed., *The Marshall Plan: Fifty Years Later* (New York: Palgrave, 2001).

21. Marc Trachtenberg, *A Constructed Peace: The Making of the European Settlement, 1945–1963* (Princeton, NJ: Princeton University Press, 1999).

22. The balance of military power between NATO and the Warsaw Pact throughout the Cold War is traced in David Miller, *The Cold War: A Military History* (New York: St. Martin's Press, 1998).

23. Robert A. Packenham, *Liberal America and the Third World* (Princeton, NJ: Princeton University Press, 1973). For an overview, see David P. Forsythe, "Human Rights in U.S. Foreign Policy: Retrospect and Prospect," *Political Science Quarterly* 105:3 (Autumn 1990): 435–54.

24. Sergei N. Goncharov, John W. Lewis, and Xue Litai, *Uncertain Partners: Stalin, Mao, and the Korean War* (Palo Alto, CA: Stanford University Press, 1999).

25. James A. Bill, *The Eagle and the Lion: The Tragedy of American–Iranian Relations* (New Haven, CT: Yale University Press, 1988).

26. Lawrence Freedman, *Kennedy's Wars: Berlin, Cuba, Laos, and Vietnam* (Oxford, UK: Oxford University Press, 2002).

27. William J. Duiker, *Sacred War: Nationalism and Revolution in a Divided Vietnam* (New York: McGraw-Hill, 1995).

28. Henry Kissinger, *Years of Upheaval* (Boston: Little, Brown, 1982); Jussi Hanhimäki, *The Flawed Architect: Henry Kissinger and American Foreign Policy* (New York: Oxford University Press, 2004).

29. Raymond Garthoff, *Détente and Confrontation: American–Soviet Relations from Nixon to Reagan* (Washington, D.C.: Brookings Institution Press, 1994).

30. Bill, *The Eagle and the Lion.*

31. Odd Arne Westad, ed., *The Fall of Détente: Soviet-American Relations during the Carter Years* (Oslo, Norway: Scandinavian University Press, 1997).

32. Garthoff, *Détente and Confrontation.*

33. Philip Hanson, *The Rise and Fall of the Soviet Economy* (London, UK: Longman, 2003).

34. Francis Fukuyama, *The End of History and the Last Man*, updated ed. (New York: Free Press, 2006).

35. For a summary of American human rights policy, see John W. Dietrich, "U.S. Human Rights Policy in the Post–Cold War Era," *Political Science Quarterly* 121:2 (Summer 2006): 269–94.

36. Samuel P. Huntington, *The Clash of Civilizations and the Remaking of World Order* (New York: Free Press, 2002).

37. Scott Wilson, "Obama Calls for Fresh Start with Muslims," *Washington Post*, June 5, 2009, p. A1.

38. For descriptions of some of these cross-cultural programs, see U.S. Department of Education, "Programs by Subject: International Education," www.ed.gov/programs/find/ subject/index.html?src=ln (accessed 8/2/08).

39. U.S. Department of Agriculture, Foreign Agricultural Service, "Market Development Programs," www.fas.usda.gov/mos/marketdev.asp, and "Issues and Policies," www.fas.usda.gov/issues_policies.asp (both accessed 8/2/08).

40. Louis Fisher, *Presidential War Power* (Lawrence, KS: University Press of Kansas, 2004).

41. Arthur M. Schlesinger, *The Imperial Presidency* (Boston: Houghton Mifflin, 1973).

42. Neil A. Lewis, "War Powers: An Old Debate Clinton May Resolve," *New York Times*, May 8, 1993, p. 14; Alison Mitchell, "Deadlocked House Denies Support for Air Campaign," *New York Times*, April 29, 1999, p. A1.

43. Terry Moe and William Howell, "Unilateral Action and Presidential Power: A Theory," *Presidential Studies Quarterly* 29:4 (1999): 850–72.

44. Laurie Goering, "Clinton Signs Pacts on Global Warming: President Acts Despite Strong Opposition to the Treaty in the Senate, Which Must Ratify It," *Chicago Tribune*, November 13, 1998, p. 4.

45. David Hoffman and David B. Ottaway, "Panel Drops Covert-Acts Notification; In Compromise, Bush Pledges to Inform Hill in All but Rare Cases," *Washington Post*, October 27, 1989, p. A1.

46. Dahlia Lithwick, "The Enemy Within," *Slate*, June 12, 2008, www.slate.com/id/2193468 (accessed 8/12/08).

47. Somini Sengupta, "As Musharraf's Woes Grow, Enter an Old Rival, Again," *New York Times*, April 6, 2007, p. A3; Leslie Wayne, "Airbus Seeks a Welcome in Alabama," *New York Times*, June 19, 2007, p. C1.

48. American Israel Public Affairs Committee, "What Is AIPAC?," www.aipac.org/about_AIPAC/default.asp (accessed 8/3/08).

49. American Israel Public Affairs Committee, "Legislation and Policy Update," www.aipac.org/Legislation_and_Policy/default.asp (accessed 8/3/08).

50. Cecilia Kang, "Huawei's U.S. Competitors among Those Pushing for Scrutiny of Chinese Tech Firm," *Washington Post*. October 10, 2012, p. D1.

51. See Pew Research Center, "The U.S. Public's Pro-Israel History," July 19, 2006, www.pewresearch.org/pubs/39/the-u.s.-publics-pro-israel-history (accessed 8/2/08).

52. Gallup Poll, "Slightly Fewer Back ISIS Military Action vs. Past Actions," September 24, 2014, www.gallup.com/poll/177263/slightly-fewer-back-isis-military-action-past-actions.aspx (accessed 10/18/14).

53. Pew Research Center "Public, Wary of Military Intervention in Libya," March 14, 2012, www.pewresearch.org/pubs/1927/strong-opposition-us-involvement-libya-military-overcommitted (accessed 9/25/12).

54. Kyle Dropp, Joshua D. Kerzer, and Thomas Zeitoff, "The Less Americans Know about Ukraine's Location, the More They Want U.S. to Intervene," *Washington Post*, www.washingtonpost.com/blogs/monkey-cage/wp/2014/04/07/the-less-americans-know-about-ukraines-location-the-more-they-want-u-s-to-intervene/ (accessed 5/5/14).

55. Pew Research Center, "Public Opinion Six Months Later," March 7, 2002, www.people-press.org/commentary/display.php3?AnalysisID=44 (accessed 8/2/08).

56. A directory of NGOs can be found at the Department of Public Information site, Nongovernmental Organization Section, www.un.org/dpi/ngosection/asp/form.asp (accessed 8/2/08).

57. See Amnesty International, "The Secretive and Illegal U.S. Programme of Rendition," April 5, 2006, www.amnesty.org/en/news-and-updates/feature-stories/secretive-and-illegal-us-programme-of-rendition-20060405 (accessed 8/12/08).

58. See the National Democratic Institute for International Affairs site at www.ndi.org and the International Republican Institute site at www.iri.org.

59. United States International Trade Commission, Harmonized Tariff Schedule of the United States (2010), Revision 2, www.usitc.gov/docs/tata/hts/bychapter/1002htsa.pdf (accessed 9/14/10).

60. Colum Lynch, "U.N. Backs Broader Sanctions on Tehran; Security Council Votes to Freeze Some Assets, Ban Arms Exports," *Washington Post*, March 25, 2007, p. A1.

61. William B. Quandt, *Camp David: Peacemaking and Politics* (Washington, D.C.: Brookings Institution Press, 1986).

62. John Lewis Gaddis, *The Cold War: A New History* (New York: Penguin Press, 2005).

63. U.S. Department of State, *Treaties in Force*, January 1, 2007, www.state.gov/s/l/treaty/treaties/2007/index.htm (accessed 8/12/08).

64. Lisa L. Martin, "The President and International Commitments: Treaties as Signaling Devices," *Presidential Studies Quarterly* 35:3 (2005): 440–65.

65. Elizabeth Bumiller, Eric Schmitt, and Thom Shanker, "U.S. Sends Top Iranian Leader a Warning on Strait Threat," *New York Times*, January 12, 2012, p. A1.

66. Johanna Neuman and Megan K. Stack, "Americans' Beirut Exodus Underway; Hundreds Are Evacuated by Ship and Helicopter," *Los Angeles Times*, July 20, 2006, p. A10. The Clinton administration resorted to cruise missile attacks five times: three against Iraq (1993, 1996, 1998), one in 1995 against Bosnian Serb forces in the former Yugoslavia, and one against targets in Afghanistan and Sudan in 1998. James Mann, "Foreign Policy of the Cruise Missile," *Los Angeles Times*, December 23, 1998, p. 5.

67. A comprehensive account of the Afghanistan invasion and its aftermath is in Barnett R. Rubin, "Saving Afghanistan," *Foreign Affairs* 86:1 (January/February, 2007): 57–78.

68. For an optimistic review, see Joseph Stiglitz, *Making Globalization Work* (New York: W. W. Norton, 2007).

69. Compiled from data released by the U. S. Office of the Special Trade Representative, www.ustr.gov/countries-regions/china-mongolia-taiwan/peoples-republic-china (accessed 5/30/14).

70. Keith Bradsher, "China Finds a Fit with Car Parts: Export Factories Are Gearing Up to Challenge Global Suppliers," *New York Times*, June 7, 2007.

71. David E. Sanger "With Spy Charges, U.S. Draws a Line That Few Others Recognize," *New York Times,* May 8, 2014, p. D8.

72. Joseph Nocera, "The Cufflinks That Went to China," *New York Times*, January 21, 2006; Jodie T. Allen, "NAFTA Math: The Faulty Arithmetic of Job Losses," *Slate*, July 13, 1997, www.slate.com/id/1889 (accessed 8/2/08).

73. Louis Uchitelle, "Retraining, but for What?" *New York Times*, March 26, 2006, p. 3.1.

74. John Mueller, "Assessing Measures Designed to Protect the Homeland," *Policy Studies Journal*, 38: 1(2010):1–21; John Mueller, *Overblown: How Politicians, the Terrorism Industry and Others Stoke National Security Fears* (New York: Free Press, 2006).

75. Mark Mazzetti, "CIA Still Awaiting Rules on Interrogating Suspects," *New York Times*, March 25, 2007, p. 14.

76. Anne Applebaum, "Cold War in a Hot Climate," *Slate*, May 28, 2002, www.slate.com/id/2066250 (accessed 8/3/08).

77. Fred Kaplan, "Let's Talk about Nukes," *Slate*, August 16, 2005, www.slate.com/id/2124544 (accessed 8/3/08).

ANSWER KEY

CHAPTER 1

1. C
2. B
3. C
4. D
5. D
6. C
7. A
8. E
9. A
10. E
11. C

CHAPTER 3

1. C
2. B
3. B
4. D
5. C
6. B
7. B
8. B
9. C
10. D
11. B
12. A
13. D
14. C
15. D

CHAPTER 5

1. A
2. C
3. B
4. E
5. E
6. B
7. D
8. C
9. E
10. A
11. B
12. C
13. C
14. A
15. D

CHAPTER 7

1. A
2. E
3. B
4. D
5. D
6. D
7. B
8. D
9. C
10. A
11. D
12. B
13. E
14. A

CHAPTER 9

1. A
2. B
3. D
4. B
5. B
6. B
7. C
8. E
9. A
10. C
11. B
12. A
13. C
14. D

CHAPTER 2

1. B
2. E
3. A
4. C
5. C
6. B
7. D
8. B
9. D
10. B
11. D
12. B
13. A
14. B
15. B

CHAPTER 4

1. D
2. B
3. A
4. D
5. B
6. C
7. A
8. B
9. A
10. A
11. B
12. C
13. C
14. B
15. C

CHAPTER 6

1. D
2. B
3. A
4. D
5. C
6. E
7. A
8. D
9. D
10. C
11. B
12. D
13. A
14. C
15. B

CHAPTER 8

1. C
2. A
3. E
4. B
5. E
6. A
7. E
8. A
9. E
10. B
11. C
12. C
13. E

CHAPTER 10

1. E
2. A
3. C
4. B
5. A
6. E
7. C
8. C
9. A
10. B
11. D
12. D
13. B
14. A

CHAPTER 11

1. D
2. E
3. C
4. B
5. A
6. D
7. D
8. B
9. D
10. A
11. C
12. E
13. B
14. B
15. A

CHAPTER 13

1. C
2. A
3. D
4. B
5. E
6. B
7. C
8. A
9. B
10. D
11. C
12. A
13. E
14. A
15. B

CHAPTER 15

1. A
2. C
3. D
4. B
5. C
6. C
7. E
8. D
9. B
10. B
11. E
12. E
13. A
14. D

CHAPTER 17

1. C
2. A
3. E
4. C
5. D
6. D
7. B
8. C
9. A
10. C
11. B
12. D
13. D
14. B
15. A

CHAPTER 12

1. A
2. A
3. C
4. D
5. A
6. D
7. C
8. E
9. B
10. A
11. C
12. B
13. D
14. B

CHAPTER 14

1. A
2. D
3. B
4. E
5. A
6. E
7. B
8. C
9. A
10. E
11. B
12. D
13. C
14. A
15. B

CHAPTER 16

1. B
2. A
3. E
4. B
5. A
6. C
7. E
8. A
9. C
10. D
11. A
12. B
13. B
14. C
15. B

CREDITS

FIGURES

Figure 1.2: Map: "2012 Presidential Election, Purple America," by Robert J. Vanderbei, Princeton University. http://www.princeton.edu/~rvdb/JAVA/election2012/. Reprinted by permission of the author.

Figure 14.4: Figure: "Current Beliefs" from Supreme Court Ideology Project, by Stephen Jessee & Alexander Tahk. http://sct.tahk.us/current.html. Reprinted by permission of the authors.

Figure 17.1: Figure: "Where's Ukraine?" by Thomas Zeitzoff / Monkey Cage, from "The Less Americans Know About Ukraine's Location, the More They Want U.S. to Intervene," by Kyle Dropp, Joshua D. Kertzer and Thomas Zeitzoff. *The Monkey Cage,* April 7, 2014. Reprinted with permission.

PHOTOGRAPHS

iii: AP Photo/Rockford Register Star, Max Gersh; **2–3:** AP Photo/Brennan Linsley; **4:** Jose Luis Magana/AP; **6 (left):** U.S. Army Photo by Staff Sgt. Russell Bassett; **6 (right):** Houston Chronicle, Brett Coomer/AP Photo; **8:** Jupiter Images; **10:** © Brooks Kraft/Corbis; **12:** Joseph Sohm/Visions of America/Corbis; **13:** © LUCAS JACKSON/Reuters/Corbis; **14 (top):** AP Photo/Ross D. Franklin, File; **14 (bottom):** Erin Siegal/Reuters/Landov; **17:** © Leigh Vogel/Corbis; **18:** Flip Schulke/CORBIS; **20:** AP Photo/The Salt Lake Tribune, Scott Sommerdorf; **23:** Win McNamee/Getty Images; **28–29:** AP Photo/J. Scott Applewhite; **30:** © Bettmann/CORBIS; **34:** © North Wind Picture Archives/Alamy; **36:** Imagno/Getty Images; **37:** North Wind Picture Archives; **38:** © Bettmann/CORBIS; **43:** Leonard de Selva/CORBIS; **45:** Corbis; **46:** Library of Congress; **47:** Library of Congress; **51:** © JOSHUA ROBERTS/Reuters/Corbis; **52:** AOC.GOV; **53:** AP Photo/Musadeq Sadeq; **54:** © B Christopher/Alamy Live News; **56:** © Porter Gifford/Corbis; **58 (right and left):** © Everett Collection Inc/Alamy; **61:** KEVIN DIETSCH/UPI/Landov; **66–67:** John Bazemore/AP; **68:** © Larry Downing/Reuters/Corbis; **72:** © MONICA M. DAVEY/epa/Corbis; **75:** © The Metropolitan Museum of Art. Image source: Art Resource, NY; **79:** Bettmann/Corbis; **80:** The Granger Collection, New York; **87:** © Will & Deni McIntyre/CORBIS; **88:** Karen Bleier/AFP/Getty Images; **94:** Kevin Maloney/Getty Images; **97:** Justin Sullivan/Getty Images; **98:** Mario Tama/Getty Images;

100: David Zalubowski/AP; **104–05:** Michael S. Williamson/The Washington Post/Getty Images; **108 (left):** AP Photo; **108 (right):** William Thomas Cain/Getty Images; **114:** Stan Shebs/Wikimedia Commons; **116:** Tom Green Defense Team/AP; **121:** © Bettmann/CORBIS; **123:** Clay good/Zuma Press; **124:** AP Photo/Bay Area News Group, Anda Chu; **126:** William Campbell/Sygma/Corbis; **127:** © B Christopher/Alamy Live News; **129:** © Stacy Walsh Rosenstock/Alamy; **131 (left):** © Scott Houston/Corbis; **131 (right):** © YURI GRIPAS/Reuters/Corbis; **135:** Gettypx/Newscom; **136:** AP Photo; **138:** © JASON REED/Reuters/Corbis; **139:** Bettmann/Corbis; **141:** Site Intelligence Handout/EPA/Newscom; **145:** AP Photo/Michael Stravato; **150–51:** AP Photo/Ross D. Franklin; **153:** © ARISTIDE ECONOMOPOULOS/Star Ledger/Corbis; **154:** Library of Congress; **157:** Michael Salas/Time Life Pictures/Getty Images; **158:** Bill Clark/CQ Roll Call/Getty Images; **159:** U.S. Army, Pfc. Scott Davis, HO/AP Photo; **160:** AFP/Getty Images; **163:** Jamie McCarthy/WireImage/Getty Images; **165 (left):** Reuters/Landov; **165 (right):** Rex Features via AP Images; **168:** Tom Williams/Roll Call/Getty Images; **169:** AP/Bill Hudson; **171:** iStockphoto; **179:** © 2012 Marilyn Humphries/Newscom; **183:** AP Photo/Ron Edmonds; **185:** Mario Tama/Getty Images; **186:** © Chuck Kennedy/White House/Handout/CNP/Corbis; **189:** AP Photo/Susan Walsh; **191:** AP Photo/The Ann Arbor News, Melanie Maxwell; **193:** Scott Olson/Getty Images; **198–99:** © Tim Clayton/TIM CLAYTON/Corbis; **200 (left):** Fox/Photofest; **200 (right):** Charles Dharapak/AP; **201:** Bill Watterson; **202:** © Kenneth D Durden | Dreamstime.com; **206:** SHAWN THEW/EPA/Newscom; **207:** Charles Dharapak/AP; **209:** JEWEL SAMAD/AFP/GettyImages; **211:** Jeff Malet Photography/Newscom; **223:** Wide World Photos/AP; **227 (left):** © Rich Pedroncelli/AP; **227 (right):** © Alex Neely/Demotix/Corbis; **230:** Pablo Martinez Monsivais-Pool/Getty Images. **236–37:** ROBERTO SCHMIDT/AFP/Getty Images; **240:** FPG/Getty Images; **241:** Alex Wong/Getty Images for Meet the Press; **243 (left):** Wide World Photos/AP; **243 (right):** Karim Kadim/AP; **244:** The National Review; **245:** AP Photo/Mother Jones Video; **246 (left):** Mary Schwalm/AP; **246 (right):** © Craig Ruttle/Alamy; **247:** www.IMAO.com; **248:** Dan Polaris/Polaris Images; **249:** Patrick Semansky/AP; **255 (left):** Ali Ali/EPA/Newscom; **255 (right):** © Eddie Gerald/Alamy; **261:** Photo by Martin H. Simon/ABC via

INDEX

Page numbers in *italics* refer to illustrations.
Page numbers in **boldface** refer to figures.

AAA, 353, 364, *364*, 365
AARP, 356, 357, **357**, *359*, 360, 362, 368, *377*, 606, 609, 630
ABC, 241, 243, 244
ABC News, 401
ABC radio network, 244
Abdullah, King of Saudi Arabia, *444*
abolition, abolitionists, 154, 166, 273
abortion, 126, 180, 293, 445
    legislation on, 12, 143, *144*
    parental consent laws and, **144**
    political parties differing views on, 291
    political process and, 145
    public opinion on, 12, 17, 19, 204, *206*
    Supreme Court and, 532, 536–37, 543, 545
    waiting periods laws and, **144**
Abramoff, Jack, 358, *358*, 401
absentee ballots, 308
activists, 281, *281*
Adams, Abigail, 158
Adams, John, 22, 31–32, 37, 75, 158, 239, 513
    compromises forged by, 437
Adams, John Quincy, 317
Adams, Samuel, 37
Adegbile, Debo, 442
administrative law, 517
adversarial system, 517
advertising, 123, 128–29, *129*, 396
    campaign, 326–28, *327*, **327**, 330, 332, 369, 377
    in lobbying campaigns, 356
affirmative action, 184–90, *191*, 204, 209, 465, 543
    in Clinton administration, 184–86
    in education, 509–10, *509*, 520, 532, 538
    future of, 187–91
    women's rights and, 175
Affordable Care Act (ACA; 2010), *10*, 67–68, *67*, 72, 74, **93**, 95, 98, 100, **223**, 225, 340, 420, 423, *424*, 441, *498*, 595–97, *596*, 617, 621, 622–24
    contraceptives and, 119
    implementation of, 478
Afghanistan, 127, 435, 443–45, 642, 645, 662, 665–66
    war in, 13, 14, 20, 105, 246, 253, 341–42, 402, 409, 460, *463*, 480, 636
    war powers and, *53*

Africa, 656
African Americans:
    civil rights of, 57, 154–56, 160–76, *160*, 181, 185–90, 192–93
    discrimination against, 111, 160–61, **221**, 274
    disenfranchisement of, 155
    hate speech against, 124–25
    party affiliation of, 274, 275, 284
    voting history of, 18, *18*, 87, 92, 155, 162–63, **162**, 411, 487, 537
age:
    political affiliation and, **283**
    political influence and, **210**
    poverty rates by, **601**
age discrimination, 176, **182**
Age Discrimination in Employment Act (1967), 91, 92, **93**, 95
aggregate limits, 124
Agnew, Spiro, 454
Agricultural Adjustment Administration (AAA), 598
agriculture, 36, 38, 80, 392
Agriculture Department, U.S., 646
    regulation and, 583
    structure of, 488–89, **489**
aid in dying, 69, 96, 97
AIDS, 97, 124
Aid to Families with Dependent Children (AFDC), 599, 605, 626, **627**
AIG (American International Group), 570
Air Force, U.S., 6, 174
Akin, Todd, 290
Alabama, 114, 190, 192
    black voting in, 155
    civil rights movement in, *169*
    desegregation in, 172
    divorce law in, 175
Alabama v. Garrett, **93**
Alden v. Maine, **93**
Aldrich, John, 272
Alexander v. Sandoval, 190
Alien and Sedition Acts (1798), 76, 120, 239
Alito, Samuel, Jr., 106, 135, 526, 541, *543*, 546
    O'Connor replaced by, 541
Alliance for Retired Americans, 377
Alliance for Student Aid, 367, 368
Al Qaeda, *141*, 435, *466*, 635, 636, 639, 644, *644*, 645, 662, 665
American Cattlemen, 379
American Civil Liberties Union (ACLU), *367*

American Crossroads, 374
American Federation of Labor and Congress of Industrial Organizations (AFL-CIO), **354**
American Hospital Association, **357**
American Independent Party, 295
American International Group (AIG), 570
American Israel Public Affairs Committee (AIPAC), 653, *653*
American Legion, 106
American Medical Association (AMA), 356, **357**
American National Election Study (ANES), 212
American Pork Federation, 379
American Recovery and Reinvestment Act (ARRA; 2009), 13, 448, 574
Americans for Prosperity, 275
Americans with Disabilities Act (1990), 88, *88*, 92, **93**, 95, 184
America's Got Talent, 165
amicus curiae, 534–35
Amish, 108, *108*, 114, 116
Amnesty International, 50, 656
anarchy, anarchists, 6, 7, 35, 112, 121
animal sacrifice, 116
Annapolis Convention, **33**, 34
Anniston, Ala., 168
Annual Economic Report of the President, 565
Anthony, Susan B., 167
anthrax attacks, 666
Antifederalist Papers, 511
Antifederalists, 153, 511
    Constitutional Convention role of, 37, 39, 41, 42, **44**
    constitutional opposition by, 46–47, 110
    separation of powers and, 54, 73, 85
antiwar protests, 105
appeals courts, 519–20, **520**
appointments, judicial:
    congressional power over, 54
    executive power of, 54, 441, 513, 523–28, **525**
    political importance of, 54, 91, 441
    to Supreme Court, 441, 513
appointments, political, 496–97
    congressional power over, 51, 60–61
    executive power of, 51, *51*, 60–61, 441
    in federal bureaucracy, 474
apportionment, 398
Arab Americans, 192

Arab-Israeli War, 642
Arab Spring, 645, 656
Argersinger v. Hamlin, **113**
aristocracy, 8
Aristotle, 8
Arizona, 74, 115, 138, 192
    school vouchers in, 629
Arizona Medical Marijuana Act, *14*
Arkansas, 95, 143, 184
Arkansas River, 531
armband wearing, as symbolic speech, 539, *539*
arms control agreements, 439, 444
Armstrong, Lance, 136
Army, U.S., 6, 120
Army Corps of Engineers, U.S., 474, 484
Arpaio, Joe, 151–52, *151*
arson, 125
Articles of Confederation, *34*, 62
    Constitutional Convention influence of, 31–34, 38, 44, 45
    duration of, **32**, **33**
    government organization under, **39**
    problems with, 32–34, 39, 46, 71
    war powers in, 52
Ashton, Catherine, *638*
Asia Foundation, 656
Asian Americans:
    civil rights of, 154, 156, 158, 185, 188, 193–94
    voting history of, 18
Assad, Bashir, 636
assassinations, 131
Associated Press (AP), 239
astroturf lobbying, 369
AT&T, 137
athletics:
    civil rights and, 156, 182–83, *183*
    regulation and, 476, *476*
Atlanta, Ga., 172
attack ads, 326, 328, *330*
attack journalism, 262, 263
attitudinalist approach, 540–41
attorneys, **113**, 140
Austin, Tex., 115
Australia, 71, 642
Austria, 71, **576**
    hyperinflation in, 581
authoritarianism, 21
automobile industry, international currency market and, 586
autonomy, under federalism, 69–70, 71, 74
Awlaki, Anwar al-, *141*
Axelrod, David, 456

baby boom generation, 611
    Social Security and, 613
Bachmann, Michele, 269
Baghdad, 127
bail, excessive, **113**
Baker, Howard, 424
Bakke, Allan, 189
balanced budgets, 558–60
balance of payments, 560, 584–88
Baldwin, Alec, 128
Baldwin, Tammy, 403, 405, **406**
Balkans, 439
ballots:
    absentee, 308
    counting of, 311

different forms of, 310–11, *310*
    see also voting
Baltimore, Md., 75
Ban Ki-moon, *638*
Bank of America, 569
bank regulations, 498
banks, 60, **70**, 75–76, **77**, 89, 579–82
    federal insuring of deposits in, 557, *557*, 581
    Federal Reserve's role in stabilization of, 567–68, 579–82
    in financial crisis of 2008, 569–72, 579, 581
    in Great Depression, 581
    lending activity regulation in, 567, 580–81
Barron v. Baltimore, **77**, 78, 111
Bartels, Larry, 603
baseball, desegregation of, 156
Bauer, Frederick W., 528
Baumgartner, Frank, 609
Bear Stearns, 569
Becerra, Xavier, *453*
Belgium, **576**
BellSouth, 137
benefits, 119
Benton v. Maryland, **113**
Berlin Wall, *643*
Bernanke, Ben, 567, 570, *570*, 581
Bible, **210**, 211
Biden, Joe, *435*, *453*, 457
"Big Brother," 138
bilateral agreements, 661
Bill of Rights, U.S., 21–22, **44**, **70**, 106, **110**, 153, 248
    creation of, 48, 59, 109–11
    privacy rights in, 142
    public awareness of, *200*
    relevance of, 55, 111, 112, 138
    states' rights and, 42, **77**, 78, 79, 109–12, 131
    see also civil liberties; *specific amendments and liberties*
bills:
    amendments to, 421–22, 425
    filibuster of, 424
    markups in, 421
bin Laden, Osama, 435, *435*, 443–44, 644, *644*, 645, 665
Biological Weapons Convention (BWC), 666
Bipartisan Campaign Reform Act (BCRA; McCain-Feingold Act; 2002), 124, 329, *329*, 427, 534
Birmingham, Ala., 168, *169*
    church bombings in, 169
    desegregation in, 172
    King's letter from jail in, 169–70
birth control, 142, 180
Black, Hugo, 127, 143, 539, 541
"black codes," *see* Jim Crow laws
black-majority districts, 174
Blackmun, Harry, 536–37
Blair, Tony, *638*
blogs, 245, 252, **254**
Blue Cross/Blue Shield, **357**
"blue states," 17, 20
Boehner, John, 271, 387, 410, *410*, 499, 547
    2013 budget and, 564
Bogle, Jack, 617
Boldin, Michael, 67
Bolsheviks, 121

bonds, government, 581
Bono, 130
books, as media news sources, **242**
Border Patrol, U.S., *193*, 648
Bork, Robert, 526
borrowing, 51, **70**, 75
Bosnia, 439, 639, 644, 649
Bossie, David, *333*
Boston, Mass., gay rights in, 179–80
Boston Tea Party, 31, 170
Bowers v. Hardwick, 145, 179–80
Bowles, Erskine, *617*
Boy Scouts of America, 180
Bradley, Joseph, 159
Bradwell, Myra, 158
Brady, Sarah and James, 131
Brady Bill, 131
Brady Handgun Violence Prevention Act (1984), 91, **93**
brand names, political, 277, 323
Brandenburg v. Ohio, 122
Brannon, Laura, 256
Braun, Ryan, 137
Brennan, John, 426, *426*
Brennan, William J., 524, 540
Brennan Center for Justice, 162
Brewer, Jan, 192
Breyer, Stephen, 115, 509–10, 526, 536, 543, *543*
"bridge to nowhere," 408, 409
briefs, 534–35
British Petroleum (BP), *475*, 476, 483
broadcast media, 240–42
    see also media
Brookfield, Wis., 126
Brown, Albert G., *389*
Brown, Monica, *159*
Brown, Scott, 305–6, 344, 345, 346, 424
Brown v. Board of Education I, 156, 167, 171, 544–45, *546*
Brown v. Board of Education II, 156, 171–72
Bryan, William Jennings, *579*
Buchanan, Pat, 310, *310*
Budget and Accounting Act (1921), 562
Budget and Impoundment Control Act (1974), 562
budgetary coercion, 95
budget deficits, 558–60, **559**, **575**, 589–90
    of 1980s, 573, **573**, 575
    see also deficits
budget making, 562, 565
budget maximizers, 491
budget process, 562–64
budget reconciliation, 562
budgets:
    state and local, 88
    see also federal budget
Burchfield, Bobby, *535*
burden of proof, 516
bureaucracy, 222–23, 465, 473–74, *475*
    budget maximizers and, 491
    control of, 497–98, *498*, 567–69
    economic policy and role of, 583, 589–90
    expertise and its consequences for, 480–83, 502
    history of, 483–87, *484*
    human face of, 493–97, **493**
    independent agencies in, 489, **489**, **490**
    legislation and, 477–78
    limits on political activity of, 495–96, *496*
    managing and directing by, 480

modern federal, 487–92, **488**

negative vs. positive aspects of, 480–83, 497–98, 502–3

political appointees and the Senior Executive Service in, 496–97

political process influence of, 9, 13, 474, 479, 482, 485

principal–agent game and, 481–82

problem of control and, 481–83

procurement handled by, 479

public opinion on, **482**

public policy and, 256

red tape and, 480

regulations issued by, 476–79, *476*, 583

regulatory capture and, 482–83

research and development work of, 479

services provided by, 479

social policy and, 605, *605*

standard operating procedures of, 480

street-level, 479

tasks of, 474–80, **475**

"turkey farms" in, 496

types of workers in, 493, **493**

see also civil servants, civil service

bureaucratic drift, 497

agency organization and, 498

correcting violations and, 501–2

monitoring and, 498–501

Bureau of Engraving and Printing, 569

Bureau of Land Management, 585

Burger, Warren, 536–37, 540

Burr, Aaron, 42

bus boycott, 167–68

Bush, George H. W., 140, **223**, 256, 439, 487

approval ratings of, **452**, 462

civil rights legislation and, 182

judges appointed by, **525**

Bush, George W., 152, 192, **223**, 250, 299, 356, 391, 425, 445, *487*, 583, *600*, 609–10

appointments made by, 442

approval ratings of, 397, **452**, 453, **461**, 462

bureaucracy and, 487, 495

Cheney's expanded role under, 457

Congress and, 14, 51

and congressional election of 2006, 397

diversity in administration of, 186

divided government of, 446

economic policy and, 572, 573

financial crisis of 2008 and, 570

foreign policy of, 637, 644, 649

Iraq War and, 639

judges appointed by, **525**, 526, 529

judges nominated by, 527

Kyoto Protocol and, 444

media and, 127

national supremacy and, 86, *87*, 88

No Child Left Behind Act and, 487, 606

pardons granted by, 449

as party leader, 453

presidential succession and, 454

September 11 attacks and, 439

social policies of, 600, 621

Social Security reform and, 605, 606, 611, 615

tax cuts of, 577

in 2000 election, 295, 317, *317*, **318**, 639

unilateral actions of, 464

war powers and, 50, 54

Bush Doctrine, 644

Bush v. Gore, **538**, 543

business:

government and, 138

procurement decisions and, 479

regulation of, 15, **15**, 16–17, **70**, 79, 90, **221**, 437, 476, 487

small, 479

state laws and, 90, 98

business cycle, 574

Business-Industry Political Action Committee (BIPAC), 360

busing, school desegregation and, *171, 172,* 545

butterfly ballots, 310, *310*

by-product theory of information transmission, 251

Byrd, Harry F., 171

Byrd, James, Jr., 165, *165*, 184

cabinet, 457–58, **457**

cabinet departments, number of employees in, 490–91, **490**

see also specific departments

cable television, 240, 241, *241,* **242**, 243–45, 251

Calhoun, John, 76

California, 73, 97, 130, 158, 179, 180, 314, 375, 522

gold rush, 158

Proposition 209 in, 188

race riots in, 165

slavery in, 154, 437

California, University of (Davis), 189

Cambodia, 53

Cameron, David, *237*, 238

campaign advertising, 326–28, *327,* **327**, 330, 332, 369, 377

campaign finance, 123–24, 286, 289, **289**, *291,* 328–32, **331**, 370, **373**, **374**, 509–10, 534, *535*

regulations on, 328–32, **329**, 330–32, 333, 358, 373

campaign platforms, 323–25, 344

Canada, 71

tax rates in, **576**

cancer, 97

Cannon, Nick, 165

Cantwell, Maria, 418

Cantwell v. Connecticut, **113**

Canyon Country Rural Alliance, 585

"cap and trade" policies, 584

capital punishment, *see* death penalty

carbon emissions, 583–84

Carpenter, Daniel, 605

Carswell, G. Harold, 526

Carter, Jimmy, 319, 439

approval ratings of, **452**, *459,* 462

foreign policy of, 642–43

Iranian Hostage Crisis and, 459

cartoons, political, 128

casework, 395, 405

Casey, Robert, 291

Catholicism, Catholics, party affiliation of, 274

Cato Institute, 602

caucus (congressional), 279, 280

caucus elections, 285, **286**, 287, 311–12, 324, 325

voter turnout in, 334

CBS Broadcasting, 130, 241, 243, 244

CBS News, 192

censorship, 123

Census, U.S., **19**, 398

of 1860, 154

Center for Responsive Politics (CRP), 245

Central America, 640

Central American Free Trade Agreement (CAFTA), 588, 658

Central Intelligence Agency (CIA), 137, 250, 449, 648, 650

secret prisons of, 249

centralized groups, 357, 359

cert pool, 533

Chaffetz, Jason, *393*

challengers, 307

Chamber of Commerce, U.S., 356, **357**

charities, 597, *599*

charter schools, 629

chat sessions, 246

Chavez, Cesar, 157, *157*

checks and balances, 7, 30, 36, 39, 41, 46, 48–55, 72, 96, 138

in Supreme Court, 511

in the War on Terror, 50

Chemical Weapons Convention (CWC), 666

chemical weapons treaty, 91

Cheney, Dick, 250, 449, 457

expanded vice presidential role of, 457

Cher, 130

Chicago Legal News, 158

Chicago Tribune, 241

child labor, 80, 119, 437

child molesters, 544

Child Nutrition Act (1966), 599

Child Online Protection Act (1997), 129

children:

in civil rights movement, 169

racial divide and, 163

China, 444, 642, 658–59, *659*

cost of labor in, 584

nuclear weapons of, 666

U.S. trading with, 341, 587–88, 654, 662–64, *663*

Chinese Americans, 158

Chinese Exclusion Act, 158

Chipman, *387*

Chisholm v. Georgia, 73, **77**, 523

chlorofluorocarbons (CFCs), *12*

Christie, Chris, *68*, 343

Christmas, 114

Churchill, Winston, 641

CIA, *see* Central Intelligence Agency

circuit courts, 512, 519

see also appeals courts

Cisco Systems, 654

citizen groups, **354**

Citizens Against Government Waste, 409

Citizens for Tax Justice, 602

citizenship, 192–93

dual, 78–79, 111

Citizens United v. Federal Election Commission, 329, 330, *333,* 373–74, 534, 546

City of Boerne v. Flores, **93**

Civilian Conservation Corps, 599

civilian control, 648

civil liberties, 8, *54,* 55, 106, 208

ambiguity of, 106

civil rights vs., 106, **107**, 153

conflict about, 106–9, *108,* 116, 119, 138

as Constitutional Convention issue, 46–47

federalism and, **77**, 79, 98, 109–11

civil liberties *(Continued)*
    origins of, 109–12
    public awareness of, *200*
    public opinion on, 109, 208, **221**
    restriction of, 36
    Supreme Court rulings on, 540
    see also Bill of Rights, U.S.; *specific*
        amendments and liberties
civil rights, *18*, 78, 80, 85–87, 98, 111–12,
    125–26, 141, 151–53, *153*, 192, 208,
    224, 274–75, 278, 408, 442
    affirmative action and, 187–91
    of African Americans, 151–56, 160–76,
        160, 181, 185–90, 192–93
    of Asian Americans, 154, 156, 158, 185, 188
    civil liberties vs., 106, **107**, 153
    color-blind society and, 160–61
    context of, 153–61
    of the disabled, 154, **182**, 184
    discrimination cases and, 177–78
    of the elderly, 154, **182**
    executive arena and, 184–87, 439
    of gays and lesbians, 154, 159–60, 166,
        169, 180, 184, 192–94
    Great Society and, 487
    judicial arena and, 170–80
    of Latinos, 154, 156–58, 163, 173, 185, 186
    legislative arena and, 181–84
    multicultural issues in, 190
    of Native Americans, 154, 156–57, 185, 188
    policy-making process and, 166–86
    racial divide today in, 162–65, **164**
    social movements for, 166–70, **166–68**,
        169
    in twenty-first century, 187–93
    violations of, 193–94
    of women, 154, 158–59, 166, 167, 169,
        174–79, 182–83, 188
Civil Rights Act (1866), 156
Civil Rights Act (1875), 79, *79*, 156
Civil Rights Act (1964), 87, 172, 181, 187, 520,
    523, 599
    Title VII of, 182
    Title VI of, 190
Civil Rights Act (1991), 182
civil rights groups, 125
civil rights movement, 156, 160, *160*, 166–70,
    169, 181
    nonviolent protest in, 168–70
    timeline for, **166–67**
civil servants, civil service, 273–74, 474
    creation of, 485
    motivations of, 493
    number of employees in, 485
    reductions in force (RIF) in, 494
    regulations for, 494–95
civil unions, 160, 228
Civil War, U.S., 45, *45*, 48, 61, 76, **77**, 78, 86, 92,
    111, 273, 426
    bureaucracy transformed after, 485
    effects of, 154–55
    federal financial support for veterans of,
        597–98
    Lincoln's setting of policy in, 437
Civil War Amendments, 111–12
Civil Works Administration, 599
Clapper, James, 426, *426*
class, politics and, 16, 36
class action lawsuits, 180, 516
    see also lawsuits

classified information, 127, *127*, 248, 260
Clawson, Rosalee, 256
Clayton Antitrust Act (1914), 437
Clean Air Act, 88
Clean Water Act, 88
clear and present danger test, 121, 248
Clear Channel Communications, 241, 244
Cleveland, Grover, 53
Cleveland, Ohio, 115
climate change, 7, 89, 96, 292, 500, 649
    see also global warming
Cline, Andrew, 262
Clinton, Bill, 131, 160, 338, 426, 487
    approval ratings of, **452**, 459, **461**, 462
    budget of, 391, 562
    civil rights and, 184–86
    divided government faced by, 446
    economic policy of, 566
    federalism and, 86
    foreign policy of, 439, 649
    Gore's relationship with, 457
    health care reform and, 605, 621, 626
    impeachment of, 467
    judges appointed by, 442, **525**, 526, 529
    Kyoto Protocol and, 444, 649
    in 1992 election, 317, *566*
    veto used by, 445
    welfare reforms and, 626
Clinton, Hillary, *435*
cloning, 96
closed primary, **286**, 287, 308
closed rules, 425
cloture, 13–14, 424
Club for Growth, 275
Clyburn, James, *453*
CNN, 13, 192, 243, **254**, **258**
Coalition for Luggage Security, *361*
Coast Guard, U.S., 6, 648
coattails, electoral, 338
coercion, 364, 365
coercive federalism, 68, 81
Coersive (Intolerable) Acts (1774), 31
Colbert, Stephen, 205, 241, *241*, 251
Colbert Report, The, 241, *241*, **254**
Cold Harbor, Va., Battle of, *45*
Cold War, 390, 641–43, 661
    end of, 643, *643*
collective action problems, 7–8, 16, 363–65, 410
    interest groups and strategies for
        solving, 364–65
colonial America, media coverage in, 239
Colorado, 531
    gay rights in, 180
Columbine High School, *94*
Columbus, Ohio, 256
commerce, 8, **70**, 116, 389
    Articles of Confederation problems with,
        32–33
    congressional authority over, 51, 57, 72,
        75–76, *75*, **77**, 79–80, **93**, 94–95, 116
    as Constitutional Convention issue, 37,
        42, **44**, 45, 46–47
    state authority over, 78
commerce clause, 30, 62
Commission on Civil Rights, U.S., 2000
    election voting findings of, 162
Commission on Presidential Debates, 325
Common Core, 628
common core curriculum, 17
common law, 517

Commons, John R., 598
Common Sense (Paine), **32**, 35
Commonwealth of Independent States (CIS), 71
Communications Act (1934), 240
Communications Decency Act (1996), 129
communism, 21, 643
Communist Party, U.S., 122
Community Development Block Grants, 85
Compassionate Use Act (Calif.; 1996), 97
compromise:
    in Constitutional Convention, 37–45,
        58–59
    difficulty of, 4, 9, 12
    forms of, 43–45
    necessity of, 12, 16
    slavery and, 437
Compromise of 1850, 155, 437
concentration, in news media, 241–42
concurrent powers, 69, **70**
concurring opinions, **538**
conditional party government, 292–94
Confederacy, *45*, 76
confederal government, 71
confederations, 8, 71
    as interest group structure, 357, 359
conference, 279, 280
conference committees, 415
Conference on Mayors, U.S., 88
conflict, 9–12, *10*, 11
    over bureaucratic expansion, 486
    in Constitutional Convention, *30*
    constitutional interpretation as cause
        of, 94–95
    between courts and other branches, 511
    cultural values as source of, 17, 97
    economic interests as source of, 16–20
    ethnicity as source of, 18–19
    federalism as source of, 4, 37, 75, 90–95, 97
    in foreign policy issues, 640–41, 654, 662
    gender as source of, 18
    in lobbying groups, 379–80
    between presidents and Congress, 442,
        466–67
    public opinion differences as cause of, 3,
        4, 10–12
    race as source of, 18–19
    religion as source of, 17
    separation of powers as source of, 75
    social policy as source of, 595–97, *596*,
        602, 612, 617, 630
    between state and national laws, 3–4,
        3, 514
conflict resolution, 21–23
Congress, U.S., 60, 62, 223, 263, 272, 294, 299,
    344, 466–67
    accountability of, 427
    advertising for, 396
    Alien and Sedition Acts enacted by, 239
    allocation of power to, 7, **39**, 42, **44**, 45,
        51–53, 57, 60, 72, 75, **77**, 80, **84**, 86,
        92, **93**, 94–95, *94*, 97, **107**, 110, 112,
        121, 123, 561
    amendments passed by, 523
    approval ratings of, 390
    Articles of Confederation structure of,
        32–34, **39**
    bailout bill of 2008 passed by, 570
    balance of power and, 511
    bicameralism of, 389
    Bill of Rights creation in, 48, 110

bureaucracy and, 474, 476, 480–83, 487, 498–501, 568
cases on appeal and, 531
caucuses and conferences in, 279
civil liberties and, 137–38
civil rights legislation of, 166, 167, 181–84; see also specific acts
collective action problems in, 410
committee system in, 414–17, **415**, 417–18, 421
compromises in, 387–88
constituency of, 393–94
constituency service in, 309–10, 396, 405–7
constitutional amendments and, **59**, 60, **60**, 72, 115
constitutional interpretation by, 59, 520
creation of laws in, 51, 75, 78–79, 86, 88, 92, 94, 98, 112, 116, 121, 123, 129, 131, 133, 137–38, 141, 142
credit claiming in, 396
cynicism about, 401–3, 427
descriptive representation in, 391
developing party agendas and, 292
economic policy and role of, 561–65, 566, 568, 570, 583, 586, 588–90
election to, 403–7
electoral connection and, 395–98
electoral process and, 42, 309–10, 317
enumerated powers of, 67
exclusive powers of, 48, 51, 57
executive orders and, 442–43
executive privilege and, 448, 449
fear of tyranny of, 511
fiscal cliff and, 414
floor debates in, 417, 421–22
foreign policy and, 649–50
fundraising in, 405, 413, 427
government shutdown and, 414
gun control and, 199, 229
health care reform and, 595–97, 619, 621–24, 621
high reelection of incumbents in, 312, 321, 403–4
home style in, 404–5
immigration laws and, 192
immigration reform in, 226
impeachment process in, 53, 446, 467
incumbency advantage in, 403–7
interest groups and lobbying of, 356, 356, 358, 358, 359, 360, 362, 365–67, 376–81, 585, 654
judicial branch and, 54, 95, 123, 139, 514–15
laws passed by, 105–6
logrolling of, 408, 416
majorities in, 13–14, 76, 86, **224**, 275, 294, 339
media and, 402
oversight by, 425–26, 490, 498–501
parties in, 410
party ideological differences and polarization in, 279–80, **279**
party unity in, 411–13, **412**
party votes in, 411, **412**
permanent campaign of members in, 319–21, 321
polarization of, 411–13, **413**
political parties in coordinating actions of government and, 292–94

position taking in, 396
power of the purse and, 561–65, 568, 650
presidential approval and, 452–53
president overridden by, 436
president's relationship with, 390, 417–18, 423, 436, 439, 452–53
public opinion and, 231
quality of life and, 427
reciprocity in, 408
reelection to, 395–97
reformation of, 427–28
regulations and, 476, 583
religion and, 112, 114
as responsible and responsive, 388, 395, **395**, 402–3
scandals in, 401–3, 402
seniority in, 408
slavery issue and, 43–45, 43, 155
social policy formation and role of, 604–5, 609, 630
Social Security reform and, 611, 613–14
specialization in, 408
spending by, 51, 86
staff of, 417
standing and, 518
State of the Union address and, 445, 453, 454
structure of, **39**, 40, **44**, 57, 407–17
substantive representation in, 391
supermajorities in, 45
Supreme Court cases overruling acts of, **518**
Supreme Court decisions enforced by, 545
term limits in, 60, **60**, 95
treaty making and, 650
two-step procedure for election to, 308–9
unilateral actions and, 465, 466–67
unitary executive theory and, 464
universalism in, 408
war powers of, 51–53, 72, 443–44, 463, 650, 651–52
welfare reform and, 626
whip system in, 410
see also House of Representatives, U.S.; legislative branch; Senate, U.S.
Congressional Black Caucus, 187
Congressional Budget Office (CBO), 86, 562, 601, 620
Congressional Pig Book, 409
Congressional Research Service, 443
Congress: The Electoral Connection (Mayhew), 396
"congruence and proportionality" test, **93**
Connecticut, 40, 40, 131, 142
Connecticut Compromise, 40, **44**
Connor, Eugene "Bull," 169
conscientious objectors, 116
consensus, 12, 12, 20, 38, 94
    lack of, 278
Conservative Political Action Committee (CPAC), 375
conservatives, 15, 19, 47, 84, 95, 97, 201, 202, 202, 203, 206, 219–21, **220**, 277, **277**, 323, 324
    in Supreme Court, 172, 540, 548
considerations, 203–4, 206, 217, 223, 225–29
    public opinion and, 205

Constitution, U.S., 367, 436, 442–43, 445, 561, 650
ambiguity of, 55, 57, 463, 467
amending of, 523
amending process of, **39**, 42, 57–59, **59**, 60, 61, **70**, 72, 110, 115
Article I of, 51, **70**, 72–73, 389
Article II of, 51, 57, 72
Article III of, 73, 511, **512**, 531
Article IV of, 73
Article V of, 57–59, 72
Article VI of, 43, 72
Article VII of, 45
balance of national and state power in, 73, 77–78, 110–11
commerce clause of, 57, 59, 76, **77**, 79, **93**, 94–95, 96, 172, 389
criticism of, 121
economic interpretation of, 36–37, 37
elastic clause of, **70**
electoral laws in, 42, 72, **311**
enumerated powers in, 57, 59, 75, 78, 91
executive orders and, 442–43
executive powers clause of, 51, 57, 59
Federalist and Antifederalist views on, 46–48
flexibility of, 51, 56, 57, 61, 112
full faith and credit clause of, 73–74
government framework in, 30–31, **39**, 48–55, 72–74
historical context of, 31–37
implied powers in, 59–61
individual rights in, **44**, 55
influence on political process of, 6, 29–31, 37–62, **39**
interpretation of, 29, 29, 42–43, 55, 56, 59–61, 61, 73, 75, 77–78, 91–95, **93**, 94, 109, 110–35, 509–10, 514–15, 520
language of, 30, 42–43, 47, 55, 57, 59–61, 111, 112, 115, 130, 133, 141, 142, 539–40
living, 55, 544
Locke's ideas in, 36, 36
national supremacy clause of, 43, 72, 76
necessary and proper clause of, 51, 57, 60, 72, 78
normative theory and, 56
opposition to, 46–47, 109
original intent of, 56, 539, 541
power of the purse in, 51, 53, 53
preamble of, 6, 71
privacy rights in, 142
privileges and immunities clause of, 73–74
public opinion and, 55, 59, 61
ratification of, **33**, **39**, 45–46, 46, 47, 109, 112, 153
recess appointment provision in, 442
relevance of, 55–62
signing of, 45
slavery and, 29
strict construction of, 539, 540, 544
supremacy clause of, 192, 514
undemocratic features of, 44–45, 48
vesting clause of, 441, 464
see also Bill of Rights, U.S.; Constitutional Convention; specific amendments

Constitutional Convention, 153, 158, 511
    civil liberties issue at, 46, 109
    compromise at, 37–45, *43*, **44**, 58–59
    conflict at, 31–37, 42–45
    economic context of, 36–37, *37*
    historical context of, 31–34, **32**, **33**
    important delegates at, 37
    political theories underlying, 35–36,
        46–48
    secrecy of, 37
    war powers issue at, 52
constitutional interpretation, 515
Constitution Party, 296
constructivism, **637**, 638–39
Consumer Financial Protection Bureau, 442,
    498
Consumer Product Safety Commission
    (CPSC), 442, 583
containment, Cold War policy of, 641–43
Continental Congress:
    First, **32**
    Second, 31–32, **32**
contractors, government, 479
contracts, government, 479
Contract with America, 626
Contras, 53
Controlled Substances Act (1970), 97, 119
cooperative federalism, 80, 83
Coots, Jamie, 108
copyrights, 51, 557, 653, 659, *659*
Cordray, Richard, 442, 498
Cornwallis, Charles, **33**
corporate taxes, 575
"corporate welfare," 602
corporations, public opinion and, **222**
cost of living adjustments (COLAs), 556
cost-plus contracts, 479
Cotton, Tom, 305–6, 307, *322*, 345, 346
Cottonseed Payment Program, 415–16
Council of Economic Advisers (CEA), 555,
    565–66
County Boards of Election, 214
Court of Appeals for the Federal Circuit, 519
Court of Appeals for the First Circuit, 519
Court of Appeals for the Ninth Circuit, 519
Court of Federal Claims, 519
Court of International Trade, 519
courts:
    abortion and, 143
    allocation of power to, **44**
    appellate, 112, 132, 135, 519–20, **520**
    cameras in, 536
    circuit, 512, 519
    civil liberties and, 107–8, *108*, 111–12,
        114–16, 120–27, 129, 135, 136–39,
        140, 145
    civil rights agenda advanced by, 168
    civil vs. criminal cases in, 140, 516–17, *516*
    in Constitution, 389
    district, 512, 519
    establishment of, **70**
    federalism and, 73, 74, 75, 519–23, **520**
    foreign policy and role of, 560, 653
    function of, 7
    fundamentals of, 515–19
    jurisdiction of, 512, **512**, 518
    of original jurisdiction, 519
    of special jurisdiction, 519
    state, 523
    structure of, 519–23

venue shopping and, 519
    see also judicial branch; Supreme Court,
        U.S.
coverage formula, 174
Craig, Larry, 401
Craig v. Boren, 178
Crapo, Mike, 309
creationism, 17
credit claiming, 396, 408, 415–16
credit markets, in financial crisis of 2008,
    569–72, 581
crime, 18, 94, 130–32, 134, 137–42, 394
    computer, 129
    gender-based, **93**, 94
    hate, 165, *165*
    punishments for, 140–43
Criminal Anarchy Act (N.Y.; 1902), 112
Criminal Justice Act (1964), 141
cross burning, 122, 125, *126*
crosscutting, 275
cross of gold, *579*
cross-ownership, 241
Crossroads, 275
Crowley, Joseph, *453*
cruel and unusual punishment, 61, *61*, 95, **113**,
    141–42, 544
Cruz, Ted, 269, *269*, 282, *293*, *424*
CSPAN, 388
Cuba, 53, 239, 642
Cuban Americans, 157
    voting history of, 18
Cuban missile crisis, 642
culture wars, political conflict as result of,
    17, 114
Cunningham, Randy "Duke," *402*
currency, 8, 32, 34, 37, **39**, 51, **70**, 72, 74–76,
    114, 569, 578, *579*, 581
    Articles of Confederation and, 32, 34, **39**
    international value of, 584–86
current account, 560, 589
    deficits and, 586–687
Czech Republic, **576**

Dahl, Robert, 38
Daily Show, The, 251, 253, **254**
"Daisy" ad, 326–27, *327*
data mining, 138
Davids, Jon, *362*
Davis, Wendy, 326
Dawson, Rosario, *163*
"death panels," 217–18, 621
death penalty, 56, 61, *61*, 95, **113**, 141–42,
    209, 544
debates, 325
Death with Dignity Act (Oreg.; 1994), 97
de Blasio, Bill, 165
Debs, Eugene V., 121, *121*
debt:
    deficits vs., 558–60, **559**
    post-Revolutionary War, 33, 34, 37, 514
decision making, 9
    of Supreme Court, 535–45
Declaration of Independence, 22, 32, **32**, 154,
    484
    Locke's ideas in, 36, *36*
    political theories in, 35–36
Deepwater Horizon, *475*
de facto segregation, 171–72
defendant, 516
defendants' rights, 112, **113**, 132–42, 145

defense, 6, *6*, 7, 69, 72, 224
    ideological views on, 19
    spending for, 492, **492**
defense appropriations bill, 408, *409*
Defense Department, U.S., 425, 443, 480
    foreign policy and role of, 648
Defense of Marriage Act (DOMA; 1996), *14*,
    73, **93**, 96, 180, 184, 522
deficits, 84, **575**, 589–90
    balance current account, 589–90
    current account and, 586–87
    cutting spending in reduction of, 573–74
    debt vs., 558–60, **559**
    of 1980s, 573, **573**, 575
    trade, 560, 561, 586–88, **587**
De Jonge v. Oregon, **113**
de jure segregation, 171
Delaware, 314
delegates, 313, 391
    allocation of, 311–12
DeMint, Jim, 29
democracy, 207, 656
    centralization in, 100
    competitive federalism and, 90, 98
    conflict resolution in, 21–23
    Constitution as blueprint for, 55
    crime and, 132–33
    interest groups as fundamental feature
        of, 353
    media in, 237–38
    populist, 38–39
    public opinion and, 221–23
    republican, 8, 35–36, 40
    U.S. as representative, 306, 307
    see also elections, U.S.; federalism
Democratic Congressional Campaign
    Committee (DCCC), 279
Democratic Governors' Association, 275
Democratic Leadership Council (DLC), 275
Democratic National Committee (DNC), *271*,
    277–78
Democratic National Conventions, 313, *313*
Democratic Party, 31, 209, 211, *224*, 263,
    270–71, **277**, 299–300, 306, *310*,
    319, 342, 411–14, 455
    activist government and, 554–55
    affiliations by race and gender with, 18,
        18, 274, 275, **283**, 284
    bailout bill of 2008 and, 570
    as brand name, 277, 323
    bureaucratic control and, 502
    campaign fundraising and support
        provided by, 289, **289**
    on civil rights issues, 274
    cloture rule and, 13–14
    congressional caucus of, 279
    Contras and, 53
    culture wars reflected in election results
        of, 17, **21**
    economic policy and, 583, 588
    founding and history of, 271–75, **272**, 437
    gun control and, 229
    health care and, 225
    House controlled by, 13, 446
    identification with, 15, 17, *18*, 19–20, **21**,
        203, 208, 209, 219, **220**
    ideology and, 15, 17, 19–20, **21**, 97,
        279–80, **279**, 291
    Iraq War funding and, 464
    judicial nominees and, 529

larger federal government favored by, 273, 274, *274*

Latinos in, 157

leadership positions in, 452

limited federal government and, 86

media and, 258

party coalitions in, 284, **284**

party identification in electorate of, 280–82, **281**, **283**

party in government of, 278–80

party organizations of, 275–78

poverty rates under leadership of, 603, **603**

presidential platforms of, 291

primaries of, 155, 537

recruiting and nominating of candidates in, 285, 287

regulation and, 16–17, 274

Senate controlled by, 13, 446

social policy approaches favored by, 595–97, 598, 615, 616–17, 629

southern, 155, 181

spending and, 16–17

superdelegates in nominating process of, 313

support of New Deal and, 486

taxes and, 16–17, 562, 572, 574

views shaped by identification with, 15

see also elections, U.S.

Democratic-Republicans, 75, 76, 120, 272, 513

Democratic Senatorial Campaign Committee (DSCC), 279

demographics, 209–11

Denmark, **576**

Department of Motor Vehicles (DMV), 610

depression, *see* economic depression; Great Depression

deregulation, of media, 241–42

Derthick, Martha, 100

descriptive representation, 391

desegregation, 166–69, 170–72

of interstate travel, 168

of schools, *see* school desegregation

see also segregation

détente, 642

Detroit, Mich., 172

devolution, 96

dictatorship, 22

Dingell, John, 14

diplomacy, as foreign policy tool, 657

direct democracy, 22

direct incitement test, 122, 126

direct lobbying, 365–66

disabled people, civil rights of, 154, **182**, 184

discount rate, 580

discretionary spending, 574, **575**

discrimination, 18, 87, 91, 92, **93**, 96, 98, 105, **107**, 111, 151–52, 160–61, **221**

disparate impact standard and, 172

in employment, 172, 181, 182, 188

gender, *see* gender discrimination

racial, *see* racial discrimination

reverse, 190

discrimination cases, civil rights and, 177–78

disparate impact standard, 172

dissents, **538**

distributive theory, 416

district courts, 512, 519

District of Columbia, 74, 132, 171, *183*

courts in, 519

districts, 87

diversity, 18, 185–86

divided government, 294, 572

social policies impacted by, 604–5, 630

DNA swabs, probable cause and, 134

Doctors without Borders, 656

domestic spying, *see* surveillance

Dominicans, 157

domino theory, 642

Donnelly, Joe, 309

"don't ask, don't tell," 184–85, *185*

Doolittle, Amos, *46*

double jeopardy, **113**, 139

Douglas, William O., 142, 531

draft, military, 51, 91, 120, 123

DREAM Act, 152, *441*

Dred Scott v. Sandford, 77–78, **77**, 111, 155, 514

drinking laws, 69, 88, 95, 175, 178

drones, 435, 499, 639, 645, *645*

Druckman, James, 256

Drug-Free Workplace Act (1988), 137

drugs, 17, 122, *123*

advertising of, 128

employment and, 119, 136–37

legalization of, 3–5, *3*, 9, *14*, 19

medical use of illegal, 96, 97, *97*

possession of, 109, 134, 135, 136

regulation of, 97, 119, 476, 479

religion and, 119

safety of, 475, 476, 480, 481–82, 502

drug-sniffing dogs, 109, 135, *135*

drug testing, 136–37

dual citizenship, 78–79, 111

dual federalism, *see* federalism, dual

due process, 47, 54, 61, **70**, 78, 92, **107**, 109, 111–12, 132–42, *141*, 145, 153

gay rights and, 180

Dukes, Betty, *179*

Duncan v. Louisiana, **113**

Dunkin' Donuts, 176

Dunne, Finley Peter, 544

Duverger's law, 296

earmarks, 408, *409*

see also pork-barrel spending

Earned Income Tax Credit (EITC), **627**

working poor and, 625

Ebola virus, 456, 460, 462, 636, 638, 648, 649, 656

economic conditions, public opinion and, **341**, **342**

economic depression, 555

economic groups, **354**, 366

see also Sallie Mae, lobbying by

economic growth, 439

as economic policy goal, 557–58, *557*

economic individualism, 16

economic interests:

Articles of Confederation and, 33–34

Constitutional Convention and, 36–37

Constitution and, 72, 73

political conflict about, 16–17

public opinion and, 203, 208, *209*, **223**, 225, 340–41

economic policy:

bureaucracy and role in, 567–69, 589–90

congressional role in, 561, 566, 568, 570, 583, 589

financial crisis of 2008 and, 569–72, *570*

fiscal theories and policies in, 572–89, **573**, 589

goals of, 555–61

government regulation and impact on, 582–84

monetary theories and polices in, 578–82, 589, 602–3

presidential role in, 256, 562, 565–66, *566*, 589–90

protectionism and, 587–88

on trade and balance of payments, 584–89, 659, 662–64

economic stimulus package, 13, 89, 292, 298, 448, 450, 462, 565, 574

economy, 71, 72, 80, 85, **85**, 94, **223**, 225

regulation of, 437

slavery and, 154

Edison High School, 94

education, 8, 13, 15, 17, 69, 74, 80, 87, *87*, 88, 91, 94, 96, 394, 439, 485

civil liberties and, 113–14, 124, 137

Common Core and, 628

conflictual issues related to, 17, 109

desegregation and, *see* school desegregation

government and, 8, 15, 69, 74, 80, 87, 91, 94, 96, 109, 115–16, *628*

ideology and, 17, 19

No Child Left Behind Act and, 487, 606, 627–28

political influence of, 207, **210**, 211

race and, 18, 87, 91

Race to the Top program and, 606, 628

social policies on, 626–29, *629*

state differences in, 91

student loans and, 351, 356, 361, 366, 367, 378

Education Amendments (1972), Title IX of, 182–83

Education Department, U.S., 8, *183*, 627, 646

Eighth Amendment, 95, **110**, **113**, 132, 141–42, 544

Eisenhower, Dwight, 184, 438, 524

civil rights and, 545

elastic clause, *see* necessary and proper clause

elderly people:

civil rights of, 154, **182**

growing population of, 611, **612**

poverty rates of, **601**, 602, 611

election cycle, 318

Election Day, 308, 334, 343, 376

elections, U.S., 5, 15, **224**, 278, 285–91, *295*, 305–45

of 1800, 76, 120, 513

of 1824, 317

of 1828, 484

of 1860, 155

of 1876, 317

of 1888, 317

of 1916, 438

of 1932, 274, 438, 598

of 1952, 319

of 1964, 326, *327*

of 1968, 319

of 1976, 319, 642

of 1980, 319, 487, 642

of 1992, 185, 317

of 1994, 338

of 2000, 162, 295, 310, *310*, *317*, 543, 639

of 2002, 329, 453

elections, U.S. *(Continued)*
    of 2004, 124, 453
    of 2006, 338, 340, 397, 446, 453
    of 2008, 13, 163, 185, **283**, 285, 292, **308**,
        320, **331**, 340, 342, 397, 404, 453, 584
    of 2010, 269, 294, **331**, 338, 340–41, 344,
        397, 404, 453, 534
    of 2012, 13, 20, **21**, 210, 216, *245*, 282,
        290, *290*, 312, *313*, 316, *320*, 322,
        324, **344**, 327, **327**, 330, **331**, 334,
        341–44, **341**, **343**, 397, 553, 572
    of 2014, 163, 238, 269, 275, **289**, 289, 300,
        305, 307, 319, *319*, **329**, 331, **331**,
        340, *344*, 344–46, **345**, 373, 374,
        377–78, 397, 413–14, *413*, *429*, 453
    accountability of incumbents and
        political parties enforced by, 299, 307
    Articles of Confederation and, 32
    campaign advertising in, 326–28, *327*,
        327, 330, 332, 369–70, 377
    campaign assistance provided by
        political parties in, 289, **329**
    campaign financing in, 289, **289**,
        328–32, **329**, 330–32, **331**, 370,
        373, **374**
    campaign platforms and, 323–25, **324**
    campaigns in, 318–32
    campaign strategies and tactics in,
        322–23
    confrontation of opponents in, 325–26
    to Congress, 403–7
    congressional districts and
        constituencies in, 309–10
    Constitutional Convention and, 42, **44**
    Constitution and, 48, **311**
    County Boards of, 214
    cultural values in, 12, 17
    fund-raising for, 289, **289**, *291*, 320, **331**
    high reelection of incumbents and low
        turnover in congressional, 321, **331**,
        403–4
    importance of, 35, 439
    indirect, **39**, 48
    influence on everyday life of, 9
    influence on political process of, 9, 13–14,
        163, 439
    for judges, 523
    laws concerning, 87
    Locke's view on, 36
    media and, 9, 14, 23, 245, *245*, 256, 306,
        321, 325–26
    national conventions in, 313
    national power over, 88
    normal vs. nationalized, 337–40
    party identifications of electorate and,
        280, **281**, **283**
    permanent campaigning of incumbents
        and, 319–21, *321*
    polls and, 212, 214
    presidential, 311–17
    primary and caucus stage in, 285, **286**,
        311–13
    process of, 306–17
    public opinion and, 200, 231
    recruiting and nominating candidates
        in, 287–88, 311–13
    rules and requirements of, 13, 163, 306,
        311–13, **311**
    spending in, 123–24, 330–31, **331**, 332,
        333, 373–74
    states' role in, 42, **70**, 74, 87
    voter turnout in, 96, 334–35, **335**
    voting cues in shaping citizen's choice in,
        336, **337**, **338**
    voting methods and ballot counting in,
        310, *310*
    voting requirements in, 308–9
electoral college, 60, 72, 313–14, 315–5, 343
    establishment of, 42, **44**
    problems with, 42
electoral connection, 395–98
electoral vote, 313–14, **314**, 315–16, 317, *317*,
    318, 343, **343**
Elementary and Secondary Education Act
    (1965), 87, 599, 627
Eleventh Amendment, 58, 73, **77**, 92, **93**, 523
Ellis Island, 531, *531*
Emancipation Proclamation, 437, 465
Emergency Economic Stabilization Act
    (2008), 570
eminent domain, 140
employment, 18, 89, 90, 95, 573
    discrimination in, 172, **173**, 181, 182, 188
    drugs and, 119, 136–37
    full, as economic policy goal, 555
    outsourcing and, 494, 664, *664*
    in selected cabinet organizations, **490**
    in selected federal organizations, 490
    social policy and, 599
    trade policy and, 586–88
    see also labor laws; workplace issues
Employment Act (1946), 555, 565
Employment Non-Discrimination Act, 184
endangered species, protection of, 515
Endangered Species Act (1973), 140, 296, 517
energy, 13, 439, 609
Energy Department, U.S., 82, 448
energy efficiency, 82
England, 71
    see also Great Britain
Engle v. Vitale, 114
English, as official language, 18, 190, 192, 227
entitlement programs, 619
environment, environmentalism, 7, 17, 19, *60*,
    71, 87, 89, 96, 98, 124, 140, 169, **221**,
    224, 445, 558
    Hudson River and, *503*
    regulations for protection of, 89, *503*,
        582–83, *582*, 585
environmental policy, federalism and, 82
Environmental Protection Agency (EPA), 82
Equal Employment Opportunity Commission
    (EEOC), **173**, 176, 181
    gender discrimination and, **182**
equality, **107**
    civil rights and, 153–54
    constitutional importance of, 35
    economic, 16–17, *17*, 22, 36, *37*, 441
    gender, 94, *479*
    political, 22–23, 43–45, 89, 111
    racial, 43–45, 87, 89, 111
    social, 22
    see also voting rights
equal protection, 58–59, 78, 91, 92, 95, **107**,
    153, 180, 193–94
    affirmative action and, 191
    blacks and, 155, 171
    women and, 158–59, 174–79
Equal Rights Amendment, 183
equal time provision, 241
Era of Good Feeling, 273
Escalante River, 585
Espionage Act (1917), 120, 127
establishment clause, 112, 114–15
estate taxes, 609
ethnicity, 18, 206
Europe, 7, 16, 36, 639–40, 641
    hyperinflation in, *581*
    see also specific countries
European Union (EU), 71, 638, 659
*Everson v. Board of Education of Ewing
    Township*, **113**
evolution, 17, 114
exchange rates, 586
excise taxes, 575–76
exclusionary rule, 136, *136*, 141
executive agreement, 444, 465
executive branch, 455–58, 511
    allocation of power to, 7, 8, 51, 57, 59, 138
    cabinet in, 457–58
    checks and balances on, 54
    drug testing in, 137
    foreign policy and role of, 647–49
    Locke's view on, 36, 41
    media and, 127
    powers allocated to, 436
    structure of, 488–89, **488**
    see also president, U.S.; vice president,
        U.S.
Executive Office of the President (EOP),
    455–56, **455**, 488, *488*, 496, 567,
    647
    federal spending and, 491
executive orders, 57, 442–43
    civil rights and, 156, 182, 184
executive privilege, 449
    limits of, 448, 449
extraordinary rendition, 107
ExxonMobil, **357**

Facebook, 245, 246, *246*
    offensive content and, 125
factions, 7
    causes and control of, 36, 38
    see also interest groups
Fair Housing Act (1968), 181
Fair Labor Standards Act (1938), **93**
fairness doctrine, 240
Fallon, Jimmy, 251
Falwell, Jerry, 128
Family Leave Act (1993), 92, **93**
Family Research Council, **354**
"family values," 17
Fannie Mae, *see* Federal National Mortgage
    Association
Farm Act (2002), 610
Farrakhan, Louis, 187
fascism, 21
fast-track authority, 444
FBI (Federal Bureau of Investigation), 6, 137,
    165, *165*
FCC, *see* Federal Communications
    Commission
FDA, *see* Food and Drug Administration
Federal Aviation Administration (FAA), 574
    regulation and, 583
federal budget, 13, 589–90, 647
    balancing of, *60*, 391, 558–60
    congressional power over, 52, 561–65,
        649, 650

deficit in, 429, 558–60, **559**, 565, 573, **573**, 574–75
ideological views on, 20
mandatory vs. discretionary spending in, 574–75, **575**
presidential power over, 562, 565
size of, 491–92, **491**
social policy and, 597–98, 602–3, 610, 620
Federal Bureau of Investigation (FBI), 6, 137, 165, *165*
federal campaign funding, 343
Federal Communications Commission (FCC), **15**, 130, 240–42, 474, 476
limits on running of, 498
Federal Deposit Insurance Corporation (FDIC), 489, 557, *557*
Federal Election Commission, 124, 328–29, 498
Federal Emergency Management Agency (FEMA), 343, 441
Hurricane Katrina and, 502
Federal Emergency Relief Administration, 599
Federal Employees Political Activities Act (1993), 495
Federal Food, Drug, and Cosmetic Act (1938), 475
federal funds rate (FFR), 580
Federal Home Loan Mortgage Corporation (Freddie Mac), 569–72
federalism, 7, 8, 68–71
advantages of, 96, 98, *100*
assessing, 95–100
balance of power under, 42, 68, 71–74
civil liberties and, 109–11
civil rights and, 166
coercive, **84**, 86–89
competing versions of, 83–90, **84**
competitive, 90, 98
constitutional framework for, 42, 73–74
cooperative, 80, 83–86, **84**, 86, 90, 98
as cornerstone of political system, 95
court structure and, 519–23
disadvantages of, 98, 100
dual, 77–80, 83, **84**, 86, 90, 514–15
early, 75–76
environmental policy and, 82
fiscal, 83, **84**, 85–86
ideological complexities of, 95–96
international forms of, 70–71
"layer cake" model of, 80, 81, **84**
"marble cake" model of, 80, 81, **84**
modern, 80, 83–95
picket fence, 80, 81, 83, **84**
sense of community under, 100
see also government, federal; states
Federalist Papers, *33*, 36, 48, 51, 389
Federalists, 272, **272**, 511
Constitutional Convention role of, 37, 39, **44**
court stacking plan of, 513
government control by, 75–76, 120
separation of powers and, 47, 54, 73, 74, 111
strategies of, 47–48
Federalist 78, 511, 514
Federalist Society, 47, 495
Federal National Mortgage Association (Fannie Mae), 569–72
federal preemptions, 88
Federal Register, 476

Federal Reserve, 8, *51*, 62, 489, 557, 561
banking system overseen by, 567–68, 579–82, 590
Board of Governors of, 567
in economic crisis of 2008, 569–72, 581
political independence of, 567
Treasury Department in cooperation with, 569–72
Federal Reserve Act (1913), 437, 567
Federal Reserve Reform Act (1977), 568
Federal Reserve System, 29, 320, 567–68
Federal Speedy Trial Act (1974), 141
Federal-State Extended Benefits Program, 625
Federal-State Unemployment Compensation Program, 624
Federal Trade Commission (FTC), 476
FedEx, 176
Feingold, Russell, 329, 427
FEMA, *see* Federal Emergency Management Agency
feminists, feminism, 18
Fenno, Richard, 393, **394**, 403, 416
feudalism, 36
Fifteenth Amendment, 59, 78, 111, 155
Fifth Amendment, **77**, 78, **110**, 111, **113**, 132–33, 138–40, 141, 142, 522
fifth party system, **272**, 274, 275
fighting words, 128
filibuster, 13–14, 424, *424*, 595, 597
to block judicial nominees, 529, *529*
budget reconciliation and, 562
Fillmore, Millard, 437
film companies, corporate ownership of, **242**
filtering, 255–57, 259–60
Financial Times, 243
Finland, **576**
fire alarm oversight, 426, 500
First Amendment, 61, 76, 105, 106, 108, 110, **110**, 112–30, **113**, 117, 128, 142, 180, 532
symbolic speech protected by, 539, *539*
First Continental Congress, **32**
first-mover advantage, 444
first party system, 272, **272**
fiscal policy, 561, 572–78, 589
see also taxes, tax policy
Fisher, Abigail, *189*
501(c) organizations, 370, **370**
527 organizations, 275, 329–30, 370, **370**, **373**
campaign finance and, 373
campaign finance regulations on, 333
flag desecration, **60**, 122–23, *124*
Flag Protection Act (1989), 123
Florida, 142, 174, 179, 188, 313, 314, 317, *317*
jury duty in, 159
school vouchers in, 629
2000 election voting problems in, 295, 310
focus groups, 212
Foley, Mark, 401
Food and Drug Administration (FDA), 8, **15**, 474, 475, 476, 479, 502
expertise in, 480, 502
regulation and, 481–82, 583
Vioxx recall and, *501*
food stamps program, 489, 597, 599, 606, 624, **627**
Forbes, 601
Ford, Gerald, 319, 439, **452**, 454, 459, 642
foreign aid, 7, 20, 217, 394, 659–60, **660**
spending for, 492, **492**

Foreign Intelligence Advisory Board, 647
Foreign Intelligence Surveillance Act (FISA), 138
Foreign Intelligence Surveillance Court, 137, 464
foreign investment, 587
Foreign Miners Tax, 158
foreign policy, 392, *439*, 444–45, 635–36, *639*
alliances and treaties as tool in, 641–42, 661
Congress and, 646, 649–50
control of, 33, 51, 59, 69, **70**
definition of, 637
diplomacy used in, 657
foreign aid in, 659–60, **660**
general principles of, 637–39
history and evolution of, 639–46
human rights as issue in, 642, 644
idealist vs. realist views in, 639
interest groups and influence on, 653–54
international organizations and, 656
international trade and, 519, 566, 584–89, 641, 644, 657–59, **658**, 662–64
Iraq War and, *see* Iraq War
key players in shaping of, 646–56
media and influence on, 654
military component of, 642, 644, 648, 661–62
peacekeeping and humanitarian operations in, 648, 649
political conflict in, 662
president's central role in, 646, 647, 648–49
public opinion and, 20, 654–56
terrorism threat and, 650, 653, 665–66
theories of, **637**
tools of, 659–62
WMDs and nuclear proliferation as issue in, 717
see also specific presidents
Forest Service, U.S., 488
Foundation for Traffic Safety, 365
Founders, 6, 30, *31*, 32, 36, 39, 52, 62
Fourteen Points, 640
Fourteenth Amendment, 30, 58–59, 77, 78–79, 92, **93**, 95, **107**, 111–12, 132, 136, 141, 143, 145, 158–59, 522
affirmative action and, 541
due process clause of, 153, 180
equal protection clause of, 153, 155, 158–59, 171, 174–79, 180, 191
Fourth Amendment, 109, **110**, **113**, 132, 133–38, 142
fourth party system, **272**, 273
Fox News Channel, **258**, 261, 262
Fox News Network, 241, 243, 244, **254**
Fox Television, 130
framing, 255–57, **257**, 259–60
France, 33, 71, 76
British war with, 463
tax rates in, **576**
Frankfurter, Felix, 537
Franklin, Benjamin, 37, 45, 239
Freddie Mac (Federal Home Loan Mortgage Corporation), 569–72
Freedmen's Bureau, 155
freedom:
civil liberties and, 153
as not absolute, 106–8

freedom of assembly, 21–22, 112, **113**, 116, 125–26
  "reasonableness" standard and, 126
freedom of religion, 7, 8, 21–22, 106, 107, *108*, 110, 112–19, **113**, 145, 153
  see also religion
freedom of speech, 8, 19, 21–22, 47, 61, 76, 79, 105, 106, 108, 110, **113**, 119–25, 145, 153, **221**, 256–57
  symbolic, 539
freedom of the press, 21–22, 47, 79, 109, 110, 112, **113**, 126–27, *127*, 145, 153, 248
Freedom Riders, 168
free exercise clause, 112, 116, 119
  corporations and, 119
free market, 16, 90
  environmentalism, 585
  government regulation of, 8, 557–58, 583, 584
  ideological views on, 19
  production of public goods by, 7
  promotion of, as economic policy goal, 557–58, *557*, 561
free riding, 7, 16, 364, 365
  strategies for solving problem of, 364, 365
free trade, 438, 439, 444, 588
  American jobs and, 586–88
  comparative advantage and, 588
  protectionist policies and, 587
French and Indian War (1754–63), 31
French Revolution, 120
frontloading, in primaries, 312
Fugitive Slave Act (1850), 155
full employment, 555
full faith and credit clause, 73–74

Gaddafi, Muammar al-, 443, 499
gambling, 17, **93**
Garner, Tyron, 145, *145*, 180
Gates, Bill, 576, *583*, 601, 616
Gates, Robert, *435*
Gates Foundation, 628
gays, gay rights, 20, 56, 69, 72, 89, 90, 95, 124, 145, 159–60, 166, 169, 179–80, 184, 202, 203, **221**, 226, 228, **229**, 522
  civil rights of, 192–94
  discrimination against, 105
  marriage and, *14*, 17, 20, 73–74, 96, 160, 180, 184, *185*, 192–93, 226, 228, 309
  military and, 105–6, 184–85, 192–93
  sex and, 179–80, 543, 544
GDP, *see* gross domestic product
Geering, John, 291
Geithner, Timothy, 571
gender:
  hate speech and, 124
  juries and, 141
  laws concerning, 92, **93**
  relationship of voting patterns to, 18, **283**
  as source of political conflict, 18
  see also women, women's rights
gender discrimination, 175, 176, *179*, 182, 516
  EEOC and, 182, **182**
"gender gap," 18
General Agreement on Trade and Tariffs (GATT), 588, 641
general election, 308, 321–26
  federal funding in, 330
General Electric, 356, **357**

General Services Administration (GSA), *479*
  number of employees in, 491
  taxpayers' money and, *480*
General Social Survey, 210, **210**, 219–20
generational effects, 208
George III, King of England, 41, 484
Georgia, 137, 172, 174, 192, 643
  sodomy in, 179
German Empire, 121
Germany, 71, 640
  exchange rate and, 586
  hyperinflation in, 581, *581*
  tax rates in, **576**
Gerry, Elbridge, 47, 109, 399
gerrymandering, 399, **400**
  types of, **399**
get-out-the-vote activities, 289, 322
Gibbons v. Ogden, 76, **77**
G.I. Bill, 555, 627
Gideon, Clarence, 140
Gideon v. Wainwright, **113**, 140
Gillibrand, Kirsten, 387–88, *387*, *429*
Gingrich, Newt, 553
Ginsburg, Ruth Bader, 526, 543, *543*
Gitlow, Benjamin, 112
Gitlow v. New York, 112, **113**
"glass ceiling," 176
globalization, 566, *586*, 663, *663*
global warming, 13, 89, 203, 284, 495, 649
  see also climate change
going public, 453
Goldman Sachs, *571*
gold standard, 579
Goldwater, Barry, 326–27, *327*
Gonzales v. Oregon, 97
Gonzales v. Raich, 97
Goodyear Tire and Rubber Company, 176
Google, 246
Gorbachev, Mikhail, *439*, 643
Gore, Al, *310*
  expanded vice presidential role of, 457
  in 2000 election, 295, 310, 317, **318**, 639
Goss, Porter, 249
government:
  definition of, 6
  divided vs. unified, 294
government, federal:
  Articles of Confederation period of, 32–34
  benefits to wealthy provided by, 601
  branches of, 7, 48–55
  criticism of, 76, 112, 120–22, *121*, 483
  debt limit and, 269
  deception by, 127
  Democrat vs. Republican views on size and role of, **272**, 273, 274, 275
  economic recovery and, 598–99
  education policies enacted by, 626–29
  Federalist and Antifederalist views of, 37
  Federalist and Democratic-Republican views of, 272, **272**
  forms of, 8, 70–71
  health care debate and, 274, 621–23
  influence on everyday life of, 11, 14–15, *14*
  interest groups and influence on, 352–53, 360–61, 377–78, *377*, 379–80
  limited, 19, 23, 32, 46–47, 62, 84, 96, 109, 201, 224, 598
  Madison's views on, 6–7, 36
  media and, 14
  order as goal of, 6

poverty programs and, 274
power of, 7, 30, 33, 36, 37, 38, 43, 46, 48–55, 57, 110–11, 121
public goods provided by, 7
public opinion on, 88–90, 202, 205–6, 219–23, **221**, **223**, **226**, 262–63
purpose of, 6–8
relationships between levels of, 80, 81, 88, 96
religion and, 109, 112–19
size of, 15, 84, 86, 224, 344, 356, 484, 487, 490–92
spending by, *see* spending, federal
state aid by, 84, 86
welfare as goal of, 7–8
workforce of, 15, 137
government, local:
  civil rights and, 166
  federalism and, 8, 38, 69, **70**, 80, 81, 84, **84**, 85, 96
  participation in, 96
  public support for, 88–89, 96
  responsibilities of, 7, 69, 85, 91, 140
  rights of, 78, 87–89, *88*, 116
  social policy formation and role of, 605–6, 626–27
  spending by, **85**
government, state:
  Articles of Confederation power of, 33, 35, 39, **39**
  civil rights and, 166
  constitutional amendments and, 58–59, **59**, **70**, 73, 110
  Constitutional Convention issues of, 37, 38, 41–46, **44**, 46
  death penalty and, 142
  drug testing by, 137
  electoral process and, 42, 72, 74
  federalism and, 80, 81
  power of, 7, 9, **39**, 46–47, 54, 110–11, 130, 137
  ratification of Constitution by, 46–47, 110
  relationships between, 73
  sovereign immunity of, 92, **93**
  spending by, 85, **85**, 88
  taxation differences among, **99**
  see also states' rights
Government Accountability Office (GAO), 138
Government Performance and Results Act (GPRA; 1993), 609–10
government surveillance, 107
GPS devices, illegal searches and, 134, 136
Grand Canyon Trust (GCT), 585
grandfather clause, 155
grand juries, **113**, 126
grants, 83, 84–86, **84**, **85**, 86
  block, 84, **84**, 86, 96
  categorical, 84, **84**, 86, 87
  general revenue sharing (GRS), 84, **84**
grassroots lobbying, 368–69, 381
Gratz, Jennifer, 191
Gratz v. Bollinger, 178
grazing rights, 585
Great Britain, 8, 31, 41, 51, 53, 71, 640, 641
  French war with, 463
  nuclear weapons of, 666
  Oregon Treaty and, 437
  tax rates in, **576**

Great Compromise, 40, **44**
Great Depression, 48, *80*, 486, 589
    bank failures in, 581
    fifth party system born out of, 274
    presidential actions in, 438
    social policies enacted in response to,
      598
Great Society, 29, 86, 87, **224**, 274, 438,
    485–86, 599, 604
Greece, **576**
Green, Donald, 209
Green, Tom, *116*
Green Party, 295, 296
Greenpeace, 495
Greensboro, N.C., sit-ins in, 168, *168*
Gregory v. Ashcroft, **93**
gridlock, 403
Griffen, Michael, 501
Grimm, Michael, 402
Griswold, Estelle, 142
Griswold v. Connecticut, **113**
gross domestic product (GDP), 85, **85**, 558
    federal spending as percent of, **491**
ground game, 322
    see also get-out-the-vote activities
Grutter, Barbara, 191
Grutter v. Bollinger, 178
Guam, 519
Guantánamo Bay, Cuba, 50, 54, *465*
Guardian, 248, 252, 260
Gulf war, *see* Persian Gulf War
gun control, 12, 13, 17, 69, 90, 91, **93**, 94, *94*,
    130–32, *131*, 145, 199–200, *199*,
    206, 211, 219, 229, 231–32, 269, 352,
    368–69, 372, 377, 380, *380*, 435,
    442–43, 609
Gun Control Act (1968), 131
Gun-Free School Zones Act (1990), 94, *94*

habeas corpus, Lincoln's suspension of, 437
Hagan, Kay, 377–78
Hagel, Chuck, 458
Hague v. CIO, **113**
Haiti, 439, *659*
Hamacher, Patrick, 191
Hamblin, Andrews, 108
Hamdan, Salim, *466*
Hamdan v. Rumsfeld, 50
Hamilton, Alexander, 34, 36, 41, 51, 60,
    75, 462
    on weakness of Supreme Court, 511, 512,
      545
Hamilton v. Regents of the University of
    California, **113**
Hancock, John, 37
Handgun Control, 352
Hannity Show, **254**
Hansen, James, 495, 500
Harding, Richard, *387*
hard money, 329, 330
hard news, 262, 263
Harkin, Tom, 624
Harley Davidson, 587
Harrison, Benjamin, 317
harsh interrogation, *see* torture
Hartnett, Tommy, 137
Hartz, Louis, 23
Hatch Act (1939), 495, 496, *496*
hate crimes, 165, *165*, 184, 187
Hawaii, 53, 73, 184, 640

Hayes, Rutherford B., 317
Haynsworth, Clement, 526
head of government, 441
head of state, 441
Head Start program, 597, 599
health, 18, **70**, 96, 97, 129
Health and Human Services Department,
    U.S., 441, 618
health care, 13, 43, 67–68, 87, 96, *98*, 203,
    225–26, **226**, 228, 278, 377, 395,
    416, 436
    Clinton and, 439
    Congress and, 595–97
    costs of, 67–70
    "death panels" and, 217–18
    fiscal problems of, 620, *621*
    government spending on, 618–20, **618**,
      620
    health insurance and, 89, 284
    reform of, *10*, 69, 89, 95, 100, 211, 217–18,
      225–26, **226**, 269, 278, 292, 293,
      298, 344, *359*, 418, 420, 422, 424,
      439, 446, 453, 460, 462, 478, 487,
      562, 595–97, *595*, 606, 617, 621–22,
      630
    social policies for, 600, 617–24, **627**
    spending for, 492, **492**
health insurance, 89, 284
Health Insurance Portability and
    Accountability Act (1996), 621
Hearst, William Randolph, 239
Hedden, Bill, 585
Henry, Patrick, 37, 46
Hibbing, John, 10, 263
Hill, Cynthia, 324
Hillary: The Movie, 333
Hispanics, *see* Latinos; *specific groups*
Hobbes, Thomas, 6–7, 35
hold, 425
Holder, Eric, 186, 449, 653
Hollings, Ernest F., 137, 587
Hollingsworth v. Perry, 522
Holmes, Oliver Wendell, 56, 121
Holocaust, 125
Homeland Security Department, U.S., 6, 86
    creation of, 648
    foreign policy and role of, 648
homes:
    constitutional protection of, 126, 133,
      135, 145
    Fourth Amendment protection of, 135
homosexuals, *see* gays, gay rights
"honest graft," 273, *273*
Hoover, Herbert, 598
horse race election coverage, 262
hotels, desegregation of, 172
House of Representatives, U.S., 29, 184,
    269–70, 340, 439
    Agriculture Committee of, 414
    apportionment of seats in, 398
    Appropriations Committee of, 416,
      422
    bailout bill of 2008 defeated in, 570
    Bill of Rights creation in, 110
    bills in, 423–25
    blacks in, 155
    Budget Committee of, 422
    caucus chair in, 410
    Committee of the Whole in, 425
    Committee on Foreign Affairs of, 649

congressional district lines in elections
    for, 309–10
Constitutional Convention organization
    of, **39**, 40, **44**
constitutional requirements of
    candidates for, **311**
creation of laws in, 94, 123, 200
Democratic Caucus of, 280
Democratic control of, 446
in economic policy making, 561
election to, 48, 308, 309–10, 389
gerrymandering of districts of, 399,
    400
impeachment in, 467
incumbents in, 393, 396, **404**
Intelligence Committee of, 650
Judiciary Committee of, 423
majority control of, 292, 293
majority whip in, 410
minority leader in, 410–11
Natural Resources Committee of, 414
Oversight Committee of, 449
party ideological differences and
    polarization in, 279–80, **279**
presidential elections and potential role
    of, 317
public knowledge of, 217
racial redistricting and, 173
redistricting and, 398, 403–4
Republican control of, **224**, 279, 446,
    487
Resolution 358 of, 418, *421*
rules and procedures in, 13
Rules Committee in, 416, 425
Select Committee on Energy
    Independence and Global Warming
    of, 414
Senate vs., 389
slave state representation in, 43
Speaker of, 271, 454
Transportation Committee of, 408
treaties approved by, 444
Veterans Affairs Committee of, 426
veto overridden by, 443, 445
Ways and Means Committee of, 416,
    561
    see also Congress, U.S.; Senate, U.S.
housing, 18, 87, 89, 601–2
    discrimination in, 161, 171
Housing and Urban Development
    Department, U.S., 439, 599
Houston, Tex., 188
Howell, William, 463
Hoyer, Steny, *453*
Huawei, 654
Hudson River, 76, *503*
Hughes, Charles, 537
Humane Society, 376
human nature, Founders' views on, 7, 36, 38
human rights, foreign policy and, 642, 644
Hungary, **576**
    hyperinflation in, 581, *581*
Huntsman, John, 214
Hustler, 128
hyperinflation, 581, *581*

Iceland, **576**
Idaho, 174, 175, 309, 428, 437
idealism, **637**, 638–39, 640
identity politics, 206, 209–11, **210**

ideology, 19–20
    federalism and, 96, 97
    inconsistency of, 20, 201, 202–3
    polarization of, 219–21
    political conflict as a result of, 12, 219–21, **221**, 570
    public opinion and, 15, 19–20, 200, 202, *202*, 203, 205, 219–21
    trade policy influenced by, 588–89
"I Have a Dream" speech, 160, *160*
IHOP, 176
Illinois, 158, 399
immigrants, legalization of, 227
immigration, 18, 78, 89, 151–52, 158, *158*, 187, 190, 192–93, 203, **221**, 226, 228, 269, 298, 344, 392, 435, 439, *441*
    ACLU and, *367*
    illegal, 190, 192, *193*
    public opinion on, **228**
    reform debates on, 190, 192, 280
immigration policy, 227, **228**
immigration reform, 12, 211, 227, **228**
impeachment, 7, 53, 222, *223*, 426, 467
    of A. Johnson, 467
    of Clinton, 467
    of judges, 546
implied powers, 59–61, 69, 76, 78
income:
    political influence of, **210**
    racial divide in, 163–65
    in South vs. North, 154
    of women vs. men, 176, **176**, 182
income inequality, 170, 553–54, 557–58, *558*, 588, 590, 600–604, **602**
income support, 624–26, **627**
income tax, 59, *60*, 61, 437, 576–77
incumbency advantage, 403–4
incumbents, 307
    election rates of, 339–40, **339**
    high reelection rates of, 321, **331**
    permanent campaign of, 319–21, *321*
    presidential nominations of, 312, 319
    retrospective evaluations of, 307, 336, **337**
indecent language, 130
independent agencies, 489, **489**
    number of employees in, 490, **490**
Independent Party, 295
independents, **220**
    candidacy of, 308
independent voters, 282
India, 666
    cost of labor in, 584
Indiana, 192, 290
Indian Removal Act (1830), 157
individualism, economic, 16
industrialization, 80, 437
industry, 16
infant mortality, 164
inflation, 439, 579, 581, 590
    Misery Index of unemployment and, **556**, 557
    prevention of, as economic policy goal, 556–57, 561
    Social Security benefits and, 616
informational theory, 416
infrastructure:
    concurrent power over, **70**
    federal authority over, 51
    federal spending on, 8, 98
    state and local spending on, 85

initiative, 375–76
In re Oliver 333 U.S. 257, **113**
inside lobbying strategies, 365–68, *367*, 371–72, 376
intelligence gathering, 648
intelligent design, 17, 114
intercontinental railroad, 158
interest groups, 7, 9, 13, 16, *88*, 318–19, 323, 351–52, *353*, **354**, *361*, *483*
    campaign ads run by, 326–28, **327**, 328, 333, 369, 377
    campaign contributions by, 330, **331**, 359, 370, 375
    collective action and free riding problems of, 363–65
    definition of, 352
    electioneering and, **370**
    financial expenditures of, 354–57, **355**, **357**, **358**, **373**, **374**, 378, 381
    foreign policy and influence of, 653–54, *653*
    as fundamental feature of democracy, 352
    funding of, 361
    growth in number of, 355
    inside lobbying strategies of, 365–68, *367*, 371–72, 376
    lobbying strategies of, *362*
    membership size and role in, 360–61
    organizational models of, 357, 359
    outside lobbying strategies of, 365, 368–76
    political influence and power of, 352, 360–62, 375, 377–78, *377*, 379–80, 585
    political parties vs., 353
    public opinion and, 14, 17, 211
    regulations imposed on, 329, 354, 358, 374
    resources used by, 361–62
    social policy formation and role of, 606, 609, 630
    staff and revolving door of, 359–60
    Supreme Court and, 534–35, 544–45
    three types of, **354**
    see also lobbying, lobbyists
interest group state, 354
interest rates, 561, 568, 579–80, 587, 589–90
intergovernmental organizations (IGOs), 71, 656
intergovernmental relations, 80, 81
Interior Department, U.S., 82, 585
    Endangered Species Act and, 517
intermediate scrutiny, 120
intermediate scrutiny test, 175, 177–78
Internal Revenue Code, 329
Internal Revenue Service (IRS), 8, 296, 490
    electioneering and, 370
international aid, *see* foreign aid
International Atomic Energy Agency (IAEA), 666
international banking system, 127
internationalism, **637**, 638, 640–41
International Monetary Fund (IMF), 71, 169, 641, 656
international organizations, 656
International Republican Institute, 656
International Trade Commission, 658
Internet, **15**, 129, 134, 214, 241, **242**, 244–47, 356, 582–83
    fabricated photos on, 247

    grassroots lobbying on, 369
    hate speech and, 125
    information gathering and availability as transformed by, 244–47, 264
    knowledge levels in users of, **254**
    Medicare Prescription Drug Benefit and, *481*
    photos on, *246*
    questionable reliability of, *246*, 247
    usage trends in, 252–53, **252**
interposition, doctrine of, 76
Interstate Commerce Act (1887), 582
Interstate Commerce Commission, 168, 437, 485, 582
investigative journalists, 240
Iowa, 312–13, 314, 324
Iran, 248, 642, 653
    nuclear program of, 659, 661, 667
Iranian Hostage Crisis, *459*, 462, 642
Iraq, 127, 250
    Persian Gulf War and, 439
    war in, 14, 105
Iraq War, 13, 250, 341, 390, 397, 409, 636, 639, 643
    funding of, 464, 565
    media coverage and, *243*, 261–62
    public opinion on, *243*, 338
    war powers and, 53, 443–45
Ireland, **576**
Irish-American Gay, Lesbian, and Bisexual Group, 179–80
ISIL (Islamic State of Iraq and Levant), 444, 460, 635, *635*, 636, 638, 644–45, *644*, 649, 654
Islam, 644
Isle of Palms, S.C., 140
isolationism, **637**, 638, 639–40
Israel, 71, 653, 659, 666
    Palestinian conflict with, *255*, 638, *638*, 657
Israel, Steve, *453*
issue scale, 212
issue voters, 335, 341–42, *344*
Italy, 71, **576**

Jack in the Box, 176
Jackman, Simon, 213
Jackson, Andrew, 273, 390, 437
    bureaucracy and, 484, *484*
Jackson, Janet, 130
Jackson, Jesse, Jr., 29
Jackson, Robert, 537
Jacobs, Lawrence, 211
James Madison University, *183*
Japan, 53, 71, 444, 640
    tax rates in, **576**
    U.S. trading with, 587–88
Japanese Americans, 156
    internment of, 175, 544
Jardines, Joelis, 135
Jarrett, Valerie, *456*
Jay, John, 36
Jefferson, Thomas, 22, 35, 37, 42, 46, 58, 60, 75, 76, 109, 114, 120, 389, 640
    compromises forged by, 437
    Marbury v. Madison and, 513–14
Jefferson, William, 401, *402*
Jehovah's Witnesses, 116
Jews, 125, 274
    in Supreme Court, 537

Jim Crow laws, 79, *79*, 156, 160
job creation, *see* employment; unemployment
Jobs Corps, 599
Joe Camel, 129, *129*
Johanns, Mike, 568
Johnson, Andrew, 426, 467
Johnson, Gary, 296
Johnson, Lyndon, 86, 274, 319, 326, 413, 439, 486, 573
    approval ratings of, **452**
    civil rights and, 181, 182, 184, 187–88, 439, 599
    Great Society and, 604
    War on Poverty program of, 599, 627
Joint Committee on Taxation, 415
joint committees, 415
Jones, Antoine, 134, 136
Jones, Bryan, 609
journalists:
    interest groups and, 375
    investigative, 240
    and leaks, sources, and shield laws, 247–51
JP Morgan Chase, 569
judicial activism, 173–74, 541–43
judicial branch, 32
    allocation of power to, 7, 8, **39**, 41, **44**, 51, 54
    appointments to, 441–42, 523–28, **525**, **527**, *529*
    checks and balances on, 51–55
    court fundamentals and, 515–19
    court structure and, 519–23
    federal, development of an independent and powerful, 511–15, **512**
    foreign policy and role of, 650, 653
    influence on political process of, 13
    structure of, 513
    see also courts; Supreme Court, U.S.
judicial restraint, 541–43
judicial review, 13, 51, 54–55, 120, 511–15, 546–47
    Marbury v. Madison and, 513–14, *513*
    in practice, 514–15
Judiciary Act (1789), 512, 514, 519
Judiciary Act (1801), 546
Juneau, Alaska, 122, *123*
juries, 159, *516*
Justice Department, U.S., 87, 138, 151, 152, 400, 425, 464, 495, 527, 582–83
    solicitor general in, 533
    Watergate investigation of, 450

Kagan, Elena, 186, 442, *524*, 526, 536, 541, *543*
Kaibab National Forest, 585
Kansas, 531, *545*
Kansas-Nebraska Act (1854), 437
Katrina, Hurricane, 603–4, 606, 609
    FEMA and, 502
Kennan, George, 641
Kennedy, Anthony M., 142, 172, 541, 543, *543*, 544
Kennedy, John F.:
    assassination of, 609
    civil rights and, 168, 169, *169*, 181, 184, 545
Kennedy, Robert F., 131, 168
Kennedy, Ted, 424
Kentucky, 76, 115, 171
Kentucky Fried Chicken, 663, *663*
Kenya, 644

Kerry, John, **318**, *638*, *647*, *653*
    in 2004 elections, 316
Keynes, John Maynard, 572
Keynesian economics, 572, 589
Kimel et al. v. Florida Board of Regents, **93**
King, Angus, 324
King, Martin Luther, Jr., 131, 160, *160*, 168, 169–70
King, Rodney, 139, 165
Kissinger, Henry, 642
knowledge, public opinion and, 205
Komorowski, Bronislaw, *649*
Kony, Joseph, 654
Korean War, 137, 390, 642
    subsidies implemented after, 610
Kosovo, 439, 639, 644, 649
Krosnick, Jon, 256
Ku Klux Klan, 122, 126, *126*, 256, *257*
Kuwait, 439
Kyoto Protocol, 444, 649

"laboratories of democracy," 95, 96
labor costs, 586, *586*, 588
Labor Department, U.S., 624
labor laws, 80, **93**
    see also employment; workplace issues
labor relations, 80
labor unions, *see* unions
Laffer, Arthur, 573
Laffer curve, 573, **573**
laissez faire capitalism, 79
Lambeau Field, *100*
Land Grant College Act (1862), 627
Landis, Floyd, 136
Landrieu, Mary, *397*
land use, 70
language:
    indecent, 130
    official, 18, 190
Laos, 53
latent groups, 364
latent opinion, 202–5
Latham, Tom, 319, *319*
Latinos, 151
    civil rights of, 154, 156–58, 163, 173, 185, 186
    G. W. Bush's overtures to, 186
    political parties and, 275
    poverty rate of, 163
    voting history of, 17, 157
Lavrov, Sergey, *638*
law clerks, 537
Lawrence, John Geddes, 145, 180
Lawrence v. Texas, 145, *145*, 180, 543
laws:
    Articles of Confederation and, 33
    creation of, 8, 13, 51, 69, **70**, 72, 73, 76, 78–79, 80, 88, 92, 94, 96, 97, 98, 112, 116, 123, 129, 130–32, 133, 137–38, 140, 141, 142, 200
    electoral, *60*
    enforcement of, 6, 8, 69, **70**, 92, **93**, 94, 134
    implementation of, 441, 465
    interpretation of, 7, 12, 13, 51, 54, 72, 75, 80, 92, 96, 97, *108*, 109, 129, 142–45, **144**, 465, 514–15
    just vs. unjust, 169
    Locke's view on, 41
    overturning of, 76, 91, 92, **93**, *94*, 96, 97, 112, 122, 129

precedence of national vs. state, 90–95, **93**, 96, 98
state and local, 73–74, 76, 79, 88, 92, **93**, 94, 95, 96–98, 108, 111, 112, 122, 126, 129, 130–32, 138–39, 140, 141, 142, 143–44, **144**
    see also specific laws
law schools, 158, 523
    affirmative action and, 189–90
    desegregation of, 170
lawsuits, 73, **77**, 122, *123*, 176
    see also class action lawsuits
lawyers:
    apprenticeship of, 523
    Supreme Court oral argument of, 535–36, *535*
    women as, 158
League of Nations, 438, 640
leaks, to media, 247–51
Ledbetter, Lily, 176
Ledbetter v. Goodyear Tire and Rubber, 520, 523
Lee, Mike, *269*
LeFevre, Dell, 585, *585*
legal aid, 124
legal system, U.S.:
    judicial system and, 515–28
    procedures of, 519
    see also courts; judicial branch; Supreme Court, U.S.
legislation:
    bureaucracy and, 477–78
    types of, **418**
legislative branch:
    allocation of power to, 7, 8, 38, **39**, 41, 48–55
    checks and balances on, 51–55
    Locke's view on, 36
    state representation in, 38
    see also Congress, U.S.; House of Representatives, U.S.; Senate, U.S.
legislative power, of president, 445–46
legislative process, 417–25
    conventional, 417–22
    deviations from, 420, 423
    differences in House and Senate, 423–25
    president's role in, 447–48
Leguizamo, John, *163*
Lehman Brothers, 569
Lemon test, 115
Lemon v. Kurtzman, 115
lesbians, *see* gays, gay rights
"Letter from the Birmingham Jail" (King), 169–70
letter-writing campaigns, 368–69
Lewinsky, Monica, 426
Lewis, John, 408
LGBTs, *see* gays, gay rights
Libby, I. Lewis "Scooter," 250, 449
libel, 128
liberals, 15, 19, 84, 95–96, 97, 201, 202, 203, 206, 219, **220**, 277, *277*, 323, 324
    in Supreme Court, 172, 537, 540, 548
Libertarian Party, 19, 295, 296
liberty, 21–23
Libya, 341, 443–45, 464, 499, *499*, 518, 650, 651–52, 654–55, 661, 665, 667
life expectancy, 164, 616
Lilly Ledbetter Fair Pay Act (2009), 176, 520, 523
Limbaugh, Rush, 244, 261

limited government, 19, 32, 46–47, 62, 84, 96, 109, 224
  activist government vs., 201
Lincoln, Abraham, 76, 155, 390
  Civil War and, 437
literacy tests, 155, 181
litigation, as lobbying strategy, 367, *367*
Little Rock, Ark., school desegregation in, 184
living Constitution, 55, 540, 544
lobbying, lobbyists, 351–52, **354**, *358*, *377*, 585
  as anti-majoritarian, 353
  astroturf, 369
  bribes used by, 358, *358*
  conflict in, 379–80
  definition of, 352–53
  direct, 365–66
  drafting legislation and regulations in, 366
  financial spending on, 354–57, **355**, **357**, **358**, 381
  grassroots, 368–69, 381
  group members as taking part in, 361
  growth in number of, 355
  inside strategies, 371
  media used in, 356, 369, 375
  outside strategies, 371
  regulations imposed on, 354, 358
  trade associations and, 357
  see also interest groups
Locke, John, 35–36, *36*, 41
Lockett, Clayton, 141
Lockheed Martin Corporation, 356
logrolling, 43–45, 408, 416
London, 204
"Looking Glass for 1787, The" (engraving), *46*
Loomis, Burdett, 402
Lopez, Alfonso, 94
Lord's Resistance Army, 654
Los Angeles, Calif., 139
  race riots in, 165
Los Angeles Times, 243
Louisiana, 174
  civil law tradition in, 517
Louisiana Purchase, 640
Louisville, Ky., 172
Low-Level Radioactive Waste Policy Act (1980), 91
loyalty, of EOP staff, 456
Lugar, Richard, 290, 309
lunch counters, desegregation of, 168, *168*
Luxembourg, **576**

Madison, James, 34, 36, 37, *38*, 58, 95, 389, 399, 462, 513
  Constitutional Convention notes of, 41
  views on government of, 6–7, 35, 36, 38–39, 41, 42, 51, 58, 75, 76, 110
magazines:
  as media news sources, **242**, 243
  online sites for, 244–45
magnet schools, 629
Maine, 74, **93**, 314
mainstream media (MSM), 242–47
  comparing differences in sources of, 242–47
  see also media
"majority-minority" districts, 400
majority opinions, **538**

majority rule:
  Constitutional Convention issue of, 38–39, 41
  see also tyranny of the majority
majority voting, 309
Malloy v. Hogan, **113**
Manchin, Joe, 372, 397
mandatory spending, 574, **575**
Mandela, Nelson, memorial service of, *237*, 238
Manning, Bradley, 127, 249, *249*
manufacturing, 38, 80
Mapp, Dollree, 136, *136*
Mapp v. Ohio, **113**, 136
Marbury, William, 513–14
Marbury v. Madison, 54–55, 513–14, *513*
Marbut, Gary, 90
March on Washington, 160, *160*, 169
marginal tax rate, 573, 578, **578**
Margolies-Mezvinsky, Marjorie, 391
marijuana, 69, 95, 96, 97
  see also drugs, medical use of illegal
Marines, U.S., 6
marketplace of ideas, 122
markups, 421
marriage, *14*, *72*, 73
  gay, *see* gays, gay rights, marriage and
  interracial, 156
Marshall, John, 55, 56, 77, *513*
  judicial review established by, 513–14
  Marbury v. Madison and, 513–14
  unanimous decisions practice of, 537
Marshall, Thurgood, 170, 536
Marshall Plan, 641, *641*
Mars rovers, 473, *473*, 474, 481
Martin, Trayvon, *124*, 165, *165*
Maryland, 60, 74, 75, 171, 528
  school desegregation in, 170
Maryland, University of, 170
Mason, George, 47, 109
Massachusetts, 34, 46, 48, 126, 129, 309
mass associations, 360–61
mass media, 238
  see also media
mass protests, 368, *368*
mass surveys, 212
Mastromonaco, Alyssa, *456*
Matthew Shepard and James Byrd, Jr. Hate
  Crimes Prevention Act (2009), 184
Mayhew, David, 395–96
McCain, John, **318**, 329, 408, 427
  2008 campaign platform of, 584
McCain-Feingold Act (Bipartisan Campaign
  Reform Act; 2002), 329, *329*, 427, 534
McCaskill, Claire, *344*, 387–88
McConnell, Mitch, *344*, *410*, *535*
McCulloch v. Maryland, 56, 60, 75–76, **77**, 78
McCutcheon v. Federal Election Commission, 329, 374, 509–10
McDonald's, 610
McDonald v. Chicago, **113**
McDonough, Denis, *456*
Mearsheimer, John, 639
Meat Inspection Act (1906), 485
media, 237–38, 356
  by-product theory of information
    transmission and, 251–52
  campaign advertising in, 326–28, *327*,
    327, 332, 369, 370, 375, 377
  classified information and, 126–27, *127*,
    145, 260

comparing differences in sources of, 242–47
  Congress and, 402
  corporate ownership in, **242**
  deregulation of, 241–42
  effects and biases in influencing citizens,
    254–63, **257**, 258–62, 263–64
  election coverage and, 306, 321, 325–26
  foreign policy and influence of, 654
  going public and, 453
  history and development of, 239–42
  Internet-based news sources in, 244–47,
    244, **253**, 264
  Internet evolution as transforming
    information gathering and, 244–47,
    246, **253**, 264, 322–23, 326
  Iraq War and, *243*, 261–62
  knowledge levels of individuals vs. their
    primary sources of, 251–54, **254**
  leaks, sources, and shield laws in,
    247–51, 260
  in lobbying campaigns, 356, 369, 375
  mainstream sources of, 242–47
  measuring effects of, 256, *257*
  news, 238–47
  "off the record" in, 250
  "on background" in, 250
  politicians and bureaucrats as shaping
    coverage in, 247–51
  politics and, 9, 13, 14, 247, 251–54,
    259–60
  public opinion and, 237–38, 654
  public policy and, 255–57
  regulation of, 17, 76, 120, 121, 238, 239,
    240–42
  short falls in coverage by, 262–63
  usage trends in, 252, **252**
  violence and, 17
  see also newspapers; publishing; *specific
    media outlets*
media conglomerates, 241, **242**
media effects, 254–57, **257**, 261
Medicaid, 67, 68, 89, 90, **93**, 274, 439, 545, 599,
  605–6, 618–19, **627**
  fiscal problems of, 620
  states' discretionary power over, 619
Medicare, 29, 274, 377, 392, 439, 575, 597, 599,
  600, 613, 618–19
  AARP and, 606
  coverage and premiums of, **619**
  "donut hole," 623
  fiscal problems of, 620, *621*
  Prescription Drug Benefit, 377, *377*, 481,
    487, 609, 619
melting pot, 18
Merkel, Angela, 137
Merrill Lynch, 569
Mexican Americans, 156, 157, 190
Mexican-American War, 157, 437, 443, 640,
  650
Mexico, **576**, 640
  U.S. barrier on border with, 190
Mica, John, *480*
Michael M. v. Superior Court, 178
Michigan, 74, 139, 172
  affirmative action in, 188, 190, 191
Michigan, University of, 124, 190, *191*, 509–10,
  509, 541
Microsoft, antitrust violations of, 582–83, *583*
Middle East, 638, 656

military, U.S., 6, 8, **70**, 116, 119, 120, 121, 130, 249, *249*, 284, 356, 435, 499, 642, *659*
  control of, 51, 123
  desegregation of, 156, 184, 465
  foreign policy and role of, 648, 661–62
  gays in, 160, 184, *185*, 192–93
  humanitarian and peacekeeping missions of, 648, 659–60
  pay increase for, 474
  Revolutionary-era support of, 33
  sexual assaults in, 387–88, 429
  women in, *159*
  see also specific branches
military funerals, protests of, 105–6
militias, state, 131
Miller, Judith, 250
Miller test, 129
Miller v. California, 129
"Millionaires" Amendment, 124
millionaire's tax, 553–54
Minerals Management Service, 476, 483
Minersville, Pa., 116
minimum wage, 91
Minnesota, 126, 256
minorities:
  in Congress, 391, **392**
  voting history of, **392**
minority-owned business, 479
minority rights, *18*
  Constitutional Convention and, 38, 41
minor political parties, 295–96, *295*
  signature requirements for presidential candidates of, 308
minors, 142
Miranda, Ernesto, 138
Miranda rights, 139, **139**
Mischiefs of Faction, 245
Misery Index, **556**, 557
Mississippi, 143, 428
  black voting in, 155, 181
  Medicaid and, 619
Mississippi River, 546–47
Missouri, 78, 91, **93**, 171, 290
Missouri Compromise (1820), **77**, 78, 154
Missouri Plan, 523
mobilization, 321–22
Model Cities Program, 486, 599
moderates, 20, 219, **220**, 228
modified rules, 425
Moe, Terry, 463, 490
"Moms Demand Action for Gun Sense in America," 368
monarchy, 8, 22, 32, 35, 41
monetarist theory, 579, 580–82
monetary policy, 561, 567–68, 578–82, 589–90, 602
money, coining of, 389
Moniz, Ernest, 458
Monkey Cage, The (blog), 245
monopolies, 76, 79, 582–83
  regulations of, 582–83
Monroe, James, 437, 640
Monroe Doctrine, 437, 640
Montana, 131, 314, 437
Montesquieu, Baron de, 36
Montgomery, Ala., 168
  bus boycott in, 167–68
Mormons, 116, *116*, 214, 217
Morrill Act (1862), 627

Morris, Gouverneur, 37
mortgage crisis, 569–72, 582
most-favored-nation status, 658
Mother Jones, *245*, 260
Motor Voter Act (1993), 88
Mourdock, Richard, 290, 309
MoveOn.org, 275, 361
Moynihan, Daniel Patrick, 109
MSNBC, **258**
muckrakers, 239–40
Mueller, John, 665
multiculturalism, 18, 190
multilateral action, 637–38
multilateral agreements, 661
multilateral organizations, 71
Murdoch, Rupert, **242**
Murphy, Walter, 62
mutually assured destruction, 642
My Story (Parks), 168

NAACP (National Association for the Advancement of Colored People), 162, 170, 187
Nabors, Rob, *456*
Nader, Ralph, 295, *295*
Nadler, Jerrold, 423
Nation, 243, 260, 261
National Aeronautics and Space Administration (NASA), 8
  bureaucratic control and, 473, *473*, 497, 501
National Association for the Advancement of Colored People (NAACP), 162, 170, 187
National Association of Counties, 88
National Association of Realtors, **357**, **374**
National Beer Wholesalers Association (NBWA), 357, **374**
National Cholesterol Education Month, 402–3
National Commission on Social Security Reform, 613–14
national committees, 275, 330
"National Conversation on Race," 186
National Democratic Institute, 656
National Economic Council (NEC), 565, 566
National Election Study, American (NES), 212
National Federation of Independent Business v. Sebelius, **93**
National Forest Service, 414
National Guard, U.S., 6, 90, 131, 184
National Highway Traffic Safety Administration (NHTSA), 583
National Independent Automobile Dealers Association (NADA), 359
National Institutes of Health, 479
nationalized elections, 337–40
National Journal, 243
National Labor Relations Act (1935), **77**, 599
National Labor Relations Board v. Jones & Laughlin Steel, **77**, 80
National Organization for Women (NOW), 182
national origins discrimination, **182**
National Public Radio (NPR), 244, **254**, **258**
National Recovery Administration (NRA), 599
National Republican Congressional Committee (NRCC), 279
National Republican Senatorial Committee (NRSC), 279
National Review, 243
National Review Online, *244*

National Rifle Association (NRA), 131, 199, 352, 353, *353*, 357, 367, 369, 372, 377, *380*, 381
National Right to Life Committee, **354**
national security, *54*, 107
National Security Agency (NSA), *54*, 127, 137, 248, 260, 426, 466–67, 648, 650, 651–52
National Security Council (NSC), 456, 647, 648
national supremacy, 43, **77**, 83, 86–89
national supremacy clause, 72
National Turkey Federation, 378, *379*
National Weather Service, **15**
National Wool Act (1954), 610
nation building, 639
Nation of Islam, 18, 187
Native Americans:
  civil rights of, 154, 156–57, 185, 188
  reservations and, 157
natural resources, 82
natural rights, constitutional importance of, 35, 36
Navy, U.S., 6, 640, 648
Nazis, 125
NBC, 241, 243
Near v. Minnesota, **113**, 126
Nebraska, 314
necessary and proper clause, 51, 57, 60, 62, 72, 78
negative campaigning, 326–28, **327**, *328*
Neighborhood Youth Corps, 599
Nelson, Thomas, 256, *257*
Netherlands, **576**
neutrality, Monroe Doctrine and, 437
Nevada, 314
Nevada Department of Human Resources v. Hibbs, **93**
New Deal, 29, 54, 57, 61, *80*, 94, 274, *274*, 390, 438, *438*, 604
  effects on bureaucracy of, 485–86, *486*
  social policies enacted by, 598–99
  Supreme Court and, 524, 543, 546
New Deal Coalition, 274
New Federalism, 84, **84**, 85–86
New Hampshire, **33**, 48, 312–13
New Haven, Conn., 189
New Jersey, *68*, 75, 76, 180
  Ellis Island and, 531, *531*
New Jersey Plan, 40, 58
New London, Conn., 140
New Mexico, 119
New Orleans, La., 502
  Hurricane Katrina and, 603–4
New Republic, 243
News Corporation, 241, **242**
news cycle, 243
news media, *see* media
newspapers, 243, 264
  corporate ownership of, **242**
  earliest forms of, 239
  knowledge levels in readers of, **254**
  media effects and biases in, 255, 259–60
  online sites for, 244–45, **254**
  usage trends in, 252–53, **252**
  wire services and, 239
Newtown, Conn., 131, *131*, 199, *199*, 219, 229, 231–32, 442
New York, N.Y., 37, 78, 128, *129*, 159, 273, *273*
  stop-and-frisk policy of, 165
New York Journal, 239

New York state, 33, **33**, 41, 46, *47*, 48, 73, *75*, 76, 80
    Ellis Island and, 531, *531*
New York State Board of Regents, 114
New York Sun, 239
New York Times, 127, 138, *169*, 240, 243, 250, **254**, **258**, 500, 585, 604
New York Tribune, 239
New Zealand, **576**
Nicaragua, 53, 640, 642
1984 (Orwell), 138
Nineteenth Amendment, *58*, *59*, 158
Ninth Amendment, **110**, **113**, 142
Nixon, Richard, 84, 85, 222, *223*, 454, 459
    affirmative action and, 184, 188
    approval ratings of, **452**
    economic policies of, 557
    executive privilege used by, 449–50
    foreign policy of, 439, 642
    justices appointed by, 526
    school desegregation and, 545
    Watergate and, 449–50
no-bid contracts, 479
No Child Left Behind Act (2001), *87*, 487, *487*, 606, 627–28, *628*
nominating conventions, 286, 313
nominations, 308, 311–13
nongovernmental organizations (NGOs), 656
nonpartisan primary, **263**
nonviolent protest, 168–70
normal elections, 337–40
normative theory, 56
North, 239
    Constitutional Convention and, 37, 43–45
    economic interests of, 37
    slavery and, 43–45, 111, 154
North America, 437, 640
North American Free Trade Agreement (NAFTA), 439, 588, 644, 658, 663
North Atlantic Treaty Organization (NATO), 71, 639, 641, 643, 650, 661
North Carolina, 48, 400
    12th District in, 174
North Carolina Supreme Court, 107
North Dakota, 143
Northern Ireland, 71
Northern Mariana Islands, 519
Northern Securities Company, 437
North Korea, 642, 661
    nuclear weapons of, 666–68, *667*
Northrup Grumman, *357*
North Vietnam, 439, 642
Norway, tax rates in, **567**
notice and comment procedure, 476
Nuclear Non-Proliferation Treaty, 666
Nuclear Test Ban Treaty, 649
nuclear weapons, 659, 666–68
    and threat of mutually assured destruction, 642
nullification, 76
NumbersUSA, **354**

Obama, Barack, 12, *13*, 20, 53, *68*, 89, 91, 97, 131, *131*, 138, 152, 160, 170, 184, 192, 203–4, 211, 212, **223**, **224**, *230*, 246, *246*, 247, 248, *271*, 282, *290*, 292, *292*, 293–94, 295, 299, 340–44, *379*, *397*, *397*, 425, 435, *435*, 439–40, *444*, 450, *460*, *463*, *524*, 617, *649*
    Affordable Care Act and, 420
    appointments made by, 442
    approval ratings of, **204**, **213**, 459–60, *461*, 462
    bureaucracy and, 497, 498
    civil rights and, 184
    Congress and, 51
    DREAM Act and, *441*
    economic policy and, 320, 565, *566*, 571, 572, 588
    economic views of, 576
    EOP staff and, *456*
    executive orders of, 442
    federal campaign funding and, 330
    foreign policy of, 443–44, 637, 639, *639*, 644–45, 654–55
    as "Fundraiser-in-Chief," 413–14
    government contracts and, 479
    Guantánamo Bay and, *465*, 466
    G. W. Bush's policies and, 50, 54
    health care reform and, 29, 211, *211*, 218, 225–26, 292, *359*, 446, 453, 460, 462, 487, 595–97, 621–23
    immigration reform and, 605
    and Iraq, 462
    judges appointed by, **525**, 526, *526*, 529
    judges nominated by, 527
    Libya and, *499*
    lobbyists and, 360
    media bias and, 261
    media coverage of, 237–38, *237*
    millionaire's tax called by, 553–54
    omnibus spending bill and, *409*
    as party leader, 452, *453*
    Race to the Top program and, 606, 628
    social policies of, 600, 616
    Supreme Court and, 509–10
    tax policy and, 589
    in 2008 election, 576, 584, **318**
    and 2010 elections, 453
    in 2012 elections, 210, **283**, 312, 314, 315, 316, **318**, 322, **324**, *326*, 553
    2013 budget and, 564
    and 2014 elections, 323, 377, *413*
    unilateral actions of, 464–65
    U.S. Supreme Court and, 546
    war powers and, 443
Obama, Michelle, *313*
Obama administration, 138
Obamacare, *see* Affordable Care Act (ACA)
obscenity, 126, 129
Occupational Safety and Health Administration (OSHA), 502, 583
Occupy Wall Street, 170, *246*
Ochs, Adolph, 240
O'Connor, Sandra Day, 97, 140, 145, 543
    expertise of, 537
    Lawrence case and, 180
    replacement of, 541
Office of Congressional Ethics, 428
Office of Economic Opportunity, 599
Office of Management and Budget (OMB), 455, 456, 488, 565, 647
Office of Personnel Management (OPM), federal retirement processing system and, 473, 474, 480, 495, 500, 501, 502, 503, 504
Office of the United States Trade Representative (USTR), 455, 456, 565, 566, 647
"off the record," 250
Ohio, 115, 119, 122, 314, 317
    school vouchers in, 629
oil, foreign, 642
Oklahoma, 141
Old-Age, Survivors, and Disability Insurance (OASDI), **614**
    trust fund of, 614–15, *615*
Oliver, John, 251
Ollie's Barbeque, 172
Olympics, 122, *123*, 642
O'Malley Dillon, Jennifer, 452
omnibus appropriations bill, 408
omnibus legislation, 423
omnibus spending bill, *409*, 427, 562
"on background," 250
O'Neill, Thomas "Tip," 337
open market operations, 581
open ("crossover") primary, **286**, 287, 308
open rules, 425
open seat, 319
Open Society Institute, 656
Operation Fast and Furious, 449, *449*
opinion writing, in Supreme Court, 536–37, *537*
opposition research, 325–26
oral argument, in Supreme Court, 535–36, *535*
Oregon, 97, 119, 308, 437
Oregon Treaty, 437
O'Reilly, Bill, 244
O'Reilly Factor, The, 244
Organization for Economic Cooperation and Development (OECD), **660**
Organization of the Petroleum Exporting Countries (OPEC), 642
original intent, 56, 539, 541
    see also strict construction
originalism, 56
    see also original intent
O'Rourke, Beto, *321*
Orwell, George, 138
Outback Steakhouse, 176
outside lobbying strategies, 365, 368–76
oversight, congressional, 490, 498–501
ownership society, 600, *600*
Oxfam International, 656
Oxley, Zoe, 256, *257*

PACs, *see* political action committees
Paine, Thomas, **32**, 35, 37
Pakistan, 23, 435, 637, 639, 645, 665, 666
Palestinians, Israeli conflict with, *255*, 638, *638*, 657
Palm Beach County, Fla., 310
Palmquist, Bradley, 209
Panama, 640
Panama Canal, 640
paradox of voting, 334–35
pardons, 41, 51, 76, 120, 449
Paris, Treaty of, 514
Parkin, Michael, 256
parks, national, 8
Parks, Rosa, 167–68
park services, 82
parliamentary system, 8, 41, 71
parties in service, 274
partisanship cues, 336
party coalitions, 282–84, **283**, **284**

party identification (party ID), 280–82, **281,** **283**
   health care and, **226**
party in government, 271, 278–80
   developing agendas and, 292
party in the electorate, 271, 280–84
party organization, 271, 275–78, 299
party platforms, 291, 313
party principle, 273
party systems, 272
   realignment in, 275
party unity, loyalty, 280, 411–13
patents, 51, 557
Patient-Centered Outcomes Research
   Institute, 622
Patriot Act, *see* USA PATRIOT Act
Patriot Guard Riders, 105
patronage, 273
Patterson, Thomas, 262
Paul, Rand, *207,* 269, 282, *375,* 466–67
Paul, Ron, *207, 320*
Paulson, Henry, 570
Pawtucket, R.I., 115
pay-as-you-go (PAYGO), 562, 565
payroll taxes, 575–76
   Social Security funded by, 613, **615,** 616,
   617
Peace Corps, 465, 599
peak associations, 360
Pearl Harbor, Hawaii, 53, 640
Pelosi, Nancy, *271,* 410, *410,* 420, *453,* 595
Pendleton Civil Service Act (1883), 485
Pennsylvania, 34, 46, 110, 291, 314, 399
   school vouchers in, 629
Pennsylvania Gazette, 239
penny press, 239
Pentagon Papers, 127
per curiam opinions, **538**
permanent campaign, 319–21, *321*
Perot, Ross, 295, 317
Perry, James, 493
Persian Gulf War, 256, 439, 443, 462
personal information, 135, 137–38
Personal Responsibility and Work
   Opportunity Act (1996), 86, 626
Peters, Gary, *413*
Pew Research Center, 204, *205,* 216, 217, 225,
   253, 492
Pharmaceutical Research & Manufacturers
   of America, **357**
Philadelphia, Pa., **33,** 34, 35, 78
Philippines, 444, 640, 642
Phoenix, Ariz., 151
photography, Internet and, *246,* 247
Pierce, Franklin, 437
Pinckney, Charles, 109
plaintiff, 516
Plame, Valerie, 449
Planned Parenthood, 142
plea bargaining, 516
Pledge of Allegiance, 116, 532
Plessy v. Ferguson, 156, 171
Plouffe, David, 455
pluralism, 39, 354
plurality opinions, **538**
plurality voting, 296, 309
pocket vetoes, 445
Pointer v. Texas, **113**
Poland, **576,** 643
   hyperinflation in, 581

polarization:
   of Congress, 411–13, **413**
   ideological, 219–21
   of political parties, 279–80, 411–13
police, 8, 69, 87, **93,** 94, 109, 126, 132, 134, 135,
   139
   brutality of, 165, 169, *169*
   patrol oversight, 426, 500
police powers, 69, 90
police raids, 159
policy agenda, 609
policy mood, 224, **224,** 231
political action committees (PACs), 275,
   329–30, *330,* 370, **370, 374,** 405
   campaign contribution limits on,
   329–32, **329**
   campaign finance and, 373
political appointees, 474
political campaigns, 9, 14, 123–24, 200, 214,
   223, 318–32
   interest groups and, 326–28, **327,** 328,
   331, 359–60, 373, 377
   political parties in providing assistance
   for, 286, 289, **289,** 321, **329, 331**
political candidates, 14, 200, 203
political cartoons, *47,* 128
political coalitions, 410
political machines, 273, *273*
political participation, 6, 13, 15–16, 36, 96,
   200, 207, 220
political parties, 14, 373
   accountability of, 294, 299
   affiliation with, 270
   as brand names, 277, 323
   campaign assistance provided by, 286,
   289, **289,** 321, **329, 331**
   coalitions in, 282–84, **284**
   developing agendas and, 292
   effects of civil service on, 485
   electoral college and, 42
   in European countries, 270
   history of U.S., 272–74, **272**
   identification with, 200, 203, 206, 209,
   219–20, **220, 221,** 336
   ideology and, 17, 19–20
   influence on electoral college of, 42
   interest groups vs., 353
   minor and independent, *295,* 296, 308, 330
   modern, 275–78
   party identification of electorate and,
   271, 280–82, **281, 283**
   party in government and, 271, 278–80
   party organizations of, 271, 275–78, 299
   polarization of, 279–80, 411–13
   political platforms of, 291, 313
   public opinion and, 15, 200, 211
   realignments in, 275
   recruiting and nomination of candidates
   by, 287–88, 297, 308, 319
   strategizing for next election and, 318–19
   see also specific parties
political process:
   appointments and, 441–42
   bureaucracy influenced by, 489, 495, 498
   bureaucrats' influence on, 9, 13, 474, 479,
   482, 485
   civil liberties and, 116, 119
   Constitution and, 109
   courts and, 511, 513
   government structure and, 71

   importance of, 440
   laws and, 75
   legal system procedures and, 519
   separation of powers and, 73
political realignments, 208
political science, role of, *see* politics, political
   scientists' role in
political scientists, role of, 442, 603
political socialization, 206, 209
politicians, public opinion and, 200, 218,
   221–23, 229–31
politicos, 392–93
Politico's Playbook, 245
politics:
   class and, 16, 36
   definition of, 9
   economic regulation and, 583–84,
   589–90
   influence on everyday life of, 69, 89–90,
   595–97
   political scientists' role in, 16, 55, 137,
   225, 257, 336, 374, 413, 545
   public awareness of, 14, 200–203, *200,*
   203, 207, 217–18, 229–31
   "red states" vs. "blue states" in, 17, 20
   role in trade policy of, 588–89
   in Supreme Court decision making,
   535–45
polity, 8
Polk, James, 437
polling, 227
polling places, *308*
polls, 200
   interpretation of, **213**
   telephone, 212
   uses of, *201*
   see also push polling; surveys
Pollster (web site), 245
polygamy, *116*
Popkin, Samuel, 336
popular vote, 317, *317,* **318,** 343
populist democracy, 38–39
pork-barrel spending, 390, 397, 408, 409, 423,
   427, 428, 429
   see also earmarks
pornography, 17, 129, 136, *136,* 145
Portugal, **576**
position taking, 396
Post Office, U.S., 8, **15,** 51, **70,** 474
   growth of, 485
poverty, 7, 17, 87, 394, 554
   charities and churches and, 597
   geographical distribution of, 163, **164**
   Great Society effect on, 487
   health care and, 619
   income support and welfare programs
   for, 624–26, **627**
   racial divide in, 163
   rates by age, **601,** 656
   social policy and, 598–99, 600–604, **603,**
   612, **627**
   war on, 627
Powell v. Alabama, **113**
power of the purse, 561, 568
precedent (*stare decisis*), 517
   Supreme Court cases overruling, 517,
   518
   in Supreme Court decision making,
   539
prerogative powers, 41

president, U.S., 62
    allocation of power to, 7, 38, **39**, 41,
        51–55, 57, 59, 440, 462–63
    appointments made by, 185–86, 441–42,
        490, 513, 523–25, **525**
    approval ratings of, 203, *204*, 208, 450,
        452, **452**, *459*, 460–62, **461**
    bureaucracy and, 479, 482, 484, 487,
        498, 501
    citizenship requirement of, 13, **311**
    civil rights and, 156, 184–86, 439
    as commander in chief, 443–44, 464
    Congress's relationship with, 390, 417–18
    constitutional authority of, 440, *440*
    constitutional requirements of
        candidates for, **311**
    creation of legislation by, 88
    economic and budgetary power of, 562,
        565–66, *566*, 568, 586, 589–90
    election of, 311–17
    executive orders issued by, 442–43
    executive privilege of, 449
    first-mover advantage of, 443
    foreign policy and central role of, 647,
        648–49
    gauging popularity of, 458–62
    going public of, 453
    as head of executive branch, 441–50, 455
    as head of government, 441
    as head of state, 441
    interpretation of Constitution by, 59, 520
    job description of, 440–54
    laws implemented by, 441
    legislative power of, 445–46
    legislative process and, 447–48
    nominations made by, 529
    other duties and powers of, 446, 449
    as party leader, 452–53
    persuasion power of, 463
    as politician, 450–53
    powers of, **440**, *441*
    signing statement of, 465
    social policy formation and role of,
        604–5, 609, 630
    statutory authority of, 440, *440*
    term limits on, *60*
    treaty making and foreign policy of,
        444–45
    unilateral action of, 463–65, 649
    unitary executive theory and, 464, 466
    U.S. public and, 458–62, **458**
    war powers of, 52, 72, 443–44, 463,
        651–52
    see also executive branch
presidential power:
    assessment of, 436, 462–67
    limits of, 438, 440, 462–63
    "two presidencies" thesis and, 445
    War Powers Resolution and, 443–44
presidential succession, 453–55, **454**, 457
presidential system (presidential republic), 8
press conferences, 250
prices:
    regulations on, 582
    stabilization of, as economic policy goal,
        556–57
primary elections, 285, **286**, 324, 325, 334,
        342
    delegate allocation in, 311–12
    federal funding in, 330

nomination in, 308
    of 2012, 334
    2012 Indiana, 290
    2012 Indiana–Republican, 309
    2012 Missouri, 290
prime interest rate, 581
prime time, 243
priming, 255–57, 259–60
principal–agent game, 481–82
principles, political, 202, 220, **221**
printing presses, 239
Printz v. United States, **93**
prior restraint, 126–27, 248
Prison Litigation Reform Act (1996), 86
prisons, 86, 119, 199
Privacy Act (1974), 138
privacy rights, **113**, 133, 135, 142–45, *145*
privileges and immunities clause, 73–74
probable cause, 134, 136
problem of control, bureaucracy and, 481–83
procedures, influence on political process of,
        9, 13
procurement, 479
product safety, 17
Progressive era, 80, 485, 486
progressive price indexing, 616
progressive taxes, 576–77
Prohibition, 58
Project Censored, 256
propaganda, 47–48
property rights, 8, 23, 36, **70**, **77**, 78, 112, 116,
        140, 557
proportional allocation, 312
Proposition, 8, 522
protection, standards for, 120
protectionism, 158–59
protectionist policies, 587–88
protests, 34, 120, 123, 124–25, *124*, 128, 204,
        206, *246*, 368–69
    prohibition of, 105–6
Pryor, Mark, 305–6, *305*, 307, 319, 345, 346
public awareness, 201
Public Citizen, 353, 367
public goods, 7, *8*
public health, 107, *108*
public interest groups, **354**
Public Interest Research Group, *362*
public knowledge, 201
public opinion:
    abortion and, 12, 17, 19, 204
    accuracy of, 217–18
    Afghanistan and, 296
    biological factors on, 207
    characteristics of, 219–29
    civil liberties and, 109
    conflict based in, 12, *12*
    consensus of, 222–23
    considerations and, 203–4
    Constitution and, 54, 61
    courts and, 141, 523
    crime and, 139
    death penalty and, 142
    early studies of, 201–2
    economic conditions and, 203, 208, 225,
        338, 340–41, **341**, **342**
    fluidity of, 202–3, 207, 208, **223**, 224
    foreign policy and, 20, 654–56
    government and, 12, 89–90, 262–64
    gun control and, 130–32, *131*, 199–200,
        199

health care and, **226**
    ideology and, 15, 19, 219–21
    on immigration, 227
    influences on, 15, 19, 47–48, 110, 202–11,
        217–18, *222*, **223**, 224–29
    Iraq War and, *243*, 338
    latency of, 202–5
    lobbying and mobilization of, 369
    lobbying success affected by, 378
    measuring of, 200–203, 212–19
    media's influence on, 237–38
    political influence of, 12, *12*, 61, 89–90,
        120, *201*, 211, 221–23, 226, 228,
        229–31, 369–70, 561, 570, 609
    president and, 458–62, **458**
    presidential approval and, 452, **452**,
        460–62, **461**
    quality of, 200
    relevance of, 229–31
    religion and, 114
    on same-sex marriage, **229**
    spending and, 88, 491–93, **492**
    studies of, 207
    Supreme Court and, 541, 544–45
    taxes and, 88
    theories of, 201–6
    voting cues and, 336–37
public order, 109
Public Policy Polling, 401
public safety, 107, *108*, 116, 133, 137
public works, 485
Public Works Administration (PWA), 599
publishing, 126, 127–30
Puerto Ricans, Puerto Rico, 157, 519
Pure Food and Drug Act (1906), 485
purposive benefits, 364
push polling, 214, 322

Quartet on the Middle East, 638, *638*
quotas, 188, 189, 587

race:
    census data on, **19**
    as defining feature, 161
    hate speech and, 124–25, *126*
    juries and, 141
    party affiliation of, **283**
    political conflict as a result of, 18–19,
        43–45
    political equality and, 43–45
    political influence of, 18–19, *18*, 204, **210**
    public opinion and, 204, **210**
    redistricting cases and, 536
    relationship of voting patterns to, 18
    Supreme Court decisions concerning,
        79, *79*, 87
    voting rights cases and, 516
race riots, 158, 165
"race to the bottom," 90, 98, 100
Race to the Top program, 606, 628
Rachel Maddow Show, 253, **254**
racial discrimination, 124–25, 126, *126*,
        160–61, 176, **182**
    in election of 2000, 162
    in employment, 172
racial profiling, 151, 165, 192
racial redistricting, 173–74, 532, 536
radio networks, 240, *240*, 244
    FCC regulations and, 240
    knowledge levels in listeners of, **254**

online sites for, 244–45
talk programs on, 244, 261
usage trends in, **252**
railroad trust, 437
"rally 'round the flag" effect, 462
Randolph, Edmund, 37, 41
random digit dialing, 214
Rangel, Charles, 547
Rasmussen Reports, 216
rational basis test, 174–75, 177–78
Rayburn, Sam, 413
Reagan, Ronald, 53, 85–86, 131, 137, **223**, **224**,
250, *439*
approval ratings and popularity of, **452**
bureaucracy and, 487
economic policies of, 573, *573*, 587–88
foreign policy of, 439, 642
judges appointed by, **525**
secret intelligence operations of, 465
social policies of, 604, 613–14
Reagan Revolution, 485, 487
realignments, in party systems, 275
realism, **637**, 638–39, 640
reasonable basis test, 174, 175, 179–80
reasonable vote, 336
recess appointments, 442
recession, 556, *566*, 579, 590, 642
Keynesian economic theory for
softening of, 572
social policy during, **627**
reconciliation process, 595, 597
Reconstruction, 78, 155, 426
recounts, 311
Redding, Savana, 133
reddit, 246
redistribution, fiscal policy's nature of, 16–17,
210, 575–78, **577**
redistricting, 398–401
Red Scare, 122
"red states," 17, 20
red tape, bureaucracy and, 480
reductions in force (RIF), 494
Reed, Stanley, 537
Reed, Thomas, 424
Reed's Rules, 424
reelection:
EOP role in, 455–56
presidential approval and, 452, **452**
referendum, 375
Reform Party, 295, 296, *310*
regional primaries, 312
regions:
economic differences among, 36
political differences among, 209, **210**
regressive taxes, 575–76, 613
regulation, 476–79, *479*
of banking system, 567–68, 579–80
business, 15, **15**, 16–17, **70**, 80, 90, **221**,
437, 476
campaign finance, 329–32, **329**, 330–32,
333, 358, 373
civil service, 494–95
commerce, 8, 57, **70**, 72, 75, 78, 80, **93**,
94–95, 116, 476, 582–83
currency, 8
drug, 97, 476, 479, 481
economic effects of, 582–84
economic vs. social, 582–83
environmental, 90, 503, *503*, 582–83,
582, 585

everyday life affected by, 14–15, 476, *479*
extent of, 439
free market, 8, 557–58, 583, 584
ideological views on, 16–17, 19, 96
Internet, 129
of lobbying groups, 358, 370
media, 17, 127–30, *129*, 238, 239, 240–42,
476
notice and comment procedure and, 476
public opinion on, **221**
role in coercive federalism of, 88
state power over, 90, 98
theories on politics of, 583–84
trade, 8, **70**, 664
regulatory capture, 482–83, 583
Rehnquist, William, 56, 97, 173, 541, 546, 548
opinion writing and, 536
Reid, Harry, *410*, 420, *570*
religion, 92, **93**
establishment of, 109
and government, 117
government and, 112–19
political affiliation and, **283**, 284
political conflict as a result of, 17
political influence of, 17, 202, 203, 207,
209–11
see also freedom of religion
religious discrimination, **182**
religious displays, 17, *114*, 115
Religious Freedom Restoration Act (1993),
92, **93**, 119
remedial legislation, 92
rendition, 107
Renteria, Amanda, *307*
reporters, *see* journalists; media
representative democracy, 22
republican democracy, 8, 35–36, 40
Republican Governors' Association, 275
Republican Lawyers' Organization, 275
Republican National Committee (RNC),
277–78
Republican National Conventions, 313
Republican Party, 31, 123, 209, **224**, 263,
270–71, **277**, 299–300, 306, 319,
342, 411–14
affiliations by race and gender with, 18,
18, **283**
bailout bill of 2008 and, 570
as brand name, 277, 323
bureaucratic control and, 502
campaign fundraising and support
provided by, 289, **289**
Civil War amendments passed by, 155
congressional conference of, 279
culture wars reflected in election results
of, 17, **21**
economic policy and, 583, 585, 588
formation of, 437
founding and history of, 271–75, **272**
gun control and, 229
health care and, 225
House controlled by, 89, 446, 487
identification with, 15, 17, *18*, 19–20, **21**,
203, 208, 209, 219, **220**
ideology and, 15, 17, 19–20, **21**, 97,
279–80, **279**, 291
judicial nominees and, 529
Latinos in, 157, 186
limited federal government and, 86, 598
limited government and, 554, 555

majority status during Bush presidency
of, 13–14
media and, 258
New Deal opposed by, 486
party coalitions in, 284, **284**
party identification in electorate of,
280–82, **283**
party in government of, 278–80
party organizations of, 275–78
position on regulation of, 16–17
position on spending of, 16–17
position on taxes of, 16–17, 572
poverty rates under leadership of, 603,
603
presidential platforms of, 291
recruiting and nominating of candidates
in, 285, 287
Senate controlled by, 446, 487
smaller federal government favored by,
274, *274*
social policy approaches favored by,
595–97, 615, 616–17, 626, 629
views shaped by identification with, 15
see also elections, U.S.
research, 16
research and development, 479
reservations, Native American, 157
reserved powers, 42–43
reserve requirement, 580
"Respect for Fallen American Heroes Act," 106
RESPECT project, 628
restaurants, desegregation of, 168, 172
restrictive covenants, 171
retirement age, 616
retrospective evaluations, 307, 336, **337**
Revenue Act (1964), 572, 574
reverse discrimination, 190
revisionary power, 511
see also judicial review
Revolutionary War, 52, 514
government during, 32–34, **32**
influence on Constitutional Convention
of, 31, 35, 38
newspaper coverage of, 239
revolving door, 360
Rhode Island, 33, 40, 41, 46, 48
Ricardo, David, 588
Richie, Nicole, 130
right to bear arms, 112, **113**, 130–32, *131*
right to die, 204
right to petition, 112, **113**
Rivkin, David, 67
R. J. Reynolds, 129
Roberts, John G., 97, 173, 526, 535, *537*, 543,
543, 546, 548
Robinson, Jackie, 156
Robinson v. California, **113**
robo-polls, 214
Rockefeller, Nelson, 454
Rock Hill, S.C., 168
Rodriguez, Alex, 136
Roe v. Wade, 143, 536–37, 543, 545
roll call votes, 411
Romney, Mitt, *13*, 20, 212, 214, 245–46, *245*,
261, 282, 290, 295, **318**, *323*, 336,
340, 342–43, 553
federal campaign funding and, 330
2012 campaign platform of, 324–26, **324**
2012 election and, 288
2012 election results of, **283**

Roosevelt, Eleanor, *599*
Roosevelt, Franklin D., 54, *80*, 274, *274*, 438, *438*, 460, 485, *486*, 509, 598
    court-packing plan of, 524, 546
    New Deal and, 604
    Supreme Court switch and, 544
Roosevelt, Theodore, 29, 437, 617
Rosen, Jeffrey, 125
Ross, Gary, 185
Rouse, Pete, *456*
Rove, Karl, 374
rubber stamping, 51
Rubio, Marco, *299*
Ruby Tuesday, 176
Ruemmler, Kathryn, *456*
rules, influence on political process of, 9, 13
"running scared," 396
runoff elections, 309
Rush Limbaugh Show, The, 244, **254**
Russia, 121, 439–40, 445, 638, 655, **655**, 657, 661
    nuclear weapons of, 666
    Ukraine and, 497
    U.S. and, 643
Rwanda, 439
Ryan, Paul, 342, *407*, *553*, 624

Safford, Arizona, 133
St. Patrick's Day parade, 179–80
St. Paul, Minn., 125
salience, 378–79, 381
Sallie Mae, lobbying by, 351, 356, 362, 367
Salt Lake City, Utah, 122
same-sex marriage, *14*, 20, 69, *72*, 73–74, 160, 180, *185*, 226, 228, **229**, 521–22
samples:
    random, 212, **213**, 214, 215–16, 218
    survey, 212, **213**, 215–16
sampling error, **213**, 215–16
Sam's Club, 179
San Antonio, Tex., 94
Sandanistas, 53, 642
Sandoval, Martha, 190
Sandy, Hurricane, *68*, 343, 600
Sandy Hook Elementary School, 131, *131*, 132, 199, *199*, 372, 442
Santeria, 108
Santorum, Rick, 290, 603
Sarbanes–Oxley Act (2002), 487
satellite television, 241
Saudi Arabia, 248, *444*
Sawyer, Diane, *313*
Scalia, Antonin, 97, 134, 515, 536, 539–40, 541, *543*
    Lawrence dissent of, 180
Schattschneider, E. E., 10
Schenck, Charles, 120–21
Schenck v. United States, 121
Schickler, Eric, 209
Schilb v. Kuebel, **113**
school desegregation, 167, 170–72, 184, 544–45
    Brown I and, 156, 167, 171, 544–45
    Brown II and, 156, 171
    busing and, *171*, 172, 545
school lunches, 518
school prayer, 17, *60*, 109, 114–15, 545, *545*
school vouchers, 17, 115, 629, *629*
Schuette, Bill, 532
Schultz, Debbie Wasserman, *271*

Scotland, 71
Scott, Dred, 78
SCOTUSblog (Supreme Court blog), 245
scrutiny, 120
searches and seizures, 87, 109, **113**, 133–38, *136*, 145
Seattle, Wash., 172, 189
Sebelius, Kathleen, 426, *498*, 623
secession, 76, 155, *389*, 437
Second Amendment, **110**, 112, **113**, 130
Second Continental Congress, 31–32, **32**
second party system, **272**, 273
Securities and Exchange Commission (SEC), 557
security, 6, 71, 72, 86, 107, 109, 126–27, 130, 137–38, 145, 248, 260
    border controls and, 227
    collective, 641
    foreign policy treaties and, 644, 661
    see also defense
Sedition Act (1918), 76, 121
segregation, 79, *79*, 87, 91, 156, 160, 167
    de jure vs. de facto, 171–72
    separate but equal doctrine and, 156, 170–71
select committees, 414
selective incentives, 364–65
selective incorporation, 111–12, *113*, **113**
self-incrimination, 87, 112, **113**, 132, 138–40, 141
self-rule:
    constitutional importance of, 35
    Locke's view on, 36
Seminole Tribe v. Florida, **93**
Senate, U.S., 184, 256, 269–70, 279, 340
    "advice and consent" of, 51, *51*, 61
    Agriculture Committee of, 414
    appointments confirmed by, 441–42, 484, 490, 496, 513, 523, 524, 526–28
    Appropriations Committee of, 416, 422
    bailout bill of 2008 retooled and passed in, 570
    Banking Committee of, *51*
    Bill of Rights creation in, 110
    bills in, 423–25
    Budget Committee of, 422
    constituencies in elections for, 309–10
    Constitutional Convention and, **39**, 40, **44**
    constitutional requirements of candidates for, **311**
    creation of laws in, 94, 123, 201
    Democratic control of, 446
    in economic policy making, 561, *567*, 568
    election to, 48, 59, 308, 309
    filibuster in, 529
    Finance Committee in, 561
    Foreign Relations Committee in, 649
    House vs., 389
    impeachment and, 467
    incumbents in, **404**
    Intelligence Committee of, 426, *426*, 650
    Judiciary Committee of, 529
    League of Nations and, 438
    majority control of, 293
    party ideological differences and polarization in, 279–80
    president pro tempore of, 411, 454
    public knowledge of, 217
    reelection to, 395–97

Republican control of, 89, 446, 487
    roll call votes in, 411
    rules and procedures in, 13
    treaties approved by, 444
    veto overridden by, 443, 445
    vice president's presiding over, 456
    see also Congress, U.S.; House of Representatives, U.S.
senatorial courtesy, 527
Seneca Falls Convention (1848), 18, 167
senior citizens, 275
Senior Executive Service (SES), 497
seniority, 408
sentencing guidelines, 54
"separate but equal" doctrine, 156, 170–71, 274, 487
separation of church and state, **113**, 114–16
    school vouchers issue and, 629, *629*
separation of powers, 7, 62, 116, 119
    Articles of Confederation structuring of, 32–34
    conflict over, 69, 75
    constitutional framework for, 48–55
    issue at Constitutional Convention of, 38, *38*, 41, 42–43, 46–47
    James Madison's view on, 36, 38, 42
    Supreme Court in, 541, 546
separatism, racial, 18
September 11, 2001 terrorist attacks, 86, 100, 133, 137–38, 204, *205*, 208, 635, 636, *644*, 648, 655, 661, 665
    foreign policy impacted by, 665
    immigration issue and, 192
    presidential approval and, 462
    spending for national security and, 409
Servicemen's Readjustment Act, *see* G.I. Bill
Seventeenth Amendment, 59, 390
Seventh Amendment, **110**, **113**
"72-Hour Task Force," 289
sexual discrimination, *see* gender discrimination
sexual harassment, 175–76, 179, 515, 526
Shaheen, Jeanne, 305–6, 307, 319, 345–46
Shapiro, Robert, 211
Shaw v. Reno, 173
Shays's Rebellion, **33**, 34
Shelby County v. Holder, **93**
Shepard, Matthew, 184
Sherman, Roger, 47
Sherman Antitrust Act (1890), 79, 437, 485, 582
shield laws, 250
Shinseki, Eric, 426, 605
Sierra Club, *354*, 357, 360, 361–62
signing statement, 465
Silver, Nate, 213
Simas, David, *456*
Simpson, Alan, *617*
Simpson, O. J., *516*
Simpsons, The, *200*
Sinclair, Barbara, 417
Sinclair, Upton, 239
Sindram, Michael, 528
single-issue groups, **354**
single-member districts, 296, 309
sit-ins, 168, *168*
Sixteenth Amendment, 59, **60**
Sixth Amendment, 56, **110**, **113**, 126, 132, 140–41, 540
sixth party system, **272**, 274, 275
60 Minutes, **258**

Skype, 246
slander, 128
slant, 255
slavery, 35, 37, 38, 42, 43–45, *43*, **44**, *45*, 48, 73, 76, **77**, 78, 111, 239, 390
    abolition of, 58
    civil rights and, 154
    compromises on, 154–55, 437
    Dred Scott and, 155, 514
    Emancipation Proclamation and, 437, 464–65
    party systems aligned over issue of, 273
Slovakia, **576**
Smith Act (1940), 122
Smoot-Hawley Act (1930), 589
Snow, Murray, 152
Snowden, Edward, *54*, 127, *127*, 137, 248, *248*, 252, 260, 393
Snowe, Olympia, 344
Snyder, Albert, 106
Snyder, Matthew, 106
Socialist Party, 112, 120, 121, *121*
social media, 246
social networking sites, 244–45
social policy, 19, 80
    agenda and, 609
    definition of, 597
    on education, 606, 626–29
    government spending and, 601–2
    government spending on, 597–98, 610, 624–26
    on health care, 595–97, 600, 617–24
    history and background of, 597–600
    income inequality and, **602**
    income support and welfare programs in, 624–26, **625**
    interest groups and, 606
    key players in formation of, 604–10
    natural disasters and, 600, 603–4, 606, 609
    and participation in mean-tested programs, **627**
    poverty impacted by, 600–604, **601**, **603**, 612
    process in formation of, 606–10
    Social Security and, 608, 610–17
    stages of process, 606–10
    types of, 598
    welfare reform and, 626
social regulation, 582–83, *582*
Social Security, 8, 29, 396, 575–76, 597, 598, 599, 610–17, **614**, 618
    AARP and, 606
    definition of, 610
    enactment and evolution of, 608
    fiscal problems of, 610–15, **615**
    intergenerational inequalities created by, 612, *613*
    1983 Amendments to, 613–14
    pay-as-you-go nature of, 611–12, *613*, 617
    privatization of, 616
    reform of, 600, *600*, 611, 613–14, 615–17, *617*
    spending for, 492, **492**, 574
    trust fund of, 614–15, **615**
Social Security Act (1935), 486
Social Security Administration, 605, 613, 626
social services:
    government provision of, 8, 80, 90, 96, 100, 204

ideological views on, 16–17, 19
    state differences in, 73–74, 96
    see also welfare
sodomy, 179–80
soft money, 124, 329–30, 332
soft news, 262, 263
solicitor general, 533
solidary benefits, 364, 365
Solyndra Corporation, 448
Somalia, 644
Sotomayor, Sonia, 186, 442, 512, *524*, 526, *526*, 536, 538, 541, *543*
sources, journalistic, 127
Souter, David, 524, 541
South, 239
    civil rights in, 154
    economic interests of, 36
    Jim Crow laws in, 156
    secession of, 76, 155, 437
    segregation in, 79, *83*, 92, 154, 156
    slavery and, 43–45, 77, **77**, 111, 154–55
    states' rights and, 77
    voting history of, *18*, 87, 92, 208, 274
South America, 437, 640
South Boston Allied War Veterans Council, 179–80
South Carolina, 76, 137, 179, 192, 313
Southern Ohio Correctional Facility, *61*
South Korea, 444, **576**, 642, 661, 666, 667
South Vietnam, 439, 642
sovereign power, 69
Soviet Union, 71, *439*
    fall of, 643, 661
    Reagan policy toward, 439, 642
    U.S. policy of containment and, 641–43
    U.S. treaties with, 642–43, 661
Spain, 53
    land dispute with U.S. and, 546–47
    tax rates in, **576**
Spanish-American War, 239, 443, 650
Speaker of the House, 410, 454
"special master" hearings, 531
speech:
    commercial, 128–29, *129*
    hate, 124–25, *126*
    less protected, 127–30
    political, 120–22, 128, *129*
    protected, 120–25
    symbolic, 122–24, *123*, 124
    see also freedom of speech
speed limits, 69
spending:
    concurrent powers of, **70**
    congressional authority over, 51, *70*, 86, 116, 561
    on defense, 642
    deficits and, **559**, 560
    federal, 15, 84, **85**, 86–89, *99*, 217, 224, 269, 280, 284, **355**, 357, **358**, 491, **491**, **492**, 554, **559**, 561, 573–75, **575**, **577**, 589, 597–98, 614
    on health care, 618–20, **618**, **620**
    ideological views on, 16–17, 19, 84
    Keynesian economic theory and, 572, 574
    on lobbying efforts, 354–57 **355**, **357**, **358**, 381
    mandatory vs. discretionary, 574, **575**
    1980s budget deficit and, 573

public opinion on, 88, 201, 203, 217, 491–92, **492**
    on social policies, **625**
    state and local, 85, **85**, 86, 100
Spirit of the Laws, The (Montesquieu), 36
split tickets, casting of, 338
spoils system, 273, 484, *484*, 485
sports, 136
Spyer, Thea, 522
spying:
    domestic, *see* surveillance
    foreign, 137
stagflation, 557, *568*
Stamp Act (1765), 31
standardized tests, 629
standard of proof, 516
Standard Oil, 582
standard operating procedures, 480
standing, 517
standing committees, 414–15
Stanton, Elizabeth Cady, 167
state capacity, 480
State Department, U.S., 484
    foreign policy and role of, 647
    spending for, 492, **492**
state laws, judicial review of, 514
State of the Union address, 445, 453, 454
    media coverage of, 251
states:
    economic differences among, *99*
    income assistance and welfare administered by, 626
    Medicaid and discretionary power of, 619
    political differences among, 17, 19, **21**, 130
    social policy formation and role of, 605–6, 626–27
states' rights, 76–77, 83, 85–86, 89–95, 96–98, 110–11, 112, 120, 125, 131, 143–44, **144**, 514
states' sovereign immunity, 92, **93**
statutory interpretation, 515
stealth democracy, 10
Steffens, Lincoln, 240
stem cell research, 20, 89
Stephanopoulos, George, *261*
Stevens, Chris, 665
Stevens, John Paul, 524, 541
Stewart, Jon, 205, 251, 252
Stewart, Potter, 129
stimulus package, *see* economic stimulus package
Stockman, David, 575
stock markets, 617
    crash of 1929 and, 598
    in financial crisis of 2008, 569–72
Stone, Harlan Fiske, 537
Stonewall Rebellion, 159
Stop Online Piracy Act (SOPA), 376
straight tickets, casting of, 338
Strategic Arms Limitation Treaty (SALT I), 642
Strauss v. Horton, 522
street-level bureaucrats, 479
strict construction, 539, 540, 544
    see also original intent
strict scrutiny, 120, 127, 175, 177–78, 191
strip searches, 133–34
Strong, Benjamin, 581

student activity fees, 124
Student Aid Alliance, 361, 362
    see also education, student loans and
Student Nonviolent Coordinating Committee
    (SNCC), 168
Stupak, Bart, 293–94
substantive due process doctrine, 145, 180
substantive representation, 391
suicide, assisted, *see* aid in dying
Summers, Charles, 324
Sunstein, Cass, 90
superdelegates, 313
supermajorities, 45
Supplemental Nutrition Assistance Program
    (SNAP), 624
Supplemental Security Income (SSI), 626, **627**
supply-side economics, 573
Supreme Court, U.S., 62, 369, 400, *510*,
    520–23, *524*, 528–48
    ACA and, 68
    access to, 528–34, **530**
    as agent of change, 545
    allocation of power to, 7, **39**, 51, 54, 73
    amicus curiae and, 534–35
    appellate jurisdiction of, 512, **512**,
        519–20
    appointments to, 54, 75–76, 92
    attitudinalist approach and, 540–41
    briefs for, 534–35
    campaign finance reforms and, 123–24,
        333
    case criteria of, 531–32
    chief justices of, 77, 109, 512–13
    civil liberties and, 109–45
    civil rights issues and, 155, 156, 158–59,
        168, 170–80, 183–84, 187, 188–89,
        190
    color-blind jurisprudence of, 173–74,
        187, 189
    constitutional amendments to overturn
        decisions of, **60**, 73–74, 122
    constitutional interpretation by, 43, 56,
        59, 60, *61*, 62, 73, 75–76, 77, 92, **93**,
        94, 96, 97, 109–45, **135**, 192, 436,
        444, 464, 514–15, 520, 540, *542*
    decision making of, 535–45, *545*
    docket of, 528, *530*, 531
    executive privilege ruling of, 449–50
    FDR's court-packing plan for, 524, 546
    federalism and, 73, 75–76, **77**, 78–80, *79*,
        86–87, *88*, 90–95, **93**, 96, 97, 98, 111,
        112–13, 119, 130, 137, 514
    hearing cases before, 534–38, *535*
    interpretation of laws by, 7, 12, 51, 54–55,
        75–76, 80, 91, 92, 96, 97, 129, 514–15
    judicial activism of, 173–74, 541–43
    judicial restraint of, 541–43
    judicial review by, 51, 54–55, 513–15, *513*,
        546–47
    justices' conference in, 536
    living Constitution and, 56
    Obama and, 509–10
    opinion writing in, 536–37, *537*
    oral argument in, 535–36, *535*
    original intent and, 56, 539, 541
    original jurisdiction of, **512**, 514, 531, *531*
    policy implications of composition of, 54,
        75–76, 92, 96
    as policy-making institution, 511,
        545–48

    as political institution, 511, 533, 535–45
    precedent overruled by, 517, **518**
    public knowledge of, *200*
    public opinion and, 541, 544–45
    "riding circuit" by justices of, 512
    Rule 10 of, 532, *533*
    rules of access for, 531
    on school voucher programs, 629
    separation of powers and, 541, 546
    "special master" hearings, and, 531
    speech protected by, 106
    strategic approach to, 541
    strict construction and, 56, 539, 540, 544
    unilateral presidential actions and, 466,
        466
    War Powers Resolution and, 443–44
    workload of, 528–30, *530*, **530**
    writ of certiorari and, 531
    writ of mandamus issued by, 514
    see also judicial branch; *specific cases*
surveillance, 56, 127, 133, 134, 135, 137–38,
    145, 208, 212, 248, 260, 280, 393,
    464, 665–66
    see also spying
surveys, 202, 227
    interpretation of, 218–21
    mass, 212, **213**
    problems with, 201–3, 214–18, **221**
    techniques of, 212–14
    wording of, 202, 212, 215, 219–21, 222
    see also polls
Sweden, 71
    tax rates in, **576**
swing states, 314, **314**, 342
Switzerland, 71, **576**
Syria, 53, 635–36, 637–38, 639, 649, 654–55,
    657

Taliban, 249, 253, 665
talk radio, 244, 261
Tammany Hall, 273, *273*
Taney, Roger, 77
Tanzania, 644
tariffs, 38, 46, 76, 390, 587, 644
    definition of, 657–58
TARP (Troubled Asset Relief Program), 391,
    570, 571
Tax Day, 170
taxes, tax policy, 392, 394, 554, 561, 565, 569,
    589
    Articles of Confederation problems with,
        33, **39**, 44
    Clinton's increase of, 391
    concurrent power over, **70**
    Constitutional Convention issue of, 38,
        42, 46–47
    corporate, 575
    cuts in, 439
    and deductions for wealthy, 601–2
    estate, 609
    excise, 575–76
    federal authority over, **39**, 51, **60**, 72,
        75–76, 88, 565–66
    fiscal theories on influencing economy
        with, 572–78, **573**
    in foreign countries, **576**
    health care programs and, 623
    ideological views on, 16–17, 19
    income, 59, *60*, 576–77
    local authority over, 70, 96

    marginal tax rate and, 578, **578**
    1962 revenue from, **577**
    payment for public goods with, 7
    payroll, 575–76, 611–12, **615**, 616, 617
    proposed constitutional amendments
        concerning, **60**
    public opinion on, 88
    redistributive, 16–17, **210**, 575–78, **577**
    regressive vs. progressive, 575–77
    religious organizations and, 115
    Social Security funding and, 613, **615**,
        616, 617
    standing and, 518
    state authority over, **70**, 72, 75–76, 90,
        96, **99**, 100
    2014 revenue from, **577**
    uses for, 124, 575, **577**
Tea Act (1773), 31
Tea Party Caucus, 269–70, 280
Tea Party movement, 29–30, *29*, 43, 56, 61–62,
    89, 170, 225, *246*, 269–70, *269*,
    275–76, 278, 282, 286, 295–96, 300,
    359, 414
technology:
    First Amendment rights and, 539
    surveillance and, 135
Tejada, Miguel, 137
Telecommunications Act (1996), 241
telegraphs, 239
television, 240–41, 243–44, 264, 356
    campaign ads on, 326–28, *327*, **327**, 332,
        369
    comedy shows as news sources on,
        251–52, 253
    corporate ownership in, **242**
    FCC regulations of, 240–41
    framing effects and, 256, *257*
    knowledge levels in viewers of, **254**
    nightly news programs on, 243–44, 251,
        253, **254**
    online sites for, 244–45
    political bias in, 258–62
    usage trends in, 252–53, **252**
Temporary Assistance to Needy Families
    (TANF), 86, 96, 605, 626, **627**
Ten Commandments, 115
Tennessee, 171
Tenth Amendment, 30, 42–43, 73, 91, **110**, 174
Tenth Amendment Center, 67
term limits, **60**, 95
territorial expansion, Mexican-American war
    and, 437
terrorism, 7, 54, 86, 100, 122, 125, 127, 133, 137,
    141, 145, 204, *205*, 208, **221**, 225,
    435, 635–36, 644, *644*, 645, 662,
    665–66
    restriction of legal rights and, *466*, 666
    see also War on Terror
Terrorist Finance Tracking Program, 127
Texas, 115, 123, 145, 174, *193*, *320*, 399
    affirmative action in, 188, 189
    annexation of, 437, 464
    sodomy in, 180
Texas, University of, 189–90, *189*
Theiss-Morse, Elizabeth, 10, 263
theocracy, 21
thermal imaging devices, 135
Thernstrom, Abigail, 187
Thernstrom, Stephan, 187
Third Amendment, **110**, **113**, 142

third party system, **272**, 273
Thirteenth Amendment, 58, 78, 111, 155, 172
Thomas, Clarence, 56, 536, 541, 543, *543*
    original intent perspective of, 539
    Supreme Court appointment of, 526
Thorning-Schmidt, Helle, *237*, 238
Three-fifths Compromise, 44, **44**, 45
Thurmond, Strom, 424
Tillis, Thom, *330*, 377–78
Time, 243, *358*
Tinker, Mary Beth, *539*
Tocqueville, Alexis de, 100
Tolstoy, Leo, 622
Toomey, Pat, 372
Top Censored Stories, 256
Tories, 31–32
torture, 54, 107
totalitarianism, 22
Tour de France, 136
trade, **70**
    Articles of Confederation and, 33–34
    Constitutional Convention and, 37, 45
    deficits, 586–88, **587**
    executive branch and power over, 566
    free, 402, 438, 439, 444, 588
    international, 519, 566, 584–89, 636, 641,
      644, 653, **658**, 662–64
    most-favored-nation status and, 658
trade agreements, 657–59
trade associations, 357
trade deficits, 560, 561
traffic violations, 151
Trail of Tears, 156
transfer payments, *see* grants
Trans-Pacific partnership, 588
transportation, 69, 80, 392, 394
    federal spending on, 408
Transportation Department, U.S., 474
Transportation Security Administration
    (TSA), U.S., 474, 648
Treasury Department, U.S., **70**, 464, 484, 489,
    567, 568–69
    economic policies and responsibilities
      of, 568–69
    Federal Reserve in cooperation with, 569
    in financial crisis of 2008, 569–72
treaties, 32, **70**, 71
    executive power to negotiate, 51, 444
    fast-track authority for, 444
Treaty of Versailles, 640
trespassing, 125
trials, rights concerning, **113**, 125–26, 132–33,
    136, 140
Tribune Company, 241
trickle-down economics, *see* supply-side
    economics
Troubled Asset Relief Program (TARP), 391,
    570, 571
Truman, Harry S., 137, 156, 184, 251, 319
Trump, Donald, 611
trustee, 391
Tunisia, 645
Turkey, **576**, 642
"turkey farms," 496
Tutu, Desmond, 128
Twain, Mark, 401, *402*
Tweed, William "Boss," *273*
Twelfth Amendment, 42, 58
Twenty-first Amendment, 58
Twenty-second Amendment, *60*

Twenty-fifth Amendment, 454
Twitter, *244*, 245, 246
"two presidencies" thesis, 445
Tyler, John, 437
tyranny, 46
tyranny of the majority, 7, 38–39, 48, 90, 98

Ukraine, 53, 439–40, 445, 497, 643, 655, **655**,
    657, 661
unalienable rights, *see* natural rights
Underground Railroad, 154
undervotes, 310
unemployment, 163, 208, 225, 438, 439, *460*,
    554, 557, 561, *571*, 572, *599*
    compensation policies for, 598–600,
      624–26
    economic bills passed for reduction of,
      555
    Misery Index of inflation and, **556**, 557
Unfunded Mandate Reform Act (1995), 86
unfunded mandates, **84**, 86, 88
unified government, 294
unilateral action (national), 637
unilateral action (presidential), 184, 463–65,
    649
Union Army, *45*
Union League, 155
unions, 274, 275, 356, 588
    interest groups and lobbying efforts of,
      354, 364, 374
    OSHA and, 502
unitary executive theory, 464, 466
unitary government, 71
unitary system, 8, 98
United Farm Workers, 157, *157*
United Kingdom, *see* Great Britain
United Nations (UN), 50, 71, 637–38, *639*, 640,
    642, 656
    Security Council of, 464, 659
United Negro College Fund, 628
United States Mint, 569
United States v. Bond, **93**
United States v. Lopez, **93**, 94, *94*
United States v. Morrison, **93**
United States v. Nixon, 449
United States v. Virginia, 178
United States v. Windsor, **93**, 522
universal health care, 618
University of California Regents v. Bakke, 189,
    190
Unorthodox Lawmaking (Sinclair), 417
urbanization, 80
Uruguay, 588
USA PATRIOT Act (2001), 133, 423
USA Today, **254**, **258**
U.S. Term Limits v. Thornton, 428
Utah, 192, 428
    school vouchers in, 629

Valadao, David, *307*
values, effect on policy of, 142
Van Buren, Martin, 437
Vandenberg, Arthur, 635
Van Hollen, Chris, *453*
verdict, 516
Verizon, 137
Vermont, 185
Versailles, Treaty of, 640
vesting clause, 441, 464
veteran-owned businesses, 479

veterans, 555
    social policy and, 597–98
Veterans Affairs Department, U.S., 396, 488, 605
Veterans of Foreign Wars, 105, 106
veto:
    Articles of Confederation rules for,
      32–33
    in confederal system, **70**
    executive power of, 7, 41, 54, 417–18, 422,
      445, 566
    overriding of, 41, 418, 422, 445
    pocket, 422
    problems with, 40
vice president, U.S., 456–57
    in presidential succession, 453–54, 457
    replacement of, 454
Vietnam War, 53, 122, 123, 127, *223*, 240, *243*,
    390, 439, 599, 642
    protest against, 169, 539, *539*
viewpoint discrimination, 124
viewpoint diversity, 191
violence, media and, 17
Violence Against Women Act (VAWA; 1995),
    93, 94, 183
Virginia, 34, *43*, 46, 48, 76, 125, 174, 317
    post-Revolutionary War debt in, 514
    slavery in, 154
Virginia Military Institute, 175
Virginia Plan, 40, 41, 58
Virgin Islands, 519
volunteering, 207
Volunteers in Service to America (VISTA),
    599
voting, 5, 9, 13, 87, 89, 96, 97, 200, 203, 208,
    212, 230, *230*, *334*
    citizen motivations for, 334–35
    citizen turnout in, 96, 334–35, **335**
    cues in shaping citizens' election
      choices, 336–37, **337**
    in Democratic primaries, 155, 537
    early or absentee, 308
    of Latinos, 157, *163*
    methods of, 310–11, *310*
    mobilization efforts for encouraging,
      321–22, 335, 343
    paradox of, 334–35
    plurality vs. majority, 309
    polling places for, *308*
    racial and gender patterns of, 18
    recounts and, 311
    requirements for, 308–9
    2000 election problems with, 162
    2008 election problems with, 163
    2014 election problems with, 163
    see also ballots
voting cues, 336–37, **337**
voting rights, 18, *18*, 22–23, *23*, 48, *58*, 59, 61,
    78, 89, 92, 111, 155, 208, 308, 439,
    515, 516
    grandfather clause and, 155
    Great Society and, 487
    of women, 158, 167
Voting Rights Act (VRA; 1965), 87, 92, **93**, 172,
    181, 599
    1982 amendments to, 173–74
Voto Latino, *163*

wage and price controls, 557
Wales, 71
Walker, Dave, 495, *496*

Wallace, George, 295
Wall Street, bailout of, 570, *571*
Wall Street Journal, 243, **254**
Walmart, 179, *179*, 516
war, public opinion and, *209*
War and Peace (Tolstoy), 622
War Department, U.S., 484
War of 1812, 53, 272, 443, 650
War on Poverty, 599, 627
War on Terror, 54, 107, 127, 341, 390, 565, 644, 666
 checks and balances in, 50
 see also terrorism
war powers, **70**, 651–52
War Powers Resolution (1973), 443–44, **443**, 464, 650, 651–52
Warren, Earl, 171, 524, 540–41, 543
Warren, Elizabeth, 309, 498
Warsaw Pact, 642, 643, 661
Washington, D.C., *see* District of Columbia
Washington, George, 33, *34*, 37, 52, *52*, 58, 59, 75, 389, 390, 639
 compromises forged by, 437
 nominations made by, 528
 as presidential ideal, *437*
 Supreme Court appointees of, 513
Washington state, 74, 188, 189, 308, 437
Washington Mutual, 570
Washington Post, 243, 248, 260, 501
Washington v. Texas, **113**
Wasserman Schultz, Debbie, 278
Watergate, 222, **223**, 450, 459
water rights, 531
Waxman, Harry, 319
wealth gap, *see* income inequality
weapons of mass destruction (WMDs), 666–68
 see also nuclear weapons
Weber, Max, 483
Weiner, Anthony, 245, 401
welfare, 7–8, 19, 74, 80, **84**, 86, 90, 96, 390, 485, 487, 597, 616, 624–26, **627**
 agencies and recipients, 605, *605*
 average monthly benefits in, **625**
 "corporate," 602
 definition of, 597
 reform of, 626

welfare reform, 439
West, Kanye, 128
Westboro Baptist Church (WBC), 105–6
"What Do Political Scientists Do?," 16, 55, 96, 137, 161, 225, 257, 280, 336, 374, 412, 442, 476, 545, 568, 603, 666
Whig Party, **272**, 273
whip system, 410–11
whistleblower laws, 127
white flight, 172
White House, 114
 Oval Office of, 456
 West Wing of, 456
white primary, 155, 156
whites, 122
 geographical distribution of, **164**
 grandfather clause and, 155
 propertyless, 154
 voting history of, 18, *18*, 162, **162**, 163, 208, 274
white supremacy, *165*
WikiLeaks, 127, 249, *249*
Wilcox, John A., *389*
Williams, George, 526
Wilson, James, 37, 41
Wilson, James Q., 610
Wilson, Woodrow, 437–38, 640
Windsor, Edith, 522
winner-take-all, 312, 314, 315
Wired magazine, 248
wire services, 239
wiretapping, 133, 464
Wisconsin, school vouchers in, 629
Wisconsin, University of, 124
Wisconsin Student Public Interest Research Group, 124
Wisconsin Territory, 78
Witte, Edwin, 598
Witte, John, 629
Wolf v. Colorado, **113**
Women, Infants, and Children (WIC), 597
women, women's rights, 18, 94, 124, **210**, 211, 275
 civil rights of, 154, 158–59, 166, 167, 169, 174–79, 182–83, 188
 in Congress, **392**

protectionism and, 158–59
 Supreme Court and, 174–79
 voting rights of, 158, 167
Woolworth's, sit-ins in, 168, *168*
working poor, Earned Income Tax Credit and, 625
workplace issues, 18, 80, 91, 96, 136–37
 see also employment; labor laws
Works Progress Administration, 599
World Bank, 641, 656
World Trade Organization (WTO), 169–70, 644, 658, 663
World War I, 120, 121, *121*, 156, 438, 443, 640, 650
 hyperinflation in Europe after, 581
World War II, 48, 390, 443, 640–41, 650
 blacks in, 156
 economic depression and, 555
 hyperinflation in Europe after, 581
 internment of Japanese Americans in, 175, 544
 Japanese Americans during, 156
 subsidies implemented after, 610
writ of certiorari, 531
writ of mandamus, 514
www.oyez.com, 536
Wyoming, 131, 437

xenophobia, *126*

Yaqui Indians, 151
Yellen, Janet, *51*, *567*, 568
yellow journalism, 239
Yemen, 435, 645, *645*
Yorktown, Va., **33**
Young, Don, 408
Young Democrats, 275
Young Republicans, 275
YouTube, 245, 251
Yugoslavia, 656

Zaller, John, 208, 252
Zimmerman, George, *124*, 165

Voting Requirements*

STATE	REGISTRATION DEADLINE BEFORE ELECTION	EARLY VOTING PERMITTED?	IDENTIFICATION REQUIRED?	MORE INFORMATION
Alabama	10 days	No	Photo ID requested	sos.state.al.us
Alaska	30 days	Yes	ID requested; photo not required	elections.alaska.gov
Arizona	29 days	Yes	ID required (nonphoto ok)	azsos.gov/election
Arkansas	30 days	Yes	ID requested; photo not required	sos.arkansas.gov
California	15 days	Yes	No	sos.ca.gov
Colorado	22 days; same-day registration permitted	Yes	ID requested; photo not required	sos.state.co.us
Connecticut	*General election*: in person, 7 days; by mail, 14 days. *Primary elections*: in person, 1 day; by mail, 5 days.	No	ID requested; photo not required	ct.gov/sots
Delaware	24 days	No	ID requested; photo not required	elections.delaware.gov
District of Columbia	30 days; same-day registration permitted	Yes	No	dcboee.org
Florida	29 days	Yes	Photo ID requested	election.dos.state.fl.us
Georgia	28 days	Yes	Photo ID required	sos.ga.gov
Hawaii	30 days	Yes	Photo ID requested	hawaii.gov/elections
Idaho	25 days; same-day registration permitted	Yes	Photo ID requested	idahovotes.gov
Illinois	27 days	Yes	No	elections.il.gov
Indiana	29 days	Yes	Photo ID required	in.gov/sos/elections
Iowa	10 days	Yes	No	sos.iowa.gov
Kansas	21 days	Yes	Photo ID required	kssos.org
Kentucky	28 days	No	ID requested; photo not required	elect.ky.gov
Louisiana	30 days	Yes	Photo ID requested	sos.la.gov
Maine	21 days; same-day registration permitted	Yes	No	maine.gov/sos
Maryland	21 days	Yes	No	elections.state.md.us
Massachusetts	20 days	No	No	www.sec.state.ma.us
Michigan	30 days	No	Photo ID requested	michigan.gov/sos
Minnesota	21 days	Yes	No	mnvotes.org
Mississippi	30 days	No	Photo ID required	sos.ms.gov
Missouri	Fourth Wednesday prior to election	No	ID requested; photo not required	sos.mo.gov

STATE	REGISTRATION DEADLINE BEFORE ELECTION	EARLY VOTING PERMITTED?	IDENTIFICATION REQUIRED?	MORE INFORMATION
Montana	30 days; same-day registration permitted	Yes	ID requested; photo not required	sos.mt.gov
Nebraska	In person: second Friday prior to election. By mail: third Friday prior to election.	Yes	No	www.sos.ne.gov
Nevada	In person: 21 days By mail: 31 days	Yes	No	nvsos.gov
New Hampshire	10 days; same-day registration permitted	No	ID requested; photo not required	sos.nh.gov
New Jersey	21 days	Yes	No	njelections.org
New Mexico	28 days	Yes	No	sos.state.nm.us
New York	25 days	No	No	www.elections.ny.gov
North Carolina	25 days	Yes	No	ncsbe.gov
North Dakota	No voter registration required	Yes	ID required (nonphoto ok)	vote.nd.gov
Ohio	30 days	Yes	ID required (nonphoto ok)	sos.state.oh.us
Oklahoma	24 days	Yes	ID requested; photo not required	ok.gov/elections
Oregon	21 days	Yes	No	sos.oregon.gov
Pennsylvania	30 days	No	No	www.votespa.com
Rhode Island	30 days	No	Photo ID requested	www.elections.state.ri.us
South Carolina	30 days	No	ID requested; photo not required	scvotes.org
South Dakota	15 days	Yes	Photo ID requested	sdsos.gov
Tennessee	30 days	Yes	Photo ID required	tn.gov/sos/election
Texas	30 days	Yes	Photo ID required	votetexas.gov
Utah	In person: 15 days By mail: 30 days	Yes	ID requested; photo not required	vote.utah.gov
Vermont	Wednesday before the election	Yes	No	www.sec.state.vt.us/elections
Virginia	22 days	No	Photo ID required	sbe.virginia.gov
Washington	In person: 8 days By mail: 30 days	Yes	ID requested; photo not required	sos.wa.gov/elections/myvote
West Virginia	21 days	Yes	No	sos.wv.gov
Wisconsin	Same-day registration permitted	Yes	No	sos.state.wi.us
Wyoming	14 days; same-day registration permitted	Yes	No	soswy.state.wy.us

* As of November 2014. Information collected from Project Vote Smart, votesmart.org/elections/voter-registration (accessed 11/4/14) and the National Conference of State Legislatures, www.ncsl.org/ (accessed 11/4/14). States often reevaluate their voting rules. Check the websites in the far right column to confirm current information.